**SOURCES AND METHODS**
LABOUR STATISTICS
VOLUME 10
ESTIMATES AND PROJECTIONS OF THE
ECONOMICALLY ACTIVE POPULATION 1950-2010

**SOURCES ET MÉTHODES**
STATISTIQUES DU TRAVAIL
VOLUME 10
ÉVALUATIONS ET PROJECTIONS
DE LA POPULATION ACTIVE 1950-2010

**FUENTES Y METODOS**
ESTADISTICAS DEL TRABAJO
VOLUMEN 10
EVALUACIONES Y PROYECCIONES DE LA
POBLACIÓN ECONÓMICAMENTE ACTIVA, 1950-2010

# SOURCES
# AND METHODS
## LABOUR STATISTICS
## VOLUME 10
### ESTIMATES AND PROJECTIONS OF THE ECONOMICALLY ACTIVE POPULATION 1950-2010

Companion to the *Yearbook of Labour Statistics*

# SOURCES
# ET MÉTHODES
## STATISTIQUES DU TRAVAIL
## VOLUME 10
### ÉVALUATIONS ET PROJECTIONS DE LA POPULATION ACTIVE 1950-2010

Complément de l'*Annuaire des statistiques du travail*

# FUENTES
# Y METODOS
## ESTADISTICAS DEL TRABAJO
## VOLUMEN 10
### EVALUACIONES Y PROYECCIONES DE LA POBLACIÒN ECONÒMICAMENTE ACTIVA, 1950-2010

Complemento del *Anuario de Estadísticas del Trabajo*

INTERNATIONAL LABOUR OFFICE   GENEVA
BUREAU INTERNATIONAL DU TRAVAIL   GENÈVE
OFICINA INTERNACIONAL DEL TRABAJO   GINEBRA

ISBN 92-2-011371-6
(the set of 2 volumes)
ISSN 0084-3857

This volume:
ISBN 92-2-012278-2
ISSN 1014-9856

Edition 2000

ISBN 92-2-011371-6
(le jeu de 2 volumes)
ISSN 0084-3857

Ce volume:
ISBN 92-2-012278-2
ISSN 1014-9856

Édition 2000

ISBN 92-2-011371-6
(el juego de 2 volúmenes)
ISSN 0084-3857

Este volumen:
ISBN 92-2-012278-2
ISSN 1014-9856

Edición 2000

Printed in France          Imprimé en France          Impreso en Francia          JOU

# Important

● In order to enhance the usefulness of the *Yearbook of Labour Statistics,* each issue is now accompanied by a methodological volume of the series *Sources and Methods: Labour Statistics* (formerly entitled *Statistical Sources and Methods*).

● This series provides methodological descriptions of the data published in the *Yearbook* and *Bulletin of Labour Statistics.* Each volume covers different subjects according to the source of the data.

● The methodological descriptions include information on the method of data collection, coverage, concepts and definitions, classifications, historical changes, technical references, etc. In each volume the information is presented by country under standard headings.

# Important

● Afin de mettre en valeur l'utilité de l'*Annuaire des statistiques du travail,* chaque édition est maintenant accompagnée d'un volume méthodologique de la série *Sources et méthodes: statistiques du travail* (intitulée précédemment *Sources et méthodes statistiques*).

● Cette série fournit des descriptions méthodologiques des données publiées dans l'*Annuaire* et dans le *Bulletin des statistiques du travail.* Chaque volume traite de sujets différents suivant la source des données.

● Les descriptions méthodologiques contiennent des informations sur la méthode de collecte des données, la portée, les concepts et définitions, les classifications, les modifications apportées aux séries, les références techniques, etc. Dans chaque volume, les informations sont présentées par pays sous des rubriques standardisées.

# Importante

● Con el fin de mejorar la utilidad del *Anuario de Estadísticas del Trabajo,* ahora cada edición va acompañada de un volumen metodológico de la serie *Fuentes y Métodos: Estadísticas del Trabajo* (titulada anteriormente *Fuentes y Métodos Estadísticos*).

● Esta serie proporciona las descripciones metodológicas de los datos que se publican en el *Anuario* y el *Boletín de Estadísticas del Trabajo.* Cada volumen abarca diferentes temas del *Anuario* de acuerdo con la fuente de los datos.

● Las descripciones metodológicas incluyen informaciones acerca del método de recolección de datos, el alcance, los conceptos y definiciones, las clasificaciones, los cambios históricos, las referencias técnicas, etc. En cada volumen, la información se presenta por país de acuerdo a encabezamientos estándar.

# Preface

This Volume 10 of the series **Sources and Methods: Labour Statistics** is a special edition, which describes the methodology of *"Economically active population 1950-2010"*[1] (Fourth edition, Geneva, 1996).

The series comprises the following volumes:
**Volume 1:**
Consumer price indices (Third edition, Geneva, 1992).
**Volume 2:**
Employment, wages, hours of work and labour cost (establishment surveys) (Second edition, Geneva, 1995).
**Volume 3:**
Economically active population, employment, unemployment and hours of work (household surveys) (Second edition, Geneva, 1990).
**Volume 4:**
Employment, unemployment, wages and hours of work (administrative records and related sources) (First published Geneva, 1989).
**Volume 5:**
Total and economically active population, employment and unemployment (population censuses) (Second edition, Geneva,1996).
**Volume 6:**
Household income and expenditure surveys (First published Geneva, 1994).
**Volume 7:**
Strikes and lockouts (First published, Geneva, 1993)
**Volume 8**
Occupational injuries (First published, Geneva, 1999).
**Volume 9**
Transition countries (First published, Geneva, 1999).

Volume 10 describes the options chosen, the principles adopted and the methods used to produce the estimates and projections of the economically active population for the periods 1950-1990 and 2000-2010 respectively. It synthesises the work of preparing and producing the estimates and projections of the economically active population for the fourth edition. Its aim is to provide readers from various backgrounds with basic information on the general methodology adopted as well as specific information about the

# Préface

Le volume 10 de la série **Sources et méthodes: statistiques du travail** est une édition spéciale qui porte sur la méthodologie de *"Population active 1950 - 2010"*[1] (quatrième édition, Genève, 1996).

La série comprend les volumes suivants:
**Volume 1:**
Indice des prix à la consommation (troisième édition, Genève 1992).
**Volume 2:**
Emploi, salaires, durée du travail et coût de la main-d'oeuvre (enquêtes auprès des établissements) (deuxième édition, Genève, 1995).
**Volume 3:**
Population active, emploi, chômage et durée du travail (enquête auprès des ménages) (deuxième, édition, Genève, 1991).
**Volume 4:**
Emploi, chômage, salaires et durée du travail (documents administratifs et sources assimilées) (première édition, Genève,1989).
**Volume 5:**
Population totale et population active, emploi et chômage (recensements de population) (deuxième édition, Genève, 1996).
**Volume 6:**
Enquêtes sur le revenu et les dépenses des ménages (première édition, Genève, 1994).
**Volume 7:**
Grèves et lock-out (première édition, Genève, 1993).
**Volume 8:**
Lésions professionnelles (première édition, Genève, 1999).
**Volume 9:**
Pays en transition (première édition, Genève, 1999).

Le volume 10 décrit les options choisies, les principes adoptés et les méthodes appliquées pour établir les évaluations et les projections de la population active, respectivement pour les périodes 1950 - 1990 et 2000 - 2010. Il est une synthèse des travaux préparatoires et d'élaboration des évaluations et projections de la population active réalisés pour la quatrième édition. Il est conçu dans le but d'offrir aux lecteurs de différents

# Prefacio

Este volumen 10 de la serie **Fuentes y Métodos: Estadísticas del Trabajo** es una edición especial que abarca a la metodología de *"Población económicamente activa, 1950-2010"*[1] (cuarta edición, Ginebra, 1996).

Esta serie comprende los siguientes volúmenes:
**Volumen 1:**
Indices de los precios del consumo (tercera edición, Ginebra, 1992).
**Volumen 2:**
Empleo, salarios, horas de trabajo y costo de la mano de obra (encuestas de establecimientos) (segunda edición, Ginebra, 1995).
**Volumen 3:**
Población económicamente activa, empleo, desempleo y horas de trabajo (encuestas de hogares) (segunda edición, Ginebra, 1992).
**Volumen 4:**
Empleo, desempleo, salarios y horas de trabajo (registros administrativos y fuentes conexas) (primera edición, Ginebra, 1989).
**Volumen 5:**
Población total y población económicamente activa, empleo y desempleo (censos de población) (segunda edición, Ginebra, 1996).
**Volumen 6:**
Encuestas de ingresos y gastos de los hogares (primera edición, Ginebra, 1994).
**Volumen 7:**
Huelgas y cierres patronales (primera edición, Ginebra, 1993).
**Volumen 8:**
Lesiones profesionales (primera edición, Ginebra, 1999).
**Volumen 9:**
Países en transicion (primera edición, Ginebra, 1999).

Esta Volumen 10 describe las opciones elegidas, los principios adoptados y los métodos aplicados con el fin de establecer evaluaciones y proyecciones de la población activa para los períodos 1950-1990 y 2000-2010, respectivamente. El presente volumen es una síntesis de los trabajos preliminares y de elaboración de las evaluaciones y proyecciones de la población activa que se han llevado a cabo para la cuarta edición. Se ha

methods applied to each country and territory considered.

A standard methodological description is given for each country and territory individually selected in the fourth edition for separate estimates and projections. Each description indicates the sources and the benchmark data and notes the estimation methods, the projection models and the assumptions specific to the country or territory concerned.

The preparation and production of the estimates and projections of the economically active population for the fourth edition was carried out by Messrs Ettore Denti and Edmond Ruhumuliza, consulting statisticians, and completed in December 1996. Mrs. Angela Martins-Oliveira of the Bureau of Statistics of the ILO was responsible for the operation and management of the estimates and projections databases (LABPROJ) until September 1999.

This publication was prepared by Mr. M. Hammouya of the ILO Bureau of Statistics.

horizons les informations essentielles sur la méthodologie générale adoptée ainsi que les informations particulières sur les méthodes appliquées à chacun des pays et territoires étudiés.

Pour chaque pays et territoire retenu individuellement dans la quatrième édition pour des évaluations et projections séparées, une description méthodologique standard a été établie. Dans chaque description y sont indiquées les sources et les données de base et y sont notés les méthodes d'évaluation, les modèles de projection et les hypothèses particulières au pays ou au territoire en question.

Le travail d'élaboration des évaluations et projections de la population active de la quatrième édition a été effectué par MM. Ettore Denti et Edmond Ruhumuliza, consultants statisticiens, et achevé en décembre 1996. Mme Angela Martins-Oliveira du Bureau de statistique du BIT a été chargée de l'exploitation et la gestion des bases de données des évaluations et projections de la population active (LABPROJ) jusqu'en septembre 1999.

La présente publication a été préparée par M. M. Hammouya, du Bureau de statistique du BIT.

preparado con el fin de ofrecer a lectores de diferentes ámbitos informaciones esenciales sobre la metodología general adoptada, así como informaciones específicas sobre los métodos aplicados respecto de cada país y territorio considerados.

Una descripción metodológica estándar se hizo para cada país y territorio considerados individualmente en las evaluaciones y proyecciones por separado que figuran en la cuarta edición. En cada descripción se indican las fuentes y los datos básicos, así como los métodos de evaluación, los modelos de proyección y las hipótesis específicas relativas al país o territorio de que se trata.

Los trabajos de elaboración de las evaluaciones y las proyecciones de la población económicamente activa de la cuarta edición se han llevado a cabo por los Sres. Ettore Denti y Edmond Ruhumuliza, consultores de estadística, y se terminaron en diciembre de 1996. La Sra. Angela Martins-Oliveira, de la Oficina de Estadística de la OIT, se encargó de la explotación y gestión de las bases de datos de las evaluaciones y proyecciones (LABPROJ) hasta septiembre de 1999.

Esta publicación fue preparada por el Sr. M. Hammouya de la Oficina de Estadística de la OIT.

---

[1] The five volumes of the publication may be requested free of charge from the Bureau of Statistics at the following address: ILO Bureau of Statistics, 4 route des Morillons, CH-1211 Geneva 22, or by e-mail: stat@ilo.org The set of diskettes containing the estimates and projections of "Economically active population 1950-2010" (fourth edition) may be obtained from the following address: ILO Publications, International Labour Office, CH-1211 Geneva 22, or by e-mail to: pubvente@ilo.org

[1] Les cinq volumes de la publication peuvent être obtenus à titre gratuit sur demande au Bureau de statistique à l'adresse suivante : Bureau de statistique du BIT, 4 route des Morillons, CH-1211 Genève 22, ou par courrier électronique : stat@ilo.org Le jeu de disquettes contenant les évaluations et projections de "Population active 1950 – 2010" (quatrième édition) peut être obtenu à l'adresse suivante : Publications du BIT, Bureau international du Travail, CH-1211 Genève 22, ou par courrier électronique: pubvente@ilo.org

[1] Los cinco volúmenes de la publicación pueden conseguirse gratuitamente pidiéndolos a la Oficina de Estadística a la dirección siguiente: Oficina de Estadística de la OIT, 4 route des Morillons, CH-1211 Ginebra 22, o por correo electrónico: stat@ilo.org El juego de disquetes con las evaluaciones y proyecciones de "Población económicamente activa 1950-2010" (cuarta edición) puede pedirse a la dirección siguiente: Publicaciones de la OIT, Oficina Internacional del Trabajo, CH-1211 Ginebra 22, o por correo electrónico: pubvente@ilo.org

# Contents | Table des matières | Indice

## Signs and Symbols Used in the tables

.. Not applicable.
… Not available.

## Signes et symboles Utilisés dans les tableaux

. Ne s'applique pas.
… Pas disponible.

## Signos y símbolos Que figuran en los cuadros

.. No se aplica.
… No disponible.

# Introduction

The programme of estimates and projections of the economically active population by sex and age group has now reached its fourth edition. The ILO Bureau of Statistics published the first edition[1] in 1971. The other two editions, the second[2] and the third,[3] were published in 1976 and 1986 respectively.

The purpose of this programme is to provide ILO member States, international agencies and private users with the most comprehensive, detailed and comparable working tool possible at the national, regional and international levels. It is part of the joint programme of the United Nations and the specialised international agencies, in particular the International Labour Office (ILO), the Food and Agriculture Organization of the United Nations (FAO) and the United Nations Educational, Scientific and Cultural Organization (UNESCO). It also aims to furnish coordinated and compatible demographic data on population, economically active population, agricultural population, school population, households, birth, fertility, mortality rates, etc.

**Figure 1: Links between the ILO programme on economically active population and other programmes**

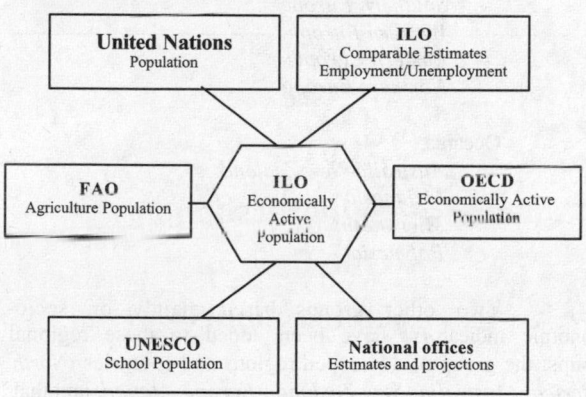

One significant feature of international estimates and projections of economically active population is that they enable comparison of levels and trends in the economically active population of various regions and countries over past and future years.

To enhance international comparability, the benchmark data on active population were standardised as far as possible, particularly with regard to concepts, coverage, scope and age group distribution. Besides, to ensure the

consistency of the estimates and projections of active population with the findings of other international demographic programmes, the estimates and projections of total population made by the United Nations Population Division were used in producing the estimates and projections of economically active population for the fourth edition.

As for the preceding editions, the estimates and projections of active population for the fourth edition were obtained by applying to the population estimates and projections (medium variant) produced by the United Nations[4], ILO estimates and projections of activity rates by sex and age groups as of the middle of each reference year, that is, the years 1950, 1960, 1970, 1980, 1990, 2000 and 2010.

By comparison with the three preceding editions, the fourth edition introduces innovations and changes in concepts, definitions and methodology.

## 1. Concepts and definitions

### 1.1 Economically active population

The concept of economically active population is outlined in the Resolution concerning statistics of the economically active population, employment, unemployment and underemployment, adopted by the Thirteenth International Conference of Labour Statisticians - ICLS 1982.

This Resolution defines the economically active population as *"all persons of either sex who furnish the supply of labour for the production of economic goods and services as defined by the United Nations systems of national accounts and balances during a specified time-reference period. According to these systems the production of economic goods and services includes all production and processing of primary products whether for the market, for barter or for own consumption, the production of all other goods and services for the market and, in the case of households which produce such goods and services for the market, the corresponding production for own consumption.*[5]

By that definition, the active population includes: persons in *"paid"* or *"unpaid"*[6] employment, members of the armed forces (including temporary members) and the *unemployed* (including first-time job-seekers.)

---

[1] ILO, *Labour force projections, 1965-85* (1st edition, Geneva, 1971)

[2] ILO, *Labour force projections, 1950-2010* (2nd edition, Geneva, 1976)

[3] *ILO, Economically Active Population: Estimates and projections, 1950-2025* (3rd edition, Geneva, 1986).

[4] United Nations, World Population Prospects, the 1994 Revisions, ST/ESA/SER.A/145, New York, 1995.

[5] ILO, *Current international recommendations on labour statistics*, Geneva, 1988 edition, Geneva 1988.

[6] Employers, own-account workers and members of producers' cooperatives; unpaid family workers, persons engaged in the production of economic goods and services for own and household consumption, and apprentices who receive pay.

**Figure 2: Conceptual framework of the economically active population**

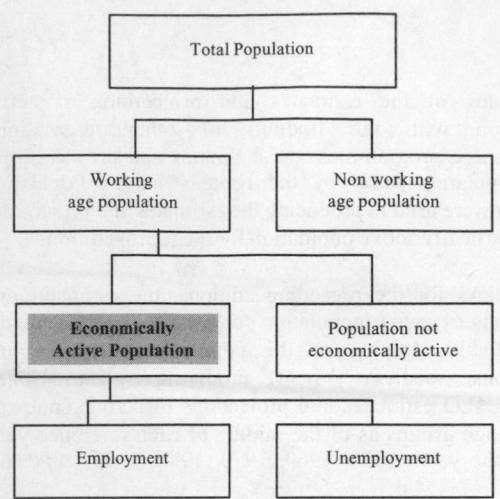

## 1.2    Activity rate

The global activity rate is the proportion of the workforce, as defined below, within the total population of working age.

$$TA = \frac{PA}{PT} \times 100$$

Activity rates are calculated for each age group, separately for men and women and for the two sexes taken together.

## 1.3    Geographic coverage

All countries and territories whose total population had reached or exceeded the threshold of 200,000 as of mid-1990 are covered by the fourth edition.

By comparison with the third edition, the number of countries and territories for which individual estimates and projections of economically active population were compiled has increased considerably. This increase is due, on the one hand, to the lowering of the threshold from 300,000 to 200,000 inhabitants and, on the other, to the separate treatment of each of the republics of the former USSR, Yugoslavia and Czechoslovakia.

## 1.4    Age limit and classification by age group

The minimum age selected is ten years. In the vast majority of countries, the legal minimum working age is above this limit. Nevertheless, in a good many developing countries a sizeable proportion of young peopleunder 15 years of age do work as unpaid family workers in agriculture. It was considered reasonable to adopt the age of ten years as the lower age limit and to adjust the data whenever necessary.

The age group distribution which comprises 12 five-year age groups, is the same as in the third edition, comprises  12 five-year age groups, except for the last one:

10-14, 15-19, 20-24, 25-29, 30-34, 35-39, 40-44, 45-49, 50-54, 55-59, 60-64 and 65+.

## 1.5    Regional classification

The regional classification adopted is the latest version established by the United Nations. It comprises six major regions and twenty areas:

Asia
  *Middle South Asia*
  *Eastern South Asia*
  *Western Asia*
  *East Asia*

Africa
  *Middle Africa*
  *Southern Africa*
  *Western Africa*
  *Eastern Africa*
  *Northern Africa*

Latin America and the Caribbean
  *Central America*
  *South America*
  *Caribbean*

Northern America

Europe
  *Southern Europe*
  *Western Europe*
  *Eastern Europe*
  *Northern Europe*

Oceania
  *Australia-New Zealand*
  *Melanesia*
  *Micronesia*
  *Polynesia*

Two other groups based mainly on socio-economic indicators[7] have been added to these regional groups: the group of developed regions and countries *(North America - Australia, New Zealand - Europe - Japan)* and that of the less developed regions *(Africa - Asia (excluding Japan) - Latin America and the Caribbean - Melanesia - Micronesia - Polynesia).*

For the World as a whole, and for each major region, area, developed region and less developed region, the respective activity rates were estimated by sex, age group and by sector of economic activity.

## 1.6    Sectors of economic activity

As in the preceding editions, the fourth edition also provides estimates of sectoral distribution rates for all economic activity. The composition of each sector is drawn

---

[7]  United Nations,  World Population Prospects, New York, 1985.

from The International Standard Industrial Classification Of All Economic Activities (ISIC - Rev.2, 1968[8])

Branch 1 (*agriculture, hunting, forestry and fishing*) is the "agriculture" sector.

The "industry" sector is composed of branches 2, 3, 4 and 5 (*extractive industries - manufacturing industries - electricity, gas and water - construction and public works*).

The "services" sector is comprised of branches 6, 7, 8 and 9 (*wholesale and retailing, restaurants and hotels - transport, warehouses and communications - banks, insurances, real estate and services provided to the companies - services provided to the community, social services and personal services*).

The fourth edition is innovative in that, for the first time, it offers separate estimates for branch 3 "manufacturing industries". Due to lack of data for most of the countries studied, these estimates are limited only to the years 1980 and 1990; for the remaining sectors, they cover the entire period 1950-1990 period.

## 2. Methodology

The general methodology adopted in the fourth edition differs from that of the other editions primarily in its "pragmatic" approach. For each country or territory studied, the choice of methods and techniques for estimating activity rates and sectoral distribution rates was based on an evaluation of certain criteria pertaining to the source and quality of the data and to national data compilation practices. This choice also took account of demographic information specific to a given country or region widely highlighted in specialised publications. It is also noteworthy that the experience of past editions has enriched the choice of estimation and projection methods and techniques.

Whenever total or partial data on these factors was unavailable, the rule was to draw on information or data on countries or territories at a similar level of socio-economic and cultural development.

The ILO programme of estimates and projections of the economically active population comprises two phases: an estimation and a projection phase.

### 2.1 Estimation phase

The estimation phase consisted of compiling harmonised chronological data series on active population by sex, age group and sector of economic activity for the period 1950-1990.

### 2.1.1 Sources and benchmark data

To collect benchmark data for use as the basis for producing estimates, it was decided to start by taking data drawn from the third edition for the years 1950, 1960 and 1970 and to supplement them with data derived from population censuses and (or) sample surveys of economically active population or similar surveys conducted between 1974 and 1994 and published by national or international statistical bodies.

To compensate for the lack of data and to verify and compare data derived from various sources, it was necessary and useful to draw on specific publications by regional or international institutions such as the Latin American Demographic Centre (CELADE), the Organisation for Economic Co-operation and Development (OECD), the Statistical Office of the European Communities (EUROSTAT), Nordic Statistics, and the regional economic commissions of the United Nations: i.e. the Economic Commission for Africa (ECA), Economic Commission for Europe (ECE), Economic Commission for Latin America and the Caribbean (ECLAC), Economic and Social Commission for Asia and the Pacific (ESCAP) and the Economic and Social Commission for Western Asia (ESCWA).

Unlike the preceding editions, the fourth edition gave priority to sample surveys of economically active population rather than to population censuses.

In many countries, sample surveys of economically active population and its main components employment and unemployment are conducted on a regular annual or infra-annual basis. This makes for the compilation of more precise and reliable figures for the economically active population. They also have the advantage of eliminating seasonal effects on the workforce when carried out at different periods of the year. These are advantages, not least of all over population censuses which cover several subjects simultaneously, relate to a single date and are generally carried out on a 10-yearly basis for the vast majority of countries.

Once the benchmark data was selected, we proceeded to the various stages indicated in figure 3, and to apply to the benchmark data the procedures and treatments appropriate to each stage. Depending on the country or the territory, one or more stages were needed to arrive at the estimates.

All told, the estimation phase comprised seven stages. Those of "Harmonisation of definitions of economically active population" and "Adjustment of age group distributions" were not applied to the estimates of sectoral distribution rates .

### 2.1.2 Harmonisation of the definitions of economically active population

It had to be ensured during this phase that the definitions of economically active population adopted in the population censuses and sample surveys of economically active population corresponded to those adopted by the ICLS 1982, and the necessary adjustments made where they did not. Volume 5, "Total population and economically active population, employment and unemployment (population

---

[8] United Nations, *Statistical Studies*, Series M, No 4, New York 1969.

censuses)"[9] of the series *"Sources and Methods: Labour Statistics"* was used as the reference for assessing the definitions.

The problems most frequently encountered at this stage stemmed from the exclusion of certain categories of the economically active population, either because they were omitted by definition or they were counted amongst the population not economically active. These were mainly the armed forces (temporary members in particular) first-time job-seekers, unpaid apprentices and family workers (mainly women active in agriculture as unpaid family workers) and seasonal workers.

When the degree of breakdown of population data by status permitted or if data for the category were available, the adjustments were effected by including the figures for the category/categories concerned in the numbers for the active population by reclassifying the economically inactive population category/categories together with the active population or by estimating the numbers to be included (case No. 1)

The example of the Republic of Korea is a good illustration of case No 1. The benchmark data selected for this country were those drawn from the third edition for the years 1950, 1960 and 1970 and those derived from the 1980 population census and from the sample surveys of the active population carried out between 1987 and 1990. For both the census and the surveys, the economically active population data all referred to the population comprised of private households. The armed forces were thus excluded from the definition as formulated by the ICLS 1982. To include the armed forces, the adjustment entailed adding the estimated difference between the total population and the civilian population to the data for the economically active civilian population.

Where no data breakdown was available, the adjustment method consisted of adding to the active population, an estimated proportion of the numbers classified in the "Others" category of the population not economically active (case No 2). The estimated proportions were based on data drawn from other sources or from the same source at another reference period, and if necessary, from data for neighbouring countries with a demographic, socio-economic and cultural situation comparable to that of the country under study.

Case No. 2 was the most frequent. Generally, the adjustment carried out was limited to the 15-29 age groups and to men only. For example, the data produced by the 1984 population census in the Congo and used as the benchmark data for the estimates were adjusted to take account of students working part-time or occasionally and not included in the active population.

The adjustment procedure consisted of adding to the economically active population rates, the estimates of

---

[9] Total population and economically active population, employment and unemployment (population censuses), Volume 5, *Labour Statistics: Sources and Methods*, 1st edition, ILO, 1990.

**Figure 3: Stages and procedures of Estimation phase**

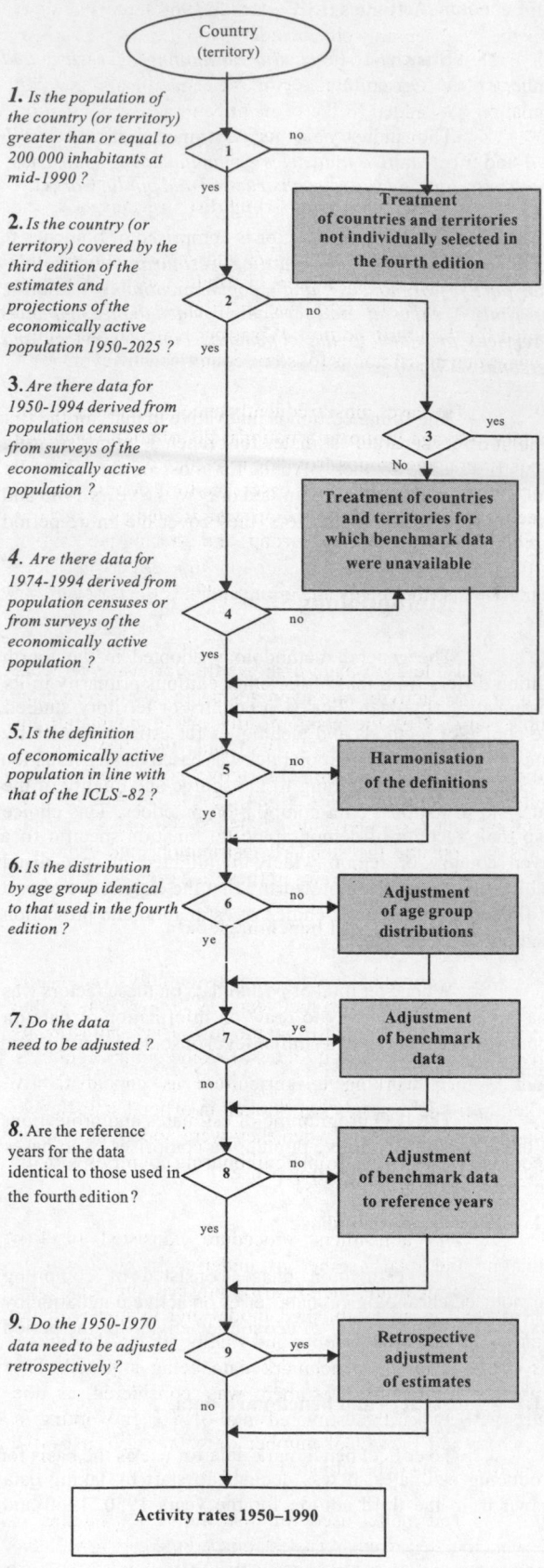

students working part-time or occasionally and classified as inactive. Besides, as the activity rates for this country thrown up by the 1984 census were considered too low in comparison with data from countries in the same situation, the total number for the "Others" category of the economically inactive population was added to the economically active population figure. Table 1 illustrates the adjustments made.

### 2.1.3    Adjustment of age group distributions

In most of the censuses and surveys studied, the economically active population distributions by age group were in line with the reference distribution by age group adopted for the fourth edition. It was necessary to harmonise the age group distributions for some countries, however.

The cases most frequently encountered were those in which one age group in a national distribution contained two or several age groups from the reference distribution. An algorithm was applied to such cases: the total population and the active economically population were treated as uniformly distributed over a given age group, and a technique applied whereby allowance was made for the effects of total population distribution by age group and the effects of activity rates.

Table 2 on page 6 shows the various treatments given to 1980 activity rate averages using data drawn from sample surveys of the economically active population in *Australia* for the years 1979, 1980 and 1981. The national distribution of the economically active population by age group was as follows: 15-19, 20-24, 25-34, 35-44, 45-54, 55-59, 60-64 and 65+. Only the 25-34, 35-44 and 45-54 age groups fall outside the standard distribution, and estimates were made of the activity rates of these age groups.

### 2.1.4    Adjustment of benchmark data

At this stage, the task was essentially to adjust the benchmark data fully for the years 1970 to 1994, as the activity rates were deemed to be too low. These adjustments were made chiefly to activity rates of women in the countries where women working in agriculture as unpaid family workers were deliberately overlooked in official statistics for socio-cultural reasons, or when they were under-enumerated by comparison with data from neighbouring countries with the same socio-economic profiles.

The adjustment procedure consisted of first estimating the total number of under-enumerated women working in agriculture, then distributing that number by age group based on an established model and in line with the country's rate of urbanisation, and finally adding the figures thus obtained to the benchmark data being adjusted. The number of unrecorded women was considered as the difference between the estimated total of women working in agriculture and the actual number of women given by the source of the data to be adjusted.

The model used for distributing the number of under-enumerated women was established in keeping with the activity rate curves for women in the agricultural sector for some countries for which very detailed and comprehensive

statistics were available; distribution was by age group and by urban and rural area. The distribution model below was uniformly applied to all the data series to be adjusted. Table 3 shows an instance of the adjustment of activity rates for women in *Mali* the data for which were drawn from the 1976 population census.

**Distribution model for under-enumerated women by age group and region**

| Age group | Urban | Rural |
|---|---|---|
| 10-14 | 3.74 | 26.68 |
| 15-19 | 3.80 | 36.76 |
| 20-24 | 4.20 | 40.36 |
| 25-29 | 3.99 | 42.46 |
| 30-34 | 7.70 | 44.02 |
| 35-39 | 8.20 | 45.29 |
| 40-44 | 10.06 | 46.33 |
| 45-49 | 7.50 | 45.36 |
| 50-54 | 10.29 | 43.47 |
| 55-59 | 9.70 | 39.18 |
| 60-64 | 6.22 | 33.48 |
| 65+ | 2.77 | 17.39 |

**Source**: Bureau of Statistics, ILO.

### 2.1.5    Adjustment of benchmark data to reference years

As was the case in the third edition, the reference period set for the estimates was the month of June of each of the reference years 1950, 1960, 1970, 1980 and 1990.

For the countries and territories for which the estimates from the third edition for the years 1950, 1960 and 1970 (and at times for 1980) were retained, with few exceptions, the benchmark data for 1974 to 1994 were all adjusted to the month of June and to each of the reference years 1980 and 1990.

An adjustment procedure was chosen depending on the number of years available for the benchmark data and the length of the interval between each of those years and the reference year. As a general rule, the procedure for a given country or territory was as follows:

- If there were two years of benchmark data available around the reference year (1979 and 1981 or 1989 and 1991), the adjustments were made by applying arithmetic averages to the activity rates from the benchmark data. This was the case for most of the countries in the developed regions.

- If there were two years of benchmark data available and relatively close to the reference year, the adjustments were done by applying weighted averages to the activity rates from the benchmark data. In the case of *Turkey*, for instance, the estimated 1990 activity rate for women in the 50-54 age group was derived by totalling the activity rates drawn from the censuses of October 1985 (1985.75) and 1990 (1990.75) weighted by the interval between those years and the reference year 1990 (1990.5): The resulting rate was: $(48.18)(0.25/5) + (44.77)(4.75/5) = 44.94$

## Table 1: Adjustment of activity rates for men derived from the Congo population census (December 1984)

| Age group | Econnomically active population in % | Population not economically active in % | | | Esimated rates of eco. Active students | Additional adjustment rates | | | Adjusted activity rates |
|---|---|---|---|---|---|---|---|---|---|
| | | Total | Students | Others | | Students | Others | Total | |
| $c_1$ | $c_2$ | $c_3$ | $c_4$ | $c_5$ | $c_6$ | $c_7 = c_4 \times c_6$ | $c_8 = c_5$ | $c_9 = c_7 + c_8$ | $c_{10} = c_2 + c_9$ |
| 10-14 | 3.10 | 94.26 | 93.14 | 2.64 | 0.25 | 23.28 | 2.64 | 25.92 | 29.02 |
| 15-19 | 18.84 | 77.89 | 75.07 | 3.28 | 0.40 | 30.03 | 3.28 | 33.30 | 52.14 |
| 20-24 | 53.49 | 43.29 | 39.88 | 3.22 | 0.70 | 27.92 | 3.22 | 31.14 | 84.63 |
| 25-29 | 86.04 | 12.16 | 9.98 | 1.81 | 0.90 | 8.98 | 1.81 | 10.79 | 96.82 |
| 30-34 | 96.60 | 2.47 | 1.16 | 0.93 | 0.00 | 0.00 | 0.93 | 0.93 | 97.53 |
| 35-39 | 97.75 | 1.57 | 0.36 | 0.68 | 0.00 | 0.00 | 0.68 | 0.68 | 98.43 |
| 40-44 | 97.61 | 1.71 | 0.20 | 0.68 | 0.00 | 0.00 | 0.68 | 0.68 | 98.29 |
| 45-49 | 96.62 | 2.74 | 0.13 | 0.64 | 0.00 | 0.00 | 0.64 | 0.64 | 97.26 |
| 50-54 | 92.95 | 6.32 | 0.06 | 0.73 | 0.00 | 0.00 | 0.73 | 0.73 | 93.68 |
| 55-59 | 80.96 | 18.19 | 0.19 | 0.85 | 0.00 | 0.00 | 0.85 | 0.85 | 81.81 |
| 60-64 | 81.05 | 17.87 | 0.50 | 1.08 | 0.00 | 0.00 | 0.00 | 0.00 | 81.05 |
| 65+ | 73.79 | 23.37 | 1.63 | 2.84 | 0.00 | 0.00 | 0.00 | 0.00 | 73.79 |

Source: Bureau of Statistics, ILO.

## Table 2: Evaluation of activity rates 1980 of the age groups from 25 to 44 years for men in Australia

| Age group | Econom. active population in 1980 | Total population in 1980 (thousands) | Activity rates 1970 | Activity rates 1980 | | | | | | | | | | | | | | | Adjusted activity rates 1980 |
|---|---|---|---|---|---|---|---|---|---|---|---|---|---|---|---|---|---|---|---|
| $c_1$ | $c_2$ | $c_3$ | $c_4$ | $c_5$ | $c_6$ | $c_7$ | $c_8$ | $c_9$ | $c_{10}$ | $c_{11}$ | $c_{12}$ | $c_{13}$ | $c_{14}$ | $c_{15}$ | $c_{16}$ | $c_{17}$ | $c_{18}$ | $c_{19}$ |
| 25-29 | 95.87 | 608 | 95.79 | 94.81 | 1196 | 1147 | 576 | 1138 | 582 | 1150 | 12 | 4 | 0.30 | 0.70 | 28.64 | 66.86 | 95.50 | 95.50 |
| 30-34 | | 588 | 96.55 | 95.54 | | | 562 | | 568 | | | | | 0.70 | 28.86 | 67.39 | 96.25 | 96.25 |
| 35-39 | 95.67 | 961 | 96.44 | 95.36 | 1778 | 1701 | 916 | 1689 | 927 | 1710 | 21 | 9 | 0.42 | 0.58 | 39.59 | 56.40 | 95.99 | 95.99 |
| 40-44 | | 817 | 95.80 | 94.55 | | | 772 | | 783 | | | | | 0.58 | 39.26 | 56.03 | 95.28 | 95.28 |

$c_6$=sum of data for two adjacent groups in $c_3$; $c_7 = (c_2 \times c_6)/100$; $c_8 = (c_3 \times c_5)/100$; $c_9$=sum of data for two adjacent groups in $c_8$;
$c_{10} = (c_3 \times c_4)/100$; $c_{11}$=sum of data for two adjacent groups in $c_{10}$; $c_{12} = c_{11} - c_9$; $c_{13} = c_{11} - c_7$;
$c_{14} = c_{13}/c_{12}$; $c_{15} = 1 - (c_{13}/c_{12})$; $c_{16} = c_5 \times c_{14}$; $c_{17} = c_4 \times c_{15}$; $c_{18} = c_{16} + c_{17}$; $c_{19} = c_{18}$.

Source: Bureau of Statistics, ILO.

## Table 3: Adjustment of activity rates for women derived from the Mali population census (December 1976)

| Age group | Total population | Econo. active population | Activity rates | Distribution model for under-enumerated women in agriculture | | Share of women in agricultural sector by region in % | | | | | | Activity rates to be add | Adjusted activity rates |
|---|---|---|---|---|---|---|---|---|---|---|---|---|---|
| | | | | Urban | Rural | Urban | Rural | | | | | | |
| $c_1$ | $c_2$ | $c_3$ | $c_4$ | $c_5$ | $c_6$ | $c_7$ | $c_8$ | $c_9$ | $c_{10}$ | $c_{11}$ | $c_{12}$ | $c_{13}$ |
| 10-14 | 321959 | 47528 | 14.76 | 3.74 | 26.68 | 16.80 | 83.20 | 22.83 | 73497 | 1.66 | 37.79 | 52.55 |
| 15-19 | 333508 | 62813 | 18.83 | 3.80 | 36.76 | 16.80 | 83.20 | 31.22 | 104125 | 1.66 | 51.68 | 70.51 |
| 20-24 | 265842 | 46428 | 17.46 | 4.20 | 40.36 | 16.80 | 83.20 | 34.28 | 91142 | 1.66 | 56.75 | 74.21 |
| 25-29 | 267018 | 48138 | 18.03 | 3.99 | 42.46 | 16.80 | 83.20 | 36.00 | 96123 | 1.66 | 59.58 | 77.61 |
| 30-34 | 225950 | 38859 | 17.20 | 7.70 | 44.02 | 16.80 | 83.20 | 37.92 | 85675 | 1.66 | 62.76 | 79.96 |
| 35-39 | 165949 | 29019 | 17.49 | 8.20 | 45.29 | 16.80 | 83.20 | 39.06 | 64817 | 1.66 | 64.65 | 82.14 |
| 40-44 | 147829 | 25618 | 17.33 | 10.06 | 46.33 | 16.80 | 83.20 | 40.24 | 59480 | 1.66 | 66.60 | 83.93 |
| 45-49 | 98453 | 17225 | 17.50 | 7.50 | 45.36 | 16.80 | 83.20 | 39.00 | 38396 | 1.66 | 64.55 | 82.05 |
| 50-54 | 103607 | 16486 | 15.91 | 10.29 | 43.47 | 16.80 | 83.20 | 37.90 | 39263 | 1.66 | 62.73 | 78.64 |
| 55-59 | 62917 | 9485 | 15.08 | 9.70 | 39.18 | 16.80 | 83.20 | 34.22 | 21532 | 1.66 | 56.65 | 71.72 |
| 60-64 | 81466 | 9897 | 12.15 | 6.22 | 33.48 | 16.80 | 83.20 | 28.90 | 23543 | 1.66 | 47.83 | 59.98 |
| 65+ | 124068 | 10366 | 8.36 | 2.77 | 17.39 | 16.80 | 83.20 | 14.93 | 18524 | 1.66 | 24.71 | 33.07 |

The men/women ratio in agriculture derived from the 1976 census is: 17.94% {(1578948/283107)*100}; the men/women new ratio estimated is: 93%;
The estimated number of under-enumerated women is: 1185315 {(15789948x0.93) - 283107}. $c_9 = (c_5 \times c_7 + c_6 \times c_8)/100$; $c_{10} = c_2 \times c_9 \times 100$ $c_{11} = 185315/716117$;
$c_{12} = c_9 \times c_{11}$; $c_{13} = c_4 + c_{12}$.

Source: Bureau of Statistics, ILO.

- In the other cases, the procedure generally followed was the interpolation and/or extrapolation of the benchmark data.

For the countries and territories whose estimates from the third edition were not retained, the adjustment of the benchmark data to the reference years was done in most cases by interpolation and/or extrapolation of the benchmark data. Next, to refine the trend of estimated rates, in many instances we applied to the interpolated and/or extrapolated rates the activity rate variations generally produced by the latest census (or latest survey) in relation to the interpolated or extrapolated rates of data from the same census (or same survey). Accordingly, for the 10-24 age groups of young people, estimated activity rates were often modified by accelerating or decelerating those trends, depending on the evaluation of the level of these rates and in accordance with the assumptions made for the country or territory in question. Table 4 depicts a typical example of the adjustment of benchmark data to the reference years.

### 2.1.6 Retrospective adjustment of estimates

Initially, adjustments were made only to benchmark data for the years 1974 to 1994 from countries and territories whose statistics largely or completely ignored the contribution of women to economic activity. To render the estimates and projections comparable for the entire 1950-2010 period and at the request of several institutions, in particular that made by the Permanent Subcommittee on Demographic Estimates and Projections of the Administrative Committee on Coordination at its meeting of 25-27 June 1996, it was decided to adjust benchmark data drawn from the third edition and retained in the fourth edition for the years 1950, 1960 and 1970.

The methods and the models used for these adjustments were similar to those used during the "Adjustment of benchmark data" stage (paragraph 2.1.4)

### 2.1.7 Treatment of countries and territories not individually selected in the fourth edition

These are the countries and territories for which separate estimates could not be established because their total population had not attained the minimum threshold of 200,000 inhabitants at mid-1990. Nevertheless, the data for these countries and territories were included in the regional totals. They were included as follows: average activity rates were computed for the region without these countries and territories, these average rates were then applied to the total population of these countries and territories; finally, the active populations of all the countries and territories comprising the region were totalled so as to arrive at the economically active population of the region.

For the World as a whole, and for each major region, area, developed region and less developed region, the procedure for estimating and projecting the economically active population was similar to that used to estimate economically regional active population.

The treatments applied during this stage were therefore effected after the treatment of countries and territories selected individually in the fourth edition.

### 2.1.8 Treatment of countries and territories for which benchmark data were unavailable

During this stage, the problems relating to the total or partial unavailability of benchmark data for producing the estimates were resolved. The countries and territories dealt with here were those not covered by the third edition and/or for which no post-1974 data were available. They were classified into three categories and the most satisfactory possible solution applied to each of those categories.

**Table 4: Evaluation of activity rates 1950-1990 for men in Peru**

| Age group | Activity rates (benchmark data) | | | | Estimated rates 1980 | Interpolation and extrapolation of activity rates 1950, 1960, 1970 et 1980 | | | Extrapolated rates 1990 after modification of the trends | Estimated activity rates 1990 |
| | 1950 | 1960 | 1970 | 1981 | | 1981 | 1985 | 1990 | | |
| c1 | c2 | c3 | c4 | c5 | c6 | c7 | c8 | c9 | c10 | c11 |
| 10-14 | 11.95 | 6.75 | 5.00 | 4.92 | 4.92 | 3.50 | 2.59 | 1.45 | 2.59 | 3.64 |
| 15-19 | 59.40 | 55.30 | 42.20 | 37.52 | 37.94 | 36.31 | 33.22 | 29.34 | 33.22 | 34.31 |
| 20-24 | 93.25 | 91.70 | 82.60 | 81.67 | 81.76 | 80.35 | 78.61 | 76.43 | 78.61 | 79.90 |
| 25-29 | 98.00 | 97.50 | 94.90 | 93.43 | 93.57 | 93.45 | 92.81 | 92.02 | 92.02 | 92.00 |
| 30-34 | 98.80 | 98.60 | 97.80 | 97.21 | 97.26 | 97.25 | 97.03 | 96.76 | 96.76 | 96.72 |
| 35-39 | 98.60 | 98.50 | 98.40 | 98.33 | 98.33 | 98.31 | 98.28 | 98.23 | 98.23 | 98.25 |
| 40-44 | 98.50 | 98.40 | 98.30 | 98.30 | 98.30 | 98.26 | 98.24 | 98.20 | 98.20 | 98.24 |
| 45-49 | 98.40 | 98.30 | 98.20 | 98.27 | 98.26 | 98.21 | 98.19 | 98.16 | 98.16 | 98.22 |
| 50-54 | 97.60 | 97.50 | 96.15 | 97.04 | 96.96 | 96.53 | 96.40 | 96.24 | 96.24 | 96.75 |
| 55-59 | 96.50 | 96.05 | 93.65 | 94.50 | 94.42 | 93.77 | 93.43 | 93.00 | 93.00 | 93.71 |
| 60-64 | 91.90 | 91.75 | 85.55 | 88.26 | 88.01 | 86.44 | 85.73 | 84.84 | 84.84 | 86.62 |
| 65+ | 75.00 | 69.30 | 62.65 | 63.46 | 63.39 | 60.95 | 59.29 | 57.21 | 57.21 | 59.57 |

$c2$, $c3$ et $c4$: activity rates derived from the third edition; $c5$: activity rates derived from the 1981 (july) census; $c6=c5(10/11)+c4(1/11)$; $c11=c10(c5/c7)$.

**Source:** Bureau of Statistics, ILO.

The first category includes the 22 republics of the former USSR *(Armenia - Azerbaijan - Belarus - Estonia - Georgia - Kazakhstan - Kirghizistan - Latvia - Lithuania - Moldova - Uzbekistan - Russia, Federation of - Tajikistan - Turkmenistan - Ukraine)*, Yugoslavia *(Bosnia-Herzegovina - Croatia - Macedonia, former Yugoslav Rep. of - Slovenia - Yugoslavia, Fed. Rep. of)* and Czechoslovakia *(Czech Republic - Slovakia)*. For these countries, the ILO Bureau of Statistics benefited from the collaboration of the national authorities, and especially of experts[10],[11] from these countries in collecting data on economically active population for each of them covering the 1950-1990 period.

The second category covers countries and territories for which no data were available. In the circumstances, the solution adopted was to use the estimates made for at least two neighbouring countries as the benchmark data for these countries. Such were the case of *Eritrea,* for instance, where the benchmark data selected for that country were the estimates for *Ethiopia* and *Somalia*.

The third category includes all the countries covered by the third edition and for which no data was available between 1974 and 1994 or some countries for which data did exist but preference was given to the data from the third edition. These countries include: *Saudi Arabia - Bhutan - Burundi - Cameroon - Gabon - Gambia - Guinea - Jordan - Kenya - Lebanon - Mauritania - Uganda - People's Dem. Rep. of Korea - Suriname - East Timor*. For these countries, the benchmark data used was either only those for the years 1950, 1960 and 1970 from the third edition, or in certain cases, 1980 and/or 1990 data were also added.

The treatments and procedures used for estimating sectoral distribution rates for agriculture, industry and services were identical to those applied to estimates of activity rates.

In the absence of data breakdowns for the industrial sector for the vast majority of countries, the procedure for estimating distribution rates for the manufacturing industries was as follows:

- If benchmark data were available for a year close to the reference years 1980 and 1990 or falling between them, the distribution rates for manufacturing industries were obtained by applying the industry/manufacturing ratio(s) drawn from the available benchmark data to the estimated distribution rates for industry.

- For the countries for which no data were available, the rule adopted was to apply the estimated industry/manufacturing ratio for a country in the same demographic and economic situation to the estimated distribution rates for industry of the country being studied.

---

[10] Popovic B. (1994), "New 1980 and 1990 estimates of activity rates by age and sectoral distribution for some countries of Eastern and Southern Europe, *Bulletin of Labour Statistics* - 1994-2, ILO, Geneva, 1994.

[11] Vorobiev A. (1994), "Estimation of the economically active population for the 15 countries of the former USSR for the years 1950, 1959, 1970, 1979 and 1989", *Bulletin of Labour Statistics* - 1994-2, ILO, Geneva, 1994.

## 2.2 Projection phase

### 2.2.1 Method

In the preceding editions, projections of activity rates of economically active population were made by applying a uniform model to all the countries and territories being considered. The method was based on the relationship between the variations of activity rates and the degree of economic development and its evolution measured by the proportion of males active in the agricultural sector. The results obtained by this method were satisfactory for a large majority of countries and territories; yet several difficulties arose when this method was applied to developed countries where the population active in agriculture was only a minute proportion. In addition to this, the largely inflexible nature of this mechanism allowed for only the partial capture of significant changes occurring on the labour market, such as the development of part-time work or the growing participation of women in economic activity.

In the fourth edition therefore, it was decided to choose another approach, the historical one. This approach is based on the projection of individual trends specific to each country or territory. The experience of several national statistical entities and the ILO Bureau of Statistics has shown that this method of projection produces results qualitatively as good as those obtained by more refined methods. Moreover it has the advantage of easy application and of quickly yielding a picture of new trends emerging for a given country.

The procedure was first of all to use extrapolation functions to project activity rate trends for each sex and age group, then, using graphs and based on the assumptions made by the country or territory concerned, to choose the appropriate function and finally to modify the trends by accelerating or decelerating them as necessary.

### 2.2.2 Assumptions

Four main assumptions were made in producing the projections:

Assumption 1: for the countries and territories in developed regions, continued reduction in activity rates for all age groups. The reduction would be more marked for the 15-19 and 55+ age groups.

Assumption 2: the pace of reduction in male activity rates in the developed regions should slow down.

Assumption 3: in the less developed regions and whatever the trend observed over the 1980-1990 decade in female activity rates for the 25-54 age groups, those rates would move closer to the male rates though not surpass them.

Assumption 4: the pace of increase in the levels of female activity rates, if such were the case, would be more appreciable for age groups with a larger gap between their rate levels and those of men.

### 2.2.3 Extrapolation functions

There are six extrapolation functions, which are listed in Table 5 on page 10.

## Conclusion

The ILO produces estimates and projections of the economically active population on average every eight years. This period proved too long for the purposes of incorporating structural changes or new demographic developments occurring in certain countries after the release of an edition. In theory, these changes and new developments will only be taken into account in preparing the following edition; which means that the quality and levels of already existing estimates and projections will have been affected in the meantime. Aware of this situation and wishing to furnish users with statistics on the economically active population with the highest degree of reliability and comparability, the Bureau of Statistics is now finalising a new integrated programme of statistics on the economically active population.

The main purpose of this integrated programme would be the continuous updating of estimates and projections of the economically active population: as new data became available or demographic or socio-economic developments occurred and affected the assumptions and the methods chosen, they would be automatically integrated into the procedures and treatments used to produce estimates and projections of the economically active population. This new programme would also be aimed at:

- Integrating estimates and projections made by national statistical offices;

- Greater co-operation between the ILO and FAO, as well as UNESCO, for better incorporating and harmonising the data produced by each of these institutions;

- Integrating the results of surveys conducted under the ILO International Programme for the Elimination of Child Labour (IPEC);

- Integrating the results of the ILO Programme on Comparable Estimates on Employment and Unemployment;

- Incorporating data on the economically active population by educational level, published in the latest editions of the ILO Yearbook of Labour Statistics;

- At the technical and IT level, by means of a graphic interface and new information technologies, integrating the various data bases, documents and methods for better managing, exploiting and publishing estimates and projections of the economically active population.

This integrated programme will take concrete form with the publication of the fifth edition of *ILO: Economically Active Population: Estimates and Projections*

**Table 5: Extrapolation functions of activity rate projections for 2000 and 2010**

| N° | Projection model | Function | Linear fonction |
|---|---|---|---|
| 1 | **Linear**<br><br>*The variation in the activity rate (y) is proportional to the variation in time (x):*<br>*(dy = adx)* | $y = ax + b$ | $y = ax + b$ |
| 2 | **Log-linear**<br><br>*The rate of variation in the activity rate (y) is proportional to the rate of variation in time (x):*<br>$\dfrac{dy}{y} = a\dfrac{dx}{x}$ | $y = Bx^a$ | $p = aq + b$<br><br>with $p = Lny$,<br>$q = Lnx$,<br>and $b = LnB$ |
| 3 | **Hyperbole**<br><br>*Possibility of introducing a threshold activity rate that cannot be surpassed* | $y = \dfrac{1}{ax + b}$ | $p = ax + b$<br><br>with $p = \dfrac{1}{y}$ |
| 4 | **Exponential**<br><br>*The rate of variation in the activity rate (y) is proportional to the variation in time (x):*<br>$\dfrac{dy}{y} = adx$ | $y = e^{ax + b}$ | $p = ax + b$<br><br>with $p = Lny$ |
| 5 | **Logarithmic**<br><br>*The variation in the activity rate (y) is proportional to the rate of variation in time (x):*<br>$dy = a\dfrac{dx}{x}$ | $y = aLnx + b$ | $y = az + b$<br><br>with $z = Lnx$ |
| 6 | **Logistic**<br><br>*Possibility of expressing the transition of activity rates from a growth phase to a self-limiting phase* | $y = y_{min} + \dfrac{y_{max} - y_{min}}{1 + e^{ax + b}}$ | $y = \alpha z + \beta$<br><br>with $z = \dfrac{1}{1 + e^{ax + b}}$,<br>$\alpha = (y_{max} - y_{min})$<br>et $\beta = y_{min}$ |

# Afghanistan

## 1. Source(s) of benchmark data

Code(s):     Title(s):

EPPA3       Economically active population: Estimates and Projections, 1950-2025, Third edition, ILO, Geneva, 1986.
ADNU84      Demographic Yearbook 1984 - Population census statistics II - Thirty-sixth Edition, United Nations, New York, 1986.
ASTER       Yearbook of Labour Statistics 1945-89 - Retrospective Edition on Population Censuses, ILO, Geneva, 1990.

## 2. Estimates of activity rates: 1950 - 1990

### 2.1 Benchmark data:

Table 1: Activity rates by sex and age group

| Age group | Year 1950 (1) | 1960 (1) | 1970 (1) | 1980 (1) | 1979 (2) |
|---|---|---|---|---|---|
| **Men** | | | | | |
| 10-14 | 38.00 | 36.00 | 34.00 | 32.00 | 30.54 |
| 15-19 | 75.85 | 72.20 | 68.55 | 64.90 | 66.00 |
| 20-24 | 92.80 | 91.35 | 89.95 | 88.50 | 88.99 |
| 25-29 | 97.65 | 97.00 | 96.35 | 95.70 | 95.70 |
| 30-34 | 98.05 | 97.55 | 97.00 | 96.50 | 96.84 |
| 35-39 | 98.55 | 98.20 | 97.85 | 97.50 | 97.19 |
| 40-44 | 98.05 | 97.55 | 96.95 | 96.40 | 96.87 |
| 45-49 | 97.55 | 97.05 | 96.60 | 96.10 | 96.48 |
| 50-54 | 96.65 | 95.85 | 95.10 | 94.30 | 94.78 |
| 55-59 | 93.90 | 93.05 | 92.25 | 91.40 | 92.44 |
| 60-64 | 90.50 | 89.35 | 88.25 | 87.10 | 87.84 |
| 65+ | 76.40 | 72.85 | 69.35 | 65.80 | 61.95 |
| **Women** | | | | | |
| 10-14 | 5.00 | 4.50 | 4.00 | 3.50 | 5.06 |
| 15-19 | 8.50 | 8.80 | 9.15 | 9.55 | 9.13 |
| 20-24 | 5.80 | 6.60 | 7.90 | 9.25 | 9.18 |
| 25-29 | 5.45 | 6.20 | 7.40 | 8.70 | 8.22 |
| 30-34 | 5.30 | 5.75 | 6.40 | 7.10 | 6.75 |
| 35-39 | 6.00 | 6.30 | 6.75 | 7.20 | 6.71 |
| 40-44 | 4.55 | 4.75 | 5.05 | 5.30 | 5.17 |
| 45-49 | 4.55 | 4.70 | 4.95 | 5.20 | 4.95 |
| 50-54 | 3.25 | 3.45 | 3.75 | 4.05 | 3.62 |
| 55-59 | 3.25 | 3.50 | 3.80 | 4.10 | 3.80 |
| 60-64 | 2.40 | 2.35 | 2.30 | 2.25 | 2.12 |
| 65+ | 1.80 | 1.75 | 1.65 | 1.60 | 1.18 |

Source(s): (1) EPPA3; (2) ADNU84.

### 2.2 Method(s): linear extrapolation

#### 2.2.1 Men:

- 1950-80, 1950-80 adjusted activity rates derived from the EPPA3;
adjustment of activity rates based on the results of the 1979 census;
- 1990, extrapolation of 1950-80 activity rates derived from the EPPA3
modification of the trends of the [25-59] age groups.

#### 2.2.2 Women:

- 1950-70, 1950-70 adjusted activity rates derived from the EPPA3;
the adjustment was made on the basis of the adjustment model for
activity rates of women working in agriculture as contributing family workers;
- 1980-90, extrapolation of 1950-70 activity rates derived from the EPPA3
and of activity rates derived from the 1979 census;
adjustment of activity rates based on the men/women ratio equal to 2/3
in agriculture and of results of the 1989 survey conducted in Bangladesh.

## 3. Estimates of distribution rates by activity sector: 1950 - 1990

### 3.1 Benchmark data:

Table 2: Distribution of economically active population by activity sector

| Year | Agriculture | Industry Total | Manufac. | Services |
|---|---|---|---|---|
| **Men** | | | | |
| 1950 (1) | 80.00 | 5.00 | .. | 15.00 |
| 1960 (1) | 76.00 | 5.50 | .. | 18.50 |
| 1970 (1) | 70.50 | 7.00 | .. | 22.50 |
| 1979 (2) | 66.61 | 7.83 | 4.61 | 25.56 |
| 1980 (1) | 65.50 | 8.50 | .. | 26.00 |
| **Women** | | | | |
| 1950 (1) | 5.00 | 83.50 | .. | 11.50 |
| 1960 (1) | 4.50 | 83.75 | .. | 11.75 |
| 1970 (1) | 4.00 | 84.00 | .. | 12.00 |
| 1979 (2) | 3.53 | 84.44 | 83.60 | 12.03 |

Source(s): (1) EPPA3; (2) ASTER.

### 3.2 Method(s): linears interpolation and extrapolation

#### 3.2.1 Men:

- 1950-80, 1950-80 distribution rates derived from the EPPA3;
- 1990, extrapolation of 1950-80 distribution rates derived from the EPPA3;
modification of the trends in all sectors;
- Application of manufacturing/industry ratio derived from the 1979 census.

#### 3.2.2 Women:

- 1950-70, 1950-70 distribution rates of agriculture sector derived
from the EPPA3;
adjustment of distribution rates on the basis of men/women ratio
equal to 2/3 in agriculture;
- 1950-90, interpolation and extrapolation of 1950-70 adjusted distribution
rates derived from the EPPA3;
modification of the trends in all sectors;
- Application of manufacturing/industry ratio derived from the 1979 census.

## 4. Projection of activity rates: 2000 - 2010

### 4.1 Model(s): linear and hyperbole

#### 4.1.1 Men:

- To the [10-49] age groups, application of function F1;
- To the [50+] age groups, application of function F3;
- Modification of the trends for the [10-64] age groups.

#### 4.1.2 Women:

- To all age groups, application of function F1;
- Modification of the trends for all age groups.

---

*Notes on adjustments of rates, see p. 3-8.*          *Notes on projection functions, see p. 10.*

# Albania

## 1. Source(s) of benchmark data

Code(s):     Title(s):

EPPA3       Economically active population: Estimates and Projections, 1950-2025, Third edition, ILO, Geneva, 1986.
BLT-94-2    Popovic B. (1994), "New 1980 and 1990 estimates of activity rates by age and sectoral distribution for some countries of Eastern and Southern Europe" in the Bulletin of Labour of Statistics - 1994-2, ILO, Geneva.

## 2. Estimates of activity rates: 1950 - 1990

### 2.1 Benchmark data:

Table 1: Activity rates by sex and age group

| Age group | Year | | | | |
|---|---|---|---|---|---|
| | 1950 (1) | 1960 (1) | 1970 (1) | 1980 (2) | 1990 (2) |
| **Men** | | | | | |
| 10-14 | 13.00 | 8.00 | 5.65 | 3.80 | 2.20 |
| 15-19 | 84.15 | 72.15 | 63.35 | 55.44 | 51.71 |
| 20-24 | 97.25 | 93.25 | 90.35 | 88.06 | 87.32 |
| 25-29 | 97.45 | 95.20 | 94.50 | 94.27 | 94.02 |
| 30-34 | 98.80 | 98.60 | 97.85 | 97.57 | 97.52 |
| 35-39 | 99.40 | 99.20 | 98.45 | 98.17 | 98.12 |
| 40-44 | 99.50 | 99.30 | 98.55 | 98.37 | 98.12 |
| 45-49 | 98.60 | 97.50 | 96.40 | 95.77 | 95.42 |
| 50-54 | 98.45 | 97.35 | 96.30 | 95.57 | 94.82 |
| 55-59 | 96.65 | 90.65 | 86.65 | 83.66 | 81.92 |
| 60-64 | 96.10 | 90.10 | 86.15 | 83.16 | 77.72 |
| 65+ | 75.50 | 60.50 | 51.90 | 43.43 | 36.21 |
| **Women** | | | | | |
| 10-14 | 12.25 | 7.15 | 4.00 | 3.37 | 1.60 |
| 15-19 | 62.15 | 46.95 | 40.25 | 31.06 | 28.73 |
| 20-24 | 75.15 | 67.75 | 65.40 | 68.16 | 70.63 |
| 25-29 | 77.45 | 69.75 | 68.40 | 74.91 | 78.01 |
| 30-34 | 79.00 | 71.15 | 69.80 | 75.70 | 78.81 |
| 35-39 | 81.90 | 73.75 | 72.35 | 77.49 | 80.60 |
| 40-44 | 83.85 | 75.50 | 74.10 | 77.99 | 80.70 |
| 45-49 | 75.75 | 68.60 | 69.40 | 71.54 | 73.62 |
| 50-54 | 74.35 | 67.30 | 68.15 | 67.47 | 68.53 |
| 55-59 | 54.30 | 45.25 | 44.85 | 29.96 | 26.93 |
| 60-64 | 52.85 | 44.05 | 43.65 | 19.65 | 16.56 |
| 65+ | 25.15 | 19.90 | 18.05 | 7.54 | 6.09 |

Source(s): (1) EPPA3; (2) BLT-94-2.

### 2.2 Method(s):   data from EPPA3 and BLT-94-2.

#### 2.2.1 Men:

- 1950-70, 1950-70 activity rates derived from the EPPA3;
- 1980-90, activity rates derived from the Bulletin of Labour Statistics 1994-2.

#### 2.2.2 Women:

Method, hypothesis and treatment identical to those used for men.

## 3. Estimates of distribution rates by activity sector: 1950 - 1990

### 3.1 Benchmark data:

Table 2: Distribution of economically active population by activity sector

| Year | Agriculture | Industry | | Services |
|---|---|---|---|---|
| | | Total | Manufac. | |
| **Men** | | | | |
| 1950 (1) | 70.00 | 18.00 | .. | 12.00 |
| 1960 (1) | 63.70 | 23.00 | .. | 13.30 |
| 1970 (1) | 57.30 | 28.10 | .. | 14.50 |
| 1980 (2) | 54.00 | 27.67 | ... | 18.33 |
| 1990 (2) | 50.81 | 25.73 | ... | 23.46 |
| **Women** | | | | |
| 1950 (1) | 85.50 | 8.00 | .. | 6.50 |
| 1960 (1) | 82.50 | 9.40 | .. | 8.00 |
| 1970 (1) | 79.30 | 10.90 | .. | 9.70 |
| 1980 (2) | 62.34 | 16.73 | ... | 20.93 |
| 1990 (2) | 60.19 | 19.35 | ... | 20.46 |

Source(s): (1) EPPA3; (2) BLT-94-2.

### 3.2 Method(s):   data from BLT-94-3

#### 3.2.1 Men:

- 1950-70, 1950-70 distribution rates derived from the EPPA3;
- 1980-90, 1980 and 1990 distribution rates derived from the Bulletin of Labour Statistics, 1994-2.

#### 3.2.2 Women:

Method, hypothesis and treatment identical to those used for men.

## 4. Projection of activity rates: 2000 - 2010

### 4.1 Model(s):   linear and hyperbole

#### 4.1.1 Men:

- To the [15-54] age groups, application of function F1;
- To the [50+] age groups, application of function F3;
- Modification of the trends for the [15-19] and [45-54] age groups.

#### 4.1.2 Women:

- To the [15-19] and [50+] age groups, application of function F3;
- To the [20-49] age groups, application of function F1;
- Modification of the trend for the [15-19] age group.

# Algeria

## 1. Source(s) of benchmark data

Code(s):     Title(s):

EPPA3     Economically active population: Estimates and Projections, 1950-2025, Third edition, ILO, Geneva, 1986.
R1977     Recensement général de la population et de l'habitat 1977, Office National des Statistiques, Alger, 1979.
R1987     Recensement général de la population et de l'habitat 1987 - Données synthétiques, Office National des Statistiques, Alger, 1989.

## 2. Estimates of activity rates: 1950 - 1990

### 2.1 Benchmark data:

Table 1: Activity rates by sex and age group

| Age group | Year 1950 (1) | 1960 (1) | 1970 (1) | 1987 (2) |
|---|---|---|---|---|
| **Men** | | | | |
| 10-14 | 28.85 | 20.00 | 13.85 | 0.48 |
| 15-19 | 74.95 | 60.90 | 46.85 | 39.20 |
| 20-24 | 94.75 | 91.75 | 88.80 | 84.44 |
| 25-29 | 97.85 | 96.80 | 95.80 | 95.67 |
| 30-34 | 97.55 | 97.05 | 96.55 | 97.39 |
| 35-39 | 97.10 | 96.80 | 96.45 | 97.70 |
| 40-44 | 96.85 | 96.25 | 95.60 | 96.65 |
| 45-49 | 96.45 | 95.80 | 95.15 | 95.15 |
| 50-54 | 95.15 | 94.40 | 93.65 | 91.99 |
| 55-59 | 93.95 | 90.85 | 87.75 | 86.83 |
| 60-64 | 92.50 | 85.90 | 79.30 | 59.07 |
| 65+ | 76.65 | 60.00 | 43.40 | 25.52 |
| **Women** | | | | |
| 10-14 | .. | .. | 1.25 | 0.08 |
| 15-19 | .. | .. | 4.05 | 3.88 |
| 20-24 | .. | .. | 5.70 | 12.94 |
| 25-29 | .. | .. | 4.95 | 12.92 |
| 30-34 | .. | .. | 4.35 | 8.92 |
| 35-39 | .. | .. | 3.90 | 7.85 |
| 40-44 | .. | .. | 4.45 | 6.78 |
| 45-49 | .. | .. | 5.10 | 6.79 |
| 50-54 | .. | .. | 5.50 | 6.56 |
| 55-59 | .. | .. | 5.30 | 5.12 |
| 60-64 | .. | .. | 3.75 | 3.54 |
| 65+ | .. | .. | 1.85 | 1.71 |

Source(s): (1) EPPA3; (2) R1987.

### 2.2 Method(s): linears interpolation and extrapolation

#### 2.2.1 Men:

- 1950-90, interpolation and extrapolation of 1950-70 activity rates derived from the EPPA3 and of adjusted activity rates derived from the 1987 census;
modification of the trends for all age groups for 1990.

#### 2.2.2 Women:

- 1950-70, 1950-70 adjusted activity rates derived from the EPPA3;
- 1980-90, interpolation and extrapolation of 1970 activity rates derived from the EPPA3 and of adjusted activity rates derived from the 1987 census;
modification of the trends of the [20+] age group for 1990;
the adjustment was made on the basis of the adjustment model for activity rates of women working in agriculture as contributing family workers.

## 3. Estimates of distribution rates by activity sector: 1950 - 1990

### 3.1 Benchmark data:

Table 2: Distribution of economically active population by activity sector

| Year | Agriculture | Industry Total | Manufac. | Services |
|---|---|---|---|---|
| **Men** | | | | |
| 1977 (1) | 32.88 | 33.14 | 11.84 | 33.98 |
| 1987 (2) | 19.54 | 35.68 | 12.76 | 44.78 |
| **Women** | | | | |
| 1977 (1) | 5.09 | 19.39 | 14.21 | 75.52 |
| 1987 (2) | 2.95 | 17.04 | 11.97 | 80.01 |

Source(s): (1) R1977; (2) R1987.

### 3.2 Method(s): linears interpolation and extrapolation

#### 3.2.1 Men:
- 1950-70, 1950-70 distribution rates derived from the EPPA3;
- 1980-90, interpolation and extrapolation of distribution rates derived from the 1977 and 1987 censuses;
modification of the trends in all sectors for 1990.

#### 3.2.2 Women:

- 1980-90, weighted averages of adjusted distribution rates derived from the 1977 and 1987 censuses;
the adjustment was made on the basis of the adjustment model for activity rates of women working in agriculture as contributing family workers;
- 1950-70, interpolation of the difference between adjusted and unadjusted distribution rates for 1980 and 1990; the results obtained have been added to the 1950-70 distribution rates.

## 4. Projection of activity rates: 2000 - 2010

### 4.1 Model(s): linear and hyperbole

#### 4.1.1 Men:
- To all age groups, application of function F1;
- Modification of the trend for the [20-24] age group.

#### 4.1.2 Women:

- To the [10-19] and [60+] age groups, application of function F1;
- To the [20-59] age groups, application of function F6;
- Modification of the trends for the [25-29] and [50-59] age groups.

---

*Notes on adjustments of rates, see p. 3-8.*      *Notes on projection functions, see p. 10.*

# Angola

## 1. Source(s) of benchmark data

Code(s):     Title(s):

EPPA3     Economically active population: Estimates and Projections, 1950-2025, Third edition, ILO, Geneva, 1986.
ADNU79     Demographic Yearbook 1979 - Population census statistics - Thirty-first Edition, United Nations, New York, 1980.

## 2. Estimates of activity rates: 1950 - 1990

### 2.1 Benchmark data:

Table 1: Activity rates by sex and age group

| Age group | Year 1950 (1) | 1960 (1) | 1970 (1) | 1970 (2) | 1980 (1) |
|---|---|---|---|---|---|
| **Men** | | | | | |
| 10-14 | 44.70 | 43.30 | 41.45 | 30.33 | 38.8 |
| 15-19 | 75.05 | 73.20 | 70.70 | 84.63 | 67.25 |
| 20-24 | 91.50 | 90.75 | 89.80 | 87.82 | 88.5 |
| 25-29 | 96.85 | 96.75 | 96.60 | 94.66 | 96.4 |
| 30-34 | 97.50 | 97.40 | 97.25 | 98.22 | 97 |
| 35-39 | 97.65 | 97.50 | 97.35 | 97.44 | 97.1 |
| 40-44 | 97.45 | 97.30 | 97.15 | 96.95 | 96.9 |
| 45-49 | 96.80 | 96.65 | 96.50 | 94.73 | 96.3 |
| 50-54 | 96.05 | 95.90 | 95.65 | 94.58 | 95.35 |
| 55-59 | 94.65 | 94.35 | 94.00 | 90.56 | 93.5 |
| 60-64 | 90.70 | 90.25 | 89.65 | 83.95 | 88.8 |
| 65+ | 75.70 | 74.90 | 73.80 | 73.41 | 72.3 |
| **Women** | | | | | |
| 10-14 | 33.80 | 32.70 | 31.30 | 28.7 | 29.35 |
| 15-19 | 55.60 | 54.00 | 51.90 | 72.05 | 48.95 |
| 20-24 | 58.85 | 57.85 | 56.55 | 76.25 | 54.7 |
| 25-29 | 63.10 | 61.95 | 60.45 | 79.45 | 58.35 |
| 30-34 | 67.05 | 65.80 | 64.20 | 78.03 | 61.95 |
| 35-39 | 68.70 | 67.55 | 66.05 | 81.74 | 63.95 |
| 40-44 | 71.15 | 70.00 | 68.50 | 84.2 | 66.4 |
| 45-49 | 70.55 | 69.40 | 67.85 | 84.8 | 65.7 |
| 50-54 | 68.15 | 66.80 | 65.05 | 82.23 | 62.5 |
| 55-59 | 65.10 | 63.65 | 61.80 | 78.47 | 59.2 |
| 60-64 | 57.05 | 55.25 | 52.90 | 69.15 | 49.55 |
| 65+ | 37.65 | 35.95 | 33.75 | 42.14 | 30.65 |

Source(s):  (1) EPPA3; (2) ADNU79.

### 2.2 Method(s): linears interpolation and extrapolation

#### 2.2.1 Men:

- 1950-90, interpolation and extrapolation of 1950-80 activity rates derived from the EPPA3;
adjustment of interpolated and extrapolated rates on the basis of variations in 1970 interpolated rates, in relation to the rates derived from the 1970 census;
modification of the trends of the [10-24] age groups for 1950 and 1960 and all age groups for 1980 and 1990.

#### 2.2.2 Women:

- 1950-90, interpolation and extrapolation of 1950-80 activity rates derived from the EPPA3;
adjustment of interpolated and extrapolated rates on the basis of variations in 1970 interpolated rates, in relation to activity rates derived from the 1970 cens
modification of the trends of the [15+] for 1950 and 1960 and for all age groups for 1980 and 1990.

## 3. Estimates of distribution rates by activity sector: 1950 - 1990

### 3.1 Benchmark data:

Table 2: Distribution of economically active population by activity sector

| Year | Agriculture | Industry Total | Manufac. | Services |
|---|---|---|---|---|
| **Men** | | | | |
| 1950 (1) | 74.00 | 11.35 | .. | 14.65 |
| 1960 (1) | 71.40 | 12.50 | .. | 16.10 |
| 1970 (1) | 68.00 | 13.50 | .. | 18.50 |
| 1970 (2) | 68.52 | 12.66 | 6.19 | 18.82 |
| 1980 (1) | 63.20 | 15.00 | .. | 21.80 |
| **Women** | | | | |
| 1950 (1) | 94.60 | 0.80 | .. | 4.60 |
| 1960 (1) | 93.30 | 1.00 | .. | 5.70 |
| 1970 (1) | 91.60 | 1.25 | .. | 7.15 |
| 1970 (2) | 88.93 | 1.10 | 1.01 | 9.97 |
| 1980 (1) | 89.20 | 1.60 | .. | 9.20 |

Source(s): (1) EPPA3; (2) ADNU79.

### 3.2 Method(s): linears interpolation and extrapolation

#### 3.2.1 Men:

- 1950-90, interpolation and extrapolation of 1950-80 distribution rates derived from the EPPA3;
adjustment of extrapolated rates on the basis of variations in 1970 interpolated rates, in relation to distribution rates derived from the 1970 census;
modification of the trends in all sectors for 1980 and 1990;
- Application of manufacturing/industry ratio derived from the 1970 census.

#### 3.2.2 Women:

Method, hypothesis and treatment identical to those used for men.

## 4. Projection of activity rates: 2000 - 2010

### 4.1 Model(s): hyperbola

#### 4.1.1 Men:

- To all age groups, application of function F3.

#### 4.1.2 Women:

- To all age groups, application of function F3;
- Modification of the trends for the [20-54] age groups.

# Argentina

## 1. Source(s) of benchmark data

Code(s):    Title(s):

EPPA3    Economically active population: Estimates and Projections, 1950-2025, Third edition, ILO, Geneva, 1986.
STAT     Database on Labour Statistics, LABORSTA - Bureau of Statistics, ILO, Geneva.

## 2. Estimates of activity rates: 1950 - 1990

### 2.1 Benchmark data:

Table 1: Activity rates by sex and age group

| Age group | Year 1970 (1) | 1990 (2) |
|---|---|---|
| **Men** | | |
| 10-14 | 11.50 | 8.84 |
| 15-19 | 62.20 | 57.54 |
| 20-24 | 87.00 | 86.26 |
| 25-29 | 95.80 | 95.66 |
| 30-34 | 97.50 | 97.77 |
| 35-39 | 98.10 | 97.98 |
| 40-44 | 97.40 | 97.14 |
| 45-49 | 95.40 | 95.04 |
| 50-54 | 91.40 | 90.60 |
| 55-59 | 80.40 | 79.39 |
| 60-64 | 57.20 | 56.07 |
| 65+ | 29.10 | 23.48 |
| **Women** | | |
| 10-14 | 6.20 | 4.41 |
| 15-19 | 31.60 | 24.46 |
| 20-24 | 43.60 | 51.21 |
| 25-29 | 36.00 | 45.09 |
| 30-34 | 31.70 | 40.65 |
| 35-39 | 29.20 | 36.90 |
| 40-44 | 27.20 | 34.89 |
| 45-49 | 25.20 | 31.70 |
| 50-54 | 22.10 | 26.85 |
| 55-59 | 16.40 | 18.41 |
| 60-64 | 10.50 | 9.90 |
| 65+ | 4.70 | 2.89 |

Source(s): (1) EPPA3; (2) STAT.

### 2.2 Method(s): arithmetic average

#### 2.2.1 Men:

- 1950-70, 1950-70 activity rates derived from the EPPA3;
- 1980, average of 1970 activity rates derived from the EPPA3
and of activity rates derived from the 1990 official estimates;
- 1990, activity rates derived from the 1990 official estimates.

#### 2.2.2 Women:

Method, hypothesis and treatment identical to those used for men.

## 3. Estimates of distribution rates by activity sector: 1950 - 1990

### 3.1 Benchmark data:

Table 2: Distribution of economically active population by activity sector

| Year | Agriculture | Industry Total | Manufac. | Services |
|---|---|---|---|---|
| **Men** | | | | |
| 1950 | 23.86 | 38.43 | 28.11 | 37.72 |
| 1970 | 20.24 | 35.67 | 22.11 | 44.09 |
| 1980 | 16.63 | 39.62 | 23.04 | 43.75 |
| **Women** | | | | |
| 1950 | 5.16 | 27.02 | 26.37 | 67.81 |
| 1970 | 4.22 | 20.81 | 19.86 | 74.97 |
| 1980 | 3.06 | 18.22 | 16.91 | 78.72 |

Source(s): STAT.

### 3.2 Method(s): linear extrapolation

#### 3.2.1 Men:

- 1950-70, 1950-70 distribution rates derived from the EPPA3;
  1980-90, extrapolation of distribution rates derived from
the 1960, 1970 and 1980 censuses;
modification of the trends in all sectors;
application of manufacturing/industry ratio derived from the 1980 census.

#### 3.2.2 Women:

Method, hypothesis and treatment identical to those used for men.

## 4. Projection of activity rates: 2000 - 2010

### 4.1 Model(s): linear and hyperbole

#### 4.1.1 Men:

- To the [10-44] age groups, application of function F1;
- To the [45+] age groups, application of function F3;
- Modification of the trend for the [10-14] age group.

#### 4.1.2 Women:

- To the [10-14] age group, application of function F1;
- To the [15+] age groups, application of function F3;
- Modification of the trends for the [10-14], [20-24] and [60-64] age groups.

---

*Notes on adjustments of rates, see p. 3-8.*    *Notes on projection functions, see p. 10.*

# Armenia

## 1. Source(s) of benchmark data

Code(s):     Title(s):

BLT-94-2     Vorobiev A. (1994), "Estimates of the economically active population for the fifteen countries of the former USSR
for the years 1950, 1959, 1970, 1979 and 1989", in the Bulletin of Labour of Statistics - 1994-2, ILO, Geneva.

## 2. Estimates of activity rates: 1950 - 1990

### 2.1 Benchmark data:

Table 1: Activity rates by sex and age group

| Age group | Year 1950 | 1959 | 1970 | 1979 | 1989 |
|---|---|---|---|---|---|
| **Men** | | | | | |
| 10-14 | 0.00 | 0.00 | 0.00 | 0.00 | 0.00 |
| 15-19 | 42.35 | 50.75 | 30.53 | 33.33 | 25.69 |
| 20-24 | 79.01 | 80.68 | 70.73 | 77.64 | 60.87 |
| 25-29 | 90.91 | 93.83 | 98.33 | 95.69 | 77.64 |
| 30-34 | 91.67 | 94.81 | 98.02 | 98.63 | 80.42 |
| 35-39 | 93.75 | 96.77 | 97.59 | 98.63 | 81.90 |
| 40-44 | 93.55 | 95.65 | 96.43 | 97.94 | 79.69 |
| 45-49 | 91.30 | 93.33 | 97.44 | 96.51 | 78.79 |
| 50-54 | 90.48 | 89.66 | 90.48 | 94.74 | 77.38 |
| 55-59 | 92.86 | 86.36 | 86.21 | 86.21 | 70.67 |
| 60-64 | 76.92 | 83.33 | 60.71 | 50.00 | 45.16 |
| 65+ | 36.67 | 33.33 | 16.07 | 16.90 | 19.05 |
| **Women** | | | | | |
| 10-14 | 0.00 | 0.00 | 0.00 | 0.00 | 0.00 |
| 15-19 | 41.57 | 44.12 | 28.00 | 32.98 | 17.91 |
| 20-24 | 58.82 | 60.00 | 63.22 | 73.10 | 50.35 |
| 25-29 | 61.36 | 65.12 | 80.60 | 86.18 | 62.50 |
| 30-34 | 55.56 | 59.26 | 82.24 | 88.31 | 68.46 |
| 35-39 | 58.50 | 59.52 | 83.13 | 91.25 | 72.32 |
| 40-44 | 57.89 | 58.82 | 83.53 | 92.08 | 72.06 |
| 45-49 | 56.76 | 55.00 | 81.25 | 91.76 | 70.42 |
| 50-54 | 40.00 | 41.67 | 64.52 | 79.52 | 62.22 |
| 55-59 | 30.00 | 28.57 | 28.89 | 41.86 | 36.25 |
| 60-64 | 26.32 | 25.00 | 12.20 | 16.22 | 21.62 |
| 65+ | 2.33 | 3.45 | 3.66 | 3.64 | 6.48 |

Source(s): BLT-94-2-2

### 2.2 Method(s): weighted average

#### 2.2.1 Men:

- 1950-90, weighted average of 1950, 1959, 1970 and 1989 activity rates
derived from the Bulletin of Labour Statistics 1994-2.

#### 2.2.2 Women:

Method, hypothesis and treatment identical to those used for men.

## 3. Estimates of distribution rates by activity sector: 1950 - 1990

### 3.1 Benchmark data:

Table 2: Distribution of economically active population by activity sector

| Year | Agriculture | Industry Total | Manufac. | Services |
|---|---|---|---|---|
| **Men** | | | | |
| 1950 | 52.63 | 24.91 | 16.84 | 22.46 |
| 1959 | 39.71 | 29.90 | 17.65 | 30.39 |
| 1970 | 25.24 | 43.26 | 26.57 | 31.50 |
| 1979 | 20.92 | 47.77 | 25.78 | 31.31 |
| 1989 | 23.41 | 47.11 | 30.20 | 29.48 |
| **Women** | | | | |
| 1950 | 37.03 | 9.46 | 7.30 | 53.51 |
| 1959 | 59.55 | 21.35 | 18.35 | 19.10 |
| 1970 | 30.02 | 30.91 | 26.71 | 39.07 |
| 1979 | 22.64 | 37.68 | 25.79 | 39.68 |
| 1989 | 12.26 | 38.51 | 34.20 | 49.22 |

Source(s): BLT-94-2.

### 3.2 Method(s): weighted average

#### 3.2.1 Men:

- 1950-90, weighted averages of 1950, 1959, 1970, 1979 and 1989
distribution rates derived from the Bulletin of Labour Statistics, 1994-2.

#### 3.2.2 Women:

Method, hypothesis and treatment identical to those used for men.

## 4. Projection of activity rates: 2000 - 2010

### 4.1 Model(s): hyperbole and logistic

#### 4.1.1 Men:

- To the [15+] age groups, application of function F3;
- Modification of the trends for the [25-54] age groups.

#### 4.1.2 Women:

- To the [15-24] age groups, application of function F3;
- To the [25-59] age groups, application of function F6;
- To the [60+] age groups, application of function F3;
- Modification of the trends for the [20-59] age groups.

---

*Notes on adjustments of rates, see p. 3-8.*          *Notes on projection functions, see p. 10.*

# Australia

## 1. Source(s) of benchmark data

Code(s):     Title(s):

EPPA3     Yearbook of Labour Statistics 1945-89 - Retrospective Edition on Population Censuses, ILO, Geneva, 1990.
STAT      Database on Labour Statistics, LABORSTA - Bureau of Statistics, ILO, Geneva.

## 2. Estimates of activity rates: 1950 - 1990

### 2.1 Benchmark data:

Table 1: Activity rates by sex and age group

| Age group | Year | | | | | |
|---|---|---|---|---|---|---|
|  | 1979 | 1980 | 1981 | 1989 | 1990 | 1991 |
| **Men** | | | | | | |
| 10-14 | 0.00 | 0.00 | 0.00 | 0.00 | 0.00 | 0.00 |
| 15-19 | 64.10 | 65.30 | 66.00 | 61.90 | 61.40 | 57.10 |
| 20-24 | 90.90 | 91.50 | 91.60 | 89.90 | 89.80 | 88.40 |
| 25-34 | 96.20 | 95.90 | 95.50 | 94.60 | 94.40 | 94.50 |
| 35-44 | 95.90 | 95.60 | 95.50 | 93.80 | 94.40 | 94.10 |
| 45-54 | 91.60 | 91.50 | 90.90 | 89.10 | 89.90 | 89.60 |
| 55-59 | 82.10 | 82.60 | 81.20 | 75.20 | 75.00 | 73.70 |
| 60-64 | 54.40 | 51.50 | 50.50 | 49.80 | 50.60 | 49.90 |
| 65+ | 11.60 | 11.20 | 10.70 | 9.10 | 9.20 | 8.90 |
| **Women** | | | | | | |
| 10-14 | .. | 0.00 | .. | .. | 0.00 | .. |
| 15-19 | .. | 61.50 | .. | .. | 59.30 | .. |
| 20-24 | .. | 71.00 | .. | .. | 78.60 | .. |
| 25-34 | .. | 52.40 | .. | .. | 65.70 | .. |
| 35-44 | .. | 58.20 | .. | .. | 72.00 | .. |
| 45-54 | .. | 47.70 | .. | .. | 61.00 | .. |
| 55-59 | .. | 28.90 | .. | .. | 33.90 | .. |
| 60-64 | .. | 13.40 | .. | .. | 18.00 | .. |
| 65+ | .. | 2.80 | .. | .. | 2.40 | .. |

Source(s): STAT.

### 2.2 Method(s):  arithmetic average

**2.2.1 Men:**

- 1950-70, 1950-70 activity rates derived from the EPPA3;
adjustment of activity rates of the [15-19] age group for 1960 and 1970;
- 1980, average of adjusted activity rates derived from
the 1979, 1980 and 1981 surveys;
- 1990, average of adjusted activity rates derived from
the 1989, 1990 and 1991 surveys.

**2.2.2 Women:**

- 1950-70, 1950-70 activity rates derived from the EPPA3;
adjustment of activity rates of the [15-19] age group;
- 1980 and 1990, average of adjusted activity rates derived from
the 1980 and 1990 surveys.

## 3. Estimates of distribution rates by activity sector: 1950 - 1990

### 3.1 Benchmark data:

Table 2: Distribution of economically active population by activity sector

| Year | Agriculture | Industry | | Services |
|---|---|---|---|---|
|  |  | Total | Manufac. |  |
| **Men** | | | | |
| 1989 (1) | 7.00 | 35.40 | 20.48 | 57.61 |
| 1990 (1) | 6.39 | 35.65 | 19.72 | 57.95 |
| 1991 (1) | 6.68 | 34.78 | 19.57 | 58.55 |
| **Women** | | | | |
| 1970 (2) | 4.55 | 22.45 | .. | 73.00 |
| 1981 (1) | 3.83 | 17.06 | 14.77 | 79.11 |
| 1989 (1) | 4.16 | 13.77 | 10.87 | 82.07 |
| 1990 (1) | 3.63 | 14.00 | 10.95 | 82.36 |
| 1991 (1) | 3.76 | 13.10 | 10.11 | 83.14 |

Source(s): (1) STAT; (2) EPPA3.

### 3.2 Method(s):  arithmetic average
weighted average

**3.2.1 Men:**

- 1950-80, 1950-80 distribution rates derived from the EPPA3;
- 1990, averages of distribution rates derived from
the 1989, 1990 and 1991 surveys.

**3.2.2 Women:**

- 1950-70, 1950-70 distribution rates derived from the EPPA3;
- 1980, weighted averages of 1970 distribution rates derived from
des EPPA3 and of distribution rates derived from the 1981 census;
- 1990, averages of distribution rates derived from the 1989, 1990
and 1991 surveys.

## 4. Projection of activity rates: 2000 - 2010

### 4.1 Model(s):  linear, hyperbole and logistic

**4.1.1 Men:**

- To the [15-24] age groups, application of function F1;
- To the [25+] age groups, application of function F3;
- Modification of the trends for the [25-59] age groups.

**4.1.2 Women:**

- To the [15-24] age groups, application of function F1;
- To the [25-59] age groups, application of function F6;
- To the [60+] age groups, application of function F3;
- Modification of the trends for the [15-59] age groups.

*Notes on adjustments of rates, see p. 3-8.*

*Notes on projection functions, see p. 10.*

# Austria

## 1. Source(s) of benchmark data

Code(s):      Title(s):
EPPA3       Yearbook of Labour Statistics 1945-89 - Retrospective Edition on Population Censuses, ILO, Geneva, 1990.
STAT         Database on Labour Statistics, LABORSTA - Bureau of Statistics, ILO, Geneva.

## 2. Estimates of activity rates: 1950 - 1990

### 2.1 Benchmark data:

Table 1: Activity rates by sex and age group

| Age group | Year 1989 | 1990 | 1991 |
|---|---|---|---|
| **Men** | | | |
| 10-14 | 0.00 | 0.00 | 0.00 |
| 15-19 | 53.39 | 52.81 | 54.46 |
| 20-24 | 76.60 | 77.11 | 76.07 |
| 25-29 | 89.97 | 88.60 | 88.71 |
| 30-34 | 96.75 | 96.98 | 96.74 |
| 35-39 | 97.76 | 98.02 | 97.70 |
| 40-44 | 96.32 | 96.46 | 97.23 |
| 45-49 | 96.04 | 96.11 | 95.05 |
| 50-54 | 89.41 | 91.03 | 91.31 |
| 55-59 | 64.52 | 62.96 | 63.45 |
| 60-64 | 14.48 | 14.13 | 13.84 |
| 65+ | 2.05 | 3.32 | 1.95 |
| **Women** | | | |
| 10-14 | 0.00 | 0.00 | 0.00 |
| 15-19 | 46.49 | 44.84 | 44.53 |
| 20-24 | 72.82 | 72.38 | 73.04 |
| 25-29 | 67.28 | 69.19 | 70.12 |
| 30-34 | 63.88 | 64.09 | 66.33 |
| 35-39 | 63.60 | 66.54 | 67.24 |
| 40-44 | 63.95 | 66.93 | 66.77 |
| 45-49 | 60.28 | 60.62 | 62.07 |
| 50-54 | 51.35 | 53.74 | 54.59 |
| 55-59 | 25.57 | 26.00 | 23.90 |
| 60-64 | 4.60 | 5.00 | 5.32 |
| 65+ | 1.40 | 1.05 | 0.74 |

Source(s): STAT.

### 2.2 Method(s): arithmetic average

#### 2.2.1 Men:

- 1950-80, 1950-80 activity rates derived from the EPPA3;
- 1990, averages of adjusted activity rates derived from the 1989, 1990 and 1991 surveys.

#### 2.2.2 Women:

Method, hypothesis and treatment identical to those used for men.

## 3. Estimates of distribution rates by activity sector: 1950 - 1990

### 3.1 Benchmark data:

Table 2: Distribution of economically active population by activity sector

| Year | Agriculture | Industry Total | Manufac. | Services |
|---|---|---|---|---|
| **Men** | | | | |
| 1979 | 8.71 | 50.68 | 34.52 | 40.61 |
| 1980 | 8.78 | 50.98 | 34.37 | 40.24 |
| 1981 | 7.49 | 50.79 | 34.88 | 41.72 |
| 1989 | 7.28 | 49.24 | 33.77 | 43.48 |
| 1990 | 7.00 | 49.03 | 33.51 | 43.97 |
| 1991 | 6.61 | 49.19 | 33.64 | 44.20 |
| **Women** | | | | |
| 1979 | 13.16 | 24.56 | 22.21 | 62.28 |
| 1980 | 13.50 | 25.06 | 22.63 | 61.44 |
| 1981 | 10.03 | 26.53 | 23.90 | 63.44 |
| 1989 | 9.13 | 21.05 | 19.02 | 69.82 |
| 1990 | 9.08 | 20.40 | 18.30 | 70.52 |
| 1991 | 8.59 | 20.29 | 18.01 | 71.12 |

Source(s): STAT.

### 3.2 Method(s): arithmetic average

#### 3.2.1 Men:

- 1950-70, 1950-70 distribution rates derived from the EPPA3;
- 1980, averages of distribution rates derived from the 1979 and 1980 surveys and of distribution rates derived from the 1981 census;
- 1990, averages of distribution rates derived from the 1989, 1990 and 1991 surveys.

#### 3.2.2 Women:

Method, hypothesis and treatment identical to those used for men.

## 4. Projection of activity rates: 2000 - 2010

### 4.1 Model(s): linear and hyperbole

#### 4.1.1 Men:

- To the [15-19] and [35-49] age groups, application of function F1;
- To the [20-34] and [50+] age groups, application of function F3;
- Modification of the trends for the [25-29] and [35-49] age groups.

#### 4.1.2 Women:

- To the [15-49] age groups, application of function F1;
- To the [50+] age groups, application of function F3;
- Modification of the trends for the [15-24] age groups.

*Notes on adjustments of rates, see p. 3-8.*        *Notes on projection functions, see p. 10.*

# Azerbaijan

## 1. Source(s) of benchmark data

Code(s): Title(s):

BLT-94-2 Vorobiev A. (1994), "Estimates of the economically active population for the fifteen countries of the former USSR for the years 1950, 1959, 1970, 1979 and 1989", in the Bulletin of Labour of Statistics - 1994-2, ILO, Geneva.

## 2. Estimates of activity rates: 1950 - 1990

### 2.1 Benchmark data:

Table 1: Activity rates by sex and age group

| Age group | 1950 | 1959 | 1970 | 1979 | 1989 |
|---|---|---|---|---|---|
| **Men** | | | | | |
| 10-14 | 0.00 | 0.00 | 0.00 | 0.00 | 0.00 |
| 15-19 | 48.91 | 47.26 | 31.67 | 35.48 | 29.59 |
| 20-24 | 82.89 | 84.21 | 80.56 | 80.39 | 75.76 |
| 25-29 | 92.96 | 92.98 | 90.00 | 95.92 | 92.86 |
| 30-34 | 94.74 | 95.04 | 96.89 | 98.33 | 95.59 |
| 35-39 | 94.44 | 96.97 | 97.04 | 98.44 | 95.77 |
| 40-44 | 93.10 | 94.23 | 95.89 | 97.34 | 95.54 |
| 45-49 | 93.33 | 94.03 | 95.71 | 96.79 | 94.31 |
| 50-54 | 91.30 | 90.91 | 90.91 | 93.33 | 90.00 |
| 55-59 | 85.29 | 85.71 | 84.48 | 84.62 | 83.21 |
| 60-64 | 77.78 | 80.49 | 50.00 | 52.50 | 47.42 |
| 65+ | 47.54 | 50.00 | 22.12 | 21.31 | 20.91 |
| **Women** | | | | | |
| 10-14 | 0.00 | 0.00 | 0.00 | 0.00 | 0.00 |
| 15-19 | 45.36 | 45.52 | 30.67 | 37.24 | 28.27 |
| 20-24 | 62.09 | 61.35 | 60.14 | 77.71 | 60.50 |
| 25-29 | 62.24 | 66.86 | 75.41 | 84.95 | 64.96 |
| 30-34 | 62.65 | 61.64 | 69.23 | 86.72 | 69.55 |
| 35-39 | 61.96 | 64.52 | 78.66 | 89.21 | 74.50 |
| 40-44 | 62.96 | 62.82 | 75.00 | 89.80 | 76.67 |
| 45-49 | 61.00 | 63.22 | 74.19 | 88.24 | 75.19 |
| 50-54 | 51.43 | 51.95 | 63.77 | 75.94 | 56.99 |
| 55-59 | 40.35 | 39.24 | 28.13 | 40.70 | 30.87 |
| 60-64 | 32.65 | 40.68 | 13.41 | 18.06 | 19.17 |
| 65+ | 7.53 | 9.38 | 3.41 | 4.50 | 6.70 |

Source(s): BLT-94-2-2

### 2.2 Method(s): weighted average

#### 2.2.1 Men:

- 1950-90, weighted average of 1950, 1959, 1970 and 1989 activity rates derived from the Bulletin of Labour Statistics 1994-2.

#### 2.2.2 Women:

Method, hypothesis and treatment identical to those used for men.

## 3. Estimates of distribution rates by activity sector: 1950 - 1990

### 3.1 Benchmark data:

Table 2: Distribution of economically active population by activity sector

| Year | Agriculture | Industry Total | Manufac. | Services |
|---|---|---|---|---|
| **Men** | | | | |
| 1950 | 48.31 | 25.93 | 11.27 | 25.76 |
| 1959 | 42.14 | 25.38 | 11.18 | 32.48 |
| 1970 | 29.01 | 34.79 | 16.84 | 36.21 |
| 1979 | 27.85 | 36.37 | 15.65 | 35.78 |
| 1989 | 27.37 | 35.06 | 14.11 | 37.57 |
| **Women** | | | | |
| 1950 | 59.47 | 17.07 | 12.76 | 23.45 |
| 1959 | 59.19 | 14.20 | 11.06 | 26.61 |
| 1970 | 41.50 | 20.05 | 15.23 | 38.45 |
| 1979 | 43.41 | 19.89 | 12.31 | 36.70 |
| 1989 | 36.85 | 20.60 | 13.31 | 42.55 |

Source(s): BLT-94-2.

### 3.2 Method(s): weighted average

#### 3.2.1 Men:

- 1950-90, weighted averages of 1950, 1959, 1970, 1979 and 1989 distribution rates derived from the Bulletin of Labour Statistics, 1994-2.

#### 3.2.2 Women:

Method, hypothesis and treatment identical to those used for men.

## 4. Projection of activity rates: 2000 - 2010

### 4.1 Model(s): linear, hyperbole and logistic

#### 4.1.1 Men:

- To the [15-24] and [55+] age groups, application of function F3;
- To the [25-54] age groups, application of function F1;
- Modification of the trends for the [20-54] age groups.

#### 4.1.2 Women:

- To the [15-24] and [50+] age groups, application of function F3;
- To the [25-49] age groups, application of function F6;
- Modification of the trends for the [20-54] age groups.

*Notes on adjustments of rates, see p. 3-8.*

*Notes on projection functions, see p. 10.*

# Bahamas

## 1. Source(s) of benchmark data

Code(s):    Title(s):

STAT        Database on Labour Statistics, LABORSTA - Bureau of Statistics, ILO, Geneva.

## 2. Estimates of activity rates: 1950 - 1990

### 2.1 Benchmark data:

Table 1: Activity rates by sex and age group

| Age group | Año 1953 | 1963 | 1970 | 1980 | 1990 |
|---|---|---|---|---|---|
| **Men** | | | | | |
| 10-14 | 1.59 | 3.93 | 2.34 | 0.00 | 0.00 |
| 15-19 | 60.26 | 74.95 | 63.82 | 46.79 | 41.29 |
| 20-24 | 92.04 | 96.42 | 93.10 | 87.23 | 85.68 |
| 25-29 | 95.57 | 97.79 | 96.11 | 92.49 | 90.67 |
| 30-34 | 96.75 | 97.27 | 96.88 | 95.42 | 91.76 |
| 35-39 | 96.92 | 97.41 | 97.04 | 95.08 | 94.11 |
| 40-44 | 96.72 | 96.94 | 96.77 | 94.49 | 94.62 |
| 45-49 | 95.97 | 96.18 | 96.02 | 92.45 | 94.35 |
| 50-54 | 94.69 | 94.35 | 94.60 | 88.79 | 92.07 |
| 55-59 | 90.81 | 94.65 | 91.74 | 83.72 | 88.35 |
| 60-64 | 81.44 | 85.90 | 82.52 | 72.56 | 73.89 |
| 65+ | 50.77 | 63.20 | 53.78 | 39.93 | 36.41 |
| **Women** | | | | | |
| 10-14 | .. | 1.75 | 2.13 | .. | 0.00 |
| 15-19 | .. | 45.04 | 44.55 | 34.54 | 31.26 |
| 20-24 | .. | 61.33 | 71.90 | 72.38 | 75.28 |
| 25-29 | .. | 58.71 | 65.07 | 75.20 | 81.25 |
| 30-34 | .. | 58.33 | 63.39 | 72.19 | 80.69 |
| 35-39 | .. | 58.31 | 62.23 | 72.29 | 80.40 |
| 40-44 | .. | 56.29 | 60.60 | 68.17 | 79.03 |
| 45-49 | .. | 55.54 | 58.38 | 63.53 | 75.94 |
| 50-54 | .. | 54.56 | 56.53 | 59.17 | 68.24 |
| 55-59 | .. | 43.68 | 53.10 | 49.22 | 64.30 |
| 60-64 | .. | 41.05 | 43.73 | 38.00 | 47.48 |
| 65+ | .. | 24.92 | 28.35 | 16.14 | 15.28 |

Source(s): STAT.

### 2.2 Method(s): linears interpolation and extrapolation
weighted average

**2.2.1 Men:**

- 1950 and 1970-90, interpolation and extrapolation of activity rates derived from 1953 and 1963 censuses and of adjusted activity rates derived from the 1980 and 1990 censuses.

**2.2.2 Women:**

- 1950-60, interpolation and extrapolation of adjusted activity rates derived from the 1953 and 1963 censuses;
modification of the trends for all age groups;
- 1970-90, weighted average of adjusted activity rates derived from the 1970 and 1980 censuses and of activity rates derived from the 1990 census.

## 3. Estimates of distribution rates by activity sector: 1950 - 1990

### 3.1 Benchmark data:

Table 2: Distribution of economically active population by activity sector

| Year | Agriculture | Industry Total | Manufac. | Services |
|---|---|---|---|---|
| **Men** | | | | |
| 1963 | 18.75 | 34.69 | 8.60 | 46.56 |
| 1970 | 8.57 | 30.84 | 6.40 | 60.59 |
| 1980 | 7.96 | 24.18 | 6.57 | 67.86 |
| 1990 | 8.36 | 24.18 | 4.31 | 67.46 |
| **Women** | | | | |
| 1963 | 11.95 | 7.46 | 6.91 | 80.60 |
| 1970 | 6.23 | 7.41 | 5.68 | 86.36 |
| 1980 | 2.91 | 7.12 | 5.89 | 89.98 |
| 1990 | 1.60 | 5.25 | 3.83 | 93.15 |

Source(s): STAT.

### 3.2 Method(s): linears interpolation and extrapolation

**3.2.1 Men:**

- 1950-90, interpolation and extrapolation of distribution rates derived from the 1963, 1970, 1980 and 1990 censuses;
modification of the trends in all sectors for 1950.

**3.2.2 Women:**

Method, hypothesis and treatment identical to those used for men.

## 4. Projection of activity rates: 2000 - 2010

### 4.1 Model(s): linear, hyperbole and logistic

**4.1.1 Men:**

- To the [15-24] age groups, application of function F1;
- To the [25+] age groups, application of function F3;
- Modification of the trends for the [50-64] age groups.

**4.1.2 Women:**

- To the [15-19] age group, application of function F1;
- To the [20-64] age groups, application of function F6;
- To the [65+] age group, application of function F3;
- Modification of the trends for the [55-64] age groups.

*Notes on adjustments of rates, see p. 3-8.*

*Notes on projection functions, see p. 10.*

# Bahrain

## 1. Source(s) of benchmark data

Code(s):    Title(s):

EPPA3      Economically active population: Estimates and Projections, 1950-2025, Third edition, ILO, Geneva, 1986.
ASTER      Yearbook of Labour Statistics 1945-89 - Retrospective Edition on Population Censuses, ILO, Geneva, 1990.

## 2. Estimates of activity rates: 1950 - 1990

### 2.1 Benchmark data:

Table 1: Activity rates by sex and age group

| Age group | Year 1971 | 1981 | 1991 |
|---|---|---|---|
| **Men** | | | |
| 10-14 | 1.87 | 0.00 | 0.00 |
| 15-19 | 42.80 | 30.01 | 24.73 |
| 20-24 | 88.38 | 89.20 | 87.91 |
| 25-29 | 97.66 | 98.10 | 98.01 |
| 30-34 | 98.68 | 99.13 | 99.22 |
| 35-39 | 98.40 | 99.09 | 99.35 |
| 40-44 | 97.29 | 98.80 | 99.35 |
| 45-49 | 96.32 | 97.88 | 98.91 |
| 50-54 | 91.89 | 94.08 | 95.94 |
| 55-59 | 84.48 | 88.17 | 88.60 |
| 60-64 | 72.00 | 69.26 | 64.72 |
| 65+ | 49.52 | 45.46 | 36.05 |
| **Women** | | | |
| 10-14 | 0.04 | 0.00 | 0.00 |
| 15-19 | 3.05 | 8.41 | 8.28 |
| 20-24 | 11.59 | 31.46 | 37.00 |
| 25-29 | 10.19 | 31.09 | 42.03 |
| 30-34 | 7.44 | 24.61 | 41.73 |
| 35-39 | 5.83 | 17.28 | 37.98 |
| 40-44 | 6.15 | 12.81 | 31.87 |
| 45-49 | 4.59 | 9.58 | 18.10 |
| 50-54 | 3.92 | 6.02 | 9.04 |
| 55-59 | 3.67 | 3.63 | 5.10 |
| 60-64 | 2.80 | 1.69 | 1.68 |
| 65+ | 1.69 | 0.78 | 0.72 |

Source(s): ASTER

### 2.2 Method(s): linear interpolation

#### 2.2.1 Men:

- 1950-70, 1950-70 activity rates derived from the EPPA3;
- 1980-90, extrapolation of activity rates derived from the 1971, 1981 and 1991 censuses.

#### 2.2.2 Women:

Method, hypothesis and treatment identical to those used for men.

## 3. Estimates of distribution rates by activity sector: 1950 - 1990

### 3.1 Benchmark data:

Table 2: Distribution of economically active population by activity sector

| Year | Agriculture | Industry Total | Manufac. | Services |
|---|---|---|---|---|
| **Men** | | | | |
| 1971 | 7.08 | 36.32 | 14.73 | 56.60 |
| 1981 | 3.04 | 39.16 | 9.15 | 57.80 |
| 1991 | 2.88 | 32.76 | 14.02 | 64.36 |
| **Women** | | | | |
| 1971 | 0.12 | 4.09 | 2.72 | 95.79 |
| 1981 | 0.16 | 5.16 | 1.89 | 94.69 |
| 1991 | 0.21 | 7.23 | 5.90 | 92.57 |

Source(s): ASTER.

### 3.2 Method(s): linear interpolation

#### 3.2.1 Men:

- 1950-70, 1950-70 distribution rates derived from the EPPA3;
- 1980-90, extrapolation of distribution rates derived from the 1971, 1981 and 1991 censuses.

#### 3.2.2 Women:

Method, hypothesis and treatment identical to those used for men.

## 4. Projection of activity rates: 2000 - 2010

### 4.1 Model(s): linear, log-linear and hyperbole

#### 4.1.1 Men:

- To the [15-19] age group, application of function F2;
- To the [20+] age groups, application of function F1;
- Modification of the trends for the [20-59] age groups.

#### 4.1.2 Women:

- To the [15-59] age groups, application of function F1;
- To the [60+] age groups, application of function F3;
- Modification of the trend for the [15-19] age group.

*Notes on adjustments of rates, see p. 3-8.*          *Notes on projection functions, see p. 10.*

# Bangladesh

## 1. Source(s) of benchmark data

| Code(s): | Title(s): |
|---|---|
| EPPA3 | Economically active population: Estimates and Projections, 1950-2025, Third edition, ILO, Geneva, 1986. |
| BY83-84 | Statistical Yearbook of Bangladesh, 1983-84, Bangladesh Bureau of Statistics. |
| LFS84-85 | Report on Labour Force Survey 1984-85, february 1988, GPRB, Bangladesh Bureau of Statistics. |
| ASTER | Yearbook of Labour Statistics 1945-89 - Retrospective Edition on Population Censuses, ILO, Geneva, 1990. |
| AST85-90 | Editions 1985-1993 of ILO Yearbook of Labour Statistics, Geneva. |

## 2. Estimates of activity rates: 1950 - 1990

### 2.1 Benchmark data:

Table 1: Activity rates by sex and age group

| Age group | Year 1980 (1) | 1983 (1) | 1984 (2) | 1985 (3) | 1989 (3) |
|---|---|---|---|---|---|
| **Men** | | | | | |
| 10-14 | 32.77 | 39.86 | 37.70 | 30.40 | 33.76 |
| 15-19 | 72.39 | 69.56 | 70.40 | 67.50 | 70.70 |
| 20-24 | 87.59 | 87.18 | 85.40 | 88.10 | 82.50 |
| 25-29 | 99.53 | 98.58 | 97.70 | 98.70 | 96.50 |
| 30-34 | 99.13 | 98.44 | 99.00 | 99.90 | 98.80 |
| 35-39 | 98.68 | 98.50 | 99.70 | 99.40 | 98.50 |
| 40-44 | 98.78 | 97.05 | 98.40 | 99.50 | 98.30 |
| 45-49 | 98.77 | 98.47 | 98.40 | 99.70 | 98.30 |
| 50-54 | 98.66 | 97.01 | 98.50 | 99.30 | 96.80 |
| 55-59 | 94.89 | 97.63 | 94.70 | 98.00 | 95.70 |
| 60-64 | 90.82 | 90.65 | 91.80 | 93.00 | 89.40 |
| 65+ | 73.34 | 65.73 | 72.90 | 70.40 | 65.00 |
| **Women** | | | | | |
| 10-14 | .. | .. | .. | .. | 31.30 |
| 15-19 | .. | .. | .. | .. | 55.20 |
| 20-24 | .. | .. | .. | .. | 64.90 |
| 25-29 | .. | .. | .. | .. | 68.90 |
| 30-34 | .. | .. | .. | .. | 75.00 |
| 35-39 | .. | .. | .. | .. | 78.00 |
| 40-44 | .. | .. | .. | .. | 76.90 |
| 45-49 | .. | .. | .. | .. | 75.60 |
| 50-54 | .. | .. | .. | .. | 73.50 |
| 55-59 | .. | .. | .. | .. | 67.80 |
| 60-64 | .. | .. | .. | .. | 57.90 |
| 65+ | .. | .. | .. | .. | 33.50 |

Source(s): (1) BY83-84; (2) LFS84-85; (3) AST85-90.

### 2.2 Method(s): linears interpolation and extrapolation

#### 2.2.1 Men:

- 1950-70, 1950-70 activity rates derived from the EPPA3;
- 1980-90, interpolation and extrapolation of activity rates derived from the 1980, 1983-84, 1984-85, 1985-86 and 1989 surveys.

#### 2.2.2 Women:

- 1950-70, 1950-70 adjusted activity rates derived from the EPPA3;
- 1980-90, application to activity rates derived from the 1980 survey, 1/4 of variations in activity rates estimated for India between 1980 and 1990.

## 3. Estimates of distribution rates by activity sector: 1950 - 1990

### 3.1 Benchmark data:

Table 2: Distribution of economically active population by activity sector

| Year | Agriculture | Industry Total | Manufac. | Services |
|---|---|---|---|---|
| **Men** | | | | |
| 1983 (1) | 64.11 | 7.93 | 6.20 | 27.96 |
| 1984 (2) | 63.02 | 10.16 | 7.77 | 26.83 |
| 1985 (3) | 62.70 | 9.48 | 7.13 | 27.83 |
| 1989 (3) | 60.00 | 13.60 | 11.41 | 26.40 |
| **Women** | | | | |
| 1989 (3) | 74.34 | 18.61 | 17.96 | 7.05 |

Source(s): (1) BY83-84; (2) LFS84-85; (3) AST85-90.

### 3.2 Method(s): linear extrapolation

#### 3.2.1 Men:

- 1950-70, 1950-70 distribution rates derived from the EPPA3;
- 1990, extrapolation of distribution rates derived from the 1983-84, 1984-85, 1985-86 and 1989 surveys.

#### 3.2.2 Women:

- 1950-70, 1950-70 distribution rates derived from the EPPA3;
- 1980-90, for agriculture sector, application to distribution rates derived from the 1989 survey, the same variations estimated for men;
for industry and services sectors, application of the industry/services ratio derived from the 1989 survey.

## 4. Projection of activity rates: 2000 - 2010

### 4.1 Model(s): linear and hyperbole

#### 4.1.1 Men:

- To the [10-59] age groups, application of function F3;
- To the [60+] age groups, application of function F1;
- Modification of the trends for the [20-44] age groups.

#### 4.1.2 Women:

- To all age groups, application of function F1;
- Modification of the trends for all age groups.

---

*Notes on adjustments of rates, see p. 3-8.*   *Notes on projection functions, see p. 10.*

# Barbados

## 1. Source(s) of benchmark data

Code(s):    Title(s):

EPPA3        Economically active population: Estimates and Projections, 1950-2025, Third edition, ILO, Geneva, 1986.

ASTER      Yearbook of Labour Statistics 1945-89 - Retrospective Edition on Population Censuses, ILO, Geneva, 1990.

AST82-93   Editions 1982-1993 of ILO Yearbook of Labour Statistics, Geneva.

## 2. Estimates of activity rates: 1950 - 1990

### 2.1 Benchmark data:

Table 1: Activity rates by sex and age group

| Age group | Year 1950 (1) | 1980 (2) | 1986 (3) | 1990 (3) | 191 (3) | 1992 (3) |
|---|---|---|---|---|---|---|
| **Men** | | | | | | |
| 10-14 | .. | 0.00 | 0.00 | 0.00 | 0.00 | 0.00 |
| 15-19 | .. | 59.54 | 39.64 | 45.16 | 42.73 | 42.20 |
| 20-24 | .. | 92.31 | 88.00 | 91.60 | 80.20 | 89.52 |
| 25-29 | .. | 94.47 | 94.44 | 94.17 | 96.19 | 95.19 |
| 30-34 | .. | 95.78 | 95.05 | 95.83 | 93.64 | 93.64 |
| 35-39 | .. | 95.59 | 94.67 | 95.56 | 95.40 | 93.55 |
| 40-44 | .. | 95.38 | 95.56 | 96.77 | 96.05 | 94.20 |
| 45-49 | .. | 94.89 | 93.33 | 95.65 | 93.33 | 95.65 |
| 50-54 | .. | 93.57 | 91.67 | 94.29 | 90.91 | 92.68 |
| 55-59 | .. | 89.52 | 97.22 | 88.57 | 82.86 | 86.49 |
| 60-64 | .. | 70.82 | 61.76 | 64.52 | 58.33 | 53.49 |
| 65+ | .. | 23.63 | 17.27 | 13.76 | 14.75 | 12.93 |
| **Women** | | | | | | |
| 10-14 | 10.20 | 0.00 | 0.00 | 0.00 | .. | 0.00 |
| 15-19 | 54.15 | 39.89 | 29.46 | 34.99 | .. | 34.62 |
| 20-24 | 63.10 | 70.49 | 79.67 | 85.12 | .. | 85.11 |
| 25-29 | 57.60 | 77.54 | 82.64 | 86.96 | .. | 85.45 |
| 30-34 | 58.10 | 75.45 | 85.45 | 87.16 | .. | 84.68 |
| 35-39 | 58.25 | 71.56 | 83.12 | 90.70 | .. | 85.71 |
| 40-44 | 57.90 | 67.74 | 72.06 | 80.82 | .. | 84.81 |
| 45-49 | 60.05 | 61.27 | 79.09 | 70.01 | .. | 76.19 |
| 50-54 | 57.90 | 53.15 | 58.00 | 67.92 | .. | 72.92 |
| 55-59 | 54.85 | 45.10 | 63.89 | 43.18 | .. | 48.15 |
| 60-64 | 43.65 | 33.53 | 28.89 | 27.45 | .. | 23.91 |
| 65+ | 19.00 | 7.15 | 7.23 | 3.68 | .. | 4.81 |

Source(s): (1) EPPA3; (2) ASTER; (3) AST82-93.

### 2.2 Method(s): linears interpolation and extrapolation

#### 2.2.1 Men:

- 1990, interpolation of activity rates derived from the 1980 census and from the 1986 to 1992 surveys;
modification of the trends of the [20-29] age groups;
- 1970, 1970 activity rates derived from the EPPA3;
- 1980, activity rates derived from the 1980 census;
- 1950-60, extrapolation of activity rates estimated for 1970, 1980 and 1990;
modification of the trends for all age groups.

#### 2.2.2 Women:

- 1950, 1950 activity rates derived from the EPPA3;
- 1970-90, interpolation of 1950 activity rates derived from the EPPA3, of activity rates derived from the 1980 census and of activity rates derived from the 1986, 1990 and 1991 surveys;
modification of the trends for all age groups.

## 3. Estimates of distribution rates by activity sector: 1950 - 1990

### 3.1 Benchmark data:

Table 2: Distribution of economically active population by activity sector

| Year | Agriculture | Industry Total | Manufac. | Services |
|---|---|---|---|---|
| **Men** | | | | |
| 1960 (1) | 26.42 | 37.74 | .. | 35.85 |
| 1970 (2) | 17.56 | 47.86 | 16.05 | 34.58 |
| 1981 (3) | 10.14 | 23.83 | 10.95 | 66.02 |
| 1989 (3) | 7.12 | 33.03 | 11.50 | 59.85 |
| 1991 (3) | 7.12 | 27.88 | 10.00 | 65.00 |
| **Women** | | | | |
| 1960 (1) | 26.32 | 13.16 | .. | 60.53 |
| 1970 (2) | 16.05 | 30.79 | 14.07 | 53.16 |
| 1981 (3) | 9.20 | 24.14 | 23.22 | 80.46 |
| 1989 (3) | 7.32 | 16.48 | 14.87 | 76.20 |
| 1991 (3) | 4.94 | 14.07 | 12.59 | 80.99 |

Source(s): (1) EPPA3; (2) ASTER; (3) AST82-93..

### 3.2 Method(s): linears interpolation and extrapolation

#### 3.2.1 Men:

- 1950-60, 1950-60 distribution rates derived from the EPPA3;
- 1970, extrapolation of 1960 distribution rates derived from the EPPA3 and of distribution rates derived from the 1970 census;
- 1980, interpolation of 1970 distribution rates estimated for 1970 and of distribution rates derived from the 1981 survey;
- 1990, averages of distribution rates derived from the 1989 and 1991 surveys.

#### 3.2.2 Women:

Method, hypothesis and treatment identical to those used for men.

## 4. Projection of activity rates: 2000 - 2010

### 4.1 Model(s): linear and hyperbole

#### 4.1.1 Men:

- To the [15-24] age groups, application of function F1;
- To the [25+] age groups, application of function F3;
- Modification of the trends for the [20-24] and [30-49] age groups.

#### 4.1.2 Women:

- To the [15-19] age group, application of function F3;
- To the [20-54] age groups, application of function F6;
- To the [55+] age groups, application of function F3;
- Modification of the trends for the [45-59] age groups.

*Notes on adjustments of rates, see p. 3-8.*

*Notes on projection functions, see p. 10.*

# Belarus

## 1. Source(s) of benchmark data

**Code(s):**     **Title(s):**

BLT-94-2     Vorobiev A. (1994), "Estimates of the economically active population for the fifteen countries of the former USSR
for the years 1950, 1959, 1970, 1979 and 1989", in the Bulletin of Labour of Statistics - 1994-2, ILO, Geneva.

## 2. Estimates of activity rates: 1950 - 1990

### 2.1 Benchmark data:

Table 1: Activity rates by sex and age group

| Age group | Year 1959 | 1970 | 1979 | 1989 |
|---|---|---|---|---|
| **Men** | | | | |
| 10-14 | 0.00 | 0.00 | 0.00 | 0.00 |
| 15-19 | 64.15 | 38.64 | 37.45 | 26.97 |
| 20-24 | 86.82 | 83.56 | 86.81 | 81.14 |
| 25-29 | 95.29 | 98.39 | 97.23 | 96.99 |
| 30-34 | 94.76 | 97.99 | 98.14 | 98.33 |
| 35-39 | 96.02 | 97.57 | 98.17 | 98.06 |
| 40-44 | 93.65 | 95.42 | 97.89 | 97.30 |
| 45-49 | 93.75 | 94.82 | 96.26 | 95.74 |
| 50-54 | 91.25 | 91.23 | 91.82 | 92.69 |
| 55-59 | 88.89 | 84.46 | 82.91 | 85.61 |
| 60-64 | 56.20 | 45.07 | 30.48 | 39.91 |
| 65+ | 47.78 | 10.07 | 8.43 | 12.89 |
| **Women** | | | | |
| 10-14 | 0.00 | 0.00 | 0.00 | 0.00 |
| 15-19 | 63.50 | 34.75 | 31.44 | 24.50 |
| 20-24 | 76.87 | 80.95 | 86.10 | 82.30 |
| 25-29 | 84.10 | 94.55 | 94.44 | 92.94 |
| 30-34 | 74.10 | 93.46 | 95.93 | 95.22 |
| 35-39 | 78.68 | 91.97 | 96.19 | 96.16 |
| 40-44 | 77.36 | 92.65 | 96.22 | 96.25 |
| 45-49 | 75.95 | 89.26 | 93.96 | 93.97 |
| 50-54 | 70.09 | 79.79 | 85.71 | 86.69 |
| 55-59 | 58.08 | 28.10 | 29.04 | 36.29 |
| 60-64 | 53.18 | 14.35 | 9.64 | 20.42 |
| 65+ | 17.45 | 2.43 | 4.40 | 4.90 |

Source(s): BLT-94-2.

### 2.2 Method(s):   linears interpolation and extrapolation
weighted average

**2.2.1 Men:**

- 1950-90, interpolation and extrapolation of 1950, 1959, 1970
and 1989 activity rates derived from the Bulletin of Labour Statistics 1994-2;
modification of the trends for all age groups for 1950.

**2.2.2 Women:**

- 1950, extrapolation of 1959 and 1970 activity rates derived from
the Bulletin of Labour Statistics 1994-2;
modification of the trends for all age groups;
- 1960-90, weighted average of 1959, 1970, 1979 and 1989 activity rates
derived from the Bulletin.

## 3. Estimates of distribution rates by activity sector: 1950 - 1990

### 3.1 Benchmark data:

Table 2: Distribution of economically active population by activity sector

| Year | Agriculture | Industry Total | Manufac. | Services |
|---|---|---|---|---|
| **Men** | | | | |
| 1950 | 65.60 | 15.43 | 8.81 | 18.97 |
| 1959 | 51.06 | 22.35 | 14.08 | 26.59 |
| 1970 | 33.84 | 39.01 | 24.58 | 27.15 |
| 1979 | 28.99 | 43.43 | 26.38 | 27.58 |
| 1989 | 26.16 | 44.62 | 27.38 | 29.23 |
| **Women** | | | | |
| 1950 | 75.37 | 9.45 | 7.36 | 15.19 |
| 1959 | 65.49 | 14.45 | 11.78 | 20.06 |
| 1970 | 36.43 | 27.77 | 22.89 | 35.80 |
| 1979 | 24.42 | 32.89 | 26.06 | 42.69 |
| 1989 | 14.84 | 35.20 | 28.44 | 49.96 |

Source(s): BLT-94-2.

### 3.2 Method(s):   data from BLT-94-16

**3.2.1 Men:**

- 1950-90, weighted averages of 1950, 1959, 1970, 1979 and 1989
distribution rates derived from the Bulletin of Labour Statistics, 1994-2.

**3.2.2 Women:**

Method, hypothesis and treatment identical to those used for men.

## 4. Projection of activity rates: 2000 - 2010

### 4.1 Model(s):   linear and hyperbole

**4.1.1 Men:**

- To the [15-24] and [60+] age groups, application of function F3;
- To the [25-59] age groups, application of function F1;
- Modification of the trends for the [15-19] and [25-54] age groups.

**4.1.2 Women:**

- To the [15+] age groups, application of function F3;
- Modification of the trends for the [15-19] and [25-54] age groups.

*Notes on adjustments of rates, see p. 3-8.*          *Notes on projection functions, see p. 10.*

# Belgium

## 1. Source(s) of benchmark data

Code(s):     Title(s):
EPPA3      Yearbook of Labour Statistics 1945-89 - Retrospective Edition on Population Censuses, ILO, Geneva, 1990.
STAT       Database on Labour Statistics, LABORSTA - Bureau of Statistics, ILO, Geneva.

## 2. Estimates of activity rates: 1950 - 1990

### 2.1 Benchmark data:

Table 1: Activity rates by sex and age group

| Age group | 1988 | 1991 |
|---|---|---|
| **Men** | | |
| 10-14 | 0.00 | 0.00 |
| 15-19 | 11.30 | 12.86 |
| 20-24 | 67.10 | 66.50 |
| 25-29 | 94.50 | 94.09 |
| 30-34 | 96.10 | 95.98 |
| 35-39 | 96.40 | 95.72 |
| 40-44 | 94.80 | 94.39 |
| 45-49 | 90.90 | 92.97 |
| 50-54 | 79.10 | 80.49 |
| 55-59 | 51.30 | 50.56 |
| 60-64 | 20.50 | 18.17 |
| 65+ | 2.30 | 1.93 |
| **Women** | | |
| 10-14 | 0.00 | 0.00 |
| 15-19 | 9.72 | 9.04 |
| 20-24 | 60.90 | 61.55 |
| 25-29 | 78.20 | 80.40 |
| 30-34 | 71.00 | 74.97 |
| 35-39 | 66.00 | 70.63 |
| 40-44 | 55.40 | 61.89 |
| 45-49 | 43.30 | 50.04 |
| 50-54 | 29.00 | 31.75 |
| 55-59 | 16.30 | 17.64 |
| 60-64 | 4.10 | 3.74 |
| 65+ | 0.70 | 0.47 |

Source(s): STAT.

### 2.2 Method(s): weighted average

#### 2.2.1 Men:

- 1950-80, 1950-80 activity rates derived from the EPPA3;
- 1990, weighted average of activity rates derived from the 1988 and 1991 surveys.

#### 2.2.2 Women:

Method, hypothesis and treatment identical to those used for men.

## 3. Estimates of distribution rates by activity sector: 1950 - 1990

### 3.1 Benchmark data:

Table 2: Distribution of economically active population by activity sector

| Year | Agriculture | Industry Total | Manufac. | Services |
|---|---|---|---|---|
| **Men** | | | | |
| 1990 | 3.21 | 37.04 | 25.94 | 59.75 |
| **Women** | | | | |
| 1990 | 1.75 | 13.62 | 12.40 | 84.63 |

Source(s): STAT.

### 3.2 Method(s): national data

#### 3.2.1 Men:

- 1950-80, 1950-80 distribution rates derived from the EPPA3;
- 1990, adjusted distribution rates derived from the 1990 survey; adjustment of rates to make allowance for conscripts.

#### 3.2.2 Women:

Method, hypothesis and treatment identical to those used for men.

## 4. Projection of activity rates: 2000 - 2010

### 4.1 Model(s): hyperbole and logistic

#### 4.1.1 Men:

- To the [15+] age groups, application of function F3;
- Modification of the trends for the [15-24] age groups.

#### 4.1.2 Women:

- To the [15-19] age group, application of function F3;
- To the [20+] age groups, application of function F6;
- Modification of the trends for the [15-29] age groups.

*Notes on adjustments of rates, see p. 3-8.*   *Notes on projection functions, see p. 10.*

# Belize

## 1. Source(s) of benchmark data

Code(s):     Title(s):

EPPA3      Economically active population: Estimates and Projections, 1950-2025, Third edition, ILO, Geneva, 1986.
ASTER      Yearbook of Labour Statistics 1945-89 - Retrospective Edition on Population Censuses, ILO, Geneva, 1990.
STAT       Database on Labour Statistics, LABORSTA - Bureau of Statistics, ILO, Geneva.

## 2. Estimates of activity rates: 1950 - 1990

### 2.1 Benchmark data:

Table 1: Activity rates by sex and age group

| Age group | Year 1960 (1) | 1970 (1) | 1980 (1) | 1991 (2) |
|---|---|---|---|---|
| **Men** | | | | |
| 10-14 | .. | 9.20 | .. | 17.34 |
| 15-19 | .. | 70.95 | .. | 54.43 |
| 20-24 | .. | 96.70 | .. | 88.92 |
| 25-29 | .. | 97.77 | .. | 93.03 |
| 30-34 | .. | 97.90 | .. | 93.00 |
| 35-39 | .. | 98.20 | .. | 93.37 |
| 40-44 | .. | 96.80 | .. | 93.88 |
| 45-49 | .. | 97.63 | .. | 92.18 |
| 50-54 | .. | 95.21 | .. | 90.63 |
| 55-59 | .. | 91.43 | .. | 81.67 |
| 60-64 | .. | 86.70 | .. | 72.79 |
| 65+ | .. | 59.39 | .. | 45.81 |
| **Women** | | | | |
| 10-14 | 0.26 | 0.99 | 0.00 | 3.26 |
| 15-19 | 19.88 | 29.10 | 27.00 | 15.13 |
| 20-24 | 24.00 | 31.20 | 34.37 | 32.82 |
| 25-29 | 19.04 | 21.70 | 28.70 | 30.69 |
| 30-34 | 18.66 | 19.80 | 26.94 | 29.62 |
| 35-39 | 18.30 | 18.70 | 22.93 | 31.52 |
| 40-44 | 17.84 | 17.70 | 23.12 | 29.03 |
| 45-49 | 19.10 | 18.20 | 20.56 | 25.31 |
| 50-54 | 18.60 | 17.50 | 17.27 | 21.62 |
| 55-59 | 18.00 | 16.90 | 17.53 | 14.64 |
| 60-64 | 17.00 | 14.30 | 15.72 | 11.63 |
| 65+ | 9.70 | 7.50 | 8.36 | 5.04 |

Source(s): (1) ASTER; (2) STAT.

### 2.2 Method(s): linears interpolation and extrapolation

#### 2.2.1 Men:

- 1950-60, 1950-60 activity rates derived from the EPPA3;
- 1970-90, interpolation and extrapolation of adjusted activity rates derived from the 1970 and 1991 censuses.

#### 2.2.2 Women:

- 1960-70, activity rates derived from the 1960 and 1970 censuses;
- 1950 and 1980-90, interpolation of adjusted activity rates derived from the 1960, 1970, 1980 and 1991 censuses.

## 3. Estimates of distribution rates by activity sector: 1950 - 1990

### 3.1 Benchmark data:

Table 2: Distribution of economically active population by activity sector

| Year | Agriculture | Industry Total | Manufac. | Services |
|---|---|---|---|---|
| **Men** | | | | |
| 1943 (1) | 51.38 | 20.69 | 13.16 | 27.92 |
| 1960 (1) | 49.00 | 26.64 | 16.09 | 24.36 |
| 1980 (1) | 46.44 | 17.71 | 10.06 | 35.85 |
| 1991 (2) | 41.06 | 20.37 | 9.11 | 38.56 |
| **Women** | | | | |
| 1943 (1) | 15.72 | 14.91 | 14.86 | 69.37 |
| 1960 (1) | 10.84 | 11.57 | 11.20 | 77.60 |
| 1980 (1) | 8.69 | 15.39 | 14.24 | 75.92 |
| 1991 (2) | 3.95 | 13.33 | 12.13 | 82.72 |

Source(s): (1) ASTER; (2) STAT.

### 3.2 Method(s): linear interpolation

#### 3.2.1 Men:

- 1960 and 1980, distribution rates derived from the 1960 and 1980 censuses;
- 1950, 1970 and 1990, interpolation of distribution rates derived from the 1946, 1960, 1980 and 1991 censuses.

#### 3.2.2 Women:

Method, hypothesis and treatment identical to those used for men.

## 4. Projection of activity rates: 2000 - 2010

### 4.1 Model(s): linear, log-linear and hyperbole

#### 4.1.1 Men:

- To the [10-14] age group, application of function F2;
- To the [15-29] age groups, application of function F1;
- To the [30+] age groups, application of function F3;
- Modification of the trends for the [25-29] and [40-44] age groups.

#### 4.1.2 Women:

- To the [10-14] age group, application of function F2;
- To the [15-19] age group, application of function F1;
- To the [20+] age groups, application of function F3;
- Modification of the trends for the [15-59] age groups.

---

*Notes on adjustments of rates, see p. 3-8.*                    *Notes on projection functions, see p. 10.*

# Benin

## 1. Source(s) of benchmark data

Code(s):     Title(s):
EPPA3       Economically active population: Estimates and Projections, 1950-2025, Third edition, ILO, Geneva, 1986.
S1960       Enquête démographique 1960-61, Institut National de la Statistique et de l'Analyse Economique, Cotonou, 1961.
ADNU84      Demographic Yearbook 1984 - Population census statistics II - Thirty-sixth Edition, United Nations, New York, 1986.
ASTER       Yearbook of Labour Statistics 1945-89 - Retrospective Edition on Population Censuses, ILO, Geneva, 1990.

## 2. Estimates of activity rates: 1950 - 1990

### 2.1 Benchmark data:

Table 1: Activity rates by sex and age group

| Age group | 1950 (1) | 1960 (2) | 1960 (1) | 1970 (1) | 1979 (3) | 1980 (1) |
|---|---|---|---|---|---|---|
| **Men** | | | | | | |
| 10-14 | 46.55 | ... | .. | 42.50 | 36.78 | 36.75 |
| 15-19 | 90.00 | 87.06 | .. | 83.60 | 62.70 | 74.60 |
| 20-24 | 97.00 | 95.95 | .. | 94.70 | 87.68 | 91.40 |
| 25-29 | 97.80 | 97.66 | .. | 97.50 | 96.29 | 97.00 |
| 30-34 | 99.00 | 98.84 | .. | 98.65 | 97.49 | 98.10 |
| 35-39 | 99.20 | 98.98 | .. | 98.75 | 97.61 | 98.20 |
| 40-44 | 98.15 | 97.94 | .. | 97.70 | 97.12 | 97.10 |
| 45-49 | 97.25 | 97.09 | .. | 96.90 | 96.39 | 96.40 |
| 50-54 | 95.65 | 95.41 | .. | 95.10 | 94.37 | 94.35 |
| 55-59 | 94.05 | 93.66 | .. | 93.20 | 92.14 | 92.00 |
| 60-64 | 90.45 | 89.78 | .. | 89.00 | 88.11 | 87.00 |
| 65+ | 81.30 | 80.11 | .. | 78.70 | 75.12 | 75.00 |
| **Women** | | | | | | |
| 10-14 | 30.50 | .. | 29.10 | 28.55 | 27.16 | 27.60 |
| 15-19 | 87.90 | .. | 84.25 | 82.75 | 33.48 | 80.30 |
| 20-24 | 93.50 | .. | 91.20 | 90.25 | 37.67 | 88.70 |
| 25-29 | 97.00 | .. | 96.50 | 96.00 | 40.93 | 95.40 |
| 30-34 | 98.50 | .. | 98.00 | 97.50 | 41.87 | 97.30 |
| 35-39 | 97.80 | .. | 96.40 | 95.45 | 43.31 | 94.80 |
| 40-44 | 94.25 | .. | 93.00 | 92.10 | 44.03 | 91.60 |
| 45-49 | 84.30 | .. | 82.30 | 81.45 | 45.10 | 80.10 |
| 50-54 | 80.30 | .. | 78.00 | 77.05 | 43.02 | 75.50 |
| 55-59 | 75.50 | .. | 73.15 | 72.15 | 42.30 | 70.55 |
| 60-64 | 60.75 | .. | 58.00 | 56.85 | 37.00 | 55.00 |
| 65+ | 44.45 | .. | 41.60 | 40.45 | 27.50 | 38.50 |

Source(s): (1) EPPA3; (2) S1960; (3) ADNU84 and ASTER.

### 2.2 Method(s): linears interpolation and extrapolation

**2.2.1 Men:**

- 1950-90, interpolation and extrapolation of activity rates derived from the 1960 survey and of activity rates derived from the 1979 census; modification of the trends for all age groups for 1950 and 1990.

**2.2.2 Women:**

- 1950-90, interpolation and extrapolation of 1950-90 activity rates derived from the EPPA3; modification of the trends for all age groups for 1950 and 1990.

## 3. Estimates of distribution rates by activity sector: 1950 - 1990

### 3.1 Benchmark data:

Table 2: Distribution of economically active population by activity sector

| Year | Agriculture | Industry Total | Manufac. | Services |
|---|---|---|---|---|
| **Men** | | | | |
| 1950 | 85.79 | 5.00 | .. | 9.25 |
| 1960 | 82.00 | 6.50 | .. | 11.50 |
| 1970 | 77.55 | 8.00 | .. | 14.45 |
| 1980 | 66.00 | 10.00 | .. | 24.00 |
| **Women** | | | | |
| 1950 | 91.60 | 1.10 | .. | 7.30 |
| 1960 | 88.40 | 1.55 | .. | 10.05 |
| 1970 | 84.55 | 2.10 | .. | 13.35 |
| 1980 | 68.80 | 3.20 | .. | 22.20 |

Source(s): EPPA3.

### 3.2 Method(s): linear extrapolation

**3.2.1 Men:**

- 1950-80, 1950-80 distribution rates derived from the EPPA3;
- 1990, extrapolation of 1950-80 distribution rates derived from the EPPA3;
- the manufacturing/industry ratio for 1980 and 1990 estimated on the basis of manufacturing/industry ratio for 1980 and 1990 in Togo.

**3.2.2 Women:**

Method, hypothesis and treatment identical to those used for men.

## 4. Projection of activity rates: 2000 - 2010

### 4.1 Model(s): logistic, linear and hyperbole

**4.1.1 Men:**

- To the [10-14] age group, application of function F6;
- To the [15-19] age group, application of function F1;
- To the [20+] age groups, application of function F3;
- Modification of the trends for the [55+] age groups.

**4.1.2 Women:**

- To the [10-14] and [20-64] age groups, application of function F3;
- To the [15-19] age group, application of function F6;
- To the [65+] age group, application of function F1;
- Modification of the trends for the [20+] age groups.

28

# Bhutan

## 1. Source(s) of benchmark data

Code(s):    Title(s):

EPPA3    Economically active population: Estimates and Projections, 1950-2025, Third edition, ILO, Geneva, 1986.
EPPA4    Economically active population 1950-2010 - Fourth edition, ILO, Geneva 1996.

## 2. Estimates of activity rates: 1950 - 1990

### 2.1 Benchmark data:

Table 1: Activity rates by sex and age group

| Age group | Year 1950 | 1975 |
|---|---|---|
| **Men** | | |
| 10-14 | 77.04 | 65.31 |
| 15-19 | 95.13 | 78.23 |
| 20-24 | 97.97 | 91.82 |
| 25-29 | 98.84 | 96.72 |
| 30-34 | 98.88 | 97.74 |
| 35-39 | 99.08 | 97.95 |
| 40-44 | 99.15 | 98.16 |
| 45-49 | 98.16 | 96.84 |
| 50-54 | 98.34 | 95.31 |
| 55-59 | 95.63 | 93.08 |
| 60-64 | 86.37 | 84.06 |
| 65+ | 71.24 | 69.35 |
| **Women** | | |
| 10-14 | 67.68 | 52.88 |
| 15-19 | 79.11 | 65.13 |
| 20-24 | 70.39 | 61.85 |
| 25-29 | 66.08 | 59.79 |
| 30-34 | 62.52 | 59.08 |
| 35-39 | 60.04 | 59.61 |
| 40-44 | 56.44 | 58.93 |
| 45-49 | 54.24 | 58.47 |
| 50-54 | 50.91 | 56.88 |
| 55-59 | 44.74 | 53.24 |
| 60-64 | 33.03 | 38.66 |
| 65+ | 14.10 | 28.59 |

Source(s): EPPA4.

### 2.2 Method(s):  linear interpolation

#### 2.2.1 Men:

- 1950 and 1990, 1950 and 1990 activity rates estimated for Nepal;
- 1960-80, interpolation of 1950 and 1990 estimated activity rates.

#### 2.2.2 Women:

Method, hypothesis and treatment identical to those used for men.

## 3. Estimates of distribution rates by activity sector: 1950 - 1990

### 3.1 Benchmark data:

Table 2: Distribution of economically active population by activity sector

| Year | Agriculture | Industry Total | Manufac. | Services |
|---|---|---|---|---|
| **Men** | | | | |
| 1950 (1) | 93.50 | 3.08 | 2.78 | 3.42 |
| 1975 (1) | 91.60 | 1.26 | 1.09 | 7.14 |
| **Women** | | | | |
| 1950 (1) | 97.83 | 1.73 | 1.69 | 0.44 |
| 1975 (1) | 98.00 | 0.37 | 0.35 | 1.64 |

Note(s): Nepal.
Source(s): EPPA4

### 3.2 Method(s):  linear interpolation

#### 3.2.1 Men:

- 1950 et 1990, 1950 and 1975 distribution rates estimated for Nepal;
- 1960-80, interpolation of distribution rates estimated for 1950 and 1990.

#### 3.2.2 Women:

Method, hypothesis and treatment identical to those used for men.

## 4. Projection of activity rates: 2000 - 2010

### 4.1 Model(s):  linear

#### 4.1.1 Men:

- To all age groups, application of function F1;
- Modification of the trends for the [10-19] and [60+] age groups.

#### 4.1.2 Women:

- To all age groups, application of function F1;
- Modification of the trends for all age groups.

*Notes on adjustments of rates, see p. 3-8.*    *Notes on projection functions, see p. 10.*

# Bolivia

## 1. Source(s) of benchmark data

| Code(s): | Title(s): |
|---|---|
| EPPA3 | Economically active population: Estimates and Projections, 1950-2025, Third edition, ILO, Geneva, 1986. |
| ASTER | Yearbook of Labour Statistics 1945-89 - Retrospective Edition on Population Censuses, ILO, Geneva, 1990. |
| AST94 | Yearbook of Labour Statistics 1994, ILO, Geneva, 1994. |

## 2. Estimates of activity rates: 1950 - 1990

### 2.1 Benchmark data:

Table 1: Activity rates by sex and age group

| Age group | Year 1950 (1) | 1976 (1) | 1992 (2) |
|---|---|---|---|
| **Men** | | | |
| 10-14 | 44.17 | 15.99 | 16.12 |
| 15-19 | 78.27 | 54.97 | 44.58 |
| 20-24 | 92.90 | 83.80 | 76.97 |
| 25-29 | 96.73 | 94.75 | 91.03 |
| 30-34 | 97.30 | 98.10 | 95.48 |
| 35-39 | 97.28 | 98.65 | 96.34 |
| 40-44 | 96.82 | 98.44 | 96.28 |
| 45-49 | 96.58 | 98.25 | 95.69 |
| 50-54 | 95.54 | 97.18 | 93.79 |
| 55-59 | 94.58 | 94.77 | 87.26 |
| 60-64 | 92.23 | 89.73 | 80.98 |
| 65+ | 78.13 | 80.49 | 69.49 |
| **Women** | | | |
| 10-14 | 51.91 | 10.09 | 15.28 |
| 15-19 | 66.74 | 22.11 | 35.61 |
| 20-24 | 64.80 | 25.16 | 45.70 |
| 25-29 | 64.22 | 25.44 | 50.16 |
| 30-34 | 66.28 | 23.62 | 52.05 |
| 35-39 | 64.56 | 22.76 | 54.27 |
| 40-44 | 68.30 | 22.88 | 55.20 |
| 45-49 | 65.36 | 22.49 | 54.27 |
| 50-54 | 66.67 | 20.58 | 51.18 |
| 55-59 | 43.29 | 18.63 | 46.97 |
| 60-64 | 29.67 | 16.75 | 43.48 |
| 65+ | 21.68 | 14.06 | 37.18 |

Source(s): (1) ASTER; (2) AST94.

### 2.2 Method(s): linears interpolation and extrapolation

#### 2.2.1 Men:

- 1950-70, 1950-70 activity rates derived from the EPPA3;
- 1980-90, extrapolation of adjusted activity rates derived from the 1976 census and of adjusted activity rates derived from the 1992 census.

#### 2.2.2 Women:

- 1950-70, interpolation of activity rates derived from the 1950 and 1976 censuses;
adjustment of activity rates based on the men/women ratio in agriculture derived from the 1992 census;
- 1980-90, interpolation of activity rates derived from the 1976 and 1992 censuses.

## 3. Estimates of distribution rates by activity sector: 1950 - 1990

### 3.1 Benchmark data:

Table 2: Distribution of economically active population by activity sector

| Year | Agriculture | Industry Total | Manufac. | Services |
|---|---|---|---|---|
| **Men** | | | | |
| 1950 (1) | 54.44 | 31.55 | 12.79 | 14.02 |
| 1976 (1) | 54.21 | 20.65 | 7.98 | 25.15 |
| 1992 (2) | 44.22 | 23.47 | 10.70 | 32.31 |
| **Women** | | | | |
| 1950 (1) | 74.34 | 11.23 | 8.42 | 14.42 |
| 1976 (1) | 27.21 | 18.51 | 17.26 | 54.28 |
| 1992 (2) | 43.57 | 9.37 | 8.62 | 47.07 |

Source(s): (1) ASTER; (2) AST94.

### 3.2 Method(s): linear interpolation

#### 3.2.1 Men:

- 1950-90, interpolation of distribution rates derived from the 1950 1976 and 1992 censuses;
adjustment of 1950-60 rates to make allowance for the under-registration of contributing family workers in agriculture.

#### 3.2.2 Women:

Method, hypothesis and treatment identical to those used for men.

## 4. Projection of activity rates: 2000 - 2010

### 4.1 Model(s): linear, log-linear and hyperbole

#### 4.1.1 Men:

- To the [10-14] and [60+] age groups, application of function F1;
- To the [15-59] age groups, application of function F3;
- Modification of the trends for the [10-14], [20-34] and [40-49].

#### 4.1.2 Women:

- To the [10-19] and [55+] age groups, application of function F1;
- To the [20-54] age groups, application of function F2;
- Modification of the trends for the [10-19] and [55+] age groups.

*Notes on adjustments of rates, see p. 3-8.*

*Notes on projection functions, see p. 10.*

# Bosnia and Herzegovina

## 1. Source(s) of benchmark data

Code(s):     Title(s):

EPPA3       Economically active population: Estimates and Projections, 1950-2025, Third edition, ILO, Geneva, 1986.
BLT-94-2     Popovic B. (1994), "New 1980 and 1990 estimates of activity rates by age and sectoral distribution for some countries of Eastern and Southern Europe"
            in the Bulletin of Labour of Statistics - 1994-2, ILO, Geneva.

## 2. Estimates of activity rates: 1950 - 1990

### 2.1 Benchmark data:

Table 1: Activity rates by sex and age group

| Age group | Year 1950 (1) | 1960 (1) | 1970 (1) | 1980 (2) | 1990 (2) |
|---|---|---|---|---|---|
| **Men** | | | | | |
| 10-14 | 24.10 | 8.85 | 3.25 | 0.31 | 0.02 |
| 15-19 | 86.80 | 67.25 | 48.45 | 25.07 | 22.47 |
| 20-24 | 94.85 | 90.75 | 85.80 | 80.53 | 81.67 |
| 25-29 | 96.10 | 96.55 | 95.80 | 95.53 | 96.06 |
| 30-34 | 97.60 | 97.90 | 98.35 | 97.79 | 98.01 |
| 35-39 | 97.80 | 97.25 | 98.30 | 97.34 | 97.97 |
| 40-44 | 97.60 | 97.00 | 95.55 | 96.11 | 96.85 |
| 45-49 | 97.20 | 96.10 | 96.00 | 92.38 | 93.97 |
| 50-54 | 94.20 | 94.00 | 92.35 | 77.71 | 80.28 |
| 55-59 | 84.65 | 85.60 | 77.05 | 59.83 | 60.51 |
| 60-64 | 79.75 | 75.50 | 65.10 | 51.19 | 38.79 |
| 65+ | 61.60 | 56.70 | 51.30 | 38.36 | 27.42 |
| **Women** | | | | | |
| 10-14 | 23.20 | 12.50 | 5.45 | 1.02 | 0.07 |
| 15-19 | 68.80 | 58.35 | 45.15 | 20.99 | 18.13 |
| 20-24 | 60.75 | 60.55 | 60.35 | 54.68 | 61.95 |
| 25-29 | 45.00 | 53.20 | 57.35 | 56.44 | 68.73 |
| 30-34 | 38.85 | 47.65 | 52.25 | 50.93 | 64.91 |
| 35-39 | 35.45 | 45.15 | 50.35 | 40.73 | 64.17 |
| 40-44 | 32.80 | 42.15 | 47.20 | 35.00 | 56.15 |
| 45-49 | 29.50 | 37.80 | 43.40 | 28.17 | 43.69 |
| 50-54 | 24.20 | 31.70 | 36.70 | 20.12 | 29.67 |
| 55-59 | 21.10 | 26.75 | 31.60 | 15.34 | 17.94 |
| 60-64 | 16.50 | 22.10 | 26.80 | 12.68 | 12.32 |
| 65+ | 10.95 | 14.10 | 14.60 | 7.45 | 7.23 |

Source(s): (1) EPPA3; (2) BLT-94-2.

### 2.2 Method(s):   data from EPPA3 and BLT-94-2.

#### 2.2.1 Men:

F
derived from the EPPA3 and of 1990 activity rates derived from
- 1980-90, 1980 and 1990 activity rates derived from the Bulletin
of Labour Statistics 1994-2.

#### 2.2.2 Women:

Method, hypothesis and treatment identical to those used for men.

## 3. Estimates of distribution rates by activity sector: 1950 - 1990

### 3.1 Benchmark data:

Table 2: Distribution of economically active population by activity sector

| Year | Agriculture | Industry Total | Manufac. | Services |
|---|---|---|---|---|
| **Men** | | | | |
| 1950 (1) | 68.30 | 17.80 | .. | 13.90 |
| 1960 (1) | 56.00 | 28.00 | .. | 16.00 |
| 1970 (1) | 45.00 | 34.40 | .. | 20.60 |
| 1980 (2) | 25.60 | 44.67 | 22.28 | 29.73 |
| 1990 (2) | 8.78 | 53.95 | 31.08 | 37.27 |
| **Women** | | | | |
| 1950 (1) | 83.00 | 5.40 | .. | 11.50 |
| 1960 (1) | 78.10 | 15.00 | .. | 6.80 |
| 1970 (1) | 58.20 | 20.00 | .. | 21.80 |
| 1980 (2) | 37.49 | 23.92 | 20.51 | 38.58 |
| 1990 (2) | 15.55 | 36.83 | 32.57 | 47.62 |

Source(s): (1) EPPA3; (2) BLT-94-2.

### 3.2 Method(s):   data from BLT-94-2

#### 3.2.1 Men:

- 1950-70, 1950-70 distribution rates for Yugoslavia
derived from the EPPA3;
- 1980-90, distribution rates derived from the Bulletin
of Labour Statistics, 1994-2.

#### 3.2.2 Women:

Method, hypothesis and treatment identical to those used for men.

## 4. Projection of activity rates: 2000 - 2010

### 4.1 Model(s):   linear and hyperbole

#### 4.1.1 Men:

- To the [15-24] and [50+] age groups, application of function F3;
- To the [25-49] age groups, application of function F1;
- Modification of the trends for the [15-24] age groups.

#### 4.1.2 Women:

- To the [15-24] and [50+] age groups, application of function F3;
- To the [25-49] age groups, application of function F1;
- Modification of the trend for the [15-19] age group.

# Botswana

## 1. Source(s) of benchmark data

Code(s):    Title(s):

ASTER    Yearbook of Labour Statistics 1945-89 - Retrospective Edition on Population Censuses, ILO, Geneva, 1990.
R1991    1991 Population and Housing Census Administrative/Technical Report and National Statistical Tables, Central Statistical Office, Gaborone, 1994.

## 2. Estimates of activity rates: 1950 - 1990

### 2.1 Benchmark data:

Table 1: Activity rates by sex and age group

| Age group | Year 1964 (1) | 1971 (1) | 1991 (2) |
|---|---|---|---|
| **Men** | | | |
| 10-14 | 37.95 | 40.18 | 18.16 |
| 15-19 | 63.98 | 66.26 | 43.78 |
| 20-24 | 92.32 | 92.92 | 86.92 |
| 25-29 | 99.15 | 99.20 | 98.71 |
| 30-34 | 99.07 | 99.10 | 98.81 |
| 35-39 | 99.03 | 99.05 | 98.87 |
| 40-44 | 98.99 | 99.01 | 98.85 |
| 45-49 | 98.82 | 98.82 | 98.82 |
| 50-54 | 98.70 | 98.70 | 98.78 |
| 55-59 | 98.44 | 98.42 | 98.69 |
| 60-64 | 89.85 | 90.70 | 82.33 |
| 65+ | 74.31 | 75.08 | 67.54 |
| **Women** | | | |
| 10-14 | .. | 27.64 | 18.14 |
| 15-19 | .. | 58.54 | 41.26 |
| 20-24 | .. | 83.12 | 75.68 |
| 25-29 | .. | 87.20 | 82.50 |
| 30-34 | .. | 87.49 | 80.84 |
| 35-39 | .. | 87.35 | 77.83 |
| 40-44 | .. | 85.69 | 73.46 |
| 45-49 | .. | 83.54 | 67.01 |
| 50-54 | .. | 80.22 | 60.05 |
| 55-59 | .. | 77.68 | 54.74 |
| 60-64 | .. | 72.40 | 46.65 |
| 65+ | .. | 59.24 | 27.12 |

Source(s): (1) ASTER; (2) R1991.

### 2.2 Method(s): linears interpolation and extrapolation

#### 2.2.1 Men:

- 1950-90, interpolation and extrapolation of activity rates derived from the 1964, 1971 and 1991 censuses;
distribution by age groups of economically active population of the 1964 and 1971 censuses based on distribution by age groups of economically active population of Namibia.

#### 2.2.2 Women:

Method, hypothesis and treatment identical to those used for men.

## 3. Estimates of distribution rates by activity sector: 1950 - 1990

### 3.1 Benchmark data:

Table 2: Distribution of economically active population by activity sector

| Year | Agriculture | Industry Total | Manufac. | Services |
|---|---|---|---|---|
| **Men** | | | | |
| 1964 (1) | 87.41 | 5.04 | 1.28 | 7.55 |
| 1981 (1) | 51.14 | 19.26 | 2.05 | 29.60 |
| 1991 (2) | 37.27 | 31.65 | 5.29 | 31.08 |
| **Women** | | | | |
| 1964 (1) | 95.11 | 0.73 | 0.66 | 4.15 |
| 1981 (1) | 72.91 | 1.75 | 0.67 | 25.34 |
| 1991 (2) | 52.85 | 9.98 | 5.97 | 37.17 |

Source(s): (1) ASTER; (2) R1991.

### 3.2 Method(s): linears interpolation and extrapolation weighted average

#### 3.2.1 Men:

- 1950-60, interpolation and extrapolation of distribution rates derived from the 1964, 1981 and 1991 censuses;
modification of the trends in all sectors;
- 1970-90, weighted averages of distribution rates derived from the 1964, 1981 and 1991 censuses.

#### 3.2.2 Women:

Method, hypothesis and treatment identical to those used for men.

## 4. Projection of activity rates: 2000 - 2010

### 4.1 Model(s): logistic, log-linear, hyperbole and logarithmic

#### 4.1.1 Men:

- To the [10-14] and [65+] age groups, application of function F6;
- To the [15-19] age group, application of function F2;
- To the [20-64] age groups, application of function F3;
- Modification of the trends for the [35-39] and [45-59] age groups.

#### 4.1.2 Women:

- To the [10-14] age group, application of function F5;
- To the [15-19] age group, application of function F2;
- To the [20+] age groups, application of function F3;
- Modification of the trends for the [20-64] age groups.

# Brazil

## 1. Source(s) of benchmark data

Code(s):    Title(s):

EPPA3    Economically active population: Estimates and Projections, 1950-2025, Third edition, ILO, Geneva, 1986.
ASTER    Yearbook of Labour Statistics 1945-89 - Retrospective Edition on Population Censuses, ILO, Geneva, 1990.
AST93    Yearbook of Labour Statistics 1993, ILO, Geneva, 1993.

## 2. Estimates of activity rates: 1950 - 1990

### 2.1 Benchmark data:

Table 1: Activity rates by sex and age group

| Age group | Year 1980 (1) | 1989 (2) | 1990 (2) |
|---|---|---|---|
| **Men** | | | |
| 10-14 | 20.24 | 25.51 | 24.32 |
| 15-19 | 64.80 | 73.27 | 71.76 |
| 20-24 | 90.03 | 92.50 | 92.14 |
| 25-29 | 96.05 | 96.30 | 96.16 |
| 30-39 | 96.53 | 97.31 | 96.85 |
| 40-49 | 93.16 | 94.62 | 94.46 |
| 50-59 | 82.30 | 81.51 | 82.33 |
| 60+ | 44.39 | 45.51 | 46.03 |
| **Women** | | | |
| 10-14 | 8.61 | 11.77 | 10.61 |
| 15-19 | 31.21 | 40.93 | 41.42 |
| 20-24 | 39.07 | 52.02 | 52.86 |
| 25-29 | 35.95 | 52.45 | 52.75 |
| 30-39 | 34.20 | 53.27 | 54.66 |
| 40-49 | 30.04 | 48.63 | 49.50 |
| 50-59 | 21.38 | 33.85 | 34.54 |
| 60+ | 7.38 | 11.29 | 11.55 |

Source(s): (1) ASTER; (2) AST93.

### 2.2 Method(s):  weighted average

#### 2.2.1 Men:

- 1950-70, 1950-70 adjusted activity rates derived from the EPPA3;
adjustment of activity rates based on the results of the 1980 census
and of the 1989 and 1990 surveys;
- 1980, weighted average of 1970 activity rates derived from the EPPA3
and of adjusted activity rates derived from the 1980 census;
- 1990, weighted average of activity rates derived from the 1989
and 1990 surveys.

#### 2.2.2 Women:

Method, hypothesis and treatment identical to those used for men.

## 3. Estimates of distribution rates by activity sector: 1950 - 1990

### 3.1 Benchmark data:

Table 2: Distribution of economically active population by activity sector

| Year | Agriculture | Industry Total | Manufac. | Services |
|---|---|---|---|---|
| **Men** | | | | |
| 1980 (1) | 37.54 | 29.32 | 19.11 | 33.14 |
| 1989 (2) | 29.36 | 29.04 | .. | 41.60 |
| 1990 (3) | 28.08 | 28.15 | 16.93 | 43.78 |
| **Women** | | | | |
| 1980 (1) | 15.27 | 15.76 | 15.27 | 68.98 |
| 1989 (2) | 14.68 | 12.72 | 0.00 | 72.60 |
| 1990 (3) | 13.34 | 12.82 | 11.94 | 73.85 |

Source(s): (1) ASTER; (2) AST93.

### 3.2 Method(s):  weighted average

#### 3.2.1 Men:

- 1950-70, 1950-70 adjusted distribution rates derived from the EPPA3;
adjustment of 1970 rates on the basis of the results of the 1975 census
and of the 1989 and 1990 surveys;
- 1980-90, weighted averages of distribution rates derived from
the 1980 census and of distribution rates derived from the 1989
and 1990 surveys.

#### 3.2.2 Women:

Method, hypothesis and treatment identical to those used for men.

## 4. Projection of activity rates: 2000 - 2010

### 4.1 Model(s):  linear, hyperbole and logistic

#### 4.1.1 Men:

- To the [10-44] age groups, application of function F1;
- To the [45+] age groups, application of function F3;
- Modification of the trends for the [10-24] and [35-49] age groups.

#### 4.1.2 Women:

- To the [10-14] age group, application of function F1;
- To the [15-64] age groups, application of function F6;
- To the [65+] age group, application of function F3;
- Modification of the trends for the [10-64] age groups.

# Brunei Darussalam

## 1. Source(s) of benchmark data

Code(s):     Title(s):

ADNU79     Demographic Yearbook 1979 - Population census statistics - Thirty-first Edition, United Nations, New York, 1980.
ASTER     Yearbook of Labour Statistics 1945-89 - Retrospective Edition on Population Censuses, ILO, Geneva, 1990.
STAT     Database on Labour Statistics, LABORSTA - Bureau of Statistics, ILO, Geneva.

## 2. Estimates of activity rates: 1950 - 1990

### 2.1 Benchmark data:

Table 1: Activity rates by sex and age group

| Age group | Year 1960 (1) | 1971 (1) | 1981 (1) | 1986 (1) | 1991 (2) |
|---|---|---|---|---|---|
| **Men** | | | | | |
| 10-14 | 0.00 | 0.00 | 0.00 | .. | 0.00 |
| 15-19 | 46.47 | 32.90 | 38.18 | .. | 23.80 |
| 20-24 | 91.30 | 86.55 | 86.40 | .. | 84.22 |
| 25-29 | 99.02 | 97.10 | 97.30 | .. | 97.10 |
| 30-34 | 99.29 | 97.33 | 98.71 | .. | 98.13 |
| 35-39 | 99.97 | 98.08 | 98.91 | .. | 98.35 |
| 40-44 | 99.36 | 97.66 | 98.32 | .. | 98.25 |
| 45-49 | 97.96 | 97.12 | 98.27 | .. | 96.34 |
| 50-54 | 95.89 | 94.87 | 96.40 | .. | 93.95 |
| 55-59 | 90.92 | 88.11 | 88.86 | .. | 72.08 |
| 60-64 | 82.44 | 80.88 | 82.70 | .. | 71.03 |
| 65+ | 56.66 | 58.61 | 51.94 | .. | 32.23 |
| **Women** | | | | | |
| 10-14 | 0.00 | 0.00 | 0.00 | 0.00 | 0.00 |
| 15-19 | 18.82 | 17.92 | 17.02 | 14.45 | 13.74 |
| 20-24 | 19.83 | 30.23 | 47.13 | 52.68 | 58.19 |
| 25-29 | 16.68 | 24.36 | 43.37 | 57.18 | 63.89 |
| 30-34 | 18.49 | 21.78 | 36.73 | 48.01 | 60.67 |
| 35-39 | 21.89 | 18.35 | 32.92 | 46.93 | 56.66 |
| 40-44 | 25.03 | 19.76 | 28.56 | 41.79 | 51.50 |
| 45-49 | 26.42 | 20.26 | 22.74 | 36.07 | 43.36 |
| 50-54 | 30.64 | 21.55 | 20.55 | 24.89 | 34.89 |
| 55-59 | 27.76 | 22.83 | 14.49 | 16.75 | 17.56 |
| 60-64 | 20.68 | 18.80 | 10.44 | 12.49 | 13.18 |
| 65+ | 7.71 | 11.48 | 5.95 | 5.77 | 4.16 |

Source(s): (1) ADNU79 and ASTER; (2) STAT.

### 2.2 Method(s): linear interpolation
weighted average

#### 2.2.1 Men:

- 1950-80, interpolation of activity rates derived from the 1960, 1971 and 1981 censuses;
modification of the trends for all age groups for 1950;
- 1990, weighted average of activity rates derived from the 1981 and 1990 censuses.

#### 2.2.2 Women:

- 1950-70, interpolation of activity rates derived from the 1960 and 1971 censuses;
- 1980-90, interpolation of activity rates derived from the 1981, 1986 and 1991 censuses;
application to activity rates of the [10-14] age group, the ratio of activity rates of the [10-14] and [15-19] age groups estimated for Kuwait.

## 3. Estimates of distribution rates by activity sector: 1950 - 1990

### 3.1 Benchmark data:

Table 2: Distribution of economically active population by activity sector

| Year | Agriculture | Industry Total | Manufac. | Services |
|---|---|---|---|---|
| **Men** | | | | |
| 1960 (1) | 28.68 | 40.69 | 5.75 | 30.63 |
| 1971 (1) | 9.84 | 39.32 | 4.37 | 50.85 |
| 1981 (1) | 4.72 | 37.23 | 4.23 | 58.05 |
| 1991 (2) | 2.21 | 31.43 | 6.44 | 66.35 |
| **Women** | | | | |
| 1960 (1) | 57.35 | 10.07 | 5.56 | 32.58 |
| 1971 (1) | 23.01 | 10.36 | 4.43 | 66.63 |
| 1981 (1) | 6.25 | 11.00 | 3.66 | 82.75 |
| 1991 (2) | 1.63 | 8.87 | 4.24 | 89.49 |

Source(s): (1) ASTER; (2) STAT.

### 3.2 Method(s): weighted average
linear extrapolation

#### 3.2.1 Men:

- 1950, extrapolation of distribution rates derived from the 1960 and 1971 censuses;
- 1960-90, weighted averages of distribution rates derived from the 1960, 1971, 1981 and 1991 censuses.

#### 3.2.2 Women:

- 1950, distribution rates of agriculture sector estimated on the basis of men/women ratio in agriculture derived from the 1960 census; distribution rates of industry sector derived from the 1960 census; distribution rates of services sector has been computed as the remainder;
- 1960-90, weighted averages of distribution rates derived from the 1960, 1971, 1981 and 1991 censuses.

## 4. Projection of activity rates: 2000 - 2010

### 4.1 Model(s): linear, log-linear, hyperbole and logistic

#### 4.1.1 Men:

- To the [15-54] age groups, application of function F1;
- To the [55+] age groups, application of function F3;
- Modification of the trends for the [15-19], [25-34], [40-44] and [55-64] age groups.

#### 4.1.2 Women:

- To the [15-24], [30-39] and [45-64] age groups, application of function F1;
- To the [25-29] age group, application of function F6;
- To the [40-44] age group, application of function F2;
- To the [65+] age group, application of function F3;
- Modification of the trends for the [15-64] age groups.

*Notes on adjustments of rates, see p. 3-8.*     *Notes on projection functions, see p. 10.*

# Bulgaria

## 1. Source(s) of benchmark data

Code(s):     Title(s):

EPPA3      Economically active population: Estimates and Projections, 1950-2025, Third edition, ILO, Geneva, 1986.
ASTER     Yearbook of Labour Statistics 1945-89 - Retrospective Edition on Population Censuses, ILO, Geneva, 1990.
BLT-94-2   Popovic B. (1994), "New 1980 and 1990 estimates of activity rates by age and sectoral distribution for some countries of Eastern and Southern Europe"
           in the Bulletin of Labour of Statistics - 1994-2, ILO, Geneva.

## 2. Estimates of activity rates: 1950 - 1990

### 2.1 Benchmark data:

Table 1: Activity rates by sex and age group

| Age group | Year | | | |
|---|---|---|---|---|
| | 1950 (1) | 1960 (1) | 1970 (1) | 1985 (2) |
| **Men** | | | | |
| 10-14 | 2.00 | 0.85 | 0.45 | 0.00 |
| 15-19 | 60.00 | 45.55 | 31.15 | 17.69 |
| 20-24 | 92.70 | 90.00 | 83.30 | 81.90 |
| 25-29 | 95.55 | 95.35 | 95.15 | 95.07 |
| 30-34 | 98.00 | 97.90 | 97.80 | 97.80 |
| 35-39 | 98.35 | 98.10 | 97.80 | 95.80 |
| 40-44 | 98.50 | 97.90 | 97.35 | 95.50 |
| 45-49 | 98.40 | 97.25 | 96.15 | 94.60 |
| 50-54 | 97.80 | 95.30 | 92.80 | 88.10 |
| 55-59 | 95.50 | 90.80 | 86.05 | 80.90 |
| 60-64 | 93.20 | 70.00 | 46.80 | 39.20 |
| 65+ | 69.00 | 38.35 | 20.60 | 15.17 |
| **Women** | | | | |
| 10-14 | 3.50 | 1.30 | 0.85 | 0.07 |
| 15-19 | 56.25 | 44.50 | 32.20 | 34.47 |
| 20-24 | 72.50 | 69.80 | 73.35 | 87.04 |
| 25-29 | 71.70 | 78.10 | 85.05 | 95.00 |
| 30-34 | 74.05 | 80.90 | 88.35 | 96.40 |
| 35-39 | 77.15 | 83.25 | 89.90 | 94.80 |
| 40-44 | 78.55 | 83.35 | 88.50 | 94.60 |
| 45-49 | 76.55 | 79.55 | 82.70 | 91.00 |
| 50-54 | 71.55 | 71.40 | 71.25 | 83.60 |
| 55-59 | 68.95 | 46.40 | 31.20 | 32.00 |
| 60-64 | 62.80 | 28.45 | 12.90 | 16.50 |
| 65+ | 20.40 | 8.60 | 3.60 | 4.35 |

Source(s): (1) EPPA3; (2) STAT.

### 2.2 Method(s):  weighted average
                    linear extrapolation

#### 2.2.1 Men:

- 1950-70, 1950-70 activity rates derived from the EPPA3;
- 1980, weighted average of activity rates of 1970 derived from the EPPA3
and of adjusted activity rates derived from the 1985 census;
- 1990, extrapolation of 1950-70 activity rates derived from the EPPA3
and of activity rates estimated for 1980 and adjusted activity rates derived
from the 1985 census; modification of the trends for all age groups;
application to extrapolated rates, variations in 1985 interpolated rates,
in relation to adjusted activity rates derived from the 1985 census.

#### 2.2.2 Women:

Method, hypothesis and treatment identical to those used for men.

## 3. Estimates of distribution rates by activity sector: 1950 - 1990

### 3.1 Benchmark data:

Table 2: Distribution of economically active population by activity sector

| Year | Agriculture | Industry | | Services |
|---|---|---|---|---|
| | | Total | Manufac. | |
| **Men** | | | | |
| 1950 (1) | 63.20 | 18.30 | .. | 18.40 |
| 1960 (1) | 47.60 | 31.30 | .. | 21.10 |
| 1970 (1) | 29.10 | 44.30 | .. | 26.60 |
| 1980 (2) | 18.72 | 49.90 | 34.99 | 31.38 |
| 1990 (2) | 13.83 | 53.96 | 40.81 | 32.21 |
| **Women** | | | | |
| 1950 (1) | 85.50 | 7.00 | .. | 7.40 |
| 1960 (1) | 68.60 | 15.60 | .. | 15.80 |
| 1970 (1) | 41.90 | 29.50 | .. | 28.50 |
| 1980 (2) | 21.94 | 38.64 | 33.90 | 39.42 |
| 1990 (2) | 13.05 | 42.09 | 36.62 | 44.86 |

Source(s): (1) EPPA3; (2) BLT-94-2.

### 3.2 Method(s):  data from BLT-94-4

#### 3.2.1 Men:

- 1950-70, 1950-70 distribution rates derived from the EPPA3;
- 1980-90, 1980 and 1990 distribution rates derived from the Bulletin
of Labour Statistics, 1994-2.

#### 3.2.2 Women:

Method, hypothesis and treatment identical to those used for men.

## 4. Projection of activity rates: 2000 - 2010

### 4.1 Model(s):  linear and hyperbole

#### 4.1.1 Men:

- To the [15+] age groups, application of function F3;
- Modification of the trends for the [20-24] and [30-34] age groups.

#### 4.1.2 Women:

- To the [15-19] age group, application of function F1;
- To the [20+] age groups, application of function F3;
- Modification des tendances du groupe d'âge [15-54] age groups.

---

*Notes on adjustments of rates, see p. 3-8.*          *Notes on projection functions, see p. 10.*

# Burkina Faso

## 1. Source(s) of benchmark data

Code(s):     Title(s):

S1960        Enquête démographique 1960-61, Institut National de la Statistique et de la Démographie, Ouagadougou, 1961.

R1985        Recensement général de la population 1985, Institut National de la Statistique et de la Démographie, Ouagadougou, 1985.

S1991        Enquête démographique, 1991, Institut National de la Statistique et de la Démographie, Ouagadougou, 1991.

## 2. Estimates of activity rates: 1950 - 1990

### 2.1 Benchmark data:

Table 1: Activity rates by sex and age group

| Age group | Year 1960 (1) | 1985 (2) | 1991 (3) |
|---|---|---|---|
| **Men** | | | |
| 10-14 | 79.00 | 71.18 | 63.25 |
| 15-19 | 87.00 | 86.02 | 77.75 |
| 20-24 | 96.05 | 92.24 | 85.99 |
| 25-29 | 97.50 | 96.78 | 93.45 |
| 30-34 | 98.25 | 97.72 | 97.60 |
| 35-39 | 98.45 | 98.06 | 98.13 |
| 40-44 | 98.30 | 97.62 | 98.33 |
| 45-49 | 97.50 | 97.47 | 98.49 |
| 50-54 | 97.15 | 95.78 | 96.24 |
| 55-59 | 96.40 | 94.05 | 93.73 |
| 60-64 | 93.65 | 91.01 | 92.33 |
| 65+ | 80.85 | 73.31 | 78.19 |
| **Women** | | | |
| 10-14 | 79.80 | 68.18 | 60.63 |
| 15-19 | 88.75 | 76.33 | 71.58 |
| 20-24 | 93.05 | 76.82 | 75.27 |
| 25-29 | 93.95 | 80.07 | 80.89 |
| 30-34 | 95.50 | 81.20 | 83.56 |
| 35-39 | 95.40 | 82.44 | 84.02 |
| 40-44 | 94.80 | 82.08 | 86.60 |
| 45-49 | 93.40 | 82.32 | 85.51 |
| 50-54 | 92.04 | 81.12 | 87.24 |
| 55-59 | 86.37 | 74.46 | 78.47 |
| 60-64 | 80.38 | 64.13 | 67.88 |
| 65+ | 65.46 | 40.32 | 44.05 |

Source(s): (1) S1960; (2) R1985; (3) S1991.

### 2.2 Method(s): linears interpolation and extrapolation

#### 2.2.1 Men:

- 1950-90, interpolation and extrapolation of activity rates derived from
the 1985 census and of activity rates derived from the 1960 and 1991 surveys;
adjustment of 1950 extrapolated rates on the basis of variations
in 1960 interpolated rates, in relation to activity rates derived from
the 1960 survey; adjustment of extrapolated rates on the basis of variations
in 1985 interpolated rates, in relation to activity rates derived from the 1985
census; modification of the trends for all age groups for 1950
and of the [10-19] age groups for 1990.

#### 2.2.2 Women:

- 1950-90, interpolation and extrapolation of activity rates derived from
the 1960 survey and of average of activity rates derived from the 1985 census
and the 1991 survey;
modification of the trends for all age groups for 1950
and the [10-14] and [20+] age groups for 1990.

## 3. Estimates of distribution rates by activity sector: 1950 - 1990

### 3.1 Benchmark data:

Table 2: Distribution of economically active population by activity sector

| Year | Agriculture | Industry Total | Manufac. | Services |
|---|---|---|---|---|
| **Men** | | | | |
| 1960 (1) | 92.00 | 3.00 | .. | 5.00 |
| 1985 (2) | 91.18 | 3.64 | .. | 5.18 |
| 1991 (3) | 91.85 | 1.84 | 1.15 | 6.31 |
| **Women** | | | | |
| 1960 (1) | 91.50 | 2.10 | .. | 6.40 |
| 1985 (2) | 92.32 | 2.08 | .. | 5.60 |
| 1991 (3) | 94.40 | 1.14 | 1.09 | 4.45 |

Source(s): (1) S1960; (2) R1985; (3) S1991.

### 3.2 Method(s): linears interpolation and extrapolation

#### 3.2.1 Men:

1950-90, interpolation of distribution rates derived from the 1960
and 1991 surveys and from the 1985 census;
Application of manufacturing/industry ratio derived from the 1991 survey.

#### 3.2.2 Women:

Method, hypothesis and treatment identical to those used for men.

## 4. Projection of activity rates: 2000 - 2010

### 4.1 Model(s): linear, hyperbole and exponential

#### 4.1.1 Men:

- To the [10-24] age groups, application of function F1;
- To the [25+] age groups, application of function F3;
- Modification of the trends for the [20-24] and [40-44] age groups.

#### 4.1.2 Women:

- To the [10-14] age group, application of function F4;
- To the [15+] age groups, application of function F3;
- Modification of the trends for the [10-14] and [20-64] age groups.

*Notes on adjustments of rates, see p. 3-8.*                    *Notes on projection functions, see p. 10.*

# Burundi

## 1. Source(s) of benchmark data

Code(s):  Title(s):

EPPA3  Economically active population: Estimates and Projections, 1950-2025, Third edition, ILO, Geneva, 1986.
ASTER  Yearbook of Labour Statistics 1945-89 - Retrospective Edition on Population Censuses, ILO, Geneva, 1990.

## 2. Estimates of activity rates: 1950 - 1990

### 2.1 Benchmark data:

Table 1: Activity rates by sex and age group

| Age group | Year | | | |
|---|---|---|---|---|
| | 1950 | 1960 | 1970 | 1980 |
| **Men** | | | | |
| 10-14 | 56.35 | 55.25 | 54.15 | 53.45 |
| 15-19 | 89.35 | 87.90 | 86.45 | 85.55 |
| 20-24 | 96.25 | 95.65 | 95.10 | 94.80 |
| 25-29 | 97.80 | 97.75 | 97.65 | 97.60 |
| 30-34 | 98.55 | 98.45 | 98.35 | 98.30 |
| 35-39 | 98.55 | 98.45 | 98.35 | 98.30 |
| 40-44 | 98.15 | 98.05 | 97.95 | 97.90 |
| 45-49 | 98.05 | 97.95 | 97.85 | 97.80 |
| 50-54 | 96.85 | 96.70 | 96.60 | 96.50 |
| 55-59 | 95.65 | 95.40 | 95.20 | 95.10 |
| 60-64 | 92.60 | 92.25 | 91.90 | 91.70 |
| 65+ | 76.25 | 75.70 | 75.10 | 74.75 |
| **Women** | | | | |
| 10-14 | 50.35 | 48.90 | 47.45 | 46.55 |
| 15-19 | 92.60 | 89.55 | 86.45 | 84.60 |
| 20-24 | 96.80 | 93.80 | 90.80 | 89.00 |
| 25-29 | 97.45 | 94.65 | 91.90 | 90.25 |
| 30-34 | 98.75 | 96.15 | 93.55 | 92.00 |
| 35-39 | 98.45 | 96.00 | 93.55 | 92.10 |
| 40-44 | 97.55 | 95.35 | 93.15 | 91.85 |
| 45-49 | 96.10 | 93.95 | 91.80 | 90.55 |
| 50-54 | 88.20 | 86.40 | 84.65 | 83.55 |
| 55-59 | 78.10 | 76.80 | 75.55 | 74.75 |
| 60-64 | 61.90 | 61.15 | 60.35 | 59.90 |
| 65+ | 35.75 | 35.45 | 35.20 | 35.05 |

Source: EPPA3.

### 2.2 Method(s): linears interpolation and extrapolation

#### 2.2.1 Men:

- 1950-90, interpolation and extrapolation of 1950-80 activity rates derived from the EPPA3;
modification of the trends for all age groups;
adjustment of 1990 extrapolated rates on the basis of variations in 1980 interpolated rates, in relation to the 1980 activity rates derived from the EPPA3.

#### 2.2.2 Women:

Method, hypothesis and treatment identical to those used for men.

## 3. Estimates of distribution rates by activity sector: 1950 - 1990

### 3.1 Benchmark data:

Table 2: Distribution of economically active population by activity sector

| Year | Agriculture | Industry | | Services |
|---|---|---|---|---|
| | | Total | Manufac. | |
| **Men** | | | | |
| 1950 (1) | 93.00 | 2.20 | .. | 4.80 |
| 1960 (1) | 91.00 | 2.85 | .. | 6.15 |
| 1970 (1) | 89.00 | 3.30 | .. | 7.70 |
| 1979 (2) | 87.90 | 3.66 | 2.11 | 8.43 |
| 1980 (1) | 87.80 | 3.70 | .. | 8.50 |
| **Women** | | | | |
| 1950 (1) | 98.30 | 0.80 | .. | 0.90 |
| 1960 (1) | 98.15 | 0.90 | .. | 0.95 |
| 1970 (1) | 98.00 | 0.95 | .. | 1.05 |
| 1979 (2) | 97.89 | 1.02 | 1.01 | 1.10 |
| 1980 (1) | 97.85 | 1.05 | .. | 1.10 |

Source(s): (1) EPPA3; (2) ASTER.

### 3.2 Method(s): linear extrapolation

#### 3.2.1 Men:

- 1950-80, 1950-80 distribution rates derived from the EPPA3;
- 1990, extrapolation of 1950-80 distribution rates derived from the EPPA3;
- Application of manufacturing/industry ratio derived from the 1979 census.

#### 3.2.2 Women:

Method, hypothesis and treatment identical to those used for men.

## 4. Projection of activity rates: 2000 - 2010

### 4.1 Model(s): linear and hyperbole

#### 4.1.1 Men:

- To all age groups, application of function F1.

#### 4.1.2 Women:

- To all age groups, application of function F3;
- Modification of the trends for the [20-54] age groups.

---

*Notes on adjustments of rates, see p. 3-8.*   *Notes on projection functions, see p. 10.*

# Cambodia

## 1. Source(s) of benchmark data

Code(s):    Title(s):

EPPA3       Economically active population: Estimates and Projections, 1950-2025, Third edition, ILO, Geneva, 1986.
STAT        Database on Labour Statistics - LABORSTA, Bureau of Statistics, ILO, Geneva.
AST93       Yearbook of Labour Statistics 1993, ILO, Geneva, 1993.

## 2. Estimates of activity rates: 1950 - 1990

### 2.1 Benchmark data:

Table 1: Activity rates by sex and age group

| Age group | Year 1962 (1) | 1992 (2) |
|---|---|---|
| **Men** | | |
| 10-14 | 17.87 | 24.31 |
| 15-19 | 58.08 | 54.00 |
| 20-24 | 87.99 | 88.00 |
| 25-29 | 97.45 | 96.77 |
| 30-34 | 98.81 | 98.30 |
| 35-39 | 98.85 | 98.75 |
| 40-44 | 98.76 | 98.12 |
| 45-49 | 98.35 | 97.42 |
| 50-54 | 96.54 | 95.83 |
| 55-59 | 91.09 | 91.43 |
| 60-64 | 78.11 | 68.11 |
| 65+ | 49.61 | 41.10 |
| **Women** | | |
| 10-14 | 28.48 | 26.49 |
| 15-19 | 66.96 | 68.82 |
| 20-24 | 63.76 | 87.89 |
| 25-29 | 58.40 | 88.82 |
| 30-34 | 58.94 | 91.73 |
| 35-39 | 61.49 | 92.28 |
| 40-44 | 62.71 | 92.76 |
| 45-49 | 63.58 | 91.41 |
| 50-54 | 57.98 | 89.29 |
| 55-60 | 49.47 | 83.48 |
| 60-64 | 32.42 | 56.01 |
| 65+ | 16.23 | 26.63 |

Source(s): (1) STAT; (2) AST93.

### 2.2 Method(s):  linears interpolation and extrapolation

**2.2.1 Men:**

- 1950-90, interpolation and extrapolation of activity rates derived from
the 1962 census and of activity rates derived from the 1992 official estimates.

**2.2.2 Women:**

- 1950-90, application to estimated activity rates for Thailand,
the variations in the 1992 estimated activity rates, in relation to activity rates
derived from the 1992 official estimates;
modification of the trends for all age groups.

## 3. Estimates of distribution rates by activity sector: 1950 - 1990

### 3.1 Benchmark data:

Table 2: Distribution of economically active population by activity sector

| Year | Agriculture | Industry Total | Manufac. | Services |
|---|---|---|---|---|
| **Men** | | | | |
| 1950 (1) | 79.90 | 2.55 | 0.00 | 17.55 |
| 1960 (1) | 77.20 | 4.65 | 0.00 | 18.15 |
| 1962 (2) | 76.74 | 5.01 | 3.34 | 18.25 |
| 1970 (1) | 73.80 | 5.35 | 0.00 | 20.85 |
| 1980 (1) | 70.30 | 6.80 | 4.77 | 22.90 |
| **Women** | | | | |
| 1950 (1) | 89.35 | 0.85 | 0.00 | 9.80 |
| 1960 (1) | 88.35 | 1.90 | 0.00 | 9.75 |
| 1962 (2) | 88.19 | 2.21 | 2.01 | 9.61 |
| 1970 (1) | 84.55 | 2.60 | 0.00 | 12.85 |
| 1980 (1) | 80.00 | 6.50 | 5.98 | 13.50 |

Source(s): (1) EPPA3; (2) STAT.

### 3.2 Method(s):  linear extrapolation

**3.2.1 Men:**

- 1950-80, 1950-80 distribution rates derived from the EPPA3;
- 1990, extrapolation of 1950-80 distribution rates derived from the EPPA3;
modification of the trends in all sectors;
- Application of manufacturing/industry ratio derived from the 1962 census.

**3.2.2 Women:**

Method, hypothesis and treatment identical to those used for men.

## 4. Projection of activity rates: 2000 - 2010

### 4.1 Model(s):  linear, log-linear, hyperbole and logistic

**4.1.1 Men:**

- To the [10-59] age groups, application of function F1;
- To the [60+] age groups, application of function F3;
- Modification of the trend for the [35-39] age group.

**4.1.2 Women:**

- To the [10-14] age group, application of function F1;
- To the [15-24] age groups, application of function F2;
- To the [25-59] age groups, application of function F6;
- To the [60+] age groups, application of function F3;
- Modification of the trend for the [10-14] age group.

*Notes on adjustments of rates, see p. 3-8.*

*Notes on projection functions, see p. 10.*

# Cameroon

## 1. Source(s) of benchmark data

Code(s):     Title(s):

EPPA3     Economically active population: Estimates and Projections, 1950-2025, Third edition, ILO, Geneva, 1986.
ASTER     Yearbook of Labour Statistics 1945-89 - Retrospective Edition on Population Censuses, ILO, Geneva, 1990.

## 2. Estimates of activity rates: 1950 - 1990

### 2.1 Benchmark data:

Table 1: Activity rates by sex and age group

| Age group | Year | | | | |
|---|---|---|---|---|---|
| | 1950 (1) | 1960 (1) | 1970 (1) | 1980 (1) | 1976 (2) |
| **Men** | | | | | |
| 10-14 | 52.05 | 50.35 | 47.35 | 40.00 | .. |
| 15-19 | 84.80 | 82.60 | 78.60 | 68.85 | .. |
| 20-24 | 95.25 | 94.35 | 92.85 | 89.10 | .. |
| 25-29 | 97.40 | 97.25 | 97.05 | 96.50 | .. |
| 30-34 | 98.15 | 98.00 | 97.75 | 97.10 | .. |
| 35-39 | 98.30 | 98.15 | 97.90 | 97.20 | .. |
| 40-44 | 98.15 | 98.00 | 97.70 | 97.00 | .. |
| 45-49 | 97.35 | 97.25 | 97.00 | 96.40 | .. |
| 50-54 | 96.95 | 96.75 | 96.35 | 95.50 | .. |
| 55-59 | 96.05 | 95.75 | 95.15 | 93.75 | .. |
| 60-64 | 93.10 | 92.55 | 91.60 | 89.15 | .. |
| 65+ | 79.90 | 78.95 | 77.20 | 73.00 | .. |
| **Women** | | | | | |
| 10-14 | 31.65 | 30.65 | 28.80 | 24.35 | 13.26 |
| 15-19 | 42.30 | 41.00 | 38.80 | 33.30 | 35.42 |
| 20-24 | 49.55 | 48.65 | 47.00 | 42.95 | 44.40 |
| 25-29 | 53.15 | 52.10 | 50.20 | 45.65 | 47.40 |
| 30-34 | 55.90 | 54.75 | 52.80 | 47.90 | 49.78 |
| 35-39 | 62.00 | 60.85 | 58.85 | 53.90 | 55.79 |
| 40-44 | 62.75 | 61.65 | 59.65 | 54.85 | 56.64 |
| 45-49 | 70.35 | 69.10 | 66.80 | 61.25 | 63.38 |
| 50-54 | 66.25 | 64.85 | 62.30 | 56.10 | 58.48 |
| 55-59 | 60.85 | 59.40 | 56.90 | 50.70 | 61.64 |
| 60-64 | 57.90 | 56.05 | 52.70 | 44.55 | 47.68 |
| 65+ | 40.80 | 39.05 | 35.90 | 28.25 | 31.21 |

Source(s): (1) EPPA3; (2) ASTER.

### 2.2 Method(s): linears interpolation and extrapolation

#### 2.2.1 Men:

- 1950-90, interpolation and extrapolation of 1950-80 activity rates
derived from the EPPA3;
modification of the trends of the [10-14] and [15-19] age groups for 1990.

#### 2.2.2 Women:

- 1950-90, interpolation and extrapolation of 1950-80 activity rates
derived from the EPPA3;
adjustment of 1980 interpolated rates on the basis of variations
in 1976 interpolated rates, in relation to adjusted activity rates derived from
the 1976 census;
modification of the trends of the [15+] age groups for 1990.

## 3. Estimates of distribution rates by activity sector: 1950 - 1990

### 3.1 Benchmark data:

Table 2: Distribution of economically active population by activity sector

| Year | Agriculture | Industry | | Services |
|---|---|---|---|---|
| | | Total | Manufac. | |
| **Men** | | | | |
| 1950 (1) | 87.50 | 4.50 | .. | 8.00 |
| 1960 (1) | 84.40 | 5.40 | .. | 10.20 |
| 1970 (1) | 78.90 | 7.00 | .. | 14.10 |
| 1976 (2) | 70.61 | 9.62 | 6.35 | 19.77 |
| 1980 (1) | 65.40 | 11.15 | .. | 23.45 |
| **Women** | | | | |
| 1950 (1) | 99.00 | 0.30 | .. | 0.70 |
| 1960 (1) | 97.00 | 1.00 | .. | 2.00 |
| 1970 (1) | 95.00 | 1.20 | .. | 3.80 |
| 1976 (2) | 92.14 | 2.56 | 2.48 | 5.29 |
| 1980 (1) | 86.50 | 2.25 | .. | 11.25 |

Source(s): (1) EPPA3; (2) ASTER.

### 3.2 Method(s): linear extrapolation

#### 3.2.1 Men:

- 1950-80, 1950-80 distribution rates derived from the EPPA3;
- 1990, extrapolation of 1950-80 distribution rates derived from the EPPA3
and of distribution rates derived from the 1976 census;
- Application of manufacturing/industry ratio derived from the 1976 census.

#### 3.2.2 Women:

Method, hypothesis and treatment identical to those used for men.

## 4. Projection of activity rates: 2000 - 2010

### 4.1 Model(s): linear and hyperbole

#### 4.1.1 Men:

- To the [10-24] age groups, application of function F1;
- To the [25+] age groups, application of function F3;
- Modification of the trends for the [25-64] age groups.

#### 4.1.2 Women:

- To the [10-14] age group, application of function F1;
- To the [15+] age groups, application of function F3;
- Modification of the trends for the [10-44] and [60-64] age groups.

# Canada

## 1. Source(s) of benchmark data

Code(s): Title(s):
EPPA3 Economically active population: Estimates and Projections, 1950-2025, Third edition, ILO, Geneva, 1986.
STAT Database on Labour Statistics, LABORSTA - Bureau of Statistics, ILO, Geneva.

## 2. Estimates of activity rates: 1950 - 1990

### 2.1 Benchmark data:

Table 1: Activity rates by sex and age group

| Age group | Year 1979 | 1980 | 1981 | 1989 | 1990 | 1991 |
|---|---|---|---|---|---|---|
| **Men** | | | | | | |
| 10-14 | 0.00 | 0.00 | 0.00 | 0.00 | 0.00 | 0.00 |
| 15-19 | 57.20 | 58.00 | 58.17 | 60.51 | 58.90 | 55.82 |
| 20-24 | 86.40 | 86.20 | 86.52 | 84.79 | 82.80 | 81.45 |
| 25-29 | 94.43 | 94.23 | 94.20 | 93.64 | 93.11 | 91.86 |
| 30-34 | 97.05 | 96.65 | 96.60 | 94.66 | 94.22 | 93.19 |
| 35-39 | 96.72 | 96.38 | 96.50 | 95.02 | 94.49 | 93.73 |
| 40-44 | 95.85 | 95.59 | 95.69 | 94.47 | 94.18 | 93.76 |
| 45-49 | 94.58 | 94.49 | 94.64 | 93.32 | 92.98 | 92.82 |
| 50-54 | 90.77 | 90.66 | 90.85 | 89.84 | 88.61 | 88.02 |
| 55-59 | 85.27 | 85.04 | 84.16 | 78.11 | 77.35 | 75.97 |
| 60-64 | 65.65 | 65.25 | 63.66 | 53.44 | 51.58 | 48.19 |
| 65+ | 15.30 | 14.70 | 14.09 | 10.97 | 11.41 | 11.33 |
| **Women** | | | | | | |
| 10-14 | 0.00 | 0.00 | 0.00 | 0.00 | 0.00 | 0.00 |
| 15-19 | 50.80 | 52.20 | 53.03 | 56.49 | 55.93 | 53.82 |
| 20-24 | 71.30 | 73.00 | 72.96 | 77.24 | 76.46 | 75.55 |
| 25-29 | 62.28 | 64.45 | 67.11 | 77.30 | 78.15 | 77.99 |
| 30-34 | 58.39 | 60.83 | 63.84 | 75.14 | 76.26 | 76.35 |
| 35-39 | 58.73 | 60.94 | 63.85 | 76.57 | 77.74 | 77.67 |
| 40-44 | 60.22 | 62.41 | 65.30 | 77.80 | 79.08 | 79.09 |
| 45-49 | 54.77 | 57.04 | 58.85 | 71.81 | 73.02 | 74.41 |
| 50-54 | 49.42 | 51.16 | 52.55 | 62.42 | 63.45 | 64.48 |
| 55-59 | 41.81 | 41.20 | 41.25 | 46.37 | 45.23 | 46.60 |
| 60-64 | 24.71 | 24.78 | 24.78 | 22.25 | 25.95 | 24.49 |
| 65+ | 4.2 | 4.3 | 4.48 | 3.96 | 3.79 | 3.50 |

Source(s): STAT.

### 2.2 Method(s): arithmetic average

#### 2.2.1 Men:

- 1950-70, 1950-70 activity rates derived from the EPPA3;
- 1980, average of activity rates derived from the 1979, 1980 and 1981 surveys;
- 1990, average of activity rates derived from the 1989, 1990 and 1991 surveys;
adjustment of activity rates to make allowance for armed forces.

#### 2.2.2 Women:

Method, hypothesis and treatment identical to those used for men.

## 3. Estimates of distribution rates by activity sector: 1950 - 1990

### 3.1 Benchmark data:

Table 2: Distribution of economically active population by activity sector

| Year | Agriculture | Industry Total | Manufac. | Services |
|---|---|---|---|---|
| **Men** | | | | |
| 1979 | 7.51 | 36.44 | 23.20 | 56.05 |
| 1980 | 6.88 | 36.20 | 23.80 | 56.92 |
| 1981 | 6.73 | 36.36 | 24.10 | 56.91 |
| 1989 | 4.08 | 35.58 | 21.41 | 60.34 |
| 1990 | 4.01 | 34.90 | 20.34 | 61.09 |
| 1991 | 4.18 | 33.89 | 19.68 | 61.93 |
| **Women** | | | | |
| 1979 | 3.37 | 15.25 | 12.96 | 81.38 |
| 1980 | 3.16 | 15.76 | 13.68 | 81.08 |
| 1981 | 11.74 | 56.40 | 47.31 | 31.86 |
| 1989 | 2.44 | 13.52 | 11.34 | 84.04 |
| 1990 | 2.38 | 12.97 | 10.69 | 84.64 |
| 1991 | 2.57 | 12.36 | 10.17 | 85.07 |

Source(s): STAT.

### 3.2 Method(s): arithmetic average

#### 3.2.1 Men:

- 1950-70, 1950-70 distribution rates derived from the EPPA3;
- 1980, averages of distribution rates derived from the 1979, 1980 and 1981 surveys;
- 1990, averages of distribution rates derived from the 1989, 1990 and 1991 surveys.

#### 3.2.2 Women:

Method, hypothesis and treatment identical to those used for men.

## 4. Projection of activity rates: 2000 - 2010

### 4.1 Model(s): linear, hyperbole and logistic

#### 4.1.1 Men:

- To the [15-19] age group, application of function F1;
- To the [20+] age groups, application of function F3;
- Modification of the trends for the [15-19] and [25-54] age groups.

#### 4.1.2 Women:

- To the [15-64] age groups, application of function F6;
- To the [65+] age group, application of function F3;
- Modification of the trends for the [15-64] age groups.

*Notes on adjustments of rates, see p. 3-8.*     *Notes on projection functions, see p. 10.*

# Cape Verde

## 1. Source(s) of benchmark data

Code(s):     Title(s):

EPPA3      Economically active population: Estimates and Projections, 1950-2025, Third edition, ILO, Geneva, 1986.
R1980      Recenseamento Geral da Populacao e Habitacao 1980, III Volume: Populacao Activa, Ministerio do Plano e das Finanças, Paraia, 1983.
R1990      Recenseamento da Populacao e Habitacao 1990, Ministerio do Plano e das Finanças, Paraia, 1992.

## 2. Estimates of activity rates: 1950 - 1990

### 2.1 Benchmark data:

Table 1: Activity rates by sex and age group

| Age group | Year 1950 (1) | 1960 (1) | 1970 (1) | 1980 (1) | 1980 (2) | 1990 (3) |
|---|---|---|---|---|---|---|
| **Men** | | | | | | |
| 10-14 | 52.05 | 52.00 | 51.85 | 51.60 | .. | 17.89 |
| 15-19 | 84.80 | 84.75 | 84.60 | 84.25 | .. | 72.65 |
| 20-24 | 95.25 | 95.20 | 95.15 | 95.00 | .. | 94.27 |
| 25-29 | 97.40 | 97.40 | 97.40 | 97.35 | .. | 96.83 |
| 30-34 | 98.15 | 98.10 | 98.10 | 98.10 | .. | 96.69 |
| 35-39 | 98.30 | 98.30 | 98.30 | 98.25 | .. | 95.78 |
| 40-44 | 98.15 | 98.15 | 98.10 | 98.10 | .. | 95.11 |
| 45-49 | 97.35 | 97.35 | 97.35 | 97.35 | .. | 95.63 |
| 50-54 | 96.95 | 96.95 | 96.90 | 96.90 | .. | 93.57 |
| 55-59 | 96.05 | 96.05 | 96.05 | 96.00 | .. | 91.54 |
| 60-64 | 93.10 | 93.10 | 93.05 | 92.95 | .. | 86.64 |
| 65+ | 79.90 | 79.85 | 79.80 | 79.65 | .. | 59.42 |
| **Women** | | | | | | |
| 10-14 | 7.50 | 6.80 | 6.20 | .. | 5.48 | 10.97 |
| 15-19 | 29.70 | 32.10 | 34.50 | .. | 36.32 | 43.19 |
| 20-24 | 31.40 | 35.70 | 40.00 | .. | 44.49 | 52.56 |
| 25-29 | 27.05 | 30.50 | 34.00 | .. | 37.98 | 51.66 |
| 30-34 | 24.80 | 28.55 | 32.20 | .. | 34.14 | 51.24 |
| 35-39 | 22.10 | 24.50 | 27.80 | .. | 30.35 | 50.02 |
| 40-44 | 19.20 | 21.20 | 23.20 | .. | 25.14 | 42.84 |
| 45-49 | 18.70 | 19.50 | 20.45 | .. | 21.20 | 38.52 |
| 50-54 | 18.00 | 19.00 | 20.00 | .. | 20.95 | 33.96 |
| 55-59 | 15.80 | 16.30 | 17.80 | .. | 17.36 | 27.95 |
| 60-64 | 13.00 | 13.10 | 13.20 | .. | 13.30 | 24.58 |
| 65+ | 11.80 | 10.50 | 9.20 | .. | 7.75 | 11.87 |

Source(s): (1) EPPA3; (2) R1980; (3) R1990.

### 2.2 Method(s): linears interpolation and extrapolation

#### 2.2.1 Men:

- 1950-80, interpolation of 1950-80 activity rates derived from the EPPA3;
adjustment of interpolated rates on the basis of variations in 1990
extrapolated rates, in relation to the adjusted activity rates derived from
the 1990 census;
- 1990, adjusted activity rates derived from the 1990 census;
modification of the trends of the [10-14] and [60+] age groups for 1980
and 1990.

#### 2.2.2 Women:

- 1950-70, extrapolation of adjusted activity rates derived from
the 1980 and 1990 censuses;
- 1980-90, adjusted activity rates derived from the 1980 and 1990 censuses;
modification of the trends for all age groups.

## 3. Estimates of distribution rates by activity sector: 1950 - 1990

### 3.1 Benchmark data:

Table 2: Distribution of economically active population by activity sector

| Year | Agriculture | Industry Total | Manufac. | Services |
|---|---|---|---|---|
| **Men** | | | | |
| 1980 (1) | 34.76 | 37.08 | 2.55 | 28.17 |
| 1990 (2) | 29.92 | 37.54 | 6.50 | 32.54 |
| **Women** | | | | |
| 1980 (1) | 40.35 | 18.63 | 2.88 | 41.03 |
| 1990 (2) | 31.63 | 17.43 | 4.18 | 50.94 |

Source(s): (1) R1980; (2) R1990.

### 3.2 Method(s): linear extrapolation

#### 3.2.1 Men:

- 1980-90, distribution rates derived from the 1980 and 1980 censuses;
- 1950-70, for services sector, extrapolation of distribution rates derived
from the 1980 and 1990 censuses;
for industry sector, application of the industry/services ratio derived from
the 1980 census; for agriculture sector, distribution rates sector has been
computed as the remainder.

#### 3.2.2 Women:

- 1980-90, distribution rates derived from the 1980 and 1990 censuses;
- 1950-70, for services sector, extrapolation of distribution rates derived
from the 1980 and 1990 censuses;
modification of the trend in sector;
for industry sector, application of the industry/services ratio derived from
the 1980 census;
for agriculture sector, distribution rates sector has been
computed as the remainder.

## 4. Projection of activity rates: 2000 - 2010

### 4.1 Model(s): linear

#### 4.1.1 Men:

- To all age groups, application of function F1;
- Modification of the trends for the [15-24] age groups.

#### 4.1.2 Women:

- To all age groups, application of function F1;
- Modification of the trends for the [60+] age groups.

---

*Notes on adjustments of rates, see p. 3-8.*          *Notes on projection functions, see p. 10.*

# Central African Rep.

## 1. Source(s) of benchmark data

Code(s):     Title(s):

EPPA3        Economically active population: Estimates and Projections, 1950-2025, Third edition, ILO, Geneva, 1986.
R1988        Recensement de la population 1988 - Tableaux statistiques, Bureau Central du Recensement, Division des Statistiques et des Etudes Economiques, Bangui
AST93        Yearbook of Labour Statistics 1993, ILO, Geneva, 1993.

## 2. Estimates of activity rates: 1950 - 1990

### 2.1 Benchmark data:

Table 1: Activity rates by sex and age group

| Age group | Year 1950 (1) | 1960 (1) | 1988 (2) |
|---|---|---|---|
| **Men** | | | |
| 10-14 | 54.50 | 53.40 | 23.06 |
| 15-19 | 88.10 | 86.65 | 59.51 |
| 20-24 | 96.50 | 95.90 | 84.42 |
| 25-29 | 97.55 | 97.50 | 94.73 |
| 30-34 | 98.35 | 98.25 | 98.15 |
| 35-39 | 98.50 | 98.40 | 98.53 |
| 40-44 | 98.35 | 98.25 | 98.31 |
| 45-49 | 97.55 | 97.50 | 97.97 |
| 50-54 | 97.25 | 97.10 | 96.71 |
| 55-59 | 96.55 | 96.35 | 94.25 |
| 60-64 | 93.90 | 93.55 | 92.23 |
| 65+ | 81.30 | 80.65 | 82.54 |
| **Women** | | | |
| 10-14 | .. | 48.15 | 28.06 |
| 15-19 | .. | 88.00 | 53.79 |
| 20-24 | .. | 92.30 | 62.27 |
| 25-29 | .. | 93.30 | 68.09 |
| 30-34 | .. | 94.85 | 72.10 |
| 35-39 | .. | 94.75 | 76.87 |
| 40-44 | .. | 94.25 | 79.35 |
| 45-49 | .. | 02.00 | 02.03 |
| 50-54 | .. | 85.50 | 81.84 |
| 55-59 | .. | 78.20 | 81.72 |
| 60-64 | .. | 60.75 | 78.22 |
| 65+ | .. | 35.35 | 64.67 |

Source(s): (1) EPPA3; (2) R1988 and AST93.

### 2.2 Method(s): linears interpolation and extrapolation

#### 2.2.1 Men:

- 1950-90, interpolation and extrapolation of 1950-60 activity rates
derived from the EPPA3 and of adjusted activity rates derived
from the 1988 census;
modification of the trends for all age groups for 1950.

#### 2.2.2 Women:

Method, hypothesis and treatment identical to those used for men.

## 3. Estimates of distribution rates by activity sector: 1950 - 1990

### 3.1 Benchmark data:

Table 2: Distribution of economically active population by activity sector

| Year | Agriculture | Industry Total | Manufac. | Services |
|---|---|---|---|---|
| **Men** | | | | |
| 1960 (1) | 90.00 | 3.00 | .. | 7.00 |
| 1988 (2) | 74.82 | 6.14 | 2.88 | 19.04 |
| **Women** | | | | |
| 1960 (1) | 96.85 | 0.95 | .. | 2.20 |
| 1988 (2) | 87.63 | 0.37 | 0.24 | 12.00 |

Source(s): (1) EPPA3; (2) R1988 and AST93.

### 3.2 Method(s): linears interpolation and extrapolation

#### 3.2.1 Men:

- 1950-90, interpolation and extrapolation of 1980 distribution rates
derived from the EPPA3 and of distribution rates derived from the 1988 census;
- Application of manufacturing/industry ratio derived from the 1988 census.

#### 3.2.2 Women:

Method, hypothesis and treatment identical to those used for men.

## 4. Projection of activity rates: 2000 - 2010

### 4.1 Model(s): linear, log-linear and hyperbole

#### 4.1.1 Men:

- To the [10-14] and [60+] age groups, application of function F1;
- To the [15-19] age group, application of function F2;
- To the [20-59] age groups, application of function F3;
- Modification of the trends for the [35-49] and [60+] age groups.

#### 4.1.2 Women:

- To the [10-14] age group, application of function F1;
- To the [15+] age groups, application of function F3;
- Modification of the trends for all age groups.

*Notes on adjustments of rates, see p. 3-8.*     *Notes on projection functions, see p. 10.*

# Chad

## 1. Source(s) of benchmark data

Code(s):     Title(s):
S1964       Enquête démographique au Tchad, 1964, Vol I et II, Bureau central du Recensement, Ndjamena, 1966.
EPPA3       Economically active population: Estimates and Projections, 1950-2025, Third edition, ILO, Geneva, 1986.
ASTER       Yearbook of Labour Statistics 1945-89 - Retrospective Edition on Population Censuses, ILO, Geneva, 1990.

## 2. Estimates of activity rates: 1950 - 1990

### 2.1 Benchmark data:

Table 1: Activity rates by sex and age group

| Age group | Year 1964 (1) | 1980 (2) |
|---|---|---|
| **Men** | | |
| 10-14 | 48.42 | 45.61 |
| 15-19 | 75.10 | 70.74 |
| 20-24 | 95.60 | 94.16 |
| 25-29 | 98.60 | 98.08 |
| 30-34 | 98.70 | 98.12 |
| 35-39 | 98.60 | 98.45 |
| 40-44 | 98.10 | 97.70 |
| 45-49 | 98.10 | 97.48 |
| 50-54 | 97.50 | 97.29 |
| 55-59 | 96.30 | 93.35 |
| 60-64 | 95.55 | 86.87 |
| 65+ | 80.82 | 73.48 |
| **Women** | | |
| 10-14 | 11.56 | 10.57 |
| 15-19 | 24.10 | 22.03 |
| 20-24 | 29.70 | 28.07 |
| 25-29 | 30.90 | 28.02 |
| 30-34 | 28.60 | 27.97 |
| 35-39 | 30.90 | 27.96 |
| 40-44 | 26.10 | 28.04 |
| 45-49 | 27.70 | 25.21 |
| 50-54 | 25.10 | 25.58 |
| 55-59 | 24.90 | 25.58 |
| 60-64 | 22.76 | 20.37 |
| 65+ | 8.07 | 7.22 |

Source(s): (1) S1964; (2) ASTER.

### 2.2 Method(s): linears interpolation and extrapolation

#### 2.2.1 Men:

- 1950-90, interpolation and extrapolation of activity rates derived from the 1964 survey and from the 1980 census;
modification of the trends of the [15-49] and [55-64] age groups for 1950;
modification of the trend for the [25-29] age group for 1990.

#### 2.2.2 Women:

- 1950-90, interpolation and extrapolation of activity rates derived from the 1964 survey and from the 1980 census;
modification of the trends of the [10-14], [30-34] and [50+] age groups for 1990.

## 3. Estimates of distribution rates by activity sector: 1950 - 1990

### 3.1 Benchmark data:

Table 2: Distribution of economically active population by activity sector

| Year | Agriculture | Industry Total | Manufac. | Services |
|---|---|---|---|---|
| **Men** | | | | |
| 1970 (1) | 89.00 | 4.10 | .. | 6.90 |
| 1980 (1) | 82.20 | 5.70 | .. | 12.10 |
| **Women** | | | | |
| 1964 (2) | 95.25 | 0.40 | .. | 4.35 |
| 1980 (3) | 86.89 | 1.09 | .. | 12.02 |

Source(s): (1) EPPA3; (2) S1964.

### 3.2 Method(s): linears interpolation and extrapolation weighted average

#### 3.2.1 Men:

- 1950-80, 1950-80 distribution rates derived from the EPPA3;
- 1990, extrapolation of 1950-80 distribution rates derived from the EPPA3.

#### 3.2.2 Women:

- 1950-90, interpolation and extrapolation of adjusted distribution rates derived from 1964 survey and from the 1983 census.

## 4. Projection of activity rates: 2000 - 2010

### 4.1 Model(s): linear, hyperbole and logistic

#### 4.1.1 Men:

- To the [10-29] age groups, application of function F1;
- To the [30+] age groups, application of function F3;
- Modification of the trends for the [10-14], [20-24], [40-44] and [60+] age groups.

#### 4.1.2 Women:

- To the [10-19] and [65+] age groups, application of function F1;
- To the [20-64] age groups, application of function F6;
- Modification of the trends for the [10-19], [35-39] and [50+] age groups.

*Notes on adjustments of rates, see p. 3-8.*     *Notes on projection functions, see p. 10.*

# Chile

## 1. Source(s) of benchmark data

Code(s):     Title(s):

EPPA3       Economically active population: Estimates and Projections, 1950-2025, Third edition, ILO, Geneva, 1986.
ASTER       Yearbook of Labour Statistics 1945-89 - Retrospective Edition on Population Censuses, ILO, Geneva, 1990.
AST90-92    Editions 1990-1992 of ILO Yearbook of Labour Statistics, Geneva.
INE         Indicatores de empleo por sexo y grupos de edad, Total Nacional, Instituto Nacional de Estadísticas, Santiago.

## 2. Estimates of activity rates: 1950 - 1990

### 2.1 Benchmark data:

Table 1: Activity rates by sex and age group

| Age group | Year | | | | | |
|---|---|---|---|---|---|---|
| | 1952 (1) | 1970 (1) | 1980 (1) | 1989 (2) | 1990 (2) | 1991 (2) |
| **Men** | | | | | | |
| 10-14 | .. | 4.17 | 0.00 | 0.00 | 0.00 | 0.00 |
| 15-19 | .. | 46.87 | 39.24 | 30.10 | 30.00 | 29.70 |
| 20-24 | .. | 86.07 | 81.94 | 79.20 | 80.90 | 78.25 |
| 25-29 | .. | 96.88 | 95.04 | 94.50 | 94.20 | 93.50 |
| 30-34 | .. | 97.92 | 97.69 | 97.40 | 97.50 | 97.10 |
| 35-39 | .. | 97.72 | 97.64 | 97.90 | 98.00 | 97.70 |
| 40-44 | .. | 96.51 | 97.33 | 97.30 | 96.80 | 97.00 |
| 45-49 | .. | 94.79 | 93.68 | 94.80 | 95.10 | 95.20 |
| 50-54 | .. | 89.72 | 87.13 | 89.50 | 89.20 | 90.30 |
| 55-59 | .. | 84.31 | 78.24 | 80.50 | 79.80 | 80.60 |
| 60-64 | .. | 75.03 | 68.64 | 67.50 | 64.60 | 62.60 |
| 65+ | .. | 48.40 | 32.51 | 29.25 | 28.69 | 28.71 |
| **Women** | | | | | | |
| 10-14 | 3.38 | 1.79 | 0.00 | 0.00 | 0.00 | 0.00 |
| 15-19 | 28.40 | 17.26 | 15.30 | 18.40 | 15.90 | 19.50 |
| 20-24 | 35.10 | 32.47 | 34.57 | 38.10 | 38.40 | 38.20 |
| 25-29 | 30.40 | 30.13 | 35.89 | 40.90 | 41.95 | 42.45 |
| 30-34 | 28.00 | 26.04 | 33.28 | 42.63 | 41.48 | 41.08 |
| 35-39 | 27.60 | 25.04 | 31.51 | 42.55 | 43.38 | 41.50 |
| 40-44 | 27.60 | 23.64 | 29.49 | 42.55 | 42.93 | 42.83 |
| 45-49 | 26.60 | 22.07 | 26.71 | 30.70 | 38.50 | 39.45 |
| 50-54 | 24.60 | 20.26 | 22.88 | 30.78 | 31.88 | 32.18 |
| 55-59 | 22.40 | 16.59 | 17.38 | 26.40 | 20.43 | 26.98 |
| 60-64 | 19.50 | 12.76 | 11.55 | 15.88 | 15.40 | 15.43 |
| 65+ | 13.24 | 6.45 | 4.51 | 3.33 | 3.95 | 4.03 |

Source(s): (1) ASTER; (2) AST90-92 and INE.

### 2.2 Method(s): linears interpolation and extrapolation weighted average

#### 2.2.1 Men:

- 1950-60, 1950-60 activity rates derived from the EPPA3;
- 1970-80, interpolation of adjusted activity rates derived from the 1970 and 1982 censuses;
- 1990, average of activity rates derived from the 1989, 1990 and 1991 surveys;
adjustment of activity rates of the [15-24] age groups.

#### 2.2.2 Women:

- 1950-70, extrapolation of activity rates derived from the 1952 census and of adjusted activity rates derived from the 1970 census;
- 1980, weighted average of adjusted activity rates derived from 1982 census and of 1990 estimated activity rates;
- 1980, average of activity rates derived from the 1989, 1990 and 1991 surveys.

## 3. Estimates of distribution rates by activity sector: 1950 - 1990

### 3.1 Benchmark data:

Table 2: Distribution of economically active population by activity sector

| Year | Agriculture | Industry | | Services |
|---|---|---|---|---|
| | | Total | Manufac. | |
| **Men** | | | | |
| 1970 (1) | 29.13 | 32.06 | 17.80 | 38.81 |
| 1982 (1) | 25.53 | 29.10 | 15.75 | 45.37 |
| 1989 (2) | 24.42 | 30.12 | 17.14 | 45.45 |
| 1991 (2) | 24.40 | 29.27 | 16.82 | 46.33 |
| 1990 (2) | 23.98 | 30.30 | 17.24 | 45.72 |
| **Femmes** | | | | |
| 1952 (1) | 8.00 | 25.87 | 25.07 | 66.12 |
| 1970 (1) | 6.81 | 19.89 | 18.79 | 73.30 |
| 1982 (1) | 6.31 | 12.45 | 11.53 | 81.24 |
| 1989 (2) | 5.89 | 15.70 | 14.81 | 78.41 |
| 1991 (2) | 5.88 | 13.93 | 13.02 | 80.20 |
| 1990 (2) | 6.02 | 14.77 | 13.72 | 79.21 |

Source(s): (1) ASTER; (2) AST90-92 and INE.

### 3.2 Method(s): weighted average arithmetic average

#### 3.2.1 Men:

- 1950-60, 1950-60 distribution rates derived from the EPPA3;
- 1970-80, weighted averages of distribution rates derived from the 1970 and 1982 censuses;
- 1990, averages of distribution rates derived from the 1989, 1990 and 1991 surveys.

#### 3.2.2 Women:

- 1960-80, weighted averages of distribution rates derived from the 1952 census and of adjusted distribution rates derived from the 1970 and 1982 censuses;
- 1990, averages of distribution rates derived from the 1989, 1990 and 1991 surveys.

## 4. Projection of activity rates: 2000 - 2010

### 4.1 Model(s): linear and hyperbole

#### 4.1.1 Men:

- To the [15+] age groups, application of function F3;
- Modification of the trends for the [15-44] age groups.

#### 4.1.2 Women:

- To the [15+] age groups, application of function F3;
- Modification of the trends for all age groups.

---

*Notes on adjustments of rates, see p. 3-8.*        *Notes on projection functions, see p. 10.*

# China

## 1. Source(s) of benchmark data

Code(s):    Title(s):

EPPA3    Economically active population: Estimates and Projections, 1950-2025, Third edition, ILO, Geneva, 1986.
ASTER    Yearbook of Labour Statistics 1945-89 - Retrospective Edition on Population Censuses, ILO, Geneva, 1990.
R1990    Population Statistics of China, I.D.A, Statistical Data Series No. 55, State Statistical Bureau, Beijing.

## 2. Estimates of activity rates: 1950 - 1990

### 2.1 Benchmark data:

Table 1: Activity rates by sex and age group

| Age group | Year 1950 (1) | 1960 (1) | 1970 (1) | 1980 (1) | 1990 (2) |
|---|---|---|---|---|---|
| **Men** | | | | | |
| 10-14 | 52.00 | 46.00 | 40.00 | 30.00 | 0.00 |
| 15-19 | 87.10 | 83.70 | 80.30 | 74.70 | 63.76 |
| 20-24 | 96.90 | 96.90 | 96.90 | 96.80 | 94.10 |
| 25-29 | 98.75 | 98.75 | 98.75 | 98.70 | 98.51 |
| 30-34 | 98.95 | 98.95 | 98.95 | 98.90 | 98.90 |
| 35-39 | 99.00 | 99.00 | 99.00 | 98.90 | 99.00 |
| 40-44 | 98.90 | 98.85 | 98.80 | 98.75 | 98.74 |
| 45-49 | 97.75 | 97.70 | 97.60 | 97.55 | 97.65 |
| 50-54 | 95.60 | 94.65 | 93.70 | 92.00 | 93.29 |
| 55-59 | 91.70 | 89.80 | 87.90 | 84.30 | 83.55 |
| 60-64 | 81.65 | 77.80 | 73.95 | 66.30 | 63.19 |
| 65+ | 56.00 | 50.45 | 44.90 | 34.00 | 32.72 |
| **Women** | | | | | |
| 10-14 | 43.00 | 40.00 | 38.00 | 31.00 | 0.00 |
| 15-19 | 72.40 | 73.90 | 75.40 | 78.60 | 70.52 |
| 20-24 | 82.30 | 84.20 | 86.10 | 89.60 | 91.22 |
| 25-29 | 79.90 | 82.20 | 83.70 | 87.40 | 91.43 |
| 30-34 | 78.00 | 80.90 | 83.00 | 87.10 | 91.29 |
| 35-39 | 77.80 | 80.00 | 82.20 | 86.60 | 91.25 |
| 40-44 | 75.50 | 77.10 | 78.70 | 81.90 | 88.36 |
| 45-49 | 64.70 | 65.90 | 67.10 | 69.50 | 81.14 |
| 50-54 | 47.10 | 47.90 | 48.70 | 50.20 | 62.00 |
| 55-59 | 36.10 | 35.50 | 34.90 | 33.50 | 45.08 |
| 60-64 | 25.50 | 23.70 | 21.90 | 18.40 | 27.29 |
| 65+ | 9.95 | 8.90 | 7.85 | 5.70 | 8.03 |

Source(s): (1) EPPA3; (2) R1990.

### 2.2 Method(s):  national data

#### 2.2.1 Men:

- 1950-80, 1950-80 activity rates derived from the EPPA3;
- 1990, activity rates derived from 1990 census;
adjustment of activity rates of the [10-14] age group.

#### 2.2.2 Women:

Method, hypothesis and treatment identical to those used for men.

## 3. Estimates of distribution rates by activity sector: 1950 - 1990

### 3.1 Benchmark data:

Table 2: Distribution of economically active population by activity sector

| Year | Agriculture | Industry Total | Manufac. | Services |
|---|---|---|---|---|
| **Men** | | | | |
| 1980 (1) | 71.00 | 15.50 | .. | 13.50 |
| 1982 (2) | 70.36 | 17.70 | 11.75 | 11.94 |
| 1990 (3) | 69.10 | 16.52 | .. | 14.38 |
| **Women** | | | | |
| 1980 (1) | 78.50 | 12.00 | .. | 9.50 |
| 1982 (2) | 78.01 | 13.82 | 11.94 | 8.17 |
| 1990 (3) | 76.09 | 13.34 | .. | 10.56 |

Source(s): (1) EPPA3; (2) ASTER; (3) R1990.

### 3.2 Method(s):  national data

#### 3.2.1 Men:

- 1950-80, 1950-80 distribution rates derived from the EPPA3;
- 1990, distribution rates of agriculture sector derived from the 1990 census;
- Application of 1980 industry/services ratio derived from the EPPA3;
- Application of manufacturing/industry ratio derived from the 1982 census.

#### 3.2.2 Women:

Method, hypothesis and treatment identical to those used for men.

## 4. Projection of activity rates: 2000 - 2010

### 4.1 Model(s):  linear, hyperbole and logistic

#### 4.1.1 Men:

- To the [10-49] age groups, application of function F1;
- To the [50+] age groups, application of function F3;
- Modification of the trends for the [10-54] and [65+] age groups.

#### 4.1.2 Women:

- To the [10-19] age groups, application of function F1;
- To the [20+] age groups, application of function F6;
- Modification of the trends for all age groups.

# Colombia

## 1. Source(s) of benchmark data

Code(s):     Title(s):

EPPA3        Economically active population: Estimates and Projections, 1950-2025, Third edition, ILO, Geneva, 1986.
CELADE       CELADE, Bulletin Démographique, No. 49, janvier 1992.
STAT         Database on Labour Statistics, LABORSTA - Bureau of Statistics, ILO, Geneva.

## 2. Estimates of activity rates: 1950 - 1990

### 2.1 Benchmark data:

Table 1: Activity rates by sex and age group

| Age group | Year 1985 (1) | 1985 (2) | 1985 (3) | 1991 (1) | 1991 (2) | 1991 (3) |
|---|---|---|---|---|---|---|
| **Men** | | | | | | |
| 10-14 | 16.36 | 10.50 | 25.50 | 12.56 | 4.35 | 37.19 |
| 15-19 | 45.71 | 37.00 | 60.50 | 47.40 | 38.17 | 75.07 |
| 20-24 | 68.22 | 63.00 | 79.50 | 84.74 | 81.78 | 93.64 |
| 25-29 | 85.81 | 85.50 | 86.50 | 95.65 | 94.86 | 97.99 |
| 30-34 | 90.22 | 91.00 | 88.50 | 98.11 | 97.75 | 99.18 |
| 35-39 | 91.03 | 92.00 | 89.00 | 97.97 | 97.99 | 97.89 |
| 40-44 | 90.32 | 91.00 | 89.00 | 97.95 | 97.58 | 99.05 |
| 45-49 | 89.64 | 90.00 | 89.00 | 96.70 | 96.65 | 96.84 |
| 50-54 | 86.10 | 85.00 | 88.00 | 90.65 | 88.57 | 96.88 |
| 55-59 | 79.24 | 75.50 | 85.50 | 83.78 | 80.50 | 93.60 |
| 60-64 | 69.41 | 63.80 | 78.50 | 74.05 | 68.42 | 90.92 |
| 65+ | 46.73 | 40.02 | 57.37 | 32.57 | 20.92 | 67.52 |
| **Women** | | | | | | |
| 10-14 | 8.77 | 7.00 | 11.90 | 4.91 | 2.17 | 11.31 |
| 15-19 | 21.86 | 21.80 | 22.00 | 30.51 | 31.51 | 28.19 |
| 20-24 | 35.83 | 37.30 | 31.50 | 54.90 | 61.30 | 39.97 |
| 25-29 | 46.67 | 49.99 | 36.63 | 58.17 | 63.96 | 44.66 |
| 30-34 | 44.17 | 46.90 | 36.26 | 60.64 | 67.03 | 45.75 |
| 35-39 | 41.04 | 43.00 | 35.90 | 57.41 | 61.67 | 47.46 |
| 40-44 | 37.48 | 38.50 | 35.06 | 52.82 | 54.52 | 48.83 |
| 45-49 | 33.32 | 33.06 | 33.91 | 49.77 | 54.80 | 38.03 |
| 50-54 | 28.93 | 27.30 | 32.70 | 33.96 | 33.73 | 34.50 |
| 55-59 | 24.25 | 21.50 | 30.70 | 29.22 | 27.73 | 32.71 |
| 60-64 | 19.51 | 15.78 | 28.50 | 22.18 | 17.16 | 33.89 |
| 65+ | 12.63 | 9.16 | 21.34 | 8.85 | 4.73 | 18.47 |

Note(s): (1) Total; (2) Uban; (3) Rural.
Source(s): CELADE and STAT.

### 2.2 Method(s):  weighted average
linears interpolation and extrapolation

#### 2.2.1 Men:

- 1950-70, 1950-70 activity rates derived from the EPPA3;
adjustment of activity rates for all age groups for 1970;
- 1980, weighted average of 1970 and 1990 estimated activity rates;
- 1990, extrapolation of activity rates for urban areas derived from
the 1990 survey and the 1991 census;
application to extrapolated rates, variations in weighted average
of activity rates in urban and rural areas derived from the 1991 census,
in relation to 1991 activity rates in urban areas.

#### 2.2.2 Women:

- 1950-70, interpolation and extrapolation of 1950-70 adjusted activity rates
derived from the EPPA3;
the adjustment was made on the basis of the adjustment model for
activity rates of women working in agriculture as contributing family workers;
- 1980-90, weighted average of activity rates estimated separately for
urban and rural areas on the basis of interpolation and extrapolation
of activity rates derived from the 1986 and 1991 censuses for urban
and rural areas.

## 3. Estimates of distribution rates by activity sector: 1950 - 1990

### 3.1 Benchmark data:

Table 2: Distribution of economically active population by activity sector

| Year | Agriculture | Industry Total | Manufac. | Services |
|---|---|---|---|---|
| **Men** | | | | |
| 1980 (1) | 46.72 | 22.81 | 15.24 | 30.47 |
| 1991 (2) | 1.94 | 34.68 | 23.97 | 63.38 |
| 1991 (3) | 70.59 | 10.70 | 4.66 | 18.71 |
| **Women** | | | | |
| 1980 (1) | 5.55 | 21.57 | 19.94 | 72.88 |
| 1991 (2) | 0.64 | 25.03 | 23.65 | 74.33 |
| 1991 (3) | 29.73 | 17.07 | 14.83 | 53.20 |

Note(s): (1) Total; (2) Urban; (3) Rural.
Source(s): STAT.

### 3.2 Method(s):  weighted average

#### 3.2.1 Men:

- 1950-70, 1950-70 distribution rates derived from the EPPA3;
- 1980, distribution rates derived from the 1980 survey;
- 1990, weighted averages of distribution rates derived from the 1980 survey and
of distribution rates derived from the 1991 official
estimates for urban and rural areas;

#### 3.2.2 Women:

- 1950-70, 1950-70 adjusted distribution rates derived from the EPPA3;
- 1980, adjusted distribution rates derived from the 1980 survey;
- 1990, weighted averages of adjusted distribution rates derived from
the 1980 survey and of distribution rates derived from the 1991 official
estimates for urban and rural areas.

## 4. Projection of activity rates: 2000 - 2010

### 4.1 Model(s):  log-linear, hyperbole and logistic

#### 4.1.1 Men:

- To the [10-14] age group, application of function F2;
- To the [20+] age groups, application of function F3;
- Modification of the trends for the [15-24] and [35-49] age groups.

#### 4.1.2 Women:

- To the [10-14] age group, application of function F2;
- To the [15-19] and [65+] age groups, application of function F3;
- To the [20-24] age group, application of function F1;
- To the [25-64] age groups, application of function F6;
- Modification of the trends for the [20-24] and [65+] age groups.

*Notes on adjustments of rates, see p. 3-8.*

*Notes on projection functions, see p. 10.*

# Comoros

## 1. Source(s) of benchmark data

Code(s):    Title(s):

EPPA3      Economically active population: Estimates and Projections, 1950-2025, Third edition, ILO, Geneva, 1986.
ASTER      Yearbook of Labour Statistics 1945-89 - Retrospective Edition on Population Censuses, ILO, Geneva, 1990.

## 2. Estimates of activity rates: 1950 - 1990

### 2.1 Benchmark data:

Table 1: Activity rates by sex and age group

| Age group | Year | | | | |
|---|---|---|---|---|---|
| | 1950 (1) | 1960 (1) | 1970 (1) | 1980 (1) | 1980 (2) |
| **Men** | | | | | |
| 10-14 | 51.75 | 50.90 | 49.65 | 47.75 | 48.12 |
| 15-19 | 84.45 | 83.30 | 81.65 | 79.10 | 60.94 |
| 20-24 | 95.10 | 94.65 | 94.00 | 93.05 | 84.25 |
| 25-29 | 97.35 | 97.30 | 97.20 | 97.05 | 96.41 |
| 30-34 | 98.10 | 98.05 | 97.90 | 97.75 | 98.35 |
| 35-39 | 98.25 | 98.20 | 98.10 | 97.90 | 98.66 |
| 40-44 | 98.10 | 98.05 | 97.90 | 97.75 | 98.24 |
| 45-49 | 97.35 | 97.30 | 97.20 | 97.05 | 97.78 |
| 50-54 | 96.90 | 96.80 | 96.65 | 96.40 | 96.89 |
| 55-59 | 96.00 | 95.85 | 95.60 | 95.25 | 96.56 |
| 60-64 | 93.00 | 92.75 | 92.35 | 91.70 | 93.43 |
| 65+ | 79.75 | 79.25 | 78.50 | 77.45 | 81.31 |
| **Women** | | | | | |
| 10-14 | 39.10 | 38.45 | 37.50 | 36.10 | 41.05 |
| 15-19 | 63.60 | 62.60 | 61.20 | 59.05 | 55.55 |
| 20-24 | 63.90 | 63.30 | 62.40 | 61.05 | 63.30 |
| 25-29 | 68.85 | 68.15 | 67.15 | 65.60 | 67.13 |
| 30-34 | 73.20 | 72.45 | 71.35 | 69.70 | 70.67 |
| 35-39 | 74.45 | 73.75 | 72.70 | 71.15 | 72.85 |
| 40-44 | 76.90 | 76.15 | 75.15 | 73.60 | 75.44 |
| 45-49 | 76.40 | 75.65 | 74.65 | 73.05 | 73.11 |
| 50-54 | 74.95 | 74.10 | 72.90 | 71.10 | 72.75 |
| 55-59 | 72.15 | 71.30 | 70.05 | 68.15 | 66.41 |
| 60-64 | 66.05 | 64.95 | 63.35 | 60.90 | 58.71 |
| 65+ | 46.00 | 45.00 | 43.50 | 41.25 | 37.59 |

Source(s): (1) EPPA3; (2) ASTER.

### 2.2 Method(s):   linears interpolation and extrapolation

#### 2.2.1 Men:

- 1950-90, interpolation and extrapolation of 1950-80 activity rates
derived from the EPPA3;
adjustment of interpolated and extrapolated rates on the basis of variations
in 1980 interpolated rates, in relation to the adjusted rates derived from
the 1980 census.

#### 2.2.2 Women:

- 1950-90, interpolation and extrapolation of 1950-80 adjusted activity rates
derived from the EPPA3;
adjustment of rates to make allowance for the under-registration
of women working in agriculture;
adjustment of interpolated and extrapolated rates on the basis of variations
in 1980 interpolated rates, in relation to activity rates derived from
the 1980 census.

## 3. Estimates of distribution rates by activity sector: 1950 - 1990

### 3.1 Benchmark data:

Table 2: Distribution of economically active population by activity sector

| Year | Agriculture | Industry | | Services |
|---|---|---|---|---|
| | | Total | Manufac. | |
| **Men** | | | | |
| 1950 (1) | 87.00 | 5.20 | .. | 7.80 |
| 1960 (1) | 85.40 | 5.85 | .. | 8.75 |
| 1970 (1) | 83.10 | 6.80 | .. | 10.10 |
| 1980 (1) | 79.60 | 8.15 | .. | 12.25 |
| 1980 (2) | 70.65 | 11.01 | 4.69 | 18.34 |
| **Women** | | | | |
| 1950 (1) | 95.70 | 0.95 | .. | 3.35 |
| 1960 (1) | 93.95 | 1.20 | .. | 4.85 |
| 1970 (1) | 91.40 | 1.70 | .. | 6.90 |
| 1980 (1) | 87.55 | 2.50 | .. | 9.95 |
| 1980 (2) | 93.33 | 3.41 | 3.34 | 3.25 |

Source(s): (1) EPPA3; (2) ASTER.

### 3.2 Method(s):   linears interpolation and extrapolation

#### 3.2.1 Men:

- 1950-90, interpolation and extrapolation of 1950-80 distribution rates
derived from the EPPA3;
modification of the trends in all sectors;
adjustment of distribution rates on the basis of variations in 1980 interpolated
rates, in relation to distribution rates derived from derived from the 1980 census.

#### 3.2.2 Women:

- 1950-90, interpolation and extrapolation of 1950-80 distribution rates
derived from the EPPA3;
modification of the trends in all sectors;
application to interpolated and extrapolated rates, variations in 1980
interpolated rates, in relation to distribution rates derived from the 1980 census.

## 4. Projection of activity rates: 2000 - 2010

### 4.1 Model(s):   linear and hyperbole

#### 4.1.1 Men:

- To all age groups, application of function F1.

#### 4.1.2 Women:

- To the [10-19] age groups, application of function F1;
- To the [20+] age groups, application of function F3;
- Modification of the trends for the [20-59] age groups.

---

*Notes on adjustments of rates, see p. 3-8.*                    *Notes on projection functions, see p. 10.*

# Congo

## 1. Source(s) of benchmark data

Code(s):     Title(s):

EPPA3       Economically active population: Estimates and Projections, 1950-2025, Third edition, ILO, Geneva, 1986.
ASTER       Yearbook of Labour Statistics 1945-89 - Retrospective Edition on Population Censuses, ILO, Geneva, 1990.
AST89-90    Yearbook of Labour Statistics 1989-90, ILO, Geneva, 1990.

## 2. Estimates of activity rates: 1950 - 1990

### 2.1 Benchmark data:

Table 1: Activity rates by sex and age group

| Age group | Année | | | |
|---|---|---|---|---|
| | 1950 (1) | 1960 (1) | 1970 (1) | 1984 (2) |
| **Men** | | | | |
| 10-14 | 32.10 | 31.45 | 30.70 | 3.10 |
| 15-19 | 58.35 | 57.45 | 56.45 | 18.84 |
| 20-24 | 84.70 | 84.35 | 83.95 | 53.49 |
| 25-29 | 97.55 | 97.50 | 97.45 | 86.04 |
| 30-34 | 99.45 | 99.35 | 99.30 | 96.60 |
| 35-39 | 99.55 | 99.50 | 99.40 | 97.75 |
| 40-44 | 99.05 | 99.00 | 98.90 | 97.61 |
| 45-49 | 98.75 | 98.70 | 98.65 | 96.62 |
| 50-54 | 96.55 | 96.50 | 96.40 | 92.95 |
| 55-59 | 93.35 | 93.20 | 93.05 | 80.96 |
| 60-64 | 90.45 | 90.20 | 89.95 | 81.05 |
| 65+ | 69.00 | 68.65 | 68.20 | 73.79 |
| **Women** | | | | |
| 10-14 | .. | .. | 22.10 | 4.67 |
| 15-19 | .. | .. | 37.65 | 17.84 |
| 20-24 | .. | .. | 40.90 | 32.98 |
| 25-29 | .. | .. | 49.00 | 51.02 |
| 30-34 | .. | .. | 55.40 | 59.26 |
| 35-39 | .. | .. | 61.40 | 64.39 |
| 40-44 | .. | .. | 69.50 | 67.97 |
| 45-49 | .. | .. | 72.95 | 70.90 |
| 50-54 | .. | .. | 75.95 | 73.56 |
| 55-59 | .. | .. | 76.55 | 72.47 |
| 60-64 | .. | .. | 71.95 | 69.74 |
| 65+ | .. | .. | 59.84 | 58.00 |

Source(s): (1) EPPA3; (2) AST89-90.

### 2.2 Method(s): linears interpolation and extrapolation

#### 2.2.1 Men:

- 1950-90, interpolation and extrapolation of 1950-70 activity rates derived from the EPPA3 and of adjusted activity rates derived from the 1984 census;
modification of the trends of the [10-19] and [25-64] age groups for 1950; and for the [20-24] and [65+] age groups for 1980.

#### 2.2.2 Women:

- 1950-90, interpolation and extrapolation of 1970 activity rates derived from the EPPA3 and of activity rates derived from the 1984 census;
modification of the trends of the [10-14] age group from 1950 to 1970.

## 3. Estimates of distribution rates by activity sector: 1950 - 1990

### 3.1 Benchmark data:

Table 2: Distribution of economically active population by activity sector

| Year | Agriculture | Industry | | Services |
|---|---|---|---|---|
| | | Total | Manufac. | |
| **Men** | | | | |
| 1974 (1) | 47.95 | 18.15 | 12.77 | 33.91 |
| 1984 (2) | 36.40 | 22.05 | 10.95 | 41.55 |
| **Women** | | | | |
| 1974 (1) | 89.55 | 1.27 | 1.20 | 9.18 |
| 1984 (2) | 73.37 | 3.08 | 2.51 | 23.56 |

Source(s): (1) ASTER; (2) AST89-90.

### 3.2 Method(s): linears interpolation and extrapolation

#### 3.2.1 Men:

- 1950-90, interpolation and extrapolation of distribution rates derived from the 1974 and 1984 censuses;
modification of the trends in all sectors for 1950-70 and 1990.

#### 3.2.2 Women:

Method, hypothesis and treatment identical to those used for men.

## 4. Projection of activity rates: 2000 - 2010

### 4.1 Model(s): log-linear, hyperbole and linear

#### 4.1.1 Men:

- To the [10-14] age group, application of function F2;
- To the [15-19] and [65+] age groups, application of function F1;
- To the [20-64] age groups, application of function F3;
- Modification of the trends for the [30-34] and [65+] age groups.

#### 4.1.2 Women:

- To the [10-14] age group, application of function F2;
- To the [15+] age groups, application of function F1;
- Modification of the trends for the [10-19], [40-44] and [55+] age groups.

*Notes on adjustments of rates, see p. 3-8.*

*Notes on projection functions, see p. 10.*

# Costa Rica

## 1. Source(s) of benchmark data

Code(s):  Title(s):

EPPA3     Economically active population: Estimates and Projections, 1950-2025, Third edition, ILO, Geneva, 1986.
ADNU88    Yearbook of Labour Statistics 1945-89 - Retrospective Edition on Population Censuses, ILO, Geneva, 1990.
ASTER     Demographic Yearbook 1988 - Population census statistics - Fortieth Edition, United Nations, New York, 1990.
AST90-92  Editions 1990-1992 of ILO Yearbook of Labour Statistics, Geneva.

## 2. Estimates of activity rates: 1950 - 1990

### 2.1 Benchmark data:

Table 1: Activity rates by sex and age group

| Age group | Year 1984 (1) | 1989 (2) | 1990 (2) | 1991 (2) |
|---|---|---|---|---|
| **Men** | | | | |
| 10-14 | 3.80 | 10.36 | 11.16 | 9.52 |
| 15-19 | 17.09 | 61.98 | 59.37 | 55.63 |
| 20-24 | 28.25 | 86.42 | 89.78 | 88.09 |
| 25-29 | 29.97 | 95.26 | 95.93 | 96.43 |
| 30-39 | 29.96 | 97.08 | 97.05 | 97.01 |
| 40-49 | 24.26 | 95.82 | 94.93 | 94.46 |
| 50-59 | 13.77 | 87.10 | 87.12 | 84.58 |
| 60-64 | 6.95 | 60.90 | 59.63 | 55.27 |
| 65+ | 3.08 | ... | ... | ... |
| **Women** | | | | |
| 10-14 | 12.72 | 3.00 | 3.05 | 3.36 |
| 15-19 | 59.43 | 27.05 | 27.14 | 23.90 |
| 20-24 | 83.74 | 42.43 | 44.04 | 44.07 |
| 25-29 | 92.65 | 40.35 | 35.49 | 38.64 |
| 30-39 | 94.53 | 43.12 | 43.22 | 42.89 |
| 40-49 | 93.11 | 34.39 | 39.60 | 37.92 |
| 50-59 | 86.16 | 19.20 | 21.04 | 22.85 |
| 60-64 | 69.63 | 9.64 | 11.94 | 7.74 |
| 65+ | 38.91 | ... | ... | ... |

Source(s): (1) ASTER and ADNU88; (2) AST90-92.

### 2.2 Method(s): weighted average
arithmetic average

**2.2.1 Men:**

- 1950-70, 1950-70 activity rates derived from the EPPA3;
- 1980, weighted average of activity rates of 1970 derived from the EPPA3 and of adjusted activity rates derived from the 1984 census;
- 1990, average of activity rates derived from the 1989, 1990 and 1991 surveys.

**2.2.2 Women:**

Method, hypothesis and treatment identical to those used for men.

## 3. Estimates of distribution rates by activity sector: 1950 - 1990

### 3.1 Benchmark data:

Table 2: Distribution of economically active population by activity sector

| Year | Agriculture | Industry Total | Manufac. | Services |
|---|---|---|---|---|
| **Men** | | | | |
| 1983 (1) | 36.26 | 22.63 | 15.25 | 41.11 |
| 1984 (1) | 43.56 | 22.74 | 13.54 | 33.70 |
| 1985 (1) | 35.44 | 29.83 | 14.87 | 34.73 |
| 1989 (2) | 34.45 | 26.67 | 16.77 | 38.88 |
| 1991 (2) | 33.39 | 27.25 | 16.87 | 39.36 |
| 1990 (2) | 33.23 | 27.36 | 17.93 | 39.41 |
| **Women** | | | | |
| 1983 (1) | 5.15 | 21.76 | 21.57 | 73.10 |
| 1984 (1) | 4.81 | 20.46 | 19.68 | 74.73 |
| 1985 (1) | 4.52 | 20.69 | 26.53 | 74.79 |
| 1989 (2) | 6.06 | 26.67 | 28.37 | 67.27 |
| 1991 (2) | 6.40 | 24.40 | 25.85 | 69.20 |
| 1990 (2) | 6.70 | 26.76 | 23.46 | 66.54 |

Source(s): (1) ASTER and ADNU88; (2) AST90-92.

### 3.2 Method(s): weighted average
arithmetic average

**3.2.1 Men:**

- 1950-60, 1950-60 distribution rates derived from the EPPA3;
- 1980, weighted averages of 1970 distribution rates derived from the EPPA3 and of averages of distribution rates derived from the 1983 and and 1985 surveys and from the 1984 census;
- 1990, averages of distribution rates derived from the 1989, 1990 and 1991 surveys.

**3.2.2 Women:**

Method, hypothesis and treatment identical to those used for men.

## 4. Projection of activity rates: 2000 - 2010

### 4.1 Model(s): linear, log-linear, hyperbole and logistic

**4.1.1 Men:**

- To the [10-14] age group, application of function F2;
- To the [15-29] age groups, application of function F1;
- To the [30+] age groups, application of function F3;
- Modification of the trends for the [10-14] and [30-34] age groups.

**4.1.2 Women:**

- To the [10-19] age groups, application of function F1;
- To the [20-49] age groups, application of function F6;
- To the [50-64] age groups, application of function F2;
- To the [65+] age group, application of function F3;
- Modification of the trends for the [10-14] and [50-64] age groups.

*Notes on adjustments of rates, see p. 3-8.*

*Notes on projection functions, see p. 10.*

# Côte d'Ivoire

## 1. Source(s) of benchmark data

Code(s):    Title(s):

EPPA3      Economically active population: Estimates and Projections, 1950-2025, Third edition, ILO, Geneva, 1986.
ADNU84     Demographic Yearbook 1984 - Population census statistics II - Thirty-sixth Edition, United Nations, New York, 1986.
AST93      Yearbook of Labour Statistics 1993, ILO, Geneva, 1993.

## 2. Estimates of activity rates: 1950 - 1990

### 2.1 Benchmark data:

Table 1: Activity rates by sex and age group

| Age group | Year | | | |
|---|---|---|---|---|
| | 1960 (1) | 1970 (1) | 1975 (2) | 1988 (3) |
| **Men** | | | | |
| 10-14 | 47.75 | .. | 32.35 | 26.20 |
| 15-19 | 84.40 | .. | 70.38 | 62.74 |
| 20-24 | 95.30 | .. | 93.94 | 87.65 |
| 25-29 | 97.65 | .. | 98.07 | 96.18 |
| 30-34 | 98.40 | .. | 98.18 | 98.14 |
| 35-39 | 98.55 | .. | 98.50 | 98.54 |
| 40-44 | 98.35 | .. | 97.80 | 98.53 |
| 45-49 | 98.15 | .. | 97.50 | 97.76 |
| 50-54 | 97.60 | .. | 97.28 | 97.17 |
| 55-59 | 96.05 | .. | 93.20 | 91.87 |
| 60-64 | 92.70 | .. | 90.22 | 89.49 |
| 65+ | 78.20 | .. | 74.78 | 74.17 |
| **Women** | | | | |
| 10-14 | 40.45 | 33.80 | 27.93 | 20.67 |
| 15-19 | 76.25 | 61.40 | 39.45 | 35.07 |
| 20-24 | 79.50 | 65.35 | 43.97 | 39.25 |
| 25-29 | 81.75 | 68.70 | 46.00 | 42.81 |
| 30-34 | 84.00 | 71.80 | 48.73 | 46.59 |
| 35-39 | 84.55 | 73.15 | 50.29 | 48.16 |
| 40-44 | 85.00 | 74.80 | 51.49 | 49.87 |
| 45-49 | 80.00 | 70.55 | 51.64 | 50.14 |
| 50-54 | 74.85 | 66.90 | 49.94 | 48.65 |
| 55-59 | 58.50 | 53.60 | 47.46 | 46.30 |
| 60-64 | 47.95 | 44.95 | 43.31 | 39.85 |
| 65+ | 28.95 | 27.95 | 26.22 | 24.19 |

Source(s): (1) EPPA3; (2) ASTER and ADNU84; (3) AST93.

### 2.2 Method(s): linears interpolation and extrapolation

**2.2.1 Men:**

- 1950-90, interpolation and extrapolation of 1960 activity rates
derived from the EPPA3 and of activity rates derived
from the 1975 and 1988 censuses;
modification of the trends for all age groups for 1950.

**2.2.2 Women:**

- 1950-90, interpolation and extrapolation of 1960-70 activity rates
derived from the EPPA3 and of activity rates derived from the 1975
and 1988 censuses.

## 3. Estimates of distribution rates by activity sector: 1950 - 1990

### 3.1 Benchmark data:

Table 2: Distribution of economically active population by activity sector

| Year | Agriculture | Industry | | Services |
|---|---|---|---|---|
| | | Total | Manufac. | |
| **Men** | | | | |
| 1950 | 86.00 | 3.50 | .. | 10.50 |
| 1960 | 79.00 | 5.25 | .. | 15.75 |
| 1970 | 70.00 | 7.50 | .. | 22.50 |
| 1980 | 60.00 | 10.00 | .. | 30.00 |
| **Women** | | | | |
| 1950 | 96.50 | 0.70 | .. | 2.80 |
| 1960 | 93.35 | 1.35 | .. | 5.30 |
| 1970 | 87.00 | 2.60 | .. | 10.40 |
| 1980 | 75.00 | 5.00 | .. | 20.00 |

Source(s): EPPA3.

### 3.2 Method(s): linear extrapolation

**3.2.1 Men:**

- 1950-80, 1950-80 distribution rates derived from the EPPA3;
- 1990, extrapolation of 1950-80 distribution rates derived from the EPPA3.
- Application of manufacturing/industry ratio estimated for Cameroon.

**3.2.2 Women:**

Method, hypothesis and treatment identical to those used for men.

## 4. Projection of activity rates: 2000 - 2010

### 4.1 Model(s): log-linear and hyperbole

**4.1.1 Men:**

- To the [10-19] age groups, application of function F2;
- To the [20+] age groups, application of function F3;
- Modification of the trends for the [30-34] and [50-54] age groups.

**4.1.2 Women:**

- To the [10-19] age groups, application of function F2;
- To the [20+] age groups, application of function F3;
- Modification of the trends for the [15+] age groups.

*Notes on adjustments of rates, see p. 3-8.*

*Notes on projection functions, see p. 10.*

# Croatia

## 1. Source(s) of benchmark data

| Code(s): | Title(s): |
|---|---|
| BLT-94-2 | Popovic B. (1994), "New 1980 and 1990 estimates of activity rates by age and sectoral distribution for some countries of Eastern and Southern Europe" in the Bulletin of Labour of Statistics - 1994-2, ILO, Geneva. |
| STAT | Database on Labour Statistics, LABORSTA - Bureau of Statistics, ILO, Geneva. |

## 2. Estimates of activity rates: 1950 - 1990

### 2.1 Benchmark data:

Table 1: Activity rates by sex and age group

| Age group | Year 1953 (1) | 1961 (1) | 1971 (1) | 1980 (2) | 1990 (2) |
|---|---|---|---|---|---|
| **Men** | | | | | |
| 10-14 | 19.19 | 2.52 | 1.46 | 0.07 | 0.00 |
| 15-19 | 82.87 | 64.93 | 38.43 | 23.90 | 21.81 |
| 20-24 | 93.57 | 90.85 | 82.88 | 78.82 | 77.23 |
| 25-29 | 95.61 | 96.45 | 95.00 | 95.25 | 92.98 |
| 30-34 | 97.34 | 97.57 | 97.60 | 97.57 | 96.52 |
| 35-39 | 96.63 | 96.61 | 97.36 | 97.53 | 96.45 |
| 40-44 | 97.19 | 96.26 | 93.77 | 96.33 | 96.17 |
| 45-49 | 96.23 | 95.36 | 84.70 | 93.93 | 93.76 |
| 50-54 | 92.76 | 92.62 | 80.75 | 82.58 | 86.04 |
| 55-59 | 82.87 | 82.66 | 68.90 | 63.39 | 60.84 |
| 60-64 | 76.95 | 71.09 | 56.70 | 49.04 | 30.26 |
| 65+ | 59.76 | 54.26 | 45.43 | 36.74 | 17.49 |
| **Women** | | | | | |
| 10-14 | 18.38 | 3.52 | 2.06 | 0.08 | 0.00 |
| 15-19 | 66.09 | 54.87 | 35.33 | 20.48 | 18.64 |
| 20-24 | 62.20 | 67.15 | 61.98 | 69.45 | 65.49 |
| 25-29 | 48.59 | 59.84 | 66.77 | 78.92 | 79.48 |
| 30-34 | 43.47 | 54.20 | 60.06 | 76.81 | 82.68 |
| 35-39 | 40.99 | 50.71 | 56.93 | 71.27 | 81.62 |
| 40-44 | 36.55 | 49.29 | 52.21 | 60.50 | 77.31 |
| 45-49 | 32.61 | 43.64 | 45.54 | 51.77 | 66.95 |
| 50-54 | 27.55 | 36.55 | 38.86 | 38.38 | 43.98 |
| 55-59 | 22.94 | 29.98 | 28.93 | 24.92 | 23.92 |
| 60-64 | 19.85 | 24.56 | 23.44 | 19.53 | 14.66 |
| 65+ | 12.69 | 15.51 | 14.76 | 10.75 | 7.85 |

Source(s): (1) STAT; (2) BLT-94-2.

### 2.2 Method(s): linear extrapolation
weighted average

#### 2.2.1 Men:

- 1950, extrapolation of adjusted activity rates derived from the 1953 and 1971 censuses, of activity rates derived from the 1961 census and of estimated activity rates for 1980;
application to extrapolated rates, variations in 1953 interpolated rates, in relation to activity rates derived from the 1953 census;
- 1960-70, weighted average of adjusted activity rates derived from the 1953 and 1971 censuses and of activity rates derived from the 1961 census;
- 1980-90, 1980 and 1990 activity rates derived from BLT-94-2.

#### 2.2.2 Women:

- 1950, extrapolation of activity rates derived from the 1953, 1961, 1971 and 1981 censuses;
application to extrapolated rates, variations in 1953 interpolated rates, in relation to activity rates derived from the 1953 census;
- 1960-70, weighted average of activity rates derived from the 1953, 1961 and 1971 censuses;
- 1980-90, 1980 and 1990 activity rates derived from the Bulletin of Labour Statistics 1994-2.

## 3. Estimates of distribution rates by activity sector: 1950 - 1990

### 3.1 Benchmark data:

Table 2: Distribution of economically active population by activity sector

| Year | Agriculture | Industry Total | Manufac. | Services |
|---|---|---|---|---|
| **Men** | | | | |
| 1953 (1) | 56.04 | 15.12 | .. | 28.83 |
| 1961 (1) | 45.81 | 22.88 | .. | 31.31 |
| 1971 (1) | 34.47 | 29.20 | .. | 36.33 |
| 1980 (2) | 23.14 | 38.36 | 24.58 | 38.50 |
| 1990 (2) | 16.68 | 37.90 | 26.97 | 45.42 |
| **Women** | | | | |
| 1953 (1) | 80.61 | 8.00 | .. | 11.39 |
| 1961 (1) | 62.74 | 14.59 | .. | 22.67 |
| 1971 (1) | 44.83 | 20.78 | .. | 34.39 |
| 1980 (2) | 27.73 | 27.45 | 24.93 | 44.83 |
| 1990 (2) | 15.21 | 28.27 | 25.72 | 56.52 |

Source(s): (1) STAT; (2) BLT-94-2.

### 3.2 Method(s): weighted average
linear extrapolation

#### 3.2.1 Men:

- 1950, extrapolation of distribution rates derived from the 1953, 1961 and 1971 and of 1980 and 1990 distribution rates derived from the Bulletin of Labour Statistics, 1994-2; modification of the trends in all sectors;
- 1960-70, weighted averages of distribution rates derived from the 1953, 1961 and 1971 censuses;
- 1980-90, 1980-90 distribution rates derived from the Bulletin.

#### 3.2.2 Women:

Method, hypothesis and treatment identical to those used for men.

## 4. Projection of activity rates: 2000 - 2010

### 4.1 Model(s): linear, hyperbole and logistic

#### 4.1.1 Men:

- To the [15+] age groups, application of function F3;
- Modification of the trends for the [15-24] and [50-54] age groups.

#### 4.1.2 Women:

- To the [15-19] and [60+] age groups, application of function F3;
- To the [25-54] age groups, application of function F6;
- To the [55-59] age group, application of function F1;
- Modification of the trends for the [15-24] and [55-59] age groups.

*Notes on adjustments of rates, see p. 3-8.*

*Notes on projection functions, see p. 10.*

# Cuba

## 1. Source(s) of benchmark data

| Code(s): | Title(s): |
|---|---|
| CB-R70 | Censo de Poblacion y viviendas, 1970, Oficina Nacional del Censo, Comité Estatal de Estadísticas, La Habana. |
| EPPA3 | Economically active population: Estimates and Projections, 1950-2025, Third edition, ILO, Geneva, 1986. |
| ASTER | Yearbook of Labour Statistics 1945-89 - Retrospective Edition on Population Censuses, ILO, Geneva, 1990. |
| STAT | Database on Labour Statistics, LABORSTA - Bureau of Statistics, ILO, Geneva. |

## 2. Estimates of activity rates: 1950 - 1990

### 2.1 Benchmark data:

Table 1: Activity rates by sex and age group

| Age group | Year 1953 (1) | 1970 (2) | 1981 (1) | 1988 (3) |
|---|---|---|---|---|
| **Men** | | | | |
| 10-14 | 8.00 | 1.04 | 0.00 | 0.00 |
| 15-19 | 76.70 | 51.03 | 32.79 | 38.60 |
| 20-24 | 91.60 | 85.73 | 82.79 | 85.65 |
| 25-29 | 94.20 | 92.45 | 94.79 | 93.74 |
| 30-34 | 94.80 | 93.54 | 96.76 | 98.41 |
| 35-39 | 95.10 | 93.80 | 96.95 | 98.28 |
| 40-44 | 94.90 | 93.19 | 96.34 | 97.63 |
| 45-49 | 94.40 | 92.07 | 95.15 | 96.45 |
| 50-54 | 92.50 | 88.83 | 92.07 | 93.68 |
| 55-59 | 89.20 | 82.22 | 86.08 | 88.28 |
| 60-64 | 82.20 | 65.45 | 60.91 | 50.63 |
| 65+ | 57.10 | 27.84 | 21.44 | 12.77 |
| **Women** | | | | |
| 10-14 | 2.00 | 0.39 | 0.00 | 0.00 |
| 15-19 | 17.20 | 16.41 | 15.53 | 15.44 |
| 20-24 | 22.30 | 25.26 | 45.59 | 51.07 |
| 25-29 | 22.10 | 24.17 | 51.73 | 57.10 |
| 30-34 | 21.30 | 23.03 | 52.79 | 65.94 |
| 35-39 | 21.10 | 22.18 | 52.06 | 65.50 |
| 40-44 | 20.90 | 21.09 | 48.89 | 61.56 |
| 45-49 | 19.60 | 18.91 | 40.83 | 53.43 |
| 50-54 | 18.20 | 15.92 | 30.95 | 41.88 |
| 55-59 | 15.50 | 12.01 | 18.11 | 22.38 |
| 60-64 | 12.90 | 6.75 | 7.78 | 8.69 |
| 65+ | 8.50 | 1.89 | 2.03 | 1.78 |

Source(s): (1) ASTER; (2) ASTER and CB-R70; (3) STAT

### 2.2 Method(s): linears interpolation and extrapolation

#### 2.2.1 Men:

- 1950-70, interpolation and extrapolation of adjusted activity rates derived from the 1953 and 1970 censuses;
- 1980-90, extrapolation of adjusted activity rates derived from the 1982 census and from the 1988 survey.

#### 2.2.2 Women:

- 1950-70, interpolation and extrapolation of adjusted activity rates derived from the 1953 and 1970 censuses;
- 1980-90, extrapolation of adjusted activity rates derived from the 1981 census and from the 1988 survey;
modification of the trends for all age groups.

## 3. Estimates of distribution rates by activity sector: 1950 - 1990

### 3.1 Benchmark data:

Table 2: Distribution of economically active population by activity sector

| Year | Agriculture | Industry Total | Manufac. | Services |
|---|---|---|---|---|
| **Men** | | | | |
| 1960 (1) | 42.00 | 24.20 | .. | 33.80 |
| 1970 (2) | 35.42 | 27.61 | 19.32 | 36.97 |
| 1981 (2) | 28.88 | 32.04 | 18.57 | 39.08 |
| **Women** | | | | |
| 1960 (1) | 6.80 | 20.80 | .. | 72.40 |
| 1970 (2) | 8.24 | 22.10 | 21.19 | 69.66 |
| 1981 (2) | 10.62 | 21.55 | 17.59 | 67.82 |

Source(s): (1) EPPA3; (2) ASTER.

### 3.2 Method(s): weighted average
linear extrapolation

#### 3.2.1 Men:

- 1950-60, 1950-60 distribution rates derived from the EPPA3;
- 1970, weighted averages of 1960 distribution rates derived from the EPPA3 and of distribution rates derived from the 1970 census;
- 1980-90, weighted averages of distribution rates derived from the 1970 and 1981 censuses.

#### 3.2.2 Women:

- 1950-60, 1950-60 distribution rates derived from the EPPA3;
- 1970, weighted averages of 1960 distribution rates derived from the EPPA3 and of distribution rates derived from the 1970 census;
- 1980, weighted averages of distribution rates derived from the 1970 and 1981 censuses;
- 1990, extrapolation of distribution rates estimated for 1970 and of distribution rates derived from the 1981 census;
modification of the trends in all sectors.

## 4. Projection of activity rates: 2000 - 2010

### 4.1 Model(s): hyperbole and logistic

#### 4.1.1 Men:

- To the [15+] age groups, application of function F3;
- Modification of the trends for the [30-59] age groups.

#### 4.1.2 Women:

- To the [15-19] and [60+] age groups, application of function F3;
- To the [20-59] age groups, application of function F6;
- Modification of the trend for the [20-24] age group.

*Notes on adjustments of rates, see p. 3-8.*

*Notes on projection functions, see p. 10.*

# Cyprus

## 1. Source(s) of benchmark data

| Code(s): | Title(s): |
|---|---|
| EPPA3 | Economically active population: Estimates and Projections, 1950-2025, Third edition, ILO, Geneva, 1986. |
| CHY-OE1 | Labour force and migration surveys, 19886/87, DSRMF, Series III, Report No. 6, Department of Statistics and Research, Nicosia. |
| CHY-OE2 | Labour Statistics 1987-1992, DSRMF, Series II, Department of Statistics and Research, Nicosia. |

## 2. Estimates of activity rates: 1950 - 1990

### 2.1 Benchmark data:

Table 1: Activity rates by sex and age group

| Age group | Year 1987 | 1988 | 1989 | 1990 |
|---|---|---|---|---|
| **Men** | | | | |
| 10-14 | 0.00 | 0.00 | 0.00 | 0.00 |
| 15-19 | 57.21 | 55.50 | 66.50 | 64.40 |
| 20-24 | 80.60 | 85.80 | 83.50 | 81.10 |
| 25-29 | 94.01 | 93.70 | 93.70 | 93.90 |
| 30-34 | 98.02 | 99.10 | 99.60 | 99.60 |
| 35-39 | 99.08 | 99.50 | 99.50 | 99.50 |
| 40-44 | 98.52 | 98.40 | 99.50 | 99.50 |
| 45-49 | 97.82 | 97.20 | 99.30 | 98.70 |
| 50-54 | 96.92 | 93.90 | 97.10 | 97.30 |
| 55-59 | 92.78 | 92.70 | 95.50 | 92.90 |
| 60-64 | 82.37 | 80.20 | 77.30 | 77.50 |
| 65+ | 27.62 | 28.00 | 28.00 | 28.00 |
| **Women** | | | | |
| 10-14 | 0.00 | 0.00 | 0.00 | 0.00 |
| 15-19 | 36.88 | 29.70 | 33.70 | 34.00 |
| 20-24 | 61.30 | 56.60 | 63.80 | 65.10 |
| 25-29 | 61.12 | 57.90 | 63.10 | 64.20 |
| 30-34 | 59.68 | 58.50 | 63.10 | 64.00 |
| 35-39 | 62.04 | 61.60 | 63.40 | 64.00 |
| 40-44 | 58.62 | 58.90 | 63.10 | 64.00 |
| 45-49 | 61.94 | 61.80 | 59.50 | 60.10 |
| 50-54 | 55.12 | 54.70 | 49.00 | 49.70 |
| 55-59 | 45.37 | 46.00 | 38.10 | 39.20 |
| 60-64 | 33.58 | 36.00 | 24.60 | 25.20 |
| 65+ | 10.82 | 10.80 | 8.80 | 8.70 |

Source(s): CHY-OE1 and CHY-OE2.

### 2.2 Method(s): linears interpolation and extrapolation

#### 2.2.1 Men:

- 1950-90, interpolation of 1950-80 activity rates derived from EPPA3 and of activity rates derived from the 1987 to 1990 official estimates; for the [10-14] age group, activity rates derived from the EPPA3.

#### 2.2.2 Women:

- 1950-80, 1950-80 activity rates derived from the EPPA3;
- 1990, extrapolation of 1950-80 activity rates derived from the EPPA3; adjustment of extrapolated rates on the basis of variations in 1980 interpolated rates, in relation to the 1980 rates derived from the EPPA3.

## 3. Estimates of distribution rates by activity sector: 1950 - 1990

### 3.1 Benchmark data:

Table 2: Distribution of economically active population by activity sector

| Year | Agriculture | Industry Total | Manufac. | Services |
|---|---|---|---|---|
| **Men** | | | | |
| 1981 | 19.15 | 36.91 | 19.33 | 43.94 |
| 1989 | 13.36 | 33.13 | 17.42 | 53.51 |
| **Women** | | | | |
| 1981 | 34.80 | 29.09 | 25.73 | 36.11 |
| 1989 | 18.00 | 26.33 | 24.72 | 55.68 |

Source(s): CHY-OE1 and CHY-OE2.

### 3.2 Method(s): arithmetic average

#### 3.2.1 Men:

- 1950-70, 1950-70 distribution rates derived from the EPPA3;
- 1980, averages of distribution rates derived from the 1979, 1980 and 1981 surveys;
- 1990, averages of distribution rates derived from the 1989, 1990 and 1991 official estimates.

#### 3.2.2 Women:

Method, hypothesis and treatment identical to those used for men.

## 4. Projection of activity rates: 2000 - 2010

### 4.1 Model(s): linear, hyperbole and logistic

#### 4.1.1 Men:

- To the [15-19] age group, application of function F1;
- To the [20+] age groups, application of function F3;
- Modification of the trends for the [15-49] and [65+] age groups.

#### 4.1.2 Women:

- To the [15-19] and [60+] age groups, application of function F3;
- To the [20-54] age groups, application of function F6;
- To the [55-59] age group, application of function F1;
- Modification of the trends for the [15-19] and [55-59] age groups.

*Notes on adjustments of rates, see p. 3-8.*

*Notes on projection functions, see p. 10.*

# Czech Republic

## 1. Source(s) of benchmark data

| Code(s): | Title(s): |
|---|---|
| BLT-94-2 | Vorobiev A. (1994), "Estimates of the economically active population for the fifteen countries of the former USSR for the years 1950, 1959, 1970, 1979 and 1989", in the Bulletin of Labour of Statistics - 1994-2, ILO, Geneva. |
| STAT | Database on Labour Statistics, LABORSTA - Bureau of Statistics, ILO, Geneva. |

## 2. Estimates of activity rates: 1950 - 1990

### 2.1 Benchmark data:

Table 1: Activity rates by sex and age group

| Age group | Year 1950 (1)(2) | 1950 (2) | 1961 (2) | 1970 (2) | 1980 (3) | 1990 (3) |
|---|---|---|---|---|---|---|
| **Men** | | | | | | |
| 10-14 | 0.90 | .. | 0.00 | 0.00 | 0.00 | 0.00 |
| 15-19 | 74.46 | | 47.32 | 34.90 | 27.25 | 34.83 |
| 20-24 | 93.09 | .. | 94.20 | 91.55 | 86.49 | 88.19 |
| 25-29 | 98.34 | .. | 98.79 | 98.61 | 98.23 | 98.02 |
| 30-34 | 98.38 | .. | 98.87 | 98.97 | 98.89 | 98.32 |
| 35-39 | 98.51 | .. | 98.42 | 98.69 | 98.66 | 97.84 |
| 40-44 | 98.10 | .. | 97.73 | 97.92 | 97.65 | 97.19 |
| 45-49 | 97.14 | .. | 96.35 | 96.52 | 96.29 | 95.62 |
| 50-54 | 93.59 | .. | 93.09 | 93.74 | 92.94 | 91.89 |
| 55-59 | 88.67 | .. | 84.32 | 85.26 | 84.31 | 80.36 |
| 60-64 | 76.58 | .. | 46.28 | 31.47 | 46.58 | 29.09 |
| 65+ | 38.38 | .. | 23.87 | 14.66 | 18.96 | 12.38 |
| **Women** | | | | | | |
| 10-14 | .. | 0.00 | 0.00 | 0.00 | 0.00 | 0.00 |
| 15-19 | .. | 69.83 | 58.21 | 44.21 | 29.77 | 33.65 |
| 20-24 | .. | 59.29 | 73.15 | 79.68 | 84.57 | 87.25 |
| 25-29 | .. | 39.30 | 62.77 | 80.91 | 91.17 | 94.36 |
| 30-34 | .. | 40.99 | 65.65 | 83.81 | 93.09 | 95.03 |
| 35-39 | .. | 46.39 | 72.27 | 86.57 | 94.31 | 95.43 |
| 40-44 | .. | 48.10 | 74.53 | 86.41 | 94.03 | 94.97 |
| 45-49 | .. | 51.82 | 72.96 | 84.05 | 91.27 | 93.21 |
| 50-54 | .. | 45.51 | 66.20 | 77.13 | 83.68 | 85.40 |
| 55-59 | .. | 34.81 | 46.81 | 39.38 | 43.11 | 32.29 |
| 60-64 | .. | 22.14 | 33.23 | 20.01 | 23.87 | 16.42 |
| 65+ | .. | 8.80 | 9.10 | 5.89 | 7.24 | 5.09 |

Note(s): (1) Slovakia.
Source(s): (2) STAT; (3) BLT-94-2.

### 2.2 Method(s): weighted average

**2.2.1 Men:**

- 1950-90, weighted average of activity rates derived from the 1961 and 1970 censuses, of 1980 and 1990 activity rates derived from the Bulletin of Labour Statistics 1994-2 and 1950 estimated activity rates based on the application to activity rates for Slovakia derived from the 1950 census, the variations in activity rates derived from the 1961 census, in relation to activity rates for Slovakia derived from the 1961 census; adjustment of 1950-70 estimated activity rates of the [10-14] age group.

**2.2.2 Women:**

- 1950-90, weighted average of activity rates derived from the 1950, 1961 and 1970 censuses and of 1980 and 1990 activity rates derived from the Bulletin of Labour Statistics 1994-2; adjustment of 1950-70 estimated activity rates of the [10-14] age group.

## 3. Estimates of distribution rates by activity sector: 1950 - 1990

### 3.1 Benchmark data:

Table 2: Distribution of economically active population by activity sector

| Year | Agriculture | Industry Total | Manufac. | Services |
|---|---|---|---|---|
| **Men** | | | | |
| 1950 | 25.00 | 46.50 | .. | 28.50 |
| 1961 | 17.75 | 57.47 | 48.22 | 24.78 |
| 1970 | 14.76 | 56.27 | .. | 28.97 |
| 1980 | 14.40 | 66.54 | 45.50 | 19.07 |
| 1991 | 13.03 | 52.55 | 35.42 | 34.41 |
| **Women** | | | | |
| 1950 | 43.72 | 32.06 | .. | 24.22 |
| 1961 | 26.99 | 40.36 | 42.31 | 32.65 |
| 1970 | 14.99 | 41.94 | 0.00 | 43.07 |
| 1980 | 11.40 | 43.58 | 38.91 | 45.02 |
| 1991 | 8.91 | 35.75 | 35.53 | 55.34 |

Source(s): STAT.

### 3.2 Method(s): weighted average

**3.2.1 Men:**

- 1950-90, weighted averages of distribution rates derived from the 1950, 1961, 1970, 1980 and 1991 censuses.

**3.2.2 Women:**

Method, hypothesis and treatment identical to those used for men.

## 4. Projection of activity rates: 2000 - 2010

### 4.1 Model(s): linear and hyperbole

**4.1.1 Men:**

- To the [15-44] and [60+] age groups, application of function F3;
- To the [45-59] age groups, application of function F1;
- Modification of the trends for the [45-59] age groups.

**4.1.2 Women:**

- To the [15+] age groups, application of function F3;
- Modification of the trends for the [15-54] age groups.

*Notes on adjustments of rates, see p. 3-8.*

*Notes on projection functions, see p. 10.*

# Dem. Rep. of the Congo

## 1. Source(s) of benchmark data

Code(s):     Title(s):

EPPA3     Economically active population: Estimates and Projections, 1950-2025, Third edition, ILO, Geneva, 1986.

## 2. Estimates of activity rates: 1950 - 1990

### 2.1 Benchmark data:

Table 1: Activity rates by sex and age group

| Age group | Year 1950 | 1960 | 1970 | 1980 |
|---|---|---|---|---|
| **Men** | | | | |
| 10-14 | 45.35 | 43.75 | 40.05 | 35.70 |
| 15-19 | 75.95 | 73.85 | 68.90 | 63.10 |
| 20-24 | 91.80 | 91.00 | 89.10 | 86.90 |
| 25-29 | 96.90 | 96.75 | 96.50 | 96.15 |
| 30-34 | 97.55 | 97.45 | 97.10 | 96.75 |
| 35-39 | 97.70 | 97.55 | 97.20 | 96.85 |
| 40-44 | 97.50 | 97.35 | 97.00 | 96.60 |
| 45-49 | 96.85 | 96.70 | 96.40 | 96.05 |
| 50-54 | 96.15 | 95.95 | 95.50 | 94.95 |
| 55-59 | 94.75 | 94.45 | 93.75 | 92.90 |
| 60-64 | 90.90 | 90.40 | 89.20 | 87.75 |
| 65+ | 76.05 | 75.15 | 73.05 | 70.55 |
| **Women** | | | | |
| 10-14 | 37.35 | 35.20 | 30.25 | 24.40 |
| 15-19 | 65.25 | 60.80 | 50.35 | 38.05 |
| 20-24 | 70.10 | 65.75 | 55.55 | 43.55 |
| 25-29 | 72.80 | 68.75 | 59.35 | 48.25 |
| 30-34 | 75.60 | 71.85 | 63.00 | 52.60 |
| 35-39 | 76.75 | 73.20 | 64.95 | 55.20 |
| 40-44 | 78.05 | 74.85 | 67.40 | 58.65 |
| 45-49 | 77.10 | 74.00 | 66.75 | 58.20 |
| 50-54 | 72.35 | 69.75 | 63.70 | 56.60 |
| 55-59 | 66.65 | 64.75 | 60.40 | 55.25 |
| 60-64 | 54.95 | 53.80 | 51.15 | 48.05 |
| 65+ | 33.40 | 33.05 | 32.15 | 31.10 |

Source(s): EPPA3.

### 2.2 Method(s):   linears interpolation and extrapolation

#### 2.2.1 Men:

- 1950-80, 1950-80 activity rates derived from the EPPA3;
- 1990, extrapolation of 1950-80 activity rates derived from the EPPA3;
adjustment of extrapolated rates on the basis of variations in 1980
interpolated rates, in relation to the 1980 rates derived from the EPPA3.

#### 2.2.2 Women:

- 1950-90, interpolation and extrapolation of 1950-80 activity rates
derived from the EPPA3;
adjustment of interpolated and extrapolated rates on the basis of variations
in 1980 interpolated rates, in relation to the 1980 rates derived the EPPA3.

## 3. Estimates of distribution rates by activity sector: 1950 - 1990

### 3.1 Benchmark data:

Table 2: Distribution of economically active population by activity sector

| Year | Agriculture | Industry Total | Manufac. | Services |
|---|---|---|---|---|
| **Men** | | | | |
| 1950 | 75.20 | 13.20 | .. | 11.60 |
| 1980 | 57.50 | 19.80 | .. | 22.70 |
| **Women** | | | | |
| 1950 | 99.8 | 0.05 | .. | 0.15 |
| 1980 | 94.7 | 1.45 | .. | 3.85 |

Source(s): EPPA3;

### 3.2 Method(s):   linears interpolation and extrapolation

#### 3.2.1 Men:

- 1950 et 1990, 1950 and 1980 distribution rates derived from the EPPA3;
- 1960-80, interpolation of distribution rates estimated for 1950 and 1990;
industry and services sectors, same proportion as in the EPPA3;
- Application of average manufacturing/industry ratio estimated
for Angola and Zimbabwe.

#### 3.2.2 Women:

- 1950-90, interpolation and extrapolation of 1950 and 1980 adjusted
distribution rates derived from the EPPA3;
adjustment of distribution rates on the basis of men/women ratio
equal to 1 in agriculture;
- 1960-80, interpolation of distribution rates estimated for 1950 and 1990;
- Application of average manufacturing/industry ratios estimated for Angola
and Zimbabwe.

## 4. Projection of activity rates: 2000 - 2010

### 4.1 Model(s):   hyperbola

#### 4.1.1 Men:

- To all age groups, application of function F3;
- Modification of the trends for the [20-54] age groups.

#### 4.1.2 Women:

- To all age groups, application of function F3;
- Modification of the trends for the [20-59] and [65+] age groups.

*Notes on adjustments of rates, see p. 3-8.*     *Notes on projection functions, see p. 10.*

# Denmark

## 1. Source(s) of benchmark data

Code(s):    Title(s):

EPPA3      Yearbook of Labour Statistics 1945-89 - Retrospective Edition on Population Censuses, ILO, Geneva, 1990.
STAT       Database on Labour Statistics, LABORSTA - Bureau of Statistics, ILO, Geneva.

## 2. Estimates of activity rates: 1950 - 1990

### 2.1 Benchmark data:

Table 1: Activity rates by sex and age group

| Age group | Year 1989 | 1990 | 1991 |
|---|---|---|---|
| **Men** | | | |
| 10-14 | 0.00 | 0.00 | 0.00 |
| 15-19 | 73.20 | 71.60 | 69.90 |
| 20-24 | 88.40 | 86.80 | 85.80 |
| 25-29 | 93.00 | 92.90 | 92.20 |
| 30-34 | 94.20 | 95.30 | 95.70 |
| 35-39 | 96.00 | 95.40 | 94.90 |
| 40-44 | 95.90 | 96.10 | 95.10 |
| 45-49 | 96.40 | 94.80 | 94.30 |
| 50-54 | 90.70 | 91.60 | 92.40 |
| 55-59 | 85.30 | 84.50 | 81.90 |
| 60-64 | 49.50 | 50.50 | 47.10 |
| 65+ | 10.32 | 12.46 | 10.97 |
| **Women** | | | |
| 10-14 | 0.00 | 0.00 | 0.00 |
| 15-19 | 65.20 | 65.20 | 64.40 |
| 20-24 | 80.10 | 79.30 | 81.70 |
| 25-29 | 86.70 | 86.90 | 85.10 |
| 30-34 | 91.90 | 90.70 | 90.30 |
| 35-39 | 89.30 | 90.30 | 90.50 |
| 40-44 | 88.70 | 89.60 | 91.00 |
| 45-49 | 82.80 | 87.30 | 87.00 |
| 50-54 | 76.60 | 79.50 | 79.40 |
| 55-59 | 59.00 | 62.10 | 64.50 |
| 60-64 | 23.40 | 26.40 | 26.80 |
| 65+ | 3.23 | 3.17 | 3.02 |

Source(s): STAT.

### 2.2 Method(s): arithmetic average

#### 2.2.1 Men:

- 1950-80, 1950-80 activity rates derived from the EPPA3;
adjustment of activity rates of the [15-19] age group for 1980;
- 1990, average of activity rates derived from the 1989, 1990
and 1991 surveys.

#### 2.2.2 Women:

Method, hypothesis and treatment identical to those used for men.

## 3. Estimates of distribution rates by activity sector: 1950 - 1990

### 3.1 Benchmark data:

Table 2: Distribution of economically active population by activity sector

| Year | Agriculture | Industry Total | Manufac. | Services |
|---|---|---|---|---|
| **Men** | | | | |
| 1979 | 10.22 | 40.96 | 27.06 | 48.81 |
| 1981 | 10.06 | 43.13 | 28.33 | 46.82 |
| 1989 | 7.83 | 38.00 | 23.87 | 54.17 |
| 1990 | 7.69 | 37.84 | 24.89 | 54.46 |
| 1991 | 7.89 | 37.94 | 25.13 | 54.18 |
| **Women** | | | | |
| 1979 | 5.27 | 16.87 | 14.87 | 77.86 |
| 1981 | 3.28 | 17.57 | 15.68 | 79.15 |
| 1989 | 2.98 | 16.47 | 14.40 | 80.55 |
| 1990 | 2.81 | 16.62 | 14.78 | 80.58 |
| 1991 | 2.99 | 17.08 | 15.14 | 79.94 |

Source(s): STAT.

### 3.2 Method(s):   weighted average
arithmetic average

#### 3.2.1 Men:

- 1950-70, 1950-70 distribution rates derived from the EPPA3;
- 1980, weighted averages of distribution rates derived from
the 1979 and 1981 surveys;
- 1990, averages of distribution rates derived from the 1989, 1990
and 1991 surveys.

#### 3.2.2 Women:

Method, hypothesis and treatment identical to those used for men.

## 4. Projection of activity rates: 2000 - 2010

### 4.1 Model(s):   linear, hyperbole and logistic

#### 4.1.1 Men:

- To the [15-24] age groups, application of function F1;
- To the [25+] age groups, application of function F3;
- Modification of the trends for the [15-39] and [45-49] age groups.

#### 4.1.2 Women:

- To the [15-34] and [60-64] age groups, application of function F1;
- To the [35-59] age groups, application of function F6;
- To the [65+] age group, application of function F3;
- Modification of the trends for the [15-64] age groups.

*Notes on adjustments of rates, see p. 3-8.*          *Notes on projection functions, see p. 10.*

# Dominican Republic

## 1. Source(s) of benchmark data

Code(s): Title(s):

EPPA3 Economically active population: Estimates and Projections, 1950-2025, Third edition, ILO, Geneva, 1986.
RDR-70 Censos Nacional de Poblacion Y habitacion 1970, Oficina Nacional de Estadistica (ONE), Santo Domingo.
ASTER Yearbook of Labour Statistics 1945-89 - Retrospective Edition on Population Censuses, ILO, Geneva, 1990.

## 2. Estimates of activity rates: 1950 - 1990

### 2.1 Benchmark data:

Table 1: Activity rates by sex and age group

| Age group | Year | | | |
|---|---|---|---|---|
| | 1950 (1) | 1960 (2) | 1970 (3) | 1981 (2) |
| **Men** | | | | |
| 10-14 | 53.75 | 48.00 | 41.87 | .. |
| 15-19 | 78.50 | 70.10 | 60.24 | .. |
| 20-24 | 97.00 | 95.05 | 84.94 | .. |
| 25-29 | 98.00 | 97.84 | 92.86 | .. |
| 30-34 | 98.80 | 98.64 | 95.00 | .. |
| 35-39 | 98.80 | 98.65 | 94.61 | .. |
| 40-44 | 98.65 | 98.47 | 93.97 | .. |
| 45-49 | 98.50 | 98.16 | 93.27 | .. |
| 50-54 | 98.25 | 97.86 | 90.95 | .. |
| 55-59 | 97.45 | 96.68 | 90.48 | .. |
| 60-64 | 96.60 | 95.12 | 88.19 | .. |
| 65+ | 84.59 | 83.27 | 79.12 | .. |
| **Women** | | | | |
| 10-14 | 2.80 | 2.21 | 25.81 | 11.00 |
| 15-19 | 9.50 | 8.97 | 23.49 | 20.40 |
| 20-24 | 11.55 | 12.23 | 26.53 | 33.30 |
| 25-29 | 11.50 | 12.25 | 25.84 | 38.30 |
| 30-34 | 11.50 | 12.23 | 25.72 | 37.10 |
| 35-39 | 11.65 | 12.39 | 24.72 | 32.40 |
| 40-44 | 11.90 | 12.64 | 25.74 | 33.30 |
| 45-49 | 12.55 | 12.87 | 23.40 | 32.30 |
| 50-54 | 10.00 | 10.25 | 22.52 | 28.90 |
| 55-59 | 11.20 | 11.13 | 21.94 | 28.10 |
| 60-64 | 9.35 | 9.26 | 22.21 | 26.90 |
| 65+ | 4.50 | 4.27 | 10.50 | 10.28 |

Source(s): (1) EPPA3; (2) RDR-70 and ASTER; (3) ASTER.

### 2.2 Method(s): linears interpolation and extrapolation

#### 2.2.1 Men:

- 1950-60, 1950-60 activity rates derived from the EPPA3;
adjustment of activity rates of the [10-14] and [65+] age groups based
on the results of the 1970 and 1981 censuses;
- 1970, adjusted activity rates derived from the 1970 census;
- 1980-90, extrapolation of the 1950 activity rates derived from the EPPA3,
of adjusted activity rates derived from the 1960 census and of activity rates
derived from the 1970 census; application to extrapolated rates, variations in
1970 interpolated rates, in relation to activity rates derived from the 1970 census

#### 2.2.2 Women:

- 1950-60, 1950-60 activity rates derived from the EPPA3;
modification of the trends of the [10-19] age groups for 1960;
- 1970-80, interpolation of activity rates derived from
the 1970 and 1981 censuses;
- 1990, extrapolation of activity rates derived from the 1970 and 1981 censuses;
application to extrapolated rates, variations in 1970 interpolated rates,
to activity rates derived from the 1970 census.

## 3. Estimates of distribution rates by activity sector: 1950 - 1990

### 3.1 Benchmark data:

Table 2: Distribution of economically active population by activity sector

| Year | Agriculture | Industry | | Services |
|---|---|---|---|---|
| | | Total | Manufac. | |
| **Men** | | | | |
| 1960 | 69.30 | 12.35 | .. | 18.35 |
| 1970 | 58.20 | 14.68 | 11.16 | 27.12 |
| 1981 | 38.61 | 26.64 | 17.02 | 34.76 |
| **Women** | | | | |
| 1960 | 13.15 | 16.15 | .. | 70.70 |
| 1970 | 11.91 | 13.02 | 12.43 | 75.07 |
| 1981 | 11.02 | 16.44 | 15.07 | 72.54 |

Source(s): ASTER.

### 3.2 Method(s): weighted average
linear interpolation and extrapolation

#### 3.2.1 Men:

- 1950-60, 1950-60 distribution rates derived from the EPPA3;
- 1970, weighted averages of 1960 distribution rates derived from
the EPPA3 and of distribution rates derived from the 1970 census;
- 1980-90, interpolation and extrapolation of distribution rates derived from
the 1970 and 1981 censuses;
modification of the trends in all sectors for 1990.

#### 3.2.2 Women:

Method, hypothesis and treatment identical to those used for men.

## 4. Projection of activity rates: 2000 - 2010

### 4.1 Model(s): linear, hyperbole and logistic

#### 4.1.1 Men:

- To the [10-24] and [55+] age groups, application of function F1;
- To the [25-54] age groups, application of function F3;
- Modification of the trends for the [10-24] and [50-59] age groups.

#### 4.1.2 Women:

- To the [10-19] and [40+] age groups, application of function F1;
- To the [20-39] age groups, application of function F6;
- Modification of the trends for the [10-39] and [50+] age groups.

Notes on adjustments of rates, see p. 3-8.          Notes on projection functions, see p. 10.

# East Timor

## 1. Source(s) of benchmark data

Code(s):     Title(s):

EPPA3     Economically active population: Estimates and Projections, 1950-2025, Third edition, ILO, Geneva, 1986.

## 2. Estimates of activity rates: 1950 - 1990

### 2.1 Benchmark data:

Table 1: Activity rates by sex and age group

|  | Year | | | | |
| Age group | 1950 | 1960 | 1970 | 1980 | 1990 |
|---|---|---|---|---|---|
| **Men** | | | | | |
| 10-14 | 28.51 | 26.60 | 24.69 | 22.78 | .. |
| 15-19 | 82.80 | 81.50 | 75.70 | 72.80 | .. |
| 20-24 | 97.50 | 97.00 | 95.25 | 94.00 | .. |
| 25-29 | 97.65 | 97.40 | 97.15 | 97.00 | .. |
| 30-34 | 97.65 | 97.40 | 97.15 | 97.00 | .. |
| 35-39 | 97.60 | 97.35 | 97.10 | 97.00 | .. |
| 40-44 | 97.50 | 97.25 | 97.00 | 96.90 | .. |
| 45-49 | 97.40 | 96.15 | 95.50 | 95.20 | .. |
| 50-54 | 97.00 | 95.70 | 95.00 | 94.65 | .. |
| 55-59 | 95.00 | 93.50 | 91.50 | 90.50 | .. |
| 60-64 | 90.00 | 88.50 | 86.00 | 84.75 | .. |
| 65+ | 78.00 | 76.00 | 70.25 | 67.40 | .. |
| **Women** | | | | | |
| 10-14 | 3.00 | .. | .. | .. | 2.20 |
| 15-19 | 10.60 | .. | .. | .. | 12.28 |
| 20-24 | 11.80 | .. | .. | .. | 18.66 |
| 25-29 | 11.45 | .. | .. | .. | 17.36 |
| 30-34 | 10.25 | .. | .. | .. | 15.69 |
| 35-39 | 10.70 | .. | .. | .. | 15.82 |
| 40-44 | 12.00 | .. | .. | .. | 17.40 |
| 45-49 | 11.20 | .. | .. | .. | 15.00 |
| 50-54 | 10.75 | .. | .. | .. | 14.02 |
| 55-59 | 10.00 | .. | .. | .. | 9.86 |
| 60-64 | 8.35 | .. | .. | .. | 7.08 |
| 65+ | 4.50 | .. | .. | .. | 4.15 |

Source(s): EPPA3.

### 2.2 Method(s): linear interpolation
weighted average

#### 2.2.1 Men:

- 1950-80, 1950-80 activity rates derived from the EPPA3;
adjustment of activity rates of the [10-14] age group;
- 1990, extrapolation of 1950-80 activity rates derived from the EPPA3;
adjustment of extrapolated rates on the basis of variations
in 1980 interpolated rates, in relation to 1980 activity rates derived from
the EPPA3;
modification of the trends for all age groups for 1970.

#### 2.2.2 Women:

- 1950 and 1990, 1950 and 1990 adjusted activity rates derived from the EPPA3
the adjustment was made on the basis of the adjustment model for
activity rates of women working in agriculture as contributing family workers;
- 1960-80, weighted average of activity rates estimated for 1950 and 1990.

## 3. Estimates of distribution rates by activity sector: 1950 - 1990

### 3.1 Benchmark data:

Table 2: Distribution of economically active population by activity sector

|  | Agriculture | Industry | | Services |
| Year | | Total | Manufac. | |
|---|---|---|---|---|
| **Men** | | | | |
| 1950 | 80.00 | 7.50 | .. | 12.50 |
| 1960 | 79.00 | 8.00 | .. | 13.00 |
| 1970 | 78.00 | 8.50 | .. | 13.50 |
| 1980 | 77.00 | 8.75 | .. | 14.25 |
| **Women** | | | | |
| 1950 | 98.00 | 0.06 | .. | 1.94 |
| 1960 | 96.75 | 0.10 | .. | 3.15 |
| 1970 | 95.50 | 0.14 | .. | 4.36 |
| 1980 | 94.25 | 0.17 | .. | 5.58 |

Source(s): EPPA3.

### 3.2 Method(s): linear extrapolation

#### 3.2.1 Men:

- 1950-80, 1950-80 distribution rates derived from the EPPA3;
- 1990, extrapolation of 1950-80 distribution rates of agriculture sector
derived from the EPP3;
- Application of 1980 industry/services derived from the EPPA3.

#### 3.2.2 Women:

- 1950-80, 1950-80 distribution rates of agriculture sector derived
from the EPPA3;
adjustment of distribution rates on the basis of men/women ratio
equal to 1 in agriculture;
application of 1950-80 industry/services derived from the EPPA3;
- 1990, extrapolation of distribution rates estimated of agriculture sector
1950-80;
application of 1980 industry/services derived from the EPPA3.

## 4. Projection of activity rates: 2000 - 2010

### 4.1 Model(s): linear, hyperbolc and logistic

#### 4.1.1 Men:

- To the [10-19] and [55+] age groups, application of function F1;
- To the [20-54] age groups, application of function F3;
- Modification of the trends for the [55+] age groups.

#### 4.1.2 Women:

- To the [10-19] age groups, application of function F1;
- To the [20+] age groups, application of function F6;
- Modification of the trends for the [10-19] age groups.

---

*Notes on adjustments of rates, see p. 3-8.*         *Notes on projection functions, see p. 10.*

# Ecuador

## 1. Source(s) of benchmark data

Code(s):    Title(s):

EPPA3    Economically active population: Estimates and Projections, 1950-2025, Third edition, ILO, Geneva, 1986.
STAT    Database on Labour Statistics, LABORSTA - Bureau of Statistics, ILO, Geneva.

## 2. Estimates of activity rates: 1950 - 1990

### 2.1 Benchmark data:

Table 1: Activity rates by sex and age group

| Age group | Year | | |
|---|---|---|---|
| | 1970 (1) | 1982 (2) | 1990 (2) |
| **Men** | | | |
| 10-14 | 25.00 | 9.34 | 17.06 |
| 15-19 | 68.00 | 47.78 | 52.43 |
| 20-24 | 88.85 | 75.31 | 79.32 |
| 25-29 | 96.70 | 90.04 | 90.83 |
| 30-34 | 98.65 | 91.98 | 94.97 |
| 35-39 | 98.90 | 92.97 | 95.87 |
| 40-44 | 98.80 | 92.98 | 95.57 |
| 45-49 | 98.45 | 92.13 | 95.02 |
| 50-54 | 97.55 | 90.53 | 93.36 |
| 55-59 | 96.00 | 88.30 | 91.02 |
| 60-64 | 93.90 | 82.69 | 85.68 |
| 65+ | 83.40 | 64.77 | 64.34 |
| **Women** | | | |
| 10-14 | 5.00 | 3.97 | 6.69 |
| 15-19 | 17.70 | 14.55 | 19.04 |
| 20-24 | 21.70 | 22.75 | 29.35 |
| 25-29 | 19.40 | 26.18 | 34.06 |
| 30-34 | 17.50 | 24.18 | 35.91 |
| 35-39 | 16.60 | 22.09 | 35.38 |
| 40-44 | 16.65 | 20.44 | 33.34 |
| 45-49 | 16.20 | 18.91 | 30.37 |
| 50-54 | 15.70 | 17.35 | 27.21 |
| 55-59 | 14.55 | 15.57 | 24.44 |
| 60-64 | 13.15 | 13.15 | 20.98 |
| 65+ | 10.15 | 9.11 | 13.95 |

Source(s): (1) EPPA3; (2) STAT.

### 2.2 Method(s): linear interpolation weighted average

#### 2.2.1 Men:

- 1950-70, 1950-70 activity rates derived from the EPPA3;
- 1980-90, weighted average of activity rates of 1970 derived from the EPPA3 and of adjusted activity rates derived from the 1982 and 1990 censuses.

#### 2.2.2 Women:

- 1950-70, 1950-70 adjusted activity rates derived from the EPPA3;
the adjustment was made on the basis of the adjustment model for
activity rates of women working in agriculture as contributing family workers;
- 1980-90, interpolation and extrapolation of adjusted activity rates
the 1982 census and adjusted activity rates derived from the 1990 census.

## 3. Estimates of distribution rates by activity sector: 1950 - 1990

### 3.1 Benchmark data:

Table 2: Distribution of economically active population by activity sector

| Year | Agriculture | Industry | | Services |
|---|---|---|---|---|
| | | Total | Manufac. | |
| **Men** | | | | |
| 1970 (1) | 57.60 | 19.60 | .. | 22.80 |
| 1982 (2) | 41.11 | 21.89 | 12.09 | 36.99 |
| 1990 (2) | 38.79 | 20.14 | 10.64 | 41.06 |
| **Women** | | | | |
| 1982 (2) | 13.02 | 17.08 | 15.96 | 69.90 |
| 1990 (2) | 15.75 | 15.73 | 14.69 | 68.52 |

Source(s): (1) EPPA3; (2) STAT.

### 3.2 Method(s): weighted average linear interpolation and extrapolation

#### 3.2.1 Men:

- 1950-70, 1950-70 distribution rates derived from the EPPA3;
- 1980-90, weighted averages of 1970 distribution rates derived from
the EPPA3 and of distribution rates derived from the 1982 and 1990 censuses.

#### 3.2.2 Women:

- 1950, 1950 distribution rates derived from the EPPA3;
- 1960-70, interpolation of distribution rates estimated for 1950 and 1980;
- 1980-90, interpolation and extrapolation of distribution rates derived from
the 1982 and 1990 censuses.

## 4. Projection of activity rates: 2000 - 2010

### 4.1 Model(s): linear, log-linear and hyperbole

#### 4.1.1 Men:

- To the [10-19] age groups, application of function F2;
- To the [20-59] age groups, application of function F3;
- To the [60+] age groups, application of function F3;
- Modification of the trends for the [20-49] age groups.

#### 4.1.2 Women:

- To the [10-24] age groups, application of function F3;
- To the [25+] age groups, application of function F2;
- Modification of the trends for the [10-14] and [20-24] age groups.

*Notes on adjustments of rates, see p. 3-8.*    *Notes on projection functions, see p. 10.*

# Egypt

## 1. Source(s) of benchmark data

| Code(s): | Title(s): |
|---|---|
| EPPA3 | Economically active population: Estimates and Projections, 1950-2025, Third edition, ILO, Geneva, 1986. |
| ASTER | Yearbook of Labour Statistics 1945-89 - Retrospective Edition on Population Censuses, ILO, Geneva, 1990. |
| AST91 | Yearbook of Labour Statistics 1991, ILO, Geneva, 1991. |
| AST93 | Yearbook of Labour Statistics 1993, ILO, Geneva, 1993. |

## 2. Estimates of activity rates: 1950 - 1990

### 2.1 Benchmark data:

Table 1: Activity rates by sex and age group

| Age group | Year 1950 (1) | 1960 (1) | 1970 (1) | 1976 (2) | 1986 (3) | 1989 (4) |
|---|---|---|---|---|---|---|
| **Men** | | | | | | |
| 10-14 | 30.50 | 26.15 | .. | 26.30 | 12.44 | .. |
| 15-19 | 78.95 | 68.75 | .. | 49.85 | 39.45 | .. |
| 20-24 | 90.35 | 86.70 | .. | 71.69 | 78.52 | .. |
| 25-29 | 97.75 | 96.05 | .. | 92.84 | 94.96 | .. |
| 30-34 | 98.25 | 97.80 | .. | 96.98 | 98.21 | .. |
| 35-39 | 98.05 | 98.10 | .. | 98.27 | 98.23 | .. |
| 40-44 | 97.90 | 97.90 | .. | 97.86 | 96.80 | .. |
| 45-49 | 97.40 | 97.70 | .. | 98.23 | 95.74 | .. |
| 50-54 | 96.00 | 96.30 | .. | 96.76 | 93.70 | .. |
| 55-59 | 94.20 | 94.50 | .. | 95.02 | 90.95 | .. |
| 60-64 | 90.00 | 85.30 | .. | 76.71 | 66.82 | .. |
| 65+ | 74.80 | 62.80 | .. | 40.92 | 25.79 | .. |
| **Women** | | | | | | |
| 10-14 | 8.50 | 8.20 | 4.90 | 7.22 | 1.44 | 5.80 |
| 15-19 | 10.20 | 8.65 | 6.25 | 5.13 | 5.91 | 17.10 |
| 20-24 | 6.15 | 7.25 | 10.05 | 12.42 | 18.85 | 38.50 |
| 25-29 | 3.70 | 4.75 | 7.85 | 10.79 | 16.83 | 38.10 |
| 30-34 | 3.75 | 4.45 | 6.30 | 7.81 | 14.17 | 40.24 |
| 35-39 | 4.10 | 4.40 | 5.05 | 5.47 | 9.56 | 38.00 |
| 40-44 | 5.65 | 5.30 | 4.65 | 4.39 | 7.47 | 37.87 |
| 45-49 | 4.75 | 4.40 | 3.85 | 3.53 | 5.36 | 29.60 |
| 50-54 | 5.20 | 4.60 | 3.60 | 3.14 | 3.51 | 26.99 |
| 55-59 | 3.05 | 3.40 | 2.95 | 2.75 | 2.64 | 24.38 |
| 60-64 | 3.60 | 3.20 | 2.55 | 2.20 | 1.40 | 13.70 |
| 65+ | 2.25 | 1.90 | 1.35 | 1.03 | 0.63 | 8.90 |

Source(s): (1) EPPA3; (2) ASTER; (3) AST91; (4) AST93.

### 2.2 Method(s): linears interpolation and extrapolation

#### 2.2.1 Men:

- 1950-90, interpolation and extrapolation of 1950-60 activity rates derived from the EPPA3 and of adjusted activity rates derived from the 1976 and 1986 censuses.

#### 2.2.2 Women:

- 1950-70, 1950-70 adjusted activity rates derived from the EPPA3;
- 1980-90, interpolation and extrapolation of adjusted activity rates derived from the 1980 and 1985 censuses and of activity rates derived from the 1988 survey; the adjustment was made on the basis of the adjustment model for activity rates of women working in agriculture as contributing family workers.

## 3. Estimates of distribution rates by activity sector: 1950 - 1990

### 3.1 Benchmark data:

Table 2: Distribution of economically active population by activity sector

| Year | Agriculture | Industry Total | Manufac. | Services |
|---|---|---|---|---|
| **Men** | | | | |
| 1976 (1) | 50.35 | 19.00 | 13.61 | 30.65 |
| 1986 (2) | 43.83 | 22.45 | 13.22 | 33.73 |
| 1989 (3) | 34.58 | 25.16 | 14.94 | 40.26 |
| **Women** | | | | |
| 1976 (1) | 23.34 | 15.40 | 13.44 | 61.26 |
| 1986 (2) | 10.82 | 12.61 | 10.43 | 76.58 |
| 1989 (3) | 63.16 | 9.09 | 8.37 | 27.75 |

Source(s): (1) ASTER; (2) AST91; (3) AST93.

### 3.2 Method(s): weighted average

#### 3.2.1 Men:

- 1950-70, 1950-70 distribution rates derived from the EPPA3;
- 1980-90, weighted averages of adjusted distribution rates derived from the 1976 census and of distribution rates derived from the 1986 census and the 1989 survey.

#### 3.2.2 Women:

Method, hypothesis and treatment identical to those used for men.

## 4. Projection of activity rates: 2000 - 2010

### 4.1 Model(s): linear and hyperbole

#### 4.1.1 Men:

- To the [10-14] age group, application of function F1;
- To the [15+] age groups, application of function F3;
- Modification of the trends for the [10-24] age groups.

#### 4.1.2 Women:

- To all age groups, application of function F1;
- Modification of the trends for the [10-19], [30-34] and [30+] age groups.

*Notes on adjustments of rates, see p. 3-8.*

*Notes on projection functions, see p. 10.*

# El Salvador

## 1. Source(s) of benchmark data

Code(s):    Title(s):

EPPA3      Economically active population: Estimates and Projections, 1950-2025, Third edition, ILO, Geneva, 1986.
CELADE    CELADE, Bulletin Démographique, No. 49, janvier 1992.
STAT       Database on Labour Statistics, LABORSTA - Bureau of Statistics, ILO, Geneva.

## 2. Estimates of activity rates: 1950 - 1990

### 2.1 Benchmark data:

Table 1: Activity rates by sex and age group

| Age group | Year 1970 (1) | 1990 (2)(3) | 1990 (4)(5) |
|---|---|---|---|
| **Men** | | | |
| 10-14 | 30.00 | 39.73 | 35.77 |
| 15-19 | 71.00 | 78.73 | 75.97 |
| 20-24 | 93.30 | 93.83 | 92.67 |
| 25-29 | 97.40 | 99.00 | 99.00 |
| 30-34 | 97.90 | 99.00 | 99.00 |
| 35-39 | 98.00 | 99.00 | 99.00 |
| 40-44 | 98.10 | 99.00 | 99.00 |
| 45-49 | 98.10 | 99.00 | 99.00 |
| 50-54 | 97.30 | 98.60 | 98.60 |
| 55-59 | 96.80 | 97.00 | 96.00 |
| 60-64 | 94.10 | 94.17 | 92.33 |
| 65+ | 71.80 | ... | 73.21 |
| **Women** | | | |
| 10-14 | 5.20 | 4.80 | 4.78 |
| 15-19 | 26.10 | 20.33 | 20.33 |
| 20-24 | 34.65 | 24.80 | 39.34 |
| 25-29 | 26.35 | 13.20 | 20.78 |
| 30-34 | 24.00 | 11.10 | 17.58 |
| 35-39 | 22.20 | 10.30 | 16.27 |
| 40-44 | 21.55 | 10.10 | 15.87 |
| 45-49 | 19.85 | 9.50 | 14.57 |
| 50-54 | 18.45 | 9.00 | 13.44 |
| 55-59 | 16.50 | 8.50 | 12.11 |
| 60-64 | 15.25 | 7.83 | 10.81 |
| 65+ | 9.70 | ... | 4.80 |

Note(s): (2) Rural; (5) Urban.
Source(s): (1) EPPA3; (2) CELADE; (4) STAT.

### 2.2 Method(s): arithmetic average

**2.2.1 Men:**

- 1950-70, 1950-70 activity rates derived from the EPPA3;
- 1980, average of estimated activity rates for 1970 and 1990;
- 1990, adjusted activity rates derived from the 1990 survey;
adjustment on the basis of estimates activity rates in rural areas.

**2.2.2 Women:**

Method, hypothesis and treatment identical to those used for men.

## 3. Estimates of distribution rates by activity sector: 1950 - 1990

### 3.1 Benchmark data:

Table 2: Distribution of economically active population by activity sector

| Year | Agriculture | Industry Total | Manufac. | Services |
|---|---|---|---|---|
| **Men** | | | | |
| 1950 (1) | 75.70 | 13.60 | .. | 10.70 |
| 1960 (1) | 72.35 | 15.65 | .. | 12.00 |
| 1970 (1) | 69.00 | 13.40 | .. | 17.60 |
| 1980 (1) | 55.80 | 19.80 | .. | 24.40 |
| **Women** | | | | |
| 1950 (1) | 12.40 | 24.85 | .. | 62.75 |
| 1961 (2) | 71.72 | 15.89 | 10.53 | 12.39 |
| 1971 (2) | 69.57 | 12.67 | 8.49 | 17.76 |
| 1991 (2) | 15.30 | 33.55 | 22.44 | 51.15 |

Source(s): (1) EPPA3; (2) STAT.

### 3.2 Method(s): linears interpolation and extrapolation

**3.2.1 Men:**

- 1950-80, 1950-80 distribution rates derived from the EPPA3;
- 1990, extrapolation of 1950-80 distribution rates derived from the EPPA3;
adjustment of extrapolated rates on the basis of variations in 1980 interpolated rates, in relation to 1980 distribution rates derived from the EPPA3.

**3.2.2 Women:**

- 1950, 1950 distribution rates derived from the EPPA3;
- 1960, 1970 and 1990, interpolation and extrapolation of distribution rates derived from the 1961 and 1971 censuses and adjusted distribution rates derived from the 1991 census;
- 1980, averages of distribution rates estimated for 1970 and 1990.

## 4. Projection of activity rates: 2000 - 2010

### 4.1 Model(s): linear, hyperbole and logistic

**4.1.1 Men:**

- To the [10-54] age groups, application of function F1;
- To the [55+] age groups, application of function F3;
- Modification of the trends for the [10-14], [25-49] and [60+].

**4.1.2 Women:**

- To the [10-14] and [20-44] age groups, application of function F1;
- To the [15-19] age group, application of function F3;
- To the [45+] age groups, application of function F6;
- Modification of the trends for all age groups.

---

*Notes on adjustments of rates, see p. 3-8.*      *Notes on projection functions, see p. 10.*

# Equatorial Guinea

## 1. Source(s) of benchmark data

Code(s):    Title(s):

EPPA3    Economically active population: Estimates and Projections, 1950-2025, Third edition, ILO, Geneva, 1986.
AST91    Yearbook of Labour Statistics 1991, ILO, Geneva, 1991.
R1983    Republica de Guinea Ecuatorial, Censos Nacionales I de Poblacion I de Vivienda, Caractristica de la Poblacion, 4/07/1983, Malabo.

## 2. Estimates of activity rates: 1950 - 1990

### 2.1 Benchmark data:

Table 1: Activity rates by sex and age group

| Age group | Year 1950 (1) | 1960 (1) | 1970 (1) | 1980 (1) | 1983 (2) |
|---|---|---|---|---|---|
| **Men** | | | | | |
| 10-14 | 49.30 | 44.95 | 39.80 | 32.75 | 8.97 |
| 15-19 | 81.20 | 75.40 | 68.55 | 59.15 | 77.54 |
| 20-24 | 93.85 | 91.60 | 89.00 | 85.35 | 96.37 |
| 25-29 | 97.20 | 96.85 | 96.45 | 95.95 | 96.92 |
| 30-34 | 97.90 | 97.55 | 97.10 | 96.50 | 96.89 |
| 35-39 | 98.05 | 97.65 | 97.20 | 96.55 | 97.03 |
| 40-44 | 97.90 | 97.45 | 97.00 | 96.30 | 97.15 |
| 45-49 | 97.15 | 96.80 | 96.40 | 95.80 | 96.68 |
| 50-54 | 96.60 | 96.10 | 95.45 | 94.60 | 96.54 |
| 55-59 | 95.55 | 94.70 | 93.70 | 92.30 | 96.00 |
| 60-64 | 92.20 | 90.80 | 89.10 | 86.80 | 93.83 |
| 65+ | 78.35 | 75.85 | 72.90 | 68.85 | 52.17 |
| **Women** | | | | | |
| 10-14 | 36.35 | 34.20 | 31.75 | 28.85 | 9.17 |
| 15-19 | 59.45 | 56.20 | 52.50 | 48.20 | 48.55 |
| 20-24 | 61.30 | 59.25 | 56.95 | 54.20 | 37.82 |
| 25-29 | 65.90 | 63.55 | 60.90 | 57.80 | 37.18 |
| 30-34 | 70.00 | 67.50 | 64.65 | 61.35 | 41.96 |
| 35-39 | 71.50 | 69.15 | 66.50 | 63.40 | 44.62 |
| 40-44 | 73.95 | 71.60 | 68.95 | 65.85 | 46.95 |
| 45-49 | 73.40 | 71.00 | 68.30 | 65.15 | 46.71 |
| 50-54 | 71.45 | 68.70 | 65.55 | 61.90 | 48.02 |
| 55-59 | 68.50 | 65.60 | 62.35 | 58.55 | 47.33 |
| 60-64 | 61.40 | 57.75 | 53.60 | 48.75 | 48.71 |
| 65+ | 41.70 | 38.25 | 34.40 | 29.90 | 22.45 |

Source(s): (1) EPPA3; (2) AST91 and R1983.

### 2.2 Method(s): linears interpolation and extrapolation

#### 2.2.1 Men:

- 1950-90, interpolation and extrapolation of 1950-80 activity rates derived from the EPPA3 and of adjusted activity rates derived from the 1983 census;
adjustment of interpolated and extrapolated rates on the basis of variations in 1983 interpolated rates, in relation to activity rates derived from the 1983 census;
modification of the trends for all age groups.

#### 2.2.2 Women:

Method, hypothesis and treatment identical to those used for men.

## 3. Estimates of distribution rates by activity sector: 1950 - 1990

### 3.1 Benchmark data:

Table 2: Distribution of economically active population by activity sector

| Year | Agriculture | Industry Total | Manufac. | Services |
|---|---|---|---|---|
| **Men** | | | | |
| 1950 (1) | 82.50 | 6.25 | .. | 11.15 |
| 1960 (1) | 74.50 | 9.25 | .. | 16.25 |
| 1970 (1) | 65.00 | 12.70 | .. | 22.30 |
| 1980 (1) | 52.00 | 17.4 | | 30.60 |
| 1983 (2) | 69.10 | 7.34 | 2.63 | 23.55 |
| **Women** | | | | |
| 1950 (1) | 96.00 | 0.70 | .. | 3.30 |
| 1960 (1) | 93.00 | 1.25 | .. | 5.75 |
| 1970 (1) | 89.00 | 2.00 | .. | 9.00 |
| 1980 (1) | 85.50 | 2.60 | .. | 11.90 |
| 1983 (2) | 92.05 | 0.88 | 0.70 | 7.07 |

Source(s): (1) EPPA3; (2) AST91.

### 3.2 Method(s): linears interpolation and extrapolation

#### 3.2.1 Men:

- 1950-90, interpolation and extrapolation of 1950-80 distribution rates derived from the EPPA3 and of distribution rates derived from the 1983 census, adjustment of 1950-90 interpolated and extrapolated rates on the basis of 1/3 of variations in 1983 interpolated rates, in relation to distribution rates derived from the 1983 census;
- Application of manufacturing/industry ratio derived from the 1983 census.

#### 3.2.2 Women:

Method, hypothesis and treatment identical to those used for men.

## 4. Projection of activity rates: 2000 - 2010

### 4.1 Model(s): linear and hyperbole

#### 4.1.1 Men:

- To the [10-29] and [55+] age groups, application of function F1;
- To the [30-54] age groups, application of function F3;
- Modification of the trend for the [10-14] age group.

#### 4.1.2 Women:

- To the [10-14] age group, application of function F1;
- To the [15+] age groups, application of function F3;
- Modification of the trends for the [15-54] age groups.

*Notes on adjustments of rates, see p. 3-8.*

*Notes on projection functions, see p. 10.*

# Eritrea

## 1. Source(s) of benchmark data

Code(s):     Title(s):

FSEE94      ILO, Foundation For Sustained Employment in Eritrea, EAMAT Addis Ababa, 1994.
EPPA4       Economically active population 1950-2010 - Fourth edition, ILO, Geneva 1996.

## 2. Estimates of activity rates: 1950 - 1990

### 2.1 Benchmark data:

Table 1: Activity rates by sex and age group

| Age group | Year 1950 (1) | 1970 (1) | 1990 (1) | 1950 (2) | 1970 (2) | 1990 (2) |
|---|---|---|---|---|---|---|
| **Men** | | | | | | |
| 10-14 | 55.69 | 51.05 | 45.02 | 47.40 | 42.80 | 38.02 |
| 15-19 | 71.92 | 67.03 | 62.13 | 78.65 | 72.55 | 66.15 |
| 20-24 | 83.93 | 81.97 | 80.45 | 92.85 | 90.50 | 88.06 |
| 25-29 | 94.75 | 94.43 | 94.10 | 97.05 | 96.70 | 96.32 |
| 30-34 | 97.21 | 96.85 | 96.49 | 97.75 | 97.35 | 96.95 |
| 35-39 | 98.26 | 97.87 | 97.52 | 97.90 | 97.45 | 97.03 |
| 40-44 | 98.19 | 97.78 | 97.38 | 97.70 | 97.25 | 96.83 |
| 45-49 | 98.00 | 97.65 | 97.29 | 97.00 | 96.65 | 96.27 |
| 50-54 | 96.29 | 95.76 | 95.24 | 96.40 | 95.80 | 95.20 |
| 55-59 | 95.66 | 94.80 | 93.94 | 95.15 | 94.25 | 93.35 |
| 60-64 | 93.95 | 92.51 | 91.07 | 91.60 | 90.10 | 88.54 |
| 65+ | 80.93 | 78.37 | 75.81 | 77.25 | 74.60 | 71.86 |
| **Women** | | | | | | |
| 10-14 | 50.19 | 46.02 | 41.85 | 41.00 | 37.00 | 31.00 |
| 15-19 | 61.10 | 57.45 | 54.54 | 65.71 | 59.76 | 56.05 |
| 20-24 | 64.17 | 61.77 | 59.86 | 68.56 | 64.51 | 61.99 |
| 25-29 | 65.16 | 62.60 | 60.54 | 73.45 | 68.93 | 66.11 |
| 30-34 | 65.21 | 62.62 | 60.54 | 77.95 | 73.15 | 70.15 |
| 35-39 | 65.85 | 63.47 | 61.56 | 79.70 | 75.15 | 72.31 |
| 40-44 | 67.12 | 64.76 | 62.86 | 82.40 | 77.89 | 75.07 |
| 45-49 | 67.66 | 65.21 | 63.26 | 81.59 | 76.97 | 74.08 |
| 50-54 | 66.09 | 63.27 | 61.02 | 79.26 | 74.11 | 70.88 |
| 55-59 | 64.45 | 61.48 | 59.10 | 75.48 | 70.16 | 66.84 |
| 60-64 | 59.79 | 55.91 | 52.81 | 67.01 | 60.48 | 56.40 |
| 65+ | 46.41 | 41.30 | 36.18 | 44.22 | 38.34 | 34.66 |

Note(s): (1) Ethiopie; (2) Somalie. Source(s): EPPA4.

### 2.2 Method(s):  arithmetic average

#### 2.2.1 Men:

- 1950-90, average of 1950-90 activity rates estimated for Somalia and Ethiopia.

#### 2.2.2 Women:

- 1990, average of 1990 activity rates estimated for Somalia and Ethiopia;
adjustment of average activity rates based on the men/women ratio
in agriculture equal to 1;
- 1950-80, adjusted average of 1950-90 activity rates estimated for Somalia
and Ethiopia;
adjustment of rates on the basis of variations in average rates, in relation
to estimated rates;
modification of the trend of the [10-14] age group for 1990.

## 3. Estimates of distribution rates by activity sector: 1950 - 1990

### 3.1 Benchmark data:

Table 2: Distribution of economically active population by activity sector

| | Year | Agriculture | Industry Total | Manufac. | Services |
|---|---|---|---|---|---|
| **Men** | | | | | |
| | 1993 | 50.13 | 14.04 | 12.39 | 35.83 |
| **Women** | | | | | |
| | 1993 | 60.87 | 15.24 | 13.35 | 23.89 |

Source(s): FSSE94.

### 3.2 Method(s):  arithmetic average

#### 3.2.1 Men:

- 1950-80, averages of 1950-70 distribution rates estimated for Somalia
and Ethiopia;
- 1990, distribution rates estimated on the basis of the FSEE94 report;
industry/services ratio based on the estimates for Somalia and Ethiopia;
- Application of manufacturing/industry ratio derived from the FSEE94 estimate

#### 3.2.2 Women:

Method, hypothesis and treatment identical to those used for men.

## 4. Projection of activity rates: 2000 - 2010

### 4.1 Model(s):  linear and hyperbole

#### 4.1.1 Men:

- To the [10-29] age groups, application of function F1;
- To the [30+] age groups, application of function F3;
- Modification of the trends for the [30-59] age groups.

#### 4.1.2 Women:

- To the [10-19] age groups, application of function F1;
- To the [20+] age groups, application of function F3;
- Modification of the trends for the [20-49] age groups.

*Notes on adjustments of rates, see p. 3-8.*                    *Notes on projection functions, see p. 10.*

# Estonia

## 1. Source(s) of benchmark data

Code(s):     Title(s):

BLT-94-2     Vorobiev A. (1994), "Estimates of the economically active population for the fifteen countries of the former USSR
for the years 1950, 1959, 1970, 1979 and 1989", in the Bulletin of Labour of Statistics - 1994-2, ILO, Geneva.

## 2. Estimates of activity rates: 1950 - 1990

### 2.1 Benchmark data:

Table 1: Activity rates by sex and age group

| Age group | Year | | | |
|---|---|---|---|---|
| | 1959 | 1970 | 1979 | 1989 |
| **Men** | | | | |
| 10-14 | 0.00 | 0.00 | 0.00 | 0.00 |
| 15-19 | 48.84 | 43.40 | 33.93 | 32.20 |
| 20-24 | 88.00 | 88.68 | 86.67 | 81.13 |
| 25-29 | 93.88 | 95.83 | 98.31 | 96.67 |
| 30-34 | 95.24 | 96.36 | 97.92 | 96.67 |
| 35-39 | 93.33 | 98.04 | 99.98 | 98.21 |
| 40-44 | 92.31 | 97.87 | 96.08 | 97.78 |
| 45-49 | 93.75 | 96.88 | 95.83 | 95.65 |
| 50-54 | 90.00 | 91.67 | 90.24 | 91.30 |
| 55-59 | 88.46 | 86.21 | 81.48 | 85.37 |
| 60-64 | 78.95 | 34.62 | 42.86 | 51.52 |
| 65+ | 38.46 | 18.37 | 15.79 | 22.22 |
| **Women** | | | | |
| 10-14 | 0.00 | 0.00 | 0.00 | 0.00 |
| 15-19 | 37.21 | 35.42 | 27.45 | 26.42 |
| 20-24 | 73.47 | 82.98 | 83.64 | 76.47 |
| 25-29 | 74.07 | 91.49 | 94.74 | 91.53 |
| 30-34 | 71.43 | 92.86 | 95.92 | 93.44 |
| 35-39 | 71.74 | 92.59 | 96.15 | 96.55 |
| 40-44 | 72.97 | 92.86 | 96.36 | 93.88 |
| 45-49 | 71.74 | 91.67 | 94.44 | 94.12 |
| 50-54 | 68.10 | 82.35 | 85.45 | 88.68 |
| 55-59 | 50.00 | 40.00 | 43.18 | 53.85 |
| 60-64 | 55.66 | 20.93 | 26.47 | 37.25 |
| 65+ | 6.90 | 8.26 | 8.73 | 12.80 |

Source(s): BLT-94-2.

### 2.2 Method(s):   linear extrapolation
weighted average

**2.2.1 Men:**

- 1950-60, extrapolation of 1970, 1979 and 1989 activity rates
derived from the Bulletin of Labour Statistics 1994-2;
modification of the trends for all age groups;
application to 1990 estimated rates, variations in 1970 interpolated rates,
in relation to 1970 activity rates derived from the Bulletin;
- 1970-90, weighted average of 1970, 1979 and 1989 activity rates
derived from the Bulletin.

**2.2.2 Women:**

- 1950-90, weighted average of 1950, 1959, 1970 and 1989 activity rates
derived from the Bulletin of Labour Statistics 1994-2;
adjustment of activity rate for the [15-19] age group for 1950;
adjustment of activity rate for the [55-64] age groups for 1959, 1970 and 1979.

## 3. Estimates of distribution rates by activity sector: 1950 - 1990

### 3.1 Benchmark data:

Table 2: Distribution of economically active population by activity sector

| Year | Agriculture | Industry | | Services |
|---|---|---|---|---|
| | | Total | Manufac. | |
| **Men** | | | | |
| 1950 | 32.42 | 33.98 | 16.41 | 33.59 |
| 1959 | 26.84 | 41.85 | 25.24 | 31.31 |
| 1970 | 20.22 | 50.69 | 31.30 | 29.09 |
| 1979 | 18.64 | 50.63 | 29.47 | 30.73 |
| 1989 | 17.88 | 48.71 | 28.00 | 33.41 |
| **Women** | | | | |
| 1950 | 51.81 | 19.20 | 14.49 | 28.99 |
| 1959 | 33.11 | 28.48 | 22.52 | 38.41 |
| 1970 | 15.79 | 36.29 | 29.92 | 47.92 |
| 1979 | 12.25 | 36.75 | 29.00 | 51.00 |
| 1989 | 11.14 | 34.36 | 27.25 | 54.50 |

Source(s): BLT-94-2.

### 3.2 Method(s):   data from BLT-94-17

**3.2.1 Men:**

- 1950-90, weighted averages of 1950, 1959, 1970, 1979 and 1989
distribution rates derived from the Bulletin of Labour Statistics, 1994-2.

**3.2.2 Women:**

Method, hypothesis and treatment identical to those used for men.

## 4. Projection of activity rates: 2000 - 2010

### 4.1 Model(s):   linear, hyperbole and logistic

**4.1.1 Men:**

- To the [15-19], [25-39] and [65+] age groups, application of function F1;
- To the [20-24] and [40-59] age groups, application of function F3;
- Modification of the trends for the [15-44] age groups.

**4.1.2 Women:**

- To the [15-19] and [65+] age groups, application of function F1;
- To the [20-24] and [55-64] age groups, application of function F3;
- To the [25-54] age groups, application of function F6;
- Modification of the trends for the [15-24] and [65+] age groups.

*Notes on adjustments of rates, see p. 3-8.*          *Notes on projection functions, see p. 10.*

# Ethiopia

## 1. Source(s) of benchmark data

Code(s):     Title(s):

EPPA3      Economically active population: Estimates and Projections, 1950-2025, Third edition, ILO, Geneva, 1986.
AST91      Yearbook of Labour Statistics 1991, ILO, Geneva, 1991.

## 2. Estimates of activity rates: 1950 - 1990

### 2.1 Benchmark data:

Table 1: Activity rates by sex and age group

| Age group | Year | | | | |
|---|---|---|---|---|---|
| | 1950 (1) | 1960 (1) | 1970 (1) | 1980 (1) | 1984 (2) |
| **Men** | | | | | |
| 10-14 | 57.85 | 55.45 | 53.65 | 50.40 | 47.80 |
| 15-19 | 85.05 | 82.20 | 80.05 | 76.10 | 63.60 |
| 20-24 | 92.85 | 91.80 | 91.00 | 89.50 | 80.60 |
| 25-29 | 96.60 | 96.45 | 96.30 | 96.10 | 94.20 |
| 30-34 | 97.75 | 97.60 | 97.45 | 97.20 | 96.60 |
| 35-39 | 97.80 | 97.80 | 97.70 | 97.40 | 97.60 |
| 40-44 | 97.30 | 97.10 | 96.90 | 96.70 | 97.50 |
| 45-49 | 96.90 | 96.70 | 96.60 | 96.35 | 97.40 |
| 50-54 | 96.00 | 95.75 | 95.55 | 95.20 | 95.40 |
| 55-59 | 94.80 | 94.40 | 94.05 | 93.50 | 94.20 |
| 60-64 | 90.65 | 89.95 | 89.45 | 88.50 | 91.50 |
| 65+ | 67.60 | 66.55 | 65.75 | 64.30 | 76.58 |
| **Women** | | | | | |
| 10-14 | 38.10 | 36.50 | 35.35 | 33.20 | 43.10 |
| 15-19 | 66.40 | 63.85 | 61.95 | 58.50 | 54.90 |
| 20-24 | 66.50 | 64.90 | 63.70 | 61.50 | 60.10 |
| 25-29 | 69.85 | 68.05 | 66.75 | 64.30 | 60.80 |
| 30-34 | 71.85 | 70.00 | 68.60 | 66.10 | 60.80 |
| 35-39 | 68.50 | 66.90 | 65.70 | 63.50 | 61.80 |
| 40-44 | 66.10 | 64.60 | 63.45 | 61.40 | 63.10 |
| 45-49 | 61.70 | 60.25 | 59.15 | 57.20 | 63.50 |
| 50-54 | 55.25 | 53.70 | 52.60 | 50.50 | 61.30 |
| 55-59 | 45.85 | 44.50 | 43.50 | 41.60 | 59.40 |
| 60-64 | 39.25 | 37.65 | 36.40 | 34.20 | 53.20 |
| 65+ | 14.10 | 13.35 | 12.75 | 11.70 | 37.71 |

Source(s):  (1) EPPA3; (2) AST91.

### 2.2 Method(s):  linears interpolation and extrapolation

#### 2.2.1 Men:

- 1950-90, interpolation and extrapolation of 1950-80 activity rates
derived from the EPPA3 and of adjusted activity rates derived
from the 1984 census;
adjustment of interpolated and extrapolated rates on the basis of variations
in 1984 extrapolated rates, in relation to the 1984 activity rates
derived from the 1984 census;
modification of the trends of the [10-14] and [20-24] age groups for 1990.

#### 2.2.2 Women:

- 1950-90, interpolation and extrapolation of 1950-80 activity rates
derived from the EPPA3 and of adjusted activity rates derived
from the 1984 census;
adjustment of interpolated and extrapolated rates on the basis of variations
in 1984 extrapolated rates, in relation to the 1984 activity rates
derived from the 1984 census;
modification of the trends of the [15-64] age groups for 1950-90.

## 3. Estimates of distribution rates by activity sector: 1950 - 1990

### 3.1 Benchmark data:

Table  2: Distribution of economically active population by activity sector

| Year | Agriculture | Industry | | Services |
|---|---|---|---|---|
| | | Total | Manufac. | |
| **Men** | | | | |
| 1950 (1) | 89.00 | 4.00 | .. | 7.00 |
| 1960 (1) | 85.00 | 5.50 | .. | 9.50 |
| 1970 (1) | 82.00 | 7.00 | .. | 11.00 |
| 1980 (1) | 76.50 | 9.00 | .. | 14.50 |
| 1984 (2) | 89.28 | 2.16 | 1.58 | 8.56 |
| **Women** | | | | |
| 1950 (1) | 93.50 | 2.80 | .. | 3.70 |
| 1960 (1) | 90.95 | 3.70 | .. | 5.35 |
| 1970 (1) | 89.40 | 4.30 | .. | 6.30 |
| 1980 (1) | 84.90 | 6.10 | .. | 9.00 |
| 1984 (2) | 87.56 | 1.70 | 1.58 | 10.74 |

Source(s): (1) EPPA3; (2) AST91

### 3.2 Method(s):  linears interpolation and extrapolation

#### 3.2.1 Men:

- 1950-90, interpolation and extrapolation of 1950-80 distribution rates
derived from the EPPA3;
for agriculture sector, adjustment of interpolated and extrapolated rates
on the basis of variations in 1984 interpolated rates, in relation to distribution
rates derived from the 1984 census; estimated distribution rates of industry
and services sectors based on the results of 1984 census.

#### 3.2.2 Women:

Method, hypothesis and treatment identical to those used for men.

## 4. Projection of activity rates: 2000 - 2010

### 4.1 Model(s):  linear and hyperbole

#### 4.1.1 Men:

- To the [10-19] age groups, application of function F1;
- To the [20+] age groups, application of function F3;
- Modification of the trend for the [20-24] age group.

#### 4.1.2 Women:

- To the [10-19] age groups, application of function F1;
- To the [20+] age groups, application of function F3;
- Modification of the trends for the [15-59] age groups.

*Notes on  adjustments of rates, see p. 3-8.*                    *Notes on  projection functions, see p. 10.*

# Fiji

## 1. Source(s) of benchmark data

Code(s):    Title(s):

EPPA3      Yearbook of Labour Statistics 1945-89 - Retrospective Edition on Population Censuses, ILO, Geneva, 1990.
STAT       Database on Labour Statistics, LABORSTA - Bureau of Statistics, ILO, Geneva.

## 2. Estimates of activity rates: 1950 - 1990

### 2.1 Benchmark data:

Table 1: Activity rates by sex and age group

| Age group | Year 1950 (1) | 1960 (1) | 1970 (1) | 1976 (2) | 1986 (2) |
|---|---|---|---|---|---|
| **Men** | | | | | |
| 10-14 | 31.00 | 21.00 | 15.00 | 0.00 | 0.00 |
| 15-19 | 86.60 | 75.90 | 65.20 | 56.84 | 57.90 |
| 20-24 | 97.00 | 96.30 | 93.60 | 91.28 | 91.00 |
| 25-29 | 98.85 | 98.00 | 97.20 | 96.34 | 95.97 |
| 30-34 | 98.75 | 98.30 | 97.85 | 97.31 | 97.32 |
| 35-39 | 98.45 | 98.15 | 97.90 | 97.37 | 97.41 |
| 40-44 | 98.55 | 98.10 | 97.60 | 97.35 | 97.57 |
| 45-49 | 97.30 | 97.70 | 96.35 | 95.39 | 95.83 |
| 50-54 | 98.05 | 95.80 | 93.55 | 92.37 | 92.04 |
| 55-59 | 96.00 | 92.65 | 89.30 | 84.94 | 83.71 |
| 60-64 | 91.50 | 86.60 | 81.75 | 76.14 | 71.64 |
| 65+ | 60.70 | 54.55 | 48.40 | 48.41 | 48.42 |
| **Women** | | | | | |
| 10-14 | 1.60 | 2.00 | 1.50 | .. | 0.00 |
| 15-19 | 4.05 | 6.30 | 10.85 | .. | 21.40 |
| 20-24 | 5.75 | 9.75 | 17.70 | .. | 29.11 |
| 25-29 | 3.95 | 7.40 | 14.35 | .. | 26.19 |
| 30-34 | 3.05 | 6.35 | 12.90 | .. | 26.32 |
| 35-39 | 2.80 | 5.80 | 11.85 | .. | 25.31 |
| 40-44 | 3.30 | 6.00 | 11.35 | .. | 23.32 |
| 45-49 | 3.20 | 5.65 | 10.50 | .. | 21.32 |
| 50-54 | 2.75 | 5.05 | 9.60 | .. | 19.14 |
| 55-59 | 2.55 | 4.50 | 8.45 | .. | 16.71 |
| 60-64 | 1.45 | 3.10 | 6.40 | .. | 13.53 |
| 65+ | 0.90 | 1.95 | 4.10 | .. | 8.32 |

Source(s): (1) EPPA3; (2) STAT.

### 2.2 Method(s): linear extrapolation
weighted average

#### 2.2.1 Men:

- 1950-70, 1950-70 activity rates derived from the EPPA3;
- 1980, weighted average of activity rates derived from
the 1976 and 1986 censuses;
- 1990, extrapolation of 1950-70 activity rates derived from the EPPA3
and of activity rates estimated for 1980 and of activity rates derived from
the 1986 census.

#### 2.2.2 Women:

- 1950-80, 1950-80 activity rates derived from the EPPA3;
- 1990, weighted average of activity rates of 1980 derived from the EPPA3
of activity rates derived from the 1986 census.

## 3. Estimates of distribution rates by activity sector: 1950 - 1990

### 3.1 Benchmark data:

Table 2: Distribution of economically active population by activity sector

| Year | Agriculture | Industry Total | Manufac. | Services |
|---|---|---|---|---|
| **Men** | | | | |
| 1976 | 50.69 | 18.45 | 8.16 | 30.86 |
| 1986 | 52.69 | 15.99 | 7.66 | 31.33 |
| **Women** | | | | |
| 1976 | 27.07 | 8.02 | 6.96 | 64.90 |
| 1986 | 28.42 | 11.28 | 10.33 | 60.30 |

Source(s): STAT.

### 3.2 Method(s): linears interpolation and extrapolation

#### 3.2.1 Men:

- 1950-70, 1950-70 distribution rates derived from the EPPA3;
- 1980, interpolation of distribution rates derived from
the 1976 and 1986 censuses;
- 1990, extrapolation of 1950-70 distribution rates derived from the EPPA3,
of 1980 estimated rates and of distribution rates derived from the 1986 census;
- Application of manufacturing/industry ratio derived from the 1986 census.

#### 3.2.2 Women:

Method, hypothesis and treatment identical to those used for men.

## 4. Projection of activity rates: 2000 - 2010

### 4.1 Model(s): linear, hyperbole and logistic

#### 4.1.1 Men:

- To the [15-19] and [30+] age groups, application of function F3;
- To the [20-29] age groups, application of function F1;
- Modification of the trends for the [15-24] and [30-44] age groups.

#### 4.1.2 Women:

- To the [15-19] and [65+] age groups, application of function F1;
- To the [20-64] age groups, application of function F6;
- Modification of the trends for the [20-59] age groups.

*Notes on adjustments of rates, see p. 3-8.*    *Notes on projection functions, see p. 10.*

# Finland

## 1. Source(s) of benchmark data

Code(s):     Title(s):

EPPA3        Yearbook of Labour Statistics 1945-89 - Retrospective Edition on Population Censuses, ILO, Geneva, 1990.
STAT         Database on Labour Statistics, LABORSTA - Bureau of Statistics, ILO, Geneva.

## 2. Estimates of activity rates: 1950 - 1990

### 2.1 Benchmark data:

Table 1: Activity rates by sex and age group

| Age group | Year | | |
|---|---|---|---|
| | 1989 | 1990 | 1991 |
| **Men** | | | |
| 10-14 | 0.00 | 0.00 | 0.00 |
| 15-19 | 42.21 | 40.26 | 36.94 |
| 20-24 | 81.97 | 80.79 | 79.07 |
| 25-29 | 92.23 | 92.23 | 91.67 |
| 30-34 | 95.48 | 95.43 | 94.87 |
| 35-39 | 95.28 | 94.71 | 94.69 |
| 40-44 | 94.93 | 94.74 | 94.64 |
| 45-49 | 91.95 | 91.50 | 90.53 |
| 50-54 | 86.03 | 84.89 | 84.40 |
| 55-59 | 59.68 | 61.79 | 61.48 |
| 60-64 | 27.83 | 28.21 | 29.66 |
| 65+ | 5.60 | 4.66 | 4.55 |
| **Women** | | | |
| 10-14 | 0.00 | 0.00 | 0.00 |
| 15-19 | 36.49 | 38.10 | 32.89 |
| 20-24 | 69.89 | 67.84 | 66.87 |
| 25-29 | 82.16 | 80.98 | 79.89 |
| 30-34 | 85.79 | 83.96 | 82.26 |
| 35-39 | 88.61 | 88.44 | 86.87 |
| 40-44 | 90.82 | 89.86 | 89.67 |
| 45-49 | 89.80 | 89.93 | 90.24 |
| 50-54 | 82.61 | 82.98 | 83.22 |
| 55-59 | 58.65 | 60.77 | 60.47 |
| 60-64 | 22.06 | 19.71 | 20.44 |
| 65+ | 1.88 | 1.62 | 1.61 |

Source(s): STAT.

### 2.2 Method(s):   arithmetic average

#### 2.2.1 Men:

- 1950-80, 1950-80 activity rates derived from the EPPA3;
adjustment of activity rates of the [15-19] age group for 1980;
- 1990, average of activity rates derived from
the 1989, 1990 and 1991 surveys;
adjustment of estimated activity rates of [15-19] age group.

#### 2.2.2 Women:

- 1950-80, 1950-80 activity rates derived from the EPPA3;
adjustment of activity rate of the [15-19] age group for 1980;
- 1990, average of activity rates derived from
the 1989, 1990 and 1991 surveys;
adjustment of estimated activity rates of [15-24] age groups.

## 3. Estimates of distribution rates by activity sector: 1950 - 1990

### 3.1 Benchmark data:

Table 2: Distribution of economically active population by activity sector

| Year | Agriculture | Industry | | Services |
|---|---|---|---|---|
| | | Total | Manufac. | |
| **Men** | | | | |
| 1989 | 10.83 | 42.59 | 23.29 | 46.57 |
| 1990 | 10.12 | 42.84 | 23.34 | 47.05 |
| 1991 | 10.02 | 42.03 | 23.64 | 47.94 |
| **Women** | | | | |
| 1989 | 6.28 | 17.77 | 12.89 | 75.95 |
| 1990 | 6.21 | 17.56 | 12.92 | 76.22 |
| 1991 | 6.23 | 16.84 | 13.13 | 76.94 |

Source(s): STAT.

### 3.2 Method(s):   arithmetic average

#### 3.2.1 Men:

- 1950-80, 1950-80 distribution rates derived from the EPPA3;
1982 distribution rates of manufacturing sector has been adjusted on the basis
of application to 1980 distribution rates in industry sector, average of
manufacturing/industry ratio derived from the 1979, 1980 and 1981 surveys;
- 1990, averages of distribution rates derived from the 1989, 1990
and 1991 surveys.

#### 3.2.2 Women:

Method, hypothesis and treatment identical to those used for men.

## 4. Projection of activity rates: 2000 - 2010

### 4.1 Model(s):   linear, hyperbole and logistic

#### 4.1.1 Men:

- To the [15-19] and [30+] age groups, application of function F3;
- To the [20-29] age groups, application of function F1;
- Modification of the trends for the [45-59] age groups.

#### 4.1.2 Women:

- To the [15-29] age groups, application of function F1;
- To the [30-59] age groups, application of function F6;
- To the [60+] age groups, application of function F3;
- Modification of the trends for the [20-59] age groups.

*Notes on adjustments of rates, see p. 3-8.*

*Notes on projection functions, see p. 10.*

# France

## 1. Source(s) of benchmark data

Code(s):    Title(s):

EPPA3     Yearbook of Labour Statistics 1945-89 - Retrospective Edition on Population Censuses, ILO, Geneva, 1990.

STAT     Database on Labour Statistics, LABORSTA - Bureau of Statistics, ILO, Geneva.

## 2. Estimates of activity rates: 1950 - 1990

### 2.1 Benchmark data:

Table 1: Activity rates by sex and age group

| Age group | Year 1979 | 1980 | 1981 | 1989 | 1990 | 1991 |
|---|---|---|---|---|---|---|
| **Men** | | | | | | |
| 10-14 | 0.00 | 0.00 | 0.00 | 0.00 | 0.00 | 0.00 |
| 15-19 | 26.50 | 25.70 | 24.30 | 14.90 | 14.60 | 12.20 |
| 20-24 | 81.10 | 80.10 | 78.10 | 69.30 | 65.00 | 62.10 |
| 25-29 | 95.40 | 95.40 | 94.90 | 94.40 | 94.00 | 93.90 |
| 30-34 | 98.10 | 98.10 | 98.00 | 97.20 | 96.80 | 96.80 |
| 35-39 | 98.10 | 98.30 | 97.90 | 97.30 | 97.00 | 97.20 |
| 40-44 | 97.60 | 97.60 | 97.60 | 97.20 | 97.00 | 96.80 |
| 45-49 | 95.60 | 96.60 | 96.40 | 95.50 | 96.10 | 95.60 |
| 50-54 | 93.00 | 92.90 | 92.40 | 90.10 | 90.00 | 89.40 |
| 55-59 | 82.30 | 81.00 | 79.80 | 68.10 | 67.70 | 68.60 |
| 60-64 | 45.30 | 47.90 | 43.10 | 24.20 | 22.80 | 19.70 |
| 65+ | 6.80 | 6.00 | 5.30 | 3.51 | 2.77 | 2.60 |
| **Women** | | | | | | |
| 10-14 | 0.00 | 0.00 | 0.00 | 0.00 | 0.00 | 0.00 |
| 15-19 | 20.00 | 18.40 | 17.30 | 9.40 | 8.10 | 6.80 |
| 20-24 | 68.90 | 68.00 | 67.50 | 59.90 | 57.60 | 54.00 |
| 25-29 | 70.10 | 70.50 | 70.30 | 76.40 | 77.70 | 78.10 |
| 30-34 | 66.50 | 66.90 | 67.70 | 73.50 | 74.60 | 74.50 |
| 35-39 | 63.70 | 65.00 | 66.90 | 73.50 | 73.10 | 74.70 |
| 40-44 | 61.30 | 63.00 | 64.80 | 74.10 | 75.40 | 76.10 |
| 45-49 | 59.20 | 59.10 | 59.30 | 69.00 | 69.10 | 71.30 |
| 50-54 | 53.80 | 55.40 | 57.20 | 62.10 | 62.70 | 64.40 |
| 55-59 | 46.60 | 47.80 | 47.20 | 44.60 | 45.30 | 45.40 |
| 60-64 | 34.00 | 27.60 | 28.00 | 17.60 | 17.00 | 16.00 |
| 65+ | 3.7 | 2.9 | 2.6 | 1.72 | 1.53 | 1.36 |

Source(s): STAT.

### 2.2 Method(s): weighted average

#### 2.2.1 Men:

- 1950-70, 1950-70 activity rates derived from the EPPA3;
- 1980, weighted average of activity rates derived from the 1979, 1980 and 1981 surveys;
- 1990, weighted average of activity rates derived from 1989, 1990 and 1991 surveys.

#### 2.2.2 Women:

Method, hypothesis and treatment identical to those used for men.

## 3. Estimates of distribution rates by activity sector: 1950 - 1990

### 3.1 Benchmark data:

Table 2: Distribution of economically active population by activity sector

| Year | Agriculture | Industry Total | Manufac. | Services |
|---|---|---|---|---|
| **Men** | | | | |
| 1979 | 9.11 | 43.36 | .. | 47.53 |
| 1980 | 8.86 | 43.16 | .. | 47.98 |
| 1981 | 8.60 | 42.65 | .. | 48.75 |
| 1989 | 6.45 | 37.49 | .. | 56.06 |
| 1990 | 6.23 | 38.13 | .. | 55.63 |
| 1991 | 6.10 | 37.79 | .. | 56.11 |
| **Women** | | | | |
| 1979 | 7.67 | 22.56 | .. | 69.78 |
| 1980 | 7.35 | 22.18 | .. | 70.47 |
| 1981 | 7.08 | 21.31 | .. | 71.62 |
| 1989 | 4.83 | 17.22 | .. | 77.95 |
| 1990 | 4.51 | 17.14 | .. | 78.35 |
| 1991 | 4.15 | 16.73 | .. | 79.12 |

Source(s): STAT.

### 3.2 Method(s): arithmetic average

#### 3.2.1 Men:

- 1950-70, 1950-70 distribution rates derived from the EPPA3;
- 1980, averages of distribution rates derived from the 1979, 1980 and 1981 surveys;
- 1990, averages of distribution rates derived from the 1989, 1990 and 1991 surveys.

#### 3.2.2 Women:

Method, hypothesis and treatment identical to those used for men.

## 4. Projection of activity rates: 2000 - 2010

### 4.1 Model(s): linear, hyperbole and logistic

#### 4.1.1 Men:

- To all age groups, application of function F3;
- Modification of the trends for the [20-24] and [30-44] age groups.

#### 4.1.2 Women:

- To the [15-24] and [60+] age groups, application of function F3;
- To the [25-54] age groups, application of function F6;
- To the [55-59] age group, application of function F1;
- Modification of the trends for the [15-59] age groups.

*Notes on adjustments of rates, see p. 3-8.*    *Notes on projection functions, see p. 10.*

# Gabon

## 1. Source(s) of benchmark data

Code(s):     Title(s):

EPPA3      Economically active population: Estimates and Projections, 1950-2025, Third edition, ILO, Geneva, 1986.

## 2. Estimates of activity rates: 1950 - 1990

### 2.1 Benchmark data:

Table 1: Activity rates by sex and age group

| Age group | Year 1950 | 1960 | 1970 | 1980 |
|---|---|---|---|---|
| **Men** | | | | |
| 10-14 | 38.90 | 36.60 | 33.60 | 31.85 |
| 15-19 | 48.35 | 46.00 | 43.00 | 41.25 |
| 20-24 | 91.10 | 89.65 | 87.75 | 86.60 |
| 25-29 | 96.20 | 96.00 | 95.70 | 95.55 |
| 30-34 | 97.25 | 97.00 | 96.70 | 96.50 |
| 35-39 | 97.25 | 97.00 | 96.65 | 96.45 |
| 40-44 | 97.30 | 97.00 | 96.65 | 96.45 |
| 45-49 | 95.35 | 95.10 | 94.80 | 94.60 |
| 50-54 | 94.35 | 94.00 | 93.55 | 93.30 |
| 55-59 | 92.25 | 91.70 | 91.00 | 90.55 |
| 60-64 | 81.85 | 81.00 | 79.90 | 79.25 |
| 65+ | 72.70 | 71.15 | 69.10 | 67.90 |
| **Women** | | | | |
| 10-14 | 41.10 | 40.40 | 39.10 | 37.75 |
| 15-19 | 66.55 | 65.50 | 63.60 | 61.55 |
| 20-24 | 65.80 | 65.10 | 63.90 | 62.65 |
| 25-29 | 71.00 | 70.25 | 68.85 | 67.40 |
| 30-34 | 75.45 | 74.65 | 73.20 | 71.65 |
| 35-39 | 76.55 | 75.80 | 74.45 | 73.00 |
| 40-44 | 79.00 | 78.25 | 76.90 | 75.40 |
| 45-49 | 78.55 | 77.80 | 76.40 | 74.90 |
| 50-54 | 77.45 | 76.55 | 74.95 | 73.20 |
| 55-59 | 74.75 | 73.85 | 72.15 | 70.35 |
| 60-64 | 69.35 | 68.20 | 66.05 | 63.75 |
| 65+ | 49.10 | 48.00 | 46.00 | 43.90 |

Source(s):  EPPA3.

### 2.2 Method(s):  linears interpolation and extrapolation

#### 2.2.1 Men:

- 1950 and 1970-90, interpolation and extrapolation of 1950-80 activity rates derived from the EPPA3;
adjustment of interpolated and extrapolated rates on the basis of variations in 1960 interpolated rates, in relation to the rates derived from the EPPA3; modification of the trends of the [10-14], [25-49] and [65+] age groups for 1980 and 1990;
- 1960, 1960 activity rates derived from the EPPA3.

#### 2.2.2 Women:

- 1960, 1960 activity rates derived from the EPPA3;
- 1950 and 1970-90, interpolation and extrapolation of 1950-80 activity rates derived from the EPPA3;
adjustment of interpolated and extrapolated rates on the basis of variations in 1960 interpolated rates, in relation to the 1960 activity rates derived from the EPPA3;
modification of the trends for all age groups for 1950 and of the [30+] age groups for 1970 and 1980.

## 3. Estimates of distribution rates by activity sector: 1950 - 1990

### 3.1 Benchmark data:

Table 2: Distribution of economically active population by activity sector

| Year | Agriculture | Industry Total | Manufac. | Services |
|---|---|---|---|---|
| **Men** | | | | |
| 1950 | 84.00 | 8.40 | .. | 7.60 |
| 1960 | 78.50 | 11.00 | .. | 10.50 |
| 1970 | 71.40 | 14.60 | .. | 14.00 |
| **Women** | | | | |
| 1950 | 97.50 | 0.35 | .. | 2.15 |
| 1960 | 95.00 | 0.70 | .. | 4.30 |
| 1970 | 92.00 | 1.40 | .. | 6.60 |

Source(s): (1) EPPA3.

### 3.2 Method(s):  weighted average

#### 3.2.1 Men:

- 1950-70, 1950-70 distribution rates derived from the EPPA3;
- 1980, weighted averages of 1970 distribution rates derived from the EPPA3 and of distribution rates estimated for 1990;
- 1990, extrapolation of 1950-70 distribution rates derived from the EPPA3; modification of the trends in all sectors.

#### 3.2.2 Women:

Method, hypothesis and treatment identical to those used for men.

## 4. Projection of activity rates: 2000 - 2010

### 4.1 Model(s):  linear and hyperbole

#### 4.1.1 Men:

- To the [10-19] and [65+] age groups, application of function F1;
- To the [20-64] age groups, application of function F3;
- Modification of the trend for the [10-14] age group.

#### 4.1.2 Women:

- To the [10-14] age group, application of function F1;
- To the [15+] age groups, application of function F3;
- Modification of the trends for the [15-64] age groups.

*Notes on adjustments of rates, see p. 3-8.*          *Notes on projection functions, see p. 10.*

# Gambia

## 1. Source(s) of benchmark data

Code(s):    Title(s):

EPPA3      Economically active population: Estimates and Projections, 1950-2025, Third edition, ILO, Geneva, 1986.
ASTER      Yearbook of Labour Statistics 1945-89 - Retrospective Edition on Population Censuses, ILO, Geneva, 1990.

## 2. Estimates of activity rates: 1950 - 1990

### 2.1 Benchmark data:

Table 1: Activity rates by sex and age group

| Age group | Year 1950 (1) | 1960 (1) | 1970 (1) | 1980 (1) | 1983 (2) |
|---|---|---|---|---|---|
| **Men** | | | | | |
| 10-14 | 50.70 | 49.70 | 48.35 | 46.55 | .. |
| 15-19 | 83.00 | 81.70 | 79.95 | 77.55 | .. |
| 20-24 | 94.55 | 94.05 | 93.35 | 92.45 | .. |
| 25-29 | 97.30 | 97.20 | 97.10 | 97.00 | .. |
| 30-34 | 98.00 | 97.95 | 97.80 | 97.65 | .. |
| 35-39 | 98.20 | 98.10 | 97.95 | 97.80 | .. |
| 40-44 | 98.00 | 97.90 | 97.80 | 97.60 | .. |
| 45-49 | 97.25 | 97.20 | 97.10 | 96.95 | .. |
| 50-54 | 96.80 | 96.65 | 96.50 | 96.30 | .. |
| 55-59 | 95.80 | 95.60 | 95.35 | 95.00 | .. |
| 60-64 | 92.65 | 92.35 | 91.90 | 91.30 | .. |
| 65+ | 79.10 | 78.55 | 77.80 | 76.75 | .. |
| **Women** | | | | | |
| 10-14 | 38.30 | 37.55 | 36.55 | 35.20 | 41.91 |
| 15-19 | 62.35 | 61.25 | 59.75 | 57.70 | 61.89 |
| 20-24 | 63.15 | 62.45 | 61.50 | 60.20 | 68.30 |
| 25-29 | 67.95 | 67.20 | 66.10 | 64.65 | 71.14 |
| 30-34 | 72.25 | 71.40 | 70.25 | 68.65 | 73.90 |
| 35-39 | 73.55 | 72.75 | 71.70 | 70.2 | 74.58 |
| 40-44 | 76.00 | 75.20 | 74.10 | 72.65 | 77.22 |
| 45-49 | 75.50 | 74.70 | 73.60 | 72.1 | 75.31 |
| 50-54 | 73.90 | 72.95 | 71.70 | 69.95 | 73.86 |
| 55-59 | 71.05 | 70.10 | 68.75 | 66.95 | 72.41 |
| 60-64 | 64.65 | 63.40 | 61.70 | 59.45 | 71.49 |
| 65+ | 44.70 | 43.55 | 42.00 | 39.85 | 60.74 |

Source(s): (1) EPPA3; (2) ASTER.

### 2.2 Method(s):   linears interpolation and extrapolation

**2.2.1 Men:**

- 1950-80, 1950-80 activity rates derived from the EPPA3;
- 1990, extrapolation of 1950-80 activity rates derived from the EPPA3;
adjustment of extrapolated rates on the basis of variations in 1980
interpolated rates, in relation to the 1980 rates derived from the EPPA3;
modification of the trends of the [10-14], [15-24]
and [65+] age groups for 1990.

**2.2.2 Women:**

- 1950-90, interpolation and extrapolation of 1950-80 activity rates
derived from the EPPA3;
adjustment of interpolated and extrapolated rates on the basis of variations
in 1983 extrapolated rates, in relation to activity rates derived from the 1983 cens
modification of the trends for all age groups for 1970 and 1980
and of the [10-14] and [60-64] age groups for 1990.

## 3. Estimates of distribution rates by activity sector: 1950 - 1990

### 3.1 Benchmark data:

Table 2: Distribution of economically active population by activity sector

| Year | Agriculture | Industry Total | Manufac. | Services |
|---|---|---|---|---|
| **Men** | | | | |
| 1950 | 85.00 | 6.60 | .. | 8.40 |
| 1960 | 83.20 | 7.40 | .. | 9.40 |
| 1970 | 80.75 | 8.50 | .. | 10.75 |
| 1980 | 77.45 | 10.00 | .. | 12.55 |
| **Women** | | | | |
| 1950 | 97.00 | 1.00 | .. | 2.00 |
| 1960 | 96.00 | 1.30 | .. | 2.70 |
| 1970 | 94.50 | 1.80 | .. | 3.70 |
| 1980 | 93.00 | 2.30 | .. | 4.70 |

Source(s): EPPA3.

### 3.2 Method(s):   linear extrapolation

**3.2.1 Men:**

- 1950-80, 1950-80 distribution rates derived from the EPPA3;
- 1990, extrapolation of 1950-80 distribution rates derived from the EPPA3;
adjustment of extrapolated rates on the basis of variations in 1980 interpolated
rates, in relation to 1980 distribution rates derived from the EPPA3;
- Application of manufacturing/industry ratios estimated for Niger.

**3.2.2 Women:**

Method, hypothesis and treatment identical to those used for men.

## 4. Projection of activity rates: 2000 - 2010

### 4.1 Model(s):   linear and hyperbole

**4.1.1 Men:**

- To all age groups, application of function F1;
- Modification of the trends for the [10-19] age groups.

**4.1.2 Women:**

- To the [10-19] age groups, application of function F1;
- To the [20+] age groups, application of function F3;
- Modification of the trends for the [20-59] age groups.

*Notes on adjustments of rates, see p. 3-8.*          *Notes on projection functions, see p. 10.*

8270

# Gaza Strip

## 1. Source(s) of benchmark data

Code(s): | Title(s):

EPPA3 Economically active population: Estimates and Projections, 1950-2025, Third edition, ILO, Geneva, 1986.
LFS-97-93 Labour Force Statistics in the West Bank and Gaza Strip, Curent Status Report Series (No.3), Palestinian Central Bureau of Statistics, Ramallah-West Bank, 1995.

## 2. Estimates of activity rates: 1950 - 1990

### 2.1 Benchmark data:

Table 1: Activity rates by sex and age group

| Age group | Year 1987 | 1989 | 1991 | 1993 |
|---|---|---|---|---|
| **Men** | | | | |
| Total | 71.00 | 67.00 | 68.00 | 68.00 |
| 15-24 | 34.00 | 32.00 | 30.00 | 30.00 |
| 25-64 | 85.00 | 83.00 | 87.00 | 86.00 |
| 65+ | 29.00 | 19.00 | 20.00 | 14.00 |
| **Women** | | | | |
| Total | 3.00 | 2.00 | 1.70 | 1.80 |
| 15-24 | 1.50 | 0.60 | 0.60 | 0.30 |
| 25-64 | 4.00 | 3.10 | 2.50 | 2.90 |
| 65+ | 1.30 | 0.10 | 0.20 | 0.30 |

Source(s): LFS-87-93.

### 2.2 Method(s): linears interpolation and extrapolation

**2.2.1 Men:**

- 1950-90, interpolation and extrapolation of adjusted activity rates derived from the 1987, 1989, 1991 and 1993 surveys;
modification of the trends for all age groups.

**2.2.2 Women:**

Method, hypothesis and treatment identical to those used for men.

## 3. Estimates of distribution rates by activity sector: 1950 - 1990

### 3.1 Benchmark data:

Table 2: Distribution of economically active population by activity sector

| Year | Agriculture | Industry Total | Manufac. | Services |
|---|---|---|---|---|
| **Men** | | | | |
| 1950 | 40.50 | 25.00 | .. | 34.50 |
| 1960 | 32.00 | 31.40 | .. | 36.60 |
| 1970 | 31.70 | 32.80 | .. | 35.50 |
| **Women** | | | | |
| 1950 | 64.00 | 22.00 | .. | 14.00 |
| 1960 | 62.00 | 18.50 | .. | 19.50 |
| 1970 | 51.90 | 18.00 | .. | 30.10 |

Source(s): EPPA3.

### 3.2 Method(s): linear extrapolation

**3.2.1 Men:**
- 1950-70, 1950-70 distribution rates derived from the EPPA3;
- 1980, averages of distribution rates derived from the 1979, 1980 and 1981 surveys;
- 1990, averages of distribution rates derived from the 1989, 1990 and 1991 official estimates.

**3.2.2 Women:**

Method, hypothesis and treatment identical to those used for men.

## 4. Projection of activity rates: 2000 - 2010

### 4.1 Model(s): linear and hyperbole

**4.1.1 Men:**
- To the [15+] age groups, application of function F3;
- Modification of the trends for all age groups.

**4.1.2 Women:**
- To the [15+] age groups, application of function F1;
- Modification of the trends for all age groups.

*Notes on adjustments of rates, see p. 3-8.* *Notes on projection functions, see p. 10.*

# Georgia

## 1. Source(s) of benchmark data

Code(s):     Title(s):

BLT-94-2     Vorobiev A. (1994), "Estimates of the economically active population for the fifteen countries of the former USSR
for the years 1950, 1959, 1970, 1979 and 1989", in the Bulletin of Labour of Statistics - 1994-2, ILO, Geneva.

## 2. Estimates of activity rates: 1950 - 1990

### 2.1 Benchmark data:

Table 1: Activity rates by sex and age group

| Age group | 1950 | 1959 | 1970 | 1979 | 1989 |
|---|---|---|---|---|---|
| **Men** | | | | | |
| 10-14 | 0.00 | 0.00 | 0.00 | 0.00 | 0.00 |
| 15-19 | 50.56 | 51.53 | 32.51 | 34.40 | 29.36 |
| 20-24 | 82.02 | 81.62 | 82.76 | 80.60 | 74.38 |
| 25-29 | 92.13 | 91.38 | 85.83 | 94.77 | 47.79 |
| 30-34 | 93.83 | 94.19 | 96.84 | 97.64 | 96.02 |
| 35-39 | 92.63 | 94.32 | 96.41 | 97.18 | 96.55 |
| 40-44 | 92.94 | 93.15 | 96.05 | 96.67 | 95.20 |
| 45-49 | 91.55 | 91.67 | 90.63 | 95.57 | 93.53 |
| 50-54 | 90.91 | 89.19 | 89.06 | 90.91 | 90.85 |
| 55-59 | 86.79 | 87.10 | 83.33 | 82.43 | 84.40 |
| 60-64 | 78.00 | 86.79 | 71.01 | 50.00 | 55.38 |
| 65+ | 42.06 | 41.83 | 14.09 | 18.90 | 25.95 |
| **Women** | | | | | |
| 10-14 | 0.00 | 0.00 | 0.00 | 0.00 | 0.00 |
| 15-19 | 42.86 | 42.20 | 31.12 | 35.86 | 27.23 |
| 20-24 | 56.68 | 56.28 | 59.87 | 75.35 | 59.05 |
| 25-29 | 62.69 | 62.50 | 83.22 | 86.17 | 70.54 |
| 30-34 | 62.18 | 61.46 | 80.00 | 89.29 | 75.93 |
| 35-39 | 62.39 | 64.18 | 81.03 | 90.30 | 80.85 |
| 40-44 | 64.08 | 65.22 | 80.75 | 90.77 | 82.35 |
| 45-49 | 62.93 | 63.16 | 82.17 | 88.55 | 81.01 |
| 50-54 | 53.49 | 57.14 | 73.27 | 81.61 | 75.27 |
| 55-59 | 48.81 | 50.00 | 40.00 | 48.03 | 50.31 |
| 60-64 | 42.50 | 48.15 | 22.94 | 23.64 | 34.13 |
| 65+ | 18.56 | 17.61 | 6.44 | 6.83 | 12.19 |

Source(s): BLT-94-2-2

### 2.2 Method(s): weighted average

**2.2.1 Men:**

- 1950-90, weighted average of 1950, 1959, 1970 and 1989 activity rates
derived from the Bulletin of Labour Statistics 1994-2.

**2.2.2 Women:**

Method, hypothesis and treatment identical to those used for men.

## 3. Estimates of distribution rates by activity sector: 1950 - 1990

### 3.1 Benchmark data:

Table 2: Distribution of economically active population by activity sector

| Year | Agriculture | Industry Total | Manufac. | Services |
|---|---|---|---|---|
| **Men** | | | | |
| 1950 | 57.65 | 20.56 | 11.87 | 21.79 |
| 1959 | 44.18 | 24.26 | 13.51 | 31.56 |
| 1970 | 33.73 | 30.71 | 18.97 | 35.56 |
| 1979 | 31.08 | 31.55 | 17.93 | 37.37 |
| 1989 | 27.91 | 37.42 | 21.17 | 34.66 |
| **Women** | | | | |
| 1950 | 66.85 | 11.14 | 8.04 | 22.00 |
| 1959 | 45.51 | 18.58 | 9.12 | 35.91 |
| 1970 | 40.85 | 19.98 | 17.01 | 39.17 |
| 1979 | 35.46 | 20.48 | 17.45 | 44.06 |
| 1989 | 25.83 | 23.01 | 19.04 | 51.16 |

Source(s): BLT-94-2.

### 3.2 Method(s): weighted average

**3.2.1 Men:**

- 1950-90, weighted averages of 1950, 1959, 1970, 1979 and 1989
distribution rates derived from the Bulletin of Labour Statistics, 1994-2.

**3.2.2 Women:**

Method, hypothesis and treatment identical to those used for men.

## 4. Projection of activity rates: 2000 - 2010

### 4.1 Model(s): linear, hyperbole and logistic

**4.1.1 Men:**

- To the [15-24] and [55+] age groups, application of function F3;
- To the [25-54] age groups, application of function F1;
- Modification of the trends for the [20-54] age groups.

**4.1.2 Women:**

- To the [15-19] and [55+] age groups, application of function F3;
- To the [20-24] and [50-54] age groups, application of function F1;
- To the [25-49] age groups, application of function F6;
- Modification of the trend for the [50-54] age group.

*Notes on adjustments of rates, see p. 3-8.*            *Notes on projection functions, see p. 10.*

# Germany

## 1. Source(s) of benchmark data

Code(s):    Title(s):
EPPA3      Yearbook of Labour Statistics 1945-89 - Retrospective Edition on Population Censuses, ILO, Geneva, 1990.
STAT       Database on Labour Statistics, LABORSTA - Bureau of Statistics, ILO, Geneva.

## 2. Estimates of activity rates: 1950 - 1990

### 2.1 Benchmark data:

Table 1: Activity rates by sex and age group

| Age group | Year 1989 (1) | 1990 (1) | 1991 (1) | 1991 | 1992 (1) | 1992 |
|---|---|---|---|---|---|---|
| **Men** | | | | | | |
| 10-14 | 0.00 | 0.00 | 0.00 | 0.00 | 0.00 | 0.00 |
| 15-19 | 43.14 | 43.22 | 40.70 | 44.56 | 39.43 | 41.72 |
| 20-24 | 79.64 | 79.81 | 77.82 | 79.70 | 77.69 | 79.36 |
| 25-29 | 87.00 | 87.38 | 86.76 | 88.50 | 86.84 | 88.24 |
| 30-34 | 95.95 | 95.77 | 95.69 | 96.31 | 95.63 | 96.19 |
| 35-39 | 97.48 | 97.48 | 97.35 | 97.71 | 97.36 | 97.60 |
| 40-44 | 97.50 | 97.41 | 97.22 | 97.56 | 97.34 | 97.56 |
| 45-49 | 96.63 | 96.55 | 95.93 | 96.43 | 95.82 | 96.23 |
| 50-54 | 92.97 | 93.23 | 92.93 | 93.37 | 92.94 | 93.28 |
| 55-59 | 78.63 | 81.09 | 81.45 | 79.75 | 81.51 | 74.21 |
| 60-64 | 34.21 | 35.05 | 34.95 | 33.49 | 34.87 | 31.31 |
| 65+ | 4.50 | 5.25 | 5.13 | 4.54 | 4.91 | 4.36 |
| **Women** | | | | | | |
| 10-14 | 0.00 | 0.00 | 0.00 | 0.00 | 0.00 | 0.00 |
| 15-19 | 38.36 | 37.29 | 34.84 | 37.20 | 34.29 | 36.01 |
| 20-24 | 74.08 | 75.65 | 73.42 | 75.86 | 72.55 | 74.58 |
| 25-29 | 69.26 | 71.58 | 70.77 | 75.57 | 72.47 | 76.56 |
| 30-34 | 62.86 | 66.90 | 66.46 | 72.79 | 67.68 | 73.59 |
| 35-39 | 64.40 | 68.03 | 68.76 | 75.07 | 70.22 | 75.93 |
| 40-44 | 64.81 | 69.46 | 70.52 | 75.35 | 72.59 | 77.12 |
| 45-49 | 61.82 | 66.71 | 67.12 | 72.79 | 68.70 | 73.77 |
| 50-54 | 54.38 | 57.82 | 58.59 | 65.32 | 60.80 | 66.75 |
| 55-59 | 40.89 | 43.82 | 44.36 | 42.84 | 45.51 | 41.70 |
| 60-64 | 11.18 | 12.49 | 12.20 | 10.70 | 11.91 | 9.99 |
| 65+ | 1.64 | 2.00 | 1.99 | 1.73 | 2.00 | 1.71 |

Note(s): (1) Fed. Rep. of Germany.
Source(s): STAT.

### 2.2 Method(s): arithmetic average

#### 2.2.1 Men:

- 1950-80, 1950-80 activity rates derived from the EPPA3;
- 1990, application to activity rates derived from the 1989, 1990 and 1991 surveys for Fed. Rep. of Germany, the variations in average activity rates; for Germany derived from the 1991 and 1992 surveys, in relation to average activity rates for Fed. Rep. of Germany derived from the 1991 and 1992 surveys.

#### 2.2.2 Women:

Method, hypothesis and treatment identical to those used for men.

## 3. Estimates of distribution rates by activity sector: 1950 - 1990

### 3.1 Benchmark data:

Table 2: Distribution of economically active population by activity sector

| Year | Agriculture | Industry Total | Manufac. | Services |
|---|---|---|---|---|
| **Men** | | | | |
| 1989 (1) | 3.39 | 48.50 | 36.59 | 48.11 |
| 1990 (1) | 3.25 | 48.79 | 36.90 | 47.97 |
| 1991 (1) | 3.00 | 46.23 | 35.09 | 50.76 |
| 1991 (2) | 7.27 | 47.95 | 30.58 | 44.79 |
| 1992 (2) | 5.64 | 50.66 | 27.74 | 43.70 |
| 1992 (1) | 3.01 | 47.97 | 36.40 | 49.02 |
| **Women** | | | | |
| 1989 (1) | 4.14 | 24.69 | 22.40 | 71.17 |
| 1990 (1) | 3.82 | 24.58 | 22.27 | 71.60 |
| 1991 (1) | 3.28 | 22.49 | 20.28 | 74.22 |
| 1991 (2) | 4.77 | 24.65 | 20.51 | 70.58 |
| 1992 (2) | 4.07 | 21.51 | 16.75 | 74.41 |
| 1992 (1) | 3.22 | 23.33 | 2.14 | 73.45 |

Notes(s): (1) German Dem. Rep.; (2) Fed. Rep. of Germany.
Source(s): STAT.

### 3.2 Method(s): arithmetic average

#### 3.2.1 Men:

- 1950-80, 1950-80 distribution rates derived from the EPPA3;
- 1980-90, application to averages of distribution rates derived from the 1989, 1990 and 1991 for Fed. Rep. of Germany, variation of average of distribution rates derived from 1991 and 1992 surveys for Germany, in relation to averages of distribution rates derived from the 1991 and 1992 surveys for Fed. Rep. of Germany.

#### 3.2.2 Women:

Method, hypothesis and treatment identical to those used for men.

## 4. Projection of activity rates: 2000 - 2010

### 4.1 Model(s): linear, log-linear, hyperbole and logistic

#### 4.1.1 Men:

- To the [15-19] age group, application of function F1;
- To the [20-24] age group, application of function F2;
- To the [25+] age groups, application of function F3;
- Modification of the trends for the [25-44] and [55+] age groups.

#### 4.1.2 Women:

- To the [15-19] age group, application of function F1;
- To the [20-24] age group, application of function F2;
- To the [25-54] age groups, application of function F6;
- To the [55+] age groups, application of function F3;
- Modification of the trends for the [15-24] age groups.

*Notes on adjustments of rates, see p. 3-8.*

*Notes on projection functions, see p. 10.*

# Ghana

## 1. Source(s) of benchmark data

Code(s):    Title(s):

EPPA3    Economically active population: Estimates and Projections, 1950-2025, Third edition, ILO, Geneva, 1986.
ADNU64    Demographic Yearbook 1964 - Population census statistics III- Sixteeenth Edition, United Nations, New York, 1965.
ASTER    Yearbook of Labour Statistics 1945-89 - Retrospective Edition on Population Censuses, ILO, Geneva, 1990.

## 2. Estimates of activity rates: 1950 - 1990

### 2.1 Benchmark data:

Table 1: Activity rates by sex and age group

| Age group | Year 1950 (1) | 1960 (2) | 1970 (3) | 1984 (3) |
|---|---|---|---|---|
| **Men** | | | | |
| 10-14 | 27.80 | 0.00 | 0.00 | 0.00 |
| 15-19 | 63.40 | 61.49 | 42.31 | 42.10 |
| 20-24 | 90.00 | 91.00 | 82.60 | 82.51 |
| 25-29 | 97.25 | 96.48 | 95.53 | 95.52 |
| 30-34 | 98.25 | 97.50 | 97.52 | 97.52 |
| 35-39 | 98.35 | 97.54 | 97.93 | 97.93 |
| 40-44 | 98.15 | 97.34 | 97.82 | 97.83 |
| 45-49 | 97.75 | 96.92 | 97.52 | 97.52 |
| 50-54 | 96.75 | 96.03 | 96.57 | 96.58 |
| 55-59 | 96.00 | 93.73 | 95.23 | 95.25 |
| 60-64 | 95.20 | 89.12 | 91.61 | 91.64 |
| 65+ | 82.00 | 71.52 | 75.41 | 75.45 |
| **Women** | | | | |
| 10-14 | .. | ... | .. | ... |
| 15-19 | .. | 53.71 | .. | 64.59 |
| 20-24 | .. | 52.32 | .. | 83.94 |
| 25-29 | .. | 51.50 | .. | 86.62 |
| 30-34 | .. | 57.05 | .. | 88.96 |
| 35-39 | .. | 59.32 | .. | 90.91 |
| 40-44 | .. | 65.35 | .. | 91.26 |
| 45-49 | .. | 67.00 | .. | 91.73 |
| 50-54 | .. | 69.63 | .. | 90.95 |
| 55-59 | .. | 70.61 | .. | 89.53 |
| 60-64 | .. | 64.03 | .. | 85.66 |
| 65+ | .. | 43.20 | .. | 73.57 |

Source(s): (1) EPPA3; (2) ASTER and ADNU64; (3) ASTER.

### 2.2 Method(s): linears interpolation and extrapolation weighted average

#### 2.2.1 Men:

- 1950-90, interpolation and extrapolation of activity rates derived from the 1960 and 1984 censuses;
application to 1950 activity rates derived from the EPPA3,
variations in 1960 extrapolated rates, in relation to activity rates derived from the 1960 census;
- 1960-90, weighted average of activity rates derived from the 1960 and 1984 censuses.

#### 2.2.2 Women:

- 1950-90, interpolation and extrapolation of activity rates derived from the 1960 and 1984 censuses;
modification of the trends of the [60+] age groups for 1950-90, for the [10-59] age groups for 1950 and for the [10-19] age groups for 1980 and 1990.

## 3. Estimates of distribution rates by activity sector: 1950 - 1990

### 3.1 Benchmark data:

Table 2: Distribution of economically active population by activity sector

| Year | Agriculture | Industry Total | Manufac. | Services |
|---|---|---|---|---|
| **Men** | | | | |
| 1960 (1) | 65.42 | 17.16 | 8.27 | 17.42 |
| 1984 (2) | 66.36 | 11.30 | 7.52 | 22.33 |
| **Women** | | | | |
| 1960 (1) | 58.26 | 10.56 | 10.01 | 31.18 |
| 1984 (2) | 56.04 | 14.26 | 14.00 | 29.70 |

Source(s): (1) ADNU64; (2) ASTER.

### 3.2 Method(s): weighted average

#### 3.2.1 Men:

- 1950-60, 1950-60 distribution rates derived from the EPPA3;
- 1980, weighted averages of 1960 distribution rates derived from the EPPA3 and of distribution rates derived from the 1984 census;
- 1970, averages of estimates for 1960 and 1980;
- 1990, estimate based on a 0.25 point/year reduction in agriculture sector; the difference has been imputed to services sector.

#### 3.2.2 Women:

- 1950-70, 1950-70 distribution rates derived from the EPPA3;
- 1980, weighted averages of 1960 distribution rates derived from the EPPA3 and of distribution rates derived from the 1984 census;
- 1990, extrapolation of distribution rates estimated for 1970 and 1980.

## 4. Projection of activity rates: 2000 - 2010

### 4.1 Model(s): linear and hyperbole

#### 4.1.1 Men:

- To the [10-59] age groups, application of function F1;
- To the [60+] age groups, application of function F3;
- Modification of the trends for the [15-59] age groups.

#### 4.1.2 Women:

- To all age groups, application of function F1;
- Modification of the trends for the [15+] age groups.

---

*Notes on adjustments of rates, see p. 3-8.*      *Notes on projection functions, see p. 10.*

# Greece

## 1. Source(s) of benchmark data

Code(s):    Title(s):
EPPA3      Yearbook of Labour Statistics 1945-89 - Retrospective Edition on Population Censuses, ILO, Geneva, 1990.
STAT       Database on Labour Statistics, LABORSTA - Bureau of Statistics, ILO, Geneva.

## 2. Estimates of activity rates: 1950 - 1990

### 2.1 Benchmark data:

Table 1: Activity rates by sex and age group

| Age group | Year | | | | |
|---|---|---|---|---|---|
| | 1970 (1) | 1981 (2) | 1989 (2) | 1990 (2) | 1991 (2) |
| **Men** | | | | | |
| 10-14 | .. | .. | 0.00 | 0.00 | 0.00 |
| 15-19 | .. | .. | 20.00 | 19.10 | 18.60 |
| 20-24 | .. | .. | 72.00 | 70.40 | 68.30 |
| 25-29 | .. | .. | 94.30 | 93.70 | 92.30 |
| 30-34 | .. | .. | 97.20 | 96.70 | 96.50 |
| 35-39 | .. | .. | 97.10 | 97.30 | 97.00 |
| 40-44 | .. | .. | 96.70 | 96.30 | 96.10 |
| 45-49 | .. | .. | 94.50 | 94.00 | 93.90 |
| 50-54 | .. | .. | 86.90 | 87.70 | 86.40 |
| 55-59 | .. | .. | 73.50 | 72.30 | 71.50 |
| 60-64 | .. | .. | 48.10 | 46.00 | 45.60 |
| 65+ | .. | .. | 11.70 | 11.80 | 11.00 |
| **Women** | | | | | |
| 10-14 | 6.50 | 3.04 | 0.00 | 0.00 | 0.00 |
| 15-19 | 28.10 | 23.24 | 15.40 | 15.60 | 14.10 |
| 20-24 | 36.00 | 39.02 | 53.90 | 54.00 | 53.00 |
| 25-29 | 31.85 | 37.50 | 59.10 | 60.20 | 58.70 |
| 30-34 | 29.80 | 33.56 | 58.40 | 58.50 | 55.70 |
| 35-39 | 29.70 | 30.82 | 57.10 | 57.10 | 54.20 |
| 40-44 | 29.55 | 30.64 | 50.00 | 49.90 | 49.10 |
| 45-49 | 27.35 | 28.80 | 45.60 | 45.40 | 41.30 |
| 50-54 | 25.40 | 25.77 | 38.90 | 37.80 | 34.70 |
| 55-59 | 21.95 | 19.91 | 30.20 | 28.50 | 26.60 |
| 60-64 | 16.40 | 13.38 | 19.60 | 19.90 | 15.90 |
| 65+ | 8.20 | 4.96 | 4.1 | 4.5 | 3.9 |

Source(s): (1) EPPA3; (2) STAT.

### 2.2 Method(s):  weighted average
arithmetic average

#### 2.2.1 Men:

- 1950-80, 1950-80 activity rates derived from the EPPA3;
- 1990, averages of adjusted activity rates derived from
the 1989, 1990 and 1991 surveys;
adjustment of estimated activity rates of the [15-29] age groups
to make allowance for conscripts.

#### 2.2.2 Women:

- 1950-70, 1950-70 activity rates derived from the EPPA3;
- 1980, weighted average of 1970 activity rates derived from the EPPA3
and of activity rates derived from the 1981 census;
- 1990, average of activity rates derived from the 1989, 1990
and 1991 surveys;
adjustment of activity rates estimated of the [15-19] age group for 1990.

## 3. Estimates of distribution rates by activity sector: 1950 - 1990

### 3.1 Benchmark data:

Table 2: Distribution of economically active population by activity sector

| Year | Agriculture | Industry | | Services |
|---|---|---|---|---|
| | | Total | Manufac. | |
| **Men** | | | | |
| 1981 | 27.46 | 34.29 | 19.52 | 38.24 |
| 1989 | 21.22 | 33.28 | 21.06 | 45.50 |
| 1990 | 20.19 | 33.60 | 20.98 | 46.21 |
| 1991 | 19.56 | 33.00 | 20.65 | 47.44 |
| **Women** | | | | |
| 1981 | 32.69 | 21.19 | 20.23 | 46.12 |
| 1989 | 31.39 | 18.22 | 17.51 | 50.39 |
| 1990 | 29.52 | 18.11 | 17.26 | 52.37 |
| 1991 | 25.85 | 18.53 | 17.67 | 55.63 |

Source(s): STAT.

### 3.2 Method(s):  arithmetic average

#### 3.2.1 Men:

- 1950-80, 1950-80 distribution rates derived from the EPPA3;
- Application of manufacturing/industry ratio derived from the 1981 census;
- 1990, adjusted averages of distribution rates derived from
the 1989, 1990 and 1991 surveys;
adjustment of rates to make allowance for conscripts.

#### 3.2.2 Women:

Method, hypothesis and treatment identical to those used for men.

## 4. Projection of activity rates: 2000 - 2010

### 4.1 Model(s):  linear, hyperbole and logistic

#### 4.1.1 Men:

- To the [15-19] and [35+] age groups, application of function F1;
- To the [20-34] age groups, application of function F3;
- Modification of the trends for the [25-34] age groups.

#### 4.1.2 Women:

- To the [15-19] and [60+] age groups, application of function F3;
- To the [20-24] age group, application of function F1;
- To the [25-59] age groups, application of function F6;
- Modification of the trends for the [15-19] and [50-64] age groups.

*Notes on adjustments of rates, see p. 3-8.*     *Notes on projection functions, see p. 10.*

# Guadeloupe

## 1. Source(s) of benchmark data

**Code(s):**    **Title(s):**

EPPA3     Economically active population: Estimates and Projections, 1950-2025, Third edition, ILO, Geneva, 1986.
ADNU     Editions 1984 and 1988 of United Nations Demographic Yearbook, New York.
ASTER     Yearbook of Labour Statistics 1945-89 - Retrospective Edition on Population Censuses, ILO, Geneva, 1990.
STAT     Database on Labour Statistics, LABORSTA - Bureau of Statistics, ILO, Geneva.

## 2. Estimates of activity rates: 1950 - 1990

### 2.1 Benchmark data:

Table 1: Activity rates by sex and age group

|  | Year | | |
|---|---|---|---|
| Age group | 1974 (1) | 1982 (1) | 1990 (2) |
| **Men** | | | |
| 10-14 | 0.00 | 0.00 | 0.00 |
| 15-19 | 37.26 | 24.12 | 18.31 |
| 20-24 | 76.83 | 83.50 | 75.69 |
| 25-29 | 94.73 | 93.44 | 92.49 |
| 30-34 | 94.75 | 95.55 | 94.06 |
| 35-39 | 94.45 | 96.11 | 93.24 |
| 40-44 | 93.58 | 94.92 | 93.05 |
| 45-49 | 90.96 | 93.32 | 91.83 |
| 50-54 | 87.31 | 90.56 | 85.04 |
| 55-59 | 79.94 | 83.11 | 72.60 |
| 60-64 | 53.03 | 52.34 | 37.50 |
| 65+ | 15.74 | 10.05 | 5.53 |
| **Women** | | | |
| 10-14 | 0.00 | 0.00 | 0.00 |
| 15-19 | 29.22 | 15.38 | 12.61 |
| 20-24 | 65.18 | 66.74 | 67.66 |
| 25-29 | 59.27 | 69.70 | 81.48 |
| 30-34 | 54.17 | 66.91 | 77.61 |
| 35-39 | 50.35 | 64.85 | 75.88 |
| 40-44 | 48.67 | 61.47 | 73.45 |
| 45-49 | 47.66 | 57.07 | 68.10 |
| 50-54 | 45.48 | 51.48 | 59.11 |
| 55-59 | 40.89 | 46.70 | 45.79 |
| 60-64 | 24.93 | 25.34 | 21.77 |
| 65+ | 6.16 | 3.82 | 2.55 |

Source(s): (1) ADNU; (2) EPPA3.

### 2.2 Method(s): linears interpolation and extrapolation
weighted average

**2.2.1 Men:**

- 1950-60, 1950-60 activity rates derived from the EPPA3;
adjustment of activity rates of the [25-29] age group;
- 1970 and 1990, interpolation and extrapolation of adjusted activity rates
derived from the 1974, 1982 and 1990 censuses.

**2.2.2 Women:**

- 1950-70, 1950-70 activity rates derived from the EPPA3;
- 1980, weighted average of activity rates derived from
the 1974 and 1982 censuses;
- 1990, weighted average of activity rates derived from
the 1982 and 1990 censuses.

## 3. Estimates of distribution rates by activity sector: 1950 - 1990

### 3.1 Benchmark data:

Table 2: Distribution of economically active population by activity sector

|  | Agriculture | Industry | | Services |
|---|---|---|---|---|
| Year | | Total | Manufac. | |
| **Men** | | | | |
| 1974 | 27.49 | 32.01 | 12.21 | 40.50 |
| 1982 | 24.06 | 24.52 | 5.14 | 51.42 |
| 1990 | 10.11 | 30.63 | 11.26 | 59.26 |
| **Women** | | | | |
| 1974 | 13.15 | 7.40 | 6.03 | 79.45 |
| 1982 | 9.78 | 3.46 | 2.10 | 86.77 |
| 1990 | 3.03 | 5.46 | 3.94 | 91.51 |

Source(s): STAT.

### 3.2 Method(s): weighted average

**3.2.1 Men:**

- 1950-70, 1950-70 distribution rates derived from the EPPA3;
1980-90, weighted averages of distribution rates derived from
the 1974, 1982 and 1990 census.

**3.2.2 Women:**

Method, hypothesis and treatment identical to those used for men.

## 4. Projection of activity rates: 2000 - 2010

### 4.1 Model(s): linear, hyperbole and logistic

**4.1.1 Men:**

- To the [15-19], [40-44] and [50+] age groups, application of function F3;
- To the [20-39] and [45-49] age groups, application of function F1;
- Modification of the trends for the [30-39] and [45-49] age groups.

**4.1.2 Women:**

- To the [15-19], [45-49] and [55+] age groups, application of function F3;
- To the [20-24] and [50-54] age groups, application of function F1;
- To the [25-44] age groups, application of function F6;
- Modification of the trends for the [20-24] and [50-54] age groups.

---

*Notes on adjustments of rates, see p. 3-8.*

*Notes on projection functions, see p. 10.*

# Guatemala

## 1. Source(s) of benchmark data

| Code(s): | Title(s): |
|---|---|
| EPPA3 | Economically active population: Estimates and Projections, 1950-2025, Third edition, ILO, Geneva, 1986. |
| INEG-81 | Censos Nacionales de 1981, Tomo I, Cifras definitivas, Instituto Nacional de Estadística, Guatemala. |
| ADNU | Editions 1979 and 1988 of United Nations Demographic Yearbook, New York. |
| ASTER | Yearbook of Labour Statistics 1945-89 - Retrospective Edition on Population Censuses, ILO, Geneva, 1990. |
| AST-93 | Yearbook of Labour Statistics 1993, ILO, Geneva, 1993. |

## 2. Estimates of activity rates: 1950 - 1990

### 2.1 Benchmark data:

Table 1: Activity rates by sex and age group

| Age group | Year 1973 (1) | 1981 (1) | 1989 (2) |
|---|---|---|---|
| **Men** | | | |
| 10-14 | 26.39 | 17.57 | 28.01 |
| 15-19 | 72.04 | 63.29 | 74.01 |
| 20-24 | 90.04 | 85.80 | 93.96 |
| 25-29 | 94.59 | 92.19 | 97.93 |
| 30-34 | 95.52 | 93.69 | 97.99 |
| 35-39 | 95.62 | 93.80 | 98.53 |
| 40-44 | 95.38 | 93.41 | 98.70 |
| 45-49 | 95.02 | 93.16 | 97.80 |
| 50-54 | 93.73 | 91.75 | 96.44 |
| 55-59 | 91.95 | 90.31 | 94.84 |
| 60-64 | 87.15 | 85.85 | 89.53 |
| 65+ | 68.60 | 66.83 | 62.93 |
| **Women** | | | |
| 10-14 | 4.10 | 3.44 | 7.80 |
| 15-19 | 14.99 | 13.27 | 25.63 |
| 20-24 | 17.38 | 17.18 | 29.83 |
| 25-29 | 15.00 | 15.96 | 29.72 |
| 30-34 | 14.09 | 15.39 | 33.81 |
| 35-39 | 13.87 | 13.99 | 31.46 |
| 40-44 | 14.05 | 13.59 | 30.89 |
| 45-49 | 13.54 | 12.26 | 30.32 |
| 50-54 | 12.92 | 11.69 | 28.93 |
| 55-59 | 11.93 | 10.05 | 23.36 |
| 60-64 | 10.13 | 8.81 | 20.62 |
| 65+ | 7.06 | 6.49 | 13.73 |

Source(s): (1) ADNU, ASTER, INEG-81; (2) AST-93.

### 2.2 Method(s): linears interpolation and extrapolation

#### 2.2.1 Men:

- 1950-60, 1950-60 activity rates derived from the EPPA3;
adjustment of activity rates of the [10-14] age group;
- 1970-90, interpolation and extrapolation of adjusted activity rates
the 1973 and 1981 censuses.

#### 2.2.2 Women:

- 1950-70, 1950-70 adjusted activity rates derived from the EPPA3;
the adjustment was made on the basis of the adjustment model for
activity rates of women working in agriculture as contributing family workers;
- 1980-90, interpolation and extrapolation of adjusted activity rates
derived from the 1981 census and of activity rates derived from the 1989 census.

## 3. Estimates of distribution rates by activity sector: 1950 - 1990

### 3.1 Benchmark data:

Table 2: Distribution of economically active population by activity sector

| Year | Agriculture | Industry Total | Manufac. | Services |
|---|---|---|---|---|
| **Men** | | | | |
| 1980 (1) | 64.45 | 16.55 | .. | 19.00 |
| 1981 (2) | 64.07 | 16.58 | 9.77 | 19.34 |
| 1989 (3) | 61.35 | 16.53 | 10.45 | 22.13 |
| **Women** | | | | |
| 1981 (2) | 9.70 | 19.68 | 18.82 | 70.62 |
| 1989 (3) | 15.99 | 23.58 | 23.24 | 60.43 |

Source(s): (1) EPPA3; (2) ASTER; (3) AST93.

### 3.2 Method(s): weighted average
linear extrapolation

#### 3.2.1 Men:

- 1950-80, 1950-80 distribution rates derived from the EPPA3;
- Application of manufacturing/industry ratio derived from the 1981 census;
- 1990, weighted averages of 1980 distribution rates derived from
the EPPA3 and of distribution rates derived from the 1989 survey;
application of manufacturing/industry ratio derived from the 1989 survey.

#### 3.2.2 Women:

- 1950-70, 1950-70 adjusted distribution rates derived from the EPPA3;
adjustment of rates based on the men/women ratio in agriculture equal to 1/10;
- 1980-90, extrapolation of adjusted distribution rates derived from
the 1981 census and of distribution rates derived from the 1989 survey.

## 4. Projection of activity rates: 2000 - 2010

### 4.1 Model(s): linear, log-linear and logistic

#### 4.1.1 Men:

- To the [10-14] and [25+] age groups, application of function F1;
- To the [19-24] age groups, application of function F6;
- Modification of the trends for the [10-54] and [65+] age groups.

#### 4.1.2 Women:

- To the [10-14] and [65+] age groups, application of function F1;
- To the [15-64] age groups, application of function F2;
- Modification of the trends for the [15+] age groups.

---

*Notes on adjustments of rates, see p. 3-8.*

*Notes on projection functions, see p. 10.*

# Guinea

## 1. Source(s) of benchmark data

Code(s):    Title(s):
EPPA3       Economically active population: Estimates and Projections, 1950-2025, Third edition, ILO, Geneva, 1986.
AST91       Yearbook of Labour Statistics 1991, ILO, Geneva, 1991.

## 2. Estimates of activity rates: 1950 - 1990

### 2.1 Benchmark data:

Table 1: Activity rates by sex and age group

| Age group | Year 1950 (1) | 1960 (1) | 1970 (1) | 1980 (1) | 1983 (2) |
|---|---|---|---|---|---|
| **Men** | | | | | |
| 10-14 | 52.30 | 50.00 | 48.05 | 45.35 | .. |
| 15-19 | 85.20 | 82.15 | 79.55 | 75.95 | .. |
| 20-24 | 95.35 | 94.20 | 93.20 | 91.85 | .. |
| 25-29 | 97.40 | 97.25 | 97.10 | 96.90 | .. |
| 30-34 | 98.15 | 97.95 | 97.80 | 97.55 | .. |
| 35-39 | 98.30 | 98.10 | 97.95 | 97.70 | .. |
| 40-44 | 98.15 | 97.95 | 97.75 | 97.50 | .. |
| 45-49 | 97.40 | 97.20 | 97.05 | 96.85 | .. |
| 50-54 | 96.95 | 96.70 | 96.45 | 96.15 | .. |
| 55-59 | 96.10 | 95.70 | 95.30 | 94.80 | .. |
| 60-64 | 93.20 | 92.45 | 91.80 | 90.95 | .. |
| 65+ | 80.05 | 78.75 | 77.60 | 76.10 | .. |
| **Women** | | | | | |
| 10-14 | 39.50 | 37.80 | 36.30 | 34.30 | 28.40 |
| 15-19 | 64.20 | 61.60 | 59.40 | 56.35 | 41.20 |
| 20-24 | 64.30 | 62.70 | 61.30 | 59.35 | 44.80 |
| 25-29 | 69.30 | 67.45 | 65.85 | 63.65 | 50.40 |
| 30-34 | 73.65 | 71.70 | 70.00 | 67.65 | 51.70 |
| 35-39 | 74.90 | 73.05 | 71.45 | 69.25 | 51.20 |
| 40-44 | 77.30 | 75.45 | 73.90 | 71.7 | 51.00 |
| 45-49 | 76.85 | 74.95 | 73.35 | 71.1 | 51.20 |
| 50-54 | 75.45 | 73.25 | 71.40 | 68.8 | 49.30 |
| 55-59 | 72.70 | 70.40 | 68.45 | 65.75 | 46.00 |
| 60-64 | 66.75 | 63.85 | 61.35 | 57.9 | 34.00 |
| 65+ | 46.65 | 43.95 | 41.60 | 38.45 | 16.95 |

Source(s): (1) EPPA3; (2) AST91.

### 2.2 Method(s):  linears interpolation and extrapolation

#### 2.2.1 Men:

- 1950-80, 1950-80 activity rates derived from the EPPA3;
- 1990, extrapolation of 1950-80 activity rates derived from the EPPA3;
adjustment of extrapolated rates on the basis of variations in 1980
interpolated rates, in relation to the 1980 rates derived from the EPPA3;
modification of the trends for all age groups for 1990.

#### 2.2.2 Women:

- 1950-90, interpolation and extrapolation of 1950-80 activity rates
derived from the EPPA3;
adjustment of interpolated and extrapolated rates on the basis of variations
in 1983 extrapolated rates, in relation to activity rates derived from the 1983 cens
modification of the trends of all age groups for 1950 to 1980.

## 3. Estimates of distribution rates by activity sector: 1950 - 1990

### 3.1 Benchmark data:

Table 2: Distribution of economically active population by activity sector

| Year | Agriculture | Industry Total | Manufac. | Services |
|---|---|---|---|---|
| **Men** | | | | |
| 1950 (1) | 88.00 | 5.80 | .. | 6.20 |
| 1960 (1) | 83.80 | 7.85 | .. | 8.35 |
| 1970 (1) | 80.20 | 9.60 | .. | 10.20 |
| 1980 (1) | 75.25 | 11.95 | .. | 12.80 |
| 1983 (2) | 85.44 | 2.11 | 0.67 | 12.45 |
| **Women** | | | | |
| 1950 (1) | 97.30 | 1.90 | .. | 0.80 |
| 1960 (1) | 96.15 | 2.70 | .. | 1.15 |
| 1970 (1) | 92.00 | 3.50 | .. | 4.50 |
| 1980 (1) | 88.30 | 4.90 | .. | 6.80 |
| 1983 (2) | 85.30 | 2.20 | 0.68 | 12.50 |

Source(s): (1) EPPA3; (2) AST91.

### 3.2 Method(s):  linears interpolation and extrapolation

#### 3.2.1 Men:

- 1950-90, interpolation and extrapolation of distribution rates derived
from the EPPA3;
adjustment of 1950-90 interpolated and extrapolated rates on the basis
of variations in 1983 interpolated rates, in relation to distribution rates
derived from the 1983 census;
- Application of manufacturing/industry ratio derived from the 1983 census.

#### 3.2.2 Women:

- 1950-90, interpolation and extrapolation of 1950 and 1980 adjusted
distribution rates derived from the EPPA3;
adjustment of distribution rates on the basis of men/women ratio
equal to 1 in agriculture;
application of industry/services ratio derived from the 1983 census;
- Application of manufacturing/industry ratio derived from the 1983 census.

## 4. Projection of activity rates: 2000 - 2010

### 4.1 Model(s):  linear and hyperbole

#### 4.1.1 Men:

- To the [10-29] age groups, application of function F1;
- Modification of the trend for the [10-14] age group.

#### 4.1.2 Women:

- To the [10-19] and [60+] age groups, application of function F1;
- To the [20-59] age groups, application of function F3;
- Modification of the trends for the [10-19] and [60+] age groups.

*Notes on adjustments of rates, see p. 3-8.*    *Notes on projection functions, see p. 10.*

# Guinea-Bissau

## 1. Source(s) of benchmark data

Code(s):    Title(s):

EPPA3      Economically active population: Estimates and Projections, 1950-2025, Third edition, ILO, Geneva, 1986.
ADNU84     Demographic Yearbook 1984 - Population census statistics II - Thirty-sixth Edition, United Nations, New York, 1986.
ASTER      Yearbook of Labour Statistics 1945-89 - Retrospective Edition on Population Censuses, ILO, Geneva, 1990.

## 2. Estimates of activity rates: 1950 - 1990

### 2.1 Benchmark data:

Table 1: Activity rates by sex and age group

| Age group | Year | | | |
|---|---|---|---|---|
| | 1950 (1) | 1960 (1) | 1970 (1) | 1979 (2) |
| **Men** | | | | |
| 10-14 | 50.95 | 49.10 | 46.75 | 48.22 |
| 15-19 | 83.40 | 80.90 | 77.80 | 55.21 |
| 20-24 | 94.65 | 93.75 | 92.55 | 86.87 |
| 25-29 | 97.30 | 97.15 | 97.00 | 97.46 |
| 30-34 | 98.05 | 97.90 | 97.70 | 98.86 |
| 35-39 | 98.20 | 98.05 | 97.80 | 99.02 |
| 40-44 | 98.05 | 97.85 | 97.65 | 98.80 |
| 45-49 | 97.30 | 97.15 | 96.95 | 98.95 |
| 50-54 | 96.80 | 96.60 | 96.30 | 98.18 |
| 55-59 | 95.85 | 95.50 | 95.05 | 97.95 |
| 60-64 | 92.75 | 92.15 | 91.40 | 96.87 |
| 65+ | 79.25 | 78.20 | 76.85 | 89.46 |
| **Women** | | | | |
| 10-14 | 38.50 | 37.10 | 35.35 | 2.63 |
| 15-19 | 62.65 | 60.55 | 57.90 | 2.22 |
| 20-24 | 63.35 | 62.00 | 60.35 | 3.96 |
| 25-29 | 68.20 | 66.70 | 64.80 | 3.22 |
| 30-34 | 72.50 | 70.85 | 68.85 | 2.68 |
| 35-39 | 73.80 | 72.25 | 70.40 | 2.35 |
| 40-44 | 76.20 | 74.70 | 72.80 | 2.26 |
| 45-49 | 75.70 | 74.20 | 72.25 | 2.25 |
| 50-54 | 74.15 | 72.40 | 70.15 | 1.83 |
| 55-59 | 71.35 | 69.50 | 67.15 | 2.18 |
| 60-64 | 65.00 | 62.65 | 59.65 | 1.70 |
| 65+ | 45.05 | 42.85 | 40.10 | 1.45 |

Source(s): (1) EPPA3; (2) ADNU84 and ASTER.

### 2.2 Method(s):   linears interpolation and extrapolation

#### 2.2.1 Men:

- 1950-90, interpolation and extrapolation of 1950-80 activity rates derived from the EPPA3 and of adjusted activity rates derived from the 1979 census;
adjustment of interpolated and extrapolated rates on the basis of variations in 1979 interpolated rates, in relation to activity rates derived from the 1979 census;
modification of the trends for all age groups.

#### 2.2.2 Women:

Method, hypothesis and treatment identical to those used for men.

## 3. Estimates of distribution rates by activity sector: 1950 - 1990

### 3.1 Benchmark data:

Table 2: Distribution of economically active population by activity sector

| Year | Agriculture | Industry | | Services |
|---|---|---|---|---|
| | | Total | Manufac. | |
| **Men** | | | | |
| 1950 (1) | 85.50 | 1.85 | .. | 12.65 |
| 1960 (1) | 82.10 | 2.55 | .. | 15.35 |
| 1970 (1) | 77.80 | 4.10 | .. | 18.10 |
| 1979 (2) | 81.08 | 2.45 | 1.42 | 16.47 |
| 1980 (1) | 75.20 | 5.00 | .. | 19.80 |
| **Women** | | | | |
| 1950 (1) | 95.00 | 0.65 | .. | 4.35 |
| 1960 (1) | 94.00 | 1.00 | .. | 5.00 |
| 1970 (1) | 92.70 | 1.40 | .. | 5.90 |
| 1979 (2) | 97.64 | 0.23 | 0.18 | 2.13 |
| 1980 (1) | 91.90 | 1.65 | .. | 6.45 |

Source(s): (1) EPPA3; (2) ASTER.

### 3.2 Method(s):   linears interpolation and extrapolation

#### 3.2.1 Men:

- 1950-90, interpolation and extrapolation of 1950-80 distribution rates derived from the EPPA3 and of distribution rates derived from the 1979 census; adjustment of 1950-90 interpolated and extrapolated rates on the basis of 1/3 of variations in 1979 interpolated rates, in relation to distribution rates derived from the 1979 census;
- Application of manufacturing/industry ratio derived from the 1979 census.

#### 3.2.2 Women:

- 1950-90, interpolation and extrapolation of 1950-80 distribution rates derived from the EPPA3 and of distribution rates derived from the 1979 census; adjustment of interpolated and extrapolated rates on the basis of half (total for 1990) of variations 1979 interpolated rates, in relation to distribution rates derived from the 1979 census;
- Application of manufacturing/industry ratio derived from the 1979 census.

## 4. Projection of activity rates: 2000 - 2010

### 4.1 Model(s):   linear and hyperbole

#### 4.1.1 Men:

- To the [10-29] age groups, application of function F1;
- To the [30+] age groups, application of function F3;
- Modification of the trend for the [10-14] age group.

#### 4.1.2 Women:

- To the [10-19] age groups, application of function F1;
- To the [20+] age groups, application of function F3;
- Modification of the trends for the [10-19] and [60+] age groups.

*Notes on adjustments of rates, see p. 3-8.*                    *Notes on projection functions, see p. 10.*

# Guyana

## 1. Source(s) of benchmark data

Code(s): Title(s):

EPPA3    Economically active population: Estimates and Projections, 1950-2025, Third edition, ILO, Geneva, 1986.
STAT     Database on Labour Statistics, LABORSTA - Bureau of Statistics, ILO, Geneva.

## 2. Estimates of activity rates: 1950 - 1990

### 2.1 Benchmark data:

Table 1: Activity rates by sex and age group

|  | Year | | |
| Age group | 1970 (1) | 1980 (2) | 1987 (2) |
|---|---|---|---|
| **Men** | | | |
| 10-14 | 4.40 | 0.00 | 0.00 |
| 15-19 | 67.00 | 64.77 | 61.42 |
| 20-24 | 94.20 | 94.22 | 91.98 |
| 25-29 | 97.90 | 97.77 | 94.40 |
| 30-34 | 98.55 | 97.96 | 97.79 |
| 35-39 | 97.95 | 97.97 | 97.81 |
| 40-44 | 97.30 | 97.70 | 97.35 |
| 45-49 | 96.75 | 96.51 | 95.66 |
| 50-54 | 93.50 | 93.72 | 93.44 |
| 55-59 | 91.90 | 88.92 | 86.79 |
| 60-64 | 67.75 | 65.66 | 64.17 |
| 65+ | 41.35 | 34.36 | 32.27 |
| **Women** | | | |
| 10-14 | 1.40 | 0.00 | |
| 15-19 | 26.25 | 21.28 | 22.56 |
| 20-24 | 29.10 | 36.57 | 42.30 |
| 25-29 | 20.50 | 33.26 | 41.70 |
| 30-34 | 18.50 | 30.21 | 43.70 |
| 35-39 | 19.95 | 27.37 | 39.61 |
| 40-44 | 22.00 | 27.04 | 37.06 |
| 45-49 | 22.25 | 26.90 | 34.50 |
| 50-54 | 20.40 | 25.44 | 31.05 |
| 55-59 | 18.05 | 21.77 | 26.82 |
| 60-64 | 12.10 | 15.07 | 17.93 |
| 65+ | 5.15 | 5.55 | 5.24 |

Source(s): (1) EPPA3; (2) STAT.

### 2.2 Method(s): weighted average

#### 2.2.1 Men:

- 1950-70, 1950-70 activity rates derived from the EPPA3;
- 1980, weighted average of activity rates of 1970 derived from the EPPA3 and of adjusted activity rates derived from the 1980 census;
modification of the trends of the [55-64] age groups;
- 1990, weighted average of adjusted activity rates derived from the 1980 census and of activity rates derived from the 1987 survey;
modification of the trend of the [65+] age group.

#### 2.2.2 Women:

- 1950-70, 1950-70 activity rates derived from the EPPA3;
- 1980, weighted average of activity rates of 1970 derived from the EPPA3 and of adjusted activity rates derived from the 1980 census;
- 1990, weighted average of adjusted activity rates derived from the 1980 census and of adjusted activity rates derived from the 1987 survey;
modification of the trends of the [65+] age group.

## 3. Estimates of distribution rates by activity sector: 1950 - 1990

### 3.1 Benchmark data:

Table 2: Distribution of economically active population by activity sector

|  | | Agriculture | Industry | | Services |
| Year | | | Total | Manufac. | |
|---|---|---|---|---|---|
| **Men** | | | | | |
| 1960 | | 40.95 | 30.25 | .. | 28.80 |
| 1970 | | 35.85 | 32.05 | .. | 32.10 |
| 1980 | | 31.60 | 28.90 | 16.39 | 39.50 |
| **Women** | | | | | |
| 1960 | | 25.80 | 15.00 | .. | 59.20 |
| 1970 | | 16.85 | 15.00 | .. | 68.15 |
| 1980 | | 11.80 | 16.25 | 12.79 | 71.95 |

Source(s): EPPA3.

### 3.2 Method(s): linear extrapolation

#### 3.2.1 Men:

- 1950-80, 1950-80 distribution rates derived from the EPPA3;
- 1990, extrapolation of 1950-80 distribution rates derived from the EPPA3;
modification of the trends in all sectors.

#### 3.2.2 Women:

Method, hypothesis and treatment identical to those used for men.

## 4. Projection of activity rates: 2000 - 2010

### 4.1 Model(s): linear, log-linear, hyperbole and logistic

#### 4.1.1 Men:

- To the [15-24] age groups, application of function F1;
- To the [25+] age groups, application of function F3.

#### 4.1.2 Women:

- To the [15-24] age groups, application of function F2;
- To the [25-64] age groups, application of function F6;
- To the [65+] age group, application of function F3.

*Notes on adjustments of rates, see p. 3-8.*

*Notes on projection functions, see p. 10.*

# Haiti

## 1. Source(s) of benchmark data

Code(s):    Title(s):

EPPA3      Economically active population: Estimates and Projections, 1950-2025, Third edition, ILO, Geneva, 1986.
ASTER      Yearbook of Labour Statistics 1945-89 - Retrospective Edition on Population Censuses, ILO, Geneva, 1990.

## 2. Estimates of activity rates: 1950 - 1990

### 2.1 Benchmark data:

Table 1: Activity rates by sex and age group

| Age group | Year 1950 (1) | 1960 (1) | 1970 (1) | 1982 (2) |
|---|---|---|---|---|
| **Men** | | | | |
| 10-14 | 53.00 | 47.50 | 42.00 | 25.70 |
| 15-19 | 83.70 | 75.00 | 66.40 | 43.87 |
| 20-24 | 95.60 | 92.60 | 89.75 | 76.99 |
| 25-29 | 98.40 | 98.00 | 97.55 | 91.85 |
| 30-34 | 98.80 | 98.80 | 98.75 | 94.13 |
| 35-39 | 99.00 | 99.10 | 99.20 | 96.18 |
| 40-44 | 98.90 | 98.90 | 98.95 | 95.23 |
| 45-49 | 98.80 | 98.75 | 98.75 | 94.21 |
| 50-54 | 98.35 | 98.25 | 98.10 | 91.14 |
| 55-59 | 97.75 | 97.60 | 97.50 | 92.68 |
| 60-64 | 96.50 | 95.90 | 95.30 | 87.47 |
| 65+ | 87.20 | 84.25 | 81.00 | 70.32 |
| **Women** | | | | |
| 10-14 | 51.50 | 45.00 | 41.00 | 22.29 |
| 15-19 | 81.10 | 73.05 | 64.85 | 35.14 |
| 20-24 | 85.80 | 80.65 | 75.40 | 53.49 |
| 25-29 | 85.25 | 80.05 | 74.75 | 56.71 |
| 30-34 | 85.70 | 80.00 | 74.20 | 55.50 |
| 35-39 | 86.30 | 80.85 | 75.35 | 58.42 |
| 40-44 | 87.15 | 82.35 | 77.50 | 57.51 |
| 45-49 | 87.10 | 82.35 | 77.45 | 60.16 |
| 50-54 | 85.15 | 81.20 | 77.20 | 57.83 |
| 55-59 | 83.50 | 79.55 | 75.50 | 54.15 |
| 60-64 | 79.75 | 74.90 | 69.85 | 46.55 |
| 65+ | 59.00 | 52.25 | 45.40 | 35.80 |

Source(s): (1) EPPA3; (2) ASTER.

### 2.2 Method(s): linear extrapolation / weighted average

**2.2.1 Men:**

- 1950-70, 1950-70 activity rates derived from the EPPA3;
- 1980, weighted average of activity rates of 1970 derived from the EPPA3 and of adjusted activity rates derived from the 1982 census;
- 1990, extrapolation of 1950-70 activity rates derived from the EPPA3 and of activity rates estimated for 1980;
application to extrapolated rates, variations in 1982 interpolated rates, in relation to adjusted activity rates derived from the 1982 census; modification of the trends for all age groups.

**2.2.2 Women:**

Method, hypothesis and treatment identical to those used for men.

## 3. Estimates of distribution rates by activity sector: 1950 - 1990

### 3.1 Benchmark data:

Table 2: Distribution of economically active population by activity sector

| Year | Agriculture | Industry Total | Manufac. | Services |
|---|---|---|---|---|
| **Men** | | | | |
| 1950 | 88.70 | 5.60 | 4.30 | 5.70 |
| 1971 | 83.97 | 6.84 | 4.96 | 9.19 |
| 1982 | 77.92 | 8.71 | 6.02 | 13.37 |
| **Women** | | | | |
| 1950 | 82.25 | 5.84 | 5.78 | 11.91 |
| 1971 | 61.85 | 7.67 | 7.62 | 30.48 |
| 1982 | 51.31 | 9.59 | 7.64 | 39.10 |

Source(s): (1) ASTER.

### 3.2 Method(s): weighted average / linear extrapolation

**3.2.1 Men:**

- 1950-70, 1950-70 distribution rates derived from the EPPA3;
- 1980, weighted averages of 1970 distribution rates derived from the EPPA3 and of distribution rates derived from the 1982 census;
- 1990, extrapolation of distribution rates derived from the 1950, 1971 and 1982 censuses;
modification of the trends in all sectors.

**3.2.2 Women:**

Method, hypothesis and treatment identical to those used for men.

## 4. Projection of activity rates: 2000 - 2010

### 4.1 Model(s): linear and hyperbole

**4.1.1 Men:**

- To the [10-14] and [20+] age groups, application of function F1;
- To the [15-19] age group, application of function F3;
- Modification of the trends for the [10-34] and [45-54] age groups.

**4.1.2 Women:**

- To the [10-14] age group, application of function F1;
- To the [15+] age groups, application of function F3;
- Modification of the trends for the [10-64] age groups.

---

Notes on adjustments of rates, see p. 3-8.          Notes on projection functions, see p. 10.

# Honduras

## 1. Source(s) of benchmark data

**Code(s):**    **Title(s):**

EPPA3    Economically active population: Estimates and Projections, 1950-2025, Third edition, ILO, Geneva, 1986.
STAT     Database on Labour Statistics, LABORSTA - Bureau of Statistics, ILO, Geneva.

## 2. Estimates of activity rates: 1950 - 1990

### 2.1 Benchmark data:

Table 1: Activity rates by sex and age group

| Age group | Year 1974 | 1991 | 1992 |
|---|---|---|---|
| **Men** | | | |
| 10-14 | 28.88 | 13.95 | 15.18 |
| 15-19 | 77.75 | 63.47 | 63.80 |
| 20-24 | 92.38 | 90.93 | 89.17 |
| 25-29 | 96.58 | 94.90 | 94.03 |
| 30-34 | 98.07 | 97.61 | 97.65 |
| 35-39 | 98.22 | 97.83 | 97.86 |
| 40-44 | 97.53 | 97.67 | 97.66 |
| 45-49 | 97.24 | 96.74 | 97.92 |
| 50-54 | 95.38 | 95.22 | 95.58 |
| 55-59 | 94.08 | 95.26 | 94.06 |
| 60-64 | 89.07 | 88.23 | 88.44 |
| 65+ | 65.21 | 57.34 | 59.24 |
| **Women** | | | |
| 10-14 | .. | 3.63 | 3.82 |
| 15-19 | .. | 21.16 | 24.51 |
| 20-24 | .. | 38.55 | 37.57 |
| 25-29 | .. | 36.11 | 35.17 |
| 30-34 | .. | 42.78 | 46.24 |
| 35-39 | .. | 43.79 | 46.60 |
| 40-44 | .. | 41.01 | 45.12 |
| 45-49 | .. | 39.10 | 41.37 |
| 50-54 | .. | 34.22 | 37.84 |
| 55-59 | .. | 29.99 | 32.31 |
| 60-64 | .. | 22.22 | 22.52 |
| 65+ | .. | 13.61 | 14.44 |

Source(s): STAT.

### 2.2 Method(s): linear interpolation / arithmetic average

#### 2.2.1 Men:

- 1950-60, 1950-60 activity rates derived from the EPPA3;
- 1970-90, interpolation of adjusted activity rates derived from the 1974 census and of average of activity rates derived from the 1991 and 1992 surveys.

#### 2.2.2 Women:

- 1950-70, 1950-70 activity rates derived from the EPPA3;
- 1980-90, application to average activity rates derived from the 1991 and 1992 surveys, 3/4 of the variations in 1980 and 1990 activity rates estimated for Mexico.

## 3. Estimates of distribution rates by activity sector: 1950 - 1990

### 3.1 Benchmark data:

Table 2: Distribution of economically active population by activity sector

| Year | Agriculture | Industry Total | Manufac. | Services |
|---|---|---|---|---|
| **Men** | | | | |
| 1974 (1) | 71.76 | 12.84 | 8.30 | 15.41 |
| 1991 (2) | 45.27 | 23.69 | 16.34 | 31.03 |
| **Women** | | | | |
| 1980 (1) | 7.10 | 30.18 | .. | 62.72 |
| 1991 (2) | 22.09 | 12.00 | 11.82 | 65.91 |

Source(s): (1) STAT; (2) EPPA3.

### 3.2 Method(s): linear interpolation / weighted average

#### 3.2.1 Men:

- 1950-70, 1950-70 distribution rates derived from the EPPA3;
- 1980-90, weighted averages of distribution rates derived from the 1974 census and of averages of distribution rates derived from the 1991 and 1992 surveys.

#### 3.2.2 Women:

- 1950-70, 1950-70 distribution rates derived from the EPPA3;
- 1980-90, interpolation of 1980 distribution rates derived from the EPPA3 and of averages of distribution rates derived from the 1991 and 1992 surveys; adjustment of distribution rates on the basis of men/women ratio in agriculture derived from the 1981 survey.

## 4. Projection of activity rates: 2000 - 2010

### 4.1 Model(s): linear, log-linear, hyperbole and logistic

#### 4.1.1 Men:

- To the [10-14] age group, application of function F2;
- To the [15+] age groups, application of function F3;
- Modification of the trend for the [10-14] age group.

#### 4.1.2 Women:

- To the [10-14] and [30+] age groups, application of function F1;
- To the [15-29] age groups, application of function F6;
- Modification of the trends for the [15+] age groups.

# Hong Kong, China

## 1. Source(s) of benchmark data

Code(s):   Title(s):
EPPA3     Economically active population: Estimates and Projections, 1950-2025, Third edition, ILO, Geneva, 1986.
STAT      Database on Labour Statistics, LABORSTA - Bureau of Statistics, ILO, Geneva.

## 2. Estimates of activity rates: 1950 - 1990

### 2.1 Benchmark data:

Table 1: Activity rates by sex and age group

| Age group | 1979 | 1980 | 1981 | 1989 | 1990 | 1991 |
|---|---|---|---|---|---|---|
| **Men** | | | | | | |
| 10-14 | 0.00 | 0.00 | 0.00 | 0.00 | 0.00 | 0.00 |
| 15-19 | 35.80 | 39.60 | 45.50 | 31.10 | 29.80 | 29.30 |
| 20-24 | 87.40 | 89.00 | 91.90 | 86.30 | 86.00 | 84.50 |
| 25-29 | 98.50 | 97.90 | 98.30 | 98.30 | 98.40 | 97.50 |
| 30-34 | 98.70 | 99.10 | 98.80 | 98.90 | 98.90 | 98.80 |
| 35-39 | 99.10 | 98.90 | 98.90 | 98.90 | 98.80 | 98.70 |
| 40-44 | 98.40 | 98.60 | 98.30 | 99.00 | 98.90 | 98.40 |
| 45-49 | 97.50 | 97.40 | 97.40 | 97.70 | 97.80 | 97.80 |
| 50-54 | 93.90 | 93.60 | 93.80 | 93.30 | 92.80 | 92.40 |
| 55-59 | 83.30 | 84.00 | 83.00 | 81.20 | 81.20 | 81.60 |
| 60-64 | 64.40 | 64.10 | 67.00 | 56.80 | 54.70 | 54.60 |
| 65+ | 32.50 | 32.10 | 35.20 | 22.50 | 21.40 | 20.80 |
| **Women** | | | | | | |
| 10-14 | 0.00 | 0.00 | 0.00 | 0.00 | 0.00 | 0.00 |
| 15-19 | 39.50 | 39.00 | 42.70 | 31.10 | 29.80 | 29.30 |
| 20-24 | 78.00 | 79.70 | 80.00 | 86.30 | 86.00 | 84.50 |
| 25-29 | 58.40 | 60.30 | 61.30 | 76.40 | 77.90 | 79.60 |
| 30-34 | 41.60 | 44.70 | 49.20 | 54.10 | 55.30 | 59.10 |
| 35-39 | 41.60 | 44.70 | 49.20 | 52.20 | 52.30 | 52.30 |
| 40-44 | 44.80 | 48.00 | 54.10 | 53.40 | 53.50 | 53.90 |
| 45-49 | 41.20 | 44.20 | 49.40 | 51.00 | 52.30 | 52.20 |
| 50-54 | 36.80 | 36.00 | 44.60 | 39.50 | 38.10 | 41.60 |
| 55-59 | 33.70 | 31.50 | 36.90 | 28.30 | 27.10 | 27.50 |
| 60-64 | 19.60 | 19.80 | 22.20 | 19.50 | 18.40 | 17.20 |
| 65+ | 11.30 | 11.90 | 13.70 | 7.60 | 5.90 | 6.40 |

Source(s): STAT.

### 2.2 Method(s): linear interpolation

#### 2.2.1 Men:
- 1950-80, 1950-80 activity rates derived from the EPPA3;
- 1990, interpolation of adjusted activity rates derived from the 1979 to 1992 surveys;
adjustment of interpolated rates on the basis of variations in 1980 interpolated rates, in relation to the 1980 activity rates derived from the EPPA3.

#### 2.2.2 Women:
- 1950-70, 1950-70 activity rates derived from the EPPA3;
- 1980-90, extrapolation of activity rates derived from the 1979 to 1992 surveys.

## 3. Estimates of distribution rates by activity sector: 1950 - 1990

### 3.1 Benchmark data:

Table 2: Distribution of economically active population by activity sector

| Year | Agriculture | Industry Total | Manufac. | Services |
|---|---|---|---|---|
| **Men** | | | | |
| 1979 | 1.42 | 46.69 | 36.02 | 51.89 |
| 1980 | 1.44 | 47.21 | 35.05 | 51.36 |
| 1981 | 1.31 | 45.52 | 31.85 | 53.18 |
| 1989 | 1.14 | 40.16 | 26.52 | 58.69 |
| 1990 | 0.95 | 38.85 | 25.31 | 60.20 |
| 1991 | 0.84 | 38.13 | 24.68 | 61.03 |
| **Women** | | | | |
| 1979 | 0.89 | 57.72 | 56.30 | 41.39 |
| 1980 | 1.08 | 56.15 | 54.76 | 42.77 |
| 1981 | 1.59 | 54.27 | 52.82 | 44.13 |
| 1989 | 1.08 | 36.39 | 35.27 | 62.53 |
| 1990 | 0.71 | 33.04 | 31.86 | 66.25 |
| 1991 | 0.43 | 29.56 | 28.39 | 70.01 |

Source(s): STAT.

### 3.2 Method(s): arithmetic average

#### 3.2.1 Men:
- 1950-70, 1950-70 distribution rates derived from the EPPA3;
- 1980, averages of distribution rates derived from the 1979, 1980 and 1981 surveys;
- 1990, averages of distribution rates derived from the 1989, 1990 and 1991 surveys.

#### 3.2.2 Women:
Method, hypothesis and treatment identical to those used for men.

## 4. Projection of activity rates: 2000 - 2010

### 4.1 Model(s): linear, hyperbole and logistic

#### 4.1.1 Men:
- To the [15-54] age groups, application of function F1;
- To the [55+] age groups, application of function F3;
- Modification of the trends for the [15+] age groups.

#### 4.1.2 Women:
- To the [15-24] age groups, application of function F1;
- To the [25-54] age groups, application of function F6;
- To the [55+] age groups, application of function F3;
- Modification of the trends for the [15-54] age groups.

*Notes on adjustments of rates, see p. 3-8.*

*Notes on projection functions, see p. 10.*

# Hungary

## 1. Source(s) of benchmark data

Code(s):     Title(s):

EPPA3     Economically active population: Estimates and Projections, 1950-2025, Third edition, ILO, Geneva, 1986.

BLT-94-2     Popovic B. (1994), "New 1980 and 1990 estimates of activity rates by age and sectoral distribution for some countries of Eastern and Southern Europe" in the Bulletin of Labour of Statistics - 1994-2, ILO, Geneva.

## 2. Estimates of activity rates: 1950 - 1990

### 2.1 Benchmark data:

Table 1: Activity rates by sex and age group

| | Year | | | | |
|---|---|---|---|---|---|
| Age group | 1950 (1) | 1960 (1) | 1970 (1) | 1980 (2) | 1990 (2) |
| **Men** | | | | | |
| 10-14 | 6.65 | 2.20 | 0.75 | 0.26 | 0.23 |
| 15-19 | 79.20 | 75.00 | 64.00 | 60.02 | 52.69 |
| 20-24 | 93.60 | 93.05 | 92.50 | 91.77 | 88.27 |
| 25-29 | 97.65 | 98.00 | 98.35 | 98.14 | 96.72 |
| 30-34 | 98.70 | 98.65 | 98.60 | 98.35 | 97.11 |
| 35-39 | 98.25 | 98.15 | 98.10 | 97.68 | 96.15 |
| 40-44 | 98.05 | 97.55 | 97.00 | 95.95 | 94.31 |
| 45-49 | 97.20 | 96.05 | 95.00 | 92.79 | 90.75 |
| 50-54 | 95.75 | 93.15 | 91.00 | 86.02 | 81.39 |
| 55-59 | 92.45 | 88.00 | 84.50 | 71.72 | 60.46 |
| 60-64 | 83.20 | 76.00 | 75.00 | 12.53 | 3.55 |
| 65+ | 64.40 | 57.00 | 54.00 | 3.82 | 0.98 |
| **Women** | | | | | |
| 10-14 | 6.50 | 3.00 | 2.50 | 0.64 | 0.47 |
| 15-19 | 55.55 | 54.00 | 53.00 | 46.81 | 41.97 |
| 20-24 | 45.00 | 55.40 | 66.00 | 59.96 | 61.22 |
| 25-29 | 35.50 | 48.70 | 65.30 | 69.61 | 64.34 |
| 30-34 | 33.00 | 49.10 | 68.70 | 80.96 | 78.86 |
| 35-39 | 30.00 | 50.70 | 71.00 | 85.03 | 86.62 |
| 40-44 | 29.00 | 51.80 | 69.40 | 83.33 | 87.74 |
| 45-49 | 28.00 | 49.70 | 64.00 | 77.74 | 83.58 |
| 50-54 | 27.00 | 40.30 | 50.00 | 07.49 | 00.49 |
| 55-59 | 28.50 | 30.60 | 29.20 | 18.22 | 5.07 |
| 60-64 | 27.00 | 26.00 | 23.00 | 8.20 | 1.63 |
| 65+ | 20.00 | 20.00 | 18.00 | 3.05 | 0.21 |

Source(s): (1) EPPA3; (2) BLT-94-2.

### 2.2 Method(s):  data from EPPA3 and BLT-94-2.

#### 2.2.1 Men:

- 1950-70, 1950-70 activity rates derived from the EPPA3;
- 1980-90, activity rates derived from the Bulletin of Labour Statistics 1994-2;
adjustment of activity rates of the [15-19] age group.

#### 2.2.2 Women:

Method, hypothesis and treatment identical to those used for men.

## 3. Estimates of distribution rates by activity sector: 1950 - 1990

### 3.1 Benchmark data:

Table 2: Distribution of economically active population by activity sector

| | Agriculture | Industry | | Services |
|---|---|---|---|---|
| Year | | Total | Manufac. | |
| **Men** | | | | |
| 1950 (1) | 51.30 | 26.40 | .. | 22.30 |
| 1960 (1) | 36.60 | 38.40 | .. | 24.90 |
| 1970 (1) | 26.80 | 47.80 | .. | 25.40 |
| 1980 (2) | 20.86 | 47.49 | 28.90 | 31.65 |
| 1990 (2) | 18.91 | 42.36 | 29.30 | 38.73 |
| **Women** | | | | |
| 1950 (1) | 52.90 | 17.30 | ... | 29.80 |
| 1960 (1) | 40.60 | 28.40 | ... | 30.90 |
| 1970 (1) | 22.60 | 40.30 | ... | 37.00 |
| 1980 (2) | 15.21 | 38.15 | 32.51 | 46.64 |
| 1990 (2) | 10.53 | 32.12 | 28.76 | 57.34 |

Source(s): (1) EPPA3; (2) BLT-94-2.

### 3.2 Method(s):  data from BLT-94-5

#### 3.2.1 Men:

- 1950-70, 1950-70 distribution rates derived from the EPPA3;
  1980-90, 1980 and 1990 distribution rates derived from the Bulletin of Labour Statistics, 1994-2.

#### 3.2.2 Women:

Method, hypothesis and treatment identical to those used for men.

## 4. Projection of activity rates: 2000 - 2010

### 4.1 Model(s):  linear, hyperbole and logistic

#### 4.1.1 Men:

- To the [15-19] age group, application of function F1;
- To the [20+] age groups, application of function F3;
- Modification of the trends for the [35+] age groups.

#### 4.1.2 Women:

- To the [15-19] age group, application of function F1;
- To the [20-54] age groups, application of function F6;
- To the [55+] age groups, application of function F3;
- Modification of the trends for the [20+] age groups.

---

*Notes on adjustments of rates, see p. 3-8.*     *Notes on projection functions, see p. 10.*

84

# Iceland

## 1. Source(s) of benchmark data

Code(s): Title(s):

EPPA3 Economically active population: Estimates and Projections, 1950-2025, Third edition, ILO, Geneva, 1986.
YNS-94 Yearbook of Nordic Statistics 1994

## 2. Estimates of activity rates: 1950 - 1990

### 2.1 Benchmark data:

Table 1: Activity rates by sex and age group

| Age group | Year 1950 (1) | 1960 (1) | 1970 (1) | 1980 (1) | 1992 (2) |
|---|---|---|---|---|---|
| **Men** | | | | | |
| 10-14 | 7.50 | 3.00 | 2.05 | 0.00 | 0.00 |
| 15-19 | 80.70 | 65.65 | 62.50 | 57.42 | 48.40 |
| 20-24 | 91.90 | 90.00 | 90.00 | 89.62 | 77.30 |
| 25-29 | 94.20 | 94.45 | 95.50 | 96.92 | 95.00 |
| 30-34 | 98.80 | 97.70 | 97.45 | 96.89 | 97.00 |
| 35-39 | 98.60 | 97.50 | 97.25 | 96.83 | 97.00 |
| 40-44 | 97.75 | 97.70 | 97.55 | 97.49 | 97.50 |
| 45-49 | 97.80 | 97.20 | 97.60 | 97.34 | 97.35 |
| 50-54 | 97.30 | 95.85 | 95.35 | 94.59 | 94.75 |
| 55-59 | 97.15 | 94.90 | 93.05 | 91.79 | 92.47 |
| 60-64 | 93.25 | 92.20 | 91.45 | 90.85 | 91.16 |
| 65+ | 63.00 | 53.00 | 43.00 | 33.00 | 43.48 |
| **Women** | | | | | |
| 10-14 | 3.00 | 1.25 | 0.80 | 0.00 | 0.00 |
| 15-19 | 61.55 | 55.20 | 57.45 | 59.80 | 60.40 |
| 20-24 | 51.35 | 45.30 | 59.30 | 79.00 | 67.60 |
| 25-29 | 34.65 | 29.00 | 46.45 | 76.50 | 76.72 |
| 30-34 | 25.90 | 24.85 | 41.00 | 70.50 | 81.60 |
| 35-39 | 27.80 | 24.85 | 41.05 | 70.70 | 85.12 |
| 40-44 | 29.65 | 28.75 | 44.00 | 68.50 | 88.47 |
| 45-49 | 32.10 | 33.75 | 47.90 | 69.00 | 87.23 |
| 50-54 | 33.35 | 35.60 | 47.75 | 65.40 | 81.23 |
| 55-59 | 34.75 | 36.50 | 43.55 | 52.00 | 79.76 |
| 60-64 | 31.90 | 33.95 | 40.90 | 50.00 | 76.87 |
| 65+ | 12.95 | 15.05 | 14.15 | 13.3 | 23.14 |

Source(s): (1) EPPA3; (2) YNS-94.

### 2.2 Method(s): linear interpolation

#### 2.2.1 Men:

- 1950-80, 1950-80 activity rates derived from the EPPA3;
- 1980, interpolation of 1980 activity rates derived from the EPPA3 and of 1992 adjusted activity rates derived from the 1994 edition of the Yearbook of Nordic Statistics.

#### 2.2.2 Women:

Method, hypothesis and treatment identical to those used for men.

## 3. Estimates of distribution rates by activity sector: 1950 - 1990

### 3.1 Benchmark data:

Table 2: Distribution of economically active population by activity sector

| Year | Agriculture | Industry Total | Manufac. | Services |
|---|---|---|---|---|
| **Men** | | | | |
| 1980 (1) | 14.71 | 45.59 | 27.35 | 39.71 |
| 1992 (2) | 16.25 | 32.50 | 18.75 | 51.25 |
| **Women** | | | | |
| 1980 (1) | 4.17 | 25.00 | 25.00 | 70.83 |
| 1992 (2) | 4.92 | 14.75 | 14.75 | 80.33 |

Source(s): (1) EPPA3; (2) YNS-94.

### 3.2 Method(s): linear interpolation

#### 3.2.1 Men:

- 1950-80, 1950-80 distribution rates derived from the EPPA3;
1983 distribution rates of manufacturing sector has been adjusted on the basis of distribution rates derived from the 1994 Yearbook of Nordic Statistics;
- 1990, interpolation of 1980 distribution rates derived from the EPPA3 and of 1992 distribution rates derived from the Yearbook.

#### 3.2.2 Women:

Method, hypothesis and treatment identical to those used for men.

## 4. Projection of activity rates: 2000 - 2010

### 4.1 Model(s): linear, hyperbole and logistic

#### 4.1.1 Men:

- To the [15-19] and [25-29] age groups, application of function F1;
- To the [20-54] and [30+] age groups, application of function F3;
- Modification of the trend for the [25-29] age group.

#### 4.1.2 Women:

- To the [15-19] age group, application of function F1;
- To the [20-24] and [60+] age groups, application of function F3;
- To the [25-59] age groups, application of function F6;
- Modification of the trends for the [15-24] and [60+] age groups.

*Notes on adjustments of rates, see p. 3-8.*

*Notes on projection functions, see p. 10.*

# India

## 1. Source(s) of benchmark data

Code(s):     Title(s):

EPPA3       Economically active population: Estimates and Projections, 1950-2025, Third edition, ILO, Geneva, 1986.
ADNU        Editions 1984 and 1988 of United Nations Demographic Yearbook, New York.
STAT        Database on Labour Statistics, LABORSTA - Bureau of Statistics, ILO, Geneva.

## 2. Estimates of activity rates: 1950 - 1990

### 2.1 Benchmark data:

Table 1: Activity rates by sex and age group

| Age group | Year 1950 (1) | 1960 (1) | 1970 (1) | 1981 (2) | 1983 (2) | 1990 (3) |
|---|---|---|---|---|---|---|
| **Men** | | | | | | |
| 10-14 | 41.40 | 33.60 | 25.80 | 22.14 | 22.77 | 12.40 |
| 15-19 | 76.95 | 69.40 | 62.40 | 61.69 | 65.18 | 54.63 |
| 20-24 | 93.55 | 90.35 | 89.20 | 88.42 | 89.65 | 86.18 |
| 25-29 | 97.50 | 97.35 | 96.65 | 96.80 | 96.89 | 96.47 |
| 30-34 | 97.80 | 97.70 | 97.70 | 98.32 | 98.54 | 97.03 |
| 35-39 | 97.80 | 97.70 | 97.70 | 98.61 | 98.80 | 98.02 |
| 40-44 | 97.70 | 97.60 | 97.60 | 98.66 | 98.69 | 97.90 |
| 45-49 | 97.35 | 96.95 | 97.20 | 97.48 | 97.48 | 97.76 |
| 50-54 | 96.60 | 95.95 | 95.50 | 95.31 | 94.99 | 96.30 |
| 55-59 | 96.00 | 94.00 | 92.50 | 91.85 | 90.81 | 92.97 |
| 60-64 | 89.60 | 85.25 | 81.65 | 75.62 | 74.32 | 76.48 |
| 65+ | 71.65 | 68.65 | 63.65 | 57.96 | 56.53 | 58.92 |
| **Women** | | | | | | |
| 10-14 | 28.05 | 25.30 | 20.75 | 15.15 | 20.16 | 11.68 |
| 15-19 | 38.25 | 35.40 | 31.00 | 32.36 | 39.70 | 25.05 |
| 20-24 | 45.40 | 42.40 | 36.35 | 35.34 | 44.33 | 34.47 |
| 25-29 | 51.40 | 48.50 | 42.15 | 35.98 | 45.52 | 34.66 |
| 30-34 | 52.40 | 49.50 | 44.30 | 37.09 | 54.71 | 38.70 |
| 35-39 | 53.40 | 51.00 | 45.65 | 38.03 | 47.78 | 36.60 |
| 40-44 | 52.05 | 49.85 | 44.60 | 37.59 | 59.68 | 42.61 |
| 45-49 | 50.25 | 48.30 | 43.50 | 36.36 | 58.52 | 45.17 |
| 50-54 | 46.25 | 44.20 | 39.60 | 31.87 | 43.77 | 36.06 |
| 55-59 | 41.25 | 38.35 | 34.55 | 28.25 | 42.46 | 31.40 |
| 60-64 | 32.70 | 30.45 | 27.15 | 22.11 | 30.07 | 24.24 |
| 65+ | 19.75 | 15.50 | 13.20 | 9.81 | 15.16 | 11.24 |

Source(s): (1) EPPA3; (2) ADNU; (3) STAT.

### 2.2 Method(s): linear interpolation

#### 2.2.1 Men:

- 1950-90, interpolation of 1950-70 activity rates derived from EPPA3 and of activity rates derived from the 1981 census and the 1983 and 1989/90 surveys.

#### 2.2.2 Women:

- 1950-70, 1950-70 adjusted activity rates derived from the EPPA3; the adjustment was made on the basis of the adjustment model for activity rates of women working in agriculture as contributing family workers;
- 1980-90, interpolation of activity rates derived from the 1981 census and of activity rates derived from the 1983 and 1989/90 surveys.

## 3. Estimates of distribution rates by activity sector: 1950 - 1990

### 3.1 Benchmark data:

Table 2: Distribution of economically active population by activity sector

| Year | Agriculture | Industry Total | Manufac. | Services |
|---|---|---|---|---|
| **Men** | | | | |
| 1981 | 65.89 | 15.05 | 12.01 | 19.07 |
| 1983 | 62.41 | 15.58 | .. | 22.00 |
| 1990 | 58.35 | 16.37 | .. | 25.28 |
| **Women** | | | | |
| 1981 | 84.07 | 8.60 | 7.58 | 7.32 |
| 1983 | 81.12 | 10.18 | .. | 8.69 |
| 1990 | 74.82 | 14.47 | .. | 10.71 |

Source(s): STAT.

### 3.2 Method(s): linears interpolation and extrapolation

#### 3.2.1 Men:

- 1970-90, interpolation of 1950-70 distribution rates derived from the EPPA3 and of distribution rates derived from the 1983 and 1989/90 surveys;
- Application of manufacturing/industry ratio derived from the 1981 census.

#### 3.2.2 Women:

- 1950-70, 1950-70 distribution rates derived from the EPPA3;
- 1980-90, interpolation and extrapolation of distribution rates derived from the 1983 census and from the 1989/90 survey;
- Application of manufacturing/industry ratio derived from the 1981 census.

## 4. Projection of activity rates: 2000 - 2010

### 4.1 Model(s): linear, log-linear and hyperbole

#### 4.1.1 Men:

- To the [10-14] age group, application of function F2;
- To the [15+] age groups, application of function F1;
- Modification of the trends for the [10-54] age groups.

#### 4.1.2 Women:

- To the [10-19] and [40-59] age groups, application of function F1;
- To the [20-39] and [60+] age groups, application of function F3;
- To the [10-59] age groups, application of function F1.

*Notes on adjustments of rates, see p. 3-8.*

*Notes on projection functions, see p. 10.*

# Indonesia

## 1. Source(s) of benchmark data

Code(s):     Title(s):

EPPA3     Economically active population: Estimates and Projections, 1950-2025, Third edition, ILO, Geneva, 1986.
STAT     Database on Labour Statistics, LABORSTA - Bureau of Statistics, ILO, Geneva.

## 2. Estimates of activity rates: 1950 - 1990

### 2.1 Benchmark data:

Table 1: Activity rates by sex and age group

| Age group | Year | | | |
|---|---|---|---|---|
| | 1978 | 1982 | 1988 | 1992 |
| **Men** | | | | |
| 10-14 | .. | .. | 13.70 | 12.52 |
| 15-19 | .. | .. | 45.60 | 47.76 |
| 20-24 | .. | .. | 77.30 | 76.75 |
| 25-29 | .. | .. | 94.10 | 93.60 |
| 30-34 | .. | .. | 97.80 | 97.52 |
| 35-39 | .. | .. | 98.60 | 98.68 |
| 40-44 | .. | .. | 98.40 | 98.04 |
| 45-49 | .. | .. | 97.80 | 97.58 |
| 50-54 | .. | .. | 95.40 | 93.84 |
| 55-59 | .. | .. | 89.10 | 89.55 |
| 60-64 | .. | .. | 79.20 | 79.67 |
| 65+ | .. | .. | 56.30 | 56.84 |
| **Women** | | | | |
| 10-14 | .. | 9.00 | 10.90 | 7.97 |
| 15-19 | 36.20 | 33.20 | 36.20 | 34.86 |
| 20-24 | 38.30 | 41.40 | 52.70 | 46.31 |
| 25-29 | 44.40 | 43.90 | 56.50 | 52.18 |
| 30-34 | 52.60 | 47.00 | 58.80 | 54.43 |
| 35-39 | .. | 51.80 | 62.10 | 58.00 |
| 40-44 | | 54.70 | 64.20 | 59.56 |
| 45-49 | .. | 56.70 | 63.60 | 60.55 |
| 50-54 | 52.90 | 51.10 | 60.70 | 57.65 |
| 55-59 | 49.20 | 50.40 | 55.60 | 52.17 |
| 60-64 | 42.30 | 39.30 | 46.10 | 42.73 |
| 65+ | 27 | 23.2 | 25.40 | 25.09 |

Source(s): STAT.

### 2.2 Method(s): arithmetic average

#### 2.2.1 Men:

- 1950-70, 1950-70 activity rates derived from the EPPA3;
- 1990, interpolation of activity rates derived from the 1988 and 1992 surveys.

#### 2.2.2 Women:

- 1950-70, 1950-70 activity rates derived from the EPPA3;
- 1980, average of adjusted activity rates derived from the 1978 and 1982 surveys;
- 1990, average of activity rates derived from the 1988 and 1992 surveys.

## 3. Estimates of distribution rates by activity sector: 1950 - 1990

### 3.1 Benchmark data:

Table 2: Distribution of economically active population by activity sector

| Year | Agriculture | Industry | | Services |
|---|---|---|---|---|
| | | Total | Manufac. | |
| **Men** | | | | |
| 1978 | 62.75 | 8.63 | 5.88 | 28.61 |
| 1982 | 55.16 | 15.16 | 8.47 | 29.68 |
| 1989 | 55.72 | 14.08 | 8.90 | 30.19 |
| 1992 | 53.74 | 15.09 | 8.92 | 31.17 |
| **Women** | | | | |
| 1978 | 57.74 | 10.37 | 10.17 | 31.89 |
| 1982 | 53.77 | 14.47 | 13.90 | 31.77 |
| 1989 | 57.09 | 12.05 | 13.01 | 30.86 |
| 1992 | 55.06 | 13.51 | 12.85 | 31.43 |

Source(s): STAT.

### 3.2 Method(s): weighted average
arithmetic average

#### 3.2.1 Men:

- 1950-70, 1950-70 distribution rates derived from the EPPA3;
- 1980, averages of distribution rates derived from the 1978 and 1982 surveys;
- 1990, weighted averages of distribution rates derived from the 1989 and 1992 surveys.

#### 3.2.2 Women:

Method, hypothesis and treatment identical to those used for men.

## 4. Projection of activity rates: 2000 - 2010

### 4.1 Model(s): linear, log-linear, hyperbole and logistic

#### 4.1.1 Men:

- To the [10-14] and [50+] age groups, application of function F1;
- To the [15-19] age group, application of function F2;
- To the [20-49] age groups, application of function F3;
- Modification of the trends for the [20-44] age groups.

#### 4.1.2 Women:

- To the [10-19] and [65+] age groups, application of function F3;
- To the [20-24] age group, application of function F1;
- To the [25-64] age groups, application of function F6;
- Modification of the trend for the [15-19] age group.

*Notes on adjustments of rates, see p. 3-8.*     *Notes on projection functions, see p. 10.*

# Iran, Islamic Rep. of

## 1. Source(s) of benchmark data

| Code(s): | Title(s): |
|---|---|
| EPPA3 | Economically active population: Estimates and Projections, 1950-2025, Third edition, ILO, Geneva, 1986. |
| ADNU84 | Editions 1984 and 1988 of United Nations Demographic Yearbook, New York. |
| ASTER | Yearbook of Labour Statistics 1945-89 - Retrospective Edition on Population Censuses, ILO, Geneva, 1990. |
| AST92 | Yearbook of Labour Statistics 1992, ILO, Geneva, 1992. |
| STAT | Database on Labour Statistics, LABORSTA - Bureau of Statistics, ILO, Geneva. |

## 2. Estimates of activity rates: 1950 - 1990

### 2.1 Benchmark data:

Table 1: Activity rates by sex and age group

| Age group | Year 1976 (1) | 1986 (2) | 1991 (3) |
|---|---|---|---|
| **Men** | | | |
| 10-14 | 18.41 | 11.44 | 6.86 |
| 15-19 | 53.34 | 50.41 | 42.49 |
| 20-24 | 86.44 | 86.34 | 82.95 |
| 25-29 | 95.74 | 94.08 | 94.28 |
| 30-34 | 97.84 | 96.14 | 97.02 |
| 35-39 | 98.38 | 96.64 | 97.46 |
| 40-44 | 97.72 | 95.84 | 96.76 |
| 45-49 | 96.02 | 93.27 | 94.86 |
| 50-54 | 92.44 | 89.65 | 90.94 |
| 55-59 | 86.25 | 84.05 | 86.96 |
| 60-64 | 77.04 | 76.34 | 78.97 |
| 65+ | 56.40 | 53.10 | 59.48 |
| **Women** | | | |
| 10-14 | 10.75 | 4.49 | 3.90 |
| 15-19 | 15.74 | 9.40 | 11.10 |
| 20-24 | 17.90 | 12.01 | 14.01 |
| 25-29 | 16.11 | 11.15 | 11.50 |
| 30-34 | 14.14 | 11.16 | 11.16 |
| 35-39 | 12.75 | 9.46 | 10.84 |
| 40-44 | 11.72 | 7.79 | 8.79 |
| 45-49 | 10.89 | 6.21 | 6.84 |
| 50-54 | 9.73 | 5.44 | 4.96 |
| 55-59 | 8.10 | 4.84 | 4.13 |
| 60-64 | 6.62 | 4.24 | 3.75 |
| 65+ | 4.48 | 2.80 | 3.45 |

Source(s): (1) ASTER and ADNU84; (2) AST92; (3) STAT.

### 2.2 Method(s): linear interpolation

#### 2.2.1 Men:

- 1950-70, 1950-70 activity rates derived from the EPPA3;
- 1980-90, extrapolation of adjusted activity rates derived from the 1976 and 1991 censuses.

#### 2.2.2 Women:

- 1950-70, 1950-70 adjusted activity rates derived from the EPPA3; the adjustment was made on the basis of the adjustment model for activity rates of women working in agriculture as contributing family workers;
- 1980-90, interpolation adjusted activity rates derived from the 1986 and 1991 censuses; adjustment of activity rates based on the men/women ratio equal to 2/3 in agriculture; modification of the trends for all age groups for 1980 and of the [10-14] and [60+] age groups for 1990.

## 3. Estimates of distribution rates by activity sector: 1950 - 1990

### 3.1 Benchmark data:

Table 2: Distribution of economically active population by activity sector

| Year | Agriculture | Industry Total | Manufac. | Services |
|---|---|---|---|---|
| **Men** | | | | |
| 1976 | 36.88 | 31.27 | 13.69 | 31.84 |
| 1986 | 30.27 | 26.33 | 12.78 | 43.40 |
| **Women** | | | | |
| 1976 | 45.45 | 36.92 | 35.65 | 17.63 |
| 1986 | 27.97 | 24.33 | 23.02 | 47.70 |

Source(s): ASTER.

### 3.2 Method(s): linears interpolation and extrapolation

#### 3.2.1 Men:

- 1950-70, 1950-70 distribution rates derived from the EPPA3;
- 1980-90, interpolation and extrapolation of distribution rates derived from the 1976 and 1986 censuses;
modification of the trends in all sectors.

#### 3.2.2 Women:

- 1950-70, 1950-70 distribution rates of agriculture sector derived from the EPPA3;
adjustment of rates to make allowance for the under-registration of contributing family workers in agriculture;
- 1980-90, interpolation and extrapolation of adjusted distribution rates derived from the 1976 and 1986 censuses; adjustment of distribution rates on the basis of men/women ratio equal to 2/3 in agriculture;
- Application of manufacturing/industry ratio derived from the 1986 census.

## 4. Projection of activity rates: 2000 - 2010

### 4.1 Model(s): linear, log-linear, hyperbolc and logistic

#### 4.1.1 Men:

- To the [10-14] age group, application of function F1;
- To the [15+] age groups, application of function F3;
- Modification of the trends for the [20-24] and [50-54] age groups.

#### 4.1.2 Women:

- To the [10-14] age group, application of function F1;
- To the [15-19] and [54+] age groups, application of function F6;
- To the [20-49] age groups, application of function F2;
- Modification of the trends for the [10-59] age groups.

---

*Notes on adjustments of rates, see p. 3-8.*

*Notes on projection functions, see p. 10.*

# Iraq

## 1. Source(s) of benchmark data

Code(s):    Title(s):

EPPA3    Economically active population: Estimates and Projections, 1950-2025, Third edition, ILO, Geneva, 1986.
ASTER    Yearbook of Labour Statistics 1945-89 - Retrospective Edition on Population Censuses, ILO, Geneva, 1990.
ADNU88    Demographic Yearbook 1988 - Population census statistics - Fortieth Edition, United Nations, New York, 1990.
STAT    Database on Labour Statistics, LABORSTA - Bureau of Statistics, ILO, Geneva.

## 2. Estimates of activity rates: 1950 - 1990

### 2.1 Benchmark data:

Table 1: Activity rates by sex and age group

| Age group | Year 1950 (1) | 1960 (1) | 1970 (1) | 1977 (2) | 1987 (3) |
|---|---|---|---|---|---|
| **Men** | | | | | |
| 10-14 | 35.50 | 29.00 | 24.00 | 10.97 | 6.18 |
| 15-19 | 80.00 | 67.00 | 50.00 | 39.87 | 41.59 |
| 20-24 | 92.00 | 88.50 | 86.00 | 84.93 | 80.70 |
| 25-29 | 96.00 | 96.25 | 96.50 | 96.65 | 94.81 |
| 30-34 | 97.60 | 97.45 | 97.35 | 97.52 | 95.52 |
| 35-39 | 96.75 | 96.75 | 96.80 | 96.79 | 95.43 |
| 40-44 | 96.50 | 96.00 | 95.50 | 94.86 | 94.27 |
| 45-49 | 96.00 | 94.65 | 93.35 | 92.17 | 87.58 |
| 50-54 | 95.00 | 93.00 | 90.00 | 87.75 | 77.98 |
| 55-59 | 94.00 | 90.00 | 86.00 | 82.88 | 72.07 |
| 60-64 | 92.50 | 86.00 | 79.50 | 74.71 | 70.00 |
| 65+ | 80.00 | 68.00 | 59.00 | 54.01 | 47.98 |
| **Women** | | | | | |
| 10-14 | .. | .. | .. | 9.84 | 1.06 |
| 15-19 | .. | .. | .. | 10.86 | 3.57 |
| 20-24 | .. | .. | .. | 15.45 | 14.16 |
| 25-29 | .. | .. | .. | 18.99 | 20.14 |
| 30-34 | .. | .. | .. | 20.84 | 15.28 |
| 35-39 | .. | .. | .. | 19.17 | 12.50 |
| 40-44 | .. | .. | .. | 19.25 | 13.33 |
| 45-49 | .. | .. | .. | 18.60 | 10.14 |
| 50-54 | .. | .. | .. | 18.31 | 7.35 |
| 55-59 | .. | .. | .. | 16.48 | 5.27 |
| 60-64 | .. | .. | .. | 12.96 | 3.81 |
| 65+ | .. | .. | .. | 6.71 | 2.54 |

Source(s): (1) EPPA3; (2) ASTER and ADNU88; (3) STAT.

### 2.2 Method(s): linear extrapolation
weighted average

#### 2.2.1 Men:

- 1950-70, 1950-70 activity rates derived from the EPPA3;
- 1980-90, extrapolation of adjusted activity rates derived from
the 1977 and 1987 censuses;
adjustment of interpolated rates on the basis of variations
in 1970 interpolated rates, in relation to the 1970 activity rates derived
from the EPPA3.

#### 2.2.2 Women:

- 1950-70, 1950-70 adjusted activity rates derived from the EPPA3;
- 1980, weighted average of activity rates derived from
the 1977 and 1987 censuses;
- 1990, application to 1980 estimated activity rates, variations in adjusted
activity rates derived from the 1977 census, in relation to adjusted activity
rates derived from the 1987 census;
adjustment of activity rates to make allowance for the under-registration
of women working in agriculture.

## 3. Estimates of distribution rates by activity sector: 1950 - 1990

### 3.1 Benchmark data:

Table 2: Distribution of economically active population by activity sector

| Year | Agriculture | Industry Total | Manufac. | Services |
|---|---|---|---|---|
| **Men** | | | | |
| 1977 (1) | 23.84 | 24.58 | 9.51 | 51.58 |
| 1987 (2) | 13.21 | 19.81 | 7.14 | 66.98 |
| **Women** | | | | |
| 1977 (1) | 67.60 | 10.89 | 9.31 | 21.52 |
| 1987 (2) | 17.35 | 13.84 | 9.50 | 68.81 |

Source(s): (1) ASTER; (2) STAT.

### 3.2 Method(s): weighted average

#### 3.2.1 Men:

- 1950-70, 1950-70 distribution rates derived from the EPPA3;
- 1980, weighted averages of adjusted distribution rates derived from
the 1977 and 1987 censuses;
- 1990, application to 1980 estimated rates, variations in adjusted rates
derived from the 1977 census, in relation to adjusted rates derived from
the 1987 census.

#### 3.2.2 Women:

Method, hypothesis and treatment identical to those used for men.

## 4. Projection of activity rates: 2000 - 2010

### 4.1 Model(s): linear, log-linear, hyperbole and logistic

#### 4.1.1 Men:

- To the [10-14] age group, application of function F2;
- To the [15-24] and [60+] age groups, application of function F3;
- To the [25-59] age groups, application of function F1;
- Modification of the trends for the [10-14] and [20-59] age groups.

#### 4.1.2 Women:

- To the [10-19] and [65+] age groups, application of function F1;
- To the [20-64] age groups, application of function F6;
- Modification of the trends for all age groups.

*Notes on adjustments of rates, see p. 3-8.*          *Notes on projection functions, see p. 10.*

# Ireland

## 1. Source(s) of benchmark data

Code(s):     Title(s):

EPPA3        Yearbook of Labour Statistics 1945-89 - Retrospective Edition on Population Censuses, ILO, Geneva, 1990.
STAT         Database on Labour Statistics, LABORSTA - Bureau of Statistics, ILO, Geneva.

## 2. Estimates of activity rates: 1950 - 1990

### 2.1 Benchmark data:

Table 1: Activity rates by sex and age group

| Age group | Year | | |
|---|---|---|---|
| | 1989 | 1990 | 1991 |
| **Men** | | | |
| 10-14 | 0.00 | 0.00 | 0.00 |
| 15-19 | 30.35 | 29.98 | 29.25 |
| 20-24 | 82.40 | 82.08 | 81.12 |
| 25-29 | 96.20 | 95.58 | 95.23 |
| 30-34 | 96.86 | 96.96 | 97.01 |
| 35-39 | 96.01 | 96.03 | 96.44 |
| 40-44 | 95.00 | 95.59 | 95.39 |
| 45-49 | 93.19 | 92.72 | 93.50 |
| 50-54 | 88.62 | 89.78 | 89.39 |
| 55-59 | 79.44 | 79.42 | 79.80 |
| 60-64 | 60.93 | 57.19 | 59.37 |
| 65+ | 16.82 | 15.88 | 15.79 |
| **Women** | | | |
| 10-14 | 0.00 | 0.00 | 0.00 |
| 15-19 | 23.39 | 23.57 | 21.11 |
| 20-24 | 73.68 | 73.28 | 73.37 |
| 25-29 | 62.14 | 64.79 | 65.96 |
| 30-34 | 42.05 | 44.65 | 49.43 |
| 35-39 | 30.75 | 34.00 | 38.53 |
| 40-44 | 27.99 | 30.83 | 32.26 |
| 45-49 | 27.00 | 29.28 | 29.50 |
| 50-54 | 23.37 | 26.19 | 27.97 |
| 55-59 | 19.83 | 21.80 | 22.13 |
| 60-64 | 13.27 | 14.51 | 14.04 |
| 65+ | 3.07 | 3.07 | 2.99 |

Source(s): STAT.

### 2.2 Method(s):  linear interpolation

#### 2.2.1 Men:

- 1950-80, 1950-80 activity rates derived from the EPPA3;
- 1990, interpolation of activity rates derived from
the 1989, 1990 and 1991 surveys;
application to interpolated rates, average of variations in activity rates
derived from 1989, 1990 and 1991 surveys, in relation to activity rates
derived from the 1990 survey.

#### 2.2.2 Women:

Method, hypothesis and treatment identical to those used for men.

## 3. Estimates of distribution rates by activity sector: 1950 - 1990

### 3.1 Benchmark data:

Table 2: Distribution of economically active population by activity sector

| Year | Agriculture | Industry | | Services |
|---|---|---|---|---|
| | | Total | Manufac. | |
| **Men** | | | | |
| 1981 | 20.68 | 39.76 | 22.22 | 39.56 |
| 1989 | 20.56 | 32.18 | 20.16 | 47.26 |
| 1990 | 20.44 | 33.17 | 20.56 | 46.38 |
| 1991 | 19.03 | 33.87 | 21.12 | 47.10 |
| **Women** | | | | |
| 1981 | 3.74 | 21.93 | 20.45 | 74.33 |
| 1989 | 3.45 | 19.58 | 18.38 | 76.97 |
| 1990 | 3.70 | 18.76 | 17.57 | 77.53 |
| 1991 | 3.27 | 18.39 | 16.92 | 78.34 |

Source(s): STAT.

### 3.2 Method(s):  arithmetic average

#### 3.2.1 Men:

- 1950-80, 1950-80 distribution rates derived from the EPPA3,
1981 distribution rates of manufacturing sector has been adjusted on the basis
of application to 1980 distribution rates in industry sector,
the manufacturing/industry ratio derived from the 1981;
- 1990, adjusted averages of distribution rates derived from the 1989,
1990 and 1991 surveys.

#### 3.2.2 Women:

Method, hypothesis and treatment identical to those used for men.

## 4. Projection of activity rates: 2000 - 2010

### 4.1 Model(s):  linear, log-linear, hyperbole and logistic

#### 4.1.1 Men:

- To the [15-24] and [55+] age groups, application of function F3;
- To the [25-54] age groups, application of function F1;
- Modification of the trends for the [35-49] age groups.

#### 4.1.2 Women:

- To the [15-19] and [55+] age groups, application of function F3;
- To the [20-29] age groups, application of function F1;
- To the [30-54] age groups, application of function F2;
- Modification of the trends for the [15-24] and [30-54] age groups.

*Notes on adjustments of rates, see p. 3-8.*          *Notes on projection functions, see p. 10.*

# Israel

## 1. Source(s) of benchmark data

Code(s):  Title(s):

EPPA3  Economically active population: Estimates and Projections, 1950-2025, Third edition, ILO, Geneva, 1986.
AST75-93  Editions 1975-1993 of ILO Yearbook of Labour Statistics, Geneva.
ISRCBS  Labour force surveys 1979, special series No. 662, CBS, Jerusalem, 1981.

## 2. Estimates of activity rates: 1950 - 1990

### 2.1 Benchmark data:

Table 1: Activity rates by sex and age group

| Age group | Year 1975 | 1980 | 1985 | 1990 | 1991 | 1992 |
|---|---|---|---|---|---|---|
| **Men** | | | | | | |
| 10-14 | 0.00 | 0.00 | 0.00 | 0.00 | 0.00 | 0.00 |
| 15-19 | 18.50 | 14.30 | 13.60 | 14.10 | 13.9 | 13.50 |
| 20-24 | 40.30 | 41.30 | 42.80 | 40.30 | 42.1 | 42.40 |
| 25-29 | 86.70 | 84.70 | 83.60 | 82.60 | 82.5 | 81.90 |
| 30-39 | 93.80 | 91.10 | 90.20 | 88.00 | 87.4 | 86.90 |
| 40-49 | 92.80 | 90.40 | 89.70 | 87.70 | 86.9 | 87.90 |
| 50-59 | 84.30 | 82.50 | 76.10 | 73.70 | 71.5 | 71.40 |
| 60+ | 29.20 | 27.90 | 21.40 | 20.20 | 18.7 | 18.70 |
| **Women** | | | | | | |
| 10-14 | 0.00 | 0.00 | 0.00 | 0.00 | 0.00 | 0.00 |
| 15-19 | 11.30 | 10.90 | 8.30 | 10.00 | 7.90 | 7.90 |
| 20-24 | 40.40 | 39.90 | 39.30 | 40.70 | 40.10 | 40.00 |
| 25-29 | 44.20 | 52.60 | 55.60 | 58.40 | 58.50 | 58.50 |
| 30-39 | 40.60 | 50.10 | 57.40 | 62.90 | 63.20 | 63.20 |
| 40-49 | 36.80 | 41.70 | 46.40 | 53.10 | 56.90 | 57.00 |
| 50-59 | 22.40 | 26.00 | 24.80 | 28.60 | 30.90 | 30.90 |
| 60+ | 6.00 | 6.60 | 5.60 | 6.30 | 5.50 | 5.60 |

Source(s): AST75-93.

### 2.2 Method(s): linear interpolation

#### 2.2.1 Men:

- 1950-80, 1950-80 activity rates derived from the EPPA3;
- 1990, interpolation of activity rates derived from
the 1975 to 1992 surveys;
adjustment of interpolated rates on the basis of variations
in 1980 interpolated rates, in relation to the 1980 activity rates derived
from the EPPA3.

#### 2.2.2 Women:

- 1950-80, 1950-80 activity rates derived from the EPPA3;
modification of the trends of the [35-54] age groups for 1980;
- 1990, interpolation of adjusted activity rates derived from
the 1975 to 1992 surveys;
adjustment of interpolated rates on the basis of variations
in 1980 interpolated rates, in relation to the 1980 activity rates derived from
the EPPA3.

## 3. Estimates of distribution rates by activity sector: 1950 - 1990

### 3.1 Benchmark data:

Table 2: Distribution of economically active population by activity sector

| Year | Agriculture | Industry Total | Manufac. | Services |
|---|---|---|---|---|
| **Men** | | | | |
| 1979 | 6.91 | 39.91 | 24.85 | 53.19 |
| 1980 | 7.52 | 39.90 | 24.51 | 52.58 |
| 1981 | 7.47 | 39.67 | 24.05 | 52.87 |
| 1989 | 5.99 | 36.72 | 21.67 | 57.29 |
| 1990 | 5.32 | 37.23 | 21.31 | 57.45 |
| 1991 | 4.53 | 38.50 | 20.12 | 56.96 |
| **Women** | | | | |
| 1979 | 3.88 | 17.65 | 12.01 | 78.47 |
| 1980 | 4.06 | 15.94 | 11.55 | 80.00 |
| 1981 | 3.41 | 15.54 | 11.26 | 81.05 |
| 1989 | 2.44 | 15.32 | 8.76 | 82.24 |
| 1990 | 2.37 | 15.39 | 8.57 | 82.24 |
| 1991 | 1.91 | 15.21 | 8.06 | 82.88 |

Source(s): (1) AST75-93.

### 3.2 Method(s): arithmetic average

#### 3.2.1 Men:

- 1950-70, 1950-70 distribution rates derived from the EPPA3;
- 1980-90, averages of distribution rates derived from
the 1979, 1980 and 1981 surveys for 1980 and from the 1989, 1990 and 1991
surveys for 1990.

#### 3.2.2 Women:

Method, hypothesis and treatment identical to those used for men.

## 4. Projection of activity rates: 2000 - 2010

### 4.1 Model(s): linear, log-linear and hyperbole

#### 4.1.1 Men:

- To the [15-24] and [65+] age groups, application of function F2;
- To the [20-64] age groups, application of function F3.

#### 4.1.2 Women:

- To the [15-19] age group, application of function F3;
- To the [20+] age groups, application of function F1.

# Italy

## 1. Source(s) of benchmark data

Code(s):       Title(s):

EPPA3        Yearbook of Labour Statistics 1945-89 - Retrospective Edition on Population Censuses, ILO, Geneva, 1990.
STAT         Database on Labour Statistics, LABORSTA - Bureau of Statistics, ILO, Geneva.

## 2. Estimates of activity rates: 1950 - 1990

### 2.1 Benchmark data:

Table 1: Activity rates by sex and age group

| Age group | Year 1979 | 1980 | 1981 | 1989 | 1990 | 1991 |
|---|---|---|---|---|---|---|
| **Men** | | | | | | |
| 10-14 | 0.00 | 0.00 | 0.00 | 1.12 | 0.00 | 0.00 |
| 15-19 | 33.04 | 33.30 | 33.10 | 30.58 | 24.73 | 23.23 |
| 20-24 | 71.65 | 72.52 | 74.10 | 71.49 | 70.16 | 69.55 |
| 25-29 | 93.72 | 93.00 | 93.00 | 90.65 | 90.39 | 89.46 |
| 30-34 | 98.50 | 98.60 | 98.30 | 96.85 | 96.65 | 96.62 |
| 35-39 | 98.50 | 98.60 | 98.50 | 97.97 | 97.59 | 97.63 |
| 40-44 | 97.90 | 97.70 | 98.00 | 97.27 | 97.31 | 97.19 |
| 45-49 | 96.50 | 96.30 | 96.50 | 95.59 | 95.19 | 95.05 |
| 50-54 | 90.70 | 90.70 | 91.10 | 87.53 | 87.35 | 87.23 |
| 55-59 | 74.20 | 74.80 | 74.90 | 67.76 | 68.51 | 68.92 |
| 60-64 | 37.56 | 39.60 | 39.60 | 35.21 | 35.87 | 37.16 |
| 65+ | 12.56 | 12.62 | 11.90 | 7.90 | 7.97 | 8.10 |
| **Women** | | | | | | |
| 10-14 | 0.00 | 0.00 | 0.00 | 0.38 | 0.00 | 0.00 |
| 15-19 | 28.59 | 28.94 | 29.00 | 26.41 | 21.38 | 19.06 |
| 20-24 | 55.42 | 57.87 | 58.50 | 63.91 | 62.75 | 61.19 |
| 25-29 | 52.94 | 54.64 | 56.50 | 64.83 | 65.29 | 65.06 |
| 30-34 | 46.50 | 48.40 | 50.20 | 62.15 | 62.04 | 62.59 |
| 35-39 | 42.20 | 44.50 | 45.30 | 58.95 | 58.84 | 59.52 |
| 40-44 | 39.20 | 40.30 | 41.90 | 51.64 | 52.76 | 53.76 |
| 45-49 | 30.50 | 30.00 | 37.50 | 44.09 | 44.07 | 45.03 |
| 50-54 | 32.10 | 32.00 | 32.20 | 34.06 | 34.98 | 36.07 |
| 55-59 | 21.10 | 21.40 | 21.30 | 20.20 | 20.38 | 21.15 |
| 60-64 | 10.50 | 11.00 | 11.50 | 9.76 | 10.05 | 10.02 |
| 65+ | 3.63 | 3.48 | 3.4 | 2.00 | 2.18 | 2.24 |

Source(s): STAT.

### 2.2 Method(s):  arithmetic average

#### 2.2.1 Men:

- 1950-70, 1950-70 activity rates derived from the EPPA3;
adjustment of activity rates of the [25+] age groups for 1970;
- 1980, average of activity rates derived from
1980 and 1981 surveys;
modification of the trends of the [10-25] age groups;
- 1990, average of activity rates derived from 1989, 1990
and 1991 surveys;
modification of the trends of the [15-24] age groups.

#### 2.2.2 Women:

- 1950-70, 1950-70 activity rates derived from the EPPA3;
- 1980, average of activity rates derived from
the 1979, 1980 and 1981 surveys;
modification of the trends of the [10-19] age groups;
- 1990, average of activity rates derived from
the 1989, 1990 and 1991 surveys;
modification of the trends of the [10-19] age groups.

## 3. Estimates of distribution rates by activity sector: 1950 - 1990

### 3.1 Benchmark data:

Table 2: Distribution of economically active population by activity sector

| Year | Agriculture | Industry Total | Manufac. | Services |
|---|---|---|---|---|
| **Men** | | | | |
| 1979 | 13.24 | 40.86 | 25.86 | 45.90 |
| 1980 | 10.07 | 41.88 | 26.43 | 48.05 |
| 1981 | 11.79 | 43.36 | 23.94 | 44.85 |
| 1989 | 8.63 | 36.20 | 22.65 | 55.18 |
| 1990 | 8.25 | 36.59 | 22.65 | 55.16 |
| 1991 | 8.14 | 36.73 | 22.35 | 55.13 |
| **Women** | | | | |
| 1979 | 17.20 | 27.38 | 26.26 | 55.42 |
| 1980 | 12.97 | 29.19 | 27.78 | 57.85 |
| 1981 | 13.20 | 28.51 | 24.57 | 58.29 |
| 1989 | 9.40 | 22.86 | 21.29 | 67.73 |
| 1990 | 8.97 | 22.93 | 21.26 | 68.10 |
| 1991 | 8.79 | 22.11 | 20.44 | 69.10 |

Source(s): STAT.

### 3.2 Method(s):  arithmetic average

#### 3.2.1 Men:
1950-80, 1950-80 distribution rates derived from the EPPA3;
- 1980, averages of distribution rates derived from the 1979, 1980
and 1981 surveys;
- 1990, averages of distribution rates derived from the 1989, 1990
and 1991 surveys.

#### 3.2.2 Women:

Method, hypothesis and treatment identical to those used for men.

## 4. Projection of activity rates: 2000 - 2010

### 4.1 Model(s):  hyperbole and logistic

#### 4.1.1 Men:

- To all age groups, application of function F3;
- Modification of the trends for the [20-54] age groups.

#### 4.1.2 Women:

- To the [10-19] and [55+] age groups, application of function F3;
- To the [20-54] age groups, application of function F6;
- Modification of the trends for the [20-24] and [55-59] age groups.

*Notes on adjustments of rates, see p. 3-8.*          *Notes on projection functions, see p. 10.*

92

# Jamaica

## 1. Source(s) of benchmark data

Code(s):     Title(s):
EPPA3     Economically active population: Estimates and Projections, 1950-2025, Third edition, ILO, Geneva, 1986.
STAT     Database on Labour Statistics, LABORSTA - Bureau of Statistics, ILO, Geneva.

## 2. Estimates of activity rates: 1950 - 1990

### 2.1 Benchmark data:

Table 1: Activity rates by sex and age group

| Age group | Year 1980 (1) | 1990 (2) |
|---|---|---|
| **Men** | | |
| 10-14 | 0.60 | 0.30 |
| 15-19 | 52.00 | 39.66 |
| 20-24 | 94.50 | 92.57 |
| 25-29 | 96.60 | 93.91 |
| 30-34 | 97.90 | 96.14 |
| 35-39 | 97.90 | 96.24 |
| 40-44 | 98.00 | 96.33 |
| 45-49 | 97.40 | 95.74 |
| 50-54 | 96.30 | 93.93 |
| 55-59 | 92.50 | 88.80 |
| 60-64 | 84.00 | 78.78 |
| 65+ | 58.90 | 53.64 |
| **Women** | | |
| 10-14 | 0.30 | 0.10 |
| 15-19 | 40.00 | 31.70 |
| 20-24 | 82.50 | 80.33 |
| 25-29 | 87.80 | 82.83 |
| 30-34 | 87.70 | 85.95 |
| 35-39 | 87.60 | 88.46 |
| 40-44 | 87.30 | 88.16 |
| 45-49 | 87.00 | 88.00 |
| 50-54 | 77.00 | 77.89 |
| 55-59 | 70.00 | 72.10 |
| 60-64 | 47.00 | 46.06 |
| 65+ | 9.90 | 23.58 |

Source(s): (1) EPPA3; (2) STAT.

### 2.2 Method(s): linear interpolation

**2.2.1 Men:**

- 1950-80, 1950-80 activity rates derived from the EPPA3;
- 1990, interpolation of 1980 activity rates derived from the EPPA3 and of adjusted activity rates derived from the 1990 survey.

**2.2.2 Women:**

- 1950-80, 1950-80 adjusted activity rates derived from the EPPA3; adjustment of activity rates of the [65+] age groups for 1970 and 1980;
- 1990, interpolation of 1980 adjusted activity rates derived from the EPPA3 and of activity rates derived from the 1990 survey.

## 3. Estimates of distribution rates by activity sector: 1950 - 1990

### 3.1 Benchmark data:

Table 2: Distribution of economically active population by activity sector

| Year | Agriculture | Industry Total | Manufac. | Services |
|---|---|---|---|---|
| **Men** | | | | |
| 1981 | 44.78 | 22.38 | 13.88 | 32.85 |
| 1990 | 33.56 | 32.04 | 18.88 | 34.39 |
| **Women** | | | | |
| 1981 | 20.78 | 7.35 | 6.90 | 71.87 |
| 1990 | 14.53 | 13.11 | 12.42 | 72.36 |

Source(s): STAT.

### 3.2 Method(s): national data

**3.2.1 Men:**

- 1950-80, 1950-80 distribution rates derived from the EPPA3;
- Application of manufacturing/industry ratio derived from the 1981 survey;
- 1990, distribution rates derived from 1981 survey.

**3.2.2 Women:**

Method, hypothesis and treatment identical to those used for men.

## 4. Projection of activity rates: 2000 - 2010

### 4.1 Model(s): linear, log-linear, hyperbole and logistic

**4.1.1 Men:**

- To the [15-19] age group, application of function F2;
- To the [20-24] and [65+] age groups, application of function F1;
- To the [25-64] age groups, application of function F3;
- Modification of the trends for the [20-59] age groups.

**4.1.2 Women:**

- To the [15-19] age group, application of function F2;
- To the [20-59] age groups, application of function F6;
- To the [60+] age groups, application of function F1;
- Modification of the trends for the [20+] age groups.

*Notes on adjustments of rates, see p. 3-8.*

*Notes on projection functions, see p. 10.*

# Japan

## 1. Source(s) of benchmark data

Code(s):     Title(s):

EPPA3        Economically active population: Estimates and Projections, 1950-2025, Third edition, ILO, Geneva, 1986.
STAT         Database on Labour Statistics, LABORSTA - Bureau of Statistics, ILO, Geneva.

## 2. Estimates of activity rates: 1950 - 1990

### 2.1 Benchmark data:

Table 1: Activity rates by sex and age group

|  | Age group | 1980 (1) | 1980 (2) | 1990 (1) | 1990 (2) |
|---|---|---|---|---|---|
| **Men** | | | | | |
| | 10-14 | 0.00 | .. | 0.00 | .. |
| | 15-19 | 20.34 | .. | 19.94 | .. |
| | 20-24 | 74.74 | .. | 75.40 | .. |
| | 25-29 | 97.58 | .. | 96.69 | .. |
| | 30-34 | 98.60 | .. | 98.06 | .. |
| | 35-39 | 98.68 | .. | 98.15 | .. |
| | 40-44 | 98.42 | .. | 98.13 | .. |
| | 45-49 | 97.99 | .. | 97.90 | .. |
| | 50-54 | 97.30 | .. | 97.05 | .. |
| | 55-59 | 93.99 | .. | 93.99 | .. |
| | 60-64 | 81.45 | .. | 76.14 | .. |
| | 65+ | 46.01 | .. | 39.44 | .. |
| **Women** | | | | | |
| | 10-14 | 0.00 | 0.00 | 0.00 | 0.00 |
| | 15-19 | 18.76 | 18.50 | 17.35 | 17.80 |
| | 20-24 | 71.13 | 70.00 | 75.54 | 75.10 |
| | 25-29 | 49.43 | 49.20 | 61.25 | 61.40 |
| | 30-34 | 46.47 | 48.35 | 50.71 | 51.70 |
| | 35-39 | 55.54 | 57.77 | 59.42 | 62.60 |
| | 40-44 | 61.82 | 64.31 | 66.74 | 69.60 |
| | 45-49 | 62.27 | 64.40 | 68.33 | 71.70 |
| | 50-54 | 58.73 | 59.30 | 62.96 | 65.50 |
| | 55-59 | 50.66 | 50.50 | 51.51 | 53.90 |
| | 60-64 | 38.85 | 38.80 | 37.35 | 39.50 |
| | 65+ | 16.14 053 | 15.50 | 14.93 | 16.20 |

Note(s): (1) census; (2) survey.
Source(s): STAT.

### 2.2 Method(s):  weighted average
arithmetic average

#### 2.2.1 Men:

- 1950-80, 1950-80 activity rates derived from the EPPA3;
- 1990, weighted average of activity rates derived from
the 1980 and 1990 censuses.

#### 2.2.2 Women:

- 1950-70, 1950-70 activity rates derived from the EPPA3;
- 1980, average of activity rates derived from
the 1980 census and the 1980 survey;
- 1990, average of activity rates derived from the 1990 survey
and the 1990 census.

## 3. Estimates of distribution rates by activity sector: 1950 - 1990

### 3.1 Benchmark data:

Table 2: Distribution of economically active population by activity sector

|  | Agriculture | Industry Total | Manufac. | Services |
|---|---|---|---|---|
| **Men** | | | | |
| 1985 (1) | 8.22 | 38.39 | 24.47 | 53.39 |
| 1990 (1) | 6.50 | 39.00 | 24.67 | 54.50 |
| **Women** | | | | |
| 1980 (1) | 13.74 | 26.37 | 22.72 | 59.89 |
| 1980 (2) | 13.24 | 28.48 | 24.65 | 58.28 |
| 1990 (1) | 8.17 | 26.45 | 22.63 | 65.39 |
| 1990 (2) | 8.51 | 27.56 | 23.56 | 63.92 |

Note(s): (1) Census; (2) Survey.
Source(s): STAT.

### 3.2 Method(s):  weighted average
arithmetic average

#### 3.2.1 Men:

- 1950-80, 1950-80 distribution rates derived from the EPPA3;
- 1980, weighted averages of adjusted distribution rates derived from
the 1985 and 1990 censuses.

#### 3.2.2 Women:

- 1950-70, 1950-70 distribution rates derived from the EPPA3;
- 1980, averages of distribution rates derived from the 1980 survey
and of from the 1980 census;
- 1990, averages of distribution rates derived from the 1989 survey
and from the 1990 census.

## 4. Projection of activity rates: 2000 - 2010

### 4.1 Model(s):  linear and hyperbole

#### 4.1.1 Men:

- To the [15-24] age groups, application of function F3;
- To the [25+] age groups, application of function F1;
- Modification of the trends for the [25+] age groups.

#### 4.1.2 Women:

- To the [15-44], [50-59] and [65+] age groups, application of function F3;
- To the [45-49] and [60-64] age groups, application of function F1;
- Modification of the trends for the [20-64] age groups.

Notes on adjustments of rates, see p. 3-8.

Notes on projection functions, see p. 10.

# Jordan

## 1. Source(s) of benchmark data

Code(s):     Title(s):

EPPA3     Economically active population: Estimates and Projections, 1950-2025, Third edition, ILO, Geneva, 1986.
ASTER     Yearbook of Labour Statistics 1945-89 - Retrospective Edition on Population Censuses, ILO, Geneva, 1990.
ESCWA     Compedium of Social Statistics Indicators, Third Issue, December 1993, Economic and Social Commission for Western Asia.

## 2. Estimates of activity rates: 1950 - 1990

### 2.1 Benchmark data:

Table 1: Activity rates by sex and age group

| Age group | Year | | | | | |
|---|---|---|---|---|---|---|
| | 1970 (1) | 1960 (1) | 1970 (1) | 1979 (2) | 1980 (1) | 1987 (3) |
| **Men** | | | | | | |
| 10-14 | 17.70 | 13.90 | 10.30 | .. | 6.40 | .. |
| 15-19 | 60.00 | 55.00 | 52.00 | .. | 37.00 | .. |
| 20-24 | 88.20 | 87.30 | 86.70 | .. | 84.50 | .. |
| 25-29 | 96.90 | 96.70 | 96.40 | .. | 96.25 | .. |
| 30-34 | 98.10 | 97.90 | 97.70 | .. | 97.50 | .. |
| 35-39 | 98.10 | 97.90 | 97.70 | .. | 97.50 | .. |
| 40-44 | 96.80 | 96.55 | 96.30 | .. | 96.30 | .. |
| 45-49 | 96.80 | 96.20 | 95.40 | .. | 94.90 | .. |
| 50-54 | 94.10 | 93.40 | 92.70 | .. | 92.20 | .. |
| 55-59 | 90.00 | 89.00 | 88.00 | .. | 87.20 | .. |
| 60-64 | 83.60 | 81.50 | 79.20 | .. | 76.00 | .. |
| 65+ | 55.80 | 51.60 | 47.90 | | 38.70 | |
| **Women** | | | | | | |
| 10-14 | .. | .. | .. | 1.20 | .. | 0.24 |
| 15-19 | .. | .. | .. | 3.44 | .. | 2.15 |
| 20-24 | .. | .. | .. | 15.69 | .. | 20.06 |
| 25-29 | .. | .. | .. | 13.51 | .. | 16.83 |
| 30-34 | .. | .. | .. | 8.66 | .. | 12.03 |
| 35-39 | .. | .. | .. | 5.15 | .. | 8.38 |
| 40-44 | .. | .. | .. | 3.26 | .. | 6.68 |
| 45-49 | .. | .. | .. | 2.38 | .. | 5.72 |
| 50-54 | .. | .. | .. | 2.04 | .. | 4.80 |
| 55-59 | .. | .. | .. | 1.81 | .. | 3.91 |
| 60-64 | .. | .. | .. | 1.06 | .. | 1.23 |
| 65+ | | | | 0.49 | | 0.54 |

Source(s): (1) EPPA3; (2) ASTER; (3) ESCWA.

### 2.2 Method(s):   linears interpolation and extrapolation

#### 2.2.1 Men:

- 1950-80, 1950-80 activity rates derived from the EPPA3;
- 1990, extrapolation of 1950-80 activity rates derived from the EPPA3;
adjustment of extrapolated rates on the basis of variations in 1980
interpolated rates, in relation to the 1980 rates derived from the EPPA3.

#### 2.2.2 Women:

- 1950-70, 1950-70 activity rates derived from the EPPA3;
- 1980-90, interpolation and extrapolation of activity rates derived
the 1979 census and from the 1986 ESCWA estimates;
the adjustment was made on the basis of the adjustment model for
activity rates of women working in agriculture as contributing family workers.

## 3. Estimates of distribution rates by activity sector: 1950 - 1990

### 3.1 Benchmark data:

Table 2: Distribution of economically active population by activity sector

| Year | Agriculture | Industry | | Services |
|---|---|---|---|---|
| | | Total | Manufac. | |
| **Men** | | | | |
| 1950 (1) | 55.00 | 25.70 | .. | 19.30 |
| 1960 (1) | 46.00 | 26.00 | .. | 28.00 |
| 1970 (1) | 28.50 | 26.60 | .. | 44.90 |
| 1979 (2) | 12.13 | 27.17 | 8.05 | 60.69 |
| 1980 (1) | 11.00 | 27.20 | .. | 61.80 |
| **Women** | | | | |
| 1950 (1) | 44.00 | 24.00 | .. | 32.00 |
| 1960 (1) | 35.00 | 24.00 | .. | 41.00 |
| 1970 (1) | 18.00 | 15.50 | .. | 66.50 |
| 1979 (2) | 1.23 | 7.42 | 6.43 | 91.34 |

Source(s): (1) EPPA3; (2) ASTER.

### 3.2 Method(s):   linear extrapolation

#### 3.2.1 Men:

- 1950-80, 1950-80 distribution rates derived from the EPPA3;
- 1990, extrapolation of 1950-80 distribution rates derived from the EPPA3
and distribution rates derived from the 1979 census;
modification of the trends in all sectors.

#### 3.2.2 Women:

- 1950-70, 1950-70 distribution rates derived from the EPPA3;
- 1980-90, extrapolation of 1950-80 distribution rates derived from the EPPA3
and of distribution rates derived from the 1979 census;
modification of the trends in all sectors.

## 4. Projection of activity rates: 2000 - 2010

### 4.1 Model(s):   linear and hyperbole

#### 4.1.1 Men:

- To the [15+] age groups, application of function F3;
- Modification of the trends for the [35-39] and [45-54] age groups.

#### 4.1.2 Women:

- To the [15+] age groups, application of function F1;
- Modification of the trends for the [15+] age groups.

*Notes on adjustments of rates, see p. 3-8.*

*Notes on projection functions, see p. 10.*

# Kazakstan

## 1. Source(s) of benchmark data

Code(s):    Title(s):

BLT-94-2    Vorobiev A. (1994), "Estimates of the economically active population for the fifteen countries of the former USSR
            for the years 1950, 1959, 1970, 1979 and 1989", in the Bulletin of Labour of Statistics - 1994-2, ILO, Geneva.

## 2. Estimates of activity rates: 1950 - 1990

### 2.1 Benchmark data:

Table 1: Activity rates by sex and age group

| Age group | Year | | | | |
|---|---|---|---|---|---|
| | 1950 | 1959 | 1970 | 1979 | 1989 |
| **Men** | | | | | |
| 10-14 | 0.00 | 0.00 | 0.00 | 0.00 | 0.00 |
| 15-19 | 51.92 | 60.15 | 41.55 | 39.04 | 34.45 |
| 20-24 | 83.05 | 87.40 | 87.53 | 88.83 | 82.82 |
| 25-29 | 94.68 | 97.61 | 96.85 | 97.55 | 96.77 |
| 30-34 | 94.22 | 95.66 | 98.30 | 98.71 | 98.09 |
| 35-39 | 93.41 | 95.58 | 98.14 | 98.30 | 98.03 |
| 40-44 | 94.01 | 93.41 | 97.20 | 97.91 | 97.95 |
| 45-49 | 91.67 | 92.13 | 96.08 | 96.72 | 96.64 |
| 50-54 | 85.83 | 86.93 | 88.51 | 90.97 | 92.50 |
| 55-59 | 16.00 | 79.28 | 80.12 | 78.23 | 80.74 |
| 60-64 | 54.69 | 70.10 | 34.56 | 24.59 | 28.94 |
| 65+ | 30.35 | 26.84 | 7.32 | 9.69 | 9.16 |
| **Women** | | | | | |
| 10-14 | 0.00 | 0.00 | 0.00 | 0.00 | 0.00 |
| 15-19 | 48.29 | 50.67 | 33.28 | 33.04 | 25.04 |
| 20-24 | 58.06 | 59.21 | 80.74 | 82.41 | 73.42 |
| 25-29 | 62.36 | 67.69 | 84.42 | 90.69 | 84.70 |
| 30-34 | 60.50 | 59.24 | 82.46 | 92.33 | 88.87 |
| 35-39 | 52.78 | 55.09 | 93.61 | 93.04 | 91.62 |
| 40-44 | 47.64 | 49.79 | 83.11 | 92.36 | 91.85 |
| 45-49 | 46.41 | 46.64 | 82.09 | 88.47 | 88.32 |
| 50-54 | 33.33 | 32.86 | 65.47 | 74.07 | 71.85 |
| 55-59 | 19.83 | 19.91 | 21.71 | 25.10 | 25.95 |
| 60-64 | 9.38 | 11.18 | 8.23 | 7.27 | 12.89 |
| 65+ | 2.94 | 2.10 | 1.76 | 1.66 | 3.12 |

Source(s): BLT-94-2-2

### 2.2 Method(s): weighted average

#### 2.2.1 Men:

- 1950-90, weighted average of 1950, 1959, 1970 and 1989 activity rates
derived from the Bulletin of Labour Statistics 1994-2.

#### 2.2.2 Women:

Method, hypothesis and treatment identical to those used for men.

## 3. Estimates of distribution rates by activity sector: 1950 - 1990

### 3.1 Benchmark data:

Table 2: Distribution of economically active population by activity sector

| Year | Agriculture | Industry | | Services |
|---|---|---|---|---|
| | | Total | Manufac. | |
| **Men** | | | | |
| 1950 | 53.30 | 21.94 | 10.57 | 24.76 |
| 1959 | 38.25 | 24.35 | 10.55 | 37.40 |
| 1970 | 29.30 | 38.08 | 16.09 | 32.62 |
| 1979 | 28.38 | 37.97 | 16.13 | 33.65 |
| 1989 | 28.16 | 37.41 | 15.03 | 34.43 |
| **Women** | | | | |
| 1950 | 58.18 | 14.68 | 9.28 | 27.14 |
| 1959 | 40.44 | 21.20 | 11.98 | 38.36 |
| 1970 | 24.34 | 21.18 | 16.69 | 54.49 |
| 1979 | 20.79 | 24.80 | 15.94 | 54.41 |
| 1989 | 16.00 | 24.78 | 15.78 | 59.22 |

Source(s): BLT-94-2.

### 3.2 Method(s): weighted average

#### 3.2.1 Men:

- 1950-90, weighted averages of 1950, 1959, 1970, 1979 and 1989
distribution rates derived from the Bulletin of Labour Statistics, 1994-2.

#### 3.2.2 Women:

Method, hypothesis and treatment identical to those used for men.

## 4. Projection of activity rates: 2000 - 2010

### 4.1 Model(s): linear, log-linear, hyperbole and logistic

#### 4.1.1 Men:

- To the [15-19] age group, application of function F2;
- To the [20-24] and [60+] age groups, application of function F3;
- To the [25-59] age groups, application of function F1;
- Modification of the trends for the [25-59] age groups.

#### 4.1.2 Women:

- To the [15-19] age group, application of function F3;
- To the [20-24] and [50+] age groups, application of function F1;
- To the [25-49] age groups, application of function F6;
- Modification of the trends for the [15+] age groups.

*Notes on adjustments of rates, see p. 3-8.*          *Notes on projection functions, see p. 10.*

# Kenya

## 1. Source(s) of benchmark data

Code(s):     Title(s):

EPPA3      Economically active population: Estimates and Projections, 1950-2025, Third edition, ILO, Geneva, 1986.

## 2. Estimates of activity rates: 1950 - 1990

### 2.1 Benchmark data:

Table 1: Activity rates by sex and age group

|  | Year | | | |
|---|---|---|---|---|
| Age group | 1950 | 1960 | 1970 | 1980 |
| **Men** | | | | |
| 10-14 | 50.70 | 49.75 | 48.40 | 46.45 |
| 15-19 | 83.00 | 81.80 | 80.00 | 77.35 |
| 20-24 | 94.55 | 94.05 | 93.35 | 92.35 |
| 25-29 | 97.30 | 97.20 | 97.10 | 96.95 |
| 30-34 | 98.00 | 97.95 | 97.80 | 97.65 |
| 35-39 | 98.20 | 98.10 | 97.95 | 97.80 |
| 40-44 | 98.00 | 97.90 | 97.80 | 97.60 |
| 45-49 | 97.25 | 97.20 | 97.10 | 96.90 |
| 50-54 | 96.80 | 96.65 | 96.50 | 96.25 |
| 55-59 | 95.80 | 95.65 | 95.35 | 95.00 |
| 60-64 | 92.65 | 92.35 | 91.90 | 91.25 |
| 65+ | 79.10 | 78.60 | 77.80 | 76.70 |
| **Women** | | | | |
| 10-14 | 38.30 | 37.60 | 36.55 | 35.10 |
| 15-19 | 62.35 | 61.30 | 59.75 | 57.55 |
| 20-24 | 63.15 | 62.50 | 61.50 | 60.10 |
| 25-29 | 67.95 | 67.20 | 66.10 | 64.55 |
| 30-34 | 72.25 | 71.45 | 70.25 | 68.55 |
| 35-39 | 73.55 | 72.80 | 71.70 | 70.10 |
| 40-44 | 76.00 | 75.25 | 74.15 | 72.55 |
| 45-49 | 75.50 | 74.75 | 73.60 | 72.00 |
| 50-54 | 73.90 | 73.00 | 71.70 | 69.85 |
| 55-59 | 71.05 | 70.15 | 68.80 | 66.80 |
| 60-64 | 64.65 | 63.50 | 61.75 | 59.25 |
| 65+ | 44.70 | 43.60 | 42.00 | 39.70 |

Source(s): EPPA3.

### 2.2 Method(s): linears interpolation and extrapolation

**2.2.1 Men:**

- 1950-80, 1950-80 activity rates derived from the EPPA3;
- 1990, extrapolation of 1950-80 activity rates derived from the EPPA3; adjustment of extrapolated rates on the basis of variations in 1980 interpolated rates, in relation to the 1980 rates derived from the EPPA3.

**2.2.2 Women:**

- 1950-90, interpolation and extrapolation of 1950-80 activity rates derived from the EPPA3; adjustment of interpolated and extrapolated rates on the basis of variations in 1980 interpolated rates, in relation to the 1980 adjusted rates derived from the EPPA3; adjustment of 1980 activity rates based on the men/women ratio equal to 1 in agriculture; modification of the trends of the [10-19] for 1990.

## 3. Estimates of distribution rates by activity sector: 1950 - 1990

### 3.1 Benchmark data:

Table 2: Distribution of economically active population by activity sector

|  | Agriculture | Industry | | Services |
|---|---|---|---|---|
| Year | | Total | Manufac. | |
| **Men** | | | | |
| 1950 | 85.00 | 6.50 | .. | 8.50 |
| 1960 | 83.30 | 7.15 | .. | 9.55 |
| 1970 | 80.80 | 8.20 | .. | 11.00 |
| 1980 | 77.20 | 9.80 | .. | 13.00 |
| **Women** | | | | |
| 1950 | 95.00 | 1.00 | .. | 4.00 |
| 1960 | 92.00 | 1.45 | .. | 5.75 |
| 1970 | 90.30 | 1.95 | .. | 7.75 |
| 1980 | 86.30 | 2.75 | .. | 10.95 |

Source(s): EPPA3.

### 3.2 Method(s): linears interpolation and extrapolation

**3.2.1 Men:**

- 1950-80, 1950-80 distribution rates derived from the EPPA3;
- 1990, extrapolation of 1950-80 distribution rates derived from the EPPA3; adjustment of extrapolated rates on the basis of variations in 1980 interpolated rates, in relation to 1980 distribution rates derived from the EPPA3;
- Application of manufacturing/industry ratio estimated for Malawi.

**3.2.2 Women:**

- 1980, distribution rates estimated on the basis of men/women ratio equal to 1 in agriculture;
- 1950-70 and 1990, interpolation and extrapolation of 1950-70 distribution rates derived from the EPPA3 and of estimated rates for 1980; adjustment of 1990 extrapolated rates on the basis of variations in 1980 interpolated rates, in relation to 1980 estimated rates;
- Application of manufacturing/industry ratio estimated for Malawi.

## 4. Projection of activity rates: 2000 - 2010

### 4.1 Model(s): linear and hyperbole

**4.1.1 Men:**

- To all age groups, application of function F1;
- Modification of the trends for the [10-24] and [60+] age groups.

**4.1.2 Women:**

- To the [10-19] age groups, application of function F1;
- To the [20+] age groups, application of function F3;
- Modification of the trends for the [10-14] and [65+] age groups.

*Notes on adjustments of rates, see p. 3-8.*     *Notes on projection functions, see p. 10.*

# Korea, Dem. People's Rep. of

## 1. Source(s) of benchmark data

Code(s):    Title(s):

EPPA3    Economically active population: Estimates and Projections, 1950-2025, Third edition, ILO, Geneva, 1986.

## 2. Estimates of activity rates: 1950 - 1990

### 2.1 Benchmark data:

Table 1: Activity rates by sex and age group

| Age group | Year | | | |
|---|---|---|---|---|
| | 1950 | 1960 | 1970 | 1980 |
| **Men** | | | | |
| 10-14 | 13.00 | 7.00 | 4.75 | 2.40 |
| 15-19 | 78.10 | 64.10 | 54.95 | 42.59 |
| 20-24 | 95.00 | 92.00 | 88.75 | 85.35 |
| 25-29 | 97.00 | 96.50 | 96.00 | 95.50 |
| 30-34 | 98.00 | 97.90 | 97.80 | 97.70 |
| 35-39 | 98.10 | 98.00 | 97.90 | 97.80 |
| 40-44 | 98.00 | 97.70 | 97.65 | 97.10 |
| 45-49 | 97.90 | 97.00 | 96.70 | 96.00 |
| 50-54 | 97.70 | 96.40 | 95.60 | 94.30 |
| 55-59 | 96.00 | 92.00 | 90.00 | 85.00 |
| 60-64 | 92.00 | 84.80 | 82.30 | 75.30 |
| 65+ | 73.10 | 61.10 | 51.40 | 37.40 |
| **Women** | | | | |
| 10-14 | .. | .. | 6.45 | 3.20 |
| 15-19 | .. | .. | 51.00 | 43.20 |
| 20-24 | .. | .. | 74.55 | 77.00 |
| 25-29 | .. | .. | 75.00 | 75.90 |
| 30-34 | .. | .. | 73.80 | 74.50 |
| 35-39 | .. | .. | 72.90 | 73.60 |
| 40-44 | .. | .. | 72.30 | 73.00 |
| 45-49 | .. | .. | 72.00 | 79.00 |
| 50-54 | .. | .. | 71.50 | 72.50 |
| 55-59 | .. | .. | 52.00 | 51.00 |
| 60-64 | .. | .. | 38.00 | 36.00 |
| 65+ | .. | .. | 25.45 | 21.50 |

Source(s): EPPA3.

### 2.2 Method(s):  linear extrapolation

#### 2.2.1 Men:

- 1950-80, 1950-80 activity rates derived from the EPPA3;
- 1990, extrapolation of 1950-80 activity rates derived from the EPPA3;
adjustment of extrapolated rates on the basis of variations in 1980
interpolated rates, in relation to the 1980 rates derived from the EPPA3;
modification of the trends of the [15-19] and [25+] age groups.

#### 2.2.2 Women:

Method, hypothesis and treatment identical to those used for men.

## 3. Estimates of distribution rates by activity sector: 1950 - 1990

### 3.1 Benchmark data:

Table 2: Distribution of economically active population by activity sector

| Year | Agriculture | Industry | | Services |
|---|---|---|---|---|
| | | Total | Manufac. | |
| **Men** | | | | |
| 1950 | 64.00 | 20.00 | .. | 16.00 |
| 1960 | 57.00 | 28.00 | .. | 19.00 |
| 1970 | 48.50 | 33.00 | .. | 22.00 |
| 1980 | 39.00 | 39.00 | .. | 26.00 |
| **Women** | | | | |
| 1950 | 79.50 | 8.60 | .. | 11.90 |
| 1960 | 71.50 | 12.50 | .. | 16.00 |
| 1970 | 62.20 | 16.80 | .. | 21.00 |
| 1980 | 52.00 | 20.00 | .. | 28.00 |

Source(s): EPPA3.

### 3.2 Method(s):  linear extrapolation

#### 3.2.1 Men:

- 1950-80, 1950-80 distribution rates derived from the EPPA3;
- 1990, extrapolation of 1950-80 distribution rates derived from the EPPA3;
modification of the trends in industry and services sectors.

#### 3.2.2 Women:

Method, hypothesis and treatment identical to those used for men.

## 4. Projection of activity rates: 2000 - 2010

### 4.1 Model(s):  log-linear and hyperbole

#### 4.1.1 Men:

- To the [15-19] age group, application of function F2;
- To the [20+] age groups, application of function F3;
- Modification of the trend for the [20-24] age group.

#### 4.1.2 Women:

- To the [15-19] age group, application of function F2;
- To the [20+] age groups, application of function F3;
- Modification of the trends for the [20-64] age groups.

*Notes on adjustments of rates, see p. 3-8.*    *Notes on projection functions, see p. 10.*

# Korea, Republic of

## 1. Source(s) of benchmark data

| Code(s): | Title(s): |
|---|---|
| EPPA3 | Economically active population: Estimates and Projections, 1950-2025, Third edition, ILO, Geneva, 1986. |
| ADNU | Editions 1979, 1984 and 1988 of United Nations Demographic Yearbook, New York. |
| ASTER | Yearbook of Labour Statistics 1945-89 - Retrospective Edition on Population Censuses, ILO, Geneva, 1990. |
| AST90-93 | Editions 1990-1993 of ILO Yearbook of Labour Statistics, Geneva. |
| KNSO | Monthly Statistcs of Korea, National Statistical Office, Séoul. |

## 2. Estimates of activity rates: 1950 - 1990

### 2.1 Benchmark data:

Table 1: Activity rates by sex and age group

| Age group | Year 1975 (1) | 1980 (2) | 1987 (3) | 1988 (3) | 1989 (3) | 1990 (3) | 1991 (3) | 1992 (3) |
|---|---|---|---|---|---|---|---|---|
| **Men** | | | | | | | | |
| 10-14 | .. | 0.70 | 0.00 | 0.00 | 0.00 | 0.00 | .. | .. |
| 15-19 | .. | 26.79 | 17.33 | 15.14 | 12.13 | 11.19 | .. | .. |
| 20-24 | .. | 79.46 | 77.06 | 77.06 | 77.60 | 77.23 | .. | .. |
| 25-29 | .. | 93.02 | 90.34 | 90.57 | 91.51 | 92.53 | .. | .. |
| 30-34 | .. | 97.38 | 96.08 | 96.67 | 97.18 | 97.37 | .. | .. |
| 35-39 | .. | 97.43 | 96.15 | 96.59 | 97.18 | 97.10 | .. | .. |
| 40-44 | .. | 96.86 | 95.30 | 95.70 | 95.40 | 95.70 | .. | .. |
| 45-49 | .. | 95.21 | 92.70 | 93.20 | 93.60 | 94.10 | .. | .. |
| 50-54 | .. | 90.63 | 87.80 | 89.20 | 89.70 | 90.90 | .. | .. |
| 55-59 | .. | 82.52 | 77.40 | 79.70 | 82.40 | 83.60 | .. | .. |
| 60-64 | .. | 68.82 | 64.40 | 65.20 | 65.60 | 67.50 | .. | .. |
| 65+ | .. | 40.63 | 36.20 | 37.00 | 39.00 | 39.60 | .. | .. |
| **Women** | | | | | | | | |
| 10-14 | 4.69 | .. | 0.00 | 0.00 | 0.00 | 0.00 | 0.00 | 0.00 |
| 15-19 | 47.48 | .. | 27.68 | 25.06 | 22.32 | 21.46 | 19.67 | 18.49 |
| 20-24 | 62.89 | .. | 63.88 | 65.32 | 67.22 | 67.16 | 67.87 | 67.26 |
| 25-29 | 35.59 | .. | 40.82 | 41.72 | 48.18 | 47.02 | 47.25 | 48.89 |
| 30-34 | 41.63 | .. | 47.53 | 49.48 | 52.42 | 53.11 | 53.98 | 54.52 |
| 35-39 | 51.15 | .. | 57.97 | 57.00 | 57.26 | 58.36 | 60.53 | 59.53 |
| 40-44 | 58.10 | .. | 60.30 | 60.20 | 61.00 | 60.50 | 60.40 | 60.40 |
| 45-49 | 60.08 | .. | 62.10 | 62.70 | 63.50 | 63.90 | 62.00 | 60.90 |
| 50-54 | 57.55 | .. | 57.00 | 58.00 | 60.40 | 60.00 | 60.00 | 60.80 |
| 55-59 | 51.43 | .. | 49.10 | 49.50 | 52.70 | 54.40 | 54.50 | 54.10 |
| 60-64 | 33.00 | .. | 40.30 | 39.70 | 41.60 | 43.60 | 43.20 | 44.90 |
| 65+ | 12.24 | .. | 15.40 | 15.50 | 18.10 | 18.40 | 18.80 | 19.60 |

Source(s): (1) (2) ADNU et ASTER; (3) KNSO and AST90-93.

### 2.2 Method(s): linears interpolation and extrapolation

#### 2.2.1 Men:

- 1950-70, 1950-70 activity rates derived from the EPPA3;
- 1980-90, extrapolation of adjusted activity rates derived from the 1980 census and 1987 to 1990 surveys;
adjustment of interpolated rates on the basis of variations in 1970 extrapolated rates, in relation to the 1970 activity rates derived from the EPPA3;
modification of the trends of the [15-29] age groups for 1990.

#### 2.2.2 Women:

- 1950-80, 1950-80 adjusted activity rates derived from the EPPA3;
- 1990, interpolation of activity rates derived from the 1975 census and from the 1987 to 1992 surveys;
adjustment of interpolated rates on the basis of variations in 1970 interpolated rates, in relation to the 1970 activity rates derived from the EPPA3.

## 3. Estimates of distribution rates by activity sector: 1950 - 1990

### 3.1 Benchmark data:

Table 2: Distribution of economically active population by activity sector

| Year | Agriculture | Industry Total | Manufac. | Services |
|---|---|---|---|---|
| **Men** | | | | |
| 1989 | 18.05 | 37.98 | 26.77 | 43.97 |
| 1980 | 16.76 | 38.67 | 26.15 | 44.56 |
| 1991 | 15.42 | 39.63 | 26.01 | 44.95 |
| **Women** | | | | |
| 1989 | 21.65 | 30.69 | 28.91 | 47.66 |
| 1990 | 20.41 | 30.00 | 27.93 | 49.60 |
| 1991 | 18.60 | 29.68 | 27.42 | 51.72 |

Source(s): KNSO and AST90-93.

### 3.2 Method(s): arithmetic average

#### 3.2.1 Men:
- 1950-80, 1950-80 distribution rates derived from the EPPA3;
- 1990, averages of distribution rates derived from the 1989, 1990 and 1991 surveys.

#### 3.2.2 Women:

Method, hypothesis and treatment identical to those used for men.

## 4. Projection of activity rates: 2000 - 2010

### 4.1 Model(s): linear, hyperbole and logistic

#### 4.1.1 Men:

- To the [15+] age groups, application of function F3;
- Modification of the trends for the [15-49] age groups.

#### 4.1.2 Women:

- To the [15-24] and [60+] age groups, application of function F1;
- To the [25-59] age groups, application of function F6;
- Modification of the trends for the [15+] age groups.

---

*Notes on adjustments of rates, see p. 3-8.*

*Notes on projection functions, see p. 10.*

# Kuwait

## 1. Source(s) of benchmark data

Code(s):    Title(s):

EPPA3    Economically active population: Estimates and Projections, 1950-2025, Third edition, ILO, Geneva, 1986.
ASTER    Yearbook of Labour Statistics 1945-89 - Retrospective Edition on Population Censuses, ILO, Geneva, 1990.
AST92    Yearbook of Labour Statistics 1992, ILO, Geneva, 1992.

## 2. Estimates of activity rates: 1950 - 1990

### 2.1 Benchmark data:

Table 1: Activity rates by sex and age group

| Age group | Year 1975 (1) | 1980 (1) | 1985 (1) | 1988 (2) |
|---|---|---|---|---|
| **Men** | | | | |
| 10-14 | .. | 0.00 | 0.00 | 0.00 |
| 15-19 | .. | 34.74 | 14.20 | 9.04 |
| 20-24 | .. | 86.16 | 79.67 | 73.32 |
| 25-29 | .. | 97.64 | 97.72 | 97.61 |
| 30-34 | .. | 98.69 | 99.15 | 99.52 |
| 35-39 | .. | 98.49 | 98.96 | 99.33 |
| 40-44 | .. | 97.52 | 96.34 | 97.59 |
| 45-49 | .. | 95.57 | 91.20 | 91.87 |
| 50-54 | .. | 90.92 | 86.61 | 84.83 |
| 55-59 | .. | 84.39 | 79.45 | 79.90 |
| 60-64 | .. | 67.20 | 63.97 | 58.46 |
| 65+ | .. | 33.61 | 20.64 | 15.71 |
| **Women** | | | | |
| 10-14 | 0.00 | 0.00 | 0.00 | 0.00 |
| 15-19 | 4.62 | 4.99 | 6.28 | 4.59 |
| 20-24 | 15.31 | 21.36 | 37.07 | 42.13 |
| 25-29 | 19.81 | 29.92 | 47.38 | 55.32 |
| 30-34 | 18.90 | 27.35 | 45.19 | 52.10 |
| 35-39 | 19.16 | 23.88 | 37.59 | 42.04 |
| 40-44 | 21.42 | 24.13 | 29.54 | 31.77 |
| 45-49 | 19.99 | 21.83 | 24.29 | 22.88 |
| 50-54 | 15.89 | 18.93 | 18.19 | 18.89 |
| 55-59 | 10.41 | 13.21 | 13.14 | 13.44 |
| 60-64 | 6.37 | 7.63 | 7.23 | 10.19 |
| 65+ | 2.61 | 2.80 | 1.48 | 0.69 |

Source(s): (1) ASTER; (2) AST92.

### 2.2 Method(s): linears interpolation and extrapolation

**2.2.1 Men:**

- 1950-70, 1950-70 activity rates derived from the EPPA3;
- 1980-90, interpolation and extrapolation of activity rates derived from the 1977 and 1986 censuses and of activity rates derived from the 1989 survey; adjustment of interpolated and extrapolated rates on the basis of variations in 1980 interpolated rates, in relation to activity rates derived from the 1980 census.

**2.2.2 Women:**

- 1950-70, 1950-70 activity rates derived from the EPPA3;
- 1980-90, interpolation and extrapolation of activity rates derived from the 1975, 1980 and 1985 censuses and from the 1988 survey; adjustment of interpolated and extrapolated rates on the basis of variations in 1980 interpolated rates, in relation to activity rates derived from the 1980 census.

## 3. Estimates of distribution rates by activity sector: 1950 - 1990

### 3.1 Benchmark data:

Table 2: Distribution of economically active population by activity sector

| Year | Agriculture | Industry Total | Manufac. | Services |
|---|---|---|---|---|
| **Men** | | | | |
| 1975 (1) | 2.84 | 25.88 | 9.15 | 71.28 |
| 1980 (1) | 2.15 | 35.93 | 9.61 | 61.92 |
| 1985 (1) | 2.35 | 35.07 | 9.35 | 62.58 |
| 1988 (2) | 1.67 | 32.99 | 9.76 | 65.34 |
| **Women** | | | | |
| 1975 (1) | 0.06 | 1.83 | 0.98 | 98.11 |
| 1980 (1) | 0.13 | 2.52 | 1.16 | 97.35 |
| 1985 (1) | 0.09 | 2.21 | 0.98 | 97.70 |
| 1988 (2) | 0.08 | 1.92 | 0.83 | 98.00 |

Source(s): (1) ASTER; (2) AST91; (3) AST93.

### 3.2 Method(s): linear extrapolation

**3.2.1 Men:**

- 1950-80, 1950-80 distribution rates derived from the EPPA3;
- 1990, extrapolation of distribution rates derived from the 1975, 1980 and 1985 censuses and from the 1988 survey; modification of the trends in all sectors;
- Application of manufacturing/industry ratio derived from the 1988 survey.

**3.2.2 Women:**

Method, hypothesis and treatment identical to those used for men.

## 4. Projection of activity rates: 2000 - 2010

### 4.1 Model(s): linear, hyperbole and logistic

**4.1.1 Men:**

- To the [15-19] age group, application of function F3;
- To the [20+] age groups, application of function F1;
- Modification of the trends for the [20-24] and [60+] age groups.

**4.1.2 Women:**

- To the [15-39] age groups, application of function F1;
- To the [40-64] age groups, application of function F6;
- To the [65+] age group, application of function F3;
- Modification of the trends for the [15-64] age groups.

*Notes on adjustments of rates, see p. 3-8.*          *Notes on projection functions, see p. 10.*

# Kyrgyzstan

## 1. Source(s) of benchmark data

**Code(s):**    **Title(s):**

BLT-94-2    Vorobiev A. (1994), "Estimates of the economically active population for the fifteen countries of the former USSR for the years 1950, 1959, 1970, 1979 and 1989", in the Bulletin of Labour of Statistics - 1994-2, ILO, Geneva.

## 2. Estimates of activity rates: 1950 - 1990

### 2.1 Benchmark data:

Table 1: Activity rates by sex and age group

| Age group | 1950 | 1959 | 1970 | 1979 | 1989 |
|---|---|---|---|---|---|
| **Men** | | | | | |
| 10-14 | 0.00 | 0.00 | 0.00 | 0.00 | 0.00 |
| 15-19 | 48.89 | 51.85 | 35.04 | 37.44 | 27.88 |
| 20-24 | 82.14 | 84.88 | 84.52 | 87.80 | 80.66 |
| 25-29 | 91.84 | 95.35 | 94.44 | 96.88 | 96.28 |
| 30-34 | 92.11 | 95.00 | 98.08 | 98.65 | 98.08 |
| 35-39 | 93.18 | 95.24 | 97.73 | 97.53 | 98.35 |
| 40-44 | 94.29 | 93.75 | 96.55 | 97.87 | 97.01 |
| 45-49 | 90.63 | 91.89 | 95.74 | 96.30 | 95.95 |
| 50-54 | 87.88 | 90.00 | 90.32 | 90.41 | 91.36 |
| 55-59 | 76.92 | 81.48 | 82.86 | 80.56 | 82.61 |
| 60-64 | 64.00 | 74.07 | 46.67 | 26.92 | 28.81 |
| 65+ | 26.79 | 33.93 | 7.25 | 6.67 | 10.29 |
| **Women** | | | | | |
| 10-14 | 0.00 | 0.00 | 0.00 | 0.00 | 0.00 |
| 15-19 | 43.75 | 47.30 | 31.21 | 33.17 | 25.50 |
| 20-24 | 61.70 | 66.67 | 79.57 | 84.05 | 74.03 |
| 25-29 | 68.57 | 76.67 | 85.92 | 90.70 | 84.29 |
| 30-34 | 66.07 | 69.32 | 87.62 | 92.00 | 87.42 |
| 35-39 | 66.10 | 70.49 | 88.76 | 92.50 | 90.32 |
| 40-44 | 59.18 | 63.83 | 87.23 | 92.55 | 91.30 |
| 45-49 | 55.00 | 56.00 | 84.85 | 89.66 | 89.19 |
| 50-54 | 40.43 | 42.86 | 70.21 | 73.86 | 62.07 |
| 55-59 | 26.32 | 28.85 | 27.59 | 26.23 | 23.17 |
| 60-64 | 15.15 | 14.63 | 10.00 | 8.51 | 12.82 |
| 65+ | 2.70 | 3.95 | 1.77 | 2.19 | 3.45 |

Source(s): BLT-94-2-2

### 2.2 Method(s): weighted average

**2.2.1 Men:**

- 1950-90, weighted average of 1950, 1959, 1970 and 1989 activity rates derived from the Bulletin of Labour Statistics 1994-2.

**2.2.2 Women:**

Method, hypothesis and treatment identical to those used for men.

## 3. Estimates of distribution rates by activity sector: 1950 - 1990

### 3.1 Benchmark data:

Table 2: Distribution of economically active population by activity sector

| Year | Agriculture | Industry Total | Manufac. | Services |
|---|---|---|---|---|
| **Men** | | | | |
| 1950 | 69.15 | 13.30 | 9.57 | 17.55 |
| 1959 | 61.37 | 3.01 | 15.89 | 35.62 |
| 1970 | 35.00 | 35.00 | 17.59 | 30.00 |
| 1979 | 34.28 | 34.28 | 15.59 | 31.44 |
| 1989 | 35.57 | 30.78 | 13.74 | 33.65 |
| **Women** | | | | |
| 1950 | 71.74 | 9.32 | 7.76 | 18.94 |
| 1959 | 57.14 | 16.17 | 11.32 | 26.68 |
| 1970 | 36.40 | 23.90 | 17.65 | 39.71 |
| 1979 | 33.66 | 23.46 | 17.32 | 42.88 |
| 1989 | 28.59 | 22.65 | 16.46 | 48.76 |

Source(s): BLT-94-2.

### 3.2 Method(s): weighted average

**3.2.1 Men:**

- 1950-90, weighted averages of 1950, 1959, 1970, 1979 and 1989 distribution rates derived from the Bulletin of Labour Statistics, 1994-2.

**3.2.2 Women:**

Method, hypothesis and treatment identical to those used for men.

## 4. Projection of activity rates: 2000 - 2010

### 4.1 Model(s): linear, hyperbole and logistic

**4.1.1 Men:**

- To the [15-24] and [60+] age groups, application of function F3;
- To the [25-59] age groups, application of function F1;
- Modification of the trends for the [25-59] age groups.

**4.1.2 Women:**

- To the [15-24] and [65+] age groups, application of function F3;
- To the [25-64] age groups, application of function F6;
- Modification of the trends for the [20+];
- Modification of the trends for the [15+] age groups.

# Lao People's Dem. Rep.

## 1. Source(s) of benchmark data

Code(s): Title(s):
EPPA4 Economically active population 1950-2010 - Fourth edition, ILO, Geneva 1996.

## 2. Estimates of activity rates: 1950 - 1990

### 2.1 Benchmark data:

Table 1: Activity rates by sex and age group

| Age group | Year 1950 (1) | 1950 (2) | 1970 (1) | 1970 (2) |
|---|---|---|---|---|
| **Men** | | | | |
| 10-14 | 37.12 | 38.56 | 28.30 | 29.66 |
| 15-19 | 81.62 | 91.66 | 74.84 | 84.50 |
| 20-24 | 90.30 | 97.38 | 88.80 | 97.38 |
| 25-29 | 95.84 | 98.00 | 96.31 | 98.00 |
| 30-34 | 97.23 | 97.93 | 97.53 | 97.93 |
| 35-39 | 97.42 | 96.85 | 97.85 | 96.85 |
| 40-44 | 97.58 | 94.64 | 97.64 | 94.55 |
| 45-49 | 97.10 | 91.62 | 97.13 | 91.48 |
| 50-54 | 95.50 | 89.96 | 95.41 | 88.17 |
| 55-59 | 92.10 | 88.04 | 91.80 | 84.39 |
| 60-64 | 82.55 | 87.72 | 76.21 | 79.45 |
| 65+ | 55.88 | 81.07 | 48.00 | 65.00 |
| **Women** | | | | |
| 10-14 | 43.31 | 29.50 | 32.15 | 26.07 |
| 15-19 | 85.90 | 68.50 | 77.05 | 71.34 |
| 20-24 | 87.06 | 77.59 | 83.57 | 81.17 |
| 25-29 | 84.57 | 76.61 | 83.75 | 80.25 |
| 30-34 | 84.25 | 74.03 | 84.69 | 78.78 |
| 35-39 | 85.81 | 73.25 | 85.98 | 77.39 |
| 40-44 | 86.42 | 72.29 | 86.01 | 75.35 |
| 45-49 | 87.71 | 66.55 | 85.94 | 69.02 |
| 50-54 | 81.61 | 68.64 | 80.24 | 60.04 |
| 55-59 | 78.86 | 53.98 | 73.78 | 52.19 |
| 60-64 | 49.03 | 50.09 | 47.71 | 43.02 |
| 65+ | 34.88 | 39.46 | 27.10 | 31.13 |

Note(s): (1) Thailand; (2) Viet Nam.
Source(s): EPPA4.

### 2.2 Method(s): linear interpolation
arithmetic average

**2.2.1 Men:**

- 1990, average of 1990 activity rates estimated for Thailand and Viet Nam;
- 1950, application to 1990 estimated activity rates, the average
variations in 1950 estimated activity rates for Thailand and Viet Nam,
in relation to 1970 estimated activity rates for these countries;
- 1960-80, interpolation of activity rates estimated for 1950 and 1990;
modification of the trends for all age groups.

**2.2.2 Women:**

Method, hypothesis and treatment identical to those used for men.

## 3. Estimates of distribution rates by activity sector: 1950 - 1990

### 3.1 Benchmark data:

Table 2: Distribution of economically active population by activity sector

| Year | Agriculture | Industry Total | Manufac. | Services |
|---|---|---|---|---|
| **Men** | | | | |
| 1950 (1) | 82.90 | 3.60 | .. | 13.50 |
| 1950 (2) | 81.30 | 4.00 | .. | 14.70 |
| 1970 (1) | 76.25 | 7.45 | .. | 16.30 |
| 1970 (2) | 75.10 | 7.35 | .. | 17.55 |
| **Women** | | | | |
| 1950 (1) | 86.60 | 1.90 | .. | 9.50 |
| 1950 (2) | 85.75 | 2.55 | .. | 11.70 |
| 1970 (1) | 83.65 | 4.45 | .. | 11.90 |
| 1970 (2) | 78.25 | 5.55 | .. | 16.20 |

Note(s): (1) Thailand; (2) Viet Nam.
Source(s): EPPA4.

### 3.2 Method(s): weighted average

**3.2.1 Men:**

- 1950, application to distribution rates estimated for 1990,
average of variations in 1950 distribution rates estimated for Thailand
and Viet Nam, in relation to 1970 distribution rates for those countries;
- 1960-80, weighted averages of estimated rates for 1950 and 1990;
- 1990, averages of 1970 distribution rates estimated for Thailand
and Viet Nam.

**3.2.2 Women:**

Method, hypothesis and treatment identical to those used for men.

## 4. Projection of activity rates: 2000 - 2010

### 4.1 Model(s): linear

**4.1.1 Men:**

- To all age groups, application of function F1;
- Modification of the trends for the [10-19] age groups.

**4.1.2 Women:**

- To all age groups, application of function F1;
- Modification of the trends for the [10-54] age groups.

*Notes on adjustments of rates, see p. 3-8.*

*Notes on projection functions, see p. 10.*

102

# Latvia

## 1. Source(s) of benchmark data

Code(s):    Title(s):

BLT-94-2    Vorobiev A. (1994), "Estimates of the economically active population for the fifteen countries of the former USSR
for the years 1950, 1959, 1970, 1979 and 1989", in the Bulletin of Labour of Statistics - 1994-2, ILO, Geneva.

## 2. Estimates of activity rates: 1950 - 1990

### 2.1 Benchmark data:

Table 1: Activity rates by sex and age group

| Age group | 1950 | 1959 | 1970 | 1979 | 1989 |
|---|---|---|---|---|---|
| **Men** | | | | | |
| 10-14 | 0.00 | 0.00 | 0.00 | 0.00 | 0.00 |
| 15-19 | 55.56 | 57.14 | 40.23 | 33.33 | 32.63 |
| 20-24 | 84.21 | 85.37 | 84.52 | 85.15 | 82.11 |
| 25-29 | 92.73 | 96.47 | 96.59 | 96.77 | 96.19 |
| 30-34 | 93.48 | 94.37 | 96.88 | 98.75 | 97.98 |
| 35-39 | 93.65 | 96.08 | 98.85 | 98.89 | 97.78 |
| 40-44 | 92.31 | 93.02 | 96.25 | 96.63 | 96.05 |
| 45-49 | 92.00 | 93.10 | 96.36 | 96.39 | 98.78 |
| 50-54 | 89.74 | 91.53 | 92.68 | 92.65 | 92.50 |
| 55-59 | 85.19 | 89.13 | 90.38 | 86.67 | 86.11 |
| 60-64 | 56.00 | 72.73 | 43.14 | 42.86 | 51.79 |
| 65+ | 28.57 | 42.47 | 21.74 | 16.67 | 20.62 |
| **Women** | | | | | |
| 10-14 | 0.00 | 0.00 | 0.00 | 0.00 | 0.00 |
| 15-19 | 43.01 | 45.24 | 35.44 | 31.52 | 29.21 |
| 20-24 | 62.50 | 67.42 | 82.28 | 83.33 | 81.11 |
| 25-29 | 71.59 | 79.35 | 92.05 | 93.48 | 90.48 |
| 30-34 | 69.57 | 71.29 | 92.93 | 95.12 | 94.06 |
| 35-39 | 69.32 | 70.37 | 92.47 | 94.79 | 94.68 |
| 40-44 | 92.77 | 69.84 | 91.09 | 95.88 | 95.06 |
| 45-49 | 67.11 | 71.25 | 89.66 | 93.55 | 93.62 |
| 50-54 | 59.70 | 63.64 | 81.36 | 88.78 | 88.17 |
| 55-59 | 41.51 | 44.44 | 40.51 | 43.59 | 50.00 |
| 60-64 | 29.17 | 32.79 | 24.00 | 22.41 | 33.33 |
| 65+ | 10.62 | 12.24 | 6.35 | 7.31 | 11.01 |

Source(s): BLT-94-2.

### 2.2 Method(s): weighted average

**2.2.1 Men:**

- 1950-90, weighted average of 1950, 1959, 1970 and 1989 activity rates
derived from the Bulletin of Labour Statistics 1994-2;
modification of the trends of the [30-34] age group for 1950 and 1960;
modification of the trends of the [60+] age groups for 1960-80.

**2.2.2 Women:**

- 1950-90, weighted average of 1950, 1959, 1970 and 1989 activity rates
derived from the Bulletin of Labour Statistics 1994-2;
modification of the trend for the [65+] age group for 1950.

## 3. Estimates of distribution rates by activity sector: 1950 - 1990

### 3.1 Benchmark data:

Table 2: Distribution of economically active population by activity sector

| Year | Agriculture | Industry Total | Manufac. | Services |
|---|---|---|---|---|
| **Men** | | | | |
| 1950 | 39.22 | 30.50 | 18.95 | 30.28 |
| 1959 | 30.84 | 39.93 | 24.42 | 29.23 |
| 1970 | 19.30 | 50.40 | 30.62 | 30.30 |
| 1979 | 18.44 | 49.41 | 31.12 | 32.15 |
| 1989 | 19.18 | 46.85 | 29.73 | 33.97 |
| **Women** | | | | |
| 1950 | 57.29 | 16.91 | 14.16 | 25.79 |
| 1959 | 38.65 | 25.77 | 21.92 | 35.58 |
| 1970 | 18.99 | 34.97 | 30.22 | 46.04 |
| 1979 | 14.27 | 35.45 | 30.69 | 50.29 |
| 1989 | 12.33 | 32.55 | 28.12 | 55.12 |

Source(s): BLT-94-2.

### 3.2 Method(s): data from BLT-94-11

**3.2.1 Men:**

- 1950, 1960, 1970, 1980 et 1990, respectively 1950, 1959, 1970, 1979
and 1989 distribution rates derived from the Bulletin of Labour Statistics, 1994-

**3.2.2 Women:**

Method, hypothesis and treatment identical to those used for men.

## 4. Projection of activity rates: 2000 - 2010

### 4.1 Model(s): linear, hyperbole and logistic

**4.1.1 Men:**

- To the [15-54] age groups, application of function F1;
- To the [55+] age groups, application of function F3;
- Modification of the trends for the [25-54] age groups.

**4.1.2 Women:**

- To the [15-19] age group, application of function F1;
- To the [20-54] age groups, application of function F6;
- To the [55+] age groups, application of function F3;
- Modification of the trends for the [20+] age groups.

*Notes on adjustments of rates, see p. 3-8.*    *Notes on projection functions, see p. 10.*

# Lebanon

## 1. Source(s) of benchmark data

**Code(s):** **Title(s):**

EPPA3    Economically active population: Estimates and Projections, 1950-2025, Third edition, ILO, Geneva, 1986.

## 2. Estimates of activity rates: 1950 - 1990

### 2.1 Benchmark data:

Table 1: Activity rates by sex and age group

| Age group | Year 1950 | 1960 | 1970 | 1980 |
|---|---|---|---|---|
| **Men** | | | | |
| 10-14 | 22.55 | 12.15 | 6.55 | 5.35 |
| 15-19 | 46.65 | 42.20 | 38.20 | 35.00 |
| 20-24 | 79.75 | 76.25 | 72.90 | 72.00 |
| 25-29 | 96.65 | 95.50 | 94.00 | 93.80 |
| 30-34 | 97.20 | 97.00 | 96.35 | 96.30 |
| 35-39 | 97.50 | 97.20 | 96.90 | 96.80 |
| 40-44 | 97.05 | 96.00 | 96.00 | 95.70 |
| 45-49 | 96.90 | 95.20 | 94.00 | 94.50 |
| 50-54 | 94.00 | 92.00 | 89.00 | 89.00 |
| 55-59 | 92.00 | 86.15 | 80.70 | 79.05 |
| 60-64 | 82.35 | 75.70 | 69.55 | 68.40 |
| 65+ | 58.50 | 46.70 | 42.20 | 41.40 |
| **Women** | | | | |
| 10-14 | 8.00 | 6.40 | 5.90 | 4.20 |
| 15-19 | 9.00 | 10.60 | 16.70 | 17.75 |
| 20-24 | 11.50 | 17.45 | 28.35 | 33.15 |
| 25-29 | 11.00 | 15.50 | 25.00 | 30.05 |
| 30-34 | 10.50 | 13.50 | 20.35 | 24.10 |
| 35-39 | 10.30 | 11.90 | 16.35 | 18.90 |
| 40-44 | 9.60 | 11.30 | 15.10 | 17.05 |
| 45-49 | 9.20 | 10.80 | 13.95 | 15.50 |
| 50-54 | 9.00 | 9.50 | 11.60 | 13.05 |
| 55-59 | 8.70 | 8.50 | 9.10 | 9.90 |
| 60-64 | 8.40 | 8.10 | 8.30 | 8.80 |
| 65+ | 4.20 | 3.40 | 2.85 | 3.00 |

Source(s): EPPA3.

### 2.2 Method(s): linear extrapolation

**2.2.1 Men:**

- 1950-90, 1950-90 adjusted activity rates derived from the EPPA3; adjustment of activity rates based on evaluation of armed forces.

**2.2.2 Women:**

- 1950-80, 1950-80 activity rates derived from the EPPA3;
- 1990, extrapolation of 1950-80 activity rates derived from the EPPA3.

## 3. Estimates of distribution rates by activity sector: 1950 - 1990

### 3.1 Benchmark data:

Table 2: Distribution of economically active population by activity sector

| Year | Agriculture | Industry Total | Manufac. | Services |
|---|---|---|---|---|
| **Men** | | | | |
| 1950 | 52.60 | 21.80 | | 25.60 |
| 1960 | 36.50 | 24.30 | | 39.20 |
| 1970 | 18.90 | 26.40 | | 54.70 |
| 1980 | 12.60 | 29.20 | | 58.20 |
| **Women** | | | | |
| 1950 | 76.20 | 8.50 | | 15.30 |
| 1960 | 49.90 | 14.25 | | 35.85 |
| 1970 | 23.60 | 20.00 | | 56.40 |
| 1980 | 20.00 | 21.00 | | 59.00 |

Source(s): EPPA3.

### 3.2 Method(s): linear extrapolation

**3.2.1 Men:**

- 1950-80, 1950-80 distribution rates derived from the EPPA3;
- 1990, extrapolation of 1950-80 distribution rates of agriculture sector derived from the EPPA3; the distribution rates for agriculture between 1980 and 1990 has been divided up between industry (80%) and services (20%).

**3.2.2 Women:**

- 1950-80, 1950-80 distribution rates derived from the EPPA3;
- 1990, extrapolation of 1950-80 distribution rates of agriculture sector derived from the EPPA3; the distribution rates for agriculture between 1980 and 1990 has been divided up between industry (10%) and services (90%).

## 4. Projection of activity rates: 2000 - 2010

### 4.1 Model(s): linear, log-linear, hyperbole and logistic

**4.1.1 Men:**

- To the [15-19] and [55+] age groups, application of function F3;
- To the [20-54] age groups, application of function F1;
- Modification of the trends for the [20-54] age groups.

**4.1.2 Women:**

- To the [15-29] age groups, application of function F6;
- To the [30-59] age groups, application of function F2;
- To the [60+] age groups, application of function F3;
- Modification of the trends for the [15-59] age groups.

*Notes on adjustments of rates, see p. 3-8.*

*Notes on projection functions, see p. 10.*

# Lesotho

## 1. Source(s) of benchmark data

Code(s):    Title(s):

EPPA3    Economically active population: Estimates and Projections, 1950-2025, Third edition, ILO, Geneva, 1986.
ASTER    Yearbook of Labour Statistics 1945-89 - Retrospective Edition on Population Censuses, ILO, Geneva, 1990.
R1986    1986 Population Census, Statistical tables, Vol II., Bureau of Statistics, Maseru, 1987.

## 2. Estimates of activity rates: 1950 - 1990

### 2.1 Benchmark data:

Table 1: Activity rates by sex and age group

| Age group | 1950 (1) | 1960 (1) | 1970 (1) | 1980 (1) | 1986 (2) |
|---|---|---|---|---|---|
| **Men** | | | | | |
| 10-14 | 51.35 | 44.10 | 40.00 | 32.30 | 34.36 |
| 15-19 | 86.75 | 83.50 | 80.45 | 74.70 | 54.24 |
| 20-24 | 97.85 | 96.80 | 96.00 | 94.30 | 88.65 |
| 25-29 | 98.90 | 98.70 | 98.50 | 98.20 | 97.58 |
| 30-34 | 99.40 | 99.20 | 99.00 | 98.65 | 98.31 |
| 35-39 | 99.45 | 99.30 | 99.10 | 98.75 | 98.22 |
| 40-44 | 99.40 | 99.20 | 99.00 | 98.70 | 97.80 |
| 45-49 | 99.35 | 99.15 | 98.95 | 98.30 | 97.23 |
| 50-54 | 99.25 | 99.05 | 98.85 | 98.20 | 95.79 |
| 55-59 | 99.20 | 97.80 | 97.10 | 95.80 | 93.56 |
| 60-64 | 98.45 | 97.10 | 96.05 | 93.75 | 89.78 |
| 65+ | 83.35 | 83.00 | 80.90 | 73.60 | 77.45 |
| **Women** | | | | | |
| 10-14 | 19.00 | 16.00 | 15.00 | 12.00 | 16.98 |
| 15-19 | 39.50 | 36.50 | 34.75 | 31.10 | 39.04 |
| 20-24 | 81.10 | 78.65 | 75.70 | 71.45 | 53.07 |
| 25-29 | 87.70 | 86.35 | 83.40 | 80.15 | 53.16 |
| 30-34 | 89.75 | 88.35 | 85.35 | 82.00 | 53.67 |
| 35-39 | 90.05 | 88.70 | 85.65 | 82.30 | 54.49 |
| 40-44 | 90.15 | 88.75 | 85.70 | 82.40 | 53.66 |
| 45-49 | 92.60 | 91.50 | 88.80 | 85.05 | 51.42 |
| 50-54 | 90.25 | 89.15 | 86.55 | 82.90 | 47.14 |
| 55-59 | 89.80 | 88.20 | 85.90 | 81.35 | 43.93 |
| 60-64 | 85.85 | 84.35 | 82.15 | 77.80 | 37.25 |
| 65+ | 81.25 | 78.80 | 75.90 | 68.00 | 22.63 |

Source(s): (1) EPPA3; (2) R1986.

### 2.2 Method(s): linears interpolation and extrapolation

#### 2.2.1 Men:
- 1950-90, interpolation and extrapolation of 1950-80 activity rates derived from the EPPA3;
adjustment of interpolated and extrapolated rates on the basis of variations in 1986 interpolated rates, in relation to the rates derived from the 1986 census;
modification of the trends for all age groups from 1950 to 1990.

#### 2.2.2 Women:
- 1950-90, interpolation and extrapolation of 1950-80 activity rates derived from the EPPA3;
adjustment of interpolated and extrapolated rates on the basis of variations in 1986 interpolated rates, in relation to the adjusted rates derived from the 1986 census.

## 3. Estimates of distribution rates by activity sector: 1950 - 1990

### 3.1 Benchmark data:

Table 2: Distribution of economically active population by activity sector

| Year | Agriculture | Industry Total | Manufac. | Services |
|---|---|---|---|---|
| **Men** | | | | |
| 1976 (1) | 23.62 | 57.92 | 2.33 | 18.46 |
| 1986 (2) | 28.87 | 43.44 | 1.76 | 27.69 |
| **Women** | | | | |
| 1976 (1) | 65.80 | 5.57 | 3.52 | 28.63 |
| 1986 (2) | 61.19 | 5.05 | 2.89 | 33.76 |

Source(s): (1) ASTER; (2) R1986.

### 3.2 Method(s): weighted average

#### 3.2.1 Men:
- 1950-90, interpolation and extrapolation of distribution rates derived from the 1976 and 1986 censuses;
modification of the trend in agriculture sector for 1950;
- Application to 1950-60 distribution rates of industry and services sectors, the same proportion in 1970 distribution rates.

#### 3.2.2 Women:
Method, hypothesis and treatment identical to those used for men.

## 4. Projection of activity rates: 2000 - 2010

### 4.1 Model(s): linear and hyperbole

#### 4.1.1 Men:
- To all age groups, application of function F1;
- Modification of the trend for the [65+] age group.

#### 4.1.2 Women:
- To the [10-19] age groups, application of function F1;
- To the [20+] age groups, application of function F3;
- Modification of the trends for the [10-49] age groups.

# Liberia

## 1. Source(s) of benchmark data

Code(s):     Title(s):

ASTER        Yearbook of Labour Statistics 1945-89 - Retrospective Edition on Population Censuses, ILO, Geneva, 1990.

## 2. Estimates of activity rates: 1950 - 1990

### 2.1 Benchmark data:

Table 1: Activity rates by sex and age group

| Age group | Year | | |
|---|---|---|---|
| | 1962 | 1974 | 1984 |
| **Men** | | | |
| 10-14 | 22.39 | 8.60 | .. |
| 15-19 | 46.45 | 21.07 | .. |
| 20-24 | 74.78 | 51.33 | .. |
| 25-29 | 87.30 | 78.36 | .. |
| 30-34 | 92.99 | 88.10 | .. |
| 35-39 | 94.44 | 91.26 | .. |
| 40-44 | 93.91 | 91.65 | .. |
| 45-49 | 93.76 | 91.75 | .. |
| 50-54 | 92.12 | 90.43 | .. |
| 55-59 | 91.13 | 89.61 | .. |
| 60-64 | 81.51 | 80.33 | .. |
| 65+ | 64.30 | 65.97 | .. |
| **Women** | | | |
| 10-14 | 20.12 | 6.75 | 14.18 |
| 15-19 | 34.93 | 15.37 | 25.37 |
| 20-24 | 41.20 | 21.57 | 37.80 |
| 25-29 | 44.25 | 25.42 | 48.47 |
| 30-34 | 47.90 | 28.65 | 56.17 |
| 35-39 | 49.76 | 30.67 | 59.03 |
| 40-44 | 51.05 | 33.51 | 63.74 |
| 45-49 | 49.87 | 33.00 | 63.00 |
| 50-54 | 46.94 | 31.44 | 62.76 |
| 55-59 | 44.35 | 30.38 | 59.09 |
| 60-64 | 31.98 | 23.69 | 49.49 |
| 65+ | 20.38 | 16.20 | 32.47 |

Source(s): ASTER.

### 2.2 Method(s):  linears interpolation and extrapolation

#### 2.2.1 Men:

- 1950-90, interpolation and extrapolation of activity rates derived from the 1962 and 1974 census;
modification of the trends of the [35-44] age groups for 1980 and for the [20-29] age groups for 1990.

#### 2.2.2 Women:

- 1950-90, interpolation and extrapolation of activity rates derived from the 1962, 1974 and 1984 censuses;
modification of the trends for all age groups.

## 3. Estimates of distribution rates by activity sector: 1950 - 1990

### 3.1 Benchmark data:

Table 2: Distribution of economically active population by activity sector

| Year | Agriculture | Industry | | Services |
|---|---|---|---|---|
| | | Total | Manufac. | |
| **Men** | | | | |
| 1962 | 74.52 | 13.03 | 2.96 | 12.45 |
| 1974 | 71.01 | 10.34 | 1.78 | 18.65 |
| 1984 | 67.08 | 9.03 | 2.74 | 23.89 |
| **Women** | | | | |
| 1962 | 95.03 | 0.72 | 0.41 | 4.26 |
| 1974 | 94.19 | 0.50 | 0.13 | 5.31 |
| 1984 | 85.89 | 0.75 | 0.24 | 13.35 |

Source(s): ASTER.

### 3.2 Method(s):  weighted average

#### 3.2.1 Men:

- 1960-80, weighted averages of rates derived from the 1962, 1974 and 1984 censuses;
- 1990, extrapolation of rates derived from the 1974 and 1984 censuses;
- 1950, application to 1950 distribution rates for agriculture sector derived from the EPPA3, 3/4 of 1980-90 trend; distribution rates for industry and services sectors as in distribution for 1960.

#### 3.2.2 Women:

- 1960-80, weighted averages of distribution rates derived from the 1962, 1974 and 1984 censuses;
- 1990, extrapolation of distribution rates derived from the 1974 and 1984 censuses;
- 1950, application to 1950 distribution rates for agriculture sector derived from the EPPA3, half of 1980-90 trend; distribution rates for industry and services sectors as in distribution for 1960.

## 4. Projection of activity rates: 2000 - 2010

### 4.1 Model(s):  log-linear, hyperbole and linear

#### 4.1.1 Men:

- To the [10-19] age groups, application of function F2;
- To the [20-64] age groups, application of function F3;
- To the [60+] age groups, application of function F1;
- Modification of the trends for the [25-29] and [35-39] age groups.

#### 4.1.2 Women:

- To the [10-54] age groups, application of function F1;
- To the [55+] age groups, application of function F3;
- Modification of the trend for the [15-19] age group.

# Libyan Arab Jamahiriya

## 1. Source(s) of benchmark data

**Code(s):** **Title(s):**

EPPA3    Economically active population: Estimates and Projections, 1950-2025, Third edition, ILO, Geneva, 1986.
ASTER    Yearbook of Labour Statistics 1945-89 - Retrospective Edition on Population Censuses, ILO, Geneva, 1990.
ADNU88    Demographic Yearbook 1988 - Population census statistics - Fortieth Edition, United Nations, New York, 1990.
STAT    Database on Labour Statistics, LABORSTA - Bureau of Statistics, ILO, Geneva.

## 2. Estimates of activity rates: 1950 - 1990

### 2.1 Benchmark data:

Table 1: Activity rates by sex and age group

| Age group | Year | | | | |
|---|---|---|---|---|---|
| | 1950 (1) | 1960 (1) | 1970 (1) | 1973 (2) | 1984 (3) |
| **Men** | | | | | |
| 10-14 | 46.75 | 26.50 | 16.00 | 1.90 | 0.00 |
| 15-19 | 72.65 | 58.50 | 57.06 | 27.21 | 20.44 |
| 20-24 | 95.00 | 88.05 | 87.19 | 75.79 | 73.25 |
| 25-29 | 96.30 | 95.40 | 96.55 | 95.96 | 95.50 |
| 30-34 | 96.85 | 96.95 | 97.05 | 97.87 | 97.96 |
| 35-39 | 97.00 | 97.20 | 97.70 | 98.48 | 98.76 |
| 40-44 | 96.70 | 97.05 | 97.40 | 98.23 | 98.53 |
| 45-49 | 96.60 | 96.55 | 96.50 | 96.96 | 97.96 |
| 50-54 | 95.55 | 94.90 | 94.25 | 94.87 | 96.83 |
| 55-59 | 93.05 | 91.40 | 89.75 | 90.63 | 94.23 |
| 60-64 | 91.80 | 86.10 | 80.40 | 80.73 | 89.35 |
| 65+ | 72.85 | 61.55 | 50.25 | 49.35 | 40.98 |
| **Women** | | | | | |
| 10-14 | 6.75 | 5.05 | 2.65 | 1.74 | 0.00 |
| 15-19 | 4.55 | 4.50 | 4.40 | 4.09 | 5.86 |
| 20-24 | 3.65 | 4.75 | 6.30 | 7.38 | 23.08 |
| 25-29 | 2.95 | 4.45 | 6.60 | 8.09 | 19.71 |
| 30-34 | 3.25 | 4.50 | 6.30 | 7.79 | 9.68 |
| 35-39 | 3.60 | 4.75 | 6.40 | 7.40 | 7.68 |
| 40-44 | 4.25 | 5.40 | 7.05 | 7.74 | 7.42 |
| 45-49 | 5.00 | 6.15 | 7.80 | 9.08 | 8.26 |
| 50-54 | 4.75 | 5.90 | 7.55 | 8.83 | 8.93 |
| 55-59 | 3.25 | 4.60 | 6.55 | 7.85 | 9.64 |
| 60-64 | 2.85 | 3.40 | 4.20 | 4.72 | 7.10 |
| 65+ | 2.00 | 1.85 | 1.65 | 1.67 | 1.55 |

**Source(s):** (1) EPPA3; (2) ASTER; (3) ADNU88 and STAT.

### 2.2 Method(s): linears interpolation and extrapolation

#### 2.2.1 Men:

- 1950-90, interpolation and extrapolation of 1950-70 activity rates derived from the EPPA3 and of adjusted activity rates derived from the 1973 census and of activity rates derived from the 1984 census.

#### 2.2.2 Women:

- 1950-70, 1950-70 adjusted activity rates derived from the EPPA3;
- 1980-90, interpolation and extrapolation of 1970 activity rates derived from the EPPA3 and of adjusted activity rates derived from the 1973 and 1984 censuses;
the adjustment was made on the basis of the adjustment model for activity rates of women working in agriculture as contributing family workers.

## 3. Estimates of distribution rates by activity sector: 1950 - 1990

### 3.1 Benchmark data:

Table 2: Distribution of economically active population by activity sector

| Year | Agriculture | Industry | | Services |
|---|---|---|---|---|
| | | Total | Manufac. | |
| **Men** | | | | |
| 1973 (1) | 22.54 | 27.21 | 4.28 | 50.24 |
| 1984 (2) | 12.60 | 29.27 | 6.12 | 58.13 |
| **Women** | | | | |
| 1976 (1) | 38.85 | 6.37 | 4.61 | 54.78 |
| 1984 (2) | 12.12 | 6.49 | 3.99 | 81.39 |

**Source(s):** (1) ASTER; (2) STAT.

### 3.2 Method(s): weighted average
linear extrapolation

#### 3.2.1 Men:

- 1950-70, 1950-70 distribution rates derived from the EPPA3;
- 1980, weighted averages of adjusted distribution rates derived from the 1973 census and of distribution rates derived from the 1984 census;
- 1990, extrapolation of adjusted distribution rates derived from the 1973 census and distribution rates derived from the 1984 census; modification of the trends in all sectors.

#### 3.2.2 Women:

Method, hypothesis and treatment identical to those used for men.

## 4. Projection of activity rates: 2000 - 2010

### 4.1 Model(s): linear and hyperbole

#### 4.1.1 Men:

- To the [15+] age groups, application of function F3;
- Modification of the trends for the [20-59] age groups.

#### 4.1.2 Women:

- To the [15+] age groups, application of function F1;
- Modification of the trends for all age groups.

---

*Notes on adjustments of rates, see p. 3-8.*     *Notes on projection functions, see p. 10.*

# Lithuania

## 1. Source(s) of benchmark data

Code(s):    Title(s):

BLT-94-2    Vorobiev A. (1994), "Estimates of the economically active population for the fifteen countries of the former USSR for the years 1950, 1959, 1970, 1979 and 1989", in the Bulletin of Labour of Statistics - 1994-2, ILO, Geneva.

## 2. Estimates of activity rates: 1950 - 1990

### 2.1 Benchmark data:

Table 1: Activity rates by sex and age group

| Age group | Year 1950 | 1959 | 1970 | 1979 | 1989 |
|---|---|---|---|---|---|
| **Men** | | | | | |
| 10-14 | 0.00 | 0.00 | 0.00 | 0.00 | 0.00 |
| 15-19 | 55.74 | 58.62 | 33.88 | 27.10 | 26.90 |
| 20-24 | 92.59 | 81.98 | 84.11 | 84.17 | 79.17 |
| 25-29 | 93.75 | 94.64 | 97.32 | 97.56 | 96.82 |
| 30-34 | 91.07 | 95.74 | 98.26 | 99.06 | 97.83 |
| 35-39 | 92.19 | 94.37 | 98.21 | 98.25 | 97.50 |
| 40-44 | 91.84 | 93.88 | 97.00 | 97.32 | 97.03 |
| 45-49 | 90.77 | 94.74 | 96.00 | 97.20 | 95.33 |
| 50-54 | 89.09 | 92.94 | 93.62 | 94.25 | 92.08 |
| 55-59 | 84.78 | 89.29 | 88.68 | 89.06 | 86.02 |
| 60-64 | 66.67 | 80.43 | 55.56 | 39.02 | 44.59 |
| 65+ | 48.08 | 52.63 | 20.34 | 12.41 | 14.71 |
| **Women** | | | | | |
| 10-14 | 0.00 | 0.00 | 0.00 | 0.00 | 0.00 |
| 15-19 | 44.60 | 49.17 | 28.70 | 21.53 | 20.00 |
| 20-24 | 68.09 | 70.73 | 80.56 | 80.30 | 72.79 |
| 25-29 | 71.17 | 74.02 | 88.70 | 95.08 | 87.74 |
| 30-34 | 65.85 | 68.00 | 88.00 | 95.54 | 91.43 |
| 35-39 | 65.66 | 66.67 | 88.71 | 95.90 | 93.65 |
| 40-44 | 63.74 | 67.14 | 87.90 | 95.20 | 93.64 |
| 45-49 | 62.96 | 65.88 | 84.31 | 93.50 | 90.83 |
| 50-54 | 57.81 | 60.24 | 75.38 | 86.44 | 85.00 |
| 55-59 | 42.37 | 46.15 | 38.10 | 36.17 | 42.37 |
| 60-64 | 23.08 | 50.75 | 16.87 | 15.63 | 25.66 |
| 65+ | 8.13 | 9.77 | 6.22 | 7.86 | 7.06 |

Source(s): BLT-94-2.

### 2.2 Method(s): weighted average

#### 2.2.1 Men:

- 1950-90, weighted average of 1950, 1959, 1970 and 1989 activity rates derived from the Bulletin of Labour Statistics 1994-2;
adjustment of 1950, 1959, 1970 and 1979 activity rate derived from the Bulletin for the [15-19] and [55+] age groups;
adjustment of estimated activity rate of the [20-24] age group for 1960.

#### 2.2.2 Women:

- 1950-90, weighted average of 1950, 1959, 1970 and 1989 activity rates derived from the Bulletin of Labour Statistics 1994-2;
adjustment of 1950, 1959, 1970 and 1979 activity rate derived from the Bulletin for the [55+] age groups.

## 3. Estimates of distribution rates by activity sector: 1950 - 1990

### 3.1 Benchmark data:

Table 2: Distribution of economically active population by activity sector

| Year | Agriculture | Industry Total | Manufac. | Services |
|---|---|---|---|---|
| **Men** | | | | |
| 1950 | 61.38 | 16.01 | 11.62 | 22.61 |
| 1959 | 48.49 | 27.20 | 16.76 | 24.31 |
| 1970 | 31.26 | 43.96 | 24.78 | 24.78 |
| 1979 | 26.36 | 46.82 | 27.05 | 26.82 |
| 1989 | 23.21 | 46.93 | 27.61 | 29.86 |
| **Women** | | | | |
| 1950 | 73.04 | 9.29 | 8.01 | 17.67 |
| 1959 | 56.80 | 16.64 | 13.76 | 26.56 |
| 1970 | 31.59 | 29.70 | 24.87 | 38.71 |
| 1979 | 29.34 | 29.55 | 24.28 | 41.12 |
| 1989 | 13.35 | 33.70 | 28.01 | 52.95 |

Source(s): BLT-94-2.

### 3.2 Method(s): data from BLT-94-12

#### 3.2.1 Men:

1950, 1960, 1970, 1980 et 1990, respectively 1950, 1959, 1970, 1980 and 1989 distribution rates derived from the Bulletin of Labour Statistics, 1994-

#### 3.2.2 Women:

Method, hypothesis and treatment identical to those used for men.

## 4. Projection of activity rates: 2000 - 2010

### 4.1 Model(s): linear, hyperbole and logistic

#### 4.1.1 Men:

- To the [15-19] and [50+] age groups, application of function F3;
- To the [20-49] age groups, application of function F1;
- Modification of the trends for the [25-54] age groups.

#### 4.1.2 Women:

- To the [15-19] and [55+] age groups, application of function F3;
- To the [20-24] age group, application of function F1;
- To the [25-54] age groups, application of function F6;
- Modification of the trends for the [20-54] age groups.

*Notes on adjustments of rates, see p. 3-8.*

*Notes on projection functions, see p. 10.*

# Luxembourg

## 1. Source(s) of benchmark data

Code(s):    Title(s):
EPPA3      Yearbook of Labour Statistics 1945-89 - Retrospective Edition on Population Censuses, ILO, Geneva, 1990.
STAT       Database on Labour Statistics, LABORSTA - Bureau of Statistics, ILO, Geneva.

## 2. Estimates of activity rates: 1950 - 1990

### 2.1 Benchmark data:

Table 1: Activity rates by sex and age group

| Age group | Year 1950 (1) | 1960 (1) | 1970 (1) | 1980 (1) | 1991 (2) |
|---|---|---|---|---|---|
| **Men** | | | | | |
| 10-14 | 3.25 | 1.65 | 1.00 | 0.00 | 0.00 |
| 15-19 | 73.05 | 58.80 | 53.10 | 47.45 | 29.63 |
| 20-24 | 90.55 | 92.75 | 86.95 | 81.15 | 75.34 |
| 25-29 | 95.15 | 96.45 | 96.05 | 95.60 | 94.02 |
| 30-34 | 96.70 | 97.95 | 98.15 | 98.35 | 97.27 |
| 35-39 | 96.05 | 96.95 | 97.80 | 98.70 | 97.80 |
| 40-44 | 95.30 | 96.90 | 97.35 | 97.80 | 96.86 |
| 45-49 | 95.10 | 95.45 | 95.70 | 95.95 | 94.78 |
| 50-54 | 91.65 | 92.35 | 91.30 | 90.30 | 85.92 |
| 55-59 | 88.45 | 85.65 | 72.75 | 59.85 | 54.78 |
| 60-64 | 58.35 | 55.70 | 43.35 | 31.00 | 19.04 |
| 65+ | 34.45 | 21.15 | 13.35 | 5.50 | 2.09 |
| **Women** | | | | | |
| 10-14 | 2.50 | 1.60 | 1.05 | 0.00 | 0.00 |
| 15-19 | 56.00 | 56.80 | 54.80 | 45.20 | 25.75 |
| 20-24 | 50.00 | 50.60 | 52.90 | 68.70 | 71.04 |
| 25-29 | 34.40 | 30.45 | 33.75 | 55.50 | 68.39 |
| 30-34 | 29.30 | 26.20 | 26.35 | 43.95 | 56.78 |
| 35-39 | 31.30 | 28.30 | 24.50 | 39.70 | 54.60 |
| 40-44 | 33.30 | 30.20 | 24.75 | 35.25 | 51.94 |
| 45-49 | 31.95 | 29.60 | 25.40 | 29.45 | 44.20 |
| 50-54 | 28.65 | 26.50 | 23.80 | 25.10 | 32.86 |
| 55-59 | 27.95 | 21.60 | 19.95 | 19.85 | 19.83 |
| 60-64 | 21.95 | 17.20 | 13.40 | 12.20 | 9.38 |
| 65+ | 13.65 | 9.8 | 4.8 | 2.75 | 0.78 |

Source(s): STAT.

### 2.2 Method(s): weighted average

#### 2.2.1 Men:

- 1950-80, 1950-80 activity rates derived from the EPPA3;
- 1990, weighted average of activity rates of 1980 derived from the EPPA3 and of activity rates derived from the 1991 census.

#### 2.2.2 Women:

Method, hypothesis and treatment identical to those used for men.

## 3. Estimates of distribution rates by activity sector: 1950 - 1990

### 3.1 Benchmark data:

Table 2: Distribution of economically active population by activity sector

| Year | Agriculture | Industry Total | Manufac. | Services |
|---|---|---|---|---|
| **Men** | | | | |
| 1981 | 4.85 | 44.97 | 30.47 | 50.18 |
| 1991 | 3.56 | 36.07 | 30.19 | 60.37 |
| **Women** | | | | |
| 1981 | 5.38 | 10.84 | 8.96 | 83.78 |
| 1991 | 3.26 | 9.27 | 7.39 | 87.47 |

Source(s): (1) STAT.

### 3.2 Method(s): weighted average

#### 3.2.1 Men:
- 1950-80, 1950-80 distribution rates derived from the EPPA3;
- 1990, weighted averages of distribution rates derived from the 1981 and 1991 censuses.

#### 3.2.2 Women:

Method, hypothesis and treatment identical to those used for men.

## 4. Projection of activity rates: 2000 - 2010

### 4.1 Model(s): linear, hyperbole and logistic

#### 4.1.1 Men:
- To the [15-34] and [50+] age groups, application of function F3;
- To the [35-49] age groups, application of function F3;
- Modification of the trends for the [30-49] age groups.

#### 4.1.2 Women:
- To the [15-19] and [50+] age groups, application of function F3;
- To the [20-29] age groups, application of function F6;
- To the [30-49] age groups, application of function F1;
- Modification of the trend for the [20-24] age group.

# Macau, China

## 1. Source(s) of benchmark data

Code(s):   Title(s):

STAT     Database on Labour Statistics, LABORSTA - Bureau of Statistics, ILO, Geneva.

## 2. Estimates of activity rates: 1950 - 1990

### 2.1 Benchmark data:

Table 1: Activity rates by sex and age group

| Age group | 1960 | 1981 | 1991 | 1992 |
|---|---|---|---|---|
| **Men** | | | | |
| 10-14 | .. | 5.97 | 3.86 | .. |
| 15-19 | .. | 57.31 | 59.50 | .. |
| 20-24 | .. | 94.62 | 92.11 | .. |
| 25-29 | .. | 98.49 | 97.94 | .. |
| 30-34 | .. | 98.76 | 98.02 | .. |
| 35-39 | .. | 98.25 | 99.98 | .. |
| 40-44 | .. | 97.17 | 97.24 | .. |
| 45-49 | .. | 95.07 | 95.54 | .. |
| 50-54 | .. | 87.95 | 86.87 | .. |
| 55-59 | .. | 79.85 | 78.08 | .. |
| 60-64 | .. | 72.01 | 57.60 | .. |
| 65+ | | ... | 29.29 | |
| **Women** | | | | |
| 10-14 | 3.95 | 8.18 | ... | ... |
| 15-19 | 16.40 | 57.32 | 29.26 | 29.26 |
| 20-24 | 20.57 | 83.50 | 56.90 | 56.90 |
| 25-29 | 17.13 | 69.71 | 59.53 | 59.53 |
| 30-34 | 18.36 | 53.98 | 53.86 | 53.86 |
| 35-39 | 21.27 | 50.00 | 59.13 | 59.13 |
| 40-44 | 22.84 | 45.97 | 50.99 | 60.93 |
| 45-49 | 21.97 | 39.58 | 52.12 | 52.12 |
| 50-54 | 22.89 | 31.39 | 47.69 | 47.69 |
| 55-59 | 19.49 | 27.58 | 23.54 | 23.54 |
| 60-64 | 17.37 | 19.97 | 21.94 | 21.94 |
| 65+ | 8.26 | 12.30 | 5.11 | 5.11 |

Source(s): STAT.

### 2.2 Method(s): weighted average

#### 2.2.1 Men:

- 1950-90, weighted average of adjusted activity rates derived from the 1981 and 1991 census;
modification of the trends of the [25-29] age groups for 1950-70.

#### 2.2.2 Women:

- 1960, 1980 and 1990, weighted average of activity rates derived from the 1960 and 1980 censuses and from the 1992 official estimates;
- 1950 and 1970, weighted average of 1960 and 1980 estimated activity rates; modification of the trends for all age groups for 1950.

## 3. Estimates of distribution rates by activity sector: 1950 - 1990

### 3.1 Benchmark data:

Table 2: Distribution of economically active population by activity sector

| Year | Agriculture | Industry Total | Manufac. | Services |
|---|---|---|---|---|
| **Men** | | | | |
| 1960 | 6.08 | 30.82 | 25.14 | 63.09 |
| 1981 | 6.50 | 47.47 | 34.46 | 46.03 |
| 1991 | 1.50 | 34.28 | 20.77 | 64.22 |
| **Women** | | | | |
| 1960 | 3.36 | 49.43 | 47.19 | 47.21 |
| 1981 | 5.25 | 64.26 | 62.80 | 30.49 |
| 1991 | 1.23 | 48.63 | 46.52 | 50.14 |

Source(s): STAT.

### 3.2 Method(s): weighted average

#### 3.2.1 Men:

- 1960 et 1980-90, weighted averages of distribution rates derived from the 1960, 1981 and 1991 censuses;
- 1950 and 1970, weighted averages of distribution rates estimated for 1960 and 1980.

#### 3.2.2 Women:

Method, hypothesis and treatment identical to those used for men.

## 4. Projection of activity rates: 2000 - 2010

### 4.1 Model(s): linear, log-linear, hyperbole and logistic

#### 4.1.1 Men:

- To the [15-19] and [55+] age groups, application of function F3;
- To the [20-24] age group, application of function F2;
- To the [25-54] age groups, application of function F1;
- Modification of the trend for the [30-34] age group.

#### 4.1.2 Women:

- To the [15-24] and [60+] age groups, application of function F1;
- To the [25-59] age groups, application of function F6;
- Modification of the trends for the [15-54] age groups.

*Notes on adjustments of rates, see p. 3-8.*    *Notes on projection functions, see p. 10.*

# Macedonia, the former Yugoslav

## 1. Source(s) of benchmark data

| Code(s): | Title(s): |
|---|---|
| BLT-94-2 | Popovic B. (1994), "New 1980 and 1990 estimates of activity rates by age and sectoral distribution for some countries of Eastern and Southern Europe" in the Bulletin of Labour of Statistics - 1994-2, ILO, Geneva. |
| STAT | Database on Labour Statistics, LABORSTA - Bureau of Statistics, ILO, Geneva. |

## 2. Estimates of activity rates: 1950 - 1990

### 2.1 Benchmark data:

Table 1: Activity rates by sex and age group

| Age group | Year 1948 (1) | 1953 (1) | 1961 (1) | 1971 (1) | 1980 (2) | 1990 (2) |
|---|---|---|---|---|---|---|
| **Men** | | | | | | |
| 10-14 | 20.84 | 17.03 | 9.84 | 3.30 | 0.63 | 0.04 |
| 15-19 | 89.34 | 79.29 | 56.27 | 40.69 | 27.13 | 21.91 |
| 20-24 | 96.01 | 93.56 | 89.27 | 77.27 | 76.89 | 76.52 |
| 25-29 | 99.87 | 97.06 | 94.67 | 95.45 | 92.01 | 92.64 |
| 30-34 | 99.99 | 98.78 | 96.95 | 98.31 | 98.12 | 96.30 |
| 35-39 | 99.82 | 98.80 | 98.42 | 97.58 | 98.69 | 96.79 |
| 40-44 | 98.92 | 97.17 | 96.47 | 96.84 | 98.04 | 96.02 |
| 45-49 | 99.18 | 99.96 | 97.98 | 90.83 | 96.28 | 94.91 |
| 50-54 | 96.42 | 96.62 | 97.08 | 87.33 | 88.83 | 85.97 |
| 55-59 | 94.44 | 92.78 | 90.61 | 83.95 | 73.93 | 64.83 |
| 60-64 | 92.46 | 88.73 | 85.01 | 67.87 | 59.77 | 41.20 |
| 65+ | 71.06 | 60.08 | 59.48 | 50.97 | 39.52 | 25.55 |
| **Women** | | | | | | |
| 10-14 | .. | 13.69 | 9.08 | 4.66 | 1.05 | 0.07 |
| 15-19 | .. | 58.59 | 54.39 | 37.98 | 22.34 | 17.73 |
| 20-24 | .. | 50.49 | 49.63 | 48.78 | 50.60 | 61.03 |
| 25-29 | .. | 37.11 | 43.52 | 45.29 | 61.65 | 67.08 |
| 30-34 | .. | 34.75 | 36.34 | 38.44 | 64.34 | 69.04 |
| 35-39 | .. | 30.52 | 32.04 | 36.88 | 59.78 | 69.03 |
| 40-44 | .. | 28.93 | 31.64 | 32.14 | 53.19 | 66.87 |
| 45-49 | .. | 22.07 | 26.52 | 28.70 | 46.39 | 60.54 |
| 50-54 | .. | 17.05 | 22.26 | 26.00 | 36.12 | 50.42 |
| 55-59 | .. | 11.58 | 18.07 | 21.72 | 28.84 | 26.43 |
| 60-64 | .. | 12.44 | 14.41 | 16.39 | 22.77 | 20.89 |
| 65+ | .. | 4.94 | 7.58 | 8.04 | 12.20 | 9.99 |

Source(s): (1) STAT; (2) BLT-94-2.

### 2.2 Method(s): linear extrapolation

#### 2.2.1 Men:

- 1950-70, extrapolation of activity rates derived from the 1948, 1953, 1961 and 1971 censuses;
- 1980-90, 1980 and 1990 activity rates derived from the Bulletin of Labour Statistics 1994-2.

#### 2.2.2 Women:

- 1950-70, extrapolation of activity rates derived from the 1953 census and of adjusted activity rates derived from the 1961 and 1971 censuses;
- 1980-90, 1980 and 1990 activity rates derived from the Bulletin of Labour Statistics 1994-2.

## 3. Estimates of distribution rates by activity sector: 1950 - 1990

### 3.1 Benchmark data:

Table 2: Distribution of economically active population by activity sector

| Year | Agriculture | Industry Total | Manufac. | Services |
|---|---|---|---|---|
| **Men** | | | | |
| 1950 (1) | 72.22 | 11.71 | 3.52 | 16.08 |
| 1960 (1) | 61.01 | 19.78 | 10.18 | 19.21 |
| 1970 (1) | 49.63 | 27.01 | .. | 23.36 |
| 1980 (2) | 29.89 | 38.10 | 20.58 | 32.01 |
| 1990 (2) | 20.84 | 39.88 | 24.46 | 39.27 |
| **Women** | | | | |
| 1950 (1) | 88.70 | 3.55 | 3.20 | 7.75 |
| 1960 (1) | 76.13 | 9.53 | 8.78 | 14.34 |
| 1970 (1) | 62.21 | 16.47 | .. | 21.32 |
| 1980 (2) | 46.88 | 23.01 | 21.04 | 30.10 |
| 1990 (2) | 22.54 | 41.05 | 37.59 | 36.41 |

Source(s): (1) EPPA3; (2) BLT-94-2.

### 3.2 Method(s): data from BLT-94-6

#### 3.2.1 Men:

- 1950-70, 1950-70 distribution rates derived from the EPPA3;
- 1980-90, 1980 and 1990 distribution rates derived from the Bulletin of Labour Statistics, 1994-2.

#### 3.2.2 Women:

Method, hypothesis and treatment identical to those used for men.

## 4. Projection of activity rates: 2000 - 2010

### 4.1 Model(s): linear, hyperbole and logistic

#### 4.1.1 Men:

- To the [15+] age groups, application of function F3;
- Modification of the trends for the [15-39] age groups.

#### 4.1.2 Women:

- To the [15-19] and [65+] age groups, application of function F3;
- To the [20-54] age groups, application of function F6;
- To the [55-64] age groups, application of function F1;
- Modification of the trends for the [15-24] and [50+] age groups.

# Madagascar

## 1. Source(s) of benchmark data

| Code(s): | Title(s): |
|---|---|
| EPPA3 | Economically active population: Estimates and Projections, 1950-2025, Third edition, ILO, Geneva, 1986. |
| ASTER | Yearbook of Labour Statistics 1945-89 - Retrospective Edition on Population Censuses, ILO, Geneva, 1990. |

## 2. Estimates of activity rates: 1950 - 1990

### 2.1 Benchmark data:

Table 1: Activity rates by sex and age group

| Age group | Year 1950 (1) | 1960 (1) | 1970 (1) | 1980 (1) | 1975 (2) | 1980 (1) |
|---|---|---|---|---|---|---|
| **Men** | | | | | | |
| 10-14 | 49.05 | 47.40 | 45.50 | 45.50 | 43.98 | 43.60 |
| 15-19 | 80.85 | 78.65 | 76.15 | 76.15 | 75.21 | 73.60 |
| 20-24 | 93.70 | 92.85 | 91.90 | 91.90 | 89.96 | 90.95 |
| 25-29 | 97.15 | 97.05 | 96.90 | 96.90 | 98.30 | 96.75 |
| 30-34 | 97.85 | 97.75 | 97.60 | 97.60 | 98.99 | 97.40 |
| 35-39 | 98.05 | 97.90 | 97.70 | 97.70 | 99.03 | 97.55 |
| 40-44 | 97.85 | 97.70 | 97.50 | 97.50 | 98.97 | 97.35 |
| 45-49 | 97.15 | 97.00 | 96.85 | 96.85 | 98.90 | 96.70 |
| 50-54 | 96.60 | 96.40 | 96.15 | 96.15 | 98.61 | 95.90 |
| 55-59 | 95.50 | 95.15 | 94.80 | 94.80 | 95.62 | 94.45 |
| 60-64 | 92.15 | 91.60 | 90.95 | 90.95 | 94.14 | 90.35 |
| 65+ | 78.20 | 77.25 | 76.15 | 76.15 | 83.84 | 75.05 |
| **Women** | | | | | | |
| 10-14 | 37.05 | 35.85 | 34.40 | 34.40 | 38.99 | 32.95 |
| 15-19 | 60.50 | 58.65 | 56.50 | 56.50 | 58.20 | 54.35 |
| 20-24 | 62.00 | 60.80 | 59.45 | 59.45 | 69.33 | 58.10 |
| 25-29 | 66.65 | 65.30 | 63.80 | 63.80 | 78.10 | 62.25 |
| 30-34 | 70.85 | 69.40 | 67.75 | 67.75 | 78.42 | 66.10 |
| 35-39 | 72.25 | 70.90 | 69.35 | 69.35 | 79.00 | 67.80 |
| 40-44 | 74.70 | 73.35 | 71.80 | 71.80 | 79.45 | 70.25 |
| 45-49 | 74.15 | 72.80 | 71.25 | 71.25 | 82.55 | 69.65 |
| 50-54 | 72.35 | 70.75 | 68.95 | 68.95 | 82.86 | 67.10 |
| 55-59 | 69.45 | 67.80 | 65.90 | 65.90 | 76.67 | 64.00 |
| 60-64 | 62.60 | 60.50 | 58.10 | 58.10 | 76.73 | 55.65 |
| 65+ | 42.80 | 40.85 | 38.60 | 38.60 | 46.32 | 36.35 |

Source(s): (1) EPPA3; (2) ASTER.

### 2.2 Method(s): linears interpolation and extrapolation

#### 2.2.1 Men:

- 1950-90, interpolation and extrapolation of 1950-80 activity rates derived from the EPPA3;
adjustment of interpolated and extrapolated rates on the basis of variations in 1975 interpolated rates, in relation to the rates derived from the 1975 census;
modification of the trends for all age groups from 1950 to 1970 and of the [10-19] and [65+] age groups for 1980 and 1990.

#### 2.2.2 Women:

- 1950-90, interpolation and extrapolation of 1950-80 activity rates derived from the EPPA3;
adjustment of interpolated and extrapolated rates on the basis of variations in 1975 interpolated rates, in relation to the rates derived from the 1975 census;
modification of the trends for all age groups from 1950 to 1970;
modification of the trends of the [20-64] age groups for 1980 and 1990.

## 3. Estimates of distribution rates by activity sector: 1950 - 1990

### 3.1 Benchmark data:

Table 2: Distribution of economically active population by activity sector

| Year | Agriculture | Industry Total | Manufac. | Services |
|---|---|---|---|---|
| **Men** | | | | |
| 1950 (1) | 82.00 | 5.00 | .. | 13.00 |
| 1960 (1) | 79.00 | 6.00 | .. | 15.00 |
| 1970 (1) | 75.50 | 7.50 | .. | 17.00 |
| 1975 (2) | 73.75 | 8.25 | .. | 18.00 |
| 1980 (1) | 72.00 | 9.00 | .. | 19.00 |
| **Women** | | | | |
| 1950 (1) | 98.50 | 0.35 | .. | 1.15 |
| 1960 (1) | 97.00 | 0.75 | .. | 2.25 |
| 1970 (1) | 95.25 | 1.20 | .. | 3.55 |
| 1975 (2) | 95.00 | 1.70 | .. | 3.30 |
| 1980 (1) | 93.50 | 1.65 | .. | 4.85 |

Source(s): (1) EPPA3; (2) ASTER.

### 3.2 Method(s): linears interpolation and extrapolation

#### 3.2.1 Men:

- 1950-90, interpolation and extrapolation of 1950-80 distribution rates derived from the EPPA3;
adjustment of extrapolated rates on the basis of 3/4 variations in 1975 interpolated rates, in relation to distribution rates derived from the 1975 census.

#### 3.2.2 Women:

- 1950-90, interpolation and extrapolation of 1950 and 1980 adjusted distribution rates derived from the EPPA3;
adjustment of distribution rates on the basis of men/women ratio in agriculture derived from the 1975 census;
distribution rates of manufacturing sector based on manufacturing/industry ratio estimated for Mauritius.

## 4. Projection of activity rates: 2000 - 2010

### 4.1 Model(s): linear

#### 4.1.1 Men:

- To all age groups, application of function F1;
- Modification of the trends for the [10-19] and [60+] age groups.

#### 4.1.2 Women:

- To all age groups, application of function F1;
- Modification of the trends for the [10-59] age groups.

---

*Notes on adjustments of rates, see p. 3-8.*

*Notes on projection functions, see p. 10.*

# Malawi

## 1. Source(s) of benchmark data

Code(s):    Title(s):

EPPA3    Economically active population: Estimates and Projections, 1950-2025, Third edition, ILO, Geneva, 1986.
ASTER    Yearbook of Labour Statistics 1945-89 - Retrospective Edition on Population Censuses, ILO, Geneva, 1990.
R1987    Population Census 1987, National Statistical Office, Zomba.

## 2. Estimates of activity rates: 1950 - 1990

### 2.1 Benchmark data:

Table 1: Activity rates by sex and age group

| Age group | Year 1950 (1) | 1960 (1) | 1970 (1) | 1977 (2) | 1980 (1) | 1987 (3) |
|---|---|---|---|---|---|---|
| **Men** | | | | | | |
| 10-14 | 49.45 | 47.65 | 45.70 | .. | 40.35 | 10.85 |
| 15-19 | 80.50 | 78.05 | 75.45 | .. | 68.25 | 34.28 |
| 20-24 | 93.05 | 92.05 | 91.00 | .. | 88.05 | 72.48 |
| 25-29 | 98.90 | 98.75 | 98.60 | .. | 98.10 | 92.42 |
| 30-34 | 99.15 | 98.95 | 98.75 | .. | 98.25 | 96.17 |
| 35-39 | 99.30 | 99.10 | 98.90 | .. | 98.35 | 96.96 |
| 40-44 | 99.40 | 99.20 | 99.00 | .. | 98.45 | 97.13 |
| 45-49 | 99.20 | 99.05 | 98.85 | .. | 98.35 | 97.14 |
| 50-54 | 99.10 | 99.00 | 98.85 | .. | 98.10 | 96.83 |
| 55-59 | 99.00 | 98.90 | 98.80 | .. | 97.65 | 96.89 |
| 60-64 | 98.55 | 97.85 | 97.10 | .. | 95.05 | 95.12 |
| 65+ | 88.80 | 87.55 | 86.20 | .. | 82.45 | 87.91 |
| **Women** | | | | | | |
| 10-14 | .. | .. | .. | 16.50 | .. | 10.72 |
| 15-19 | .. | .. | .. | 43.81 | .. | 49.57 |
| 20-24 | .. | .. | .. | 60.71 | .. | 73.51 |
| 25-29 | .. | .. | .. | 65.24 | .. | 78.72 |
| 30-34 | .. | .. | .. | 69.00 | .. | 82.23 |
| 35-39 | .. | .. | .. | 71.42 | .. | 84.59 |
| 40-44 | .. | .. | .. | 73.49 | .. | 87.04 |
| 45-49 | .. | .. | .. | 73.29 | .. | 88.72 |
| 50-54 | .. | .. | .. | 72.96 | .. | 89.50 |
| 55-59 | .. | .. | .. | 76.45 | .. | 89.94 |
| 60-64 | .. | .. | .. | 68.60 | .. | 83.93 |
| 65+ | .. | .. | .. | 55.19 | .. | 71.35 |

Source(s): (1) EPPA3; (2) ASTER; (3) R1987.

### 2.2 Method(s): linears interpolation and extrapolation

#### 2.2.1 Men:

- 1950-90, interpolation and extrapolation of 1950-80 activity rates
derived from the EPPA3;
adjustment of interpolated and extrapolated rates on the basis of variations
in 1987 interpolated rates, in relation to the rates derived from
the 1987 census;
modification of the trends of the [10+] age groups for 1990.

#### 2.2.2 Women:

- 1950-90, interpolation and extrapolation of adjusted activity rates derived from
the 1977 and 1987 censuses.

## 3. Estimates of distribution rates by activity sector: 1950 - 1990

### 3.1 Benchmark data:

Table 2: Distribution of economically active population by activity sector

| Year | Agriculture | Industry Total | Manufac. | Services |
|---|---|---|---|---|
| **Men** | | | | |
| 1950 (1) | 93.75 | 2.60 | .. | 3.65 |
| 1960 (1) | 90.00 | 4.00 | .. | 6.00 |
| 1970 (1) | 86.00 | 6.00 | .. | 8.00 |
| 1977 (2) | 78.08 | 9.91 | 5.65 | 12.00 |
| 1987 (3) | 78.39 | 8.46 | 4.81 | 13.15 |
| **Women** | | | | |
| 1950 (1) | 98.50 | 0.50 | .. | 1.00 |
| 1960 (1) | 97.50 | 0.80 | .. | 1.70 |
| 1970 (1) | 96.00 | 1.30 | .. | 2.70 |
| 1977 (2) | 96.31 | 1.38 | 1.17 | 2.31 |
| 1987 (3) | 95.66 | 1.20 | 1.06 | 3.14 |

Source(s): (1) EPPA3; (2) ASTER; (3) R1987.

### 3.2 Method(s): linears interpolation and extrapolation weighted average

#### 3.2.1 Men:

- 1950-70, 1950-70 distribution rates derived from the EPPA3;
- 1980, weighted averages of distribution rates derived from
the 1977 and 1987 censuses;
- 1990, distribution rates of agriculture sector based on the results
of 1987 census and application to distribution rates of industry and services
the same proportion as in the 1987 census.

#### 3.2.2 Women:

- 1950-90, interpolation and extrapolation of distribution rates derived
from the 1977 and 1987 censuses;
modification of the trends in all sectors for 1950 and 1960.

## 4. Projection of activity rates: 2000 - 2010

### 4.1 Model(s): linear and hyperbole

#### 4.1.1 Men:

- To the [10-14] age group, application of function F1;
- To the [15+] age groups, application of function F3;
- Modification of the trend for the [65+] age group.

#### 4.1.2 Women:

- To the [10-19] and [60+] age groups, application of function F1;
- To the [20-59] age groups, application of function F3;
- Modification of the trends for all age groups.

# Malaysia

## 1. Source(s) of benchmark data

Code(s):    Title(s):

EPPA3    Economically active population: Estimates and Projections, 1950-2025, Third edition, ILO, Geneva, 1986.
STAT    Database on Labour Statistics, LABORSTA - Bureau of Statistics, ILO, Geneva.

## 2. Estimates of activity rates: 1950 - 1990

### 2.1 Benchmark data:

Table 1: Activity rates by sex and age group

| Age group | 1950 (3) | 1960 (3) | 1970 (3) | 1980 (1)(4) | 1980 (2)(4) | 1990 (4) |
|---|---|---|---|---|---|---|
| **Men** | | | | | | |
| 10-14 | .. | .. | .. | 8.84 | ... | ... |
| 15-19 | .. | .. | .. | 49.05 | 50.10 | 40.20 |
| 20-24 | .. | .. | .. | 89.76 | 92.20 | 83.20 |
| 25-29 | .. | .. | .. | 95.55 | 97.70 | 95.10 |
| 30-34 | .. | .. | .. | 96.29 | 98.30 | 97.10 |
| 35-39 | .. | .. | .. | 96.54 | 97.80 | 97.80 |
| 40-44 | .. | .. | .. | 96.24 | 98.30 | 97.20 |
| 45-49 | .. | .. | .. | 95.19 | 97.60 | 96.60 |
| 50-54 | .. | .. | .. | 91.47 | 94.80 | 92.60 |
| 55-59 | .. | .. | .. | 77.63 | 79.90 | 71.40 |
| 60-64 | .. | .. | .. | 69.03 | 70.50 | 61.40 |
| 65+ | .. | .. | .. | 49.37 | ... | ... |
| **Women** | | | | | | |
| 10-14 | 10.90 | 9.20 | 8.55 | .. | ... | ... |
| 15-19 | 33.20 | 33.75 | 34.25 | .. | 33.70 | 27.60 |
| 20-24 | 35.20 | 38.90 | 42.65 | .. | 56.70 | 57.70 |
| 25-29 | 30.00 | 30.70 | 37.80 | .. | 46.50 | 51.40 |
| 30-34 | 32.95 | 33.70 | 39.25 | .. | 44.30 | 49.30 |
| 35-39 | 36.95 | 37.80 | 42.85 | .. | 48.20 | 48.30 |
| 40-44 | 38.25 | 39.15 | 42.30 | .. | 50.20 | 49.60 |
| 45-49 | 39.90 | 41.10 | 42.30 | .. | 49.40 | 49.60 |
| 50-54 | 37.00 | 37.75 | 38.45 | .. | 44.10 | 42.40 |
| 55-59 | 32.00 | 31.95 | 31.90 | .. | 35.40 | 32.50 |
| 60-64 | 24.25 | 24.25 | 24.20 | .. | 27.90 | 26.60 |
| 65+ | 12.85 | 11.85 | 13.70 | .. | ... | ... |

Note(s): (1) Census; (2) Survey.
Source(s): (3) EPPA3; (4) STAT.

### 2.2 Method(s): linear interpolation
arithmetic average

#### 2.2.1 Men:

- 1950-70, 1950-70 activity rates derived from the EPPA3;
adjustment of activity rates of the [20-24] age group;
- 1980, average of activity rates derived from
the 1980 census and from the 1980 survey;
activity rates of [10-14] and [65+] age groups derived from the 1980 census;
- 1990, adjusted activity rates derived from the 1990 survey.

#### 2.2.2 Women:

- 1950-80, 1950-80 activity rates derived from the EPPA3;
- 1990, interpolation of 1950-70 activity rates derived from the EPPA3
and of activity rates derived from the 1980 and 1990 surveys.

## 3. Estimates of distribution rates by activity sector: 1950 - 1990

### 3.1 Benchmark data:

Table 2: Distribution of economically active population by activity sector

| Year | Agriculture | Industry Total | Industry Manufac. | Services |
|---|---|---|---|---|
| **Men** | | | | |
| 1980 | 37.49 | 19.86 | 11.83 | 42.65 |
| 1988 | 29.95 | 22.57 | 13.12 | 47.48 |
| **Women** | | | | |
| 1980 | 49.33 | 17.69 | 16.31 | 32.98 |
| 1988 | 30.31 | 21.68 | 20.61 | 48.01 |

Source(s): STAT.

### 3.2 Method(s): linear extrapolation

#### 3.2.1 Men:

- 1950-70, 1950-70 distribution rates derived from the EPPA3;
- 1980, adjusted distribution rates derived from the 1980 census;
- 1990, extrapolation of adjusted distribution rates derived from
the 1980 and of distribution rates derived from the 1988 survey.

#### 3.2.2 Women:

- 1950-70, 1950-70 distribution rates derived from the EPPA3;
- 1980, distribution rates derived from the 1980 census;
- 1990, extrapolation of distribution rates derived from
the 1980 census and the 1988 survey.

## 4. Projection of activity rates: 2000 - 2010

### 4.1 Model(s): linear, log-linear and hyperbole

#### 4.1.1 Men:

- To the [10-24] age groups, application of function F1;
- To the [25+] age groups, application of function F3;
- Modification of the trends for the [10-49] age groups.

#### 4.1.2 Women:

- To the [10-39] age groups, application of function F1;
- To the [40-59] age groups, application of function F2;
- To the [60+] age groups, application of function F3;
- Modification of the trends for the [10-14], [20-44] and [65+] age groups.

*Notes on adjustments of rates, see p. 3-8.*     *Notes on projection functions, see p. 10.*

# Maldives

## 1. Source(s) of benchmark data

Code(s):     Title(s):
ADNU84     Demographic Yearbook 1984 - Population census statistics II - Thirty-sixth Edition, United Nations, New York, 1986.
ADNU88     Demographic Yearbook 1988 - Population census statistics - Fortieth Edition, United Nations, New York, 1990.

## 2. Estimates of activity rates: 1950 - 1990

### 2.1 Benchmark data:

Table 1: Activity rates by sex and age group

| Age group | Year | |
|---|---|---|
| | 1977 | 1985 |
| **Men** | | |
| 10-14 | 37.23 | 5.08 |
| 15-19 | 77.95 | 56.40 |
| 20-24 | 93.39 | 84.59 |
| 25-29 | 95.04 | 87.83 |
| 30-34 | 95.69 | 88.89 |
| 35-39 | 96.50 | 88.93 |
| 40-44 | 96.80 | 86.84 |
| 45-49 | 97.05 | 86.87 |
| 50-54 | 95.54 | 83.33 |
| 55-59 | 93.77 | 80.55 |
| 60-64 | 87.47 | 72.89 |
| 65+ | 65.13 | 49.38 |
| **Women** | | |
| 10-14 | 24.13 | 1.81 |
| 15-19 | 52.23 | 19.80 |
| 20-24 | 62.14 | 23.76 |
| 25-29 | 64.73 | 23.27 |
| 30-34 | 64.76 | 25.48 |
| 35-39 | 70.70 | 26.53 |
| 40-44 | 71.93 | 27.82 |
| 45-49 | 73.33 | 28.34 |
| 50-54 | 68.14 | 28.15 |
| 55-59 | 61.47 | 26.87 |
| 60-64 | 52.26 | 22.44 |
| 65+ | 35.07 | 16.37 |

Source(s): ADNU88 and STAT.

### 2.2 Method(s):  weighted average

#### 2.2.1 Men:

- 1980, weighted average of adjusted activity rates derived from
the 1977 and 1985 censuses;
modification of the trends of the [10-14] and [60+] age groups;
- 1990, application to 1980 estimated activity rates, variations resulted on
interpolation of adjusted activity rates derived from the 1975 and 1985 censuses;
- 1950-70, application to 1980 estimated rates, variations estimated
for Indonesia.

#### 2.2.2 Women:

- 1980, weighted average of activity rates derived from
the 1977 census and of adjusted activity rates derived from the 1985 census;
modification of the trends of the [10-14] and [60+] age groups;
- 1990, application to 1980 estimated activity rates, variations resulted
on interpolation of activity rates derived from the 1975 census
and adjusted activity rates derived from the 1985 census;
- 1950-70, application to 1980 estimated rates, variations estimated for Indonesia

## 3. Estimates of distribution rates  by activity sector: 1950 - 1990

### 3.1 Benchmark data:

Table  2: Distribution of economically active population by activity sector

| Year | Agriculture | Industry | | Services |
|---|---|---|---|---|
| | | Total | Manufac. | |
| **Men** | | | | |
| 1975 | 63.32 | 13.39 | 7.89 | 23.29 |
| 1985 | 43.01 | 19.46 | 11.38 | 37.52 |
| **Women** | | | | |
| 1975 | 44.02 | 48.13 | 47.90 | 7.84 |
| 1985 | 32.49 | 56.65 | 55.97 | 10.86 |

Source(s): STAT.

### 3.2 Method(s):  linears interpolation and extrapolation

#### 3.2.1 Men:

- 1950-90, interpolation and extrapolation of distribution rates derived from
the 1977 and 1985 censuses;
modification of the trends in all sectors.

#### 3.2.2 Women:

- 1950-90, interpolation and extrapolation of distribution rates derived from
the 1977 and 1985 censuses;
distribution rates of agriculture sector estimated on the basis of the
men/women ratio in agriculture derived from the 1977 census;
- Application of manufacturing/industry ratio derived from 1977 census.

## 4. Projection of activity rates: 2000 - 2010

### 4.1 Model(s):  linear, log-linear, hyperbole and logistic

#### 4.1.1 Men:

- To the [10-14], [20-29] and [60+] age groups, application of function F1;
- To the [15-19] and [30-59] age groups, application of function F3;
- Modification of the trends for the [10-29] age groups.

#### 4.1.2 Women:

- To the [10-19] age groups, application of function F2;
- To the [20-59] age groups, application of function F6;
- To the [60+] age groups, application of function F3;
- Modification of the trends for the [10-64] age groups.

---

*Notes on  adjustments of rates, see p. 3-8.*          *Notes on  projection functions, see p. 10.*

# Mali

## 1. Source(s) of benchmark data

**Code(s):**     **Title(s):**

EPPA3     Economically active population: Estimates and Projections, 1950-2025, Third edition, ILO, Geneva, 1986.
ASTER     Yearbook of Labour Statistics 1945-89 - Retrospective Edition on Population Censuses, ILO, Geneva, 1990.

## 2. Estimates of activity rates: 1950 - 1990

### 2.1 Benchmark data:

Table 1: Activity rates by sex and age group

| Age group | Year 1950 (1) | 1960 (1) | 1970 (1) | 1976 (2) |
|---|---|---|---|---|
| **Men** | | | | |
| 10-14 | 70.75 | 69.05 | 67.35 | 66.17 |
| 15-19 | 86.20 | 84.50 | 82.75 | 81.59 |
| 20-24 | 92.60 | 91.95 | 91.30 | 90.84 |
| 25-29 | 97.55 | 97.45 | 97.35 | 97.27 |
| 30-34 | 98.25 | 98.10 | 98.00 | 97.92 |
| 35-39 | 98.25 | 98.15 | 98.00 | 97.93 |
| 40-44 | 98.00 | 97.85 | 97.75 | 97.64 |
| 45-49 | 97.75 | 97.65 | 97.55 | 97.47 |
| 50-54 | 96.65 | 96.50 | 96.35 | 96.22 |
| 55-59 | 95.20 | 94.95 | 94.70 | 94.49 |
| 60-64 | 90.30 | 89.90 | 89.45 | 89.17 |
| 65+ | 74.40 | 73.70 | 73.00 | 72.51 |
| **Women** | | | | |
| 10-14 | 15.80 | 15.40 | 15.00 | 14.76 |
| 15-19 | 20.00 | 19.55 | 19.10 | 18.83 |
| 20-24 | 18.15 | 17.90 | 17.65 | 17.46 |
| 25-29 | 18.80 | 18.50 | 18.20 | 18.03 |
| 30-34 | 17.95 | 17.65 | 17.40 | 17.20 |
| 35-39 | 18.20 | 17.95 | 17.65 | 17.49 |
| 40-44 | 18.00 | 17.75 | 17.50 | 17.33 |
| 45-49 | 18.20 | 17.95 | 17.70 | 17.50 |
| 50-54 | 16.65 | 16.35 | 16.10 | 15.91 |
| 55-59 | 15.85 | 15.55 | 15.30 | 15.08 |
| 60-64 | 13.00 | 12.65 | 12.35 | 12.15 |
| 65+ | 9.10 | 8.85 | 8.55 | 8.36 |

**Source(s):** (1) EPPA3; (2) ASTER.

### 2.2 Method(s):   linears interpolation and extrapolation

#### 2.2.1 Men:

- 1950-70, 1950-70 activity rates derived from the EPPA3;
- 1980-90, interpolation of 1950-70 activity rates derived from the EPPA3 of activity rates derived from the 1976 census;
adjustment of extrapolated rates on the basis of variations in 1976 interpolated rates, in relation to activity rates derived from the 1976 census.

#### 2.2.2 Women:

- 1950-90, interpolation and extrapolation of 1950-80 activity rates derived from the EPPA3 and of adjusted activity rates derived from the 1976 census;
adjustment of interpolated and extrapolated rates on the basis of variations in 1976 interpolated rates, in relation to activity rates derived from the 1976 census.

## 3. Estimates of distribution rates by activity sector: 1950 - 1990

### 3.1 Benchmark data:

Table 2: Distribution of economically active population by activity sector

| Year | Agriculture | Industry Total | Manufac. | Services |
|---|---|---|---|---|
| **Men** | | | | |
| 1976 | 88.99 | 1.32 | 0.39 | 9.69 |
| **Women** | | | | |
| 1976 | 43.15 | 8.00 | .. | 48.85 |

**Source(s):** ASTER.

### 3.2 Method(s):   linears interpolation and extrapolation

#### 3.2.1 Men:

- 1950-90, interpolation and extrapolation of 1990 distribution rates derived from the EPPA3 and of distribution rates derived from the 1976 census;
- Application of manufacturing/industry ratio derived from the 1976 census.

#### 3.2.2 Women:

Method, hypothesis and treatment identical to those used for men.

## 4. Projection of activity rates: 2000 - 2010

### 4.1 Model(s):   linear

#### 4.1.1 Men:

- To all age groups, application of function F1;
- Modification of the trends for the [10-19], [30-34] and [65+] age groups.

#### 4.1.2 Women:

- To the [10-19] and [45+] age groups, application of function F1;
- To the [20-44] age groups, application of function F3;
- Modification of the trends for the [20-34] and [45+] age groups.

*Notes on adjustments of rates, see p. 3-8.*

*Notes on projection functions, see p. 10.*

# Malta

## 1. Source(s) of benchmark data

Code(s):     Title(s):
EPPA3        Yearbook of Labour Statistics 1945-89 - Retrospective Edition on Population Censuses, ILO, Geneva, 1990.
STAT         Database on Labour Statistics, LABORSTA - Bureau of Statistics, ILO, Geneva.

## 2. Estimates of activity rates: 1950 - 1990

### 2.1 Benchmark data:

Table 1: Activity rates by sex and age group

| Age group | 1950 (1) | 1960 (1) | 1970 (1) | 1980 (1) | 1985 (2) |
|---|---|---|---|---|---|
| **Men** | | | | | |
| 10-14 | 4.30 | 3.00 | 1.80 | 1.50 | 0.00 |
| 15-19 | 68.65 | 64.35 | 60.30 | 56.50 | 23.20 |
| 20-24 | 92.30 | 91.15 | 90.05 | 88.90 | 72.15 |
| 25-29 | 96.35 | 95.90 | 95.50 | 95.05 | 81.89 |
| 30-34 | 97.35 | 97.60 | 97.90 | 98.15 | 87.19 |
| 35-39 | 96.20 | 97.05 | 97.90 | 98.75 | 87.82 |
| 40-44 | 96.35 | 96.65 | 96.95 | 97.25 | 88.16 |
| 45-49 | 93.65 | 94.05 | 94.45 | 94.80 | 85.68 |
| 50-54 | 91.25 | 90.30 | 89.35 | 88.45 | 78.67 |
| 55-59 | 86.95 | 84.80 | 82.70 | 80.65 | 66.98 |
| 60-64 | 63.30 | 62.10 | 60.90 | 59.70 | 19.51 |
| 65+ | 31.45 | 23.60 | 17.70 | 13.30 | 2.49 |
| **Women** | | | | | |
| 10-14 | 1.35 | 1.35 | 0.95 | 0.75 | 0.00 |
| 15-19 | 24.00 | 30.05 | 32.20 | 30.35 | 36.99 |
| 20-24 | 22.75 | 29.15 | 32.95 | 34.25 | 59.60 |
| 25-29 | 14.85 | 18.25 | 21.75 | 25.35 | 28.36 |
| 30-34 | 13.50 | 13.50 | 15.60 | 19.85 | 14.62 |
| 35-39 | 14.80 | 13.25 | 13.55 | 15.65 | 13.31 |
| 40-44 | 16.30 | 13.70 | 13.15 | 14.75 | 13.94 |
| 45-49 | 16.60 | 15.00 | 14.85 | 16.30 | 12.59 |
| 50-54 | 15.65 | 12.40 | 12.90 | 17.05 | 9.78 |
| 55-59 | 14.60 | 12.75 | 13.00 | 15.45 | 7.24 |
| 60-64 | 12.10 | 9.95 | 10.00 | 12.20 | 1.40 |
| 65+ | 6.45 | 4.05 | 2.75 | 2.50 | 0.42 |

Source(s): (1) EPPA3; (2) STAT.

### 2.2 Method(s): linear extrapolation

#### 2.2.1 Men:

- 1950-80, 1950-80 activity rates derived from the EPPA3;
- 1990, extrapolation of 1950-80 activity rates derived from the EPPA3 and of activity rates derived from 1985 census;
modification of the trends for all age groups;
application to extrapolated rates, variations in 1985 interpolated rates, in relation to activity rates derived from the 1985 census.

#### 2.2.2 Women:

Method, hypothesis and treatment identical to those used for men.

## 3. Estimates of distribution rates by activity sector: 1950 - 1990

### 3.1 Benchmark data:

Table 2: Distribution of economically active population by activity sector

| Year | Agriculture | Industry Total | Manufac. | Services |
|---|---|---|---|---|
| **Men** | | | | |
| 1968 | 10.38 | 54.17 | 32.30 | 35.45 |
| 1972 | 6.98 | 38.93 | 26.61 | 54.09 |
| 1979 | 10.14 | 48.47 | 37.95 | 41.39 |
| 1980 | 9.64 | 48.36 | 37.27 | 42.00 |
| 1981 | 8.87 | 48.84 | 37.52 | 42.29 |
| 1990 | 3.01 | 34.66 | 25.88 | 62.33 |
| **Women** | | | | |
| 1968 | 4.85 | 29.82 | 29.76 | 65.32 |
| 1972 | 3.10 | 35.89 | 35.87 | 61.01 |
| 1979 | 2.88 | 55.87 | 55.45 | 41.26 |
| 1980 | 2.88 | 54.99 | 54.59 | 42.13 |
| 1981 | 3.66 | 54.32 | 53.83 | 42.02 |
| 1990 | 1.25 | 34.35 | 33.64 | 64.40 |

Source(s): STAT.

### 3.2 Method(s): arithmetic average

#### 3.2.1 Men:

- 1950-60, 1950-60 distribution rates derived from the EPPA3;
- 1970, averages of distribution rates derived from the 1968 and 1970 official estimates and of distribution rates derived from the 1972 survey;
- 1980, averages of distribution rates derived from the 1979, 1980 and 1981 official estimates;
- 1990, distribution rates derived from the 1990 survey.

#### 3.2.2 Women:

Method, hypothesis and treatment identical to those used for men.

## 4. Projection of activity rates: 2000 - 2010

### 4.1 Model(s): linear, hyperbole and logistic

#### 4.1.1 Men:

- To the [15-19] age group, application of function F1;
- To the [20+] age groups, application of function F3;
- Modification of the trends for the [25-59] age groups.

#### 4.1.2 Women:

- To the [15-64] age groups, application of function F6;
- To the [65+] age group, application of function F3;
- Modification of the trends for the [15-54] age groups.

*Notes on adjustments of rates, see p. 3-8.*    *Notes on projection functions, see p. 10.*

# Martinique

## 1. Source(s) of benchmark data

Code(s):     Title(s):

EPPA3        Economically active population: Estimates and Projections, 1950-2025, Third edition, ILO, Geneva, 1986.
STAT         Database on Labour Statistics, LABORSTA - Bureau of Statistics, ILO, Geneva.

## 2. Estimates of activity rates: 1950 - 1990

### 2.1 Benchmark data:

Table 1: Activity rates by sex and age group

| Age group | Year 1950 (1) | 1970 (1) | 1974 (2) | 1980 (1) | 1982 (2) | 1990 (2) |
|---|---|---|---|---|---|---|
| **Men** | | | | | | |
| 10-14 | 4.00 | 1.05 | .. | .. | 0.00 | .. |
| 15-19 | 55.00 | 43.20 | .. | .. | 25.24 | .. |
| 20-24 | 87.60 | 86.70 | .. | .. | 81.85 | .. |
| 25-29 | 96.50 | 94.60 | .. | .. | 91.37 | .. |
| 30-34 | 97.90 | 95.95 | .. | .. | 93.51 | .. |
| 35-39 | 97.95 | 96.00 | .. | .. | 93.97 | .. |
| 40-44 | 97.45 | 95.55 | .. | .. | 91.81 | .. |
| 45-49 | 96.70 | 93.25 | .. | .. | 88.87 | .. |
| 50-54 | 93.60 | 90.25 | .. | .. | 83.91 | .. |
| 55-59 | 88.35 | 82.10 | .. | .. | 74.44 | .. |
| 60-64 | 72.00 | 66.90 | .. | .. | 43.08 | .. |
| 65+ | 52.90 | 28.70 | .. | .. | 6.16 | .. |
| **Women** | | | | | | |
| 10-14 | 2.00 | 0.55 | 0.00 | 0.35 | 0.00 | 0.00 |
| 15-19 | 33.70 | 29.20 | 29.35 | 28.10 | 17.61 | 9.49 |
| 20-24 | 47.55 | 57.60 | 69.34 | 69.10 | 70.03 | 66.25 |
| 25-29 | 48.50 | 53.00 | 64.73 | 72.50 | 76.96 | 85.08 |
| 30-34 | 49.35 | 47.40 | 59.22 | 69.35 | 74.19 | 83.85 |
| 35-39 | 51.85 | 44.70 | 53.22 | 66.50 | 71.94 | 82.13 |
| 40-44 | 53.65 | 45.10 | 50.01 | 62.10 | 66.66 | 80.52 |
| 45-49 | 53.15 | 44.60 | 46.91 | 56.70 | 60.83 | 75.39 |
| 50-54 | 54.30 | 40.45 | 45.50 | 48.95 | 52.11 | 65.60 |
| 55-59 | 45.45 | 37.10 | 35.90 | 40.30 | 44.82 | 49.89 |
| 60-64 | 32.15 | 18.45 | 18.36 | 20.60 | 25.26 | 22.28 |
| 65+ | 16.95 | 4.50 | 4.08 | 4.05 | 3.32 | 2.40 |

Source(s): (1) EPPA3; (2) STAT.

### 2.2 Method(s): linears interpolation and extrapolation

#### 2.2.1 Men:

- 1950-70, 1950-70 activity rates derived from the EPPA3;
- 1980, extrapolation of 1970 activity rates derived from the EPPA3 and of adjusted activity rates derived from the 1982 census;
- 1990, extrapolation of 1950-80 activity rates derived from the EPPA3 and adjusted activity rates derived from the 1982 census; adjustment of activity rates on the basis of variations in 1982 interpolated rates, in relation to adjusted activity rates derived from the 1982 census; modification of the trend for the [65+] age group.

#### 2.2.2 Women:

- 1950-60, 1950-60 activity rates derived from the EPPA3;
- 1970-90, interpolation and extrapolation of 1960 activity rates derived from the EPPA3 and of activity rates derived from the 1974, 1982 and 1990 censuses.

## 3. Estimates of distribution rates by activity sector: 1950 - 1990

### 3.1 Benchmark data:

Table 2: Distribution of economically active population by activity sector

| Year | Agriculture | Industry Total | Manufac. | Services |
|---|---|---|---|---|
| **Men** | | | | |
| 1960 (1) | 45.16 | 27.42 | .. | 27.42 |
| 1974 (2) | 23.35 | 27.64 | 9.59 | 49.01 |
| 1982 (2) | 14.92 | 26.40 | 5.04 | 58.68 |
| 1990 (2) | 10.20 | 26.37 | 12.07 | 63.43 |
| **Women** | | | | |
| 1960 (1) | 33.33 | 11.11 | 0.00 | 55.56 |
| 1974 (2) | 10.83 | 7.09 | 5.69 | 82.09 |
| 1982 (2) | 6.87 | 5.11 | 4.06 | 88.03 |
| 1990 (2) | 4.62 | 6.29 | 4.90 | 89.09 |

Source(s): (1) EPPA3; (2) STAT.

### 3.2 Method(s): linears interpolation and extrapolation

#### 3.2.1 Men:

- 1950-70, 1950-70 distribution rates derived from the EPPA3;
- 1980-90, interpolation and extrapolation of 1960 distribution rates derived from the EPPA3 and distribution rates derived from the 1974, 1982 and 1990 censuses.

#### 3.2.2 Women:

Method, hypothesis and treatment identical to those used for men.

## 4. Projection of activity rates: 2000 - 2010

### 4.1 Model(s): linear, log-linear, hyperbole and logistic

#### 4.1.1 Men:

- To the [10-14] age group, application of function F2;
- To the [15-29] age groups, application of function F1;
- To the [30+] age groups, application of function F3;
- Modification of the trends for the [40-49] age groups.

#### 4.1.2 Women:

- To the [15-19] and [55+] age groups, application of function F3;
- To the [20-24] age group, application of function F1;
- To the [25-54] age groups, application of function F6;
- Modification of the trends for the [20-29] and [40-49] age groups.

*Notes on adjustments of rates, see p. 3-8.*          *Notes on projection functions, see p. 10.*

# Mauritania

## 1. Source(s) of benchmark data

Code(s):      Title(s):

EPPA3         Economically active population: Estimates and Projections, 1950-2025, Third edition, ILO, Geneva, 1986.
R1977         Recensement de la population 1977, Direction de la Statistique et de la Comptabilité Nationale, Nouakchott.

## 2. Estimates of activity rates: 1950 - 1990

### 2.1 Benchmark data:

Table 1: Activity rates by sex and age group

| Age group | Year | | | |
|---|---|---|---|---|
| | 1950 | 1960 | 1970 | 1980 |
| **Men** | | | | |
| 10-14 | 39.60 | 38.60 | 35.15 | 28.20 |
| 15-19 | 91.75 | 89.90 | 83.25 | 70.00 |
| 20-24 | 97.75 | 98.30 | 95.35 | 91.10 |
| 25-29 | 99.00 | 98.50 | 97.55 | 96.80 |
| 30-34 | 99.25 | 99.15 | 98.70 | 97.90 |
| 35-39 | 99.45 | 99.30 | 98.85 | 97.95 |
| 40-44 | 99.50 | 99.35 | 98.90 | 97.95 |
| 45-49 | 98.80 | 98.70 | 98.30 | 97.50 |
| 50-54 | 97.35 | 97.15 | 96.60 | 95.40 |
| 55-59 | 97.25 | 96.95 | 96.00 | 94.10 |
| 60-64 | 81.15 | 80.80 | 79.40 | 76.65 |
| 65+ | 66.75 | 66.10 | 63.85 | 59.30 |
| **Women** | | | | |
| 10-14 | 16.50 | 16.10 | 14.65 | 11.75 |
| 15-19 | 31.20 | 30.50 | 27.95 | 22.90 |
| 20-24 | 27.35 | 26.95 | 25.50 | 22.65 |
| 25-29 | 25.25 | 24.85 | 23.45 | 20.70 |
| 30-34 | 25.85 | 25.45 | 24.05 | 21.15 |
| 35-39 | 24.20 | 23.85 | 22.65 | 20.15 |
| 40-44 | 25.50 | 25.15 | 23.85 | 21.35 |
| 45-49 | 24.20 | 23.85 | 22.60 | 20.15 |
| 50-54 | 25.50 | 25.10 | 23.55 | 20.50 |
| 55-59 | 23.10 | 22.70 | 21.20 | 18.25 |
| 60-64 | 17.55 | 17.10 | 15.60 | 12.50 |
| 65+ | 14.05 | 13.60 | 12.00 | 8.80 |

Source(s): EPPA3.

### 2.2 Method(s): linears interpolation and extrapolation

#### 2.2.1 Men:

- 1950-80, 1950-80 activity rates derived from the EPPA3;
- 1990, extrapolation of 1950-80 activity rates derived from the EPPA3;
adjustment of extrapolated rates on the basis of variations in 1980
interpolated rates, in relation to the 1980 rates derived from the EPPA3;
modification of the trends of the [25-54] age groups for 1990.

#### 2.2.2 Women:

- 1950-90, interpolation and extrapolation of 1950-80 activity rates
derived from the EPPA3;
adjustment of rates to make allowance for the under-registration
of women working in agriculture;
adjustment based on the men/women ratio in agriculture equal to 1.

## 3. Estimates of distribution rates by activity sector: 1950 - 1990

### 3.1 Benchmark data:

Table 2: Distribution of economically active population by activity sector

| Year | Agriculture | Industry | | Services |
|---|---|---|---|---|
| | | Total | Manufac. | |
| **Men** | | | | |
| 1950 (1) | 94.50 | 1.60 | .. | 3.90 |
| 1960 (1) | 92.00 | 2.40 | .. | 5.60 |
| 1970 (1) | 83.00 | 5.00 | .. | 12.00 |
| 1977 (2) | 65.82 | 8.88 | 4.38 | 25.31 |
| 1980 (1) | 65.00 | 10.50 | .. | 24.50 |
| **Women** | | | | |
| 1977 (2) | 70.67 | 2.92 | 0.00 | 26.41 |

Source(s): (1) EPPA3; (2) R1977.

### 3.2 Method(s): linears interpolation and extrapolation

#### 3.2.1 Men:
- 1950-80, 1950-80 distribution rates derived from the EPPA3;
- 1990, extrapolation of 1950-80 distribution rates derived from the EPPA3;
modification of the trends in all sectors.

#### 3.2.2 Women:

- 1950 et 1980-90, distribution rates of agriculture sector estimated
on the basis of men/women ration in agriculture equal to 1;
distribution rates of industry and services sectors estimated on the basis of the
industry/services ratio derived from the 1977 census;
- Application of manufacturing/industry ratio estimated for Morocco;
- 1960-70, interpolation of distribution rates estimated for 1950
and of distribution rates derived from the 1977 census.

## 4. Projection of activity rates: 2000 - 2010

### 4.1 Model(s): linear

#### 4.1.1 Men:

- To all age groups, application of function F1;
- Modification of the trends for the [10-19] and [60+] age groups.

#### 4.1.2 Women:

- To all age groups, application of function F1;
- Modification of the trends for the [15-54] age groups.

*Notes on adjustments of rates, see p. 3-8.*          *Notes on projection functions, see p. 10.*

119

# Mauritius

## 1. Source(s) of benchmark data

Code(s):     Title(s):

EPPA3       Economically active population: Estimates and Projections, 1950-2025, Third edition, ILO, Geneva, 1986.
ASTER       Yearbook of Labour Statistics 1945-89 - Retrospective Edition on Population Censuses, ILO, Geneva, 1990.
R1983       1983 Housing and Population Census, Analysis Report, Vol IV, Central Statistical Office, Port Louis, April 1987.
R1990       1990 Housing and Population Census of Mauritius - Economic Characteristics, Central Statistical Office, Port Louis, 1991.

## 2. Estimates of activity rates: 1950 - 1990

### 2.1 Benchmark data:

Table 1: Activity rates by sex and age group

| Age group | Year 1950 (1) | 1960 (1) | 1970 (1) | 1972 (2) | 1983 (3) | 1990 (4) |
|---|---|---|---|---|---|---|
| **Men** | | | | | | |
| 10-14 | 11.80 | 10.40 | 9.05 | 15.73 | 10.13 | 11.21 |
| 15-19 | 82.45 | 73.30 | 65.75 | 64.72 | 61.88 | 50.71 |
| 20-24 | 97.80 | 96.30 | 94.75 | 94.58 | 95.98 | 90.43 |
| 25-29 | 98.60 | 97.90 | 97.25 | 97.60 | 97.85 | 95.46 |
| 30-34 | 98.70 | 98.00 | 97.35 | 97.36 | 97.65 | 96.79 |
| 35-39 | 98.60 | 97.90 | 97.25 | 97.25 | 97.28 | 97.10 |
| 40-44 | 98.55 | 97.85 | 97.20 | 96.54 | 95.81 | 96.55 |
| 45-49 | 97.70 | 96.65 | 95.65 | 95.22 | 94.49 | 94.61 |
| 50-54 | 94.60 | 93.30 | 92.00 | 91.68 | 91.05 | 91.19 |
| 55-59 | 93.55 | 90.00 | 88.00 | 85.25 | 82.30 | 81.70 |
| 60-64 | 91.00 | 68.00 | 50.00 | 41.93 | 22.53 | 29.74 |
| 65+ | 49.07 | 34.80 | 24.15 | 22.37 | 12.13 | 16.39 |
| **Women** | | | | | | |
| 10-14 | 4.20 | 3.25 | 2.30 | 3.69 | 3.15 | 3.41 |
| 15-19 | 13.95 | 14.35 | 14.75 | 15.15 | 24.30 | 25.72 |
| 20-24 | 18.10 | 19.80 | 21.50 | 21.97 | 38.68 | 43.63 |
| 25-29 | 19.10 | 19.25 | 19.40 | 20.20 | 33.33 | 41.90 |
| 30-34 | 22.15 | 22.30 | 22.45 | 23.20 | 31.21 | 45.58 |
| 35-39 | 25.80 | 26.00 | 26.15 | 26.01 | 32.87 | 45.94 |
| 40-44 | 26.50 | 26.70 | 26.90 | 27.81 | 32.87 | 41.81 |
| 45-49 | 31.60 | 29.95 | 28.30 | 28.22 | 31.26 | 37.04 |
| 50-54 | 31.25 | 29.60 | 28.00 | 27.98 | 27.89 | 32.42 |
| 55-59 | 29.00 | 27.00 | 25.00 | 24.31 | 23.48 | 24.61 |
| 60-64 | 27.00 | 21.00 | 15.00 | 12.95 | 6.03 | 9.00 |
| 65+ | 7.55 | 6.85 | 5.35 | 5.26 | 2.57 | 4.09 |

Source(s): (1) EPPA3; (2) ASTER; (3) ASTER and R1983; (4) R1990.

### 2.2 Method(s): linear interpolation

**2.2.1 Men:**

- 1950-70, 1950-70 activity rates derived from the EPPA3;
- 1980, interpolation of activity rates derived from the 1972, 1983 and 1990 censuses;
modification of the trends for all age groups;
- 1990, activity rates derived from the 1990 census.

**2.2.2 Women:**

Method, hypothesis and treatment identical to those used for men.

## 3. Estimates of distribution rates by activity sector: 1950 - 1990

### 3.1 Benchmark data:

Table 2: Distribution of economically active population by activity sector

| Year | Agriculture | Industry Total | Manufac. | Services |
|---|---|---|---|---|
| **Men** | | | | |
| 1972 (1) | 31.99 | 28.23 | 14.40 | 39.77 |
| 1983 (2) | 25.36 | 27.45 | 15.84 | 47.18 |
| 1990 (3) | 17.75 | 40.14 | 24.51 | 42.11 |
| **Women** | | | | |
| 1972 (1) | 37.18 | 11.02 | 10.41 | 51.80 |
| 1983 (2) | 23.33 | 33.58 | 32.94 | 43.09 |
| 1990 (3) | 14.32 | 50.19 | 49.72 | 35.50 |

Source(s): (1) ASTER; (2) R1983; (3) R1990.

### 3.2 Method(s): weighted average

**3.2.1 Men:**

- 1950-70, 1950-70 distribution rates derived from the EPPA3;
- 1980, weighted averages of distribution rates derived from the 1972 and 1983 censuses;
- 1990, distribution rates derived from 1990 census.

**3.2.2 Women:**

Method, hypothesis and treatment identical to those used for men.

## 4. Projection of activity rates: 2000 - 2010

### 4.1 Model(s): linear, log-linear and hyperbole

**4.1.1 Men:**

- To the [10-14] and [20-29] age groups, application of function F1;
- To the [15-19] age group, application of function F2;
- To the [30+] age groups, application of function F3;
- Modification of the trends for the [15-19] and [30-49] age groups.

**4.1.2 Women:**

- To the [10-19] and [45-49] age groups, application of function F1;
- To the [20-44] age groups, application of function F2;
- To the [50+] age groups, application of function F3;
- Modification of the trend for the [20-24] age group.

Notes on adjustments of rates, see p. 3-8.

Notes on projection functions, see p. 10.

# Mexico

## 1. Source(s) of benchmark data

| Code(s): | Title(s): |
|---|---|
| EPPA3 | Economically active population: Estimates and Projections, 1950-2025, Third edition, ILO, Geneva, 1986. |
| ASTER | Yearbook of Labour Statistics 1945-89 - Retrospective Edition on Population Censuses, ILO, Geneva, 1990. |
| AST93 | Yearbook of Labour Statistics 1993, ILO, Geneva, 1993. |

## 2. Estimates of activity rates: 1950 - 1990

### 2.1 Benchmark data:

Table 1: Activity rates by sex and age group

| Age group | Year | | |
|---|---|---|---|
| | 1980 (1) | 1990 (2) | 1991 (2) |
| **Men** | | | |
| 10-14 | 11.69 | 6.72 | .. |
| 15-19 | 55.89 | 47.05 | .. |
| 20-24 | 83.45 | 77.10 | .. |
| 25-29 | 94.16 | 89.32 | .. |
| 30-34 | 96.12 | 92.11 | .. |
| 35-39 | 96.20 | 92.18 | .. |
| 40-44 | 95.92 | 91.17 | .. |
| 45-49 | 95.27 | 89.04 | .. |
| 50-54 | 93.83 | 84.68 | .. |
| 55-59 | 91.42 | 78.75 | .. |
| 60-64 | 85.64 | 68.55 | .. |
| 65+ | 68.58 | 45.90 | .. |
| **Women** | | | |
| 10-14 | 2.09 | .. | 6.19 |
| 15-19 | 17.95 | .. | 30.11 |
| 20-24 | 29.10 | .. | 40.42 |
| 25-29 | 28.42 | .. | 37.92 |
| 30-34 | 26.87 | .. | 40.71 |
| 35-39 | 24.85 | .. | 42.48 |
| 40-44 | 22.56 | .. | 38.40 |
| 45-49 | 18.71 | .. | 36.27 |
| 50-54 | 15.20 | .. | 28.85 |
| 55-59 | 12.01 | .. | 26.54 |
| 60-64 | 9.33 | .. | 21.77 |
| 65+ | 5.42 | .. | 12.40 |

Source(s): (1) ASTER; (2) AST93,

### 2.2 Method(s): weighted average

#### 2.2.1 Men:

- 1950-70, 1950-70 activity rates derived from the EPPA3;
adjustment of activity rates of the [10-19] and [40-59] age groups for 1970;
- 1980, adjusted activity rates derived from the 1980 census;
- 1990, weighted average of adjusted activity rates derived from the 1980 and 1990 censuses.

#### 2.2.2 Women:

- 1950-70, 1950-70 activity rates derived from the EPPA3;
- 1980, activity rates derived from census 1980;
- 1990, weighted average of activity rates derived from the 1980 census and from the 1991 survey.

## 3. Estimates of distribution rates by activity sector: 1950 - 1990

### 3.1 Benchmark data:

Table 2: Distribution of economically active population by activity sector

| Year | Agriculture | Industry | | Services |
|---|---|---|---|---|
| | | Total | Manufac. | |
| **Men** | | | | |
| 1980 (1) | 42.58 | 29.53 | 16.31 | 27.89 |
| 1990 (2) | 29.40 | 30.81 | 19.77 | 39.79 |
| 1991 (2) | 34.05 | 24.98 | 14.84 | 40.97 |
| **Women** | | | | |
| 1980 (1) | 19.18 | 27.87 | 17.60 | 52.95 |
| 1990 (2) | 3.63 | 22.00 | 20.26 | 74.38 |
| 1991 (2) | 10.86 | 19.20 | 18.11 | 69.94 |

Source(s): (1) ASTER; (2) AST93.

### 3.2 Method(s): weighted average

#### 3.2.1 Men:

- 1950-70, 1950-70 distribution rates derived from the EPPA3;
- 1980, distribution rates derived from the 1980 census;
- 1970-90, weighted averages of distribution rates derived from the 1980 census and from the 1991 survey.

#### 3.2.2 Women:

Method, hypothesis and treatment identical to those used for men.

## 4. Projection of activity rates: 2000 - 2010

### 4.1 Model(s): linear, hyperbole and logistic

#### 4.1.1 Men:

- To the [10-54] and [65+] age groups, application of function F1;
- To the [55-64] age groups, application of function F3;
- Modification of the trends for the [20-24] and [40-54] age groups.

#### 4.1.2 Women:

- To the [10-29] and [50-59] age groups, application of function F6;
- To the [30-49] and [60+] age groups, application of function F1;
- Modification of the trends for the [10-34] and [50+] age groups.

# Moldova, Rep. of

## 1. Source(s) of benchmark data

Code(s):     Title(s):

BLT-94-2    Vorobiev A. (1994), "Estimates of the economically active population for the fifteen countries of the former USSR
            for the years 1950, 1959, 1970, 1979 and 1989", in the Bulletin of Labour of Statistics - 1994-2, ILO, Geneva.

## 2. Estimates of activity rates: 1950 - 1990

### 2.1 Benchmark data:

Table 1: Activity rates by sex and age group

| Age group | Year 1950 | 1959 | 1970 | 1979 | 1989 |
|---|---|---|---|---|---|
| **Men** | | | | | |
| 10-14 | 0.00 | 0.00 | 0.00 | 0.00 | 0.00 |
| 15-19 | 53.04 | 75.86 | 46.99 | 40.93 | 29.94 |
| 20-24 | 91.02 | 88.98 | 86.92 | 89.53 | 82.76 |
| 25-29 | 95.65 | 99.08 | 95.33 | 97.66 | 96.07 |
| 30-34 | 93.94 | 96.12 | 82.68 | 98.00 | 97.19 |
| 35-39 | 96.10 | 97.70 | 99.13 | 99.13 | 97.63 |
| 40-44 | 94.83 | 98.39 | 97.25 | 98.39 | 96.77 |
| 45-49 | 95.65 | 97.22 | 96.70 | 97.22 | 95.28 |
| 50-54 | 91.18 | 94.55 | 94.92 | 92.93 | 92.66 |
| 55-59 | 92.31 | 93.02 | 91.43 | 87.18 | 84.95 |
| 60-64 | 77.27 | 87.10 | 58.82 | 31.37 | 28.75 |
| 65+ | 32.35 | 60.00 | 15.48 | 8.70 | 9.23 |
| **Women** | | | | | |
| 10-14 | 0.00 | 0.00 | 0.00 | 0.00 | 0.00 |
| 15-19 | 71.32 | 80.00 | 49.72 | 40.00 | 28.93 |
| 20-24 | 81.34 | 84.03 | 86.40 | 90.27 | 80.39 |
| 25-29 | 81.51 | 89.76 | 95.20 | 96.69 | 90.00 |
| 30-34 | 81.18 | 81.89 | 93.92 | 96.33 | 93.05 |
| 35-39 | 79.35 | 81.08 | 96.12 | 98.46 | 94.44 |
| 40-44 | 76.06 | 79.49 | 91.60 | 95.77 | 94.23 |
| 45-49 | 72.60 | 76.74 | 89.74 | 92.68 | 90.98 |
| 50-54 | 70.18 | 70.77 | 80.00 | 78.74 | 75.78 |
| 55-59 | 59.52 | 61.19 | 38.95 | 22.73 | 21.37 |
| 60-64 | 38.89 | 64.00 | 14.49 | 8.11 | 9.65 |
| 65+ | 9.09 | 13.19 | 5.63 | 1.61 | 3.15 |

Source(s): BLT-94-2.

### 2.2 Method(s):   linears interpolation and extrapolation
                     weighted average

#### 2.2.1 Men:

- 1950-90, for the [10-19] and [60+] age groups, weighted average
of 1950, 1959, 1970, 1979 and 1989 activity rates derived from
the Bulletin of Labour Statistics 1994-2;
adjustment of 1950-80 estimated activity rates of the [10-14] age group;
for the [10-59] age groups, interpolation and extrapolation of 1950, 1959,
1970, 1979 and 1989 derived from the Bulletin;
adjustment of activity rates of the [60+] age groups for 1959.

#### 2.2.2 Women:

- 1950-90, weighted average of 1950, 1959, 1970 and 1989 activity rates
derived from the Bulletin of Labour Statistics 1994-2;
adjustment of activity rates of the [15-19] and [60+] age groups for 1959;
modification of the trends of the [10-14] age groups for 1950 to 1980.

## 3. Estimates of distribution rates by activity sector: 1950 - 1990

### 3.1 Benchmark data:

Table 2: Distribution of economically active population by activity sector

| Year | Agriculture | Industry Total | Manufac. | Services |
|---|---|---|---|---|
| **Men** | | | | |
| 1950 | 75.99 | 8.78 | 5.73 | 15.23 |
| 1959 | 66.23 | 13.35 | 8.64 | 20.42 |
| 1970 | 52.07 | 25.46 | 15.44 | 22.47 |
| 1979 | 45.51 | 29.49 | 17.29 | 25.00 |
| 1989 | 38.13 | 33.58 | 18.09 | 28.29 |
| **Women** | | | | |
| 1950 | 86.61 | 3.15 | 2.52 | 10.24 |
| 1959 | 77.90 | 7.58 | 6.57 | 14.52 |
| 1970 | 56.41 | 17.17 | 13.91 | 26.41 |
| 1979 | 40.91 | 22.73 | 18.09 | 36.36 |
| 1989 | 27.56 | 26.00 | 20.06 | 46.45 |

Source(s): BLT-94-2.

### 3.2 Method(s):   data from BLT-94-13

#### 3.2.1 Men:

- 1950, 1960, 1970, 1980 et 1990, respectively 1950, 1959, 1970, 1981
and 1989 distribution rates derived from the Bulletin of Labour Statistics, 1994-

#### 3.2.2 Women:

Method, hypothesis and treatment identical to those used for men.

## 4. Projection of activity rates: 2000 - 2010

### 4.1 Model(s):   hyperbole and logistic

#### 4.1.1 Men:

- To the [15+] age groups, application of function F3;
- Modification of the trends for the [20-49] age groups.

#### 4.1.2 Women:

- To the [15-24] and [55+] age groups, application of function F3;
- To the [25-54] age groups, application of function F6;
- Modification of the trends for the [20-54] age groups.

*Notes on adjustments of rates, see p. 3-8.*        *Notes on projection functions, see p. 10.*

# Mongolia

## 1. Source(s) of benchmark data

Code(s):  Title(s):

EPPA3  Economically active population: Estimates and Projections, 1950-2025, Third edition, ILO, Geneva, 1986.

## 2. Estimates of activity rates: 1950 - 1990

### 2.1 Benchmark data:

Table 1: Activity rates by sex and age group

| Age group | Year 1950 | 1960 | 1970 | 1980 |
|---|---|---|---|---|
| **Men** | | | | |
| 10-14 | 5.75 | 5.40 | 4.65 | 4.00 |
| 15-19 | 84.90 | 82.40 | 76.50 | 71.45 |
| 20-24 | 95.40 | 94.70 | 93.05 | 91.65 |
| 25-29 | 96.80 | 96.80 | 96.85 | 96.90 |
| 30-34 | 98.00 | 98.00 | 98.05 | 98.10 |
| 35-39 | 98.25 | 98.20 | 98.15 | 98.05 |
| 40-44 | 98.40 | 98.30 | 98.05 | 97.80 |
| 45-49 | 98.35 | 98.15 | 97.65 | 97.20 |
| 50-54 | 98.35 | 97.90 | 96.75 | 95.75 |
| 55-59 | 98.35 | 97.30 | 94.90 | 92.85 |
| 60-64 | 95.80 | 92.60 | 85.25 | 78.95 |
| 65+ | 69.20 | 65.90 | 58.35 | 51.85 |
| **Women** | | | | |
| 10-14 | 6.45 | 4.90 | 3.80 | 3.05 |
| 15-19 | 88.50 | 72.90 | 66.75 | 60.80 |
| 20-24 | 78.40 | 79.15 | 79.45 | 79.70 |
| 25-29 | 67.95 | 75.50 | 78.50 | 81.40 |
| 30-34 | 66.00 | 75.05 | 78.60 | 82.10 |
| 35-39 | 68.20 | 76.65 | 80.00 | 83.20 |
| 40-44 | 70.00 | 77.40 | 80.35 | 83.20 |
| 45-49 | 70.50 | 76.80 | 79.30 | 81.75 |
| 50-54 | 71.50 | 75.25 | 76.70 | 78.15 |
| 55-59 | 79.75 | 74.10 | 72.00 | 69.80 |
| 60-64 | 83.90 | 66.95 | 60.30 | 53.80 |
| 65+ | 58.40 | 43.05 | 37.00 | 31.10 |

Source(s): EPPA3.

### 2.2 Method(s): linear extrapolation

#### 2.2.1 Men:

- 1950-80, 1950-80 activity rates derived from the EPPA3;
- 1990, extrapolation of 1950-80 activity rates derived from the EPPA3;
modification of the trends of the [10-24] and [65+] age groups.

#### 2.2.2 Women:

- 1950-80, 1950-80 activity rates derived from the EPPA3;
- 1990, extrapolation of 1950-80 activity rates derived from the EPPA3;
adjustment of extrapolated rates on the basis of variations in 1980
interpolated rates, in relation to the 1980 rates derived from the EPPA3;
modification of the trends of the [10-19] and [65+] age groups.

## 3. Estimates of distribution rates by activity sector: 1950 - 1990

### 3.1 Benchmark data:

Table 2: Distribution of economically active population by activity sector

| Year | Agriculture | Industry Total | Manufac. | Services |
|---|---|---|---|---|
| **Men** | | | | |
| 1950 | 70.00 | 17.00 | .. | 13.00 |
| 1960 | 64.00 | 19.00 | .. | 17.00 |
| 1970 | 51.00 | 21.00 | .. | 28.00 |
| 1980 | 43.00 | 21.00 | .. | 36.00 |
| **Women** | | | | |
| 1950 | 67.00 | 17.00 | .. | 16.00 |
| 1960 | 57.00 | 19.00 | .. | 24.00 |
| 1970 | 44.00 | 21.00 | .. | 25.00 |
| 1980 | 36.00 | 21.00 | .. | 43.00 |

Source(s): EPPA3.

### 3.2 Method(s): linear extrapolation

#### 3.2.1 Men:

- 1950-80, 1950-80 distribution rates derived from the EPPA3;
- 1990, extrapolation of 1950-80 distribution rates derived from the EPPA3.

#### 3.2.2 Women:

- 1950-80, 1950-80 distribution rates derived from the EPPA3;
- 1980-90, extrapolation of 1950-80 distribution rates derived from the EPPA3;
modification of the trends in all sectors.

## 4. Projection of activity rates: 2000 - 2010

### 4.1 Model(s): linear, log-linear, hyperbole and logistic

#### 4.1.1 Men:

- To the [10-59] age groups, application of function F1;
- To the [60+] age groups, application of function F3;
- Modification of the trends for the [10-34] age groups.

#### 4.1.2 Women:

- To the [10-19] age groups, application of function F2;
- To the [20-49] age groups, application of function F6;
- To the [50+] age groups, application of function F3;
- Modification of the trend for the [10-14] age group.

*Notes on adjustments of rates, see p. 3-8.*

*Notes on projection functions, see p. 10.*

# Morocco

## 1. Source(s) of benchmark data

Code(s):     Title(s):

EPPA3      Economically active population: Estimates and Projections, 1950-2025, Third edition, ILO, Geneva, 1986.
R1971      Recensement général de la population et de l'habitat 1971: résultats de l'exhaustif, niveau national, Direction de la statistique, Rabat, 1976.
R1982      Caractéristiques socio-économiques de la population d'après le recensement général de la population et de l'habitat de 1982,
           Direction de la statistique, Rabat, 1984.

## 2. Estimates of activity rates: 1950 - 1990

### 2.1 Benchmark data:

Table 1: Activity rates by sex and age group

| Age group | Year | | | | |
|---|---|---|---|---|---|
| | 1950 (1) | 1960 (1) | 1970 (1) | 1980 (1) | 1982 (2) |
| **Men** | | | | | |
| 10-14 | 33.50 | 25.50 | 17.50 | 16.50 | 16.51 |
| 15-19 | 80.00 | 70.00 | 60.00 | 57.00 | 57.03 |
| 20-24 | 95.40 | 93.00 | 85.40 | 81.10 | 80.32 |
| 25-29 | 97.20 | 97.10 | 96.20 | 95.30 | 95.17 |
| 30-34 | 97.40 | 97.50 | 97.25 | 97.70 | 98.14 |
| 35-39 | 97.00 | 97.00 | 97.00 | 98.00 | 98.37 |
| 40-44 | 96.50 | 96.60 | 96.70 | 97.80 | 98.06 |
| 45-49 | 96.20 | 96.30 | 96.40 | 96.60 | 96.56 |
| 50-54 | 95.80 | 95.00 | 94.30 | 93.60 | 93.27 |
| 55-59 | 95.10 | 94.00 | 92.00 | 90.00 | 89.53 |
| 60-64 | 94.00 | 91.00 | 86.00 | 81.00 | 68.94 |
| 65+ | 84.00 | 68.00 | 55.70 | 43.50 | 42.12 |
| **Women** | | | | | |
| 10-14 | 5.30 | 5.80 | 8.70 | 11.95 | 11.91 |
| 15-19 | 6.00 | 8.80 | 15.70 | 18.40 | 18.97 |
| 20-24 | 5.80 | 6.20 | 13.00 | 19.00 | 20.42 |
| 25-29 | 5.60 | 6.00 | 9.90 | 19.00 | 20.94 |
| 30-34 | 6.00 | 7.30 | 9.90 | 16.50 | 17.72 |
| 35-39 | 6.00 | 8.50 | 10.70 | 15.00 | 16.16 |
| 40-44 | 6.30 | 9.70 | 12.70 | 14.50 | 14.65 |
| 45-49 | 7.00 | 10.60 | 12.30 | 14.50 | 14.09 |
| 50-54 | 7.20 | 10.60 | 12.60 | 14.50 | 14.64 |
| 55-59 | 7.20 | 10.60 | 12.60 | 14.50 | 14.63 |
| 60-64 | 7.00 | 9.20 | 10.20 | 11.00 | 11.16 |
| 65+ | 6.50 | 6.30 | 5.90 | 5.50 | 5.30 |

Source(s): (1) EPPA3; (2) R1982.

### 2.2 Method(s):  linears interpolation and extrapolation

#### 2.2.1 Men:

- 1950-80, 1950-80 activity rates derived from the EPPA3;
- 1990, extrapolation of 1950-80 activity rates derived from the EPPA3 and of adjusted activity rates derived from the 1982 census;
modification of the trends of the [10-14], [25-54] and [65+] age groups.

#### 2.2.2 Women:

- 1950-80, 1950-80 adjusted activity rates derived from the EPPA3;
- 1990, extrapolation of 1950-80 activity rates derived from the EPPA3 and of activity rates derived from 1982 census;
adjustment of extrapolated rates on the basis of variations in 1980 interpolated rates, in relation to the 1980 activity rates derived from the EPPA3;
modification of the trends of the [10-14], [20-49] and [55+] age groups;
the adjustment was made on the basis of the adjustment model for activity rates of women working in agriculture as contributing family workers.

## 3. Estimates of distribution rates  by activity sector: 1950 - 1990

### 3.1 Benchmark data:

Table 2: Distribution of economically active population by activity sector

| Year | Agriculture | Industry | | Services |
|---|---|---|---|---|
| | | Total | Manufac. | |
| **Men** | | | | |
| 1971 (1) | 59.44 | 16.51 | .. | 24.05 |
| 1982 (2) | 44.84 | 25.02 | 13.38 | 30.14 |
| **Women** | | | | |
| 1971 (1) | 44.23 | 23.20 | .. | 32.56 |
| 1982 (2) | 35.70 | 33.87 | 33.19 | 30.43 |

Source(s): (1) R1971; (2) R1982.

### 3.2 Method(s):  linears interpolation and extrapolation

#### 3.2.1 Men:

- 1950-70, 1950-70 distribution rates derived from the EPPA3;
- 1980-90, interpolation and extrapolation of adjusted distribution rates derived from the 1971 census and of distribution rates derived from the 1982 census;
modification of the trends in all sectors.

#### 3.2.2 Women:

- 1950-70, 1950-70 distribution rates derived from the EPPA3;
- 1980-90, interpolation and extrapolation of adjusted distribution rates derived from the 1971 census and of distribution rates derived from the 1982 census;
modification of the trends in all sectors;
adjustment of 1950-90 rates to make allowance for the under-registration of contributing family workers in agriculture.

## 4. Projection of activity rates: 2000 - 2010

### 4.1 Model(s):  linear and hyperbole

#### 4.1.1 Men:

- To the [10-24] age groups, application of function F1;
- To the [25+] age groups, application of function F3;
- Modification of the trends for the [20-24] and [30-49] age groups.

#### 4.1.2 Women:

- To all age groups, application of function F1;
- Modification of the trends for all age groups.

---

*Notes on  adjustments of rates, see p. 3-8.*          *Notes on  projection functions, see p. 10.*

124

# Mozambique

## 1. Source(s) of benchmark data

Code(s):  Title(s):
EPPA3  Economically active population: Estimates and Projections, 1950-2025, Third edition, ILO, Geneva, 1986.
ASTER  Yearbook of Labour Statistics 1945-89 - Retrospective Edition on Population Censuses, ILO, Geneva, 1990.
ADNU88  Demographic Yearbook 1988 - Population census statistics - Fortieth Edition, United Nations, New York, 1990.
STAT  Database on Labour Statistics, LABORSTA - Bureau of Statistics, ILO, Geneva.

## 2. Estimates of activity rates: 1950 - 1990

### 2.1 Benchmark data:

Table 1: Activity rates by sex and age group

| Age group | 1950 (1) | 1960 (1) | 1970 (1) | 1980 (1) | 1980 (2) |
|---|---|---|---|---|---|
| **Men** | | | | | |
| 10-14 | 57.90 | 55.80 | 53.65 | 51.50 | 24.52 |
| 15-19 | 79.35 | 77.00 | 74.60 | 72.25 | 52.90 |
| 20-24 | 94.20 | 93.25 | 92.35 | 91.40 | 91.41 |
| 25-29 | 98.60 | 98.50 | 98.35 | 98.20 | 97.73 |
| 30-34 | 98.85 | 98.70 | 98.55 | 98.40 | 98.74 |
| 35-39 | 99.10 | 98.95 | 98.75 | 98.60 | 98.87 |
| 40-44 | 99.30 | 99.15 | 98.95 | 98.80 | 98.86 |
| 45-49 | 99.35 | 99.20 | 99.05 | 98.90 | 98.85 |
| 50-54 | 99.30 | 99.15 | 98.95 | 98.70 | 98.53 |
| 55-59 | 99.20 | 99.00 | 98.70 | 98.60 | 98.16 |
| 60-64 | 98.90 | 98.25 | 97.65 | 97.00 | 97.01 |
| 65+ | 94.75 | 93.50 | 92.25 | 91.00 | 92.06 |
| **Women** | | | | | |
| 10-14 | 52.50 | 51.65 | 50.85 | 50.00 | 33.33 |
| 15-19 | 83.10 | 81.40 | 79.70 | 78.00 | 68.88 |
| 20-24 | 92.50 | 90.85 | 89.15 | 87.50 | 87.56 |
| 25-29 | 93.60 | 92.05 | 90.55 | 89.00 | 90.02 |
| 30-34 | 95.35 | 93.90 | 92.45 | 91.00 | 91.47 |
| 35-39 | 95.55 | 94.20 | 92.85 | 91.50 | 93.05 |
| 40-44 | 95.65 | 94.45 | 93.20 | 92.00 | 93.01 |
| 45-49 | 96.05 | 94.85 | 93.70 | 92.50 | 93.43 |
| 50-54 | 94.50 | 93.50 | 92.50 | 91.50 | 92.28 |
| 55-59 | 91.65 | 90.95 | 90.20 | 89.50 | 91.41 |
| 60-64 | 88.10 | 87.75 | 87.35 | 87.00 | 87.80 |
| 65+ | 76.45 | 76.30 | 76.15 | 76.00 | 78.46 |

Source(s): (1) EPPA3; (2) ASTER and ADNU88.

### 2.2 Method(s): linears interpolation and extrapolation

#### 2.2.1 Men:

- 1980, adjusted activity rates derived from the 1980 census;
- 1950-70 and 1990, interpolation and extrapolation of 1950-70 and 1990 activity rates derived from the EPPA3;
adjustment of interpolated and extrapolated rates on the basis of variations in 1980 interpolated rates, in relation to the 1980 activity rates derived from the EPPA3; modification of the trends for all age groups for 1950-80 and of the [60+] age groups for 1990.

#### 2.2.2 Women:

Method, hypothesis and treatment identical to those used for men.

## 3. Estimates of distribution rates by activity sector: 1950 - 1990

### 3.1 Benchmark data:

Table 2: Distribution of economically active population by activity sector

| Year | Agriculture | Industry Total | Manufac. | Services |
|---|---|---|---|---|
| **Men** | | | | |
| 1950 (1) | 82.00 | 7.10 | .. | 10.90 |
| 1960 (1) | 78.70 | 9.40 | .. | 11.90 |
| 1970 (1) | 75.40 | 11.60 | .. | 13.00 |
| 1980 (1) | 72.00 | 13.90 | .. | 14.10 |
| 1980 (2) | 71.99 | 13.93 | 12.35 | 14.08 |
| **Women** | | | | |
| 1950 (1) | 98.15 | 0.40 | .. | 1.45 |
| 1960 (1) | 97.80 | 0.50 | .. | 1.70 |
| 1970 (1) | 97.40 | 0.70 | .. | 1.90 |
| 1980 (1) | 97.05 | 0.80 | .. | 2.15 |
| 1980 (2) | 97.05 | 0.80 | 0.78 | 2.15 |

Source(s): (1) EPPA3; (2) STAT.

### 3.2 Method(s): linear extrapolation

#### 3.2.1 Men:

- 1950-80, 1950-80 distribution rates derived from the EPPA3;
- 1990, distribution rates estimated on the basis of extrapolation of 1950-80 distribution rates derived from the EPPA3;
modification of the trends in all sectors;
- Application of manufacturing/industry ratio derived from the 1980 census.

#### 3.2.2 Women:

Method, hypothesis and treatment identical to those used for men.

## 4. Projection of activity rates: 2000 - 2010

### 4.1 Model(s): linear

#### 4.1.1 Men:

- To all age groups, application of function F1;
- Modification of the trends for the [10-29] and [60+] age groups.

#### 4.1.2 Women:

- To all age groups, application of function F1;
- Modification of the trends for the [25-49] and [60+] age groups.

*Notes on adjustments of rates, see p. 3-8.*  *Notes on projection functions, see p. 10.*

# Myanmar

## 1. Source(s) of benchmark data

Code(s):     Title(s):

ADNU84     Demographic Yearbook 1984 - Population census statistics II - Thirty-sixth Edition, United Nations, New York, 1986.
STAT     Database on Labour Statistics - LABORSTA, Bureau of Statistics, ILO, Geneva.
EPPA4     Economically active population 1950-2010 - Fourth edition, ILO, Geneva 1996.

## 2. Estimates of activity rates: 1950 - 1990

### 2.1 Benchmark data:

Table 1: Activity rates by sex and age group

| Age group | Year 1983 (1) | 1983 (2) | 1983 (3) |
|---|---|---|---|
| **Men** | | | |
| 10-14 | 2.24 | 8.62 | 89.75 |
| 15-19 | 26.31 | 47.32 | 51.68 |
| 20-24 | 64.39 | 73.76 | 25.03 |
| 25-29 | 80.72 | 79.34 | 16.82 |
| 30-34 | 86.53 | 82.27 | 14.45 |
| 35-39 | 88.92 | 83.14 | 14.55 |
| 40-44 | 88.68 | 84.18 | 15.11 |
| 45-49 | 86.59 | 82.71 | 16.25 |
| 50-54 | 80.98 | 81.30 | 18.12 |
| 55-59 | 77.62 | 80.19 | 20.08 |
| 60-64 | 63.06 | 72.67 | 29.24 |
| 65+ | 48.42 | 57.09 | 45.56 |
| **Women** | | | |
| 10-14 | 2.76 | 8.37 | 88.53 |
| 15-19 | 18.08 | 36.70 | 64.21 |
| 20-24 | 34.15 | 49.10 | 59.92 |
| 25-29 | 43.11 | 50.00 | 59.37 |
| 30-34 | 46.14 | 51.30 | 59.10 |
| 35-39 | 46.15 | 53.40 | 58.36 |
| 40-44 | 48.56 | 53.87 | 57.77 |
| 45-49 | 50.39 | 52.29 | 57.66 |
| 50-54 | 49.00 | 53.64 | 57.90 |
| 55-59 | 47.47 | 51.01 | 59.21 |
| 60-64 | 35.68 | 43.58 | 63.35 |
| 65+ | 20.81 | 27.57 | 75.43 |

Note(s): (1) Urban; (2) Rural; (3) Total.
Source(s): ADNU88 and STAT.

### 2.2 Method(s): linear interpolation

**2.2.1 Men:**

- 1950-90, application to 1950-90 activity rates derived from the urban-rural mod
the variations in adjusted activity rates derived from the 1983 census,
in relation to 1983 interpolated rates.

**2.2.2 Women:**

- 1950-90, application to estimated activity rates for Thailand,
the variations in the 1983 estimated activity rates, in relation to adjusted
activity rates derived from the 1983 census;
modification of the trends of the [10-14] age group.

## 3. Estimates of distribution rates by activity sector: 1950 - 1990

### 3.1 Benchmark data:

Table 2: Distribution of economically active population by activity sector

| Year | Agriculture | Industry Total | Manufac. | Services |
|---|---|---|---|---|
| **Men** | | | | |
| 1950 (1) | 81.30 | 4.00 | .. | 14.70 |
| 1960 (1) | 78.70 | 6.05 | .. | 15.25 |
| 1970 (1) | 75.10 | 7.35 | .. | 17.55 |
| 1980 (1) | 71.24 | 16.15 | 13.11 | 12.61 |
| 1983 (2) | 71.69 | 9.41 | 6.80 | 18.90 |
| **Women** | | | | |
| 1950 (1) | 85.75 | 2.55 | .. | 11.70 |
| 1960 (1) | 84.70 | 3.55 | .. | 11.75 |
| 1970 (1) | 78.25 | 5.55 | .. | 16.20 |
| 1980 (1) | 75.31 | 9.96 | 8.98 | 14.73 |
| 1983 (2) | 79.52 | 7.71 | 7.29 | 12.77 |

Note(s): (1) Viet Nam.
Source(s): (1) EPPA4; (2) STAT.

### 3.2 Method(s): linear interpolation

**3.2.1 Men:**

- 1950-90, interpolation of 1950-90 distribution rates estimated for Viet Nam;
adjustment of interpolated rates on the basis of 3/4 of variations in 1983
interpolated rates, in relation to adjusted distribution rates derived from
the 1983 census.

**3.2.2 Women:**

Method, hypothesis and treatment identical to those used for men.

## 4. Projection of activity rates: 2000 - 2010

### 4.1 Model(s): linear, hyperbole and logistic

**4.1.1 Men:**

- To all age groups, application of function F1;
- Modification of the trends for the [10-24] and [60+] age groups.

**4.1.2 Women:**

- To the [10-19] age groups, application of function F1;
- To the [20-64] age groups, application of function F6;
- To the [65+] age group, application of function F3;
- Modification of the trends for the [10-64] age groups.

*Notes on adjustments of rates, see p. 3-8.*     *Notes on projection functions, see p. 10.*

# Namibia

## 1. Source(s) of benchmark data

Code(s):     Title(s):

EPPA3     Economically active population: Estimates and Projections, 1950-2025, Third edition, ILO, Geneva, 1986.
ASTER     Yearbook of Labour Statistics 1945-89 - Retrospective Edition on Population Censuses, ILO, Geneva, 1990.
R1991     Republic of Namibia, 1991 Population and Housing Census, Report A, Statistical tables, Central Statistical Office, Windhoek, 1993.

## 2. Estimates of activity rates: 1950 - 1990

### 2.1 Benchmark data:

Table 1: Activity rates by sex and age group

| Age group | Year 1960 (1) | 1991 (2) |
|---|---|---|
| **Men** | | |
| 10-14 | 45.00 | 29.31 |
| 15-19 | 75.00 | 52.96 |
| 20-24 | 95.90 | 80.46 |
| 25-29 | 99.40 | 95.04 |
| 30-34 | 99.25 | 97.29 |
| 35-39 | 99.10 | 97.04 |
| 40-44 | 99.05 | 97.01 |
| 45-49 | 98.75 | 96.61 |
| 50-54 | 98.50 | 94.12 |
| 55-59 | 98.00 | 90.94 |
| 60-64 | 95.60 | 65.16 |
| 65+ | 79.00 | 36.27 |
| **Women** | | |
| 10-14 | 43.42 | 18.96 |
| 15-19 | 58.78 | 31.03 |
| 20-24 | 62.84 | 59.51 |
| 25-29 | 54.45 | 67.88 |
| 30-34 | 54.07 | 66.21 |
| 35-39 | 53.09 | 65.69 |
| 40-44 | 53.16 | 64.34 |
| 45-49 | 54.25 | 63.08 |
| 50-54 | 53.01 | 58.67 |
| 55-59 | 48.63 | 52.85 |
| 60-64 | 42.95 | 36.55 |
| 65+ | 30.69 | 20.59 |

Source(s): (1) EPPA3; (2) R1991.

### 2.2 Method(s): linears interpolation and extrapolation

**2.2.1 Men:**

- 1950-90, interpolation and extrapolation of 1960 activity rates
derived from the EPPA3 and of adjusted activity rates derived
from the 1991 census;
modification of the trends of the [10-14] and [20+] age groups for 1950
and for the [20+] age groups for 1960-90.

**2.2.2 Women:**

Method, hypothesis and treatment identical to those used for men.

## 3. Estimates of distribution rates by activity sector: 1950 - 1990

### 3.1 Benchmark data:

Table 2: Distribution of economically active population by activity sector

| Year | Agriculture | Industry Total | Manufac. | Services |
|---|---|---|---|---|
| **Men** | | | | |
| 1960 (1) | 62.68 | 21.71 | 5.34 | 15.61 |
| 1991 (2) | 45.30 | 20.65 | 4.88 | 34.06 |
| **Women** | | | | |
| 1960 (1) | 58.62 | 1.94 | 1.38 | 39.43 |
| 1991 (2) | 52.10 | 7.88 | 7.02 | 40.01 |

Source(s): (1) ASTER; (2) R1991.

### 3.2 Method(s): weighted average

**3.2.1 Men:**

- 1950-90, interpolation and extrapolation of 1950-80 distribution rates
derived from the EPPA3 and of distribution rates derived from the 1991 census;
- Application of manufacturing/industry ratio derived from the 1991 census.

**3.2.2 Women:**

Method, hypothesis and treatment identical to those used for men.

## 4. Projection of activity rates: 2000 - 2010

### 4.1 Model(s): linear, hyperbole and log-linear

**4.1.1 Men:**

- To the [10-19] age groups, application of function F1;
- To the [20+] age groups, application of function F3;
- Modification of the trends for the [10-14] and [20+] age groups.

**4.1.2 Women:**

- To the [10-14] age group, application of function F2;
- To the [15-24] and [60+] age groups, application of function F3;
- To the [25-59] age groups, application of function F1;
- Modification of the trends for the [10-14], [25-29] and [55-59] age groups.

*Notes on adjustments of rates, see p. 3-8.*     *Notes on projection functions, see p. 10.*

# Nepal

## 1. Source(s) of benchmark data

| Code(s): | Title(s): |
|---|---|
| ADNU84 | Demographic Yearbook 1984 - Population census statistics II - Thirty-sixth Edition, United Nations, New York, 1986. |
| STAT | Database on Labour Statistics - LABORSTA, Bureau of Statistics, ILO, Geneva. |

## 2. Estimates of activity rates: 1950 - 1990

### 2.1 Benchmark data:

Table 1: Activity rates by sex and age group

| Age group | Year 1961 | 1971 | 1981 |
|---|---|---|---|
| **Men** | | | |
| 10-14 | 74.69 | .. | 61.28 |
| 15-19 | 91.75 | .. | 72.44 |
| 20-24 | 96.74 | .. | 89.71 |
| 25-29 | 98.41 | .. | 96.00 |
| 30-34 | 98.65 | .. | 97.35 |
| 35-39 | 98.85 | .. | 97.56 |
| 40-44 | 98.95 | .. | 97.83 |
| 45-49 | 97.90 | .. | 96.39 |
| 50-54 | 97.74 | .. | 94.27 |
| 55-59 | 95.12 | .. | 92.21 |
| 60-64 | 85.90 | .. | 83.27 |
| 65+ | 70.86 | .. | 68.69 |
| **Women** | | | |
| 10-14 | 67.20 | 51.30 | 50.29 |
| 15-19 | 77.47 | 66.00 | 61.50 |
| 20-24 | 69.33 | 62.51 | 59.57 |
| 25-29 | 64.77 | 61.33 | 57.59 |
| 30-34 | 61.04 | 61.45 | 57.11 |
| 35-39 | 59.04 | 61.54 | 58.54 |
| 40-44 | 56.03 | 60.16 | 58.88 |
| 45-49 | 54.00 | 60.60 | 58.87 |
| 50-54 | 51.42 | 56.90 | 58.24 |
| 55-59 | 46.06 | 52.05 | 55.78 |
| 60-64 | 33.49 | 38.72 | 39.92 |
| 65+ | 18.44 | 22.40 | 35.00 |

Source(s): STAT.

### 2.2 Method(s): linears interpolation and extrapolation

**2.2.1 Men:**

- 1950-90, interpolation and extrapolation of activity rates derived from the 1961 and 1981 censuses;
modification of the trends for all age groups for 1950 and 1990.

**2.2.2 Women:**

- 1950-90, interpolation and extrapolation of adjusted activity rates derived from the 1961, 1971 and 1981 censuses;
adjustment of activity rates based on the men/women ratio in agriculture derived from the 1961 census;
modification of the trends for all age groups for 1950 and 1990.

## 3. Estimates of distribution rates by activity sector: 1950 - 1990

### 3.1 Benchmark data:

Table 2: Distribution of economically active population by activity sector

| Year | Agriculture | Industry Total | Manufac. | Services |
|---|---|---|---|---|
| **Men** | | | | |
| 1961 | 92.54 | 2.59 | 2.33 | 4.87 |
| 1971 | 92.81 | 1.51 | 1.32 | 5.68 |
| 1981 | 90.64 | 0.77 | 0.64 | 8.60 |
| **Women** | | | | |
| 1961 | 97.48 | 1.28 | 1.24 | 1.24 |
| 1971 | 98.17 | 0.47 | 0.46 | 1.36 |
| 1981 | 97.06 | 0.23 | 0.21 | 2.71 |

Source(s): STAT.

### 3.2 Method(s): linears interpolation and extrapolation

**3.2.1 Men:**

- 1950-90, interpolation and extrapolation of distribution rates derived from the 1961, 1971 and 1981 censuses;
modification of the trends in all sectors for 1980 and 1990.

**3.2.2 Women:**

- 1950-80, interpolation and extrapolation of distribution rates derived the 1961, 1971 and 1981 censuses;
- 1990, distribution rates estimated for 1980.

## 4. Projection of activity rates: 2000 - 2010

### 4.1 Model(s): linear and logistic

**4.1.1 Men:**

- To the [10-54] age groups, application of function F1;
- To the [55+] age groups, application of function F3;
- Modification of the trends for the [20+] age groups.

**4.1.2 Women:**

- To the [10-39] and [60+] age groups, application of function F1;
- To the [40-59] age groups, application of function F6;
- Modification of the trends for all age groups.

---

*Notes on adjustments of rates, see p. 3-8.*     *Notes on projection functions, see p. 10.*

128

# Netherlands

## 1. Source(s) of benchmark data

Code(s):    Title(s):

EPPA3     Yearbook of Labour Statistics 1945-89 - Retrospective Edition on Population Censuses, ILO, Geneva, 1990.
STAT      Database on Labour Statistics, LABORSTA - Bureau of Statistics, ILO, Geneva.

## 2. Estimates of activity rates: 1950 - 1990

### 2.1 Benchmark data:

Table 1: Activity rates by sex and age group

| Age group | Year 1987 | 1988 | 1989 | 1990 | 1991 |
|---|---|---|---|---|---|
| **Men** | | | | | |
| 10-14 | 0.00 | 0.00 | 0.00 | 0.00 | 0.00 |
| 15-19 | 41.11 | 42.83 | 42.93 | 44.36 | 45.66 |
| 20-24 | 79.20 | 78.05 | 78.37 | 76.74 | 76.97 |
| 25-29 | 93.32 | 93.25 | 93.21 | 94.14 | 94.42 |
| 30-34 | 96.36 | 96.19 | 96.39 | 96.12 | 96.28 |
| 35-39 | 95.81 | 95.95 | 96.16 | 96.20 | 96.07 |
| 40-44 | 94.64 | 94.91 | 95.02 | 94.40 | 94.44 |
| 45-49 | 91.71 | 91.28 | 91.25 | 91.93 | 92.16 |
| 50-54 | 83.51 | 94.06 | 84.20 | 83.92 | 84.71 |
| 55-59 | 66.17 | 66.57 | 65.27 | 66.30 | 63.66 |
| 60-64 | 27.66 | 26.81 | 24.45 | 22.67 | 21.69 |
| 65+ | 2.96 | 3.32 | 3.20 | 3.08 | 2.96 |
| **Women** | | | | | |
| 10-14 | .. | .. | 0.00 | 0.00 | 0.00 |
| 15-19 | .. | .. | 39.18 | 41.86 | 42.89 |
| 20-24 | .. | .. | 75.49 | 77.06 | 76.01 |
| 25-29 | .. | .. | 67.15 | 69.90 | 72.96 |
| 30-34 | .. | .. | 58.35 | 61.30 | 62.52 |
| 35-39 | .. | .. | 59.51 | 61.20 | 62.65 |
| 40-44 | .. | .. | 56.33 | 58.35 | 61.32 |
| 45-49 | .. | .. | 49.38 | 52.49 | 54.31 |
| 50-54 | .. | .. | 37.66 | 38.72 | 42.04 |
| 55-59 | .. | .. | 23.96 | 25.56 | 22.78 |
| 60-64 | .. | .. | 8.94 | 7.82 | 7.80 |
| 65+ | .. | .. | ... | 0.30 | ... |

Source(s): STAT.

### 2.2 Method(s):  linear interpolation
arithmetic average

#### 2.2.1 Men:

- 1950-80, 1960-80 adjusted activity rates derived from the EPPA3;
adjustment of activity rates of the [15-29] and [50+] age groups based on
the interpolation of activity rates derived from the 1960, 1971 and 1981 censuses
- 1990, interpolation of adjusted activity rates derived from
the 1987, 1988, 1989, 1990 and 1991 surveys;
modification of the trend of the [65+] age group.

#### 2.2.2 Women:

- 1950-80, 1950-80 activity rates derived from the EPPA3;
adjustment of activity rate of the [15-19] age group;
- 1990, average of activity rates derived from
the 1989, 1990 and 1991 surveys;
modification of the trend of the [65+] age group.

## 3. Estimates of distribution rates by activity sector: 1950 - 1990

### 3.1 Benchmark data:

Table 2: Distribution of economically active population by activity sector

| Year | Agriculture | Industry Total | Manufac. | Services |
|---|---|---|---|---|
| **Men** | | | | |
| 1989 | 5.45 | 35.05 | 24.19 | 59.50 |
| 1990 | 5.29 | 35.13 | 24.17 | 59.58 |
| 1991 | 5.30 | 34.47 | 23.45 | 60.23 |
| **Women** | | | | |
| 1989 | 3.35 | 11.16 | 9.66 | 85.49 |
| 1990 | 3.40 | 11.35 | 10.04 | 85.25 |
| 1991 | 3.28 | 10.96 | 9.48 | 85.76 |

Source(s): (1) STAT.

### 3.2 Method(s):  arithmetic average

#### 3.2.1 Men:
- 1950-80, 1950-80 distribution rates derived from the EPPA3;
- 1990, averages of distribution rates derived from
the 1989, 1990 and 1991 surveys.

#### 3.2.2 Women:
- 1950-70, 1950-70 distribution rates derived from the EPPA3;
- 1980, averages of distribution rates derived from the 1979
and 1981 surveys;
- 1990, averages of distribution rates derived from the 1989, 1990
and 1991 surveys.

## 4. Projection of activity rates: 2000 - 2010

### 4.1 Model(s):  linear, log-linear, hyperbole and logistic

#### 4.1.1 Men:
- To the [15-19] age group, application of function F2;
- To the [20+] age groups, application of function F3;
- Modification of the trends for the [30-54] age groups.

#### 4.1.2 Women:
- To the [15-19] age group, application of function F1;
- To the [20-59] age groups, application of function F6;
- To the [60+] age groups, application of function F3;
- Modification of the trend for the [20-24] age group.

*Notes on adjustments of rates, see p. 3-8.*

*Notes on projection functions, see p. 10.*

# Netherlands Antilles

## 1. Source(s) of benchmark data

Code(s):     Title(s):

STAT        Database on Labour Statistics, LABORSTA - Bureau of Statistics, ILO, Geneva.

## 2. Estimates of activity rates: 1950 - 1990

### 2.1 Benchmark data:

Table 1: Activity rates by sex and age group

| Age group | Year | | |
|---|---|---|---|
| | 1972 | 1981 | 1992 |
| **Men** | | | |
| 10-14 | .. | 0.32 | 0.00 |
| 15-19 | .. | 34.10 | 29.76 |
| 20-24 | .. | 85.33 | 80.75 |
| 25-29 | .. | 94.93 | 91.46 |
| 30-34 | .. | 95.79 | 92.59 |
| 35-39 | .. | 96.01 | 93.10 |
| 40-44 | .. | 95.70 | 93.09 |
| 45-49 | .. | 94.83 | 91.54 |
| 50-54 | .. | 89.94 | 86.40 |
| 55-59 | .. | 80.46 | 67.78 |
| 60-64 | .. | 48.37 | 34.32 |
| 65+ | .. | 20.16 | 13.62 |
| **Women** | | | |
| 10-14 | 0.41 | 0.16 | 0.00 |
| 15-19 | 32.11 | 26.20 | 22.00 |
| 20-24 | 66.83 | 73.42 | 70.68 |
| 25-29 | 51.57 | 70.36 | 77.50 |
| 30-34 | 41.25 | 61.34 | 75.90 |
| 35-39 | 35.99 | 53.90 | 73.43 |
| 40-44 | 31.81 | 44.71 | 68.37 |
| 45-49 | 28.51 | 37.66 | 57.96 |
| 50-54 | 24.67 | 29.73 | 43.84 |
| 55-59 | 22.86 | 22.00 | 29.78 |
| 60-64 | 13.54 | 12.73 | 14.31 |
| 65+ | 5.41 | 4.12 | 3.59 |

Source(s): STAT.

### 2.2 Method(s):  linears interpolation and extrapolation

#### 2.2.1 Men:

- 1950-80, extrapolation of adjusted activity rates derived from
the 1981 and 1992 censuses;
modification of the trends of the [50-54] age group;
- 1990, interpolation of adjusted activity rates derived from
the 1981 and 1992 censuses.

#### 2.2.2 Women:

- 1950-70, extrapolation of adjusted activity rates derived from
the 1972 and 1981 censuses;
modification of the trends for all age groups;
- 1980, interpolation of adjusted activity rates derived from
the 1972 and 1981 censuses;
modification of the trend of the [50-54] age group;
- 1990, interpolation of activity rates derived from the 1981 and 1992 censuses.

## 3. Estimates of distribution rates by activity sector: 1950 - 1990

### 3.1 Benchmark data:

Table 2: Distribution of economically active population by activity sector

| Year | Agriculture | Industry | | Services |
|---|---|---|---|---|
| | | Total | Manufac. | |
| **Men** | | | | |
| 1960 | 2.83 | 56.86 | 40.51 | 40.31 |
| 1972 | 1.34 | 37.42 | 20.28 | 61.24 |
| 1981 | 0.55 | 30.54 | 14.38 | 68.91 |
| 1992 | 1.07 | 31.37 | 13.57 | 67.56 |
| **Women** | | | | |
| 1960 | 0.21 | 8.09 | 7.32 | 91.70 |
| 1972 | 0.20 | 13.34 | 11.68 | 86.46 |
| 1981 | 0.13 | 5.83 | 3.66 | 94.04 |
| 1992 | 0.28 | 5.20 | 3.76 | 94.52 |

Source(s): STAT

### 3.2 Method(s):  linears interpolation and extrapolation

#### 3.2.1 Men:

1950, extrapolation of distribution rates derived from the 1960
and 1972 censuses;
- 1970-90, interpolation of distribution rates derived from
the 1960, 1972, 1981 and 1992 censuses.

#### 3.2.2 Women:

Method, hypothesis and treatment identical to those used for men.

## 4. Projection of activity rates: 2000 - 2010

### 4.1 Model(s):  linear, hyperbole and logistic

#### 4.1.1 Men:

- To the [10-19] age groups, application of function F1;
- To the [20+] age groups, application of function F3;
- Modification of the trends for all age groups.

#### 4.1.2 Women:

- To the [15-19] age group, application of function F1;
- To the [20-64] age groups, application of function F6;
- To the [65+] age group, application of function F3;
- Modification of the trends for all age groups.

*Notes on adjustments of rates, see p. 3-8.*          *Notes on projection functions, see p. 10.*

# New Zealand

## 1. Source(s) of benchmark data

Code(s):     Title(s):

EPPA3     Yearbook of Labour Statistics 1945-89 - Retrospective Edition on Population Censuses, ILO, Geneva, 1990.
STAT     Database on Labour Statistics, LABORSTA - Bureau of Statistics, ILO, Geneva.

## 2. Estimates of activity rates: 1950 - 1990

### 2.1 Benchmark data:

Table 1: Activity rates by sex and age group

| Age group | Year 1980 (1) | 1989 (2) | 1990 (2) | 1991 (2) |
|---|---|---|---|---|
| **Men** | | | | |
| 10-14 | 0.00 | 0.00 | 0.00 | 0.00 |
| 15-19 | 55.65 | 55.81 | 56.09 | 53.79 |
| 20-24 | 89.80 | 86.02 | 84.46 | 82.90 |
| 25-29 | 95.65 | 94.23 | 92.25 | 92.43 |
| 30-34 | 96.90 | 94.98 | 93.02 | 93.86 |
| 35-39 | 97.10 | 94.97 | 93.64 | 94.50 |
| 40-44 | 97.10 | 94.95 | 94.02 | 94.98 |
| 45-49 | 96.30 | 93.33 | 92.73 | 93.17 |
| 50-54 | 94.35 | 91.94 | 90.18 | 91.14 |
| 55-59 | 88.10 | 78.13 | 78.39 | 80.67 |
| 60-64 | 48.50 | 33.76 | 35.34 | 33.19 |
| 65+ | 12.30 | 10.60 | 10.94 | 9.42 |
| **Women** | | | | |
| 10-14 | 0.00 | 0.00 | 0.00 | 0.00 |
| 15-19 | 48.80 | 49.38 | 56.68 | 52.22 |
| 20-24 | 62.50 | 69.46 | 69.81 | 71.70 |
| 25-29 | 41.30 | 61.25 | 61.80 | 61.62 |
| 30-34 | 39.70 | 60.49 | 61.54 | 63.05 |
| 35-39 | 49.10 | 72.86 | 71.58 | 72.54 |
| 40-44 | 54.10 | 77.92 | 78.45 | 79.38 |
| 45-49 | 51.80 | 75.78 | 77.32 | 77.73 |
| 50-54 | 43.35 | 69.80 | 69.54 | 69.08 |
| 55-59 | 30.55 | 47.05 | 44.56 | 47.46 |
| 60-64 | 12.40 | 14.41 | 17.34 | 15.48 |
| 65+ | 2.10 | 3.53 | 3.60 | 3.29 |

Source(s): (1) EPPA3; (2) STAT.

### 2.2 Method(s): arithmetic average

**2.2.1 Men:**

- 1950-80, 1950-80 activity rates derived from the EPPA3;
adjustment of activity rates of the [15-19] age group for 1980;
- 1990, average of activity rates derived from
the 1989, 1990 and 1991 surveys.

**2.2.2 Women:**

Method, hypothesis and treatment identical to those used for men.

## 3. Estimates of distribution rates by activity sector: 1950 - 1990

### 3.1 Benchmark data:

Table 2: Distribution of economically active population by activity sector

| Year | Agriculture | Industry Total | Manufac. | Services |
|---|---|---|---|---|
| **Men** | | | | |
| 1980 | 13.40 | 39.23 | 26.89 | 47.37 |
| 1991 | 12.59 | 32.32 | 20.81 | 55.09 |
| **Women** | | | | |
| 1980 | 6.19 | 21.75 | 19.95 | 72.06 |
| 1991 | 7.42 | 13.43 | 11.61 | 79.15 |

Source(s): STAT.

### 3.2 Method(s): weighted average

**3.2.1 Men:**

- 1950-80, 1950-80 distribution rates derived from the EPPA3;
- 1990, weighted averages of distribution rates derived from
the 1980 and 1991 surveys.

**3.2.2 Women:**

Method, hypothesis and treatment identical to those used for men.

## 4. Projection of activity rates: 2000 - 2010

### 4.1 Model(s): linear, hyperbole and logistic

**4.1.1 Men:**

- To the [15-19] age group, application of function F1;
- To the [20+] age groups, application of function F3;
- Modification of the trends for the [20-24] and [30-49] age groups.

**4.1.2 Women:**

- To the [15-24] age groups, application of function F1;
- To the [25-64] age groups, application of function F6;
- To the [65+] age group, application of function F3.

---

*Notes on adjustments of rates, see p. 3-8.*     *Notes on projection functions, see p. 10.*

# Nicaragua

## 1. Source(s) of benchmark data

| Code(s): | Title(s): |
|---|---|
| EPPA3 | Economically active population: Estimates and Projections, 1950-2025, Third edition, ILO, Geneva, 1986. |
| ASTER | Yearbook of Labour Statistics 1945-89 - Retrospective Edition on Population Censuses, ILO, Geneva, 1990. |
| AST91 | Yearbook of Labour Statistics 1991, ILO, Geneva, 1991. |
| STAT | Database on Labour Statistics, LABORSTA - Bureau of Statistics, ILO, Geneva. |

## 2. Estimates of activity rates: 1950 - 1990

### 2.1 Benchmark data:

Table 1: Activity rates by sex and age group

| Age group | 1950 (1) | 1960 (1) | 1971 (2) | 1985 (3) | 1990 (3) |
|---|---|---|---|---|---|
| **Men** | | | | | |
| 10-14 | 45.00 | 34.70 | 18.74 | .. | .. |
| 15-19 | 91.10 | 78.85 | 54.55 | .. | .. |
| 20-24 | 96.95 | 94.60 | 81.21 | .. | .. |
| 25-29 | 98.65 | 97.60 | 89.78 | .. | .. |
| 30-34 | 98.80 | 97.90 | 91.51 | .. | .. |
| 35-39 | 99.00 | 98.05 | 92.17 | .. | .. |
| 40-44 | 98.90 | 98.00 | 91.43 | .. | .. |
| 45-49 | 98.50 | 97.75 | 91.38 | .. | .. |
| 50-54 | 98.30 | 96.65 | 88.48 | .. | .. |
| 55-59 | 97.80 | 94.60 | 87.30 | .. | .. |
| 60-64 | 96.80 | 93.35 | 80.70 | .. | .. |
| 65+ | 86.30 | 75.05 | 60.73 | .. | .. |
| **Women** | | | | | |
| 10-14 | | | 4.01 | 6.34 | 6.92 |
| 15-19 | .. | .. | 17.44 | 23.62 | 25.62 |
| 20-24 | .. | .. | 25.62 | 38.75 | 42.10 |
| 25-29 | .. | .. | 23.70 | 45.61 | 49.45 |
| 30-34 | .. | .. | 22.99 | 50.03 | 54.99 |
| 35-39 | .. | .. | 22.86 | 45.95 | 51.72 |
| 40-44 | .. | .. | 22.32 | 45.79 | 47.69 |
| 45-49 | .. | .. | 20.59 | 41.70 | 40.04 |
| 50-54 | .. | .. | 18.64 | 37.46 | 42.86 |
| 55-59 | .. | .. | 17.27 | 33.84 | 35.43 |
| 60-64 | .. | .. | 13.99 | 22.06 | 23.71 |
| 65+ | .. | .. | 9.05 | 13.30 | 14.77 |

**Source(s)**: (1) EPPA3; (2) ASTER; (3) AST91.

### 2.2 Method(s): linears interpolation and extrapolation

#### 2.2.1 Men:

- 1950-60, 1950-60 activity rates derived from the EPPA3;
- 1970-90, interpolation and extrapolation of 1950-60 activity rates derived from the EPPA3 and of adjusted activity rates derived from the 1971 census; application to interpolated and extrapolated rates, variations in 1971 interpolated rates, in relation to adjusted activity rates derived from the 1971 census.

#### 2.2.2 Women:

- 1950-70, 1950-70 adjusted activity rates derived from the EPPA3; the adjustment was made on the basis of the adjustment model for activity rates of women working in agriculture as contributing family workers;
- 1980-90, interpolation and extrapolation of activity rates derived from the 1971 census, of activity rates derived from the 1985 survey and of 1990 official estimates; application to interpolated rates, variations in 1985 interpolated rates, in relation to activity rates derived from the 1985 census.

## 3. Estimates of distribution rates by activity sector: 1950 - 1990

### 3.1 Benchmark data:

Table 2: Distribution of economically active population by activity sector

| Year | Agriculture | Industry Total | Manufac. | Services |
|---|---|---|---|---|
| **Men** | | | | |
| 1960 (1) | 72.25 | 15.20 | .. | 12.55 |
| 1971 (2) | 58.83 | 18.05 | 11.45 | 23.12 |
| 1977 (3) | 53.49 | 22.02 | 14.49 | 24.50 |
| **Women** | | | | |
| 1960 (1) | 14.20 | 19.70 | .. | 66.10 |
| 1971 (2) | 8.20 | 17.22 | 16.68 | 74.58 |
| 1977 (3) | 15.73 | 20.85 | 20.32 | 63.42 |

**Source(s)**: (1) EPPA3; (2) ASTER; (3) STAT.

### 3.2 Method(s): weighted average linear extrapolation

#### 3.2.1 Men:

- 1950-60, 1950-60 distribution rates derived from the EPPA3;
- 1970, weighted averages of 1960 distribution rates derived from the EPPA3 and of distribution rates derived from the 1971 census;
- 1980-90, extrapolation of distribution rates derived from the 1971 census and of distribution rates derived from the 1977 official estimates; modification of the trends in all sectors.

#### 3.2.2 Women:

Method, hypothesis and treatment identical to those used for men.

## 4. Projection of activity rates: 2000 - 2010

### 4.1 Model(s): linear

#### 4.1.1 Men:

- To all age groups, application of function F1;
- Modification of the trends for the [10-19], [30-34], [40-44] and [65+] age groups.

#### 4.1.2 Women:

- To all age groups, application of function F1;
- Modification of the trends for the [10-24], [45-54] and [65+] age groups.

*Notes on adjustments of rates, see p. 3-8.*     *Notes on projection functions, see p. 10.*

# Niger

## 1. Source(s) of benchmark data

Code(s):     Title(s):

EPPA3     Economically active population: Estimates and Projections, 1950-2025, Third edition, ILO, Geneva, 1986.
ASTER     Yearbook of Labour Statistics 1945-89 - Retrospective Edition on Population Censuses, ILO, Geneva, 1990.
STAT     Database on Labour Statistics, LABORSTA - Bureau of Statistics, ILO, Geneva.

## 2. Estimates of activity rates: 1950 - 1990

### 2.1 Benchmark data:

Table 1: Activity rates by sex and age group

| Age group | 1959 (1) | 1950 (2) | 1960 (2) | 1970 (2) | 1977 (3) | 1980 (2) | 1988 (1) |
|---|---|---|---|---|---|---|---|
| **Men** | | | | | | | |
| 10-14 | 56.10 | .. | .. | .. | 20.63 | .. | 53.87 |
| 15-19 | 90.25 | .. | .. | .. | 83.88 | .. | 89.55 |
| 20-24 | 97.30 | .. | .. | .. | 95.90 | .. | 92.64 |
| 25-29 | 97.70 | .. | .. | .. | 98.15 | .. | 97.23 |
| 30-34 | 98.45 | .. | .. | .. | 98.68 | .. | 97.79 |
| 35-39 | 98.65 | .. | .. | .. | 98.95 | .. | 98.29 |
| 40-44 | 98.55 | .. | .. | .. | 98.57 | .. | 98.04 |
| 45-49 | 97.70 | .. | .. | .. | 98.56 | .. | 97.51 |
| 50-54 | 97.45 | .. | .. | .. | 97.05 | .. | 96.91 |
| 55-59 | 96.85 | .. | .. | .. | 96.15 | .. | 95.74 |
| 60-64 | 94.45 | .. | .. | .. | 89.80 | .. | 94.00 |
| 65+ | 82.25 | .. | .. | .. | 72.44 | .. | 87.86 |
| **Women** | | | | | | | |
| 10-14 | 50.15 | 50.35 | 50.15 | 49.90 | 2.83 | 46.90 | .. |
| 15-19 | 92.15 | 92.60 | 92.15 | 91.70 | 6.33 | 85.30 | .. |
| 20-24 | 96.35 | 96.80 | 96.35 | 95.90 | 6.49 | 89.70 | .. |
| 25-29 | 97.00 | 97.45 | 97.00 | 96.60 | 6.48 | 90.85 | .. |
| 30-34 | 98.40 | 98.75 | 98.40 | 98.00 | 7.07 | 92.60 | .. |
| 35-39 | 98.05 | 98.45 | 98.05 | 97.70 | 8.02 | 92.65 | .. |
| 40-44 | 97.20 | 97.55 | 97.20 | 96.90 | 9.08 | 92.35 | .. |
| 45-49 | 95.75 | 96.10 | 95.75 | 95.45 | 10.24 | 91.00 | .. |
| 50-54 | 87.90 | 88.20 | 87.90 | 87.65 | 10.13 | 83.95 | .. |
| 55-59 | 77.90 | 78.10 | 77.90 | 77.70 | 10.36 | 75.05 | .. |
| 60-64 | 61.80 | 61.90 | 61.80 | 61.70 | 8.01 | 60.05 | .. |
| 65+ | 35.70 | 35.75 | 35.70 | 35.65 | 6.40 | 35.10 | .. |

Source(s): (1) STAT; (2) EPPA3; (3) ASTER.

### 2.2 Method(s): linears interpolation and extrapolation

#### 2.2.1 Men:

- 1950-90, interpolation and extrapolation of activity rates derived from the 1959-60 survey and of activity rates derived from the 1977 and 1988 censuses.

#### 2.2.2 Women:

- 1950-90, interpolation and extrapolation of 1950-80 activity rates derived from the EPPA3;
adjustment of interpolated and extrapolated rates on the basis of variations in 1977 interpolated rates, in relation to the rates derived from the 1977 census; modification of the trends of the [20-34] age groups for 1950 to 1990.

## 3. Estimates of distribution rates by activity sector: 1950 - 1990

### 3.1 Benchmark data:

Table 2: Distribution of economically active population by activity sector

| Year | Agriculture | Industry Total | Industry Manufac. | Services |
|---|---|---|---|---|
| **Men** | | | | |
| 1950 (1) | 96.00 | 1.20 | .. | 2.80 |
| 1960 (1) | 95.00 | 1.50 | .. | 3.50 |
| 1970 (1) | 92.40 | 2.20 | .. | 5.40 |
| 1977 (2) | 91.91 | 2.83 | 1.73 | 5.26 |
| 1980 (1) | 88.25 | 3.00 | .. | 8.75 |
| **Women** | | | | |
| 1950 (1) | 98.00 | 0.05 | .. | 1.95 |
| 1960 (1) | 97.50 | 0.05 | .. | 2.45 |
| 1970 (1) | 96.20 | 0.10 | .. | 3.70 |
| 1977 (2) | 97.40 | 1.39 | 1.36 | 1.21 |
| 1980 (1) | 94.15 | 0.15 | .. | 5.7 |

Source(s): (1) EPPA3; (2) ASTER.

### 3.2 Method(s): linears interpolation and extrapolation

#### 3.2.1 Men:
- 1950-90, interpolation and extrapolation of 1950-80 distribution rates derived from the EPPA3 and of distribution rates derived from the 1977 census; modification of the trends in all sectors.

#### 3.2.2 Women:
Method, hypothesis and treatment identical to those used for men.

## 4. Projection of activity rates: 2000 - 2010

### 4.1 Model(s): linear and hyperbole

#### 4.1.1 Men:
- To all age groups, application of function F1;
- Modification of the trends for the [10-24] and [65+] age groups.

#### 4.1.2 Women:
- To the [10-19] age groups, application of function F1;
- To the [20+] age groups, application of function F3;
- Modification of the trends for the [20-59] age groups.

*Notes on adjustments of rates, see p. 3-8.*     *Notes on projection functions, see p. 10.*

# Nigeria

## 1. Source(s) of benchmark data

Code(s):    Title(s):
EPPA3      Economically active population: Estimates and Projections, 1950-2025, Third edition, ILO, Geneva, 1986.
ASTER     Yearbook of Labour Statistics 1945-89 - Retrospective Edition on Population Censuses, ILO, Geneva, 1990.
AST87      Yearbook of Labour Statistics 1987, ILO, Geneva, 1987.
AST93      Yearbook of Labour Statistics 1993, ILO, Geneva, 1993.

## 2. Estimates of activity rates: 1950 - 1990

### 2.1 Benchmark data:

Table 1: Activity rates by sex and age group

| Age group | 1950 (1) | 1960 (1) | 1970 (1) | 1983 (2) |
|---|---|---|---|---|
| **Men** | | | | |
| 10-14 | 46.85 | 44.60 | 43.10 | 62.04 |
| 15-19 | 77.95 | 74.95 | 72.90 | 29.79 |
| 20-24 | 92.60 | 91.45 | 90.65 | 69.12 |
| 25-29 | 97.00 | 96.85 | 96.70 | 92.52 |
| 30-34 | 97.70 | 97.50 | 97.35 | 96.16 |
| 35-39 | 97.85 | 97.65 | 97.50 | 97.56 |
| 40-44 | 97.65 | 97.45 | 97.30 | 97.94 |
| 45-49 | 96.95 | 96.80 | 96.65 | 98.79 |
| 50-54 | 96.30 | 96.05 | 95.85 | 96.66 |
| 55-59 | 95.05 | 94.65 | 94.35 | 94.63 |
| 60-64 | 91.40 | 90.70 | 90.20 | 91.48 |
| 65+ | 76.95 | 75.65 | 74.75 | 73.57 |
| **Women** | | | | |
| 10-14 | 21.25 | 20.20 | 19.50 | 5.36 |
| 15-19 | 46.30 | 44.25 | 42.85 | 13.58 |
| 20-24 | 50.30 | 48.95 | 48.05 | 24.57 |
| 25-29 | 53.90 | 52.40 | 51.35 | 37.21 |
| 30-34 | 57.20 | 55.55 | 54.45 | 40.25 |
| 35-39 | 59.25 | 57.70 | 56.65 | 47.77 |
| 40-44 | 61.60 | 60.05 | 59.00 | 49.31 |
| 45-49 | 65.55 | 63.85 | 62.70 | 55.30 |
| 50-54 | 70.00 | 67.85 | 66.70 | 57.08 |
| 55-59 | 67.15 | 64.90 | 63.35 | 52.55 |
| 60-64 | 59.50 | 56.65 | 54.70 | 43.61 |
| 65+ | 43.85 | 40.90 | 38.95 | 20.57 |

Source(s): (1) EPPA3; (2) AST87.

### 2.2 Method(s): linears interpolation and extrapolation

#### 2.2.1 Men:

- 1950-90, interpolation and extrapolation of 1950-70 activity rates derived from the EPPA3 and of adjusted activity rates derived from the 1983 survey;
modification of the trends for all age groups for 1950.

#### 2.2.2 Women:

- 1950-90, interpolation and extrapolation of 1950-70 activity rates derived from the EPPA3 and of adjusted activity rates derived from the 1983 survey;
adjustment of activity rates of the [10-24] age groups.

## 3. Estimates of distribution rates by activity sector: 1950 - 1990

### 3.1 Benchmark data:

Table 2: Distribution of economically active population by activity sector

| Year | Agriculture | Industry Total | Manufac. | Services |
|---|---|---|---|---|
| **Men** | | | | |
| 1970 (1) | 71.05 | 13.00 | .. | 15.95 |
| 1983 (2) | 38.74 | 10.74 | 4.35 | 50.52 |
| 1986 (3) | 49.98 | 7.58 | 4.11 | 42.44 |
| **Women** | | | | |
| 1970 (1) | 70.80 | 6.25 | .. | 22.95 |
| 1983 (2) | 22.77 | 7.44 | 6.09 | 69.79 |

Source(s): (1) EPPA3; (2) AST87; (3) AST93.

### 3.2 Method(s): linears interpolation and extrapolation

#### 3.2.1 Men:
- 1950-70, 1950-70 distribution rates derived from the EPPA3;
- 1980-90, interpolation and extrapolation of 1970 distribution rates derived from the EPPA3 and of averages of distribution rates derived from the 1983 and 1986 surveys;
modification of the trends in all sectors for 1990.

#### 3.2.2 Women:
- 1950-70, 1950-70 distribution rates derived from the EPPA3;
- 1980-90, interpolation and extrapolation of 1970 distribution rates derived from the EPPA3 and of distribution rates derived from the 1983 survey.

## 4. Projection of activity rates: 2000 - 2010

### 4.1 Model(s): linear and hyperbole

#### 4.1.1 Men:
- To the [10-19] age groups, application of function F1;
- To the [20+] age groups, application of function F3;
- Modification of the trends for the [10-14], [20-24], [40-44] and [60-64] age groups.

#### 4.1.2 Women:
- To all age groups, application of function F3;
- Modification of the trends for the [10-34] and [45-49] age groups.

*Notes on adjustments of rates, see p. 3-8.*    *Notes on projection functions, see p. 10.*

# Norway

## 1. Source(s) of benchmark data

Code(s):    Title(s):

EPPA3    Yearbook of Labour Statistics 1945-89 - Retrospective Edition on Population Censuses, ILO, Geneva, 1990.
STAT    Database on Labour Statistics, LABORSTA - Bureau of Statistics, ILO, Geneva.

## 2. Estimates of activity rates: 1950 - 1990

### 2.1 Benchmark data:

Table 1: Activity rates by sex and age group

| Age group | Year | | | | | |
|---|---|---|---|---|---|---|
|  | 1979 | 1980 | 1981 | 1989 | 1990 | 1991 |
| **Men** | | | | | | |
| 10-14 | 0.00 | 0.00 | 0.00 | 0.00 | 0.00 | 0.00 |
| 15-19 | ... | ... | ... | 46.97 | 44.62 | 39.20 |
| 20-24 | 79.49 | 78.52 | 80.29 | 79.89 | 78.49 | 74.42 |
| 25-29 | 88.89 | 88.51 | 89.60 | 90.06 | 88.55 | 86.78 |
| 30-34 | 96.25 | 96.02 | 95.24 | 95.15 | 93.87 | 93.17 |
| 35-39 | 97.76 | 96.73 | 95.72 | 94.97 | 93.51 | 94.12 |
| 40-44 | 96.23 | 96.73 | 96.79 | 94.44 | 93.98 | 93.83 |
| 45-49 | 94.00 | 93.62 | 95.15 | 93.80 | 93.94 | 92.57 |
| 50-54 | 90.91 | 92.63 | 93.67 | 90.53 | 89.22 | 87.13 |
| 55-59 | 88.70 | 86.63 | 87.71 | 83.16 | 82.02 | 81.18 |
| 60-64 | 74.07 | 75.74 | 73.67 | 64.95 | 64.21 | 62.24 |
| 65+ |  |  |  | 14.84 | 13.29 | 11.62 |
| **Women** | | | | | | |
| 10-14 | .. | .. | .. | 0.00 | 0.00 | 0.00 |
| 15-19 | .. | .. | .. | 46.03 | 43.55 | 40.83 |
| 20-24 | .. | .. | .. | 70.30 | 67.07 | 66.46 |
| 25-29 | .. | .. | .. | 75.50 | 75.00 | 73.46 |
| 30-34 | .. | .. | .. | 76.92 | 78.21 | 79.74 |
| 35-39 | .. | .. | .. | 82.00 | 81.05 | 80.89 |
| 40-44 | .. | .. | .. | 81.05 | 81.94 | 83.22 |
| 45-49 | .. | .. | .. | 81.97 | 83.46 | 81.34 |
| 50-54 | .. | .. | .. | 75.79 | 74.49 | 75.00 |
| 55-59 | .. | .. | .. | 63.16 | 61.96 | 63.04 |
| 60-64 | .. | .. | .. | 44.12 | 46.53 | 47.47 |
| 65+ | .. | .. | .. | 6.44 | 6.43 | 5.92 |

Source(s): STAT.

### 2.2 Method(s): linear interpolation
arithmetic average

#### 2.2.1 Men:

- 1950-70, 1950-70 activity rates derived from the EPPA3;
- 1980, interpolation of adjusted activity rates derived from the 1980, 1981 and 1982 surveys;
adjustment of activity rate of the [15-19] age group;
- 1990, average of adjusted activity rates derived from the 1989, 1990 and 1991 surveys;
adjustment of activity rate of the [15-19] age group.

#### 2.2.2 Women:

- 1950-80, 1950-80 activity rates derived from the EPPA3;
- 1990, averages of adjusted activity rates derived from the 1989, 1990 and 1991 surveys;
adjustment of activity rate of the [15-19] age group.

## 3. Estimates of distribution rates by activity sector: 1950 - 1990

### 3.1 Benchmark data:

Table 2: Distribution of economically active population by activity sector

| Year | Agriculture | Industry | | Services |
|---|---|---|---|---|
|  |  | Total | Manufac. |  |
| **Men** | | | | |
| 1979 | 10.04 | 41.23 | 21.43 | 48.73 |
| 1980 | 9.98 | 40.11 | 20.14 | 49.91 |
| 1981 | 9.86 | 40.31 | 19.72 | 49.83 |
| 1989 | 8.45 | 36.38 | 19.30 | 55.17 |
| 1990 | 8.03 | 37.16 | 19.44 | 54.81 |
| 1991 | 8.27 | 35.77 | 19.67 | 55.96 |
| **Women** | | | | |
| 1979 | 6.46 | 14.10 | 11.20 | 79.45 |
| 1980 | 5.98 | 13.74 | 9.92 | 80.28 |
| 1981 | 5.81 | 12.98 | 9.77 | 81.21 |
| 1989 | 4.05 | 11.82 | 8.41 | 84.13 |
| 1990 | 3.73 | 11.67 | 8.21 | 84.60 |
| 1991 | 3.84 | 11.42 | 8.43 | 84.74 |

Source(s): STAT.

### 3.2 Method(s): arithmetic average

#### 3.2.1 Men:

- 1950-70, 1950-70 distribution rates derived from the EPPA3;
- 1980, averages of adjusted distribution rates derived from the 1979, 1980 and 1981 surveys;
adjustment of rates to make allowance for conscripts;
- 1990, averages of distribution rates derived from the 1989, 1990 and 1991 surveys.

#### 3.2.2 Women:

- 1950-70, 1950-70 distribution rates derived from the EPPA3;
- 1980, averages of distribution rates derived from the 1979, 1980 and 1981 surveys;
- 1990, averages of distribution rates derived from the 1989, 1990 and 1991 surveys.

## 4. Projection of activity rates: 2000 - 2010

### 4.1 Model(s): hyperbole and logistic

#### 4.1.1 Men:

- To the [15+] age groups, application of function F3;
- Modification of the trends for the [25-49] age groups.

#### 4.1.2 Women:

- To the [15-64] age groups, application of function F6;
- To the [65+] age group, application of function F3;
- Modification of the trends for the [15-24] age groups.

*Notes on adjustments of rates, see p. 3-8.*     *Notes on projection functions, see p. 10.*

# Oman

**Code(s):**   **Title(s):**

EPPA3   Economically active population: Estimates and Projections, 1950-2025, Third edition, ILO, Geneva, 1986.

## 2. Estimates of activity rates: 1950 - 1990

### 2.1 Benchmark data:

Table 1: Activity rates by sex and age group

| Age group | Year 1950 | 1960 | 1970 | 1980 |
|---|---|---|---|---|
| **Men** | | | | |
| 10-14 | 27.00 | 22.00 | 17.00 | 9.00 |
| 15-19 | 87.40 | 73.70 | 60.00 | 46.30 |
| 20-24 | 96.20 | 95.95 | 95.65 | 95.40 |
| 25-29 | 99.20 | 99.25 | 99.25 | 99.30 |
| 30-34 | 99.20 | 99.15 | 99.05 | 99.00 |
| 35-39 | 99.20 | 99.05 | 98.85 | 98.70 |
| 40-44 | 98.20 | 98.00 | 97.80 | 97.60 |
| 45-49 | 97.00 | 96.55 | 96.15 | 95.70 |
| 50-54 | 94.50 | 93.45 | 92.45 | 91.40 |
| 55-59 | 91.00 | 89.35 | 87.75 | 86.10 |
| 60-64 | 80.55 | 78.55 | 76.60 | 74.60 |
| 65+ | 63.00 | 60.10 | 57.20 | 54.30 |
| **Women** | | | | |
| 10-14 | 1.00 | 1.35 | 1.70 | 2.05 |
| 15-19 | 2.00 | 2.70 | 3.40 | 4.10 |
| 20-24 | 2.60 | 3.95 | 5.35 | 6.70 |
| 25-29 | 3.00 | 5.50 | 7.90 | 10.30 |
| 30-34 | 3.20 | 5.95 | 8.65 | 11.40 |
| 35-39 | 3.45 | 5.65 | 7.85 | 10.10 |
| 40-44 | 3.55 | 5.15 | 6.80 | 8.40 |
| 45-49 | 3.55 | 4.80 | 6.10 | 7.40 |
| 50-54 | 2.80 | 4.00 | 5.20 | 6.40 |
| 55-59 | 2.70 | 3.40 | 4.10 | 4.80 |
| 60-64 | 2.60 | 2.95 | 3.25 | 3.60 |
| 65+ | 2.50 | 2.65 | 2.75 | 2.90 |

Source(s): EPPA3.

### 2.2 Method(s):   linear extrapolation

#### 2.2.1 Men:

- 1950-80, 1950-80 activity rates derived from the EPPA3;
- 1990, extrapolation of 1950-80 activity rates derived from the EPPA3;
modification of the trends for all age groups.

#### 2.2.2 Women:

Method, hypothesis and treatment identical to those used for men.

## 3. Estimates of distribution rates by activity sector: 1950 - 1990

### 3.1 Benchmark data:

Table 2: Distribution of economically active population by activity sector

| Year | Agriculture | Industry Total | Manufac. | Services |
|---|---|---|---|---|
| **Men** | | | | |
| 1950 | 77.00 | 8.50 | .. | 14.50 |
| 1960 | 68.50 | 12.00 | .. | 19.50 |
| 1970 | 58.50 | 17.00 | .. | 24.50 |
| 1980 | 52.00 | 21.00 | .. | 27.00 |
| **Women** | | | | |
| 1950 | 55.00 | 15.00 | .. | 30.00 |
| 1960 | 43.00 | 20.00 | .. | 37.00 |
| 1970 | 33.00 | 27.00 | .. | 40.00 |
| 1980 | 25.00 | 33.00 | .. | 42.00 |

Source(s): EPPA3.

### 3.2 Method(s):   linear extrapolation

#### 3.2.1 Men:

- 1950-80, 1950-80 distribution rates derived from the EPPA3;
- 1990, extrapolation of 1950-80 distribution rates derived from the EPPA3;
modification of the trends in all sectors.

#### 3.2.2 Women:

Method, hypothesis and treatment identical to those used for men.

## 4. Projection of activity rates: 2000 - 2010

### 4.1 Model(s):   linear, log-linear and hyperbole

#### 4.1.1 Men:

- To the [15-19] and [25-64] age groups, application of function F3;
- To the [20-24] age group, application of function F2;
- To the [65+] age group, application of function F1;
- Modification of the trends for the [15-34] age groups.

#### 4.1.2 Women:

- To the [15-19] and [65+] age groups, application of function F1;
- To the [20-64] age groups, application of function F2;
- Modification of the trends for all age groups.

*Notes on adjustments of rates, see p. 3-8.*     *Notes on projection functions, see p. 10.*

# Other Melanesia

## 1. Source(s) of benchmark data

Code(s):    Title(s):

EPPA3    Yearbook of Labour Statistics 1945-89 - Retrospective Edition on Population Censuses, ILO, Geneva, 1990.
STAT    Database on Labour Statistics, LABORSTA - Bureau of Statistics, ILO, Geneva.

## 2. Estimates of activity rates: 1950 - 1990

### 2.1 Benchmark data:

Table 1: Activity rates by sex and age group

| Age group | Year | | | | |
|---|---|---|---|---|---|
| | 1976 (1) | 1979 (2) | 1983 (1) | 1989 (1) | 1989 (2) |
| **Men** | | | | | |
| 10-14 | 1.51 | 0.00 | 0.00 | ... | 0.00 |
| 15-19 | 36.03 | 61.72 | 38.70 | ... | 73.16 |
| 20-24 | 74.53 | 92.87 | 82.99 | 86.34 | 91.19 |
| 25-29 | 93.98 | 97.33 | 91.62 | 93.25 | 95.03 |
| 30-34 | 95.48 | 98.69 | 95.11 | 95.13 | 95.33 |
| 35-39 | 95.77 | 98.65 | 95.31 | 94.81 | 94.93 |
| 40-44 | 95.21 | 98.70 | 94.57 | 94.56 | 94.53 |
| 45-49 | 93.76 | 98.78 | 93.43 | 92.23 | 93.76 |
| 50-54 | 90.91 | 98.17 | 81.23 | 81.36 | 94.75 |
| 55-59 | 79.17 | 97.11 | 61.90 | 56.18 | 94.11 |
| 60-64 | 56.18 | 93.97 | 36.67 | 26.72 | 88.63 |
| 65+ | 36.12 | 85.88 | ... | 11.99 | 74.45 |
| **Women** | | | | | |
| 10-14 | 1.58 | 0.00 | 0.00 | ... | 0.00 |
| 15-19 | 29.57 | 64.90 | 17.87 | ... | 70.66 |
| 20-24 | 55.94 | 80.12 | 50.63 | 65.53 | 80.42 |
| 25-29 | 53.17 | 79.81 | 54.76 | 61.94 | 81.64 |
| 30-34 | 50.75 | 81.26 | 53.24 | 59.45 | 79.67 |
| 35-39 | 48.97 | 84.32 | 50.95 | 58.19 | 84.01 |
| 40-44 | 47.80 | 83.30 | 48.41 | 54.97 | 85.04 |
| 45-49 | 47.02 | 85.70 | 44.68 | 50.19 | 86.98 |
| 50-54 | 47.48 | 85.83 | 37.06 | 41.06 | 87.11 |
| 55-59 | 41.46 | 86.07 | 33.19 | 29.32 | 83.82 |
| 60-64 | 32.14 | 82.35 | 12.15 | 16.07 | 79.42 |
| 65+ | 19.43 | 71.87 | ... | 5.74 | 64.48 |

Note(s): (1) New Caledonia; (2) Vanuatu.
Source(s): STAT.

### 2.2 Method(s): linears interpolation and extrapolation
weighted average

#### 2.2.1 Men:

- 1950-90, weighted average of activity rates estimated separately
for New Caledonia and Vanuatu;
estimated activity rates were based on the interpolation and extrapolation of
adjusted activity rates for New Caledonia derived from the 1976, 1983
and 1989 censuses and of activity rates for Vanuatu derived from the 1979
and 1989 census.

#### 2.2.2 Women:

Method, hypothesis and treatment identical to those used for men.

## 3. Estimates of distribution rates by activity sector: 1950 - 1990

### 3.1 Benchmark data:

Table 2: Distribution of economically active population by activity sector

| Year | Agriculture | Industry | | Services |
|---|---|---|---|---|
| | | Total | Manufac. | |
| **Men** | | | | |
| 1976 (1) | 25.93 | 37.70 | 15.89 | 36.37 |
| 1979 (2) | 71.56 | 6.18 | 2.01 | 22.26 |
| 1983 (1) | 21.45 | 25.08 | 14.01 | 53.47 |
| 1989 (1) | 14.38 | 27.72 | 13.51 | 57.89 |
| 1989 (2) | 70.56 | 6.27 | 2.35 | 23.16 |
| **Women** | | | | |
| 1976 (1) | 35.32 | 6.24 | 3.64 | 58.44 |
| 1979 (2) | 84.71 | 2.06 | 1.87 | 13.23 |
| 1983 (1) | 23.24 | 4.98 | 3.80 | 71.78 |
| 1989 (1) | 14.20 | 6.26 | 4.92 | 79.54 |
| 1989 (2) | 83.65 | 1.35 | 1.25 | 15.00 |

Note(s): (1) New Caledonia; (2) Vanuatu.
Source(s): STAT.

### 3.2 Method(s): weighted average
linear interpolation and extrapolation

#### 3.2.1 Men:

- 1950-90, weighted averages of distribution rates estimated
separately for New Caledonia and Vanuatu;
estimated rates based on interpolation and extrapolation of distribution rates
derived from the 1976, 1983 and 1989 censuses for New Caledonia,
and from the 1979 and 1989 censuses for Vanuatu.

#### 3.2.2 Women:

Method, hypothesis and treatment identical to those used for men.

## 4. Projection of activity rates: 2000 - 2010

### 4.1 Model(s): linear and hyperbole

#### 4.1.1 Men:

- To the [10-29] age groups, application of function F1;
- To the [30+] age groups, application of function F3;
- Modification of the trends for the [10-14], [20-24] and [30-49] age groups.

#### 4.1.2 Women:

- To all age groups, application of function F1;
- Modification of the trends for the [20+] age groups.

---

*Notes on adjustments of rates, see p. 3-8.*    *Notes on projection functions, see p. 10.*

# Pakistan

## 1. Source(s) of benchmark data

Code(s):   Title(s):

EPPA3   Economically active population: Estimates and Projections, 1950-2025, Third edition, ILO, Geneva, 1986.
STAT    Database on Labour Statistics, LABORSTA - Bureau of Statistics, ILO, Geneva.

## 2. Estimates of activity rates: 1950 - 1990

### 2.1 Benchmark data:

Table 1: Activity rates by sex and age group

| Age group | Year 1950 | 1960 | 1970 | 1978 | 1981 | 1990 | 1991 |
|---|---|---|---|---|---|---|---|
| **Men** | | | | | | | |
| 10-14 | 45.05 | 38.90 | 31.10 | 29.49 | 30.90 | 26.60 | 19.20 |
| 15-19 | 84.65 | 78.80 | 71.25 | 64.60 | 67.70 | 59.40 | 55.20 |
| 20-24 | 93.50 | 90.80 | 90.25 | 88.40 | 88.20 | 86.90 | 87.70 |
| 25-29 | 97.65 | 97.15 | 96.55 | 96.20 | 96.00 | 97.30 | 97.70 |
| 30-34 | 97.70 | 97.50 | 97.30 | 97.94 | 97.10 | 98.80 | 97.80 |
| 35-39 | 97.90 | 97.75 | 97.60 | 98.24 | 97.40 | 98.70 | 97.90 |
| 40-44 | 97.50 | 97.35 | 97.15 | 97.84 | 97.00 | 97.80 | 98.20 |
| 45-49 | 97.25 | 97.15 | 97.00 | 97.50 | 96.80 | 97.40 | 97.60 |
| 50-54 | 96.00 | 95.55 | 95.10 | 95.70 | 94.50 | 94.10 | 94.80 |
| 55-59 | 95.50 | 94.40 | 93.25 | 92.10 | 91.80 | 91.20 | 90.40 |
| 60-64 | 89.70 | 87.45 | 95.20 | 86.70 | 82.30 | 81.00 | 78.50 |
| 65+ | 80.25 | 75.15 | 67.40 | 59.70 | 56.90 | 55.70 | 52.03 |
| **Women** | | | | | | | |
| 10-14 | 7.05 | 5.70 | 4.45 | .. | 6.30 | .. | 6.90 |
| 15-19 | 7.65 | 7.45 | 7.25 | .. | 12.10 | .. | 13.10 |
| 20-24 | 7.95 | 8.50 | 9.15 | .. | 12.90 | .. | 14.00 |
| 25-29 | 9.60 | 10.05 | 10.40 | .. | 14.00 | .. | 13.20 |
| 30-34 | 10.75 | 11.25 | 11.65 | .. | 15.70 | .. | 14.10 |
| 35-39 | 9.45 | 9.90 | 10.25 | .. | 13.80 | .. | 13.90 |
| 40-44 | 9.60 | 10.05 | 10.40 | .. | 14.00 | .. | 17.50 |
| 45-49 | 10.95 | 11.05 | 11.15 | .. | 12.70 | .. | 17.00 |
| 50-54 | 10.40 | 10.50 | 10.60 | .. | 11.70 | .. | 16.50 |
| 55-59 | 10.00 | 10.15 | 10.30 | .. | 12.40 | .. | 13.90 |
| 60-64 | 8.20 | 7.95 | 7.60 | .. | 7.40 | .. | 10.70 |
| 65+ | 6.45 | 5.55 | 4.55 | .. | 5.40 | .. | 7.40 |

Source(s): STAT.

### 2.2 Method(s): linear interpolation

#### 2.2.1 Men:

- 1950-90, interpolation of 1950-70 activity rates derived from EPPA3
and of activity rates derived from the 1978 to 1992 surveys.

#### 2.2.2 Women:

- 1950-70, 1950-70 adjusted activity rates derived from the EPPA3;
the adjustment was made on the basis of the adjustment model for
activity rates of women working in agriculture as contributing family workers;
- 1980-90, interpolation of activity rates derived from
the 1981 and 1991 surveys;
adjustment of rates to make allowance for the under-registration
of women working in agriculture.

## 3. Estimates of distribution rates by activity sector: 1950 - 1990

### 3.1 Benchmark data:

Table 2: Distribution of economically active population by activity sector

| Year | Agriculture | Industry Total | Manufac. | Services |
|---|---|---|---|---|
| **Men** | | | | |
| 1981 | 55.98 | 14.94 | 9.40 | 29.08 |
| 1982 | 44.80 | 20.59 | 12.08 | 34.61 |
| **Women** | | | | |
| 1981 | 41.18 | 19.02 | 15.98 | 39.80 |
| 1982 | 66.02 | 14.69 | 13.33 | 19.29 |

Source(s): STAT.

### 3.2 Method(s): linears interpolation and extrapolation

#### 3.2.1 Men:

- 1950-80, 1950-80 distribution rates derived from the EPPA3;
- 1990, extrapolation of distribution rates derived from
the 1981 survey and from the 1991 official estimates;
modification of the trends in all sectors.

#### 3.2.2 Women:

- 1950-70, 1950-70 adjusted distribution rates derived from the EPPA3;
- 1980-90, interpolation and extrapolation of distribution rates derived from
the 1981 survey and from the 1991 official estimates;
adjustment of 1950-90 rates to make allowance for the under-registration
of contributing family workers in agriculture.

## 4. Projection of activity rates: 2000 - 2010

### 4.1 Model(s): linear, hyperbole and logistic

#### 4.1.1 Men:

- To the [10-14] age group, application of function F1;
- To the [15+] age groups, application of function F3;
- Modification of the trends for the [10-14] and [30-49] age groups.

#### 4.1.2 Women:

- To the [10-19] and [60+] age groups, application of function F1;
- To the [20-59] age groups, application of function F6;
- Modification of the trends for the [10-19] and [65+] age groups.

*Notes on adjustments of rates, see p. 3-8.*

*Notes on projection functions, see p. 10.*

# Panama

## 1. Source(s) of benchmark data

Code(s):    Title(s):

EPPA3    Economically active population: Estimates and Projections, 1950-2025, Third edition, ILO, Geneva, 1986.
STAT    Database on Labour Statistics, LABORSTA - Bureau of Statistics, ILO, Geneva.
PAN90    Censos Nacionales de Poblacion y Vivienda, 13 de mayo 1990, Dirección de Estadística y Censo, Controloria General de la República, Panamá.

## 2. Estimates of activity rates: 1950 - 1990

### 2.1 Benchmark data:

Table 1: Activity rates by sex and age group

| Age group | Year 1979 | 1980 | 1985 | 1989 | 1990 | 1991 |
|---|---|---|---|---|---|---|
| **Men** | | | | | | |
| 10-14 | .. | .. | .. | ... | 6.49 | ... |
| 15-19 | .. | .. | .. | 46.91 | 42.69 | 45.11 |
| 20-24 | .. | .. | .. | 85.75 | 80.31 | 82.32 |
| 25-29 | .. | .. | .. | 95.82 | 91.39 | 94.93 |
| 30-39 | .. | .. | .. | 96.99 | 94.50 | 96.95 |
| 40-49 | .. | .. | .. | 96.21 | 93.99 | 96.31 |
| 50-59 | .. | .. | .. | 88.93 | 84.89 | 83.65 |
| 60-64 | .. | .. | .. | 43.40 | 47.33 | 42.09 |
| 65+ | .. | .. | .. | ... | ... | ... |
| **Women** | | | | | | |
| 10-14 | ... | 2.58 | ... | ... | 2.48 | |
| 15-19 | 19.98 | 16.78 | 19.12 | 21.17 | 18.88 | 21.69 |
| 20-24 | 49.49 | 38.29 | 42.44 | 45.71 | 34.66 | 45.70 |
| 25-29 | 50.44 | 41.63 | 50.61 | 52.42 | 40.84 | 51.65 |
| 30-39 | 46.18 | 39.25 | 52.02 | 54.51 | 46.65 | 55.19 |
| 40-49 | 38.54 | 33.28 | 43.06 | 49.75 | 42.36 | 50.90 |
| 50-59 | 24.41 | 19.17 | 24.95 | 25.94 | 23.90 | 25.00 |
| 60-64 | 11.95 | 23.01 | 12.41 | 8.04 | 7.47 | 7.79 |
| 65+ | ... | ... | ... | ... | ... | ... |

Source(s): STAT.

### 2.2 Method(s):  linear interpolation
arithmetic average

#### 2.2.1 Men:

- 1950-80, 1950-80 activity rates derived from the EPPA3;
- 1990, averages of adjusted activity rates derived from
the 1989 and 1991 surveys;
for the [10-14] age group, activity rates derived from 1990 the census.

#### 2.2.2 Women:

- 1950-70, 1950-70 activity rates derived from the EPPA3;
- 1980-90, extrapolation of adjusted activity rates derived from
the 1979, 1985, 1989 and 1991 surveys;
for the [10-14] age group, activity rates derived from the 1980 and 1990 censuses

## 3. Estimates of distribution rates by activity sector: 1950 - 1990

### 3.1 Benchmark data:

Table 2: Distribution of economically active population by activity sector

| Year | Agriculture | Industry Total | Manufac. | Services |
|---|---|---|---|---|
| **Men** | | | | |
| 1980 | 39.31 | 22.43 | 11.92 | 38.26 |
| 1989 | 39.23 | 19.03 | 11.27 | 41.74 |
| 1991 | 35.08 | 17.78 | 10.14 | 47.13 |
| **Women** | | | | |
| 1979 | 4.61 | 12.49 | 11.26 | 82.90 |
| 1985 | 4.53 | 12.34 | 10.70 | 83.13 |
| 1989 | 4.08 | 11.30 | 9.82 | 84.61 |
| 1991 | 2.43 | 10.98 | 9.97 | 86.59 |

Source(s): STAT.

### 3.2 Method(s):  linears interpolation and extrapolation
arithmetic average

#### 3.2.1 Men:

- 1950-70, 1950-70 distribution rates derived from the EPPA3;
- 1980, interpolation of distribution rates derived from
the 1980 census and of distribution rates estimated for 1990;
- 1990, averages of distribution rates derived from the 1989 and 1991 surveys.

#### 3.2.2 Women:

- 1950-70, 1950-70 distribution rates derived from the EPPA3;
- 1980-90, extrapolation of distribution rates derived from
the 1979, 1985, 1989 and 1991 surveys.

## 4. Projection of activity rates: 2000 - 2010

### 4.1 Model(s):  linear, log-linear, hyperbole and logistic

#### 4.1.1 Men:

- To the [10-19] age groups, application of function F1;
- To the [20-59] age groups, application of function F3;
- To the [60+] age groups, application of function F2;
- Modification of the trends for the [10-19] age groups.

#### 4.1.2 Women:

- To the [10-59] age groups, application of function F6;
- To the [60-64] age group, application of function F1;
- To the [65+] age group, application of function F3;
- Modification of the trends for the [20-24] and [60-64] age groups.

*Notes on adjustments of rates, see p. 3-8.*          *Notes on projection functions, see p. 10.*

# Papua New Guinea

## 1. Source(s) of benchmark data

Code(s):      Title(s):

EPPA3        Yearbook of Labour Statistics 1945-89 - Retrospective Edition on Population Censuses, ILO, Geneva, 1990.
STAT         Database on Labour Statistics, LABORSTA - Bureau of Statistics, ILO, Geneva.

## 2. Estimates of activity rates: 1950 - 1990

### 2.1 Benchmark data:

Table 1: Activity rates by sex and age group

| Age group | Year 1950 (1) | 1960 (1) | 1970 (1) | 1980 (2) |
|---|---|---|---|---|
| **Men** | | | | |
| 10-14 | 48.20 | 46.05 | 43.15 | 9.17 |
| 15-19 | 81.20 | 78.25 | 74.25 | 35.45 |
| 20-24 | 97.00 | 95.80 | 95.24 | 59.21 |
| 25-29 | 98.25 | 98.10 | 98.05 | 64.07 |
| 30-34 | 98.50 | 98.30 | 98.30 | 59.65 |
| 35-39 | 98.75 | 98.55 | 98.25 | 57.85 |
| 40-44 | 98.65 | 98.40 | 98.10 | 54.50 |
| 45-49 | 97.15 | 96.95 | 96.70 | 51.35 |
| 50-54 | 94.55 | 94.25 | 93.85 | 47.44 |
| 55-59 | 89.90 | 89.50 | 88.90 | 42.77 |
| 60-64 | 81.90 | 81.20 | 80.30 | 33.20 |
| 65+ | 63.60 | 62.50 | 61.05 | 24.65 |
| **Women** | | | | |
| 10-14 | 46.55 | 44.50 | 34.56 | 11.27 |
| 15-19 | 73.60 | 70.60 | 63.76 | 30.04 |
| 20-24 | 77.00 | 75.00 | 71.32 | 35.38 |
| 25-29 | 77.35 | 75.20 | 73.13 | 35.59 |
| 30-34 | 79.35 | 77.15 | 77.67 | 38.14 |
| 35-39 | 80.70 | 78.65 | 78.67 | 38.48 |
| 40-44 | 81.45 | 79.45 | 80.48 | 39.71 |
| 45-49 | 80.60 | 78.55 | 79.53 | 38.69 |
| 50-54 | 78.30 | 76.00 | 76.74 | 36.74 |
| 55-59 | 70.65 | 68.40 | 69.25 | 32.69 |
| 60-64 | 62.15 | 59.40 | 56.59 | 23.52 |
| 65+ | 45.55 | 42.90 | 40.44 | 17.18 |

Source(s): (1) EPPA3; (2) STAT.

### 2.2 Method(s):   linear extrapolation
                    weighted average

**2.2.1 Men:**

- 1950-70, 1950-70 activity rates derived from the EPPA3;
- 1980, weighted average of activity rates of 1970 derived from the EPPA3
and of activity rates derived from the 1980 census;
- 1990, extrapolation of 1950-80 activity rates derived from the EPPA3
and of activity rates estimated for 1980;
modification of the trends for all age groups;
application to extrapolated rates, variations in 1980 interpolated rates,
in relation to activity rates estimated for 1980.

**2.2.2 Women:**

Method, hypothesis and treatment identical to those used for men.

## 3. Estimates of distribution rates by activity sector: 1950 - 1990

### 3.1 Benchmark data:

Table 2: Distribution of economically active population by activity sector

| Year | Agriculture | Industry Total | Manufac. | Services |
|---|---|---|---|---|
| **Men** | | | | |
| 1971 | 79.85 | 7.58 | 2.37 | 12.56 |
| 1982 | 75.75 | 8.44 | 3.59 | 15.81 |
| **Women** | | | | |
| 1971 | 94.11 | 0.81 | 0.65 | 5.09 |
| 1982 | 91.56 | 2.10 | 1.87 | 6.34 |

Source(s): STAT.

### 3.2 Method(s):   linears interpolation and extrapolation

**3.2.1 Men:**

- 1950-90, interpolation and extrapolation of distribution rates derived
from the 1971 and 1981 censuses;
modification of the trends in all sectors for 1990.

**3.2.2 Women:**

- 1950-90, interpolation and extrapolation of distribution rates derived from
the 1971 and 1981 censuses.

## 4. Projection of activity rates: 2000 - 2010

### 4.1 Model(s):   linear and hyperbole

**4.1.1 Men:**

- To all age groups, application of function F3;
- Modification of the trends for the [15-49] age groups.

**4.1.2 Women:**

- To the [10-14] and [20-54] age groups, application of function F3;
- To the [15-19] and [55+] age groups, application of function F1;
- Modification of the trends for the [20-39] and [50-59] age groups.

# Paraguay

## 1. Source(s) of benchmark data

Code(s):     Title(s):
EPPA3        Economically active population: Estimates and Projections, 1950-2025, Third edition, ILO, Geneva, 1986.
ASTER        Yearbook of Labour Statistics 1945-89 - Retrospective Edition on Population Censuses, ILO, Geneva, 1990.

## 2. Estimates of activity rates: 1950 - 1990

### 2.1 Benchmark data:

Table 1: Activity rates by sex and age group

| Age group | Year 1962 | 1972 | 1982 |
|---|---|---|---|
| **Men** | | | |
| 10-14 | 16.69 | 25.28 | 19.74 |
| 15-19 | 81.71 | 76.81 | 74.47 |
| 20-24 | 95.74 | 93.28 | 92.14 |
| 25-29 | 98.17 | 97.22 | 97.37 |
| 30-34 | 98.74 | 98.04 | 98.58 |
| 35-39 | 98.86 | 98.11 | 98.84 |
| 40-44 | 98.43 | 97.49 | 98.21 |
| 45-49 | 97.99 | 96.63 | 97.69 |
| 50-54 | 97.32 | 95.30 | 96.47 |
| 55-59 | 95.62 | 91.89 | 94.58 |
| 60-64 | 92.96 | 87.20 | 90.10 |
| 65+ | 74.29 | 65.14 | 54.59 |
| **Women** | | | |
| 10-14 | .. | 8.01 | 3.99 |
| 15-19 | .. | 24.67 | 19.99 |
| 20-24 | .. | 30.70 | 27.46 |
| 25-29 | .. | 28.01 | 27.45 |
| 30-34 | .. | 25.67 | 26.35 |
| 35-39 | .. | 23.23 | 24.84 |
| 40-44 | .. | 22.71 | 23.22 |
| 45-49 | .. | 20.69 | 20.66 |
| 50-54 | .. | 18.31 | 18.23 |
| 55-59 | .. | 16.25 | 15.95 |
| 60-64 | .. | 13.89 | 12.70 |
| 65+ | .. | 7.21 | 6.93 |

Source(s): ASTER.

### 2.2 Method(s): linear extrapolation / weighted average

**2.2.1 Men:**
- 1950, 1950 activity rates derived from the EPPA3;
- 1960-80, weighted average of activity rates derived from the 1972 and 1982 censuses and of adjusted activity rates derived from the 1962 census;
- 1990, extrapolation of 1950-80 activity rates derived from the EPPA3; application to extrapolated rates, variations in 1982 interpolated rates, in relation to activity rates derived from the 1982 census; modification of the trends for all age groups on the basis of the surveys conducted in 1989 to 1992.

**2.2.2 Women:**
- 1950-80, 1950-80 adjusted activity rates derived from the EPPA3; the adjustment was made on the basis of the adjustment model for activity rates of women working in agriculture as contributing family workers;
- 1990, weighted average of activity rates derived from the 1972 and 1982 censuses.

## 3. Estimates of distribution rates by activity sector: 1950 - 1990

### 3.1 Benchmark data:

Table 2: Distribution of economically active population by activity sector

| Year | Agriculture | Industry Total | Manufac. | Services |
|---|---|---|---|---|
| **Men** | | | | |
| 1962 | 65.76 | 15.77 | 11.27 | 18.46 |
| 1972 | 62.60 | 15.92 | 10.39 | 21.48 |
| 1982 | 55.38 | 20.18 | 10.59 | 24.44 |
| **Women** | | | | |
| 1962 | 22.66 | 30.42 | 29.47 | 46.93 |
| 1972 | 13.75 | 28.70 | 28.54 | 57.55 |
| 1982 | 11.97 | 23.52 | 23.16 | 64.51 |

Source(s): ASTER.

### 3.2 Method(s): linear extrapolation / weighted average

**3.2.1 Men:**
- 1950-80, 1950-80 distribution rates derived from the EPPA3;
- 1990, extrapolation of distribution rates derived from the 1972 and 1982 censuses; modification of the trends in all sectors;
- Application of manufacturing/industry ratio derived from the 1982 census.

**3.2.2 Women:**
- 1950-60, 1950-60 distribution rates derived from the EPPA3;
- 1970, weighted averages of distribution rates derived from the 1962 and 1972 censuses;
- 1980-90, extrapolation of distribution rates derived from the 1962, 1972 and 1982 censuses; modification of the trends in all sectors;
- Application of manufacturing/industry ratio derived from the 1982 census.

## 4. Projection of activity rates: 2000 - 2010

### 4.1 Model(s): linear, log-linear and hyperbole

**4.1.1 Men:**
- To the [10-49] age groups, application of function F1;
- To the [50-59] age groups, application of function F3;
- To the [60+] age groups, application of function F2;
- Modification of the trends for the [10-49] age groups.

**4.1.2 Women:**
- To the [10-19] and [55+] age groups, application of function F1;
- To the [20-54] age groups, application of function F2;
- Modification of the trends for the [10-24], [40-44] and [60+] age groups.

Notes on adjustments of rates, see p. 3-8.     Notes on projection functions, see p. 10.

# Peru

## 1. Source(s) of benchmark data

**Code(s):**   **Title(s):**

EPPA3    Economically active population: Estimates and Projections, 1950-2025, Third edition, ILO, Geneva, 1986.
ASTER    Yearbook of Labour Statistics 1945-89 - Retrospective Edition on Population Censuses, ILO, Geneva, 1990.

## 2. Estimates of activity rates: 1950 - 1990

### 2.1 Benchmark data:

Table 1: Activity rates by sex and age group

| Age group | 1950 (1) | 1960 (1) | 1970 (1) | 1981 (2) |
|---|---|---|---|---|
| **Men** | | | | |
| 10-14 | 11.95 | 6.75 | 5.00 | 4.92 |
| 15-19 | 59.40 | 55.30 | 42.20 | 37.52 |
| 20-24 | 93.25 | 91.70 | 82.60 | 81.67 |
| 25-29 | 98.00 | 97.50 | 94.90 | 93.43 |
| 30-34 | 98.80 | 98.60 | 97.80 | 97.21 |
| 35-39 | 98.60 | 98.50 | 98.40 | 98.33 |
| 40-44 | 98.50 | 98.40 | 98.30 | 98.30 |
| 45-49 | 98.40 | 98.30 | 98.20 | 98.27 |
| 50-54 | 97.60 | 97.50 | 96.15 | 97.04 |
| 55-59 | 96.50 | 96.05 | 93.65 | 94.50 |
| 60-64 | 91.90 | 91.75 | 85.55 | 88.26 |
| 65+ | 75.00 | 69.30 | 62.65 | 63.46 |
| **Women** | | | | |
| 10-14 | 9.50 | 6.60 | 4.10 | 3.94 |
| 15-19 | 29.00 | 27.60 | 19.10 | 18.06 |
| 20-24 | 26.40 | 26.30 | 26.10 | 29.27 |
| 25-29 | 23.50 | 23.50 | 24.15 | 31.09 |
| 30-34 | 20.10 | 21.00 | 21.75 | 30.75 |
| 35-39 | 18.90 | 20.40 | 20.55 | 28.69 |
| 40-44 | 19.80 | 20.60 | 21.10 | 27.28 |
| 45-49 | 20.00 | 20.40 | 19.70 | 26.15 |
| 50-54 | 20.50 | 20.10 | 18.40 | 25.43 |
| 55-59 | 19.70 | 19.40 | 16.60 | 23.23 |
| 60-64 | 19.10 | 18.80 | 14.20 | 22.99 |
| 65+ | 14.25 | 12.10 | 9.00 | 12.02 |

**Source(s):** (1) EPPA3; (2) ASTER.

### 2.2 Method(s): linear extrapolation
weighted average

**2.2.1 Men:**

- 1950-70, 1950-70 activity rates derived from the EPPA3;
- 1980, weighted average of activity rates of 1970 derived from the EPPA3 and of adjusted activity rates derived from the 1981 census;
- 1990, extrapolation of 1950-70 activity rates derived from the EPPA3 and of activity rates estimated for 1980;
application to extrapolated rates, variations in 1981 interpolated rates, in relation to adjusted activity rates derived from the 1981 census;
modification of the trends for all age groups.

**2.2.2 Women:**

- 1950-70, 1950-70 activity rates derived from the EPPA3;
adjustment of 1970 activity rates based on the men/women ratio in agriculture derived from the 1981 census;
- 1980, weighted average of 1970 activity rates derived from the EPPA3 and of adjusted activity rates derived from the 1981 census;
- 1990, extrapolation of 1970 activity rates derived from the EPPA3 and adjusted activity rates derived from the 1981 census;
modification of the trends for all age groups.

## 3. Estimates of distribution rates by activity sector: 1950 - 1990

### 3.1 Benchmark data:

Table 2: Distribution of economically active population by activity sector

| Year | Agriculture | Industry Total | Manufac. | Services |
|---|---|---|---|---|
| **Men** | | | | |
| 1950 (1) | 63.85 | 17.95 | .. | 18.20 |
| 1960 (1) | 57.25 | 20.30 | .. | 22.45 |
| 1970 (1) | 53.30 | 17.60 | .. | 29.10 |
| 1980 (1) | 45.05 | 19.75 | .. | 35.20 |
| 1981 (2) | 43.43 | 19.63 | 11.43 | 36.94 |
| **Women** | | | | |
| 1972 (2) | 19.28 | 18.89 | 18.41 | 61.82 |
| 1981 (2) | 24.57 | 13.48 | 12.51 | 61.95 |

**Source(s):** (1) EPPA3; (2) ASTER.

### 3.2 Method(s): linears interpolation and extrapolation

**3.2.1 Men:**

- 1950-80, 1950-80 distribution rates derived from the EPPA3;
- 1980-90, extrapolation of 1950-80 distribution rates derived from the EPPA3; application to extrapolated rates, variations in 1980 interpolated rates, in relation to 1980 distribution rates derived from the EPPA3;
- Application of manufacturing/industry ratio derived from the 1981 census.

**3.2.2 Women:**

- 1950-60, 1950-60 distribution rates derived from the EPPA3;
- 1970-90, interpolation and extrapolation of adjusted distribution rates derived from the 1972 and of distribution rates derived from the 1981 census; distribution rates of manufacturing sector estimated on the basis of manufacturing/industry ratio derived from the 1981 census.

## 4. Projection of activity rates: 2000 - 2010

### 4.1 Model(s): linear, hyperbole and logistic

**4.1.1 Men:**

- To the [10-14] and [50+] age groups, application of function F1;
- To the [15-49] age groups, application of function F3;
- Modification of the trends for the [15-34], [40-49] and [65+] age groups.

**4.1.2 Women:**

- To the [10-14] age group, application of function F1;
- To the [15-19] age group, application of function F3;
- To the [20+] age groups, application of function F6;
- Modification of the trends for the [20-59] age groups.

*Notes on adjustments of rates, see p. 3-8.*    *Notes on projection functions, see p. 10.*

# Philippines

## 1. Source(s) of benchmark data

Code(s):   Title(s):
EPPA3      Economically active population: Estimates and Projections, 1950-2025, Third edition, ILO, Geneva, 1986.
STAT       Database on Labour Statistics, LABORSTA - Bureau of Statistics, ILO, Geneva.

## 2. Estimates of activity rates: 1950 - 1990

### 2.1 Benchmark data:

Table 1: Activity rates by sex and age group

| Age group | Year | | | | |
|---|---|---|---|---|---|
| | 1958 | 1960 | 1970 | 1975 | 1990 |
| **Men** | | | | | |
| 10-14 | .. | 30.85 | 28.85 | 20.44 | .. |
| 15-19 | .. | 69.11 | 57.18 | 52.63 | 42.30 |
| 20-24 | .. | 87.89 | 86.35 | 84.35 | 70.74 |
| 25-29 | .. | 95.54 | 95.03 | 93.12 | 86.60 |
| 30-34 | .. | 98.09 | 97.70 | 97.17 | 91.46 |
| 35-39 | .. | 98.18 | 97.91 | 98.29 | 92.69 |
| 40-44 | .. | 98.32 | 97.95 | 98.62 | 92.64 |
| 45-49 | .. | 98.21 | 97.75 | 98.07 | 92.01 |
| 50-54 | .. | 97.95 | 97.34 | 97.28 | 89.94 |
| 55-59 | .. | 95.86 | 96.97 | 95.87 | 86.61 |
| 60-64 | .. | 87.81 | 87.31 | 84.25 | 78.00 |
| 65+ | .. | 69.22 | 63.41 | 62.56 | 59.88 |
| **Women** | | | | | |
| 10-14 | 10.12 | .. | .. | .. | .. |
| 15-19 | 21.30 | .. | .. | .. | 31.32 |
| 20-24 | 50.80 | .. | .. | .. | 42.53 |
| 25-29 | 44.00 | .. | .. | .. | 43.25 |
| 30-34 | 47.00 | .. | .. | .. | 42.22 |
| 35-39 | 46.50 | .. | .. | .. | 42.45 |
| 40-44 | 47.00 | .. | .. | .. | 44.27 |
| 45-49 | 50.00 | .. | .. | .. | 42.64 |
| 50-54 | 54.00 | .. | .. | .. | 40.68 |
| 55-59 | 46.00 | .. | .. | .. | 38.87 |
| 60-64 | 33.00 | .. | .. | .. | 35.39 |
| 65+ | 19.20 | .. | .. | .. | 24.85 |

Source(s): STAT.

### 2.2 Method(s): linears interpolation and extrapolation

#### 2.2.1 Men:

- 1950-90, interpolation and extrapolation of activity rates derived from the 1960, 1970 and 1975 censuses and of adjusted activity rates derived from the 1990 census.

#### 2.2.2 Women:

- 1950-90, interpolation and extrapolation of activity rates derived from the 1958 survey and of adjusted activity rates derived from the 1990 census; adjustment of activity rates based on the results of the 1989, 1990 and 1991 surveys conducted in Pakistan; modification of the trends for all age groups.

## 3. Estimates of distribution rates by activity sector: 1950 - 1990

### 3.1 Benchmark data:

Table 2: Distribution of economically active population by activity sector

| Year | Agriculture | Industry | | Services |
|---|---|---|---|---|
| | | Total | Manufac. | |
| **Men** | | | | |
| 1960 | 74.55 | 10.09 | 6.54 | 15.35 |
| 1965 | 66.60 | 12.77 | 7.97 | 20.64 |
| 1974 | 64.71 | 13.80 | 8.47 | 21.49 |
| 1975 | 64.45 | 13.93 | 8.56 | 21.62 |
| 1985 | 58.26 | 14.47 | 7.75 | 27.27 |
| 1989 | 53.19 | 16.69 | 8.78 | 30.12 |
| 1990 | 56.57 | 24.56 | 14.88 | 18.87 |
| 1991 | 53.96 | 17.28 | 8.53 | 28.76 |
| **Women** | | | | |
| 1989 | 30.94 | 14.20 | 13.58 | 54.87 |
| 1990 | 31.35 | 12.80 | 12.24 | 55.85 |
| 1991 | 30.06 | 13.88 | 13.28 | 56.06 |

Source(s): STAT.

### 3.2 Method(s): linears interpolation and extrapolation

#### 3.2.1 Men:

- 1950-90, interpolation and extrapolation of distribution rates derived from the 1960 and 1975 censuses and from the 1965, 1974, 1985, 1990 and 1991 surveys; modification of the trends in all sectors for 1950.

#### 3.2.2 Women:

- 1950-80, 1950-80 distribution rates derived from the EPPA3;
- 1990, averages of distribution rates derived from the 1989, 1990 and 1991 surveys.

## 4. Projection of activity rates: 2000 - 2010

### 4.1 Model(s): linear, hyperbole and logistic

#### 4.1.1 Men:

- To the [10-14] age group, application of function F2;
- To the [15+] age groups, application of function F3;
- Modification of the trends for the [10-14], [35-49] and [65+] age groups.

#### 4.1.2 Women:

- To the [10-14] age group, application of function F2;
- To the [15-34] and [50+] age groups, application of function F3;
- To the [35-49] age groups, application of function F1;
- Modification of the trends for all age groups.

---

*Notes on adjustments of rates, see p. 3-8.*                *Notes on projection functions, see p. 10.*

# Poland

## 1. Source(s) of benchmark data

Code(s):     Title(s):

EPPA3     Economically active population: Estimates and Projections, 1950-2025, Third edition, ILO, Geneva, 1986.
BLT-94-2     Popovic B. (1994), "New 1980 and 1990 estimates of activity rates by age and sectoral distribution for some countries of Eastern and Southern Europe" in the Bulletin of Labour of Statistics - 1994-2, ILO, Geneva.

## 2. Estimates of activity rates: 1950 - 1990

### 2.1 Benchmark data:

Table 1: Activity rates by sex and age group

| Age group | Year 1950 (1) | 1960 (1) | 1970 (1) | 1980 (1) | 1980 (2) | 1990 (2) |
|---|---|---|---|---|---|---|
| **Men** | | | | | | |
| 10-14 | 2.25 | 0.90 | 0.50 | 0.00 | 0.00 | 0.00 |
| 15-19 | 63.00 | 54.50 | 49.50 | 46.00 | 28.20 | 20.72 |
| 20-24 | 92.90 | 90.40 | 88.95 | 82.50 | 82.25 | 78.19 |
| 25-29 | 97.05 | 96.40 | 96.35 | 96.20 | 95.96 | 93.99 |
| 30-34 | 97.80 | 97.20 | 97.15 | 97.10 | 96.92 | 96.02 |
| 35-39 | 97.80 | 97.15 | 96.90 | 96.20 | 96.07 | 95.53 |
| 40-44 | 97.55 | 96.90 | 96.15 | 94.80 | 94.68 | 94.02 |
| 45-49 | 97.40 | 96.20 | 95.15 | 92.20 | 91.80 | 89.17 |
| 50-54 | 97.00 | 94.85 | 94.05 | 87.30 | 86.36 | 81.70 |
| 55-59 | 96.40 | 91.60 | 90.95 | 82.00 | 79.71 | 70.88 |
| 60-64 | 86.40 | 82.10 | 83.05 | 58.00 | 60.31 | 52.83 |
| 65+ | 59.75 | 57.60 | 55.45 | 30.00 | 34.56 | 32.09 |
| **Women** | | | | | | |
| 10-14 | 2.15 | 1.20 | 0.65 | 0.00 | 0.00 | 0.00 |
| 15-19 | 51.10 | 43.25 | 36.65 | 31.20 | 20.71 | 15.92 |
| 20-24 | 68.65 | 69.20 | 69.80 | 68.40 | 67.91 | 63.05 |
| 25-29 | 60.30 | 62.75 | 74.55 | 76.00 | 74.42 | 69.05 |
| 30-34 | 60.85 | 63.30 | 77.15 | 81.00 | 78.92 | 76.37 |
| 35-39 | 64.20 | 66.80 | 79.20 | 82.50 | 82.15 | 83.08 |
| 40-44 | 66.40 | 69.10 | 79.45 | 83.20 | 82.19 | 85.94 |
| 45-49 | 63.20 | 68.10 | 78.70 | 79.00 | 78.87 | 81.78 |
| 50-54 | 60.65 | 65.35 | 75.40 | 72.60 | 71.54 | 71.07 |
| 55-59 | 55.70 | 60.00 | 67.85 | 56.00 | 56.64 | 49.63 |
| 60-64 | 45.25 | 48.70 | 50.90 | 35.00 | 36.65 | 33.99 |
| 65+ | 28.95 | 30.00 | 32.90 | 17.50 | 19.31 | 19.00 |

Source(s): (1) EPPA3; (2) BLT-94-2.

### 2.2 Method(s): data from EPPA3 and BLT-94-2.

**2.2.1 Men:**

- 1950-80, 1950-80 activity rates derived from the EPPA3;
- 1990, application to 1990 activity rates derived from the Bulletin of Labour Statistics 1994-2, the variations in 1980 activity rates derived from the EPPA3, in relation to 1980 activity rates derived from the Bulletin.

**2.2.2 Women:**

Method, hypothesis and treatment identical to those used for men.

## 3. Estimates of distribution rates by activity sector: 1950 - 1990

### 3.1 Benchmark data:

Table 2: Distribution of economically active population by activity sector

| Year | Agriculture | Industry Total | Manufac. | Services |
|---|---|---|---|---|
| **Men** | | | | |
| 1950 (1) | 49.00 | 30.00 | .. | 20.90 |
| 1960 (1) | 39.50 | 37.80 | .. | 22.60 |
| 1970 (1) | 32.60 | 43.40 | .. | 24.00 |
| 1980 (2) | 28.04 | 45.63 | 28.44 | 26.33 |
| 1990 (2) | 27.44 | 44.88 | 26.86 | 27.68 |
| **Women** | | | | |
| 1950 (1) | 69.40 | 13.70 | .. | 16.80 |
| 1960 (1) | 59.40 | 16.90 | .. | 23.70 |
| 1970 (1) | 46.50 | 23.20 | .. | 30.30 |
| 1980 (2) | 31.91 | 28.13 | 24.20 | 39.96 |
| 1990 (2) | 27.50 | 25.01 | 21.19 | 47.49 |

Source(s): (1) EPPA3; (2) BLT-94-2.

### 3.2 Method(s):   data from BLT-94-7

**3.2.1 Men:**

- 1950-70, 1950-70 distribution rates derived from the EPPA3,
- 1980-90, 1980 and 1990 distribution rates derived from the Bulletin of Labour Statistics, 1994-2.

**3.2.2 Women:**

Method, hypothesis and treatment identical to those used for men.

## 4. Projection of activity rates: 2000 - 2010

### 4.1 Model(s):   hyperbole and logistic

**4.1.1 Men:**

- To all age groups, application of function F3;
- Modification of the trends for the [20-24] and [30-49] age groups.

**4.1.2 Women:**

- To the [15-24] and [55+] age groups, application of function F3;
- To the [25-54] age groups, application of function F6;
- Modification of the trends for the [15-24] and [55-59] age groups.

*Notes on adjustments of rates, see p. 3-8.*          *Notes on projection functions, see p. 10.*

# Portugal

## 1. Source(s) of benchmark data

Code(s):    Title(s):
EPPA3       Yearbook of Labour Statistics 1945-89 - Retrospective Edition on Population Censuses, ILO, Geneva, 1990.
STAT        Database on Labour Statistics, LABORSTA - Bureau of Statistics, ILO, Geneva.

## 2. Estimates of activity rates: 1950 - 1990

### 2.1 Benchmark data:

Table 1: Activity rates by sex and age group

| Age group | Year 1950 (1) | 1960 (1) | 1970 (1) | 1980 (1) | 1980 (2) | 1990 (12 |
|---|---|---|---|---|---|---|
| **Men** | | | | | | |
| 10-14 | 43.90 | 35.10 | 17.05 | 12.40 | .. | 4.86 |
| 15-19 | 90.70 | 86.85 | 78.85 | 76.15 | .. | 51.12 |
| 20-24 | 94.00 | 92.00 | 93.15 | 92.15 | .. | 73.20 |
| 25-29 | 94.65 | 97.20 | 97.05 | 97.00 | .. | 93.92 |
| 30-34 | 96.35 | 98.40 | 97.70 | 97.50 | .. | 96.32 |
| 35-39 | 96.65 | 98.35 | 97.30 | 96.75 | .. | 96.58 |
| 40-44 | 96.30 | 97.65 | 96.35 | 96.70 | .. | 96.17 |
| 45-49 | 94.55 | 96.00 | 95.05 | 92.40 | .. | 93.57 |
| 50-54 | 92.20 | 93.45 | 92.35 | 88.35 | .. | 86.93 |
| 55-59 | 88.30 | 89.10 | 87.65 | 79.15 | .. | 75.24 |
| 60-64 | 84.10 | 82.55 | 78.95 | 60.60 | .. | 57.08 |
| 65+ | 67.45 | 62.85 | 53.20 | 29.65 | .. | 20.03 |
| **Women** | | | | | | |
| 10-14 | 11.30 | 8.70 | 9.50 | .. | 3.01 | 4.84 |
| 15-19 | 34.70 | 27.60 | 44.00 | .. | 54.39 | 39.70 |
| 20-24 | 31.45 | 26.75 | 44.60 | .. | 69.35 | 68.46 |
| 25-29 | 23.15 | 19.95 | 32.50 | .. | 67.49 | 76.53 |
| 30-34 | 20.20 | 16.75 | 25.20 | .. | 63.09 | 77.66 |
| 35-39 | 19.30 | 15.50 | 22.75 | .. | 59.13 | 74.05 |
| 40-44 | 18.70 | 14.95 | 21.20 | .. | 50.51 | 67.77 |
| 45-49 | 19.05 | 14.45 | 19.60 | .. | 44.19 | 61.66 |
| 50-54 | 18.75 | 13.85 | 17.55 | .. | 42.36 | 50.49 |
| 55-59 | 18.05 | 13.55 | 14.60 | .. | 34.46 | 39.84 |
| 60-64 | 16.80 | 12.35 | 12.85 | .. | 29.03 | 24.72 |
| 65+ | 12.40 | 8.05 | 8.05 | .. | 8.50 | 7.77 |

Source(s): (1) EPPA3; (2) STAT.

### 2.2 Method(s):  national data

#### 2.2.1 Men:

- 1950-80, 1950-80 activity rates derived from the EPPA3;
adjustment of activity rates of the [45-49] age group for 1980;
- 1990, adjusted activity rates derived from the 1990 survey;
adjustment of activity rates to make allowance for conscripts.

#### 2.2.2 Women:

- 1950-70, 1950-70 activity rates derived from the EPPA3;
adjustment of activity rates of the [65+] age groups for 1970;
- 1980, adjusted activity rates derived from the 1980 survey;
- 1990, activity rates derived from the 1990 survey.

## 3. Estimates of distribution rates  by activity sector: 1950 - 1990

### 3.1 Benchmark data:

Table  2: Distribution of economically active population by activity sector

| Year | Agriculture | Industry Total | Manufac. | Services |
|---|---|---|---|---|
| **Men** | | | | |
| 1980 | 21.27 | 42.53 | 26.18 | 36.20 |
| 1990 | 15.38 | 40.06 | 24.02 | 44.57 |
| **Women** | | | | |
| 1980 | 33.42 | 26.40 | 25.72 | 40.18 |
| 1990 | 21.09 | 25.92 | 24.95 | 52.99 |

Source(s): (1) STAT.

### 3.2 Method(s):  national data

#### 3.2.1 Men:
- 1950-70, 1950-70 distribution rates derived from the EPPA3;
- 1980, distribution rates derived from the 1980 survey;
- 1980, adjusted distribution rates from the 1980 survey;
adjustment of rates to make allowance for conscripts.

#### 3.2.2 Women:

Method, hypothesis and treatment identical to those used for men.

## 4. Projection of activity rates: 2000 - 2010

### 4.1 Model(s):  linear, hyperbole and logistic

#### 4.1.1 Men:

- To the [15-19] age group, application of function F1;
- To the [20+] age groups, application of function F3;
- Modification of the trends for the [25-29] and [45-49] age groups.

#### 4.1.2 Women:

- To the [10-14] age group, application of function F1;
- To the [15-59] age groups, application of function F6;
- To the [60+] age groups, application of function F3;
- Modification of the trends for the [15-64] age groups.

---

*Notes on  adjustments of rates, see p. 3-8.*     *Notes on  projection functions, see p. 10.*

# Puerto Rico

## 1. Source(s) of benchmark data

Code(s):     Title(s):

EPPA3      Economically active population: Estimates and Projections, 1950-2025, Third edition, ILO, Geneva, 1986.
ASTER      Yearbook of Labour Statistics 1945-89 - Retrospective Edition on Population Censuses, ILO, Geneva, 1990.
AST91-93   Editions 1991-1993 of ILO Yearbook of Labour Statistics, Geneva.

## 2. Estimates of activity rates: 1950 - 1990

### 2.1 Benchmark data:

Table 1: Activity rates by sex and age group

| Age group | Year 1980 (1) | 1990 (2) | 1991 (2) | 1992 (2) |
|---|---|---|---|---|
| **Men** | | | | |
| 10-14 | 0.00 | 0.00 | 0.00 | 0.00 |
| 15-19 | 14.81 | 15.24 | 20.16 | 16.84 |
| 20-24 | 58.04 | 67.20 | 67.72 | 65.22 |
| 25-29 | 75.49 | 85.71 | 85.32 | 85.59 |
| 30-34 | 77.34 | 86.73 | 87.13 | 88.57 |
| 35-39 | 77.41 | 86.60 | 86.46 | 86.14 |
| 40-44 | 73.98 | 82.83 | 86.27 | 85.71 |
| 45-49 | 69.00 | 83.33 | 79.31 | 80.21 |
| 50-54 | 62.28 | 72.37 | 77.63 | 75.00 |
| 55-59 | 53.57 | 61.29 | 64.18 | 63.89 |
| 60-64 | 35.93 | 36.21 | 38.98 | 39.06 |
| 65+ | 12.40 | 14.47 | 13.92 | 13.77 |
| **Women** | | | | |
| 10-14 | 0.00 | 0.00 | 0.00 | 0.00 |
| 15-19 | 10.15 | 6.87 | 7.22 | 6.40 |
| 20-24 | 37.42 | 34.06 | 31.39 | 33.10 |
| 25-29 | 47.45 | 48.03 | 50.79 | 50.74 |
| 30-34 | 43.34 | 46.77 | 48.39 | 51.52 |
| 35-39 | 40.73 | 51.26 | 51.67 | 48.44 |
| 40-44 | 37.95 | 44.26 | 46.22 | 44.72 |
| 45-49 | 33.46 | 38.00 | 43.69 | 45.09 |
| 50-54 | 25.26 | 35.96 | 33.70 | 36.00 |
| 55-59 | 17.62 | 20.27 | 22.08 | 24.69 |
| 60-64 | 9.96 | 11.76 | 8.82 | 12.99 |
| 65+ | 2.8 | 3.41 | 2.14 | 2.56 |

Source(s): (1) ASTER; (2) AST91-93.

### 2.2 Method(s): linears interpolation and extrapolation

#### 2.2.1 Men:

- 1950-80, 1950-80 activity rates derived from the EPPA3;
adjustment of activity rates of the [55+] age groups based on the results of the 1979 and 1981 surveys;
- 1990, extrapolation of activity rates derived from
and the 1990, 1991 and 1992 surveys;
application to extrapolated rates, variations in 1980 interpolated rates, to 1980 activity rates derived from the EPPA3.

#### 2.2.2 Women:

- 1950-70, 1950-70 activity rates derived from the EPPA3;
- 1980-90, extrapolation of activity rates derived from
the 1980 census and of average of activity rates derived from
the 1990, 1991 and 1992 surveys.

## 3. Estimates of distribution rates by activity sector: 1950 - 1990

### 3.1 Benchmark data:

Table 2: Distribution of economically active population by activity sector

| Year | Agriculture | Industry Total | Manufac. | Services |
|---|---|---|---|---|
| **Men** | | | | |
| 1979 (1) | 8.57 | 29.43 | 15.82 | 62.00 |
| 1980 (2) | 5.58 | 33.46 | 17.98 | 60.95 |
| 1981 (1) | 8.09 | 30.38 | 15.88 | 61.53 |
| 1990 (1) | 6.95 | 29.00 | 15.41 | 64.05 |
| 1991 (1) | 6.15 | 28.40 | 15.96 | 65.45 |
| 1992 (1) | 5.60 | 29.31 | 15.61 | 65.10 |
| **Women** | | | | |
| 1979 (1) | 0.31 | 27.80 | 26.94 | 71.89 |
| 1980 (2) | 0.48 | 26.14 | 24.40 | 73.38 |
| 1981 (1) | 0.58 | 24.86 | 24.28 | 74.57 |
| 1990 (1) | 0.51 | 21.54 | 20.77 | 77.95 |
| 1991 (1) | 0.51 | 20.51 | 19.24 | 78.99 |
| 1992 (1) | 0.25 | 21.57 | 20.34 | 78.19 |

Source(s): ASTER.

### 3.2 Method(s): linear interpolation

#### 3.2.1 Men:

- 1950-70, 1950-70 distribution rates derived from the EPPA3;
- 1980-90, extrapolation of distribution rates derived from
the 1980 census and from the 1979, 1981, 1990, 1991 and 1992 surveys.

#### 3.2.2 Women:

Method, hypothesis and treatment identical to those used for men.

## 4. Projection of activity rates: 2000 - 2010

### 4.1 Model(s): log-linear, hyperbole and logistic

#### 4.1.1 Men:

- To the [15+] age groups, application of function F3;
- Modification of the trends for all age groups.

#### 4.1.2 Women:

- To the [15-19] age group, application of function F3;
- To the [20-49] age groups, application of function F2;
- To the [50+] age groups, application of function F6;
- Modification of the trends for the [20+] age groups.

*Notes on adjustments of rates, see p. 3-8.*    *Notes on projection functions, see p. 10.*

# Qatar

## 1. Source(s) of benchmark data

Code(s):  Title(s):

EPPA3      Economically active population: Estimates and Projections, 1950-2025, Third edition, ILO, Geneva, 1986.
EPPA4      Economically active population 1950-2010 - Fourth edition, ILO, Geneva 1996.
STAT       Database on Labour Statistics, LABORSTA - Bureau of Statistics, ILO, Geneva.

## 2. Estimates of activity rates: 1950 - 1990

### 2.1 Benchmark data:

Table 1: Activity rates by sex and age group

| Age group | Year | | | | | | |
|---|---|---|---|---|---|---|---|
| | 1950 (1) | 1970 (1) | 1990 (1) | 1986 (3) | 1950 (2) | 1970 (2) | 1990 (2) |
| **Men** | | | | | | | |
| 10-14 | 14.00 | 7.00 | 0.00 | 0.00 | 13.18 | 6.88 | 0.00 |
| 15-19 | 57.35 | 44.50 | 27.84 | 32.16 | 54.00 | 43.75 | 25.44 |
| 20-24 | 92.85 | 88.15 | 84.52 | 88.44 | 87.70 | 88.35 | 87.92 |
| 25-29 | 98.05 | 97.40 | 97.60 | 98.70 | 97.35 | 97.65 | 98.00 |
| 30-34 | 99.45 | 98.90 | 98.67 | 99.61 | 98.35 | 98.65 | 99.20 |
| 35-39 | 99.00 | 98.70 | 98.50 | 99.68 | 97.80 | 98.35 | 99.31 |
| 40-44 | 98.50 | 98.05 | 97.33 | 99.61 | 96.00 | 97.20 | 99.23 |
| 45-49 | 97.00 | 96.40 | 94.89 | 99.04 | 94.90 | 96.20 | 98.81 |
| 50-54 | 92.20 | 91.75 | 90.10 | 96.72 | 90.00 | 91.75 | 95.79 |
| 55-59 | 86.55 | 85.55 | 83.53 | 93.76 | 81.25 | 84.20 | 88.44 |
| 60-64 | 61.75 | 65.70 | 67.16 | 82.32 | 74.35 | 72.20 | 64.99 |
| 65+ | 34.00 | 34.35 | 31.12 | 59.61 | 53.00 | 49.80 | 36.55 |
| **Women** | | | | | | | |
| 10-14 | .. | .. | 0.00 | 0.00 | .. | .. | .. |
| 15-19 | .. | .. | 4.66 | 1.37 | .. | .. | .. |
| 20-24 | .. | .. | 46.42 | 13.67 | .. | .. | .. |
| 25-29 | .. | .. | 60.87 | 28.73 | .. | .. | .. |
| 30-34 | .. | .. | 57.34 | 46.91 | .. | .. | .. |
| 35-39 | .. | .. | 45.72 | 47.47 | .. | .. | .. |
| 40-44 | .. | .. | 33.40 | 37.59 | .. | .. | .. |
| 45-49 | .. | .. | 23.39 | 27.09 | .. | .. | .. |
| 50-54 | .. | .. | 19.27 | 15.95 | .. | .. | .. |
| 55-59 | .. | .. | 13.85 | 11.46 | .. | .. | .. |
| 60-64 | .. | .. | 10.70 | 6.83 | .. | .. | .. |
| 65+ | .. | .. | 0.46 | 2.72 | .. | .. | .. |

Note(s): (1) Kuwait; (2) Bahrain.
Source(s): (1)(2) EPPA4; (3) STAT.

### 2.2 Method(s): arithmetic average

#### 2.2.1 Men:

- 1950-90, application to adjusted activity rates derived from the 1986 census,
of average variations in estimated activity rates for Kuwait and Bahrain,
in relation to the 1986 estimated activity rates for these countries;
modification of the trends of the [10-14] and [50+] age groups.

#### 2.2.2 Women:

- 1950-80, 1950-80 activity rates derived from the EPPA3;
- 1990, application to 1990 activity rates estimated for Kuwait,
1/4 of variations in adjusted activity rates derived from the 1986 census,
in relation to 1986 activity rates estimated for Kuwait.

## 3. Estimates of distribution rates by activity sector: 1950 - 1990

### 3.1 Benchmark data:

Table 2: Distribution of economically active population by activity sector

| Year | Agriculture | Industry | | Services |
|---|---|---|---|---|
| | | Total | Manufac. | |
| **Men** | | | | |
| 1950 (1) | 30.00 | 22.00 | .. | 48.00 |
| 1960 (1) | 18.00 | 24.70 | .. | 57.30 |
| 1970 (1) | 10.00 | 27.30 | .. | 62.70 |
| 1980 (1) | 3.00 | 30.00 | .. | 67.00 |
| 1986 (2) | 3.48 | 35.56 | 7.65 | 60.96 |
| **Women** | | | | |
| 1950 (1) | 7.60 | 0.00 | .. | 92.40 |
| 1960 (1) | 4.10 | 0.00 | .. | 95.90 |
| 1970 (1) | 0.25 | 0.00 | .. | 99.75 |
| 1980 (1) | 0.00 | 0.00 | .. | 100.00 |
| 1986 (2) | 0.02 | 2.13 | 0.63 | 97.85 |

Source(s): (1) EPPA3; (2) STAT.

### 3.2 Method(s): linear extrapolation

#### 3.2.1 Men:

- 1950-80, 1950-80 distribution rates derived from the EPPA3;
- 1990, extrapolation of 1950-80 distribution rates of agriculture sector
derived from the EPP3;
modification of the trend in the sector;
distribution rates of industry, manufacturing and services sectors based
on distribution by sector derived from the 1986 census.

#### 3.2.2 Women:

Method, hypothesis and treatment identical to those used for men.

## 4. Projection of activity rates: 2000 - 2010

### 4.1 Model(s): linear, hyperbole and logistic

#### 4.1.1 Men:

- To the [15-19] and [25-54] age groups, application of function F3;
- To the [20-24] and [55+] age groups, application of function F6;
- Modification of the trends for the [20-49] age groups.

#### 4.1.2 Women:

- To the [15-19], [30-39] and [50-64] age groups, application of function F1;
- To the [20-29] and [40-49] age groups, application of function F6;
- To the [65+] age group, application of function F3;
- Modification of the trends for the [20-29] age groups.

*Notes on adjustments of rates, see p. 3-8.*

*Notes on projection functions, see p. 10.*

# Réunion

## 1. Source(s) of benchmark data

Code(s):     Title(s):

EPPA3     Economically active population: Estimates and Projections, 1950-2025, Third edition, ILO, Geneva, 1986.
ASTER     Yearbook of Labour Statistics 1945-89 - Retrospective Edition on Population Censuses, ILO, Geneva, 1990.
AST92     Yearbook of Labour Statistics 1992, ILO, Geneva, 1992.

## 2. Estimates of activity rates: 1950 - 1990

### 2.1 Benchmark data:

Table 1: Activity rates by sex and age group

| Age group | Year 1982 (1) | 1990 (2) |
|---|---|---|
| **Men** | | |
| 10-14 | 0.00 | 0.00 |
| 15-19 | 32.85 | 19.60 |
| 20-24 | 87.28 | 77.50 |
| 25-29 | 93.83 | 92.30 |
| 30-34 | 94.28 | 92.30 |
| 35-39 | 93.82 | 91.50 |
| 40-44 | 91.38 | 89.40 |
| 45-49 | 88.45 | 85.40 |
| 50-54 | 82.81 | 77.50 |
| 55-59 | 72.66 | 58.40 |
| 60-64 | 33.65 | 19.30 |
| 65+ | 22.51 | 3.05 |
| **Women** | | |
| 10-14 | 0.00 | 0.00 |
| 15-19 | 25.90 | 14.60 |
| 20-24 | 56.70 | 63.90 |
| 25-29 | 50.30 | 68.10 |
| 30-34 | 46.90 | 63.00 |
| 35-39 | 43.70 | 60.30 |
| 40-44 | 40.40 | 57.40 |
| 45-49 | 37.00 | 51.20 |
| 50-54 | 32.40 | 40.50 |
| 55-59 | 27.90 | 27.50 |
| 60-64 | 11.90 | 8.70 |
| 65+ | 1.34 | 0.80 |

Source(s): (1) ASTER; (2) AST92.

### 2.2 Method(s): weighted average

#### 2.2.1 Men:

- 1950-70, 1950-70 activity rates derived from the EPPA3;
- 1980-90, weighted average of adjusted activity rates derived from the 1982 and 1990 censuses;
modification of the trends of the [20-34] age groups for 1980.

#### 2.2.2 Women:

- 1950-80, 1950-80 activity rates derived from the EPPA3;
- 1990, weighted average of activity rates derived from the 1982 and 1990 censuses.

## 3. Estimates of distribution rates by activity sector: 1950 - 1990

### 3.1 Benchmark data:

Table 2: Distribution of economically active population by activity sector

| Year | Agriculture | Industry Total | Manufac. | Services |
|---|---|---|---|---|
| **Men** | | | | |
| 1982 (1) | 36.99 | 29.42 | 8.92 | 33.59 |
| 1990 (2) | 11.12 | 27.64 | 9.51 | 61.25 |
| **Women** | | | | |
| 1982 (1) | 7.14 | 4.80 | 3.62 | 88.07 |
| 1990 (2) | 1.94 | 5.09 | 3.64 | 92.97 |

Source(s): (1) ASTER; (2) AST92.

### 3.2 Method(s): linears interpolation and extrapolation

#### 3.2.1 Men:

- 1950-70, 1950-70 distribution rates derived from the EPPA3;
- 1980-90, interpolation and extrapolation of distribution rates derived from the 1982 and 1990 censuses;
modification of the trends in all sectors for 1980.

#### 3.2.2 Women:

Method, hypothesis and treatment identical to those used for men.

## 4. Projection of activity rates: 2000 - 2010

### 4.1 Model(s): linear, hyperbole and logistic

#### 4.1.1 Men:

- To the [15-19] age group, application of function F1;
- To the [20+] age groups, application of function F3.

#### 4.1.2 Women:

- To the [15-19] and [50-54] age groups, application of function F1;
- To the [20-49] age groups, application of function F6;
- Modification of the trend for the [25-29] age group.

---

*Notes on adjustments of rates, see p. 3-8.*

*Notes on projection functions, see p. 10.*

# Romania

## 1. Source(s) of benchmark data

| Code(s): | Title(s): |
|---|---|
| EPPA3 | Economically active population: Estimates and Projections, 1950-2025, Third edition, ILO, Geneva, 1986. |
| ASTER | Yearbook of Labour Statistics 1945-89 - Retrospective Edition on Population Censuses, ILO, Geneva, 1990. |
| BLT-94-2 | Popovic B. (1994), "New 1980 and 1990 estimates of activity rates by age and sectoral distribution for some countries of Eastern and Southern Europe" in the Bulletin of Labour of Statistics - 1994-2, ILO, Geneva. |
| AST94 | Yearbook of Labour Statistics 1994, ILO, Geneva, 1994. |

## 2. Estimates of activity rates: 1950 - 1990

### 2.1 Benchmark data:

Table 1: Activity rates by sex and age group

| Age group | Year 1950 (1) | 1960 (1) | 1970 (1) | 1977 (2) | 1992 (2) |
|---|---|---|---|---|---|
| **Men** | | | | | |
| 10-14 | 1.50 | 0.85 | 0.50 | 0.40 | 0.42 |
| 15-19 | 90.00 | 74.10 | 62.10 | 37.50 | 38.60 |
| 20-24 | 95.60 | 93.20 | 90.10 | 87.10 | 86.80 |
| 25-29 | 97.90 | 97.35 | 96.85 | 97.00 | 95.70 |
| 30-34 | 98.40 | 98.35 | 97.90 | 97.90 | 96.70 |
| 35-39 | 98.75 | 98.50 | 98.00 | 97.20 | 96.60 |
| 40-44 | 98.45 | 98.00 | 97.50 | 95.80 | 95.80 |
| 45-49 | 97.95 | 97.70 | 97.50 | 93.80 | 93.20 |
| 50-54 | 96.95 | 95.30 | 94.80 | 88.80 | 79.60 |
| 55-59 | 94.50 | 92.90 | 88.00 | 78.70 | 45.80 |
| 60-64 | 90.85 | 80.40 | 65.00 | 44.70 | 21.00 |
| 65+ | 74.10 | 62.50 | 54.85 | 13.23 | 5.37 |
| **Women** | | | | | |
| 10-14 | 2.00 | 1.45 | 0.90 | 0.50 | 0.21 |
| 15-19 | 79.45 | 69.95 | 45.20 | 32.10 | 32.70 |
| 20-24 | 78.55 | 75.90 | 74.15 | 75.60 | 72.10 |
| 25-29 | 74.85 | 76.15 | 80.35 | 83.10 | 78.50 |
| 30-34 | 74.20 | 75.70 | 80.45 | 83.50 | 81.30 |
| 35-39 | 74.05 | 75.85 | 80.80 | 83.60 | 81.60 |
| 40-44 | 75.80 | 76.40 | 79.45 | 81.70 | 79.00 |
| 45-49 | 74.75 | 74.90 | 75.85 | 77.60 | 72.80 |
| 50-54 | 73.85 | 72.10 | 70.70 | 69.70 | 51.00 |
| 55-59 | 67.95 | 63.50 | 55.90 | 72.50 | 28.70 |
| 60-64 | 61.40 | 52.10 | 34.45 | 25.20 | 10.20 |
| 65+ | 40.35 | 29.90 | 15.85 | 10.04 | 4.69 |

Source(s): (1) EPPA3; (2) AST94.

### 2.2 Method(s): linear interpolation

#### 2.2.1 Men:

- 1950-70, 1950-70 activity rates derived from the EPPA3;
- 1980-90, extrapolation of activity rates derived from the 1977 and 1992 censuses.

#### 2.2.2 Women:

Method, hypothesis and treatment identical to those used for men.

## 3. Estimates of distribution rates by activity sector: 1950 - 1990

### 3.1 Benchmark data:

Table 2: Distribution of economically active population by activity sector

| Year | Agriculture | Industry Total | Manufac. | Services |
|---|---|---|---|---|
| **Men** | | | | |
| 1950 (1) | 61.80 | 21.70 | .. | 16.50 |
| 1960 (1) | 53.00 | 29.50 | .. | 17.40 |
| 1970 (1) | 37.10 | 41.60 | .. | 21.30 |
| 1980 (2) | 25.93 | 50.14 | 33.92 | 23.93 |
| 1990 (2) | 20.95 | 52.91 | 37.39 | 26.14 |
| **Women** | | | | |
| 1950 (1) | 84.30 | 6.50 | .. | 9.20 |
| 1960 (1) | 78.40 | 9.40 | .. | 12.10 |
| 1970 (1) | 63.70 | 17.50 | .. | 18.80 |
| 1980 (2) | 45.33 | 29.45 | 26.43 | 25.21 |
| 1990 (2) | 27.75 | 40.04 | 35.94 | 32.21 |

Source(s): (1) EPPA3; (2) BLT-94-2.

### 3.2 Method(s): data from BLT-94-8

#### 3.2.1 Men:

- 1950-70, 1950-70 distribution rates derived from the EPPA3;
- 1980-90, 1980 and 1990 distribution rates derived from the Bulletin of Labour Statistics, 1994-2.

#### 3.2.2 Women:

Method, hypothesis and treatment identical to those used for men.

## 4. Projection of activity rates: 2000 - 2010

### 4.1 Model(s): linear and hyperbole

#### 4.1.1 Men:

- To the [15-19] and [25+] age groups, application of function F3;
- To the [20-24] age groups, application of function F1;
- Modification of the trends for the [35-39] and [50-64] age groups.

#### 4.1.2 Women:

- To the [15+] age groups, application of function F3;
- Modification of the trends for the [20-24] and [30-39] age groups.

---

*Notes on adjustments of rates, see p. 3-8.*     *Notes on projection functions, see p. 10.*

# Russian Federation

## 1. Source(s) of benchmark data

Code(s):     Title(s):

BLT-94-2     Vorobiev A. (1994), "Estimates of the economically active population for the fifteen countries of the former USSR
for the years 1950, 1959, 1970, 1979 and 1989", in the Bulletin of Labour of Statistics - 1994-2, ILO, Geneva.

## 2. Estimates of activity rates: 1950 - 1990

### 2.1 Benchmark data:

Table 1: Activity rates by sex and age group

|  | Year | | | | |
|---|---|---|---|---|---|
| Age group | 1950 | 1959 | 1970 | 1979 | 1989 |
| **Men** | | | | | |
| 10-14 | 0.00 | 0.00 | 0.00 | 0.00 | 0.00 |
| 15-19 | 52.20 | 63.65 | 43.79 | 38.71 | 31.02 |
| 20-24 | 84.87 | 86.31 | 85.24 | 87.28 | 80.97 |
| 25-29 | 96.82 | 97.09 | 96.59 | 96.87 | 96.36 |
| 30-34 | 96.72 | 95.52 | 97.14 | 98.04 | 97.68 |
| 35-39 | 94.99 | 92.85 | 97.69 | 97.97 | 97.69 |
| 40-44 | 94.18 | 94.27 | 97.12 | 97.51 | 97.25 |
| 45-49 | 90.99 | 90.45 | 93.33 | 96.11 | 95.67 |
| 50-54 | 84.98 | 85.56 | 89.86 | 89.68 | 91.49 |
| 55-59 | 71.93 | 77.11 | 78.41 | 75.90 | 78.82 |
| 60-64 | 51.97 | 57.83 | 23.26 | 28.22 | 35.31 |
| 65+ | 21.08 | 25.52 | 10.99 | 10.09 | 13.49 |
| **Women** | | | | | |
| 10-14 | 0.00 | 0.00 | 0.00 | 0.00 | 0.00 |
| 15-19 | 50.83 | 44.12 | 37.41 | 33.42 | 24.93 |
| 20-24 | 73.68 | 77.09 | 82.86 | 85.04 | 78.12 |
| 25-29 | 71.61 | 76.16 | 92.01 | 94.42 | 90.14 |
| 30-34 | 68.10 | 72.09 | 93.81 | 95.78 | 93.58 |
| 35-39 | 67.62 | 74.50 | 92.62 | 96.35 | 95.24 |
| 40-44 | 67.46 | 68.18 | 90.32 | 95.72 | 95.47 |
| 45-49 | 62.86 | 64.50 | 90.99 | 92.32 | 92.81 |
| 50-54 | 51.61 | 52.36 | 75.58 | 81.13 | 82.59 |
| 55-59 | 23.57 | 25.81 | 22.47 | 29.11 | 34.30 |
| 60-64 | 20.09 | 21.08 | 9.41 | 11.12 | 20.06 |
| 65+ | 2.35 | 2.35 | 2.01 | 3.01 | 5.86 |

Source(s): BLT-94-2.

### 2.2 Method(s): weighted average

#### 2.2.1 Men:

- 1950-90, weighted average of 1950, 1959, 1970 and 1989 activity rates
derived from the Bulletin of Labour Statistics 1994-2;
adjustment of 1959, 1970 and 1979 activity rate derived
from the Bulletin for the [15-19] and [60+] age groups.

#### 2.2.2 Women:

- 1950-90, weighted average of 1950, 1959, 1970 and 1989 activity rates
derived from the Bulletin of Labour Statistics 1994-2;
adjustment of 1959 activity rate derived from the Bulletin
for the [15-19] age group.

## 3. Estimates of distribution rates by activity sector: 1950 - 1990

### 3.1 Benchmark data:

Table 2: Distribution of economically active population by activity sector

|  | Agriculture | Industry | | Services |
|---|---|---|---|---|
| Year |  | Total | Manufac. |  |
| **Men** | | | | |
| 1950 | 36.27 | 36.23 | 20.01 | 27.50 |
| 1959 | 27.23 | 39.65 | 25.68 | 33.12 |
| 1970 | 20.17 | 49.68 | 31.74 | 30.15 |
| 1979 | 18.81 | 50.33 | 28.71 | 30.86 |
| 1989 | 17.43 | 48.24 | 26.76 | 34.33 |
| **Women** | | | | |
| 1950 | 42.63 | 27.67 | 20.30 | 29.70 |
| 1959 | 33.71 | 31.35 | 23.65 | 34.94 |
| 1970 | 17.68 | 35.82 | 28.75 | 46.50 |
| 1979 | 13.19 | 37.00 | 26.86 | 49.81 |
| 1989 | 9.75 | 34.76 | 24.61 | 55.50 |

Source(s): BLT-94-2.

### 3.2 Method(s):   data from BLT-94-14

#### 3.2.1 Men:

- 1950, 1960, 1970, 1980 et 1990, respectively 1950, 1959, 1970, 1982
and 1989 distribution rates derived from the Bulletin of Labour Statistics, 1994-

#### 3.2.2 Women:

Method, hypothesis and treatment identical to those used for men.

## 4. Projection of activity rates: 2000 - 2010

### 4.1 Model(s):   log-linear, hyperbole and logistic

#### 4.1.1 Men:

- To the [15-24] age groups, application of function F2;
- To the [25+] age groups, application of function F3;
- Modification of the trends for the [20+] age groups.

#### 4.1.2 Women:

- To the [15-19] and [60+] age groups, application of function F3;
- To the [20-59] age groups, application of function F6;
- Modification of the trends for the [20-59] age groups.

*Notes on adjustments of rates, see p. 3-8.*        *Notes on projection functions, see p. 10.*

# Rwanda

## 1. Source(s) of benchmark data

Code(s):    Title(s):
EPPA3       Economically active population: Estimates and Projections, 1950-2025, Third edition, ILO, Geneva, 1986.
ASTER       Yearbook of Labour Statistics 1945-89 - Retrospective Edition on Population Censuses, ILO, Geneva, 1990.

## 2. Estimates of activity rates: 1950 - 1990

### 2.1 Benchmark data:

Table 1: Activity rates by sex and age group

| Age group | Year | | | | |
|---|---|---|---|---|---|
| | 1950 (1) | 1960 (1) | 1970 (1) | 1978 (2) | 1980 (1) |
| **Men** | | | | | |
| 10-14 | 40.35 | 39.70 | 39.05 | 32.34 | 38.50 |
| 15-19 | 90.00 | 88.85 | 87.60 | 86.85 | 86.65 |
| 20-24 | 98.15 | 97.70 | 97.20 | 96.51 | 96.85 |
| 25-29 | 98.35 | 98.30 | 98.20 | 98.16 | 98.15 |
| 30-34 | 98.75 | 98.70 | 98.60 | 98.50 | 98.55 |
| 35-39 | 98.55 | 98.50 | 98.40 | 98.55 | 98.35 |
| 40-44 | 98.50 | 98.45 | 98.35 | 98.27 | 98.30 |
| 45-49 | 98.00 | 97.90 | 97.85 | 97.77 | 97.80 |
| 50-54 | 96.95 | 96.85 | 96.75 | 96.64 | 96.65 |
| 55-59 | 95.00 | 94.85 | 94.65 | 94.55 | 94.55 |
| 60-64 | 89.30 | 89.00 | 88.75 | 88.55 | 88.50 |
| 65+ | 70.15 | 69.75 | 69.30 | 69.00 | 68.95 |
| **Women** | | | | | |
| 10-14 | 49.85 | 48.70 | 47.45 | 33.32 | 46.50 |
| 15-19 | 91.55 | 89.15 | 86.55 | 88.19 | 84.55 |
| 20-24 | 95.75 | 93.45 | 90.90 | 96.14 | 88.95 |
| 25-29 | 96.45 | 94.30 | 91.95 | 97.08 | 90.15 |
| 30-34 | 97.85 | 95.85 | 93.65 | 97.43 | 91.95 |
| 35-39 | 97.60 | 95.70 | 93.60 | 97.97 | 92.05 |
| 40-44 | 96.75 | 95.05 | 93.20 | 97.96 | 91.80 |
| 45-49 | 95.35 | 93.70 | 91.85 | 97.25 | 90.50 |
| 50-54 | 87.55 | 86.20 | 84.65 | 95.26 | 83.50 |
| 55-59 | 77.65 | 76.65 | 75.55 | 90.92 | 74.75 |
| 60-64 | 61.65 | 61.05 | 60.35 | 81.67 | 59.85 |
| 65+ | 35.65 | 35.45 | 35.20 | 58.61 | 35.05 |

Source(s): (1) EPPA3; (2) ASTER.

### 2.2 Method(s): linear extrapolation

#### 2.2.1 Men:

- 1950-80, 1950-80 activity rates derived from the EPPA3;
- 1990, extrapolation of 1950-80 activity rates derived from the EPPA3;
and of activity rates derived from 1978 census;
modification of the trends for all age groups for 1990;
adjustment of 1990 extrapolated rates on the basis of variations
in 1980 interpolated rates, in relation to the 1980 activity rates derived from
the EPPA3.

#### 2.2.2 Women:

Method, hypothesis and treatment identical to those used for men.

## 3. Estimates of distribution rates by activity sector: 1950 - 1990

### 3.1 Benchmark data:

Table 2: Distribution of economically active population by activity sector

| Year | Agriculture | Industry | | Services |
|---|---|---|---|---|
| | | Total | Manufac. | |
| **Men** | | | | |
| 1950 (1) | 92.30 | 3.25 | .. | 4.45 |
| 1960 (1) | 90.75 | 3.90 | .. | 5.35 |
| 1970 (1) | 89.05 | 4.65 | .. | 6.30 |
| 1978 (2) | 88.01 | 5.09 | 2.14 | 6.90 |
| 1980 (1) | 87.75 | 5.20 | .. | 7.05 |
| **Women** | | | | |
| 1950 (1) | 99.10 | 0.30 | .. | 0.60 |
| 1960 (1) | 98.70 | 0.40 | .. | 0.90 |
| 1970 (1) | 98.30 | 0.55 | .. | 1.15 |
| 1978 (2) | 97.96 | 0.63 | 0.60 | 1.40 |
| 1980 (1) | 97.95 | 0.65 | .. | 1.40 |

Source(s): (1) EPPA3; (2) ASTER.

### 3.2 Method(s): linear extrapolation

#### 3.2.1 Men:

- 1950-80, 1950-80 distribution rates derived from the EPPA3;
- 1990, extrapolation of 1950-80 distribution rates derived from the EPPA3;
- Application of manufacturing/industry ratio derived from the 1978 census.

#### 3.2.2 Women:

Method, hypothesis and treatment identical to those used for men.

## 4. Projection of activity rates: 2000 - 2010

### 4.1 Model(s): linear and hyperbole

#### 4.1.1 Men:

- To all age groups, application of function F1.

#### 4.1.2 Women:

- To all age groups, application of function F3;
- Modification of the trends for the [25-64] age groups.

# Saudi Arabia

## 1. Source(s) of benchmark data

Code(s):     Title(s):

EPPA3       Economically active population: Estimates and Projections, 1950-2025, Third edition, ILO, Geneva, 1986.

## 2. Estimates of activity rates: 1950 - 1990

### 2.1 Benchmark data:

Table 1: Activity rates by sex and age group

| Age group | Year 1975 (1) | 1980 (2) | 1987 (3) | 1988 (3) |
|---|---|---|---|---|
| **Men** | | | | |
| 10-14 | 22.00 | 19.30 | 16.20 | 8.10 |
| 15-19 | 86.75 | 81.85 | 69.30 | 49.30 |
| 20-24 | 95.40 | 94.50 | 91.30 | 86.65 |
| 25-29 | 98.00 | 97.80 | 97.30 | 96.55 |
| 30-34 | 98.40 | 98.35 | 98.20 | 98.00 |
| 35-39 | 97.25 | 97.40 | 97.65 | 98.10 |
| 40-44 | 96.80 | 96.85 | 97.00 | 97.20 |
| 45-49 | 96.40 | 96.30 | 96.00 | 97.55 |
| 50-54 | 93.60 | 93.35 | 92.80 | 91.90 |
| 55-59 | 90.35 | 89.90 | 88.50 | 86.40 |
| 60-64 | 81.75 | 80.85 | 78.50 | 74.75 |
| 65+ | 56.15 | 55.30 | 53.05 | 49.50 |
| **Women** | | | | |
| 10-14 | .. | .. | .. | .. |
| 15-19 | .. | .. | .. | .. |
| 20-24 | .. | .. | .. | .. |
| 25-29 | .. | .. | .. | .. |
| 30-34 | .. | .. | .. | .. |
| 35-39 | .. | .. | .. | .. |
| 40-44 | .. | .. | .. | .. |
| 45-49 | .. | .. | .. | .. |
| 50-54 | .. | .. | .. | .. |
| 55-59 | .. | .. | .. | .. |
| 60-64 | .. | .. | .. | .. |
| 65+ | .. | .. | .. | .. |

Source(s): EPPA3.

### 2.2 Method(s):  linear extrapolation

#### 2.2.1 Men:

- 1950-80, 1950-80 activity rates derived from the EPPA3;
- 1990, extrapolation of 1950-80 activity rates derived from the EPPA3;
adjustment of extrapolated rates on the basis of variations in 1980
interpolated rates, in relation to the 1980 rates derived from the EPPA3;
modification of the trends of the [10-14], [25-54] and [60+] age groups.

#### 2.2.2 Women:

- 1950-70, 1950-70 activity rates derived from the EPPA3;
- 1980-90, application to 1970 activity rates derived from the EPPA3,
the average of variations in 1980 and 1990 activity rates estimated for Bahrain,
Kuwait and Oman, in relation to the 1970 activity rates estimated
for these countries.

## 3. Estimates of distribution rates by activity sector: 1950 - 1990

### 3.1 Benchmark data:

Table 2: Distribution of economically active population by activity sector

| Year | Agriculture | Industry Total | Manufac. | Services |
|---|---|---|---|---|
| **Men** | | | | |
| 1950 | 76.00 | 9.00 | .. | 15.00 |
| 1960 | 71.00 | 10.00 | .. | 19.00 |
| 1970 | 65.00 | 12.50 | .. | 22.50 |
| 1980 | 45.00 | 16.50 | 5.33 | 38.50 |
| **Women** | | | | |
| 1950 | 87.00 | 2.80 | .. | 10.20 |
| 1960 | 76.00 | 3.60 | .. | 20.40 |
| 1970 | 48.60 | 4.40 | .. | 47.00 |
| 1980 | 25.00 | 5.00 | 2.82 | 70.00 |

Source(s): EPPA3.

### 3.2 Method(s):  linear extrapolation

#### 3.2.1 Men:

- 1950-80, 1950-80 distribution rates derived from the EPPA3;
- 1990, extrapolation of 1950-80 distribution rates derived from the EPPA3;
modification of the trends in all sectors.

#### 3.2.2 Women:

Method, hypothesis and treatment identical to those used for men.

## 4. Projection of activity rates: 2000 - 2010

### 4.1 Model(s):  linear, log-linear, hyperbole and logistic

#### 4.1.1 Men:

- To the [15-19] age group, application of function F2;
- To the [20-59] age groups, application of function F3;
- To the [60+] age groups, application of function F1;
- Modification of the trends for the [20-24] and [35-54] age groups.

#### 4.1.2 Women:

- To the [15-24] age groups, application of function F2;
- To the [25-39] age groups, application of function F6;
- To the [40-64] age groups, application of function F2;
- To the [65+] age group, application of function F1;
- Modification of the trend for the [15-19] age group.

*Notes on adjustments of rates, see p. 3-8.*

*Notes on projection functions, see p. 10.*

# Senegal

## 1. Source(s) of benchmark data

Code(s):    Title(s):

EPPA3    Economically active population: Estimates and Projections, 1950-2025, Third edition, ILO, Geneva, 1986.
R1976    République du Sénégal, Ministère de l'Economie et des Finances, Recensement Général de la Population, avril 1976.
AST93    Yearbook of Labour Statistics 1993, ILO, Geneva, 1993.

## 2. Estimates of activity rates: 1950 - 1990

### 2.1 Benchmark data:

Table 1: Activity rates by sex and age group

| Age group | Year | | | | | |
|---|---|---|---|---|---|---|
| | 1950 (1) | 1960 (1) | 1970 (1) | 1976 (2) | 1980 (1) | 1988 (3) |
| **Men** | | | | | | |
| 10-14 | .. | 58.55 | .. | 47.40 | .. | 37.25 |
| 15-19 | .. | 76.35 | .. | 72.75 | .. | 64.76 |
| 20-24 | .. | 87.25 | .. | 88.39 | .. | 88.39 |
| 25-29 | .. | 95.20 | .. | 96.35 | .. | 94.51 |
| 30-34 | .. | 96.35 | .. | 98.34 | .. | 96.04 |
| 35-39 | .. | 96.90 | .. | 98.63 | .. | 97.07 |
| 40-44 | .. | 96.15 | .. | 98.81 | .. | 96.86 |
| 45-49 | .. | 95.25 | .. | 98.72 | .. | 96.15 |
| 50-54 | .. | 94.10 | .. | 97.37 | .. | 93.99 |
| 55-59 | .. | 86.60 | .. | 90.31 | .. | 86.93 |
| 60-64 | .. | 79.10 | .. | 85.40 | .. | 79.87 |
| 65+ | .. | 59.80 | .. | 74.80 | .. | 61.64 |
| **Women** | | | | | | |
| 10-14 | 44.65 | 44.10 | 43.55 | 5.18 | 42.55 | .. |
| 15-19 | 54.40 | 53.80 | 53.20 | 7.26 | 52.10 | .. |
| 20-24 | 57.00 | 56.65 | 56.25 | 5.96 | 55.55 | .. |
| 25-29 | 63.30 | 62.85 | 62.40 | 4.86 | 61.60 | .. |
| 30-34 | 67.30 | 66.85 | 66.35 | 3.84 | 65.45 | .. |
| 35-39 | 69.65 | 69.20 | 68.70 | 3.89 | 67.90 | .. |
| 40-44 | 72.10 | 71.70 | 71.20 | 4.07 | 70.40 | .. |
| 45-49 | 70.80 | 70.35 | 69.85 | 4.75 | 69.00 | .. |
| 50-54 | 67.25 | 66.75 | 66.20 | 4.57 | 65.25 | .. |
| 55-59 | 62.50 | 62.00 | 61.40 | 4.45 | 60.45 | .. |
| 60-64 | 50.05 | 49.50 | 48.85 | 4.61 | 47.75 | .. |
| 65+ | 27.45 | 27.00 | 26.55 | 3.84 | 25.70 | .. |

Source(s): (1) EPPA3; (2) R1976; (3) AST93.

### 2.2 Method(s): linears interpolation and extrapolation

#### 2.2.1 Men:

- 1950-90, interpolation and extrapolation of 1960 activity rates
derived from the EPPA3 and of adjusted activity rates derived
from the 1976 and 1988 censuses;
modification of the trends of the [10-14] age group for 1960 and 1980.

#### 2.2.2 Women:

- 1950-90, interpolation and extrapolation of 1950-80 activity rates
derived from the EPPA3;
adjustment of interpolated and extrapolated rates on the basis of variations
in 1976 interpolated rates, in relation to the rates derived from
the 1976 census;
modification of the trends for all age groups for 1980 and 1990.

## 3. Estimates of distribution rates by activity sector: 1950 - 1990

### 3.1 Benchmark data:

Table 2: Distribution of economically active population by activity sector

| Year | Agriculture | Industry | | Services |
|---|---|---|---|---|
| | | Total | Manufac. | |
| **Men** | | | | |
| 1950 | 78.00 | 7.65 | .. | 14.35 |
| 1960 | 77.00 | 8.00 | .. | 15.00 |
| 1970 | 75.90 | 8.40 | .. | 15.70 |
| 1980 | 74.00 | 9.05 | .. | 16.95 |
| **Women** | | | | |
| 1950 | 95.00 | 1.15 | .. | 3.85 |
| 1960 | 93.60 | 1.45 | .. | 4.95 |
| 1970 | 92.30 | 1.75 | .. | 5.95 |
| 1980 | 89.95 | 2.30 | .. | 7.75 |

Source(s): EPPA3.

### 3.2 Method(s): linear extrapolation

#### 3.2.1 Men:

- 1950-80, 1950-80 distribution rates derived from the EPPA3;
- 1990, extrapolation of 1950-80 distribution rates derived from the EPPA3;
modification of the trends in all sectors;
- Application of manufacturing/industry ratio estimated for Niger.

#### 3.2.2 Women:

Method, hypothesis and treatment identical to those used for men.

## 4. Projection of activity rates: 2000 - 2010

### 4.1 Model(s): linear and hyperbole

#### 4.1.1 Men:

- To the [10-24] age groups, application of function F1;
- To the [25+] age groups, application of function F3;
- Modification of the trends for the [10-14] and [20-54] age groups.

#### 4.1.2 Women:

- To the [10-14] age group, application of function F1;
- To the [15+] age groups, application of function F3;
- Modification of the trends for the [15-54] age groups.

*Notes on adjustments of rates, see p. 3-8.*    *Notes on projection functions, see p. 10.*

8

153

# Sierra Leone

## 1. Source(s) of benchmark data

Code(s):     Title(s):

EPPA3       Economically active population: Estimates and Projections, 1950-2025, Third edition, ILO, Geneva, 1986.

## 2. Estimates of activity rates: 1950 - 1990

### 2.1 Benchmark data:

Table 1: Activity rates by sex and age group

| Age group | Year 1950 | 1960 | 1970 |
|---|---|---|---|
| **Men** | | | |
| 10-14 | 39.00 | 33.00 | 24.55 |
| 15-19 | 71.20 | 66.35 | 59.85 |
| 20-24 | 89.85 | 88.90 | 86.80 |
| 25-29 | 97.15 | 96.95 | 96.70 |
| 30-34 | 97.90 | 97.60 | 97.35 |
| 35-39 | 98.05 | 97.75 | 97.45 |
| 40-44 | 97.90 | 97.55 | 97.25 |
| 45-49 | 97.50 | 97.40 | 96.75 |
| 50-54 | 97.00 | 96.70 | 95.90 |
| 55-59 | 92.90 | 92.80 | 91.00 |
| 60-64 | 88.00 | 87.50 | 84.60 |
| 65+ | 73.45 | 70.35 | 64.30 |
| **Women** | | | |
| 10-14 | 26.80 | 23.85 | 19.00 |
| 15-19 | 46.80 | 41.70 | 36.80 |
| 20-24 | 54.00 | 49.00 | 45.25 |
| 25-29 | 54.50 | 50.15 | 47.90 |
| 30-34 | 54.90 | 50.60 | 48.35 |
| 35-39 | 55.40 | 51.00 | 48.80 |
| 40-44 | 55.00 | 51.25 | 49.15 |
| 45-49 | 56.20 | 52.45 | 51.15 |
| 50-54 | 54.40 | 50.75 | 49.50 |
| 55-59 | 48.45 | 47.55 | 46.65 |
| 60-64 | 36.35 | 34.25 | 33.55 |
| 65+ | 23.40 | 22.20 | 20.75 |

Source(s): EPPA3.

### 2.2 Method(s):  linear extrapolation

#### 2.2.1 Men:

- 1950-70, 1950-70 activity rates derived from the EPPA3;
- 1980-90, extrapolation of 1950-70 activity rates derived from the EPPA3;
adjustment of interpolated and extrapolated rates on the basis of variations
in 1970 interpolated rates, in relation to the 1970 rates derived from
the EPPA3;
modification of the trends for all age groups from 1980 to 1990.

#### 2.2.2 Women:

Method, hypothesis and treatment identical to those used for men.

## 3. Estimates of distribution rates by activity sector: 1950 - 1990

### 3.1 Benchmark data:

Table 2: Distribution of economically active population by activity sector

| Year | Agriculture | Industry Total | Manufac. | Services |
|---|---|---|---|---|
| **Men** | | | | |
| 1950 | 82.00 | 10.55 | .. | 7.45 |
| 1960 | 77.00 | 13.50 | .. | 9.50 |
| 1970 | 70.00 | 17.60 | .. | 12.40 |
| 1980 | 63.00 | 19.65 | .. | 17.35 |
| **Women** | | | | |
| 1950 | 91.50 | 1.70 | .. | 6.80 |
| 1960 | 89.00 | 2.20 | .. | 8.80 |
| 1970 | 85.50 | 2.90 | .. | 11.60 |
| 1980 | 82.00 | 3.60 | .. | 14.40 |

Source(s): EPPA3.

### 3.2 Method(s):  linear extrapolation

#### 3.2.1 Men:

- 1950-80, 1950-80 distribution rates derived from the EPPA3;
- 1990, extrapolation of 1950-80 distribution rates derived from the EPPA3;
- Application of manufacturing/industry ratio estimated for Liberia.

#### 3.2.2 Women:

Method, hypothesis and treatment identical to those used for men.

## 4. Projection of activity rates: 2000 - 2010

### 4.1 Model(s):  log-linear and hyperbole

#### 4.1.1 Men:

- To the [10-14] age group, application of function F2;
- To the [15+] age groups, application of function F3.

#### 4.1.2 Women:

- To the [10-14] age group, application of function F2;
- To the [15+] age groups, application of function F3;
- Modification of the trends for the [20+] age groups.

*Notes on adjustments of rates, see p. 3-8.*          *Notes on projection functions, see p. 10.*

## Singapore

### 1. Source(s) of benchmark data

Code(s):    Title(s):

EPPA3    Economically active population: Estimates and Projections, 1950-2025, Third edition, ILO, Geneva, 1986.
STAT    Database on Labour Statistics, LABORSTA - Bureau of Statistics, ILO, Geneva.

### 2. Estimates of activity rates: 1950 - 1990

#### 2.1 Benchmark data:

Table 1: Activity rates by sex and age group

| Age group | 1980 (1) | 1980 (2) | 1989 (2) | 1990 (1) | 1991 (2) |
|---|---|---|---|---|---|
| **Men** | | | | | |
| 10-14 | 1.64 | 1.64 | 0.00 | 0.00 | 0.00 |
| 15-19 | 47.49 | 45.80 | 25.50 | 28.39 | 31.10 |
| 20-24 | 93.35 | 92.50 | 84.80 | 84.35 | 83.10 |
| 25-29 | 97.23 | 97.30 | 96.60 | 95.42 | 97.00 |
| 30-34 | 97.94 | 98.32 | 98.30 | 96.56 | 98.70 |
| 35-39 | 98.03 | 98.41 | 99.00 | 97.22 | 99.10 |
| 40-44 | 97.62 | 98.00 | 97.80 | 97.65 | 98.40 |
| 45-49 | 95.72 | 96.30 | 96.10 | 95.19 | 96.50 |
| 50-54 | 89.57 | 90.40 | 89.20 | 88.19 | 92.50 |
| 55-59 | 70.69 | 73.20 | 66.60 | 68.35 | 71.00 |
| 60-64 | 52.53 | 55.80 | 48.20 | 31.86 | 46.90 |
| 65+ | 28.61 | 29.80 | 20.74 | ... | 19.80 |
| **Women** | | | | | |
| 10-14 | 1.65 | 1.64 | 0.00 | 0.00 | 0.00 |
| 15-19 | 50.73 | 45.80 | 25.50 | 27.84 | 31.10 |
| 20-24 | 78.40 | 92.50 | 84.80 | 79.57 | 83.10 |
| 25-29 | 58.67 | 97.30 | 96.60 | 76.31 | 97.00 |
| 30-34 | 44.20 | 98.32 | 98.30 | 63.06 | 98.70 |
| 35-39 | 37.13 | 98.41 | 99.00 | 54.95 | 99.10 |
| 40-44 | 33.16 | 98.00 | 97.80 | 51.86 | 98.40 |
| 45-49 | 26.47 | 96.30 | 96.10 | 45.01 | 96.50 |
| 50-54 | 20.43 | 90.40 | 89.20 | 34.15 | 92.50 |
| 55-59 | 14.50 | 73.20 | 66.60 | 21.48 | 71.00 |
| 60-64 | 11.30 | 55.80 | 48.20 | 7.70 | 46.90 |
| 65+ | 6.40 | 29.80 | 20.74 | ... | 19.80 |

Note(s): (1) Census; (2) Survey.
Source(s): STAT.

#### 2.2 Method(s): arithmetic average

**2.2.1 Men:**

- 1950-70, 1950-70 activity rates derived from the EPPA3;
- 1980, average of activity rates derived from the 1980 census and the 1980 survey;
- 1990, average of activity rates derived from the 1990 census and of activity rates derived from the 1989 and 1990 surveys.

**2.2.2 Women:**

Method, hypothesis and treatment identical to those used for men.

### 3. Estimates of distribution rates by activity sector: 1950 - 1990

#### 3.1 Benchmark data:

Table 2: Distribution of economically active population by activity sector

| Year | Agriculture | Industry Total | Manufac. | Services |
|---|---|---|---|---|
| **Men** | | | | |
| 1980 (1) | 1.54 | 33.48 | 24.42 | 64.98 |
| 1980 (2) | 1.97 | 35.32 | 24.66 | 62.71 |
| 1989 (1) | 0.62 | 36.81 | 25.93 | 62.56 |
| 1991 (1) | 0.39 | 36.72 | 26.18 | 62.89 |
| **Women** | | | | |
| 1980 (1) | 0.95 | 40.33 | 38.56 | 58.72 |
| 1980 (2) | 1.67 | 86.31 | 8.25 | 12.02 |
| 1989 (1) | 0.19 | 35.28 | 33.68 | 64.54 |
| 1991 (1) | 0.11 | 32.85 | 31.22 | 67.04 |

Note(s): (1) Survey; (2) Census.
Source(s): STAT.

#### 3.2 Method(s): arithmetic average

**3.2.1 Men:**

- 1950-70, 1950-70 distribution rates derived from the EPPA3;
- 1980, averages of distribution rates derived from 1980 census and from the 1980 survey;
- 1990, averages of distribution rates derived from the 1989 and 1990 surveys.

**3.2.2 Women:**

Method, hypothesis and treatment identical to those used for men.

### 4. Projection of activity rates: 2000 - 2010

#### 4.1 Model(s): linear, hyperbole and logistic

**4.1.1 Men:**

- To the [15-19] age group, application of function F1;
- To the [20+] age groups, application of function F6;
- Modification of the trends for the [55-64] age groups.

**4.1.2 Women:**

- To the [15-19] and [35-54] age groups, application of function F1;
- To the [20-34] age groups, application of function F6;
- To the [55+] age groups, application of function F3;
- Modification of the trends for the [15-59] age groups.

*Notes on adjustments of rates, see p. 3-8.*      *Notes on projection functions, see p. 10.*

# Slovakia

## 1. Source(s) of benchmark data

Code(s):  Title(s):

BLT-94-2  Vorobiev A. (1994), "Estimates of the economically active population for the fifteen countries of the former USSR for the years 1950, 1959, 1970, 1979 and 1989", in the Bulletin of Labour of Statistics - 1994-2, ILO, Geneva.

## 2. Estimates of activity rates: 1950 - 1990

### 2.1 Benchmark data:

Table 1: Activity rates by sex and age group

| Age group | 1950 (1) | 1961 | 1970 (1) | 1980 | 1991 (1) |
|---|---|---|---|---|---|
| **Men** | | | | | |
| 10-14 | 0.00 | 0.00 | 0.00 | 0.00 | 0.00 |
| 15-19 | 77.05 | 45.71 | 34.90 | 31.58 | 35.28 |
| 20-24 | 94.95 | 91.92 | 91.55 | 86.49 | 88.32 |
| 25-29 | 98.93 | 97.10 | 98.61 | 98.21 | 98.01 |
| 30-34 | 99.14 | 97.53 | 98.97 | 98.36 | 98.26 |
| 35-39 | 98.42 | 97.20 | 98.69 | 97.89 | 97.78 |
| 40-44 | 97.50 | 96.40 | 97.92 | 97.66 | 97.16 |
| 45-49 | 94.75 | 95.25 | 96.52 | 95.45 | 95.58 |
| 50-54 | 91.95 | 92.30 | 93.74 | 92.37 | 91.80 |
| 55-59 | 84.88 | 86.34 | 85.26 | 84.25 | 80.00 |
| 60-64 | 44.19 | 64.53 | 31.47 | 47.83 | 28.22 |
| 65+ | 20.28 | 30.15 | 14.66 | 20.27 | 11.63 |
| **Women** | | | | | |
| 10-14 | 0.00 | 0.00 | 0.00 | 0.00 | 0.00 |
| 15-19 | 69.83 | 47.73 | 44.21 | 29.65 | 33.88 |
| 20-24 | 59.29 | 61.32 | 79.68 | 81.43 | 87.46 |
| 25-29 | 39.30 | 47.99 | 80.91 | 89.81 | 94.66 |
| 30-34 | 40.99 | 46.03 | 83.81 | 89.50 | 95.22 |
| 35-39 | 46.39 | 50.74 | 86.57 | 89.12 | 95.50 |
| 40-44 | 48.10 | 52.46 | 86.41 | 86.76 | 95.01 |
| 45-49 | 51.82 | 48.84 | 84.05 | 81.43 | 93.33 |
| 50-54 | 45.51 | 41.90 | 77.13 | 71.33 | 85.56 |
| 55-59 | 34.81 | 32.10 | 39.38 | 36.11 | 31.25 |
| 60-64 | 22.14 | 21.49 | 20.01 | 16.46 | 16.04 |
| 65+ | 8.80 | 6.79 | 5.89 | 4.59 | 4.93 |

Note(s): (1) Czech Republic.
Source(s): STAT.

### 2.2 Method(s): weighted average

#### 2.2.1 Men:

- 1950-90, weighted average of activity rates derived from the 1961 and 1980 census and of activity rates for the Czech Republic derived from the 1950, 1970 and 1991 censuses; adjustment of 1950-70 estimated activity rates of the [10-14] age group.

#### 2.2.2 Women:

Method, hypothesis and treatment identical to those used for men.

## 3. Estimates of distribution rates by activity sector: 1950 - 1990

### 3.1 Benchmark data:

Table 2: Distribution of economically active population by activity sector

| Year | Agriculture | Industry Total | Manufac. | Services |
|---|---|---|---|---|
| **Men** | | | | |
| 1950 | 44.56 | 33.11 | .. | 22.32 |
| 1961 | 30.12 | 46.54 | .. | 23.34 |
| 1970 | 21.00 | 51.33 | .. | 27.68 |
| 1980 | 14.76 | 37.42 | 30.73 | 47.82 |
| 1991 | 14.39 | 35.32 | 28.66 | 50.29 |
| **Women** | | | | |
| 1950 | 62.26 | 18.35 | .. | 19.39 |
| 1961 | 40.70 | 26.84 | .. | 32.46 |
| 1970 | 20.04 | 36.39 | .. | 43.56 |
| 1980 | 12.39 | 33.81 | 30.04 | 53.81 |
| 1991 | 9.20 | 30.62 | 26.93 | 60.18 |

Source(s): STAT.

### 3.2 Method(s): weighted average

#### 3.2.1 Men:

- 1950-90, weighted averages of distribution rates derived from the 1950, 1961, 1970, 1980 and 1991 censuses.

#### 3.2.2 Women:

Method, hypothesis and treatment identical to those used for men.

## 4. Projection of activity rates: 2000 - 2010

### 4.1 Model(s): linear, hyperbole and logistic

#### 4.1.1 Men:

- To the [15-19] and [60+] age groups, application of function F3;
- To the [20-59] age groups, application of function F1;
- Modification of the trends for the [25-34] age groups.

#### 4.1.2 Women:

- To the [15-19] and [55+] age groups, application of function F3;
- To the [20-54] age groups, application of function F6;
- Modification of the trends for the [20-54] age groups.

Notes on adjustments of rates, see p. 3-8.
Notes on projection functions, see p. 10.

# Slovenia

## 1. Source(s) of benchmark data

**Code(s):** **Title(s):**

BLT-94-2    Popovic B. (1994), "New 1980 and 1990 estimates of activity rates by age and sectoral distribution for some countries of Eastern and Southern Europe" in the Bulletin of Labour of Statistics - 1994-2, ILO, Geneva.

STAT    Database on Labour Statistics, LABORSTA - Bureau of Statistics, ILO, Geneva.

## 2. Estimates of activity rates: 1950 - 1990

### 2.1 Benchmark data:

Table 1: Activity rates by sex and age group

| Age group | Year | | | | |
|---|---|---|---|---|---|
| | 1953 (1) | 1961 (1) | 1971 (1) | 1980 (2) | 1990 (2) |
| **Men** | | | | | |
| 10-14 | 9.27 | 1.02 | 0.32 | 0.01 | 0.00 |
| 15-19 | 84.70 | 71.57 | 44.88 | 33.54 | 25.75 |
| 20-24 | 92.77 | 90.57 | 88.33 | 86.09 | 79.08 |
| 25-29 | 95.99 | 96.52 | 85.32 | 97.30 | 94.50 |
| 30-34 | 97.51 | 97.74 | 90.24 | 98.36 | 97.20 |
| 35-39 | 98.01 | 97.23 | 92.40 | 98.23 | 97.06 |
| 40-44 | 97.85 | 96.83 | 91.50 | 97.17 | 96.28 |
| 45-49 | 96.62 | 96.11 | 95.32 | 94.54 | 93.69 |
| 50-54 | 93.34 | 92.24 | 86.80 | 81.35 | 84.60 |
| 55-59 | 72.85 | 74.50 | 61.55 | 59.18 | 49.85 |
| 60-64 | 60.78 | 58.83 | 41.89 | 31.41 | 30.64 |
| 65+ | 45.85 | 42.31 | 33.52 | 19.27 | 14.45 |
| **Women** | | | | | |
| 10-14 | 7.87 | 0.85 | 0.27 | 0.01 | 0.00 |
| 15-19 | 71.52 | 62.50 | 38.32 | 28.27 | 21.07 |
| 20-24 | 72.19 | 77.30 | 68.23 | 82.35 | 75.70 |
| 25-29 | 54.59 | 67.39 | 74.63 | 91.65 | 92.89 |
| 30-34 | 45.79 | 59.35 | 71.34 | 90.91 | 93.93 |
| 35-39 | 43.15 | 55.10 | 68.49 | 88.59 | 92.56 |
| 40-44 | 41.88 | 51.98 | 64.08 | 82.30 | 89.94 |
| 45-49 | 41.82 | 48.91 | 56.27 | 73.37 | 82.10 |
| 50-54 | 37.33 | 42.14 | 44.45 | 57.07 | 45.36 |
| 55-59 | 34.00 | 35.92 | 30.89 | 28.13 | 22.98 |
| 60-64 | 31.46 | 31.31 | 25.37 | 19.94 | 17.96 |
| 65+ | 21.45 | 22.09 | 18.88 | 9.85 | 9.42 |

**Source(s):** (1) STAT; (2) BLT-94-2.

### 2.2 Method(s): linear interpolation

**2.2.1 Men:**

- 1950-70, interpolation and extrapolation of activity rates derived from the 1953, 1961 and 1971 censuses;
- 1980-90, 1980 and 1990 activity rates derived from the Bulletin of Labour Statistics 1994-2.

**2.2.2 Women:**

Method, hypothesis and treatment identical to those used for men.

## 3. Estimates of distribution rates by activity sector: 1950 - 1990

### 3.1 Benchmark data:

Table 2: Distribution of economically active population by activity sector

| Year | Agriculture | Industry | | Services |
|---|---|---|---|---|
| | | Total | Manufac. | |
| **Men** | | | | |
| 1953 (1) | 46.40 | 31.59 | 15.48 | 22.01 |
| 1961 (1) | 35.48 | 39.60 | 34.21 | 24.93 |
| 1971 (1) | 23.93 | 46.67 | 41.15 | 29.40 |
| 1980 (2) | 14.02 | 48.51 | 34.98 | 37.47 |
| 1990 (2) | 5.13 | 52.07 | 41.10 | 42.81 |
| **Women** | | | | |
| 1953 (1) | 64.15 | 17.39 | 16.62 | 18.45 |
| 1961 (1) | 45.05 | 28.28 | 27.18 | 26.67 |
| 1971 (1) | 31.49 | 35.12 | 33.80 | 33.39 |
| 1980 (2) | 17.13 | 37.37 | 34.70 | 45.49 |
| 1990 (2) | 6.35 | 39.22 | 36.79 | 54.44 |

**Source(s):** (1) STAT; (2) BLT-94-2.

### 3.2 Method(s): weighted average
linear extrapolation

**3.2.1 Men:**

- 1950, weighted averages of distribution rates derived from the 1953 and 1961 censuses;
- 1960-70, interpolation and extrapolation of distribution rates derived from the 1961 and 1971 censuses;
- 1980-90, 1980-90 distribution rates derived from the Bulletin of Labour Statistics, 1994-2.

**3.2.2 Women:**

Method, hypothesis and treatment identical to those used for men.

## 4. Projection of activity rates: 2000 - 2010

### 4.1 Model(s): linear, hyperbole and logistic

**4.1.1 Men:**

- To the [15+] age groups, application of function F3;
- Modification of the trends for the [40-49] age groups.

**4.1.2 Women:**

- To the [15-19] age group, application of function F3;
- To the [20-49] age groups, application of function F6;
- To the [50+] age groups, application of function F1;
- Modification of the trends for the [15-64] age groups.

---

*Notes on adjustments of rates, see p. 3-8.*    *Notes on projection functions, see p. 10.*

# Solomon Islands

## 1. Source(s) of benchmark data

**Code(s):**    **Title(s):**

EPPA3    Yearbook of Labour Statistics 1945-89 - Retrospective Edition on Population Censuses, ILO, Geneva, 1990.

STAT    Database on Labour Statistics, LABORSTA - Bureau of Statistics, ILO, Geneva.

## 2. Estimates of activity rates: 1950 - 1990

### 2.1 Benchmark data:

Table 1: Activity rates by sex and age group

| Age group | Year | | | | |
|---|---|---|---|---|---|
| | 1950 (1) | 1960 (1) | 1970 (1) | 1980 (1) | 1986 (2) |
| **Men** | | | | | |
| 10-14 | 45.48 | 41.48 | 37.49 | 33.61 | 33.60 |
| 15-19 | 81.99 | 77.86 | 72.45 | 65.23 | 77.27 |
| 20-24 | 97.00 | 95.88 | 94.01 | 91.23 | 96.33 |
| 25-29 | 98.33 | 98.09 | 97.74 | 97.24 | 97.50 |
| 30-34 | 98.54 | 98.30 | 97.98 | 97.52 | 97.57 |
| 35-39 | 98.71 | 98.49 | 98.20 | 97.72 | 97.52 |
| 40-44 | 98.64 | 98.36 | 98.03 | 97.53 | 96.54 |
| 45-49 | 97.17 | 97.06 | 96.65 | 96.04 | 96.01 |
| 50-54 | 94.99 | 94.44 | 93.80 | 92.98 | 92.24 |
| 55-59 | 90.73 | 89.91 | 88.96 | 87.61 | 86.26 |
| 60-64 | 83.42 | 81.90 | 80.49 | 78.43 | 79.31 |
| 65+ | 63.18 | 61.14 | 59.04 | 62.39 | 68.98 |
| **Women** | | | | | |
| 10-14 | 38.84 | 36.20 | 33.33 | 31.03 | 41.86 |
| 15-19 | 62.38 | 58.54 | 54.99 | 50.60 | 81.77 |
| 20-24 | 66.44 | 63.56 | 61.43 | 59.13 | 87.81 |
| 25-29 | 66.86 | 64.58 | 61.16 | 58.34 | 86.15 |
| 30-34 | 68.09 | 66.33 | 63.26 | 60.85 | 89.49 |
| 35-39 | 70.01 | 67.90 | 65.04 | 60.76 | 88.54 |
| 40-44 | 72.15 | 68.36 | 66.65 | 63.24 | 88.50 |
| 45-49 | 71.75 | 68.61 | 65.01 | 61.46 | 88.70 |
| 50-54 | 70.48 | 67.89 | 63.18 | 60.28 | 87.10 |
| 55-59 | 63.48 | 61.55 | 56.08 | 53.33 | 86.27 |
| 60-64 | 54.56 | 54.04 | 48.61 | 43.77 | 74.11 |
| 65+ | 42.92 | 37.78 | 33.57 | 24.81 | 56.38 |

Source(s): (1) EPPA3; (2) STAT.

### 2.2 Method(s): linears interpolation and extrapolation

#### 2.2.1 Men:

- 1950-90, interpolation and extrapolation of 1950-80 activity rates
derived from the EPPA3;
modification of the trends for all age groups;
application to 1990 extrapolated rates, variations in 1986 extrapolated rates,
in relation to activity rates of the 1986 census.

#### 2.2.2 Women:

Method, hypothesis and treatment identical to those used for men.

## 3. Estimates of distribution rates by activity sector: 1950 - 1990

### 3.1 Benchmark data:

Table 2: Distribution of economically active population by activity sector

| Year | Agriculture | Industry | | Services |
|---|---|---|---|---|
| | | Total | Manufac. | |
| **Men** | | | | |
| 1986 | 69.05 | 10.15 | 4.22 | 20.80 |
| **Women** | | | | |
| 1986 | 86.19 | 2.96 | 2.36 | 10.85 |

Source(s): STAT.

### 3.2 Method(s): linear interpolation

#### 3.2.1 Men:

- 1950-90, interpolation of 1950-90 distribution rates estimated for
Papua New Guinea;
modification of the trends in all sectors for 1980 and 1990;
application to 1950-90 interpolated rates, variations in 1986 interpolated
rates, in relation to distribution rates derived from the 1986 census;
- Application of manufacturing/industry ratio derived from the 1966 census.

#### 3.2.2 Women:

Method, hypothesis and treatment identical to those used for men.

## 4. Projection of activity rates: 2000 - 2010

### 4.1 Model(s): linear and hyperbole

#### 4.1.1 Men:

- To all age groups, application of function F3;
- Modification of the trends for the [10-44] age groups.

#### 4.1.2 Women:

- To the [10-19] and [60+] age groups, application of function F1;
- To the [20-59] age groups, application of function F3;
- Modification of the trends for the [10-19] and [50+] age groups.

158

# Somalia

## 1. Source(s) of benchmark data

Code(s):  Title(s):

EPPA3    Economically active population: Estimates and Projections, 1950-2025, Third edition, ILO, Geneva, 1986.

## 2. Estimates of activity rates: 1950 - 1990

### 2.1 Benchmark data:

Table 1: Activity rates by sex and age group

| Age group | Year 1950 | 1960 | 1970 | 1980 |
|---|---|---|---|---|
| **Men** | | | | |
| 10-14 | 47.40 | 44.95 | 42.80 | 40.35 |
| 15-19 | 78.65 | 75.40 | 72.55 | 69.25 |
| 20-24 | 92.85 | 91.60 | 90.50 | 89.25 |
| 25-29 | 97.05 | 96.85 | 96.70 | 96.50 |
| 30-34 | 97.75 | 97.55 | 97.35 | 97.15 |
| 35-39 | 97.90 | 97.65 | 97.45 | 97.25 |
| 40-44 | 97.70 | 97.45 | 97.25 | 97.05 |
| 45-49 | 97.00 | 96.80 | 96.65 | 96.45 |
| 50-54 | 96.40 | 96.10 | 95.80 | 95.50 |
| 55-59 | 95.15 | 94.70 | 94.25 | 93.80 |
| 60-64 | 91.60 | 90.80 | 90.10 | 89.30 |
| 65+ | 77.25 | 75.85 | 74.60 | 73.20 |
| **Women** | | | | |
| 10-14 | 35.85 | 34.00 | 32.35 | 30.50 |
| 15-19 | 58.65 | 55.90 | 53.40 | 50.65 |
| 20-24 | 60.80 | 59.05 | 57.50 | 55.75 |
| 25-29 | 65.30 | 63.35 | 61.55 | 59.60 |
| 30-34 | 69.40 | 67.30 | 65.40 | 63.25 |
| 35-39 | 70.90 | 68.90 | 67.15 | 65.15 |
| 40-44 | 73.35 | 71.35 | 69.60 | 67.65 |
| 45-49 | 72.80 | 70.80 | 69.00 | 66.95 |
| 50-54 | 70.75 | 68.40 | 66.35 | 64.00 |
| 55-59 | 67.80 | 65.35 | 63.15 | 60.70 |
| 60-64 | 60.50 | 57.40 | 54.60 | 51.50 |
| 65+ | 40.85 | 37.95 | 35.35 | 32.45 |

Source(s): EPPA3.

### 2.2 Method(s): linears interpolation and extrapolation

#### 2.2.1 Men:

- 1950-80, 1950-80 activity rates derived from the EPPA3;
- 1990, extrapolation of 1950-80 activity rates derived from the EPPA3; adjustment of extrapolated rates on the basis of variations in 1980 interpolated rates, in relation to the 1980 rates derived from the EPPA3.

#### 2.2.2 Women:

- 1950-90, interpolation and extrapolation of 1950 and 1980 adjusted activity rates derived from the EPPA; adjustment of average activity rates based on the men/women ratio in agriculture equal to 1; adjustment of interpolated and extrapolated rates on the basis of variations in 1980 interpolated rates, in relation to the 1980 adjusted activity rates derived from the EPPA3.

## 3. Estimates of distribution rates by activity sector: 1950 - 1990

### 3.1 Benchmark data:

Table 2: Distribution of economically active population by activity sector

| | Year | Agriculture | Industry Total | Manufac. | Services |
|---|---|---|---|---|---|
| **Men** | | | | | |
| | 1950 | 79.00 | 7.00 | .. | 14.00 |
| | 1980 | 66.00 | 13.00 | .. | 21.00 |
| **Women** | | | | | |
| | 1950 | 97.00 | 0.50 | .. | 2.50 |
| | 1980 | 89.00 | 1.70 | .. | 8.80 |

Source(s): EPPA3.

### 3.2 Method(s): linears interpolation and extrapolation

#### 3.2.1 Men:

- 1950-80, 1950-80 distribution rates derived from the EPPA3;
- 1990, extrapolation of 1950-80 distribution rates derived from the EPPA3;
- Application of manufacturing/industry ratio estimated for Eritrea.

#### 3.2.2 Women:

- 1950-90, interpolation and extrapolation of 1950 and 1980 adjusted distribution rates derived from the EPPA3; adjustment of distribution rates on the basis of men/women ratio equal to 1 in agriculture; distribution rates of manufacturing sector based on manufacturing/industry ratio estimated for Eritrea.

## 4. Projection of activity rates: 2000 - 2010

### 4.1 Model(s): linear and hyperbole

#### 4.1.1 Men:

- To the [10-19] age groups, application of function F1;
- To the [20+] age groups, application of function F3;
- Modification of the trends for the [20-49] age groups.

#### 4.1.2 Women:

- To all age groups, application of function F3;
- Modification of the trends for the [20-59] age groups.

*Notes on adjustments of rates, see p. 3-8.*     *Notes on projection functions, see p. 10.*

# South Africa

## 1. Source(s) of benchmark data

| Code(s): | Title(s): |
|---|---|
| EPPA3 | Economically active population: Estimates and Projections, 1950-2025, Third edition, ILO, Geneva, 1986. |
| ASTER | Yearbook of Labour Statistics 1945-89 - Retrospective Edition on Population Censuses, ILO, Geneva, 1990. |
| ADNU88 | Demographic Yearbook 1988 - Population census statistics - Fortieth Edition, United Nations, New York, 1990. |
| AST93 | Yearbook of Labour Statistics 1993, ILO, Geneva, 1993. |

## 2. Estimates of activity rates: 1950 - 1990

### 2.1 Benchmark data:

Table 1: Activity rates by sex and age group

| Age group | Year 1950 (1) | 1960 (1) | 1970 (1) | 1980 (1) | 1985 (2) |
|---|---|---|---|---|---|
| **Men** | | | | | |
| 10-14 | 22.30 | 7.80 | 3.85 | 0.30 | 0.00 |
| 15-19 | 74.40 | 67.60 | 59.50 | 35.90 | 47.94 |
| 20-24 | 95.70 | 98.00 | 92.65 | 83.45 | 81.70 |
| 25-29 | 97.50 | 96.60 | 95.45 | 93.35 | 95.37 |
| 30-34 | 99.25 | 98.60 | 97.85 | 96.40 | 97.79 |
| 35-39 | 99.40 | 98.75 | 98.00 | 96.50 | 97.85 |
| 40-44 | 98.90 | 98.25 | 97.65 | 96.40 | 97.49 |
| 45-49 | 98.55 | 98.00 | 97.25 | 94.50 | 97.13 |
| 50-54 | 98.00 | 97.00 | 95.85 | 91.50 | 95.62 |
| 55-59 | 95.55 | 94.65 | 90.35 | 80.00 | 87.09 |
| 60-64 | 90.00 | 87.15 | 80.25 | 62.10 | 73.75 |
| 65+ | 69.65 | 53.05 | 44.30 | 14.30 | 30.29 |
| **Women** | | | | | |
| 10-14 | 4.00 | 2.60 | 1.50 | 0.15 | 0.00 |
| 15-19 | 35.45 | 35.30 | 46.80 | 28.25 | 41.91 |
| 20-24 | 35.40 | 38.60 | 58.45 | 59.65 | 54.07 |
| 25-29 | 23.40 | 29.55 | 49.65 | 50.50 | 58.92 |
| 30-34 | 20.20 | 25.55 | 43.50 | 44.30 | 51.69 |
| 35-39 | 19.95 | 25.25 | 39.55 | 40.25 | 51.19 |
| 40-44 | 19.75 | 24.95 | 37.55 | 38.20 | 48.25 |
| 45-49 | 18.40 | 23.50 | 36.85 | 37.55 | 47.84 |
| 50-54 | 17.90 | 22.85 | 34.40 | 35.55 | 44.36 |
| 55-59 | 15.15 | 18.90 | 25.95 | 25.30 | 29.43 |
| 60-64 | 11.25 | 13.80 | 20.05 | 14.90 | 22.72 |
| 65+ | 8.15 | 6.00 | 5.60 | 2.00 | 5.61 |

Source(s): (1) EPPA3; (2) ADNU88 and ASTER.

### 2.2 Method(s): linear extrapolation
weighted average

**2.2.1 Men:**

- 1950-70, 1950-70 activity rates derived from the EPPA3;
- 1980, weighted average of activity rates of 1970 derived from the EPPA3 and of adjusted activity rates derived from the 1985 census;
- 1990, extrapolation of 1950-70 activity rates derived from the EPPA3 and of adjusted activity rates derived from the 1985 census; adjustment of extrapolated rates on the basis of variations in 1985 interpolated rates, in relation to adjusted activity rates derived from the 1985 census.

**2.2.2 Women:**

- 1950-70, 1950-70 activity rates derived from the EPPA3; adjustment of 1950 and 1960 activity rates;
- 1980, weighted average of 1970 activity rates derived from the EPPA3 and of adjusted activity rates derived from the 1985 census;
- 1990, extrapolation of the 1950-70 activity rates derived from the EPPA3 and of adjusted activity rates derived from the 1985 census; adjustment of extrapolated rates on the basis of variations in 1985 interpolated rates, in relation to adjustment activity rates derived from the 1985 census; modification of the trends of the [20-24] and [40-44] age groups.

## 3. Estimates of distribution rates by activity sector: 1950 - 1990

### 3.1 Benchmark data:

Table 2: Distribution of economically active population by activity sector

| Year | Agriculture | Industry Total | Manufac. | Services |
|---|---|---|---|---|
| **Men** | | | | |
| 1980 (1) | 18.12 | 44.69 | 20.25 | 37.19 |
| 1985 (1) | 17.07 | 46.55 | 19.79 | 36.38 |
| 1991 (2) | 15.42 | 41.58 | 17.41 | 43.00 |
| **Women** | | | | |
| 1985 (1) | 12.49 | 17.16 | 14.94 | 70.35 |
| 1991 (2) | 9.99 | 14.44 | 12.31 | 75.57 |

Source(s): (1) ASTER; (2) AST93.

### 3.2 Method(s): weighted average

**3.2.1 Men:**

- 1950-70, 1950-70 distribution rates derived from the EPPA3;
- 1980-90, weighted averages of distribution rates derived from the 1980, 1985 and 1991 censuses.

**3.2.2 Women:**

- 1950-80, 1950-80 distribution rates derived from the EPPA3; adjustment of rates to take account of contributing family workers in agriculture;
- 1990, weighted averages of distribution rates derived from the 1985 and 1991 censuses.

## 4. Projection of activity rates: 2000 - 2010

### 4.1 Model(s): linear, log-linear, hyperbole and logistic

**4.1.1 Men:**

- To the [15-19] age group, application of function F2;
- To the [20+] age groups, application of function F3.

**4.1.2 Women:**

- To the [15-19] and [60+] age groups, application of function F3;
- To the [20-24] age groups, application of function F1;
- To the [25-59] age groups, application of function F6;
- Modification of the trends for the [15-19], [25-29] and [60-64] age groups.

*Notes on adjustments of rates, see p. 3-8.*

*Notes on projection functions, see p. 10.*

# Spain

## 1. Source(s) of benchmark data

Code(s):    Title(s):

EPPA3    Yearbook of Labour Statistics 1945-89 - Retrospective Edition on Population Censuses, ILO, Geneva, 1990.
STAT    Database on Labour Statistics, LABORSTA - Bureau of Statistics, ILO, Geneva.

## 2. Estimates of activity rates: 1950 - 1990

### 2.1 Benchmark data:

Table 1: Activity rates by sex and age group

| Age group | Year | | | | | |
|---|---|---|---|---|---|---|
| | 1970 (1) | 1980 (2) | 1981 (2) | 1989 (2) | 1990 (2) | 1991 (2) |
| **Men** | | | | | | |
| 10-14 | .. | .. | .. | 0.00 | 0.00 | 0.00 |
| 15-19 | .. | .. | .. | 34.82 | 33.31 | 32.25 |
| 20-24 | .. | .. | .. | 71.87 | 72.53 | 71.15 |
| 25-29 | .. | .. | .. | 91.58 | 91.99 | 91.82 |
| 30-34 | .. | .. | .. | 96.08 | 96.55 | 96.08 |
| 35-39 | .. | .. | .. | 96.20 | 96.70 | 96.88 |
| 40-44 | .. | .. | .. | 95.46 | 95.67 | 95.76 |
| 45-49 | .. | .. | .. | 94.14 | 94.06 | 93.57 |
| 50-54 | .. | .. | .. | 88.43 | 89.30 | 88.96 |
| 55-59 | .. | .. | .. | 75.70 | 76.53 | 76.26 |
| 60-64 | .. | .. | .. | 48.19 | 46.94 | 46.59 |
| 65+ | .. | .. | .. | 4.27 | 3.77 | 3.68 |
| **Women** | | | | | | |
| 10-14 | 3.45 | 0.00 | 0.00 | 0.00 | 0.00 | 0.00 |
| 15-19 | 36.15 | 40.52 | 38.67 | 32.70 | 31.20 | 27.80 |
| 20-24 | 38.90 | 55.21 | 55.42 | 62.22 | 61.45 | 60.62 |
| 25-29 | 20.70 | 42.13 | 42.91 | 64.00 | 65.15 | 65.90 |
| 30-34 | 13.75 | 30.34 | 31.25 | 53.79 | 56.26 | 58.51 |
| 35-39 | 13.35 | 30.01 | 28.72 | 45.14 | 48.96 | 51.95 |
| 40-44 | 14.15 | 28.26 | 27.87 | 38.92 | 41.11 | 42.72 |
| 45-49 | 14.65 | 27.82 | 28.40 | 33.27 | 34.53 | 35.96 |
| 50-54 | 15.25 | 26.79 | 25.15 | 28.16 | 29.15 | 30.60 |
| 55-59 | 14.90 | 24.61 | 23.05 | 23.64 | 23.24 | 22.66 |
| 60-64 | 12.00 | 17.27 | 17.29 | 15.34 | 15.54 | 15.84 |
| 65+ | 4.4 | 7.88 | 6.73 | 1.84 | 1.66 | 1.46 |

Source(s): (1) EPPA3; (2) STAT.

### 2.2 Method(s): linears interpolation and extrapolation
arithmetic average

#### 2.2.1 Men:

- 1950-80, 1950-80 activity rates derived from the EPPA3;
adjustment of activity rates of the [30+] age groups for 1980;
- 1990, adjusted average of activity rates derived from
the 1989, 1990 and 1991 surveys;
adjustment of estimated activity rates to make allowance for conscripts.

#### 2.2.2 Women:

- 1950-80, interpolation and extrapolation of 1970 activity rates
derived from the EPPA3 and of activity rates derived from the 1980
and 1982 surveys;
modification of the trends for all age groups;
- 1990, average of activity rates derived from
the 1990 and 1991 surveys;
adjustment of activity rate of the [15-19] age group.

## 3. Estimates of distribution rates by activity sector: 1950 - 1990

### 3.1 Benchmark data:

Table 2: Distribution of economically active population by activity sector

| Year | Agriculture | Industry | | Services |
|---|---|---|---|---|
| | | Total | Manufac. | |
| **Men** | | | | |
| 1950 | 54.75 | 25.20 | .. | 20.05 |
| 1960 | 46.80 | 32.05 | .. | 21.15 |
| 1970 | 28.90 | 39.05 | .. | 32.05 |
| **Women** | | | | |
| 1950 | 24.94 | 25.00 | .. | 50.06 |
| 1960 | 20.81 | 28.50 | .. | 50.69 |
| 1970 | 13.93 | 31.36 | .. | 54.70 |

Source(s): EPPA3.

### 3.2 Method(s): linears interpolation and extrapolation

#### 3.2.1 Men:
- 1950-90, weighted averages of interpolated and extrapolated rates
resulted on of interpolation and extrapolation of 1950-70 distribution rates
derived from the EPPA3.

#### 3.2.2 Women:

Method, hypothesis and treatment identical to those used for men.

## 4. Projection of activity rates: 2000 - 2010

### 4.1 Model(s): linear, hyperbole and logistic

#### 4.1.1 Men:

- To the [15+] age groups, application of function F3;
- Modification of the trend for the [45-49] age group.

#### 4.1.2 Women:

- To the [15-54] age groups, application of function F6;
- To the [55-64] age groups, application of function F1;
- To the [65+] age group, application of function F3;
- Modification of the trends for the [15-19] and [55-64] age groups.

# Sri Lanka

## 1. Source(s) of benchmark data

| Code(s): | Title(s): |
|---|---|
| EPPA3 | Economically active population: Estimates and Projections, 1950-2025, Third edition, ILO, Geneva, 1986. |
| STAT | Database on Labour Statistics, LABORSTA - Bureau of Statistics, ILO, Geneva. |

## 2. Estimates of activity rates: 1950 - 1990

### 2.1 Benchmark data:

Table 1: Activity rates by sex and age group

| Age group | Year 1990 | 1992 | 1993 |
|---|---|---|---|
| **Men** | | | |
| 10-14 | 5.30 | 1.80 | .. |
| 15-19 | 36.20 | 30.30 | .. |
| 20-24 | 84.90 | 89.50 | .. |
| 25-29 | 96.40 | 95.20 | .. |
| 30-34 | 97.70 | 98.10 | .. |
| 35-39 | 96.70 | 96.00 | .. |
| 40-44 | 97.90 | 96.20 | .. |
| 45-49 | 95.80 | 91.90 | .. |
| 50-54 | 94.60 | 82.70 | .. |
| 55-59 | 73.90 | 73.90 | .. |
| 60-64 | 49.00 | 38.60 | .. |
| 65+ | 52.90 | 28.70 | .. |
| **Women** | | | |
| 10-14 | 4.60 | 1.40 | 1.80 |
| 15-19 | 26.90 | 21.10 | 19.70 |
| 20-24 | 63.80 | 57.10 | 58.47 |
| 25-29 | 58.30 | 56.50 | 50.02 |
| 30-34 | 62.30 | 47.60 | 47.80 |
| 35-39 | 55.60 | 48.70 | 53.71 |
| 40-44 | 51.80 | 43.30 | 45.49 |
| 45-49 | 47.90 | 42.30 | 37.34 |
| 50-54 | 34.50 | 27.10 | 35.13 |
| 55-59 | 31.30 | 20.60 | 19.24 |
| 60-64 | 13.30 | 6.10 | 6.31 |
| 65+ | | | |

Source(s): STAT.

### 2.2 Method(s): linear interpolation

**2.2.1 Men:**

- 1950-80, 1950-80 activity rates derived from the EPPA3;
- 1990, interpolation of 1950-80 activity rates derived from the EPPA3 and of average activity rates derived from the 1990 and 1992 surveys; adjustment of interpolated rates on the basis of variations in 1980 interpolated rates, in relation to the 1980 activity rates derived from the EPPA3.

**2.2.2 Women:**

- 1950-80, 1950-80 activity rates derived from the EPPA3;
- 1990, interpolation of 1980 activity rates derived from the EPPA3 and of average of activity rates derived from the 1990, 1992 and 1993 surveys.

## 3. Estimates of distribution rates by activity sector: 1950 - 1990

### 3.1 Benchmark data:

Table 2: Distribution of economically active population by activity sector

| Year | Agriculture | Industry Total | Manufac. | Services |
|---|---|---|---|---|
| **Men** | | | | |
| 1981 | 49.37 | 18.97 | 10.42 | 31.66 |
| 1985 | 49.75 | 19.27 | 10.58 | 30.98 |
| 1993 | 40.01 | 19.43 | 9.11 | 40.56 |
| **Women** | | | | |
| 1981 | 57.30 | 15.84 | 14.61 | 26.86 |
| 1985 | 55.04 | 20.22 | 18.92 | 24.74 |
| 1993 | 39.18 | 26.15 | 23.28 | 34.67 |

Source(s): STAT.

### 3.2 Method(s): linear interpolation

**3.2.1 Men:**

- 1950-70, 1950-70 distribution rates derived from the EPPA3;
- 1980-90, extrapolation of distribution rates derived from the 1981, 1985 and 1991 censuses; modification of the trends in all sectors.

**3.2.2 Women:**

Method, hypothesis and treatment identical to those used for men.

## 4. Projection of activity rates: 2000 - 2010

### 4.1 Model(s): linear, log-linear and hyperbole

**4.1.1 Men:**

- To the [10-14] age group, application of function F2;
- To the [15+] age groups, application of function F3;
- Modification of the trends for the [10-14] and [35-49] age groups.

**4.1.2 Women:**

- To the [10-34] age groups, application of function F2;
- To the [35-59] age groups, application of function F1;
- To the [60+] age groups, application of function F3;
- Modification of the trends for the [10-19] and [30-59] age groups.

*Notes on adjustments of rates, see p. 3-8.*

*Notes on projection functions, see p. 10.*

# Sudan

## 1. Source(s) of benchmark data

Code(s):    Title(s):

EPPA3    Economically active population: Estimates and Projections, 1950-2025, Third edition, ILO, Geneva, 1986.
R1983    Population and Housing Census of the Sudan 1989, Ministry of Finance and Economic Planning, Department of Statistics, Khartoum, 1989.
ASTER    Yearbook of Labour Statistics 1945-89 - Retrospective Edition on Population Censuses, ILO, Geneva, 1990.

## 2. Estimates of activity rates: 1950 - 1990

### 2.1 Benchmark data:

Table 1: Activity rates by sex and age group

| Age group | Year 1950 (1) | 1960 (1) | 1970 (1) | 1973 (2) | 1983 (3) |
|---|---|---|---|---|---|
| **Men** | | | | | |
| 10-14 | 46.15 | 42.90 | 42.84 | .. | 39.01 |
| 15-19 | 74.95 | 70.60 | 64.40 | .. | 58.92 |
| 20-24 | 95.55 | 93.60 | 90.85 | .. | 81.27 |
| 25-29 | 97.90 | 97.60 | 97.20 | .. | 92.90 |
| 30-34 | 99.05 | 98.75 | 98.25 | .. | 95.58 |
| 35-39 | 99.50 | 99.15 | 98.65 | .. | 96.90 |
| 40-44 | 99.50 | 99.15 | 98.60 | .. | 96.74 |
| 45-49 | 99.30 | 99.00 | 98.55 | .. | 97.33 |
| 50-54 | 98.40 | 97.95 | 97.25 | .. | 95.63 |
| 55-59 | 98.05 | 97.30 | 96.20 | .. | 95.00 |
| 60-64 | 95.85 | 94.55 | 92.75 | .. | 91.47 |
| 65+ | 78.25 | 76.15 | 78.55 | .. | 78.55 |
| **Women** | | | | | |
| 10-14 | 12.15 | 11.30 | 10.05 | ... | 25.29 |
| 15-19 | 19.75 | 18.50 | 16.65 | 16.08 | 28.62 |
| 20-24 | 20.95 | 20.10 | 18.85 | 18.47 | 29.58 |
| 25-29 | 23.25 | 22.20 | 20.75 | 20.32 | 30.49 |
| 30-34 | 24.50 | 23.40 | 21.85 | 21.41 | 31.13 |
| 35-39 | 27.25 | 26.15 | 24.55 | 24.08 | 32.09 |
| 40-44 | 30.40 | 29.20 | 27.50 | 26.98 | 33.44 |
| 45-49 | 31.80 | 30.50 | 28.70 | 28.14 | 35.20 |
| 50-54 | 33.40 | 31.80 | 29.55 | 28.85 | 36.72 |
| 55-59 | 32.15 | 30.50 | 28.15 | 27.45 | 33.22 |
| 60-64 | 33.70 | 31.30 | 27.90 | 26.40 | 33.80 |
| 65+ | 27.60 | 25.00 | 21.35 | ... | 25.44 |

Source(s): (1) EPPA3; (2) ASTER; (3) R1983.

### 2.2 Method(s): linears interpolation and extrapolation
weighted average

#### 2.2.1 Men:

- 1950-90, interpolation and extrapolation of 1950-70 activity rates derived from the EPPA3 and of adjusted activity rates derived from the 1983 census;
modification of the trends of the [45-49] and [65+] age groups from 1950 to 1990.

#### 2.2.2 Women:

- 1950-70, 1950-70 adjusted activity rates derived from the EPPA3; the adjustment was made on the basis of the adjustment model for activity rates of women working in agriculture as contributing family workers;
- 1980, weighted average of adjusted activity rates derived from the 1973 census and of activity rates derived from the 1983 census;
adjustment of activity rates based on the men/women ratio in agriculture derived from the 1983 census;
- 1990, application to 1980 estimated rates, variations in 1980 estimated rates for Egypt, in relation to 1990 estimated rates for the same country.

## 3. Estimates of distribution rates by activity sector: 1950 - 1990

### 3.1 Benchmark data:

Table 2: Distribution of economically active population by activity sector

| Year | Agriculture | Industry Total | Manufac. | Services |
|---|---|---|---|---|
| **Men** | | | | |
| 1973 (1) | 65.49 | 8.78 | 4.50 | 25.73 |
| 1983 (2) | 66.47 | 9.68 | 5.17 | 23.85 |
| **Women** | | | | |
| 1973 (1) | 88.81 | 3.38 | 3.25 | 7.81 |
| 1983 (2) | 87.11 | 4.51 | 3.85 | 8.38 |

Source(s): (1) ASTER; (2) R1983.

### 3.2 Method(s): weighted average

#### 3.2.1 Men:

- 1950-70, 1950-70 distribution rates derived from the EPPA3;
- 1980, weighted averages of distribution rates derived from the 1973 and 1983 censuses;
- 1990, same variations in percentages as in distribution rates for Egypt between 1980 and 1990.

#### 3.2.2 Women:

- 1950-70, 1950-70 distribution rates derived from the EPPA3;
- 1980, weighted averages of distribution rates derived from the 1973 and 1983 censuses;
- 1990, same variations in percentages as in distribution rates for Egypt between 1980 and 1990;
adjustment of rates to make allowance for the under-registration of contributing family workers in agriculture.

## 4. Projection of activity rates: 2000 - 2010

### 4.1 Model(s): linear, hyperbole and logistic

#### 4.1.1 Men:

- To the [10-14] age group, application of function F1;
- To the [15+] age groups, application of function F3;
- Modification of the trends for the [10-14], [20-24], [50-54] and [65+] age groups.

#### 4.1.2 Women:

- To the [10-19] age groups, application of function F1;
- To the [20+] age groups, application of function F6;
- Modification of the trends for all age groups.

---

*Notes on adjustments of rates, see p. 3-8.*

*Notes on projection functions, see p. 10.*

# Suriname

## 1. Source(s) of benchmark data

Code(s):      Title(s):

EPPA3      Economically active population: Estimates and Projections, 1950-2025, Third edition, ILO, Geneva, 1986.

ASTER      Yearbook of Labour Statistics 1945-89 - Retrospective Edition on Population Censuses, ILO, Geneva, 1990.

## 2. Estimates of activity rates: 1950 - 1990

### 2.1 Benchmark data:

Table 1: Activity rates by sex and age group

| Age group | Year 1950 (1) | 1960 (1) | 1964 (2) | 1970 (1) | 1980 (1) | 1980 (2) |
|---|---|---|---|---|---|---|
| **Men** | | | | | | |
| 10-14 | 1.80 | 1.00 | .. | 0.70 | 0.50 | .. |
| 15-19 | 66.95 | 48.00 | .. | 43.00 | 35.00 | .. |
| 20-24 | 93.55 | 90.80 | .. | 87.00 | 80.00 | .. |
| 25-29 | 98.25 | 97.05 | .. | 96.90 | 93.50 | .. |
| 30-34 | 98.95 | 97.75 | .. | 97.60 | 97.00 | .. |
| 35-39 | 99.50 | 98.35 | .. | 98.20 | 97.50 | .. |
| 40-44 | 98.30 | 96.85 | .. | 97.00 | 95.00 | .. |
| 45-49 | 96.90 | 96.30 | .. | 95.75 | 93.00 | .. |
| 50-54 | 95.50 | 93.45 | .. | 92.90 | 90.00 | .. |
| 55-59 | 90.65 | 89.00 | .. | 85.00 | 81.00 | .. |
| 60-64 | 80.00 | 75.00 | .. | 72.00 | 65.00 | .. |
| 65+ | 65.60 | 51.90 | .. | 40.60 | 22.00 | .. |
| **Women** | | | | | | |
| 10-14 | .. | .. | 0.80 | .. | .. | 0.20 |
| 15-19 | .. | .. | 11.20 | .. | .. | 3.80 |
| 20-24 | .. | .. | 23.90 | .. | .. | 25.30 |
| 25-29 | .. | .. | 20.90 | .. | .. | 32.10 |
| 30-34 | .. | .. | 20.60 | .. | .. | 30.60 |
| 35-39 | .. | .. | 21.40 | .. | .. | 31.80 |
| 40-44 | .. | .. | 22.30 | .. | .. | 29.80 |
| 45-49 | .. | .. | 23.10 | .. | .. | 28.60 |
| 50-54 | .. | .. | 23.20 | .. | .. | 24.50 |
| 55-59 | .. | .. | 16.90 | .. | .. | 20.80 |
| 60-64 | .. | .. | 14.20 | .. | .. | 12.70 |
| 65+ | .. | .. | 8.64 | .. | .. | 4.00 |

Source(s): (1) EPPA3; (2) ASTER.

### 2.2 Method(s):  linears interpolation and extrapolation

#### 2.2.1 Men:

- 1950-80, 1950-80 activity rates derived from the EPPA3;
- 1990, extrapolation of 1950-80 activity rates derived from the EPPA3; adjustment of extrapolated rates on the basis of variations in 1980 interpolated rates, in relation to the 1980 rates derived from the EPPA3; modification of the trends for all age groups.

#### 2.2.2 Women:

- 1950-90, interpolation and extrapolation of activity rates derived from the 1977 census and of adjusted activity rates derived from the 1985 census; adjustment of activity rates based on the men/women ratio in agriculture derived from the 1964 census; modification of the trends for all age groups for 1950, 1960 and 1990.

## 3. Estimates of distribution rates by activity sector: 1950 - 1990

### 3.1 Benchmark data:

Table 2: Distribution of economically active population by activity sector

| Year | Agriculture | Industry Total | Manufac. | Services |
|---|---|---|---|---|
| **Men** | | | | |
| 1964 | 28.64 | 26.91 | 11.41 | 44.44 |
| 1980 | 24.83 | 24.94 | 9.42 | 50.22 |
| **Women** | | | | |
| 1989 | 27.36 | 7.95 | 6.14 | 64.69 |
| 1990 | 17.50 | 5.39 | 3.62 | 77.12 |

Source(s): ASTER.

### 3.2 Method(s):  linears interpolation and extrapolation

#### 3.2.1 Men:

1950-90, interpolation and extrapolation of distribution rates derived from the 1964 census and adjusted activity rates derived from the 1980 census.

#### 3.2.2 Women:

Method, hypothesis and treatment identical to those used for men.

## 4. Projection of activity rates: 2000 - 2010

### 4.1 Model(s):  log-linear, hyperbole and logistic

#### 4.1.1 Men:

- To the [15+] age groups, application of function F3;
- Modification of the trends for the [15-49] age groups.

#### 4.1.2 Women:

- To the [15-19] and [60+] age groups, application of function F3;
- To the [20-24] age group, application of function F2;
- To the [25-59] age groups, application of function F6;
- Modification of the trends for the [20-24] and [40-59] age groups.

---

*Notes on adjustments of rates, see p. 3-8.*     *Notes on projection functions, see p. 10.*

# Swaziland

## 1. Source(s) of benchmark data

**Code(s):**    **Title(s):**

EPPA3      Economically active population: Estimates and Projections, 1950-2025, Third edition, ILO, Geneva, 1986.
R1966      Report on the 1966 Swaziland Population Census, Swaziland Government, Mbabane, 1968.
ADNU72    Demographic Yearbook 1972 - Population census statistics III - Twenty-fourth Edition, United Nations, New York, 1973.
R1986      Report on the 1986 Swaziland Population Census, 3 Vol., Central Statistical Office, Mbabane, 1986.

## 2. Estimates of activity rates: 1950 - 1990

### 2.1 Benchmark data:

Table 1: Activity rates by sex and age group

| Age group | Année 1950 (1) | 1960 (1) | 1966 (2) | 1970 (1) | 1980 (1) | 1986 (3) |
|---|---|---|---|---|---|---|
| **Men** | | | | | | |
| 10-14 | .. | .. | 26.48 | .. | .. | 20.02 |
| 15-19 | .. | .. | 66.14 | .. | .. | 50.00 |
| 20-24 | .. | .. | 92.53 | .. | .. | 89.18 |
| 25-29 | .. | .. | 98.20 | .. | .. | 97.56 |
| 30-34 | .. | .. | 98.57 | .. | .. | 98.20 |
| 35-39 | .. | .. | 98.62 | .. | .. | 98.25 |
| 40-44 | .. | .. | 97.76 | .. | .. | 97.43 |
| 45-49 | .. | .. | 97.46 | .. | .. | 96.49 |
| 50-54 | .. | .. | 96.04 | .. | .. | 92.55 |
| 55-59 | .. | .. | 94.95 | .. | .. | 85.07 |
| 60-64 | .. | .. | 93.04 | .. | .. | 77.09 |
| 65+ | .. | .. | 83.91 | .. | .. | 40.94 |
| **Women** | | | | | | |
| 10-14 | 39.40 | 37.55 | 3.97 | 33.60 | 30.10 | 12.12 |
| 15-19 | 64.05 | 61.30 | 45.63 | 55.45 | 50.15 | 33.08 |
| 20-24 | 64.20 | 62.60 | 51.68 | 59.15 | 55.95 | 49.51 |
| 25-29 | 69.15 | 67.35 | 49.38 | 63.45 | 59.70 | 50.47 |
| 30-34 | 73.50 | 71.55 | 49.66 | 67.40 | 63.40 | 48.35 |
| 35-39 | 74.70 | 72.95 | 49.63 | 69.10 | 65.40 | 44.95 |
| 40-44 | 77.15 | 75.40 | 52.82 | 71.55 | 67.90 | 42.51 |
| 45-49 | 76.70 | 74.90 | 53.05 | 70.95 | 67.20 | 38.25 |
| 50-54 | 75.30 | 73.15 | 53.66 | 68.45 | 64.10 | 34.28 |
| 55-59 | 72.55 | 70.25 | 55.35 | 65.30 | 60.70 | 30.28 |
| 60-64 | 66.60 | 63.45 | 54.28 | 56.70 | 50.75 | 18.90 |
| 65+ | 46.65 | 43.25 | 45.86 | 36.45 | 30.70 | 9.80 |

**Source(s):** (1) EPPA3; (2) R1966 and ADNU72; (3) R1986.

### 2.2 Method(s): linears interpolation and extrapolation

**2.2.1 Men:**

- 1950-90, interpolation and extrapolation of adjusted activity rates derived from the 1966 and 1986 censuses;
modification of the trends of the [10-14] and [45+] age groups for 1950 and 1960;
modification of the trends of the [55+] age groups for 1990.

**2.2.2 Women:**

- 1950-90, interpolation and extrapolation of 1950-80 activity rates des EPPA3 and of adjusted activity rates derived from the 1986 census; adjustment of interpolated and extrapolated rates on the basis of variations in 1986 interpolated rates, in relation to adjusted activity rates derived from the 1986 census.

## 3. Estimates of distribution rates by activity sector: 1950 - 1990

### 3.1 Benchmark data:

Table 2: Distribution of economically active population by activity sector

| Year | Agriculture | Industry Total | Manufac. | Services |
|---|---|---|---|---|
| **Men** | | | | |
| 1966 (1) | 66.49 | 13.60 | 6.09 | 19.91 |
| 1986 (2) | 33.49 | 29.71 | 12.61 | 36.80 |
| **Women** | | | | |
| 1966 (1) | 80.53 | 3.68 | 3.57 | 15.79 |
| 1986 (2) | 55.34 | 7.59 | 6.94 | 37.07 |

**Source(s):** (1) R1966; (2) R1986.

### 3.2 Method(s): linears interpolation and extrapolation

**3.2.1 Men:**
- 1950-90, interpolation and extrapolation of adjusted distribution rates derived from the 1966 and 1986 censuses;
modification of the trends in all sectors for 1950, 1960 and 1990.

**3.2.2 Women:**

Method, hypothesis and treatment identical to those used for men.

## 4. Projection of activity rates: 2000 - 2010

### 4.1 Model(s): linear and hyperbole

**4.1.1 Men:**
- To the [10-14] age group, application of function F1;
- To the [15+] age groups, application of function F3;
- Modification of the trends for the [15-19], [45-49] and [65+].

**4.1.2 Women:**
- To all age groups, application of function F3;
- Modification of the trends for the [10-14] and [20-59] age groups.

Notes on adjustments of rates, see p. 3-8.      Notes on projection functions, see p. 10.

# Sweden

## 1. Source(s) of benchmark data

Code(s):     Title(s):

EPPA3        Yearbook of Labour Statistics 1945-89 - Retrospective Edition on Population Censuses, ILO, Geneva, 1990.

STAT         Database on Labour Statistics, LABORSTA - Bureau of Statistics, ILO, Geneva.

## 2. Estimates of activity rates: 1950 - 1990

### 2.1 Benchmark data:

Table 1: Activity rates by sex and age group

| Age group | Year 1970 (1) | 1980 (1) | 1989 (2) | 1990 (2) | 1991 (2) |
|---|---|---|---|---|---|
| **Men** | | | | | |
| 10-14 | .. | .. | 0.00 | 0.00 | 0.00 |
| 15-19 | .. | .. | 48.05 | 47.64 | 42.24 |
| 20-24 | .. | .. | 84.86 | 84.57 | 82.89 |
| 25-29 | .. | .. | 92.62 | 92.60 | 91.61 |
| 30-34 | .. | .. | 95.25 | 95.61 | 94.92 |
| 35-39 | .. | .. | 96.05 | 95.33 | 94.98 |
| 40-44 | .. | .. | 96.78 | 96.74 | 96.34 |
| 45-49 | .. | .. | 95.82 | 96.39 | 96.00 |
| 50-54 | .. | .. | 92.92 | 93.59 | 93.72 |
| 55-59 | .. | .. | 86.96 | 87.86 | 86.41 |
| 60-64 | .. | .. | 62.86 | 63.11 | 64.22 |
| 65+ | .. | .. | 8.07 | 7.32 | 8.75 |
| **Women** | | | | | |
| 10-14 | 0.35 | 0.00 | 0.00 | 0.00 | 0.00 |
| 15-19 | | | 51.36 | 50.45 | 47.06 |
| 20-24 | 64.05 | 71.30 | 82.00 | 80.68 | 77.32 |
| 25-29 | 55.45 | 73.60 | 87.94 | 87.07 | 86.14 |
| 30-34 | 52.35 | 74.60 | 90.75 | 91.10 | 88.97 |
| 35-39 | 52.85 | 78.60 | 92.10 | 90.03 | 91.06 |
| 40-44 | 53.90 | 82.60 | 93.31 | 93.85 | 93.38 |
| 45-49 | 53.40 | 82.80 | 92.07 | 93.10 | 92.88 |
| 50-54 | 51.15 | 77.80 | 88.34 | 89.08 | 89.27 |
| 55-59 | 44.95 | 66.40 | 78.50 | 79.25 | 80.00 |
| 60-64 | 29.25 | 41.40 | 50.67 | 53.85 | 54.79 |
| 65+ | 3.20 | 2.60 | 3.00 | 2.62 | 2.60 |

Source(s): (1) EPPA3; (2) STAT.

### 2.2 Method(s):  arithmetic average

#### 2.2.1 Men:

- 1950-80, 1950-80 activity rates derived from the EPPA3;
adjustment of activity rates of the [20-24] age group for 1950 and 1960
and of the [15-19] age group for 1980;
- 1990, average of activity rates derived from the 1989, 1990
and 1991 surveys;
modification of the trend of the [15-19] age group.

#### 2.2.2 Women:

- 1950-80, 1950-80 activity rates derived from the EPPA3;
adjustment of activity rates of the [15-19] age group for 1970 and 1980;
- 1990, average of activity rates derived from
the 1989, 1990 and 1991 surveys.

## 3. Estimates of distribution rates by activity sector: 1950 - 1990

### 3.1 Benchmark data:

Table 2: Distribution of economically active population by activity sector

| Year | Agriculture | Industry Total | Manufac. | Services |
|---|---|---|---|---|
| **Men** | | | | |
| 1979 | 8.26 | 49.28 | 34.70 | 42.46 |
| 1980 | 7.89 | 47.72 | 32.54 | 44.39 |
| 1981 | 8.11 | 46.12 | 32.64 | 45.77 |
| 1989 | 7.02 | 42.85 | 32.42 | 50.13 |
| 1990 | 5.64 | 44.30 | 30.96 | 50.07 |
| 1991 | 5.45 | 43.97 | 30.98 | 50.58 |
| **Women** | | | | |
| 1979 | 3.94 | 19.01 | 16.73 | 77.05 |
| 1980 | 3.65 | 16.98 | 15.15 | 79.37 |
| 1981 | 3.52 | 16.51 | 15.20 | 79.96 |
| 1989 | 2.98 | 14.16 | 12.96 | 82.86 |
| 1990 | 2.61 | 14.63 | 13.20 | 82.76 |
| 1991 | 2.31 | 14.38 | 13.37 | 83.32 |

Source(s): STAT.

### 3.2 Method(s):  arithmetic average

#### 3.2.1 Men:

- 1950-70, 1950-70 distribution rates derived from the EPPA3;
- 1980, averages of distribution rates derived from the 1979, 1980
and 1981 surveys;
- 1990, averages of distribution rates derived from the 1989, 1990
and 1991 surveys.

#### 3.2.2 Women:

Method, hypothesis and treatment identical to those used for men.

## 4. Projection of activity rates: 2000 - 2010

### 4.1 Model(s):  linear, hyperbole and logistic

#### 4.1.1 Men:

- To the [15-19] and [55+] age groups, application of function F3;
- To the [20-54] age groups, application of function F1;
- Modification of the trends for the [15-39] age groups.

#### 4.1.2 Women:

- To the [15-19] and [65+] age groups, application of function F3;
- To the [20-64] age groups, application of function F6;
- Modification of the trends for all age groups.

*Notes on adjustments of rates, see p. 3-8.*          *Notes on projection functions, see p. 10.*

# Switzerland

## 1. Source(s) of benchmark data

Code(s):     Title(s):
EPPA3        Yearbook of Labour Statistics 1945-89 - Retrospective Edition on Population Censuses, ILO, Geneva, 1990.
STAT         Database on Labour Statistics, LABORSTA - Bureau of Statistics, ILO, Geneva.

## 2. Estimates of activity rates: 1950 - 1990

### 2.1 Benchmark data:

Table 1: Activity rates by sex and age group

| Age group | Year 1950 (1) | 1960 (1) | 1970 (1) | 1980 (1) | 1990 (2) |
|---|---|---|---|---|---|
| **Men** | | | | | |
| 10-14 | 1.10 | 0.35 | 0.20 | 0.00 | 0.00 |
| 15-19 | 74.10 | 69.10 | 63.40 | 57.05 | 55.98 |
| 20-24 | 91.00 | 90.50 | 88.55 | 85.20 | 83.80 |
| 25-29 | 96.15 | 96.85 | 96.40 | 94.90 | 93.87 |
| 30-34 | 98.40 | 98.75 | 98.75 | 98.35 | 97.84 |
| 35-39 | 98.70 | 99.00 | 99.10 | 98.95 | 98.56 |
| 40-44 | 98.55 | 98.80 | 98.90 | 98.80 | 98.68 |
| 45-49 | 98.15 | 98.50 | 98.55 | 98.25 | 98.35 |
| 50-54 | 97.15 | 97.55 | 97.45 | 96.85 | 97.44 |
| 55-59 | 94.95 | 95.65 | 95.15 | 93.60 | 94.84 |
| 60-64 | 87.75 | 88.90 | 87.30 | 82.95 | 79.78 |
| 65+ | 50.70 | 43.05 | 31.50 | 16.05 | 9.18 |
| **Women** | | | | | |
| 10-14 | 0.65 | 0.35 | 0.20 | 0.00 | 0.00 |
| 15-19 | 64.10 | 63.10 | 58.95 | 51.65 | 49.21 |
| 20-24 | 67.85 | 69.10 | 71.80 | 75.95 | 80.38 |
| 25-29 | 40.45 | 43.70 | 49.75 | 58.70 | 71.39 |
| 30-34 | 27.70 | 33.50 | 40.80 | 49.55 | 60.88 |
| 35-39 | 26.20 | 32.25 | 40.50 | 51.00 | 62.92 |
| 40-44 | 26.85 | 32.40 | 41.20 | 53.20 | 66.79 |
| 45-49 | 27.30 | 33.50 | 41.60 | 51.75 | 66.56 |
| 50-54 | 27.35 | 33.40 | 40.15 | 47.55 | 60.57 |
| 55-59 | 26.15 | 32.00 | 37.20 | 41.75 | 49.88 |
| 60-64 | 22.90 | 27.20 | 27.95 | 25.20 | 24.91 |
| 65+ | 11.65 | 11.50 | 9.35 | 5.15 | 3.22 |

Source(s): (1) EPPA3; (2) STAT.

### 2.2 Method(s): weighted average

#### 2.2.1 Men:

- 1950-80, 1950-80 activity rates derived from the EPPA3;
- 1990, weighted average of activity rates of 1980 derived from the EPPA3 and of activity rates derived from the 1990 census.

#### 2.2.2 Women:

Method, hypothesis and treatment identical to those used for men.

## 3. Estimates of distribution rates by activity sector: 1950 - 1990

### 3.1 Benchmark data:

Table 2: Distribution of economically active population by activity sector

| Year | Agriculture | Industry Total | Manufac. | Services |
|---|---|---|---|---|
| **Men** | | | | |
| 1990 | 6.31 | 43.94 | 32.34 | 49.75 |
| **Women** | | | | |
| 1990 | 4.29 | 20.31 | 19.38 | 75.40 |

Source(s): (1) STAT.

### 3.2 Method(s): national data

#### 3.2.1 Men:

- 1950-80, 1950-80 distribution rates derived from the EPPA3;
- 1990, distribution rates derived from the 1990 official estimates.

#### 3.2.2 Women:

Method, hypothesis and treatment identical to those used for men.

## 4. Projection of activity rates: 2000 - 2010

### 4.1 Model(s): linear, hyperbole and logistic

#### 4.1.1 Men:

- To the [15-54] age groups, application of function F1;
- To the [55+] age groups, application of function F3;
- Modification of the trends for the [15-19] and [40-49] age groups.

#### 4.1.2 Women:

- To the [15-59] age groups, application of function F6;
- To the [60+] age groups, application of function F3;
- Modification of the trends for the [15-24] and [60-64] age groups.

*Notes on adjustments of rates, see p. 3-8.*     *Notes on projection functions, see p. 10.*

# Syrian Arab Republic

## 1. Source(s) of benchmark data

Code(s):   Title(s):
EPPA3      Economically active population: Estimates and Projections, 1950-2025, Third edition, ILO, Geneva, 1986.
STAT       Database on Labour Statistics, LABORSTA - Bureau of Statistics, ILO, Geneva.

## 2. Estimates of activity rates: 1950 - 1990

### 2.1 Benchmark data:

Table 1: Activity rates by sex and age group

| Age group | 1950 (1) | 1960 (1) | 1970 (1) | 1981 (2) |
|---|---|---|---|---|
| **Men** | | | | |
| 10-14 | 23.25 | 20.65 | .. | 12.53 |
| 15-19 | 71.20 | 65.50 | .. | 53.15 |
| 20-24 | 89.45 | 87.30 | .. | 82.08 |
| 25-29 | 96.45 | 95.95 | .. | 95.50 |
| 30-34 | 97.25 | 97.35 | .. | 98.07 |
| 35-39 | 96.20 | 96.90 | .. | 98.21 |
| 40-44 | 95.55 | 96.10 | .. | 97.15 |
| 45-49 | 94.65 | 94.90 | .. | 94.46 |
| 50-54 | 90.50 | 91.35 | .. | 89.78 |
| 55-59 | 86.95 | 87.30 | .. | 85.27 |
| 60-64 | 75.85 | 76.65 | .. | 68.56 |
| 65+ | 43.35 | 45.55 | .. | 37.44 |
| **Women** | | | | |
| 10-14 | .. | .. | 6.90 | .. |
| 15-19 | .. | .. | 13.35 | .. |
| 20-24 | .. | .. | 16.45 | .. |
| 25-29 | .. | .. | 14.55 | .. |
| 30-34 | .. | .. | 12.60 | .. |
| 35-39 | .. | .. | 12.40 | .. |
| 40-44 | .. | .. | 12.35 | .. |
| 45-49 | .. | .. | 12.65 | .. |
| 50-54 | .. | .. | 11.00 | .. |
| 55-59 | .. | .. | 7.00 | .. |
| 60-64 | .. | .. | 5.50 | .. |
| 65+ | .. | .. | 2.7 | .. |

Source(s): (1) EPPA3; (2) STAT.

### 2.2 Method(s): linears interpolation and extrapolation
weighted average

#### 2.2.1 Men:
- 1950-80, interpolation of 1950-60 activity rates derived from the EPPA3 and of activity rates derived from the 1981 census;
- 1990, application to 1980 estimated rates, average of the variations of 1990 estimated activity rates for Egypt and Jordan.

#### 2.2.2 Women:
- 1950-70, 1950-70 adjusted activity rates derived from the EPPA3; the adjustment was made on the basis of the adjustment model for activity rates of women working in agriculture as contributing family workers;
- 1980, weighted average of 1970 activity rates derived from the EPPA3 and of activity rates derived from the 1983 census;
- 1990, extrapolation of activity rates estimated for 1970 and 1980; adjustment of activity rates to make allowance for the under-registration of women working in agriculture.

## 3. Estimates of distribution rates by activity sector: 1950 - 1990

### 3.1 Benchmark data:

Table 2: Distribution of economically active population by activity sector

| Year | Agriculture | Industry Total | Manufac. | Services |
|---|---|---|---|---|
| **Men** | | | | |
| 1979 | 27.48 | 34.70 | 16.63 | 37.82 |
| 1983 | 22.17 | 36.53 | 15.38 | 41.30 |
| 1989 | 19.64 | 31.47 | 15.96 | 48.89 |
| 1991 | 23.06 | 28.42 | 15.55 | 48.52 |
| **Women** | | | | |
| 1979 | 60.26 | 14.18 | 12.39 | 25.55 |
| 1983 | 47.80 | 13.83 | 11.47 | 38.37 |
| 1989 | 41.43 | 13.81 | 12.14 | 44.76 |
| 1991 | 54.10 | 7.71 | 6.42 | 38.18 |

Source(s): STAT.

### 3.2 Method(s): weighted average
linear interpolation and extrapolation

#### 3.2.1 Men:
1950-70, 1950-70 distribution rates derived from the EPPA3;
- 1980, weighted averages of distribution rates derived from the 1979 and 1983 surveys;
- 1990, weighted averages of distribution rates derived from des the 1989 and 1991 surveys.

#### 3.2.2 Women:
- 1950-70, 1950-70 distribution rates of agriculture sector derived from the EPPA3;
adjustment of rates to make allowance for the under-registration of contributing family workers in agriculture;
- 1980-90, interpolation and extrapolation of adjusted distribution rates derived from the 1979, 1983, 1989 and 1991 surveys;
adjustment of rates to make allowance for the under-registration of contributing family workers in agriculture.

## 4. Projection of activity rates: 2000 - 2010

### 4.1 Model(s): linear and hyperbole

#### 4.1.1 Men:
- To the [10-14], [30-44] and [50+] age groups, application of function F1;
- To the [15-29] and [45-49] age groups, application of function F3;
- Modification of the trends for the [10-14], [20-44] and [50-59] age groups.

#### 4.1.2 Women:
- To all age groups, application of function F1;
- Modification of the trends for all age groups.

# Tajikistan

## 1. Source(s) of benchmark data

Code(s):    Title(s):

BLT-94-2    Vorobiev A. (1994), "Estimates of the economically active population for the fifteen countries of the former USSR for the years 1950, 1959, 1970, 1979 and 1989", in the Bulletin of Labour of Statistics - 1994-2, ILO, Geneva.

## 2. Estimates of activity rates: 1950 - 1990

### 2.1 Benchmark data:

Table 1: Activity rates by sex and age group

| Age group | Year | | | | |
|---|---|---|---|---|---|
| | 1950 | 1959 | 1970 | 1979 | 1989 |
| **Men** | | | | | |
| 10-14 | 0.00 | 0.00 | 0.00 | 0.00 | 0.00 |
| 15-19 | 54.44 | 57.14 | 35.11 | 37.28 | 28.90 |
| 20-24 | 83.33 | 86.75 | 83.12 | 85.19 | 79.39 |
| 25-29 | 91.49 | 93.98 | 92.11 | 97.58 | 95.91 |
| 30-34 | 94.29 | 97.44 | 97.66 | 98.70 | 98.77 |
| 35-39 | 92.11 | 97.67 | 98.78 | 98.85 | 98.31 |
| 40-44 | 91.43 | 96.88 | 98.72 | 98.91 | 97.22 |
| 45-49 | 90.32 | 91.43 | 95.24 | 98.70 | 97.50 |
| 50-54 | 89.66 | 93.75 | 92.86 | 95.45 | 93.90 |
| 55-59 | 90.00 | 89.66 | 87.10 | 88.24 | 88.24 |
| 60-64 | 76.47 | 80.00 | 66.67 | 36.00 | 37.50 |
| 65+ | 37.04 | 37.21 | 7.69 | 9.21 | 12.16 |
| **Women** | | | | | |
| 10-14 | 0.00 | 0.00 | 0.00 | 0.00 | 0.00 |
| 15-19 | 43.43 | 59.15 | 41.35 | 45.18 | 31.30 |
| 20-24 | 69.05 | 71.43 | 73.86 | 84.21 | 63.14 |
| 25-29 | 70.00 | 73.63 | 76.06 | 86.61 | 66.67 |
| 30-34 | 68.09 | 70.51 | 75.79 | 87.67 | 70.73 |
| 35-39 | 62.79 | 66.07 | 77.38 | 88.46 | 76.86 |
| 40-44 | 58.54 | 63.64 | 76.00 | 88.89 | 77.94 |
| 45-49 | 52.27 | 56.41 | 74.07 | 87.34 | 76.39 |
| 50-54 | 41.18 | 42.11 | 65.00 | 72.86 | 54.22 |
| 55-59 | 23.08 | 26.83 | 26.09 | 27.78 | 22.97 |
| 60-64 | 13.64 | 11.76 | 10.00 | 10.00 | 12.50 |
| 65+ | 5.26 | 5.56 | 2.44 | 2.94 | 5.08 |

Source(s): BLT-94-2-2

### 2.2 Method(s): weighted average

#### 2.2.1 Men:

- 1950-90, weighted average of 1950, 1959, 1970 and 1989 activity rates derived from the Bulletin of Labour Statistics 1994-2.

#### 2.2.2 Women:

Method, hypothesis and treatment identical to those used for men.

## 3. Estimates of distribution rates by activity sector: 1950 - 1990

### 3.1 Benchmark data:

Table 2: Distribution of economically active population by activity sector

| Year | Agriculture | Industry | | Services |
|---|---|---|---|---|
| | | Total | Manufac. | |
| **Men** | | | | |
| 1950 | 73.95 | 8.96 | 6.16 | 17.09 |
| 1959 | 57.11 | 17.83 | 7.22 | 25.05 |
| 1970 | 41.30 | 25.91 | 12.86 | 32.79 |
| 1979 | 35.98 | 28.94 | 13.06 | 35.08 |
| 1989 | 37.01 | 27.97 | 10.66 | 35.01 |
| **Women** | | | | |
| 1950 | 77.01 | 8.03 | 6.93 | 14.96 |
| 1959 | 68.73 | 11.83 | 8.73 | 19.44 |
| 1970 | 52.65 | 16.81 | 11.28 | 30.53 |
| 1979 | 55.27 | 16.03 | 9.56 | 28.69 |
| 1989 | 46.74 | 17.19 | 12.24 | 36.07 |

Source(s): BLT-94-2.

### 3.2 Method(s): weighted average

#### 3.2.1 Men:

- 1950-90, weighted averages of 1950, 1959, 1970, 1979 and 1989 distribution rates derived from the Bulletin of Labour Statistics, 1994-2.

#### 3.2.2 Women:

Method, hypothesis and treatment identical to those used for men.

## 4. Projection of activity rates: 2000 - 2010

### 4.1 Model(s): linear, hyperbole and logistic

#### 4.1.1 Men:

- To the [15-24] and [60+] age groups, application of function F3;
- To the [25-59] age groups, application of function F1;
- Modification of the trends for the [20-64] age groups.

#### 4.1.2 Women:

- To the [15-19] age group, application of function F1;
- To the [20-24] and [60+] age groups, application of function F3;
- To the [25-59] age groups, application of function F6;
- Modification of the trends for the [20-49] age groups.

*Notes on adjustments of rates, see p. 3-8.*

*Notes on projection functions, see p. 10.*

# Tanzania, United Rep. of

## 1. Source(s) of benchmark data

Code(s):    Title(s):

EPPA3    Economically active population: Estimates and Projections, 1950-2025, Third edition, ILO, Geneva, 1986.

## 2. Estimates of activity rates: 1950 - 1990

### 2.1 Benchmark data:

Table 1: Activity rates by sex and age group

| Age group | Year 1950 | 1960 | 1970 | 1980 |
|---|---|---|---|---|
| **Men** | | | | |
| 10-14 | 49.00 | 47.95 | 46.55 | 43.45 |
| 15-19 | 78.70 | 77.35 | 75.45 | 71.40 |
| 20-24 | 87.15 | 86.65 | 85.90 | 84.35 |
| 25-29 | 96.25 | 96.15 | 96.05 | 95.80 |
| 30-34 | 98.15 | 98.05 | 97.90 | 97.60 |
| 35-39 | 99.05 | 98.95 | 98.80 | 98.50 |
| 40-44 | 99.15 | 99.05 | 98.90 | 98.60 |
| 45-49 | 99.35 | 99.25 | 99.15 | 98.85 |
| 50-54 | 98.90 | 98.75 | 98.55 | 98.15 |
| 55-59 | 98.60 | 98.50 | 98.40 | 97.95 |
| 60-64 | 97.75 | 97.35 | 96.85 | 95.65 |
| 65+ | 91.70 | 90.95 | 89.95 | 87.75 |
| **Women** | | | | |
| 10-14 | 46.45 | 45.70 | 44.60 | 42.25 |
| 15-19 | 85.80 | 84.25 | 82.00 | 77.20 |
| 20-24 | 90.90 | 89.40 | 87.20 | 82.50 |
| 25-29 | 94.85 | 93.45 | 91.45 | 87.10 |
| 30-34 | 97.35 | 96.05 | 94.15 | 90.05 |
| 35-39 | 98.20 | 97.00 | 95.20 | 91.40 |
| 40-44 | 98.50 | 97.40 | 95.80 | 92.35 |
| 45-49 | 98.30 | 97.20 | 95.65 | 92.30 |
| 50-54 | 95.95 | 95.05 | 93.75 | 90.95 |
| 55-59 | 92.90 | 92.25 | 91.30 | 89.30 |
| 60-64 | 85.30 | 84.90 | 84.35 | 83.10 |
| 65+ | 61.45 | 61.30 | 61.10 | 60.70 |

Source(s): EPPA3.

### 2.2 Method(s): linear extrapolation

#### 2.2.1 Men:

- 1950-80, 1950-80 activity rates derived from the EPPA3;
- 1990, extrapolation of 1950-80 activity rates derived from the EPPA3; adjustment of extrapolated rates on the basis of variations in 1980 interpolated rates, in relation to the 1980 rates derived from the EPPA3; modification of the trends for all age groups.

#### 2.2.2 Women:

Method, hypothesis and treatment identical to those used for men.

## 3. Estimates of distribution rates by activity sector: 1950 - 1990

### 3.1 Benchmark data:

Table 2: Distribution of economically active population by activity sector

| Year | Agriculture | Industry Total | Manufac. | Services |
|---|---|---|---|---|
| **Men** | | | | |
| 1950 | 90.60 | 3.40 | .. | 6.00 |
| 1960 | 88.55 | 4.10 | .. | 7.35 |
| 1970 | 85.00 | 5.40 | .. | 9.60 |
| 1980 | 79.75 | 7.25 | .. | 13.00 |
| **Women** | | | | |
| 1950 | 97.50 | 0.50 | .. | 2.00 |
| 1960 | 96.45 | 0.75 | .. | 2.80 |
| 1970 | 95.00 | 1.00 | .. | 4.00 |
| 1980 | 91.85 | 1.65 | .. | 6.50 |

Source(s): EPPA3.

### 3.2 Method(s): linear extrapolation

#### 3.2.1 Men:

1950-80, 1950-80 distribution rates derived from the EPPA3;
- 1990, extrapolation of 1950-80 distribution rates derived from the EPPA3; modification of the trends in all sectors;
- Application of manufacturing/industry ratio estimated for Ethiopia.

#### 3.2.2 Women:

Method, hypothesis and treatment identical to those used for men.

## 4. Projection of activity rates: 2000 - 2010

### 4.1 Model(s): linear and hyperbole

#### 4.1.1 Men:

- To the [10-24] age groups, application of function F1;
- To the [25+] age groups, application of function F3;
- Modification of the trends for the [10-14] and [60+] age groups.

#### 4.1.2 Women:

- To the [10-19] age groups, application of function F1;
- To the [20+] age groups, application of function F3;
- Modification of the trends for all age groups.

*Notes on adjustments of rates, see p. 3-8.*          *Notes on projection functions, see p. 10.*

# Thailand

## 1. Source(s) of benchmark data

Code(s):    Title(s):
EPPA3       Economically active population: Estimates and Projections, 1950-2025, Third edition, ILO, Geneva, 1986.
STAT        Database on Labour Statistics, LABORSTA - Bureau of Statistics, ILO, Geneva.

## 2. Estimates of activity rates: 1950 - 1990

### 2.1 Benchmark data:

Table 1: Activity rates by sex and age group

| Age group | Year 1979 | 1980 | 1989 | 1990 |
|---|---|---|---|---|
| **Men** | | | | |
| 10-19 | 70.60 | 70.90 | 71.20 | 67.70 |
| 20-24 | 88.80 | 87.80 | 92.80 | 91.60 |
| 25-29 | 97.50 | 97.20 | 97.30 | 96.60 |
| 30-39 | 98.70 | 98.80 | 98.00 | 98.00 |
| 40-49 | 98.40 | 98.50 | 98.10 | 97.90 |
| 50-59 | 94.70 | 95.50 | 94.40 | 94.80 |
| 60+ | 59.20 | 56.70 | 49.50 | 53.00 |
| **Women** | | | | |
| 10-19 | 69.90 | 71.00 | 72.20 | 69.40 |
| 20-24 | 81.20 | 80.30 | 83.00 | 81.70 |
| 25-29 | 83.50 | 84.70 | 84.70 | 83.60 |
| 30-39 | 86.00 | 86.80 | 87.00 | 86.60 |
| 40-49 | 85.30 | 87.80 | 86.10 | 86.30 |
| 50-59 | 74.80 | 77.70 | 76.40 | 76.50 |
| 60+ | 29.10 | 31.40 | 28.50 | 32.20 |

Source(s): STAT.

### 2.2 Method(s): linear interpolation

#### 2.2.1 Men:

- 1950-90, interpolation of 1950-80 activity rates derived from EPPA3,
of average of adjusted activity rates derived from the 1979 and 1980 surveys
and of average of adjusted activity rates derived from the 1989
and 1990 surveys.

#### 2.2.2 Women:

Method, hypothesis and treatment identical to those used for men.

## 3. Estimates of distribution rates by activity sector: 1950 - 1990

### 3.1 Benchmark data:

Table 2: Distribution of economically active population by activity sector

| Year | Agriculture | Industry Total | Manufac. | Services |
|---|---|---|---|---|
| **Men** | | | | |
| 1980 (1) | 67.95 | 12.50 | .. | 19.55 |
| 1990 (2) | 63.13 | 15.55 | 9.54 | 21.32 |
| **Women** | | | | |
| 1980 (1) | 74.20 | 7.75 | .. | 18.05 |
| 1990 (2) | 65.00 | 12.27 | 10.88 | 22.73 |

Source(s): (1) EPPA3; (2) STAT.

### 3.2 Method(s): linear interpolation

#### 3.2.1 Men:

- 1950-80, 1950-80 distribution rates derived from the EPPA3;
- 1990, interpolation of 1980 distribution rates derived from the EPPA3
and of distribution rates derived from the 1990 survey;
modification of the trends in all sectors;
- Application of manufacturing/industry ratio derived from the 1990 survey.

#### 3.2.2 Women:

Method, hypothesis and treatment identical to those used for men.

## 4. Projection of activity rates: 2000 - 2010

### 4.1 Model(s): linear, log-linear, hyperbole and logistic

#### 4.1.1 Men:

- To the [10-14] age group, application of function F1;
- To the [15-19] age group, application of function F2;
- To the [20+] age groups, application of function F3;
- Modification of the trends for the [10-49] age groups.

#### 4.1.2 Women:

- To the [10-19] age groups, application of function F1;
- To the [20-64] age groups, application of function F6;
- To the [65+] age group, application of function F3;
- Modification of the trends for the [10-59] age groups.

*Notes on adjustments of rates, see p. 3-8.*          *Notes on projection functions, see p. 10.*

# Togo

## 1. Source(s) of benchmark data

Code(s):     Title(s):

EPPA3        Economically active population: Estimates and Projections, 1950-2025, Third edition, ILO, Geneva, 1986.
STAT         Database on Labour Statistics, LABORSTA - Bureau of Statistics, ILO, Geneva.
R1970        Recensement général de la Population (mars-avril 1970), Direction de la Statistique, Lomé, 1974.
AST87        Yearbook of Labour Statistics 1987, ILO, Geneva, 1987.

## 2. Estimates of activity rates: 1950 - 1990

### 2.1 Benchmark data:

Table 1: Activity rates by sex and age group

| Age group | 1950 (1) | 1960 (1) | 1961 (2) | 1970 (1) | 1970 (3) | 1981 (4) |
|---|---|---|---|---|---|---|
| **Men** | | | | | | |
| 10-14 | 50.60 | 49.30 | .. | 47.70 | .. | 12.72 |
| 15-19 | 74.00 | 72.50 | .. | 70.55 | .. | 36.61 |
| 20-24 | 93.15 | 92.50 | .. | 91.70 | .. | 70.05 |
| 25-29 | 97.20 | 97.10 | .. | 96.95 | .. | 94.59 |
| 30-34 | 97.35 | 97.25 | .. | 97.10 | .. | 98.14 |
| 35-39 | 97.70 | 97.60 | .. | 97.45 | .. | 98.60 |
| 40-44 | 97.45 | 97.30 | .. | 97.15 | .. | 98.12 |
| 45-49 | 97.05 | 96.95 | .. | 96.85 | .. | 97.59 |
| 50-54 | 95.55 | 95.40 | .. | 95.20 | .. | 92.70 |
| 55-59 | 94.30 | 94.05 | .. | 93.75 | .. | 90.12 |
| 60-64 | 90.55 | 90.15 | .. | 89.60 | .. | 87.54 |
| 65+ | 78.30 | 77.55 | .. | 76.65 | .. | 71.52 |
| **Women** | | | | | | |
| 10-14 | .. | .. | 36.59 | .. | 47.86 | 12.73 |
| 15-19 | .. | .. | 51.97 | .. | 51.85 | 35.83 |
| 20-24 | .. | .. | 51.73 | .. | 54.01 | 47.66 |
| 25-29 | .. | .. | 55.43 | .. | 57.80 | 55.15 |
| 30-34 | .. | .. | 56.99 | .. | 58.90 | 58.03 |
| 35-39 | .. | .. | 58.50 | .. | 60.52 | 59.59 |
| 40-44 | .. | .. | 60.44 | .. | 60.88 | 60.27 |
| 45-49 | .. | .. | 60.05 | .. | 61.00 | 60.13 |
| 50-54 | .. | .. | 58.76 | .. | 58.86 | 59.94 |
| 55-59 | .. | .. | 55.73 | .. | 55.34 | 56.46 |
| 60-64 | .. | .. | 53.85 | .. | 49.54 | 50.85 |
| 65+ | .. | .. | 37.21 | .. | 33.95 | 34.95 |

Source(s): (1) EPPA3; (2) STAT; (3) R1970; (4) AST87.

### 2.2 Method(s): linears interpolation and extrapolation

2.2.1 Men:

- 1950-70, 1950-70 activity rates derived from the EPPA3;
adjustment of activity rates of the [30-49] age groups for 1950 and 1960;
- 1980-90, extrapolation of 1950-70 activity rates derived from the EPPA3
and of activity rates derived from the 1981 census;
adjustment of interpolated and extrapolated rates on the basis of variations
in 1970 interpolated rates, in relation to the 1970 activity rates derived from
the EPPA3; modification of the trends of the [10-19] age groups for 1990.

2.2.2 Women:

- 1950-90, interpolation and extrapolation of activity rates derived from
the 1961 census and of adjusted activity rates derived from the 1970
and 1981 censuses;
modification of the trends for all age groups for 1950.

## 3. Estimates of distribution rates by activity sector: 1950 - 1990

### 3.1 Benchmark data:

Table 2: Distribution of economically active population by activity sector

| Year | Agriculture | Industry Total | Manufac. | Services |
|---|---|---|---|---|
| **Men** | | | | |
| 1961 (1) | 83.50 | 9.50 | .. | 7.00 |
| 1981 (2) | 69.11 | 11.71 | 6.23 | 19.18 |
| **Women** | | | | |
| 1961 (1) | 73.50 | 6.00 | .. | 20.50 |
| 1981 (2) | 66.75 | 6.70 | 6.57 | 26.55 |

Source(s): (1) STAT; (2) AST87.

### 3.2 Method(s): linears interpolation and extrapolation

3.2.1 Men:
- 1950-90, interpolation and extrapolation of distribution rates derived
from the 1961 survey and from the 1981 census;
modification of the trends in all sectors;
- Application of manufacturing/industry ratio derived from the 1981 census.

3.2.2 Women:

Method, hypothesis and treatment identical to those used for men.

## 4. Projection of activity rates: 2000 - 2010

### 4.1 Model(s): log-linear and hyperbole

4.1.1 Men:

- To the [10-14] age group, application of function F2;
- To the [15+] age groups, application of function F1;
- Modification of the trends for the [30-39] age groups.

4.1.2 Women:

- To the [10-14] age group, application of function F2;
- To the [15+] age groups, application of function F1;
- Modification of the trends for the [10-59] age groups.

*Notes on adjustments of rates, see p. 3-8.*      *Notes on projection functions, see p. 10.*

# Trinidad and Tobago

## 1. Source(s) of benchmark data

Code(s):   Title(s):

EPPA3     Economically active population: Estimates and Projections, 1950-2025, Third edition, ILO, Geneva, 1986.
AST75-93   Editions 1975-1993 of ILO Yearbook of Labour Statistics, Geneva.
TET-LFS   Continuous Sample Survey of Population; Labour Force Report 1989.

## 2. Estimates of activity rates: 1950 - 1990

### 2.1 Benchmark data:

Table 1: Activity rates by sex and age group

| Age group | 1980 (1) | 1987 (2) | 1988 (2) | 1989 (2) |
|---|---|---|---|---|
| **Men** | | | | |
| 10-14 | 1.10 | 0.00 | 0.00 | 0.00 |
| 15-19 | 50.90 | 45.50 | 41.00 | 39.00 |
| 20-24 | 90.20 | 90.30 | 89.40 | 87.70 |
| 25-29 | 95.40 | 96.10 | 93.10 | 94.30 |
| 30-34 | 96.50 | 94.80 | 95.40 | 94.00 |
| 35-39 | 97.00 | 96.40 | 94.70 | 93.60 |
| 40-44 | 95.50 | 93.80 | 94.80 | 94.10 |
| 45-49 | 95.40 | 95.50 | 94.60 | 92.00 |
| 50-54 | 94.00 | 89.50 | 89.70 | 89.00 |
| 55-59 | 89.60 | 85.10 | 81.50 | 79.90 |
| 60-64 | 71.40 | 55.50 | 55.90 | 49.00 |
| 65+ | 21.80 | 20.30 | 21.80 | 18.40 |
| **Women** | | | | |
| 10-14 | 0.00 | 0.00 | 0.00 | 0.00 |
| 15-19 | 20.10 | 21.00 | 18.10 | 16.30 |
| 20-24 | 50.03 | 52.20 | 52.10 | 50.70 |
| 25-29 | 49.58 | 51.70 | 50.60 | 51.40 |
| 30-34 | 48.27 | 52.60 | 51.00 | 48.80 |
| 35-39 | 49.01 | 49.30 | 52.50 | 52.50 |
| 40-44 | 43.11 | 52.00 | 50.60 | 49.00 |
| 45-49 | 47.80 | 45.00 | 45.10 | 48.60 |
| 50-54 | 38.95 | 40.70 | 40.20 | 36.90 |
| 55-59 | 34.10 | 30.70 | 33.30 | 26.40 |
| 60-64 | 23.08 | 20.00 | 18.70 | 13.90 |
| 65+ | 7.77 | 6.00 | 5.70 | 5.40 |

Source(s): (1) EPPA3; (2) AST75-93 and TET-LFS.

### 2.2 Method(s): linear extrapolation

**2.2.1 Men:**

- 1950-80, 1950-80 activity rates derived from the EPPA3;
adjustment of activity rates of the [15-24] and [65+] age groups for 1980;
- 1990, extrapolation of 1980 activity rates derived from the EPPA3
and of activity rates derived from the 1987, 1988 and 1989 censuses;
modification of the trends for all age groups.

**2.2.2 Women:**

- 1950-80, 1950-80 activity rates derived from the EPPA3;
modification of the trends for all age groups for 1980;
- 1990, extrapolation of 1980 estimated activity rates and of average of
activity rates derived from the 1987, 1988 and 1989 surveys.

## 3. Estimates of distribution rates by activity sector: 1950 - 1990

### 3.1 Benchmark data:

Table 2: Distribution of economically active population by activity sector

| Year | Agriculture | Industry Total | Manufac. | Services |
|---|---|---|---|---|
| **Men** | | | | |
| 1980 | 10.70 | 45.55 | 16.34 | 43.75 |
| 1989 | 14.81 | 39.69 | 10.73 | 45.50 |
| 1990 | 13.78 | 37.59 | 10.23 | 48.64 |
| 1991 | 13.36 | 39.89 | 11.04 | 46.76 |
| **Women** | | | | |
| 1979 | 7.69 | 26.85 | 15.62 | 65.46 |
| 1980 | 7.88 | 24.49 | 14.48 | 67.63 |
| 1981 | 9.96 | 22.51 | 12.47 | 67.53 |
| 1989 | 6.13 | 16.48 | 9.39 | 77.39 |
| 1990 | 5.25 | 16.32 | 9.80 | 78.43 |
| 1991 | 5.16 | 19.61 | 10.54 | 75.23 |

Source(s): AST75-93.

### 3.2 Method(s): arithmetic average

**3.2.1 Men:**

- 1950-80, 1950-80 distribution rates derived from the EPPA3;
- Application of manufacturing/industry ratio derived from the 1980 survey;
- 1990, averages of distribution rates derived from
the 1989, 1990 and 1991 surveys.

**3.2.2 Women:**

- 1950-70, 1950-70 distribution rates derived from the EPPA3;
- 1980, averages of distribution rates derived from the 1979, 1980
and 1981 surveys;
- 1990, averages of distribution rates derived from the 1989, 1990
and 1991 surveys.

## 4. Projection of activity rates: 2000 - 2010

### 4.1 Model(s): linear, log-linear, hyperbole and logistic

**4.1.1 Men:**

- To the [15-54] age groups, application of function F1;
- To the [55+] age groups, application of function F3;
- Modification of the trends for the [15-54] age groups.

**4.1.2 Women:**

- To the [15-19] and [55+] age groups, application of function F3;
- To the [20-24] age group, application of function F6;
- To the [25-54] age groups, application of function F2.

# Tunisia

## 1. Source(s) of benchmark data

| Code(s): | Title(s): |
|---|---|
| EPPA3 | Economically active population: Estimates and Projections, 1950-2025, Third edition, ILO, Geneva, 1986. |
| R1984 | Recencement général de la population et de l'habitat, 30 mars 1984, Institut National de la Statistique, Tunis, 1984. |
| ASTER | Yearbook of Labour Statistics 1945-89 - Retrospective Edition on Population Censuses, ILO, Geneva, 1990. |
| ADNU88 | Demographic Yearbook 1988 - Population census statistics - Fortieth Edition, United Nations, New York, 1990. |

## 2. Estimates of activity rates: 1950 - 1990

### 2.1 Benchmark data:

Table 1: Activity rates by sex and age group

| Age group | Year 1950 (1) | 1960 (1) | 1970 (1) | 1975 (2) | 1984 (3) |
|---|---|---|---|---|---|
| **Men** | | | | | |
| 10-14 | .. | .. | 18.00 | 17.33 | 0.00 |
| 15-19 | .. | .. | 57.45 | 64.03 | 20.44 |
| 20-24 | .. | .. | 89.40 | 85.39 | 73.25 |
| 25-29 | .. | .. | 97.30 | 99.29 | 95.50 |
| 30-34 | .. | .. | 98.40 | 96.90 | 97.96 |
| 35-39 | .. | .. | 98.30 | 96.90 | 98.76 |
| 40-44 | .. | .. | 97.85 | 99.20 | 98.53 |
| 45-49 | .. | .. | 96.75 | 98.10 | 97.96 |
| 50-54 | .. | .. | 93.60 | 89.70 | 96.83 |
| 55-59 | .. | .. | 86.80 | 68.20 | 94.23 |
| 60-64 | .. | .. | 70.85 | 53.90 | 89.35 |
| 65+ | .. | .. | 49.70 | 38.70 | 40.98 |
| **Women** | | | | | |
| 10-14 | 0.00 | 0.00 | 0.00 | 11.80 | 0.00 |
| 15-19 | 9.45 | 11.80 | 16.50 | 29.50 | 25.18 |
| 20-24 | 8.15 | 10.70 | 15.75 | 27.50 | 38.12 |
| 25-29 | 4.00 | 6.65 | 11.85 | 21.80 | 29.41 |
| 30-34 | 2.40 | 4.80 | 9.50 | 15.00 | 23.66 |
| 35-39 | 2.60 | 4.60 | 8.65 | 14.00 | 18.97 |
| 40-44 | 3.35 | 5.25 | 0.00 | 14.60 | 14.57 |
| 45-49 | 3.00 | 4.95 | 8.90 | 14.10 | 12.87 |
| 50-54 | 3.25 | 4.90 | 8.15 | 11.60 | 11.60 |
| 55-59 | 3.05 | 4.35 | 6.95 | 9.20 | 9.83 |
| 60-64 | 3.25 | 4.00 | 5.45 | 7.00 | 4.43 |
| 65+ | 2.10 | 2.40 | 3.00 | 5.40 | 3.46 |

Source(s): (1) EPPA3; (2) ASTER; (3) ADNU88 and R1984.

### 2.2 Method(s): linear extrapolation

#### 2.2.1 Men:

- 1950-70, 1950-70 activity rates derived from the EPPA3;
- 1980-90, extrapolation of 1970 activity rates derived from the EPPA3 of activity rates derived from the 1975 and 1984 censuses;
modification of the trends of the [15-24] age groups for 1990.

#### 2.2.2 Women:

- 1950-70, 1950-70 adjusted activity rates derived from the EPPA3;
- 1980, weighted average of adjusted activity rates derived from the 1975 and 1984 censuses;
- 1990, extrapolation of adjusted activity rates derived from the 1975 and 1984 censuses;
adjustment of extrapolated rates on the basis of variations in 1980 interpolated rates, in relation to activity rates estimated for 1980;
adjustment of rates to make allowance for the under-registration of women working in agriculture.

## 3. Estimates of distribution rates by activity sector: 1950 - 1990

### 3.1 Benchmark data:

Table 2: Distribution of economically active population by activity sector

| Year | Agriculture | Industry Total | Manufac. | Services |
|---|---|---|---|---|
| **Men** | | | | |
| 1975 (1) | 45.10 | 22.60 | | 32.30 |
| 1984 (2) | 40.73 | 26.17 | 10.33 | 33.10 |
| **Women** | | | | |
| 1975 (1) | 27.10 | 49.56 | 48.73 | 23.34 |
| 1984 (2) | 25.86 | 49.08 | 47.69 | 25.06 |

Source(s): (1) ASTER; (2) R1984.

### 3.2 Method(s): weighted average
linear extrapolation

#### 3.2.1 Men:

- 1950-70, 1950-70 distribution rates derived from the EPPA3;
- 1980, weighted averages of adjusted distribution rates derived from the 1975 and 1984 censuses;
- 1990, extrapolation of distribution rates derived from the 1975 and 1984 censuses;
modification of the trends in all sectors.

#### 3.2.2 Women:

- 1950-70, 1950-70 distribution rates derived from the EPPA3;
- 1980, weighted averages of adjusted distribution rates derived from the 1975 and 1984 censuses;
- 1990, extrapolation of distribution rates derived from the 1975 and 1984 censuses;
modification of the trends in all sectors;
adjustment of rates to make allowance for the under-registration of contributing family workers in agriculture.

## 4. Projection of activity rates: 2000 - 2010

### 4.1 Model(s): linear, log-linear and hyperbole

#### 4.1.1 Men:

- To the [15-19] age group, application of function F2;
- To the [20-59] age groups, application of function F1;
- To the [60+] age groups, application of function F3.

#### 4.1.2 Women:

- To all age groups, application of function F1;
- Modification of the trends for the [15-24] and [50+] age groups.

---

*Notes on adjustments of rates, see p. 3-8.*                    *Notes on projection functions, see p. 10.*

# Turkey

## 1. Source(s) of benchmark data

Code(s):    Title(s):

EPPA3      Economically active population: Estimates and Projections, 1950-2025, Third edition, ILO, Geneva, 1986.
STAT       Database on Labour Statistics, LABORSTA - Bureau of Statistics, ILO, Geneva.

## 2. Estimates of activity rates: 1950 - 1990

### 2.1 Benchmark data:

Table 1: Activity rates by sex and age group

| Age group | Year | |
|---|---|---|
| | 1985 | 1990 |
| **Men** | | |
| 10-14 | 22.67 | 29.40 |
| 15-19 | 68.12 | 66.11 |
| 20-24 | 90.23 | 89.67 |
| 25-29 | 96.48 | 97.45 |
| 30-34 | 97.41 | 98.34 |
| 35-39 | 97.22 | 98.18 |
| 40-44 | 93.72 | 95.63 |
| 45-49 | 87.05 | 88.00 |
| 50-54 | 79.99 | 77.43 |
| 55-59 | 72.16 | 69.12 |
| 60-64 | 62.95 | 60.60 |
| 65+ | 41.73 | 46.05 |
| **Women** | | |
| 10-14 | 22.64 | 22.60 |
| 15-19 | 49.94 | 48.34 |
| 20-24 | 48.18 | 48.27 |
| 25-29 | 43.43 | 43.11 |
| 30-34 | 42.28 | 42.80 |
| 35-39 | 43.33 | 43.43 |
| 40-44 | 46.21 | 43.99 |
| 45-49 | 46.79 | 44.21 |
| 50-54 | 48.18 | 44.77 |
| 55-59 | 44.88 | 44.33 |
| 60-64 | 39.84 | 39.25 |
| 65+ | 23.17 | 27.97 |

Source(s): STAT.

### 2.2 Method(s):  weighted average

**2.2.1 Men:**

- 1950-80, 1950-80 activity rates derived from the EPPA3;
- 1990, weighted average of activity rates derived from
the 1985 and 1990 censuses.

**2.2.2 Women:**

Method, hypothesis and treatment identical to those used for men.

## 3. Estimates of distribution rates  by activity sector: 1950 - 1990

### 3.1 Benchmark data:

Table  2: Distribution of economically active population by activity sector

| Year | Agriculture | Industry | | Services |
|---|---|---|---|---|
| | | Total | Manufac. | |
| **Men** | | | | |
| 1975 | 56.40 | 16.85 | 10.90 | 26.75 |
| 1980 | 44.54 | 22.42 | 14.45 | 33.04 |
| 1985 | 43.44 | 21.24 | 14.29 | 35.33 |
| 1990 | 38.02 | 24.23 | 14.96 | 37.75 |
| **Women** | | | | |
| 1975 | 89.31 | 4.33 | 4.19 | 6.36 |
| 1980 | 87.86 | 4.60 | 4.48 | 7.55 |
| 1985 | 86.70 | 4.57 | 4.44 | 8.73 |
| 1990 | 82.27 | 6.89 | 6.68 | 10.84 |

Source(s): STAT.

### 3.2 Method(s):  weighted average

**3.2.1 Men:**

- 1950-70, 1950-70 distribution rates derived from the EPPA3;
- 1980-90, weighted averages of distribution rates derived from
the 1975, 1980, 1985 and 1990 censuses.

**3.2.2 Women:**

Method, hypothesis and treatment identical to those used for men.

## 4. Projection of activity rates: 2000 - 2010

### 4.1 Model(s):  linear and hyperbole

**4.1.1 Men:**

- To the [10-44] age groups, application of function F1;
- To the [45+] age groups, application of function F3;
- Modification of the trends for the [10-14], [30-34] and [40+] age groups.

**4.1.2 Women:**

- To the [10-14] age group, application of function F1;
- To the [15+] age groups, application of function F3;
- Modification of the trends for the [10-14] and [20+] age groups.

Notes on  adjustments of rates, see p. 3-8.

Notes on  projection functions, see p. 10.

# Turkmenistan

## 1. Source(s) of benchmark data

Code(s):     Title(s):

BLT-94-2     Vorobiev A. (1994), "Estimates of the economically active population for the fifteen countries of the former USSR
             for the years 1950, 1959, 1970, 1979 and 1989", in the Bulletin of Labour of Statistics - 1994-2, ILO, Geneva.

## 2. Estimates of activity rates: 1950 - 1990

### 2.1 Benchmark data:

Table 1: Activity rates by sex and age group

| Age group | Year 1950 | 1959 | 1970 | 1979 | 1989 |
|---|---|---|---|---|---|
| **Men** | | | | | |
| 10-14 | 0.00 | 0.00 | 0.00 | 0.00 | 0.00 |
| 15-19 | 50.75 | 52.38 | 42.86 | 41.32 | 35.64 |
| 20-24 | 82.26 | 85.07 | 85.92 | 90.00 | 85.09 |
| 25-29 | 94.29 | 96.77 | 98.25 | 97.98 | 96.84 |
| 30-34 | 93.10 | 96.49 | 98.63 | 98.36 | 98.39 |
| 35-39 | 90.32 | 93.75 | 98.33 | 98.36 | 97.80 |
| 40-44 | 92.59 | 92.31 | 94.74 | 97.01 | 98.08 |
| 45-49 | 91.30 | 93.10 | 96.88 | 98.18 | 98.15 |
| 50-54 | 89.47 | 91.67 | 91.30 | 93.62 | 94.64 |
| 55-59 | 82.35 | 85.00 | 84.62 | 84.00 | 89.13 |
| 60-64 | 66.67 | 68.42 | 50.00 | 35.00 | 40.54 |
| 65+ | 25.00 | 29.41 | 9.52 | 10.42 | 15.22 |
| **Women** | | | | | |
| 10-14 | 0.00 | 0.00 | 0.00 | 0.00 | 0.00 |
| 15-19 | 45.07 | 46.30 | 41.41 | 40.99 | 34.27 |
| 20-24 | 60.87 | 62.32 | 67.65 | 84.85 | 74.55 |
| 25-29 | 62.00 | 66.15 | 92.59 | 88.12 | 77.44 |
| 30-34 | 63.41 | 63.49 | 78.57 | 89.83 | 79.84 |
| 35-39 | 62.50 | 63.04 | 84.48 | 91.53 | 83.16 |
| 40-44 | 62.86 | 62.16 | 81.03 | 90.00 | 80.00 |
| 45-49 | 54.05 | 56.76 | 81.40 | 87.50 | 83.33 |
| 50-54 | 44.00 | 45.16 | 72.73 | 74.07 | 58.62 |
| 55-59 | 28.57 | 26.47 | 29.27 | 30.00 | 27.45 |
| 60-64 | 17.65 | 16.00 | 12.50 | 12.12 | 14.89 |
| 65+ | 4.88 | 4.88 | 3.39 | 4.00 | 4.65 |

Source(s): BLT-94-2-2

### 2.2 Method(s): weighted average

#### 2.2.1 Men:

- 1950-90, weighted average of 1950, 1959, 1970 and 1989 activity rates
derived from the Bulletin of Labour Statistics 1994-2.

#### 2.2.2 Women:

Method, hypothesis and treatment identical to those used for men.

## 3. Estimates of distribution rates by activity sector: 1950 - 1990

### 3.1 Benchmark data:

Table 2: Distribution of economically active population by activity sector

| Year | Agriculture | Industry Total | Manufac. | Services |
|---|---|---|---|---|
| **Men** | | | | |
| 1950 | 58.36 | 17.84 | 9.29 | 23.79 |
| 1959 | 43.84 | 23.21 | 8.60 | 32.95 |
| 1970 | 33.26 | 29.59 | 9.40 | 37.16 |
| 1979 | 32.83 | 31.83 | 8.50 | 35.33 |
| 1989 | 33.76 | 30.04 | 8.34 | 36.20 |
| **Women** | | | | |
| 1950 | 60.91 | 13.64 | 9.55 | 25.45 |
| 1959 | 54.72 | 14.57 | 11.02 | 30.71 |
| 1970 | 43.01 | 17.81 | 10.96 | 39.18 |
| 1979 | 46.48 | 16.67 | 9.07 | 36.85 |
| 1989 | 42.01 | 14.58 | 7.84 | 43.42 |

Source(s): BLT-94-2.

### 3.2 Method(s): weighted average

#### 3.2.1 Men:

- 1950-90, weighted averages of 1950, 1959, 1970, 1979 and 1989
distribution rates derived from the Bulletin of Labour Statistics, 1994-2.

#### 3.2.2 Women:

Method, hypothesis and treatment identical to those used for men.

## 4. Projection of activity rates: 2000 - 2010

### 4.1 Model(s): linear, hyperbole and logistic

#### 4.1.1 Men:

- To the [15-64] age groups, application of function F1;
- To the [65+] age group, application of function F3;
- Modification of the trends for the [20-64] age groups.

#### 4.1.2 Women:

- To the [15-19] age group, application of function F1;
- To the [20-59] age groups, application of function F6;
- To the [60+] age groups, application of function F3;
- Modification of the trends for the [15-54] age groups.

*Notes on adjustments of rates, see p. 3-8.*          *Notes on projection functions, see p. 10.*

# Uganda

## 1. Source(s) of benchmark data

Code(s):    Title(s):

EPPA3    Economically active population: Estimates and Projections, 1950-2025, Third edition, ILO, Geneva, 1986.

## 2. Estimates of activity rates: 1950 - 1990

### 2.1 Benchmark data:

Table 1: Activity rates by sex and age group

| Age group | Year 1950 | 1960 | 1970 | 1980 |
|---|---|---|---|---|
| **Men** | | | | |
| 10-14 | 54.40 | 53.45 | 51.75 | 49.95 |
| 15-19 | 87.95 | 86.70 | 84.45 | 82.05 |
| 20-24 | 96.40 | 95.95 | 95.10 | 94.15 |
| 25-29 | 97.55 | 97.50 | 97.35 | 97.25 |
| 30-34 | 98.30 | 98.25 | 98.10 | 97.95 |
| 35-39 | 98.50 | 98.45 | 98.25 | 98.10 |
| 40-44 | 98.35 | 98.25 | 98.10 | 97.95 |
| 45-49 | 97.55 | 97.50 | 97.35 | 97.20 |
| 50-54 | 97.20 | 97.10 | 96.90 | 96.70 |
| 55-59 | 96.50 | 96.35 | 96.00 | 95.65 |
| 60-64 | 93.90 | 93.55 | 93.00 | 92.45 |
| 65+ | 81.25 | 80.70 | 79.75 | 78.70 |
| **Women** | | | | |
| 10-14 | 41.10 | 40.40 | 39.10 | 37.75 |
| 15-19 | 66.55 | 65.50 | 63.60 | 61.55 |
| 20-24 | 65.80 | 65.10 | 63.90 | 62.65 |
| 25-29 | 71.00 | 70.25 | 68.85 | 67.40 |
| 30-34 | 75.45 | 74.65 | 73.20 | 71.65 |
| 35-39 | 76.55 | 75.80 | 74.45 | 73.00 |
| 40-44 | 79.00 | 78.25 | 76.90 | 75.40 |
| 45-49 | 78.55 | 77.80 | 76.40 | 74.90 |
| 50-54 | 77.45 | 76.55 | 74.95 | 73.20 |
| 55-59 | 74.75 | 73.85 | 72.15 | 70.35 |
| 60-64 | 69.35 | 68.20 | 66.05 | 63.75 |
| 65+ | 49.10 | 48.00 | 46.00 | 43.90 |

Source(s): EPPA3.

### 2.2 Method(s): linears interpolation and extrapolation

#### 2.2.1 Men:

- 1950-80, 1950-80 activity rates derived from the EPPA3;
- 1990, extrapolation of 1950-80 activity rates derived from the EPPA3; adjustment of extrapolated rates on the basis of variations in 1980 interpolated rates, in relation to the 1980 rates derived from the EPPA3.

#### 2.2.2 Women:

- 1950-90, interpolation and extrapolation of 1950 and 1980 adjusted activity rates derived from the EPPA; adjustment of average activity rates based on the men/women ratio in agriculture equal to 1.

## 3. Estimates of distribution rates by activity sector: 1950 - 1990

### 3.1 Benchmark data:

Table 2: Distribution of economically active population by activity sector

| Year | Agriculture | Industry Total | Manufac. | Services |
|---|---|---|---|---|
| **Men** | | | | |
| 1950 | 91.80 | 3.15 | .. | 5.05 |
| 1960 | 90.10 | 3.80 | .. | 6.10 |
| 1970 | 87.00 | 5.00 | .. | 8.00 |
| 1980 | 83.70 | 6.30 | .. | 10.00 |
| **Women** | | | | |
| 1950 | 97.85 | 0.36 | .. | 1.79 |
| 1960 | 95.49 | 0.76 | .. | 3.75 |
| 1970 | 93.13 | 1.16 | .. | 5.71 |
| 1980 | 90.77 | 1.56 | .. | 7.67 |

Source(s): EPPA3.

### 3.2 Method(s): linears interpolation and extrapolation

#### 3.2.1 Men:

- 1950-80, 1950-80 distribution rates derived from the EPPA3;
- 1990, extrapolation of 1950-80 distribution rates derived from the EPPA3; adjustment of extrapolated rates on the basis of variations in 1980 interpolated rates, in relation to 1980 distribution rates derived from the EPPA3;
- Application of manufacturing/industry ratio estimated for Rwanda.

#### 3.2.2 Women:

- 1950-90, interpolation and extrapolation of 1950 and 1980 adjusted distribution rates derived from the EPPA3; adjustment of distribution rates on the basis of men/women ratio equal to 1 in agriculture; distribution rates of manufacturing sector based on manufacturing/industry ratio estimated for Rwanda.

## 4. Projection of activity rates: 2000 - 2010

### 4.1 Model(s): linear and hyperbole

#### 4.1.1 Men:

- To all age groups, application of function F1;
- Modification of the trends for the [10-14] and [20-24] age groups.

#### 4.1.2 Women:

- To the [10-19] age groups, application of function F1;
- To the [20+] age groups, application of function F3;
- Modification of the trends for the [20-54] age groups.

*Notes on adjustments of rates, see p. 3-8.*    *Notes on projection functions, see p. 10.*

# Ukraine

## 1. Source(s) of benchmark data

Code(s):     Title(s):

BLT-94-2     Vorobiev A. (1994), "Estimates of the economically active population for the fifteen countries of the former USSR for the years 1950, 1959, 1970, 1979 and 1989", in the Bulletin of Labour of Statistics - 1994-2, ILO, Geneva.

## 2. Estimates of activity rates: 1950 - 1990

### 2.1 Benchmark data:

Table 1: Activity rates by sex and age group

| Age group | 1959 | 1970 | 1979 | 1989 |
|---|---|---|---|---|
| **Men** | | | | |
| 10-14 | 0.00 | 0.00 | 0.00 | 0.00 |
| 15-19 | 62.57 | 40.71 | 36.28 | 27.71 |
| 20-24 | 86.88 | 85.15 | 86.32 | 79.76 |
| 25-29 | 96.22 | 96.37 | 96.77 | 96.09 |
| 30-34 | 95.77 | 98.14 | 98.30 | 97.77 |
| 35-39 | 93.61 | 97.01 | 98.17 | 97.75 |
| 40-44 | 94.96 | 96.39 | 97.73 | 97.22 |
| 45-49 | 90.91 | 94.09 | 96.14 | 95.41 |
| 50-54 | 87.02 | 88.31 | 88.09 | 89.69 |
| 55-59 | 81.38 | 78.71 | 78.73 | 77.74 |
| 60-64 | 60.29 | 31.11 | 26.29 | 31.69 |
| 65+ | 35.31 | 11.14 | 7.09 | 10.54 |
| **Women** | | | | |
| 10-14 | 0.00 | 0.00 | 0.00 | 0.00 |
| 15-19 | 60.26 | 38.69 | 34.60 | 25.90 |
| 20-24 | 68.94 | 80.86 | 85.71 | 78.18 |
| 25-29 | 84.82 | 94.38 | 94.01 | 89.33 |
| 30-34 | 71.99 | 91.69 | 95.32 | 92.76 |
| 35-39 | 72.27 | 90.01 | 95.94 | 94.47 |
| 40-44 | 72.47 | 91.94 | 95.34 | 94.41 |
| 45-49 | 62.27 | 81.17 | 91.67 | 92.08 |
| 50-54 | 54.22 | 73.68 | 83.91 | 84.18 |
| 55-59 | 31.62 | 21.59 | 24.92 | 28.43 |
| 60-64 | 22.79 | 10.53 | 7.38 | 14.35 |
| 65+ | 2.73 | 0.89 | 1.66 | 3.66 |

Source(s): BLT-94-2.

### 2.2 Method(s): weighted average

#### 2.2.1 Men:

- 1950-70, interpolation and extrapolation of 1950, 1959, 1970, 1979 and 1989 activity rates derived from the Bulletin of Labour Statistics 1994-2; application to interpolated and extrapolated rates, variations in 1990 extrapolated rates, in relation to activity rates derived from the 1989 census.

#### 2.2.2 Women:

Method, hypothesis and treatment identical to those used for men.

## 3. Estimates of distribution rates by activity sector: 1950 - 1990

### 3.1 Benchmark data:

Table 2: Distribution of economically active population by activity sector

| Year | Agriculture | Industry Total | Manufac. | Services |
|---|---|---|---|---|
| **Men** | | | | |
| 1950 | 52.91 | 26.77 | 16.53 | 20.32 |
| 1959 | 39.52 | 32.18 | 18.79 | 28.31 |
| 1970 | 28.74 | 44.50 | 28.65 | 26.76 |
| 1979 | 25.93 | 46.18 | 28.35 | 27.89 |
| 1989 | 23.60 | 45.76 | 28.56 | 30.64 |
| **Women** | | | | |
| 1950 | 66.31 | 14.53 | 10.81 | 19.16 |
| 1959 | 55.74 | 19.32 | 14.18 | 24.94 |
| 1970 | 32.81 | 28.85 | 22.73 | 38.34 |
| 1979 | 23.64 | 32.55 | 26.12 | 43.81 |
| 1989 | 16.20 | 33.51 | 27.37 | 50.29 |

Source(s): BLT-94-2.

### 3.2 Method(s):   data from BLT-94-15

#### 3.2.1 Men:

- 1950, 1960, 1970, 1980 et 1990, respectively 1950, 1959, 1970, 1983 and 1989 distribution rates derived from the Bulletin of Labour Statistics, 1994-

#### 3.2.2 Women:

Method, hypothesis and treatment identical to those used for men.

## 4. Projection of activity rates: 2000 - 2010

### 4.1 Model(s):   linear, hyperbole and logistic

#### 4.1.1 Men:

- To the [15-24] and [55+] age groups, application of function F3;
- To the [25-54] age groups, application of function F1;
- Modification of the trends for the [25-54] age groups.

#### 4.1.2 Women:

- To the [15-19] and [55+] age groups, application of function F3;
- To the [20-54] age groups, application of function F6;
- Modification of the trends for the [20-54] age groups.

*Notes on adjustments of rates, see p. 3-8.*          *Notes on projection functions, see p. 10.*

# United Arab Emirates

## 1. Source(s) of benchmark data

Code(s):     Title(s):
EPPA3       Economically active population: Estimates and Projections, 1950-2025, Third edition, ILO, Geneva, 1986.
STAT        Database on Labour Statistics, LABORSTA - Bureau of Statistics, ILO, Geneva.

## 2. Estimates of activity rates: 1950 - 1990

### 2.1 Benchmark data:

Table 1: Activity rates by sex and age group

| Age group | Year | | |
|---|---|---|---|
| | 1975 | 1980 | 1985 |
| **Men** | | | |
| 10-14 | 12.54 | 0.00 | 0.00 |
| 15-19 | 65.81 | 45.32 | 28.03 |
| 20-24 | 96.38 | 94.57 | 88.88 |
| 25-29 | 99.01 | 99.03 | 98.60 |
| 30-34 | 99.18 | 99.50 | 99.40 |
| 35-39 | 98.88 | 99.38 | 99.46 |
| 40-44 | 98.37 | 99.04 | 99.27 |
| 45-49 | 96.87 | 97.94 | 98.62 |
| 50-54 | 92.05 | 94.39 | 96.24 |
| 55-59 | 86.74 | 90.74 | 91.99 |
| 60-64 | 72.81 | 76.02 | 78.06 |
| 65+ | 31.78 | 27.90 | 25.98 |
| **Women** | | | |
| 10-14 | 0.95 | 0.00 | 0.00 |
| 15-19 | 3.94 | 4.47 | 5.99 |
| 20-24 | 12.12 | 14.63 | 26.43 |
| 25-29 | 16.51 | 21.91 | 30.34 |
| 30-34 | 14.59 | 24.74 | 33.21 |
| 35-39 | 11.73 | 19.41 | 31.34 |
| 40-44 | 9.62 | 18.32 | 27.13 |
| 45-49 | 7.70 | 13.18 | 19.18 |
| 50-54 | 6.54 | 9.47 | 12.61 |
| 55-59 | 4.95 | 5.89 | 6.60 |
| 60-64 | 2.75 | 3.39 | 3.26 |
| 65+ | 1.36 | 1.07 | 0.86 |

Source(s): STAT.

### 2.2 Method(s): linear extrapolation
weighted average

#### 2.2.1 Men:

- 1950-70, 1950-70 activity rates derived from the EPPA3;
- 1980, weighted average of activity rates of 1970 derived from the EPPA3
and of activity rates derived from the 1980 census
- 1990, extrapolation of activity rates derived from the 1980, 1975
and 1985 censuses; adjustment of extrapolated rates on the basis
of variations in 1985 interpolated rates, in relation to activity rates derived from
the 1985 census; modification of the trends for all age groups.

#### 2.2.2 Women:

- 1950-80, 1950-80 activity rates derived from the EPPA3;
- 1990, extrapolation of activity rates derived from
the 1975, 1980 and 1985 censuses;
adjustment of extrapolated rates on the basis of variations
in 1985 interpolated rates, in relation to activity rates derived from
the 1985 census.

## 3. Estimates of distribution rates by activity sector: 1950 - 1990

### 3.1 Benchmark data:

Table 2: Distribution of economically active population by activity sector

| Year | Agriculture | Industry | | Services |
|---|---|---|---|---|
| | | Total | Manufac. | |
| **Men** | | | | |
| 1975 | 4.76 | 43.98 | 6.08 | 51.26 |
| 1980 | 4.83 | 39.81 | 6.51 | 55.35 |
| 1985 | 8.43 | 30.86 | 8.13 | 60.72 |
| **Women** | | | | |
| 1975 | 0.32 | 5.80 | 1.06 | 93.88 |
| 1980 | 0.08 | 6.71 | 1.48 | 93.21 |
| 1985 | 0.06 | 3.32 | 1.05 | 96.62 |

Source(s): STAT.

### 3.2 Method(s): linear extrapolation

#### 3.2.1 Men:

- 1950-80, 1950-80 distribution rates derived from the EPPA3;
adjustment of 1970 rates on the basis of the results of the 1975 census;
- 1990, extrapolation of distribution rates derived from the 1980
and 1985 censuses;
modification of the trends in all sectors.

#### 3.2.2 Women:

- 1950-80, 1950-80 distribution rates derived from the EPPA3;
- 1990, extrapolation of distribution rates derived from
the 1980 and 1985 censuses;
modification of the trends in all sectors.

## 4. Projection of activity rates: 2000 - 2010

### 4.1 Model(s): linear, log-linear and hyperbole

#### 4.1.1 Men:

- To the [15-19] age group, application of function F2;
- To the [20-59] age groups, application of function F1;
- To the [60+] age groups, application of function F3;
- Modification of the trends for the [20-59] age groups.

#### 4.1.2 Women:

- To the [15+] age groups, application of function F1;
- Modification of the trend for the [15-19] age group.

---

*Notes on adjustments of rates, see p. 3-8.*          *Notes on projection functions, see p. 10.*

# United Kingdom

## 1. Source(s) of benchmark data

Code(s):     Title(s):

EPPA3       Yearbook of Labour Statistics 1945-89 - Retrospective Edition on Population Censuses, ILO, Geneva, 1990.
STAT        Database on Labour Statistics, LABORSTA - Bureau of Statistics, ILO, Geneva.

## 2. Estimates of activity rates: 1950 - 1990

### 2.1 Benchmark data:

Table 1: Activity rates by sex and age group

| Age group | Year 1950 (1) | 1960 (1) | 1970 (1) | 1980 (1) | 1991 (2) |
|---|---|---|---|---|---|
| **Men** | | | | | |
| 10-14 | 0.10 | 0.05 | 0.00 | 0.00 | 0.00 |
| 15-19 | 87.25 | 77.95 | 68.60 | 59.25 | 68.20 |
| 20-24 | 95.40 | 93.65 | 91.85 | 90.10 | 71.55 |
| 25-29 | 98.15 | 97.60 | 97.10 | 96.60 | 95.34 |
| 30-34 | 99.20 | 98.65 | 98.10 | 97.55 | 95.65 |
| 35-39 | 99.35 | 98.75 | 98.10 | 97.50 | 95.31 |
| 40-44 | 99.15 | 98.70 | 98.20 | 97.75 | 94.86 |
| 45-49 | 99.10 | 98.45 | 97.75 | 97.10 | 93.39 |
| 50-54 | 98.60 | 97.55 | 96.45 | 95.40 | 89.23 |
| 55-59 | 97.35 | 95.50 | 93.65 | 91.75 | 79.82 |
| 60-64 | 93.60 | 87.40 | 81.20 | 75.00 | 56.67 |
| 65+ | 34.40 | 26.60 | 18.80 | 11.00 | 8.04 |
| **Women** | | | | | |
| 10-14 | 0.10 | 0.05 | 0.05 | 0.00 | 0.00 |
| 15-19 | 80.75 | 71.65 | 62.50 | 53.35 | 61.36 |
| 20-24 | 64.85 | 64.75 | 64.65 | 64.55 | 59.08 |
| 25-29 | 39.55 | 44.25 | 49.00 | 53.70 | 69.09 |
| 30-34 | 26.85 | 36.50 | 46.15 | 55.80 | 65.19 |
| 35-39 | 28.70 | 39.30 | 49.90 | 60.45 | 70.40 |
| 40-44 | 28.50 | 41.45 | 54.40 | 67.35 | 75.24 |
| 45-49 | 29.60 | 42.40 | 55.15 | 67.95 | 74.21 |
| 50-54 | 28.20 | 40.45 | 52.75 | 65.00 | 66.85 |
| 55-59 | 24.60 | 35.00 | 45.45 | 55.85 | 52.61 |
| 60-64 | 15.00 | 18.20 | 21.45 | 24.70 | 22.01 |
| 65+ | 6.05 | 5.40 | 4.75 | 4.15 | 2.95 |

Source(s): (1) EPPA3; (2) STAT.

### 2.2 Method(s): linear interpolation

#### 2.2.1 Men:

- 1950-80, 1950-80 activity rates derived from the EPPA3;
- 1990, interpolation of 1980 activity rates derived from the EPPA3
and of activity rates derived from the 1991 survey;
modification of the trends of the [10-19] age groups.

#### 2.2.2 Women:

Method, hypothesis and treatment identical to those used for men.

## 3. Estimates of distribution rates by activity sector: 1950 - 1990

### 3.1 Benchmark data:

Table 2: Distribution of economically active population by activity sector

| Year | Agriculture | Industry Total | Manufac. | Services |
|---|---|---|---|---|
| **Men** | | | | |
| 1979 | 3.38 | 48.36 | 33.98 | 48.26 |
| 1980 | 3.51 | 47.58 | 33.05 | 48.91 |
| 1981 | 3.24 | 47.40 | 26.75 | 49.36 |
| 1990 | 3.02 | 39.27 | 25.67 | 57.71 |
| **Women** | | | | |
| 1979 | 1.22 | 23.52 | 21.57 | 75.26 |
| 1980 | 1.37 | 22.49 | 20.47 | 76.14 |
| 1981 | 0.98 | 22.19 | 17.51 | 76.83 |
| 1990 | 1.01 | 15.33 | 12.93 | 83.67 |

Source(s): (1) STAT.

### 3.2 Method(s): national data

#### 3.2.1 Men:

- 1950-80, 1950-80 distribution rates derived from the EPPA3;
1980 distribution rates of manufacturing sector has been adjusted on the basis
of application to 1980 distribution rates in industry sector, average of
manufacturing/industry ratio derived from the 1979 and 1980 official
estimates and from the 1981 census;
- 1990, distribution rates derived from the 1990 official estimates.

#### 3.2.2 Women:

Method, hypothesis and treatment identical to those used for men.

## 4. Projection of activity rates: 2000 - 2010

### 4.1 Model(s): linear, hyperbole and logistic

#### 4.1.1 Men:

- To the [15-29] and [55+] age groups, application of function F1;
- To the [30-54] age groups, application of function F3;
- Modification of the trends for the [15-44] and [55-64] age groups.

#### 4.1.2 Women:

- To the [15-19] and [55-64] age groups, application of function F1;
- To the [20-54] age groups, application of function F6;
- To the [65+] age group, application of function F3;
- Modification of the trends for the [15-29] and [55-64] age groups.

*Notes on adjustments of rates, see p. 3-8.*

*Notes on projection functions, see p. 10.*

# United States

## 1. Source(s) of benchmark data

Code(s):     Title(s):

EPPA3        Economically active population: Estimates and Projections, 1950-2025, Third edition, ILO, Geneva, 1986.
STAT         Database on Labour Statistics, LABORSTA - Bureau of Statistics, ILO, Geneva.

## 2. Estimates of activity rates: 1950 - 1990

### 2.1 Benchmark data:

Table 1: Activity rates by sex and age group

| Age group | Year 1989 | 1990 | 1991 |
|---|---|---|---|
| **Men** | | | |
| 10-14 | 0.00 | 0.00 | 0.00 |
| 15-19 | 45.50 | 44.52 | 40.62 |
| 20-24 | 79.61 | 84.30 | 74.37 |
| 25-29 | 89.56 | 93.80 | 89.32 |
| 30-34 | 91.84 | 94.60 | 93.03 |
| 35-39 | 92.25 | 94.90 | 92.99 |
| 40-44 | 92.18 | 93.90 | 90.66 |
| 45-49 | 91.61 | 92.30 | 93.02 |
| 50-54 | 88.44 | 88.80 | 89.02 |
| 55-59 | 78.75 | 79.80 | 79.65 |
| 60-64 | 54.14 | 55.50 | 55.15 |
| 65+ | 15.96 | | 15.55 |
| **Women** | | | |
| 10-14 | 0.00 | 0.00 | 0.00 |
| 15-19 | 43.78 | 41.40 | 39.78 |
| 20-24 | 72.01 | 71.60 | 68.37 |
| 25-29 | 73.41 | 73.80 | 73.48 |
| 30-34 | 72.69 | 73.40 | 73.66 |
| 35-39 | 74.67 | 75.50 | 75.73 |
| 40-44 | 76.79 | 77.60 | 76.74 |
| 45-49 | 74.28 | 74.80 | 76.96 |
| 50-54 | 65.75 | 66.90 | 68.88 |
| 55-59 | 54.50 | 55.30 | 56.49 |
| 60-64 | 35.23 | 35.50 | 35.14 |
| 65+ | 7.79 | ... | 7.97 |

Source(s): STAT.

### 2.2 Method(s): arithmetic average

#### 2.2.1 Men:

- 1950-80, 1950-80 activity rates derived from the EPPA3;
- 1990, weighted average of activity rates derived from
the 1989, 1990 and 1991 surveys;
adjustment of activity rates to make allowance for armed forces.

#### 2.2.2 Women:

Method, hypothesis and treatment identical to those used for men.

## 3. Estimates of distribution rates by activity sector: 1950 - 1990

### 3.1 Benchmark data:

Table 2: Distribution of economically active population by activity sector

| Year | Agriculture | Industry Total | Manufac. | Services |
|---|---|---|---|---|
| **Men** | | | | |
| 1989 | 3.99 | 35.12 | 21.61 | 60.89 |
| 1990 | 3.96 | 34.98 | 21.28 | 61.06 |
| 1991 | 4.09 | 33.70 | 20.83 | 62.20 |
| **Women** | | | | |
| 1989 | 1.38 | 15.61 | 13.54 | 83.01 |
| 1990 | 1.35 | 15.13 | 13.09 | 83.53 |
| 1991 | 1.34 | 14.85 | 12.86 | 83.81 |

Source(s): STAT.

### 3.2 Method(s): arithmetic average

#### 3.2.1 Men:

- 1950-70, 1950-70 distribution rates derived from the EPPA3;
- 1990, averages of distribution rates derived from
the 1989, 1990 and 1991 surveys.

#### 3.2.2 Women:

Method, hypothesis and treatment identical to those used for men.

## 4. Projection of activity rates: 2000 - 2010

### 4.1 Model(s): linear, hyperbole and logistic

#### 4.1.1 Men:

- To the [15-19] age group, application of function F1;
- To the [20+] age groups, application of function F3;
- Modification of the trends for the [15-19] and [25-54] age groups.

#### 4.1.2 Women:

- To the [15-64] age groups, application of function F6;
- To the [65+] age group, application of function F3;
- Modification of the trends for the [15-64] age groups.

*Notes on adjustments of rates, see p. 3-8.*     *Notes on projection functions, see p. 10.*

# Uruguay

## 1. Source(s) of benchmark data

| Code(s): | Title(s): |
|---|---|
| EPPA3 | Economically active population: Estimates and Projections, 1950-2025, Third edition, ILO, Geneva, 1986. |
| STAT | Database on Labour Statistics, LABORSTA - Bureau of Statistics, ILO, Geneva. |

## 2. Estimates of activity rates: 1950 - 1990

### 2.1 Benchmark data:

Table 1: Activity rates by sex and age group

| Age group | Year 1975 (1) | 1975 (2) | 1985 (1) | 1985 (2) | 1991 (1) | 1992 (1) | 1993 (1) |
|---|---|---|---|---|---|---|---|
| **Men** | | | | | | | |
| 10-14 | ... | ... | ... | ... | 2.16 | 1.97 | 3.15 |
| 15-19 | 56.50 | 81.50 | 55.04 | 79.64 | 56.69 | 57.05 | 54.18 |
| 20-24 | 88.80 | 92.50 | 86.50 | 95.30 | 88.52 | 88.76 | 88.25 |
| 25-29 | 95.10 | 94.50 | 95.40 | 97.00 | 97.17 | 96.63 | 96.77 |
| 30-34 | 97.20 | 95.90 | 96.70 | 97.00 | 97.32 | 98.10 | 97.54 |
| 35-39 | 97.20 | 96.60 | 96.50 | 96.70 | 98.02 | 97.44 | 97.45 |
| 40-44 | 96.50 | 96.70 | 96.00 | 96.60 | 97.28 | 97.81 | 97.50 |
| 45-49 | 94.50 | 96.00 | 93.50 | 95.20 | 96.90 | 97.40 | 96.33 |
| 50-54 | 89.10 | 94.30 | 87.30 | 94.50 | 94.06 | 94.09 | 92.64 |
| 55-59 | 78.10 | 90.90 | 78.00 | 81.40 | 87.67 | 87.42 | 86.85 |
| 60-64 | 54.30 | 75.50 | 48.20 | 70.20 | 59.12 | 60.41 | 56.11 |
| 65+ | 17.70 | 35.90 | 13.90 | 33.50 | 17.75 | 17.38 | 16.21 |
| **Women** | | | | | | | |
| 10-14 | ... | ... | ... | ... | 1.00 | 1.01 | 1.84 |
| 15-19 | 27.80 | 23.80 | 23.76 | 23.09 | 31.26 | 33.01 | 32.98 |
| 20-24 | 45.00 | 26.50 | 49.60 | 32.30 | 66.60 | 68.39 | 67.61 |
| 25-29 | 45.00 | 24.40 | 55.50 | 31.30 | 67.82 | 71.43 | 70.59 |
| 30-34 | 43.50 | 21.70 | 54.10 | 32.20 | 68.68 | 71.60 | 71.62 |
| 35-39 | 43.30 | 19.80 | 53.60 | 32.10 | 69.75 | 73.00 | 71.25 |
| 40-44 | 41.20 | 20.60 | 52.20 | 29.90 | 66.82 | 69.89 | 67.21 |
| 45-49 | 37.30 | 20.30 | 48.80 | 28.60 | 61.36 | 65.93 | 64.77 |
| 50-54 | 31.10 | 17.90 | 38.30 | 26.10 | 54.49 | 56.30 | 55.22 |
| 55-59 | 22.60 | 14.90 | 26.50 | 19.80 | 37.00 | 36.47 | 37.73 |
| 60-64 | 12.40 | 10.00 | 13.40 | 11.40 | 21.50 | 21.05 | 20.83 |
| 65+ | 3.50 | 4.10 | 3.60 | 4.90 | 5.75 | 6.30 | 5.82 |

Note(s): (1) Urban; (2) Rural.
Source(s): STAT.

### 2.2 Method(s): weighted average
linears interpolation and extrapolation

#### 2.2.1 Men:

- 1950-70, 1950-70 activity rates derived from the EPPA3;
- 1980-90, weighted average of activity rates estimated separately for the urban and rural areas; for the urban areas, the rate estimates were obtained on the basis of interpolation of adjusted activity rates derived from the 1975 and 1985 censuses and of average of activity rates derived from the 1991, 1992 and 1993 surveys; for rural areas, the rate estimates were obtained on the basis of interpolation and extrapolation of activity rates derived from 1975 and 1985 censuses.

#### 2.2.2 Women:

Method, hypothesis and treatment identical to those used for men.

## 3. Estimates of distribution rates by activity sector: 1950 - 1990

### 3.1 Benchmark data:

Table 2: Distribution of economically active population by activity sector

| Year | Agriculture | Industry Total | Manufac. | Services |
|---|---|---|---|---|
| **Men** | | | | |
| 1975 (1) | 23.09 | 30.41 | 19.84 | 46.50 |
| 1985 (1) | 21.64 | 30.83 | 19.74 | 47.53 |
| 1985 (2) | 8.13 | 35.93 | 23.09 | 55.94 |
| 1991 (2) | 7.02 | 33.21 | 21.97 | 59.77 |
| 1992 (2) | 7.12 | 36.20 | 22.36 | 56.68 |
| **Women** | | | | |
| 1975 (1) | 3.61 | 23.93 | 23.09 | 72.46 |
| 1985 (1) | 4.00 | 21.30 | 20.27 | 74.70 |
| 1985 (2) | 1.07 | 21.36 | 20.32 | 77.57 |
| 1991 (2) | 1.13 | 22.23 | 21.98 | 76.64 |
| 1992 (2) | 1.07 | 20.89 | 19.82 | 78.04 |

Note(s): (1) Total; (2) Urban.
Source(s): STAT.

### 3.2 Method(s): weighted average

#### 3.2.1 Men:

- 1950-60, 1950-60 distribution rates derived from the EPPA3;
- 1980, weighted averages of distribution rates derived from the 1975 and 1985 censuses;
- 1990, weighted averages of estimated distribution rates separately for urban and rural areas; estimated rates on the basis of the results of the 1985 census and of the 1991 and 1992 surveys.

#### 3.2.2 Women:

Method, hypothesis and treatment identical to those used for men.

## 4. Projection of activity rates: 2000 - 2010

### 4.1 Model(s): linear, hyperbole and logistic

#### 4.1.1 Men:

- To the [10-14] age group, application of function F1;
- To the [15+] age groups, application of function F3;
- Modification of the trends for the [15-19] and [25-49] age groups.

#### 4.1.2 Women:

- To the [10-14] age group, application of function F1;
- To the [15-19] and [65+] age groups, application of function F3;
- Modification of the trends for the [10-19] and [65+] age groups.

---

*Notes on adjustments of rates, see p. 3-8.*

*Notes on projection functions, see p. 10.*

# Uzbekistan

## 1. Source(s) of benchmark data

Code(s):  Title(s):

BLT-94-2  Vorobiev A. (1994), "Estimates of the economically active population for the fifteen countries of the former USSR for the years 1950, 1959, 1970, 1979 and 1989", in the Bulletin of Labour of Statistics - 1994-2, ILO, Geneva.

## 2. Estimates of activity rates: 1950 - 1990

### 2.1 Benchmark data:

Table 1: Activity rates by sex and age group

| Age group | Year | | | | |
|---|---|---|---|---|---|
| | 1950 | 1959 | 1970 | 1979 | 1989 |
| **Men** | | | | | |
| 10-14 | 0.00 | 0.00 | 0.00 | 0.00 | 0.00 |
| 15-19 | 53.02 | 52.08 | 37.13 | 37.18 | 28.81 |
| 20-24 | 81.94 | 82.34 | 80.50 | 84.52 | 80.02 |
| 25-29 | 94.80 | 95.99 | 94.75 | 97.00 | 95.96 |
| 30-34 | 95.62 | 95.77 | 97.50 | 98.42 | 97.84 |
| 35-39 | 95.57 | 96.13 | 98.46 | 98.54 | 97.82 |
| 40-44 | 94.19 | 93.28 | 96.13 | 98.10 | 97.55 |
| 45-49 | 91.45 | 92.20 | 97.56 | 97.36 | 96.23 |
| 50-54 | 88.11 | 89.93 | 90.57 | 93.21 | 92.57 |
| 55-59 | 83.33 | 86.36 | 82.54 | 82.17 | 84.59 |
| 60-64 | 71.13 | 72.36 | 45.19 | 30.21 | 34.72 |
| 65+ | 30.91 | 29.25 | 10.33 | 6.97 | 10.60 |
| **Women** | | | | | |
| 10-14 | 0.00 | 0.00 | 0.00 | 0.00 | 0.00 |
| 15-19 | 50.76 | 56.86 | 42.55 | 41.42 | 32.53 |
| 20-24 | 72.22 | 78.79 | 78.67 | 86.41 | 75.60 |
| 25-29 | 68.56 | 67.62 | 86.99 | 93.03 | 81.12 |
| 30-34 | 67.19 | 67.61 | 83.72 | 93.23 | 83.33 |
| 35-39 | 68.18 | 69.51 | 88.24 | 93.29 | 85.49 |
| 40-44 | 59.04 | 62.92 | 84.29 | 92.96 | 85.31 |
| 45-49 | 53.21 | 54.40 | 80.89 | 90.42 | 81.49 |
| 50-54 | 40.66 | 41.67 | 97.86 | 68.46 | 52.44 |
| 55-59 | 26.58 | 25.96 | 27.23 | 24.77 | 20.95 |
| 60-64 | 13.74 | 11.98 | 9.14 | 8.00 | 11.57 |
| 65+ | 4.64 | 4.56 | 2.80 | 2.04 | 3.65 |

Source(s): BLT-94-2-2

### 2.2 Method(s): weighted average

#### 2.2.1 Men:

- 1950-90, weighted average of 1950, 1959, 1970 and 1989 activity rates derived from the Bulletin of Labour Statistics 1994-2.

#### 2.2.2 Women:

Method, hypothesis and treatment identical to those used for men.

## 3. Estimates of distribution rates by activity sector: 1950 - 1990

### 3.1 Benchmark data:

Table 2: Distribution of economically active population by activity sector

| Year | Agriculture | Industry | | Services |
|---|---|---|---|---|
| | | Total | Manufac. | |
| **Men** | | | | |
| 1950 | 70.22 | 12.57 | 11.13 | 17.21 |
| 1959 | 53.44 | 20.23 | 9.21 | 26.34 |
| 1970 | 38.72 | 28.36 | 14.79 | 32.93 |
| 1979 | 34.60 | 34.44 | 12.76 | 30.96 |
| 1989 | 34.49 | 30.67 | 12.11 | 34.84 |
| **Women** | | | | |
| 1950 | 73.71 | 10.26 | 9.58 | 16.03 |
| 1959 | 65.99 | 13.16 | 9.80 | 20.85 |
| 1970 | 50.57 | 17.32 | 12.83 | 32.12 |
| 1979 | 47.01 | 18.68 | 11.50 | 34.31 |
| 1989 | 36.98 | 19.19 | 12.51 | 43.83 |

Source(s): BLT-94-2.

### 3.2 Method(s): weighted average

#### 3.2.1 Men:
- 1950-90, weighted averages of 1950, 1959, 1970, 1979 and 1989 distribution rates derived from the Bulletin of Labour Statistics, 1994-2.

#### 3.2.2 Women:

Method, hypothesis and treatment identical to those used for men.

## 4. Projection of activity rates: 2000 - 2010

### 4.1 Model(s): linear, log-linear, hyperbole and logistic

#### 4.1.1 Men:

- To the [15-24] and [55+] age groups, application of function F3;
- To the [25-54] age groups, application of function F1;
- Modification of the trends for the [25-64] age groups.

#### 4.1.2 Women:

- To the [15-19] age group, application of function F2;
- To the [20-24] and [55+] age groups, application of function F3;
- To the [25-54] age groups, application of function F6;
- Modification of the trends for the [20-59] age groups.

*Notes on adjustments of rates, see p. 3-8.*   *Notes on projection functions, see p. 10.*

# Venezuela

## 1. Source(s) of benchmark data

| Code(s): | Title(s): |
|---|---|
| EPPA3 | Economically active population: Estimates and Projections, 1950-2025, Third edition, ILO, Geneva, 1986. |
| ADNU84 | Demographic Yearbook 1984 - Population census statistics II - Thirty-sixth Edition, United Nations, New York, 1986. |
| ASTER | Yearbook of Labour Statistics 1945-89 - Retrospective Edition on Population Censuses, ILO, Geneva, 1990. |
| AST91-93 | Editions 1991-1993 of ILO Yearbook of Labour Statistics, Geneva. |

## 2. Estimates of activity rates: 1950 - 1990

### 2.1 Benchmark data:

Table 1: Activity rates by sex and age group

| Age group | Year 1971 (1) | 1981 (2) | 1990 (3) |
|---|---|---|---|
| **Men** | | | |
| 10-14 | 0.00 | 5.30 | .. |
| 15-19 | 50.20 | 47.32 | .. |
| 20-24 | 81.85 | 80.88 | .. |
| 25-29 | 93.58 | 91.15 | .. |
| 30-34 | 95.99 | 93.54 | .. |
| 35-39 | 96.40 | 93.87 | .. |
| 40-44 | 95.74 | 93.47 | .. |
| 45-49 | 94.91 | 91.23 | .. |
| 50-54 | 91.39 | 87.68 | .. |
| 55-59 | 87.24 | 81.16 | .. |
| 60-64 | 63.38 | 70.03 | .. |
| 65+ | 50.14 | 41.94 | .. |
| **Women** | | | |
| 10-14 | 0.00 | 1.69 | 0.00 |
| 15-19 | 20.30 | 18.47 | 17.86 |
| 20-24 | 29.40 | 35.78 | 35.80 |
| 25-29 | 29.50 | 39.50 | 42.46 |
| 30-34 | 26.80 | 39.85 | 46.17 |
| 35-39 | 25.00 | 39.02 | 46.02 |
| 40-44 | 23.80 | 35.66 | 43.76 |
| 45-49 | 20.00 | 28.88 | 37.78 |
| 50-54 | 17.00 | 23.35 | 28.78 |
| 55-59 | 13.50 | 16.56 | 20.26 |
| 60-64 | 9.80 | 10.73 | 12.66 |
| 65+ | 5.80 | 5.46 | 6.00 |

Source(s): (1) ASTER; (2) ADNU84 and ASTER; (3) AST91-93.

### 2.2 Method(s): linears interpolation and extrapolation weighted average

**2.2.1 Men:**

- 1950-60, 1950-60 activity rates derived from the EPPA3;
- 1970, weighted average of 1960 activity rates derived from the EPPA3 and of adjusted activity rates derived from the 1971 census;
- 1980, interpolation of adjusted rates derived from the 1971 and 1981 censuses;
- 1990, extrapolation of 1950-60 rates derived from the EPPA3 and of activity rates estimated for 1970 and 1980; adjustment of extrapolated rates on the basis of variations in 1980 estimated rates, in relation to 1980 extrapolated rates.

**2.2.2 Women:**

- 1950-70, 1950-70 adjusted activity rates derived from the EPPA3;
- 1980, weighted average of activity rates derived from the 1971 and 1981 censuses;
- 1990, weighted average of activity rates derived from the 1981 and 1990 censuses.

## 3. Estimates of distribution rates by activity sector: 1950 - 1990

### 3.1 Benchmark data:

Table 2: Distribution of economically active population by activity sector

| Year | Agriculture | Industry Total | Manufac. | Services |
|---|---|---|---|---|
| **Men** | | | | |
| 1981 | 17.48 | 32.76 | 16.74 | 49.75 |
| 1989 | 17.31 | 31.49 | 17.20 | 51.20 |
| 1990 | 16.56 | 32.06 | 16.93 | 51.38 |
| 1991 | 15.95 | 33.00 | 17.48 | 51.05 |
| **Women** | | | | |
| 1981 | 1.70 | 16.04 | 12.91 | 82.27 |
| 1989 | 1.82 | 17.19 | 15.30 | 80.99 |
| 1990 | 1.94 | 16.04 | 14.00 | 82.02 |
| 1991 | 1.79 | 16.48 | 14.31 | 81.72 |

Source(s): AST91-93.

### 3.2 Method(s): arithmetic average

**3.2.1 Men:**

- 1950-70, 1950-70 distribution rates derived from the EPPA3;
- 1980-90, averages of distribution rates derived from the 1981 census and of averages of distribution rates derived from the 1989, 1990 and 1991 surveys.

**3.2.2 Women:**

Method, hypothesis and treatment identical to those used for men.

## 4. Projection of activity rates: 2000 - 2010

### 4.1 Model(s): hyperbole, exponential and logistic

**4.1.1 Men:**

- To the [15+] age groups, application of function F3;
- Modification of the trends for the [20-24] and [30-59] age groups.

**4.1.2 Women:**

- To the [15-19] and [55+] age groups, application of function F3;
- To the [20-24] age group, application of function F4;
- To the [25-54] age groups, application of function F6;
- Modification of the trend for the [20-24] age group.

---

*Notes on adjustments of rates, see p. 3-8.*

*Notes on projection functions, see p. 10.*

# Viet Nam

## 1. Source(s) of benchmark data

Code(s):    Title(s):

EPPA3    Economically active population: Estimates and Projections, 1950-2025, Third edition, ILO, Geneva, 1986.
STAT    Database on Labour Statistics, LABORSTA - Bureau of Statistics, ILO, Geneva.
EPPA4    Economically active population 1950-2010 - Fourth edition, ILO, Geneva 1996.

## 2. Estimates of activity rates: 1950 - 1990

### 2.1 Benchmark data:

Table 1: Activity rates by sex and age group

| Age group | Year 1950 (1) | 1960 (1) | 1970 (1) | 1980 (1) | 1989 (2) |
|---|---|---|---|---|---|
| **Men** | | | | | |
| 10-14 | 52.00 | 46.00 | 40.00 | 30.00 | 11.73 |
| 15-19 | 87.10 | 83.70 | 80.30 | 74.70 | 67.42 |
| 20-24 | 96.90 | 96.90 | 96.90 | 96.80 | 94.36 |
| 25-29 | 98.75 | 98.75 | 98.75 | 98.70 | 97.41 |
| 30-34 | 98.95 | 98.95 | 98.95 | 98.90 | 97.26 |
| 35-39 | 99.00 | 99.00 | 99.00 | 98.90 | 95.70 |
| 40-44 | 98.90 | 98.85 | 98.80 | 98.75 | 91.78 |
| 45-49 | 97.75 | 97.70 | 97.60 | 97.55 | 86.92 |
| 50-54 | 95.60 | 94.65 | 93.70 | 92.00 | 81.21 |
| 55-59 | 91.70 | 89.80 | 87.90 | 84.30 | 70.86 |
| 60-64 | 81.65 | 77.80 | 73.95 | 66.30 | 53.04 |
| 65+ | 56.00 | 50.45 | 44.90 | 34.00 | 27.19 |
| **Women** | | | | | |
| 10-14 | 43.00 | 40.00 | 38.00 | 31.00 | 14.82 |
| 15-19 | 72.40 | 73.90 | 75.40 | 78.60 | 73.33 |
| 20-24 | 82.30 | 84.20 | 86.10 | 89.60 | 88.75 |
| 25-29 | 79.90 | 82.20 | 83.70 | 87.40 | 89.26 |
| 30-34 | 78.00 | 80.90 | 83.00 | 87.10 | 88.11 |
| 35-39 | 77.80 | 80.00 | 82.20 | 86.60 | 86.90 |
| 40-44 | 75.50 | 77.10 | 78.70 | 81.90 | 83.92 |
| 45-49 | 64.70 | 65.90 | 67.10 | 69.50 | 78.67 |
| 50-54 | 47.10 | 47.90 | 48.70 | 50.20 | 69.42 |
| 55-59 | 36.10 | 35.50 | 34.90 | 33.50 | 54.22 |
| 60-64 | 25.50 | 23.70 | 21.90 | 18.40 | 35.54 |
| 65+ | 9.95 | 8.90 | 7.85 | 5.70 | 13.14 |

Note(s): (1) China.
Source(s): (1) EPPA4; (2) STAT.

### 2.2 Method(s): linears interpolation and extrapolation

#### 2.2.1 Men:

- 1950-90, interpolation and extrapolation of 1980-90 activity rates
estimated for China;
application to 1950-80 activity rates estimated for China,
variations in 1989 interpolated rates, in relation to adjusted activity rates
derived from the 1989 census.

#### 2.2.2 Women:

Method, hypothesis and treatment identical to those used for men.

## 3. Estimates of distribution rates by activity sector: 1950 - 1990

### 3.1 Benchmark data:

Table 2: Distribution of economically active population by activity sector

| Year | Agriculture | Industry Total | Manufac. | Services |
|---|---|---|---|---|
| **Men** | | | | |
| 1950 (1) | 86.00 | 5.00 | .. | 9.00 |
| 1960 (1) | 81.00 | 6.50 | .. | 12.50 |
| 1970 (1) | 75.00 | 12.00 | .. | 13.00 |
| 1989 (2) | 69.53 | 17.11 | 13.89 | 13.36 |
| **Women** | | | | |
| 1950 (1) | 92.00 | 4.00 | .. | 4.00 |
| 1960 (1) | 86.50 | 6.00 | .. | 7.50 |
| 1970 (1) | 83.00 | 7.50 | .. | 9.50 |
| 1989 (2) | 73.15 | 10.84 | 9.77 | 16.02 |

Source(s): (1) EPPA3; (2) STAT.

### 3.2 Method(s): rapport proportionnel

#### 3.2.1 Men:
- 1950-70, 1950-70 distribution rates derived from the EPPA3;
- 1980-90, application to distribution rates of agriculture sector derived from
the 1989 census, the same variations in distribution rates estimated
for China for 1980 and 1990; distribution rates of industry and manufacturing
and services sectors estimated on the basis of composition by sector
derived from the 1989 census.

#### 3.2.2 Women:

Method, hypothesis and treatment identical to those used for men.

## 4. Projection of activity rates: 2000 - 2010

### 4.1 Model(s): linear and hyperbole

#### 4.1.1 Men:

- To the [10-34] and [65+] age groups, application of function F1;
- To the [35-64] age groups, application of function F3;
- Modification of the trends for the [15-34] and [65+] age groups.

#### 4.1.2 Women:

- To all age groups, application of function F1;
- Modification of the trends for the [10-54] age groups.

*Notes on adjustments of rates, see p. 3-8.*      *Notes on projection functions, see p. 10.*

# Yemen

## 1. Source(s) of benchmark data

Code(s):     Title(s):

EPPA3      Economically active population: Estimates and Projections, 1950-2025, Third edition, ILO, Geneva, 1986.
ESCWA     Compedium of Social Statistics Indicators, Third Issue, December 1993, Economic and Social Commission for Western Asia.
EPPA4      Economically active population 1950-2010 - Fourth edition, ILO, Geneva 1996.
STAT       Database on Labour Statistics, LABORSTA - Bureau of Statistics, ILO, Geneva.

## 2. Estimates of activity rates: 1950 - 1990

### 2.1 Benchmark data:

Table 1: Activity rates by sex and age group

| Age group | Year 1950 (1) | 1960 (1) | 1970 (1) | 1980 (1) | 1986 (2) | 1990 (1) |
|---|---|---|---|---|---|---|
| **Men** | | | | | | |
| 10-14 | 31.55 | 27.84 | 24.12 | 20.41 | 24.87 | 18.56 |
| 15-19 | 79.48 | 69.03 | 58.58 | 48.12 | 52.49 | 42.89 |
| 20-24 | 90.07 | 86.70 | 83.33 | 79.96 | 87.48 | 78.28 |
| 25-29 | 97.41 | 96.86 | 96.31 | 95.76 | 96.61 | 95.49 |
| 30-34 | 97.98 | 97.89 | 97.79 | 97.70 | 97.84 | 97.65 |
| 35-39 | 98.06 | 98.11 | 98.17 | 98.23 | 98.14 | 98.26 |
| 40-44 | 98.08 | 97.82 | 97.57 | 97.32 | 97.71 | 97.19 |
| 45-49 | 97.86 | 97.53 | 97.21 | 96.89 | 97.39 | 96.73 |
| 50-54 | 96.56 | 96.08 | 95.61 | 95.13 | 95.86 | 94.89 |
| 55-59 | 94.92 | 94.23 | 93.55 | 92.86 | 93.92 | 92.52 |
| 60-64 | 90.94 | 84.79 | 78.63 | 72.47 | 79.86 | 69.39 |
| 65+ | 75.53 | 62.13 | 48.73 | 35.33 | 51.41 | 28.63 |
| **Women** | | | | | | |
| 10-14 | .. | .. | .. | 16.09 | 21.43 | 7.50 |
| 15-19 | .. | .. | .. | 22.80 | 26.50 | 18.90 |
| 20-24 | .. | .. | .. | 34.33 | 26.91 | 39.17 |
| 25-29 | .. | .. | .. | 33.53 | 32.31 | 38.44 |
| 30-34 | .. | .. | .. | 32.89 | 32.47 | 39.68 |
| 35-39 | .. | .. | .. | 30.77 | 31.44 | 36.43 |
| 40-44 | .. | .. | .. | 30.59 | 31.96 | 35.79 |
| 45-49 | .. | .. | .. | 27.60 | 29.44 | 29.04 |
| 50-54 | .. | .. | .. | 26.78 | 27.96 | 26.52 |
| 55-59 | .. | .. | .. | 24.10 | 24.15 | 23.74 |
| 60-64 | .. | .. | .. | 18.87 | 22.31 | 14.83 |
| 65+ | .. | .. | .. | 9.77 | 6.60 | 8.86 |

Note(s): (1) Egypt.
Source(s): (1) EPPA4; (2) ESCWA and STAT.

### 2.2 Method(s): linears interpolation and extrapolation

**2.2.1 Men:**

- 1950-90, application to the 1986 activity rates estimates of the ESCWA, the half of estimated trends for Egypt.

**2.2.2 Women:**

- 1950-70, 1950-70 adjusted activity rates derived from the EPPA3;
- 1980-90, application to the 1986 activity rates estimates of the ESCWA, half of the estimated trends for Egypt.

## 3. Estimates of distribution rates by activity sector: 1950 - 1990

### 3.1 Benchmark data:

Table 2: Distribution of economically active population by activity sector

| Year | Agriculture | Industry Total | Manufac. | Services |
|---|---|---|---|---|
| **Men** | | | | |
| 1986 | 59.10 | 18.30 | .. | 22.60 |
| **Women** | | | | |
| 1986 | 95.66 | 1.96 | .. | 2.38 |

Source(s): ESCWA and STAT.

### 3.2 Method(s): linear extrapolation

**3.2.1 Men:**

- 1950-70, 1950-70 distribution rates derived from the EPPA3;
- 1980-90, application to distribution rates derived from the 1986 estimates of ESCWA, the half of trends computed for Egypt in the same period.

**3.2.2 Women:**

- 1950-70, 1950-70 distribution rates derived from the EPPA3;
- 1980-90, application to distribution rates derived from the 1986 estimates of ESCWA, the same variations of distribution rates estimated for men in Yemen.

## 4. Projection of activity rates: 2000 - 2010

### 4.1 Model(s): linear and hyperbole

**4.1.1 Men:**

- To the [10-14] age group, application of function F1;
- To the [15+] age groups, application of function F3;
- Modification of the trends for the [10-14] and [30-39] age groups.

**4.1.2 Women:**

- To all age groups, application of function F1;
- Modification of the trends for all age groups.

# Yugoslavia, Fed. Rep. of

## 1. Source(s) of benchmark data

Code(s):    Title(s):

EPPA3       Economically active population: Estimates and Projections, 1950-2025, Third edition, ILO, Geneva, 1986.
BLT-94-2    Popovic B. (1994), "New 1980 and 1990 estimates of activity rates by age and sectoral distribution for some countries of Eastern and Southern Europe"
            in the Bulletin of Labour of Statistics - 1994-2, ILO, Geneva.

## 2. Estimates of activity rates: 1950 - 1990

### 2.1 Benchmark data:

Table 1: Activity rates by sex and age group

| Age group | Year | | | | |
|---|---|---|---|---|---|
| | 1950 (1) | 1960 (1) | 1970 (1) | 1980 (2) | 1990 (2) |
| **Men** | | | | | |
| 10-14 | 24.10 | 8.85 | 3.25 | 0.25 | 0.01 |
| 15-19 | 86.80 | 67.25 | 48.45 | 21.59 | 25.04 |
| 20-24 | 94.85 | 90.75 | 85.80 | 72.02 | 77.31 |
| 25-29 | 96.10 | 96.55 | 95.80 | 92.87 | 92.16 |
| 30-34 | 97.60 | 97.90 | 98.35 | 97.57 | 98.18 |
| 35-39 | 97.80 | 97.25 | 98.30 | 97.76 | 98.33 |
| 40-44 | 97.60 | 97.00 | 95.55 | 97.05 | 96.39 |
| 45-49 | 97.20 | 96.10 | 96.00 | 95.03 | 91.97 |
| 50-54 | 94.20 | 94.00 | 92.35 | 84.40 | 83.20 |
| 55-59 | 84.65 | 85.60 | 77.05 | 65.39 | 61.20 |
| 60-64 | 79.75 | 75.50 | 65.10 | 55.26 | 40.13 |
| 65+ | 61.60 | 56.70 | 51.30 | 43.30 | 30.63 |
| **Women** | | | | | |
| 10-14 | 23.20 | 12.50 | 5.45 | 0.45 | 0.03 |
| 15-19 | 68.80 | 58.35 | 45.15 | 16.18 | 19.15 |
| 20-24 | 60.75 | 60.55 | 60.35 | 53.43 | 60.77 |
| 25-29 | 45.00 | 53.20 | 57.35 | 66.65 | 76.03 |
| 30-34 | 38.85 | 47.65 | 52.25 | 67.14 | 79.56 |
| 35-39 | 35.45 | 45.15 | 50.35 | 58.72 | 78.64 |
| 40-44 | 32.80 | 42.15 | 47.20 | 54.44 | 72.22 |
| 45-49 | 29.50 | 37.80 | 43.40 | 50.19 | 58.33 |
| 50-54 | 24.20 | 31.70 | 36.70 | 41.32 | 42.36 |
| 55-59 | 21.10 | 26.75 | 31.60 | 34.62 | 29.89 |
| 60-64 | 16.50 | 22.10 | 26.80 | 28.84 | 24.58 |
| 65+ | 10.95 | 14.10 | 14.60 | 18.55 | 17.09 |

Source(s): (1) EPPA3; (2) BLT-94-2.

### 2.2 Method(s):  data from EPPA3 and BLT-94-2.

#### 2.2.1 Men:

- 1950-70, weighted average of 1950-70 activity rates for Yugoslavia
derived from the EPPA3 and of 1990 activity rates derived from
the Bulletin of Labour Statistics 1994-2;
modification of the trends for all age groups;
- 1980-90, 1980-90 activity rates derived from the Bulletin.

#### 2.2.2 Women:

- 1950-70, 1950-70 activity rates for Yugoslavia
derived from the EPPA3;
adjustment of activity rates of the [10-19] age groups;
- 1980-90, 1980-90 activity rates derived from the Bulletin
of Labour Statistics 1994-2.

## 3. Estimates of distribution rates by activity sector: 1950 - 1990

### 3.1 Benchmark data:

Table 2: Distribution of economically active population by activity sector

| Year | Agriculture | Industry | | Services |
|---|---|---|---|---|
| | | Total | Manufac. | |
| **Men** | | | | |
| 1950 (1) | 68.30 | 17.80 | .. | 13.90 |
| 1960 (1) | 56.00 | 28.00 | .. | 16.00 |
| 1970 (1) | 45.00 | 34.40 | .. | 20.60 |
| 1980 (2) | 33.86 | 34.99 | 21.41 | 31.14 |
| 1990 (2) | 27.82 | 37.97 | 26.31 | 34.22 |
| **Women** | | | | |
| 1950 (1) | 83.00 | 5.40 | .. | 11.50 |
| 1960 (1) | 78.10 | 15.00 | .. | 6.80 |
| 1970 (1) | 58.20 | 20.00 | .. | 21.80 |
| 1980 (2) | 47.39 | 19.24 | 16.99 | 33.37 |
| 1990 (2) | 32.33 | 26.25 | 23.15 | 41.42 |

Source(s): (1) EPPA3; (2) BLT-94-2.

### 3.2 Method(s):  data from BLT-94-9

#### 3.2.1 Men:

- 1950-70, 1950-70 distribution rates derived from the EPPA3;
- 1980-90, 1980 and 1990 distribution rates derived from the Bulletin
of Labour Statistics, 1994-2.

#### 3.2.2 Women:

- 1950-90, weighted averages of 1950-70 distribution rates derived
from the EPPA3 and of 1980-90 distribution rates derived from the Bulletin
of Labour Statistics, 1994-2.

## 4. Projection of activity rates: 2000 - 2010

### 4.1 Model(s):  linear, hyperbole and logistic

#### 4.1.1 Men:

- To the [15+] age groups, application of function F3;
- Modification of the trends for the [15+] age groups.

#### 4.1.2 Women:

- To the [15-19] and [25-54] age groups, application of function F6;
- To the [20-24] age group, application of function F3;
- To the [55+] age groups, application of function F1;
- Modification of the trends for the [15-24] and [35+] age groups.

# Zambia

## 1. Source(s) of benchmark data

Code(s):    Title(s):

EPPA3    Economically active population: Estimates and Projections, 1950-2025, Third edition, ILO, Geneva, 1986.
ASTER    Yearbook of Labour Statistics 1945-89 - Retrospective Edition on Population Censuses, ILO, Geneva, 1990.
ADNU88    Demographic Yearbook 1988 - Population census statistics - Fortieth Edition, United Nations, New York, 1990.
STAT    Database on Labour Statistics, LABORSTA - Bureau of Statistics, ILO, Geneva.

## 2. Estimates of activity rates: 1950 - 1990

### 2.1 Benchmark data:

Table 1: Activity rates by sex and age group

| Age group | Year 1950 (1) | 1960 (1) | 1970 (1) | 1980 (2) | 1980 (1) | 1990 (3) |
|---|---|---|---|---|---|---|
| **Men** | | | | | | |
| 10-14 | 27.60 | 26.40 | 24.85 | 19.39 | .. | 17.90 |
| 15-19 | 74.10 | 71.45 | 68.15 | 37.73 | .. | 69.70 |
| 20-24 | 87.80 | 86.75 | 85.45 | 82.78 | .. | 90.20 |
| 25-29 | 98.65 | 98.50 | 98.30 | 96.76 | .. | 96.40 |
| 30-34 | 99.60 | 99.40 | 99.20 | 98.10 | .. | 97.00 |
| 35-39 | 99.65 | 99.45 | 99.20 | 98.29 | .. | 97.20 |
| 40-44 | 99.55 | 99.35 | 99.05 | 98.23 | .. | 96.00 |
| 45-49 | 99.40 | 99.20 | 99.00 | 98.37 | .. | 95.20 |
| 50-54 | 99.00 | 98.70 | 98.35 | 97.72 | .. | 93.30 |
| 55-59 | 98.75 | 98.30 | 97.75 | 97.77 | .. | 91.30 |
| 60-64 | 97.20 | 96.45 | 95.50 | 96.50 | .. | 78.22 |
| 65+ | 85.90 | 84.55 | 82.85 | 58.68 | .. | 58.68 |
| **Women** | | | | | | |
| 10-14 | 23.20 | 22.15 | 20.85 | .. | 19.85 | 15.93 |
| 15-19 | 44.65 | 42.85 | 40.55 | .. | 38.75 | 62.03 |
| 20-24 | 29.80 | 29.05 | 28.10 | .. | 27.35 | 73.29 |
| 25-29 | 25.55 | 24.85 | 24.00 | .. | 23.35 | 73.23 |
| 30-34 | 24.50 | 23.85 | 23.00 | .. | 22.35 | 74.76 |
| 35-39 | 25.65 | 25.00 | 24.20 | .. | 23.60 | 74.24 |
| 40-44 | 28.85 | 28.15 | 27.30 | .. | 26.65 | 68.29 |
| 45-49 | 33.85 | 33.00 | 32.00 | .. | 31.20 | 62.64 |
| 50-54 | 44.30 | 43.05 | 41.45 | .. | 40.15 | 58.20 |
| 55-59 | 53.90 | 52.20 | 50.10 | .. | 48.40 | 49.93 |
| 60-64 | 43.85 | 41.90 | 39.45 | .. | 37.50 | 43.70 |
| 65+ | 21.20 | 19.95 | 18.35 | .. | 17.05 | 32.79 |

Source(s): (1) EPPA3; (2) ADNU88 and ASTER; (3) STAT.

### 2.2 Method(s):   linears interpolation and extrapolation

#### 2.2.1 Men:

- 1950-90, interpolation and extrapolation of 1950-70 activity rates derived from the EPPA3 and of adjusted activity rates derived from the 1980 and 1990 censuses;
adjustment of extrapolated rates on the basis of variations in 1990 interpolated rates, in relation to adjusted activity rates derived from the 1990 census.

#### 2.2.2 Women:

- 1950-90, interpolation and extrapolation of 1950-80 activity rates derived from the EPPA3;
adjustment of interpolated and extrapolated rates on the basis of variations in 1990 interpolated rates, in relation to the adjusted rates derived from the 1990 census;
modification of the trends for all age groups.

## 3. Estimates of distribution rates by activity sector: 1950 - 1990

### 3.1 Benchmark data:

Table 2: Distribution of economically active population by activity sector

| Year | Agriculture | Industry Total | Manufac. | Services |
|---|---|---|---|---|
| **Men** | | | | |
| 1950 (1) | 82.00 | 8.00 | .. | 10.00 |
| 1960 (1) | 78.00 | 9.50 | .. | 12.50 |
| 1970 (1) | 73.00 | 11.00 | .. | 16.00 |
| 1980 (1) | 69.00 | 12.50 | .. | 18.50 |
| 1980 (2) | 47.98 | 18.91 | 6.36 | 33.11 |
| **Women** | | | | |
| 1950 (1) | 90.00 | 1.50 | .. | 8.50 |
| 1980 (1) | 84.00 | 2.75 | .. | 13.25 |
| 1980 (2) | 79.22 | 2.63 | 1.97 | 18.15 |

Source(s): (1) EPPA3; (2) STAT.

### 3.2 Method(s):   linears interpolation and extrapolation

#### 3.2.1 Men:

- 1950-80, 1950-80 distribution rates derived from the EPPA3;
- 1990, extrapolation of 1950-80 distribution rates derived from the EPPA3;
adjustment of extrapolated rates on the basis of 1/4 variations in 1980 interpolated rates, in relation to 1980 distribution rates derived from the EPPA3

#### 3.2.2 Women:

- 1950-90, interpolation and extrapolation of 1950 and 1980 adjusted distribution rates derived from the EPPA3;
adjustment of distribution rates on the basis of men/women ratio equal to 1 in agriculture;
distribution rates of manufacturing sector based on manufacturing/industry ratio derived from the 1980 census.

## 4. Projection of activity rates: 2000 - 2010

### 4.1 Model(s):   linear and hyperbole

#### 4.1.1 Men:

- To the [10-14] and [25+] age groups, application of function F3;
- To the [15-19] age group, application of function F1;
- Modification of the trends for the [15-24] and [30-54] age groups.

#### 4.1.2 Women:

- To all age groups, application of function F3;
- Modification of the trends for the [20-54] age groups.

*Notes on adjustments of rates, see p. 3-8.*

*Notes on projection functions, see p. 10.*

# Zimbabwe

## 1. Source(s) of benchmark data

Code(s):    Title(s):

EPPA3    Economically active population: Estimates and Projections, 1950-2025, Third edition, ILO, Geneva, 1986.
R1982    Main Demographic Features of Zimbabwe, Population Census 1982, Central Statistical Office, Causeway, 1985.
ASTER    Yearbook of Labour Statistics 1945-89 - Retrospective Edition on Population Censuses, ILO, Geneva, 1990.
AST93    Yearbook of Labour Statistics 1993, ILO, Geneva, 1993.

## 2. Estimates of activity rates: 1950 - 1990

### 2.1 Benchmark data:

Table 1: Activity rates by sex and age group

| Age group | Year 1950 (1) | 1960 (1) | 1970 (1) | 1980 (1) | 1982 (2) | 1987 (3) |
|---|---|---|---|---|---|---|
| **Men** | | | | | | |
| 10-14 | 48.25 | 46.75 | 44.20 | 41.15 | 36.52 | .. |
| 15-19 | 79.75 | 77.80 | 74.40 | 70.35 | 48.16 | .. |
| 20-24 | 93.30 | 92.55 | 91.25 | 89.70 | 83.35 | .. |
| 25-29 | 97.10 | 97.00 | 96.80 | 96.55 | 93.07 | .. |
| 30-34 | 97.80 | 97.70 | 97.45 | 97.20 | 93.96 | .. |
| 35-39 | 97.95 | 97.80 | 97.60 | 97.30 | 94.29 | .. |
| 40-44 | 97.80 | 97.65 | 97.40 | 97.10 | 94.14 | .. |
| 45-49 | 97.05 | 96.95 | 96.75 | 96.50 | 93.85 | .. |
| 50-54 | 96.50 | 96.30 | 96.00 | 95.60 | 92.47 | .. |
| 55-59 | 95.35 | 95.05 | 94.55 | 93.95 | 90.43 | .. |
| 60-64 | 91.85 | 91.40 | 90.55 | 89.55 | 68.97 | .. |
| 65+ | 77.70 | 76.85 | 75.40 | 73.65 | ... | .. |
| **Women** | | | | | | |
| 10-14 | .. | .. | .. | .. | .. | 0.00 |
| 15-19 | .. | .. | .. | .. | .. | 44.50 |
| 20-24 | .. | .. | .. | .. | .. | 64.50 |
| 25-29 | .. | .. | .. | .. | .. | 68.70 |
| 30-34 | .. | .. | .. | .. | .. | 83.20 |
| 35-39 | .. | .. | .. | .. | .. | 81.00 |
| 40-44 | .. | .. | .. | .. | .. | 79.28 |
| 45-49 | .. | .. | .. | .. | .. | 78.50 |
| 50-54 | .. | .. | .. | .. | .. | 76.00 |
| 55-59 | .. | .. | .. | .. | .. | 73.12 |
| 60-64 | .. | .. | .. | .. | .. | 67.95 |
| 65+ | .. | .. | .. | .. | .. | 58.84 |

Source(s): (1) EPPA3; (2) R1982 and ASTER; (3) AST93.

### 2.2 Method(s): linears interpolation and extrapolation

**2.2.1 Men:**

- 1950-90, interpolation and extrapolation of 1950-80 activity rates
derived from the EPPA3 and of adjusted activity rates derived
from the 1982 census;
adjustment of interpolated and extrapolated rates on the basis of variations
in 1982 interpolated rates, in relation to adjusted activity rates derived from
the 1982 census;
modification of the trends of the [10-19] and [65+] age groups for 1950 à 1990.

**2.2.2 Women:**

- 1950-90, interpolation and extrapolation of 1950-90 activity rates
estimated for Malawi;
adjustment of interpolated and extrapolated rates on the basis of variations
in 1986 interpolated rates, in relation to activity rates derived from
the 1986/87 survey;
modification of the trends of the [10-14] age group for 1950 to 1990.

## 3. Estimates of distribution rates by activity sector: 1950 - 1990

### 3.1 Benchmark data:

Table 2: Distribution of economically active population by activity sector

| Year | Agriculture | Industry Total | Manufac. | Services |
|---|---|---|---|---|
| **Men** | | | | |
| 1982 (1) | 54.61 | 23.60 | .. | 21.80 |
| 1986 (2) | 59.87 | 13.67 | 9.01 | 26.45 |
| **Women** | | | | |
| 1982 (1) | 76.68 | 5.56 | .. | 17.75 |
| 1986 (2) | 82.71 | 2.33 | 1.83 | 14.96 |

Source(s): R1982; (2) AST93.

### 3.2 Method(s): linear extrapolation

**3.2.1 Men:**
- 1950-70, 1950-70 distribution rates derived from the EPPA3;
- 1980-90, extrapolation of 1950-80 distribution rates derived from the EPPA3
and of distribution rates derived from the 1982 census
and from the 1986-87 survey;
modification of the trends in all sectors.

**3.2.2 Women:**

Method, hypothesis and treatment identical to those used for men.

## 4. Projection of activity rates: 2000 - 2010

### 4.1 Model(s): linear and hyperbole

**4.1.1 Men:**

- To the [10-14] age group, application of function F1;
- To the [15+] age groups, application of function F3;
- Modification of the trends for the [10-14] and [60+] age groups.

**4.1.2 Women:**

- To the [10-59] age groups, application of function F3;
- To the [60+] age groups, application of function F1;
- Modification of the trends for the [25-54] and [60+] age groups.

Notes on adjustments of rates, see p. 3-8.

Notes on projection functions, see p. 10.

# Introduction

Le programme des évaluations et projections de la population active selon le sexe et les groupes d'âge en est aujourd'hui à sa quatrième édition. La première édition[1] a été publiée par le Bureau de statistique du BIT en 1971. Quant aux deux autres éditions, la deuxième[2] et la troisième[3], ont été respectivement publiées en 1976 et 1986.

Ce programme vise à mettre à la disposition des Etats membres de l'Organisation internationale du Travail (OIT), des institutions internationales et des utilisateurs particuliers un outil de travail aussi complet, détaillé et comparable que possible sur les plans national, régional et international. Il s'inscrit dans le cadre du programme commun des Nations Unies et des institutions internationales spécialisées, particulièrement le BIT, l'organisation des Nations Unies pour l'alimentation et l'agriculture (FAO) et l'organisation des Nations Unies pour l'éducation, la science et la culture (UNESCO). Il vise également à fournir des données démographiques coordonnées et compatibles sur la population, la population active, la population agricole, la population scolaire, les ménages, la natalité, la fécondité, la mortalité, etc.

**Figure 1 : Liens entre le programme de la population active du du BIT et d'autres programmes**

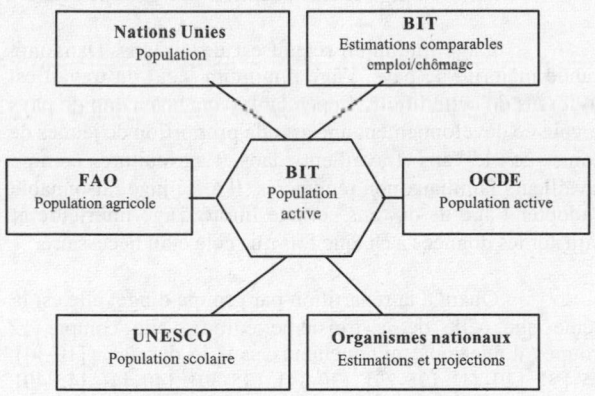

Une des caractéristiques importantes des estimations et projections internationales de la population active réside dans le fait qu'elles permettent de comparer les niveaux et les tendances de la population active des différentes régions et des différents pays au cours des années passées et à venir. Afin d'améliorer la comparabilité internationale, les données de base relatives à la population active ont été uniformisées dans toute la mesure du possible, particulièrement en ce qui concerne les concepts, le champ couvert, la portée et la répartition par groupes d'âge. En outre, pour assurer la cohérence des évaluations et projections de la population active avec les résultats des autres programmes démographiques internationaux, on a utilisé les évaluations et projections de la population totale établie par la Division de la population des Nations Unies dans l'élaboration des évaluations et projections de la population active pour la quatrième édition.

Comme cela a été le cas pour les précédentes éditions, dans la quatrième édition, les évaluations et les projections de la population active ont été obtenues par l'application aux évaluations et projections de la population (variante moyenne) élaborées par les Nations Unies[4], des évaluations et projections des taux d'activité du BIT selon le sexe et les groupes d'âge au milieu de chacune des années de référence retenus, à savoir, les années 1950, 1960, 1970, 1980, 1990, 2000 et 2010. Par rapport aux trois précédentes éditions, la quatrième édition comporte des innovations et des changements au niveau des concepts, des définitions et de la méthodologie.

## 1. Concepts et définitions

### 1.1 Population active

Le concept de la population active est contenu dans la Résolution relative aux statistiques de la population active, de l'emploi, du chômage et du sous-emploi, adoptée par la treizième Conférence internationale des statisticiens du travail - CIST 1982.

**Figure 2 : Cadre conceptuel de la population active.**

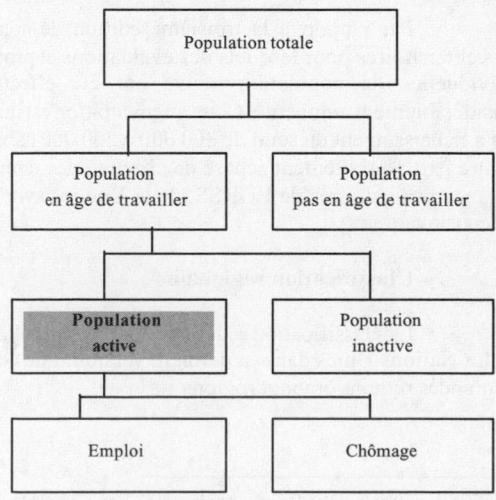

---

[1] BIT, Projections de la main-d'œuvre 1965 – 1985, première édition, Genève, 1971.

[2] BIT, Projections de la main-d'œuvre 1950 – 2010, deuxième édition, Genève, 1976.

[3] BIT, Evaluations et projections de la population active 1950 -2025, troisième édition, Genève, 1986.

[4] Nations Unies, World Population Prospects, the 1994 Revisions, ST/ESA/SER.A/145, New York, 1995.

Dans cette Résolution, la population active est définie comme étant l'ensemble de *«toutes les personnes des deux sexes qui fournissent, durant une période de référence spécifiée, la main-d'œuvre disponible pour la production de biens et services, comme définis par les systèmes de comptabilité et bilans nationaux des Nations Unies. Selon ces systèmes, la production de biens et services comprend toute la production et la transformation des produits primaires, que ceux-ci soient destinés au marché, ou troc ou à l'autoconsommation, ainsi que la production pour le marché de tous les autres biens et services et, dans le cas de ménages produisant de tels biens et services pour le marché, la production correspondante qui fait l'objet d'autoconsommation»* [5].

Ainsi définie, la population active comprend : les personnes pourvues d'un *«emploi salarié»* ou *«non salarié»*[6], les *membres des forces armées* (y compris les militaires du contingent) et les *chômeurs* (y compris les personnes en quête d'un premier emploi).

## 1.2 Taux d'activité

Le taux d'activité global (TA) est la proportion d'actifs (PA), comme définis ci-dessous, dans la population totale en âge de travailler (PT).

$$TA = \frac{PA}{PT} \times 100$$

Les taux d'activité sont calculés pour chaque groupe d'âge, pour les hommes et les femmes séparément et pour l'ensemble des deux sexes.

## 1.3 Couverture géographique

Tous les pays et territoires dont la population totale a atteint ou a dépassé le seuil de 200 000 habitants au milieu de l'année 1990, sont couverts par la quatrième édition.

Par rapport à la troisième édition, le nombre de pays et territoires pour lesquels des évaluations et projections individuelles de population active ont été effectuées, a considérablement augmenté. Cette augmentation est due d'une part à l'abaissement du seuil de 300 000 à 200 000 habitants et d'autre part au traitement séparé de chacune des républiques des anciens territoires de l'URSS, de la Yougoslavie et de la Tchécoslovaquie.

## 1.4 Classification régionale

La classification régionale adoptée est celle établie par les Nations Unies dans sa dernière version. Elle comporte six grandes régions et vingt régions :

Asie
*Asie méridionale centrale*
*Asie méridionale orientale*
*Asie occidentale*
*Asie orientale*

Afrique
*Afrique centrale*
*Afrique méridionale*
*Afrique occidentale*
*Afrique orientale*
*Afrique septentrionale*

Amérique latine et les Caraïbes
*Amérique centrale*
*Amérique du Sud*
*Caraïbes*

Amérique du Nord

Europe
*Europe méridionale*
*Europe occidentale*
*Europe orientale*
*Europe septentrionale*

Océanie
*Australie, Nouvelle-Zélande*
*Mélanésie*
*Micronésie*
*Polynésie*

## 1.5 Limite d'âge et classification par groupe d'âge

L'âge minimum retenu est de dix ans. Dans une grande majorité de pays, l'âge minimum légal du travail est au-dessus de cette limite. Cependant, dans beaucoup de pays en voie de développement une grande proportion de jeunes de moins de 15 ans travaillent dans l'agriculture comme travailleurs familiaux non rémunérés. Il a été jugé raisonnable d'adopter l'âge de dix ans comme limite d'âge inférieure et d'ajuster les données à chaque fois que cela était nécessaire.

Quant à la répartition par groupe d'âge, elle est la même que celle de la troisième édition, elle compte 12 groupes d'âge tous quinquennaux sauf le dernier : [10-14], [15-19], [20-24], [25-29], [30-34], [35-39], [40-44], [45-49], [50-54], [55-59], [60-64] et [65+].

A ces groupements régionaux, deux autres groupements basés principalement sur des indicateurs socio-économiques[7] ont été ajoutés : le groupement des régions et des pays développés (*Amérique du Nord – Australie, Nouvelle-Zélande – Europe – Japon*) et le groupement des régions moins développées (*Afrique – Asie (non compris le Japon) – Amérique latine et les Caraïbes – Mélanésie – Micronésie – Polynésie*).

Pour l'ensemble du Monde ainsi que pour chaque grande région, région, régions développées et régions moins développées, les taux d'activité respectifs ont été évalués par sexe, par groupe d'âge et par secteur d'activité économique.

[5] BIT, Recommandations internationales en vigueur sur les statistiques du travail, édition 1988, Genève, 1988.

[6] Les employeurs, les personnes travaillant pour leur propre compte, les membres des coopératives de producteurs, les travailleurs familiaux non-rémunérés, les personnes engagées dans la production de biens et services pour leur propre consommation ou celles des ménages, les apprentis rémunérés.

[7] Nations Unies, les perspectives d'avenir de la population mondiale, New York, 1985.

## 1.6    Secteurs d'activité économique

Comme dans les éditions précédentes, la quatrième édition présente également des évaluations des taux de répartition sectorielle pour l'ensemble de l'activité économique. La composition de chaque secteur est tirée de la Classification internationale type, par industrie, de toutes les branches d'activité économique[8]) (CITI - Rév. 2, 1968):

le secteur "agriculture" englobe la branche 1 (*Agriculture, Chasse, Sylviculture et pêche*) constitue

Le secteur "industrie" est composé des branches 2, 3, 4 et 5 (*Industries extractives - industries manufacturières - Electricité, gaz et eau - Bâtiment et travaux publics*).

Le secteur "services" est constitué des branches 6, 7, 8 et 9 (*Commerce de gros et de détail, restaurants et hôtels - Transports, entrepôts et communications - Banques, assurances, affaires immobilières et services fournis aux entreprises - Services fournis à la collectivité, services sociaux et services personnels*).

La quatrième édition innove en présentant pour la première fois des évaluations séparées pour la branche 3 "industries manufacturières". Faute de données pour la majorité des pays étudiés, ces évaluations sont limitées seulement aux années 1980 et 1990; pour les autres secteurs, elles couvrent toute la période 1950-1990.

## 2.    Méthodologie

La méthodologie générale adoptée dans la quatrième édition se distingue essentiellement des autres éditions par son caractère "pragmatique".

Pour chaque pays ou territoire étudié, afin d'évaluer les taux d'activité et les taux de répartition sectorielle, le choix des méthodes et des techniques à appliquer a été fonction de l'appréciation d'un certain nombre de critères qui sont en rapport avec la source et la qualité des données et les pratiques nationales de collecte de données. Ce choix tient compte aussi des informations démographiques particulières sur un pays donné ou une région donnée qui ont été largement soulignées dans des publications spécialisées.

Il est aussi à noter que les expériences des éditions passées ont enrichi le choix des méthodes et des techniques d'évaluation et de projection.

Dans les cas où il y avait une absence totale ou partielle d'information sur ces facteurs, le recours à des informations ou à des données sur des pays ou territoires de développement socio-économique et culturel similaire a été la règle.

Le programme des évaluations et projections de la population active du BIT comporte deux phases: une phase d'évaluation et une phase de projection

---

[8]  Nations Unies, *Etudes statistique*, série M, n° 4, New York 1969.

## 2.1    Phase d'évaluation

La phase d'évaluation a consisté à établir des séries chronologiques harmonisées de la population active par sexe, groupe d'âge et secteur d'activité économique couvrant la période 1950-1990.

### 2.1.1    Sources et données de base

Il a été décidé de prendre comme point de départ pour rassembler les données de base qui serviront à établir les évaluations, les données tirées de la troisième édition pour les années 1950, 1960 et 1970 et de les compléter par des données issues de recensements de population et (ou) d'enquêtes par sondage sur la population active ou enquêtes similaires effectué(e)s entre 1974 et 1994 et publiées par les organismes nationaux ou internationaux de statistiques.

Afin de palier au manque de données ainsi que de vérifier et confronter les données issues de différentes sources, il a été nécessaire et utile de recourir à des publications spécifiques d'institutions régionales ou internationales telles que le Centre de démographie de l'Amérique latine (CELADE), l'Organisation de coopération et de développement économique (OECD), l'Office de statistique des communautés européennes (EUROSTAT), le Nordic Statistics et les commissions économiques régionales des Nations Unies: la Commission économique pour l'Afrique (CEA), la Commission économique pour l'Europe (CEE), la Commission économique pour l'Amérique latine et les Caraïbes (CEPAL), la Commission économique et sociale pour l'Asie et le Pacifique (CESAP) et la Commission économique et sociale pour l'Asie occidentale (CESAO).

Par rapport aux éditions précédentes, la quatrième édition a accordé la priorité aux enquêtes par sondage sur la population active plutôt qu'aux recensements de population

Dans beaucoup de pays, les enquêtes par sondage sur la population active et ses composantes principales l'emploi et le chômage, sont régulières et conduites à des fréquences annuelles ou infra-annuelles Ainsi, elles permettent de rassembler des données plus précises et plus fiables sur les effectifs de la population active.

Elles offrent aussi l'avantage d'épurer les effets saisonniers sur les effectifs quand elles sont conduites à des périodes différentes de l'année. Ce sont là des avantages et non des moindres par rapport aux recensements de population qui traitent plusieurs sujets à la fois, se réfèrent à une date unique et s'effectuent généralement sur une fréquence décennale pour une grande majorité de pays.

Une fois les données de base sélectionnées, la démarche a consisté à suivre les différentes étapes comme indiqué dans la figure 3, et d'appliquer aux données de base, les procédures et traitements propres à chacune de ces étapes. Selon le pays ou le territoire une ou plusieurs étapes ont été nécessaires aux fins des évaluations.

Au total, la phase d'évaluation comptait sept étapes; les étapes "Harmonisation des définitions de la population active" et "Ajustement des répartitions par groupes d'âge" ne s'appliquaient pas aux évaluations des taux de répartition sectorielle.

### 2.1.2 Harmonisation des définitions

Au cours de cette étape, il fallait s'assurer que les définitions de la population active adoptées dans les recensements de population et d'enquêtes par sondage sur la population active, correspondent bien à celle adoptée par la CIST 1982 et dans le cas contraire, d'effectuer les ajustements nécessaires. Le volume 5 "Population totale et population active, emploi et chômage (recensements de population)"[9] de la série "*Sources et méthodes: statistiques du travail*" a servi de base de référence pour l'appréciation des définitions.

Les difficultés le plus souvent rencontrées à ce stade ont trait à l'exclusion de certaines catégories de personnes de la population active soit parce qu'elles étaient omises par définition ou qu'elles étaient incluses dans la population inactive. Il s'agit principalement des forces armées (notamment les militaires du contingent) les personnes en quête d'un premier emploi, les apprentis et les travailleurs familiaux sans rémunération (principalement les femmes travaillant dans l'agriculture comme aides familiales) et les saisonniers.

Quand le degré de ventilation des données de la population par statut le permettait ou les données de la catégorie étaient disponibles, les ajustements ont été effectués en incorporant les effectifs de(s) la catégorie(s) en question aux effectifs de la population active par déplacement de(s) la catégorie(s) de la population inactive vers la population active ou par estimation des effectifs à incorporer (cas n° 1).

L'exemple de la République de Corée illustre bien le cas n° 1. Les données de base retenues pour ce pays sont celles tirées de la troisième édition pour les années 1950, 1960 et 1970 et celles issues du recensement de la population de 1980 et des enquêtes par sondage sur la population active effectuées entre 1987 et 1990. Qu'il s'agisse du recensement ou des enquêtes, les données de la population active se réfèrent toutes à la population des ménages privés. Les militaires sont donc exclus de la définition telle qu'elle est formulée par la CIST 1982. Pour inclure les forces armées, l'ajustement a consisté à ajouter aux données de la population active civile les données estimées de la différence entre la population totale et la population civile.

Dans les cas où on ne dispose pas de données ventilées, la méthode d'ajustement a consisté à ajouter à la population active, une proportion estimée des effectifs classée dans la catégorie "Autres" des inactifs (cas n° 2). Les proportions estimés sont fondées sur des données issues d'autres sources ou de la même source à une autre période de référence, et le cas échéant, aux données des pays voisins ayant une situation démographique, socio-économique et culturelle comparable à celle du pays étudié.

---

[9] Population totale et population active, emploi et chômage (recensements de population), Volume 5, *Sources et méthodes: Statistiques du travail,* première édition, BIT, 1990.

**Figure 3 : Etapes et procédures de la phase d'évaluation des taux d'activité 1950 - 1990**

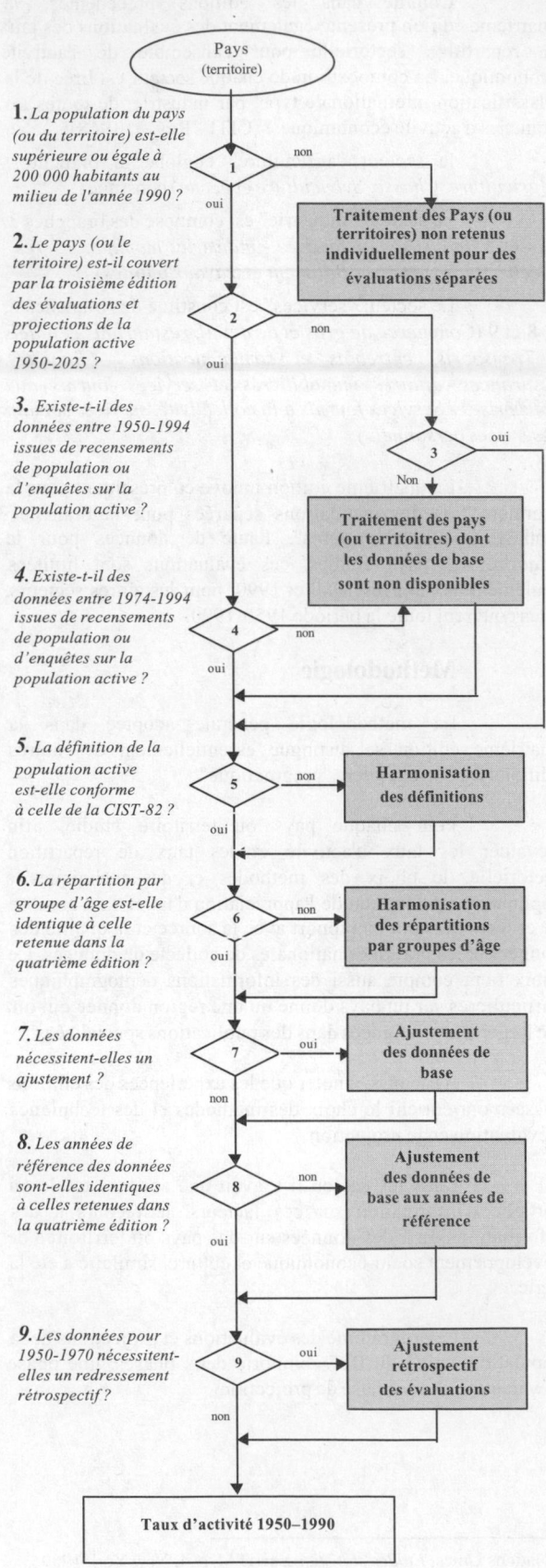

Le cas n° 2 était le plus fréquent. Généralement, l'ajustement effectué était limité aux groupes d'age [15-29] et seulement pour les hommes. Par exemple, Les données issues du recensement de 1984 de la population du *Congo* et dont les données ont servi comme données de base pour les évaluations, ont été ajustées pour tenir compte des étudiants travaillant à temps partiel ou occasionnellement qui n'ont pas été inclus dans la population active.

La procédure d'ajustement a consisté à ajouter aux taux des actifs, les taux estimés des étudiants travaillant à temps partiel ou occasionnellement qui ont été classées non actifs. En outre, comme pour ce pays les taux d'activité du recensement de 1984 ont été jugés trop faibles comparativement aux données de pays de même situation; la totalité des effectifs de la catégorie « Autres » des personnes inactives a été ajoutée aux effectifs des personnes actives. Le tableau 1 (page 194) donne un aperçu des ajustements effectués.

### 2.1.3 Ajustement des répartitions par groupes d'âge

Dans la majorité des recensements et des enquêtes étudiés, les répartitions de la population active par groupe d'âge correspondent à la répartition de référence par groupes d'âge retenue dans la quatrième édition. Néanmoins, pour quelques pays il a été nécessaire d'harmoniser les répartitions par groupes d'âge. Les cas les plus souvent rencontrés ont été les cas où un groupe d'âge d'une répartition nationale renferme deux ou plusieurs groupes d'âge de la répartition de référence. A ces cas un algorithme a été appliqué : on considère que la population totale et la population active sont uniformément distribuées sur un groupe d'âge donné, et on applique une technique qui consiste à prendre en considération les effets des répartitions de la population totale par groupe d'âge et les effets des taux d'activité.

Dans le Tableau 2 (page 194) sont indiqués les différents traitements qui ont été appliqués à la moyenne des taux d'activité 1980 calculée à partir des données tirées des enquêtes par sondage de la population active en *Australie* pour les années 1979, 1980 et 1981. La répartition nationale de la population active par groupe d'âge était la suivante: [15-19], [20-24], [25-34], [35-44], [45-54], [55-59], [60-64] et [65+]. Seuls les groupes d'âge [25-34], [35-44] et [45-54] n'appartiennent pas à la répartition standard, ce sont les taux d'activité de ces groupes d'âge qui ont été évalués.

### 2.1.4 Ajustement des données de base

L'essentiel du travail au cours de cette étape a consisté à redresser complètement les données de base entre les années 1970 et 1994 lorsque les taux d'activité ont été jugés trop faibles. Ces redressements ont été opérés principalement, sur les taux d'activité des femmes dans les pays où les femmes travaillant dans l'agriculture comme aides familiales sans rémunération ont été pour des raisons socio-culturelles volontairement omises des statistiques officielles ou quand elles ont été sous-énumérées comparativement à des données de même portée et de même nature pour des pays voisins de mêmes profils socio-économiques.

La procédure d'ajustement a consisté tout d'abord à évaluer le nombre total des femmes sous-énumérées travaillant dans l'agriculture, puis à répartir ce nombre par groupes d'âge suivant un modèle établi et selon le taux d'urbanisation du pays et enfin, les résultas ainsi obtenus, ont été ajoutés aux données de base faisant objet de redressement. Le nombre de la sous-énumération des femmes a été considéré comme étant la différence entre le nombre total estimatif de femmes travaillant dans l'agriculture et le nombre effectif des femmes tel qu'il est donné par la source dont les données sont à redresser.

Le modèle suivant lequel a été réparti le nombre de la sous-énumération des femmes a été établi d'après les courbes des taux d'activité des femmes dans le secteur agricole pour un certain nombre de pays pour lesquels on possède des statistiques très détaillées et très complètes; la répartition s'effectue par groupes d'âge et par régions urbaines et rurales.

Le modèle de répartition ci-dessous a été appliqué uniformément à toutes les séries de données à redresser.

Modèle de répartition de la sous-énumération des femmes par groupe d'âge et par région

| Groupe d'âge | Urbain | Rural |
|---|---|---|
| 10-14 | 3.74 | 26.68 |
| 15-19 | 3.80 | 36.76 |
| 20-24 | 4.20 | 40.36 |
| 25-29 | 3.99 | 42.46 |
| 30-34 | 7.70 | 44.02 |
| 35-39 | 8.20 | 45.29 |
| 40-44 | 10.06 | 46.33 |
| 45-49 | 7.50 | 45.36 |
| 50-54 | 10.29 | 43.47 |
| 55-59 | 9.70 | 39.18 |
| 60-64 | 6.22 | 33.48 |
| 65+ | 2.77 | 17.39 |

**Source**: Bureau de statistique, BIT.

Le Tableau 3 (page 194) montre un exemple d'ajustement des taux d'activité des femmes du *Mali* dont les données ont été tirées du recensement de la population de 1976.

### 2.1.5 Ajustement des données de base aux années de référence

Comme c'était le cas dans la troisième édition, la période de référence des évaluations a été fixée au mois de juin pour chacune des années de référence 1950, 1960, 1970, 1980 et 1990

Pour les pays et territoires dont on a maintenu les évaluations issues de la troisième édition pour les années 1950, 1960 et 1970 (et aussi parfois 1980), les données de base entre 1974 et 1994 à quelques rares exceptions, ont été toutes ajustées au mois de juin et à chacune des années de référence 1980 et 1990.

Selon le nombre d'années disponibles pour les données de base et l'importance de l'intervalle entre chacune de ces années et l'année de référence, une procédure d'ajustement a été choisie. En règle générale, pour un pays ou un territoire donné on a opéré ainsi:

## Tableau 1: Ajustement des taux d'activité masculins tirés du recensement de la population du Congo (décembre 1984)

| Groupe d'âge | Population active en % | Population inactive en % | | | Taux estimés d'étudiants actifs | Taux additionnels d'ajustement | | | Taux d'activité ajustés |
| | | Total | Etudiants | Autres | | Etudiants | Autres | Total | |
| $c_1$ | $c_2$ | $c_3$ | $c_4$ | $c_5$ | $c_6$ | $c_7=c_4 \times c_6$ | $c_8=c_5$ | $c_9=c_7+c_8$ | $c_{10}=c_2+c_9$ |
|---|---|---|---|---|---|---|---|---|---|
| 10-14 | 3.10 | 94.26 | 93.14 | 2.64 | 0.25 | 23.28 | 2.64 | 25.92 | 29.02 |
| 15-19 | 18.84 | 77.89 | 75.07 | 3.28 | 0.40 | 30.03 | 3.28 | 33.30 | 52.14 |
| 20-24 | 53.49 | 43.29 | 39.88 | 3.22 | 0.70 | 27.92 | 3.22 | 31.14 | 84.63 |
| 25-29 | 86.04 | 12.16 | 9.98 | 1.81 | 0.90 | 8.98 | 1.81 | 10.79 | 96.82 |
| 30-34 | 96.60 | 2.47 | 1.16 | 0.93 | 0.00 | 0.00 | 0.93 | 0.93 | 97.53 |
| 35-39 | 97.75 | 1.57 | 0.36 | 0.68 | 0.00 | 0.00 | 0.68 | 0.68 | 98.43 |
| 40-44 | 97.61 | 1.71 | 0.20 | 0.68 | 0.00 | 0.00 | 0.68 | 0.68 | 98.29 |
| 45-49 | 96.62 | 2.74 | 0.13 | 0.64 | 0.00 | 0.00 | 0.64 | 0.64 | 97.26 |
| 50-54 | 92.95 | 6.32 | 0.06 | 0.73 | 0.00 | 0.00 | 0.73 | 0.73 | 93.68 |
| 55-59 | 80.96 | 18.19 | 0.19 | 0.85 | 0.00 | 0.00 | 0.85 | 0.85 | 81.81 |
| 60-64 | 81.05 | 17.87 | 0.50 | 1.08 | 0.00 | 0.00 | 0.00 | 0.00 | 81.05 |
| 65+ | 73.79 | 23.37 | 1.63 | 2.84 | 0.00 | 0.00 | 0.00 | 0.00 | 73.79 |

**Source**: Bureau de statistique, BIT.

## Tableau 2: Evaluation des taux d'activité masculins des groupes d'âge de 25 à 44 ans en Australie pour 1980

| Groupe d'âge | Population active en % en 1980 | Population totale en 1980 (milliers) | Taux d'activité 1970 | Taux d'activité 1980 | $c_6$ | $c_7$ | $c_8$ | $c_9$ | $c_{10}$ | $c_{11}$ | $c_{12}$ | $c_{13}$ | $c_{14}$ | $c_{15}$ | $c_{16}$ | $c_{17}$ | $c_{18}$ | Taux d'activité ajustés 1980 |
| $c_1$ | $c_2$ | $c_3$ | $c_4$ | $c_5$ | $c_6$ | $c_7$ | $c_8$ | $c_9$ | $c_{10}$ | $c_{11}$ | $c_{12}$ | $c_{13}$ | $c_{14}$ | $c_{15}$ | $c_{16}$ | $c_{17}$ | $c_{18}$ | $c_{19}$ |
|---|---|---|---|---|---|---|---|---|---|---|---|---|---|---|---|---|---|---|
| 25-29 | 95.87 | 608 | 95.79 | 94.81 | 1196 | 1147 | 576 | 1138 | 582 | 1150 | 12 | 4 | 0.30 | 0.70 | 28.64 | 66.86 | 95.50 | 95.50 |
| 30-34 | | 588 | 96.55 | 95.54 | | | 562 | | 568 | | | | | 0.70 | 28.86 | 67.39 | 96.25 | 96.25 |
| 35-39 | 95.67 | 961 | 96.44 | 95.36 | 1778 | 1701 | 916 | 1689 | 927 | 1710 | 21 | 9 | 0.42 | 0.58 | 39.59 | 56.40 | 95.99 | 95.99 |
| 40-44 | | 817 | 95.80 | 94.55 | | | 772 | | 783 | | | | | 0.58 | 39.26 | 56.03 | 95.28 | 95.28 |

$c_6$ = somme des données de deux groupes d'âge adjacents de la $c_3$; $c_7$ =(c2xc6)/100; $c_8$ =(c3xc5)/100; $c_9$ = somme des données de deux groupes d'âg adjacents de la c8; $c_{10}$ =(c3xc4)/100; $c_{11}$=somme des données de deux groupes d'âge adjacents de c10; $c_{12}$=c11-c9; $c_{13}$ =c11-c7; $c_{14}$=c13/c12; $c_{15}$=1-(c13/c12); $c_{16}$=c5xc14; $c_{17}$=c4xc15; $c_{18}$=c16+c17; $c_{19}$=c18.

**Source:** Bureau de statistique, BIT.

## Tableau 3: Ajustement des taux d'activité féminins tirés du recensement de la population du Mali (décembre 1976)

| Groupe d'âge | Population totale | Population active | Taux d'activité | Modèle de répartition de la sous-énumération des femmes par région | | Part des femmes dans le seteur agricole en % par région | | | | | Taux d'activité à ajouter | Taux d'activité ajustés |
| | | | | Urbain | Rural | Urbain | Rural | | | | | |
| $c_1$ | $c_2$ | $c_3$ | $c_4$ | $c_5$ | $c_6$ | $c_7$ | $c_8$ | $c_9$ | $c_{10}$ | $c_{11}$ | $c_{12}$ | $c_{13}$ |
|---|---|---|---|---|---|---|---|---|---|---|---|---|
| 10-14 | 321959 | 47528 | 14.76 | 3.74 | 26.68 | 16.80 | 83.20 | 22.83 | 73497 | 1.66 | 37.79 | 52.55 |
| 15-19 | 333508 | 62813 | 18.83 | 3.80 | 36.76 | 16.80 | 83.20 | 31.22 | 104125 | 1.66 | 51.68 | 70.51 |
| 20-24 | 265842 | 46428 | 17.46 | 4.20 | 40.36 | 16.80 | 83.20 | 34.28 | 91142 | 1.66 | 56.75 | 74.21 |
| 25-29 | 267018 | 48138 | 18.03 | 3.99 | 42.46 | 16.80 | 83.20 | 36.00 | 96123 | 1.66 | 59.58 | 77.61 |
| 30-34 | 225950 | 38859 | 17.20 | 7.70 | 44.02 | 16.80 | 83.20 | 37.92 | 85675 | 1.66 | 62.76 | 79.96 |
| 35-39 | 165949 | 29019 | 17.49 | 8.20 | 45.29 | 16.80 | 83.20 | 39.06 | 64817 | 1.66 | 64.65 | 82.14 |
| 40-44 | 147829 | 25618 | 17.33 | 10.06 | 46.33 | 16.80 | 83.20 | 40.24 | 59480 | 1.66 | 66.60 | 83.93 |
| 45-49 | 98453 | 17225 | 17.50 | 7.50 | 45.36 | 16.80 | 83.20 | 39.00 | 38396 | 1.66 | 64.55 | 82.05 |
| 50-54 | 103607 | 16486 | 15.91 | 10.29 | 43.47 | 16.80 | 83.20 | 37.90 | 39263 | 1.66 | 62.73 | 78.64 |
| 55-59 | 62917 | 9485 | 15.08 | 9.70 | 39.18 | 16.80 | 83.20 | 34.22 | 21532 | 1.66 | 56.65 | 71.72 |
| 60-64 | 81466 | 9897 | 12.15 | 6.22 | 33.48 | 16.80 | 83.20 | 28.90 | 23543 | 1.66 | 47.83 | 59.98 |
| 65+ | 124068 | 10366 | 8.36 | 2.77 | 17.39 | 16.80 | 83.20 | 14.93 | 18524 | 1.66 | 24.71 | 33.07 |

Le rapport femmes/hommes dans l'agriculture tiré du recensement de 1976 est de 17.94% {(1578948/283107)*100}; le nouveau rapport femmes/hommes estimé a été fixé à 93%;
Le nombre de femmes sous-énumérées est estimé à: 1185315 {(15789948x0.93) - 283107}. $c_9$=(c5xc7+c6xc8)/100; $c_{10}$=c2xc9x100 $c_{11}$=185315/716117; $c_{12}$=c9xc11; $c_{13}$=c4+c12.

**Source**: Bureau de statistique, BIT.

- s'il y deux années de données de base disponibles autour de l'année de référence (1979 et 1981 ou 1989 et 1991), les ajustements ont été effectués par application de moyennes arithmétiques aux taux d'activité des données de base. C'était le cas de la majorité des pays des régions développées.

- s'il y deux années de données de base disponibles et relativement proches de l'année de référence, les ajustements ont été effectués par application de moyennes pondérées aux taux d'activité des données de base. Par exemple pour la *Turquie*, l'évaluation du taux d'activité 1990 du groupe d'âge [50-54] pour les femmes a été obtenue en additionnant les taux d'activité tirés des recensements des mois d'octobre 1985 (1985.75) et 1990 (1990.75) pondérés par les distances relatives à l'année de référence 1990 (1990.5): Ce taux calculé ainsi est de:

$$(48.18)(0.25/5) + (44.77)(4.75/5) = 44.94$$

- Dans les autres cas, le plus souvent on a procédé par interpolation et/ou extrapolation des données de base.

Pour les pays et territoires dont on n'a pas maintenu les évaluations issues de la troisième édition, l'ajustement des données de base aux années de référence s'est opéré en majorité pour ces pays par interpolation et/ou extrapolation des données de base. Ensuite, dans bien de cas, pour peaufiner la tendance des taux estimés, on a appliqué aux taux interpolés et/ou extrapolés les variations des taux d'activité issus généralement du dernier recensement (ou dernière enquête) par rapport aux taux interpolés ou extrapolés des données du même recensement (ou de la même enquête). Aussi, pour les groupes d'âge des jeunes âgés de 10 à 24 ans, on a eu souvent recours à des modifications de tendance des taux d'activité estimés en accélérant ou en décélérant ces tendances selon l'appréciation du niveau de ces taux et conformément aux hypothèses prises pour le pays ou le territoire en question.

Le tableau 4 (page 196) donne un exemple type d'ajustement des données de base aux années de référence.

### 2.1.6 Ajustement rétrospectif des évaluations

Initialement, seulement les données de base entre les années 1974 et 1994 des pays et territoires dont les statistiques passablement ou totalement ignoraient l'apport des femmes à l'activité économique ont été ajustées. Pour que les les évaluations et projections soient comparables sur toute la période 1950-2010 et suite à la demande de plusieurs institutions et notamment celle du Comité permanent sur les évaluations et projections démographiques du Comité administratif lors de sa réunion du 25 au 27 juin 1996, il a été décidé de procéder au redressement des données de base tirées de la troisième édition et retenues dans la quatrième édition pour les années 1950, 1960 et 1970.

Les méthodes et les modèles utilisés pour ces ajustements ont été semblables à ceux utilisés au cours de l'étape "ajustement des données de base" (point 2.1.4).

### 2.1.7 Traitement des pays et territoires non retenus individuellement dans la quatrième édition

Ce sont les pays et territoires pour lesquels des évaluations séparées n'ont pu être établies du fait que leur population totale n'a pas atteint au milieu de l'année 1990 le seuil minimum fixé à 200 000 habitants. Néanmoins, les données de ces pays et territoires ont été incluses dans les totaux régionaux. Elles étaient incluses de la manière suivante : on calcul les taux d'activité moyens de la région sans ces pays et territoires, on applique ensuite ces taux moyens à la population totale de ces pays et territoires et enfin, par addition des populations actives de tous les pays et territoires qui constituent la région, on obtient la population active de la région.

Pour l'ensemble du Monde, pour chaque grande région et pour les régions développées et moins développées, la procédure des évaluations et projections de la population active est similaire dans son déroulement à celle appliquée à l'évaluation de la population active régionale.

Les traitements appliqués au cours de cette étape s'effectuent donc après les traitements relatifs aux pays et territoires retenus individuellement dans la quatrième édition.

### 2.1.8 Traitement des pays et territoires dont les données de base sont non disponibles

Au cours de cette étape, sont résolus les problèmes qui sont liés à la non-disponibilité totale ou partielle des données de base servant à l'élaboration des évaluations. Les pays et territoires qui y sont traités, sont les pays et territoires qui n'ont pas été couverts par la troisième édition ou/et pour lesquels on ne dispose pas de données postérieures à 1974. Ils ont été classés dans trois catégories et à chacune de ces catégories une solution autant que possible satisfaisante a été apportée

Dans la première catégorie, sont regroupées les vingt-deux républiques issues des territoires de l'URSS (*Arménie - Azerbaïdjan - Bélarus - Estonie - Géorgie - Kazakhstan - Kirghizistan - Lettonie - Lituanie - Moldova - Ouzbékistan - Russie, Fédération de - Tadjikistan - Turkménistan - Ukraine*), de la Yougoslavie (*Bosnie-Herzégovine - Croatie - Macédoine, Ex-Rép. yougoslave de - Slovénie - Yougoslavie, Rép. féd. de*) et de la Tchécoslovaquie (*République tchèque – Slovaquie*). Pour ces pays, le Bureau de statistique du BIT a bénéficié du concours des autorités nationales et surtout d'experts[10,11] de ces pays pour rassembler des données relatives à la population active pour chacun de ces pays couvrant la période 1950-1990.

---

[10] Popovic B. (1994), "New 1980 and 1990 estimates of activity rates by age and sectoral distribution for some countries of Eastern and Southern Europe, dans le *Bulletin des statistiques du travail* - 1994-2, BIT, Genève, 1994.

[11] Vorobiev A. (1994), "Estimation de la population active pour les quinze pays de l'ex-URSS pour les années 1950, 1959, 1970, 1979 et 1989", dans le *Bulletin des statistiques du travail* - 1994-2, BIT, Genève, 1994.

## Tableau 4: Evaluation des taux d'activité masculin pour le Pérou, 1950 - 1990

| Groupe d'âge | Taux d'activité (données de base) | | | | Taux estimés 1980 | Interpolation et extrapolation des taux d'activité 1950, 1960, 1970 et 1980 | | | Taux extrapolés 1990 après modification de tendances | Taux d'activité estimés 1990 |
| | 1950 | 1960 | 1970 | 1981 | | 1981 | 1985 | 1990 | | |
| c1 | c2 | c3 | c4 | c5 | c6 | c7 | c8 | c9 | c10 | c11 |
|---|---|---|---|---|---|---|---|---|---|---|
| 10-14 | 11.95 | 6.75 | 5.00 | 4.92 | 4.92 | 3.50 | 2.59 | 1.45 | 2.59 | 3.64 |
| 15-19 | 59.40 | 55.30 | 42.20 | 37.52 | 37.94 | 36.31 | 33.22 | 29.34 | 33.22 | 34.31 |
| 20-24 | 93.25 | 91.70 | 82.60 | 81.67 | 81.76 | 80.35 | 78.61 | 76.43 | 78.61 | 79.90 |
| 25-29 | 98.00 | 97.50 | 94.90 | 93.43 | 93.57 | 93.45 | 92.81 | 92.02 | 92.02 | 92.00 |
| 30-34 | 98.80 | 98.60 | 97.80 | 97.21 | 97.26 | 97.25 | 97.03 | 96.76 | 96.76 | 96.72 |
| 35-39 | 98.60 | 98.50 | 98.40 | 98.33 | 98.33 | 98.31 | 98.28 | 98.23 | 98.23 | 98.25 |
| 40-44 | 98.50 | 98.40 | 98.30 | 98.30 | 98.30 | 98.26 | 98.24 | 98.20 | 98.20 | 98.24 |
| 45-49 | 98.40 | 98.30 | 98.20 | 98.27 | 98.26 | 98.21 | 98.19 | 98.16 | 98.16 | 98.22 |
| 50-54 | 97.60 | 97.50 | 96.15 | 97.04 | 96.96 | 96.53 | 96.40 | 96.24 | 96.24 | 96.75 |
| 55-59 | 96.50 | 96.05 | 93.65 | 94.50 | 94.42 | 93.77 | 93.43 | 93.00 | 93.00 | 93.71 |
| 60-64 | 91.90 | 91.75 | 85.55 | 88.26 | 88.01 | 86.44 | 85.73 | 84.84 | 84.84 | 86.62 |
| 65+ | 75.00 | 69.30 | 62.65 | 63.46 | 63.39 | 60.95 | 59.29 | 57.21 | 57.21 | 59.57 |

$c_2$, $c_3$ et $c_4$: taux d'activité tirés de la troisième édition; $c_5$: taux d'activité tirés du recensement de juillet 1981; $c_6 = c_5(10/11) + c_4(1/11)$; $c_{11} = c_{10}(c_5/c_7)$.

**Source**: Bureau de statistique, BIT.

La deuxième catégorie regroupe les pays et territoires pour lesquels on ne dispose d'aucune donnée. Dans cette situation, la solution adoptée a consisté de prendre comme données de base pour ces pays, les évaluations établies pour au moins deux pays proches. Par exemple, tel a été le cas de l'*Erythrée;* les données de base sélectionnées pour ce pays ont été celles estimées pour l'*Ethiopie* et la *Somalie*.

La troisième catégorie regroupe tous les pays qui sont couverts par la troisième édition et pour lesquels on ne dispose pas de données entre 1974 et 1994 ou pour certains d'entre eux, des données existent mais la préférence a été accordée aux données de la troisième édition. Parmi ces pays, on trouve: *Arabie saoudite - Bhoutan - Burundi - Cameroun - Gabon - Gambie - Guinée - Jordanie - Kenya - Liban - Mauritanie - Ouganda - Rép. pop. dém. de Corée - Suriname - Timor oriental*. Pour ces pays, soit seules les données des années 1950, 1960 et 1970 de la troisième édition ont servi de données de base; ou dans certains cas, on a rajouté aussi les données de 1980 et/ou de 1990.

Les traitements et procédures des évaluations des taux de répartition sectorielle de l'agriculture, de l'industrie et des services ont été identiques à ceux appliqués aux évaluations des taux d'activité.

A défaut de données disponibles ventilées du secteur industriel pour une grande majorité de pays, la procédure d'évaluation des taux de répartition des industries manufacturières s'est effectuée ainsi:

- s'il y des données de base disponibles pour une année proche des années de référence 1980 et 1990 ou entre celles-ci, les taux de répartition des industries manufacturières sont obtenus par application aux taux de répartition estimés de l'industrie du (ou des) rapport(s) industrie/manufacture tiré(s) des données de base disponibles

- Pour les pays pour lesquels on ne dispose d'aucune donnée, la règle adoptée était de prendre le rapport industrie/manufacture estimé pour un pays de même situation démographique et économique et de l'appliquer aux taux de répartition estimés de l'industrie du pays considéré.

### 2.2 Phase de projection

### 2.2.1 Méthode

Dans les éditions précédentes, les projections des taux d'activité de la population active ont été effectuées par application d'un modèle uniforme à tous les pays et territoires pris en considération. La méthode se fondait sur la relation entre les variations des taux d'activité et le degré de développement économique et son évolution mesurés par la proportion d'actifs masculins dans le secteur agricole. Les résultats obtenus par cette méthode étaient satisfaisants pour une grande majorité de pays et territoires; cependant, principalement pour les pays développés où la population active dans l'agriculture ne représentait qu'une proportion très faible, plusieurs difficultés sont apparues lors de l'application de cette méthode. En plus celle-ci, par son mécanisme peu flexible, ne permettait de saisir que partiellement des changements importants survenus sur le marché du travail tel que le développement du travail à temps partiel ou la participation grandissante des femmes à l'activité économique.

Dans la quatrième édition, il a été donc décidé d'opter pour une autre approche, l'approche historique. Cette approche est fondée sur la projection des tendances individuelles propres à chaque pays ou territoire. Les expériences de plusieurs organismes nationaux de statistiques et le Bureau de statistique du BIT ont montré que cette méthode de projection produit des résultats aussi bons qualitativement que ceux obtenus par des méthodes plus fines. De plus elle a l'avantage d'être d'application facile et de

refléter rapidement les nouvelles tendances qui se dégagent pour un pays déterminé.

La démarche a consisté tout d'abord, à l'aide de fonctions extrapolatrices, à projeter les tendances des taux d'activité pour chaque sexe et groupe d'âge, ensuite à l'aide de graphique et selon les hypothèses prises par le pays ou territoire considéré, de choisir la fonction appropriée et enfin si nécessaire, d'apporter des modifications aux tendances en les accélérant ou en les décélérant.

### 2.2.2 Hypothèses

Les principales hypothèses prises dans l'élaboration des projections sont en nombre de quatre:

Hypothèse 1: pour les pays et territoires des régions développées, poursuite de la diminution des taux d'activité pour tous les groupes d'âge. La diminution serait plus marquée pour les groupes d'âge [15-19] et [55+].

Hypothèse 2: le rythme de diminution des taux d'activité des hommes dans les régions moins développées devrait s'estomper.

Hypothèse 3: dans les régions moins développées et quelle que soit la tendance observée au cours de la décennie 1980-1990 des taux d'activité des femmes pour les groupes d'âge [25-54], ces taux évolueraient vers ceux des hommes sans pour autant les dépasser.

Hypothèse 4: le rythme d'augmentation des niveaux des taux d'activité des femmes s'il y avait lieu, serait plus important pour les groupes d'âge où les écarts des niveaux des taux avec ceux des hommes étaient plus grands.

### 2.2.3 Fonctions extrapolatrices

Les fonctions extrapolatrices sont en nombre de six et sont listées dans le tableau 5 à la page 198. Dans l'ensemble, les modéles linéaire, hyperbole et logistique ont été les modèles les plus utilisés dans la phase d'élaboration des des projections des taux d'activité pour 2000 et 2010.

## Conclusion

Les fréquences d'élaboration des évaluations et projections de la population active du BIT se font en moyenne tous les huit ans. Cette période s'est avérée trop longue au vu de l'intégration des changements structurels ou de faits démographiques nouveaux survenus dans certains pays après l'apparition d'une édition. En principe, ces changements et ces faits nouveaux ne seront pris en considération qu'au cours de l'édition suivante ; entre-temps, la qualité et les niveaux des évaluations et projections déjà élaborées en sont affectées. Le Bureau de statistique, conscient de cette situation et dans le souci de mettre à disposition des utilisateurs des statistiques fiables et comparables autant que possible sur la population active, est sur le point de finaliser un nouveau programme intégré des statistiques de la population active.

Ce programme intégré aurait pour objectif principal la mise à jour continue des évaluations et projections de la population active : au fur et à mesure que des nouvelles données seraient disponibles ou que des faits démographiques ou socio-économiques surviendraient et affecteraient les hypothèses et les méthodes choisies, ils seraient automatiquement intégrés aux procédures et traitements des évaluations et projections de la population active. Il viserait également :

- l'intégration des évaluations et projections établies par les organismes nationaux de statistiques ;

- une coopération accrue entre le BIT et la FAO, ainsi que l'UNESCO, pour mieux intégrer et harmoniser les données produites par chacune de ces institutions ;

- une intégration des résultats des enquêtes menées dans le cadre du Programme international pour l'abolition du travail des enfants (IPEC) du BIT ;

- une l'intégration des résultats du programme sur les estimations comparables sur l'emploi et le chômage du BIT ;

- une intégration des données de la population active par niveaux d'éducation publiées dans les dernières éditions de l'Annuaire des statistiques du travail du BIT ;

- sur le plan technique et informatique, intégration des différentes bases de données, de documents et de méthodes pour mieux gérer, exploiter et diffuser les évaluations et projections de la population active.

La réalisation de ce programme intégré se concrétisera par la parution de la cinquième édition des évaluations et projections de la population active du BIT.

**Tableau 5: Fonctions extrapolatrices de la phase des projections des taux d'activité pour 2000 et 2010**

| N° | Modèle de projection | Fonction | Fonction linéaire |
|---|---|---|---|
| 1 | **Linéaire**<br><br>*La variation du taux d'activité (y) est proportionnelle à la variation du temps (x) : ($dy = adx$)* | $y = ax + b$ | $y = ax + b$ |
| 2 | **Log-linéaire**<br><br>*Le taux de variation du taux d'activité (y) est proportionnelle au taux de variation du temps (x) :* $\dfrac{dy}{y} = a\dfrac{dx}{x}$ | $y = Bx^a$ | $p = aq + b$<br><br>*avec* $p = Lny$,<br>$q = Lnx$,<br>*et* $b = LnB$ |
| 3 | **Hyperbole**<br><br>*Possibilité d'introduire un seuil de taux d'activité non franchissable* | $y = \dfrac{1}{ax + b}$ | $p = ax + b$<br><br>*avec* $p = \dfrac{1}{y}$ |
| 4 | **Exponentiel**<br><br>*Le taux de variation du taux d'activité (y) est proportionnelle à la variation du temps (x) :* $\dfrac{dy}{y} = adx$ | $y = e^{ax+b}$ | $p = ax + b$<br><br>*avec* $p = Lny$ |
| 5 | **Logarithmique**<br><br>*La variation du taux d'activité (y) est proportionnelle au taux de variation du temps (x) :* $dy = a\dfrac{dx}{x}$ | $y = aLnx + b$ | $y = az + b$<br><br>*avec* $z = Lnx$ |
| 6 | **Logistique**<br><br>*Possibilité de traduire la transition des taux d'activité d'une phase de croissance à une phase auto-freinée* | $y = y_{min} + \dfrac{y_{max} - y_{min}}{1 + e^{ax+b}}$ | $y = \alpha z + \beta$<br><br>*avec* $z = \dfrac{1}{1 + e^{ax+b}}$,<br>$\alpha = (y_{max} - y_{min})$<br>*et* $\beta = y_{min}$ |

# Afghanistan

## 1. Source(s) des données de base

Code(s):    Titre(s):

EPPA3    Evaluations et projections de la population active 1950-2025 - troisième édition, BIT, Genève, 1986.
ADNU84    Annuaire démographique 1984 - Statistiques des recensements de population II, trente-sixième édition, Nations Unies, New York, 1986.
ASTER    Annuaire des statistiques du travail 1945-89 - Edition rétrospective sur les recensements de population, BIT, Genève, 1990.

## 2. Evaluation des taux d'activité: 1950 - 1990

### 2.1 Données de base:

Tableau 1: Taux d'activité par sexe et par groupe d'âge

| Groupe d'âge | Année 1950 (1) | 1960 (1) | 1970 (1) | 1980 (1) | 1979 (2) |
|---|---|---|---|---|---|
| **Hommes** | | | | | |
| 10-14 | 38.00 | 36.00 | 34.00 | 32.00 | 30.54 |
| 15-19 | 75.85 | 72.20 | 68.55 | 64.90 | 66.00 |
| 20-24 | 92.80 | 91.35 | 89.95 | 88.50 | 88.99 |
| 25-29 | 97.65 | 97.00 | 96.35 | 95.70 | 95.70 |
| 30-34 | 98.05 | 97.55 | 97.00 | 96.50 | 96.84 |
| 35-39 | 98.55 | 98.20 | 97.85 | 97.50 | 97.19 |
| 40-44 | 98.05 | 97.55 | 96.95 | 96.40 | 96.87 |
| 45-49 | 97.55 | 97.05 | 96.60 | 96.10 | 96.48 |
| 50-54 | 96.65 | 95.85 | 95.10 | 94.30 | 94.78 |
| 55-59 | 93.90 | 93.05 | 92.25 | 91.40 | 92.44 |
| 60-64 | 90.50 | 89.35 | 88.25 | 87.10 | 87.84 |
| 65+ | 76.40 | 72.85 | 69.35 | 65.80 | 61.95 |
| **Femmes** | | | | | |
| 10-14 | 5.00 | 4.50 | 4.00 | 3.50 | 5.06 |
| 15-19 | 8.50 | 8.80 | 9.15 | 9.55 | 9.13 |
| 20-24 | 5.80 | 6.60 | 7.90 | 9.25 | 9.18 |
| 25-29 | 5.45 | 6.20 | 7.40 | 8.70 | 8.22 |
| 30-34 | 5.30 | 5.75 | 6.40 | 7.10 | 6.75 |
| 35-39 | 6.00 | 6.30 | 6.75 | 7.20 | 6.71 |
| 40-44 | 4.55 | 4.75 | 5.05 | 5.30 | 5.17 |
| 45-49 | 4.55 | 4.70 | 4.95 | 5.20 | 4.95 |
| 50-54 | 3.25 | 3.45 | 3.75 | 4.05 | 3.62 |
| 55-59 | 3.25 | 3.50 | 3.80 | 4.10 | 3.80 |
| 60-64 | 2.40 | 2.35 | 2.30 | 2.25 | 2.12 |
| 65+ | 1.80 | 1.75 | 1.65 | 1.60 | 1.18 |

Source(s): (1) EPPA3; (2) ADNU84.

### 2.2 Méthode(s): extrapolation linéaires

#### 2.2.1 Hommes:

- 1950-80, taux d'activité 1950-80 ajustés tirés des EPPA3;
ajustement des taux d'activité sur la base des résultats du recensement de 1979;
- 1990, extrapolation des taux d'activité ajustés 1950-80 tirés des EPPA3;
modification des tendances des groupes d'âge [25-59].

#### 2.2.2 Femmes:

- 1950-70, taux d'activité ajustés 1950-70 tirés des EPPA3;
ajustement des taux sur la base du modèle d'ajustement des taux d'activité des femmes travaillant dans l'agriculture comme aides familiales;
- 1980-90, extrapolation des taux d'activité 1950-70 tirés des EPPA3 et des taux du recensement de 1979;
ajustement des taux sur la base d'un rapport hommes/femmes égal à 2/3 dans l'agri
de la courbe par âge des taux d'activité tirés de l'enquête de 1989 au Bangladesh.

## 3. Evaluation des taux de répartition par secteur d'activité: 1950 - 1990

### 3.1 Données de base:

Tableau 2: Répartition de la population active en % par secteur d'activité

| Année | Agriculture | Industrie Total | Manufac. | Services |
|---|---|---|---|---|
| **Hommes** | | | | |
| 1950 (1) | 80.00 | 5.00 | .. | 15.00 |
| 1960 (1) | 76.00 | 5.50 | .. | 18.50 |
| 1970 (1) | 70.50 | 7.00 | .. | 22.50 |
| 1979 (2) | 66.61 | 7.83 | 4.61 | 25.56 |
| 1980 (1) | 65.50 | 8.50 | .. | 26.00 |
| **Femmes** | | | | |
| 1950 (1) | 5.00 | 83.50 | .. | 11.50 |
| 1960 (1) | 4.50 | 83.75 | .. | 11.75 |
| 1970 (1) | 4.00 | 84.00 | .. | 12.00 |
| 1979 (2) | 3.53 | 84.44 | 83.60 | 12.03 |

Source(s): (1) EPPA3; (2) ASTER.

### 3.2 Méthode(s): interpolation et extrapolation linéaires

#### 3.2.1 Hommes:

- 1950-80, taux de répartition 1950-80 tirés des EPPA3;
- 1990, extrapolation des taux de répartition 1950-80 tirés des EPPA3;
modification des tendances de tous les secteurs;
- Application du rapport manufacture/industrie tiré du recensement de 1979.

#### 3.2.2 Femmes:

- 1950-70, taux de répartition de l'agriculture 1950-70 tirés des EPPA3;
ajustement des taux sur la base d'un rapport hommes/femmes égal à 2/3 dans l'agriculture;
- 1950-90, interpolation et extrapolation des taux de répartition ajustés 1950-70 tirés des EPPA3; modification des tendances de tous les secteurs; les taux de répartition de manufacture ont été estimés sur la base du rapport manufacture/industrie tiré du recensement de 1979.

## 4. Projection des taux d'activité: 2000 - 2010

### 4.1 Modèle(s): linéaire et hyperbole

#### 4.1.1 Hommes:

- Aux groupes d'âge [10-49], application de la fonction F1;
- Aux groupes d'âge [50+], application de la fonction F3;
- Modification des tendances des groupes d'âge [10-64].

#### 4.1.2 Femmes:

- A tous les groupes d'âge, application de la fonction F1;
- Modification des tendances de tous les groupes d'âge.

*Notes sur les ajustements des taux, voir p. 192-195.*    *Notes sur les fonctions de projection, voir p. 198.*

# Afrique du Sud

## 1. Source(s) des données de base

Code(s):    Titre(s):

EPPA3      Evaluations et projections de la population active 1950-2025 - troisième édition, BIT, Genève, 1986.
ASTER      Annuaire des statistiques du travail 1945-89 - Edition rétrospective sur les recensements de population, BIT, Genève, 1990.
ADNU88     Annuaire démographique 1988 - Statistiques des recensements de population, quarantième édition, Nations Unies, New York, 1990.
AST93      Annuaire des statistiques du travail 1993, BIT, Genève, 1993.

## 2. Evaluation des taux d'activité: 1950 - 1990

### 2.1 Données de base:

Tableau 1: Taux d'activité par sexe et par groupe d'âge

| Groupe d'âge | Année 1950 (1) | 1960 (1) | 1970 (1) | 1980 (1) | 1985 (2) |
|---|---|---|---|---|---|
| **Hommes** | | | | | |
| 10-14 | 22.30 | 7.80 | 3.85 | 0.30 | 0.00 |
| 15-19 | 74.40 | 67.60 | 59.50 | 35.90 | 47.94 |
| 20-24 | 95.70 | 98.00 | 92.65 | 83.45 | 81.70 |
| 25-29 | 97.50 | 96.60 | 95.45 | 93.35 | 95.37 |
| 30-34 | 99.25 | 98.60 | 97.85 | 96.40 | 97.79 |
| 35-39 | 99.40 | 98.75 | 98.00 | 96.50 | 97.85 |
| 40-44 | 98.90 | 98.25 | 97.65 | 96.40 | 97.49 |
| 45-49 | 98.55 | 98.00 | 97.25 | 94.50 | 97.13 |
| 50-54 | 98.00 | 97.00 | 95.85 | 91.50 | 95.62 |
| 55-59 | 95.55 | 94.65 | 90.35 | 80.00 | 87.09 |
| 60-64 | 90.00 | 87.15 | 80.25 | 62.10 | 73.75 |
| 65+ | 69.65 | 53.05 | 44.30 | 14.30 | 30.29 |
| **Femmes** | | | | | |
| 10-14 | 4.00 | 2.60 | 1.50 | 0.15 | 0.00 |
| 15-19 | 35.45 | 35.30 | 46.80 | 28.25 | 41.91 |
| 20-24 | 35.40 | 38.60 | 58.45 | 59.65 | 54.07 |
| 25-29 | 23.40 | 29.55 | 49.65 | 50.50 | 58.92 |
| 30-34 | 20.20 | 25.55 | 43.50 | 44.30 | 51.69 |
| 35-39 | 19.95 | 25.25 | 39.55 | 40.25 | 51.19 |
| 40-44 | 19.75 | 24.95 | 37.55 | 38.20 | 48.25 |
| 45-49 | 18.40 | 23.50 | 36.85 | 37.55 | 47.84 |
| 50-54 | 17.90 | 22.85 | 34.40 | 35.55 | 44.36 |
| 55-59 | 15.15 | 18.90 | 25.95 | 25.30 | 29.43 |
| 60-64 | 11.25 | 13.80 | 20.05 | 14.90 | 22.72 |
| 65+ | 8.15 | 6.00 | 5.60 | 2.00 | 5.61 |

Source(s): (1) EPPA3; (2) ADNU88 et ASTER.

### 2.2 Méthode(s): extrapolation linéaire
moyenne pondérée

**2.2.1 Hommes:**

- 1950-70, taux d'activité 1950-70 tirés des EPPA3;
- 1980, moyennes pondérées des taux d'activité 1970 tirés des EPPA3
et des taux ajustés tirés du recensement de 1985;
- 1990, extrapolation des taux d'activité 1950-70 tirés des EPPA3 et des
taux ajustés du recensement de 1985;
ajustement des taux extrapolés sur la base des variations d
es taux interpolés 1985 par rapport aux taux ajustés du recensement de 1985.

**2.2.2 Femmes:**

- 1950-70, taux d'activité 1950-70 tirés des EPPA3;
ajustement des taux 1950 et 1960 en tenant compte des aides familiales en agricul
- Pour 1980, moyennes pondérées des taux d'activité 1970 tirés des EPPA3
et des taux ajustés tirés du recensement de 1985;
- 1990, extrapolation des taux d'activité 1950-70 tirés des EPPA3
et des taux ajustés du recensement de 1985;
ajustement des taux extrapolés sur la base des variations des
taux interpolés 1985 par rapport aux taux ajustés du recensement de 1985;
modification des tendances des groupes d'âge [20-24] et [40-44].

## 3. Evaluation des taux de répartition par secteur d'activité: 1950 - 1990

### 3.1 Données de base:

Tableau 2: Répartition de la population active en % par secteur d'activité

| Année | Agriculture | Industrie Total | Manufac. | Services |
|---|---|---|---|---|
| **Hommes** | | | | |
| 1980 (1) | 18.12 | 44.69 | 20.25 | 37.19 |
| 1985 (1) | 17.07 | 46.55 | 19.79 | 36.38 |
| 1991 (2) | 15.42 | 41.58 | 17.41 | 43.00 |
| **Femmes** | | | | |
| 1985 (1) | 12.49 | 17.16 | 14.94 | 70.35 |
| 1991 (2) | 9.99 | 14.44 | 12.31 | 75.57 |

Source(s): (1) ASTER; (2) AST93.

### 3.2 Méthode(s): moyenne pondérée

**3.2.1 Hommes:**

- 1950-70, taux de répartition 1950-70 tirés des EPPA3;
- 1980-90, moyennes pondérées des taux de répartition tirés des
recensements de 1980, 1985 et 1991.

**3.2.2 Femmes:**

- 1950-80, taux de répartition tirés des EPPA3;
ajustement des taux pour tenir compte des aides familiales en agriculture;
- 1990, moyennes pondérées des taux de répartition tirés des
recensements de 1985 et 1991.

## 4. Projection des taux d'activité: 2000 - 2010

### 4.1 Modèle(s): linéaire, log-linéaire, hyperbole et logistique

**4.1.1 Hommes:**

- Au groupe d'âge [15-19], application de la fonction F2;
- Aux groupes d'âge [20+], application de la fonction F3.

**4.1.2 Femmes:**

- Aux groupes d'âge [15-19] et [60+], application de la fonction F3;
- Aux groupes d'âge [20-24], application de la fonction F1;
- Aux groupes d'âge [25-59], application de la fonction F6;
- Modification des tendances des groupes d'âge [15-19], [25-29] et [60-64].

*Notes sur les ajustements des taux, voir p. 192-195.*    *Notes sur les fonctions de projection, voir p. 198.*

# Albanie

## 1. Source(s) des données de base

Code(s):    Titre(s):

EPPA3    Evaluations et projections de la population active 1950-2025 - troisième édition, BIT, Genève, 1986.

BLT-94-2    Popovic B. (1994), "Nouvelles estimations pour 1980 et 1990 des taux d'activité par âge et répartition sectorielle pour certains pays d'Europe orientale et méridionale" dans le Bulletin des statistiques du travail - 1994-2, BIT, Genève.

## 2. Evaluation des taux d'activité: 1950 - 1990

### 2.1 Données de base:

Tableau 1: Taux d'activité par sexe et par groupe d'âge

| Groupe d'âge | Année 1950 (1) | 1960 (1) | 1970 (1) | 1980 (2) | 1990 (2) |
|---|---|---|---|---|---|
| **Hommes** | | | | | |
| 10-14 | 13.00 | 8.00 | 5.65 | 3.80 | 2.20 |
| 15-19 | 84.15 | 72.15 | 63.35 | 55.44 | 51.71 |
| 20-24 | 97.25 | 93.25 | 90.35 | 88.06 | 87.32 |
| 25-29 | 97.45 | 95.20 | 94.50 | 94.27 | 94.02 |
| 30-34 | 98.80 | 98.60 | 97.85 | 97.57 | 97.52 |
| 35-39 | 99.40 | 99.20 | 98.45 | 98.17 | 98.12 |
| 40-44 | 99.50 | 99.30 | 98.55 | 98.37 | 98.12 |
| 45-49 | 98.60 | 97.50 | 96.40 | 95.77 | 95.42 |
| 50-54 | 98.45 | 97.35 | 96.30 | 95.57 | 94.82 |
| 55-59 | 96.65 | 90.65 | 86.65 | 83.66 | 81.92 |
| 60-64 | 96.10 | 90.10 | 86.15 | 83.16 | 77.72 |
| 65+ | 75.50 | 60.50 | 51.90 | 43.43 | 36.21 |
| **Femmes** | | | | | |
| 10-14 | 12.25 | 7.15 | 4.00 | 3.37 | 1.60 |
| 15-19 | 62.15 | 46.95 | 40.25 | 31.06 | 28.73 |
| 20-24 | 75.15 | 67.75 | 65.40 | 68.16 | 70.63 |
| 25-29 | 77.45 | 69.75 | 68.40 | 74.91 | 78.01 |
| 30-34 | 79.00 | 71.15 | 69.80 | 75.70 | 78.81 |
| 35-39 | 81.90 | 73.75 | 72.35 | 77.49 | 80.60 |
| 40-44 | 83.86 | 76.50 | 74.10 | 77.99 | 80.70 |
| 45-49 | 75.75 | 68.60 | 69.40 | 71.54 | 73.62 |
| 50-54 | 74.35 | 67.30 | 68.16 | 67.47 | 68.53 |
| 55-59 | 54.30 | 45.25 | 44.85 | 29.96 | 26.93 |
| 60-64 | 52.85 | 44.05 | 43.65 | 19.65 | 16.56 |
| 65+ | 25.15 | 19.90 | 18.05 | 7.54 | 6.09 |

Source(s): (1) EPPA3; (2) BLT-94-2.

### 2.2 Méthode(s): Données tirées des EPPA3 et du BLT-94-2.

#### 2.2.1 Hommes:

- 1950-70, taux d'activité 1950-70 tirés des EPPA3;
- 1980-90, taux d'activité tirés du Bulletin des statistiques du travail 1994-2.

#### 2.2.2 Femmes:

Méthode, hypothèses et traitements identiques à ceux appliqués aux hommes.

## 3. Evaluation des taux de répartition par secteur d'activité: 1950 - 1990

### 3.1 Données de base:

Tableau 2: Répartition de la population active en % par secteur d'activité

| Année | Agriculture | Industrie Total | Manufac. | Services |
|---|---|---|---|---|
| **Hommes** | | | | |
| 1950 (1) | 70.00 | 18.00 | .. | 12.00 |
| 1960 (1) | 63.70 | 23.00 | .. | 13.30 |
| 1970 (1) | 57.30 | 28.10 | .. | 14.50 |
| 1980 (2) | 54.00 | 27.67 | ... | 18.33 |
| 1990 (2) | 50.81 | 25.73 | ... | 23.46 |
| **Femmes** | | | | |
| 1950 (1) | 85.50 | 8.00 | .. | 6.50 |
| 1960 (1) | 82.50 | 9.40 | .. | 8.00 |
| 1970 (1) | 79.30 | 10.90 | .. | 9.70 |
| 1980 (2) | 62.34 | 16.73 | ... | 20.93 |
| 1990 (2) | 60.19 | 19.35 | ... | 20.46 |

Source(s): (1) EPPA3; (2) BLT-94-2.

### 3.2 Méthode(s): données du BLT-94-2

#### 3.2.1 Hommes:

- 1950-70, taux de répartition 1950-70 tirés des EPPA3;
- 1980-90, taux de répartition tirés du Bulletin des statistiques du travail - 1994-2.

#### 3.2.2 Femmes:

Méthode, hypothèses et traitements identiques à ceux appliqués aux hommes.

## 4. Projection des taux d'activité: 2000 - 2010

### 4.1 Modèle(s): linéaire et hyperbole

#### 4.1.1 Hommes:

- Aux groupes d'âge [15-54], application de la fonction F1;
- Aux groupes d'âge [50+], application de la fonction F3;
- Modification des tendances des groupes d'âge [15-19] et [45-54].

#### 4.1.2 Femmes:

- Aux groupes d'âge [15-19] et [50+], application de la fonction F3;
- Aux groupes d'âge [20-49], application de la fonction F1;
- Modification de la tendance du groupe d'âge [15-19].

---

*Notes sur les ajustements des taux, voir p. 192-195.*      *Notes sur les fonctions de projection, voir p. 198.*

# Algérie

## 1. Source(s) des données de base

Code(s):      Titre(s):

EPPA3      Evaluations et projections de la population active 1950-2025 - troisième édition, BIT, Genève, 1986.
R1977      Recensement général de la population et de l'habitat 1977, Office National des Statistiques, Alger, 1979.
R1987      Recensement général de la population et de l'habitat 1987 - Données synthétiques, Office National des Statistiques, Alger, 1989.

## 2. Evaluation des taux d'activité: 1950 - 1990

### 2.1 Données de base:

Tableau 1: Taux d'activité par sexe et par groupe d'âge

| Groupe d'âge | Année 1950 (1) | 1960 (1) | 1970 (1) | 1987 (2) |
|---|---|---|---|---|
| **Hommes** | | | | |
| 10-14 | 28.85 | 20.00 | 13.85 | 0.48 |
| 15-19 | 74.95 | 60.90 | 46.85 | 39.20 |
| 20-24 | 94.75 | 91.75 | 88.80 | 84.44 |
| 25-29 | 97.85 | 96.80 | 95.80 | 95.67 |
| 30-34 | 97.55 | 97.05 | 96.55 | 97.39 |
| 35-39 | 97.10 | 96.80 | 96.45 | 97.70 |
| 40-44 | 96.85 | 96.25 | 95.60 | 96.65 |
| 45-49 | 96.45 | 95.80 | 95.15 | 95.15 |
| 50-54 | 95.15 | 94.40 | 93.65 | 91.99 |
| 55-59 | 93.95 | 90.85 | 87.75 | 86.83 |
| 60-64 | 92.50 | 85.90 | 79.30 | 59.07 |
| 65+ | 76.65 | 60.00 | 43.40 | 25.52 |
| **Femmes** | | | | |
| 10-14 | .. | .. | 1.25 | 0.08 |
| 15-19 | .. | .. | 4.05 | 3.88 |
| 20-24 | .. | .. | 5.70 | 12.94 |
| 25-29 | .. | .. | 4.95 | 12.92 |
| 30-34 | .. | .. | 4.35 | 8.92 |
| 35-39 | .. | .. | 3.90 | 7.85 |
| 40-44 | .. | .. | 4.45 | 6.78 |
| 45-49 | .. | .. | 5.10 | 6.79 |
| 50-54 | .. | .. | 5.50 | 5.56 |
| 55-59 | .. | .. | 5.30 | 5.12 |
| 60-64 | .. | .. | 3.75 | 3.54 |
| 65+ | .. | .. | 1.85 | 1.71 |

Source(s): (1) EPPA3; (2) R1987.

### 2.2 Méthode(s): interpolation et extrapolation linéaires

#### 2.2.1 Hommes:

- 1950-90, interpolation et extrapolation des taux d'activité 1950-70 tirés des EPPA3 et des taux d'activité tirés du recensement de 1987;
modification des tendances de tous les groupes d'âge pour 1990.

#### 2.2.2 Femmes:

- 1950-70, taux d'activité ajustés 1950-70 tirés des EPPA3;
- 1980-90, interpolation et extrapolation des taux d'activité 1970 tirés des EPPA3 et des taux ajustés du recensement de 1987;
modification tendances des groupes d'âge [20+] pour 1990;
ajustement des taux d'activité sur la base du modèle d'ajustement des taux d'activité des femmes travaillant dans l'agriculture comme aides familiales.

## 3. Evaluation des taux de répartition par secteur d'activité: 1950 - 1990

### 3.1 Données de base:

Tableau 2: Répartition de la population active en % par secteur d'activité

| Année | Agriculture | Industrie Total | Manufac. | Services |
|---|---|---|---|---|
| **Hommes** | | | | |
| 1977 (1) | 32.88 | 33.14 | 11.84 | 33.98 |
| 1987 (2) | 19.54 | 35.68 | 12.76 | 44.78 |
| **Femmes** | | | | |
| 1977 (1) | 5.09 | 19.39 | 14.21 | 75.52 |
| 1987 (2) | 2.95 | 17.04 | 11.97 | 80.01 |

Source(s): (1) R1977; (2) R1987.

### 3.2 Méthode(s): interpolation et extrapolation linéaires

#### 3.2.1 Hommes:

- 1950-70, taux de répartition 1950-70 tirés des EPPA3;
- 1980-90, interpolation et extrapolation des taux de répartition tirés des recensements de 1977 et 1987;
modification des tendances de tous les secteurs pour 1990.

#### 3.2.2 Femmes:

- 1980-90, moyennes pondérées des taux de répartition ajustés tirés des recensements de 1977 et 1987;
ajustement des taux pour tenir compte des aides familiales en agriculture;
- 1950-70, interpolation de la différence des taux de répartition ajustés et non ajustés pour 1980 et 1990; les résultats obtenus ont été ajoutés aux taux de répartition non ajustés de la même période.

## 4. Projection des taux d'activité: 2000 - 2010

### 4.1 Modèle(s): linéaire et hyperbole

#### 4.1.1 Hommes:

- A tous les groupes d'âge, application de la fonction F1;
- Modification de la tendance du groupe d'âge [20-24].

#### 4.1.2 Femmes:

- Aux groupes d'âge [10-19] et [60+], application de la fonction F1;
- Aux groupes d'âge [20-59], application de la fonction F6;
- Modification des tendances des groupes d'âge [25-29] et [50-59].

*Notes sur les ajustements des taux, voir p. 192-195.*      *Notes sur les fonctions de projection, voir p. 198.*

# Allemagne

## 1. Source(s) des données de base

Code(s):     Titre(s):

EPPA3     Annuaire des statistiques du travail 1945-89 - Edition rétrospective sur les recensements de population, BIT, Genève, 1990.
STAT     Base de données sur les statistiques du travail - LABORSTA, Bureau de statistique, BIT, Genève.

## 2. Evaluation des taux d'activité: 1950 - 1990

### 2.1 Données de base:

Tableau 1: Taux d'activité par sexe et par groupe d'âge

| Groupe d'âge | Année | | | | | |
|---|---|---|---|---|---|---|
| | 1989 (1) | 1990 (1) | 1991 (1) | 1991 | 1992 (1) | 1992 |
| **Hommes** | | | | | | |
| 10-14 | 0.00 | 0.00 | 0.00 | 0.00 | 0.00 | 0.00 |
| 15-19 | 43.14 | 43.22 | 40.70 | 44.56 | 39.43 | 41.72 |
| 20-24 | 79.64 | 79.81 | 77.82 | 79.70 | 77.69 | 79.36 |
| 25-29 | 87.00 | 87.38 | 86.76 | 88.50 | 86.84 | 88.24 |
| 30-34 | 95.95 | 95.77 | 95.69 | 96.31 | 95.63 | 96.19 |
| 35-39 | 97.48 | 97.48 | 97.35 | 97.71 | 97.36 | 97.60 |
| 40-44 | 97.50 | 97.41 | 97.22 | 97.56 | 97.34 | 97.56 |
| 45-49 | 96.63 | 96.55 | 95.93 | 96.43 | 95.82 | 96.23 |
| 50-54 | 92.97 | 93.23 | 92.93 | 93.37 | 92.94 | 93.28 |
| 55-59 | 78.63 | 81.09 | 81.45 | 79.75 | 81.51 | 74.21 |
| 60-64 | 34.21 | 35.05 | 34.95 | 33.49 | 34.87 | 31.31 |
| 65+ | 4.50 | 5.25 | 5.13 | 4.54 | 4.91 | 4.36 |
| **Femmes** | | | | | | |
| 10-14 | 0.00 | 0.00 | 0.00 | 0.00 | 0.00 | 0.00 |
| 15-19 | 38.36 | 37.29 | 34.84 | 37.20 | 34.29 | 36.01 |
| 20-24 | 74.08 | 75.65 | 73.42 | 75.86 | 72.55 | 74.58 |
| 25-29 | 69.26 | 71.58 | 70.77 | 75.57 | 72.47 | 76.56 |
| 30-34 | 62.86 | 66.90 | 66.46 | 72.79 | 67.68 | 73.59 |
| 35-39 | 64.40 | 68.03 | 68.76 | 75.07 | 70.22 | 75.93 |
| 40-44 | 64.81 | 69.46 | 70.52 | 75.35 | 72.59 | 77.12 |
| 45-49 | 61.82 | 66.71 | 67.12 | 72.79 | 68.70 | 73.77 |
| 50-54 | 54.38 | 57.82 | 68.60 | 65.32 | 60.80 | 66.75 |
| 55-59 | 40.89 | 43.82 | 44.36 | 42.84 | 45.51 | 41.70 |
| 60-64 | 11.18 | 12.49 | 12.20 | 10.70 | 11.91 | 9.99 |
| 65+ | 1.64 | 2.00 | 1.99 | 1.73 | 2.00 | 1.71 |

**Note(s)**: (1) Rép. Féd. d'Allemagne.
**Source(s)**: STAT.

### 2.2 Méthode(s): moyenne arithmétique

#### 2.2.1 Hommes:

- 1950-80, taux d'activité 1950-80 tirés des EPPA3;
- 1990, aux moyennes des taux d'activité tirés des enquêtes de 1989, 1990, et 1991 pour la Rép. Féd. d'Allemagne, application des variations des moyennes des taux d'activité tirés des enquêtes de 1991 et 1992 pour l'Allemagne par rapport aux moyennes des taux d'activité tirés des enquêtes de 1991 et 1992 pour la Rép. Féd. d'Allemagne.

#### 2.2.2 Femmes:

Méthode, hypothèses et traitements identiques à ceux appliqués aux hommes.

## 3. Evaluation des taux de répartition par secteur d'activité: 1950 - 1990

### 3.1 Données de base:

Tableau 2: Répartition de la population active en % par secteur d'activité

| Année | Agriculture | Industrie | | Services |
|---|---|---|---|---|
| | | Total | Manufac. | |
| **Hommes** | | | | |
| 1989 (1) | 3.39 | 48.50 | 36.59 | 48.11 |
| 1990 (1) | 3.25 | 48.79 | 36.90 | 47.97 |
| 1991 (1) | 3.00 | 46.23 | 35.09 | 50.76 |
| 1991 (2) | 7.27 | 47.95 | 30.58 | 44.79 |
| 1992 (2) | 5.64 | 50.66 | 27.74 | 43.70 |
| 1992 (1) | 3.01 | 47.97 | 36.40 | 49.02 |
| **Femmes** | | | | |
| 1989 (1) | 4.14 | 24.69 | 22.40 | 71.17 |
| 1990 (1) | 3.82 | 24.58 | 22.27 | 71.60 |
| 1991 (1) | 3.28 | 22.49 | 20.28 | 74.22 |
| 1991 (2) | 4.77 | 24.65 | 20.51 | 70.58 |
| 1992 (2) | 4.07 | 21.51 | 16.75 | 74.41 |
| 1992 (1) | 3.22 | 23.33 | 2.14 | 73.45 |

**Notes(s)**: (1) Rép. Dém. d'Allemagne; (2) Rép. Féd. d'Allemagne.
**Source(s)**: STAT.

### 3.2 Méthode(s): moyenne arithmétique

#### 3.2.1 Hommes:

- 1950-80, taux de répartition 1950-80 tirés des EPPA3;
- 1990, aux moyennes des taux de répartition tirés des enquêtes de 1989, 1990 et 1991 pour la Rép. Féd. D'Allemagne, application des variations des moyennes des taux tirés des enquêtes de 1991 et 1992 pour l'ensemble de l'Allemagne par rapport aux moyennes des taux tirés des enquêtes de 1991 et 1992 pour la Rép. Féd. d'Allemagne.

#### 3.2.2 Femmes:

Méthode, hypothèses et traitements identiques à ceux appliqués aux hommes.

## 4. Projection des taux d'activité: 2000 - 2010

### 4.1 Modèle(s): linéaire, log-linéaire, hyperbole et logistique

#### 4.1.1 Hommes:

- Au groupe d'âge [15-19], application de la fonction F1;
- Au groupe d'âge [20-24], application de la fonction F2;
- Aux groupes d'âge [25+], application de la fonction F3;
- Modification des tendances des groupes d'âge [25-44] et [55+].

#### 4.1.2 Femmes:

- Au groupe d'âge [15-19], application de la fonction F1;
- Au groupe d'âge [20-24], application de la fonction F2;
- Aux groupes d'âge [25-54], application de la fonction F6;
- Aux groupes d'âge [55+], application de la fonction F3;
- Modification des tendances des groupes d'âge [15-24].

*Notes sur les ajustements des taux, voir p. 192-195.*

*Notes sur les fonctions de projection, voir p. 198.*

# Angola

## 1. Source(s) des données de base

Code(s):     Titre(s):

EPPA3      Evaluations et projections de la population active 1950-2025 - troisième édition, BIT, Genève, 1986.
ADNU79     Annuaire démographique 1979 - Statistiques des recensements de population, trente et unième édition, Nations Unies, New York, 1980.

## 2. Evaluation des taux d'activité: 1950 - 1990

### 2.1 Données de base:

Tableau 1: Taux d'activité par sexe et par groupe d'âge

| Groupe d'âge | Année 1950 (1) | 1960 (1) | 1970 (1) | 1970 (2) | 1980 (1) |
|---|---|---|---|---|---|
| **Hommes** | | | | | |
| 10-14 | 44.70 | 43.30 | 41.45 | 30.33 | 38.8 |
| 15-19 | 75.05 | 73.20 | 70.70 | 84.63 | 67.25 |
| 20-24 | 91.50 | 90.75 | 89.80 | 87.82 | 88.5 |
| 25-29 | 96.85 | 96.75 | 96.60 | 94.66 | 96.4 |
| 30-34 | 97.50 | 97.40 | 97.25 | 98.22 | 97 |
| 35-39 | 97.65 | 97.50 | 97.35 | 97.44 | 97.1 |
| 40-44 | 97.45 | 97.30 | 97.15 | 96.95 | 96.9 |
| 45-49 | 96.80 | 96.65 | 96.50 | 94.73 | 96.3 |
| 50-54 | 96.05 | 95.90 | 95.65 | 94.58 | 95.35 |
| 55-59 | 94.65 | 94.35 | 94.00 | 90.56 | 93.5 |
| 60-64 | 90.70 | 90.25 | 89.65 | 83.95 | 88.8 |
| 65+ | 75.70 | 74.90 | 73.80 | 73.41 | 72.3 |
| **Femmes** | | | | | |
| 10-14 | 33.80 | 32.70 | 31.30 | 28.7 | 29.35 |
| 15-19 | 55.60 | 54.00 | 51.90 | 72.05 | 48.95 |
| 20-24 | 58.85 | 57.85 | 56.55 | 76.25 | 54.7 |
| 25-29 | 63.10 | 61.95 | 60.45 | 79.45 | 58.35 |
| 30-34 | 67.05 | 65.80 | 64.20 | 78.03 | 61.95 |
| 35-39 | 68.70 | 67.55 | 66.05 | 81.74 | 63.95 |
| 40-44 | 71.15 | 70.00 | 68.50 | 84.2 | 66.4 |
| 45-49 | 70.55 | 69.40 | 67.85 | 84.8 | 65.7 |
| 50-54 | 68.15 | 66.80 | 65.05 | 82.23 | 62.5 |
| 55-59 | 65.10 | 63.65 | 61.80 | 78.47 | 59.2 |
| 60-64 | 57.05 | 55.25 | 52.90 | 69.15 | 49.55 |
| 65+ | 37.65 | 35.95 | 33.75 | 42.14 | 30.65 |

Source(s):  (1) EPPA3; (2) ADNU79.

### 2.2 Méthode(s): interpolation et extrapolation linéaires

#### 2.2.1 Hommes:

- 1950-90, interpolation et extrapolation des taux d'activité 1950-80
tirés des EPPA3;
ajustement des taux interpolés et extrapolés sur la base des
variations des taux interpolés 1970 par rapport aux taux tirés du recensement
de 1970;
modification des tendances des groupes d'âge [10-24] pour 1950 et 1960
et de tous les groupes d'âge pour 1980 et 1990.

#### 2.2.2 Femmes:

- 1950-90, interpolation et extrapolation des taux d'activité 1950-80 tirés
des EPPA3;
ajustement des taux interpolés et extrapolés sur la base des variations
des taux interpolés 1970 par rapport aux taux tirés du recensement de 1970;
modification des tendances des groupes d'âge [15+] pour 1950 et 1960
et de tous les groupes d'âge pour 1980 et 1990.

## 3. Evaluation des taux de répartition par secteur d'activité: 1950 - 1990

### 3.1 Données de base:

Tableau 2: Répartition de la population active en % par secteur d'activité

| Année | Agriculture | Industrie Total | Manufac. | Services |
|---|---|---|---|---|
| **Hommes** | | | | |
| 1950 (1) | 74.00 | 11.35 | .. | 14.65 |
| 1960 (1) | 71.40 | 12.50 | .. | 16.10 |
| 1970 (1) | 68.00 | 13.50 | .. | 18.50 |
| 1970 (2) | 68.52 | 12.66 | 6.19 | 18.82 |
| 1980 (1) | 63.20 | 15.00 | .. | 21.80 |
| **Femmes** | | | | |
| 1950 (1) | 94.60 | 0.80 | .. | 4.60 |
| 1960 (1) | 93.30 | 1.00 | .. | 5.70 |
| 1970 (1) | 91.60 | 1.25 | .. | 7.15 |
| 1970 (2) | 88.93 | 1.10 | 1.01 | 9.97 |
| 1980 (1) | 89.20 | 1.60 | .. | 9.20 |

Source(s): (1) EPPA3; (2) ADNU79.

### 3.2 Méthode(s): interpolation et extrapolation linéaires

#### 3.2.1 Hommes:

- 1950-90, interpolation et extrapolation des taux de répartition 1950-80
tirés des EPPA3;
ajustement des taux sur la base des variations des taux interpolés 1970
par rapport aux taux tirés du recensement de 1970;
modification des tendances de tous les secteurs pour 1980 et 1990;
- Application du rapport manufacture/industrie tiré du recensement de 1970.

#### 3.2.2 Femmes:

Méthode, hypothèses et traitements identiques à ceux appliqués aux hommes.

## 4. Projection des taux d'activité: 2000 - 2010

### 4.1 Modèle(s): hyperbole

#### 4.1.1 Hommes:

- A tous les groupes d'âge, application de la fonction F3.

#### 4.1.2 Femmes:

- A tous les groupes d'âge, application de la fonction F3;
- Modification des tendances des groupes d'âge [20-54].

---

*Notes sur les ajustements des taux, voir p. 192-195.*          *Notes sur les fonctions de projection, voir p. 198.*

# Antilles néerlandaises

## 1. Source(s) des données de base

Code(s):    Titre(s):
STAT       Base de données sur les statistiques du travail - LABORSTA, Bureau de statistique, BIT, Genève.

## 2. Evaluation des taux d'activité: 1950 - 1990

### 2.1 Données de base:

Tableau 1: Taux d'activité par sexe et par groupe d'âge

| Groupe d'âge | 1972 | 1981 | 1992 |
|---|---|---|---|
| **Hommes** | | | |
| 10-14 | .. | 0.32 | 0.00 |
| 15-19 | .. | 34.10 | 29.76 |
| 20-24 | .. | 85.33 | 80.75 |
| 25-29 | .. | 94.93 | 91.46 |
| 30-34 | .. | 95.79 | 92.59 |
| 35-39 | .. | 96.01 | 93.10 |
| 40-44 | .. | 95.70 | 93.09 |
| 45-49 | .. | 94.83 | 91.54 |
| 50-54 | .. | 89.94 | 86.40 |
| 55-59 | .. | 80.46 | 67.78 |
| 60-64 | .. | 48.37 | 34.32 |
| 65+ | .. | 20.16 | 13.62 |
| **Femmes** | | | |
| 10-14 | 0.41 | 0.16 | 0.00 |
| 15-19 | 32.11 | 26.20 | 22.00 |
| 20-24 | 66.83 | 73.42 | 70.68 |
| 25-29 | 51.57 | 70.36 | 77.50 |
| 30-34 | 41.25 | 61.34 | 75.90 |
| 35-39 | 35.99 | 53.90 | 73.43 |
| 40-44 | 31.81 | 44.71 | 68.37 |
| 45-49 | 28.51 | 37.66 | 57.96 |
| 50-54 | 24.07 | 29.73 | 43.84 |
| 55-59 | 22.86 | 22.00 | 29.78 |
| 60-64 | 13.54 | 12.73 | 14.31 |
| 65+ | 5.41 | 4.12 | 3.59 |

Source(s): STAT.

### 2.2 Méthode(s): interpolation et extrapolation linéaires

#### 2.2.1 Hommes:
- 1950-80, extrapolation des taux d'activité ajustés tirés des recensements de 1981 et 1992;
modification de la tendance du groupe d'âge [50-54];
- 1990, interpolation des taux d'activité ajustés tirés des recensements de 1981 et 1992.

#### 2.2.2 Femmes:
- 1950-70, extrapolation des taux d'activité ajustés tirés des recensements de 1972 et 1981;
modification des tendances de tous les groupes d'âge;
- 1980, interpolation des taux d'activité ajustés tirés des recensements de 1972 et 1981;
modification de la tendance du groupe d'âge [50-54];
- 1990, interpolation des taux d'activité ajustés tirés des recensements de 1981 et 1992.

## 3. Evaluation des taux de répartition par secteur d'activité: 1950 - 1990

### 3.1 Données de base:

Tableau 2: Répartition de la population active en % par secteur d'activité

| Année | Agriculture | Industrie Total | Manufac. | Services |
|---|---|---|---|---|
| **Hommes** | | | | |
| 1960 | 2.83 | 56.86 | 40.51 | 40.31 |
| 1972 | 1.34 | 37.42 | 20.28 | 61.24 |
| 1981 | 0.55 | 30.54 | 14.38 | 68.91 |
| 1992 | 1.07 | 31.37 | 13.57 | 67.56 |
| **Femmes** | | | | |
| 1960 | 0.21 | 8.09 | 7.32 | 91.70 |
| 1972 | 0.20 | 13.34 | 11.68 | 86.46 |
| 1981 | 0.13 | 5.83 | 3.66 | 94.04 |
| 1992 | 0.28 | 5.20 | 3.76 | 94.52 |

Source(s): STAT

### 3.2 Méthode(s): interpolation et extrapolation linéaires

#### 3.2.1 Hommes:
- 1950, extrapolation des taux de répartition tirés des recensements de 1960 et 1972,
- 1970-90, interpolation des taux de répartition tirés des recensements de 1960, 1972, 1981 et 1992.

#### 3.2.2 Femmes:
Méthode, hypothèses et traitements identiques à ceux appliqués aux hommes.

## 4. Projection des taux d'activité: 2000 - 2010

### 4.1 Modèle(s): linéaire, hyperbole et logistique

#### 4.1.1 Hommes:
- Aux groupes d'âge [10-19], application de la fonction F1;
- Aux groupes d'âge [20+], application de la fonction F3;
- Modification des tendances de tous les groupes d'âge.

#### 4.1.2 Femmes:
- Au groupe d'âge [15-19], application de la fonction F1;
- Aux groupes d'âge [20-64], application de la fonction F6;
- Au groupe d'âge [65+], application de la fonction F3;
- Modification des tendances de tous les groupes d'âge.

*Notes sur les ajustements des taux, voir p. 192-195.*

*Notes sur les fonctions de projection, voir p. 198.*

# Arabie saoudite

## 1. Source(s) des données de base

Code(s):     Titre(s):

EPPA3     Evaluations et projections de la population active 1950-2025 - troisième édition, BIT, Genève, 1986.

## 2. Evaluation des taux d'activité: 1950 - 1990

### 2.1 Données de base:

Tableau 1: Taux d'activité par sexe et par groupe d'âge

| Groupe d'âge | Année 1975 (1) | 1980 (2) | 1987 (3) | 1988 (3) |
|---|---|---|---|---|
| **Hommes** | | | | |
| 10-14 | 22.00 | 19.30 | 16.20 | 8.10 |
| 15-19 | 86.75 | 81.85 | 69.30 | 49.30 |
| 20-24 | 95.40 | 94.50 | 91.30 | 86.65 |
| 25-29 | 98.00 | 97.80 | 97.30 | 96.55 |
| 30-34 | 98.40 | 98.35 | 98.20 | 98.00 |
| 35-39 | 97.25 | 97.40 | 97.65 | 98.10 |
| 40-44 | 96.80 | 96.85 | 97.00 | 97.20 |
| 45-49 | 96.40 | 96.30 | 96.00 | 97.55 |
| 50-54 | 93.60 | 93.35 | 92.80 | 91.90 |
| 55-59 | 90.35 | 89.90 | 88.50 | 86.40 |
| 60-64 | 81.75 | 80.85 | 78.50 | 74.75 |
| 65+ | 56.15 | 55.30 | 53.05 | 49.50 |
| **Femmes** | | | | |
| 10-14 | .. | .. | .. | .. |
| 15-19 | .. | .. | .. | .. |
| 20-24 | .. | .. | .. | .. |
| 25-29 | .. | .. | .. | .. |
| 30-34 | .. | .. | .. | .. |
| 35-39 | .. | .. | .. | .. |
| 40-44 | .. | .. | .. | .. |
| 45-49 | .. | .. | .. | .. |
| 50-54 | .. | .. | .. | .. |
| 55-59 | .. | .. | .. | .. |
| 60-64 | .. | .. | .. | .. |
| 65+ | .. | .. | .. | .. |

Source(s): EPPA3.

### 2.2 Méthode(s): extrapolation linéaire

#### 2.2.1 Hommes:

- 1950-80, taux d'activité 1950-80 tirés des EPPA3;
- 1990, extrapolation des taux d'activité 1950-80 tirés des EPPA3;
ajustement des taux extrapolés sur la base des variations des taux interpolés 1980 par rapport aux taux 1980 tirés des EPPA3;
modification des tendances des groupes d'âge [10-14], [25-54] et [60+].

#### 2.2.2 Femmes:

- 1950-70, taux d'activité 1950-70 tirés des EPPA3;
- 1980-90, aux taux d'activité 1970 tirés des EPPA3, application de la moyenne des variations des taux d'activité estimés pour Bahreïn, le Koweït et Oman pour 1980 et 1990 par rapport aux taux estimés 1970 pour ces pays.

## 3. Evaluation des taux de répartition par secteur d'activité: 1950 - 1990

### 3.1 Données de base:

Tableau 2: Répartition de la population active en % par secteur d'activité

| Année | Agriculture | Industrie Total | Manufac. | Services |
|---|---|---|---|---|
| **Hommes** | | | | |
| 1950 | 76.00 | 9.00 | .. | 15.00 |
| 1960 | 71.00 | 10.00 | .. | 19.00 |
| 1970 | 65.00 | 12.50 | .. | 22.50 |
| 1980 | 45.00 | 16.50 | 5.33 | 38.50 |
| **Femmes** | | | | |
| 1950 | 87.00 | 2.80 | .. | 10.20 |
| 1960 | 76.00 | 3.60 | .. | 20.40 |
| 1970 | 48.60 | 4.40 | .. | 47.00 |
| 1980 | 25.00 | 5.00 | 2.82 | 70.00 |

Source(s): EPPA3.

### 3.2 Méthode(s): extrapolation linéaire

#### 3.2.1 Hommes:

- 1950-80, taux de répartition 1950-80 tirés des EPPA3;
- 1990, extrapolation des taux de répartition 1950-80 tirés des EPPA3;
modification des tendances de tous les secteurs.

#### 3.2.2 Femmes:

Méthode, hypothèses et traitements identiques à ceux appliqués aux hommes.

## 4. Projection des taux d'activité: 2000 - 2010

### 4.1 Modèle(s): linéaire, log-linéaire, hyperbole et logistique

#### 4.1.1 Hommes:

- Au groupe d'âge [15-19], application de la fonction F2;
- Aux groupes d'âge [20-59], application de la fonction F3;
- Aux groupes d'âge [60+], application de la fonction F1;
- Modification des tendances des groupes d'âge [20-24] et [35-54].

#### 4.1.2 Femmes:

- Aux groupes d'âge [15-24], application de la fonction F2;
- Aux groupes d'âge [25-39], application de la fonction F6;
- Aux groupes d'âge [40-64], application de la fonction F2;
- Au groupe d'âge [65+], application de la fonction F1;
- Modification de la tendance du groupe d'âge [15-19].

---

*Notes sur les ajustements des taux, voir p. 192-195.*     *Notes sur les fonctions de projection, voir p. 198.*

# Argentine

## 1. Source(s) des données de base

| Code(s): | Titre(s): |
|---|---|
| EPPA3 | Evaluations et projections de la population active 1950-2025 - troisième édition, BIT, Genève, 1986. |
| STAT | Base de données sur les statistiques du travail - LABORSTA, Bureau de statistique, BIT, Genève. |

## 2. Evaluation des taux d'activité: 1950 - 1990

### 2.1 Données de base:

Tableau 1: Taux d'activité par sexe et par groupe d'âge

| Groupe d'âge | Année 1970 (1) | 1990 (2) |
|---|---|---|
| **Hommes** | | |
| 10-14 | 11.50 | 8.84 |
| 15-19 | 62.20 | 57.54 |
| 20-24 | 87.00 | 86.26 |
| 25-29 | 95.80 | 95.66 |
| 30-34 | 97.50 | 97.77 |
| 35-39 | 98.10 | 97.98 |
| 40-44 | 97.40 | 97.14 |
| 45-49 | 95.40 | 95.04 |
| 50-54 | 91.40 | 90.60 |
| 55-59 | 80.40 | 79.39 |
| 60-64 | 57.20 | 56.07 |
| 65+ | 29.10 | 23.48 |
| **Femmes** | | |
| 10-14 | 6.20 | 4.41 |
| 15-19 | 31.60 | 24.46 |
| 20-24 | 43.60 | 51.21 |
| 25-29 | 36.00 | 45.09 |
| 30-34 | 31.70 | 40.65 |
| 35-39 | 29.20 | 36.90 |
| 40-44 | 27.20 | 34.89 |
| 45-49 | 25.20 | 31.70 |
| 50-54 | 22.10 | 26.85 |
| 55-59 | 16.40 | 18.41 |
| 60-64 | 10.50 | 9.90 |
| 65+ | 4.70 | 2.89 |

Source(s): (1) EPPA3; (2) STAT.

### 2.2 Méthode(s): moyenne arithmétique

#### 2.2.1 Hommes:

- 1950-70, taux d'activité 1950-70 tirés des EPPA3;
- 1980, moyennes des taux d'activité 1970 tirés des EPPA3 et des taux d'activité tirés des évaluations officielles de 1990;
- 1990, taux d'activité tirés des évaluations officielles de 1990.

#### 2.2.2 Femmes:

Méthode, hypothèses et traitements identiques à ceux appliqués aux hommes.

## 3. Evaluation des taux de répartition par secteur d'activité: 1950 - 1990

### 3.1 Données de base:

Tableau 2: Répartition de la population active en % par secteur d'activité

| Année | Agriculture | Industrie Total | Manufac. | Services |
|---|---|---|---|---|
| **Hommes** | | | | |
| 1950 | 23.86 | 38.43 | 28.11 | 37.72 |
| 1970 | 20.24 | 35.67 | 22.11 | 44.09 |
| 1980 | 16.63 | 39.62 | 23.04 | 43.75 |
| **Femmes** | | | | |
| 1950 | 5.16 | 27.02 | 26.37 | 67.81 |
| 1970 | 4.22 | 20.81 | 19.86 | 74.97 |
| 1980 | 3.06 | 18.22 | 16.91 | 78.72 |

Source(s): STAT.

### 3.2 Méthode(s): extrapolation linéaire

#### 3.2.1 Hommes:

- 1950-70, taux de répartition 1950-70 tirés des EPPA3;
- 1980-90, extrapolation des taux de répartition tirés des recensements de 1960, 1970 et 1980;
modification des tendances de tous les secteurs;
application du rapport manufacture/industrie tiré du recensement de 1980.

#### 3.2.2 Femmes:

Méthode, hypothèses et traitements identiques à ceux appliqués aux hommes.

## 4. Projection des taux d'activité: 2000 - 2010

### 4.1 Modèle(s): linéaire et hyperbole

#### 4.1.1 Hommes:

- Aux groupes d'âge [10-44], application de la fonction F1;
- Aux groupes d'âge [45+], application de la fonction F3;
- Modification de la tendance du groupe d'âge [10-14].

#### 4.1.2 Femmes:

- Au groupe d'âge [10-14], application de la fonction F1;
- Aux groupes d'âge [15+], application de la fonction F3;
- Modification des tendances des groupes d'âge [10-14], [20-24] et [60-64].

*Notes sur les ajustements des taux, voir p. 192-195.*

*Notes sur les fonctions de projection, voir p. 198.*

# Arménie

## 1. Source(s) des données de base

Code(s): Titre(s):

BLT-94-2    Vorobiev A. (1994), "Estimation de la population active pour les quinze pays de l'ex-URSS pour les années 1950, 1959, 1970, 1979 et 1989", dans le Bulletin des statistiques du travail - 1994-2, BIT, Genève.

## 2. Evaluation des taux d'activité: 1950 - 1990

### 2.1 Données de base:

Tableau 1: Taux d'activité par sexe et par groupe d'âge

| Groupe d'âge | Année 1950 | 1959 | 1970 | 1979 | 1989 |
|---|---|---|---|---|---|
| **Hommes** | | | | | |
| 10-14 | 0.00 | 0.00 | 0.00 | 0.00 | 0.00 |
| 15-19 | 42.35 | 50.75 | 30.53 | 33.33 | 25.69 |
| 20-24 | 79.01 | 80.68 | 70.73 | 77.64 | 60.87 |
| 25-29 | 90.91 | 93.83 | 98.33 | 95.69 | 77.64 |
| 30-34 | 91.67 | 94.81 | 98.02 | 98.63 | 80.42 |
| 35-39 | 93.75 | 96.77 | 97.59 | 98.63 | 81.90 |
| 40-44 | 93.55 | 95.65 | 96.43 | 97.94 | 79.69 |
| 45-49 | 91.30 | 93.33 | 97.44 | 96.51 | 78.79 |
| 50-54 | 90.48 | 89.66 | 90.48 | 94.74 | 77.38 |
| 55-59 | 92.86 | 86.36 | 86.21 | 86.21 | 70.67 |
| 60-64 | 76.92 | 83.33 | 60.71 | 50.00 | 45.16 |
| 65+ | 36.67 | 33.33 | 16.07 | 16.90 | 19.05 |
| **Femmes** | | | | | |
| 10-14 | 0.00 | 0.00 | 0.00 | 0.00 | 0.00 |
| 15-19 | 41.57 | 44.12 | 28.00 | 32.98 | 17.91 |
| 20-24 | 58.82 | 60.00 | 63.22 | 73.10 | 50.35 |
| 25-29 | 61.36 | 65.12 | 80.60 | 86.18 | 62.50 |
| 30-34 | 55.56 | 59.26 | 82.24 | 88.31 | 68.46 |
| 35-39 | 58.50 | 59.52 | 83.13 | 91.25 | 72.32 |
| 40-44 | 57.89 | 58.82 | 83.53 | 92.08 | 72.06 |
| 45-49 | 56.76 | 55.00 | 81.25 | 91.76 | 70.42 |
| 50-54 | 40.00 | 41.67 | 64.52 | 79.52 | 62.22 |
| 55-59 | 30.00 | 28.57 | 28.89 | 41.86 | 36.25 |
| 60-64 | 26.32 | 25.00 | 12.20 | 16.22 | 21.62 |
| 65+ | 2.33 | 3.45 | 3.66 | 3.64 | 6.48 |

Source(s): BLT-94-2-2

### 2.2 Méthode(s): moyenne pondérée

#### 2.2.1 Hommes:
- 1950-90, moyennes pondérées des taux d'activité 1950, 1959, 1970 et 1989 tirés du Bulletin des statistiques du travail, 1994-2.

#### 2.2.2 Femmes:
Méthode, hypothèses et traitements identiques à ceux appliqués aux hommes.

## 3. Evaluation des taux de répartition par secteur d'activité: 1950 - 1990

### 3.1 Données de base:

Tableau 2: Répartition de la population active en % par secteur d'activité

| Année | Agriculture | Industrie Total | Manufac. | Services |
|---|---|---|---|---|
| **Hommes** | | | | |
| 1950 | 52.63 | 24.91 | 16.84 | 22.46 |
| 1959 | 39.71 | 29.90 | 17.65 | 30.39 |
| 1970 | 25.24 | 43.26 | 26.57 | 31.50 |
| 1979 | 20.92 | 47.77 | 25.78 | 31.31 |
| 1989 | 23.41 | 47.11 | 30.20 | 29.48 |
| **Femmes** | | | | |
| 1950 | 37.03 | 9.46 | 7.30 | 53.51 |
| 1959 | 59.55 | 21.35 | 18.35 | 19.10 |
| 1970 | 30.02 | 30.91 | 26.71 | 39.07 |
| 1979 | 22.64 | 37.68 | 25.79 | 39.68 |
| 1989 | 12.26 | 38.51 | 34.20 | 49.22 |

Source(s): BLT-94-2.

### 3.2 Méthode(s): moyenne pondérée

#### 3.2.1 Hommes:
- 1950-90, moyennes pondérées des taux de répartition 1950, 1959, 1970, 1979 et 1989 tirés du Bulletin des statistiques du travail - 1994-2.

#### 3.2.2 Femmes:
Méthode, hypothèses et traitements identiques à ceux appliqués aux hommes.

## 4. Projection des taux d'activité: 2000 - 2010

### 4.1 Modèle(s): hyperbole et logistique

#### 4.1.1 Hommes:
- Aux groupes d'âge [15+], application de la fonction F3;
- Modification des tendances des groupes d'âge [25-54].

#### 4.1.2 Femmes:
- Aux groupes d'âge [15-24], application de la fonction F3;
- Aux groupes d'âge [25-59], application de la fonction F6;
- Aux groupes d'âge [60+], application de la fonction F3;
- Modification des tendances des groupes d'âge [20-59].

---

*Notes sur les ajustements des taux, voir p. 192-195.*    *Notes sur les fonctions de projection, voir p. 198.*

# Australie

## 1. Source(s) des données de base

Code(s):    Titre(s):

EPPA3    Annuaire des statistiques du travail 1945-89 - Edition rétrospective sur les recensements de population, BIT, Genève, 1990.

STAT    Base de données sur les statistiques du travail - LABORSTA, Bureau de statistique, BIT, Genève.

## 2. Evaluation des taux d'activité: 1950 - 1990

### 2.1 Données de base:

Tableau 1: Taux d'activité par sexe et par groupe d'âge

| Groupe d'âge | Année | | | | | |
|---|---|---|---|---|---|---|
| | 1979 | 1980 | 1981 | 1989 | 1990 | 1991 |
| **Hommes** | | | | | | |
| 10-14 | 0.00 | 0.00 | 0.00 | 0.00 | 0.00 | 0.00 |
| 15-19 | 64.10 | 65.30 | 66.00 | 61.90 | 61.40 | 57.10 |
| 20-24 | 90.90 | 91.50 | 91.60 | 89.90 | 89.80 | 88.40 |
| 25-34 | 96.20 | 95.90 | 95.50 | 94.60 | 94.40 | 94.50 |
| 35-44 | 95.90 | 95.60 | 95.50 | 93.80 | 94.40 | 94.10 |
| 45-54 | 91.60 | 91.50 | 90.90 | 89.10 | 89.90 | 89.60 |
| 55-59 | 82.10 | 82.60 | 81.20 | 75.20 | 75.00 | 73.70 |
| 60-64 | 54.40 | 51.50 | 50.50 | 49.80 | 50.60 | 49.90 |
| 65+ | 11.60 | 11.20 | 10.70 | 9.10 | 9.20 | 8.90 |
| **Femmes** | | | | | | |
| 10-14 | .. | 0.00 | .. | .. | 0.00 | .. |
| 15-19 | .. | 61.50 | .. | .. | 59.30 | .. |
| 20-24 | .. | 71.00 | .. | .. | 78.60 | .. |
| 25-34 | .. | 52.40 | .. | .. | 65.70 | .. |
| 35-44 | .. | 58.20 | .. | .. | 72.00 | .. |
| 45-54 | .. | 47.70 | .. | .. | 61.00 | .. |
| 55-59 | .. | 28.90 | .. | .. | 33.90 | .. |
| 60-64 | .. | 13.40 | .. | .. | 10.00 | .. |
| 65+ | .. | 2.80 | .. | .. | 2.40 | .. |

Source(s): STAT.

### 2.2 Méthode(s): moyenne arithmétique

#### 2.2.1 Hommes:

- 1950-70, taux d'activité 1950-70 tirés des EPPA3;
ajustement du taux d'activité du groupe d'âge [15-19] pour 1960 et 1970;
- 1980, moyennes des taux d'activité ajustés tirés des enquêtes de 1979, 1980 et 1981;
- 1990, moyennes des taux d'activité ajustés tirés des enquêtes de 1989, 1990 et 1991.

#### 2.2.2 Femmes:

- 1950-70, taux d'activité 1950-70 tirés des EPPA3;
ajustement des taux d'activité du groupe d'âge [15-19];
- 1980 et 1990, taux d'activité ajustés tirés respectivement des enquêtes de 1980 et 1990.

## 3. Evaluation des taux de répartition par secteur d'activité: 1950 - 1990

### 3.1 Données de base:

Tableau 2: Répartition de la population active en % par secteur d'activité

| Année | Agriculture | Industrie | | Services |
|---|---|---|---|---|
| | | Total | Manufac. | |
| **Hommes** | | | | |
| 1989 (1) | 7.00 | 35.40 | 20.48 | 57.61 |
| 1990 (1) | 6.39 | 35.65 | 19.72 | 57.95 |
| 1991 (1) | 6.68 | 34.78 | 19.57 | 58.55 |
| **Femmes** | | | | |
| 1970 (2) | 4.55 | 22.45 | .. | 73.00 |
| 1981 (1) | 3.83 | 17.06 | 14.77 | 79.11 |
| 1989 (1) | 4.16 | 13.77 | 10.87 | 82.07 |
| 1990 (1) | 3.63 | 14.00 | 10.95 | 82.36 |
| 1991 (1) | 3.76 | 13.10 | 10.11 | 83.14 |

Source(s): (1) STAT; (2) EPPA3.

### 3.2 Méthode(s): moyenne arithmétique
moyenne pondérée

#### 3.2.1 Hommes:

- 1950-80, taux de répartition 1950-80 tirés des EPPA3;
- 1990, moyennes des taux de répartition tirés des enquêtes de 1989, 1990 et 1991.

#### 3.2.2 Femmes:

- 1950-70, taux de répartition 1950-70 tirés des EPPA3;
- 1980, moyennes pondérées des taux de répartition 1970 tirés des des EPPA3 et des taux de répartition tirés du recensement de 1981;
- 1990, moyennes des taux de répartition tirés des enquêtes de 1989, 1990 et 1991.

## 4. Projection des taux d'activité: 2000 - 2010

### 4.1 Modèle(s): linéaire, hyperbole et logistique

#### 4.1.1 Hommes:

- Aux groupes d'âge [15-24], application de la fonction F1;
- Aux groupes d'âge [25+], application de la fonction F3;
- Modification des tendances des groupes d'âge [25-59].

#### 4.1.2 Femmes:

- Aux groupes d'âge [15-24], application de la fonction F1;
- Aux groupes d'âge [25-59], application de la fonction F6;
- Aux groupes d'âge [60+], application de la fonction F3;
- Modification des tendances des groupes d'âge [15-59].

*Notes sur les ajustements des taux, voir p. 192-195.*

*Notes sur les fonctions de projection, voir p. 198.*

# Autres Mélanésie

## 1. Source(s) des données de base

| Code(s): | Titre(s): |
|---|---|
| EPPA3 | Annuaire des statistiques du travail 1945-89 - Edition rétrospective sur les recensements de population, BIT, Genève, 1990. |
| STAT | Base de données sur les statistiques du travail - LABORSTA, Bureau de statistique, BIT, Genève. |

## 2. Evaluation des taux d'activité: 1950 - 1990

### 2.1 Données de base:

Tableau 1: Taux d'activité par sexe et par groupe d'âge

| Groupe d'âge | 1976 (1) | 1979 (2) | 1983 (1) | 1989 (1) | 1989 (2) |
|---|---|---|---|---|---|
| **Hommes** | | | | | |
| 10-14 | 1.51 | 0.00 | 0.00 | ... | 0.00 |
| 15-19 | 36.03 | 61.72 | 38.70 | ... | 73.16 |
| 20-24 | 74.53 | 92.87 | 82.99 | 86.34 | 91.19 |
| 25-29 | 93.98 | 97.33 | 91.62 | 93.25 | 95.03 |
| 30-34 | 95.48 | 98.69 | 95.11 | 95.13 | 95.33 |
| 35-39 | 95.77 | 98.65 | 95.31 | 94.81 | 94.93 |
| 40-44 | 95.21 | 98.70 | 94.57 | 94.56 | 94.53 |
| 45-49 | 93.76 | 98.78 | 93.43 | 92.23 | 93.76 |
| 50-54 | 90.91 | 98.17 | 81.23 | 81.36 | 94.75 |
| 55-59 | 79.17 | 97.11 | 61.90 | 56.18 | 94.11 |
| 60-64 | 56.18 | 93.97 | 36.67 | 26.72 | 88.63 |
| 65+ | 36.12 | 85.88 | ... | 11.99 | 74.45 |
| **Femmes** | | | | | |
| 10-14 | 1.58 | 0.00 | 0.00 | ... | 0.00 |
| 15-19 | 29.57 | 64.90 | 17.87 | ... | 70.66 |
| 20-24 | 55.94 | 80.12 | 50.63 | 65.53 | 80.42 |
| 25-29 | 53.17 | 79.81 | 54.76 | 61.94 | 81.64 |
| 30-34 | 50.75 | 81.26 | 53.24 | 59.45 | 79.67 |
| 35-39 | 48.97 | 84.32 | 50.95 | 58.19 | 84.01 |
| 40-44 | 47.80 | 83.30 | 48.41 | 54.97 | 85.04 |
| 45-49 | 47.02 | 85.70 | 44.68 | 50.19 | 86.98 |
| 50-54 | 47.48 | 85.83 | 37.06 | 41.06 | 87.11 |
| 55-59 | 41.46 | 86.07 | 33.19 | 29.32 | 83.82 |
| 60-64 | 32.14 | 82.35 | 12.15 | 16.07 | 79.42 |
| 65+ | 19.43 | 71.87 | ... | 5.74 | 64.48 |

Note(s): (1) Nouvelle-Calédonie; (2) Vanuatu.
Source(s): STAT.

### 2.2 Méthode(s): interpolation et extrapolation linéaires
moyenne pondérée

#### 2.2.1 Hommes:

- 1950-90, moyennes pondérées des taux d'activité estimés séparément pour la Nouvelle-Calédonie et Vanuatu; les taux estimés ont été obtenus sur la base d'interpolation et extrapolation des taux d'activité ajustés tirés des recensements de 1976, 1983 et 1989 pour la Nouvelle-Calédonie et des taux d'activité tirés des recensements de 1979 et 1989 pour Vanuatu.

#### 2.2.2 Femmes:

Méthode, hypothèses et traitements identiques à ceux appliqués aux hommes.

## 3. Evaluation des taux de répartition par secteur d'activité: 1950 - 1990

### 3.1 Données de base:

Tableau 2: Répartition de la population active en % par secteur d'activité

| Année | Agriculture | Industrie Total | Manufac. | Services |
|---|---|---|---|---|
| **Hommes** | | | | |
| 1976 (1) | 25.93 | 37.70 | 15.89 | 36.37 |
| 1979 (2) | 71.56 | 6.18 | 2.01 | 22.26 |
| 1983 (1) | 21.45 | 25.08 | 14.01 | 53.47 |
| 1989 (1) | 14.38 | 27.72 | 13.51 | 57.89 |
| 1989 (2) | 70.56 | 6.27 | 2.35 | 23.16 |
| **Femmes** | | | | |
| 1976 (1) | 35.32 | 6.24 | 3.64 | 58.44 |
| 1979 (2) | 84.71 | 2.06 | 1.87 | 13.23 |
| 1983 (1) | 23.24 | 4.98 | 3.80 | 71.78 |
| 1989 (1) | 14.20 | 6.26 | 4.92 | 79.54 |
| 1989 (2) | 83.65 | 1.35 | 1.25 | 15.00 |

Note(s): (1) Nouvelle-Calédonie; (2) Vanuatu.
Source(s): STAT.

### 3.2 Méthode(s): moyenne pondérée
interpolation et extrapolation linéaires

#### 3.2.1 Hommes:
- 1950-90, moyennes pondérées des taux de répartition estimés séparément pour la Nouvelle-Calédonie et Vanuatu; les taux estimés ont été obtenus sur la base d'interpolation et extrapolation des taux de répartition tirés des recensements de 1976, 1983 et 1989 pour la Nouvelle-Calédonie et des recensements de 1979 et 1989 pour Vanuatu.

#### 3.2.2 Femmes:
Méthode, hypothèses et traitements identiques à ceux appliqués aux hommes.

## 4. Projection des taux d'activité: 2000 - 2010

### 4.1 Modèle(s): linéaire et hyperbole

#### 4.1.1 Hommes:
- Aux groupes d'âge [10-29], application de la fonction F1;
- Aux groupes d'âge [30+], application de la fonction F3;
- Modification des tendances des groupes d'âge [10-14], [20-24] et [30-49].

#### 4.1.2 Femmes:
- A tous les groupes d'âge, application de la fonction F1;
- Modification des tendances des groupes d'âge [20+].

# Autriche

## 1. Source(s) des données de base

| Code(s): | Titre(s): |
|---|---|
| EPPA3 | Annuaire des statistiques du travail 1945-89 - Edition rétrospective sur les recensements de population, BIT, Genève, 1990. |
| STAT | Base de données sur les statistiques du travail - LABORSTA, Bureau de statistique, BIT, Genève. |

## 2. Evaluation des taux d'activité: 1950 - 1990

### 2.1 Données de base:

Tableau 1: Taux d'activité par sexe et par groupe d'âge

| Groupe d'âge | Année 1989 | 1990 | 1991 |
|---|---|---|---|
| **Hommes** | | | |
| 10-14 | 0.00 | 0.00 | 0.00 |
| 15-19 | 53.39 | 52.81 | 54.46 |
| 20-24 | 76.60 | 77.11 | 76.07 |
| 25-29 | 89.97 | 88.60 | 88.71 |
| 30-34 | 96.75 | 96.98 | 96.74 |
| 35-39 | 97.76 | 98.02 | 97.70 |
| 40-44 | 96.32 | 96.46 | 97.23 |
| 45-49 | 96.04 | 96.11 | 95.05 |
| 50-54 | 89.41 | 91.03 | 91.31 |
| 55-59 | 64.52 | 62.96 | 63.45 |
| 60-64 | 14.48 | 14.13 | 13.84 |
| 65+ | 2.05 | 3.32 | 1.95 |
| **Femmes** | | | |
| 10-14 | 0.00 | 0.00 | 0.00 |
| 15-19 | 46.49 | 44.84 | 44.53 |
| 20-24 | 72.82 | 72.38 | 73.04 |
| 25-29 | 67.28 | 69.19 | 70.12 |
| 30-34 | 63.88 | 64.09 | 66.33 |
| 35-39 | 63.60 | 66.54 | 67.24 |
| 40-44 | 63.95 | 66.93 | 66.77 |
| 45-49 | 60.28 | 60.62 | 62.07 |
| 50-54 | 51.35 | 53.74 | 54.59 |
| 55-59 | 25.57 | 26.00 | 23.90 |
| 60-64 | 4.60 | 5.00 | 5.32 |
| 65+ | 1.40 | 1.05 | 0.74 |

Source(s): STAT.

### 2.2 Méthode(s): moyenne arithmétique

#### 2.2.1 Hommes:

- 1950-80, taux d'activité 1950-80 tirés des EPPA3;
- 1990, moyennes des taux d'activité tirés des enquêtes de 1989, 1990 et 1991.

#### 2.2.2 Femmes:

Méthode, hypothèses et traitements identiques à ceux appliqués aux hommes.

## 3. Evaluation des taux de répartition par secteur d'activité: 1950 - 1990

### 3.1 Données de base:

Tableau 2: Répartition de la population active en % par secteur d'activité

| Année | Agriculture | Industrie Total | Manufac. | Services |
|---|---|---|---|---|
| **Hommes** | | | | |
| 1979 | 8.71 | 50.68 | 34.52 | 40.61 |
| 1980 | 8.78 | 50.98 | 34.37 | 40.24 |
| 1981 | 7.49 | 50.79 | 34.88 | 41.72 |
| 1989 | 7.28 | 49.24 | 33.77 | 43.48 |
| 1990 | 7.00 | 49.03 | 33.51 | 43.97 |
| 1991 | 6.61 | 49.19 | 33.64 | 44.20 |
| **Femmes** | | | | |
| 1979 | 13.16 | 24.56 | 22.21 | 62.28 |
| 1980 | 13.50 | 25.06 | 22.63 | 61.44 |
| 1981 | 10.03 | 26.53 | 23.90 | 63.44 |
| 1989 | 9.13 | 21.05 | 19.02 | 69.82 |
| 1990 | 9.08 | 20.40 | 18.30 | 70.52 |
| 1991 | 8.59 | 20.29 | 18.01 | 71.12 |

Source(s): STAT.

### 3.2 Méthode(s): moyenne arithmétique

#### 3.2.1 Hommes:

- 1950-70, taux de répartition 1950-70 tirés des EPPA3;
- 1980, moyennes des taux de répartition tirés des enquêtes de 1979, et 1980 et des taux de répartition tirés du recensement de 1981;
- 1990, moyennes des taux de répartition tirés des enquêtes de 1989, 1990 et 1991.

#### 3.2.2 Femmes:

Méthode, hypothèses et traitements identiques à ceux appliqués aux hommes.

## 4. Projection des taux d'activité: 2000 - 2010

### 4.1 Modèle(s): linéaire et hyperbole

#### 4.1.1 Hommes:

- Aux groupes d'âge [15-19] et [35-49], application de la fonction F1;
- Aux groupes d'âge [20-34] et [50+], application de la fonction F3;
- Modification des tendances des groupes d'âge [25-29] et [35-49].

#### 4.1.2 Femmes:

- Aux groupes d'âge [15-49], application de la fonction F1;
- Aux groupes d'âge [50+], application de la fonction F3;
- Modification des tendances des groupes d'âge [15-24].

*Notes sur les ajustements des taux, voir p. 192-195.*

*Notes sur les fonctions de projection, voir p. 198.*

# Azerbaïdjan

## 1. Source(s) des données de base

Code(s):     Titre(s):

BLT-94-2     Vorobiev A. (1994), "Estimation de la population active pour les quinze pays de l'ex-URSS pour les années 1950, 1959, 1970, 1979 et 1989",
dans le Bulletin des statistiques du travail - 1994-2, BIT, Genève.

## 2. Evaluation des taux d'activité: 1950 - 1990

### 2.1 Données de base:

Tableau 1: Taux d'activité par sexe et par groupe d'âge

| Groupe d'âge | Année | | | | |
|---|---|---|---|---|---|
| | 1950 | 1959 | 1970 | 1979 | 1989 |
| **Hommes** | | | | | |
| 10-14 | 0.00 | 0.00 | 0.00 | 0.00 | 0.00 |
| 15-19 | 48.91 | 47.26 | 31.67 | 35.48 | 29.59 |
| 20-24 | 82.89 | 84.21 | 80.56 | 80.39 | 75.76 |
| 25-29 | 92.96 | 92.98 | 90.00 | 95.92 | 92.86 |
| 30-34 | 94.74 | 95.04 | 96.89 | 98.33 | 95.59 |
| 35-39 | 94.44 | 96.97 | 97.04 | 98.44 | 95.77 |
| 40-44 | 93.10 | 94.23 | 95.89 | 97.34 | 95.54 |
| 45-49 | 93.33 | 94.03 | 95.71 | 96.79 | 94.31 |
| 50-54 | 91.30 | 90.91 | 90.91 | 93.33 | 90.00 |
| 55-59 | 85.29 | 85.71 | 84.48 | 84.62 | 83.21 |
| 60-64 | 77.78 | 80.49 | 50.00 | 52.50 | 47.42 |
| 65+ | 47.54 | 50.00 | 22.12 | 21.31 | 20.91 |
| **Femmes** | | | | | |
| 10-14 | 0.00 | 0.00 | 0.00 | 0.00 | 0.00 |
| 15-19 | 45.36 | 45.52 | 30.67 | 37.24 | 28.27 |
| 20-24 | 62.09 | 61.35 | 60.14 | 77.71 | 60.50 |
| 25-29 | 62.24 | 66.86 | 75.41 | 84.95 | 64.96 |
| 30-34 | 62.65 | 61.64 | 69.23 | 86.72 | 69.55 |
| 35-39 | 61.96 | 64.52 | 78.66 | 89.21 | 74.50 |
| 40-44 | 62.96 | 62.82 | 75.00 | 89.80 | 76.67 |
| 45-49 | 61.90 | 63.22 | 74.19 | 88.24 | 75.19 |
| 50-54 | 51.43 | 51.95 | 63.77 | 75.94 | 56.99 |
| 55-59 | 40.35 | 39.24 | 28.13 | 40.70 | 30.87 |
| 60-64 | 32.65 | 40.68 | 13.41 | 18.06 | 19.17 |
| 65+ | 7.53 | 9.38 | 3.41 | 4.50 | 6.70 |

Source(s): BLT-94-2-2

### 2.2 Méthode(s): moyenne pondérée

#### 2.2.1 Hommes:

- 1950-90, moyennes pondérées des taux d'activité 1950, 1959, 1970 et 1989
tirés du Bulletin des statistiques du travail, 1994-2.

#### 2.2.2 Femmes:

Méthode, hypothèses et traitements identiques à ceux appliqués aux hommes.

## 3. Evaluation des taux de répartition par secteur d'activité: 1950 - 1990

### 3.1 Données de base:

Tableau 2: Répartition de la population active en % par secteur d'activité

| Année | Agriculture | Industrie | | Services |
|---|---|---|---|---|
| | | Total | Manufac. | |
| **Hommes** | | | | |
| 1950 | 48.31 | 25.93 | 11.27 | 25.76 |
| 1959 | 42.14 | 25.38 | 11.18 | 32.48 |
| 1970 | 29.01 | 34.79 | 16.84 | 36.21 |
| 1979 | 27.85 | 36.37 | 15.65 | 35.78 |
| 1989 | 27.37 | 35.06 | 14.11 | 37.57 |
| **Femmes** | | | | |
| 1950 | 59.47 | 17.07 | 12.76 | 23.45 |
| 1959 | 59.19 | 14.20 | 11.06 | 26.61 |
| 1970 | 41.50 | 20.05 | 15.23 | 38.45 |
| 1979 | 43.41 | 19.89 | 12.31 | 36.70 |
| 1989 | 36.85 | 20.60 | 13.31 | 42.55 |

Source(s): BLT-94-2.

### 3.2 Méthode(s): moyenne pondérée

#### 3.2.1 Hommes:

- 1950-90, moyennes pondérées des taux de répartition 1950, 1959,
1970, 1979 et 1989 tirés du Bulletin des statistiques du travail - 1994-2.

#### 3.2.2 Femmes:

Méthode, hypothèses et traitements identiques à ceux appliqués aux hommes.

## 4. Projection des taux d'activité: 2000 - 2010

### 4.1 Modèle(s): linéaire, hyperbole et logistique

#### 4.1.1 Hommes:

- Aux groupes d'âge [15-24] et [55+], application de la fonction F3;
- Aux groupes d'âge [25-54], application de la fonction F1;
- Modification des tendances des groupes d'âge [20-54].

#### 4.1.2 Femmes:

- Aux groupes d'âge [15-24] et [50+], application de la fonction F3;
- Aux groupes d'âge [25-49], application de la fonction F6;
- Modification des tendances des groupes d'âge [20-54].

*Notes sur les ajustements des taux, voir p. 192-195.*     *Notes sur les fonctions de projection, voir p. 198.*

# Bahamas

## 1. Source(s) des données de base

Code(s):    Titre(s):

STAT      Base de données sur les statistiques du travail - LABORSTA, Bureau de statistique, BIT, Genève.

## 2. Evaluation des taux d'activité: 1950 - 1990

### 2.1 Données de base:

Tableau 1: Taux d'activité par sexe et par groupe d'âge

| Groupe d'âge | Année | | | | |
|---|---|---|---|---|---|
| | 1953 | 1963 | 1970 | 1980 | 1990 |
| **Hommes** | | | | | |
| 10-14 | 1.59 | 3.93 | 2.34 | 0.00 | 0.00 |
| 15-19 | 60.26 | 74.95 | 63.82 | 46.79 | 41.29 |
| 20-24 | 92.04 | 96.42 | 93.10 | 87.23 | 85.68 |
| 25-29 | 95.57 | 97.79 | 96.11 | 92.49 | 90.67 |
| 30-34 | 96.75 | 97.27 | 96.88 | 95.42 | 91.76 |
| 35-39 | 96.92 | 97.41 | 97.04 | 95.08 | 94.11 |
| 40-44 | 96.72 | 96.94 | 96.77 | 94.49 | 94.62 |
| 45-49 | 95.97 | 96 18 | 96.02 | 92.45 | 94.35 |
| 50-54 | 94.69 | 94.35 | 94.60 | 88.79 | 92.07 |
| 55-59 | 90.81 | 94.65 | 91.74 | 83.72 | 88.35 |
| 60-64 | 81.44 | 85.90 | 82.52 | 72.56 | 73.89 |
| 65+ | 50.77 | 63.20 | 53.78 | 39.93 | 36.41 |
| **Femmes** | | | | | |
| 10-14 | .. | 1.75 | 2.13 | .. | 0.00 |
| 15-19 | .. | 45.04 | 44.55 | 34.54 | 31.26 |
| 20-24 | .. | 61.33 | 71.90 | 72.38 | 75.28 |
| 25-29 | .. | 58.71 | 65.07 | 75.20 | 81.25 |
| 30-34 | .. | 58.33 | 63.39 | 72.19 | 80.69 |
| 35-39 | .. | 58.31 | 62.23 | 72.29 | 80.40 |
| 40-44 | .. | 56.29 | 60.60 | 68.17 | 79.03 |
| 45-49 | .. | 55.54 | 58.38 | 63.53 | 75.94 |
| 50-54 | .. | 54.56 | 56.63 | 59 17 | 68.24 |
| 55-59 | .. | 43.68 | 53.10 | 49.22 | 64.30 |
| 60-64 | .. | 41.05 | 43.73 | 38.00 | 47.48 |
| 65+ | .. | 24.92 | 28.35 | 16.14 | 15.28 |

Source(s): STAT.

### 2.2 Méthode(s): interpolation et extrapolation linéaires moyenne pondérée

**2.2.1 Hommes:**

- 1950 et 1970-90, interpolation et extrapolation des taux d'activité tirés des recensements de 1953 et 1963 et des taux d'activité ajustés tirés des recensements de 1980 et 1990.

**2.2.2 Femmes:**

- 1950-60, interpolation et extrapolation des taux d'activité ajustés tirés des recensements de 1953 et 1963;
modification des tendances de tous les groupes d'âge;
- 1970-90, moyennes pondérées des taux d'activité ajustés tirés des recensements de 1970 et 1980 et des taux d'activité tirés du recensement de 1990.

## 3. Evaluation des taux de répartition par secteur d'activité: 1950 - 1990

### 3.1 Données de base:

Tableau 2: Répartition de la population active en % par secteur d'activité

| Année | Agriculture | Industrie | | Services |
|---|---|---|---|---|
| | | Total | Manufac. | |
| **Hommes** | | | | |
| 1963 | 18.75 | 34.69 | 8.60 | 46.56 |
| 1970 | 8.57 | 30.84 | 6.40 | 60.59 |
| 1980 | 7.96 | 24.18 | 6.57 | 67.86 |
| 1990 | 8.36 | 24.18 | 4.31 | 67.46 |
| **Femmes** | | | | |
| 1963 | 11.95 | 7.46 | 6.91 | 80.60 |
| 1970 | 6.23 | 7.41 | 5.68 | 86.36 |
| 1980 | 2.91 | 7.12 | 5.89 | 89.98 |
| 1990 | 1.60 | 5.25 | 3.83 | 93.15 |

Source(s): STAT.

### 3.2 Méthode(s): interpolation et extrapolation linéaires

**3.2.1 Hommes:**

- 1950-90, interpolation et extrapolation des aux taux de répartition tirés des recensements de 1963, 1970, 1980 et 1990,
modification des tendances de tous les secteurs pour 1950.

**3.2.2 Femmes:**

Méthode, hypothèses et traitements identiques à ceux appliqués aux hommes.

## 4. Projection des taux d'activité: 2000 - 2010

### 4.1 Modèle(s): linéaire, hyperbole et logistique

**4.1.1 Hommes:**

- Aux groupes d'âge [15-24], application de la fonction F1;
- Aux groupes d'âge [25+], application de la fonction F3;
- Modification des tendances des groupes d'âge [50-64].

**4.1.2 Femmes:**

- Au groupe d'âge [15-19], application de la fonction F1;
- Aux groupes d'âge [20-64], application de la fonction F6;
- Au groupe d'âge [65+], application de la fonction F3;
- Modification des tendances des groupes d'âge [55-64].

*Notes sur les ajustements des taux, voir p. 192-195.*

*Notes sur les fonctions de projection, voir p. 198.*

# Bahreïn

## 1. Source(s) des données de base

Code(s):    Titre(s):

EPPA3      Evaluations et projections de la population active 1950-2025 - troisième édition, BIT, Genève, 1986.
ASTER      Annuaire des statistiques du travail 1945-89 - Edition rétrospective sur les recensements de population, BIT, Genève, 1990.

## 2. Evaluation des taux d'activité: 1950 - 1990

### 2.1 Données de base:

Tableau 1: Taux d'activité par sexe et par groupe d'âge

| | Année | | |
|---|---|---|---|
| Groupe d'âge | 1971 | 1981 | 1991 |
| **Hommes** | | | |
| 10-14 | 1.87 | 0.00 | 0.00 |
| 15-19 | 42.80 | 30.01 | 24.73 |
| 20-24 | 88.38 | 89.20 | 87.91 |
| 25-29 | 97.66 | 98.10 | 98.01 |
| 30-34 | 98.68 | 99.13 | 99.22 |
| 35-39 | 98.40 | 99.09 | 99.35 |
| 40-44 | 97.29 | 98.80 | 99.35 |
| 45-49 | 96.32 | 97.88 | 98.91 |
| 50-54 | 91.89 | 94.08 | 95.94 |
| 55-59 | 84.48 | 88.17 | 88.60 |
| 60-64 | 72.00 | 69.26 | 64.72 |
| 65+ | 49.52 | 45.46 | 36.05 |
| **Femmes** | | | |
| 10-14 | 0.04 | 0.00 | 0.00 |
| 15-19 | 3.05 | 8.41 | 8.28 |
| 20-24 | 11.59 | 31.46 | 37.00 |
| 25-29 | 10.19 | 31.09 | 42.03 |
| 30-34 | 7.44 | 24.61 | 41.73 |
| 35-39 | 5.83 | 17.28 | 37.98 |
| 40-44 | 6.15 | 12.81 | 31.87 |
| 45-49 | 4.59 | 9.58 | 18.10 |
| 50-54 | 3.92 | 6.02 | 9.04 |
| 55-59 | 3.67 | 3.63 | 5.10 |
| 60-64 | 2.80 | 1.69 | 1.68 |
| 65+ | 1.69 | 0.78 | 0.72 |

Source(s): ASTER

### 2.2 Méthode(s): interpolation linéaire

#### 2.2.1 Hommes:

- 1950-70, taux d'activité 1950-70 tirés des EPPA3;
- 1980-90, interpolation des taux d'activité tirés des recensements de 1971, 1981 et 1991.

#### 2.2.2 Femmes:

Méthode, hypothèses et traitements identiques à ceux appliqués aux hommes.

## 3. Evaluation des taux de répartition par secteur d'activité: 1950 - 1990

### 3.1 Données de base:

Tableau 2: Répartition de la population active en % par secteur d'activité

| | Agriculture | Industrie | | Services |
|---|---|---|---|---|
| Année | | Total | Manufac. | |
| **Hommes** | | | | |
| 1971 | 7.08 | 36.32 | 14.73 | 56.60 |
| 1981 | 3.04 | 39.16 | 9.15 | 57.80 |
| 1991 | 2.88 | 32.76 | 14.02 | 64.36 |
| **Femmes** | | | | |
| 1971 | 0.12 | 4.09 | 2.72 | 95.79 |
| 1981 | 0.16 | 5.16 | 1.89 | 94.69 |
| 1991 | 0.21 | 7.23 | 5.90 | 92.57 |

Source(s): ASTER.

### 3.2 Méthode(s): interpolation linéaire

#### 3.2.1 Hommes:

- 1950-70, taux de répartition 1950-70 tirés des EPPA3;
- 1980-90, interpolation des taux de répartition tirés des recensements de 1971, 1981 et 1991.

#### 3.2.2 Femmes:

Méthode, hypothèses et traitements identiques à ceux appliqués aux hommes.

## 4. Projection des taux d'activité: 2000 - 2010

### 4.1 Modèle(s): linéaire, log-linéaire et hyperbole

#### 4.1.1 Hommes:

- Au groupe d'âge [15-19], application de la fonction F2;
- Aux groupes d'âge [20+], application de la fonction F1;
- Modification des tendances des groupes d'âge [20-59].

#### 4.1.2 Femmes:

- Aux groupes d'âge [15-59], application de la fonction F1;
- Aux groupes d'âge [60+], application de la fonction F3;
- Modification de la tendance du groupe d'âge [15-19].

*Notes sur les ajustements des taux, voir p. 192-195.*     *Notes sur les fonctions de projection, voir p. 198.*

# Bangladesh

## 1. Source(s) des données de base

Code(s):     Titre(s):

EPPA3       Evaluations et projections de la population active 1950-2025 - troisième édition, BIT, Genève, 1986.
BY83-84     Statistical Yearbook of Bangladesh, 1983-84, Bangladesh Bureau of Statistics.
LFS84-85    Report on Labour Force Survey 1984-85, february 1988, GPRB, Bangladesh Bureau of Statistics.
ASTER       Annuaire des statistiques du travail 1945-89 - Edition rétrospective sur les recensements de population, BIT, Genève, 1990.
AST85-90    Editions de 1985 à 1993 de l'Annuaire des statistiques du travail du BIT, Genève.

## 2. Evaluation des taux d'activité: 1950 - 1990

### 2.1 Données de base:

Tableau 1: Taux d'activité par sexe et par groupe d'âge

| Groupe d'âge | Année 1980 (1) | 1983 (1) | 1984 (2) | 1985 (3) | 1989 (3) |
|---|---|---|---|---|---|
| **Hommes** | | | | | |
| 10-14 | 32.77 | 39.86 | 37.70 | 30.40 | 33.76 |
| 15-19 | 72.39 | 69.56 | 70.40 | 67.50 | 70.70 |
| 20-24 | 87.59 | 87.18 | 85.40 | 88.10 | 82.50 |
| 25-29 | 99.53 | 98.58 | 97.70 | 98.70 | 96.50 |
| 30-34 | 99.13 | 98.44 | 99.00 | 99.90 | 98.80 |
| 35-39 | 98.68 | 98.50 | 99.70 | 99.40 | 98.50 |
| 40-44 | 98.78 | 97.05 | 98.40 | 99.50 | 98.30 |
| 45-49 | 98.77 | 98.47 | 98.40 | 99.70 | 98.30 |
| 50-54 | 98.66 | 97.01 | 98.50 | 99.30 | 96.80 |
| 55-59 | 94.89 | 97.63 | 94.70 | 98.00 | 95.70 |
| 60-64 | 90.82 | 90.65 | 91.80 | 93.00 | 89.40 |
| 65+ | 73.34 | 65.73 | 72.90 | 70.40 | 65.00 |
| **Femmes** | | | | | |
| 10-14 | .. | .. | .. | .. | 31.30 |
| 15-19 | .. | .. | .. | .. | 55.20 |
| 20-24 | .. | .. | .. | .. | 64.90 |
| 25-29 | .. | .. | .. | .. | 68.90 |
| 30-34 | .. | .. | .. | .. | 75.00 |
| 35-39 | .. | .. | .. | .. | 78.00 |
| 40-44 | .. | .. | .. | .. | 76.90 |
| 45-49 | .. | .. | .. | .. | 75.60 |
| 50-54 | .. | .. | .. | .. | 73.50 |
| 55-59 | .. | .. | .. | .. | 87.80 |
| 60-64 | .. | .. | .. | .. | 57.90 |
| 65+ | .. | .. | .. | .. | 33.50 |

Source(s): (1) BY83-84; (2) LFS84-85; (3) AST85-90.

### 2.2 Méthode(s): interpolation et extrapolation linéaires

#### 2.2.1 Hommes:

- 1950-70, taux d'activité 1950-70 tirés des EPPA3;
- 1980-90, interpolation et extrapolation des taux d'activité tirés des
des enquêtes de 1980, 1983-84, 1984-85, 1985-86 et 1989.

#### 2.2.2 Femmes:

- 1950-70, taux d'activité ajustés 1950-70 tirés des EPPA3;
- 1980-90, aux taux d'activité tirés de l'enquête de 1980 application
du quart des variations des taux d'activité estimés pour l'Inde entre 1980 et 1990.

## 3. Evaluation des taux de répartition par secteur d'activité: 1950 - 1990

### 3.1 Données de base:

Tableau 2: Répartition de la population active en % par secteur d'activité

| Année | Agriculture | Industrie Total | Manufac. | Services |
|---|---|---|---|---|
| **Hommes** | | | | |
| 1983 (1) | 64.11 | 7.93 | 6.20 | 27.96 |
| 1984 (2) | 63.02 | 10.16 | 7.77 | 26.83 |
| 1985 (3) | 62.70 | 9.48 | 7.13 | 27.83 |
| 1989 (3) | 60.00 | 13.60 | 11.41 | 26.40 |
| **Femmes** | | | | |
| 1989 (3) | 74.34 | 18.61 | 17.96 | 7.05 |

Source(s): (1) BY83-84; (2) LFS84-85; (3) AST85-90.

### 3.2 Méthode(s): extrapolation linéaire

#### 3.2.1 Hommes:

- 1950-70, taux de répartition 1950-70 tirés des EPPA3;
- 1990, extrapolation des taux de répartition tirés des enquêtes
de 1983-84, 1984-85, 1985-86 et 1989.

#### 3.2.2 Femmes:

- 1950-70, taux de répartition 1950-70 tirés des EPPA3;
- 1980-90, pour l'agriculture, application aux taux de répartition
tirés de l'enquête de 1989 des mêmes variations que celles estimées
pour les hommes pour la même période; pour l'industrie et les services,
maintien du rapport industrie/services tiré de l'enquête de 1989.

## 4. Projection des taux d'activité: 2000 - 2010

### 4.1 Modèle(s): linéaire et hyperbole

#### 4.1.1 Hommes:

- Aux groupes d'âge [10-59], application de la fonction F3;
- Aux groupes d'âge [60+], application de la fonction F1;
- Modification des tendances des groupes d'âge [20-44].

#### 4.1.2 Femmes:

- A tous les groupes d'âge, application de la fonction F1;
- Modification des tendances de tous les groupes d'âge.

*Notes sur les ajustements des taux, voir p. 192-195.*         *Notes sur les fonctions de projection, voir p. 198.*

216

# Barbade

## 1. Source(s) des données de base

Code(s):    Titre(s):

EPPA3      Evaluations et projections de la population active 1950-2025 - troisième édition, BIT, Genève, 1986.
ASTER     Annuaire des statistiques du travail 1945-89 - Edition rétrospective sur les recensements de population, BIT, Genève, 1990.
AST82-93  Editions de 1982 à 1993 de l'Annuaire des statistiques du travail du BIT, Genève.

## 2. Evaluation des taux d'activité: 1950 - 1990

### 2.1 Données de base:

Tableau 1: Taux d'activité par sexe et par groupe d'âge

| Groupe d'âge | Année 1950 (1) | 1980 (2) | 1986 (3) | 1990 (3) | 191 (3) | 1992 (3) |
|---|---|---|---|---|---|---|
| **Hommes** | | | | | | |
| 10-14 | .. | 0.00 | 0.00 | 0.00 | 0.00 | 0.00 |
| 15-19 | .. | 59.54 | 39.64 | 45.16 | 42.73 | 42.20 |
| 20-24 | .. | 92.31 | 88.00 | 91.60 | 80.20 | 89.52 |
| 25-29 | .. | 94.47 | 94.44 | 94.17 | 96.19 | 95.19 |
| 30-34 | .. | 95.78 | 95.05 | 95.83 | 93.64 | 93.64 |
| 35-39 | .. | 95.59 | 94.67 | 95.56 | 95.40 | 93.55 |
| 40-44 | .. | 95.38 | 95.56 | 96.77 | 96.05 | 94.20 |
| 45-49 | .. | 94.89 | 93.33 | 95.65 | 93.33 | 95.65 |
| 50-54 | .. | 93.57 | 91.67 | 94.29 | 90.91 | 92.68 |
| 55-59 | .. | 89.52 | 97.22 | 88.57 | 82.86 | 86.49 |
| 60-64 | .. | 70.82 | 61.76 | 64.52 | 58.33 | 53.49 |
| 65+ | .. | 23.63 | 17.27 | 13.76 | 14.75 | 12.93 |
| **Femmes** | | | | | | |
| 10-14 | 10.20 | 0.00 | 0.00 | 0.00 | .. | 0.00 |
| 15-19 | 54.15 | 39.89 | 29.46 | 34.99 | .. | 34.62 |
| 20-24 | 63.10 | 70.49 | 79.67 | 85.12 | .. | 85.11 |
| 25-29 | 57.60 | 77.54 | 82.64 | 86.96 | .. | 85.45 |
| 30-34 | 58.10 | 75.45 | 85.45 | 87.16 | .. | 84.68 |
| 35-39 | 58.25 | 71.56 | 83.12 | 90.70 | .. | 85.71 |
| 40-44 | 57.90 | 67.74 | 72.06 | 80.82 | .. | 84.81 |
| 45-49 | 60.05 | 61.27 | 73.08 | 70.91 | .. | 76.19 |
| 50-54 | 57.90 | 53.15 | 58.00 | 67.92 | .. | 72.92 |
| 55-59 | 54.85 | 45.10 | 63.89 | 43.18 | .. | 48.15 |
| 60-64 | 43.65 | 33.53 | 28.89 | 27.45 | .. | 23.91 |
| 65+ | 19.00 | 7.15 | 7.23 | 3.68 | .. | 4.81 |

Source(s): (1) EPPA3; (2) ASTER; (3) AST82-93.

### 2.2 Méthode(s): interpolation et extrapolation linéaires

#### 2.2.1 Hommes:

- 1990, interpolation des taux d'activité tirés du recensement de 1980 et des enquêtes de 1986 à 1992;
modification des tendances des groupes d'âge [20-29];
- 1970 et 1980, taux de d'activité tirés respectivement des EPPA3 et du recensement de 1980;
- 1950-60, extrapolation des taux d'activité 1970-90 estimés;
modification des tendances de tous les groupes d'âge.

#### 2.2.2 Femmes:

- 1950, taux d'activité 1950 tirés des EPPA3;
- 1970-90, interpolation des taux d'activité 1950 tirés des EPPA3, des taux d'activité tirés du recensement de 1980 et des enquêtes de 1986, 1990 et 1991;
modification des tendances de tous les groupes d'âge.

## 3. Evaluation des taux de répartition par secteur d'activité: 1950 - 1990

### 3.1 Données de base:

Tableau 2: Répartition de la population active en % par secteur d'activité

| Année | Agriculture | Industrie Total | Manufac. | Services |
|---|---|---|---|---|
| **Hommes** | | | | |
| 1960 (1) | 26.42 | 37.74 | .. | 35.85 |
| 1970 (2) | 17.56 | 47.86 | 16.05 | 34.58 |
| 1981 (3) | 10.14 | 23.83 | 10.95 | 66.02 |
| 1989 (3) | 7.12 | 33.03 | 11.50 | 59.85 |
| 1991 (3) | 7.12 | 27.88 | 10.00 | 65.00 |
| **Femmes** | | | | |
| 1960 (1) | 26.32 | 13.16 | .. | 60.53 |
| 1970 (2) | 16.05 | 30.79 | 14.07 | 53.16 |
| 1981 (3) | 9.20 | 24.14 | 23.22 | 80.46 |
| 1989 (3) | 7.32 | 16.48 | 14.87 | 76.20 |
| 1991 (3) | 4.94 | 14.07 | 12.59 | 80.99 |

Source(s): (1) EPPA3; (2) ASTER; (3) AST82-93..

### 3.2 Méthode(s): interpolation et extrapolation linéaires

#### 3.2.1 Hommes:

- 1950-60, taux de répartition 1950-60 tirés des EPPA3;
- 1970, extrapolation des taux de répartition 1960 tirés des EPPA3 et des taux de répartition du recensement de 1970;
- 1980, interpolation des taux de répartition estimés pour 1970 et des taux de répartition de l'enquête de 1981;
- 1990, moyennes des taux tirés des enquêtes de 1989 et 1991.

#### 3.2.2 Femmes:

Méthode, hypothèses et traitements identiques à ceux appliqués aux hommes.

## 4. Projection des taux d'activité: 2000 - 2010

### 4.1 Modèle(s): linéaire et hyperbole

#### 4.1.1 Hommes:

- Aux groupes d'âge [15-24], application de la fonction F1;
- Aux groupes d'âge [25+], application de la fonction F3;
- Modification des tendances des groupes d'âge [20-24] et [30-49].

#### 4.1.2 Femmes:

- Au groupe d'âge [15-19], application de la fonction F3;
- Aux groupes d'âge [20-54], application de la fonction F6;
- Aux groupes d'âge [55+], application de la fonction F3;
- Modification des tendances des groupes d'âge [45-59].

*Notes sur les ajustements des taux, voir p. 192-195.*    *Notes sur les fonctions de projection, voir p. 198.*

# Bélarus

## 1. Source(s) des données de base

Code(s):     Titre(s):

BLT-94-2     Vorobiev A. (1994), "Estimation de la population active pour les quinze pays de l'ex-URSS pour les années 1950, 1959, 1970, 1979 et 1989", dans le Bulletin des statistiques du travail - 1994-2, BIT, Genève.

## 2. Evaluation des taux d'activité: 1950 - 1990

### 2.1 Données de base:

Tableau 1: Taux d'activité par sexe et par groupe d'âge

| Groupe d'âge | Année 1959 | 1970 | 1979 | 1989 |
|---|---|---|---|---|
| **Hommes** | | | | |
| 10-14 | 0.00 | 0.00 | 0.00 | 0.00 |
| 15-19 | 64.15 | 38.64 | 37.45 | 26.97 |
| 20-24 | 86.82 | 83.56 | 86.81 | 81.14 |
| 25-29 | 95.29 | 98.39 | 97.23 | 96.99 |
| 30-34 | 94.76 | 97.99 | 98.14 | 98.33 |
| 35-39 | 96.02 | 97.57 | 98.17 | 98.06 |
| 40-44 | 93.65 | 95.42 | 97.89 | 97.30 |
| 45-49 | 93.75 | 94.82 | 96.26 | 95.74 |
| 50-54 | 91.25 | 91.23 | 91.82 | 92.69 |
| 55-59 | 88.89 | 84.46 | 82.91 | 85.61 |
| 60-64 | 56.20 | 45.07 | 30.48 | 39.91 |
| 65+ | 47.78 | 10.07 | 8.43 | 12.89 |
| **Femmes** | | | | |
| 10-14 | 0.00 | 0.00 | 0.00 | 0.00 |
| 15-19 | 63.50 | 34.75 | 31.44 | 24.50 |
| 20-24 | 76.87 | 80.95 | 86.10 | 82.30 |
| 25-29 | 84.10 | 94.55 | 94.44 | 92.94 |
| 30-34 | 74.10 | 93.46 | 95.93 | 95.22 |
| 35-39 | 78.68 | 91.97 | 96.19 | 96.16 |
| 40-44 | 77.36 | 92.65 | 96.22 | 96.25 |
| 45-49 | 75.95 | 89.26 | 93.96 | 93.97 |
| 50-54 | 70.09 | 79.79 | 85.71 | 86.69 |
| 55-59 | 58.08 | 28.10 | 20.04 | 36.29 |
| 60-64 | 53.10 | 14.35 | 9.64 | 20.42 |
| 65+ | 17.45 | 2.43 | 4.40 | 4.90 |

Source(s): BLT-94-2.

### 2.2 Méthode(s): interpolation et extrapolation linéaires
                 moyenne pondérée

#### 2.2.1 Hommes:

- 1950-90, interpolation et extrapolation des taux d'activité 1959, 1970, 1979, et 1989 tirés du Bulletin des statistiques du travail 1994-2; modification des tendances de tous les groupes d'âge pour 1950.

#### 2.2.2 Femmes:

- 1950, extrapolation des taux d'activité 1959 et 1970 tirés du Bulletin des statistiques du travail 1994-2;
modification des tendances de tous les groupes d'âge;
- 1960-90, moyennes pondérées des taux d'activité 1959, 1970, 1979 et 1989 tirés du Bulletin.

## 3. Evaluation des taux de répartition par secteur d'activité: 1950 - 1990

### 3.1 Données de base:

Tableau 2: Répartition de la population active en % par secteur d'activité

| Année | Agriculture | Industrie Total | Manufac. | Services |
|---|---|---|---|---|
| **Hommes** | | | | |
| 1950 | 65.60 | 15.43 | 8.81 | 18.97 |
| 1959 | 51.06 | 22.35 | 14.08 | 26.59 |
| 1970 | 33.84 | 39.01 | 24.58 | 27.15 |
| 1979 | 28.99 | 43.43 | 26.38 | 27.58 |
| 1989 | 26.16 | 44.62 | 27.38 | 29.23 |
| **Femmes** | | | | |
| 1950 | 75.37 | 9.45 | 7.36 | 15.19 |
| 1959 | 65.49 | 14.45 | 11.78 | 20.06 |
| 1970 | 36.43 | 27.77 | 22.89 | 35.80 |
| 1979 | 24.42 | 32.89 | 26.06 | 42.69 |
| 1989 | 14.84 | 35.20 | 28.44 | 49.96 |

Source(s): BLT-94-2.

### 3.2 Méthode(s): données du BLT-94-2

#### 3.2.1 Hommes:

- 1950-90, moyennes pondérées des taux de répartition 1950, 1959, 1970, 1979 et 1990 tirés du Bulletin des statistiques du travail - 1994-2.

#### 3.2.2 Femmes:

Méthode, hypothèses et traitements identiques à ceux appliqués aux hommes.

## 4. Projection des taux d'activité: 2000 - 2010

### 4.1 Modèle(s): linéaire et hyperbole

#### 4.1.1 Hommes:

- Aux groupes d'âge [15-24] et [60+], application de la fonction F3;
- Aux groupes d'âge [25-59], application de la fonction F1;
- Modification des tendances des groupes d'âge [15-19] et [25-54].

#### 4.1.2 Femmes:

- Aux groupes d'âge [15+], application de la fonction F3;
- Modification des tendances des groupes d'âge [15-19] et [25-54].

---

*Notes sur les ajustements des taux, voir p. 192-195.*
        *Notes sur les fonctions de projection, voir p. 198.*

# Belgique

## 1. Source(s) des données de base

Code(s):     Titre(s):
EPPA3       Annuaire des statistiques du travail 1945-89 - Edition rétrospective sur les recensements de population, BIT, Genève, 1990.
STAT        Base de données sur les statistiques du travail - LABORSTA, Bureau de statistique, BIT, Genève.

## 2. Evaluation des taux d'activité: 1950 - 1990

### 2.1 Données de base:

Tableau 1: Taux d'activité par sexe et par groupe d'âge

| Groupe d'âge | Année 1988 | 1991 |
|---|---|---|
| **Hommes** | | |
| 10-14 | 0.00 | 0.00 |
| 15-19 | 11.30 | 12.86 |
| 20-24 | 67.10 | 66.50 |
| 25-29 | 94.50 | 94.09 |
| 30-34 | 96.10 | 95.98 |
| 35-39 | 96.40 | 95.72 |
| 40-44 | 94.80 | 94.39 |
| 45-49 | 90.90 | 92.97 |
| 50-54 | 79.10 | 80.49 |
| 55-59 | 51.30 | 50.56 |
| 60-64 | 20.50 | 18.17 |
| 65+ | 2.30 | 1.93 |
| **Femmes** | | |
| 10-14 | 0.00 | 0.00 |
| 15-19 | 9.72 | 9.04 |
| 20-24 | 60.90 | 61.55 |
| 25-29 | 78.20 | 80.40 |
| 30-34 | 71.00 | 74.97 |
| 35-39 | 66.00 | 70.63 |
| 40-44 | 55.40 | 61.89 |
| 45-49 | 43.30 | 50.04 |
| 50-54 | 29.00 | 31.75 |
| 55-59 | 16.30 | 17.64 |
| 60-64 | 4.10 | 3.74 |
| 65+ | 0.70 | 0.47 |

Source(s): STAT.

### 2.2 Méthode(s): moyenne pondérée

#### 2.2.1 Hommes:

- 1950-80, taux d'activité 1950-80 tirés des EPPA3;
- 1990, moyennes pondérées des taux d'activité tirés des enquêtes de 1988 et 1991.

#### 2.2.2 Femmes:

Méthode, hypothèses et traitements identiques à ceux appliqués aux hommes.

## 3. Evaluation des taux de répartition par secteur d'activité: 1950 - 1990

### 3.1 Données de base:

Tableau 2: Répartition de la population active en % par secteur d'activité

| Année | Agriculture | Industrie Total | Manufac. | Services |
|---|---|---|---|---|
| **Hommes** | | | | |
| 1990 | 3.21 | 37.04 | 25.94 | 59.75 |
| **Femmes** | | | | |
| 1990 | 1.75 | 13.62 | 12.40 | 84.63 |

Source(s): STAT.

### 3.2 Méthode(s): données nationales

#### 3.2.1 Hommes:

- 1950-80, taux de répartition 1950-80 tirés des EPPA3;
- 1990, taux de répartition ajustés tirés de l'enquête de 1990; ajustement des taux de répartition pour tenir compte des militaires du contingent.

#### 3.2.2 Femmes:

Méthode, hypothèses et traitements identiques à ceux appliqués aux hommes.

## 4. Projection des taux d'activité: 2000 - 2010

### 4.1 Modèle(s): hyperbole et logistique

#### 4.1.1 Hommes:

- Aux groupes d'âge [15+], application de la fonction F3;
- Modification des tendances des groupes d'âge [15-24].

#### 4.1.2 Femmes:

- Au groupe d'âge [15-19], application de la fonction F3;
- Aux groupes d'âge [20+], application de la fonction F6;
- Modification des tendances des groupes d'âge [15-29].

*Notes sur les ajustements des taux, voir p. 192-195.*

*Notes sur les fonctions de projection, voir p. 198.*

# Belize

## 1. Source(s) des données de base

Code(s):  Titre(s):

EPPA3   Evaluations et projections de la population active 1950-2025 - troisième édition, BIT, Genève, 1986.
ASTER   Annuaire des statistiques du travail 1945-89 - Edition rétrospective sur les recensements de population, BIT, Genève, 1990.
STAT    Base de données sur les statistiques du travail - LABORSTA, Bureau de statistique, BIT, Genève.

## 2. Evaluation des taux d'activité: 1950 - 1990

### 2.1 Données de base:

Tableau 1: Taux d'activité par sexe et par groupe d'âge

| Groupe d'âge | Année | | | |
|---|---|---|---|---|
| | 1960 (1) | 1970 (1) | 1980 (1) | 1991 (2) |
| **Hommes** | | | | |
| 10-14 | .. | 9.20 | .. | 17.34 |
| 15-19 | .. | 70.95 | .. | 54.43 |
| 20-24 | .. | 96.70 | .. | 88.92 |
| 25-29 | .. | 97.77 | .. | 93.03 |
| 30-34 | .. | 97.90 | .. | 93.00 |
| 35-39 | .. | 98.20 | .. | 93.37 |
| 40-44 | .. | 96.80 | .. | 93.88 |
| 45-49 | .. | 97.63 | .. | 92.18 |
| 50-54 | .. | 95.21 | .. | 90.63 |
| 55-59 | .. | 91.43 | .. | 81.67 |
| 60-64 | .. | 86.70 | .. | 72.79 |
| 65+ | .. | 59.39 | .. | 45.81 |
| **Femmes** | | | | |
| 10-14 | 0.26 | 0.99 | 0.00 | 3.26 |
| 15-19 | 19.88 | 29.10 | 27.00 | 15.13 |
| 20-24 | 24.00 | 31.20 | 34.37 | 32.82 |
| 25-29 | 19.04 | 21.70 | 28.70 | 30.69 |
| 30-34 | 18.66 | 19.80 | 26.94 | 29.62 |
| 35-39 | 18.30 | 18.70 | 22.93 | 31.52 |
| 40-44 | 17.84 | 17.70 | 23.12 | 29.03 |
| 45-49 | 19.10 | 18.20 | 20.56 | 25.31 |
| 50-54 | 18.60 | 17.50 | 17.27 | 21.62 |
| 55-59 | 18.00 | 16.90 | 17.60 | 14.64 |
| 60-64 | 17.00 | 14.30 | 15.72 | 11.63 |
| 65+ | 9.70 | 7.50 | 8.36 | 5.04 |

Source(s): (1) ASTER; (2) STAT.

### 2.2 Méthode(s): interpolation et extrapolation linéaires

#### 2.2.1 Hommes:

- 1950-60, taux d'activité 1950-60 tirés des EPPA3;
- 1970-90, interpolation et extrapolation des taux d'activité ajustés tirés des recensements de 1970 et 1991.

#### 2.2.2 Femmes:

- 1960-70, taux d'activité tirés des recensements de 1960 et 1970;
- 1950 et 1980-90, interpolation des taux d'activité ajustés tirés des recensements de 1960, 1970, 1980 et 1991.

## 3. Evaluation des taux de répartition par secteur d'activité: 1950 - 1990

### 3.1 Données de base:

Tableau 2: Répartition de la population active en % par secteur d'activité

| Année | Agriculture | Industrie | | Services |
|---|---|---|---|---|
| | | Total | Manufac. | |
| **Hommes** | | | | |
| 1943 (1) | 51.38 | 20.69 | 13.16 | 27.92 |
| 1960 (1) | 49.00 | 26.64 | 16.09 | 24.36 |
| 1980 (1) | 46.44 | 17.71 | 10.06 | 35.85 |
| 1991 (2) | 41.06 | 20.37 | 9.11 | 38.56 |
| **Femmes** | | | | |
| 1943 (1) | 15.72 | 14.91 | 14.86 | 69.37 |
| 1960 (1) | 10.84 | 11.57 | 11.20 | 77.60 |
| 1980 (1) | 8.69 | 15.39 | 14.24 | 75.92 |
| 1991 (2) | 3.95 | 13.33 | 12.13 | 82.72 |

Source(s): (1) ASTER; (2) STAT.

### 3.2 Méthode(s): interpolation linéaire

#### 3.2.1 Hommes:

- 1960 et 1980, taux de répartition tirés des recensements de 1960 et 1980;
- 1950, 1970 et 1990, interpolation des taux de répartition tirés des recensements de 1946, 1960, 1980 et 1991.

#### 3.2.2 Femmes:

Méthode, hypothèses et traitements identiques à ceux appliqués aux hommes.

## 4. Projection des taux d'activité: 2000 - 2010

### 4.1 Modèle(s): linéaire, log-linéaire et hyperbole

#### 4.1.1 Hommes:

- Au groupe d'âge [10-14], application de la fonction F2;
- Aux groupes d'âge [15-29], application de la fonction F1;
- Aux groupes d'âge [30+], application de la fonction F3;
- Modification des tendances des groupes d'âge [25-29] et [40-44].

#### 4.1.2 Femmes:

- Au groupe d'âge [10-14], application de la fonction F2;
- Au groupe d'âge [15-19], application de la fonction F1;
- Aux groupes d'âge [20+], application de la fonction F3;
- Modification des tendances des groupes d'âge [15-59].

*Notes sur les ajustements des taux, voir p. 192-195.*

*Notes sur les fonctions de projection, voir p. 198.*

# Bénin

## 1. Source(s) des données de base

Code(s):     Titre(s):

EPPA3      Evaluations et projections de la population active 1950-2025 - troisième édition, BIT, Genève, 1986.
S1960       Enquête démographique 1960-61, Institut National de la Statistique et de l'Analyse Economique, Cotonou, 1961.
ADNU84    Annuaire démographique 1984 - Statistiques des recensements de population II, trente-sixième édition, Nations Unies, New York, 1986.
ASTER      Annuaire des statistiques du travail 1945-89 - Edition rétrospective sur les recensements de population, BIT, Genève, 1990.

## 2. Evaluation des taux d'activité: 1950 - 1990

### 2.1 Données de base:

Tableau 1: Taux d'activité par sexe et par groupe d'âge

| Groupe d'âge | Année | | | | | |
|---|---|---|---|---|---|---|
| | 1950 (1) | 1960 (2) | 1960 (1) | 1970 (1) | 1979 (3) | 1980 (1) |
| **Hommes** | | | | | | |
| 10-14 | 46.55 | ... | .. | 42.50 | 36.78 | 36.75 |
| 15-19 | 90.00 | 87.06 | .. | 83.60 | 62.70 | 74.60 |
| 20-24 | 97.00 | 95.95 | .. | 94.70 | 87.68 | 91.40 |
| 25-29 | 97.80 | 97.66 | .. | 97.50 | 96.29 | 97.00 |
| 30-34 | 99.00 | 98.84 | .. | 98.65 | 97.49 | 98.10 |
| 35-39 | 99.20 | 98.98 | .. | 98.75 | 97.61 | 98.20 |
| 40-44 | 98.15 | 97.94 | .. | 97.70 | 97.12 | 97.10 |
| 45-49 | 97.25 | 97.09 | .. | 96.90 | 96.39 | 96.40 |
| 50-54 | 95.65 | 95.41 | .. | 95.10 | 94.37 | 94.35 |
| 55-59 | 94.05 | 93.66 | .. | 93.20 | 92.14 | 92.00 |
| 60-64 | 90.45 | 89.78 | .. | 89.00 | 88.11 | 87.00 |
| 65+ | 81.30 | 80.11 | .. | 78.70 | 75.12 | 75.00 |
| **Femmes** | | | | | | |
| 10-14 | 30.50 | .. | 29.10 | 28.55 | 27.16 | 27.60 |
| 15-19 | 87.90 | .. | 84.25 | 82.75 | 33.48 | 80.30 |
| 20-24 | 93.50 | .. | 91.20 | 90.25 | 37.67 | 88.70 |
| 25-29 | 97.00 | .. | 96.50 | 96.00 | 40.93 | 95.40 |
| 30-34 | 98.50 | .. | 98.00 | 97.50 | 41.87 | 97.30 |
| 35-39 | 97.80 | .. | 96.40 | 95.45 | 43.31 | 94.80 |
| 40-44 | 94.25 | .. | 93.00 | 92.10 | 44.03 | 91.60 |
| 45-49 | 84.30 | .. | 82.30 | 81.45 | 45.10 | 80.10 |
| 50-54 | 80.30 | .. | 78.00 | 77.05 | 43.02 | 75.50 |
| 55-59 | 75.50 | .. | 73.15 | 72.15 | 42.30 | 70.55 |
| 60-64 | 60.75 | .. | 58.00 | 56.85 | 37.00 | 55.00 |
| 65+ | 44.45 | .. | 41.60 | 40.45 | 27.50 | 38.50 |

Source(s): (1) EPPA3; (2) S1960; (3) ADNU84 et ASTER.

### 2.2 Méthode(s): interpolation et extrapolation linéaires

#### 2.2.1 Hommes:

- 1950-90, interpolation et extrapolation des taux d'activité tirés de l'enquête de 1960 et des taux d'activité tirés du recensement de 1979; modification des tendances de tous les groupes d'âge de 1950 et 1990.

#### 2.2.2 Femmes:

- 1950-90 interpolation et extrapolation des taux d'activité 1950-90 tirés des EPPA3; modification des tendances de tous les groupes d'âge de 1950 et 1990.

## 3. Evaluation des taux de répartition par secteur d'activité: 1950 - 1990

### 3.1 Données de base:

Tableau 2: Répartition de la population active en % par secteur d'activité

| Année | Agriculture | Industrie | | Services |
|---|---|---|---|---|
| | | Total | Manufac. | |
| **Hommes** | | | | |
| 1950 | 85.79 | 5.00 | .. | 9.25 |
| 1960 | 82.00 | 6.50 | .. | 11.50 |
| 1970 | 77.55 | 8.00 | .. | 14.45 |
| 1980 | 66.00 | 10.00 | .. | 24.00 |
| **Femmes** | | | | |
| 1950 | 91.60 | 1.10 | .. | 7.30 |
| 1960 | 88.40 | 1.55 | .. | 10.05 |
| 1970 | 84.55 | 2.10 | .. | 13.35 |
| 1980 | 68.80 | 3.20 | .. | 22.20 |

Source(s): EPPA3.

### 3.2 Méthode(s): extrapolation linéaire

#### 3.2.1 Hommes:

- 1950-80, taux de répartition 1950-80 tirés des EPPA3;
- 1990, extrapolation des taux 1950-80 tirés des EPPA3;
- Les rapports manufacture/industrie pour 1980 et 1990 ont été évalués sur la base des rapports manufacture/industrie observés pour les mêmes années au Togo.

#### 3.2.2 Femmes:

Méthode, hypothèses et traitements identiques à ceux appliqués aux hommes.

## 4. Projection des taux d'activité: 2000 - 2010

### 4.1 Modèle(s): logistique, linéaire et hyperbole

#### 4.1.1 Hommes:

- Au groupe d'âge [10-14], application de la fonction F6;
- Au groupe d'âge [15-19], application de la fonction F1;
- Aux groupes d'âge [20+], application de la fonction F3;
- Modification des tendances des groupes d'âge [55+].

#### 4.1.2 Femmes:

- Aux groupes d'âge [10-14] et [20-64], application de la fonction F3;
- Au groupe d'âge [15-19], application de la fonction F6;
- Au groupe d'âge [65+], application de la fonction F1;
- Modification des tendances des groupes d'âge [20+].

*Notes sur les ajustements des taux, voir p. 192-195.*            *Notes sur les fonctions de projection, voir p. 198.*

# Bhoutan

## 1. Source(s) des données de base

| Code(s): | Titre(s): |
|---|---|
| EPPA3 | Evaluations et projections de la population active 1950-2025 - troisième édition, BIT, Genève, 1986. |
| EPPA4 | Population active 1950-2010 - quatrième édition, BIT, Genève 1996. |

## 2. Evaluation des taux d'activité: 1950 - 1990

### 2.1 Données de base:

Tableau 1: Taux d'activité par sexe et par groupe d'âge

| Groupe d'âge | Année 1950 | 1975 |
|---|---|---|
| **Hommes** | | |
| 10-14 | 77.04 | 65.31 |
| 15-19 | 95.13 | 78.23 |
| 20-24 | 97.97 | 91.82 |
| 25-29 | 98.84 | 96.72 |
| 30-34 | 98.88 | 97.74 |
| 35-39 | 99.08 | 97.95 |
| 40-44 | 99.15 | 98.16 |
| 45-49 | 98.16 | 96.84 |
| 50-54 | 98.34 | 95.31 |
| 55-59 | 95.63 | 93.08 |
| 60-64 | 86.37 | 84.06 |
| 65+ | 71.24 | 69.35 |
| **Femmes** | | |
| 10-14 | 67.68 | 52.88 |
| 15-19 | 79.11 | 65.13 |
| 20-24 | 70.39 | 61.85 |
| 25-29 | 66.08 | 59.79 |
| 30-34 | 62.52 | 59.08 |
| 35-39 | 60.04 | 59.61 |
| 40-44 | 56.44 | 58.93 |
| 45-49 | 54.24 | 58.47 |
| 50-54 | 50.91 | 56.88 |
| 55-59 | 44.74 | 53.24 |
| 60-64 | 33.03 | 38.66 |
| 65+ | 14.10 | 28.59 |

Source(s): EPPA4.

### 2.2 Méthode(s): interpolation linéaire

#### 2.2.1 Hommes:

- 1950 et 1990, taux d'activité 1950 et 1975 estimés pour le Népal;
- 1960-80, interpolation des taux d'activité estimés pour 1950 et 1990.

#### 2.2.2 Femmes:

Méthode, hypothèses et traitements identiques à ceux appliqués aux hommes.

## 3. Evaluation des taux de répartition par secteur d'activité: 1950 - 1990

### 3.1 Données de base:

Tableau 2: Répartition de la population active en % par secteur d'activité

| Année | Agriculture | Industrie Total | Manufac. | Services |
|---|---|---|---|---|
| **Hommes** | | | | |
| 1950 (1) | 93.50 | 3.08 | 2.78 | 3.42 |
| 1975 (1) | 91.60 | 1.26 | 1.09 | 7.14 |
| **Femmes** | | | | |
| 1950 (1) | 97.83 | 1.73 | 1.69 | 0.44 |
| 1975 (1) | 98.00 | 0.37 | 0.35 | 1.64 |

Note(s): (1) Népal.
Source(s): EPPA4.

### 3.2 Méthode(s): interpolation linéaire

#### 3.2.1 Hommes:

- 1950 et 1990, taux de répartition 1950 et 1975 estimés pour le Népal;
- 1960-80, interpolation des taux de répartition estimés pour 1950 et 1990.

#### 3.2.2 Femmes:

Méthode, hypothèses et traitements identiques à ceux appliqués aux hommes.

## 4. Projection des taux d'activité: 2000 - 2010

### 4.1 Modèle(s): linéaire

#### 4.1.1 Hommes:

- A tous les groupes d'âge, application de la fonction F1;
- Modification des tendances des groupes d'âge [10-19] et [60+].

#### 4.1.2 Femmes:

- A tous les groupes d'âge, application de la fonction F1;
- Modification des tendances de tous les groupes d'âge.

*Notes sur les ajustements des taux, voir p. 192-195.*

*Notes sur les fonctions de projection, voir p. 198.*

# Bolivie

## 1. Source(s) des données de base

| Code(s): | Titre(s): |
|---|---|
| EPPA3 | Evaluations et projections de la population active 1950-2025 - troisième édition, BIT, Genève, 1986. |
| ASTER | Annuaire des statistiques du travail 1945-89 - Edition rétrospective sur les recensements de population, BIT, Genève, 1990. |
| AST94 | Annuaire des statistiques du travail 1994, BIT, Genève, 1994. |

## 2. Evaluation des taux d'activité: 1950 - 1990

### 2.1 Données de base:

Tableau 1: Taux d'activité par sexe et par groupe d'âge

| Groupe d'âge | Année 1950 (1) | 1976 (1) | 1992 (2) |
|---|---|---|---|
| **Hommes** | | | |
| 10-14 | 44.17 | 15.99 | 16.12 |
| 15-19 | 78.27 | 54.97 | 44.58 |
| 20-24 | 92.90 | 83.80 | 76.97 |
| 25-29 | 96.73 | 94.75 | 91.03 |
| 30-34 | 97.30 | 98.10 | 95.48 |
| 35-39 | 97.28 | 98.65 | 96.34 |
| 40-44 | 96.82 | 98.44 | 96.28 |
| 45-49 | 96.58 | 98.25 | 95.69 |
| 50-54 | 95.54 | 97.18 | 93.79 |
| 55-59 | 94.58 | 94.77 | 87.26 |
| 60-64 | 92.23 | 89.73 | 80.98 |
| 65+ | 78.13 | 80.49 | 69.49 |
| **Femmes** | | | |
| 10-14 | 51.91 | 10.09 | 15.28 |
| 15-19 | 66.74 | 22.11 | 35.61 |
| 20-24 | 64.80 | 25.16 | 45.70 |
| 25-29 | 64.22 | 25.44 | 50.16 |
| 30-34 | 66.28 | 23.62 | 52.05 |
| 35-39 | 64.56 | 22.76 | 54.27 |
| 40-44 | 68.30 | 22.88 | 55.20 |
| 45-49 | 65.36 | 22.49 | 54.27 |
| 50-54 | 66.67 | 20.58 | 51.18 |
| 55-59 | 43.29 | 18.63 | 46.97 |
| 60-64 | 29.67 | 16.75 | 43.48 |
| 65+ | 21.68 | 14.06 | 37.18 |

Source(s): (1) ASTER; (2) AST94.

### 2.2 Méthode(s): interpolation et extrapolation linéaires

#### 2.2.1 Hommes:

- 1950-70, taux d'activité 1950-70 tirés des EPPA3;
- 1980-90, extrapolation des taux d'activité tirés du recensement de 1976 et des taux ajustés tirés de recensement de 1992.

#### 2.2.2 Femmes:

- 1950-70, interpolation des taux d'activité tirés des recensements de 1950 et 1976;
ajustement des taux estimés sur la base du rapport hommes/femmes dans l'agriculture tiré du recensement de 1992;
- 1980-90, interpolation des taux d'activité tirés des recensements de 1976 et 1992.

## 3. Evaluation des taux de répartition par secteur d'activité: 1950 - 1990

### 3.1 Données de base:

Tableau 2: Répartition de la population active en % par secteur d'activité

| Année | Agriculture | Industrie Total | Manufac. | Services |
|---|---|---|---|---|
| **Hommes** | | | | |
| 1950 (1) | 54.44 | 31.55 | 12.79 | 14.02 |
| 1976 (1) | 54.21 | 20.65 | 7.98 | 25.15 |
| 1992 (2) | 44.22 | 23.47 | 10.70 | 32.31 |
| **Femmes** | | | | |
| 1950 (1) | 74.34 | 11.23 | 8.42 | 14.42 |
| 1976 (1) | 27.21 | 18.51 | 17.26 | 54.28 |
| 1992 (2) | 43.57 | 9.37 | 8.62 | 47.07 |

Source(s): (1) ASTER; (2) AST94.

### 3.2 Méthode(s): interpolation linéaire

#### 3.2.1 Hommes:

- 1950-90, interpolation des taux de répartition tirés des recensements de 1950, 1976 et 1992;
ajustement des taux de répartition estimés pour 1950-60 pour tenir compte des aides familiales en agriculture.

#### 3.2.2 Femmes:

Méthode, hypothèses et traitements identiques à ceux appliqués aux hommes.

## 4. Projection des taux d'activité: 2000 - 2010

### 4.1 Modèle(s): linéaire, log-linéaire et hyperbole

#### 4.1.1 Hommes:

- Aux groupes d'âge [10-14] et [60+], application de la fonction F1;
- Aux groupes d'âge [15-59], application de la fonction F3;
- Modification des tendances des groupes d'âge [10-14], [20-34] et [40-49].

#### 4.1.2 Femmes:

- Aux groupes d'âge [10-19] et [55+], application de la fonction F1;
- Aux groupes d'âge [20-54], application de la fonction F2;
- Modification des tendances des groupes d'âge [10-19] et [55+].

*Notes sur les ajustements des taux, voir p. 192-195.*

*Notes sur les fonctions de projection, voir p. 198.*

# Bosnie-Herzégovine

## 1. Source(s) des données de base

**Code(s):** **Titre(s):**

EPPA3  Evaluations et projections de la population active 1950-2025 - troisième édition, BIT, Genève, 1986.

BLT-94-2  Popovic B. (1994), "Nouvelles estimations pour 1980 et 1990 des taux d'activité par âge et répartition sectorielle
pour certains pays d'Europe orientale et méridionale" dans le Bulletin des statistiques du travail - 1994-2, BIT, Genève.

## 2. Evaluation des taux d'activité: 1950 - 1990

### 2.1 Données de base:

Tableau 1: Taux d'activité par sexe et par groupe d'âge

| | | Année | | | | |
|---|---|---|---|---|---|---|
| | Groupe d'âge | 1950 (1) | 1960 (1) | 1970 (1) | 1980 (2) | 1990 (2) |
| **Hommes** | | | | | | |
| | 10-14 | 24.10 | 8.85 | 3.25 | 0.31 | 0.02 |
| | 15-19 | 86.80 | 67.25 | 48.45 | 25.07 | 22.47 |
| | 20-24 | 94.85 | 90.75 | 85.80 | 80.53 | 81.67 |
| | 25-29 | 96.10 | 96.55 | 95.53 | 95.53 | 96.06 |
| | 30-34 | 97.60 | 97.90 | 98.35 | 97.79 | 98.01 |
| | 35-39 | 97.80 | 97.25 | 98.30 | 97.34 | 97.97 |
| | 40-44 | 97.60 | 97.00 | 95.55 | 96.11 | 96.85 |
| | 45-49 | 97.20 | 96.10 | 96.00 | 92.38 | 93.97 |
| | 50-54 | 94.20 | 94.00 | 92.35 | 77.71 | 80.28 |
| | 55-59 | 84.65 | 85.60 | 77.05 | 59.83 | 60.51 |
| | 60-64 | 79.75 | 75.50 | 65.10 | 51.19 | 38.79 |
| | 65+ | 61.60 | 56.70 | 51.30 | 38.36 | 27.42 |
| **Femmes** | | | | | | |
| | 10-14 | 23.20 | 12.50 | 5.45 | 1.02 | 0.07 |
| | 15-19 | 68.80 | 58.35 | 45.15 | 20.99 | 18.13 |
| | 20-24 | 60.75 | 60.55 | 60.35 | 54.68 | 61.95 |
| | 25-29 | 45.00 | 53.20 | 57.35 | 56.44 | 68.73 |
| | 30-34 | 38.85 | 47.65 | 52.25 | 50.93 | 64.91 |
| | 35-39 | 35.45 | 45.15 | 50.35 | 40.73 | 64.17 |
| | 40-44 | 32.80 | 42.15 | 47.20 | 35.00 | 56.15 |
| | 45-49 | 29.50 | 37.80 | 43.40 | 28.17 | 43.69 |
| | 50-54 | 24.20 | 31.70 | 36.70 | 20.12 | 29.67 |
| | 55-59 | 21.10 | 26.75 | 31.60 | 15.34 | 17.04 |
| | 60-64 | 16.50 | 22.10 | 26.80 | 12.68 | 12.32 |
| | 65+ | 10.95 | 14.10 | 14.60 | 7.45 | 7.23 |

**Source(s):** (1) EPPA3; (2) BLT-94-2.

### 2.2 Méthode(s): Données tirées des EPPA3 et du BLT-94-2.

#### 2.2.1 Hommes:

- 1950-70, taux d'activité 1950-70 pour la Yougoslavie tirés des EPPA3;
- 1980-90, taux d'activité tirés du Bulletin des statistiques
du travail 1994-2.

#### 2.2.2 Femmes:

Méthode, hypothèses et traitements identiques à ceux appliqués aux hommes.

## 3. Evaluation des taux de répartition par secteur d'activité: 1950 - 1990

### 3.1 Données de base:

Tableau 2: Répartition de la population active en % par secteur d'activité

| | Agriculture | Industrie | | Services |
|---|---|---|---|---|
| Année | | Total | Manufac. | |
| **Hommes** | | | | |
| 1950 (1) | 68.30 | 17.80 | .. | 13.90 |
| 1960 (1) | 56.00 | 28.00 | .. | 16.00 |
| 1970 (1) | 45.00 | 34.40 | .. | 20.60 |
| 1980 (2) | 25.60 | 44.67 | 22.28 | 29.73 |
| 1990 (2) | 8.78 | 53.95 | 31.08 | 37.27 |
| **Femmes** | | | | |
| 1950 (1) | 83.00 | 5.40 | .. | 11.50 |
| 1960 (1) | 78.10 | 15.00 | .. | 6.80 |
| 1970 (1) | 58.20 | 20.00 | .. | 21.80 |
| 1980 (2) | 37.49 | 23.92 | 20.51 | 38.58 |
| 1990 (2) | 15.55 | 36.83 | 32.57 | 47.62 |

**Source(s):** (1) EPPA3; (2) BLT-94-2.

### 3.2 Méthode(s): données du BLT-94-2

#### 3.2.1 Hommes:

- 1950-70, taux de répartition 1950-70 pour la Yougoslavie,
tirés des EPPA3;
   1980-90, taux de répartition tirés du Bulletin des statistiques
du travail - 1994-2.

#### 3.2.2 Femmes:

Méthode, hypothèses et traitements identiques à ceux appliqués aux hommes.

## 4. Projection des taux d'activité: 2000 - 2010

### 4.1 Modèle(s): linéaire et hyperbole

#### 4.1.1 Hommes:

- Aux groupes d'âge [15-24] et [50+], application de la fonction F3;
- Aux groupes d'âge [25-49], application de la fonction F1;
- Modification des tendances des groupes d'âge [15-24].

#### 4.1.2 Femmes:

- Aux groupes d'âge [15-24] et [50+], application de la fonction F3;
- Aux groupes d'âge [25-49], application de la fonction F1;
- Modification de la tendance du groupe d'âge [15-19].

*Notes sur les ajustements des taux, voir p. 192-195.*     *Notes sur les fonctions de projection, voir p. 198.*

# Botswana

## 1. Source(s) des données de base

Code(s):     Titre(s):

ASTER        Annuaire des statistiques du travail 1945-89 - Edition rétrospective sur les recensements de population, BIT, Genève, 1990.
R1991        1991 Population and Housing Census Administrative/Technical Report and National Statistical Tables, Central Statistical Office, Gaborone, 1994.

## 2. Evaluation des taux d'activité: 1950 - 1990

### 2.1 Données de base:

Tableau 1: Taux d'activité par sexe et par groupe d'âge

|  | Année | | |
|---|---|---|---|
| Groupe d'âge | 1964 (1) | 1971 (1) | 1991 (2) |
| **Hommes** | | | |
| 10-14 | 37.95 | 40.18 | 18.16 |
| 15-19 | 63.98 | 66.26 | 43.78 |
| 20-24 | 92.32 | 92.92 | 86.92 |
| 25-29 | 99.15 | 99.20 | 98.71 |
| 30-34 | 99.07 | 99.10 | 98.81 |
| 35-39 | 99.03 | 99.05 | 98.87 |
| 40-44 | 98.99 | 99.01 | 98.85 |
| 45-49 | 98.82 | 98.82 | 98.82 |
| 50-54 | 98.70 | 98.70 | 98.78 |
| 55-59 | 98.44 | 98.42 | 98.69 |
| 60-64 | 89.85 | 90.70 | 82.33 |
| 65+ | 74.31 | 75.08 | 67.54 |
| **Femmes** | | | |
| 10-14 | .. | 27.64 | 18.14 |
| 15-19 | .. | 58.54 | 41.26 |
| 20-24 | .. | 83.12 | 75.68 |
| 25-29 | .. | 87.20 | 82.50 |
| 30-34 | .. | 87.49 | 80.84 |
| 35-39 | .. | 87.35 | 77.83 |
| 40-44 | .. | 85.69 | 73.46 |
| 45-49 | .. | 83.54 | 67.01 |
| 50-54 | .. | 80.22 | 60.05 |
| 55-59 | .. | 77.68 | 54.74 |
| 60-64 | .. | 72.40 | 46.65 |
| 65+ | .. | 59.24 | 27.12 |

Source(s): (1) ASTER; (2) R1991.

### 2.2 Méthode(s): interpolation et extrapolation linéaires

#### 2.2.1 Hommes:

- 1950-90, interpolation et extrapolation des taux d'activité tirés des recensements de 1964, 1971 et 1991; la répartition de la population active par groupe d'âge pour les recensements de 1964 et 1971 a été évaluée sur la base de la répartition par groupe d'âge de la population active en Namibie.

#### 2.2.2 Femmes:

Méthode, hypothèses et traitements identiques à ceux appliqués aux hommes.

## 3. Evaluation des taux de répartition par secteur d'activité: 1950 - 1990

### 3.1 Données de base:

Tableau 2: Répartition de la population active en % par secteur d'activité

|  | Agriculture | Industrie | | Services |
|---|---|---|---|---|
| Année | | Total | Manufac. | |
| **Hommes** | | | | |
| 1964 (1) | 87.41 | 5.04 | 1.28 | 7.55 |
| 1981 (1) | 51.14 | 19.26 | 2.05 | 29.60 |
| 1991 (2) | 37.27 | 31.65 | 5.29 | 31.08 |
| **Femmes** | | | | |
| 1964 (1) | 95.11 | 0.73 | 0.66 | 4.15 |
| 1981 (1) | 72.91 | 1.75 | 0.67 | 25.34 |
| 1991 (2) | 52.85 | 9.98 | 5.97 | 37.17 |

Source(s): (1) ASTER; (2) R1991.

### 3.2 Méthode(s): interpolation et extrapolation linéaires
moyenne pondérée

#### 3.2.1 Hommes:

- 1950-60, interpolation et extrapolation des taux de répartition tirés des recensements de 1964, 1981 et 1991;
modification des tendances de tous les secteurs;
- 1970-90, moyennes pondérées des taux de répartition tirés des recensements de 1964, 1981 et 1991.

#### 3.2.2 Femmes:

Méthode, hypothèses et traitements identiques à ceux appliqués aux hommes.

## 4. Projection des taux d'activité: 2000 - 2010

### 4.1 Modèle(s): logistique, log-linéaire, hyperbole et logarithmique

#### 4.1.1 Hommes:

- Aux groupes d'âge [10-14] et [65+], application de la fonction F6;
- Au groupe d'âge [15-19], application de la fonction F2;
- Aux groupes d'âge [20-64], application de la fonction F3;
- Modification des tendances des groupes d'âge [35-39] et [45-59].

#### 4.1.2 Femmes:

- Au groupe d'âge [10-14], application de la fonction F5;
- Au groupe d'âge [15-19], application de la fonction F2;
- Aux groupes d'âge [20+], application de la fonction F3;
- Modification des tendances des groupes d'âge [20-64].

*Notes sur les ajustements des taux, voir p. 192-195.*     *Notes sur les fonctions de projection, voir p. 198.*

# Brésil

## 1. Source(s) des données de base

Code(s):   Titre(s):
EPPA3   Evaluations et projections de la population active 1950-2025 - troisième édition, BIT, Genève, 1986.
ASTER   Annuaire des statistiques du travail 1945-89 - Edition rétrospective sur les recensements de population, BIT, Genève, 1990.
AST93   Annuaire des statistiques du travail 1993, BIT, Genève, 1993.

## 2. Evaluation des taux d'activité: 1950 - 1990

### 2.1 Données de base:

Tableau 1: Taux d'activité par sexe et par groupe d'âge

| Groupe d'âge | Année 1980 (1) | 1989 (2) | 1990 (2) |
|---|---|---|---|
| **Hommes** | | | |
| 10-14 | 20.24 | 25.51 | 24.32 |
| 15-19 | 64.80 | 73.27 | 71.76 |
| 20-24 | 90.03 | 92.50 | 92.14 |
| 25-29 | 96.05 | 96.30 | 96.16 |
| 30-39 | 96.53 | 97.31 | 96.85 |
| 40-49 | 93.16 | 94.62 | 94.46 |
| 50-59 | 82.30 | 81.51 | 82.33 |
| 60+ | 44.39 | 45.51 | 46.03 |
| **Femmes** | | | |
| 10-14 | 8.61 | 11.77 | 10.61 |
| 15-19 | 31.21 | 40.93 | 41.42 |
| 20-24 | 39.07 | 52.02 | 52.86 |
| 25-29 | 35.95 | 52.45 | 52.75 |
| 30-39 | 34.20 | 53.27 | 54.66 |
| 40-49 | 30.04 | 48.63 | 49.50 |
| 50-59 | 21.38 | 33.85 | 34.54 |
| 60+ | 7.38 | 11.29 | 11.55 |

Source(s): (1) ASTER; (2) AST93.

### 2.2 Méthode(s): moyenne pondérée

#### 2.2.1 Hommes:
- 1950-70, taux d'activité 1950-70 ajustés tirés des EPPA3;
ajustement des taux d'activité sur la base des résultats du recensement
de 1980 et des enquêtes de 1989 et 1990;
- 1980, moyennes pondérées des taux d'activité 1970 tirés des EPPA3
et des taux d'activité ajustés tirés du recensement de 1980;
- 1990, moyennes pondérées des taux d'activité tirés des enquêtes
de 1989 et 1990.

#### 2.2.2 Femmes:
Méthode, hypothèses et traitements identiques à ceux appliqués aux hommes.

## 3. Evaluation des taux de répartition par secteur d'activité: 1950 - 1990

### 3.1 Données de base:

Tableau 2: Répartition de la population active en % par secteur d'activité

| Année | Agriculture | Industrie Total | Manufac. | Services |
|---|---|---|---|---|
| **Hommes** | | | | |
| 1980 (1) | 37.54 | 29.32 | 19.11 | 33.14 |
| 1989 (2) | 29.36 | 29.04 | .. | 41.60 |
| 1990 (3) | 28.08 | 28.15 | 16.93 | 43.78 |
| **Femmes** | | | | |
| 1980 (1) | 15.27 | 15.76 | 15.27 | 68.98 |
| 1989 (2) | 14.68 | 12.72 | 0.00 | 72.60 |
| 1990 (3) | 13.34 | 12.82 | 11.94 | 73.85 |

Source(s): (1) ASTER; (2) AST93.

### 3.2 Méthode(s): moyenne pondérée

#### 3.2.1 Hommes:
- 1950-70, taux de répartition ajustés 1950-70 tirés des EPPA3;
ajustement des taux sur la base des résultats du recensement de 1980
et des enquêtes de 1989 et 1990;
- 1980-90, moyennes pondérées des taux de répartition tirés du
recensement de 1980 et des taux de répartition tirés des enquête de 1989
et 1990.

#### 3.2.2 Femmes:
Méthode, hypothèses et traitements identiques à ceux appliqués aux hommes.

## 4. Projection des taux d'activité: 2000 - 2010

### 4.1 Modèle(s): linéaire, hyperbole et logistique

#### 4.1.1 Hommes:
- Aux groupes d'âge [10-44], application de la fonction F1;
- Aux groupes d'âge [45+], application de la fonction F3;
- Modification des tendances des groupes d'âge [10-24] et [35-49].

#### 4.1.2 Femmes:
- Au groupe d'âge [10-14], application de la fonction F1;
- Aux groupes d'âge [15-64], application de la fonction F6;
- Au groupe d'âge [65+], application de la fonction F3;
- Modification des tendances des groupes d'âge [10-64].

# Brunéi Darussalam

## 1. Source(s) des données de base

Code(s):    Titre(s):

ADNU79    Annuaire démographique 1979 - Statistiques des recensements de population, trente et unième édition, Nations Unies, New York, 1980.
ASTER     Annuaire des statistiques du travail 1945-89 - Edition rétrospective sur les recensements de population, BIT, Genève, 1990.
ADNU93    Annuaire démographique 1993 - Statistiques des recensements de population, trente et unième édition, Nations Unies, New York.
STAT      Base de données sur les statistiques du travail - LABORSTA, Bureau de statistique, BIT, Genève.

## 2. Evaluation des taux d'activité: 1950 - 1990

### 2.1 Données de base:

Tableau 1: Taux d'activité par sexe et par groupe d'âge

| Groupe d'âge | Année | | | | |
|---|---|---|---|---|---|
| | 1960 (1) | 1971 (1) | 1981 (1) | 1986 (1) | 1991 (2) |
| **Hommes** | | | | | |
| 10-14 | 0.00 | 0.00 | 0.00 | .. | 0.00 |
| 15-19 | 46.47 | 32.90 | 38.18 | .. | 23.80 |
| 20-24 | 91.30 | 86.55 | 86.40 | .. | 84.22 |
| 25-29 | 99.02 | 97.10 | 97.30 | .. | 97.10 |
| 30-34 | 99.29 | 97.33 | 98.71 | .. | 98.13 |
| 35-39 | 99.97 | 98.08 | 98.91 | .. | 98.35 |
| 40-44 | 99.36 | 97.66 | 98.32 | .. | 98.25 |
| 45-49 | 97.96 | 97.12 | 98.27 | .. | 96.34 |
| 50-54 | 95.89 | 94.87 | 96.40 | .. | 93.95 |
| 55-59 | 90.92 | 88.11 | 88.86 | .. | 72.08 |
| 60-64 | 82.44 | 80.88 | 82.70 | .. | 71.03 |
| 65+ | 56.66 | 58.61 | 51.94 | .. | 32.23 |
| **Femmes** | | | | | |
| 10-14 | 0.00 | 0.00 | 0.00 | 0.00 | 0.00 |
| 15-19 | 18.82 | 17.92 | 17.02 | 14.45 | 13.74 |
| 20-24 | 19.83 | 30.23 | 47.13 | 52.68 | 58.19 |
| 25-29 | 16.68 | 24.36 | 43.37 | 57.18 | 63.89 |
| 30-34 | 18.49 | 21.78 | 36.73 | 48.01 | 60.67 |
| 35-39 | 21.89 | 18.35 | 32.92 | 46.93 | 56.66 |
| 40-44 | 25.03 | 19.76 | 28.56 | 41.79 | 51.50 |
| 45-49 | 26.42 | 20.26 | 22.74 | 36.07 | 43.36 |
| 50-54 | 30.64 | 21.55 | 20.55 | 24.89 | 34.89 |
| 55-59 | 27.76 | 22.83 | 14.49 | 16.75 | 17.56 |
| 60-64 | 20.68 | 18.80 | 10.44 | 12.49 | 13.18 |
| 65+ | 7.71 | 11.48 | 5.95 | 5.77 | 4.16 |

Source(s): (1) ADNU79 et ASTER; (2) STAT.

### 2.2 Méthode(s): interpolation linéaire
moyenne pondérée

**2.2.1 Hommes:**

- 1950-80, interpolation des taux d'activité tirés des recensements de de 1960, 1971 et 1981;
modification des tendances de tous les groupes d'âge pour 1950;
- 1990, moyennes pondérées des taux d'activité tirés des recensements de 1981 et 1991.

**2.2.2 Femmes:**

- 1950-70, interpolation des taux d'activité tirés des recensements de 1960 et 1971;
- 1980-90, interpolation des taux d'activité tirés des recensements de 1981, 1986 et 1991;
aux taux d'activité du groupe d'âge [10-14], application du rapport des taux d'activité des groupes d'âge [10-14] et [15-19] estimés pour le Koweït.

## 3. Evaluation des taux de répartition par secteur d'activité: 1950 - 1990

### 3.1 Données de base:

Tableau 2: Répartition de la population active en % par secteur d'activité

| Année | Agriculture | Industrie | | Services |
|---|---|---|---|---|
| | | Total | Manufac. | |
| **Hommes** | | | | |
| 1960 (1) | 28.68 | 40.69 | 5.75 | 30.63 |
| 1971 (1) | 9.84 | 39.32 | 4.37 | 50.85 |
| 1981 (1) | 4.72 | 37.23 | 4.23 | 58.05 |
| 1991 (2) | 2.21 | 31.43 | 6.44 | 66.35 |
| **Femmes** | | | | |
| 1960 (1) | 57.35 | 10.07 | 5.56 | 32.58 |
| 1971 (1) | 23.01 | 10.36 | 4.43 | 66.63 |
| 1981 (1) | 6.25 | 11.00 | 3.66 | 82.75 |
| 1991 (2) | 1.63 | 8.87 | 4.24 | 89.49 |

Source(s): (1) ASTER; (2) STAT.

### 3.2 Méthode(s): moyenne pondérée
extrapolation linéaire

**3.2.1 Hommes:**

- 1950, extrapolation des taux de répartition tirés des recensements de 1960 et 1971;
- 1960-90, moyennes pondérées des taux de répartition tirés des recensements de 1960, 1971, 1981 et 1991.

**3.2.2 Femmes:**

- 1950, taux de répartition de l'agriculture estimé sur la base du rapport hommes/femmes dans l'agriculture tiré du recensement de 1960, le taux de répartition de l'industrie a été maintenu au même niveau que celui du recensement de 1960 et celui des services a été calculé en tant que résidu;
- 1960-90, moyennes pondérées des taux de répartition tirés des recensements de 1960, 1971, 1981 et 1991.

## 4. Projection des taux d'activité: 2000 - 2010

### 4.1 Modèle(s): linéaire, log-linéaire, hyperbole et logistique

**4.1.1 Hommes:**

- Aux groupes d'âge [15-54], application de la fonction F1;
- Aux groupes d'âge [55+], application de la fonction F3;
- Modification des tendances des groupes d'âge [15-19], [25-34], [40-44] et [55-64].

**4.1.2 Femmes:**

- Aux groupes d'âge [15-24], [30-39] et [45-64], application de la fonction F1;
- Au groupe d'âge [25-29], application de la fonction F6;
- Au groupe d'âge [40-44], application de la fonction F2;
- Au groupe d'âge [65+], application de la fonction F3;
- Modification des tendances des groupes d'âge [15-64].

---

*Notes sur les ajustements des taux, voir p. 192-195.*          *Notes sur les fonctions de projection, voir p. 198.*

# Bulgarie

## 1. Source(s) des données de base

**Code(s):**  **Titre(s):**

EPPA3  Evaluations et projections de la population active 1950-2025 - troisième édition, BIT, Genève, 1986.
ASTER  Annuaire des statistiques du travail 1945-89 - Edition rétrospective sur les recensements de population, BIT, Genève, 1990.
BLT-94-2  Popovic B. (1994), "Nouvelles estimations pour 1980 et 1990 des taux d'activité par âge et répartition sectorielle
  pour certains pays d'Europe orientale et méridionale" dans le Bulletin des statistiques du travail - 1994-2, BIT, Genève.

## 2. Evaluation des taux d'activité: 1950 - 1990

### 2.1 Données de base:

Tableau 1: Taux d'activité par sexe et par groupe d'âge

| Groupe d'âge | Année 1950 (1) | 1960 (1) | 1970 (1) | 1985 (2) |
|---|---|---|---|---|
| **Hommes** | | | | |
| 10-14 | 2.00 | 0.85 | 0.45 | 0.00 |
| 15-19 | 60.00 | 45.55 | 31.15 | 17.69 |
| 20-24 | 92.70 | 90.00 | 83.30 | 81.90 |
| 25-29 | 95.55 | 95.35 | 95.15 | 95.07 |
| 30-34 | 98.00 | 97.90 | 97.80 | 97.80 |
| 35-39 | 98.35 | 98.10 | 97.80 | 95.80 |
| 40-44 | 98.50 | 97.90 | 97.35 | 95.50 |
| 45-49 | 98.40 | 97.25 | 96.15 | 94.60 |
| 50-54 | 97.80 | 95.30 | 92.80 | 88.10 |
| 55-59 | 95.50 | 90.80 | 86.05 | 80.90 |
| 60-64 | 93.20 | 70.00 | 46.80 | 39.20 |
| 65+ | 69.00 | 38.35 | 20.60 | 15.17 |
| **Femmes** | | | | |
| 10-14 | 3.50 | 1.30 | 0.85 | 0.07 |
| 15-19 | 56.25 | 44.50 | 32.20 | 34.47 |
| 20-24 | 72.50 | 69.80 | 73.35 | 87.04 |
| 25-29 | 71.70 | 78.10 | 85.05 | 95.00 |
| 30-34 | 74.05 | 80.90 | 88.35 | 96.40 |
| 35-39 | 77.15 | 83.25 | 89.90 | 94.80 |
| 40-44 | 78.55 | 83.35 | 88.50 | 94.60 |
| 45-49 | 76.55 | 79.55 | 82.70 | 91.00 |
| 50-54 | 71.65 | 71.40 | 71.25 | 83.60 |
| 55-59 | 68.95 | 46.40 | 31.20 | 32.00 |
| 60-64 | 62.80 | 28.45 | 12.90 | 16.50 |
| 65+ | 20.40 | 8.60 | 3.60 | 4.35 |

Source(s): (1) EPPA3; (2) STAT.

### 2.2 Méthode(s): moyenne pondérée
extrapolation linéaire

**2.2.1 Hommes:**

- 1950-70, taux d'activité 1950-70 tirés des EPPA3;
- 1980, moyennes pondérées des taux d'activité 1970 tirés des EPPA3
et des taux d'activité ajustés tirés du recensement de 1985;
- 1990, extrapolation des taux d'activité 1950-1970 tirés des EPPA3,
des taux estimés pour 1980 et des taux ajustés tirés du recensement de 1985;
modification des tendances de tous les groupes d'âge;
aux taux extrapolés, application des variations des taux interpolés 1985
par rapport aux taux ajustés tirés du recensement1985.

**2.2.2 Femmes:**

Méthode, hypothèses et traitements identiques à ceux appliqués aux hommes.

## 3. Evaluation des taux de répartition par secteur d'activité: 1950 - 1990

### 3.1 Données de base:

Tableau 2: Répartition de la population active en % par secteur d'activité

| Année | Agriculture | Industrie Total | Manufac. | Services |
|---|---|---|---|---|
| **Hommes** | | | | |
| 1950 (1) | 63.20 | 18.30 | .. | 18.40 |
| 1960 (1) | 47.60 | 31.30 | .. | 21.10 |
| 1970 (1) | 29.10 | 44.30 | .. | 26.60 |
| 1980 (2) | 18.72 | 49.90 | 34.99 | 31.38 |
| 1990 (2) | 13.83 | 53.96 | 40.81 | 32.21 |
| **Femmes** | | | | |
| 1950 (1) | 85.50 | 7.00 | .. | 7.40 |
| 1960 (1) | 68.60 | 15.60 | .. | 15.80 |
| 1970 (1) | 41.90 | 29.50 | .. | 28.50 |
| 1980 (2) | 21.94 | 38.64 | 33.90 | 39.42 |
| 1990 (2) | 13.05 | 42.09 | 36.62 | 44.86 |

Source(s): (1) EPPA3; (2) BLT-94-2.

### 3.2 Méthode(s): données du BLT-94-2

**3.2.1 Hommes:**

- 1950-70, taux de répartition 1950-70 tirés des EPPA3;
- 1980-90, taux de répartition tirés du Bulletin des statistiques du travail - 1994-2

**3.2.2 Femmes:**

Méthode, hypothèses et traitements identiques à ceux appliqués aux hommes.

## 4. Projection des taux d'activité: 2000 - 2010

### 4.1 Modèle(s): linéaire et hyperbole

**4.1.1 Hommes:**

- Aux groupes d'âge [15+], application de la fonction F3;
- Modification des tendances des groupes d'âge [20-24] et [30-34].

**4.1.2 Femmes:**

- Au groupe d'âge [15-19], application de la fonction F1;
- Aux groupes d'âge [20+], application de la fonction F3;
- Modification des tendances du groupe d'âge [15-54].

*Notes sur les ajustements des taux, voir p. 192-195.*

*Notes sur les fonctions de projection, voir p. 198.*

# Burkina Faso

## 1. Source(s) des données de base

Code(s):    Titre(s):

S1960       Enquête démographique 1960-61, Institut National de la Statistique et de la Démographie, Ouagadougou, 1961.
R1985       Recensement général de la population 1985, Institut National de la Statistique et de la Démographie, Ouagadougou, 1985.
S1991       Enquête démographique, 1991, Institut National de la Statistique et de la Démographie, Ouagadougou, 1991.

## 2. Evaluation des taux d'activité: 1950 - 1990

### 2.1 Données de base:

Tableau 1: Taux d'activité par sexe et par groupe d'âge

| Groupe d'âge | Année 1960 (1) | 1985 (2) | 1991 (3) |
|---|---|---|---|
| **Hommes** | | | |
| 10-14 | 79.00 | 71.18 | 63.25 |
| 15-19 | 87.00 | 86.02 | 77.75 |
| 20-24 | 96.05 | 92.24 | 85.99 |
| 25-29 | 97.50 | 96.78 | 93.45 |
| 30-34 | 98.25 | 97.72 | 97.60 |
| 35-39 | 98.45 | 98.06 | 98.13 |
| 40-44 | 98.30 | 97.62 | 98.33 |
| 45-49 | 97.50 | 97.47 | 98.49 |
| 50-54 | 97.15 | 95.78 | 96.24 |
| 55-59 | 96.40 | 94.05 | 93.73 |
| 60-64 | 93.65 | 91.01 | 92.33 |
| 65+ | 80.85 | 73.31 | 78.19 |
| **Femmes** | | | |
| 10-14 | 79.80 | 68.18 | 60.63 |
| 15-19 | 88.75 | 76.33 | 71.58 |
| 20-24 | 93.05 | 76.82 | 75.27 |
| 25-29 | 93.95 | 80.07 | 80.89 |
| 30-34 | 95.50 | 81.20 | 83.56 |
| 35-39 | 95.40 | 82.44 | 84.02 |
| 40-44 | 94.80 | 82.08 | 86.60 |
| 45-49 | 93.40 | 82.32 | 85.51 |
| 50-54 | 92.04 | 81.12 | 87.24 |
| 55-59 | 86.37 | 74.46 | 78.47 |
| 60-64 | 80.38 | 64.13 | 67.88 |
| 65+ | 65.46 | 40.32 | 44.05 |

Source(s):  (1) S1960; (2) R1985; (3) S1991.

### 2.2 Méthode(s): interpolation et extrapolation linéaires

#### 2.2.1 Hommes:

- 1950-90, interpolation et extrapolation des taux d 'activité tirés du
recensement de 1985 et des taux d'activité tirés des enquêtes de 1960 et 1991;
ajustement des taux extrapolés 1950 sur la base des variations des taux
interpolés 1960 par rapport aux taux de l'enquête de 1960;
ajustement des taux interpolés 1990 sur la base des variations
des taux interpolés 1985 par rapport aux taux du recensement de 1985;
modification des tendances de tous les groupes d'âge pour 1950
et des groupes d'âge [10-19] pour 1990.

#### 2.2.2 Femmes:

- 1950-90, interpolation et extrapolation des taux d'activité tirés de
l'enquête de 1960 et des moyennes des taux d'activité tirés du recensement
de 1985 et de l'enquête de 1991;
modification des tendances de tous les groupes d'âge pour 1950
et des groupes d'âge [10-14] et [20+] pour 1990.

## 3. Evaluation des taux de répartition par secteur d'activité: 1950 - 1990

### 3.1 Données de base:

Tableau 2: Répartition de la population active en % par secteur d'activité

| Année | Agriculture | Industrie Total | Manufac. | Services |
|---|---|---|---|---|
| **Hommes** | | | | |
| 1960 (1) | 92.00 | 3.00 | .. | 5.00 |
| 1985 (2) | 91.18 | 3.64 | .. | 5.18 |
| 1991 (3) | 91.85 | 1.84 | 1.15 | 6.31 |
| **Femmes** | | | | |
| 1960 (1) | 91.50 | 2.10 | .. | 6.40 |
| 1985 (2) | 92.32 | 2.08 | .. | 5.60 |
| 1991 (3) | 94.40 | 1.14 | 1.09 | 4.45 |

Source(s): (1) S1960; (2) R1985; (3) S1991.

### 3.2 Méthode(s): interpolation et extrapolation linéaires

#### 3.2.1 Hommes:

- 1950-90, interpolation des taux de répartition tirés des enquêtes
de 1960 et 1991 et du recensement de 1985;
- Application du rapport manufacture/industrie tiré de l'enquête de 1991.

#### 3.2.2 Femmes:

Méthode, hypothèses et traitements identiques à ceux appliqués aux hommes.

## 4. Projection des taux d'activité: 2000 - 2010

### 4.1 Modèle(s): linéaire, hyperbole et exponentiel

#### 4.1.1 Hommes:

- Aux groupes d'âge [10-24], application de la fonction F1;
- Aux groupes d'âge [25+], application de la fonction F3;
- Modification des tendances des groupes d'âge [20-24] et [40-44].

#### 4.1.2 Femmes:

- Au groupe d'âge [10-14], application de la fonction F4;
- Aux groupes d'âge [15+], application de la fonction F3;
- Modification des tendances des groupes d'âge [10-14] et [20-64].

*Notes sur les ajustements des taux, voir p. 192-195.*    *Notes sur les fonctions de projection, voir p. 198.*

# Burundi

## 1. Source(s) des données de base

Code(s):    Titre(s):

EPPA3    Evaluations et projections de la population active 1950-2025 - troisième édition, BIT, Genève, 1986.

ASTER    Annuaire des statistiques du travail 1945-89 - Edition rétrospective sur les recensements de population, BIT, Genève, 1990.

## 2. Evaluation des taux d'activité: 1950 - 1990

### 2.1 Données de base:

Tableau 1: Taux d'activité par sexe et par groupe d'âge

| Groupe d'âge | Année 1950 | 1960 | 1970 | 1980 |
|---|---|---|---|---|
| **Hommes** | | | | |
| 10-14 | 56.35 | 55.25 | 54.15 | 53.45 |
| 15-19 | 89.35 | 87.90 | 86.45 | 85.55 |
| 20-24 | 96.25 | 95.65 | 95.10 | 94.80 |
| 25-29 | 97.80 | 97.75 | 97.65 | 97.60 |
| 30-34 | 98.55 | 98.45 | 98.35 | 98.30 |
| 35-39 | 98.55 | 98.45 | 98.35 | 98.30 |
| 40-44 | 98.15 | 98.05 | 97.95 | 97.90 |
| 45-49 | 98.05 | 97.95 | 97.85 | 97.80 |
| 50-54 | 96.85 | 96.70 | 96.60 | 96.50 |
| 55-59 | 95.65 | 95.40 | 95.20 | 95.10 |
| 60-64 | 92.60 | 92.25 | 91.90 | 91.70 |
| 65+ | 76.25 | 75.70 | 75.10 | 74.75 |
| **Femmes** | | | | |
| 10-14 | 50.35 | 48.90 | 47.45 | 46.55 |
| 15-19 | 92.60 | 89.55 | 86.45 | 84.60 |
| 20-24 | 96.80 | 93.80 | 90.80 | 89.00 |
| 25-29 | 97.45 | 94.65 | 91.90 | 90.25 |
| 30-34 | 98.75 | 96.15 | 93.55 | 92.00 |
| 35-39 | 98.45 | 96.00 | 93.55 | 92.10 |
| 40-44 | 97.55 | 95.35 | 93.15 | 91.85 |
| 45-49 | 96.10 | 93.95 | 91.80 | 90.55 |
| 50-54 | 88.20 | 86.40 | 84.65 | 83.55 |
| 55-59 | 78.10 | 76.80 | 75.55 | 74.75 |
| 60-64 | 61.90 | 61.15 | 60.35 | 59.90 |
| 65+ | 35.75 | 35.45 | 35.20 | 35.05 |

Source: EPPA3.

### 2.2 Méthode(s): interpolation et extrapolation linéaires

#### 2.2.1 Hommes:

- 1950-90, interpolation et extrapolation des taux d'activité 1950-80
tirés des EPPA3;
modification des tendances de tous les groupes d'âge
pour 1990;
ajustement des taux extrapolés 1990 sur la base des variations
des taux interpolés 1980 par rapport aux taux 1980 tirés des EPPA3.

#### 2.2.2 Femmes:

Méthode, hypothèses et traitements identiques à ceux appliqués aux hommes.

## 3. Evaluation des taux de répartition par secteur d'activité: 1950 - 1990

### 3.1 Données de base:

Tableau 2: Répartition de la population active en % par secteur d'activité

| Année | Agriculture | Industrie Total | Manufac. | Services |
|---|---|---|---|---|
| **Hommes** | | | | |
| 1950 (1) | 93.00 | 2.20 | .. | 4.80 |
| 1960 (1) | 91.00 | 2.85 | .. | 6.15 |
| 1970 (1) | 89.00 | 3.30 | .. | 7.70 |
| 1979 (2) | 87.90 | 3.66 | 2.11 | 8.43 |
| 1980 (1) | 87.80 | 3.70 | .. | 8.50 |
| **Femmes** | | | | |
| 1950 (1) | 98.30 | 0.80 | .. | 0.90 |
| 1960 (1) | 98.15 | 0.90 | .. | 0.95 |
| 1970 (1) | 98.00 | 0.95 | .. | 1.05 |
| 1979 (2) | 97.89 | 1.02 | 1.01 | 1.10 |
| 1980 (1) | 97.85 | 1.05 | .. | 1.10 |

Source(s): (1) EPPA3; (2) ASTER.

### 3.2 Méthode(s): extrapolation linéaire

#### 3.2.1 Hommes:

- 1950-80, taux de répartition 1950-80 tirés des EPPA3;
- 1990, extrapolation des taux de répartition 1950-80 tirés des EPPA3;
- Application du rapport manufacturé/industrie tiré du recensement de 1979.

#### 3.2.2 Femmes:

Méthode, hypothèses et traitements identiques à ceux appliqués aux hommes.

## 4. Projection des taux d'activité: 2000 - 2010

### 4.1 Modèle(s): linéaire et hyperbole

#### 4.1.1 Hommes:

- A tous les groupes d'âge, application de la fonction F1.

#### 4.1.2 Femmes:

- A tous les groupes d'âge, application de la fonction F3;
- Modification des tendances des groupes d'âge [20-54].

*Notes sur les ajustements des taux, voir p. 192-195.*    *Notes sur les fonctions de projection, voir p. 198.*

# Cambodge

## 1. Source(s) des données de base

Code(s):    Titre(s):

EPPA3    Evaluations et projections de la population active 1950-2025 - troisième édition, BIT, Genève, 1986.
STAT    Base de données sur les statistiques du travail - LABORSTA, Bureau de statistique, BIT, Genève.
AST93    Annuaire des statistiques du travail 1993, BIT, Genève, 1993.

## 2. Evaluation des taux d'activité: 1950 - 1990

### 2.1 Données de base:

Tableau 1: Taux d'activité par sexe et par groupe d'âge

| Groupe d'âge | Année 1962 (1) | 1992 (2) |
|---|---|---|
| **Hommes** | | |
| 10-14 | 17.87 | 24.31 |
| 15-19 | 58.08 | 54.00 |
| 20-24 | 87.99 | 88.00 |
| 25-29 | 97.45 | 96.77 |
| 30-34 | 98.81 | 98.30 |
| 35-39 | 98.85 | 98.75 |
| 40-44 | 98.76 | 98.12 |
| 45-49 | 98.35 | 97.42 |
| 50-54 | 96.54 | 95.83 |
| 55-59 | 91.09 | 91.43 |
| 60-64 | 78.11 | 68.11 |
| 65+ | 49.61 | 41.10 |
| **Femmes** | | |
| 10-14 | 28.48 | 26.49 |
| 15-19 | 66.96 | 68.82 |
| 20-24 | 63.76 | 87.89 |
| 25-29 | 58.40 | 88.82 |
| 30-34 | 58.94 | 91.73 |
| 35-39 | 61.49 | 92.28 |
| 40-44 | 62.71 | 92.76 |
| 45-49 | 63.58 | 91.41 |
| 50-54 | 57.98 | 89.29 |
| 55-59 | 49.47 | 85.46 |
| 60-64 | 32.42 | 56.01 |
| 65+ | 16.23 | 26.63 |

Source(s): (1) STAT; (2) AST93.

### 2.2 Méthode(s): interpolation et extrapolation linéaires

#### 2.2.1 Hommes:

- 1950-90, interpolation et extrapolation des taux d'activité tirés du recensement de 1962 et des taux d'activité tirés des estimations officielles de 1992.

#### 2.2.2 Femmes:

- 1950-90, aux taux d'activité estimés pour la Thaïlande, application des variations des taux d'activité estimés pour 1992 par rapport aux taux des estimations officielles de 1992;
modification des tendances de tous les groupes d'âge.

## 3. Evaluation des taux de répartition par secteur d'activité: 1950 - 1990

### 3.1 Données de base:

Tableau 2: Répartition de la population active en % par secteur d'activité

| Année | Agriculture | Industrie Total | Manufac. | Services |
|---|---|---|---|---|
| **Hommes** | | | | |
| 1950 (1) | 79.90 | 2.55 | 0.00 | 17.55 |
| 1960 (1) | 77.20 | 4.65 | 0.00 | 18.15 |
| 1962 (2) | 76.74 | 5.01 | 3.34 | 18.25 |
| 1970 (1) | 73.80 | 5.35 | 0.00 | 20.85 |
| 1980 (1) | 70.30 | 6.80 | 4.77 | 22.90 |
| **Femmes** | | | | |
| 1950 (1) | 89.35 | 0.85 | 0.00 | 9.80 |
| 1960 (1) | 88.35 | 1.90 | 0.00 | 9.75 |
| 1962 (2) | 88.19 | 2.21 | 2.01 | 9.61 |
| 1970 (1) | 84.55 | 2.60 | 0.00 | 12.85 |
| 1980 (1) | 80.00 | 6.50 | 5.98 | 13.50 |

Source(s): (1) EPPA3; (2) STAT.

### 3.2 Méthode(s): extrapolation linéaire

#### 3.2.1 Hommes:

- 1950-80, taux de répartition 1950-80 tirés des EPPA3;
- 1990, extrapolation des taux de répartition 1950-80 tirés des EPPA3;
modification des tendances de tous les secteurs;
- Application du rapport manufacture/industrie tiré du recensement de 1962.

#### 3.2.2 Femmes:

Méthode, hypothèses et traitements identiques à ceux appliqués aux hommes.

## 4. Projection des taux d'activité: 2000 - 2010

### 4.1 Modèle(s): linéaire, log-linéaire, hyperbole et logistique

#### 4.1.1 Hommes:

- Aux groupes d'âge [10-59], application de la fonction F1;
- Aux groupes d'âge [60+], application de la fonction F3;
- Modification de la tendance du groupe d'âge [35-39].

#### 4.1.2 Femmes:

- Au groupe d'âge [10-14], application de la fonction F1;
- Aux groupes d'âge [15-24], application de la fonction F2;
- Aux groupes d'âge [25-59], application de la fonction F6;
- Aux groupes d'âge [60+], application de la fonction F3;
- Modification de la tendance du groupe d'âge [10-14].

---

*Notes sur les ajustements des taux, voir p. 192-195.*

*Notes sur les fonctions de projection, voir p. 198.*

# Cameroun

## 1. Source(s) des données de base

Code(s):     Titre(s):

EPPA3     Evaluations et projections de la population active 1950-2025 - troisième édition, BIT, Genève, 1986.
ASTER     Annuaire des statistiques du travail 1945-89 - Edition rétrospective sur les recensements de population, BIT, Genève, 1990.

## 2. Evaluation des taux d'activité: 1950 - 1990

### 2.1 Données de base:

Tableau 1: Taux d'activité par sexe et par groupe d'âge

| Groupe d'âge | Année 1950 (1) | 1960 (1) | 1970 (1) | 1980 (1) | 1976 (2) |
|---|---|---|---|---|---|
| **Hommes** | | | | | |
| 10-14 | 52.05 | 50.35 | 47.35 | 40.00 | .. |
| 15-19 | 84.80 | 82.60 | 78.60 | 68.85 | .. |
| 20-24 | 95.25 | 94.35 | 92.85 | 89.10 | .. |
| 25-29 | 97.40 | 97.25 | 97.05 | 96.50 | .. |
| 30-34 | 98.15 | 98.00 | 97.75 | 97.10 | .. |
| 35-39 | 98.30 | 98.15 | 97.90 | 97.20 | .. |
| 40-44 | 98.15 | 98.00 | 97.70 | 97.00 | .. |
| 45-49 | 97.35 | 97.25 | 97.00 | 96.40 | .. |
| 50-54 | 96.95 | 96.75 | 96.35 | 95.50 | .. |
| 55-59 | 96.05 | 95.75 | 95.15 | 93.75 | .. |
| 60-64 | 93.10 | 92.55 | 91.60 | 89.15 | .. |
| 65+ | 79.90 | 78.95 | 77.20 | 73.00 | .. |
| **Femmes** | | | | | |
| 10-14 | 31.65 | 30.65 | 28.80 | 24.35 | 13.26 |
| 15-19 | 42.30 | 41.00 | 38.80 | 33.30 | 35.42 |
| 20-24 | 49.55 | 48.65 | 47.00 | 42.95 | 44.40 |
| 25-29 | 53.15 | 52.10 | 50.20 | 45.65 | 47.40 |
| 30-34 | 55.90 | 54.75 | 52.80 | 47.90 | 49.78 |
| 35-39 | 62.00 | 60.85 | 58.85 | 53.90 | 55.79 |
| 40-44 | 62.75 | 61.65 | 59.65 | 54.85 | 56.64 |
| 45-49 | 70.35 | 69.10 | 66.80 | 61.25 | 63.38 |
| 50-54 | 66.25 | 64.85 | 62.30 | 56.10 | 58.48 |
| 55-59 | 60.85 | 59.40 | 56.90 | 50.70 | 61.64 |
| 60-64 | 57.90 | 56.05 | 52.70 | 44.55 | 47.68 |
| 65+ | 40.80 | 39.05 | 35.90 | 28.25 | 31.21 |

Source(s): (1) EPPA3; (2) ASTER.

### 2.2 Méthode(s): interpolation et extrapolation linéaires

#### 2.2.1 Hommes:

- 1950-90, interpolation et extrapolation des taux d'activité 1950-80
tirés des EPPA3;
modification des tendances des groupes d'âge [10-14]
et [15-19] pour 1990.

#### 2.2.2 Femmes:

- 1950-90, interpolation et extrapolation des taux d'activité 1950-80 tirés
des EPPA3;
ajustement des taux interpolés 1980 et extrapolés 1990 sur la base
des variations des taux interpolés 1976 par rapport aux taux ajustés
du recensement de 1976;
modification des tendances des groupes d'âge [15+] pour 1990.

## 3. Evaluation des taux de répartition par secteur d'activité: 1950 - 1990

### 3.1 Données de base:

Tableau 2: Répartition de la population active en % par secteur d'activité

| Année | Agriculture | Industrie Total | Manufac. | Services |
|---|---|---|---|---|
| **Hommes** | | | | |
| 1950 (1) | 87.50 | 4.50 | .. | 8.00 |
| 1960 (1) | 84.40 | 5.40 | .. | 10.20 |
| 1970 (1) | 78.90 | 7.00 | .. | 14.10 |
| 1976 (2) | 70.61 | 9.62 | 6.35 | 19.77 |
| 1980 (1) | 65.40 | 11.15 | .. | 23.45 |
| **Femmes** | | | | |
| 1950 (1) | 99.00 | 0.30 | .. | 0.70 |
| 1960 (1) | 97.00 | 1.00 | .. | 2.00 |
| 1970 (1) | 95.00 | 1.20 | .. | 3.80 |
| 1976 (2) | 92.14 | 2.56 | 2.48 | 5.29 |
| 1980 (1) | 86.50 | 2.25 | .. | 11.25 |

Source(s): (1) EPPA3; (2) ASTER.

### 3.2 Méthode(s): extrapolation linéaire

#### 3.2.1 Hommes:

- 1950-80, taux de répartition 1950-80 tirés des EPPA3;
- 1990, extrapolation des taux de répartition 1950-80 et 1976
tirés respectivement des EPPA3 et du recensement de 1976;
- Application du rapport manufacture/industrie tiré du recensement de 1976.

#### 3.2.2 Femmes:

Méthode, hypothèses et traitements identiques à ceux appliqués aux hommes.

## 4. Projection des taux d'activité: 2000 - 2010

### 4.1 Modèle(s): linéaire et hyperbole

#### 4.1.1 Hommes:

- Aux groupes d'âge [10-24], application de la fonction F1;
- Aux groupes d'âge [25+], application de la fonction F3;
- Modification des tendances des groupes d'âge [25-64].

#### 4.1.2 Femmes:

- Au groupe d'âge [10-14], application de la fonction F1;
- Aux groupes d'âge [15+], application de la fonction F3;
- Modification des tendances des groupes d'âge [10-44] et [60-64].

*Notes sur les ajustements des taux, voir p. 192-195.*     *Notes sur les fonctions de projection, voir p. 198.*

232

# Canada

## 1. Source(s) des données de base

Code(s):     Titre(s):

EPPA3     Evaluations et projections de la population active 1950-2025 - troisième édition, BIT, Genève, 1986.
STAT      Base de données sur les statistiques du travail - LABORSTA, Bureau de statistique, BIT, Genève.

## 2. Evaluation des taux d'activité: 1950 - 1990

### 2.1 Données de base:

Tableau 1: Taux d'activité par sexe et par groupe d'âge

| Groupe d'âge | Année 1979 | 1980 | 1981 | 1989 | 1990 | 1991 |
|---|---|---|---|---|---|---|
| **Hommes** | | | | | | |
| 10-14 | 0.00 | 0.00 | 0.00 | 0.00 | 0.00 | 0.00 |
| 15-19 | 57.20 | 58.00 | 58.17 | 60.51 | 58.90 | 55.82 |
| 20-24 | 86.40 | 86.20 | 86.52 | 84.79 | 82.80 | 81.45 |
| 25-29 | 94.43 | 94.23 | 94.20 | 93.64 | 93.11 | 91.86 |
| 30-34 | 97.05 | 96.65 | 96.60 | 94.66 | 94.22 | 93.19 |
| 35-39 | 96.72 | 96.38 | 96.50 | 95.02 | 94.49 | 93.73 |
| 40-44 | 95.85 | 95.59 | 95.69 | 94.47 | 94.18 | 93.76 |
| 45-49 | 94.58 | 94.49 | 94.64 | 93.32 | 92.98 | 92.82 |
| 50-54 | 90.77 | 90.66 | 90.85 | 89.84 | 88.61 | 88.02 |
| 55-59 | 85.27 | 85.04 | 84.16 | 78.11 | 77.35 | 75.97 |
| 60-64 | 65.65 | 65.25 | 63.66 | 53.44 | 51.58 | 48.19 |
| 65+ | 15.30 | 14.70 | 14.09 | 10.97 | 11.41 | 11.33 |
| **Femmes** | | | | | | |
| 10-14 | 0.00 | 0.00 | 0.00 | 0.00 | 0.00 | 0.00 |
| 15-19 | 50.80 | 52.20 | 53.03 | 56.49 | 55.93 | 53.82 |
| 20-24 | 71.30 | 73.00 | 72.96 | 77.24 | 76.46 | 75.55 |
| 25-29 | 62.28 | 64.45 | 67.11 | 77.30 | 78.15 | 77.99 |
| 30-34 | 58.39 | 60.83 | 63.84 | 75.14 | 76.26 | 76.35 |
| 35-39 | 58.73 | 60.94 | 63.85 | 76.57 | 77.74 | 77.67 |
| 40-44 | 60.22 | 62.41 | 65.30 | 77.80 | 79.08 | 79.09 |
| 45-49 | 54.77 | 57.04 | 58.85 | 71.81 | 73.02 | 74.41 |
| 50-54 | 49.42 | 51.16 | 52.55 | 62.42 | 63.45 | 64.48 |
| 55-59 | 41.81 | 41.20 | 41.25 | 46.37 | 45.23 | 46.60 |
| 60-64 | 24.71 | 24.78 | 24.78 | 22.25 | 25.95 | 24.49 |
| 65+ | 4.2 | 4.3 | 4.48 | 3.96 | 3.79 | 3.50 |

Source(s): STAT.

### 2.2 Méthode(s): moyenne arithmétique

#### 2.2.1 Hommes:

- 1950-70, taux d'activité 1950-70 tirés des EPPA3;
- 1980, moyennes des taux d'activité ajustés tirés des enquêtes de 1979, 1980 et 1981;
- 1990, moyennes des taux d'activité tirés des enquêtes de 1989, 1990 et 1991;
Les taux estimés ont été ajustés pour tenir compte des forces armés.

#### 2.2.2 Femmes:

Méthode, hypothèses et traitements identiques à ceux appliqués aux hommes.

## 3. Evaluation des taux de répartition par secteur d'activité: 1950 - 1990

### 3.1 Données de base:

Tableau 2: Répartition de la population active en % par secteur d'activité

| Année | Agriculture | Industrie Total | Manufac. | Services |
|---|---|---|---|---|
| **Hommes** | | | | |
| 1979 | 7.51 | 36.44 | 23.20 | 56.05 |
| 1980 | 6.88 | 36.20 | 23.80 | 56.92 |
| 1981 | 6.73 | 36.36 | 24.10 | 56.91 |
| 1989 | 4.08 | 35.58 | 21.41 | 60.34 |
| 1990 | 4.01 | 34.90 | 20.34 | 61.09 |
| 1991 | 4.18 | 33.89 | 19.68 | 61.93 |
| **Femmes** | | | | |
| 1979 | 3.37 | 15.25 | 12.96 | 81.38 |
| 1980 | 3.16 | 15.76 | 13.68 | 81.08 |
| 1981 | 11.74 | 56.40 | 47.31 | 31.86 |
| 1989 | 2.44 | 13.52 | 11.34 | 84.04 |
| 1990 | 2.38 | 12.97 | 10.69 | 84.64 |
| 1991 | 2.57 | 12.36 | 10.17 | 85.07 |

Source(s): STAT.

### 3.2 Méthode(s): moyenne arithmétique

#### 3.2.1 Hommes:

- 1950-70, taux de répartition 1950-70 tirés des EPPA3;
- 1980, moyennes des taux de répartition tirés des enquêtes de 1979, 1980 et 1981;
- 1990, moyennes des taux de répartition tirés des enquêtes de 1989, 1990 et 1991.

#### 3.2.2 Femmes:

Méthode, hypothèses et traitements identiques à ceux appliqués aux hommes.

## 4. Projection des taux d'activité: 2000 - 2010

### 4.1 Modèle(s): linéaire, hyperbole et logistique

#### 4.1.1 Hommes:

- Au groupe d'âge [15-19], application de la fonction F1;
- Aux groupes d'âge [20+], application de la fonction F3;
- Modification des tendances des groupes d'âge [15-19] et [25-54].

#### 4.1.2 Femmes:

- Aux groupes d'âge [15-64], application de la fonction F6;
- Au groupe d'âge [65+], application de la fonction F3;
- Modification des tendances des groupes d'âge [15-64].

*Notes sur les ajustements des taux, voir p. 192-195.*     *Notes sur les fonctions de projection, voir p. 198.*

# Cap-Vert

## 1. Source(s) des données de base

| Code(s): | Titre(s): |
|---|---|
| EPPA3 | Evaluations et projections de la population active 1950-2025 - troisième édition, BIT, Genève, 1986. |
| R1980 | Recenseamento Geral da Populacao e Habitacao 1980, III Volume: Populacao Activa, Ministerio do Plano e das Finanças, Paraia, 1983. |
| R1990 | Recenseamento da Populacao e Habitacao 1990, Ministerio do Plano e das Finanças, Paraia, 1992. |

## 2. Evaluation des taux d'activité: 1950 - 1990

### 2.1 Données de base:

Tableau 1: Taux d'activité par sexe et par groupe d'âge

| Groupe d'âge | Année 1950 (1) | 1960 (1) | 1970 (1) | 1980 (1) | 1980 (2) | 1990 (3) |
|---|---|---|---|---|---|---|
| **Hommes** | | | | | | |
| 10-14 | 52.05 | 52.00 | 51.85 | 51.60 | .. | 17.89 |
| 15-19 | 84.80 | 84.75 | 84.60 | 84.25 | .. | 72.65 |
| 20-24 | 95.25 | 95.20 | 95.15 | 95.00 | .. | 94.27 |
| 25-29 | 97.40 | 97.40 | 97.40 | 97.35 | .. | 96.83 |
| 30-34 | 98.15 | 98.10 | 98.10 | 98.10 | .. | 96.69 |
| 35-39 | 98.30 | 98.30 | 98.30 | 98.25 | .. | 95.78 |
| 40-44 | 98.15 | 98.15 | 98.10 | 98.10 | .. | 95.11 |
| 45-49 | 97.35 | 97.35 | 97.35 | 97.35 | .. | 95.63 |
| 50-54 | 96.95 | 96.95 | 96.90 | 96.90 | .. | 93.57 |
| 55-59 | 96.05 | 96.05 | 96.05 | 96.00 | .. | 91.54 |
| 60-64 | 93.10 | 93.10 | 93.05 | 92.95 | .. | 86.64 |
| 65+ | 79.90 | 79.85 | 79.80 | 79.65 | .. | 59.42 |
| **Femmes** | | | | | | |
| 10-14 | 7.50 | 6.80 | 6.20 | .. | 5.48 | 10.97 |
| 15-19 | 29.70 | 32.10 | 34.50 | .. | 36.32 | 43.19 |
| 20-24 | 31.40 | 35.70 | 40.00 | .. | 44.49 | 52.56 |
| 25-29 | 27.05 | 30.50 | 34.00 | .. | 37.98 | 51.66 |
| 30-34 | 24.80 | 28.55 | 32.20 | .. | 34.14 | 51.24 |
| 35-39 | 22.10 | 24.50 | 27.80 | .. | 30.35 | 50.02 |
| 40-44 | 19.20 | 21.20 | 23.20 | .. | 25.14 | 42.84 |
| 45-49 | 18.70 | 19.50 | 20.45 | .. | 21.20 | 38.52 |
| 50-54 | 18.00 | 19.00 | 20.00 | .. | 20.95 | 33.96 |
| 55-59 | 15.80 | 16.30 | 17.80 | .. | 17.36 | 27.95 |
| 60-64 | 13.00 | 13.10 | 13.20 | .. | 13.30 | 24.58 |
| 65+ | 11.80 | 10.50 | 9.20 | .. | 7.75 | 11.87 |

Source(s): (1) EPPA3; (2) R1980; (3) R1990.

### 2.2 Méthode(s): interpolation et extrapolation linéaires

#### 2.2.1 Hommes:

- 1950-80, interpolation des taux d'activité 1950-80 tirés des EPPA3;
ajustement des taux interpolés 1950-80 sur la base des variations des
taux extrapolés 1990 par rapport aux taux ajustés du recensement de 1990;
- 1990, taux d'activité ajustés tirés du recensement de 1990;
modification des tendances des groupes d'âge [10-14] et [60+]
pour 1980 et 1990.

#### 2.2.2 Femmes:

- 1950-70, extrapolation des taux d'activité ajustés tirés des
recensements de 1980 et 1990;
- 1980-90, taux d'activité ajustés tirés des recensements de 1980 et 1990;
modification des tendances de tous les groupes d'âge.

## 3. Evaluation des taux de répartition par secteur d'activité: 1950 - 1990

### 3.1 Données de base:

Tableau 2: Répartition de la population active en % par secteur d'activité

| Année | Agriculture | Industrie Total | Manufac. | Services |
|---|---|---|---|---|
| **Hommes** | | | | |
| 1980 (1) | 34.76 | 37.08 | 2.55 | 28.17 |
| 1990 (2) | 29.92 | 37.54 | 6.50 | 32.54 |
| **Femmes** | | | | |
| 1980 (1) | 40.35 | 18.63 | 2.88 | 41.03 |
| 1990 (2) | 31.63 | 17.43 | 4.18 | 50.94 |

Source(s): (1) R1980; (2) R1990.

### 3.2 Méthode(s): extrapolation linéaire

#### 3.2.1 Hommes:
- 1980 et 90, taux de répartition tirés des recensements de 1980 et 1990;
- 1950-70, pour les services, extrapolation des taux de répartition
tirés des recensements de 1980 et 1990; pour l'industrie, application
du rapport industrie/services tiré du recensement de 1980 et pour l'agriculture,
par calcul des taux en tant que résidus.

#### 3.2.2 Femmes:
- 1980-90, taux de répartition tirés des recensements de 1980 et 1990;
- 1950-70, pour les services, extrapolation des taux de répartition tirés
des recensements de 1980 et 1990;
modification de la tendances du secteur;
pour l'industrie, application du rapport industrie/services tiré du recensement
de 1980 et pour l'agriculture, calcul des taux en tant que résidus.

## 4. Projection des taux d'activité: 2000 - 2010

### 4.1 Modèle(s): linéaire

#### 4.1.1 Hommes:
- A tous les groupes d'âge, application de la fonction F1;
- Modification des tendances des groupes d'âge [15-24].

#### 4.1.2 Femmes:
- A tous les groupes d'âge, application de la fonction F1;
- Modification des tendances des groupes d'âge [60+].

*Notes sur les ajustements des taux, voir p. 192-195.*

*Notes sur les fonctions de projection, voir p. 198.*

# Chili

## 1. Source(s) des données de base

| Code(s): | Titre(s): |
|---|---|
| EPPA3 | Evaluations et projections de la population active 1950-2025 - troisième édition, BIT, Genève, 1986. |
| ASTER | Annuaire des statistiques du travail 1945-89 - Edition rétrospective sur les recensements de population, BIT, Genève, 1990. |
| AST90-92 | Editions de 1990 à 1992 de l'Annuaire des statistiques du travail du BIT, Genève. |
| INE | Indicatores de empleo por sexo y grupos de edad, Total Nacional, Instituto Nacional de Estadísticas, Santiago. |

## 2. Evaluation des taux d'activité: 1950 - 1990

### 2.1 Données de base:

Tableau 1: Taux d'activité par sexe et par groupe d'âge

| Groupe d'âge | Année | | | | | |
|---|---|---|---|---|---|---|
| | 1952 (1) | 1970 (1) | 1980 (1) | 1989 (2) | 1990 (2) | 1991 (2) |
| **Hommes** | | | | | | |
| 10-14 | .. | 4.17 | 0.00 | 0.00 | 0.00 | 0.00 |
| 15-19 | .. | 46.87 | 39.24 | 30.10 | 30.00 | 29.70 |
| 20-24 | .. | 86.07 | 81.94 | 79.20 | 80.90 | 78.25 |
| 25-29 | .. | 96.88 | 95.04 | 94.50 | 94.20 | 93.50 |
| 30-34 | .. | 97.92 | 97.69 | 97.40 | 97.50 | 97.10 |
| 35-39 | .. | 97.72 | 97.64 | 97.90 | 98.00 | 97.70 |
| 40-44 | .. | 96.51 | 97.33 | 97.30 | 96.80 | 97.00 |
| 45-49 | .. | 94.79 | 93.68 | 94.80 | 95.10 | 95.20 |
| 50-54 | .. | 89.72 | 87.13 | 89.50 | 89.20 | 90.30 |
| 55-59 | .. | 84.31 | 78.24 | 80.50 | 79.80 | 80.60 |
| 60-64 | .. | 75.03 | 68.64 | 67.50 | 64.60 | 62.60 |
| 65+ | .. | 48.40 | 32.51 | 29.25 | 28.69 | 28.71 |
| **Femmes** | | | | | | |
| 10-14 | 3.38 | 1.79 | 0.00 | 0.00 | 0.00 | 0.00 |
| 15-19 | 28.40 | 17.26 | 15.30 | 18.40 | 15.90 | 19.50 |
| 20-24 | 35.10 | 32.47 | 34.57 | 38.10 | 38.40 | 38.20 |
| 25-29 | 30.40 | 30.13 | 35.89 | 40.90 | 41.95 | 42.45 |
| 30-34 | 28.00 | 26.04 | 33.28 | 42.63 | 41.48 | 41.08 |
| 35-39 | 27.60 | 25.04 | 31.51 | 42.55 | 43.38 | 41.50 |
| 40-44 | 27.60 | 23.64 | 29.49 | 42.55 | 42.93 | 42.83 |
| 45-49 | 26.60 | 22.07 | 26.71 | 38.70 | 38.50 | 39.45 |
| 50-54 | 24.60 | 20.26 | 22.88 | 30.78 | 31.88 | 32.18 |
| 55-59 | 22.40 | 16.59 | 17.38 | 25.40 | 28.45 | 26.98 |
| 60-64 | 19.50 | 12.76 | 11.55 | 15.88 | 15.40 | 15.43 |
| 65+ | 13.24 | 6.45 | 4.51 | 3.33 | 3.95 | 4.03 |

Source(s): (1) ASTER; (2) AST90-92 et INE.

### 2.2 Méthode(s): interpolation et extrapolation linéaires
moyenne pondérée

#### 2.2.1 Hommes:

- 1950-60, taux d'activité 1950-60 tirés des EPPA3;
- 1970-80, interpolation des taux d'activité ajustés tirés des recensements de 1970 et 1982;
- 1990, moyennes des taux d'activité tirés des enquêtes trimestrielles de 1989, 1990 et 1991;
ajustement des taux d'activité des groupes d'âge [15-24].

#### 2.2.2 Femmes:

- 1950-70, extrapolation des taux d'activité tirés du recensement de 1952 et des taux ajustés du recensement de 1970;
- 1980, moyennes pondérées des taux d'activité ajustés tirés du recensement de 1982 et des taux estimés pour 1990;
- 1980, moyennes des taux d'activité tirés des enquêtes trimestrielles de 1989, 1990 et 1991.

## 3. Evaluation des taux de répartition par secteur d'activité: 1950 - 1990

### 3.1 Données de base:

Tableau 2: Répartition de la population active en % par secteur d'activité

| Année | Agriculture | Industrie | | Services |
|---|---|---|---|---|
| | | Total | Manufac. | |
| **Hommes** | | | | |
| 1970 (1) | 29.13 | 32.06 | 17.80 | 38.81 |
| 1982 (1) | 25.53 | 29.10 | 15.75 | 45.37 |
| 1989 (2) | 24.42 | 30.12 | 17.14 | 45.45 |
| 1991 (2) | 24.40 | 29.27 | 16.82 | 46.33 |
| 1990 (2) | 23.98 | 30.30 | 17.24 | 45.72 |
| **Femmes** | | | | |
| 1952 (1) | 8.00 | 25.87 | 25.07 | 66.12 |
| 1970 (1) | 6.81 | 19.89 | 18.79 | 73.30 |
| 1982 (1) | 6.31 | 12.45 | 11.53 | 81.24 |
| 1989 (2) | 5.89 | 15.70 | 14.81 | 78.41 |
| 1991 (2) | 5.88 | 13.93 | 13.02 | 80.20 |
| 1990 (2) | 6.02 | 14.77 | 13.72 | 79.21 |

Source(s): (1) ASTER; (2) AST90-92 et INE.

### 3.2 Méthode(s): moyenne pondérée
moyenne arithmétique

#### 3.2.1 Hommes:

- 1950-60, taux de répartition 1950-60 tirés des EPPA3;
- 1970-80, moyennes pondérées des taux de répartition tirés des recensements de 1970 et 1982;
- 1990, moyennes des taux de répartition tirés des enquêtes de 1989, 1990 et 1991.

#### 3.2.2 Femmes:

- 1960-80, moyennes pondérées des taux de répartition tirés du recensement de 1952 et des taux ajustés des recensements de 1970 et 1982;
- 1990, moyennes des taux de répartition tirés des enquêtes de 1989, 1990 et 1991.

## 4. Projection des taux d'activité: 2000 - 2010

### 4.1 Modèle(s): linéaire et hyperbole

#### 4.1.1 Hommes:

- Aux groupes d'âge [15+], application de la fonction F3;
- Modification des tendances des groupes d'âge [15-44].

#### 4.1.2 Femmes:

- Aux groupes d'âge [15+], application de la fonction F3;
- Modification des tendances de tous les groupes d'âge.

*Notes sur les ajustements des taux, voir p. 192-195.*     *Notes sur les fonctions de projection, voir p. 198.*

# Chine

## 1. Source(s) des données de base

**Code(s):**    **Titre(s):**

EPPA3    Evaluations et projections de la population active 1950-2025 - troisième édition, BIT, Genève, 1986.
ASTER    Annuaire des statistiques du travail 1945-89 - Edition rétrospective sur les recensements de population, BIT, Genève, 1990.
R1990    Population Statistics of China, I.D.A, Statistical Data Series No. 55, State Statistical Bureau, Beijing.

## 2. Evaluation des taux d'activité: 1950 - 1990

### 2.1 Données de base:

Tableau 1: Taux d'activité par sexe et par groupe d'âge

| | Année | | | | |
|---|---|---|---|---|---|
| Groupe d'âge | 1950 (1) | 1960 (1) | 1970 (1) | 1980 (1) | 1990 (2) |
| **Hommes** | | | | | |
| 10-14 | 52.00 | 46.00 | 40.00 | 30.00 | 0.00 |
| 15-19 | 87.10 | 83.70 | 80.30 | 74.70 | 63.76 |
| 20-24 | 96.90 | 96.90 | 96.90 | 96.80 | 94.10 |
| 25-29 | 98.75 | 98.75 | 98.75 | 98.70 | 98.51 |
| 30-34 | 98.95 | 98.95 | 98.95 | 98.90 | 98.90 |
| 35-39 | 99.00 | 99.00 | 99.00 | 98.90 | 99.00 |
| 40-44 | 98.90 | 98.85 | 98.80 | 98.75 | 98.74 |
| 45-49 | 97.75 | 97.70 | 97.60 | 97.55 | 97.65 |
| 50-54 | 95.60 | 94.65 | 93.70 | 92.00 | 93.29 |
| 55-59 | 91.70 | 89.80 | 87.90 | 84.30 | 83.55 |
| 60-64 | 81.65 | 77.80 | 73.95 | 66.30 | 63.19 |
| 65+ | 56.00 | 50.45 | 44.90 | 34.00 | 32.72 |
| **Femmes** | | | | | |
| 10-14 | 43.00 | 40.00 | 38.00 | 31.00 | 0.00 |
| 15-19 | 72.40 | 73.90 | 75.40 | 78.60 | 70.52 |
| 20-24 | 82.30 | 84.20 | 86.10 | 89.60 | 91.22 |
| 25-29 | 79.90 | 82.20 | 83.70 | 87.40 | 91.43 |
| 30-34 | 78.00 | 80.90 | 83.00 | 87.10 | 91.29 |
| 35-39 | 77.80 | 80.00 | 82.20 | 86.60 | 91.25 |
| 40-44 | 75.50 | 77.10 | 78.70 | 81.90 | 88.36 |
| 45-49 | 64.70 | 65.90 | 67.10 | 69.50 | 81.14 |
| 50-54 | 47.10 | 47.90 | 48.70 | 50.20 | 62.00 |
| 55-59 | 36.10 | 35.50 | 34.90 | 33.50 | 45.08 |
| 60-64 | 25.50 | 23.70 | 21.90 | 18.40 | 27.29 |
| 65+ | 9.95 | 8.90 | 7.85 | 5.70 | 8.03 |

**Source(s):** (1) EPPA3; (2) R1990.

### 2.2 Méthode(s): données nationales

#### 2.2.1 Hommes:

- 1950-80, taux d'activité 1950-80 tirés des EPPA3;
- 1990, taux d'activité tirés du recensement de 1990;
ajustement du taux du groupe d'âge [10-14].

#### 2.2.2 Femmes:

Méthode, hypothèses et traitements identiques à ceux appliqués aux hommes.

## 3. Evaluation des taux de répartition par secteur d'activité: 1950 - 1990

### 3.1 Données de base:

Tableau 2: Répartition de la population active en % par secteur d'activité

| | | Agriculture | Industrie | | Services |
|---|---|---|---|---|---|
| | Année | | Total | Manufac. | |
| **Hommes** | | | | | |
| | 1980 (1) | 71.00 | 15.50 | .. | 13.50 |
| | 1982 (2) | 70.36 | 17.70 | 11.75 | 11.94 |
| | 1990 (3) | 69.10 | 16.52 | .. | 14.38 |
| **Femmes** | | | | | |
| | 1980 (1) | 78.50 | 12.00 | .. | 9.50 |
| | 1982 (2) | 78.01 | 13.82 | 11.94 | 8.17 |
| | 1990 (3) | 76.09 | 13.34 | .. | 10.56 |

**Source(s):** (1) EPPA3; (2) ASTER; (3) R1990.

### 3.2 Méthode(s): données nationales

#### 3.2.1 Hommes:

- 1950-80, taux de répartition 1950-80 tirés des EPPA3;
- 1990, taux de répartition de l'agriculture tiré du recensement de 1990;
- Application du rapport industrie/services 1980 tiré des EPPA3;
- Application du rapport manufacture/industrie tiré du recensement de 1982.

#### 3.2.2 Femmes:

Méthode, hypothèses et traitements identiques à ceux appliqués aux hommes.

## 4. Projection des taux d'activité: 2000 - 2010

### 4.1 Modèle(s): linéaire, hyperbole et logistique

#### 4.1.1 Hommes:

- Aux groupes d'âge [10-49], application de la fonction F1;
- Aux groupes d'âge [50+], application de la fonction F3;
- Modification des tendances des groupes d'âge [10-54] et [65+].

#### 4.1.2 Femmes:

- Aux groupes d'âge [10-19], application de la fonction F1;
- Aux groupes d'âge [20+], application de la fonction F6;
- Modification des tendances de tous les groupes d'âge.

*Notes sur les ajustements des taux, voir p. 192-195.*    *Notes sur les fonctions de projection, voir p. 198.*

# Chypre

## 1. Source(s) des données de base

Code(s):     Titre(s):

EPPA3       Evaluations et projections de la population active 1950-2025 - troisième édition, BIT, Genève, 1986.
CHY-OE1     Labour force and migration surveys, 19886/87, DSRMF, Series III, Report No. 6, Department of Statistics and Research, Nicosia.
CHY-OE2     Labour Statistics 1987-1992, DSRMF, Series II, Department of Statistics and Research, Nicosia.

## 2. Evaluation des taux d'activité: 1950 - 1990

### 2.1 Données de base:

Tableau 1: Taux d'activité par sexe et par groupe d'âge

| Groupe d'âge | Année 1987 | 1988 | 1989 | 1990 |
|---|---|---|---|---|
| **Hommes** | | | | |
| 10-14 | 0.00 | 0.00 | 0.00 | 0.00 |
| 15-19 | 57.21 | 55.50 | 66.50 | 64.40 |
| 20-24 | 80.60 | 85.80 | 83.50 | 81.10 |
| 25-29 | 94.01 | 93.70 | 93.70 | 93.90 |
| 30-34 | 98.02 | 99.10 | 99.60 | 99.60 |
| 35-39 | 99.08 | 99.50 | 99.50 | 99.50 |
| 40-44 | 98.52 | 98.40 | 99.50 | 99.50 |
| 45-49 | 97.82 | 97.20 | 99.30 | 98.70 |
| 50-54 | 96.92 | 93.90 | 97.10 | 97.30 |
| 55-59 | 92.78 | 92.70 | 95.50 | 92.90 |
| 60-64 | 82.37 | 80.20 | 77.30 | 77.50 |
| 65+ | 27.62 | 28.00 | 28.00 | 28.00 |
| **Femmes** | | | | |
| 10-14 | 0.00 | 0.00 | 0.00 | 0.00 |
| 15-19 | 36.88 | 29.70 | 33.70 | 34.00 |
| 20-24 | 61.30 | 56.60 | 63.80 | 65.10 |
| 25-29 | 61.12 | 57.90 | 63.10 | 64.20 |
| 30-34 | 59.68 | 58.50 | 63.10 | 64.00 |
| 35-39 | 62.04 | 61.60 | 63.40 | 64.00 |
| 40-44 | 58.62 | 58.90 | 63.10 | 64.00 |
| 45-49 | 61.94 | 61.80 | 59.50 | 60.10 |
| 50-54 | 55.12 | 54.70 | 49.00 | 49.70 |
| 55-59 | 45.37 | 46.00 | 38.10 | 39.20 |
| 60-64 | 33.58 | 36.00 | 24.60 | 25.20 |
| 65+ | 10.82 | 10.80 | 8.80 | 8.70 |

Source(s): CHY-OE1 et CHY-OE2.

### 2.2 Méthode(s): interpolation et extrapolation linéaires

#### 2.2.1 Hommes:

- 1950-90, interpolation des taux d'activité 1950-80 tirés des EPPA3
et des évaluations officielles de 1987 à 1990; pour le groupe d'âge [10-14],
maintien des taux d'activité tirés des EPPA3.

#### 2.2.2 Femmes:

- 1950-80, taux d'activité 1950-80 tirés des EPPA3;
- 1990, extrapolation des taux d'activité 1950-1980 tirés des EPPA3;
ajustement des taux extrapolés sur la base des variations des taux interpolés
1980 par rapport aux taux 1980 tirés des EPPA3.

## 3. Evaluation des taux de répartition par secteur d'activité: 1950 - 1990

### 3.1 Données de base:

Tableau 2: Répartition de la population active en % par secteur d'activité

| Année | Agriculture | Industrie Total | Manufac. | Services |
|---|---|---|---|---|
| **Hommes** | | | | |
| 1981 | 19.15 | 36.91 | 19.33 | 43.94 |
| 1989 | 13.36 | 33.13 | 17.42 | 53.51 |
| **Femmes** | | | | |
| 1981 | 34.80 | 29.09 | 25.73 | 36.11 |
| 1989 | 18.00 | 26.33 | 24.72 | 55.68 |

Source(s): CHY-OE1 et CHY-OE2.

### 3.2 Méthode(s): moyenne arithmétique

#### 3.2.1 Hommes:

- 1950-70, taux de répartition 1950-70 tirés des EPPA3;
- 1980, moyennes des taux de répartition tirés des enquêtes de 1979,
1980 et 1981;
- 1990, moyennes des taux de répartition tirés des estimations
officielles de 1989, 1990 et 1991.

#### 3.2.2 Femmes:

Méthode, hypothèses et traitements identiques à ceux appliqués aux hommes.

## 4. Projection des taux d'activité: 2000 - 2010

### 4.1 Modèle(s): linéaire, hyperbole et logistique

#### 4.1.1 Hommes:

- Au groupe d'âge [15-19], application de la fonction F1;
- Aux groupes d'âge [20+], application de la fonction F3;
- Modification des tendances des groupes d'âge [15-49] et [65+].

#### 4.1.2 Femmes:

- Aux groupes d'âge [15-19] et [60+], application de la fonction F3;
- Aux groupes d'âge [20-54], application de la fonction F6;
- Au groupe d'âge [55-59], application de la fonction F1;
- Modification des tendances des groupes d'âge [15-19] et [55-59].

*Notes sur les ajustements des taux, voir p. 192-195.* ·     *Notes sur les fonctions de projection, voir p. 198.*

# Colombie

## 1. Source(s) des données de base

| Code(s): | Titre(s): |
|---|---|
| EPPA3 | Evaluations et projections de la population active 1950-2025 - troisième édition, BIT, Genève, 1986. |
| CELADE | CELADE, Bulletin Démographique, No. 49, janvier 1992. |
| STAT | Base de données sur les statistiques du travail - LABORSTA, Bureau de statistique, BIT, Genève. |

## 2. Evaluation des taux d'activité: 1950 - 1990

### 2.1 Données de base:

Tableau 1: Taux d'activité par sexe et par groupe d'âge

| Groupe d'âge | Année 1985 (1) | 1985 (2) | 1985 (3) | 1991 (1) | 1991 (2) | 1991 (3) |
|---|---|---|---|---|---|---|
| **Hommes** | | | | | | |
| 10-14 | 16.36 | 10.50 | 25.50 | 12.56 | 4.35 | 37.19 |
| 15-19 | 45.71 | 37.00 | 60.50 | 47.40 | 38.17 | 75.07 |
| 20-24 | 68.22 | 63.00 | 79.50 | 84.74 | 81.78 | 93.64 |
| 25-29 | 85.81 | 85.50 | 86.50 | 95.65 | 94.86 | 97.99 |
| 30-34 | 90.22 | 91.00 | 88.50 | 98.11 | 97.75 | 99.18 |
| 35-39 | 91.03 | 92.00 | 89.00 | 97.97 | 97.99 | 97.89 |
| 40-44 | 90.32 | 91.00 | 89.00 | 97.95 | 97.58 | 99.05 |
| 45-49 | 89.64 | 90.00 | 89.00 | 96.70 | 96.65 | 96.84 |
| 50-54 | 86.10 | 85.00 | 88.00 | 90.65 | 88.57 | 96.88 |
| 55-59 | 79.24 | 75.50 | 85.50 | 83.78 | 80.50 | 93.60 |
| 60-64 | 69.41 | 63.80 | 78.50 | 74.05 | 68.42 | 90.92 |
| 65+ | 46.73 | 40.02 | 57.37 | 32.57 | 20.92 | 67.52 |
| **Femmes** | | | | | | |
| 10-14 | 8.77 | 7.00 | 11.90 | 4.91 | 2.17 | 11.31 |
| 15-19 | 21.86 | 21.80 | 22.00 | 30.51 | 31.51 | 28.19 |
| 20-24 | 35.83 | 37.30 | 31.50 | 54.90 | 61.30 | 39.97 |
| 25-29 | 46.67 | 49.99 | 36.63 | 58.17 | 63.96 | 44.66 |
| 30-34 | 44.17 | 46.90 | 36.26 | 60.64 | 67.03 | 45.75 |
| 35-39 | 41.04 | 43.00 | 35.90 | 57.41 | 61.67 | 47.46 |
| 40-44 | 37.48 | 38.50 | 35.06 | 52.82 | 54.52 | 48.83 |
| 45-49 | 33.32 | 33.06 | 33.91 | 49.77 | 54.80 | 38.03 |
| 50-54 | 28.93 | 27.30 | 32.70 | 33.96 | 33.73 | 34.50 |
| 55-59 | 24.25 | 21.50 | 30.70 | 29.22 | 27.73 | 32.71 |
| 60-64 | 19.51 | 15.78 | 28.60 | 22.18 | 17.16 | 33.89 |
| 65+ | 12.63 | 9.16 | 21.34 | 8.85 | 4.73 | 18.47 |

**Note(s)**: (1) Total; (2) Urbain; (3) Rural.
**Source(s)**: CELADE et STAT.

### 2.2 Méthode(s): moyenne pondérée
interpolation et extrapolation linéaires

**2.2.1 Hommes:**

- 1950-70, taux d'activité 1950-70 tirés des EPPA3;
ajustement des taux d'activité de tous les groupes d'âge pour 1970;
- 1980, moyennes pondérées des taux d'activité estimés 1970 et 1990;
- 1990, extrapolation des taux d'activité pour les zones urbaines tirés
de l'enquête de 1990 et du recensement de 1991; aux taux extrapolés 1990,
application des variations des moyennes pondérées des taux d'activité pour
les zones urbaines et rural tirés du recensement de 1991 par rapport aux
taux d'activité 1991 pour les zones urbaines.

**2.2.2 Femmes:**

- 1950-70, interpolation extrapolation des taux d'activité ajustés 1950-70
tirés des EPPA3;
ajustement des taux sur la base du modèle d'ajustement des taux d'activité
des femmes travaillant dans l'agriculture comme aides familiales;
- 1980-90, moyennes pondérées des taux estimés séparément pour
les zones urbaines et rurales sur la base d'une interpolation et extrapolation
des taux d'activité tirés des recensements de 1986 et 1991 pour les zones
urbaines et rurales.

## 3. Evaluation des taux de répartition par secteur d'activité: 1950 - 1990

### 3.1 Données de base:

Tableau 2: Répartition de la population active en % par secteur d'activité

| Année | Agriculture | Industrie Total | Manufac. | Services |
|---|---|---|---|---|
| **Hommes** | | | | |
| 1980 (1) | 46.72 | 22.81 | 15.24 | 30.47 |
| 1991 (2) | 1.94 | 34.68 | 23.97 | 63.38 |
| 1991 (3) | 70.59 | 10.70 | 4.66 | 18.71 |
| **Femmes** | | | | |
| 1980 (1) | 5.55 | 21.57 | 19.94 | 72.88 |
| 1991 (2) | 0.64 | 25.03 | 23.65 | 74.33 |
| 1991 (3) | 29.73 | 17.07 | 14.83 | 53.20 |

**Note(s)**: (1) Total; (2) Urbain; (3) Rural.
**Source(s)**: STAT.

### 3.2 Méthode(s): moyenne pondérée

**3.2.1 Hommes:**

- 1950-70, taux de répartition 1950-70 tirés des EPPA3;
- 1980, taux de répartition tirés de l'enquête de 1980;
- 1990, moyennes pondérées des taux de répartition tirés de l'enquête
de 1980 et des estimations officielles de 1991 pour les zones urbaines et rurales.

**3.2.2 Femmes:**

- 1950-70, taux de répartition ajustés 1950-70 tirés des EPPA3;
- 1980, taux de répartition ajustés tirés de l'enquête de 1980;
- 1990, moyennes pondérées des taux de répartition ajustés tirés
de l'enquête de 1980 et des taux de répartition tirés des estimations
officielles de 1991 pour les zones urbaines et rurales.

## 4. Projection des taux d'activité: 2000 - 2010

### 4.1 Modèle(s): log-linéaire, hyperbole et logistique

**4.1.1 Hommes:**

- Au groupe d'âge [10-14], application de la fonction F2;
- Aux groupes d'âge [20+], application de la fonction F3;
- Modification des tendances des groupes d'âge [15-24] et [35-49].

**4.1.2 Femmes:**

- Au groupe d'âge [10-14], application de la fonction F2;
- Aux groupes d'âge [15-19] et [65+], application de la fonction F3;
- Au groupe d'âge [20-24], application de la fonction F1;
- Aux groupes d'âge [25-64], application de la fonction F6;
- Modification des tendances des groupes d'âge [20-24] et [65+].

---

*Notes sur les ajustements des taux, voir p. 192-195.*     *Notes sur les fonctions de projection, voir p. 198.*

# Comores

## 1. Source(s) des données de base

Code(s):     Titre(s):

EPPA3      Evaluations et projections de la population active 1950-2025 - troisième édition, BIT, Genève, 1986.
ASTER      Annuaire des statistiques du travail 1945-89 - Edition rétrospective sur les recensements de population, BIT, Genève, 1990.

## 2. Evaluation des taux d'activité: 1950 - 1990

### 2.1 Données de base:

Tableau 1: Taux d'activité par sexe et par groupe d'âge

| Groupe d'âge | Année | | | | |
|---|---|---|---|---|---|
| | 1950 (1) | 1960 (1) | 1970 (1) | 1980 (1) | 1980 (2) |
| **Hommes** | | | | | |
| 10-14 | 51.75 | 50.90 | 49.65 | 47.75 | 48.12 |
| 15-19 | 84.45 | 83.30 | 81.65 | 79.10 | 60.94 |
| 20-24 | 95.10 | 94.65 | 94.00 | 93.05 | 84.25 |
| 25-29 | 97.35 | 97.30 | 97.20 | 97.05 | 96.41 |
| 30-34 | 98.10 | 98.05 | 97.90 | 97.75 | 98.35 |
| 35-39 | 98.25 | 98.20 | 98.10 | 97.90 | 98.66 |
| 40-44 | 98.10 | 98.05 | 97.90 | 97.75 | 98.24 |
| 45-49 | 97.35 | 97.30 | 97.20 | 97.05 | 97.78 |
| 50-54 | 96.90 | 96.80 | 96.65 | 96.40 | 96.89 |
| 55-59 | 96.00 | 95.85 | 95.60 | 95.25 | 96.56 |
| 60-64 | 93.00 | 92.75 | 92.35 | 91.70 | 93.43 |
| 65+ | 79.75 | 79.25 | 78.50 | 77.45 | 81.31 |
| **Femmes** | | | | | |
| 10-14 | 39.10 | 38.45 | 37.50 | 36.10 | 41.05 |
| 15-19 | 63.60 | 62.60 | 61.20 | 59.05 | 55.55 |
| 20-24 | 63.90 | 63.30 | 62.40 | 61.05 | 63.30 |
| 25-29 | 68.85 | 68.15 | 67.15 | 65.60 | 67.13 |
| 30-34 | 73.20 | 72.45 | 71.35 | 69.70 | 70.67 |
| 35-39 | 74.45 | 73.75 | 72.70 | 71.15 | 72.85 |
| 40-44 | 76.90 | 76.15 | 75.15 | 73.60 | 75.44 |
| 45-49 | 76.40 | 75.65 | 74.65 | 73.05 | 73.11 |
| 50-54 | 74.95 | 74.10 | 72.90 | 71.10 | 72.75 |
| 55-59 | 72.15 | 71.30 | 70.05 | 68.15 | 66.41 |
| 60-64 | 66.05 | 64.95 | 63.35 | 60.90 | 58.71 |
| 65+ | 46.00 | 45.00 | 43.50 | 41.25 | 37.59 |

Source(s): (1) EPPA3; (2) ASTER.

### 2.2 Méthode(s): interpolation et extrapolation linéaires

#### 2.2.1 Hommes:

- 1950-90, interpolation et extrapolation des taux d'activité 1950-80 tirés des EPPA3;
ajustement des taux interpolés et extrapolés sur la base des variations des taux interpolés 1980 par rapport aux taux ajustés du recensement de 1980.

#### 2.2.2 Femmes:

- 1950-90, interpolation et extrapolation des taux d'activité 1950-80 tirés des EPPA3;
ajustement des taux interpolés et extrapolés en tenant compte de la sous-énumération des femmes travaillant dans l'agriculture;
ajustement des taux interpolés et extrapolés sur la base des variations des taux interpolés 1980 par rapport aux taux ajustés du recensement de 1980.

## 3. Evaluation des taux de répartition par secteur d'activité: 1950 - 1990

### 3.1 Données de base:

Tableau 2: Répartition de la population active en % par secteur d'activité

| Année | Agriculture | Industrie | | Services |
|---|---|---|---|---|
| | | Total | Manufac. | |
| **Hommes** | | | | |
| 1950 (1) | 87.00 | 5.20 | .. | 7.80 |
| 1960 (1) | 85.40 | 5.85 | .. | 8.75 |
| 1970 (1) | 83.10 | 6.80 | .. | 10.10 |
| 1980 (1) | 79.60 | 8.15 | .. | 12.25 |
| 1980 (2) | 70.65 | 11.01 | 4.69 | 18.34 |
| **Femmes** | | | | |
| 1950 (1) | 95.70 | 0.95 | .. | 3.35 |
| 1960 (1) | 93.95 | 1.20 | .. | 4.85 |
| 1970 (1) | 91.40 | 1.70 | .. | 6.90 |
| 1980 (1) | 87.55 | 2.50 | .. | 9.95 |
| 1980 (2) | 93.33 | 3.41 | 3.34 | 3.25 |

Source(s): (1) EPPA3; (2) ASTER.

### 3.2 Méthode(s): interpolation et extrapolation linéaires

#### 3.2.1 Hommes:

- 1950-90, interpolation et extrapolation des taux de répartition 1950-80 tirés des EPPA3;
modification des tendances de tous les secteurs;
ajustement des taux sur la base des variations des taux interpolés 1980 par rapport aux taux de répartition tirés du recensement de 1980.

#### 3.2.2 Femmes:

- 1950-90, interpolation et extrapolation des taux de répartition 1950-80 tirés des EPPA3;
modification des tendances de tous les secteurs;
aux taux interpolés et extrapolés, application variations des taux interpolés 1980 par rapport aux taux de répartition tirés du recensement de 1980.

## 4. Projection des taux d'activité: 2000 - 2010

### 4.1 Modèle(s): linéaire et hyperbole

#### 4.1.1 Hommes:

- A tous les groupes d'âge, application de la fonction F1.

#### 4.1.2 Femmes:

- Aux groupes d'âge [10-19], application de la fonction F1;
- Aux groupes d'âge [20+], application de la fonction F3;
- Modification des tendances des groupes d'âge [20-59].

---

*Notes sur les ajustements des taux, voir p. 192-195.*        *Notes sur les fonctions de projection, voir p. 198.*

# Congo

## 1. Source(s) des données de base

Code(s):      Titre(s):

EPPA3        Evaluations et projections de la population active 1950-2025 - troisième édition, BIT, Genève, 1986.
ASTER        Annuaire des statistiques du travail 1945-89 - Edition rétrospective sur les recensements de population, BIT, Genève, 1990.
AST89-90     Annuaire des statistiques du travail 1989-90, BIT, Genève, 1990.

## 2. Evaluation des taux d'activité: 1950 - 1990

### 2.1 Données de base:

Tableau 1: Taux d'activité par sexe et par groupe d'âge

| Groupe d'âge | Année 1950 (1) | 1960 (1) | 1970 (1) | 1984 (2) |
|---|---|---|---|---|
| **Hommes** | | | | |
| 10-14 | 32.10 | 31.45 | 30.70 | 3.10 |
| 15-19 | 58.35 | 57.45 | 56.45 | 18.84 |
| 20-24 | 84.70 | 84.35 | 83.95 | 53.49 |
| 25-29 | 97.55 | 97.50 | 97.45 | 86.04 |
| 30-34 | 99.45 | 99.35 | 99.30 | 96.60 |
| 35-39 | 99.55 | 99.50 | 99.40 | 97.75 |
| 40-44 | 99.05 | 99.00 | 98.90 | 97.61 |
| 45-49 | 98.75 | 98.70 | 98.65 | 96.62 |
| 50-54 | 96.55 | 96.50 | 96.40 | 92.95 |
| 55-59 | 93.35 | 93.20 | 93.05 | 80.96 |
| 60-64 | 90.45 | 90.20 | 89.95 | 81.05 |
| 65+ | 69.00 | 68.65 | 68.20 | 73.79 |
| **Femmes** | | | | |
| 10-14 | .. | .. | 22.10 | 4.67 |
| 15-19 | .. | .. | 37.65 | 17.84 |
| 20-24 | .. | .. | 40.90 | 32.98 |
| 25-29 | .. | .. | 49.00 | 51.02 |
| 30-34 | .. | .. | 55.40 | 59.26 |
| 35-39 | .. | .. | 61.40 | 64.39 |
| 40-44 | .. | .. | 69.50 | 67.97 |
| 45-49 | .. | .. | 72.95 | 70.90 |
| 50-54 | .. | .. | 75.95 | 73.56 |
| 55-59 | .. | .. | 70.55 | 72.47 |
| 60-64 | .. | .. | 71.95 | 69.74 |
| 65+ | .. | .. | 59.84 | 58.00 |

Source(s): (1) EPPA3; (2) AST89-90.

### 2.2 Méthode(s): interpolation et extrapolation linéaires

#### 2.2.1 Hommes:

- 1950-90, interpolation et extrapolation des taux d'activité 1950-70 tirés des EPPA3 et des taux d'activité tirés du recensement de 1984; modification des tendances des groupes d'âge [10-19] et [25-64] pour 1950; et des tendances des groupes d'âge [20-24] et [65+] pour 1980.

#### 2.2.2 Femmes:

- 1950-90, interpolation et extrapolation des taux d'activité 1970 et 1984 tirés respectivement des EPPA3 et du recensement de 1984; modification de la tendance du groupe d'âge [10-14] de 1950 à 1970.

## 3. Evaluation des taux de répartition par secteur d'activité: 1950 - 1990

### 3.1 Données de base:

Tableau 2: Répartition de la population active en % par secteur d'activité

| Année | Agriculture | Industrie Total | Manufac. | Services |
|---|---|---|---|---|
| **Hommes** | | | | |
| 1974 (1) | 47.95 | 18.15 | 12.77 | 33.91 |
| 1984 (2) | 36.40 | 22.05 | 10.95 | 41.55 |
| **Femmes** | | | | |
| 1974 (1) | 89.55 | 1.27 | 1.20 | 9.18 |
| 1984 (2) | 73.37 | 3.08 | 2.51 | 23.56 |

Source(s): (1) ASTER; (2) AST89-90.

### 3.2 Méthode(s): interpolation et extrapolation linéaires

#### 3.2.1 Hommes:
- 1950-90, interpolation et extrapolation des taux de répartition tirés des recensements de 1974 et 1984; modification des tendances de tous les secteurs pour 1950-70 et 1990.

#### 3.2.2 Femmes:

Méthode, hypothèses et traitements identiques à ceux appliqués aux hommes.

## 4. Projection des taux d'activité: 2000 - 2010

### 4.1 Modèle(s): log-linéaire, hyperbole et linéaire

#### 4.1.1 Hommes:

- Au groupe d'âge [10-14], application de la fonction F2;
- Aux groupes d'âge [15-19] et [65+], application de la fonction F1;
- Aux groupes d'âge [20-64], application de la fonction F3;
- Modification des tendances des groupes d'âge [30-34] et [65+].

#### 4.1.2 Femmes:

- Au groupe d'âge [10-14], application de la fonction F2;
- Aux groupes d'âge [15+], application de la fonction F1;
- Modification des tendances des groupes d'âge [10-19], [40-44] et [55+].

---

*Notes sur les ajustements des taux, voir p. 192-195.*

*Notes sur les fonctions de projection, voir p. 198.*

# Costa Rica

## 1. Source(s) des données de base

Code(s):     Titre(s):

EPPA3     Evaluations et projections de la population active 1950-2025 - troisième édition, BIT, Genève, 1986.
ADNU88     Annuaire des statistiques du travail 1945-89 - Edition rétrospective sur les recensements de population, BIT, Genève, 1990.
ASTER     Annuaire démographique 1988 - Statistiques des recensements de population, quarantième édition, Nations Unies, New York, 1990.
AST90-92     Editions de 1990 à 1992 de l'Annuaire des statistiques du travail du BIT, Genève.

## 2. Evaluation des taux d'activité: 1950 - 1990

### 2.1 Données de base:

Tableau 1: Taux d'activité par sexe et par groupe d'âge

| Groupe d'âge | Année 1984 (1) | 1989 (2) | 1990 (2) | 1991 (2) |
|---|---|---|---|---|
| **Hommes** | | | | |
| 10-14 | 3.80 | 10.36 | 11.16 | 9.52 |
| 15-19 | 17.09 | 61.98 | 59.37 | 55.63 |
| 20-24 | 28.25 | 86.42 | 89.78 | 88.09 |
| 25-29 | 29.97 | 95.26 | 95.93 | 96.43 |
| 30-39 | 29.96 | 97.08 | 97.05 | 97.01 |
| 40-49 | 24.26 | 95.82 | 94.93 | 94.46 |
| 50-59 | 13.77 | 87.10 | 87.12 | 84.58 |
| 60-64 | 6.95 | 60.90 | 59.63 | 55.27 |
| 65+ | 3.08 | ... | ... | ... |
| **Femmes** | | | | |
| 10-14 | 12.72 | 3.00 | 3.05 | 3.36 |
| 15-19 | 59.43 | 27.05 | 27.14 | 23.90 |
| 20-24 | 83.74 | 42.43 | 44.04 | 44.07 |
| 25-29 | 92.65 | 40.35 | 35.49 | 38.64 |
| 30-39 | 94.53 | 43.12 | 43.22 | 42.89 |
| 40-49 | 93.11 | 34.39 | 39.60 | 37.92 |
| 50-59 | 86.16 | 19.20 | 21.04 | 22.85 |
| 60-64 | 69.63 | 9.64 | 11.94 | 7.74 |
| 65+ | 38.91 | ... | ... | ... |

**Source(s):** (1) ASTER et ADNU88; (2) AST90-92.

### 2.2 Méthode(s): moyenne pondérée
moyenne arithmétique

**2.2.1 Hommes:**

- 1950-70, taux d'activité 1950-70 tirés des EPPA3;
- 1980, moyennes pondérées des taux d'activité 1970 tirés des EPPA3 et des taux ajustés des recensements de 1984;
- 1990, moyennes des taux d'activité tirés des enquêtes de 1989, 1990 et 1991.

**2.2.2 Femmes:**

Méthode, hypothèses et traitements identiques à ceux appliqués aux hommes.

## 3. Evaluation des taux de répartition par secteur d'activité: 1950 - 1990

### 3.1 Données de base:

Tableau 2: Répartition de la population active en % par secteur d'activité

| Année | Agriculture | Industrie Total | Manufac. | Services |
|---|---|---|---|---|
| **Hommes** | | | | |
| 1983 (1) | 36.26 | 22.63 | 15.25 | 41.11 |
| 1984 (1) | 43.56 | 22.74 | 13.54 | 33.70 |
| 1985 (1) | 35.44 | 29.83 | 14.87 | 34.73 |
| 1989 (2) | 34.45 | 26.67 | 16.77 | 38.88 |
| 1991 (2) | 33.39 | 27.25 | 16.87 | 39.36 |
| 1990 (2) | 33.23 | 27.36 | 17.93 | 39.41 |
| **Femmes** | | | | |
| 1983 (1) | 5.15 | 21.76 | 21.57 | 73.10 |
| 1984 (1) | 4.81 | 20.46 | 19.68 | 74.73 |
| 1985 (1) | 4.52 | 20.69 | 26.53 | 74.79 |
| 1989 (2) | 6.06 | 26.67 | 28.37 | 67.27 |
| 1991 (2) | 6.40 | 24.40 | 25.85 | 69.20 |
| 1990 (2) | 6.70 | 26.76 | 23.46 | 66.54 |

**Source(s):** (1) ASTER et ADNU88; (2) AST90-92.

### 3.2 Méthode(s): moyenne pondérée
moyenne arithmétique

**3.2.1 Hommes:**

- 1950-60, taux de répartition 1950-60 tirés des EPPA3;
- 1980, moyennes pondérées des taux de répartition 1970 tirés des EPPA3 et des moyennes des taux de répartition tirés des enquêtes de 1983 et 1985 et du recensement de 1984;
- 1990, moyennes des taux de répartition tirés des enquêtes de 1989, 1990 et 1991.

**3.2.2 Femmes:**

Méthode, hypothèses et traitements identiques à ceux appliqués aux hommes.

## 4. Projection des taux d'activité: 2000 - 2010

### 4.1 Modèle(s): linéaire, log-linéaire, hyperbole et logistique

**4.1.1 Hommes:**

- Au groupe d'âge [10-14], application de la fonction F2;
- Aux groupes d'âge [15-29], application de la fonction F1;
- Aux groupes d'âge [30+], application de la fonction F3;
- Modification des tendances des groupes d'âge [10-14] et [30-34].

**4.1.2 Femmes:**

- Aux groupes d'âge [10-19], application de la fonction F1;
- Aux groupes d'âge [20-49], application de la fonction F6;
- Aux groupes d'âge [50-64], application de la fonction F2;
- Au groupe d'âge [65+], application de la fonction F3;
- Modification des tendances des groupes d'âge [10-14] et [50-64].

*Notes sur les ajustements des taux, voir p. 192-195.*     *Notes sur les fonctions de projection, voir p. 198.*

# Côte d'Ivoire

## 1. Source(s) des données de base

Code(s):     Titre(s):

EPPA3     Evaluations et projections de la population active 1950-2025 - troisième édition, BIT, Genève, 1986.
ADNU84     Annuaire démographique 1984 - Statistiques des recensements de population II, trente-sixième édition, Nations Unies, New York, 1986.
AST93     Annuaire des statistiques du travail 1993, BIT, Genève, 1993.

## 2. Evaluation des taux d'activité: 1950 - 1990

### 2.1 Données de base:

Tableau 1: Taux d'activité par sexe et par groupe d'âge

| Groupe d'âge | Année | | | |
| --- | --- | --- | --- | --- |
| | 1960 (1) | 1970 (1) | 1975 (2) | 1988 (3) |
| **Hommes** | | | | |
| 10-14 | 47.75 | .. | 32.35 | 26.20 |
| 15-19 | 84.40 | .. | 70.38 | 62.74 |
| 20-24 | 95.30 | .. | 93.94 | 87.65 |
| 25-29 | 97.65 | .. | 98.07 | 96.18 |
| 30-34 | 98.40 | .. | 98.18 | 98.14 |
| 35-39 | 98.55 | .. | 98.50 | 98.54 |
| 40-44 | 98.35 | .. | 97.80 | 98.53 |
| 45-49 | 98.15 | .. | 97.50 | 97.76 |
| 50-54 | 97.60 | .. | 97.28 | 97.17 |
| 55-59 | 96.05 | .. | 93.20 | 91.87 |
| 60-64 | 92.70 | .. | 90.22 | 89.49 |
| 65+ | 78.20 | .. | 74.78 | 74.17 |
| **Femmes** | | | | |
| 10-14 | 40.45 | 33.80 | 27.93 | 20.67 |
| 15-19 | 76.25 | 61.40 | 39.45 | 35.07 |
| 20-24 | 79.50 | 65.35 | 43.97 | 39.25 |
| 25-29 | 81.75 | 68.70 | 46.00 | 42.81 |
| 30-34 | 84.00 | 71.80 | 48.73 | 46.59 |
| 35-39 | 84.55 | 73.15 | 50.29 | 48.16 |
| 40-44 | 85.00 | 74.80 | 51.49 | 49.87 |
| 45-49 | 80.00 | 70.55 | 51.64 | 50.14 |
| 50-54 | 74.85 | 66.90 | 49.94 | 48.65 |
| 55-59 | 58.50 | 53.00 | 47.46 | 46.30 |
| 60-64 | 47.95 | 44.95 | 43.31 | 39.85 |
| 65+ | 28.95 | 27.95 | 26.22 | 24.19 |

Source(s): (1) EPPA3; (2) ASTER et ADNU84; (3) AST93.

### 2.2 Méthode(s): interpolation et extrapolation linéaires

#### 2.2.1 Hommes:

- 1950-90, interpolation et extrapolation des taux d'activité 1960
tirés des EPPA3 et des taux d'activité tirés des recensements de 1975 et 1988;
modification des tendances de tous les groupes d'âge pour 1950.

#### 2.2.2 Femmes:

- 1950-90, interpolation et extrapolation des taux d'activité 1960-70, 1975
et 1988 tirés respectivement des EPPA3 et des recensements de 1975 et 1988.

## 3. Evaluation des taux de répartition par secteur d'activité: 1950 - 1990

### 3.1 Données de base:

Tableau 2: Répartition de la population active en % par secteur d'activité

| Année | Agriculture | Industrie | | Services |
| --- | --- | --- | --- | --- |
| | | Total | Manufac. | |
| **Hommes** | | | | |
| 1950 | 86.00 | 3.50 | .. | 10.50 |
| 1960 | 79.00 | 5.25 | .. | 15.75 |
| 1970 | 70.00 | 7.50 | .. | 22.50 |
| 1980 | 60.00 | 10.00 | .. | 30.00 |
| **Femmes** | | | | |
| 1950 | 96.50 | 0.70 | .. | 2.80 |
| 1960 | 93.35 | 1.35 | .. | 5.30 |
| 1970 | 87.00 | 2.60 | .. | 10.40 |
| 1980 | 75.00 | 5.00 | .. | 20.00 |

Source(s): EPPA3.

### 3.2 Méthode(s): extrapolation linéaire

#### 3.2.1 Hommes:

- 1950-80, taux de répartition 1950-80 tirés des EPPA3;
- 1990, extrapolation des taux de répartition 1950-80 tirés des EPPA3;
- 1980-90, application des rapports manufacture/industrie observés
pour les mêmes années au Cameroun.

#### 3.2.2 Femmes:

Méthode, hypothèses et traitements identiques à ceux appliqués aux hommes.

## 4. Projection des taux d'activité: 2000 - 2010

### 4.1 Modèle(s): log-linéaire et hyperbole

#### 4.1.1 Hommes:

- Aux groupes d'âge [10-19], application de la fonction F2;
- Aux groupes d'âge [20+], application de la fonction F3;
- Modification des tendances des groupes d'âge [30-34] et [50-54].

#### 4.1.2 Femmes:

- Aux groupes d'âge [10-19], application de la fonction F2;
- Aux groupes d'âge [20+], application de la fonction F3;
- Modification des tendances des groupes d'âge [15+].

*Notes sur les ajustements des taux, voir p. 192-195.*      *Notes sur les fonctions de projection, voir p. 198.*

# Croatie

## 1. Source(s) des données de base

Code(s):      Titre(s):

BLT-94-2     Popovic B. (1994), "Nouvelles estimations pour 1980 et 1990 des taux d'activité par âge et répartition sectorielle
             pour certains pays d'Europe orientale et méridionale" dans le Bulletin des statistiques du travail - 1994-2, BIT, Genève.
STAT         Base de données sur les statistiques du travail - LABORSTA, Bureau de statistique, BIT, Genève.

## 2. Evaluation des taux d'activité: 1950 - 1990

### 2.1 Données de base:

Tableau 1: Taux d'activité par sexe et par groupe d'âge

| Groupe d'âge | Année 1953 (1) | 1961 (1) | 1971 (1) | 1980 (2) | 1990 (2) |
|---|---|---|---|---|---|
| **Hommes** | | | | | |
| 10-14 | 19.19 | 2.52 | 1.46 | 0.07 | 0.00 |
| 15-19 | 82.87 | 64.93 | 38.43 | 23.90 | 21.81 |
| 20-24 | 93.57 | 90.85 | 82.88 | 78.82 | 77.23 |
| 25-29 | 95.61 | 96.45 | 95.00 | 95.25 | 92.98 |
| 30-34 | 97.34 | 97.57 | 97.60 | 97.57 | 96.52 |
| 35-39 | 96.63 | 96.61 | 97.36 | 97.53 | 96.45 |
| 40-44 | 97.19 | 96.26 | 93.77 | 96.33 | 96.17 |
| 45-49 | 96.23 | 95.36 | 84.70 | 93.93 | 93.76 |
| 50-54 | 92.76 | 92.62 | 80.75 | 82.58 | 86.04 |
| 55-59 | 82.87 | 82.66 | 68.90 | 63.39 | 60.84 |
| 60-64 | 76.95 | 71.09 | 56.70 | 49.04 | 30.26 |
| 65+ | 59.76 | 54.26 | 45.43 | 36.74 | 17.49 |
| **Femmes** | | | | | |
| 10-14 | 18.38 | 3.52 | 2.06 | 0.08 | 0.00 |
| 15-19 | 66.09 | 54.87 | 35.33 | 20.48 | 18.64 |
| 20-24 | 62.20 | 67.15 | 61.98 | 69.45 | 65.49 |
| 25-29 | 48.59 | 59.84 | 66.77 | 78.92 | 79.48 |
| 30-34 | 43.47 | 54.20 | 60.06 | 76.81 | 82.68 |
| 35-39 | 40.99 | 50.71 | 56.93 | 71.27 | 81.62 |
| 40-44 | 36.55 | 49.29 | 52.21 | 60.50 | 77.31 |
| 45-49 | 32.61 | 43.64 | 45.54 | 51.77 | 66.95 |
| 50-54 | 27.55 | 36.55 | 38.86 | 38.38 | 43.98 |
| 55-59 | 22.94 | 29.98 | 28.93 | 24.92 | 23.92 |
| 60-64 | 19.85 | 24.56 | 23.44 | 19.53 | 14.66 |
| 65+ | 12.69 | 15.51 | 14.76 | 10.75 | 7.85 |

Source(s): (1) STAT; (2) BLT-94-2.

### 2.2 Méthode(s): extrapolation linéaire
moyenne pondérée

#### 2.2.1 Hommes:

- 1950, extrapolation des taux d'activité ajustés tirés des recensements
1953 et 1971, des taux d'activité tirés du recensement de 1961 et des taux
estimés pour 1980;
aux taux extrapolés, application des variations des taux interpolés 1953
par rapport aux taux d'activité tirés du recensement de 1953;
- 1960-70, moyennes pondérées des taux d'activité ajustés tirés des recensements
de 1953 et 1971 et des taux d'activité tirés du recensement de 1961;
- 1980-90, taux d'activité tirés du Bulletin des statistiques du travail 1994-2.

#### 2.2.2 Femmes:

- 1950, extrapolation des taux d'activité tirés des recensements
1953, 1961, 1971 et 1981;
aux taux extrapolés, application des variations des taux interpolés 1953
par rapport aux taux tirés du recensement de 1953;
- 1960-70, moyennes pondérées des taux d'activité tirés des
recensements de 1953, 1961 et 1971;
- 1980-90, taux d'activité tirés du Bulletin des statistiques
du travail 1994-2.

## 3. Evaluation des taux de répartition par secteur d'activité: 1950 - 1990

### 3.1 Données de base:

Tableau 2: Répartition de la population active en % par secteur d'activité

| Année | Agriculture | Industrie Total | Manufac. | Services |
|---|---|---|---|---|
| **Hommes** | | | | |
| 1953 (1) | 56.04 | 15.12 | .. | 28.83 |
| 1961 (1) | 45.81 | 22.88 | .. | 31.31 |
| 1971 (1) | 34.47 | 29.20 | .. | 36.33 |
| 1980 (2) | 23.14 | 38.36 | 24.58 | 38.50 |
| 1990 (2) | 16.68 | 37.90 | 26.97 | 45.42 |
| **Femmes** | | | | |
| 1953 (1) | 80.61 | 8.00 | .. | 11.39 |
| 1961 (1) | 62.74 | 14.59 | .. | 22.67 |
| 1971 (1) | 44.83 | 20.78 | .. | 34.39 |
| 1980 (2) | 27.73 | 27.45 | 24.93 | 44.83 |
| 1990 (2) | 15.21 | 28.27 | 25.72 | 56.52 |

Source(s): (1) STAT; (2) BLT-94-2.

### 3.2 Méthode(s): moyenne pondérée
extrapolation linéaire

#### 3.2.1 Hommes:

- 1950, extrapolation des taux de répartition tirés des recensements de
1953, 1961 et 1971 et des taux de répartition tirés du Bulletin des statistiques
du travail - 1994-2; modification des tendances de tous les secteurs;
- 1960-70, moyennes pondérées des taux de répartition tirés des
recensements de 1953, 1961 et 1971;
- 1980-90, taux de répartition tirés du Bulletin.

#### 3.2.2 Femmes:

Méthode, hypothèses et traitements identiques à ceux appliqués aux hommes.

## 4. Projection des taux d'activité: 2000 - 2010

### 4.1 Modèle(s): linéaire, hyperbole et logistique

#### 4.1.1 Hommes:

- Aux groupes d'âge [15+], application de la fonction F3;
- Modification des tendances des groupes d'âge [15-24] et [50-54].

#### 4.1.2 Femmes:

- Aux groupes d'âge [15-19] et [60+], application de la fonction F3;
- Aux groupes d'âge [25-54], application de la fonction F6;
- Au groupe d'âge [55-59], application de la fonction F1;
- Modification des tendances des groupes d'âge [15-24] et [55-59].

---

*Notes sur les ajustements des taux, voir p. 192-195.*    *Notes sur les fonctions de projection, voir p. 198.*

# Cuba

## 1. Source(s) des données de base

| Code(s): | Titre(s): |
|---|---|
| CB-R70 | Censo de Poblacion y viviendas, 1970, Oficina Nacional del Censo, Comité Estatal de Estadísticas, La Habana. |
| EPPA3 | Evaluations et projections de la population active 1950-2025 - troisième édition, BIT, Genève, 1986. |
| ASTER | Annuaire des statistiques du travail 1945-89 - Edition rétrospective sur les recensements de population, BIT, Genève, 1990. |
| STAT | Base de données sur les statistiques du travail - LABORSTA, Bureau de statistique, BIT, Genève. |

## 2. Evaluation des taux d'activité: 1950 - 1990

### 2.1 Données de base:

Tableau 1: Taux d'activité par sexe et par groupe d'âge

| Groupe d'âge | Année 1953 (1) | 1970 (2) | 1981 (1) | 1988 (3) |
|---|---|---|---|---|
| **Hommes** | | | | |
| 10-14 | 8.00 | 1.04 | 0.00 | 0.00 |
| 15-19 | 76.70 | 51.03 | 32.79 | 38.60 |
| 20-24 | 91.60 | 85.73 | 82.79 | 85.65 |
| 25-29 | 94.20 | 92.45 | 94.79 | 93.74 |
| 30-34 | 94.80 | 93.54 | 96.76 | 98.41 |
| 35-39 | 95.10 | 93.80 | 96.95 | 98.28 |
| 40-44 | 94.90 | 93.19 | 96.34 | 97.63 |
| 45-49 | 94.40 | 92.07 | 95.15 | 96.45 |
| 50-54 | 92.50 | 88.83 | 92.07 | 93.68 |
| 55-59 | 89.20 | 82.22 | 86.08 | 88.28 |
| 60-64 | 82.20 | 65.45 | 60.91 | 50.63 |
| 65+ | 57.10 | 27.84 | 21.44 | 12.77 |
| **Femmes** | | | | |
| 10-14 | 2.00 | 0.39 | 0.00 | 0.00 |
| 15-19 | 17.20 | 16.41 | 15.53 | 15.44 |
| 20-24 | 22.30 | 25.26 | 45.59 | 51.07 |
| 25-29 | 22.10 | 24.17 | 51.73 | 57.10 |
| 30-34 | 21.30 | 23.03 | 52.79 | 65.94 |
| 35-39 | 21.10 | 22.18 | 52.06 | 65.50 |
| 40-44 | 20.90 | 21.09 | 48.89 | 61.56 |
| 45-49 | 19.60 | 18.51 | 40.83 | 53.43 |
| 50-54 | 18.20 | 15.92 | 30.95 | 41.88 |
| 55-59 | 15.50 | 12.01 | 18.11 | 22.38 |
| 60-64 | 12.90 | 6.75 | 7.78 | 8.69 |
| 65+ | 8.50 | 1.89 | 2.03 | 1.78 |

Source(s): (1) ASTER; (2) ASTER et CB-R70; (3) STAT

### 2.2 Méthode(s): interpolation et extrapolation linéaires

#### 2.2.1 Hommes:

- 1950-70, interpolation et extrapolation des taux d'activité ajustés tirés des recensements de 1953 et 1970;
- 1980-90, extrapolation des taux d'activité ajustés tirés du recensement de 1981 et de l'enquête de 1988.

#### 2.2.2 Femmes:

- 1950-70, interpolation et extrapolation des taux d'activité ajustés tirés des recensements de 1953 et 1970;
- 1980-90, extrapolation des taux d'activité ajustés tirés du recensement de 1981 et de l'enquête de 1988;
modification des tendances de tous les groupes d'âge.

## 3. Evaluation des taux de répartition par secteur d'activité: 1950 - 1990

### 3.1 Données de base:

Tableau 2: Répartition de la population active en % par secteur d'activité

| Année | Agriculture | Industrie Total | Manufac. | Services |
|---|---|---|---|---|
| **Hommes** | | | | |
| 1960 (1) | 42.00 | 24.20 | .. | 33.80 |
| 1970 (2) | 35.42 | 27.61 | 19.32 | 36.97 |
| 1981 (2) | 28.88 | 32.04 | 18.57 | 39.08 |
| **Femmes** | | | | |
| 1960 (1) | 6.80 | 20.80 | .. | 72.40 |
| 1970 (2) | 8.24 | 22.10 | 21.19 | 69.66 |
| 1981 (2) | 10.62 | 21.55 | 17.59 | 67.82 |

Source(s): (1) EPPA3; (2) ASTER.

### 3.2 Méthode(s): moyenne pondérée
extrapolation linéaire

#### 3.2.1 Hommes:
- 1950-60, taux de répartition 1950-60 tirés des EPPA3;
- 1970, moyennes pondérées des taux de répartition 1960 tirés des EPPA3 et des taux de répartition tirés du recensement de 1970;
- 1980-90, moyennes pondérées des taux de répartition tirés des recensements de 1970 et 1981.

#### 3.2.2 Femmes:
- 1950-60, taux de répartition 1950-60 tirés des EPPA3;
- 1970, moyennes pondérées des taux de répartition 1960 tirés des EPPA3 et des taux de répartition tirés du recensement de 1970;
- 1980, moyennes pondérées des taux tirés des recensements de 1970 et 1981;
- 1990, extrapolation des taux de répartition 1970 estimés et des taux de répartition tirés du recensement de 1981;
modification des tendances de tous les secteurs

## 4. Projection des taux d'activité: 2000 - 2010

### 4.1 Modèle(s): hyperbole et logistique

#### 4.1.1 Hommes:
- Aux groupes d'âge [15+], application de la fonction F3;
- Modification des tendances des groupes d'âge [30-59].

#### 4.1.2 Femmes:
- Aux groupes d'âge [15-19] et [60+], application de la fonction F3;
- Aux groupes d'âge [20-59], application de la fonction F6;
- Modification de la tendance du groupe d'âge [20-24].

*Notes sur les ajustements des taux, voir p. 192-195.*     *Notes sur les fonctions de projection, voir p. 198.*

# Danemark

## 1. Source(s) des données de base

Code(s):    Titre(s):
EPPA3    Annuaire des statistiques du travail 1945-89 - Edition rétrospective sur les recensements de population, BIT, Genève, 1990.
STAT    Base de données sur les statistiques du travail - LABORSTA, Bureau de statistique, BIT, Genève.

## 2. Evaluation des taux d'activité: 1950 - 1990

### 2.1 Données de base:

Tableau 1: Taux d'activité par sexe et par groupe d'âge

| Groupe d'âge | 1989 | 1990 | 1991 |
|---|---|---|---|
| **Hommes** | | | |
| 10-14 | 0.00 | 0.00 | 0.00 |
| 15-19 | 73.20 | 71.60 | 69.90 |
| 20-24 | 88.40 | 86.80 | 85.80 |
| 25-29 | 93.00 | 92.90 | 92.20 |
| 30-34 | 94.20 | 95.30 | 95.70 |
| 35-39 | 96.00 | 95.40 | 94.90 |
| 40-44 | 95.90 | 96.10 | 95.10 |
| 45-49 | 96.40 | 94.80 | 94.30 |
| 50-54 | 90.70 | 91.60 | 92.40 |
| 55-59 | 85.30 | 84.50 | 81.90 |
| 60-64 | 49.50 | 50.50 | 47.10 |
| 65+ | 10.32 | 12.46 | 10.97 |
| **Femmes** | | | |
| 10-14 | 0.00 | 0.00 | 0.00 |
| 15-19 | 65.20 | 65.20 | 64.40 |
| 20-24 | 80.10 | 79.30 | 81.70 |
| 25-29 | 86.70 | 86.90 | 85.10 |
| 30-34 | 91.90 | 90.70 | 90.30 |
| 35-39 | 89.30 | 90.30 | 90.50 |
| 40-44 | 88.70 | 89.60 | 91.00 |
| 45-49 | 82.80 | 87.30 | 87.00 |
| 50-54 | 76.60 | 79.50 | 79.40 |
| 55-59 | 59.00 | 62.10 | 64.50 |
| 60-64 | 23.40 | 26.40 | 26.80 |
| 65+ | 3.23 | 3.17 | 3.02 |

Source(s): STAT.

### 2.2 Méthode(s): moyenne arithmétique

**2.2.1 Hommes:**

- 1950-80, taux d'activité 1950-80 tirés des EPPA3;
ajustement du taux d'activité du groupe d'âge [15-19] pour 1980;
- 1990, moyennes des taux d'activité tirés des enquêtes de 1989, 1990 et 1991.

**2.2.2 Femmes:**

Méthode, hypothèses et traitements identiques à ceux appliqués aux hommes.

## 3. Evaluation des taux de répartition par secteur d'activité: 1950 - 1990

### 3.1 Données de base:

Tableau 2: Répartition de la population active en % par secteur d'activité

| Année | Agriculture | Industrie Total | Manufac. | Services |
|---|---|---|---|---|
| **Hommes** | | | | |
| 1979 | 10.22 | 40.96 | 27.06 | 48.81 |
| 1981 | 10.06 | 43.13 | 28.33 | 46.82 |
| 1989 | 7.83 | 38.00 | 23.87 | 54.17 |
| 1990 | 7.69 | 37.84 | 24.89 | 54.46 |
| 1991 | 7.89 | 37.94 | 25.13 | 54.18 |
| **Femmes** | | | | |
| 1979 | 5.27 | 16.87 | 14.87 | 77.86 |
| 1981 | 3.28 | 17.57 | 15.68 | 79.15 |
| 1989 | 2.98 | 16.47 | 14.40 | 80.55 |
| 1990 | 2.81 | 16.62 | 14.78 | 80.58 |
| 1991 | 2.99 | 17.08 | 15.14 | 79.94 |

Source(s): STAT.

### 3.2 Méthode(s): moyenne pondérée / moyenne arithmétique

**3.2.1 Hommes:**

- 1950-70, taux de répartition 1950-70 tirés des EPPA3;
- 1980, moyennes pondérées des taux de répartition tirés des enquêtes de 1979 et 1981;
- 1990, moyennes des taux de répartition tirés des enquêtes de 1989, 1990 et 1991.

**3.2.2 Femmes:**

Méthode, hypothèses et traitements identiques à ceux appliqués aux hommes.

## 4. Projection des taux d'activité: 2000 - 2010

### 4.1 Modèle(s): linéaire, hyperbole et logistique

**4.1.1 Hommes:**

- Aux groupes d'âge [15-24], application de la fonction F1;
- Aux groupes d'âge [25+], application de la fonction F3;
- Modification des tendances des groupes d'âge [15-39] et [45-49].

**4.1.2 Femmes:**

- Aux groupes d'âge [15-34] et [60-64], application de la fonction F1;
- Aux groupes d'âge [35-59], application de la fonction F6;
- Au groupe d'âge [65+], application de la fonction F3;
- Modification des tendances des groupes d'âge [15-64].

*Notes sur les ajustements des taux, voir p. 192-195.*

*Notes sur les fonctions de projection, voir p. 198.*

# Egypte

## 1. Source(s) des données de base

Code(s):     Titre(s):

EPPA3        Evaluations et projections de la population active 1950-2025 - troisième édition, BIT, Genève, 1986.
ASTER        Annuaire des statistiques du travail 1945-89 - Edition rétrospective sur les recensements de population, BIT, Genève, 1990.
AST91        Annuaire des statistiques du travail 1991, BIT, Genève, 1991.
AST93        Annuaire des statistiques du travail 1993, BIT, Genève, 1993.

## 2. Evaluation des taux d'activité: 1950 - 1990

### 2.1 Données de base:

Tableau 1: Taux d'activité par sexe et par groupe d'âge

| Groupe d'âge | Année 1950 (1) | 1960 (1) | 1970 (1) | 1976 (2) | 1986 (3) | 1989 (4) |
|---|---|---|---|---|---|---|
| **Hommes** | | | | | | |
| 10-14 | 30.50 | 26.15 | .. | 26.30 | 12.44 | .. |
| 15-19 | 78.95 | 68.75 | .. | 49.85 | 39.45 | .. |
| 20-24 | 90.35 | 86.70 | .. | 71.69 | 78.52 | .. |
| 25-29 | 97.75 | 96.05 | .. | 92.84 | 94.96 | .. |
| 30-34 | 98.25 | 97.80 | .. | 96.98 | 98.21 | .. |
| 35-39 | 98.05 | 98.10 | .. | 98.27 | 98.23 | .. |
| 40-44 | 97.90 | 97.90 | .. | 97.86 | 96.80 | .. |
| 45-49 | 97.40 | 97.70 | .. | 98.23 | 95.74 | .. |
| 50-54 | 96.00 | 96.30 | .. | 96.76 | 93.70 | .. |
| 55-59 | 94.20 | 94.50 | .. | 95.02 | 90.95 | .. |
| 60-64 | 90.00 | 85.30 | .. | 76.71 | 66.82 | .. |
| 65+ | 74.80 | 62.80 | .. | 40.92 | 25.79 | .. |
| **Femmes** | | | | | | |
| 10-14 | 8.50 | 8.20 | 4.90 | 7.22 | 1.44 | 5.80 |
| 15-19 | 10.20 | 8.65 | 6.25 | 5.13 | 5.91 | 17.10 |
| 20-24 | 6.15 | 7.25 | 10.05 | 12.42 | 18.85 | 38.50 |
| 25-29 | 3.70 | 4.75 | 7.85 | 10.79 | 16.83 | 38.10 |
| 30-34 | 3.75 | 4.45 | 6.30 | 7.81 | 14.17 | 40.24 |
| 35-39 | 4.10 | 4.40 | 5.05 | 5.47 | 9.56 | 38.00 |
| 40-44 | 5.65 | 5.30 | 4.65 | 4.39 | 7.47 | 37.87 |
| 45-49 | 4.75 | 4.40 | 3.85 | 3.53 | 5.36 | 29.60 |
| 50-54 | 5.20 | 4.60 | 3.60 | 3.14 | 3.51 | 26.99 |
| 55-59 | 3.65 | 3.40 | 3.05 | 2.73 | 2.64 | 24.38 |
| 60-64 | 3.60 | 3.20 | 2.55 | 2.20 | 1.40 | 13.70 |
| 65+ | 2.25 | 1.90 | 1.35 | 1.03 | 0.63 | 8.90 |

Source(s): (1) EPPA3; (2) ASTER; (3) AST91; (4) AST93.

### 2.2 Méthode(s): interpolation et extrapolation linéaires

#### 2.2.1 Hommes:

- 1950-90, interpolation et extrapolation des taux d'activité 1950-60
tirés des EPPA3 et des taux ajustés des recensements de 1976 et 1986.

#### 2.2.2 Femmes:

- 1950-70, taux d'activité ajustés 1950-70 tirés des EPPA3;
- 1980-90, interpolation et extrapolation des taux d'activité ajustés des
recensements de 1976 et 1986 et des taux de l'enquête de 1989;
ajustement des taux d'activité sur la base du modèle d'ajustement des taux
d'activité des femmes travaillant dans l'agriculture comme aides familiales.

## 3. Evaluation des taux de répartition par secteur d'activité: 1950 - 1990

### 3.1 Données de base:

Tableau 2: Répartition de la population active en % par secteur d'activité

| Année | Agriculture | Industrie Total | Manufac. | Services |
|---|---|---|---|---|
| **Hommes** | | | | |
| 1976 (1) | 50.35 | 19.00 | 13.61 | 30.65 |
| 1986 (2) | 43.83 | 22.45 | 13.22 | 33.73 |
| 1989 (3) | 34.58 | 25.16 | 14.94 | 40.26 |
| **Femmes** | | | | |
| 1976 (1) | 23.34 | 15.40 | 13.44 | 61.26 |
| 1986 (2) | 10.82 | 12.61 | 10.43 | 76.58 |
| 1989 (3) | 63.16 | 9.09 | 8.37 | 27.75 |

Source(s): (1) ASTER; (2) AST91; (3) AST93.

### 3.2 Méthode(s): moyenne pondérée

#### 3.2.1 Hommes:

- 1950-70, taux de répartition 1950-70 tirés des EPPA3;
- 1980-90, moyennes pondérées des taux de répartition ajustés du
recensement de 1976, des taux du recensement de 1986 et des taux
de l'enquête de 1989.

#### 3.2.2 Femmes:

Méthode, hypothèses et traitements identiques à ceux appliqués aux hommes.

## 4. Projection des taux d'activité: 2000 - 2010

### 4.1 Modèle(s): linéaire et hyperbole

#### 4.1.1 Hommes:

- Au groupe d'âge [10-14], application de la fonction F1;
- Aux groupes d'âge [15+], application de la fonction F3;
- Modification des tendances des groupes d'âge [10-24].

#### 4.1.2 Femmes:

- A tous les groupes d'âge, application de la fonction F1;
- Modification des tendances des groupes d'âge [10-19], [30-34]
et [30+].

---

*Notes sur les ajustements des taux, voir p. 192-195.*     *Notes sur les fonctions de projection, voir p. 198.*

# El Salvador

## 1. Source(s) des données de base

| Code(s): | Titre(s): |
|---|---|
| EPPA3 | Evaluations et projections de la population active 1950-2025 - troisième édition, BIT, Genève, 1986. |
| CELADE | CELADE, Bulletin Démographique, No. 49, janvier 1992. |
| STAT | Base de données sur les statistiques du travail - LABORSTA, Bureau de statistique, BIT, Genève. |

## 2. Evaluation des taux d'activité: 1950 - 1990

### 2.1 Données de base:

Tableau 1: Taux d'activité par sexe et par groupe d'âge

| | Année | | |
|---|---|---|---|
| Groupe d'âge | 1970 (1) | 1990 (2)(3) | 1990 (4)(5) |
| **Hommes** | | | |
| 10-14 | 30.00 | 39.73 | 35.77 |
| 15-19 | 71.00 | 78.73 | 75.97 |
| 20-24 | 93.30 | 93.83 | 92.67 |
| 25-29 | 97.40 | 99.00 | 99.00 |
| 30-34 | 97.90 | 99.00 | 99.00 |
| 35-39 | 98.00 | 99.00 | 99.00 |
| 40-44 | 98.10 | 99.00 | 99.00 |
| 45-49 | 98.10 | 99.00 | 99.00 |
| 50-54 | 97.30 | 98.60 | 98.60 |
| 55-59 | 96.80 | 97.00 | 96.00 |
| 60-64 | 94.10 | 94.17 | 92.33 |
| 65+ | 71.80 | ... | 73.21 |
| **Femmes** | | | |
| 10-14 | 5.20 | 4.80 | 4.78 |
| 15-19 | 26.10 | 20.33 | 20.33 |
| 20-24 | 34.65 | 24.80 | 39.34 |
| 25-29 | 26.35 | 13.20 | 20.78 |
| 30-34 | 24.00 | 11.10 | 17.58 |
| 35-39 | 22.20 | 10.30 | 16.27 |
| 40-44 | 21.55 | 10.10 | 15.87 |
| 45-49 | 19.85 | 9.50 | 14.57 |
| 50-54 | 18.45 | 9.00 | 13.44 |
| 55-59 | 16.50 | 8.50 | 12.11 |
| 60-64 | 15.25 | 7.83 | 10.81 |
| 65+ | 9.70 | ... | 4.80 |

Note(s): (2) Rural; (5) Urbain.
Source(s): (1) EPPA3; (2) CELADE; (4) STAT.

### 2.2 Méthode(s): moyenne arithmétique

#### 2.2.1 Hommes:

- 1950-70, taux d'activité 1950-70 tirés des EPPA3;
- 1980, moyennes des taux d'activité estimés pour 1970 et 1990;
- 1990, taux d'activité ajustés tirés de l'enquête de 1990;
ajustement sur la base des évaluations des taux d'activité dans les zones rurales.

#### 2.2.2 Femmes:

Méthode, hypothèses et traitements identiques à ceux appliqués aux hommes.

## 3. Evaluation des taux de répartition par secteur d'activité: 1950 - 1990

### 3.1 Données de base:

Tableau 2: Répartition de la population active en % par secteur d'activité

| | Agriculture | Industrie | | Services |
|---|---|---|---|---|
| Année | | Total | Manufac. | |
| **Hommes** | | | | |
| 1950 (1) | 75.70 | 13.60 | .. | 10.70 |
| 1960 (1) | 72.35 | 15.65 | .. | 12.00 |
| 1970 (1) | 69.00 | 13.40 | .. | 17.60 |
| 1980 (1) | 55.80 | 19.80 | .. | 24.40 |
| **Femmes** | | | | |
| 1950 (1) | 12.40 | 24.85 | .. | 62.75 |
| 1961 (2) | 71.72 | 15.89 | 10.53 | 12.39 |
| 1971 (2) | 69.57 | 12.67 | 8.49 | 17.76 |
| 1991 (2) | 15.30 | 33.55 | 22.44 | 51.15 |

Source(s): (1) EPPA3; (2) STAT.

### 3.2 Méthode(s): interpolation et extrapolation linéaires

#### 3.2.1 Hommes:

- 1950-80, taux de répartition 1950-80 tirés des EPPA3;
- 1990, extrapolation des taux de répartition 1950-80 tirés des EPPA3; ajustement des taux extrapolés sur la base des variations des taux interpolés 1980 par rapport aux taux 1980 tirés des EPPA3.

#### 3.2.2 Femmes:

- 1950, taux de répartition 1950 tirés des EPPA3;
- 1960, 1970 et 1990, interpolation et extrapolation des taux de répartition tirés des recensements de 1961 et 1971 et des taux de répartition ajustés du recensement de 1991;
- 1980, moyennes des taux de répartition estimés pour 1970 et 1990.

## 4. Projection des taux d'activité: 2000 - 2010

### 4.1 Modèle(s): linéaire, hyperbole et logistique

#### 4.1.1 Hommes:

- Aux groupes d'âge [10-54], application de la fonction F1;
- Aux groupes d'âge [55+], application de la fonction F3;
- Modification des tendances des groupes d'âge [10-14], [25-49] et [60+].

#### 4.1.2 Femmes:

- Aux groupes d'âge [10-14] et [20-44], application de la fonction F1;
- Au groupe d'âge [15-19], application de la fonction F3;
- Aux groupes d'âge [45+], application de la fonction F6;
- Modification des tendances de tous les groupes d'âge.

---

*Notes sur les ajustements des taux, voir p. 192-195.*

*Notes sur les fonctions de projection, voir p. 198.*

# Emirats arabes unis

## 1. Source(s) des données de base

**Code(s):** **Titre(s):**

EPPA3    Evaluations et projections de la population active 1950-2025 - troisième édition, BIT, Genève, 1986.
STAT    Base de données sur les statistiques du travail - LABORSTA, Bureau de statistique, BIT, Genève.

## 2. Evaluation des taux d'activité: 1950 - 1990

### 2.1 Données de base:

Tableau 1: Taux d'activité par sexe et par groupe d'âge

| Groupe d'âge | 1975 | 1980 | 1985 |
|---|---|---|---|
| **Hommes** | | | |
| 10-14 | 12.54 | 0.00 | 0.00 |
| 15-19 | 65.81 | 45.32 | 28.03 |
| 20-24 | 96.38 | 94.57 | 88.88 |
| 25-29 | 99.01 | 99.03 | 98.60 |
| 30-34 | 99.18 | 99.50 | 99.40 |
| 35-39 | 98.88 | 99.38 | 99.46 |
| 40-44 | 98.37 | 99.04 | 99.27 |
| 45-49 | 96.87 | 97.94 | 98.62 |
| 50-54 | 92.05 | 94.39 | 96.24 |
| 55-59 | 86.74 | 90.74 | 91.99 |
| 60-64 | 72.81 | 76.02 | 78.06 |
| 65+ | 31.78 | 27.90 | 25.98 |
| **Femmes** | | | |
| 10-14 | 0.95 | 0.00 | 0.00 |
| 15-19 | 3.94 | 4.47 | 5.99 |
| 20-24 | 12.12 | 14.63 | 26.43 |
| 25-29 | 16.51 | 21.91 | 30.34 |
| 30-34 | 14.59 | 24.74 | 33.21 |
| 35-39 | 11.73 | 19.41 | 31.34 |
| 40-44 | 9.62 | 18.32 | 27.13 |
| 45-49 | 7.70 | 13.18 | 19.18 |
| 50-54 | 6.54 | 9.47 | 12.61 |
| 55-59 | 4.95 | 5.89 | 8.60 |
| 60-64 | 2.75 | 3.39 | 3.26 |
| 65+ | 1.36 | 1.07 | 0.86 |

Source(s): STAT.

### 2.2 Méthode(s): extrapolation linéaire moyenne pondérée

#### 2.2.1 Hommes:

- 1950-70, taux d'activité 1950-70 tirés des EPPA3;
- 1980, moyennes pondérées des taux d'activité 1970 tirés des EPPA3 et des taux du recensement de 1980;
- 1990, extrapolation des taux d'activité tirés des recensements de 1975, 1980 et 1985;
ajustement des taux extrapolés sur la base des variations des taux interpolés 1985 par rapport aux taux du recensement de 1985;
modification des tendances de tous les groupes d'âge.

#### 2.2.2 Femmes:

- 1950-80, taux d'activité 1950-80 tirés des EPPA3;
- 1990, extrapolation des taux d'activité tirés des recensements de 1975, 1980 et 1985;
ajustement des taux extrapolés sur la base des variations des taux interpolés 1985 par rapport aux taux du recensement de 1985.

## 3. Evaluation des taux de répartition par secteur d'activité: 1950 - 1990

### 3.1 Données de base:

Tableau 2: Répartition de la population active en % par secteur d'activité

| Année | Agriculture | Industrie Total | Manufac. | Services |
|---|---|---|---|---|
| **Hommes** | | | | |
| 1975 | 4.76 | 43.98 | 6.08 | 51.26 |
| 1980 | 4.83 | 39.81 | 6.51 | 55.35 |
| 1985 | 8.43 | 30.86 | 8.13 | 60.72 |
| **Femmes** | | | | |
| 1975 | 0.32 | 5.80 | 1.06 | 93.88 |
| 1980 | 0.08 | 6.71 | 1.48 | 93.21 |
| 1985 | 0.06 | 3.32 | 1.05 | 96.62 |

Source(s): STAT.

### 3.2 Méthode(s): extrapolation linéaire

#### 3.2.1 Hommes:

- 1950-80, taux de répartition 1950-80 tirés des EPPA3;
ajustement des taux de 1970 en tenant compte des résultats du recensement de 1975;
- 1990, extrapolation des taux de répartition des recensements de 1980 et 1985;
modification des tendances de tous les secteurs.

#### 3.2.2 Femmes:

- 1950-80, taux de répartition 1950-80 tirés des EPPA3;
- 1990, extrapolation des taux de répartition tirés des recensements de 1980 et 1985;
modification des tendances de tous les secteurs.

## 4. Projection des taux d'activité: 2000 - 2010

### 4.1 Modèle(s): linéaire, log-linéaire et hyperbole

#### 4.1.1 Hommes:

- Au groupe d'âge [15-19], application de la fonction F2;
- Aux groupes d'âge [20-59], application de la fonction F1;
- Aux groupes d'âge [60+], application de la fonction F3;
- Modification des tendances des groupes d'âge [20-59].

#### 4.1.2 Femmes:

- Aux groupes d'âge [15+], application de la fonction F1;
- Modification de la tendance du groupe d'âge [15-19].

---

*Notes sur les ajustements des taux, voir p. 192-195.*

*Notes sur les fonctions de projection, voir p. 198.*

# Equateur

## 1. Source(s) des données de base

**Code(s):** **Titre(s):**

EPPA3 — Evaluations et projections de la population active 1950-2025 - troisième édition, BIT, Genève, 1986.
STAT — Base de données sur les statistiques du travail - LABORSTA, Bureau de statistique, BIT, Genève.

## 2. Evaluation des taux d'activité: 1950 - 1990

### 2.1 Données de base:

Tableau 1: Taux d'activité par sexe et par groupe d'âge

| Groupe d'âge | 1970 (1) | 1982 (2) | 1990 (2) |
|---|---|---|---|
| **Hommes** | | | |
| 10-14 | 25.00 | 9.34 | 17.06 |
| 15-19 | 68.00 | 47.78 | 52.43 |
| 20-24 | 88.85 | 75.31 | 79.32 |
| 25-29 | 96.70 | 90.04 | 90.83 |
| 30-34 | 98.65 | 91.98 | 94.97 |
| 35-39 | 98.90 | 92.97 | 95.87 |
| 40-44 | 98.80 | 92.98 | 95.57 |
| 45-49 | 98.45 | 92.13 | 95.02 |
| 50-54 | 97.55 | 90.53 | 93.36 |
| 55-59 | 96.00 | 88.30 | 91.02 |
| 60-64 | 93.90 | 82.69 | 85.68 |
| 65+ | 83.40 | 64.77 | 64.34 |
| **Femmes** | | | |
| 10-14 | 5.00 | 3.97 | 6.69 |
| 15-19 | 17.70 | 14.55 | 19.04 |
| 20-24 | 21.70 | 22.75 | 29.35 |
| 25-29 | 19.40 | 26.18 | 34.06 |
| 30-34 | 17.50 | 24.18 | 35.91 |
| 35-39 | 16.60 | 22.09 | 35.38 |
| 40-44 | 16.65 | 20.44 | 33.34 |
| 45-49 | 16.20 | 18.91 | 30.37 |
| 50-54 | 15.70 | 17.35 | 27.21 |
| 55-59 | 14.55 | 15.57 | 24.44 |
| 60-64 | 13.15 | 13.15 | 20.98 |
| 65+ | 10.15 | 9.11 | 13.95 |

**Source(s):** (1) EPPA3; (2) STAT.

### 2.2 Méthode(s): interpolation linéaire
moyenne pondérée

**2.2.1 Hommes:**

- 1950-70, taux d'activité 1950-70 tirés des EPPA3;
- 1980-90, moyennes pondérées des taux d'activité 1970 tirés des EPPA3 et des taux ajustés tirés des recensements de 1982 et 1990.

**2.2.2 Femmes:**

- 1950-70, taux d'activité ajustés 1950-70 tirés des EPPA3; ajustement des taux sur la base du modèle d'ajustement des taux d'activité des femmes travaillant dans l'agriculture comme aides familiales;
- 1980-90, interpolation des taux d'activité ajustés tirés du recensement de 1982 et des taux d'activité tirés du recensement de 1990.

## 3. Evaluation des taux de répartition par secteur d'activité: 1950 - 1990

### 3.1 Données de base:

Tableau 2: Répartition de la population active en % par secteur d'activité

| Année | Agriculture | Industrie Total | Manufac. | Services |
|---|---|---|---|---|
| **Hommes** | | | | |
| 1970 (1) | 57.60 | 19.60 | .. | 22.80 |
| 1982 (2) | 41.11 | 21.89 | 12.09 | 36.99 |
| 1990 (2) | 38.79 | 20.14 | 10.64 | 41.06 |
| **Femmes** | | | | |
| 1982 (2) | 13.02 | 17.08 | 15.96 | 69.90 |
| 1990 (2) | 15.75 | 15.73 | 14.69 | 68.52 |

**Source(s):** (1) EPPA3; (2) STAT.

### 3.2 Méthode(s): moyenne pondérée
interpolation et extrapolation linéaires

**3.2.1 Hommes:**

- 1950-70, taux de répartition 1950-70 tirés des EPPA3;
- 1980-90, moyennes pondérées des taux de répartition 1970 tirés des EPPA3 et des taux de répartition tirés des recensements de 1982 et 1990.

**3.2.2 Femmes:**

- 1950, taux de répartition 1950 tirés des EPPA3;
- 1960-70, interpolation des taux de répartition estimés pour 1950 et 1980;
- 1980-90, interpolation et extrapolation des taux de répartition tirés des recensements de 1982 et 1990.

## 4. Projection des taux d'activité: 2000 - 2010

### 4.1 Modèle(s): linéaire, log-linéaire et hyperbole

**4.1.1 Hommes:**

- Aux groupes d'âge [10-19], application de la fonction F2;
- Aux groupes d'âge [20-59], application de la fonction F3;
- Aux groupes d'âge [60+], application de la fonction F3;
- Modification des tendances des groupes d'âge [20-49].

**4.1.2 Femmes:**

- Aux groupes d'âge [10-24], application de la fonction F3;
- Aux groupes d'âge [25+], application de la fonction F2;
- Modification des tendances des groupes d'âge [10-14] et [20-24].

*Notes sur les ajustements des taux, voir p. 192-195.*   *Notes sur les fonctions de projection, voir p. 198.*

# Erythrée

## 1. Source(s) des données de base

Code(s):    Titre(s):

FSEE94      ILO, Foundation For Sustained Employment in Eritrea, EAMAT Addis Ababa, 1994.
EPPA4       Population active 1950-2010 - quatrième édition, BIT, Genève 1996.

## 2. Evaluation des taux d'activité: 1950 - 1990

### 2.1 Données de base:

Tableau 1: Taux d'activité par sexe et par groupe d'âge

| Groupe d'âge | Année 1950 (1) | 1970 (1) | 1990 (1) | 1950 (2) | 1970 (2) | 1990 (2) |
|---|---|---|---|---|---|---|
| **Hommes** | | | | | | |
| 10-14 | 55.69 | 51.05 | 45.02 | 47.40 | 42.80 | 38.02 |
| 15-19 | 71.92 | 67.03 | 62.13 | 78.65 | 72.55 | 66.15 |
| 20-24 | 83.93 | 81.97 | 80.45 | 92.85 | 90.50 | 88.06 |
| 25-29 | 94.75 | 94.43 | 94.10 | 97.05 | 96.70 | 96.32 |
| 30-34 | 97.21 | 96.85 | 96.49 | 97.75 | 97.35 | 96.95 |
| 35-39 | 98.26 | 97.87 | 97.52 | 97.90 | 97.45 | 97.03 |
| 40-44 | 98.19 | 97.78 | 97.38 | 97.70 | 97.25 | 96.83 |
| 45-49 | 98.00 | 97.65 | 97.29 | 97.00 | 96.65 | 96.27 |
| 50-54 | 96.29 | 95.76 | 95.24 | 96.40 | 95.80 | 95.20 |
| 55-59 | 95.66 | 94.80 | 93.94 | 95.15 | 94.25 | 93.35 |
| 60-64 | 93.95 | 92.51 | 91.07 | 91.60 | 90.10 | 88.54 |
| 65+ | 80.93 | 78.37 | 75.81 | 77.25 | 74.60 | 71.86 |
| **Femmes** | | | | | | |
| 10-14 | 50.19 | 46.02 | 41.85 | 41.00 | 37.00 | 31.00 |
| 15-19 | 61.10 | 57.45 | 54.54 | 65.71 | 59.76 | 56.05 |
| 20-24 | 64.17 | 61.77 | 59.86 | 68.56 | 64.51 | 61.99 |
| 25-29 | 65.16 | 62.60 | 60.54 | 73.45 | 68.93 | 66.11 |
| 30-34 | 65.21 | 62.62 | 60.54 | 77.95 | 73.15 | 70.15 |
| 35-39 | 65.85 | 63.47 | 61.56 | 79.70 | 75.15 | 72.31 |
| 40-44 | 67.12 | 64.76 | 62.86 | 82.40 | 77.89 | 75.07 |
| 45-49 | 67.66 | 65.21 | 63.26 | 81.59 | 76.97 | 74.08 |
| 50-54 | 66.09 | 63.27 | 61.02 | 79.26 | 74.11 | 70.88 |
| 55-59 | 64.15 | 61.40 | 58.10 | 75.48 | 70.16 | 66.84 |
| 60-64 | 59.79 | 55.91 | 52.81 | 67.01 | 60.48 | 56.40 |
| 65+ | 46.41 | 41.30 | 36.18 | 44.22 | 38.34 | 34.66 |

Note(s): (1) Ethiopie; (2) Somalie. **Source(s)**: EPPA4.

### 2.2 Méthode(s): moyenne arithmétique

#### 2.2.1 Hommes:

- 1950-90, moyennes des taux d'activité estimés pour la Somalie et l'Ethiopie.

#### 2.2.2 Femmes:

- 1990, moyennes des taux d'activité estimés pour la Somalie et l'Ethiopie; ajustement des moyennes afin d'obtenir un rapport hommes/femmes égal à 1 dans l'agriculture;
- 1950-80, moyennes ajustées des taux d'activité estimés pour la Somalie et l'Ethiopie;
ajustement sur la base des variations des taux moyens 1990 par rapport aux taux estimés pour les mêmes années;
modification de la tendance du groupe d'âge [10-14] pour 1990.

## 3. Evaluation des taux de répartition par secteur d'activité: 1950 - 1990

### 3.1 Données de base:

Tableau 2: Répartition de la population active en % par secteur d'activité

| Année | Agriculture | Industrie Total | Manufac. | Services |
|---|---|---|---|---|
| **Hommes** | | | | |
| 1993 | 50.13 | 14.04 | 12.39 | 35.83 |
| **Femmes** | | | | |
| 1993 | 60.87 | 15.24 | 13.35 | 23.89 |

**Source(s)**: FSSE94.

### 3.2 Méthode(s): moyenne arithmétique

#### 3.2.1 Hommes:

- 1950-80, moyenne des taux estimés pour la Somalie et l'Ethiopie pour la période 1950-80,
- 1990, taux estimés sur la base du rapport FSEE94;
- Le rapport industrie/services a été évalué sur la base des estimations faites pour la Somalie et l'Ethiopie;
- Application du rapport manufacture/industrie tiré des estimations FSEE94.

#### 3.2.2 Femmes:

Méthode, hypothèses et traitements identiques à ceux appliqués aux hommes.

## 4. Projection des taux d'activité: 2000 - 2010

### 4.1 Modèle(s): linéaire et hyperbole

#### 4.1.1 Hommes:

- Aux groupes d'âge [10-29], application de la fonction F1;
- Aux groupes d'âge [30+], application de la fonction F3;
- Modification des tendances des groupes d'âge [30-59].

#### 4.1.2 Femmes:

- Aux groupes d'âge [10-19], application de la fonction F1;
- Aux groupes d'âge [20+], application de la fonction F3;
- Modification des tendances des groupes d'âge [20-49].

*Notes sur les ajustements des taux, voir p. 192-195.*

*Notes sur les fonctions de projection, voir p. 198.*

# Espagne

## 1. Source(s) des données de base

Code(s):     Titre(s):

EPPA3        Annuaire des statistiques du travail 1945-89 - Edition rétrospective sur les recensements de population, BIT, Genève, 1990.
STAT         Base de données sur les statistiques du travail - LABORSTA, Bureau de statistique, BIT, Genève.

## 2. Evaluation des taux d'activité: 1950 - 1990

### 2.1 Données de base:

Tableau 1: Taux d'activité par sexe et par groupe d'âge

| Groupe d'âge | Année | | | | | |
|---|---|---|---|---|---|---|
| | 1970 (1) | 1980 (2) | 1981 (2) | 1989 (2) | 1990 (2) | 1991 (2) |
| **Hommes** | | | | | | |
| 10-14 | .. | .. | .. | 0.00 | 0.00 | 0.00 |
| 15-19 | .. | .. | .. | 34.82 | 33.31 | 32.25 |
| 20-24 | .. | .. | .. | 71.87 | 72.53 | 71.15 |
| 25-29 | .. | .. | .. | 91.58 | 91.99 | 91.82 |
| 30-34 | .. | .. | .. | 96.08 | 96.55 | 96.08 |
| 35-39 | .. | .. | .. | 96.20 | 96.70 | 96.88 |
| 40-44 | .. | .. | .. | 95.46 | 95.67 | 95.76 |
| 45-49 | .. | .. | .. | 94.14 | 94.06 | 93.57 |
| 50-54 | .. | .. | .. | 88.43 | 89.30 | 88.96 |
| 55-59 | .. | .. | .. | 75.70 | 76.53 | 76.26 |
| 60-64 | .. | .. | .. | 48.19 | 46.94 | 46.59 |
| 65+ | .. | .. | .. | 4.27 | 3.77 | 3.68 |
| **Femmes** | | | | | | |
| 10-14 | 3.45 | 0.00 | 0.00 | 0.00 | 0.00 | 0.00 |
| 15-19 | 36.15 | 40.52 | 38.67 | 32.70 | 31.20 | 27.80 |
| 20-24 | 38.90 | 55.21 | 55.42 | 62.22 | 61.45 | 60.62 |
| 25-29 | 20.70 | 42.13 | 42.91 | 64.00 | 65.15 | 65.90 |
| 30-34 | 13.75 | 30.34 | 31.25 | 53.79 | 56.26 | 58.51 |
| 35-39 | 13.35 | 30.01 | 28.72 | 45.14 | 48.96 | 51.95 |
| 40-44 | 14.15 | 28.26 | 27.87 | 38.92 | 41.11 | 42.72 |
| 45-49 | 14.65 | 27.82 | 28.40 | 33.27 | 34.53 | 35.96 |
| 50-54 | 15.25 | 26.79 | 25.15 | 28.16 | 29.15 | 30.60 |
| 55-59 | 14.90 | 24.61 | 23.05 | 23.64 | 23.24 | 22.66 |
| 60-64 | 12.00 | 17.27 | 17.29 | 15.34 | 15.54 | 15.84 |
| 65+ | 4.4 | 7.88 | 6.73 | 1.84 | 1.66 | 1.46 |

Source(s): (1) EPPA3; (2) STAT.

### 2.2 Méthode(s): interpolation et extrapolation linéaires
moyenne arithmétique

**2.2.1 Hommes:**

- 1950-80, taux d'activité 1950-80 tirés des EPPA3;
ajustement des taux d'activité des groupes d'âge [30+] pour 1980;
- 1990, moyennes ajustées des taux d'activité tirés des enquêtes
de 1989, 1990 et 1991; l'ajustement a été accompli pour tenir compte des
militaires du contingent.

**2.2.2 Femmes:**

- 1950-80, interpolation et extrapolation des taux d'activité 1970
tirés des EPPA3 et des taux d'activité tirés des enquêtes de 1980 et 1982;
modification des tendances de tous les groupes d'âge;
- 1990, moyennes des taux d'activité tirés des enquêtes de 1989,
1990 et 1991;
ajustement du taux d'activité du groupe d'âge [15-19].

## 3. Evaluation des taux de répartition par secteur d'activité: 1950 - 1990

### 3.1 Données de base:

Tableau 2: Répartition de la population active en % par secteur d'activité

| Année | Agriculture | Industrie | | Services |
|---|---|---|---|---|
| | | Total | Manufac. | |
| **Hommes** | | | | |
| 1950 | 54.75 | 25.20 | .. | 20.05 |
| 1960 | 46.80 | 32.05 | .. | 21.15 |
| 1970 | 28.90 | 39.05 | .. | 32.05 |
| **Femmes** | | | | |
| 1950 | 24.94 | 25.00 | .. | 50.06 |
| 1960 | 20.81 | 28.50 | .. | 50.69 |
| 1970 | 13.93 | 31.36 | .. | 54.70 |

Source(s): EPPA3.

### 3.2 Méthode(s): interpolation et extrapolation linéaires

**3.2.1 Hommes:**
- 1950-90, moyennes pondérées des taux interpolés et extrapolés
résultant de l'interpolation et extrapolation des taux de répartition
1950-70 tirés des EPPA3.

**3.2.2 Femmes:**

Méthode, hypothèses et traitements identiques à ceux appliqués aux hommes.

## 4. Projection des taux d'activité: 2000 - 2010

### 4.1 Modèle(s): linéaire, hyperbole et logistique

**4.1.1 Hommes:**

- Aux groupes d'âge [15+], application de la fonction F3;
- Modification de la tendance du groupe d'âge [45-49].

**4.1.2 Femmes:**

- Aux groupes d'âge [15-54], application de la fonction F6;
- Aux groupes d'âge [55-64], application de la fonction F1;
- Au groupe d'âge [65+], application de la fonction F3;
- Modification des tendances des groupes d'âge [15-19] et [55-64].

*Notes sur les ajustements des taux, voir p. 192-195.*

*Notes sur les fonctions de projection, voir p. 198.*

# Estonie

## 1. Source(s) des données de base

**Code(s):**    **Titre(s):**

BLT-94-2     Vorobiev A. (1994), "Estimation de la population active pour les quinze pays de l'ex-URSS pour les années 1950, 1959, 1970, 1979 et 1989", dans le Bulletin des statistiques du travail - 1994-2, BIT, Genève.

## 2. Evaluation des taux d'activité: 1950 - 1990

### 2.1 Données de base:

Tableau 1: Taux d'activité par sexe et par groupe d'âge

| Groupe d'âge | Année | | | |
|---|---|---|---|---|
| | 1959 | 1970 | 1979 | 1989 |
| **Hommes** | | | | |
| 10-14 | 0.00 | 0.00 | 0.00 | 0.00 |
| 15-19 | 48.84 | 43.40 | 33.93 | 32.20 |
| 20-24 | 88.00 | 88.68 | 86.67 | 81.13 |
| 25-29 | 93.88 | 95.83 | 98.31 | 96.67 |
| 30-34 | 95.24 | 96.36 | 97.92 | 96.67 |
| 35-39 | 93.33 | 98.04 | 99.98 | 98.21 |
| 40-44 | 92.31 | 97.87 | 96.08 | 97.78 |
| 45-49 | 93.75 | 96.88 | 95.83 | 95.65 |
| 50-54 | 90.00 | 91.67 | 90.24 | 91.30 |
| 55-59 | 88.46 | 86.21 | 81.48 | 85.37 |
| 60-64 | 78.95 | 34.62 | 42.86 | 51.52 |
| 65+ | 38.46 | 18.37 | 15.79 | 22.22 |
| **Femmes** | | | | |
| 10-14 | 0.00 | 0.00 | 0.00 | 0.00 |
| 15-19 | 37.21 | 35.42 | 27.45 | 26.42 |
| 20-24 | 73.47 | 82.98 | 83.64 | 76.47 |
| 25-29 | 74.07 | 91.49 | 94.74 | 91.53 |
| 30-34 | 71.43 | 92.86 | 95.92 | 93.44 |
| 35-39 | 71.74 | 92.59 | 96.15 | 96.55 |
| 40-44 | 72.97 | 92.86 | 96.36 | 03.00 |
| 45-49 | 71.74 | 91.67 | 94.44 | 94.12 |
| 50-54 | 68.18 | 82.35 | 85.45 | 98.60 |
| 55-59 | 41.00 | 40.00 | 43.18 | 53.85 |
| 60-64 | 55.56 | 20.93 | 26.47 | 37.25 |
| 65+ | 6.90 | 8.26 | 8.73 | 12.80 |

**Source(s):** BLT-94-2.

### 2.2 Méthode(s): extrapolation linéaire
moyenne pondérée

**2.2.1 Hommes:**

- 1950-60, extrapolation des taux d'activité 1970, 1979 et 1989
tirés du Bulletin des statistiques du travail 1994-2;
modification des tendances de tous les groupes d'âge;
aux taux estimés pour 1970, application des variations des taux d'activité
interpolés 1960 et 1970 par rapport aux taux d'activité 1970 interpolés;
- 1970-90, moyennes pondérées des taux d'activité 1970, 1979
et 1989 tirés du Bulletin.

**2.2.2 Femmes:**

- 1950-90, moyennes pondérées des taux d'activité 1950, 1959, 1970 et 1989
tirés du Bulletin des statistiques du travail, 1994-2
les taux d'activité des groupes d'âge [15-19]
et [55-64] respectivement pour 1950 et 1959, 1970 et 1979 ont été ajustés.

## 3. Evaluation des taux de répartition par secteur d'activité: 1950 - 1990

### 3.1 Données de base:

Tableau 2: Répartition de la population active en % par secteur d'activité

| Année | Agriculture | Industrie | | Services |
|---|---|---|---|---|
| | | Total | Manufac. | |
| **Hommes** | | | | |
| 1950 | 32.42 | 33.98 | 16.41 | 33.59 |
| 1959 | 26.84 | 41.85 | 25.24 | 31.31 |
| 1970 | 20.22 | 50.69 | 31.30 | 29.09 |
| 1979 | 18.64 | 50.63 | 29.47 | 30.73 |
| 1989 | 17.88 | 48.71 | 28.00 | 33.41 |
| **Femmes** | | | | |
| 1950 | 51.81 | 19.20 | 14.49 | 28.99 |
| 1959 | 33.11 | 28.48 | 22.52 | 38.41 |
| 1970 | 15.79 | 36.29 | 29.92 | 47.92 |
| 1979 | 12.25 | 36.75 | 29.00 | 51.00 |
| 1989 | 11.14 | 34.36 | 27.25 | 54.50 |

**Source(s):** BLT-94-2.

### 3.2 Méthode(s): données du BLT-94-2

**3.2.1 Hommes:**

- 1950-90, moyennes pondérées des taux de répartition 1950, 1959,
1970, 1979 et 1990 tirés du Bulletin des statistiques du travail - 1994-2.

**3.2.2 Femmes:**

Méthode, hypothèses et traitements identiques à ceux appliqués aux hommes.

## 4. Projection des taux d'activité: 2000 - 2010

### 4.1 Modèle(s): linéaire, hyperbole et logistique

**4.1.1 Hommes:**

- Aux groupes d'âge [15-19], [25-39] et [65+], application de la fonction F1;
- Aux groupes d'âge [20-24] et [40-59], application de la fonction F3;
- Modification des tendances des groupes d'âge [15-44].

**4.1.2 Femmes:**

- Aux groupes d'âge [15-19] et [65+], application de la fonction F1;
- Aux groupes d'âge [20-24] et [55-64], application de la fonction F3;
- Aux groupes d'âge [25-54], application de la fonction F6;
- Modification des tendances des groupes d'âge [15-24] et [65+].

*Notes sur les ajustements des taux, voir p. 192-195.*

*Notes sur les fonctions de projection, voir p. 198.*

# Etats-Unis

## 1. Source(s) des données de base

Code(s):     Titre(s):

EPPA3        Evaluations et projections de la population active 1950-2025 - troisième édition, BIT, Genève, 1986.
STAT         Base de données sur les statistiques du travail - LABORSTA, Bureau de statistique, BIT, Genève.

## 2. Evaluation des taux d'activité: 1950 - 1990

### 2.1 Données de base:

Tableau 1: Taux d'activité par sexe et par groupe d'âge

| Groupe d'âge | Année | | |
| | 1989 | 1990 | 1991 |
| --- | --- | --- | --- |
| **Hommes** | | | |
| 10-14 | 0.00 | 0.00 | 0.00 |
| 15-19 | 45.50 | 44.52 | 40.62 |
| 20-24 | 79.61 | 84.30 | 74.37 |
| 25-29 | 89.56 | 93.80 | 89.32 |
| 30-34 | 91.84 | 94.60 | 93.03 |
| 35-39 | 92.25 | 94.90 | 92.99 |
| 40-44 | 92.18 | 93.90 | 90.66 |
| 45-49 | 91.61 | 92.30 | 93.02 |
| 50-54 | 88.44 | 88.80 | 89.02 |
| 55-59 | 78.75 | 79.80 | 79.65 |
| 60-64 | 54.14 | 55.50 | 55.15 |
| 65+ | 15.96 | | 15.55 |
| **Femmes** | | | |
| 10-14 | 0.00 | 0.00 | 0.00 |
| 15-19 | 43.78 | 41.40 | 39.78 |
| 20-24 | 72.01 | 71.60 | 68.37 |
| 25-29 | 73.41 | 73.80 | 73.48 |
| 30-34 | 72.69 | 73.40 | 73.66 |
| 35-39 | 74.67 | 75.50 | 75.73 |
| 40-44 | 76.79 | 77.60 | 76.74 |
| 45-49 | 74.28 | 74.80 | 76.96 |
| 50-54 | 65.75 | 66.90 | 68.88 |
| 55-59 | 54.50 | 55.30 | 56.49 |
| 60-64 | 35.23 | 35.50 | 35.14 |
| 65+ | 7.79 | … | 7.97 |

Source(s): STAT.

### 2.2 Méthode(s): moyenne arithmétique

**2.2.1 Hommes:**

- 1950-80, taux d'activité 1950-80 tirés des EPPA3;
- 1990, moyennes des taux d'activité tirés des enquêtes de 1989, 1990 et 1991;
ajustement des taux estimés pour tenir compte des forces armées.

**2.2.2 Femmes:**

Méthode, hypothèses et traitements identiques à ceux appliqués aux hommes.

## 3. Evaluation des taux de répartition par secteur d'activité: 1950 - 1990

### 3.1 Données de base:

Tableau 2: Répartition de la population active en % par secteur d'activité

| Année | Agriculture | Industrie | | Services |
| | | Total | Manufac. | |
| --- | --- | --- | --- | --- |
| **Hommes** | | | | |
| 1989 | 3.99 | 35.12 | 21.61 | 60.89 |
| 1990 | 3.96 | 34.98 | 21.28 | 61.06 |
| 1991 | 4.09 | 33.70 | 20.83 | 62.20 |
| **Femmes** | | | | |
| 1989 | 1.38 | 15.61 | 13.54 | 83.01 |
| 1990 | 1.35 | 15.13 | 13.09 | 83.53 |
| 1991 | 1.34 | 14.85 | 12.86 | 83.81 |

Source(s): STAT.

### 3.2 Méthode(s): moyenne arithmétique

**3.2.1 Hommes:**

- 1950-70, taux de répartition 1950-70 tirés des EPPA3;
- 1990, moyennes des taux de répartition tirés des enquêtes de 1989, 1990 et 1991.

**3.2.2 Femmes:**

Méthode, hypothèses et traitements identiques à ceux appliqués aux hommes.

## 4. Projection des taux d'activité: 2000 - 2010

### 4.1 Modèle(s): linéaire, hyperbole et logistique

**4.1.1 Hommes:**

- Au groupe d'âge [15-19], application de la fonction F1;
- Aux groupes d'âge [20+], application de la fonction F3;
- Modification des tendances des groupes d'âge [15-19] et [25-54].

**4.1.2 Femmes:**

- Aux groupes d'âge [15-64], application de la fonction F6;
- Au groupe d'âge [65+], application de la fonction F3;
- Modification des tendances des groupes d'âge [15-64].

---

*Notes sur les ajustements des taux, voir p. 192-195.*     *Notes sur les fonctions de projection, voir p. 198.*

# Ethiopie

**Code(s):**     **Titre(s):**

EPPA3     Evaluations et projections de la population active 1950-2025 - troisième édition, BIT, Genève, 1986.

AST91     Annuaire des statistiques du travail 1991, BIT, Genève, 1991.

## 2. Evaluation des taux d'activité: 1950 - 1990

### 2.1 Données de base:

Tableau 1: Taux d'activité par sexe et par groupe d'âge

| Groupe d'âge | Année 1950 (1) | 1960 (1) | 1970 (1) | 1980 (1) | 1984 (2) |
|---|---|---|---|---|---|
| **Hommes** | | | | | |
| 10-14 | 57.85 | 55.45 | 53.65 | 50.40 | 47.80 |
| 15-19 | 85.05 | 82.20 | 80.05 | 76.10 | 63.60 |
| 20-24 | 92.85 | 91.80 | 91.00 | 89.50 | 80.60 |
| 25-29 | 96.60 | 96.45 | 96.30 | 96.10 | 94.20 |
| 30-34 | 97.75 | 97.60 | 97.45 | 97.20 | 96.60 |
| 35-39 | 97.80 | 97.80 | 97.70 | 97.40 | 97.60 |
| 40-44 | 97.30 | 97.10 | 96.90 | 96.70 | 97.50 |
| 45-49 | 96.90 | 96.70 | 96.60 | 96.35 | 97.40 |
| 50-54 | 96.00 | 95.75 | 95.55 | 95.20 | 95.40 |
| 55-59 | 94.80 | 94.40 | 94.05 | 93.50 | 94.20 |
| 60-64 | 90.65 | 89.95 | 89.45 | 88.50 | 91.50 |
| 65+ | 67.60 | 66.55 | 65.75 | 64.30 | 76.58 |
| **Femmes** | | | | | |
| 10-14 | 38.10 | 36.50 | 35.35 | 33.20 | 43.10 |
| 15-19 | 66.40 | 63.85 | 61.95 | 58.50 | 54.90 |
| 20-24 | 66.50 | 64.90 | 63.70 | 61.50 | 60.10 |
| 25-29 | 69.85 | 68.05 | 66.75 | 64.30 | 60.80 |
| 30-34 | 71.85 | 70.00 | 68.60 | 66.10 | 60.80 |
| 35-39 | 68.50 | 66.90 | 65.70 | 63.50 | 61.80 |
| 40-44 | 66.10 | 64.60 | 63.45 | 61.40 | 63.10 |
| 45-49 | 61.70 | 60.25 | 59.15 | 57.20 | 63.50 |
| 50-54 | 55.25 | 53.70 | 52.60 | 50.50 | 61.30 |
| 55-59 | 45.85 | 44.50 | 43.50 | 41.60 | 59.40 |
| 60-64 | 39.25 | 37.65 | 36.40 | 34.20 | 53.20 |
| 65+ | 14.10 | 13.35 | 12.75 | 11.70 | 37.71 |

**Source(s):**   (1) EPPA3; (2) AST91.

### 2.2 Méthode(s): interpolation et extrapolation linéaires

**2.2.1 Hommes:**

- 1950-90, interpolation et extrapolation des taux d'activité 1950-80 tirés des EPPA3 et des taux d'activité tirés du recensement de 1984; ajustement des taux interpolés et extrapolés sur la base des variations des taux extrapolés 1984 par rapport aux taux du recensement de 1984; modification des tendances des groupes d'âge [10-14] et [20-24] pour 1990.

**2.2.2 Femmes:**

- 1950-90, interpolation et extrapolation des taux d'activité 1950-80 tirés des EPPA3 et des taux d'activité tirés du recensement de 1984; ajustement des taux interpolés et extrapolés sur la base des variations des taux extrapolés 1984 par rapport aux taux du recensement de 1984; modification des tendances des groupes d'âge [15-64] pour 1950-90.

## 3. Evaluation des taux de répartition par secteur d'activité: 1950 - 1990

### 3.1 Données de base:

Tableau 2: Répartition de la population active en % par secteur d'activité

| Année | Agriculture | Industrie Total | Manufac. | Services |
|---|---|---|---|---|
| **Hommes** | | | | |
| 1950 (1) | 89.00 | 4.00 | .. | 7.00 |
| 1960 (1) | 85.00 | 5.50 | .. | 9.50 |
| 1970 (1) | 82.00 | 7.00 | .. | 11.00 |
| 1980 (1) | 76.50 | 9.00 | .. | 14.50 |
| 1984 (2) | 89.28 | 2.16 | 1.58 | 8.56 |
| **Femmes** | | | | |
| 1950 (1) | 93.50 | 2.80 | .. | 3.70 |
| 1960 (1) | 90.95 | 3.70 | .. | 5.35 |
| 1970 (1) | 89.40 | 4.30 | .. | 6.30 |
| 1980 (1) | 84.90 | 6.10 | .. | 9.00 |
| 1984 (2) | 87.56 | 1.70 | 1.58 | 10.74 |

**Source(s):** (1) EPPA3; (2) AST91

### 3.2 Méthode(s): interpolation et extrapolation linéaires

**3.2.1 Hommes:**

- 1950-90, interpolation et extrapolation des taux de répartition 1950-80 tirés des EPPA3; pour l'agriculture, ajustement des taux interpolés et extrapolés sur la base des variations des taux interpolés 1984 par rapport aux taux tirés du recensement de 1984; les taux de répartition dans l'industrie et les services ont été évalués sur la base des résultats du recensement de 1984.

**3.2.2 Femmes:**

Méthode, hypothèses et traitements identiques à ceux appliqués aux hommes.

## 4. Projection des taux d'activité: 2000 - 2010

### 4.1 Modèle(s): linéaire et hyperbole

**4.1.1 Hommes:**

- Aux groupes d'âge [10-19], application de la fonction F1;
- Aux groupes d'âge [20+], application de la fonction F3;
- Modification de la tendance du groupe d'âge [20-24].

**4.1.2 Femmes:**

- Aux groupes d'âge [10-19], application de la fonction F1;
- Aux groupes d'âge [20+], application de la fonction F3;
- Modification des tendances des groupes d'âge [15-59].

*Notes sur les ajustements des taux, voir p. 192-195.*      *Notes sur les fonctions de projection, voir p. 198.*

# Fidji

## 1. Source(s) des données de base

Code(s):     Titre(s):

EPPA3        Annuaire des statistiques du travail 1945-89 - Edition rétrospective sur les recensements de population, BIT, Genève, 1990.
STAT         Base de données sur les statistiques du travail - LABORSTA, Bureau de statistique, BIT, Genève.

## 2. Evaluation des taux d'activité: 1950 - 1990

### 2.1 Données de base:

Tableau 1: Taux d'activité par sexe et par groupe d'âge

| Groupe d'âge | Année 1950 (1) | 1960 (1) | 1970 (1) | 1976 (2) | 1986 (2) |
|---|---|---|---|---|---|
| **Hommes** | | | | | |
| 10-14 | 31.00 | 21.00 | 15.00 | 0.00 | 0.00 |
| 15-19 | 86.60 | 75.90 | 65.20 | 56.84 | 57.90 |
| 20-24 | 97.00 | 96.30 | 93.60 | 91.28 | 91.00 |
| 25-29 | 98.85 | 98.00 | 97.20 | 96.34 | 95.97 |
| 30-34 | 98.75 | 98.30 | 97.85 | 97.31 | 97.32 |
| 35-39 | 98.45 | 98.15 | 97.90 | 97.37 | 97.41 |
| 40-44 | 98.55 | 98.10 | 97.60 | 97.35 | 97.57 |
| 45-49 | 97.30 | 97.70 | 96.35 | 95.39 | 95.83 |
| 50-54 | 98.05 | 95.80 | 93.55 | 92.37 | 92.04 |
| 55-59 | 96.00 | 92.65 | 89.30 | 84.94 | 83.71 |
| 60-64 | 91.50 | 86.60 | 81.75 | 76.14 | 71.64 |
| 65+ | 60.70 | 54.55 | 48.40 | 48.41 | 48.42 |
| **Femmes** | | | | | |
| 10-14 | 1.60 | 2.00 | 1.50 | .. | 0.00 |
| 15-19 | 4.05 | 6.30 | 10.85 | .. | 21.40 |
| 20-24 | 5.75 | 9.75 | 17.70 | .. | 29.11 |
| 25-29 | 3.95 | 7.40 | 14.35 | .. | 26.19 |
| 30-34 | 3.05 | 6.35 | 12.90 | .. | 26.32 |
| 35-39 | 2.80 | 5.80 | 11.85 | .. | 25.31 |
| 40-44 | 3.30 | 6.00 | 11.35 | .. | 23.32 |
| 45-49 | 3.20 | 5.65 | 10.50 | .. | 21.32 |
| 50-54 | 2.75 | 5.05 | 9.60 | .. | 19.14 |
| 55-59 | 2.55 | 4.50 | 8.45 | .. | 16.71 |
| 60-64 | 1.45 | 3.10 | 6.40 | .. | 13.53 |
| 65+ | 0.90 | 1.95 | 4.10 | .. | 8.32 |

Source(s): (1) EPPA3; (2) STAT.

### 2.2 Méthode(s): extrapolation linéaire
                   moyenne pondérée

#### 2.2.1 Hommes:

- 1950-70, taux d'activité 1950-70 tirés des EPPA3;
- 1980, moyennes pondérées des taux d'activité tirés des recensements de 1976 et 1986;
- 1990, extrapolation des taux d'activité 1950-1970 tirés des EPPA3, des taux d'activité estimés pour 1980 et des taux d'activité tirés du recensement de 1986.

#### 2.2.2 Femmes:

- 1950-80, taux d'activité 1950-80 tirés des EPPA3;
- 1990, moyennes pondérées des taux d'activité 1980 tirés des EPPA3 et des taux d'activité tirés du recensement de 1986.

## 3. Evaluation des taux de répartition par secteur d'activité: 1950 - 1990

### 3.1 Données de base:

Tableau 2: Répartition de la population active en % par secteur d'activité

| Année | Agriculture | Industrie Total | Manufac. | Services |
|---|---|---|---|---|
| **Hommes** | | | | |
| 1976 | 50.69 | 18.45 | 8.16 | 30.86 |
| 1986 | 52.69 | 15.99 | 7.66 | 31.33 |
| **Femmes** | | | | |
| 1976 | 27.07 | 8.02 | 6.96 | 64.90 |
| 1986 | 28.42 | 11.28 | 10.33 | 60.30 |

Source(s): STAT.

### 3.2 Méthode(s): interpolation et extrapolation linéaires

#### 3.2.1 Hommes:

- 1950-70, taux de répartition 1950-70 tirés des EPPA3;
- 1980, interpolation des taux de répartition tirés des recensements de 1976 et 1986;
- 1990, extrapolation des taux de répartition 1950-70 tirés des EPPA3, des taux estimés pour 1980 et des taux tirés du recensement de 1986;
- Application du rapport manufacture/industrie tiré du recensement de 1986.

#### 3.2.2 Femmes:

Méthode, hypothèses et traitements identiques à ceux appliqués aux hommes.

## 4. Projection des taux d'activité: 2000 - 2010

### 4.1 Modèle(s): linéaire, hyperbole et logistique

#### 4.1.1 Hommes:

- Aux groupes d'âge [15-19] et [30+], application de la fonction F3;
- Aux groupes d'âge [20-29], application de la fonction F1;
- Modification des tendances des groupes d'âge [15-24] et [30-44].

#### 4.1.2 Femmes:

- Aux groupes d'âge [15-19] et [65+], application de la fonction F1;
- Aux groupes d'âge [20-64], application de la fonction F6;
- Modification des tendances des groupes d'âge [20-59].

---

*Notes sur les ajustements des taux, voir p. 192-195.*      *Notes sur les fonctions de projection, voir p. 198.*

# Finlande

## 1. Source(s) des données de base

Code(s):    Titre(s):

EPPA3    Annuaire des statistiques du travail 1945-89 - Edition rétrospective sur les recensements de population, BIT, Genève, 1990.
STAT    Base de données sur les statistiques du travail - LABORSTA, Bureau de statistique, BIT, Genève.

## 2. Evaluation des taux d'activité: 1950 - 1990

### 2.1 Données de base:

Tableau 1: Taux d'activité par sexe et par groupe d'âge

| Groupe d'âge | Année | | |
|---|---|---|---|
| | 1989 | 1990 | 1991 |
| **Hommes** | | | |
| 10-14 | 0.00 | 0.00 | 0.00 |
| 15-19 | 42.21 | 40.26 | 36.94 |
| 20-24 | 81.97 | 80.79 | 79.07 |
| 25-29 | 92.23 | 92.23 | 91.67 |
| 30-34 | 95.48 | 95.43 | 94.87 |
| 35-39 | 95.28 | 94.71 | 94.69 |
| 40-44 | 94.93 | 94.74 | 94.64 |
| 45-49 | 91.95 | 91.50 | 90.53 |
| 50-54 | 86.03 | 84.89 | 84.40 |
| 55-59 | 59.68 | 61.79 | 61.48 |
| 60-64 | 27.83 | 28.21 | 29.66 |
| 65+ | 5.60 | 4.66 | 4.55 |
| **Femmes** | | | |
| 10-14 | 0.00 | 0.00 | 0.00 |
| 15-19 | 36.49 | 38.10 | 32.89 |
| 20-24 | 69.89 | 67.84 | 66.87 |
| 25-29 | 82.16 | 80.98 | 79.89 |
| 30-34 | 85.79 | 83.96 | 82.26 |
| 35-39 | 88.61 | 88.44 | 86.87 |
| 40-44 | 90.82 | 89.86 | 89.67 |
| 45-49 | 89.80 | 89.93 | 90.24 |
| 50-54 | 82.61 | 82.98 | 83.22 |
| 55-59 | 58.85 | 60.77 | 60.47 |
| 60-64 | 22.06 | 19.71 | 20.44 |
| 65+ | 1.88 | 1.62 | 1.61 |

Source(s): STAT.

### 2.2 Méthode(s): moyenne arithmétique

#### 2.2.1 Hommes:

- 1950-80, taux d'activité 1950-80 tirés des EPPA3;
ajustement du taux d'activité du groupe d'âge [15-19] pour 1980;
- 1990, moyennes des taux d'activité tirés des enquêtes de 1989, 1990 et 1991;
ajustement du taux estimé pour le groupe d'âge [15-19].

#### 2.2.2 Femmes:

- 1950-80, taux d'activité 1950-80 tirés des EPPA3;
ajustement du taux d'activité du groupe d'âge [15-19] pour 1980;
- 1990, moyennes des taux d'activité tirés des enquêtes de 1989, 1990 et 1991;
ajustement des taux estimés pour les groupe d'âge [15-24].

## 3. Evaluation des taux de répartition par secteur d'activité: 1950 - 1990

### 3.1 Données de base:

Tableau 2: Répartition de la population active en % par secteur d'activité

| Année | Agriculture | Industrie | | Services |
|---|---|---|---|---|
| | | Total | Manufac. | |
| **Hommes** | | | | |
| 1989 | 10.83 | 42.59 | 23.29 | 46.57 |
| 1990 | 10.12 | 42.84 | 23.34 | 47.05 |
| 1991 | 10.02 | 42.03 | 23.64 | 47.94 |
| **Femmes** | | | | |
| 1989 | 6.28 | 17.77 | 12.89 | 75.95 |
| 1990 | 6.21 | 17.56 | 12.92 | 76.22 |
| 1991 | 6.23 | 16.84 | 13.13 | 76.94 |

Source(s): STAT.

### 3.2 Méthode(s): moyenne arithmétique

#### 3.2.1 Hommes:

- 1950-80, taux de répartition 1950-80 tirés des EPPA3;
le taux de répartition 1980 de manufacture a été ajusté sur la base
de l'application aux taux de 1980 de l'industrie du rapport moyen
manufacture/industrie tiré des enquêtes de 1979, 1980 et 1981;
- 1990, moyennes des taux de répartition tirés des enquêtes de 1989,
1990 et 1991.

#### 3.2.2 Femmes:

Méthode, hypothèses et traitements identiques à ceux appliqués aux hommes.

## 4. Projection des taux d'activité: 2000 - 2010

### 4.1 Modèle(s): linéaire, hyperbole et logistique

#### 4.1.1 Hommes:

- Aux groupes d'âge [15-19] et [30+], application de la fonction F3;
- Aux groupes d'âge [20-29], application de la fonction F1;
- Modification des tendances des groupes d'âge [45-59].

#### 4.1.2 Femmes:

- Aux groupes d'âge [15-29], application de la fonction F1;
- Aux groupes d'âge [30-59], application de la fonction F6;
- Aux groupes d'âge [60+], application de la fonction F3;
- Modification des tendances des groupes d'âge [20-59].

---

*Notes sur les ajustements des taux, voir p. 192-195.*    *Notes sur les fonctions de projection, voir p. 198.*

# France

## 1. Source(s) des données de base

**Code(s):** **Titre(s):**

EPPA3    Annuaire des statistiques du travail 1945-89 - Edition rétrospective sur les recensements de population, BIT, Genève, 1990.
STAT     Base de données sur les statistiques du travail - LABORSTA, Bureau de statistique, BIT, Genève.

## 2. Evaluation des taux d'activité: 1950 - 1990

### 2.1 Données de base:

Tableau 1: Taux d'activité par sexe et par groupe d'âge

| Groupe d'âge | 1979 | 1980 | 1981 | 1989 | 1990 | 1991 |
|---|---|---|---|---|---|---|
| **Hommes** | | | | | | |
| 10-14 | 0.00 | 0.00 | 0.00 | 0.00 | 0.00 | 0.00 |
| 15-19 | 26.50 | 25.70 | 24.30 | 14.90 | 14.60 | 12.20 |
| 20-24 | 81.10 | 80.10 | 78.10 | 69.30 | 65.00 | 62.10 |
| 25-29 | 95.40 | 95.40 | 94.90 | 94.40 | 94.00 | 93.90 |
| 30-34 | 98.10 | 98.10 | 98.00 | 97.20 | 96.80 | 96.80 |
| 35-39 | 98.10 | 98.30 | 97.90 | 97.30 | 97.00 | 97.20 |
| 40-44 | 97.60 | 97.60 | 97.60 | 97.20 | 97.00 | 96.80 |
| 45-49 | 95.60 | 96.60 | 96.40 | 95.50 | 96.10 | 95.60 |
| 50-54 | 93.00 | 92.90 | 92.40 | 90.10 | 90.00 | 89.40 |
| 55-59 | 82.30 | 81.00 | 79.80 | 68.10 | 67.70 | 68.60 |
| 60-64 | 45.30 | 47.90 | 43.10 | 24.20 | 22.80 | 19.70 |
| 65+ | 6.80 | 6.00 | 5.30 | 3.51 | 2.77 | 2.60 |
| **Femmes** | | | | | | |
| 10-14 | 0.00 | 0.00 | 0.00 | 0.00 | 0.00 | 0.00 |
| 15-19 | 20.00 | 18.40 | 17.30 | 9.40 | 8.10 | 6.80 |
| 20-24 | 68.90 | 68.00 | 67.50 | 59.90 | 57.60 | 54.00 |
| 25-29 | 70.10 | 70.50 | 70.30 | 76.40 | 77.70 | 78.10 |
| 30-34 | 66.50 | 66.90 | 67.70 | 73.50 | 74.60 | 74.50 |
| 35-39 | 63.70 | 65.00 | 66.90 | 73.50 | 73.10 | 74.70 |
| 40-44 | 61.30 | 63.00 | 64.80 | 74.10 | 75.40 | 76.10 |
| 45-49 | 59.20 | 59.10 | 59.30 | 69.00 | 69.10 | 71.30 |
| 50-54 | 53.80 | 55.40 | 57.20 | 62.10 | 62.70 | 64.40 |
| 55-59 | 46.60 | 47.80 | 47.20 | 44.60 | 45.30 | 45.40 |
| 60-64 | 24.60 | 27.60 | 26.00 | 17.60 | 17.00 | 16.00 |
| 65+ | 3.7 | 2.9 | 2.6 | 1.72 | 1.53 | 1.36 |

**Source(s):** STAT.

### 2.2 Méthode(s): moyenne pondérée

#### 2.2.1 Hommes:

- 1950-70, taux d'activité 1950-70 tirés des EPPA3;
- 1980, moyennes pondérées des taux d'activité tirés des enquêtes de 1979, 1980 et 1981;
- 1990, moyennes pondérées des taux d'activité tirés des enquêtes de 1989, 1990 et 1991.

#### 2.2.2 Femmes:

Méthode, hypothèses et traitements identiques à ceux appliqués aux hommes.

## 3. Evaluation des taux de répartition par secteur d'activité: 1950 - 1990

### 3.1 Données de base:

Tableau 2: Répartition de la population active en % par secteur d'activité

| Année | Agriculture | Industrie Total | Manufac. | Services |
|---|---|---|---|---|
| **Hommes** | | | | |
| 1979 | 9.11 | 43.36 | .. | 47.53 |
| 1980 | 8.86 | 43.16 | .. | 47.98 |
| 1981 | 8.60 | 42.65 | .. | 48.75 |
| 1989 | 6.45 | 37.49 | .. | 56.06 |
| 1990 | 6.23 | 38.13 | .. | 55.63 |
| 1991 | 6.10 | 37.79 | .. | 56.11 |
| **Femmes** | | | | |
| 1979 | 7.67 | 22.56 | .. | 69.78 |
| 1980 | 7.35 | 22.18 | .. | 70.47 |
| 1981 | 7.08 | 21.31 | .. | 71.62 |
| 1989 | 4.83 | 17.22 | .. | 77.95 |
| 1990 | 4.51 | 17.14 | .. | 78.35 |
| 1991 | 4.15 | 16.73 | .. | 79.12 |

**Source(s):** STAT.

### 3.2 Méthode(s): moyenne arithmétique

#### 3.2.1 Hommes:

- 1950-70, taux de répartition 1950-70 tirés des EPPA3;
- 1980, moyennes des taux de répartition tirés des enquêtes de 1979, 1980 et 1981;
- 1990, moyennes des taux de répartition tirés des enquêtes de 1989, 1990 et 1991.

#### 3.2.2 Femmes:

Méthode, hypothèses et traitements identiques à ceux appliqués aux hommes.

## 4. Projection des taux d'activité: 2000 - 2010

### 4.1 Modèle(s): linéaire, hyperbole et logistique

#### 4.1.1 Hommes:

- A tous les groupes d'âge, application de la fonction F3;
- Modification des tendances des groupes d'âge [20-24] et [30-44].

#### 4.1.2 Femmes:

- Aux groupes d'âge [15-24] et [60+], application de la fonction F3;
- Aux groupes d'âge [25-54], application de la fonction F6;
- Au groupe d'âge [55-59], application de la fonction F1;
- Modification des tendances des groupes d'âge [15-59].

*Notes sur les ajustements des taux, voir p. 192-195.*        *Notes sur les fonctions de projection, voir p. 198.*

# Gabon

## 1. Source(s) des données de base

**Code(s):** **Titre(s):**

EPPA3 Evaluations et projections de la population active 1950-2025 - troisième édition, BIT, Genève, 1986.

## 2. Evaluation des taux d'activité: 1950 - 1990

### 2.1 Données de base:

Tableau 1: Taux d'activité par sexe et par groupe d'âge

| Groupe d'âge | Année 1950 | 1960 | 1970 | 1980 |
|---|---|---|---|---|
| **Hommes** | | | | |
| 10-14 | 38.90 | 36.60 | 33.60 | 31.85 |
| 15-19 | 48.35 | 46.00 | 43.00 | 41.25 |
| 20-24 | 91.10 | 89.65 | 87.75 | 86.60 |
| 25-29 | 96.20 | 96.00 | 95.70 | 95.55 |
| 30-34 | 97.25 | 97.00 | 96.70 | 96.50 |
| 35-39 | 97.25 | 97.00 | 96.65 | 96.45 |
| 40-44 | 97.30 | 97.00 | 96.65 | 96.45 |
| 45-49 | 95.35 | 95.10 | 94.80 | 94.60 |
| 50-54 | 94.35 | 94.00 | 93.55 | 93.30 |
| 55-59 | 92.25 | 91.70 | 91.00 | 90.55 |
| 60-64 | 81.85 | 81.00 | 79.90 | 79.25 |
| 65+ | 72.70 | 71.15 | 69.10 | 67.90 |
| **Femmes** | | | | |
| 10-14 | 41.10 | 40.40 | 39.10 | 37.75 |
| 15-19 | 66.55 | 65.50 | 63.60 | 61.55 |
| 20-24 | 65.80 | 65.10 | 63.90 | 62.65 |
| 25-29 | 71.00 | 70.25 | 68.85 | 67.40 |
| 30-34 | 75.45 | 74.65 | 73.20 | 71.65 |
| 35-39 | 76.55 | 75.80 | 74.45 | 73.00 |
| 40-44 | 79.00 | 78.25 | 76.90 | 75.40 |
| 45-49 | 78.55 | 77.80 | 76.40 | 74.90 |
| 50-54 | 77.45 | 76.55 | 74.95 | 73.20 |
| 55-59 | 74.75 | 73.85 | 72.15 | 70.35 |
| 60-64 | 69.35 | 68.20 | 66.05 | 63.75 |
| 65+ | 49.10 | 48.00 | 46.00 | 43.90 |

**Source(s):** EPPA3.

### 2.2 Méthode(s): interpolation et extrapolation linéaires

#### 2.2.1 Hommes:

- 1950 et 1970-90, interpolation et extrapolation des taux d'activité 1950-80 tirés des EPPA3;
ajustement des taux interpolés et extrapolés sur la base des variations des taux interpolés 1960 par rapport aux taux 1960 tirés des EPPA3; modification des tendances des groupes d'âge [10-14], [25-49] et [65+] pour 1980 et 1990;
- 1960, taux d'activité 1960 tirés des EPPA3.

#### 2.2.2 Femmes:

- 1960, taux d'activité tirés des EPPA3;
- 1950 et 1970-90, interpolation et extrapolation des taux d'activité 1950-80 tirés des EPPA3;
ajustement des taux interpolés et extrapolés sur la base des variations des taux interpolés 1960 par rapport aux taux 1960 des EPPA3; modification des tendances de tous les groupes d'âge pour 1950 et des groupes d'âge [30+] pour 1970 et 1980.

## 3. Evaluation des taux de répartition par secteur d'activité: 1950 - 1990

### 3.1 Données de base:

Tableau 2: Répartition de la population active en % par secteur d'activité

| Année | Agriculture | Industrie Total | Manufac. | Services |
|---|---|---|---|---|
| **Hommes** | | | | |
| 1950 | 84.00 | 8.40 | .. | 7.60 |
| 1960 | 78.50 | 11.00 | .. | 10.50 |
| 1970 | 71.40 | 14.60 | .. | 14.00 |
| **Femmes** | | | | |
| 1950 | 97.50 | 0.35 | .. | 2.15 |
| 1960 | 95.00 | 0.70 | .. | 4.30 |
| 1970 | 92.00 | 1.40 | .. | 6.60 |

**Source(s):** (1) EPPA3.

### 3.2 Méthode(s): moyenne pondérée

#### 3.2.1 Hommes:

- 1950-70, taux de répartition 1950-70 tirés des EPPA3;
- 1980, moyennes pondérées des taux de répartition 1970 tirés des EPPA3 et des taux estimés pour 1990;
- 1990, extrapolation des taux de répartition 1950-70 tirés des EPPA3; modification des tendances de tous les secteurs.

#### 3.2.2 Femmes:

Méthode, hypothèses et traitements identiques à ceux appliqués aux hommes.

## 4. Projection des taux d'activité: 2000 - 2010

### 4.1 Modèle(s): linéaire et hyperbole

#### 4.1.1 Hommes:

- Aux groupes d'âge [10-19] et [65+], application de la fonction F1;
- Aux groupes d'âge [20-64], application de la fonction F3;
- Modification de la tendance du groupe d'âge [10-14].

#### 4.1.2 Femmes:

- Au groupe d'âge [10-14], application de la fonction F1;
- Aux groupes d'âge [15+], application de la fonction F3;
- Modification des tendances des groupes d'âge [15-64].

*Notes sur les ajustements des taux, voir p. 192-195.*

*Notes sur les fonctions de projection, voir p. 198.*

# Gambie

## 1. Source(s) des données de base

Code(s):    Titre(s):

EPPA3    Evaluations et projections de la population active 1950-2025 - troisième édition, BIT, Genève, 1986.
ASTER    Annuaire des statistiques du travail 1945-89 - Edition rétrospective sur les recensements de population, BIT, Genève, 1990.

## 2. Evaluation des taux d'activité: 1950 - 1990

### 2.1 Données de base:

Tableau 1: Taux d'activité par sexe et par groupe d'âge

| Groupe d'âge | Année 1950 (1) | 1960 (1) | 1970 (1) | 1980 (1) | 1983 (2) |
|---|---|---|---|---|---|
| **Hommes** | | | | | |
| 10-14 | 50.70 | 49.70 | 48.35 | 46.55 | .. |
| 15-19 | 83.00 | 81.70 | 79.95 | 77.55 | .. |
| 20-24 | 94.55 | 94.05 | 93.35 | 92.45 | .. |
| 25-29 | 97.30 | 97.20 | 97.10 | 97.00 | .. |
| 30-34 | 98.00 | 97.95 | 97.80 | 97.65 | .. |
| 35-39 | 98.20 | 98.10 | 97.95 | 97.80 | .. |
| 40-44 | 98.00 | 97.90 | 97.80 | 97.60 | .. |
| 45-49 | 97.25 | 97.20 | 97.10 | 96.95 | .. |
| 50-54 | 96.80 | 96.65 | 96.50 | 96.30 | .. |
| 55-59 | 95.80 | 95.60 | 95.35 | 95.00 | .. |
| 60-64 | 92.65 | 92.35 | 91.90 | 91.30 | .. |
| 65+ | 79.10 | 78.55 | 77.80 | 76.75 | .. |
| **Femmes** | | | | | |
| 10-14 | 38.30 | 37.55 | 36.55 | 35.20 | 41.91 |
| 15-19 | 62.35 | 61.25 | 59.75 | 57.70 | 61.89 |
| 20-24 | 63.15 | 62.45 | 61.50 | 60.20 | 68.30 |
| 25-29 | 67.95 | 67.20 | 66.10 | 64.65 | 71.14 |
| 30-34 | 72.25 | 71.40 | 70.25 | 68.65 | 73.90 |
| 35-39 | 73.55 | 72.75 | 71.70 | 70.2 | 74.58 |
| 40-44 | 76.00 | 75.20 | 74.10 | 72.65 | 77.22 |
| 45-49 | 75.50 | 74.70 | 73.60 | 72.1 | 75.31 |
| 50-54 | 73.90 | 72.95 | 71.70 | 69.95 | 73.86 |
| 55-59 | 71.05 | 70.10 | 68.75 | 66.95 | 72.41 |
| 60-64 | 64.65 | 63.40 | 61.70 | 59.45 | 71.49 |
| 65+ | 44.70 | 43.55 | 42.00 | 39.85 | 60.74 |

Source(s): (1) EPPA3; (2) ASTER.

### 2.2 Méthode(s): interpolation et extrapolation linéaires

**2.2.1 Hommes:**

- 1950-80, taux d'activité 1950-80 tirés des EPPA3;
- 1990, extrapolation des taux d'activité 1950-1980 tirés des EPPA3;
ajustement des taux extrapolés 1990 sur la base des variations des taux
interpolés 1980 par rapport aux taux 1980 tirés des EPPA3;
modification des tendances des groupes d'âge [10-14], [15-24] et [65+] pour 199(

**2.2.2 Femmes:**

- 1950-90, interpolation et extrapolation des taux d'activité 1950-80 tirés
des EPPA3;
ajustement des taux interpolés et extrapolés sur la base des variations
des taux extrapolés 1983 par rapport aux taux tirés du recensement de 1983;
modification des tendances de tous les groupes d'âge pour 1970 et 1980
et des groupes d'âge [10-14] et [60-64] pour 1990.

## 3. Evaluation des taux de répartition par secteur d'activité: 1950 - 1990

### 3.1 Données de base:

Tableau 2: Répartition de la population active en % par secteur d'activité

| Année | Agriculture | Industrie Total | Manufac. | Services |
|---|---|---|---|---|
| **Hommes** | | | | |
| 1950 | 85.00 | 6.60 | .. | 8.40 |
| 1960 | 83.20 | 7.40 | .. | 9.40 |
| 1970 | 80.75 | 8.50 | .. | 10.75 |
| 1980 | 77.45 | 10.00 | .. | 12.55 |
| **Femmes** | | | | |
| 1950 | 97.00 | 1.00 | .. | 2.00 |
| 1960 | 96.00 | 1.30 | .. | 2.70 |
| 1970 | 94.50 | 1.80 | .. | 3.70 |
| 1980 | 93.00 | 2.30 | .. | 4.70 |

Source(s): EPPA3.

### 3.2 Méthode(s): extrapolation linéaire

**3.2.1 Hommes:**

- 1950-80, taux de répartition 1950-80 tirés des EPPA3;
- 1990, extrapolation des taux de répartition 1950-80 tirés des EPPA3;
ajustement des taux extrapolés 1990 sur la base des variations des taux
interpolés 1980 par rapport aux taux 1980 tirés des EPPA3;
- Application des rapports manufacture/industrie observés au Niger.

**3.2.2 Femmes:**

Méthode, hypothèses et traitements identiques à ceux appliqués aux hommes.

## 4. Projection des taux d'activité: 2000 - 2010

### 4.1 Modèle(s): linéaire et hyperbole

**4.1.1 Hommes:**

- A tous les groupes d'âge, application de la fonction F1;
- Modification des tendances des groupes d'âge [10-19].

**4.1.2 Femmes:**

- Aux groupes d'âge [10-19], application de la fonction F1;
- Aux groupes d'âge [20+], application de la fonction F3;
- Modification des tendances des groupes d'âge [20-59].

*Notes sur les ajustements des taux, voir p. 192-195.*    *Notes sur les fonctions de projection, voir p. 198.*

# Géorgie

## 1. Source(s) des données de base

Code(s):     Titre(s):

BLT-94-2     Vorobiev A. (1994), "Estimation de la population active pour les quinze pays de l'ex-URSS pour les années 1950, 1959, 1970, 1979 et 1989", dans le Bulletin des statistiques du travail - 1994-2, BIT, Genève.

## 2. Evaluation des taux d'activité: 1950 - 1990

### 2.1 Données de base:

Tableau 1: Taux d'activité par sexe et par groupe d'âge

| Groupe d'âge | Année | | | | |
|---|---|---|---|---|---|
| | 1950 | 1959 | 1970 | 1979 | 1989 |
| **Hommes** | | | | | |
| 10-14 | 0.00 | 0.00 | 0.00 | 0.00 | 0.00 |
| 15-19 | 50.56 | 51.53 | 32.51 | 34.40 | 29.36 |
| 20-24 | 82.02 | 81.62 | 82.76 | 80.60 | 74.38 |
| 25-29 | 92.13 | 91.38 | 85.83 | 94.77 | 47.79 |
| 30-34 | 93.83 | 94.19 | 96.84 | 97.64 | 96.02 |
| 35-39 | 92.63 | 94.32 | 96.41 | 97.18 | 96.55 |
| 40-44 | 92.94 | 93.15 | 96.05 | 96.67 | 95.20 |
| 45-49 | 91.55 | 91.67 | 90.63 | 95.57 | 93.53 |
| 50-54 | 90.91 | 89.19 | 89.06 | 90.91 | 90.85 |
| 55-59 | 86.79 | 87.10 | 83.33 | 82.43 | 84.40 |
| 60-64 | 78.00 | 86.79 | 71.01 | 50.00 | 55.38 |
| 65+ | 42.06 | 41.83 | 14.09 | 18.90 | 25.95 |
| **Femmes** | | | | | |
| 10-14 | 0.00 | 0.00 | 0.00 | 0.00 | 0.00 |
| 15-19 | 42.86 | 42.20 | 31.12 | 35.86 | 27.23 |
| 20-24 | 56.68 | 56.28 | 59.87 | 75.35 | 59.05 |
| 25-29 | 62.69 | 62.50 | 83.22 | 86.17 | 70.54 |
| 30-34 | 62.18 | 61.46 | 80.00 | 89.29 | 75.93 |
| 35-39 | 62.39 | 64.18 | 81.03 | 90.30 | 80.85 |
| 40-44 | 64.08 | 65.22 | 80.75 | 90.77 | 82.35 |
| 45-49 | 62.93 | 63.16 | 82.17 | 88.55 | 81.01 |
| 50-54 | 53.49 | 57.14 | 73.27 | 81.61 | 75.27 |
| 55-59 | 48.81 | 50.00 | 40.00 | 48.03 | 50.31 |
| 60-64 | 42.50 | 48.15 | 22.94 | 23.64 | 34.13 |
| 65+ | 18.56 | 17.61 | 6.44 | 6.83 | 12.19 |

Source(s): BLT-94-2-2

### 2.2 Méthode(s): moyenne pondérée

#### 2.2.1 Hommes:

- 1950-90, moyennes pondérées des taux d'activité 1950, 1959, 1970 et 1989 tirés du Bulletin des statistiques du travail, 1994-2.

#### 2.2.2 Femmes:

Méthode, hypothèses et traitements identiques à ceux appliqués aux hommes.

## 3. Evaluation des taux de répartition par secteur d'activité: 1950 - 1990

### 3.1 Données de base:

Tableau 2: Répartition de la population active en % par secteur d'activité

| Année | Agriculture | Industrie | | Services |
|---|---|---|---|---|
| | | Total | Manufac. | |
| **Hommes** | | | | |
| 1950 | 57.65 | 20.56 | 11.87 | 21.79 |
| 1959 | 44.18 | 24.26 | 13.51 | 31.56 |
| 1970 | 33.73 | 30.71 | 18.97 | 35.56 |
| 1979 | 31.08 | 31.55 | 17.93 | 37.37 |
| 1989 | 27.91 | 37.42 | 21.17 | 34.66 |
| **Femmes** | | | | |
| 1950 | 66.85 | 11.14 | 8.04 | 22.00 |
| 1959 | 45.51 | 18.58 | 9.12 | 35.91 |
| 1970 | 40.85 | 19.98 | 17.01 | 39.17 |
| 1979 | 35.46 | 20.48 | 17.45 | 44.06 |
| 1989 | 25.83 | 23.01 | 19.04 | 51.16 |

Source(s): BLT-94-2.

### 3.2 Méthode(s): moyenne pondérée

#### 3.2.1 Hommes:

- 1950-90, moyennes pondérées des taux de répartition 1950, 1959, 1970, 1979 et 1989 tirés du Bulletin des statistiques du travail 1994-2.

#### 3.2.2 Femmes:

Méthode, hypothèses et traitements identiques à ceux appliqués aux hommes.

## 4. Projection des taux d'activité: 2000 - 2010

### 4.1 Modèle(s): linéaire, hyperbole et logistique

#### 4.1.1 Hommes:

- Aux groupes d'âge [15-24] et [55+], application de la fonction F3;
- Aux groupes d'âge [25-54], application de la fonction F1;
- Modification des tendances des groupes d'âge [20-54].

#### 4.1.2 Femmes:

- Aux groupes d'âge [15-19] et [55+], application de la fonction F3;
- Aux groupes d'âge [20-24] et [50-54], application de la fonction F1;
- Aux groupes d'âge [25-49], application de la fonction F6;
- Modification de la tendance du groupe d'âge [50-54].

*Notes sur les ajustements des taux, voir p. 192-195.*

*Notes sur les fonctions de projection, voir p. 198.*

# Ghana

## 1. Source(s) des données de base

Code(s):    Titre(s):

EPPA3      Evaluations et projections de la population active 1950-2025 - troisième édition, BIT, Genève, 1986.
ADNU64     Annuaire démographique 1964 - Statistiques des recensements de population III, seizième édition, Nations Unies, New York, 1965.
ASTER      Annuaire des statistiques du travail 1945-89 - Edition rétrospective sur les recensements de population, BIT, Genève, 1990.

## 2. Evaluation des taux d'activité: 1950 - 1990

### 2.1 Données de base:

Tableau 1: Taux d'activité par sexe et par groupe d'âge

|              | Année |        |        |        |
|--------------|-------|--------|--------|--------|
| Groupe d'âge | 1950 (1) | 1960 (2) | 1970 (3) | 1984 (3) |
| **Hommes**   |       |        |        |        |
| 10-14        | 27.80 | 0.00   | 0.00   | 0.00   |
| 15-19        | 63.40 | 61.49  | 42.31  | 42.10  |
| 20-24        | 90.00 | 91.00  | 82.60  | 82.51  |
| 25-29        | 97.25 | 96.48  | 95.53  | 95.52  |
| 30-34        | 98.25 | 97.50  | 97.52  | 97.52  |
| 35-39        | 98.35 | 97.54  | 97.93  | 97.93  |
| 40-44        | 98.15 | 97.34  | 97.82  | 97.83  |
| 45-49        | 97.75 | 96.92  | 97.52  | 97.52  |
| 50-54        | 96.75 | 96.03  | 96.57  | 96.58  |
| 55-59        | 96.00 | 93.73  | 95.23  | 95.25  |
| 60-64        | 95.20 | 89.12  | 91.61  | 91.64  |
| 65+          | 82.00 | 71.52  | 75.41  | 75.45  |
| **Femmes**   |       |        |        |        |
| 10-14        | ..    | ...    | ..     | ...    |
| 15-19        | ..    | 53.71  | ..     | 64.59  |
| 20-24        | ..    | 52.32  | ..     | 83.94  |
| 25-29        | ..    | 51.50  | ..     | 86.62  |
| 30-34        | ..    | 57.05  | ..     | 88.96  |
| 35-39        | ..    | 59.32  | ..     | 90.91  |
| 40-44        | ..    | 65.35  | ..     | 91.26  |
| 45-49        | ..    | 67.00  | ..     | 91.73  |
| 50-54        | ..    | 69.63  | ..     | 90.95  |
| 55-59        | ..    | 70.61  | ..     | 89.53  |
| 60-64        | ..    | 64.03  | ..     | 85.66  |
| 65+          | ..    | 43.20  | ..     | 73.57  |

Source(s): (1) EPPA3; (2) ASTER et ADNU64; (3) ASTER.

### 2.2 Méthode(s): interpolation et extrapolation linéaires
moyenne pondérée

#### 2.2.1 Hommes:

- 1950-90, interpolation et extrapolation des taux d'activité tirés des recensements de 1960 et 1984;
aux taux 1950 tirés des EPPA3, application des variations des taux extrapolés 19 par rapport aux taux du recensement de 1960;
- 1960-90, moyennes pondérées des taux d'activité tirés des recensements de 1960 et 1984.

#### 2.2.2 Femmes:

- 1950-90, interpolation et extrapolation des taux d'activité tirés des recensements de 1960 et 1984;
modification des tendances des groupes d'âge [60+] pour 1950 à 1990, des groupes d'âge [10-59] pour 1950 et des [10-19] pour 1980 et 1990.

## 3. Evaluation des taux de répartition par secteur d'activité: 1950 - 1990

### 3.1 Données de base:

Tableau 2: Répartition de la population active en % par secteur d'activité

|            | Agriculture | Industrie |         | Services |
|------------|-------------|-----------|---------|----------|
| Année      |             | Total     | Manufac.|          |
| **Hommes** |             |           |         |          |
| 1960 (1)   | 65.42       | 17.16     | 8.27    | 17.42    |
| 1984 (2)   | 66.36       | 11.30     | 7.52    | 22.33    |
| **Femmes** |             |           |         |          |
| 1960 (1)   | 58.26       | 10.56     | 10.01   | 31.18    |
| 1984 (2)   | 56.04       | 14.26     | 14.00   | 29.70    |

Source(s): (1) ADNU64; (2) ASTER.

### 3.2 Méthode(s): moyenne pondérée

#### 3.2.1 Hommes:

- 1950-60, taux de répartition 1950-60 tirés des EPPA3;
- 1980, moyennes pondérées des taux de répartition 1960 et 1984 tirés des EPPA3 et du recensement de 1984;
- 1970, moyennes des estimations pour 1960 et 1980;
- 1990, estimation basée sur une diminution de 0.25 point par année dans l'agriculture; la différence a été attribuée aux services.

#### 3.2.2 Femmes:

- 1950-70, taux de répartition 1950-70 tirés des EPPA3;
- 1980, moyennes pondérées des taux de répartition 1960 et 1984 tirés des EPPA3 et du recensement de 1984;
- 1990, extrapolation des taux estimés 1970 et 1980.

## 4. Projection des taux d'activité: 2000 - 2010

### 4.1 Modèle(s): linéaire et hyperbole

#### 4.1.1 Hommes:

- Aux groupes d'âge [10-59], application de la fonction F1;
- Aux groupes d'âge [60+], application de la fonction F3;
- Modification des tendances des groupes d'âge [15-59].

#### 4.1.2 Femmes:

- A tous les groupes d'âge, application de la fonction F1;
- Modification des tendances des groupes d'âge [15+].

*Notes sur les ajustements des taux, voir p. 192-195.*          *Notes sur les fonctions de projection, voir p. 198.*

# Grèce

## 1. Source(s) des données de base

| Code(s): | Titre(s): |
|---|---|
| EPPA3 | Annuaire des statistiques du travail 1945-89 - Edition rétrospective sur les recensements de population, BIT, Genève, 1990. |
| STAT | Base de données sur les statistiques du travail - LABORSTA, Bureau de statistique, BIT, Genève. |

## 2. Evaluation des taux d'activité: 1950 - 1990

### 2.1 Données de base:

Tableau 1: Taux d'activité par sexe et par groupe d'âge

| Groupe d'âge | Année | | | | |
|---|---|---|---|---|---|
| | 1970 (1) | 1981 (2) | 1989 (2) | 1990 (2) | 1991 (2) |
| **Hommes** | | | | | |
| 10-14 | .. | .. | 0.00 | 0.00 | 0.00 |
| 15-19 | .. | .. | 20.00 | 19.10 | 18.60 |
| 20-24 | .. | .. | 72.00 | 70.40 | 68.30 |
| 25-29 | .. | .. | 94.30 | 93.70 | 92.30 |
| 30-34 | .. | .. | 97.20 | 96.70 | 96.50 |
| 35-39 | .. | .. | 97.10 | 97.30 | 97.00 |
| 40-44 | .. | .. | 96.70 | 96.30 | 96.10 |
| 45-49 | .. | .. | 94.50 | 94.00 | 93.90 |
| 50-54 | .. | .. | 86.90 | 87.70 | 86.40 |
| 55-59 | .. | .. | 73.50 | 72.30 | 71.50 |
| 60-64 | .. | .. | 48.10 | 46.00 | 45.60 |
| 65+ | .. | .. | 11.70 | 11.80 | 11.00 |
| **Femmes** | | | | | |
| 10-14 | 6.50 | 3.04 | 0.00 | 0.00 | 0.00 |
| 15-19 | 28.10 | 23.24 | 15.40 | 15.60 | 14.10 |
| 20-24 | 36.00 | 39.02 | 53.90 | 54.00 | 53.00 |
| 25-29 | 31.85 | 37.50 | 59.10 | 60.20 | 58.70 |
| 30-34 | 29.80 | 33.56 | 58.40 | 58.50 | 55.70 |
| 35-39 | 29.70 | 30.82 | 57.10 | 57.10 | 54.20 |
| 40-44 | 29.55 | 30.64 | 50.00 | 49.90 | 49.10 |
| 45-49 | 27.35 | 28.80 | 45.60 | 45.40 | 41.30 |
| 50-54 | 25.40 | 25.77 | 38.90 | 37.80 | 34.70 |
| 55-59 | 21.95 | 19.91 | 30.20 | 28.50 | 26.60 |
| 60-64 | 16.40 | 13.38 | 19.60 | 19.90 | 15.90 |
| 65+ | 8.20 | 4.96 | 4.1 | 4.5 | 3.9 |

Source(s): (1) EPPA3; (2) STAT.

### 2.2 Méthode(s): moyenne pondérée
moyenne arithmétique

#### 2.2.1 Hommes:

- 1950-80, taux d'activité 1950-80 tirés des EPPA3;
- 1990, moyennes ajustées des taux d'activité tirés des enquêtes de 1989, 1990 et 1991;
ajustement des taux d'activité 1990 estimés pour les groupes d'âge [15-29] pour tenir compte des militaires du contingent.

#### 2.2.2 Femmes:

- 1950-70, taux d'activité 1950-70 tirés des EPPA3;
- 1980, moyennes pondérées des taux d'activité 1970 tirés des EPPA3 et des taux d'activité tirés du recensement de 1981;
- 1990, moyennes des taux d'activité tirés des enquêtes de 1989, 1990 et 1991;
ajustement du taux d'activité estimé du groupe d'âge [15-19] pour 1990.

## 3. Evaluation des taux de répartition par secteur d'activité: 1950 - 1990

### 3.1 Données de base:

Tableau 2: Répartition de la population active en % par secteur d'activité

| Année | Agriculture | Industrie | | Services |
|---|---|---|---|---|
| | | Total | Manufac. | |
| **Hommes** | | | | |
| 1981 | 27.46 | 34.29 | 19.52 | 38.24 |
| 1989 | 21.22 | 33.28 | 21.06 | 45.50 |
| 1990 | 20.19 | 33.60 | 20.98 | 46.21 |
| 1991 | 19.56 | 33.00 | 20.65 | 47.44 |
| **Femmes** | | | | |
| 1981 | 32.69 | 21.19 | 20.23 | 46.12 |
| 1989 | 31.39 | 18.22 | 17.51 | 50.39 |
| 1990 | 29.52 | 18.11 | 17.26 | 52.37 |
| 1991 | 25.85 | 18.53 | 17.67 | 55.63 |

Source(s): STAT.

### 3.2 Méthode(s): moyenne arithmétique

#### 3.2.1 Hommes:

- 1950-80, taux de répartition 1950-80 tirés des EPPA3;
- Application du rapport manufacture/industrie tiré du recensement de 1981;
- 1990, moyennes ajustées des taux de répartition tirés des enquêtes de 1989, 1990 et 1991;
ajustement des taux pour tenir compte des militaires du contingent.

#### 3.2.2 Femmes:

Méthode, hypothèses et traitements identiques à ceux appliqués aux hommes.

## 4. Projection des taux d'activité: 2000 - 2010

### 4.1 Modèle(s): linéaire, hyperbole et logistique

#### 4.1.1 Hommes:

- Aux groupes d'âge [15-19] et [35+], application de la fonction F1;
- Aux groupes d'âge [20-34], application de la fonction F3;
- Modification des tendances des groupes d'âge [25-34].

#### 4.1.2 Femmes:

- Aux groupes d'âge [15-19] et [60+], application de la fonction F3;
- Au groupe d'âge [20-24], application de la fonction F1;
- Aux groupes d'âge [25-59], application de la fonction F6;
- Modification des tendances des groupes d'âge [15-19] et [50-64].

*Notes sur les ajustements des taux, voir p. 192-195.*

*Notes sur les fonctions de projection, voir p. 198.*

# Guadeloupe

## 1. Source(s) des données de base

| Code(s): | Titre(s): |
|---|---|
| EPPA3 | Evaluations et projections de la population active 1950-2025 - troisième édition, BIT, Genève, 1986. |
| ADNU | Editions de 1984 et 1988 de l'Annuaire démographique des Nations Unies, New York. |
| ASTER | Annuaire des statistiques du travail 1945-89 - Edition rétrospective sur les recensements de population, BIT, Genève, 1990. |
| STAT | Base de données sur les statistiques du travail - LABORSTA, Bureau de statistique, BIT, Genève. |

## 2. Evaluation des taux d'activité: 1950 - 1990

### 2.1 Données de base:

Tableau 1: Taux d'activité par sexe et par groupe d'âge

| Groupe d'âge | Année 1974 (1) | 1982 (1) | 1990 (2) |
|---|---|---|---|
| **Hommes** | | | |
| 10-14 | 0.00 | 0.00 | 0.00 |
| 15-19 | 37.26 | 24.12 | 18.31 |
| 20-24 | 76.83 | 83.50 | 75.69 |
| 25-29 | 94.73 | 93.44 | 92.49 |
| 30-34 | 94.75 | 95.55 | 94.06 |
| 35-39 | 94.45 | 96.11 | 93.24 |
| 40-44 | 93.58 | 94.92 | 93.05 |
| 45-49 | 90.96 | 93.32 | 91.83 |
| 50-54 | 87.31 | 90.56 | 85.04 |
| 55-59 | 79.94 | 83.11 | 72.60 |
| 60-64 | 53.03 | 52.34 | 37.50 |
| 65+ | 15.74 | 10.05 | 5.53 |
| **Femmes** | | | |
| 10-14 | 0.00 | 0.00 | 0.00 |
| 15-19 | 29.22 | 15.38 | 12.61 |
| 20-24 | 65.18 | 66.74 | 67.66 |
| 25-29 | 59.27 | 69.70 | 81.48 |
| 30-34 | 54.17 | 66.91 | 77.61 |
| 35-39 | 50.35 | 64.85 | 75.88 |
| 40-44 | 48.67 | 61.47 | 73.45 |
| 45-49 | 47.66 | 57.07 | 68.10 |
| 50-54 | 45.48 | 51.48 | 59.11 |
| 55-59 | 40.89 | 46.70 | 45.79 |
| 60-64 | 24.93 | 25.34 | 21.77 |
| 65+ | 6.16 | 3.82 | 2.55 |

Source(s): (1) ADNU; (2) EPPA3.

**2.2 Méthode(s):** interpolation et extrapolation linéaires
moyenne pondérée

### 2.2.1 Hommes:

- 1950-60, taux d'activité 1950-60 tirés des EPPA3;
ajustement des taux d'activité du groupe d'âge [25-29];
- 1970 et 1990, interpolation et extrapolation des taux d'activité ajustés
tirés des recensements de 1974, 1982 et 1990.

### 2.2.2 Femmes:

- 1950-70, taux d'activité 1950-70 tirés des EPPA3;
- 1980, moyennes pondérées des taux d'activité tirés des
recensements de 1974 et 1982;
- 1990, moyennes pondérées des taux d'activité tirés des
recensements de 1982 et 1990.

## 3. Evaluation des taux de répartition par secteur d'activité: 1950 - 1990

### 3.1 Données de base:

Tableau 2: Répartition de la population active en % par secteur d'activité

| Année | Agriculture | Industrie Total | Manufac. | Services |
|---|---|---|---|---|
| **Hommes** | | | | |
| 1974 | 27.49 | 32.01 | 12.21 | 40.50 |
| 1982 | 24.06 | 24.52 | 5.14 | 51.42 |
| 1990 | 10.11 | 30.63 | 11.26 | 59.26 |
| **Femmes** | | | | |
| 1974 | 13.15 | 7.40 | 6.03 | 79.45 |
| 1982 | 9.78 | 3.46 | 2.10 | 86.77 |
| 1990 | 3.03 | 5.46 | 3.94 | 91.51 |

Source(s): STAT.

**3.2 Méthode(s):** moyenne pondérée

### 3.2.1 Hommes:

- 1950-70, taux de répartition 1950-70 tirés des EPPA3;
- 1980-90, moyennes pondérées des taux de répartition tiré des
recensements de 1974, 1982 et 1990.

### 3.2.2 Femmes:

Méthode, hypothèses et traitements identiques à ceux appliqués aux hommes.

## 4. Projection des taux d'activité: 2000 - 2010

**4.1 Modèle(s):** linéaire, hyperbole et logistique

### 4.1.1 Hommes:

- Aux groupes d'âge [15-19], [40-44] et [50+], application de la fonction F3;
- Aux groupes d'âge [20-39] et [45-49], application de la fonction F1;
- Modification des tendances des groupes d'âge [30-39] et [45-49].

### 4.1.2 Femmes:

- Aux groupes d'âge [15-19], [45-49] et [55+], application de la fonction F3;
- Aux groupes d'âge [20-24] et [50-54], application de la fonction F1;
- Aux groupes d'âge [25-44], application de la fonction F6;
- Modification des tendances des groupes d'âge [20-24] et [50-54].

*Notes sur les ajustements des taux, voir p. 192-195.*

*Notes sur les fonctions de projection, voir p. 198.*

# Guatemala

## 1. Source(s) des données de base

Code(s):  Titre(s):

EPPA3    Evaluations et projections de la population active 1950-2025 - troisième édition, BIT, Genève, 1986.
INEG-81  Censos Nacionales de 1981, Tomo I, Cifras definitivas, Instituto Nacional de Estadistica, Guatemala.
ADNU     Editions de 1979 et 1988 de l'Annuaire démographique des Nations Unies, New York.
ASTER    Annuaire des statistiques du travail 1945-89 - Edition rétrospective sur les recensements de population, BIT, Genève, 1990.
AST-93   Annuaire des statistiques du travail 1993, BIT, Genève, 1993.

## 2. Evaluation des taux d'activité: 1950 - 1990

### 2.1 Données de base:

Tableau 1: Taux d'activité par sexe et par groupe d'âge

| Groupe d'âge | Année 1973 (1) | 1981 (1) | 1989 (2) |
|---|---|---|---|
| **Hommes** | | | |
| 10-14 | 26.39 | 17.57 | 28.01 |
| 15-19 | 72.04 | 63.29 | 74.01 |
| 20-24 | 90.04 | 85.80 | 93.96 |
| 25-29 | 94.59 | 92.19 | 97.93 |
| 30-34 | 95.52 | 93.69 | 97.99 |
| 35-39 | 95.62 | 93.80 | 98.53 |
| 40-44 | 95.38 | 93.41 | 98.70 |
| 45-49 | 95.02 | 93.16 | 97.80 |
| 50-54 | 93.73 | 91.75 | 96.44 |
| 55-59 | 91.95 | 90.31 | 94.84 |
| 60-64 | 87.15 | 85.85 | 89.53 |
| 65+ | 68.60 | 66.83 | 62.93 |
| **Femmes** | | | |
| 10-14 | 4.10 | 3.44 | 7.80 |
| 15-19 | 14.99 | 13.27 | 25.63 |
| 20-24 | 17.38 | 17.18 | 29.83 |
| 25-29 | 15.00 | 15.96 | 29.72 |
| 30-34 | 14.09 | 15.39 | 33.81 |
| 35-39 | 13.87 | 13.99 | 31.46 |
| 40-44 | 14.05 | 13.59 | 30.89 |
| 45-49 | 13.54 | 12 26 | 30.32 |
| 50-54 | 12.92 | 11.69 | 28.93 |
| 55-59 | 11.93 | 10.05 | 23.36 |
| 60-64 | 10.13 | 8.81 | 20.62 |
| 65+ | 7.06 | 6.49 | 13.73 |

Source(s): (1) ADNU, ASTER, INEG-81; (2) AST-93.

### 2.2 Méthode(s): interpolation et extrapolation linéaires

#### 2.2.1 Hommes:

- 1950-60, taux d'activité 1950-60 tirés des EPPA3;
ajustement des taux d'activité du groupe d'âge [10-14];
- 1970-90, interpolation et extrapolation des taux d'activité ajustés tirés des recensements de 1973 et 1981.

#### 2.2.2 Femmes:

- 1950-70, taux d'activité ajustés 1950-70 tirés des EPPA3;
ajustement des taux sur la base du modèle d'ajustement des taux d'activité des femmes travaillant dans l'agriculture comme aides familiales;
- 1980-90, interpolation et extrapolation des taux d'activité ajustés tirés des recensements de 1981 et des taux d'activité tirés de l'enquête de 1989.

## 3. Evaluation des taux de répartition par secteur d'activité: 1950 - 1990

### 3.1 Données de base:

Tableau 2: Répartition de la population active en % par secteur d'activité

| Année | Agriculture | Industrie Total | Manufac. | Services |
|---|---|---|---|---|
| **Hommes** | | | | |
| 1980 (1) | 64.45 | 16.55 | .. | 19.00 |
| 1981 (2) | 64.07 | 16.58 | 9.77 | 19.34 |
| 1989 (3) | 61.35 | 16.53 | 10.45 | 22.13 |
| **Femmes** | | | | |
| 1981 (2) | 9.70 | 19.68 | 18.82 | 70.62 |
| 1989 (3) | 15.99 | 23.58 | 23.24 | 60.43 |

Source(s): (1) EPPA3; (2) ASTER; (3) AST93.

### 3.2 Méthode(s): moyenne pondérée
extrapolation linéaire

#### 3.2.1 Hommes:

- 1950-80, taux de répartition 1950-80 tirés des EPPA3;
- Application du rapport manufacture/industrie tiré du recensement de 1981;
- 1990, moyennes pondérées des taux de répartition 1980 tirés des EPPA3 et des taux de répartition tirés de l'enquête de 1989;
application du rapport manufacture/industrie tiré de l'enquête de 1989.

#### 3.2.2 Femmes:

- 1950-70, taux de répartition ajustés 1950-70 tirés des EPPA3;
ajustement effectué sur la base d'un rapport femmes/hommes dans l'agriculture égal à 1/10;
- 1980-90, extrapolation des taux de répartition ajustés tirés du recensement de 1981 et des taux de répartition tirés de l'enquête de 1989.

## 4. Projection des taux d'activité: 2000 - 2010

### 4.1 Modèle(s): linéaire, log-linéaire et logistique

#### 4.1.1 Hommes:

- Aux groupes d'âge [10-14] et [25+], application de la fonction F1;
- Aux groupes d'âge [19-24], application de la fonction F6;
- Modification des tendances des groupes d'âge [10-54] et [65+].

#### 4.1.2 Femmes:

- Aux groupes d'âge [10-14] et [65+], application de la fonction F1;
- Aux groupes d'âge [15-64], application de la fonction F2;
- Modification des tendances des groupes d'âge [15+].

*Notes sur les ajustements des taux, voir p. 192-195.*          *Notes sur les fonctions de projection, voir p. 198.*

# Guinée

## 1. Source(s) des données de base

**Code(s):**      **Titre(s):**

EPPA3      Evaluations et projections de la population active 1950-2025 - troisième édition, BIT, Genève, 1986.
AST91      Annuaire des statistiques du travail 1991, BIT, Genève, 1991.

## 2. Evaluation des taux d'activité: 1950 - 1990

### 2.1 Données de base:

Tableau 1: Taux d'activité par sexe et par groupe d'âge

| Groupe d'âge | Année 1950 (1) | 1960 (1) | 1970 (1) | 1980 (1) | 1983 (2) |
|---|---|---|---|---|---|
| **Hommes** | | | | | |
| 10-14 | 52.30 | 50.00 | 48.05 | 45.35 | .. |
| 15-19 | 85.20 | 82.15 | 79.55 | 75.95 | .. |
| 20-24 | 95.35 | 94.20 | 93.20 | 91.85 | .. |
| 25-29 | 97.40 | 97.25 | 97.10 | 96.90 | .. |
| 30-34 | 98.15 | 97.95 | 97.80 | 97.55 | .. |
| 35-39 | 98.30 | 98.10 | 97.95 | 97.70 | .. |
| 40-44 | 98.15 | 97.95 | 97.75 | 97.50 | .. |
| 45-49 | 97.40 | 97.20 | 97.05 | 96.85 | .. |
| 50-54 | 96.95 | 96.70 | 96.45 | 96.15 | .. |
| 55-59 | 96.10 | 95.70 | 95.30 | 94.80 | .. |
| 60-64 | 93.20 | 92.45 | 91.80 | 90.95 | .. |
| 65+ | 80.05 | 78.75 | 77.60 | 76.10 | .. |
| **Femmes** | | | | | |
| 10-14 | 39.50 | 37.80 | 36.30 | 34.30 | 28.40 |
| 15-19 | 64.20 | 61.60 | 59.40 | 56.35 | 41.20 |
| 20-24 | 64.30 | 62.70 | 61.30 | 59.35 | 44.80 |
| 25-29 | 69.30 | 67.45 | 65.85 | 63.65 | 50.40 |
| 30-34 | 73.65 | 71.70 | 70.00 | 67.65 | 51.70 |
| 35-39 | 74.90 | 73.05 | 71.45 | 69.25 | 51.20 |
| 40-44 | 77.30 | 75.45 | 73.90 | 71.7 | 51.00 |
| 45-49 | 76.85 | 74.95 | 73.35 | 71.1 | 51.20 |
| 50-54 | 75.45 | 73.25 | 71.40 | 68.8 | 49.30 |
| 55-59 | 72.70 | 70.40 | 68.45 | 65.75 | 46.00 |
| 60-64 | 66.75 | 63.85 | 61.35 | 57.9 | 34.00 |
| 65+ | 46.65 | 43.95 | 41.60 | 38.45 | 16.95 |

**Source(s):** (1) EPPA3; (2) AST91.

### 2.2 Méthode(s): interpolation et extrapolation linéaires

**2.2.1 Hommes:**

- 1950-80, taux d'activité 1950-80 tirés des EPPA3;
- 1990, extrapolation des taux d'activité 1950-1980 tirés des EPPA3;
ajustement des taux extrapolés 1990 sur la base des variations des taux
interpolés 1980 par rapport aux taux 1980 tirés des EPPA3;
modification des tendances de tous les groupes d'âge pour 1990.

**2.2.2 Femmes:**

- 1950-90, interpolation et extrapolation des taux d'activité 1950-80 tirés
des EPPA3;
ajustement des taux interpolés et extrapolés sur la base des variations
des taux extrapolés 1983 par rapport aux taux tirés du recensement de 1983;
modification des tendances de tous les groupes d'âge de 1950 à 1980.

## 3. Evaluation des taux de répartition par secteur d'activité: 1950 - 1990

### 3.1 Données de base:

Tableau 2: Répartition de la population active en % par secteur d'activité

| Année | Agriculture | Industrie Total | Manufac. | Services |
|---|---|---|---|---|
| **Hommes** | | | | |
| 1950 (1) | 88.00 | 5.80 | .. | 6.20 |
| 1960 (1) | 83.80 | 7.85 | .. | 8.35 |
| 1970 (1) | 80.20 | 9.60 | .. | 10.20 |
| 1980 (1) | 75.25 | 11.95 | .. | 12.80 |
| 1983 (2) | 85.44 | 2.11 | 0.67 | 12.45 |
| **Femmes** | | | | |
| 1950 (1) | 97.30 | 1.90 | .. | 0.80 |
| 1960 (1) | 96.15 | 2.70 | .. | 1.15 |
| 1970 (1) | 92.00 | 3.50 | .. | 4.50 |
| 1980 (1) | 88.30 | 4.90 | .. | 6.80 |
| 1983 (2) | 85.30 | 2.20 | 0.68 | 12.50 |

**Source(s):** (1) EPPA3; (2) AST91.

### 3.2 Méthode(s): interpolation et extrapolation linéaires

**3.2.1 Hommes:**
- 1950-90, interpolation et extrapolation des taux de répartition tirés des
EPPA3;
ajustement des taux interpolés et extrapolés 1950-90 sur la base des
variations des taux interpolés 1983 par rapport aux taux de répartition
tirés du recensement de 1983;
- Application du rapport manufacture/industrie tiré du recensement de 1983.

**3.2.2 Femmes:**
- 1950-90, interpolation extrapolation des taux de répartition ajustés
1950 et 1980 tirés des EPPA3;
ajustement des taux de répartition sur la base du rapport hommes/femmes
égal à 1 dans l'agriculture; aux taux de répartition de l'industrie et des services,
application du rapport industrie/services tiré du recensement de 1983;
les taux de répartition de manufacture sont estimés sur la base du rapport
manufacture/industrie tiré du recensement de 1983.

## 4. Projection des taux d'activité: 2000 - 2010

### 4.1 Modèle(s): linéaire et hyperbole

**4.1.1 Hommes:**

- Aux groupes d'âge [10-29], application de la fonction F1;
- Modification de la tendance du groupe d'âge [10-14].

**4.1.2 Femmes:**

- Aux groupes d'âge [10-19] et [60+], application de la fonction F1;
- Aux groupes d'âge [20-59], application de la fonction F3;
- Modification des tendances des groupes d'âge [10-19] et [60+].

*Notes sur les ajustements des taux, voir p. 192-195.*          *Notes sur les fonctions de projection, voir p. 198.*

# Guinée équatoriale

## 1. Source(s) des données de base

Code(s):     Titre(s):

EPPA3     Evaluations et projections de la population active 1950-2025 - troisième édition, BIT, Genève, 1986.
AST91     Annuaire des statistiques du travail 1991, BIT, Genève, 1991.
R1983     Republica de Guinea Ecuatorial, Censos Nacionales I de Poblacion I de Vivienda, Caractristica de la Poblacion, 4/07/1983, Malabo.

## 2. Evaluation des taux d'activité: 1950 - 1990

### 2.1 Données de base:

Tableau 1: Taux d'activité par sexe et par groupe d'âge

| Groupe d'âge | Année 1950 (1) | 1960 (1) | 1970 (1) | 1980 (1) | 1983 (2) |
|---|---|---|---|---|---|
| **Hommes** | | | | | |
| 10-14 | 49.30 | 44.95 | 39.80 | 32.75 | 8.97 |
| 15-19 | 81.20 | 75.40 | 68.55 | 59.15 | 77.54 |
| 20-24 | 93.85 | 91.60 | 89.00 | 85.35 | 96.37 |
| 25-29 | 97.20 | 96.85 | 96.45 | 95.95 | 96.92 |
| 30-34 | 97.90 | 97.55 | 97.10 | 96.50 | 96.89 |
| 35-39 | 98.05 | 97.65 | 97.20 | 96.55 | 97.03 |
| 40-44 | 97.90 | 97.45 | 97.00 | 96.30 | 97.15 |
| 45-49 | 97.15 | 96.80 | 96.40 | 95.80 | 96.68 |
| 50-54 | 96.60 | 96.10 | 95.45 | 94.60 | 96.54 |
| 55-59 | 95.55 | 94.70 | 93.70 | 92.30 | 96.00 |
| 60-64 | 92.20 | 90.80 | 89.10 | 86.80 | 93.83 |
| 65+ | 78.35 | 75.85 | 72.90 | 68.85 | 52.17 |
| **Femmes** | | | | | |
| 10-14 | 36.35 | 34.20 | 31.75 | 28.85 | 9.17 |
| 15-19 | 59.45 | 56.20 | 52.50 | 48.20 | 48.55 |
| 20-24 | 61.30 | 59.25 | 56.95 | 54.20 | 37.82 |
| 25-29 | 65.90 | 63.55 | 60.90 | 57.80 | 37.18 |
| 30-34 | 70.00 | 67.50 | 64.65 | 61.35 | 41.96 |
| 35-39 | 71.50 | 69.15 | 66.50 | 63.40 | 44.62 |
| 40-44 | 73.95 | 71.60 | 68.95 | 65.85 | 46.95 |
| 45-49 | 73.40 | 71.00 | 68.30 | 65.15 | 46.71 |
| 50-54 | 71.45 | 69.70 | 65.55 | 61.00 | 40.02 |
| 55-59 | 68.50 | 65.60 | 62.35 | 58.55 | 47.55 |
| 60-64 | 61.40 | 57.75 | 53.60 | 48.75 | 48.71 |
| 65+ | 41.70 | 38.25 | 34.40 | 29.90 | 22.45 |

Source(s): (1) EPPA3; (2) AST91 et R1983.

### 2.2 Méthode(s): interpolation et extrapolation linéaires

#### 2.2.1 Hommes:

- 1950-90, interpolation et extrapolation des taux d'activité 1950-80
tirés des EPPA3 et des taux d'activité tirés du recensement de 1983;
ajustement des taux interpolés et extrapolés sur la base des variations des
taux interpolés 1983 par rapport aux taux du recensement de 1983;
modification des tendances de tous les groupes d'âge.

#### 2.2.2 Femmes:

Méthode, hypothèses et traitements identiques à ceux appliqués aux hommes.

## 3. Evaluation des taux de répartition par secteur d'activité: 1950 - 1990

### 3.1 Données de base:

Tableau 2: Répartition de la population active en % par secteur d'activité

| Année | Agriculture | Industrie Total | Manufac. | Services |
|---|---|---|---|---|
| **Hommes** | | | | |
| 1950 (1) | 82.50 | 6.25 | .. | 11.15 |
| 1960 (1) | 74.50 | 9.25 | .. | 16.25 |
| 1970 (1) | 65.00 | 12.70 | .. | 22.30 |
| 1980 (1) | 52.00 | 17.4 | | 30.60 |
| 1983 (2) | 69.10 | 7.34 | 2.63 | 23.55 |
| **Femmes** | | | | |
| 1950 (1) | 96.00 | 0.70 | .. | 3.30 |
| 1960 (1) | 93.00 | 1.25 | .. | 5.75 |
| 1970 (1) | 89.00 | 2.00 | .. | 9.00 |
| 1980 (1) | 85.50 | 2.60 | .. | 11.90 |
| 1983 (2) | 92.05 | 0.88 | 0.70 | 7.07 |

Source(s): (1) EPPA3; (2) AST91.

### 3.2 Méthode(s): interpolation et extrapolation linéaires

#### 3.2.1 Hommes:

- 1950-90, interpolation et extrapolation des taux de répartition 1950-80
tirés des EPPA3 et des taux du recensement de 1983;
ajustement des taux interpolés et extrapolés sur la base de 1/3 des variations
des taux interpolés 1983 par rapport aux taux de répartition tirés
du recensement de 1983;
- Application du rapport manufacture/industrie tiré du recensement de 1983.

#### 3.2.2 Femmes:

Méthode, hypothèses et traitements identiques à ceux appliqués aux hommes.

## 4. Projection des taux d'activité: 2000 - 2010

### 4.1 Modèle(s): linéaire et hyperbole

#### 4.1.1 Hommes:

- Aux groupes d'âge [10-29] et [55+], application de la fonction F1;
- Aux groupes d'âge [30-54], application de la fonction F3;
- Modification de la tendance du groupe d'âge [10-14].

#### 4.1.2 Femmes:

- Au groupe d'âge [10-14], application de la fonction F1;
- Aux groupes d'âge [15+], application de la fonction F3;
- Modification des tendances des groupes d'âge [15-54].

*Notes sur les ajustements des taux, voir p. 192-195.*     *Notes sur les fonctions de projection, voir p. 198.*

# Guinée-Bissau

## 1. Source(s) des données de base

Code(s):    Titre(s):

EPPA3    Evaluations et projections de la population active 1950-2025 - troisième édition, BIT, Genève, 1986.
ADNU84    Annuaire démographique 1984 - Statistiques des recensements de population II, trente-sixième édition, Nations Unies, New York, 1986.
ASTER    Annuaire des statistiques du travail 1945-89 - Edition rétrospective sur les recensements de population, BIT, Genève, 1990.

## 2. Evaluation des taux d'activité: 1950 - 1990

### 2.1 Données de base:

Tableau 1: Taux d'activité par sexe et par groupe d'âge

|  | Année | | | |
|---|---|---|---|---|
| Groupe d'âge | 1950 (1) | 1960 (1) | 1970 (1) | 1979 (2) |
| **Hommes** | | | | |
| oct.14 | 50.95 | 49.10 | 46.75 | 48.22 |
| 15-19 | 83.40 | 80.90 | 77.80 | 55.21 |
| 20-24 | 94.65 | 93.75 | 92.55 | 86.87 |
| 25-29 | 97.30 | 97.15 | 97.00 | 97.46 |
| 30-34 | 98.05 | 97.90 | 97.70 | 98.86 |
| 35-39 | 98.20 | 98.05 | 97.80 | 99.02 |
| 40-44 | 98.05 | 97.85 | 97.65 | 98.80 |
| 45-49 | 97.30 | 97.15 | 96.95 | 98.95 |
| 50-54 | 96.80 | 96.60 | 96.30 | 98.18 |
| 55-59 | 95.85 | 95.50 | 95.05 | 97.95 |
| 60-64 | 92.75 | 92.15 | 91.40 | 96.87 |
| 65+ | 79.25 | 78.20 | 76.85 | 89.46 |
| **Femmes** | | | | |
| oct.14 | 38.50 | 37.10 | 35.35 | 2.63 |
| 15-19 | 62.65 | 60.55 | 57.90 | 2.22 |
| 20-24 | 63.35 | 62.00 | 60.35 | 3.96 |
| 25-29 | 68.20 | 66.70 | 64.80 | 3.22 |
| 30-34 | 72.50 | 70.85 | 68.85 | 2.68 |
| 35-39 | 73.80 | 72.25 | 70.40 | 2.35 |
| 40-44 | 76.20 | 74.70 | 72.80 | 2.26 |
| 45-49 | 75.70 | 74.20 | 72.25 | 2.25 |
| 50-54 | 74.15 | 72.40 | 70.15 | 1.83 |
| 55-59 | 71.35 | 69.50 | 67.15 | 2.18 |
| 60-64 | 65.00 | 62.65 | 59.65 | 1.70 |
| 65+ | 45.05 | 42.85 | 40.10 | 1.45 |

Source(s): (1) EPPA3; (2) ADNU84 et ASTER.

### 2.2 Méthode(s): interpolation et extrapolation linéaires

#### 2.2.1 Hommes:

- 1950-90, interpolation et extrapolation des taux d'activité 1950-80
tirés des EPPA3 et des taux d'activité ajustés tirés du recensement de 1979;
ajustement des taux interpolés et extrapolés sur la base des variations des
taux interpolés 1979 par rapport aux taux ajustés du recensement de 1979;
modification des tendances de tous les groupes d'âge.

#### 2.2.2 Femmes:

Méthode, hypothèses et traitements identiques à ceux appliqués aux hommes.

## 3. Evaluation des taux de répartition par secteur d'activité: 1950 - 1990

### 3.1 Données de base:

Tableau 2: Répartition de la population active en % par secteur d'activité

|  | Agriculture | Industrie | | Services |
|---|---|---|---|---|
| Année | | Total | Manufac. | |
| **Hommes** | | | | |
| 1950 (1) | 85.50 | 1.85 | .. | 12.65 |
| 1960 (1) | 82.10 | 2.55 | .. | 15.35 |
| 1970 (1) | 77.80 | 4.10 | .. | 18.10 |
| 1979 (2) | 81.08 | 2.45 | 1.42 | 16.47 |
| 1980 (1) | 75.20 | 5.00 | .. | 19.80 |
| **Femmes** | | | | |
| 1950 (1) | 95.00 | 0.65 | . | 4.35 |
| 1960 (1) | 94.00 | 1.00 | .. | 5.00 |
| 1970 (1) | 92.70 | 1.40 | .. | 5.90 |
| 1979 (2) | 97.64 | 0.23 | 0.18 | 2.13 |
| 1980 (1) | 91.90 | 1.65 | .. | 6.45 |

Source(s): (1) EPPA3; (2) ASTER.

### 3.2 Méthode(s): interpolation et extrapolation linéaires

#### 3.2.1 Hommes:

- 1950-90, interpolation et extrapolation des taux de répartition 1950-80
tirés EPPA3 et des taux du recensement de 1979;
ajustement des taux interpolés et extrapolés sur la base de 1/3 des variations
des taux interpolés 1979 par rapport aux taux de répartition tirés
du recensement de 1979;
- Application du rapport manufacture/industrie tiré du recensement de 1979.

#### 3.2.2 Femmes:

- 1950-90, interpolation et extrapolation des taux de répartition 1950-80
des EPPA3 et des taux tirés du recensement de 1979;
ajustement des taux interpolés et extrapolés sur la base de la moitié
(la totalité pour 1990) des variations des taux interpolés 1979
par rapport aux taux de répartition tirés du recensement de 1979;
- Application du rapport manufacture/industrie tiré du recensement de 1979.

## 4. Projection des taux d'activité: 2000 - 2010

### 4.1 Modèle(s): linéaire et hyperbole

#### 4.1.1 Hommes:

- Aux groupes d'âge [10-29], application de la fonction F1;
- Aux groupes d'âge [30+], application de la fonction F3;
- Modification de la tendance du groupe d'âge [10-14].

#### 4.1.2 Femmes:

- Aux groupes d'âge [10-19], application de la fonction F1;
- Aux groupes d'âge [20+], application de la fonction F3;
- Modification des tendances des groupes d'âge [10-19] et [60+].

*Notes sur les ajustements des taux, voir p. 192-195.*    *Notes sur les fonctions de projection, voir p. 198.*

# Guyana

## 1. Source(s) des données de base

| Code(s): | Titre(s): |
|---|---|
| EPPA3 | Evaluations et projections de la population active 1950-2025 - troisième édition, BIT, Genève, 1986. |
| STAT | Base de données sur les statistiques du travail - LABORSTA, Bureau de statistique, BIT, Genève. |

## 2. Evaluation des taux d'activité: 1950 - 1990

### 2.1 Données de base:

Tableau 1: Taux d'activité par sexe et par groupe d'âge

| Groupe d'âge | Année 1970 (1) | 1980 (2) | 1987 (2) |
|---|---|---|---|
| **Hommes** | | | |
| 10-14 | 4.40 | 0.00 | 0.00 |
| 15-19 | 67.00 | 64.77 | 61.42 |
| 20-24 | 94.20 | 94.22 | 91.98 |
| 25-29 | 97.90 | 97.77 | 94.40 |
| 30-34 | 98.55 | 97.96 | 97.79 |
| 35-39 | 97.95 | 97.97 | 97.81 |
| 40-44 | 97.30 | 97.70 | 97.35 |
| 45-49 | 96.75 | 96.51 | 95.66 |
| 50-54 | 93.50 | 93.72 | 93.44 |
| 55-59 | 91.90 | 88.92 | 86.79 |
| 60-64 | 67.75 | 65.66 | 64.17 |
| 65+ | 41.35 | 34.36 | 32.27 |
| **Femmes** | | | |
| 10-14 | 1.40 | 0.00 | |
| 15-19 | 26.25 | 21.28 | 22.56 |
| 20-24 | 29.10 | 36.57 | 42.30 |
| 25-29 | 20.50 | 33.26 | 41.70 |
| 30-34 | 18.50 | 30.21 | 43.70 |
| 35-39 | 19.95 | 27.37 | 39.61 |
| 40-44 | 22.00 | 27.04 | 37.06 |
| 45-49 | 22.25 | 26.90 | 34.50 |
| 50-54 | 20.40 | 25.44 | 31.05 |
| 55-59 | 18.05 | 21.77 | 26.82 |
| 60-64 | 12.10 | 15.07 | 17.93 |
| 65+ | 5.15 | 5.55 | 5.24 |

Source(s): (1) EPPA3; (2) STAT.

### 2.2 Méthode(s): moyenne pondérée

#### 2.2.1 Hommes:

- 1950-70, taux d'activité 1950-70 tirés des EPPA3;
- 1980, moyennes pondérées des taux d'activité 1970 tirés des EPPA3 et des taux ajustés du recensement de 1980;
modification des tendances des groupes d'âge [55-64];
- 1990, moyennes pondérées des taux d'activité ajustés tirés du recensement de 1980 et des taux de l'enquête de 1987;
modification des tendances des groupes d'âge [65+].

#### 2.2.2 Femmes:

- 1950-70, taux d'activité 1950-70 tirés des EPPA3;
- 1980, moyennes pondérées des taux d'activité 1970 tirés des EPPA3 et des taux ajustés du recensement de 1980;
- 1990, moyennes pondérées des taux d'activité ajustés tirés du recensement de 1980 et des taux d'activité tirés de l'enquête de 1987;
modification des tendances des groupes d'âge [65+]

## 3. Evaluation des taux de répartition par secteur d'activité: 1950 - 1990

### 3.1 Données de base:

Tableau 2: Répartition de la population active en % par secteur d'activité

| Année | Agriculture | Industrie Total | Manufac. | Services |
|---|---|---|---|---|
| **Hommes** | | | | |
| 1960 | 40.95 | 30.25 | .. | 28.80 |
| 1970 | 35.85 | 32.05 | .. | 32.10 |
| 1980 | 31.60 | 28.90 | 16.39 | 39.50 |
| **Femmes** | | | | |
| 1960 | 25.80 | 15.00 | | 59.20 |
| 1970 | 16.85 | 15.00 | .. | 68.15 |
| 1980 | 11.80 | 16.25 | 12.79 | 71.95 |

Source(s): EPPA3.

### 3.2 Méthode(s): extrapolation linéaire

#### 3.2.1 Hommes:

- 1950-80, taux de répartition 1950-80 tirés des EPPA3;
- 1990, extrapolation des taux de répartition 1960-80 tirés des EPPA3;
modification des tendances de tous les secteurs.

#### 3.2.2 Femmes:

Méthode, hypothèses et traitements identiques à ceux appliqués aux hommes.

## 4. Projection des taux d'activité: 2000 - 2010

### 4.1 Modèle(s): linéaire, log-linéaire, hyperbole et logistique

#### 4.1.1 Hommes:

- Aux groupes d'âge [15-24], application de la fonction F1;
- Aux groupes d'âge [25+], application de la fonction F3.

#### 4.1.2 Femmes:

- Aux groupes d'âge [15-24], application de la fonction F2;
- Aux groupes d'âge [25-64], application de la fonction F6;
- Au groupe d'âge [65+], application de la fonction F3.

*Notes sur les ajustements des taux, voir p. 192-195.*

*Notes sur les fonctions de projection, voir p. 198.*

# Haïti

## 1. Source(s) des données de base

Code(s):     Titre(s):

EPPA3      Evaluations et projections de la population active 1950-2025 - troisième édition, BIT, Genève, 1986.
ASTER      Annuaire des statistiques du travail 1945-89 - Edition rétrospective sur les recensements de population, BIT, Genève, 1990.

## 2. Evaluation des taux d'activité: 1950 - 1990

### 2.1 Données de base:

Tableau 1: Taux d'activité par sexe et par groupe d'âge

| Groupe d'âge | Année 1950 (1) | 1960 (1) | 1970 (1) | 1982 (2) |
|---|---|---|---|---|
| **Hommes** | | | | |
| 10-14 | 53.00 | 47.50 | 42.00 | 25.70 |
| 15-19 | 83.70 | 75.00 | 66.40 | 43.87 |
| 20-24 | 95.60 | 92.60 | 89.75 | 76.99 |
| 25-29 | 98.40 | 98.00 | 97.55 | 91.85 |
| 30-34 | 98.80 | 98.80 | 98.75 | 94.13 |
| 35-39 | 99.00 | 99.10 | 99.20 | 96.18 |
| 40-44 | 98.90 | 98.90 | 98.95 | 95.23 |
| 45-49 | 98.80 | 98.75 | 98.75 | 94.21 |
| 50-54 | 98.35 | 98.25 | 98.10 | 91.14 |
| 55-59 | 97.75 | 97.60 | 97.50 | 92.68 |
| 60-64 | 96.50 | 95.90 | 95.30 | 87.47 |
| 65+ | 87.20 | 84.25 | 81.00 | 70.32 |
| **Femmes** | | | | |
| 10-14 | 51.50 | 45.00 | 41.00 | 22.29 |
| 15-19 | 81.10 | 73.05 | 64.85 | 35.14 |
| 20-24 | 85.80 | 80.65 | 75.40 | 53.49 |
| 25-29 | 85.25 | 80.05 | 74.75 | 56.71 |
| 30-34 | 85.70 | 80.00 | 74.20 | 55.50 |
| 35-39 | 86.30 | 80.85 | 75.35 | 58.42 |
| 40-44 | 87.15 | 82.35 | 77.50 | 57.51 |
| 45-49 | 87.10 | 82.35 | 77.45 | 60.16 |
| 50-54 | 85.15 | 81.20 | 77.20 | 57.83 |
| 55-59 | 83.50 | 79.55 | 75.50 | 54.15 |
| 60-64 | 79.75 | 74.90 | 69.85 | 46.55 |
| 65+ | 59.00 | 52.25 | 45.40 | 35.80 |

Source(s): (1) EPPA3; (2) ASTER.

### 2.2 Méthode(s): extrapolation linéaire
moyenne pondérée

**2.2.1 Hommes:**

- 1950-70, taux d'activité 1950-70 tirés des EPPA3;
- 1980, moyennes pondérées des taux d'activité 1970 tirés des EPPA3
et des taux d'activité ajustés tirés du recensement de 1982;
- 1990, extrapolation des taux d'activité 1950-70 tirés des EPPA3 et des
taux 1980 estimés;
aux taux extrapolés, application des variations des taux interpolés 1982
par rapport aux taux ajustés tirés du recensement de 1982;
modification des tendances de tous les groupes d'âge.

**2.2.2 Femmes:**

Méthode, hypothèses et traitements identiques à ceux appliqués aux hommes.

## 3. Evaluation des taux de répartition par secteur d'activité: 1950 - 1990

### 3.1 Données de base:

Tableau 2: Répartition de la population active en % par secteur d'activité

| Année | Agriculture | Industrie Total | Manufac. | Services |
|---|---|---|---|---|
| **Hommes** | | | | |
| 1950 | 88.70 | 5.60 | 4.30 | 5.70 |
| 1971 | 83.97 | 6.84 | 4.96 | 9.19 |
| 1982 | 77.92 | 8.71 | 6.02 | 13.37 |
| **Femmes** | | | | |
| 1950 | 82.25 | 5.84 | 5.78 | 11.91 |
| 1971 | 61.85 | 7.67 | 7.62 | 30.48 |
| 1982 | 51.31 | 9.59 | 7.64 | 39.10 |

Source(s): (1) ASTER.

### 3.2 Méthode(s): moyenne pondérée
extrapolation linéaire

**3.2.1 Hommes:**

- 1950-70, taux de répartition 1950-70 tirés des EPPA3;
- 1980, moyennes pondérées des taux de répartition 1970 tirés
des EPPA3 et des taux de répartition du recensement de 1982;
- 1990, extrapolation des taux de répartition tirés des recensements
de 1950, 1971 et 1982;
modification des tendances de tous les secteurs.

**3.2.2 Femmes:**

Méthode, hypothèses et traitements identiques à ceux appliqués aux hommes.

## 4. Projection des taux d'activité: 2000 - 2010

### 4.1 Modèle(s): linéaire et hyperbole

**4.1.1 Hommes:**

- Aux groupes d'âge [10-14] et [20+], application de la fonction F1;
- Au groupe d'âge [15-19], application de la fonction F3;
- Modification des tendances des groupes d'âge [10-34] et [45-54].

**4.1.2 Femmes:**

- Au groupe d'âge [10-14], application de la fonction F1;
- Aux groupes d'âge [15+], application de la fonction F3;
- Modification des tendances des groupes d'âge [10-64].

*Notes sur les ajustements des taux, voir p. 192-195.*          *Notes sur les fonctions de projection, voir p. 198.*

# Honduras

## 1. Source(s) des données de base

| Code(s): | Titre(s): |
|---|---|
| EPPA3 | Evaluations et projections de la population active 1950-2025 - troisième édition, BIT, Genève, 1986. |
| STAT | Base de données sur les statistiques du travail - LABORSTA, Bureau de statistique, BIT, Genève. |

## 2. Evaluation des taux d'activité: 1950 - 1990

### 2.1 Données de base:

Tableau 1: Taux d'activité par sexe et par groupe d'âge

| Groupe d'âge | Année 1974 | 1991 | 1992 |
|---|---|---|---|
| **Hommes** | | | |
| 10-14 | 28.88 | 13.95 | 15.18 |
| 15-19 | 77.75 | 63.47 | 63.80 |
| 20-24 | 92.38 | 90.93 | 89.17 |
| 25-29 | 96.58 | 94.90 | 94.03 |
| 30-34 | 98.07 | 97.61 | 97.65 |
| 35-39 | 98.22 | 97.83 | 97.86 |
| 40-44 | 97.53 | 97.67 | 97.66 |
| 45-49 | 97.24 | 96.74 | 97.92 |
| 50-54 | 95.38 | 95.22 | 95.58 |
| 55-59 | 94.08 | 95.26 | 94.06 |
| 60-64 | 89.07 | 88.23 | 88.44 |
| 65+ | 65.21 | 57.34 | 59.24 |
| **Femmes** | | | |
| 10-14 | .. | 3.63 | 3.82 |
| 15-19 | .. | 21.16 | 24.51 |
| 20-24 | .. | 38.55 | 37.57 |
| 25-29 | .. | 36.11 | 35.17 |
| 30-34 | .. | 42.78 | 46.24 |
| 35-39 | .. | 43.79 | 46.60 |
| 40-44 | .. | 41.01 | 45.12 |
| 45-49 | .. | 39.10 | 41.37 |
| 50-54 | .. | 34.22 | 37.84 |
| 55-59 | .. | 29.99 | 32.31 |
| 60-64 | .. | 22.22 | 22.52 |
| 65+ | .. | 13.61 | 14.44 |

Source(s): STAT.

### 2.2 Méthode(s): interpolation linéaire
moyenne arithmétique

**2.2.1 Hommes:**

- 1950-60, taux d'activité 1950-60 tirés des EPPA3;
- 1970-90, interpolation des taux d'activité ajustés tirés du recensement de 1974 et des moyennes des taux tirés des enquêtes de 1991 et 1992.

**2.2.2 Femmes:**

- 1950-70, taux d'activité 1950-70 tirés des EPPA3;
- 1980-90, aux moyennes des taux d'activité tirés des enquêtes de 1991 et 1992, application de 3/4 des variations des taux d'activité estimés pour le Mexique entre 1980 et 1990.

## 3. Evaluation des taux de répartition par secteur d'activité: 1950 - 1990

### 3.1 Données de base:

Tableau 2: Répartition de la population active en % par secteur d'activité

| Année | Agriculture | Industrie Total | Manufac. | Services |
|---|---|---|---|---|
| **Hommes** | | | | |
| 1974 (1) | 71.76 | 12.84 | 8.30 | 15.41 |
| 1991 (2) | 45.27 | 23.69 | 16.34 | 31.03 |
| **Femmes** | | | | |
| 1980 (1) | 7.10 | 30.18 | .. | 62.72 |
| 1991 (2) | 22.09 | 12.00 | 11.82 | 65.91 |

Source(s): (1) STAT; (2) EPPA3.

### 3.2 Méthode(s): interpolation linéaire
moyenne pondérée

**3.2.1 Hommes:**

- 1950-70, taux de répartition 1950-70 tirés des EPPA3;
- 1980-90, moyennes pondérées des taux de répartition tirés du recensement de 1974 et des moyennes des taux des enquêtes de 1991 et 1992.

**3.2.2 Femmes:**

- 1950-70, taux de répartition 1950-70 tirés des EPPA3;
- 1980-90, interpolation des taux de répartition 1980 tirés des EPPA3 et de la moyenne des taux tirés des enquêtes de 1991 et 1992; ajustement des taux sur la base du rapport hommes/femmes dans l'agriculture tiré de l'enquête de 1991.

## 4. Projection des taux d'activité: 2000 - 2010

### 4.1 Modèle(s): linéaire, log-linéaire, hyperbole et logistique

**4.1.1 Hommes:**

- Au groupe d'âge [10-14], application de la fonction F2;
- Aux groupes d'âge [15+], application de la fonction F3;
- Modification de la tendance du groupe d'âge [10-14].

**4.1.2 Femmes:**

- Aux groupes d'âge [10-14] et [30+], application de la fonction F1;
- Aux groupes d'âge [15-29], application de la fonction F6;
- Modification des tendances des groupes d'âge [15+].

*Notes sur les ajustements des taux, voir p. 192-195.*

*Notes sur les fonctions de projection, voir p. 198.*

# Hong-kong, Chine

## 1. Source(s) des données de base

Code(s):      Titre(s):

EPPA3      Evaluations et projections de la population active 1950-2025 - troisième édition, BIT, Genève, 1986.
STAT      Base de données sur les statistiques du travail - LABORSTA, Bureau de statistique, BIT, Genève.

## 2. Evaluation des taux d'activité: 1950 - 1990

### 2.1 Données de base:

Tableau 1: Taux d'activité par sexe et par groupe d'âge

| Groupe d'âge | Année 1979 | 1980 | 1981 | 1989 | 1990 | 1991 |
|---|---|---|---|---|---|---|
| **Hommes** | | | | | | |
| 10-14 | 0.00 | 0.00 | 0.00 | 0.00 | 0.00 | 0.00 |
| 15-19 | 35.80 | 39.60 | 45.50 | 31.10 | 29.80 | 29.30 |
| 20-24 | 87.40 | 89.00 | 91.90 | 86.30 | 86.00 | 84.50 |
| 25-29 | 98.50 | 97.90 | 98.30 | 98.30 | 98.40 | 97.50 |
| 30-34 | 98.70 | 99.10 | 98.80 | 98.90 | 98.90 | 98.80 |
| 35-39 | 99.10 | 98.90 | 98.90 | 98.90 | 98.80 | 98.70 |
| 40-44 | 98.40 | 98.60 | 98.30 | 99.00 | 98.90 | 98.40 |
| 45-49 | 97.50 | 97.40 | 97.40 | 97.70 | 97.80 | 97.80 |
| 50-54 | 93.90 | 93.60 | 93.80 | 93.30 | 92.80 | 92.40 |
| 55-59 | 83.30 | 84.00 | 83.00 | 81.20 | 81.20 | 81.60 |
| 60-64 | 64.40 | 64.10 | 67.00 | 56.80 | 54.70 | 54.60 |
| 65+ | 32.50 | 32.10 | 35.20 | 22.50 | 21.40 | 20.80 |
| **Femmes** | | | | | | |
| 10-14 | 0.00 | 0.00 | 0.00 | 0.00 | 0.00 | 0.00 |
| 15-19 | 39.50 | 39.00 | 42.70 | 31.10 | 29.80 | 29.30 |
| 20-24 | 78.00 | 79.70 | 80.00 | 86.30 | 86.00 | 84.50 |
| 25-29 | 58.40 | 60.30 | 61.30 | 76.40 | 77.90 | 79.60 |
| 30-34 | 41.60 | 44.70 | 49.20 | 54.10 | 55.30 | 59.10 |
| 35-39 | 41.60 | 44.70 | 49.20 | 52.20 | 52.30 | 52.30 |
| 40-44 | 44.80 | 48.00 | 54.10 | 53.40 | 53.50 | 53.90 |
| 45-49 | 41.20 | 44.20 | 49.40 | 51.00 | 52.30 | 52.20 |
| 50-54 | 36.80 | 36.00 | 44.60 | 39.50 | 38.10 | 41.60 |
| 55-59 | 33.70 | 31.50 | 36.90 | 28.30 | 27.10 | 27.50 |
| 60-64 | 19.60 | 19.80 | 22.20 | 19.50 | 18.40 | 17.20 |
| 65+ | 11.30 | 11.90 | 13.70 | 7.60 | 5.90 | 6.40 |

Source(s): STAT.

### 2.2 Méthode(s): interpolation linéaire

#### 2.2.1 Hommes:

- 1950-80, taux d'activité 1950-80 tirés des EPPA3;
- 1990, interpolation des taux d'activité ajustés tirés des enquêtes de 1979 à 1992;
ajustement des taux interpolés sur la base des variations des taux interpolés 1980 par rapport aux taux 1980 tirés des EPPA3.

#### 2.2.2 Femmes:

- 1950-70, taux d'activité 1950-70 tirés des EPPA3;
- 1980-90, interpolation des taux d'activité tirés des enquêtes de 1979 à 1992.

## 3. Evaluation des taux de répartition par secteur d'activité: 1950 - 1990

### 3.1 Données de base:

Tableau 2: Répartition de la population active en % par secteur d'activité

| Année | Agriculture | Industrie Total | Manufac. | Services |
|---|---|---|---|---|
| **Hommes** | | | | |
| 1979 | 1.42 | 46.69 | 36.02 | 51.89 |
| 1980 | 1.44 | 47.21 | 35.05 | 51.36 |
| 1981 | 1.31 | 45.52 | 31.85 | 53.18 |
| 1989 | 1.14 | 40.16 | 26.52 | 58.69 |
| 1990 | 0.95 | 38.85 | 25.31 | 60.20 |
| 1991 | 0.84 | 38.13 | 24.68 | 61.03 |
| **Femmes** | | | | |
| 1979 | 0.89 | 57.72 | 56.30 | 41.39 |
| 1980 | 1.08 | 56.15 | 54.76 | 42.77 |
| 1981 | 1.59 | 54.27 | 52.82 | 44.13 |
| 1989 | 1.08 | 36.39 | 35.27 | 62.53 |
| 1990 | 0.71 | 33.04 | 31.86 | 66.25 |
| 1991 | 0.43 | 29.56 | 28.39 | 70.01 |

Source(s): STAT.

### 3.2 Méthode(s): moyenne arithmétique

#### 3.2.1 Hommes:

- 1950-70, taux de répartition 1950-70 tirés des EPPA3;
- 1980, moyennes des taux de répartition tirés des enquêtes de 1979, 1980 et 1981;
- 1990, moyennes des taux de répartition tirés des enquêtes de 1989, 1990 et 1991.

#### 3.2.2 Femmes:

Méthode, hypothèses et traitements identiques à ceux appliqués aux hommes.

## 4. Projection des taux d'activité: 2000 - 2010

### 4.1 Modèle(s): linéaire, hyperbole et logistique

#### 4.1.1 Hommes:

- Aux groupes d'âge [15-54], application de la fonction F1;
- Aux groupes d'âge [55+], application de la fonction F3;
- Modification des tendances des groupes d'âge [15+].

#### 4.1.2 Femmes:

- Aux groupes d'âge [15-24], application de la fonction F1;
- Aux groupes d'âge [25-54], application de la fonction F6;
- Aux groupes d'âge [55+], application de la fonction F3;
- Modification des tendances des groupes d'âge [15-54].

---

*Notes sur les ajustements des taux, voir p. 192-195.*      *Notes sur les fonctions de projection, voir p. 198.*

# Hongrie

## 1. Source(s) des données de base

Code(s):    Titre(s):

EPPA3       Evaluations et projections de la population active 1950-2025 - troisième édition, BIT, Genève, 1986.
BLT-94-2    Popovic B. (1994), "Nouvelles estimations pour 1980 et 1990 des taux d'activité par âge et répartition sectorielle
            pour certains pays d'Europe orientale et méridionale" dans le Bulletin des statistiques du travail - 1994-2, BIT, Genève.

## 2. Evaluation des taux d'activité: 1950 - 1990

### 2.1 Données de base:

Tableau 1: Taux d'activité par sexe et par groupe d'âge

| Groupe d'âge | Année 1950 (1) | 1960 (1) | 1970 (1) | 1980 (2) | 1990 (2) |
|---|---|---|---|---|---|
| **Hommes** | | | | | |
| 10-14 | 6.65 | 2.20 | 0.75 | 0.26 | 0.23 |
| 15-19 | 79.20 | 75.00 | 64.00 | 60.02 | 52.69 |
| 20-24 | 93.60 | 93.05 | 92.50 | 91.77 | 88.27 |
| 25-29 | 97.65 | 98.00 | 98.35 | 98.14 | 96.72 |
| 30-34 | 98.70 | 98.65 | 98.60 | 98.35 | 97.11 |
| 35-39 | 98.25 | 98.15 | 98.10 | 97.68 | 96.15 |
| 40-44 | 98.05 | 97.55 | 97.00 | 95.95 | 94.31 |
| 45-49 | 97.20 | 96.05 | 95.00 | 92.79 | 90.75 |
| 50-54 | 95.75 | 93.15 | 91.00 | 86.02 | 81.39 |
| 55-59 | 92.45 | 88.00 | 84.50 | 71.72 | 60.46 |
| 60-64 | 83.20 | 76.00 | 75.00 | 12.53 | 3.55 |
| 65+ | 64.40 | 57.00 | 54.00 | 3.82 | 0.98 |
| **Femmes** | | | | | |
| 10-14 | 6.50 | 3.00 | 2.50 | 0.64 | 0.47 |
| 15-19 | 55.55 | 54.00 | 53.00 | 46.81 | 41.97 |
| 20-24 | 45.00 | 55.40 | 66.00 | 59.96 | 61.22 |
| 25-29 | 35.50 | 48.70 | 65.30 | 69.61 | 64.34 |
| 30-34 | 33.00 | 49.10 | 68.70 | 80.96 | 78.86 |
| 35-39 | 30.00 | 50.70 | 71.00 | 85.03 | 86.62 |
| 40-44 | 29.00 | 51.80 | 69.40 | 83.33 | 87.74 |
| 45-49 | 28.00 | 49.70 | 64.00 | 77.74 | 83.60 |
| 50-54 | 27.00 | 46.30 | 56.60 | 67.49 | 68.49 |
| 55-59 | 28.50 | 30.60 | 29.20 | 18.22 | 5.07 |
| 60-64 | 27.00 | 26.00 | 23.00 | 8.20 | 1.63 |
| 65+ | 20.00 | 20.00 | 18.00 | 3.05 | 0.21 |

Source(s): (1) EPPA3; (2) BLT-94-2.

### 2.2 Méthode(s): Données tirées des EPPA3 et du BLT-94-2.

#### 2.2.1 Hommes:

- 1950-70, taux d'activité 1950-70 tirés des EPPA3;
- 1980-90, taux d'activité tirés du Bulletin des statistiques du travail 1994-2; ajustement des taux d'activité des groupes d'âge [15-19] pour tenir compte des jeunes apprentis.

#### 2.2.2 Femmes:

Méthode, hypothèses et traitements identiques à ceux appliqués aux hommes.

## 3. Evaluation des taux de répartition par secteur d'activité: 1950 - 1990

### 3.1 Données de base:

Tableau 2: Répartition de la population active en % par secteur d'activité

| Année | Agriculture | Industrie Total | Manufac. | Services |
|---|---|---|---|---|
| **Hommes** | | | | |
| 1950 (1) | 51.30 | 26.40 | .. | 22.30 |
| 1960 (1) | 36.60 | 38.40 | .. | 24.90 |
| 1970 (1) | 26.80 | 47.80 | .. | 25.40 |
| 1980 (2) | 20.86 | 47.49 | 28.90 | 31.65 |
| 1990 (2) | 18.91 | 42.36 | 29.30 | 38.73 |
| **Femmes** | | | | |
| 1950 (1) | 52.90 | 17.30 | ... | 29.80 |
| 1960 (1) | 40.60 | 28.40 | ... | 30.90 |
| 1970 (1) | 22.60 | 40.30 | ... | 37.00 |
| 1980 (2) | 15.21 | 38.15 | 32.51 | 46.64 |
| 1990 (2) | 10.53 | 32.12 | 28.76 | 57.34 |

Source(s): (1) EPPA3; (2) BLT-94-2.

### 3.2 Méthode(s): données du BLT-94-2

#### 3.2.1 Hommes:

- 1950-70, taux de répartition 1950-70 tirés des EPPA3;
- 1980-90, taux de répartition tirés du Bulletin des statistiques du travail - 1994-2.

#### 3.2.2 Femmes:

Méthode, hypothèses et traitements identiques à ceux appliqués aux hommes.

## 4. Projection des taux d'activité: 2000 - 2010

### 4.1 Modèle(s): linéaire, hyperbole et logistique

#### 4.1.1 Hommes:

- Au groupe d'âge [15-19], application de la fonction F1;
- Aux groupes d'âge [20+], application de la fonction F3;
- Modification des tendances des groupes d'âge [35+].

#### 4.1.2 Femmes:

- Au groupe d'âge [15-19], application de la fonction F1;
- Aux groupes d'âge [20-54], application de la fonction F6;
- Aux groupes d'âge [55+], application de la fonction F3;
- Modification des tendances des groupes d'âge [20+].

*Notes sur les ajustements des taux, voir p. 192-195.*     *Notes sur les fonctions de projection, voir p. 198.*

# Iles Salomon

## 1. Source(s) des données de base

| Code(s): | Titre(s): |
|---|---|
| EPPA3 | Annuaire des statistiques du travail 1945-89 - Edition rétrospective sur les recensements de population, BIT, Genève, 1990. |
| STAT | Base de données sur les statistiques du travail - LABORSTA, Bureau de statistique, BIT, Genève. |

## 2. Evaluation des taux d'activité: 1950 - 1990

### 2.1 Données de base:

Tableau 1: Taux d'activité par sexe et par groupe d'âge

| Groupe d'âge | Année 1950 (1) | 1960 (1) | 1970 (1) | 1980 (1) | 1986 (2) |
|---|---|---|---|---|---|
| **Hommes** | | | | | |
| 10-14 | 45.48 | 41.48 | 37.49 | 33.61 | 33.60 |
| 15-19 | 81.99 | 77.86 | 72.45 | 65.23 | 77.27 |
| 20-24 | 97.00 | 95.88 | 94.01 | 91.23 | 96.33 |
| 25-29 | 98.33 | 98.09 | 97.74 | 97.24 | 97.50 |
| 30-34 | 98.54 | 98.30 | 97.98 | 97.52 | 97.57 |
| 35-39 | 98.71 | 98.49 | 98.20 | 97.72 | 97.52 |
| 40-44 | 98.64 | 98.36 | 98.03 | 97.53 | 96.54 |
| 45-49 | 97.17 | 97.06 | 96.65 | 96.04 | 96.01 |
| 50-54 | 94.99 | 94.44 | 93.80 | 92.98 | 92.24 |
| 55-59 | 90.73 | 89.91 | 88.96 | 87.61 | 86.26 |
| 60-64 | 83.42 | 81.90 | 80.49 | 78.43 | 79.31 |
| 65+ | 63.18 | 61.14 | 59.04 | 62.39 | 68.98 |
| **Femmes** | | | | | |
| 10-14 | 38.84 | 36.20 | 33.33 | 31.03 | 41.86 |
| 15-19 | 62.38 | 58.54 | 54.99 | 50.60 | 81.77 |
| 20-24 | 66.44 | 63.56 | 61.43 | 59.13 | 87.81 |
| 25-29 | 66.86 | 64.58 | 61.16 | 58.34 | 86.15 |
| 30-34 | 68.09 | 66.33 | 63.26 | 60.85 | 89.49 |
| 35-39 | 70.01 | 67.90 | 65.04 | 60.76 | 88.54 |
| 40-44 | 72.15 | 68.36 | 66.65 | 63.24 | 88.50 |
| 45-49 | 71.75 | 68.61 | 65.31 | 61.45 | 88.70 |
| 50-54 | 70.48 | 67.89 | 63.18 | 60.28 | 87.10 |
| 55-59 | 63.48 | 61.55 | 56.08 | 53.33 | 86.27 |
| 60-64 | 54.56 | 54.04 | 48.61 | 43.77 | 74.11 |
| 65+ | 42.92 | 37.78 | 33.57 | 24.81 | 56.38 |

Source(s): (1) EPPA3; (2) STAT.

### 2.2 Méthode(s): interpolation et extrapolation linéaires

#### 2.2.1 Hommes:

- 1950-90, interpolation et extrapolation des taux d'activité 1950-80 tirés des EPPA3;
modification des tendances de tous les groupes d'âge;
aux taux d'activité extrapolés 1990, application des variations des taux taux extrapolés 1986 par rapport aux taux tirés du recensement de 1986.

#### 2.2.2 Femmes:

Méthode, hypothèses et traitements identiques à ceux appliqués aux hommes.

## 3. Evaluation des taux de répartition par secteur d'activité: 1950 - 1990

### 3.1 Données de base:

Tableau 2: Répartition de la population active en % par secteur d'activité

| Année | Agriculture | Industrie Total | Manufac. | Services |
|---|---|---|---|---|
| **Hommes** | | | | |
| 1986 | 69.05 | 10.15 | 4.22 | 20.80 |
| **Femmes** | | | | |
| 1986 | 86.19 | 2.96 | 2.36 | 10.85 |

Source(s): STAT.

### 3.2 Méthode(s): interpolation linéaire

#### 3.2.1 Hommes:

- 1950-90, interpolation des aux taux estimés 1950-90 pour la Papouasie-Nouvelle-Guinée;
modification des tendances de tous les secteurs pour 1980 et 1990;
aux taux interpolés 1950-90, application des variations des taux interpolés pour 1986 par rapport aux taux tirés du recensement de 1986;
- Application du rapport manufacture/industrie tiré du recensement de 1966.

#### 3.2.2 Femmes:

Méthode, hypothèses et traitements identiques à ceux appliqués aux hommes.

## 4. Projection des taux d'activité: 2000 - 2010

### 4.1 Modèle(s): linéaire et hyperbole

#### 4.1.1 Hommes:

- A tous les groupes d'âge, application de la fonction F3;
- Modification des tendances des groupes d'âge [10-44].

#### 4.1.2 Femmes:

- Aux groupes d'âge [10-19] et [60+], application de la fonction F1;
- Aux groupes d'âge [20-59], application de la fonction F3;
- Modification des tendances des groupes d'âge [10-19] et [50+].

# Inde

## 1. Source(s) des données de base

| Code(s): | Titre(s): |
|---|---|
| EPPA3 | Evaluations et projections de la population active 1950-2025 - troisième édition, BIT, Genève, 1986. |
| ADNU | Editions de 1984 et 1988 de l'Annuaire démographique des Nations Unies, New York. |
| STAT | Base de données sur les statistiques du travail - LABORSTA, Bureau de statistique, BIT, Genève. |

## 2. Evaluation des taux d'activité: 1950 - 1990

### 2.1 Données de base:

Tableau 1: Taux d'activité par sexe et par groupe d'âge

| Groupe d'âge | Année 1950 (1) | 1960 (1) | 1970 (1) | 1981 (2) | 1983 (2) | 1990 (3) |
|---|---|---|---|---|---|---|
| **Hommes** | | | | | | |
| 10-14 | 41.40 | 33.60 | 25.80 | 22.14 | 22.77 | 12.40 |
| 15-19 | 76.95 | 69.40 | 62.40 | 61.69 | 65.18 | 54.63 |
| 20-24 | 93.55 | 90.35 | 89.20 | 88.42 | 89.65 | 86.18 |
| 25-29 | 97.50 | 97.35 | 96.65 | 96.80 | 96.89 | 96.47 |
| 30-34 | 97.80 | 97.70 | 97.70 | 98.32 | 98.54 | 97.03 |
| 35-39 | 97.80 | 97.70 | 97.70 | 98.61 | 98.80 | 98.02 |
| 40-44 | 97.70 | 97.60 | 97.60 | 98.66 | 98.69 | 97.90 |
| 45-49 | 97.35 | 96.95 | 97.10 | 97.48 | 97.48 | 97.76 |
| 50-54 | 96.60 | 95.95 | 95.50 | 95.31 | 94.99 | 96.30 |
| 55-59 | 96.00 | 94.00 | 92.50 | 91.85 | 90.81 | 92.97 |
| 60-64 | 89.60 | 85.25 | 81.65 | 75.62 | 74.32 | 76.48 |
| 65+ | 71.65 | 68.65 | 63.65 | 57.96 | 56.53 | 58.92 |
| **Femmes** | | | | | | |
| 10-14 | 28.05 | 25.30 | 20.75 | 15.15 | 20.16 | 11.68 |
| 15-19 | 38.25 | 35.40 | 31.00 | 32.36 | 39.70 | 25.05 |
| 20-24 | 45.40 | 42.40 | 36.35 | 35.34 | 44.33 | 34.47 |
| 25-29 | 51.40 | 48.50 | 42.15 | 35.98 | 45.52 | 34.66 |
| 30-34 | 52.40 | 49.50 | 44.30 | 37.09 | 54.71 | 38.70 |
| 35-39 | 53.40 | 51.00 | 45.65 | 38.03 | 47.78 | 36.60 |
| 40-44 | 52.05 | 49.85 | 44.60 | 37.59 | 59.68 | 42.61 |
| 45-49 | 50.25 | 48.30 | 43.50 | 36.36 | 58.52 | 45.17 |
| 50-54 | 40.25 | 44.20 | 39.60 | 31.87 | 43.77 | 36.06 |
| 55-59 | 41.25 | 38.35 | 34.55 | 28.25 | 42.46 | 31.40 |
| 60-64 | 32.70 | 30.45 | 27.15 | 22.11 | 30.07 | 24.24 |
| 65+ | 19.75 | 15.50 | 13.20 | 9.81 | 15.16 | 11.24 |

Source(s): (1) EPPA3; (2) ADNU; (3) STAT.

### 2.2 Méthode(s): interpolation linéaire

#### 2.2.1 Hommes:

- 1950-90, interpolation des taux d'activité 1950-70 tirés des EPPA3 et des taux tirés du recensement de 1981 et des enquêtes de 1983 et 1989/90.

#### 2.2.2 Femmes:

- 1950-70, taux d'activité ajustés 1950-70 tirés des EPPA3; ajustement des taux sur la base du modèle d'ajustement des taux d'activité des femmes travaillant dans l'agriculture comme aides familiales;
- 1980-90, interpolation des taux d'activité tirés du recensement de 1981 et des enquêtes de 1983 et 1989/90.

## 3. Evaluation des taux de répartition par secteur d'activité: 1950 - 1990

### 3.1 Données de base:

Tableau 2: Répartition de la population active en % par secteur d'activité

| Année | Agriculture | Industrie Total | Manufac. | Services |
|---|---|---|---|---|
| **Hommes** | | | | |
| 1981 | 65.89 | 15.05 | 12.01 | 19.07 |
| 1983 | 62.41 | 15.58 | .. | 22.00 |
| 1990 | 58.35 | 16.37 | .. | 25.28 |
| **Femmes** | | | | |
| 1981 | 84.07 | 8.60 | 7.58 | 7.32 |
| 1983 | 81.12 | 10.18 | .. | 8.69 |
| 1990 | 74.82 | 14.47 | .. | 10.71 |

Source(s): STAT.

### 3.2 Méthode(s): interpolation et extrapolation linéaires

#### 3.2.1 Hommes:

- 1970-90, interpolation des taux de répartition 1950-70 tirés des des EPPA3 et des taux de répartition tirés des enquêtes de 1983 et 1989/90;
- Application du rapport manufacture/industrie tiré du recensement de 1981.

#### 3.2.2 Femmes:

- 1950-70, taux de répartition 1950-70 tirés des EPPA3;
- 1980-90, interpolation et extrapolation des taux de répartition tirés du recensement de 1983 et de l'enquête de 1989/90;
- Application du rapport manufacture/industrie tiré du recensement de 1981.

## 4. Projection des taux d'activité: 2000 - 2010

### 4.1 Modèle(s): linéaire, log-linéaire et hyperbole

#### 4.1.1 Hommes:

- Au groupe d'âge [10-14], application de la fonction F2;
- Aux groupes d'âge [15+], application de la fonction F1;
- Modification des tendances des groupes d'âge [10-54].

#### 4.1.2 Femmes:

- Aux groupes d'âge [10-19] et [40-59], application de la fonction F1;
- Aux groupes d'âge [20-39] et [60+], application de la fonction F3;
- Aux groupes d'âge [10-59], application de la fonction F1.

*Notes sur les ajustements des taux, voir p. 192-195.*

*Notes sur les fonctions de projection, voir p. 198.*

# Indonésie

## 1. Source(s) des données de base

Code(s):     Titre(s):

EPPA3      Evaluations et projections de la population active 1950-2025 - troisième édition, BIT, Genève, 1986.
STAT       Base de données sur les statistiques du travail - LABORSTA, Bureau de statistique, BIT, Genève.

## 2. Evaluation des taux d'activité: 1950 - 1990

### 2.1 Données de base:

Tableau 1: Taux d'activité par sexe et par groupe d'âge

| Groupe d'âge | Année | | | |
|---|---|---|---|---|
| | 1978 | 1982 | 1988 | 1992 |
| **Hommes** | | | | |
| 10-14 | .. | .. | 13.70 | 12.52 |
| 15-19 | .. | .. | 45.60 | 47.76 |
| 20-24 | .. | .. | 77.30 | 76.75 |
| 25-29 | .. | .. | 94.10 | 93.60 |
| 30-34 | .. | .. | 97.80 | 97.52 |
| 35-39 | .. | .. | 98.60 | 98.68 |
| 40-44 | .. | .. | 98.40 | 98.04 |
| 45-49 | .. | .. | 97.80 | 97.58 |
| 50-54 | .. | .. | 95.40 | 93.84 |
| 55-59 | .. | .. | 89.10 | 89.55 |
| 60-64 | .. | .. | 79.20 | 79.67 |
| 65+ | .. | .. | 56.30 | 56.84 |
| **Femmes** | | | | |
| 10-14 | .. | 9.00 | 10.90 | 7.97 |
| 15-19 | 36.20 | 33.20 | 36.20 | 34.86 |
| 20-24 | 38.30 | 41.40 | 52.70 | 46.31 |
| 25-29 | 44.40 | 43.90 | 56.50 | 52.18 |
| 30-34 | 52.60 | 47.00 | 58.80 | 54.43 |
| 35-39 | .. | 51.80 | 62.10 | 58.00 |
| 40-44 | | 54.70 | 64.20 | 59.56 |
| 45-49 | .. | 56.70 | 63.60 | 60.55 |
| 50-54 | 52.90 | 51.10 | 60.70 | 57.65 |
| 55-59 | 49.20 | 50.40 | 55.60 | 52.17 |
| 60-64 | 42.30 | 39.30 | 46.10 | 42.73 |
| 65+ | 27 | 23.2 | 25.40 | 25.09 |

Source(s): STAT.

### 2.2 Méthode(s): moyenne arithmétique

#### 2.2.1 Hommes:

- 1950-80, taux d'activité 1950-80 tirés des EPPA3;
- 1990, moyennes des taux d'activité tirés des enquêtes de 1988 et 1992.

#### 2.2.2 Femmes:

- 1950-70, taux d'activité 1950-70 tirés des EPPA3;
- 1980, moyennes des taux d'activité ajustés tirés des enquêtes de 1978 et 1982;
- 1990, moyennes des taux d'activité ajustés tirés des enquêtes de 1988 et 1992.

## 3. Evaluation des taux de répartition par secteur d'activité: 1950 - 1990

### 3.1 Données de base:

Tableau 2: Répartition de la population active en % par secteur d'activité

| Année | Agriculture | Industrie | | Services |
|---|---|---|---|---|
| | | Total | Manufac. | |
| **Hommes** | | | | |
| 1978 | 62.75 | 8.63 | 5.88 | 28.61 |
| 1982 | 55.16 | 15.16 | 8.47 | 29.68 |
| 1989 | 55.72 | 14.08 | 8.90 | 30.19 |
| 1992 | 53.74 | 15.09 | 8.92 | 31.17 |
| **Femmes** | | | | |
| 1978 | 57.74 | 10.37 | 10.17 | 31.89 |
| 1982 | 53.77 | 14.47 | 13.90 | 31.77 |
| 1989 | 57.09 | 12.05 | 13.01 | 30.86 |
| 1992 | 55.06 | 13.51 | 12.85 | 31.43 |

Source(s): STAT.

### 3.2 Méthode(s): moyenne pondérée
moyenne arithmétique

#### 3.2.1 Hommes:

- 1950-70, taux de répartition 1950-70 tirés des EPPA3;
- 1980, moyennes des taux de répartition tirés des enquêtes de 1978 et 1982;
- 1990, moyennes pondérées des taux de répartition tirés des enquêtes de 1989 et 1992.

#### 3.2.2 Femmes:

Méthode, hypothèses et traitements identiques à ceux appliqués aux hommes.

## 4. Projection des taux d'activité: 2000 - 2010

### 4.1 Modèle(s): linéaire, log-linéaire, hyperbole et logistique

#### 4.1.1 Hommes:

- Aux groupes d'âge [10-14] et [50+], application de la fonction F1;
- Au groupe d'âge [15-19], application de la fonction F2;
- Aux groupes d'âge [20-49], application de la fonction F3;
- Modification des tendances des groupes d'âge [20-44].

#### 4.1.2 Femmes:

- Aux groupes d'âge [10-19] et [65+], application de la fonction F3;
- Au groupe d'âge [20-24], application de la fonction F1;
- Aux groupes d'âge [25-64], application de la fonction F6;
- Modification de la tendance du groupe d'âge [15-19].

*Notes sur les ajustements des taux, voir p. 192-195.*          *Notes sur les fonctions de projection, voir p. 198.*

# Iran, Rép. islamique d'

## 1. Source(s) des données de base

| Code(s): | Titre(s): |
|---|---|
| EPPA3 | Evaluations et projections de la population active 1950-2025 - troisième édition, BIT, Genève, 1986. |
| ADNU84 | Editions de 1984 et 1988 de l'Annuaire démographique des Nations Unies, New York. |
| ASTER | Annuaire des statistiques du travail 1945-89 - Edition rétrospective sur les recensements de population, BIT, Genève, 1990. |
| AST92 | Annuaire des statistiques du travail 1992, BIT, Genève, 1992. |
| STAT | Base de données sur les statistiques du travail - LABORSTA, Bureau de statistique, BIT, Genève. |

## 2. Evaluation des taux d'activité: 1950 - 1990

### 2.1 Données de base:

Tableau 1: Taux d'activité par sexe et par groupe d'âge

| Groupe d'âge | Année 1976 (1) | 1986 (2) | 1991 (3) |
|---|---|---|---|
| **Hommes** | | | |
| 10-14 | 18.41 | 11.44 | 6.86 |
| 15-19 | 53.34 | 50.41 | 42.49 |
| 20-24 | 86.44 | 86.34 | 82.95 |
| 25-29 | 95.74 | 94.08 | 94.28 |
| 30-34 | 97.84 | 96.14 | 97.02 |
| 35-39 | 98.38 | 96.64 | 97.46 |
| 40-44 | 97.72 | 95.84 | 96.76 |
| 45-49 | 96.02 | 93.27 | 94.86 |
| 50-54 | 92.44 | 89.65 | 90.94 |
| 55-59 | 86.25 | 84.05 | 86.96 |
| 60-64 | 77.04 | 76.34 | 78.97 |
| 65+ | 56.40 | 53.10 | 59.48 |
| **Femmes** | | | |
| 10-14 | 10.75 | 4.49 | 3.90 |
| 15-19 | 15.74 | 9.40 | 11.10 |
| 20-24 | 17.90 | 12.01 | 14.01 |
| 25-29 | 16.11 | 11.15 | 11.50 |
| 30-34 | 14.14 | 11.16 | 11.16 |
| 35-39 | 12.75 | 9.46 | 10.84 |
| 40-44 | 11.72 | 7.79 | 8.79 |
| 45-49 | 10.89 | 6.21 | 6.84 |
| 50-54 | 9.73 | 5.44 | 4.98 |
| 55-59 | 8.10 | 4.84 | 4.13 |
| 60-64 | 6.62 | 4.24 | 3.75 |
| 65+ | 4.48 | 2.80 | 3.45 |

Source(s): (1) ASTER et ADNU84; (2) AST92; (3) STAT.

### 2.2 Méthode(s): interpolation linéaire

#### 2.2.1 Hommes:

- 1950-70, taux d'activité 1950-70 tirés des EPPA3;
- 1980-90, interpolation des taux d'activité ajustés tirés des recensements de 1976 et 1991.

#### 2.2.2 Femmes:

- 1950-70, taux d'activité ajustés 1950-70 tirés des EPPA3; ajustement des taux sur la base du modèle d'ajustement des taux d'activité des femmes travaillant dans l'agriculture comme aides familiales;
- 1980-90, interpolation des taux d'activité ajustés tirés des recensements de 1986 et 1991; l'ajustement a été accompli sur la base d'un rapport hommes/femmes égal à 2/3 dans l'agriculture; modification des tendances de tous les groupes d'âge pour 1980 et des groupes d'âge [10-14] et [60+] pour 1990.

## 3. Evaluation des taux de répartition par secteur d'activité: 1950 - 1990

### 3.1 Données de base:

Tableau 2: Répartition de la population active en % par secteur d'activité

| Année | Agriculture | Industrie Total | Manufac. | Services |
|---|---|---|---|---|
| **Hommes** | | | | |
| 1976 | 36.88 | 31.27 | 13.69 | 31.84 |
| 1986 | 30.27 | 26.33 | 12.78 | 43.40 |
| **Femmes** | | | | |
| 1976 | 45.45 | 36.92 | 35.65 | 17.63 |
| 1986 | 27.97 | 24.33 | 23.02 | 47.70 |

Source(s): ASTER.

### 3.2 Méthode(s): interpolation et extrapolation linéaires

#### 3.2.1 Hommes:
- 1950-70, taux de répartition 1950-70 tirés des EPPA3;
- 1980-90, interpolation et extrapolation des taux de répartition tirés des recensements de 1976 et 1986; modification des tendances de tous les secteurs.

#### 3.2.2 Femmes:
- 1950-70, taux de répartition de l'agriculture 1950-70 tirés des EPPA3; ajustement des taux en tenant compte de la sous-énumération des femmes travaillant dans l'agriculture;
- 1980-90, interpolation et extrapolation des taux de répartition ajustés tirés des recensements de 1976 et 1986; ajustement des taux sur la base d'un rapport hommes/femmes dans l'agriculture égal à 2/3;
- Application du rapport manufacture/industrie tiré du recensement de 1986.

## 4. Projection des taux d'activité: 2000 - 2010

### 4.1 Modèle(s): linéaire, log-linéaire, hyperbole et logistique

#### 4.1.1 Hommes:
- Au groupe d'âge [10-14], application de la fonction F1;
- Aux groupes d'âge [15+], application de la fonction F3;
- Modification des tendances des groupes d'âge [20-24] et [50-54].

#### 4.1.2 Femmes:
- Au groupe d'âge [10-14], application de la fonction F1;
- Aux groupes d'âge [15-19] et [54+], application de la fonction F6;
- Aux groupes d'âge [20-49], application de la fonction F2;
- Modification des tendances des groupes d'âge [10-59].

*Notes sur les ajustements des taux, voir p. 192-195.*

*Notes sur les fonctions de projection, voir p. 198.*

# Iraq

## 1. Source(s) des données de base

Code(s):    Titre(s):

EPPA3      Evaluations et projections de la population active 1950-2025 - troisième édition, BIT, Genève, 1986.
ASTER      Annuaire des statistiques du travail 1945-89 - Edition rétrospective sur les recensements de population, BIT, Genève, 1990.
ADNU88     Annuaire démographique 1988 - Statistiques des recensements de population, quarantième édition, Nations Unies, New York, 1990.
STAT       Base de données sur les statistiques du travail - LABORSTA, Bureau de statistique, BIT, Genève.

## 2. Evaluation des taux d'activité: 1950 - 1990

### 2.1 Données de base:

Tableau 1: Taux d'activité par sexe et par groupe d'âge

| Groupe d'âge | Année | | | | |
|---|---|---|---|---|---|
| | 1950 (1) | 1960 (1) | 1970 (1) | 1977 (2) | 1987 (3) |
| **Hommes** | | | | | |
| 10-14 | 35.50 | 29.00 | 24.00 | 10.97 | 6.18 |
| 15-19 | 80.00 | 67.00 | 50.00 | 39.87 | 41.59 |
| 20-24 | 92.00 | 88.50 | 86.00 | 84.93 | 80.70 |
| 25-29 | 96.00 | 96.25 | 96.50 | 96.65 | 94.81 |
| 30-34 | 97.60 | 97.45 | 97.35 | 97.52 | 95.52 |
| 35-39 | 96.75 | 96.75 | 96.80 | 96.79 | 95.43 |
| 40-44 | 96.50 | 96.00 | 95.50 | 94.86 | 94.27 |
| 45-49 | 96.00 | 94.65 | 93.35 | 92.17 | 87.58 |
| 50-54 | 95.00 | 93.00 | 90.00 | 87.75 | 77.98 |
| 55-59 | 94.00 | 90.00 | 86.00 | 82.88 | 72.07 |
| 60-64 | 92.50 | 86.00 | 79.50 | 74.71 | 70.00 |
| 65+ | 80.00 | 68.00 | 59.00 | 54.01 | 47.98 |
| **Femmes** | | | | | |
| 10-14 | .. | .. | .. | 9.84 | 1.06 |
| 15-19 | .. | .. | .. | 10.86 | 3.57 |
| 20-24 | .. | .. | .. | 15.45 | 14.16 |
| 25-29 | .. | .. | .. | 18.99 | 20.14 |
| 30-34 | .. | .. | .. | 20.84 | 15.28 |
| 35-39 | .. | .. | .. | 19.17 | 12.50 |
| 40-44 | .. | .. | .. | 19.25 | 13.33 |
| 45-49 | .. | .. | .. | 18.60 | 10.14 |
| 50-54 | .. | .. | .. | 18.31 | 7.35 |
| 55-59 | .. | .. | .. | 16.48 | 5.27 |
| 60-64 | .. | .. | .. | 12.96 | 3.81 |
| 65+ | .. | .. | .. | 6.71 | 2.54 |

Source(s): (1) EPPA3; (2) ASTER et ADNU88; (3) STAT.

### 2.2 Méthode(s): extrapolation linéaire
moyenne pondérée

**2.2.1 Hommes:**

- 1950-70, taux d'activité 1950-70 tirés des EPPA3;
- 1980-90, extrapolation des taux d'activité ajustés tirés des recensements de 1977 et 1987;
ajustement des taux interpolés sur la base des variations des taux interpolés 1970 par rapport aux taux 1970 tirés des EPPA3.

**2.2.2 Femmes:**

- 1950-70, taux d'activité ajustés 1950-70 tirés des EPPA3;
- 1980, moyennes pondérées des taux d'activité ajustés tirés des recensements de 1977 et 1987;
- 1990, aux taux estimés 1980 application des variations des taux ajustés du recensement de 1977 par rapport aux taux ajustés du recensement de 1987; ajustement des taux d'activité sur la base du modèle d'ajustement des taux d'activité des femmes travaillant dans l'agriculture comme aides familiales.

## 3. Evaluation des taux de répartition par secteur d'activité: 1950 - 1990

### 3.1 Données de base:

Tableau 2: Répartition de la population active en % par secteur d'activité

| Année | Agriculture | Industrie | | Services |
|---|---|---|---|---|
| | | Total | Manufac. | |
| **Hommes** | | | | |
| 1977 (1) | 23.84 | 24.58 | 9.51 | 51.58 |
| 1987 (2) | 13.21 | 19.81 | 7.14 | 66.98 |
| **Femmes** | | | | |
| 1977 (1) | 67.60 | 10.89 | 9.31 | 21.52 |
| 1987 (2) | 17.35 | 13.84 | 9.50 | 68.81 |

Source(s): (1) ASTER; (2) STAT.

### 3.2 Méthode(s): moyenne pondérée

**3.2.1 Hommes:**

- 1950-70, taux de répartition 1950-70 tirés des EPPA3;
- 1980, moyennes pondérées des taux de répartition ajustés tirés des recensements de 1977 et 1987;
- Pour 1990, application aux taux estimés 1980 des variations des taux ajustés du recensement de 1977 par rapport aux taux ajustés du recensement de 1987.

**3.2.2 Femmes:**

Méthode, hypothèses et traitements identiques à ceux appliqués aux hommes.

## 4. Projection des taux d'activité: 2000 - 2010

### 4.1 Modèle(s): linéaire, log-linéaire, hyperbole et logistique

**4.1.1 Hommes:**

- Au groupe d'âge [10-14], application de la fonction F2;
- Aux groupes d'âge [15-24] et [60+], application de la fonction F3;
- Aux groupes d'âge [25-59], application de la fonction F1;
- Modification des tendances des groupes d'âge [10-14] et [20-59].

**4.1.2 Femmes:**

- Aux groupes d'âge [10-19] et [65+], application de la fonction F1;
- Aux groupes d'âge [20-64], application de la fonction F6;
- Modification des tendances de tous les groupes d'âge.

*Notes sur les ajustements des taux, voir p. 192-195.*          *Notes sur les fonctions de projection, voir p. 198.*

# Irlande

## 1. Source(s) des données de base

Code(s):     Titre(s):

EPPA3       Annuaire des statistiques du travail 1945-89 - Edition rétrospective sur les recensements de population, BIT, Genève, 1990.
STAT        Base de données sur les statistiques du travail - LABORSTA, Bureau de statistique, BIT, Genève.

## 2. Evaluation des taux d'activité: 1950 - 1990

### 2.1 Données de base:

Tableau 1: Taux d'activité par sexe et par groupe d'âge

| | Année | | |
| Groupe d'âge | 1989 | 1990 | 1991 |
|---|---|---|---|
| **Hommes** | | | |
| 10-14 | 0.00 | 0.00 | 0.00 |
| 15-19 | 30.35 | 29.98 | 29.25 |
| 20-24 | 82.40 | 82.08 | 81.12 |
| 25-29 | 96.20 | 95.58 | 95.23 |
| 30-34 | 96.86 | 96.96 | 97.01 |
| 35-39 | 96.01 | 96.03 | 96.44 |
| 40-44 | 95.00 | 95.59 | 95.39 |
| 45-49 | 93.19 | 92.72 | 93.50 |
| 50-54 | 88.62 | 89.78 | 89.39 |
| 55-59 | 79.44 | 79.42 | 79.80 |
| 60-64 | 60.93 | 57.19 | 59.37 |
| 65+ | 16.82 | 15.88 | 15.79 |
| **Femmes** | | | |
| 10-14 | 0.00 | 0.00 | 0.00 |
| 15-19 | 23.39 | 23.57 | 21.11 |
| 20-24 | 73.68 | 73.28 | 73.37 |
| 25-29 | 62.14 | 64.79 | 65.96 |
| 30-34 | 42.05 | 44.65 | 49.43 |
| 35-39 | 30.75 | 34.00 | 38.53 |
| 40-44 | 27.99 | 30.03 | 32.26 |
| 45-49 | 27.00 | 29.28 | 29.50 |
| 50-54 | 23.57 | 26.10 | 27.97 |
| 55-59 | 19.83 | 21.80 | 22.13 |
| 60-64 | 13.27 | 14.51 | 14.04 |
| 65+ | 3.07 | 3.07 | 2.99 |

Source(s): STAT.

### 2.2 Méthode(s): interpolation linéaire

#### 2.2.1 Hommes:

- 1950-80, taux d'activité 1950-80 tirés des EPPA3;
- 1990, interpolation des taux d'activité tirés des enquêtes des mois d'avril 1989, 1990 et 1991;
aux taux interpolés, application des variations des moyennes des taux des enquêtes de 1989, 1990 et 1991 par rapport aux taux de l'enquête de 1990.

#### 2.2.2 Femmes:

Méthode, hypothèses et traitements identiques à ceux appliqués aux hommes.

## 3. Evaluation des taux de répartition par secteur d'activité: 1950 - 1990

### 3.1 Données de base:

Tableau 2: Répartition de la population active en % par secteur d'activité

| | | Agriculture | Industrie | | Services |
| | Année | | Total | Manufac. | |
|---|---|---|---|---|---|
| **Hommes** | | | | | |
| | 1981 | 20.68 | 39.76 | 22.22 | 39.56 |
| | 1989 | 20.56 | 32.18 | 20.16 | 47.26 |
| | 1990 | 20.44 | 33.17 | 20.56 | 46.38 |
| | 1991 | 19.03 | 33.87 | 21.12 | 47.10 |
| **Femmes** | | | | | |
| | 1981 | 3.74 | 21.93 | 20.45 | 74.33 |
| | 1989 | 3.45 | 19.58 | 18.38 | 76.97 |
| | 1990 | 3.70 | 18.76 | 17.57 | 77.53 |
| | 1991 | 3.27 | 18.39 | 16.92 | 78.34 |

Source(s): STAT.

### 3.2 Méthode(s): moyenne arithmétique

#### 3.2.1 Hommes:

- 1950-80, taux de répartition 1950-80 tirés des EPPA3;
le taux de répartition 1980 de manufacture a été ajusté sur la base de l'application au taux de répartition 1980 de l'industrie du rapport manufacture/industrie tiré du recensement de 1981;
- 1990, moyennes ajustées des taux de répartition tirés des enquêtes des mois d'avril de 1989, 1990 et 1991.

#### 3.2.2 Femmes:

Méthode, hypothèses et traitements identiques à ceux appliqués aux hommes.

## 4. Projection des taux d'activité: 2000 - 2010

### 4.1 Modèle(s): linéaire, log-linéaire, hyperbole et logistique

#### 4.1.1 Hommes:

- Aux groupes d'âge [15-24] et [55+], application de la fonction F3;
- Aux groupes d'âge [25-54], application de la fonction F1;
- Modification des tendances des groupes d'âge [35-49].

#### 4.1.2 Femmes:

- Aux groupes d'âge [15-19] et [55+], application de la fonction F3;
- Aux groupes d'âge [20-29], application de la fonction F1;
- Aux groupes d'âge [30-54], application de la fonction F2;
- Modification des tendances des groupes d'âge [15-24] et [30-54].

*Notes sur les ajustements des taux, voir p. 192-195.*

*Notes sur les fonctions de projection, voir p. 198.*

# Islande

## 1. Source(s) des données de base

Code(s): Titre(s):

EPPA3  Evaluations et projections de la population active 1950-2025 - troisième édition, BIT, Genève, 1986.
YNS-94  Yearbook of Nordic Statistics 1994

## 2. Evaluation des taux d'activité: 1950 - 1990

### 2.1 Données de base:

Tableau 1: Taux d'activité par sexe et par groupe d'âge

| Groupe d'âge | 1950 (1) | 1960 (1) | 1970 (1) | 1980 (1) | 1992 (2) |
|---|---|---|---|---|---|
| **Hommes** | | | | | |
| 10-14 | 7.50 | 3.00 | 2.05 | 0.00 | 0.00 |
| 15-19 | 80.70 | 65.65 | 62.50 | 57.42 | 48.40 |
| 20-24 | 91.90 | 90.00 | 90.00 | 89.62 | 77.30 |
| 25-29 | 94.20 | 94.45 | 95.50 | 96.92 | 95.00 |
| 30-34 | 98.80 | 97.70 | 97.45 | 96.89 | 97.00 |
| 35-39 | 98.60 | 97.50 | 97.25 | 96.83 | 97.00 |
| 40-44 | 97.75 | 97.70 | 97.55 | 97.49 | 97.50 |
| 45-49 | 97.80 | 97.20 | 97.60 | 97.34 | 97.35 |
| 50-54 | 97.30 | 95.85 | 95.35 | 94.59 | 94.75 |
| 55-59 | 97.15 | 94.90 | 93.05 | 91.79 | 92.47 |
| 60-64 | 93.25 | 92.20 | 91.45 | 90.85 | 91.16 |
| 65+ | 63.00 | 53.00 | 43.00 | 33.00 | 43.48 |
| **Femmes** | | | | | |
| 10-14 | 3.00 | 1.25 | 0.80 | 0.00 | 0.00 |
| 15-19 | 61.55 | 55.20 | 57.45 | 59.80 | 60.40 |
| 20-24 | 51.35 | 45.30 | 59.30 | 79.00 | 67.60 |
| 25-29 | 34.65 | 29.00 | 46.45 | 76.50 | 76.72 |
| 30-34 | 25.90 | 24.85 | 41.00 | 70.50 | 81.60 |
| 35-39 | 27.80 | 24.85 | 41.05 | 70.70 | 85.12 |
| 40-44 | 29.65 | 28.75 | 44.00 | 68.50 | 88.47 |
| 45-49 | 32.10 | 33.75 | 47.90 | 69.00 | 87.23 |
| 50-54 | 33.35 | 35.60 | 47.75 | 65.40 | 81.23 |
| 55-59 | 34.75 | 36.50 | 43.55 | 52.00 | 79.76 |
| 60-64 | 31.90 | 33.95 | 40.90 | 50.00 | 76.87 |
| 65+ | 12.95 | 15.05 | 14.15 | 13.3 | 23.14 |

Source(s): (1) EPPA3; (2) YNS-94.

### 2.2 Méthode(s): interpolation linéaire

#### 2.2.1 Hommes:

- 1950-80, taux d'activité 1950-80 tirés des EPPA3;
- 1980, interpolation des taux d'activité 1980 tirés des EPPA3 et des taux d'activité 1992 ajustés tirés de l'édition 1994 du Yearbook of Nordic Statistics.

#### 2.2.2 Femmes:

Méthode, hypothèses et traitements identiques à ceux appliqués aux hommes.

## 3. Evaluation des taux de répartition par secteur d'activité: 1950 - 1990

### 3.1 Données de base:

Tableau 2: Répartition de la population active en % par secteur d'activité

| Année | Agriculture | Industrie Total | Manufac. | Services |
|---|---|---|---|---|
| **Hommes** | | | | |
| 1980 (1) | 14.71 | 45.59 | 27.35 | 39.71 |
| 1992 (2) | 16.25 | 32.50 | 18.75 | 51.25 |
| **Femmes** | | | | |
| 1980 (1) | 4.17 | 25.00 | 25.00 | 70.83 |
| 1992 (2) | 4.92 | 14.75 | 14.75 | 80.33 |

Source(s): (1) EPPA3; (2) YNS-94.

### 3.2 Méthode(s): interpolation linéaire

#### 3.2.1 Hommes:

- 1950-80, taux de répartition 1950-80 tirés des EPPA3;
le taux de répartition 1980 de manufacture a été ajusté sur la base du taux de répartition tiré de l'édition 1994 du Yearbook of Nordic Statistics;
- 1990, interpolation des taux de répartition 1980 tirés des EPPA3 et des taux de répartition 1992 tirés du Yearbook.

#### 3.2.2 Femmes:

Méthode, hypothèses et traitements identiques à ceux appliqués aux hommes.

## 4. Projection des taux d'activité: 2000 - 2010

### 4.1 Modèle(s): linéaire, hyperbole et logistique

#### 4.1.1 Hommes:

- Aux groupes d'âge [15-19] et [25-29], application de la fonction F1;
- Aux groupes d'âge [20-54] et [30+], application de la fonction F3;
- Modification de la tendance du groupe d'âge [25-29].

#### 4.1.2 Femmes:

- Au groupe d'âge [15-19], application de la fonction F1;
- Aux groupes d'âge [20-24] et [60+], application de la fonction F3;
- Aux groupes d'âge [25-59], application de la fonction F6;
- Modification des tendances des groupes d'âge [15-24] et [60+].

*Notes sur les ajustements des taux, voir p. 192-195.*    *Notes sur les fonctions de projection, voir p. 198.*

# Israël

## 1. Source(s) des données de base

**Code(s):**    **Titre(s):**

EPPA3      Evaluations et projections de la population active 1950-2025 - troisième édition, BIT, Genève, 1986.
AST75-93    Editions de 1975 à 1993 de l'Annuaire des statistiques du travail du BIT, Genève.
ISRCBS     Labour force surveys 1979, special series No. 662, CBS, Jerusalem, 1981.

## 2. Evaluation des taux d'activité: 1950 - 1990

### 2.1 Données de base:

Tableau 1: Taux d'activité par sexe et par groupe d'âge

| Groupe d'âge | Année | | | | | |
|---|---|---|---|---|---|---|
| | 1975 | 1980 | 1985 | 1990 | 1991 | 1992 |
| **Hommes** | | | | | | |
| 10-14 | 0.00 | 0.00 | 0.00 | 0.00 | 0.00 | 0.00 |
| 15-19 | 18.50 | 14.30 | 13.60 | 14.10 | 13.9 | 13.50 |
| 20-24 | 40.30 | 41.30 | 42.80 | 40.30 | 42.1 | 42.40 |
| 25-29 | 86.70 | 84.70 | 83.60 | 82.60 | 82.5 | 81.90 |
| 30-39 | 93.80 | 91.10 | 90.20 | 88.00 | 87.4 | 86.90 |
| 40-49 | 92.80 | 90.40 | 89.70 | 87.70 | 86.9 | 87.90 |
| 50-59 | 84.30 | 82.50 | 76.10 | 73.70 | 71.5 | 71.40 |
| 60+ | 29.20 | 27.90 | 21.40 | 20.20 | 18.7 | 18.70 |
| **Femmes** | | | | | | |
| 10-14 | 0.00 | 0.00 | 0.00 | 0.00 | 0.00 | 0.00 |
| 15-19 | 11.30 | 10.90 | 8.30 | 10.00 | 7.90 | 7.90 |
| 20-24 | 40.40 | 39.90 | 39.30 | 40.70 | 40.10 | 40.00 |
| 25-29 | 44.20 | 52.60 | 55.60 | 58.40 | 58.50 | 58.50 |
| 30-39 | 40.60 | 50.10 | 57.40 | 62.90 | 63.20 | 63.20 |
| 40-49 | 36.80 | 41.70 | 46.40 | 53.10 | 56.00 | 57.00 |
| 50-59 | 22.40 | 26.00 | 24.80 | 28.60 | 30.90 | 30.90 |
| 60+ | 6.00 | 6.60 | 5.60 | 6.30 | 5.50 | 5.60 |

Source(s): AST75-93.

### 2.2 Méthode(s): interpolation linéaire

#### 2.2.1 Hommes:

- 1950-80, taux d'activité 1950-80 tirés des EPPA3;
- 1990, interpolation des taux d'activité ajustés tirés des enquêtes
de 1975 à 1992;
ajustement des taux interpolés sur la base des variations des
taux interpolés 1980 par rapport aux taux 1980 tirés des EPPA3.

#### 2.2.2 Femmes:

- 1950-80, taux d'activité 1950-80 tirés des EPPA3;
modification des tendances des groupes d'âge [35-54] de 1980;
- 1990, interpolation des taux d'activité ajustés tirés des enquêtes
de 1975 à 1992;
ajustement des taux interpolés sur la base des variations
des taux interpolés 1980 par rapport aux taux 1980 tirés des EPPA3.

## 3. Evaluation des taux de répartition par secteur d'activité: 1950 - 1990

### 3.1 Données de base:

Tableau 2: Répartition de la population active en % par secteur d'activité

| Année | Agriculture | Industrie | | Services |
|---|---|---|---|---|
| | | Total | Manufac. | |
| **Hommes** | | | | |
| 1979 | 6.91 | 39.91 | 24.85 | 53.19 |
| 1980 | 7.52 | 39.90 | 24.51 | 52.58 |
| 1981 | 7.47 | 39.67 | 24.05 | 52.87 |
| 1989 | 5.99 | 36.72 | 21.67 | 57.29 |
| 1990 | 5.32 | 37.23 | 21.31 | 57.45 |
| 1991 | 4.53 | 38.50 | 20.12 | 56.96 |
| **Femmes** | | | | |
| 1979 | 3.88 | 17.65 | 12.01 | 78.47 |
| 1980 | 4.06 | 15.94 | 11.55 | 80.00 |
| 1981 | 3.41 | 15.54 | 11.26 | 81.05 |
| 1989 | 2.44 | 15.32 | 8.76 | 82.24 |
| 1990 | 2.37 | 15.39 | 8.57 | 82.24 |
| 1991 | 1.91 | 15.21 | 8.06 | 82.88 |

Source(s): (1) AST75-93.

### 3.2 Méthode(s): moyenne arithmétique

#### 3.2.1 Hommes:

- 1950-70, taux de répartition 1950-70 tirés des EPPA3;
- 1980-90, moyennes des taux de répartition tirés des enquêtes
de 1979 à 1981 pour 1980 et celles de 1989 à 1991 pour 1990.

#### 3.2.2 Femmes:

Méthode, hypothèses et traitements identiques à ceux appliqués aux hommes.

## 4. Projection des taux d'activité: 2000 - 2010

### 4.1 Modèle(s): linéaire, log-linéaire et hyperbole

#### 4.1.1 Hommes:

- Aux groupes d'âge [15-24] et [65+], application de la fonction F2;
- Aux groupes d'âge [20-64], application de la fonction F3.

#### 4.1.2 Femmes:

- Au groupe d'âge [15-19], application de la fonction F3;
- Aux groupes d'âge [20+], application de la fonction F1.

*Notes sur les ajustements des taux, voir p. 192-195.*      *Notes sur les fonctions de projection, voir p. 198.*

# Italie

## 1. Source(s) des données de base

Code(s):     Titre(s):
EPPA3      Annuaire des statistiques du travail 1945-89 - Edition rétrospective sur les recensements de population, BIT, Genève, 1990.
STAT       Base de données sur les statistiques du travail - LABORSTA, Bureau de statistique, BIT, Genève.

## 2. Evaluation des taux d'activité: 1950 - 1990

### 2.1 Données de base:

Tableau 1: Taux d'activité par sexe et par groupe d'âge

| Groupe d'âge | Année 1979 | 1980 | 1981 | 1989 | 1990 | 1991 |
|---|---|---|---|---|---|---|
| **Hommes** | | | | | | |
| 10-14 | 0.00 | 0.00 | 0.00 | 1.12 | 0.00 | 0.00 |
| 15-19 | 33.04 | 33.30 | 33.10 | 30.58 | 24.73 | 23.23 |
| 20-24 | 71.65 | 72.52 | 74.10 | 71.49 | 70.16 | 69.55 |
| 25-29 | 93.72 | 93.00 | 93.00 | 90.65 | 90.39 | 89.46 |
| 30-34 | 98.50 | 98.60 | 98.30 | 96.85 | 96.65 | 96.62 |
| 35-39 | 98.50 | 98.60 | 98.50 | 97.97 | 97.59 | 97.63 |
| 40-44 | 97.90 | 97.70 | 98.00 | 97.27 | 97.31 | 97.19 |
| 45-49 | 96.50 | 96.30 | 96.50 | 95.59 | 95.19 | 95.05 |
| 50-54 | 90.70 | 90.70 | 91.10 | 87.53 | 87.35 | 87.23 |
| 55-59 | 74.20 | 74.80 | 74.90 | 67.76 | 68.51 | 68.92 |
| 60-64 | 37.56 | 39.60 | 39.60 | 35.21 | 35.87 | 37.16 |
| 65+ | 12.56 | 12.62 | 11.90 | 7.90 | 7.97 | 8.10 |
| **Femmes** | | | | | | |
| 10-14 | 0.00 | 0.00 | 0.00 | 0.38 | 0.00 | 0.00 |
| 15-19 | 28.59 | 28.94 | 29.00 | 26.41 | 21.38 | 19.06 |
| 20-24 | 55.42 | 57.87 | 58.50 | 63.91 | 62.75 | 61.19 |
| 25-29 | 52.94 | 54.64 | 56.50 | 64.83 | 65.29 | 65.06 |
| 30-34 | 46.50 | 48.40 | 50.20 | 62.15 | 62.04 | 62.59 |
| 35-39 | 42.20 | 44.50 | 45.30 | 58.95 | 58.84 | 59.52 |
| 40-44 | 39.20 | 40.30 | 41.90 | 51.64 | 52.76 | 53.76 |
| 45-49 | 36.50 | 36.00 | 37.50 | 44.69 | 44.87 | 45.83 |
| 50-54 | 32.10 | 32.00 | 32.20 | 34.06 | 34.98 | 36.07 |
| 55-59 | 21.10 | 21.40 | 21.30 | 20.20 | 20.38 | 21.15 |
| 60-64 | 10.50 | 11.00 | 11.50 | 9.76 | 10.05 | 10.02 |
| 65+ | 3.63 | 3.48 | 3.4 | 2.00 | 2.18 | 2.24 |

Source(s): STAT.

### 2.2 Méthode(s): moyenne arithmétique

#### 2.2.1 Hommes:

- 1950-70, taux d'activité 1950-70 tirés des EPPA3;
ajustement des taux d'activité des groupes d'âge [25+] pour 1970;
- 1980, moyennes des taux d'activité tirés des enquêtes de 1979, 1980 et 1981;
modification des tendances des groupes d'âge [15-24];
- 1990, moyennes des taux d'activité tirés des enquêtes de 1989, 1990 et 1991;
modification des tendances des groupes d'âge [10-25].

#### 2.2.2 Femmes:

- 1950-70, taux d'activité 1950-70 tirés des EPPA3;
- 1980, moyennes des taux d'activité tirés des enquêtes de 1979, 1980 et 1981;
modification des tendances des groupes d'âge [10-19];
- 1990, moyennes des taux d'activité tirés des enquêtes de 1989, 1990 et 1991;
modification des tendances des groupes d'âge [10-19].

## 3. Evaluation des taux de répartition par secteur d'activité: 1950 - 1990

### 3.1 Données de base:

Tableau 2: Répartition de la population active en % par secteur d'activité

| Année | Agriculture | Industrie Total | Manufac. | Services |
|---|---|---|---|---|
| **Hommes** | | | | |
| 1979 | 13.24 | 40.86 | 25.86 | 45.90 |
| 1980 | 10.07 | 41.88 | 26.43 | 48.05 |
| 1981 | 11.79 | 43.36 | 23.94 | 44.85 |
| 1989 | 8.63 | 36.20 | 22.65 | 55.18 |
| 1990 | 8.25 | 36.59 | 22.65 | 55.16 |
| 1991 | 8.14 | 36.73 | 22.35 | 55.13 |
| **Femmes** | | | | |
| 1979 | 17.20 | 27.38 | 26.26 | 55.42 |
| 1980 | 12.97 | 29.19 | 27.78 | 57.85 |
| 1981 | 13.20 | 28.51 | 24.57 | 58.29 |
| 1989 | 9.40 | 22.86 | 21.29 | 67.73 |
| 1990 | 8.97 | 22.93 | 21.26 | 68.10 |
| 1991 | 8.79 | 22.11 | 20.44 | 69.10 |

Source(s): STAT.

### 3.2 Méthode(s): moyenne arithmétique

#### 3.2.1 Hommes:

- 1950-80, taux de répartition 1950-80 tirés des EPPA3;
- 1980, moyennes des taux de répartition tirés des enquêtes de 1979, 1980 et 1981;
- 1990, moyennes des taux de répartition tirés des enquêtes de 1989, 1990 et 1991.

#### 3.2.2 Femmes:

Méthode, hypothèses et traitements identiques à ceux appliqués aux hommes.

## 4. Projection des taux d'activité: 2000 - 2010

### 4.1 Modèle(s): hyperbole et logistique

#### 4.1.1 Hommes:

- A tous les groupes d'âge, application de la fonction F3;
- Modification des tendances des groupes d'âge [20-54].

#### 4.1.2 Femmes:

- Aux groupes d'âge [10-19] et [55+], application de la fonction F3;
- Aux groupes d'âge [20-54], application de la fonction F6;
- Modification des tendances des groupes d'âge [20-24] et [55-59].

*Notes sur les ajustements des taux, voir p. 192-195.*     *Notes sur les fonctions de projection, voir p. 198.*

# Jamahiriya arabe libyenne

## 1. Source(s) des données de base

Code(s):     Titre(s):

EPPA3     Evaluations et projections de la population active 1950-2025 - troisième édition, BIT, Genève, 1986.
ASTER     Annuaire des statistiques du travail 1945-89 - Edition rétrospective sur les recensements de population, BIT, Genève, 1990.
ADNU88     Annuaire démographique 1988 - Statistiques des recensements de population, quarantième édition, Nations Unies, New York, 1990.
STAT     Base de données sur les statistiques du travail - LABORSTA, Bureau de statistique, BIT, Genève.

## 2. Evaluation des taux d'activité: 1950 - 1990

### 2.1 Données de base:

Tableau 1: Taux d'activité par sexe et par groupe d'âge

| Groupe d'âge | Année | | | | |
|---|---|---|---|---|---|
| | 1950 (1) | 1960 (1) | 1970 (1) | 1973 (2) | 1984 (3) |
| **Hommes** | | | | | |
| 10-14 | 46.75 | 26.50 | 16.00 | 1.90 | 0.00 |
| 15-19 | 72.65 | 58.50 | 57.06 | 27.21 | 20.44 |
| 20-24 | 95.00 | 88.05 | 87.19 | 75.79 | 73.25 |
| 25-29 | 96.30 | 95.40 | 96.55 | 95.96 | 95.50 |
| 30-34 | 96.85 | 96.95 | 97.05 | 97.87 | 97.96 |
| 35-39 | 97.00 | 97.20 | 97.70 | 98.48 | 98.76 |
| 40-44 | 96.70 | 97.05 | 97.40 | 98.23 | 98.53 |
| 45-49 | 96.60 | 96.55 | 96.50 | 96.96 | 97.96 |
| 50-54 | 95.55 | 94.90 | 94.25 | 94.87 | 96.83 |
| 55-59 | 93.05 | 91.40 | 89.75 | 90.63 | 94.23 |
| 60-64 | 91.80 | 86.10 | 80.40 | 80.73 | 89.35 |
| 65+ | 72.85 | 61.55 | 50.25 | 49.35 | 40.98 |
| **Femmes** | | | | | |
| 10-14 | 6.75 | 5.05 | 2.65 | 1.74 | 0.00 |
| 15-19 | 4.55 | 4.50 | 4.40 | 4.09 | 5.86 |
| 20-24 | 3.65 | 4.75 | 6.30 | 7.38 | 23.08 |
| 25-29 | 2.95 | 4.45 | 6.60 | 8.09 | 19.71 |
| 30-34 | 3.25 | 4.50 | 6.30 | 7.79 | 9.68 |
| 35-39 | 3.60 | 4.75 | 6.40 | 7.40 | 7.68 |
| 40-44 | 4.25 | 5.40 | 7.05 | 7.74 | 7.42 |
| 45-49 | 5.00 | 6.15 | 7.80 | 9.08 | 8.26 |
| 50-54 | 4.75 | 5.90 | 7.55 | 8.83 | 8.93 |
| 55-59 | 3.25 | 4.60 | 6.55 | 7.85 | 9.64 |
| 60-64 | 2.85 | 3.40 | 4.20 | 4.72 | 7.10 |
| 65+ | 2.00 | 1.85 | 1.65 | 1.67 | 1.55 |

Source(s): (1) EPPA3; (2) ASTER; (3) ADNU88 et STAT.

### 2.2 Méthode(s): interpolation et extrapolation linéaires

#### 2.2.1 Hommes:

- 1950-90, interpolation et extrapolation des taux d'activité 1950-70 tirés des EPPA3, des taux ajustés tirés du recensement de 1973 et des taux du recensement de 1984.

#### 2.2.2 Femmes:

- 1950-70, taux d'activité ajustés 1950-70 tirés des EPPA3;
- 1980-90, interpolation et extrapolation des taux d'activité 1970 tirés des EPPA3 et des taux ajustés des recensements de 1973 et 1984; ajustement des taux d'activité sur la base du modèle d'ajustement des taux d'activité des femmes travaillant dans l'agriculture comme aides familiales.

## 3. Evaluation des taux de répartition par secteur d'activité: 1950 - 1990

### 3.1 Données de base:

Tableau 2: Répartition de la population active en % par secteur d'activité

| Année | Agriculture | Industrie | | Services |
|---|---|---|---|---|
| | | Total | Manufac. | |
| **Hommes** | | | | |
| 1973 (1) | 22.54 | 27.21 | 4.28 | 50.24 |
| 1984 (2) | 12.60 | 29.27 | 6.12 | 58.13 |
| **Femmes** | | | | |
| 1976 (1) | 38.85 | 6.37 | 4.61 | 54.78 |
| 1984 (2) | 12.12 | 6.49 | 3.99 | 81.39 |

Source(s): (1) ASTER; (2) STAT.

### 3.2 Méthode(s): moyenne pondérée
extrapolation linéaire

#### 3.2.1 Hommes:
- 1950-70, taux de répartition 1950-70 tirés des EPPA3;
- 1980, moyennes pondérées des taux de répartition ajustés tirés du recensement de 1973 et des taux du recensement de 1984;
- 1990, extrapolation des taux de répartition ajustés du recensement de 1973 et des taux du recensement de 1984; modification des tendances de tous les secteurs.

#### 3.2.2 Femmes:

Méthode, hypothèses et traitements identiques à ceux appliqués aux hommes.

## 4. Projection des taux d'activité: 2000 - 2010

### 4.1 Modèle(s): linéaire et hyperbole

#### 4.1.1 Hommes:

- Aux groupes d'âge [15+], application de la fonction F3;
- Modification des tendances des groupes d'âge [20-59].

#### 4.1.2 Femmes:

- Aux groupes d'âge [15+], application de la fonction F1;
- Modification des tendances de tous les groupes d'âge.

*Notes sur les ajustements des taux, voir p. 192-195.*     *Notes sur les fonctions de projection, voir p. 198.*

# Jamaïque

## 1. Source(s) des données de base

Code(s):     Titre(s):
EPPA3       Evaluations et projections de la population active 1950-2025 - troisième édition, BIT, Genève, 1986.
STAT        Base de données sur les statistiques du travail - LABORSTA, Bureau de statistique, BIT, Genève.

## 2. Evaluation des taux d'activité: 1950 - 1990

### 2.1 Données de base:

Tableau 1: Taux d'activité par sexe et par groupe d'âge

| Groupe d'âge | Année 1980 (1) | 1990 (2) |
|---|---|---|
| **Hommes** | | |
| 10-14 | 0.60 | 0.30 |
| 15-19 | 52.00 | 39.66 |
| 20-24 | 94.50 | 92.57 |
| 25-29 | 96.60 | 93.91 |
| 30-34 | 97.90 | 96.14 |
| 35-39 | 97.90 | 96.24 |
| 40-44 | 98.00 | 96.33 |
| 45-49 | 97.40 | 95.74 |
| 50-54 | 96.30 | 93.93 |
| 55-59 | 92.50 | 88.80 |
| 60-64 | 84.00 | 78.78 |
| 65+ | 58.90 | 53.64 |
| **Femmes** | | |
| 10-14 | 0.30 | 0.10 |
| 15-19 | 40.00 | 31.70 |
| 20-24 | 82.50 | 80.33 |
| 25-29 | 87.80 | 82.83 |
| 30-34 | 87.70 | 85.95 |
| 35-39 | 87.60 | 88.46 |
| 40-44 | 87.30 | 88.16 |
| 45-49 | 87.00 | 88.00 |
| 50-54 | 77.00 | 77.89 |
| 55-59 | 70.00 | 72.10 |
| 60-64 | 47.00 | 46.06 |
| 65+ | 9.90 | 23.58 |

Source(s): (1) EPPA3; (2) STAT.

### 2.2 Méthode(s): interpolation linéaire

#### 2.2.1 Hommes:

- 1950-80, taux d'activité 1950-80 tirés des EPPA3;
- 1990, interpolation des taux d'activité 1980 tirés des EPPA3 et des taux ajustés tirés de l'enquête de 1990.

#### 2.2.2 Femmes:

- 1950-80, taux d'activité 1950-80 ajustés tirés des EPPA3; ajustement des taux d'activité des groupes d'âge [65+] pour 1970 et 1980;
- 1990, interpolation des taux d'activité ajustés 1980 tirés des EPPA3 et des taux d'activité tirés de l'enquête de 1990.

## 3. Evaluation des taux de répartition par secteur d'activité: 1950 - 1990

### 3.1 Données de base:

Tableau 2: Répartition de la population active en % par secteur d'activité

| Année | Agriculture | Industrie Total | Manufac. | Services |
|---|---|---|---|---|
| **Hommes** | | | | |
| 1981 | 44.78 | 22.38 | 13.88 | 32.85 |
| 1990 | 33.56 | 32.04 | 18.88 | 34.39 |
| **Femmes** | | | | |
| 1981 | 20.78 | 7.35 | 6.90 | 71.87 |
| 1990 | 14.53 | 13.11 | 12.42 | 72.36 |

Source(s): STAT.

### 3.2 Méthode(s): données nationales

#### 3.2.1 Hommes:

- 1950-80, taux de répartition 1950-80 tirés des EPPA3;
- 1990, taux de répartition tirés de l'enquête de 1981;
- Application du rapport manufacture/industrie tiré de l'enquête de 1981.

#### 3.2.2 Femmes:

Méthode, hypothèses et traitements identiques à ceux appliqués aux hommes.

## 4. Projection des taux d'activité: 2000 - 2010

### 4.1 Modèle(s): linéaire, log-linéaire, hyperbole et logistique

#### 4.1.1 Hommes:

- Au groupe d'âge [15-19], application de la fonction F2;
- Aux groupes d'âge [20-24] et [65+], application de la fonction F1;
- Aux groupes d'âge [25-64], application de la fonction F3;
- Modification des tendances des groupes d'âge [20-59].

#### 4.1.2 Femmes:

- Au groupe d'âge [15-19], application de la fonction F2;
- Aux groupes d'âge [20-59], application de la fonction F6;
- Aux groupes d'âge [60+], application de la fonction F1;
- Modification des tendances des groupes d'âge [20+].

---

*Notes sur les ajustements des taux, voir p. 192-195.*     *Notes sur les fonctions de projection, voir p. 198.*

# Japon

## 1. Source(s) des données de base

| Code(s): | Titre(s): |
|---|---|
| EPPA3 | Evaluations et projections de la population active 1950-2025 - troisième édition, BIT, Genève, 1986. |
| STAT | Base de données sur les statistiques du travail - LABORSTA, Bureau de statistique, BIT, Genève. |

## 2. Evaluation des taux d'activité: 1950 - 1990

### 2.1 Données de base:

Tableau 1: Taux d'activité par sexe et par groupe d'âge

| Groupe d'âge | Année 1980 (1) | 1980 (2) | 1990 (1) | 1990 (2) |
|---|---|---|---|---|
| **Hommes** | | | | |
| 10-14 | 0.00 | .. | 0.00 | .. |
| 15-19 | 20.34 | .. | 19.94 | .. |
| 20-24 | 74.74 | .. | 75.40 | .. |
| 25-29 | 97.58 | .. | 96.69 | .. |
| 30-34 | 98.60 | .. | 98.06 | .. |
| 35-39 | 98.68 | .. | 98.15 | .. |
| 40-44 | 98.42 | .. | 98.13 | .. |
| 45-49 | 97.99 | .. | 97.90 | .. |
| 50-54 | 97.30 | .. | 97.05 | .. |
| 55-59 | 93.99 | .. | 93.99 | .. |
| 60-64 | 81.45 | .. | 76.14 | .. |
| 65+ | 46.01 | .. | 39.44 | .. |
| **Femmes** | | | | |
| 10-14 | 0.00 | 0.00 | 0.00 | 0.00 |
| 15-19 | 18.76 | 18.50 | 17.35 | 17.80 |
| 20-24 | 71.13 | 70.00 | 75.54 | 75.10 |
| 25-29 | 49.43 | 49.20 | 61.25 | 61.40 |
| 30-34 | 46.47 | 48.35 | 50.71 | 51.70 |
| 35-39 | 55.54 | 57.77 | 59.42 | 62.60 |
| 40-44 | 61.82 | 64.31 | 66.74 | 69.60 |
| 45-49 | 62.27 | 64.40 | 68.33 | 71.70 |
| 50-54 | 58.73 | 59.30 | 62.90 | 65.50 |
| 55-59 | 50.66 | 50.50 | 51.51 | 53.90 |
| 60-64 | 38.85 | 38.80 | 37.35 | 39.50 |
| 65+ | 16.14053 | 15.50 | 14.93 | 16.20 |

Note(s): (1) Recensement; (2) Enquête.
Source(s): STAT.

### 2.2 Méthode(s): moyenne pondérée
moyenne arithmétique

**2.2.1 Hommes:**
- 1950-80, taux d'activité 1950-80 tirés des EPPA3;
- 1990, moyennes pondérées des taux d'activité tirés des recensements de 1980 et 1990.

**2.2.2 Femmes:**
- 1950-70, taux d'activité 1950-70 tirés des EPPA3;
- 1980, moyennes des taux d'activité tirés de l'enquête de 1980 et du recensement de 1980;
- 1990, moyennes des taux d'activité tirés de l'enquête de 1990 et du recensement de 1990.

## 3. Evaluation des taux de répartition par secteur d'activité: 1950 - 1990

### 3.1 Données de base:

Tableau 2: Répartition de la population active en % par secteur d'activité

| Année | Agriculture | Industrie Total | Manufac. | Services |
|---|---|---|---|---|
| **Hommes** | | | | |
| 1985 (1) | 8.22 | 38.39 | 24.47 | 53.39 |
| 1990 (1) | 6.50 | 39.00 | 24.67 | 54.50 |
| **Femmes** | | | | |
| 1980 (1) | 13.74 | 26.37 | 22.72 | 59.89 |
| 1980 (2) | 13.24 | 28.48 | 24.65 | 58.28 |
| 1990 (1) | 8.17 | 26.45 | 22.63 | 65.39 |
| 1990 (2) | 8.51 | 27.56 | 23.56 | 63.92 |

Note(s): (1) Recensement; (2) Enquête.
Source(s): STAT.

### 3.2 Méthode(s): moyenne pondérée
moyenne arithmétique

**3.2.1 Hommes:**
- 1950-80, taux de répartition 1950-80 tirés des EPPA3.
1990, moyennes pondérées des taux de répartition ajustés tirés des recensements de 1985 et 1990.

**3.2.2 Femmes:**
- 1950-70, taux de répartition 1950-70 tirés des EPPA3;
- 1980, moyennes des taux de répartition tirés de l'enquête de 1980 et du recensement de 1980;
- 1990, moyennes des taux de répartition tirés de l'enquête de 1990 et du recensement de 1990.

## 4. Projection des taux d'activité: 2000 - 2010

### 4.1 Modèle(s): linéaire et hyperbole

**4.1.1 Hommes:**
- Aux groupes d'âge [15-24], application de la fonction F3;
- Aux groupes d'âge [25+], application de la fonction F1;
- Modification des tendances des groupes d'âge [25+].

**4.1.2 Femmes:**
- Aux groupes d'âge [15-44], [50-59] et [65+], application de la fonction F3;
- Aux groupes d'âge [45-49] et [60-64], application de la fonction F1;
- Modification des tendances des groupes d'âge [20-64].

*Notes sur les ajustements des taux, voir p. 192-195.*

*Notes sur les fonctions de projection, voir p. 198.*

# Jordanie

## 1. Source(s) des données de base

Code(s):     Titre(s):

EPPA3       Evaluations et projections de la population active 1950-2025 - troisième édition, BIT, Genève, 1986.
ASTER       Annuaire des statistiques du travail 1945-89 - Edition rétrospective sur les recensements de population, BIT, Genève, 1990.
ESCWA       Compedium of Social Statistics Indicators, Third Issue, December 1993, Economic and Social Commission for Western Asia.

## 2. Evaluation des taux d'activité: 1950 - 1990

### 2.1 Données de base:

Tableau 1: Taux d'activité par sexe et par groupe d'âge

| Groupe d'âge | Année | | | | | |
|---|---|---|---|---|---|---|
| | 1970 (1) | 1960 (1) | 1970 (1) | 1979 (2) | 1980 (1) | 1987 (3) |
| **Hommes** | | | | | | |
| 10-14 | 17.70 | 13.90 | 10.30 | .. | 6.40 | .. |
| 15-19 | 60.00 | 55.00 | 52.00 | .. | 37.00 | .. |
| 20-24 | 88.20 | 87.30 | 86.70 | .. | 84.50 | .. |
| 25-29 | 96.90 | 96.70 | 96.40 | .. | 96.25 | .. |
| 30-34 | 98.10 | 97.90 | 97.70 | .. | 97.50 | .. |
| 35-39 | 98.10 | 97.90 | 97.70 | .. | 97.50 | .. |
| 40-44 | 96.80 | 96.55 | 96.30 | .. | 96.30 | .. |
| 45-49 | 96.80 | 96.20 | 95.40 | .. | 94.90 | .. |
| 50-54 | 94.10 | 93.40 | 92.70 | .. | 92.20 | .. |
| 55-59 | 90.00 | 89.00 | 88.00 | .. | 87.20 | .. |
| 60-64 | 83.60 | 81.50 | 79.20 | .. | 76.00 | .. |
| 65+ | 55.80 | 51.60 | 47.90 | | 38.70 | |
| **Femmes** | | | | | | |
| 10-14 | .. | .. | .. | 1.20 | .. | 0.24 |
| 15-19 | .. | .. | .. | 3.44 | .. | 2.15 |
| 20-24 | .. | .. | .. | 15.69 | .. | 20.06 |
| 25-29 | .. | .. | .. | 13.51 | .. | 16.83 |
| 30-34 | .. | .. | .. | 8.66 | .. | 12.03 |
| 35-39 | .. | .. | .. | 5.15 | .. | 8.38 |
| 40-44 | .. | .. | .. | 3.26 | .. | 6.68 |
| 45-49 | .. | .. | .. | 2.38 | .. | 5.72 |
| 50-54 | .. | .. | .. | 2.04 | .. | 4.80 |
| 55-59 | .. | .. | .. | 1.81 | .. | 3.91 |
| 60-64 | .. | .. | .. | 1.06 | .. | 1.23 |
| 65+ | | | | 0.49 | | 0.54 |

**Source(s)**: (1) EPPA3; (2) ASTER; (3) ESCWA.

### 2.2 Méthode(s): interpolation et extrapolation linéaires

#### 2.2.1 Hommes:

- 1950-80, taux d'activité 1950-80 tirés des EPPA3;
- 1990, extrapolation des taux d'activité 1950-80 tirés des EPPA3;
ajustement des taux extrapolés sur la base des variations des taux
interpolés 1980 par rapport aux taux 1980 tirés des EPPA3.

#### 2.2.2 Femmes:

- 1950-70, taux d'activité 1950-70 tirés des EPPA3;
- 1980-90, interpolation et extrapolation des taux d'activité tirés
du recensement de 1979 et des évaluations de la ESCWA pour 1986;
ajustement des taux d'activité sur la base du modèle d'ajustement des taux
d'activité des femmes travaillant dans l'agriculture comme aides familiales.

## 3. Evaluation des taux de répartition par secteur d'activité: 1950 - 1990

### 3.1 Données de base:

Tableau 2: Répartition de la population active en % par secteur d'activité

| Année | Agriculture | Industrie | | Services |
|---|---|---|---|---|
| | | Total | Manufac. | |
| **Hommes** | | | | |
| 1950 (1) | 55.00 | 25.70 | .. | 19.30 |
| 1960 (1) | 46.00 | 26.00 | .. | 28.00 |
| 1970 (1) | 28.50 | 26.60 | .. | 44.90 |
| 1979 (2) | 12.13 | 27.17 | 8.05 | 60.69 |
| 1980 (1) | 11.00 | 27.20 | .. | 61.80 |
| **Femmes** | | | | |
| 1950 (1) | 44.00 | 24.00 | .. | 32.00 |
| 1960 (1) | 35.00 | 24.00 | .. | 41.00 |
| 1970 (1) | 18.00 | 15.50 | .. | 66.50 |
| 1979 (2) | 1.23 | 7.42 | 6.43 | 91.34 |

**Source(s)**: (1) EPPA3; (2) ASTER.

### 3.2 Méthode(s): extrapolation linéaire

#### 3.2.1 Hommes:

- 1950-80, taux de répartition 1950-80 tirés des EPPA3;
- 1990, extrapolation des taux de répartition 1950-80 tirés des EPPA3
et du recensement de 1979;
modification des tendances de tous les secteurs.

#### 3.2.2 Femmes:

- 1950-70, taux de répartition 1950-70 tirés des EPPA3;
- 1980-90, extrapolation des taux de répartition 1950-70 tirés des EPPA3
et des taux du recensement de 1979;
modification des tendances de tous les secteurs.

## 4. Projection des taux d'activité: 2000 - 2010

### 4.1 Modèle(s): linéaire et hyperbole

#### 4.1.1 Hommes:

- Aux groupes d'âge [15+], application de la fonction F3;
- Modification des tendances des groupes d'âge [35-39] et [45-54].

#### 4.1.2 Femmes:

- Aux groupes d'âge [15+], application de la fonction F1;
- Modification des tendances des groupes d'âge [15+].

*Notes sur les ajustements des taux, voir p. 192-195.*     *Notes sur les fonctions de projection, voir p. 198.*

# Kazakstan

## 1. Source(s) des données de base

Code(s):     Titre(s):

BLT-94-2     Vorobiev A. (1994), "Estimation de la population active pour les quinze pays de l'ex-URSS pour les années 1950, 1959, 1970, 1979 et 1989", dans le Bulletin des statistiques du travail - 1994-2, BIT, Genève.

## 2. Evaluation des taux d'activité: 1950 - 1990

### 2.1 Données de base:

Tableau 1: Taux d'activité par sexe et par groupe d'âge

|  | Année | | | | |
| Groupe d'âge | 1950 | 1959 | 1970 | 1979 | 1989 |
|---|---|---|---|---|---|
| **Hommes** | | | | | |
| 10-14 | 0.00 | 0.00 | 0.00 | 0.00 | 0.00 |
| 15-19 | 51.92 | 60.15 | 41.55 | 39.04 | 34.45 |
| 20-24 | 83.05 | 87.40 | 87.53 | 88.83 | 82.82 |
| 25-29 | 94.68 | 97.61 | 96.85 | 97.55 | 96.77 |
| 30-34 | 94.22 | 95.66 | 98.30 | 98.71 | 98.09 |
| 35-39 | 93.41 | 95.58 | 98.14 | 98.30 | 98.03 |
| 40-44 | 94.01 | 93.41 | 97.20 | 97.91 | 97.95 |
| 45-49 | 91.67 | 92.13 | 96.08 | 96.72 | 96.64 |
| 50-54 | 85.83 | 86.93 | 88.51 | 90.97 | 92.50 |
| 55-59 | 16.00 | 79.28 | 80.12 | 78.23 | 80.74 |
| 60-64 | 54.69 | 70.10 | 34.56 | 24.59 | 28.94 |
| 65+ | 30.35 | 26.84 | 7.32 | 9.69 | 9.16 |
| **Femmes** | | | | | |
| 10-14 | 0.00 | 0.00 | 0.00 | 0.00 | 0.00 |
| 15-19 | 48.29 | 50.67 | 33.28 | 33.04 | 25.04 |
| 20-24 | 58.06 | 59.21 | 80.74 | 82.41 | 73.42 |
| 25-29 | 62.36 | 67.69 | 84.42 | 90.69 | 84.70 |
| 30-34 | 60.50 | 59.24 | 82.46 | 92.33 | 88.87 |
| 35-39 | 52.78 | 55.09 | 93.61 | 93.04 | 91.62 |
| 40-44 | 47.64 | 49.79 | 83.11 | 92.36 | 91.85 |
| 45-49 | 46.41 | 46.64 | 82.09 | 88.47 | 88.32 |
| 50-54 | 33.33 | 32.86 | 65.47 | 74.07 | 71.86 |
| 55-59 | 19.83 | 10.01 | 21.71 | 25.10 | 25.95 |
| 60-64 | 9.38 | 11.18 | 8.23 | 7.27 | 12.89 |
| 65+ | 2.94 | 2.10 | 1.76 | 1.66 | 3.12 |

Source(s): BLT-94-2-2

### 2.2 Méthode(s): moyenne pondérée

#### 2.2.1 Hommes:

- 1950-90, moyennes pondérées des taux d'activité 1950, 1959, 1970 et 1989 tirés du Bulletin des statistiques du travail, 1994-2.

#### 2.2.2 Femmes:

Méthode, hypothèses et traitements identiques à ceux appliqués aux hommes.

## 3. Evaluation des taux de répartition par secteur d'activité: 1950 - 1990

### 3.1 Données de base:

Tableau 2: Répartition de la population active en % par secteur d'activité

|  | Agriculture | Industrie | | Services |
| Année | | Total | Manufac. | |
|---|---|---|---|---|
| **Hommes** | | | | |
| 1950 | 53.30 | 21.94 | 10.57 | 24.76 |
| 1959 | 38.25 | 24.35 | 10.55 | 37.40 |
| 1970 | 29.30 | 38.08 | 16.09 | 32.62 |
| 1979 | 28.38 | 37.97 | 16.13 | 33.65 |
| 1989 | 28.16 | 37.41 | 15.03 | 34.43 |
| **Femmes** | | | | |
| 1950 | 58.18 | 14.68 | 9.28 | 27.14 |
| 1959 | 40.44 | 21.20 | 11.98 | 38.36 |
| 1970 | 24.34 | 21.18 | 16.69 | 54.49 |
| 1979 | 20.79 | 24.80 | 15.94 | 54.41 |
| 1989 | 16.00 | 24.78 | 15.78 | 59.22 |

Source(s): BLT-94-2.

### 3.2 Méthode(s): moyenne pondérée

#### 3.2.1 Hommes:

- 1950-90, moyennes pondérées des taux de répartition 1950, 1959, 1970, 1979 et 1989 tiré du Bulletin des statistiques du travail - 1994-2.

#### 3.2.2 Femmes:

Méthode, hypothèses et traitements identiques à ceux appliqués aux hommes.

## 4. Projection des taux d'activité: 2000 - 2010

### 4.1 Modèle(s): linéaire, log-linéaire, hyperbole et logistique

#### 4.1.1 Hommes:

- Au groupe d'âge [15-19], application de la fonction F2;
- Aux groupes d'âge [20-24] et [60+], application de la fonction F3;
- Aux groupes d'âge [25-59], application de la fonction F1;
- Modification des tendances des groupes d'âge [25-59].

#### 4.1.2 Femmes:

- Au groupe d'âge [15-19], application de la fonction F3;
- Aux groupes d'âge [20-24] et [50+], application de la fonction F1;
- Aux groupes d'âge [25-49], application de la fonction F6;
- Modification des tendances des groupes d'âge [15+].

---

*Notes sur les ajustements des taux, voir p. 192-195.*     *Notes sur les fonctions de projection, voir p. 198.*

# Kenya

## 1. Source(s) des données de base

Code(s):      Titre(s):

EPPA3      Evaluations et projections de la population active 1950-2025 - troisième édition, BIT, Genève, 1986.

## 2. Evaluation des taux d'activité: 1950 - 1990

### 2.1 Données de base:

Tableau 1: Taux d'activité par sexe et par groupe d'âge

| Groupe d'âge | Année 1950 | 1960 | 1970 | 1980 |
|---|---|---|---|---|
| **Hommes** | | | | |
| 10-14 | 50.70 | 49.75 | 48.40 | 46.45 |
| 15-19 | 83.00 | 81.80 | 80.00 | 77.35 |
| 20-24 | 94.55 | 94.05 | 93.35 | 92.35 |
| 25-29 | 97.30 | 97.20 | 97.10 | 96.95 |
| 30-34 | 98.00 | 97.95 | 97.80 | 97.65 |
| 35-39 | 98.20 | 98.10 | 97.95 | 97.80 |
| 40-44 | 98.00 | 97.90 | 97.80 | 97.60 |
| 45-49 | 97.25 | 97.20 | 97.10 | 96.90 |
| 50-54 | 96.80 | 96.65 | 96.50 | 96.25 |
| 55-59 | 95.80 | 95.65 | 95.35 | 95.00 |
| 60-64 | 92.65 | 92.35 | 91.90 | 91.25 |
| 65+ | 79.10 | 78.60 | 77.80 | 76.70 |
| **Femmes** | | | | |
| 10-14 | 38.30 | 37.60 | 36.55 | 35.10 |
| 15-19 | 62.35 | 61.30 | 59.75 | 57.55 |
| 20-24 | 63.15 | 62.50 | 61.50 | 60.10 |
| 25-29 | 67.95 | 67.20 | 66.10 | 64.55 |
| 30-34 | 72.25 | 71.45 | 70.25 | 68.55 |
| 35-39 | 73.55 | 72.80 | 71.70 | 70.10 |
| 40-44 | 76.00 | 75.25 | 74.15 | 72.55 |
| 45-49 | 75.50 | 74.75 | 73.60 | 72.00 |
| 50-54 | 73.90 | 73.00 | 71.70 | 69.85 |
| 55-59 | 71.05 | 70.15 | 68.80 | 66.80 |
| 60-64 | 64.65 | 63.50 | 61.75 | 59.25 |
| 65+ | 44.70 | 43.60 | 42.00 | 39.70 |

Source(s): EPPA3.

### 2.2 Méthode(s): interpolation et extrapolation linéaires

#### 2.2.1 Hommes:

- 1950-80, taux d'activité 1950-80 tirés des EPPA3;
- 1990, extrapolation des taux d'activité 1950-1980 tirés des EPPA3;
ajustement des taux extrapolés 1990 sur la base des variations des taux
interpolés 1980 par rapport aux taux 1980 tirés des EPPA3.

#### 2.2.2 Femmes:

- 1950-90, interpolation et extrapolation des taux d'activité 1950-80
tirés des EPPA3;
ajustement des taux interpolés et extrapolés sur la base des
variations des taux interpolés 1980 par rapport aux taux ajustés 1980 tirés
des EPPA3;
ajustement des taux d'activité 1980 tirés des EPPA3 sur la base
du rapport hommes/femmes égal à 1;
modification des tendances des groupes d'âge [10-19] pour 1990.

## 3. Evaluation des taux de répartition par secteur d'activité: 1950 - 1990

### 3.1 Données de base:

Tableau 2: Répartition de la population active en % par secteur d'activité

| Année | Agriculture | Industrie Total | Manufac. | Services |
|---|---|---|---|---|
| **Hommes** | | | | |
| 1950 | 85.00 | 6.50 | .. | 8.50 |
| 1960 | 83.30 | 7.15 | .. | 9.55 |
| 1970 | 80.80 | 8.20 | .. | 11.00 |
| 1980 | 77.20 | 9.80 | .. | 13.00 |
| **Femmes** | | | | |
| 1950 | 95.00 | 1.00 | .. | 4.00 |
| 1960 | 92.00 | 1.45 | .. | 5.75 |
| 1970 | 90.30 | 1.95 | .. | 7.75 |
| 1980 | 86.30 | 2.75 | .. | 10.95 |

Source(s): EPPA3.

### 3.2 Méthode(s): interpolation et extrapolation linéaires

#### 3.2.1 Hommes:

- 1950-80, taux de répartition 1950-80 tirés des EPPA3;
- 1990, extrapolation des taux de répartition 1950-80 tirés des EPPA3;
ajustement des taux extrapolés 1990 sur la base des variations des taux
interpolés 1980 par rapport aux taux 1980 tirés des EPPA3;
- Application du rapport manufacture/industrie du Malawi.

#### 3.2.2 Femmes:

- 1980, taux de répartition estimés sur la base du rapport
hommes/femmes égal à 1 dans l'agriculture;
- 1950-70 et 1990, interpolation et extrapolation des taux de répartition
1950-70 tirés des EPPA3 et des taux estimés 1980;
ajustement des taux extrapolés 1990 sur la base des variations des taux
interpolés 1980 par rapport aux taux 1980 estimés;
- Application du rapport manufacture/industrie du Malawi.

## 4. Projection des taux d'activité: 2000 - 2010

### 4.1 Modèle(s): linéaire et hyperbole

#### 4.1.1 Hommes:

- A tous les groupes d'âge, application de la fonction F1;
- Modification des tendances des groupes d'âge [10-24] et [60+].

#### 4.1.2 Femmes:

- Aux groupes d'âge [10-19], application de la fonction F1;
- Aux groupes d'âge [20+], application de la fonction F3;
- Modification des tendances des groupes d'âge [10-14] et [65+].

*Notes sur les ajustements des taux, voir p. 192-195.*          *Notes sur les fonctions de projection, voir p. 198.*

# Kirghizistan

## 1. Source(s) des données de base

Code(s):     Titre(s):

BLT-94-2    Vorobiev A. (1994), "Estimation de la population active pour les quinze pays de l'ex-URSS pour les années 1950, 1959, 1970, 1979 et 1989", dans le Bulletin des statistiques du travail - 1994-2, BIT, Genève.

## 2. Evaluation des taux d'activité: 1950 - 1990

### 2.1 Données de base:

Tableau 1: Taux d'activité par sexe et par groupe d'âge

| Groupe d'âge | Année 1950 | 1959 | 1970 | 1979 | 1989 |
|---|---|---|---|---|---|
| **Hommes** | | | | | |
| 10-14 | 0.00 | 0.00 | 0.00 | 0.00 | 0.00 |
| 15-19 | 48.89 | 51.85 | 35.04 | 37.44 | 27.88 |
| 20-24 | 82.14 | 84.88 | 84.52 | 87.80 | 80.66 |
| 25-29 | 91.84 | 95.35 | 94.44 | 96.88 | 96.28 |
| 30-34 | 92.11 | 95.00 | 98.08 | 98.65 | 98.08 |
| 35-39 | 93.18 | 95.24 | 97.73 | 97.53 | 98.35 |
| 40-44 | 94.29 | 93.75 | 96.55 | 97.87 | 97.01 |
| 45-49 | 90.63 | 91.89 | 95.74 | 96.30 | 95.95 |
| 50-54 | 87.88 | 90.00 | 90.32 | 90.41 | 91.36 |
| 55-59 | 76.92 | 81.48 | 82.86 | 80.56 | 82.61 |
| 60-64 | 64.00 | 74.07 | 46.67 | 26.92 | 28.81 |
| 65+ | 26.79 | 33.93 | 7.25 | 6.67 | 10.29 |
| **Femmes** | | | | | |
| 10-14 | 0.00 | 0.00 | 0.00 | 0.00 | 0.00 |
| 15-19 | 43.75 | 47.30 | 31.21 | 33.17 | 25.50 |
| 20-24 | 61.70 | 66.67 | 79.57 | 84.05 | 74.03 |
| 25-29 | 68.57 | 76.67 | 85.92 | 90.70 | 84.29 |
| 30-34 | 66.07 | 69.32 | 87.62 | 92.00 | 87.42 |
| 35-39 | 66.10 | 70.49 | 88.76 | 92.50 | 90.32 |
| 40-44 | 59.18 | 63.83 | 87.23 | 92.55 | 91.30 |
| 45-49 | 55.00 | 56.00 | 84.85 | 89.66 | 89.19 |
| 50-54 | 40.43 | 42.86 | 70.21 | 73.86 | 62.07 |
| 55-59 | 20.32 | 24.85 | 27.59 | 26.23 | 23.17 |
| 60-64 | 15.15 | 14.63 | 10.00 | 8.51 | 12.82 |
| 65+ | 2.70 | 3.95 | 1.77 | 2.19 | 3.45 |

Source(s): BLT-94-2-2

### 2.2 Méthode(s): moyenne pondérée

#### 2.2.1 Hommes:

- 1950-90, moyennes pondérées des taux d'activité 1950, 1959, 1970 et 1989 tirés du Bulletin des statistiques du travail, 1994-2.

#### 2.2.2 Femmes:

Méthode, hypothèses et traitements identiques à ceux appliqués aux hommes.

## 3. Evaluation des taux de répartition par secteur d'activité: 1950 - 1990

### 3.1 Données de base:

Tableau 2: Répartition de la population active en % par secteur d'activité

| Année | Agriculture | Industrie Total | Manufac. | Services |
|---|---|---|---|---|
| **Hommes** | | | | |
| 1950 | 69.15 | 13.30 | 9.57 | 17.55 |
| 1959 | 61.37 | 3.01 | 15.89 | 35.62 |
| 1970 | 35.00 | 35.00 | 17.59 | 30.00 |
| 1979 | 34.28 | 34.28 | 15.59 | 31.44 |
| 1989 | 35.57 | 30.78 | 13.74 | 33.65 |
| **Femmes** | | | | |
| 1950 | 71.74 | 9.32 | 7.76 | 18.94 |
| 1959 | 57.14 | 16.17 | 11.32 | 26.68 |
| 1970 | 36.40 | 23.90 | 17.65 | 39.71 |
| 1979 | 33.66 | 23.46 | 17.32 | 42.88 |
| 1989 | 28.59 | 22.65 | 16.46 | 48.76 |

Source(s): BLT-94-2.

### 3.2 Méthode(s): moyenne pondérée

#### 3.2.1 Hommes:

- 1950-90, moyennes pondérées des taux de répartition 1950, 1959, 1970, 1979 et 1989 tirés du Bulletin des statistiques du travail - 1994-2.

#### 3.2.2 Femmes:

Méthode, hypothèses et traitements identiques à ceux appliqués aux hommes.

## 4. Projection des taux d'activité: 2000 - 2010

### 4.1 Modèle(s): linéaire, hyperbole et logistique

#### 4.1.1 Hommes:

- Aux groupes d'âge [15-24] et [60+], application de la fonction F3;
- Aux groupes d'âge [25-59], application de la fonction F1;
- Modification des tendances des groupes d'âge [25-59].

#### 4.1.2 Femmes:

- Aux groupes d'âge [15-24] et [65+], application de la fonction F3;
- Aux groupes d'âge [25-64], application de la fonction F6;
- Modification des tendances des groupes d'âge [20+];
- Modification des tendances des groupes d'âge [15+].

*Notes sur les ajustements des taux, voir p. 192-195.*     *Notes sur les fonctions de projection, voir p. 198.*

# Koweït

## 1. Source(s) des données de base

Code(s): Titre(s):

EPPA3    Evaluations et projections de la population active 1950-2025 - troisième édition, BIT, Genève, 1986.
ASTER    Annuaire des statistiques du travail 1945-89 - Edition rétrospective sur les recensements de population, BIT, Genève, 1990.
AST92    Annuaire des statistiques du travail 1992, BIT, Genève, 1992.

## 2. Evaluation des taux d'activité: 1950 - 1990

### 2.1 Données de base:

Tableau 1: Taux d'activité par sexe et par groupe d'âge

| Groupe d'âge | Année 1975 (1) | 1980 (1) | 1985 (1) | 1988 (2) |
|---|---|---|---|---|
| **Hommes** | | | | |
| 10-14 | .. | 0.00 | 0.00 | 0.00 |
| 15-19 | .. | 34.74 | 14.20 | 9.04 |
| 20-24 | .. | 86.16 | 79.67 | 73.32 |
| 25-29 | .. | 97.64 | 97.72 | 97.61 |
| 30-34 | .. | 98.69 | 99.15 | 99.52 |
| 35-39 | .. | 98.49 | 98.96 | 99.33 |
| 40-44 | .. | 97.52 | 96.34 | 97.59 |
| 45-49 | .. | 95.57 | 91.20 | 91.87 |
| 50-54 | .. | 90.92 | 86.61 | 84.83 |
| 55-59 | .. | 84.39 | 79.45 | 79.90 |
| 60-64 | .. | 67.20 | 63.97 | 58.46 |
| 65+ | .. | 33.61 | 20.64 | 15.71 |
| **Femmes** | | | | |
| 10-14 | 0.00 | 0.00 | 0.00 | 0.00 |
| 15-19 | 4.62 | 4.99 | 6.28 | 4.59 |
| 20-24 | 15.31 | 21.36 | 37.07 | 42.13 |
| 25-29 | 19.81 | 29.92 | 47.38 | 55.32 |
| 30-34 | 18.90 | 27.35 | 45.19 | 52.10 |
| 35-39 | 19.16 | 23.88 | 37.59 | 42.04 |
| 40-44 | 21.42 | 24.13 | 29.54 | 31.77 |
| 45-49 | 19.99 | 21.83 | 24.29 | 22.88 |
| 50-54 | 15.89 | 18.93 | 18.19 | 18.89 |
| 55-59 | 10.41 | 13.21 | 13.14 | 13.44 |
| 60-64 | 6.37 | 7.63 | 7.23 | 10.19 |
| 65+ | 2.61 | 2.80 | 1.48 | 0.69 |

Source(s): (1) ASTER; (2) AST92.

### 2.2 Méthode(s): interpolation et extrapolation linéaires

#### 2.2.1 Hommes:

- 1950-70, taux d'activité 1950-70 tirés des EPPA3;
- 1980-90, interpolation et extrapolation des taux d'activité tirés des recensements de 1980 et 1985 et de l'enquête de 1988; ajustement des taux interpolés et extrapolés sur la base des variations des taux interpolés 1980 par rapport aux taux du recensement de 1980.

#### 2.2.2 Femmes:

- 1950-70, taux d'activité 1950-70 tirés des EPPA3;
- 1980-90, interpolation et extrapolation des taux d'activité tirés des recensements de 1975, 1980 et 1985 et de l'enquête de 1988; ajustement des taux interpolés et extrapolés sur la base des variations des taux interpolés 1980 par rapport aux taux du recensement de 1980.

## 3. Evaluation des taux de répartition par secteur d'activité: 1950 - 1990

### 3.1 Données de base:

Tableau 2: Répartition de la population active en % par secteur d'activité

| Année | Agriculture | Industrie Total | Manufac. | Services |
|---|---|---|---|---|
| **Hommes** | | | | |
| 1975 (1) | 2.84 | 25.88 | 9.15 | 71.28 |
| 1980 (1) | 2.15 | 35.93 | 9.61 | 61.92 |
| 1985 (1) | 2.35 | 35.07 | 9.35 | 62.58 |
| 1988 (2) | 1.67 | 32.99 | 9.76 | 65.34 |
| **Femmes** | | | | |
| 1975 (1) | 0.06 | 1.83 | 0.98 | 98.11 |
| 1980 (1) | 0.13 | 2.52 | 1.16 | 97.35 |
| 1985 (1) | 0.09 | 2.21 | 0.98 | 97.70 |
| 1988 (2) | 0.08 | 1.92 | 0.83 | 98.00 |

Source(s): (1) ASTER; (2) AST91; (3) AST93.

### 3.2 Méthode(s): extrapolation linéaire

#### 3.2.1 Hommes:

- 1950-80, taux de répartition 1950-80 tirés des EPPA3;
- 1990, extrapolation des taux de répartition tirés des recensements de 1975, 1980 et 1985 et des taux de l'enquête de 1988; modification des tendances de tous les secteurs;
- Application du rapport manufacture/industrie tiré de l'enquête de 1988.

#### 3.2.2 Femmes:

Méthode, hypothèses et traitements identiques à ceux appliqués aux hommes.

## 4. Projection des taux d'activité: 2000 - 2010

### 4.1 Modèle(s): linéaire, hyperbole et logistique

#### 4.1.1 Hommes:

- Au groupe d'âge [15-19], application de la fonction F3;
- Aux groupes d'âge [20+], application de la fonction F1;
- Modification des tendances des groupes d'âge [20-24] et [60+].

#### 4.1.2 Femmes:

- Aux groupes d'âge [15-39], application de la fonction F1;
- Aux groupes d'âge [40-64], application de la fonction F6;
- Au groupe d'âge [65+], application de la fonction F3;
- Modification des tendances des groupes d'âge [15-64].

*Notes sur les ajustements des taux, voir p. 192-195.*

*Notes sur les fonctions de projection, voir p. 198.*

289

# La bande de Gaza

## 1. Source(s) des données de base

Code(s):   Titre(s):

EPPA3   Evaluations et projections de la population active 1950-2025 - troisième édition, BIT, Genève, 1986.
LFS-97-93   Labour Force Statistics in the West Bank and Gaza Strip, Curent Status Report Series (No.3), Palestinian Central Bureau of Statistics, Ramallah-West Bank, 1995.

## 2. Evaluation des taux d'activité: 1950 - 1990

### 2.1 Données de base:

Tableau 1: Taux d'activité par sexe et par groupe d'âge

| Groupe d'âge | Année 1987 | 1989 | 1991 | 1993 |
|---|---|---|---|---|
| **Hommes** | | | | |
| Total | 71.00 | 67.00 | 68.00 | 68.00 |
| 15-24 | 34.00 | 32.00 | 30.00 | 30.00 |
| 25-64 | 85.00 | 83.00 | 87.00 | 86.00 |
| 65+ | 29.00 | 19.00 | 20.00 | 14.00 |
| **Femmes** | | | | |
| Total | 3.00 | 2.00 | 1.70 | 1.80 |
| 15-24 | 1.50 | 0.60 | 0.60 | 0.30 |
| 25-64 | 4.00 | 3.10 | 2.50 | 2.90 |
| 65+ | 1.30 | 0.10 | 0.20 | 0.30 |

Source(s): LFS-87-93.

### 2.2 Méthode(s): interpolation et extrapolation linéaires

#### 2.2.1 Hommes:

- 1950-90, interpolation et extrapolation des taux d'activité ajustés tirés des enquêtes de 1987, 1989, 1991 et 1993; modification des tendances de tous les groupes d'âge.

#### 2.2.2 Femmes:

Méthode, hypothèses et traitements identiques à ceux appliqués aux hommes.

## 3. Evaluation des taux de répartition par secteur d'activité: 1950 - 1990

### 3.1 Données de base:

Tableau 2: Répartition de la population active en % par secteur d'activité

| Année | Agriculture | Industrie Total | Manufac. | Services |
|---|---|---|---|---|
| **Hommes** | | | | |
| 1950 | 40.50 | 25.00 | .. | 34.50 |
| 1960 | 32.00 | 31.40 | .. | 36.60 |
| 1970 | 31.70 | 32.80 | .. | 35.50 |
| **Femmes** | | | | |
| 1950 | 64.00 | 22.00 | .. | 14.00 |
| 1960 | 62.00 | 18.50 | .. | 19.50 |
| 1970 | 51.90 | 18.00 | .. | 30.10 |

Source(s): EPPA3.

### 3.2 Méthode(s): extrapolation linéaire

#### 3.2.1 Hommes:

- 1950-70, taux de répartition 1950-70 tirés des EPPA3;
- 1980, moyennes des taux de répartition tirés des enquêtes de 1979, 1980 et 1981;
- 1990, moyennes des taux de répartition tirés des estimations officielles de 1989, 1990 et 1991.

#### 3.2.2 Femmes:

Méthode, hypothèses et traitements identiques à ceux appliqués aux hommes.

## 4. Projection des taux d'activité: 2000 - 2010

### 4.1 Modèle(s): linéaire et hyperbole

#### 4.1.1 Hommes:

- Aux groupes d'âge [15+], application de la fonction F3;
- Modification des tendances de tous les groupes d'âge.

#### 4.1.2 Femmes:

- Aux groupes d'âge [15+], application de la fonction F1;
- Modification des tendances de tous les groupes d'âge.

*Notes sur les ajustements des taux, voir p. 192-195.*   *Notes sur les fonctions de projection, voir p. 198.*

# Lesotho

## 1. Source(s) des données de base

Code(s):    Titre(s):

EPPA3      Evaluations et projections de la population active 1950-2025 - troisième édition, BIT, Genève, 1986.
ASTER      Annuaire des statistiques du travail 1945-89 - Edition rétrospective sur les recensements de population, BIT, Genève, 1990.
R1986      1986 Population Census, Statistical tables, Vol II., Bureau of Statistics, Maseru, 1987.

## 2. Evaluation des taux d'activité: 1950 - 1990

### 2.1 Données de base:

Tableau 1: Taux d'activité par sexe et par groupe d'âge

| Groupe d'âge | Année 1950 (1) | 1960 (1) | 1970 (1) | 1980 (1) | 1986 (2) |
|---|---|---|---|---|---|
| **Hommes** | | | | | |
| 10-14 | 51.35 | 44.10 | 40.00 | 32.30 | 34.36 |
| 15-19 | 86.75 | 83.50 | 80.45 | 74.70 | 54.24 |
| 20-24 | 97.85 | 96.80 | 96.00 | 94.30 | 88.65 |
| 25-29 | 98.90 | 98.70 | 98.50 | 98.20 | 97.58 |
| 30-34 | 99.40 | 99.20 | 99.00 | 98.65 | 98.31 |
| 35-39 | 99.45 | 99.30 | 99.10 | 98.75 | 98.22 |
| 40-44 | 99.40 | 99.20 | 99.00 | 98.70 | 97.80 |
| 45-49 | 99.35 | 99.15 | 98.95 | 98.30 | 97.23 |
| 50-54 | 99.25 | 99.05 | 98.85 | 98.20 | 95.79 |
| 55-59 | 99.20 | 97.80 | 97.10 | 95.80 | 93.56 |
| 60-64 | 98.45 | 97.10 | 96.05 | 93.75 | 89.78 |
| 65+ | 83.35 | 83.00 | 80.90 | 73.60 | 77.45 |
| **Femmes** | | | | | |
| 10-14 | 19.00 | 16.00 | 15.00 | 12.00 | 16.98 |
| 15-19 | 39.50 | 36.50 | 34.75 | 31.10 | 39.04 |
| 20-24 | 81.10 | 78.65 | 75.70 | 71.45 | 53.07 |
| 25-29 | 87.70 | 86.35 | 83.40 | 80.15 | 53.16 |
| 30-34 | 89.75 | 88.35 | 85.35 | 82.00 | 53.67 |
| 35-39 | 90.05 | 88.70 | 85.65 | 82.30 | 54.49 |
| 40-44 | 90.15 | 88.75 | 85.70 | 82.40 | 53.66 |
| 45-49 | 92.60 | 91.50 | 88.80 | 85.05 | 51.42 |
| 50-54 | 90.25 | 89.15 | 86.55 | 82.90 | 47.14 |
| 55-59 | 89.80 | 88.20 | 85.90 | 81.35 | 43.93 |
| 60-64 | 85.85 | 84.35 | 82.15 | 77.80 | 37.25 |
| 65+ | 81.25 | 78.80 | 75.90 | 68.00 | 22.63 |

Source(s): (1) EPPA3; (2) R1986.

### 2.2 Méthode(s): interpolation et extrapolation linéaires

#### 2.2.1 Hommes:

- 1950-90, interpolation et extrapolation des taux d'activité 1950-80 tirés des EPPA3;
ajustement des taux interpolés et extrapolés sur la base des variations des taux interpolés 1980 par rapport aux taux ajustés tirés recensement de 1986;
modification des tendances de tous les groupes d'âge pour 1950-90.

#### 2.2.2 Femmes:

- 1950-90, interpolation et extrapolation des taux d'activité 1950-80 tirés des EPPA3;
ajustement des taux interpolés et extrapolés sur la base des variations des taux interpolés 1986 par rapport aux taux ajustés du recensement de 1986.

## 3. Evaluation des taux de répartition par secteur d'activité: 1950 - 1990

### 3.1 Données de base:

Tableau 2: Répartition de la population active en % par secteur d'activité

| Année | Agriculture | Industrie Total | Manufac. | Services |
|---|---|---|---|---|
| **Hommes** | | | | |
| 1976 (1) | 23.62 | 57.92 | 2.33 | 18.46 |
| 1986 (2) | 28.87 | 43.44 | 1.76 | 27.69 |
| **Femmes** | | | | |
| 1976 (1) | 65.80 | 5.57 | 3.52 | 28.63 |
| 1986 (2) | 61.19 | 5.05 | 2.89 | 33.76 |

Source(s): (1) ASTER; (2) R1986.

### 3.2 Méthode(s): moyenne pondérée

#### 3.2.1 Hommes:

- 1950-90, interpolation et extrapolation des taux de répartition tirés des recensements de 1976 et 1986;
modification de la tendance du secteur agricole pour 1950;
- Application à l'industrie et aux services pour 1950-60 les mêmes proportions qu'en 1970.

#### 3.2.2 Femmes:

Méthode, hypothèses et traitements identiques à ceux appliqués aux hommes.

## 4. Projection des taux d'activité: 2000 - 2010

### 4.1 Modèle(s): linéaire et hyperbole

#### 4.1.1 Hommes:

- A tous les groupes d'âge, application de la fonction F1;
- Modification de la tendance du groupe d'âge [65+].

#### 4.1.2 Femmes:

- Aux groupes d'âge [10-19], application de la fonction F1;
- Aux groupes d'âge [20+], application de la fonction F3;
- Modification des tendances des groupes d'âge [10-49].

*Notes sur les ajustements des taux, voir p. 192-195.*        *Notes sur les fonctions de projection, voir p. 198.*

# Lettonie

## 1. Source(s) des données de base

Code(s):     Titre(s):

BLT-94-2     Vorobiev A. (1994), "Estimation de la population active pour les quinze pays de l'ex-URSS pour les années 1950, 1959, 1970, 1979 et 1989", dans le Bulletin des statistiques du travail - 1994-2, BIT, Genève.

## 2. Evaluation des taux d'activité: 1950 - 1990

### 2.1 Données de base:

Tableau 1: Taux d'activité par sexe et par groupe d'âge

| Groupe d'âge | Année 1950 | 1959 | 1970 | 1979 | 1989 |
|---|---|---|---|---|---|
| **Hommes** | | | | | |
| 10-14 | 0.00 | 0.00 | 0.00 | 0.00 | 0.00 |
| 15-19 | 55.56 | 57.14 | 40.23 | 33.33 | 32.63 |
| 20-24 | 84.21 | 85.37 | 84.52 | 85.15 | 82.11 |
| 25-29 | 92.73 | 96.47 | 96.59 | 96.77 | 96.19 |
| 30-34 | 93.48 | 94.37 | 96.88 | 98.75 | 97.98 |
| 35-39 | 93.65 | 96.08 | 98.85 | 98.89 | 97.78 |
| 40-44 | 92.31 | 93.02 | 96.25 | 96.63 | 96.05 |
| 45-49 | 92.00 | 93.10 | 96.36 | 96.39 | 98.78 |
| 50-54 | 89.74 | 91.53 | 92.68 | 92.65 | 92.50 |
| 55-59 | 85.19 | 89.13 | 90.38 | 86.67 | 86.11 |
| 60-64 | 56.00 | 72.73 | 43.14 | 42.86 | 51.79 |
| 65+ | 28.57 | 42.47 | 21.74 | 16.67 | 20.62 |
| **Femmes** | | | | | |
| 10-14 | 0.00 | 0.00 | 0.00 | 0.00 | 0.00 |
| 15-19 | 43.01 | 45.24 | 35.44 | 31.52 | 29.21 |
| 20-24 | 62.50 | 67.42 | 82.28 | 83.33 | 81.11 |
| 25-29 | 71.59 | 79.35 | 92.05 | 93.48 | 90.48 |
| 30-34 | 69.57 | 71.29 | 92.93 | 95.12 | 94.06 |
| 35-39 | 69.32 | 70.37 | 92.47 | 94.79 | 94.68 |
| 40-44 | 92.77 | 69.84 | 91.09 | 95.88 | 95.06 |
| 45-49 | 67.11 | 71.25 | 89.66 | 93.55 | 93.62 |
| 50-54 | 59.70 | 63.64 | 81.36 | 88.78 | 88.17 |
| 55-59 | 41.61 | 44.44 | 40.51 | 43.59 | 50.00 |
| 60-64 | 29.17 | 32.79 | 24.00 | 22.41 | 33.33 |
| 65+ | 10.62 | 12.24 | 6.35 | 7.31 | 11.01 |

Source(s): BLT-94-2.

### 2.2 Méthode(s): moyenne pondérée

#### 2.2.1 Hommes:

- 1950-90, moyennes pondérées des taux d'activité 1950, 1959, 1970 et 1989 tirés du Bulletin des statistiques du travail, 1994-2;
modification des tendances des groupes d'âge [30-34] et [60+] respectivement pour 1950-60 et 1960-80.

#### 2.2.2 Femmes:

- 1950-90, moyennes pondérées des taux d'activité 1950, 1959, 1970 et 1989 tirés du Bulletin des statistiques du travail, 1994-2;
modification de la tendance du groupe d'âge [65+] pour 1950.

## 3. Evaluation des taux de répartition par secteur d'activité: 1950 - 1990

### 3.1 Données de base:

Tableau 2: Répartition de la population active en % par secteur d'activité

| Année | Agriculture | Industrie Total | Manufac. | Services |
|---|---|---|---|---|
| **Hommes** | | | | |
| 1950 | 39.22 | 30.50 | 18.95 | 30.28 |
| 1959 | 30.84 | 39.93 | 24.42 | 29.23 |
| 1970 | 19.30 | 50.40 | 30.62 | 30.30 |
| 1979 | 18.44 | 49.41 | 31.12 | 32.15 |
| 1989 | 19.18 | 46.85 | 29.73 | 33.97 |
| **Femmes** | | | | |
| 1950 | 57.29 | 16.91 | 14.16 | 25.79 |
| 1959 | 38.65 | 25.77 | 21.92 | 35.58 |
| 1970 | 18.99 | 34.97 | 30.22 | 46.04 |
| 1979 | 14.27 | 35.45 | 30.69 | 50.29 |
| 1989 | 12.33 | 32.55 | 28.12 | 55.12 |

Source(s): BLT-94-2.

### 3.2 Méthode(s): données du BLT-94-2

#### 3.2.1 Hommes:

- 1950, 1960, 1970, 1980 et 1990, respectivement les taux de répartition 1950, 1959, 1970, 1979 et 1989 tirés du Bulletin des statistiques du travail - 1994-2.

#### 3.2.2 Femmes:

Méthode, hypothèses et traitements identiques à ceux appliqués aux hommes.

## 4. Projection des taux d'activité: 2000 - 2010

### 4.1 Modèle(s): linéaire, hyperbole et logistique

#### 4.1.1 Hommes:

- Aux groupes d'âge [15-54], application de la fonction F1;
- Aux groupes d'âge [55+], application de la fonction F3;
- Modification des tendances des groupes d'âge [25-54].

#### 4.1.2 Femmes:

- Au groupe d'âge [15-19], application de la fonction F1;
- Aux groupes d'âge [20-54], application de la fonction F6;
- Aux groupes d'âge [55+], application de la fonction F3;
- Modification des tendances des groupes d'âge [20+].

*Notes sur les ajustements des taux, voir p. 192-195.*

*Notes sur les fonctions de projection, voir p. 198.*

# Liban

## 1. Source(s) des données de base

Code(s):     Titre(s):

EPPA3     Evaluations et projections de la population active 1950-2025 - troisième édition, BIT, Genève, 1986.

## 2. Evaluation des taux d'activité: 1950 - 1990

### 2.1 Données de base:

Tableau 1: Taux d'activité par sexe et par groupe d'âge

| Groupe d'âge | Année 1950 | 1960 | 1970 | 1980 |
|---|---|---|---|---|
| **Hommes** | | | | |
| 10-14 | 22.55 | 12.15 | 6.55 | 5.35 |
| 15-19 | 46.65 | 42.20 | 38.20 | 35.00 |
| 20-24 | 79.75 | 76.25 | 72.90 | 72.00 |
| 25-29 | 96.65 | 95.50 | 94.00 | 93.80 |
| 30-34 | 97.20 | 97.00 | 96.35 | 96.30 |
| 35-39 | 97.50 | 97.20 | 96.90 | 96.80 |
| 40-44 | 97.05 | 96.00 | 96.00 | 95.70 |
| 45-49 | 96.90 | 95.20 | 94.00 | 94.50 |
| 50-54 | 94.00 | 92.00 | 89.00 | 89.00 |
| 55-59 | 92.00 | 86.15 | 80.70 | 79.05 |
| 60-64 | 82.35 | 75.70 | 69.55 | 68.40 |
| 65+ | 58.50 | 46.70 | 42.20 | 41.40 |
| **Femmes** | | | | |
| 10-14 | 8.00 | 6.40 | 5.90 | 4.20 |
| 15-19 | 9.00 | 10.60 | 16.70 | 17.75 |
| 20-24 | 11.50 | 17.45 | 28.35 | 33.15 |
| 25-29 | 11.00 | 15.50 | 25.00 | 30.05 |
| 30-34 | 10.50 | 13.50 | 20.35 | 24.10 |
| 35-39 | 10.30 | 11.90 | 16.35 | 18.90 |
| 40-44 | 9.50 | 11.30 | 15.10 | 17.05 |
| 45-49 | 9.20 | 10.80 | 13.95 | 15.50 |
| 50-54 | 9.00 | 9.50 | 11.60 | 13.05 |
| 55-59 | 8.70 | 8.50 | 9.10 | 9.90 |
| 60-64 | 8.40 | 8.10 | 8.30 | 8.80 |
| 65+ | 4.20 | 3.40 | 2.85 | 3.00 |

Source(s): EPPA3.

### 2.2 Méthode(s): extrapolation linéaire

#### 2.2.1 Hommes:

- 1950-90, taux d'activité ajustés tirés des EPPA3;
ajustement des taux sur la base d'une évaluation des militaires.

#### 2.2.2 Femmes:

- 1950-80, taux d'activité 1950-80 tirés des EPPA3;
- 1990, extrapolation des taux d'activité 1950-1980 tirés des EPPA3.

## 3. Evaluation des taux de répartition par secteur d'activité: 1950 - 1990

### 3.1 Données de base:

Tableau 2: Répartition de la population active en % par secteur d'activité

| Année | Agriculture | Industrie Total | Manufac. | Services |
|---|---|---|---|---|
| **Hommes** | | | | |
| 1950 | 52.60 | 21.80 | | 25.60 |
| 1960 | 36.50 | 24.30 | | 39.20 |
| 1970 | 18.90 | 26.40 | | 54.70 |
| 1980 | 12.60 | 29.20 | | 58.20 |
| **Femmes** | | | | |
| 1950 | 76.20 | 8.50 | | 15.30 |
| 1960 | 49.90 | 14.25 | | 35.85 |
| 1970 | 23.60 | 20.00 | | 56.40 |
| 1980 | 20.00 | 21.00 | | 59.00 |

Source(s): EPPA3.

### 3.2 Méthode(s): extrapolation linéaire

#### 3.2.1 Hommes:

- 1950-80, taux de répartition 1950-80 tirés des EPPA3;
- 1990, extrapolation des taux de répartition de l'agriculture 1970-80 des EPPA3; la différence des taux de répartition de l'agriculture entre 1980 et 1990 a été répartie entre l'industrie (80%) et les services (20%).

#### 3.2.2 Femmes:

- 1950-80, taux de répartition 1950-80 tirés des EPPA3;
- 1990, extrapolation des taux de répartition de l'agriculture 1970-80 des EPPA3; la différence des taux de répartition de l'agriculture entre 1980 et 1990 a été répartie entre l'industrie (10%) et les services (90%).

## 4. Projection des taux d'activité: 2000 - 2010

### 4.1 Modèle(s): linéaire, log-linéaire, hyperbole et logistique

#### 4.1.1 Hommes:

- Aux groupes d'âge [15-19] et [55+], application de la fonction F3;
- Aux groupes d'âge [20-54], application de la fonction F1;
- Modification des tendances des groupes d'âge [20-54].

#### 4.1.2 Femmes:

- Aux groupes d'âge [15-29], application de la fonction F6;
- Aux groupes d'âge [30-59], application de la fonction F2;
- Aux groupes d'âge [60+], application de la fonction F3;
- Modification des tendances des groupes d'âge [15-59].

---

*Notes sur les ajustements des taux, voir p. 192-195.*     *Notes sur les fonctions de projection, voir p. 198.*

# Libéria

## 1. Source(s) des données de base

Code(s):     Titre(s):

ASTER       Annuaire des statistiques du travail 1945-89 - Edition rétrospective sur les recensements de population, BIT, Genève, 1990.

## 2. Evaluation des taux d'activité: 1950 - 1990

### 2.1 Données de base:

Tableau 1: Taux d'activité par sexe et par groupe d'âge

| | | Année | | |
|---|---|---|---|---|
| | Groupe d'âge | 1962 | 1974 | 1984 |
| **Hommes** | | | | |
| | 10-14 | 22.39 | 8.60 | .. |
| | 15-19 | 46.45 | 21.07 | .. |
| | 20-24 | 74.78 | 51.33 | .. |
| | 25-29 | 87.30 | 78.36 | .. |
| | 30-34 | 92.99 | 88.10 | .. |
| | 35-39 | 94.44 | 91.26 | .. |
| | 40-44 | 93.91 | 91.65 | .. |
| | 45-49 | 93.76 | 91.75 | .. |
| | 50-54 | 92.12 | 90.43 | .. |
| | 55-59 | 91.13 | 89.61 | .. |
| | 60-64 | 81.51 | 80.33 | .. |
| | 65+ | 64.30 | 65.97 | .. |
| **Femmes** | | | | |
| | 10-14 | 20.12 | 6.75 | 14.18 |
| | 15-19 | 34.93 | 15.37 | 25.37 |
| | 20-24 | 41.20 | 21.57 | 37.80 |
| | 25-29 | 44.25 | 25.42 | 48.47 |
| | 30-34 | 47.90 | 28.65 | 56.17 |
| | 35-39 | 49.76 | 30.67 | 59.93 |
| | 40-44 | 51.05 | 33.51 | 63.74 |
| | 45-49 | 49.87 | 33.86 | 63.90 |
| | 50-54 | 46.94 | 31.44 | 62.76 |
| | 55-59 | 44.35 | 30.38 | 59.09 |
| | 60-64 | 31.98 | 23.69 | 49.49 |
| | 65+ | 20.38 | 16.20 | 32.47 |

Source(s): ASTER.

### 2.2 Méthode(s): interpolation et extrapolation linéaires

#### 2.2.1 Hommes:

- 1950-90, interpolation et extrapolation des taux d'activité tirés des recensements de 1962 et 1974;
modification des tendances des groupes d'âge [35-44] pour 1980 et des groupes d'âge [20-29] pour 1990.

#### 2.2.2 Femmes:

- 1950-90, interpolation et extrapolation des taux d'activité tirés des recensements de 1962, 1974 et 1984;
modification des tendances de tous les groupes d'âge.

## 3. Evaluation des taux de répartition par secteur d'activité: 1950 - 1990

### 3.1 Données de base:

Tableau 2: Répartition de la population active en % par secteur d'activité

| | | Agriculture | Industrie | | Services |
|---|---|---|---|---|---|
| | Année | | Total | Manufac. | |
| **Hommes** | | | | | |
| | 1962 | 74.52 | 13.03 | 2.96 | 12.45 |
| | 1974 | 71.01 | 10.34 | 1.78 | 18.65 |
| | 1984 | 67.08 | 9.03 | 2.74 | 23.89 |
| **Femmes** | | | | | |
| | 1962 | 95.03 | 0.72 | 0.41 | 4.26 |
| | 1974 | 94.19 | 0.50 | 0.13 | 5.31 |
| | 1984 | 85.89 | 0.75 | 0.24 | 13.35 |

Source(s): ASTER.

### 3.2 Méthode(s): moyenne pondérée

#### 3.2.1 Hommes:

- 1960-80, moyennes pondérées des taux de répartition tirés des recensements de 1962, 1974 et 1984;
- 1990, extrapolation des taux tirés des recensements de 1974 et 1984;
- 1950, application au taux de répartition 1980 pour l'agriculture tiré des EPPA de 3/4 de la tendance estimée pour 1980-90; pour l'industrie et les services les mêmes proportions qu'en 1960.

#### 3.2.2 Femmes:

- 1960-80, moyennes pondérées des taux de répartition tirés des recensements de 1962, 1974 et 1984;
- 1990, extrapolation des taux tirés des recensements de 1974 et 1984;
- 1950, application au taux de répartition 1980 pour l'agriculture tiré des EPPA de la moitié de la tendance estimée pour 1980-90; pour l'industrie et les services les mêmes proportions qu'en 1960.

## 4. Projection des taux d'activité: 2000 - 2010

### 4.1 Modèle(s): log-linéaire, hyperbole et linéaire

#### 4.1.1 Hommes:

- Aux groupes d'âge [10-19], application de la fonction F2;
- Aux groupes d'âge [20-64], application de la fonction F3;
- Aux groupes d'âge [60+], application de la fonction F1;
- Modification des tendances des groupes d'âge [25-29] et [35-39].

#### 4.1.2 Femmes:

- Aux groupes d'âge [10-54], application de la fonction F1;
- Aux groupes d'âge [55+], application de la fonction F3;
- Modification de la tendance du groupe d'âge [15-19].

*Notes sur les ajustements des taux, voir p. 192-195.*

*Notes sur les fonctions de projection, voir p. 198.*

# Lituanie

## 1. Source(s) des données de base

Code(s):     Titre(s):

BLT-94-2    Vorobiev A. (1994), "Estimation de la population active pour les quinze pays de l'ex-URSS pour les années 1950, 1959, 1970, 1979 et 1989", dans le Bulletin des statistiques du travail - 1994-2, BIT, Genève.

## 2. Evaluation des taux d'activité: 1950 - 1990

### 2.1 Données de base:

Tableau 1: Taux d'activité par sexe et par groupe d'âge

| Groupe d'âge | Année 1950 | 1959 | 1970 | 1979 | 1989 |
|---|---|---|---|---|---|
| **Hommes** | | | | | |
| 10-14 | 0.00 | 0.00 | 0.00 | 0.00 | 0.00 |
| 15-19 | 55.74 | 58.62 | 33.88 | 27.10 | 26.90 |
| 20-24 | 92.59 | 81.98 | 84.11 | 84.17 | 79.17 |
| 25-29 | 93.75 | 94.64 | 97.32 | 97.56 | 96.82 |
| 30-34 | 91.07 | 95.74 | 98.26 | 99.06 | 97.83 |
| 35-39 | 92.19 | 94.37 | 98.21 | 98.25 | 97.50 |
| 40-44 | 91.84 | 93.88 | 97.00 | 97.32 | 97.03 |
| 45-49 | 90.77 | 94.74 | 96.00 | 97.20 | 95.33 |
| 50-54 | 89.09 | 92.94 | 93.62 | 94.25 | 92.08 |
| 55-59 | 84.78 | 89.29 | 88.68 | 89.06 | 86.02 |
| 60-64 | 66.67 | 80.43 | 55.56 | 39.02 | 44.59 |
| 65+ | 48.08 | 52.63 | 20.34 | 12.41 | 14.71 |
| **Femmes** | | | | | |
| 10-14 | 0.00 | 0.00 | 0.00 | 0.00 | 0.00 |
| 15-19 | 44.60 | 49.17 | 28.70 | 21.53 | 20.00 |
| 20-24 | 68.09 | 70.73 | 80.56 | 80.30 | 72.79 |
| 25-29 | 71.17 | 74.02 | 88.70 | 95.08 | 87.74 |
| 30-34 | 65.85 | 68.00 | 88.00 | 95.54 | 91.43 |
| 35-39 | 65.66 | 66.67 | 88.71 | 95.90 | 93.65 |
| 40-44 | 63.74 | 67.14 | 87.90 | 95.20 | 93.64 |
| 45-49 | 62.96 | 65.88 | 84.31 | 93.50 | 90.83 |
| 50-54 | 57.81 | 60.24 | 75.38 | 86.44 | 85.00 |
| 55-59 | 42.37 | 46.15 | 38.10 | 36.17 | 42.37 |
| 60-64 | 23.08 | 50.75 | 16.87 | 15.63 | 25.66 |
| 65+ | 8.13 | 9.77 | 6.22 | 7.86 | 7.06 |

Source(s): BLT-94-2.

### 2.2 Méthode(s): moyenne pondérée

#### 2.2.1 Hommes:

- 1950-90, moyennes pondérées des taux d'activité 1950, 1959, 1970 et 1989 tirés du Bulletin des statistiques du travail, 1994-2;
les taux d'activité 1950, 1959, 1970, 1979 tirés du Bulletin ont été ajustés pour les groupes d'âge [15-19] et [55+];
ajustement du taux d'activé estimé 1960 pour le groupe d'âge [20-24].

#### 2.2.2 Femmes:

- 1950-90, moyennes pondérées des taux d'activité 1950, 1959, 1970 et 1989 tirés du Bulletin des statistiques du travail, 1994-2;
les taux d'activité 1950, 1959, 1970, 1979 tirés du Bulletin ont été ajustés pour les groupes d'âge [55+]

## 3. Evaluation des taux de répartition par secteur d'activité: 1950 - 1990

### 3.1 Données de base:

Tableau 2: Répartition de la population active en % par secteur d'activité

| Année | Agriculture | Industrie Total | Manufac. | Services |
|---|---|---|---|---|
| **Hommes** | | | | |
| 1950 | 61.38 | 16.01 | 11.62 | 22.61 |
| 1959 | 48.49 | 27.20 | 16.76 | 24.31 |
| 1970 | 31.26 | 43.96 | 24.78 | 24.78 |
| 1979 | 26.36 | 46.82 | 27.05 | 26.82 |
| 1989 | 23.21 | 46.93 | 27.61 | 29.86 |
| **Femmes** | | | | |
| 1950 | 73.04 | 9.29 | 8.01 | 17.67 |
| 1959 | 56.80 | 16.64 | 13.76 | 26.56 |
| 1970 | 31.59 | 29.70 | 24.87 | 38.71 |
| 1979 | 29.34 | 29.55 | 24.28 | 41.12 |
| 1989 | 13.35 | 33.70 | 28.01 | 52.95 |

Source(s): BLT-94-2.

### 3.2 Méthode(s): données du BLT-94-2

#### 3.2.1 Hommes:

- 1950, 1960, 1970, 1980 et 1990, respectivement les taux de répartition 1950, 1959, 1970, 1979 et 1989 tirés du Bulletin des statistiques du travail - 1994-2.

#### 3.2.2 Femmes:

Méthode, hypothèses et traitements identiques à ceux appliqués aux hommes.

## 4. Projection des taux d'activité: 2000 - 2010

### 4.1 Modèle(s): linéaire, hyperbole et logistique

#### 4.1.1 Hommes:

- Aux groupes d'âge [15-19] et [50+], application de la fonction F3;
- Aux groupes d'âge [20-49], application de la fonction F1;
- Modification des tendances des groupes d'âge [25-54].

#### 4.1.2 Femmes:

- Aux groupes d'âge [15-19] et [55+], application de la fonction F3;
- Au groupe d'âge [20-24], application de la fonction F1;
- Aux groupes d'âge [25-54], application de la fonction F6;
- Modification des tendances des groupes d'âge [20-54].

*Notes sur les ajustements des taux, voir p. 192-195.*

*Notes sur les fonctions de projection, voir p. 198.*

# Luxembourg

## 1. Source(s) des données de base

Code(s):     Titre(s):
EPPA3       Annuaire des statistiques du travail 1945-89 - Edition rétrospective sur les recensements de population, BIT, Genève, 1990.
STAT        Base de données sur les statistiques du travail - LABORSTA, Bureau de statistique, BIT, Genève.

## 2. Evaluation des taux d'activité: 1950 - 1990

### 2.1 Données de base:

Tableau 1: Taux d'activité par sexe et par groupe d'âge

| Groupe d'âge | Année 1950 (1) | 1960 (1) | 1970 (1) | 1980 (1) | 1991 (2) |
|---|---|---|---|---|---|
| **Hommes** | | | | | |
| 10-14 | 3.25 | 1.65 | 1.00 | 0.00 | 0.00 |
| 15-19 | 73.05 | 58.80 | 53.10 | 47.45 | 29.63 |
| 20-24 | 90.55 | 92.75 | 86.95 | 81.15 | 75.34 |
| 25-29 | 95.15 | 96.45 | 96.05 | 95.60 | 94.02 |
| 30-34 | 96.70 | 97.95 | 98.15 | 98.35 | 97.27 |
| 35-39 | 96.05 | 96.95 | 97.80 | 98.70 | 97.80 |
| 40-44 | 95.30 | 96.90 | 97.35 | 97.80 | 96.86 |
| 45-49 | 95.10 | 95.45 | 95.70 | 95.95 | 94.78 |
| 50-54 | 91.65 | 92.35 | 91.30 | 90.30 | 85.92 |
| 55-59 | 88.45 | 85.65 | 72.75 | 59.85 | 54.78 |
| 60-64 | 58.35 | 55.70 | 43.35 | 31.00 | 19.04 |
| 65+ | 34.45 | 21.15 | 13.35 | 5.50 | 2.09 |
| **Femmes** | | | | | |
| 10-14 | 2.50 | 1.60 | 1.05 | 0.00 | 0.00 |
| 15-19 | 56.00 | 56.80 | 54.80 | 45.20 | 25.75 |
| 20-24 | 50.00 | 50.60 | 52.90 | 68.70 | 71.04 |
| 25-29 | 34.40 | 30.45 | 33.75 | 55.50 | 68.39 |
| 30-34 | 29.30 | 26.20 | 26.35 | 43.95 | 56.78 |
| 35-39 | 31.30 | 28.30 | 24.50 | 39.70 | 54.60 |
| 40-44 | 33.30 | 30.20 | 24.75 | 36.25 | 51.94 |
| 45-49 | 31.95 | 29.60 | 25.40 | 29.45 | 44.20 |
| 50-54 | 28.65 | 26.50 | 23.80 | 25.10 | 32.00 |
| 55-59 | 27.95 | 21.60 | 19.95 | 19.85 | 19.83 |
| 60-64 | 21.95 | 17.20 | 13.40 | 12.20 | 9.38 |
| 65+ | 13.65 | 9.8 | 4.8 | 2.75 | 0.78 |

Source(s): STAT.

### 2.2 Méthode(s): moyenne pondérée

#### 2.2.1 Hommes:

- 1950-80, taux d'activité 1950-80 tirés des EPPA3;
- 1990, moyennes pondérées des taux d'activité 1980 tirés des EPPA3 et des taux d'activité tirés du recensement de 1991.

#### 2.2.2 Femmes:

Méthode, hypothèses et traitements identiques à ceux appliqués aux hommes.

## 3. Evaluation des taux de répartition par secteur d'activité: 1950 - 1990

### 3.1 Données de base:

Tableau 2: Répartition de la population active en % par secteur d'activité

| Année | Agriculture | Industrie Total | Manufac. | Services |
|---|---|---|---|---|
| **Hommes** | | | | |
| 1981 | 4.85 | 44.97 | 30.47 | 50.18 |
| 1991 | 3.56 | 36.07 | 30.19 | 60.37 |
| **Femmes** | | | | |
| 1981 | 5.38 | 10.84 | 8.96 | 83.78 |
| 1991 | 3.26 | 9.27 | 7.39 | 87.47 |

Source(s): (1) STAT.

### 3.2 Méthode(s): moyenne pondérée

#### 3.2.1 Hommes:

- 1950-80, taux de répartition 1950-80 tirés des EPPA3;
- 1990, moyennes pondérées des taux de répartition tirés des recensements de 1981 et 1991.

#### 3.2.2 Femmes:

Méthode, hypothèses et traitements identiques à ceux appliqués aux hommes.

## 4. Projection des taux d'activité: 2000 - 2010

### 4.1 Modèle(s): linéaire, hyperbole et logistique

#### 4.1.1 Hommes:

- Aux groupes d'âge [15-34] et [50+], application de la fonction F3;
- Aux groupes d'âge [35-49], application de la fonction F3;
- Modification des tendances des groupes d'âge [30-49].

#### 4.1.2 Femmes:

- Aux groupes d'âge [15-19] et [50+], application de la fonction F3;
- Aux groupes d'âge [20-29], application de la fonction F6;
- Aux groupes d'âge [30-49], application de la fonction F1;
- Modification de la tendance du groupe d'âge [20-24].

*Notes sur les ajustements des taux, voir p. 192-195.*

*Notes sur les fonctions de projection, voir p. 198.*

# Macao, chine

## 1. Source(s) des données de base

Code(s):    Titre(s):

STAT        Base de données sur les statistiques du travail - LABORSTA, Bureau de statistique, BIT, Genève.

## 2. Evaluation des taux d'activité: 1950 - 1990

### 2.1 Données de base:

Tableau 1: Taux d'activité par sexe et par groupe d'âge

| | Année | | | |
|---|---|---|---|---|
| Groupe d'âge | 1960 | 1981 | 1991 | 1992 |
| **Hommes** | | | | |
| 10-14 | .. | 5.97 | 3.86 | .. |
| 15-19 | .. | 57.31 | 59.50 | .. |
| 20-24 | .. | 94.62 | 92.11 | .. |
| 25-29 | .. | 98.49 | 97.94 | .. |
| 30-34 | .. | 98.76 | 98.02 | .. |
| 35-39 | .. | 98.25 | 99.98 | .. |
| 40-44 | .. | 97.17 | 97.24 | .. |
| 45-49 | .. | 95.07 | 95.54 | .. |
| 50-54 | .. | 87.95 | 86.87 | .. |
| 55-59 | .. | 79.85 | 78.08 | .. |
| 60-64 | .. | 72.01 | 57.60 | .. |
| 65+ | | ... | 29.29 | |
| **Femmes** | | | | |
| 10-14 | 3.95 | 8.18 | ... | ... |
| 15-19 | 16.40 | 57.32 | 29.26 | 29.26 |
| 20-24 | 20.57 | 83.50 | 56.90 | 56.90 |
| 25-29 | 17.13 | 69.71 | 59.53 | 59.53 |
| 30-34 | 18.36 | 53.98 | 53.86 | 53.86 |
| 35-39 | 21.27 | 50.00 | 59.13 | 59.13 |
| 40-44 | 22.84 | 45.97 | 58.33 | 58.33 |
| 45-49 | 21.97 | 39.58 | 52.12 | 52.12 |
| 50-54 | 22.89 | 31.39 | 47.69 | 47.69 |
| 55-59 | 19.49 | 27.58 | 23.54 | 23.54 |
| 60-64 | 17.37 | 19.97 | 21.94 | 21.94 |
| 65+ | 8.26 | 12.30 | 5.11 | 5.11 |

Source(s): STAT.

### 2.2 Méthode(s): moyenne pondérée

#### 2.2.1 Hommes:

- 1950-90, moyennes pondérées des taux d'activité ajustés tirés
des recensements de 1981 et 1991;
modification des tendances des groupes d'âge [25-29] pour 1950-70.

#### 2.2.2 Femmes:

- 1960, 1980 et 1990, moyennes pondérées des taux d'activité tirés
des recensements de 1960 et 1980 et des estimations officielles de 1992;
- 1950 et 1970, moyennes pondérées des taux d'activité
estimés pour 1960 et 1980;
modification des tendances de tous les groupes d'âge pour 1950.

## 3. Evaluation des taux de répartition par secteur d'activité: 1950 - 1990

### 3.1 Données de base:

Tableau 2: Répartition de la population active en % par secteur d'activité

| | | Agriculture | Industrie | | Services |
|---|---|---|---|---|---|
| | Année | | Total | Manufac. | |
| **Hommes** | | | | | |
| | 1960 | 6.08 | 30.82 | 25.14 | 63.09 |
| | 1981 | 6.50 | 47.47 | 34.46 | 46.03 |
| | 1991 | 1.50 | 34.28 | 20.77 | 64.22 |
| **Femmes** | | | | | |
| | 1960 | 3.36 | 49.43 | 47.19 | 47.21 |
| | 1981 | 5.25 | 64.26 | 62.80 | 30.49 |
| | 1991 | 1.23 | 48.63 | 46.52 | 50.14 |

Source(s): STAT.

### 3.2 Méthode(s): moyenne

#### 3.2.1 Hommes:

- 1960 et 1980-90, moyennes pondérées des taux de répartition
tirés des recensements de 1960, 1981 et 1991;
- 1950 et 1970, moyennes pondérées des taux de répartition estimés
pour 1960 et 1980.

#### 3.2.2 Femmes:

Méthode, hypothèses et traitements identiques à ceux appliqués aux hommes.

## 4. Projection des taux d'activité: 2000 - 2010

### 4.1 Modèle(s): linéaire, log-linéaire, hyperbole et logistique

#### 4.1.1 Hommes:

- Aux groupes d'âge [15-19] et [55+], application de la fonction F3;
- Au groupe d'âge [20-24], application de la fonction F2;
- Aux groupes d'âge [25-54], application de la fonction F1;
- Modification de la tendance du groupe d'âge [30-34].

#### 4.1.2 Femmes:

- Aux groupes d'âge [15-24] et [60+], application de la fonction F1;
- Aux groupes d'âge [25-59], application de la fonction F6;
- Modification des tendances des groupes d'âge [15-54].

*Notes sur les ajustements des taux, voir p. 192-195.*    *Notes sur les fonctions de projection, voir p. 198.*

# Macédoine, Ex-République youg

## 1. Source(s) des données de base

Code(s):     Titre(s):

BLT-94-2     Popovic B. (1994), "Nouvelles estimations pour 1980 et 1990 des taux d'activité par âge et répartition sectorielle
             pour certains pays d'Europe orientale et méridionale" dans le Bulletin des statistiques du travail - 1994-2, BIT, Genève.
STAT         Base de données sur les statistiques du travail - LABORSTA, Bureau de statistique, BIT, Genève.

## 2. Evaluation des taux d'activité: 1950 - 1990

### 2.1 Données de base:

Tableau 1: Taux d'activité par sexe et par groupe d'âge

| Groupe d'âge | Année 1948 (1) | 1953 (1) | 1961 (1) | 1971 (1) | 1980 (2) | 1990 (2) |
|---|---|---|---|---|---|---|
| **Hommes** | | | | | | |
| 10-14 | 20.84 | 17.03 | 9.84 | 3.30 | 0.63 | 0.04 |
| 15-19 | 89.34 | 79.29 | 56.27 | 40.69 | 27.13 | 21.91 |
| 20-24 | 96.01 | 93.56 | 89.27 | 77.27 | 76.89 | 76.52 |
| 25-29 | 99.87 | 97.06 | 94.67 | 95.45 | 92.01 | 92.64 |
| 30-34 | 99.99 | 98.78 | 96.95 | 98.31 | 98.12 | 96.30 |
| 35-39 | 99.82 | 98.80 | 98.42 | 97.58 | 98.69 | 96.79 |
| 40-44 | 98.92 | 97.17 | 96.47 | 96.84 | 98.04 | 96.02 |
| 45-49 | 99.18 | 99.96 | 97.98 | 90.83 | 96.28 | 94.91 |
| 50-54 | 96.42 | 96.62 | 97.08 | 87.33 | 88.83 | 85.97 |
| 55-59 | 94.44 | 92.78 | 90.61 | 83.95 | 73.93 | 64.83 |
| 60-64 | 92.46 | 88.73 | 85.01 | 67.87 | 59.77 | 41.20 |
| 65+ | 71.06 | 60.08 | 59.48 | 50.97 | 39.52 | 25.55 |
| **Femmes** | | | | | | |
| 10-14 | .. | 13.69 | 9.08 | 4.66 | 1.05 | 0.07 |
| 15-19 | .. | 58.59 | 54.39 | 37.98 | 22.34 | 17.73 |
| 20-24 | .. | 50.49 | 49.63 | 48.78 | 50.60 | 61.03 |
| 25-29 | .. | 37.11 | 43.52 | 45.29 | 61.65 | 67.08 |
| 30-34 | .. | 34.75 | 36.34 | 38.44 | 64.34 | 69.04 |
| 35-39 | .. | 30.52 | 32.04 | 36.88 | 59.78 | 69.03 |
| 40-44 | .. | 28.93 | 31.64 | 32.14 | 53.19 | 66.87 |
| 45-49 | .. | 22.07 | 26.52 | 28.70 | 46.39 | 60.54 |
| 50-54 | .. | 17.05 | 22.26 | 20.00 | 36.12 | 50.42 |
| 55-59 | .. | 11.58 | 18.07 | 21.72 | 28.84 | 26.43 |
| 60-64 | .. | 12.44 | 14.41 | 16.39 | 22.77 | 20.89 |
| 65+ | .. | 4.94 | 7.58 | 8.04 | 12.20 | 9.99 |

Source(s): (1) STAT; (2) BLT-94-2.

### 2.2 Méthode(s): extrapolation linéaire

#### 2.2.1 Hommes:

- 1950-70, extrapolation des taux d'activité tirés des recensements
de 1948, 1953, 1961 et 1971;
- 1980-90, taux d'activité tirés du Bulletin des statistiques
du travail 1994-2.

#### 2.2.2 Femmes:

- 1950-70, extrapolation des taux d'activité tirés des recensements
de 1953 et des taux d'activité ajustés tirés des recensements de 1961 et 1971;
- 1980-90, taux d'activité tirés du Bulletin des statistiques
du travail 1994-2.

## 3. Evaluation des taux de répartition par secteur d'activité: 1950 - 1990

### 3.1 Données de base:

Tableau 2: Répartition de la population active en % par secteur d'activité

| Année | Agriculture | Industrie Total | Manufac. | Services |
|---|---|---|---|---|
| **Hommes** | | | | |
| 1950 (1) | 72.22 | 11.71 | 3.52 | 16.08 |
| 1960 (1) | 61.01 | 19.78 | 10.18 | 19.21 |
| 1970 (1) | 49.63 | 27.01 | .. | 23.36 |
| 1980 (2) | 29.89 | 38.10 | 20.58 | 32.01 |
| 1990 (2) | 20.84 | 39.88 | 24.46 | 39.27 |
| **Femmes** | | | | |
| 1950 (1) | 88.70 | 3.55 | 3.20 | 7.75 |
| 1960 (1) | 76.13 | 9.53 | 8.78 | 14.34 |
| 1970 (1) | 62.21 | 16.47 | .. | 21.32 |
| 1980 (2) | 46.88 | 23.01 | 21.04 | 30.10 |
| 1990 (2) | 22.54 | 41.05 | 37.59 | 36.41 |

Source(s): (1) EPPA3; (2) BLT-94-2.

### 3.2 Méthode(s): données du BLT-94-2

#### 3.2.1 Hommes:

- 1950-70, taux de répartition 1950-70 tirés des EPPA3;
- 1980-90, taux de répartition tirés du Bulletin des statistiques
du travail - 1994-2.

#### 3.2.2 Femmes:

Méthode, hypothèses et traitements identiques à ceux appliqués aux hommes.

## 4. Projection des taux d'activité: 2000 - 2010

### 4.1 Modèle(s): linéaire, hyperbole et logistique

#### 4.1.1 Hommes:

- Aux groupes d'âge [15+], application de la fonction F3;
- Modification des tendances des groupes d'âge [15-39].

#### 4.1.2 Femmes:

- Aux groupes d'âge [15-19] et [65+], application de la fonction F3;
- Aux groupes d'âge [20-54], application de la fonction F6;
- Aux groupes d'âge [55-64], application de la fonction F1;
- Modification des tendances des groupes d'âge [15-24] et [50+].

---

*Notes sur les ajustements des taux, voir p. 192-195.*     *Notes sur les fonctions de projection, voir p. 198.*

# Madagascar

## 1. Source(s) des données de base

Code(s):    Titre(s):

EPPA3      Evaluations et projections de la population active 1950-2025 - troisième édition, BIT, Genève, 1986.
ASTER      Annuaire des statistiques du travail 1945-89 - Edition rétrospective sur les recensements de population, BIT, Genève, 1990.

## 2. Evaluation des taux d'activité: 1950 - 1990

### 2.1 Données de base:

Tableau 1: Taux d'activité par sexe et par groupe d'âge

| | | Année | | | | | |
|---|---|---|---|---|---|---|---|
| | Groupe d'âge | 1950 (1) | 1960 (1) | 1970 (1) | 1980 (1) | 1975 (2) | 1980 (1) |
| **Hommes** | | | | | | | |
| | 10-14 | 49.05 | 47.40 | 45.50 | 45.50 | 43.98 | 43.60 |
| | 15-19 | 80.85 | 78.65 | 76.15 | 76.15 | 75.21 | 73.60 |
| | 20-24 | 93.70 | 92.85 | 91.90 | 91.90 | 89.96 | 90.95 |
| | 25-29 | 97.15 | 97.05 | 96.90 | 96.90 | 98.30 | 96.75 |
| | 30-34 | 97.85 | 97.75 | 97.60 | 97.60 | 98.99 | 97.40 |
| | 35-39 | 98.05 | 97.90 | 97.70 | 97.70 | 99.03 | 97.55 |
| | 40-44 | 97.85 | 97.70 | 97.50 | 97.50 | 98.97 | 97.35 |
| | 45-49 | 97.15 | 97.00 | 96.85 | 96.85 | 98.90 | 96.70 |
| | 50-54 | 96.60 | 96.40 | 96.15 | 96.15 | 98.61 | 95.90 |
| | 55-59 | 95.50 | 95.15 | 94.80 | 94.80 | 95.62 | 94.45 |
| | 60-64 | 92.15 | 91.60 | 90.95 | 90.95 | 94.14 | 90.35 |
| | 65+ | 78.20 | 77.25 | 76.15 | 76.15 | 83.84 | 75.05 |
| **Femmes** | | | | | | | |
| | 10-14 | 37.05 | 35.85 | 34.40 | 34.40 | 38.99 | 32.95 |
| | 15-19 | 60.50 | 58.65 | 56.50 | 56.50 | 58.20 | 54.35 |
| | 20-24 | 62.00 | 60.80 | 59.45 | 59.45 | 69.33 | 58.10 |
| | 25-29 | 66.65 | 65.30 | 63.80 | 63.80 | 78.10 | 62.25 |
| | 30-34 | 70.85 | 69.40 | 67.75 | 67.75 | 78.42 | 66.10 |
| | 35-39 | 72.25 | 70.90 | 69.35 | 69.35 | 79.00 | 67.80 |
| | 40-44 | 74.70 | 73.35 | 71.80 | 71.80 | 79.45 | 70.25 |
| | 45-49 | 74.15 | 72.80 | 71.25 | 71.25 | 82.55 | 69.65 |
| | 50-54 | 72.35 | 70.75 | 68.95 | 68.95 | 82.86 | 67.10 |
| | 55-59 | 69.45 | 67.80 | 65.90 | 65.90 | 76.67 | 64.00 |
| | 60-64 | 62.60 | 60.50 | 58.10 | 58.10 | 76.73 | 55.65 |
| | 65+ | 42.80 | 40.85 | 38.60 | 38.60 | 46.32 | 36.35 |

Source(s): (1) EPPA3; (2) ASTER.

### 2.2 Méthode(s): interpolation et extrapolation linéaires

#### 2.2.1 Hommes:

- 1950-90, interpolation et extrapolation des taux d'activité 1950-80
tirés des EPPA3;
ajustement des taux interpolés et extrapolés sur la base
des variations des taux interpolés 1975 par rapport aux taux tirés du
recensement de 1975;
modification des tendances de tous les groupes d'âge pour 1950-70
et des groupes d'âge [10-19] et [65+] pour 1980 et 1990.

#### 2.2.2 Femmes:

- 1950-90, interpolation et extrapolation des taux d'activité 1950-80
tirés des EPPA3;
ajustement des taux interpolés et extrapolés sur la base des variations des
taux interpolés 1975 par rapport aux taux tirés du recensement de 1975;
modification des tendances de tous les groupes d'âge de 1950 à 1970;
modification des tendances des groupes d'âge [20-64] de 1980 et 1990.

## 3. Evaluation des taux de répartition par secteur d'activité: 1950 - 1990

### 3.1 Données de base:

Tableau 2: Répartition de la population active en % par secteur d'activité

| | | Agriculture | Industrie | | Services |
|---|---|---|---|---|---|
| | Année | | Total | Manufac. | |
| **Hommes** | | | | | |
| | 1950 (1) | 82.00 | 5.00 | .. | 13.00 |
| | 1960 (1) | 79.00 | 6.00 | .. | 15.00 |
| | 1970 (1) | 75.50 | 7.50 | .. | 17.00 |
| | 1975 (2) | 73.75 | 8.25 | .. | 18.00 |
| | 1980 (1) | 72.00 | 9.00 | .. | 19.00 |
| **Femmes** | | | | | |
| | 1950 (1) | 98.50 | 0.35 | .. | 1.15 |
| | 1960 (1) | 97.00 | 0.75 | .. | 2.25 |
| | 1970 (1) | 95.25 | 1.20 | .. | 3.55 |
| | 1975 (2) | 95.00 | 1.70 | .. | 3.30 |
| | 1980 (1) | 93.50 | 1.65 | .. | 4.85 |

Source(s): (1) EPPA3; (2) ASTER.

### 3.2 Méthode(s): interpolation et extrapolation linéaires

#### 3.2.1 Hommes:

- 1950-90, interpolation et extrapolation des taux de répartition 1950-80
tirés des EPPA3;
ajustement des taux interpolés et extrapolés sur la base des 3/4 des
variations des taux interpolés 1975 par rapport aux taux de répartition tirés du
recensement de 1975.

#### 3.2.2 Femmes:

- 1950-90, interpolation extrapolation des taux de répartition ajustés
1950 et 1980 tirés des EPPA3;
ajustement des taux de répartition sur la base
du rapport hommes/femmes dans l'agriculture tiré du recensement de 1975;
les taux de répartition de manufacture ont été estimés sur la base des
rapports manufacture/industrie estimés pour Maurice.

## 4. Projection des taux d'activité: 2000 - 2010

### 4.1 Modèle(s): linéaire

#### 4.1.1 Hommes:

- A tous les groupes d'âge, application de la fonction F1;
- Modification des tendances des groupes d'âge [10-19] et [60+].

#### 4.1.2 Femmes:

- A tous les groupes d'âge, application de la fonction F1;
- Modification des tendances des groupes d'âge [10-59].

*Notes sur les ajustements des taux, voir p. 192-195.*    *Notes sur les fonctions de projection, voir p. 198.*

# Malaisie

## 1. Source(s) des données de base

Code(s):    Titre(s):

EPPA3    Evaluations et projections de la population active 1950-2025 - troisième édition, BIT, Genève, 1986.

STAT    Base de données sur les statistiques du travail - LABORSTA, Bureau de statistique, BIT, Genève.

## 2. Evaluation des taux d'activité: 1950 - 1990

### 2.1 Données de base:

Tableau 1: Taux d'activité par sexe et par groupe d'âge

| Groupe d'âge | Année 1950 (3) | 1960 (3) | 1970 (3) | 1980 (1)(4) | 1980 (2)(4) | 1990 (4) |
|---|---|---|---|---|---|---|
| **Hommes** | | | | | | |
| 10-14 | .. | .. | .. | 8.84 | ... | ... |
| 15-19 | .. | .. | .. | 49.05 | 50.10 | 40.20 |
| 20-24 | .. | .. | .. | 89.76 | 92.20 | 83.20 |
| 25-29 | .. | .. | .. | 95.55 | 97.70 | 95.10 |
| 30-34 | .. | .. | .. | 96.29 | 98.30 | 97.10 |
| 35-39 | .. | .. | .. | 96.54 | 97.80 | 97.80 |
| 40-44 | .. | .. | .. | 96 24 | 98.30 | 97.20 |
| 45-49 | .. | .. | .. | 95.19 | 97.60 | 96.60 |
| 50-54 | .. | .. | .. | 91.47 | 94.80 | 92.60 |
| 55-59 | .. | .. | .. | 77.63 | 79.90 | 71.40 |
| 60-64 | .. | .. | .. | 69.03 | 70.50 | 61.40 |
| 65+ | .. | .. | .. | 49.37 | ... | ... |
| **Femmes** | | | | | | |
| 10-14 | 10.90 | 9.20 | 8.55 | .. | ... | ... |
| 15-19 | 33.20 | 33.75 | 34.25 | .. | 33.70 | 27.60 |
| 20-24 | 35.20 | 38.90 | 42.65 | .. | 56.70 | 57.70 |
| 25-29 | 30.00 | 30.70 | 37.80 | .. | 46.50 | 51.40 |
| 30-34 | 32.95 | 33.70 | 39.25 | .. | 44.30 | 49.30 |
| 35-39 | 36.95 | 37.80 | 42.85 | .. | 48.20 | 48.30 |
| 40-44 | 38.25 | 39.15 | 42.30 | .. | 50.20 | 49.60 |
| 45-49 | 39.90 | 41.10 | 42.30 | .. | 49.40 | 49.60 |
| 50-54 | 37.00 | 37.75 | 38.45 | | 44.10 | 42.40 |
| 55-59 | 32.00 | 31.95 | 31.90 | .. | 35.40 | 32.50 |
| 60-64 | 24.25 | 24.25 | 24.20 | .. | 27.90 | 26.60 |
| 65+ | 12.85 | 11.85 | 13.70 | .. | ... | ... |

Note(s): (1) Recensement; (2) Enquête.
Source(s): (3) EPPA3; (4) STAT.

### 2.2 Méthode(s): interpolation linéaire
moyenne arithmétique

**2.2.1 Hommes:**

- 1950-70, taux d'activité 1950-70 tirés des EPPA3;
ajustement des taux d'activité des groupes d'âge [20-24];
- 1980, moyennes des taux d'activité tirés du recensement de 1980
et de l'enquête de 1980; taux d'activité tirés du recensement de 1980
pour les groupes d'âge [10-14] et [65+];
- 1990, taux d'activité ajustés tirés de l'enquête de 1990.

**2.2.2 Femmes:**

- 1950-80, taux d'activité 1950-80 tirés des EPPA3;
- 1990, interpolation des taux d'activité 1950-1970 tirés des EPPA3,
et des enquêtes de 1980 et 1990.

## 3. Evaluation des taux de répartition par secteur d'activité: 1950 - 1990

### 3.1 Données de base:

Tableau 2: Répartition de la population active en % par secteur d'activité

| Année | Agriculture | Industrie Total | Manufac. | Services |
|---|---|---|---|---|
| **Hommes** | | | | |
| 1980 | 37.49 | 19.86 | 11.83 | 42.65 |
| 1988 | 29.95 | 22.57 | 13.12 | 47.48 |
| **Femmes** | | | | |
| 1980 | 49.33 | 17.69 | 16.31 | 32.98 |
| 1988 | 30.31 | 21.68 | 20.61 | 48.01 |

Source(s): STAT.

### 3.2 Méthode(s): extrapolation linéaire

**3.2.1 Hommes:**

- 1950-70, taux de répartition 1950-70 tirés des EPPA3;
- 1980, taux de répartition ajustés tirés du recensement de 1980;
- 1990, extrapolation des taux de répartition ajustés du recensement
de 1980 et des taux de répartition de l'enquête de 1988.

**3.2.2 Femmes:**

- 1950-70, taux de répartition 1950-70 tirés des EPPA3;
- 1980, taux de répartition tirés du recensement de 1980;
- 1990, extrapolation des taux de répartition du recensement
de 1980 et de l'enquête de 1988.

## 4. Projection des taux d'activité: 2000 - 2010

### 4.1 Modèle(s): linéaire, log-linéaire et hyperbole

**4.1.1 Hommes:**

- Aux groupes d'âge [10-24], application de la fonction F1;
- Aux groupes d'âge [25+], application de la fonction F3;
- Modification des tendances des groupes d'âge [10-49].

**4.1.2 Femmes:**

- Aux groupes d'âge [10-39], application de la fonction F1;
- Aux groupes d'âge [40-59], application de la fonction F2;
- Aux groupes d'âge [60+], application de la fonction F3;
- Modification des tendances des groupes d'âge [10-14], [20-44] et [65+].

*Notes sur les ajustements des taux, voir p. 192-195.*   *Notes sur les fonctions de projection, voir p. 198.*

# Malawi

## 1. Source(s) des données de base

| Code(s): | Titre(s): |
|---|---|
| EPPA3 | Evaluations et projections de la population active 1950-2025 - troisième édition, BIT, Genève, 1986. |
| ASTER | Annuaire des statistiques du travail 1945-89 - Edition rétrospective sur les recensements de population, BIT, Genève, 1990. |
| R1987 | Population Census 1987, National Statistical Office, Zomba. |

## 2. Evaluation des taux d'activité: 1950 - 1990

### 2.1 Données de base:

Tableau 1: Taux d'activité par sexe et par groupe d'âge

| Groupe d'âge | Année 1950 (1) | 1960 (1) | 1970 (1) | 1977 (2) | 1980 (1) | 1987 (3) |
|---|---|---|---|---|---|---|
| **Hommes** | | | | | | |
| 10-14 | 49.45 | 47.65 | 45.70 | .. | 40.35 | 10.85 |
| 15-19 | 80.50 | 78.05 | 75.45 | .. | 68.25 | 34.28 |
| 20-24 | 93.05 | 92.05 | 91.00 | .. | 88.05 | 72.48 |
| 25-29 | 98.90 | 98.75 | 98.60 | .. | 98.10 | 92.42 |
| 30-34 | 99.15 | 98.95 | 98.75 | .. | 98.25 | 96.17 |
| 35-39 | 99.30 | 99.10 | 98.90 | .. | 98.35 | 96.96 |
| 40-44 | 99.40 | 99.20 | 99.00 | .. | 98.45 | 97.13 |
| 45-49 | 99.20 | 99.05 | 98.85 | .. | 98.35 | 97.14 |
| 50-54 | 99.10 | 99.00 | 98.85 | .. | 98.10 | 96.83 |
| 55-59 | 99.00 | 98.90 | 98.80 | .. | 97.65 | 96.89 |
| 60-64 | 98.55 | 97.85 | 97.10 | .. | 95.05 | 95.12 |
| 65+ | 88.80 | 87.55 | 86.20 | .. | 82.45 | 87.91 |
| **Femmes** | | | | | | |
| 10-14 | .. | .. | .. | 16.50 | .. | 10.72 |
| 15-19 | .. | .. | .. | 43.81 | .. | 49.57 |
| 20-24 | .. | .. | .. | 60.71 | .. | 73.51 |
| 25-29 | .. | .. | .. | 65.24 | .. | 78.72 |
| 30-34 | .. | .. | .. | 69.00 | .. | 82.23 |
| 35-39 | .. | .. | .. | 71.42 | .. | 84.59 |
| 40-44 | .. | .. | .. | 73.49 | .. | 87.04 |
| 45-49 | .. | .. | .. | 73.29 | .. | 88.72 |
| 50-54 | .. | .. | .. | 72.96 | .. | 89.50 |
| 55-59 | .. | .. | .. | 76.45 | .. | 89.94 |
| 60-64 | .. | .. | .. | 68.60 | .. | 83.93 |
| 65+ | .. | .. | .. | 55.19 | .. | 71.35 |

Source(s): (1) EPPA3; (2) ASTER; (3) R1987.

### 2.2 Méthode(s): interpolation et extrapolation linéaires

#### 2.2.1 Hommes:

- 1950-90, interpolation et extrapolation des taux d'activité 1950-80 tirés des EPPA3;
ajustement des taux interpolés et extrapolés sur la base des variations des taux interpolés 1987 par rapport aux taux tirés du recensement de 1987;
modification des tendances des groupes d'âge [10+] pour 1990.

#### 2.2.2 Femmes:

- 1950-90, interpolation et extrapolation des taux d'activité ajustés tirés des recensements de 1977 et 1987.

## 3. Evaluation des taux de répartition par secteur d'activité: 1950 - 1990

### 3.1 Données de base:

Tableau 2: Répartition de la population active en % par secteur d'activité

| Année | Agriculture | Industrie Total | Manufac. | Services |
|---|---|---|---|---|
| **Hommes** | | | | |
| 1950 (1) | 93.75 | 2.60 | .. | 3.65 |
| 1960 (1) | 90.00 | 4.00 | .. | 6.00 |
| 1970 (1) | 86.00 | 6.00 | .. | 8.00 |
| 1977 (2) | 78.08 | 9.91 | 5.65 | 12.00 |
| 1987 (3) | 78.39 | 8.46 | 4.81 | 13.15 |
| **Femmes** | | | | |
| 1950 (1) | 98.50 | 0.50 | .. | 1.00 |
| 1960 (1) | 97.50 | 0.80 | .. | 1.70 |
| 1970 (1) | 96.00 | 1.30 | .. | 2.70 |
| 1977 (2) | 96.31 | 1.38 | 1.17 | 2.31 |
| 1987 (3) | 95.66 | 1.20 | 1.06 | 3.14 |

Source(s): (1) EPPA3; (2) ASTER; (3) R1987.

### 3.2 Méthode(s): interpolation et extrapolation linéaires moyenne pondérée

#### 3.2.1 Hommes:

- 1950-70, taux de répartition 1950-70 tirés des EPPA3;
- 1980, moyennes pondérées des taux tirés des recensements de 1977 et 1987;
- 1990, estimation du taux de répartition dans l'agriculture basé sur les résultats du recensement de 1987 et application à l'industrie et aux services les mêmes proportions que dans le recensement de 1987.

#### 3.2.2 Femmes:

- 1950-90, interpolation et extrapolation des taux de répartition tirés des recensements de 1977 et 1987;
modification des tendances de tous les secteurs pour 1950 et 1960.

## 4. Projection des taux d'activité: 2000 - 2010

### 4.1 Modèle(s): linéaire et hyperbole

#### 4.1.1 Hommes:

- Au groupe d'âge [10-14], application de la fonction F1;
- Aux groupes d'âge [15+], application de la fonction F3;
- Modification de la tendance du groupe d'âge [65+].

#### 4.1.2 Femmes:

- Aux groupes d'âge [10-19] et [60+], application de la fonction F1;
- Aux groupes d'âge [20-59], application de la fonction F3;
- Modification des tendances de tous les groupes d'âge.

*Notes sur les ajustements des taux, voir p. 192-195.*     *Notes sur les fonctions de projection, voir p. 198.*

# Maldives

## 1. Source(s) des données de base

Code(s):    Titre(s):

ADNU84    Annuaire démographique 1984 - Statistiques des recensements de population II, trente-sixième édition, Nations Unies, New York, 1986.
ADNU88    Annuaire démographique 1988 - Statistiques des recensements de population, quarantième édition, Nations Unies, New York, 1990.

## 2. Evaluation des taux d'activité: 1950 - 1990

### 2.1 Données de base:

Tableau 1: Taux d'activité par sexe et par groupe d'âge

| Groupe d'âge | 1977 | 1985 |
|---|---|---|
| **Hommes** | | |
| 10-14 | 37.23 | 5.08 |
| 15-19 | 77.95 | 56.40 |
| 20-24 | 93.39 | 84.59 |
| 25-29 | 95.04 | 87.83 |
| 30-34 | 95.69 | 88.89 |
| 35-39 | 96.50 | 88.93 |
| 40-44 | 96.80 | 86.84 |
| 45-49 | 97.05 | 86.87 |
| 50-54 | 95.54 | 83.33 |
| 55-59 | 93.77 | 80.55 |
| 60-64 | 87.47 | 72.89 |
| 65+ | 65.13 | 49.38 |
| **Femmes** | | |
| 10-14 | 24.13 | 1.81 |
| 15-19 | 52.23 | 19.80 |
| 20-24 | 62.14 | 23.76 |
| 25-29 | 64.73 | 23.27 |
| 30-34 | 64.76 | 25.48 |
| 35-39 | 70.70 | 26.53 |
| 40-44 | 71.93 | 27.82 |
| 45-49 | 73.33 | 28.34 |
| 50-54 | 68.14 | 28.15 |
| 55-59 | 61.47 | 26.87 |
| 60-64 | 52.26 | 22.44 |
| 65+ | 35.07 | 16.37 |

Source(s): ADNU88 et STAT.

### 2.2 Méthode(s): moyenne pondérée

#### 2.2.1 Hommes:

- 1980, moyennes pondérées des taux d'activité ajustés tirés des recensements de 1977 et 1985;
modification des tendances des groupes d'âge [10-14] et [60+];
- 1990, aux taux d'activité estimés 1980, application des variations résultant de l'interpolation des taux d'activité ajustés tirés des recensements de 1975 et 1985;
- 1950-70, aux taux d'activité estimés pour 1980, application des variations estimées pour l'Indonésie pour la même période.

#### 2.2.2 Femmes:

- 1980, moyennes pondérées des taux d'activité tirés du recensement de 1977 et des taux d'activité ajustés tirés du recensement de 1985;
modification des tendances des groupes d'âge [10-14] et [60+];
- 1990, aux taux d'activité estimés 1980, application des variations résultant de l'interpolation des taux d'activité tirés du recensement de 1975 et des taux d'activité ajustés tirés du recensement de 1985;
- 1950-70, aux taux d'activité estimés pour 1980, application des variations estimées pour l'Indonésie pour la même période.

## 3. Evaluation des taux de répartition par secteur d'activité: 1950 - 1990

### 3.1 Données de base:

Tableau 2: Répartition de la population active en % par secteur d'activité

| Année | Agriculture | Industrie Total | Manufac. | Services |
|---|---|---|---|---|
| **Hommes** | | | | |
| 1975 | 63.32 | 13.39 | 7.89 | 23.29 |
| 1985 | 43.01 | 19.46 | 11.38 | 37.52 |
| **Femmes** | | | | |
| 1975 | 44.02 | 48.13 | 47.90 | 7.84 |
| 1985 | 32.49 | 56.65 | 55.97 | 10.86 |

Source(s): STAT.

### 3.2 Méthode(s): interpolation et extrapolation linéaires

#### 3.2.1 Hommes:

- 1950-90, interpolation et extrapolation des taux de répartition tirés des recensements de 1977 et 1985;
modification des tendances de tous les secteurs.

#### 3.2.2 Femmes:

- 1950-90, interpolation et extrapolation des taux de répartition tirés des recensements de 1977 et 1985;
les taux de répartition de l'agriculture ont été estimés sur la base du rapport hommes/femmes tiré du recensement de 1977;
- Application du rapport manufacture/industrie tiré du recensement de 1977.

## 4. Projection des taux d'activité: 2000 - 2010

### 4.1 Modèle(s): linéaire, log-linéaire, hyperbole et logistique

#### 4.1.1 Hommes:

- Aux groupes d'âge [10-14], [20-29] et [60+], application de la fonction F1;
- Aux groupes d'âge [15-19] et [30-59], application de la fonction F3;
- Modification des tendances des groupes d'âge [10-29].

#### 4.1.2 Femmes:

- Aux groupes d'âge [10-19], application de la fonction F2;
- Aux groupes d'âge [20-59], application de la fonction F6;
- Aux groupes d'âge [60+], application de la fonction F3;
- Modification des tendances des groupes d'âge [10-64].

*Notes sur les ajustements des taux, voir p. 192-195.*

*Notes sur les fonctions de projection, voir p. 198.*

# Mali

Code(s):      Titre(s):
EPPA3        Evaluations et projections de la population active 1950-2025 - troisième édition, BIT, Genève, 1986.
ASTER        Annuaire des statistiques du travail 1945-89 - Edition rétrospective sur les recensements de population, BIT, Genève, 1990.

## 2. Evaluation des taux d'activité: 1950 - 1990

### 2.1 Données de base:

Tableau 1: Taux d'activité par sexe et par groupe d'âge

| Groupe d'âge | Année 1950 (1) | 1960 (1) | 1970 (1) | 1976 (2) |
|---|---|---|---|---|
| **Hommes** | | | | |
| 10-14 | 70.75 | 69.05 | 67.35 | 66.17 |
| 15-19 | 86.20 | 84.50 | 82.75 | 81.59 |
| 20-24 | 92.60 | 91.95 | 91.30 | 90.84 |
| 25-29 | 97.55 | 97.45 | 97.35 | 97.27 |
| 30-34 | 98.25 | 98.10 | 98.00 | 97.92 |
| 35-39 | 98.25 | 98.15 | 98.00 | 97.93 |
| 40-44 | 98.00 | 97.85 | 97.75 | 97.64 |
| 45-49 | 97.75 | 97.65 | 97.55 | 97.47 |
| 50-54 | 96.65 | 96.50 | 96.35 | 96.22 |
| 55-59 | 95.20 | 94.95 | 94.70 | 94.49 |
| 60-64 | 90.30 | 89.90 | 89.45 | 89.17 |
| 65+ | 74.40 | 73.70 | 73.00 | 72.51 |
| **Femmes** | | | | |
| 10-14 | 15.80 | 15.40 | 15.00 | 14.76 |
| 15-19 | 20.00 | 19.55 | 19.10 | 18.83 |
| 20-24 | 18.15 | 17.90 | 17.65 | 17.46 |
| 25-29 | 18.80 | 18.50 | 18.20 | 18.03 |
| 30-34 | 17.95 | 17.65 | 17.40 | 17.20 |
| 35-39 | 18.20 | 17.95 | 17.65 | 17.49 |
| 40-44 | 18.00 | 17.75 | 17.50 | 17.33 |
| 45-49 | 18.20 | 17.95 | 17.70 | 17.50 |
| 50-54 | 16.65 | 16.35 | 16.10 | 15.91 |
| 55-59 | 15.85 | 15.55 | 15.30 | 15.08 |
| 60-64 | 13.00 | 12.65 | 12.35 | 12.15 |
| 65+ | 9.10 | 8.85 | 8.55 | 8.36 |

Source(s): (1) EPPA3; (2) ASTER.

### 2.2 Méthode(s): interpolation et extrapolation linéaires

#### 2.2.1 Hommes:

- 1950-70, taux d'activité 1950-70 tirés des EPPA3;
- 1980-90, extrapolation des taux d'activité 1950-70 et 1976 tirés respectivement des EPPA3 et du recensement de 1976; ajustement des taux extrapolés sur la base des variations des taux interpolés 1976 par rapport aux taux du recensement de 1976.

#### 2.2.2 Femmes:

- 1950-90, interpolation et extrapolation des taux d'activité 1950-80 tirés des EPPA3 et des taux ajustés tirés du recensement de 1976; ajustement des taux interpolés et extrapolés sur la base des variations des taux interpolés 1976 par rapport aux taux du recensement de 1976.

## 3. Evaluation des taux de répartition par secteur d'activité: 1950 - 1990

### 3.1 Données de base:

Tableau 2: Répartition de la population active en % par secteur d'activité

| Année | Agriculture | Industrie Total | Manufac. | Services |
|---|---|---|---|---|
| **Hommes** | | | | |
| 1976 | 88.99 | 1.32 | 0.39 | 9.69 |
| **Femmes** | | | | |
| 1976 | 43.15 | 8.00 | .. | 48.85 |

Source(s): ASTER.

### 3.2 Méthode(s): interpolation et extrapolation linéaires

#### 3.2.1 Hommes:

- 1950-90, interpolation et extrapolation des taux de répartition 1976 et 1990 tirés respectivement du recensement de 1976 et des EPPA3;
- Application du rapport manufacture/industrie tiré du recensement de 1976.

#### 3.2.2 Femmes:

Méthode, hypothèses et traitements identiques à ceux appliqués aux hommes.

## 4. Projection des taux d'activité: 2000 - 2010

### 4.1 Modèle(s): linéaire

#### 4.1.1 Hommes:

- A tous les groupes d'âge, application de la fonction F1;
- Modification des tendances des groupes d'âge [10-19], [30-34] et [65+].

#### 4.1.2 Femmes:

- Aux groupes d'âge [10-19] et [45+], application de la fonction F1;
- Aux groupes d'âge [20-44], application de la fonction F3;
- Modification des tendances des groupes d'âge [20-34] et [45+].

*Notes sur les ajustements des taux, voir p. 192-195.*

*Notes sur les fonctions de projection, voir p. 198.*

# Malte

## 1. Source(s) des données de base

Code(s):      Titre(s):

EPPA3      Annuaire des statistiques du travail 1945-89 - Edition rétrospective sur les recensements de population, BIT, Genève, 1990.
STAT       Base de données sur les statistiques du travail - LABORSTA, Bureau de statistique, BIT, Genève.

## 2. Evaluation des taux d'activité: 1950 - 1990

### 2.1 Données de base:

Tableau 1: Taux d'activité par sexe et par groupe d'âge

| Groupe d'âge | Année 1950 (1) | 1960 (1) | 1970 (1) | 1980 (1) | 1985 (2) |
|---|---|---|---|---|---|
| **Hommes** | | | | | |
| 10-14 | 4.30 | 3.00 | 1.80 | 1.50 | 0.00 |
| 15-19 | 68.65 | 64.35 | 60.30 | 56.50 | 23.20 |
| 20-24 | 92.30 | 91.15 | 90.05 | 88.90 | 72.15 |
| 25-29 | 96.35 | 95.90 | 95.50 | 95.05 | 81.89 |
| 30-34 | 97.35 | 97.60 | 97.90 | 98.15 | 87.19 |
| 35-39 | 96.20 | 97.05 | 97.90 | 98.75 | 87.82 |
| 40-44 | 96.35 | 96.65 | 96.95 | 97.25 | 88.16 |
| 45-49 | 93.65 | 94.05 | 94.45 | 94.80 | 85.68 |
| 50-54 | 91.25 | 90.30 | 89.35 | 88.45 | 78.67 |
| 55-59 | 86.95 | 84.80 | 82.70 | 80.65 | 66.98 |
| 60-64 | 63.30 | 62.10 | 60.90 | 59.70 | 19.51 |
| 65+ | 31.45 | 23.60 | 17.70 | 13.30 | 2.49 |
| **Femmes** | | | | | |
| 10-14 | 1.35 | 1.35 | 0.95 | 0.75 | 0.00 |
| 15-19 | 24.00 | 30.05 | 32.20 | 30.35 | 36.99 |
| 20-24 | 22.75 | 29.15 | 32.95 | 34.25 | 59.60 |
| 25-29 | 14.85 | 18.25 | 21.75 | 25.35 | 28.36 |
| 30-34 | 13.50 | 13.50 | 15.60 | 19.85 | 14.62 |
| 35-39 | 14.80 | 13.25 | 13.55 | 15.65 | 13.31 |
| 40-44 | 16.30 | 13.70 | 13.15 | 14.75 | 13.94 |
| 45-49 | 16.60 | 15.00 | 14.85 | 16.30 | 12.59 |
| 50-54 | 15.65 | 12.40 | 12.90 | 17.05 | 9.78 |
| 55-59 | 14.60 | 12.75 | 13.00 | 15.45 | 7.24 |
| 60-64 | 12.10 | 9.95 | 10.00 | 12.20 | 1.40 |
| 65+ | 6.45 | 4.05 | 2.75 | 2.50 | 0.42 |

Source(s): (1) EPPA3; (2) STAT.

### 2.2 Méthode(s): extrapolation linéaire

#### 2.2.1 Hommes:

- 1950-80, taux d'activité 1950-80 tirés des EPPA3;
- 1990, extrapolation des taux d'activité 1970-80 tirés des EPPA3
et des taux d'activité tirés du recensement de 1985;
modification tendances de tous les groupes d'âge;
aux taux d'activité extrapolés 1990, application des variations des taux
interpolés 1985 par rapport aux taux tirés du recensement de1985.

#### 2.2.2 Femmes:

Méthode, hypothèses et traitements identiques à ceux appliqués aux hommes.

## 3. Evaluation des taux de répartition par secteur d'activité: 1950 - 1990

### 3.1 Données de base:

Tableau 2: Répartition de la population active en % par secteur d'activité

| Année | Agriculture | Industrie Total | Manufac. | Services |
|---|---|---|---|---|
| **Hommes** | | | | |
| 1968 | 10.38 | 54.17 | 32.30 | 35.45 |
| 1972 | 6.98 | 38.93 | 26.61 | 54.09 |
| 1979 | 10.14 | 48.47 | 37.95 | 41.39 |
| 1980 | 9.64 | 48.36 | 37.27 | 42.00 |
| 1981 | 8.87 | 48.84 | 37.52 | 42.29 |
| 1990 | 3.01 | 34.66 | 25.88 | 62.33 |
| **Femmes** | | | | |
| 1968 | 4.85 | 29.82 | 29.76 | 65.32 |
| 1972 | 3.10 | 35.89 | 35.87 | 61.01 |
| 1979 | 2.88 | 55.87 | 55.45 | 41.26 |
| 1980 | 2.88 | 54.99 | 54.59 | 42.13 |
| 1981 | 3.66 | 54.32 | 53.83 | 42.02 |
| 1990 | 1.25 | 34.35 | 33.64 | 64.40 |

Source(s): STAT.

### 3.2 Méthode(s): moyenne arithmétique

#### 3.2.1 Hommes:

- 1950-60, taux de répartition 1950-60 tirés des EPPA3;
- 1970, moyennes des taux de répartition tirés des estimations
officielles de 1968 et 1970 et des taux de répartition tirés de l'enquête de 1972;
- 1980, moyennes des taux de répartition tirés des estimations
officielles de 1979, 1980 et 1981;
- 1990, taux de répartition tirés de l'enquête de 1990.

#### 3.2.2 Femmes:

Méthode, hypothèses et traitements identiques à ceux appliqués aux hommes.

## 4. Projection des taux d'activité: 2000 - 2010

### 4.1 Modèle(s): linéaire, hyperbole et logistique

#### 4.1.1 Hommes:

- Au groupe d'âge [15-19], application de la fonction F1;
- Aux groupes d'âge [20+], application de la fonction F3;
- Modification des tendances des groupes d'âge [25-59].

#### 4.1.2 Femmes:

- Aux groupes d'âge [15-64], application de la fonction F6;
- Au groupe d'âge [65+], application de la fonction F3;
- Modification des tendances des groupes d'âge [15-54].

*Notes sur les ajustements des taux, voir p. 192-195.*      *Notes sur les fonctions de projection, voir p. 198.*

# Maroc

## 1. Source(s) des données de base

Code(s):     Titre(s):

EPPA3       Evaluations et projections de la population active 1950-2025 - troisième édition, BIT, Genève, 1986.
R1971       Recensement général de la population et de l'habitat 1971: résultats de l'exhaustif, niveau national, Direction de la statistique, Rabat, 1976.
R1982       Caractéristiques socio-économiques de la population d'après le recensement général de la population et de l'habitat de 1982,
            Direction de la statistique, Rabat, 1984.

## 2. Evaluation des taux d'activité: 1950 - 1990

### 2.1 Données de base:

Tableau 1: Taux d'activité par sexe et par groupe d'âge

| Groupe d'âge | Année 1950 (1) | 1960 (1) | 1970 (1) | 1980 (1) | 1982 (2) |
|---|---|---|---|---|---|
| **Hommes** | | | | | |
| 10-14 | 33.50 | 25.50 | 17.50 | 16.50 | 16.51 |
| 15-19 | 80.00 | 70.00 | 60.00 | 57.00 | 57.03 |
| 20-24 | 95.40 | 93.00 | 85.40 | 81.10 | 80.32 |
| 25-29 | 97.20 | 97.10 | 96.20 | 95.30 | 95.17 |
| 30-34 | 97.40 | 97.50 | 97.25 | 97.70 | 98.14 |
| 35-39 | 97.00 | 97.00 | 97.00 | 98.00 | 98.37 |
| 40-44 | 96.50 | 96.60 | 96.70 | 97.80 | 98.06 |
| 45-49 | 96.20 | 96.30 | 96.40 | 96.60 | 96.56 |
| 50-54 | 95.80 | 95.00 | 94.30 | 93.60 | 93.27 |
| 55-59 | 95.10 | 94.00 | 92.00 | 90.00 | 89.53 |
| 60-64 | 94.00 | 91.00 | 86.00 | 81.00 | 68.94 |
| 65+ | 84.00 | 68.00 | 55.70 | 43.50 | 42.12 |
| **Femmes** | | | | | |
| 10-14 | 5.30 | 5.80 | 8.70 | 11.95 | 11.91 |
| 15-19 | 6.00 | 8.80 | 15.70 | 18.40 | 18.97 |
| 20-24 | 5.80 | 6.20 | 13.00 | 19.00 | 20.42 |
| 25-29 | 5.60 | 6.00 | 9.90 | 19.00 | 20.94 |
| 30-34 | 5.90 | 7.30 | 9.90 | 16.50 | 17.72 |
| 35-39 | 6.00 | 8.50 | 10.70 | 15.00 | 16.16 |
| 40-44 | 6.30 | 9.70 | 12.70 | 14.50 | 14.65 |
| 45-49 | 7.00 | 10.60 | 12.30 | 14.50 | 14.09 |
| 50-54 | 7.20 | 10.60 | 12.60 | 14.50 | 14.64 |
| 55-59 | 7.20 | 10.60 | 12.60 | 14.50 | 14.63 |
| 60-64 | 7.00 | 9.20 | 10.20 | 11.00 | 11.16 |
| 65+ | 6.50 | 6.30 | 5.90 | 5.50 | 5.30 |

Source(s): (1) EPPA3; (2) R1982.

### 2.2 Méthode(s): interpolation et extrapolation linéaires

#### 2.2.1 Hommes:

- 1950-80, taux d'activité 1950-80 tirés des EPPA3;
- 1990, extrapolation des taux d'activité 1950-80 tirés des EPPA3
et des taux ajustés du recensement de 1982;
modification des tendances des groupes d'âge [10-14], [25-54] et [65+].

#### 2.2.2 Femmes:

- 1950-80, taux d'activité ajustés 1950-80 tirés des EPPA3;
- 1990, extrapolation des taux d'activité 1950-80 tirés des EPPA3
et des taux ajustés du recensement de 1982;
ajustement des taux sur la base des variations des taux interpolés 1980
par rapport aux taux des EPPA3 de 1980;
modification des tendances des groupes d'âge [10-14], [20-49] et [55+];
ajustement des taux d'activité sur la base du modèle d'ajustement des taux
d'activité des femmes travaillant dans l'agriculture comme aides familiales.

## 3. Evaluation des taux de répartition par secteur d'activité: 1950 - 1990

### 3.1 Données de base:

Tableau 2: Répartition de la population active en % par secteur d'activité

| Année | Agriculture | Industrie Total | Manufac. | Services |
|---|---|---|---|---|
| **Hommes** | | | | |
| 1971 (1) | 59.44 | 16.51 | .. | 24.05 |
| 1982 (2) | 44.84 | 25.02 | 13.38 | 30.14 |
| **Femmes** | | | | |
| 1971 (1) | 44.23 | 23.20 | .. | 32.56 |
| 1982 (2) | 35.70 | 33.87 | 33.19 | 30.43 |

Source(s): (1) R1971; (2) R1982.

### 3.2 Méthode(s): interpolation et extrapolation linéaires

#### 3.2.1 Hommes:

- 1950-70, taux de répartition 1950-70 tirés des EPPA3;
- 1980-90, interpolation et extrapolation des taux de répartition
ajustés tirés du recensement de 1971 et des taux du recensement de 1982;
modification des tendances de tous les secteurs.

#### 3.2.2 Femmes:

- 1950-70, taux de répartition 1950-70 tirés des EPPA3;
- 1980-90, interpolation et extrapolation des taux de répartition
ajustés tirés du recensement de 1971 et des taux du recensement de 1982;
modification des tendances de tous les secteurs;
ajustement des taux estimés 1950-90 pour tenir compte de la
sous-énumération des femmes travaillant dans l'agriculture.

## 4. Projection des taux d'activité: 2000 - 2010

### 4.1 Modèle(s): linéaire et hyperbole

#### 4.1.1 Hommes:

- Aux groupes d'âge [10-24], application de la fonction F1;
- Aux groupes d'âge [25+], application de la fonction F3;
- Modification des tendances des groupes d'âge [20-24] et [30-49].

#### 4.1.2 Femmes:

- A tous les groupes d'âge, application de la fonction F1;
- Modification des tendances de tous les groupes d'âge.

---

*Notes sur les ajustements des taux, voir p. 192-195.*     *Notes sur les fonctions de projection, voir p. 198.*

# Martinique

**Code(s):**    **Titre(s):**

EPPA3    Evaluations et projections de la population active 1950-2025 - troisième édition, BIT, Genève, 1986.

STAT    Base de données sur les statistiques du travail - LABORSTA, Bureau de statistique, BIT, Genève.

## 2. Evaluation des taux d'activité: 1950 - 1990

### 2.1 Données de base:

Tableau 1: Taux d'activité par sexe et par groupe d'âge

| Groupe d'âge | Année 1950 (1) | 1970 (1) | 1974 (2) | 1980 (1) | 1982 (2) | 1990 (2) |
|---|---|---|---|---|---|---|
| **Hommes** | | | | | | |
| 10-14 | 4.00 | 1.05 | .. | .. | 0.00 | .. |
| 15-19 | 55.00 | 43.20 | .. | .. | 25.24 | .. |
| 20-24 | 87.60 | 86.70 | .. | .. | 81.85 | .. |
| 25-29 | 96.50 | 94.60 | .. | .. | 91.37 | .. |
| 30-34 | 97.90 | 95.95 | .. | .. | 93.51 | .. |
| 35-39 | 97.95 | 96.00 | .. | .. | 93.97 | .. |
| 40-44 | 97.45 | 95.55 | .. | .. | 91.81 | .. |
| 45-49 | 96.70 | 93.25 | .. | .. | 88.87 | .. |
| 50-54 | 93.60 | 90.25 | .. | .. | 83.91 | .. |
| 55-59 | 88.35 | 82.10 | .. | .. | 74.44 | .. |
| 60-64 | 72.00 | 66.90 | .. | .. | 43.08 | .. |
| 65+ | 52.90 | 28.70 | .. | .. | 6.16 | .. |
| **Femmes** | | | | | | |
| 10-14 | 2.00 | 0.55 | 0.00 | 0.35 | 0.00 | 0.00 |
| 15-19 | 33.70 | 29.20 | 29.35 | 28.10 | 17.61 | 9.49 |
| 20-24 | 47.55 | 57.60 | 69.34 | 69.10 | 70.03 | 66.25 |
| 25-29 | 48.50 | 53.00 | 64.73 | 72.50 | 76.96 | 85.08 |
| 30-34 | 49.35 | 47.40 | 59.22 | 69.35 | 74.19 | 83.85 |
| 35-39 | 51.85 | 44.70 | 53.22 | 66.50 | 71.94 | 82.13 |
| 40-44 | 53.65 | 45.10 | 50.01 | 62.10 | 66.66 | 80.52 |
| 45-49 | 53.15 | 44.60 | 46.91 | 56.70 | 60.83 | 75.39 |
| 50-54 | 54.30 | 40.45 | 45.50 | 48.95 | 52.11 | 65.60 |
| 55-59 | 45.45 | 37.10 | 35.90 | 40.30 | 44.82 | 49.89 |
| 60-64 | 32.15 | 18.45 | 18.36 | 20.60 | 25.26 | 22.28 |
| 65+ | 16.95 | 4.50 | 4.08 | 4.05 | 3.32 | 2.40 |

Source(s): (1) EPPA3; (2) STAT.

### 2.2 Méthode(s): interpolation et extrapolation linéaires

#### 2.2.1 Hommes:

- 1950-70, taux d'activité 1950-70 tirés des EPPA3;
- 1980, extrapolation des taux d'activité 1970 tirés des EPPA3
et des taux ajustés du recensement de 1982;
- 1990, extrapolation des taux d'activité 1950-1980 tirés des EPPA3
et des taux ajustés du recensement de 1982;
ajustement des taux d'activité sur la base des variations
des taux interpolés 1982 par rapport aux taux ajustés du recensement de 1982;
modification des tendances des groupes d'âge [65+].

#### 2.2.2 Femmes:

- 1950-60, taux d'activité tirés des EPPA3;
- 1970-90, interpolation et extrapolation des taux d'activité 1960 tirés
des EPPA3 et des taux des recensements de 1974, 1982 et 1990.

## 3. Evaluation des taux de répartition par secteur d'activité: 1950 - 1990

### 3.1 Données de base:

Tableau 2: Répartition de la population active en % par secteur d'activité

| Année | Agriculture | Industrie Total | Manufac. | Services |
|---|---|---|---|---|
| **Hommes** | | | | |
| 1960 (1) | 45.16 | 27.42 | .. | 27.42 |
| 1974 (2) | 23.35 | 27.64 | 9.59 | 49.01 |
| 1982 (2) | 14.92 | 26.40 | 5.04 | 58.68 |
| 1990 (2) | 10.20 | 26.37 | 12.07 | 63.43 |
| **Femmes** | | | | |
| 1960 (1) | 33.33 | 11.11 | 0.00 | 55.56 |
| 1974 (2) | 10.83 | 7.09 | 5.69 | 82.09 |
| 1982 (2) | 6.87 | 5.11 | 4.06 | 88.03 |
| 1990 (2) | 4.62 | 6.29 | 4.90 | 89.09 |

Source(s): (1) EPPA3; (2) STAT.

### 3.2 Méthode(s): interpolation et extrapolation linéaires

#### 3.2.1 Hommes:

- 1950-70, taux de répartition 1950-70 tirés des EPPA3;
- 1980-90, interpolation et extrapolation des taux de répartition 1960
tirés des EPPA3 et des taux des recensements de 1974, 1982 et 1990.

#### 3.2.2 Femmes:

Méthode, hypothèses et traitements identiques à ceux appliqués aux hommes.

## 4. Projection des taux d'activité: 2000 - 2010

### 4.1 Modèle(s): linéaire, log-linéaire, hyperbole et logistique

#### 4.1.1 Hommes:

- Au groupe d'âge [10-14], application de la fonction F2;
- Aux groupes d'âge [15-29], application de la fonction F1;
- Aux groupes d'âge [30+], application de la fonction F3;
- Modification des tendances des groupes d'âge [40-49].

#### 4.1.2 Femmes:

- Aux groupes d'âge [15-19] et [55+], application de la fonction F3;
- Au groupe d'âge [20-24], application de la fonction F1;
- Aux groupes d'âge [25-54], application de la fonction F6;
- Modification des tendances des groupes d'âge [20-29] et [40-49].

# Maurice

## 1. Source(s) des données de base

Code(s):     Titre(s):

EPPA3     Evaluations et projections de la population active 1950-2025 - troisième édition, BIT, Genève, 1986.
ASTER     Annuaire des statistiques du travail 1945-89 - Edition rétrospective sur les recensements de population, BIT, Genève, 1990.
R1983     1983 Housing and Population Census, Analysis Report, Vol IV, Central Statistical Office, Port Louis, April 1987.
R1990     1990 Housing and Population Census of Mauritius - Economic Characteristics, Central Statistical Office, Port Louis, 1991.

## 2. Evaluation des taux d'activité: 1950 - 1990

### 2.1 Données de base:

Tableau 1: Taux d'activité par sexe et par groupe d'âge

| Groupe d'âge | Année 1950 (1) | 1960 (1) | 1970 (1) | 1972 (2) | 1983 (3) | 1990 (4) |
|---|---|---|---|---|---|---|
| **Hommes** | | | | | | |
| 10-14 | 11.80 | 10.40 | 9.05 | 15.73 | 10.13 | 11.21 |
| 15-19 | 82.45 | 73.30 | 65.75 | 64.72 | 61.88 | 50.71 |
| 20-24 | 97.80 | 96.30 | 94.75 | 94.58 | 95.98 | 90.43 |
| 25-29 | 98.60 | 97.90 | 97.25 | 97.60 | 97.85 | 95.46 |
| 30-34 | 98.70 | 98.00 | 97.35 | 97.36 | 97.65 | 96.79 |
| 35-39 | 98.60 | 97.90 | 97.25 | 97.25 | 97.28 | 97.10 |
| 40-44 | 98.55 | 97.85 | 97.20 | 96.54 | 95.81 | 96.55 |
| 45-49 | 97.70 | 96.65 | 95.65 | 95.22 | 94.49 | 94.61 |
| 50-54 | 94.60 | 93.30 | 92.00 | 91.68 | 91.05 | 91.19 |
| 55-59 | 93.55 | 90.00 | 88.00 | 85.25 | 82.30 | 81.70 |
| 60-64 | 91.00 | 68.00 | 50.00 | 41.93 | 22.53 | 29.74 |
| 65+ | 49.07 | 34.80 | 24.15 | 22.37 | 12.13 | 16.39 |
| **Femmes** | | | | | | |
| 10-14 | 4.20 | 3.25 | 2.30 | 3.69 | 3.15 | 3.41 |
| 15-19 | 13.95 | 14.35 | 14.75 | 15.15 | 24.30 | 25.72 |
| 20-24 | 18.10 | 19.80 | 21.50 | 21.97 | 38.68 | 43.63 |
| 25-29 | 19.10 | 19.25 | 19.40 | 20.20 | 33.33 | 41.90 |
| 30-34 | 22.15 | 22.30 | 22.45 | 23.20 | 31.21 | 45.58 |
| 35-39 | 25.80 | 26.00 | 26.15 | 26.01 | 32.87 | 45.94 |
| 40-44 | 26.50 | 26.70 | 26.90 | 27.81 | 32.87 | 41.81 |
| 45-49 | 31.60 | 29.95 | 28.30 | 28.22 | 31.26 | 37.04 |
| 50-54 | 31.25 | 29.60 | 28.00 | 27.98 | 27.89 | 32.42 |
| 55-59 | 29.00 | 27.00 | 25.00 | 24.31 | 23.48 | 24.61 |
| 60-64 | 27.00 | 21.00 | 15.00 | 12.95 | 6.03 | 9.00 |
| 65+ | 7.55 | 6.85 | 5.35 | 5.26 | 2.57 | 4.09 |

Source(s): (1) EPPA3; (2) ASTER; (3) ASTER et R1983; (4) R1990.

### 2.2 Méthode(s): interpolation linéaire

#### 2.2.1 Hommes:

- 1950-70, taux d'activité 1950-70 tirés des EPPA3;
- 1980, interpolation des taux d'activité tirés des recensements de 1972, 1983 et 1990;
modification des tendances de tous les groupes d'âge;
- 1990, taux d'activité tirés du recensement de 1990.

#### 2.2.2 Femmes:

Méthode, hypothèses et traitements identiques à ceux appliqués aux hommes.

## 3. Evaluation des taux de répartition par secteur d'activité: 1950 - 1990

### 3.1 Données de base:

Tableau 2: Répartition de la population active en % par secteur d'activité

| Année | Agriculture | Industrie Total | Manufac. | Services |
|---|---|---|---|---|
| **Hommes** | | | | |
| 1972 (1) | 31.99 | 28.23 | 14.40 | 39.77 |
| 1983 (2) | 25.36 | 27.45 | 15.84 | 47.18 |
| 1990 (3) | 17.75 | 40.14 | 24.51 | 42.11 |
| **Femmes** | | | | |
| 1972 (1) | 37.18 | 11.02 | 10.41 | 51.80 |
| 1983 (2) | 23.33 | 33.58 | 32.94 | 43.09 |
| 1990 (3) | 14.32 | 50.19 | 49.72 | 35.50 |

Source(s): (1) ASTER; (2) R1983; (3) R1990.

### 3.2 Méthode(s): moyenne pondérée

#### 3.2.1 Hommes:

- 1950-70, taux de répartition 1950-70 tirés des EPPA3;
- 1980, moyennes pondérées des taux de répartition tirés des recensements de 1972 et 1983;
- 1990, taux de répartition tirés du recensement de 1990.

#### 3.2.2 Femmes:

Méthode, hypothèses et traitements identiques à ceux appliqués aux hommes.

## 4. Projection des taux d'activité: 2000 - 2010

### 4.1 Modèle(s): linéaire, log-linéaire et hyperbole

#### 4.1.1 Hommes:

- Aux groupes d'âge [10-14] et [20-29], application de la fonction F1;
- Au groupe d'âge [15-19], application de la fonction F2;
- Aux groupes d'âge [30+], application de la fonction F3;
- Modification des tendances des groupes d'âge [15-19] et [30-49].

#### 4.1.2 Femmes:

- Aux groupes d'âge [10-19] et [45-49], application de la fonction F1;
- Aux groupes d'âge [20-44], application de la fonction F2;
- Aux groupes d'âge [50+], application de la fonction F3;
- Modification de la tendance du groupe d'âge [20-24].

*Notes sur les ajustements des taux, voir p. 192-195.*

*Notes sur les fonctions de projection, voir p. 198.*

# Mauritanie

## 1. Source(s) des données de base

Code(s):     Titre(s):

EPPA3        Evaluations et projections de la population active 1950-2025 - troisième édition, BIT, Genève, 1986.
R1977        Recensement de la population 1977, Direction de la Statistique et de la Comptabilité Nationale, Nouakchott.

## 2. Evaluation des taux d'activité: 1950 - 1990

### 2.1 Données de base:

Tableau 1: Taux d'activité par sexe et par groupe d'âge

|  | Année | | | |
|---|---|---|---|---|
| Groupe d'âge | 1950 | 1960 | 1970 | 1980 |
| **Hommes** | | | | |
| 10-14 | 39.60 | 38.60 | 35.15 | 28.20 |
| 15-19 | 91.75 | 89.90 | 83.25 | 70.00 |
| 20-24 | 97.75 | 98.30 | 95.35 | 91.10 |
| 25-29 | 99.00 | 98.50 | 97.55 | 96.80 |
| 30-34 | 99.25 | 99.15 | 98.70 | 97.90 |
| 35-39 | 99.45 | 99.30 | 98.85 | 97.95 |
| 40-44 | 99.50 | 99.35 | 98.90 | 97.95 |
| 45-49 | 98.80 | 98.70 | 98.30 | 97.50 |
| 50-54 | 97.35 | 97.15 | 96.60 | 95.40 |
| 55-59 | 97.25 | 96.95 | 96.00 | 94.10 |
| 60-64 | 81.15 | 80.80 | 79.40 | 76.65 |
| 65+ | 66.75 | 66.10 | 63.85 | 59.30 |
| **Femmes** | | | | |
| 10-14 | 16.50 | 16.10 | 14.65 | 11.75 |
| 15-19 | 31.20 | 30.50 | 27.95 | 22.90 |
| 20-24 | 27.35 | 26.95 | 25.50 | 22.65 |
| 25-29 | 25.25 | 24.85 | 23.45 | 20.70 |
| 30-34 | 25.85 | 25.45 | 24.05 | 21.15 |
| 35-39 | 24.20 | 23.85 | 22.65 | 20.15 |
| 40-44 | 25.50 | 25.15 | 23.85 | 21.35 |
| 45-49 | 24.20 | 23.85 | 22.60 | 20.15 |
| 50-54 | 25.50 | 25.10 | 23.55 | 20.50 |
| 55-59 | 23.10 | 22.70 | 21.20 | 18.25 |
| 60-64 | 17.55 | 17.10 | 15.60 | 12.50 |
| 65+ | 14.05 | 13.60 | 12.00 | 8.80 |

Source(s): EPPA3.

### 2.2 Méthode(s): interpolation et extrapolation linéaires

#### 2.2.1 Hommes:

- 1950-80, taux d'activité 1950-80 tirés des EPPA3;
- 1990, extrapolation des taux d'activité 1950-80 tirés des EPPA3;
ajustement des taux extrapolés sur la base des variations des taux
interpolés 1980 par rapport aux taux 1980 tirés des EPPA3;
modification des tendances des groupes d'âge [25-54] pour 1990.

#### 2.2.2 Femmes:

- 1950-90, interpolation et extrapolation des taux d'activité 1950-80
tirés des EPPA3;
ajustement des taux interpolés et extrapolés en tenant
compte de la sous-énumération des femmes travaillant dans l'agriculture
en maintenant un rapport hommes/femmes égal à 1 sur toute la période.

## 3. Evaluation des taux de répartition par secteur d'activité: 1950 - 1990

### 3.1 Données de base:

Tableau 2: Répartition de la population active en % par secteur d'activité

|  | Agriculture | Industrie | | Services |
|---|---|---|---|---|
| Année | | Total | Manufac. | |
| **Hommes** | | | | |
| 1950 (1) | 94.50 | 1.60 | .. | 3.90 |
| 1960 (1) | 92.00 | 2.40 | .. | 5.60 |
| 1970 (1) | 83.00 | 5.00 | .. | 12.00 |
| 1977 (2) | 65.82 | 8.88 | 4.38 | 25.31 |
| 1980 (1) | 65.00 | 10.50 | .. | 24.50 |
| **Femmes** | | | | |
| 1977 (2) | 70.67 | 2.92 | 0.00 | 26.41 |

Source(s): (1) EPPA3; (2) R1977.

### 3.2 Méthode(s): interpolation et extrapolation linéaires

#### 3.2.1 Hommes:

- 1950-80, taux de répartition 1950-80 tirés des EPPA3;
- 1990, extrapolation des taux de répartition 1950-80 tirés des EPPA3;
modification des tendances de tous les secteurs.

#### 3.2.2 Femmes:

- 1950 et 1980-90, les taux de répartition de l'agriculture ont été estimés
sur la base du rapport hommes/femmes égal à 1 dans l'agriculture; les taux de
répartition de l'industrie et des services ont été estimés sur la base du rapport
industrie/service tiré du recensement de 1977;
- Application du rapport manufacture/industrie estimé pour le Maroc;
- 1960-70, interpolation des taux estimés 1950 et des taux tirés
du recensement de 1977.

## 4. Projection des taux d'activité: 2000 - 2010

### 4.1 Modèle(s): linéaire

#### 4.1.1 Hommes:

- A tous les groupes d'âge, application de la fonction F1;
- Modification des tendances des groupes d'âge [10-19] et [60+].

#### 4.1.2 Femmes:

- A tous les groupes d'âge, application de la fonction F1;
- Modification des tendances des groupes d'âge [15-54].

---

*Notes sur les ajustements des taux, voir p. 192-195.*                    *Notes sur les fonctions de projection, voir p. 198.*

# Mexique

## 1. Source(s) des données de base

Code(s): Titre(s):
EPPA3     Evaluations et projections de la population active 1950-2025 - troisième édition, BIT, Genève, 1986.
ASTER     Annuaire des statistiques du travail 1945-89 - Edition rétrospective sur les recensements de population, BIT, Genève, 1990.
AST93     Annuaire des statistiques du travail 1993, BIT, Genève, 1993.

## 2. Evaluation des taux d'activité: 1950 - 1990

### 2.1 Données de base:

Tableau 1: Taux d'activité par sexe et par groupe d'âge

| Groupe d'âge | Année 1980 (1) | 1990 (2) | 1991 (2) |
|---|---|---|---|
| **Hommes** | | | |
| 10-14 | 11.69 | 6.72 | .. |
| 15-19 | 55.89 | 47.05 | .. |
| 20-24 | 83.45 | 77.10 | .. |
| 25-29 | 94.16 | 89.32 | .. |
| 30-34 | 96.12 | 92.11 | .. |
| 35-39 | 96.20 | 92.18 | .. |
| 40-44 | 95.92 | 91.17 | .. |
| 45-49 | 95.27 | 89.04 | .. |
| 50-54 | 93.83 | 84.68 | .. |
| 55-59 | 91.42 | 78.75 | .. |
| 60-64 | 85.64 | 68.55 | .. |
| 65+ | 68.58 | 45.90 | .. |
| **Femmes** | | | |
| 10-14 | 2.09 | .. | 6.19 |
| 15-19 | 17.95 | .. | 30.11 |
| 20-24 | 29.10 | .. | 40.42 |
| 25-29 | 28.42 | .. | 37.92 |
| 30-34 | 26.87 | .. | 40.71 |
| 35-39 | 24.85 | .. | 42.48 |
| 40-44 | 22.56 | .. | 38.40 |
| 45-49 | 18.71 | .. | 36.27 |
| 50-54 | 15.20 | .. | 28.85 |
| 55-59 | 12.01 | .. | 26.54 |
| 60-64 | 9.33 | .. | 21.77 |
| 65+ | 5.42 | .. | 12.40 |

Source(s): (1) ASTER; (2) AST93,

### 2.2 Méthode(s): moyenne pondérée

#### 2.2.1 Hommes:

- 1950-70, taux d'activité 1950-70 tirés des EPPA3;
ajustement des taux d'activité des groupes d'âge [10-19] et [40-59] pour 1970;
- 1980, taux d'activité ajustés tirés du recensement de 1980;
- 1990, moyennes pondérées des taux d'activité ajustés tirés des recensements de 1980 et 1990.

#### 2.2.2 Femmes:

- 1950-70, taux d'activité 1950-70 tirés des EPPA3;
- 1980, taux d'activité ajustés tirés du recensement de 1980;
- 1990, moyennes pondérées des taux d'activité tirés du recensement de 1980 et de l'enquête de 1991.

## 3. Evaluation des taux de répartition par secteur d'activité: 1950 - 1990

### 3.1 Données de base:

Tableau 2: Répartition de la population active en % par secteur d'activité

| Année | Agriculture | Industrie Total | Manufac. | Services |
|---|---|---|---|---|
| **Hommes** | | | | |
| 1980 (1) | 42.58 | 29.53 | 16.31 | 27.89 |
| 1990 (2) | 29.40 | 30.81 | 19.77 | 39.79 |
| 1991 (2) | 34.05 | 24.98 | 14.84 | 40.97 |
| **Femmes** | | | | |
| 1980 (1) | 19.18 | 27.87 | 17.60 | 52.95 |
| 1990 (2) | 3.63 | 22.00 | 20.26 | 74.38 |
| 1991 (2) | 10.86 | 19.20 | 18.11 | 69.94 |

Source(s): (1) ASTER; (2) AST93.

### 3.2 Méthode(s): moyenne pondérée

#### 3.2.1 Hommes:

- 1950-70, taux de répartition 1950-70 tirés des EPPA3;
- 1980, taux de répartition tirés du recensement de 1980;
- 1970-90, moyennes pondérées des taux de répartition tirés du recensement de 1980 et de l'enquête de 1991.

#### 3.2.2 Femmes:

Méthode, hypothèses et traitements identiques à ceux appliqués aux hommes.

## 4. Projection des taux d'activité: 2000 - 2010

### 4.1 Modèle(s): linéaire, hyperbole et logistique

#### 4.1.1 Hommes:

- Aux groupes d'âge [10-54] et [65+], application de la fonction F1;
- Aux groupes d'âge [55-64], application de la fonction F3;
- Modification des tendances des groupes d'âge [20-24] et [40-54].

#### 4.1.2 Femmes:

- Aux groupes d'âge [10-29] et [50-59], application de la fonction F6;
- Aux groupes d'âge [30-49] et [60+], application de la fonction F1;
- Modification des tendances des groupes d'âge [10-34] et [50+].

---

*Notes sur les ajustements des taux, voir p. 192-195.*      *Notes sur les fonctions de projection, voir p. 198.*

# Moldava, Rép. de

## 1. Source(s) des données de base

Code(s):    Titre(s):

BLT-94-2    Vorobiev A. (1994), "Estimation de la population active pour les quinze pays de l'ex-URSS pour les années 1950, 1959, 1970, 1979 et 1989", dans le Bulletin des statistiques du travail - 1994-2, BIT, Genève.

## 2. Evaluation des taux d'activité: 1950 - 1990

### 2.1 Données de base:

Tableau 1: Taux d'activité par sexe et par groupe d'âge

| Groupe d'âge | Année 1950 | 1959 | 1970 | 1979 | 1989 |
|---|---|---|---|---|---|
| **Hommes** | | | | | |
| 10-14 | 0.00 | 0.00 | 0.00 | 0.00 | 0.00 |
| 15-19 | 53.04 | 75.86 | 46.99 | 40.93 | 29.94 |
| 20-24 | 91.02 | 88.98 | 86.92 | 89.53 | 82.76 |
| 25-29 | 95.65 | 99.08 | 95.33 | 97.66 | 96.07 |
| 30-34 | 93.94 | 96.12 | 82.68 | 98.00 | 97.19 |
| 35-39 | 96.10 | 97.70 | 99.13 | 99.13 | 97.63 |
| 40-44 | 94.83 | 98.39 | 97.25 | 98.39 | 96.77 |
| 45-49 | 95.65 | 97.22 | 96.70 | 97.22 | 95.28 |
| 50-54 | 91.18 | 94.55 | 94.92 | 92.93 | 92.66 |
| 55-59 | 92.31 | 93.02 | 91.43 | 87.18 | 84.95 |
| 60-64 | 77.27 | 87.10 | 58.82 | 31.37 | 28.75 |
| 65+ | 32.35 | 60.00 | 15.48 | 8.70 | 9.23 |
| **Femmes** | | | | | |
| 10-14 | 0.00 | 0.00 | 0.00 | 0.00 | 0.00 |
| 15-19 | 71.32 | 80.00 | 49.72 | 40.00 | 28.93 |
| 20-24 | 81.34 | 84.03 | 86.40 | 90.27 | 80.39 |
| 25-29 | 81.51 | 89.76 | 95.20 | 96.69 | 90.00 |
| 30-34 | 81.18 | 81.89 | 93.92 | 96.33 | 93.05 |
| 35-39 | 79.35 | 81.08 | 96.12 | 98.46 | 94.44 |
| 40-44 | 76.06 | 79.49 | 91.60 | 95.77 | 94.23 |
| 45-49 | 72.60 | 76.74 | 89.74 | 92.68 | 90.98 |
| 50-54 | 70.18 | 70.77 | 80.00 | 78.74 | 76.70 |
| 55-59 | 59.52 | 61.19 | 38.95 | 22.73 | 21.37 |
| 60-64 | 38.89 | 64.00 | 14.49 | 8.11 | 9.65 |
| 65+ | 9.09 | 13.19 | 5.63 | 1.61 | 3.15 |

Source(s): BLT-94-2.

### 2.2 Méthode(s): interpolation et extrapolation linéaires
moyenne pondérée

**2.2.1 Hommes:**

- 1950-90, pour les groupes d'âge [10-19] et [60+], moyennes pondérées des taux d'activité 1950, 1959, 1970, 1979 et 1989 tirés du Bulletin des statistiques du travail 1994-2;
ajustement des taux d'activé 1950-80 estimés pour les groupes d'âge [10-14];
pour les groupes d'âge [10-59], interpolation et extrapolation des taux d'activité 1950, 1959, 1970, 1979 et 1989 tirés du Bulletin;
les taux d'activité 1959 tirés du Bulletin ont été ajusté pour les groupes d'âge [60

**2.2.2 Femmes:**

- 1950-90, moyennes pondérées des taux d'activité 1950, 1959, 1970 et 1989 tirés du Bulletin des statistiques du travail, 1994-2;
modification des taux d'activé 1950-80
estimés pour le groupe d'âge [10-14]; les taux d'activité 1959 tirés du Bulletin ont été ajustés pour les groupes d'âge [15-19] et [60+]

## 3. Evaluation des taux de répartition par secteur d'activité: 1950 - 1990

### 3.1 Données de base:

Tableau 2: Répartition de la population active en % par secteur d'activité

| Année | Agriculture | Industrie Total | Manufac. | Services |
|---|---|---|---|---|
| **Hommes** | | | | |
| 1950 | 75.99 | 8.78 | 5.73 | 15.23 |
| 1959 | 66.23 | 13.35 | 8.64 | 20.42 |
| 1970 | 52.07 | 25.46 | 15.44 | 22.47 |
| 1979 | 45.51 | 29.49 | 17.29 | 25.00 |
| 1989 | 38.13 | 33.58 | 18.09 | 28.29 |
| **Femmes** | | | | |
| 1950 | 86.61 | 3.15 | 2.52 | 10.24 |
| 1959 | 77.90 | 7.58 | 6.57 | 14.52 |
| 1970 | 56.41 | 17.17 | 13.91 | 26.41 |
| 1979 | 40.91 | 22.73 | 18.09 | 36.36 |
| 1989 | 27.56 | 26.00 | 20.06 | 46.45 |

Source(s): BLT-94-2.

### 3.2 Méthode(s): données du BLT-94-2

**3.2.1 Hommes:**

- 1950, 1960, 1970, 1980 et 1990, respectivement les taux de répartition 1950, 1959, 1970, 1979 et 1989 tirés du Bulletin des statistiques du travail - 1994-2.

**3.2.2 Femmes:**

Méthode, hypothèses et traitements identiques à ceux appliqués aux hommes.

## 4. Projection des taux d'activité: 2000 - 2010

### 4.1 Modèle(s): hyperbole et logistique

**4.1.1 Hommes:**

- Aux groupes d'âge [15+], application de la fonction F3;
- Modification des tendances des groupes d'âge [20-49].

**4.1.2 Femmes:**

- Aux groupes d'âge [15-24] et [55+], application de la fonction F3;
- Aux groupes d'âge [25-54], application de la fonction F6;
- Modification des tendances des groupes d'âge [20-54].

*Notes sur les ajustements des taux, voir p. 192-195.*

*Notes sur les fonctions de projection, voir p. 198.*

# Mongolie

## 1. Source(s) des données de base

Code(s):     Titre(s):

EPPA3     Evaluations et projections de la population active 1950-2025 - troisième édition, BIT, Genève, 1986.

## 2. Evaluation des taux d'activité: 1950 - 1990

### 2.1 Données de base:

Tableau 1: Taux d'activité par sexe et par groupe d'âge

| Groupe d'âge | Année 1950 | 1960 | 1970 | 1980 |
|---|---|---|---|---|
| **Hommes** | | | | |
| 10-14 | 5.75 | 5.40 | 4.65 | 4.00 |
| 15-19 | 84.90 | 82.40 | 76.50 | 71.45 |
| 20-24 | 95.40 | 94.70 | 93.05 | 91.65 |
| 25-29 | 96.80 | 96.80 | 96.85 | 96.90 |
| 30-34 | 98.00 | 98.00 | 98.05 | 98.10 |
| 35-39 | 98.25 | 98.20 | 98.15 | 98.05 |
| 40-44 | 98.40 | 98.30 | 98.05 | 97.80 |
| 45-49 | 98.35 | 98.15 | 97.65 | 97.20 |
| 50-54 | 98.35 | 97.90 | 96.75 | 95.75 |
| 55-59 | 98.35 | 97.30 | 94.90 | 92.85 |
| 60-64 | 95.80 | 92.60 | 85.25 | 78.95 |
| 65+ | 69.20 | 65.90 | 58.35 | 51.85 |
| **Femmes** | | | | |
| 10-14 | 6.45 | 4.90 | 3.80 | 3.05 |
| 15-19 | 88.50 | 72.90 | 66.75 | 60.80 |
| 20-24 | 78.40 | 79.15 | 79.45 | 79.70 |
| 25-29 | 67.95 | 75.50 | 78.50 | 81.40 |
| 30-34 | 66.00 | 75.05 | 78.60 | 82.10 |
| 35-39 | 68.20 | 76.65 | 80.00 | 83.20 |
| 40-44 | 70.00 | 77.40 | 80.35 | 83.20 |
| 45-49 | 70.50 | 76.80 | 79.30 | 81.75 |
| 50-54 | 71.50 | 75.25 | 76.70 | 78.15 |
| 55-59 | 79.75 | 74.10 | 72.00 | 69.80 |
| 60-64 | 83.90 | 66.95 | 60.30 | 53.80 |
| 65+ | 58.40 | 43.05 | 37.00 | 31.10 |

Source(s): EPPA3.

### 2.2 Méthode(s): extrapolation linéaire

#### 2.2.1 Hommes:

- 1950-80, taux d'activité 1950-80 tirés des EPPA3;
- 1990, extrapolation des taux d'activité 1950-80 tirés des EPPA3;
modification des tendances des groupes d'âge [10-24] et [65+].

#### 2.2.2 Femmes:

- 1950-80, taux d'activité 1950-80 tirés des EPPA3;
- 1990, extrapolation des taux d'activité 1950-1980 tirés des EPPA3;
ajustement des taux extrapolés sur la base des variations des taux
interpolés 1980 par rapport aux taux 1980 tirés des EPPA3;
modification des tendances des groupes d'âge [10-19] et [65+]

## 3. Evaluation des taux de répartition par secteur d'activité: 1950 - 1990

### 3.1 Données de base:

Tableau 2: Répartition de la population active en % par secteur d'activité

| Année | Agriculture | Industrie Total | Manufac. | Services |
|---|---|---|---|---|
| **Hommes** | | | | |
| 1950 | 70.00 | 17.00 | .. | 13.00 |
| 1960 | 64.00 | 19.00 | .. | 17.00 |
| 1970 | 51.00 | 21.00 | .. | 28.00 |
| 1980 | 43.00 | 21.00 | .. | 36.00 |
| **Femmes** | | | | |
| 1950 | 67.00 | 17.00 | .. | 16.00 |
| 1960 | 57.00 | 19.00 | .. | 24.00 |
| 1970 | 44.00 | 21.00 | .. | 25.00 |
| 1980 | 36.00 | 21.00 | .. | 43.00 |

Source(s): EPPA3.

### 3.2 Méthode(s): extrapolation linéaire

#### 3.2.1 Hommes:

- 1950-80, taux de répartition 1950-80 tirés des EPPA3;
- 1990, extrapolation des taux de répartition 1950-80 tirés des EPPA3.

#### 3.2.2 Femmes:

- 1950-80, taux de répartition 1950-80 tirés des EPPA3;
- 1980-90, extrapolation des taux de répartition 1950-80 tirés des EPPA3;
modification des tendances de tous les secteurs.

## 4. Projection des taux d'activité: 2000 - 2010

### 4.1 Modèle(s): linéaire, log-linéaire, hyperbole et logistique

#### 4.1.1 Hommes:

- Aux groupes d'âge [10-59], application de la fonction F1;
- Aux groupes d'âge [60+], application de la fonction F3;
- Modification des tendances des groupes d'âge [10-34].

#### 4.1.2 Femmes:

- Aux groupes d'âge [10-19], application de la fonction F2;
- Aux groupes d'âge [20-49], application de la fonction F6;
- Aux groupes d'âge [50+], application de la fonction F3;
- Modification de la tendance du groupe d'âge [10-14].

*Notes sur les ajustements des taux, voir p. 192-195.*

*Notes sur les fonctions de projection, voir p. 198.*

# Mozambique

## 1. Source(s) des données de base

**Code(s):**    **Titre(s):**

EPPA3    Evaluations et projections de la population active 1950-2025 - troisième édition, BIT, Genève, 1986.
ASTER    Annuaire des statistiques du travail 1945-89 - Edition rétrospective sur les recensements de population, BIT, Genève, 1990.
ADNU88    Annuaire démographique 1988 - Statistiques des recensements de population, quarantième édition, Nations Unies, New York, 1990.
STAT    Base de données sur les statistiques du travail - LABORSTA, Bureau de statistique, BIT, Genève.

## 2. Evaluation des taux d'activité: 1950 - 1990

### 2.1 Données de base:

Tableau 1: Taux d'activité par sexe et par groupe d'âge

| | | Année | | | | |
|---|---|---|---|---|---|---|
| | Groupe d'âge | 1950 (1) | 1960 (1) | 1970 (1) | 1980 (1) | 1980 (2) |
| **Hommes** | | | | | | |
| | 10-14 | 57.90 | 55.80 | 53.65 | 51.50 | 24.52 |
| | 15-19 | 79.35 | 77.00 | 74.60 | 72.25 | 52.90 |
| | 20-24 | 94.20 | 93.25 | 92.35 | 91.40 | 91.41 |
| | 25-29 | 98.60 | 98.50 | 98.35 | 98.20 | 97.73 |
| | 30-34 | 98.85 | 98.70 | 98.55 | 98.40 | 98.74 |
| | 35-39 | 99.10 | 98.95 | 98.75 | 98.60 | 98.87 |
| | 40-44 | 99.30 | 99.15 | 98.95 | 98.80 | 98.86 |
| | 45-49 | 99.35 | 99.20 | 99.05 | 98.90 | 98.85 |
| | 50-54 | 99.30 | 99.15 | 98.95 | 98.70 | 98.53 |
| | 55-59 | 99.20 | 99.00 | 98.70 | 98.60 | 98.16 |
| | 60-64 | 98.90 | 98.25 | 97.65 | 97.00 | 97.01 |
| | 65+ | 94.75 | 93.50 | 92.25 | 91.00 | 92.06 |
| **Femmes** | | | | | | |
| | 10-14 | 52.50 | 51.65 | 50.85 | 50.00 | 33.33 |
| | 15-19 | 83.10 | 81.40 | 79.70 | 78.00 | 68.88 |
| | 20-24 | 92.50 | 90.85 | 89.15 | 87.50 | 87.56 |
| | 25-29 | 93.60 | 92.05 | 90.55 | 89.00 | 90.02 |
| | 30-34 | 95.35 | 93.90 | 92.45 | 91.00 | 91.47 |
| | 35-39 | 95.55 | 94.20 | 92.85 | 91.50 | 93.05 |
| | 40-44 | 95.65 | 94.45 | 93.20 | 92.00 | 93.01 |
| | 45-49 | 96.05 | 94.85 | 93.70 | 92.50 | 93.43 |
| | 50-54 | 94.50 | 93.50 | 92.50 | 91.50 | 92.28 |
| | 55-59 | 91.65 | 90.95 | 90.20 | 89.50 | 91.41 |
| | 60-64 | 88.10 | 87.75 | 87.35 | 87.00 | 87.80 |
| | 65+ | 76.45 | 76.30 | 76.15 | 76.00 | 78.46 |

**Source(s):** (1) EPPA3; (2) ASTER et ADNU88.

### 2.2 Méthode(s): interpolation et extrapolation linéaires

#### 2.2.1 Hommes:

- 1980, taux d'activité ajustés tirés du recensement de 1980;
- 1950-70 et 1990, interpolation et extrapolation des taux d'activité 1950-70 et 1990 tirés des EPPA3;
ajustement des taux interpolés et extrapolés sur la base des variations des taux interpolés 1980 par rapport aux taux du recensement de 1980; modification des tendances de tous les groupes d'âge pour 1950-80; et des tendances des groupes d'âge [60+] pour 1990.

#### 2.2.2 Femmes:

Méthode, hypothèses et traitements identiques à ceux appliqués aux hommes.

## 3. Evaluation des taux de répartition par secteur d'activité: 1950 - 1990

### 3.1 Données de base:

Tableau 2: Répartition de la population active en % par secteur d'activité

| | | Agriculture | Industrie | | Services |
|---|---|---|---|---|---|
| | Année | | Total | Manufac. | |
| **Hommes** | | | | | |
| | 1950 (1) | 82.00 | 7.10 | .. | 10.90 |
| | 1960 (1) | 78.70 | 9.40 | .. | 11.90 |
| | 1970 (1) | 75.40 | 11.60 | .. | 13.00 |
| | 1980 (1) | 72.00 | 13.90 | .. | 14.10 |
| | 1980 (2) | 71.99 | 13.93 | 12.35 | 14.08 |
| **Femmes** | | | | | |
| | 1950 (1) | 98.15 | 0.40 | .. | 1.45 |
| | 1960 (1) | 97.80 | 0.50 | .. | 1.70 |
| | 1970 (1) | 97.40 | 0.70 | .. | 1.90 |
| | 1980 (1) | 97.05 | 0.80 | .. | 2.15 |
| | 1980 (2) | 97.05 | 0.80 | 0.78 | 2.15 |

**Source(s):** (1) EPPA3; (2) STAT.

### 3.2 Méthode(s): extrapolation linéaire

#### 3.2.1 Hommes:

- 1950-80, taux de répartition 1950-80 tirés des EPPA3;
1990, taux de répartition estimés sur la base de l'extrapolation des taux de répartition 1950-80 tirés des EPPA3;
modification des tendances de tous les secteurs;
- Application du rapport manufacture/industrie tiré du recensement de 1980.

#### 3.2.2 Femmes:

Méthode, hypothèses et traitements identiques à ceux appliqués aux hommes.

## 4. Projection des taux d'activité: 2000 - 2010

### 4.1 Modèle(s): linéaire

#### 4.1.1 Hommes:

- A tous les groupes d'âge, application de la fonction F1;
- Modification des tendances des groupes d'âge [10-29] et [60+].

#### 4.1.2 Femmes:

- A tous les groupes d'âge, application de la fonction F1;
- Modification des tendances des groupes d'âge [25-49] et [60+].

---

*Notes sur les ajustements des taux, voir p. 192-195.*      *Notes sur les fonctions de projection, voir p. 198.*

# Myanmar

## 1. Source(s) des données de base

Code(s):     Titre(s):

ADNU84     Annuaire démographique 1984 - Statistiques des recensements de population II, trente-sixième édition, Nations Unies, New York, 1986.
STAT          Base de données sur les statistiques du travail - LABORSTA, Bureau de statistique, BIT, Genève.
EPPA4        Population active 1950-2010 - quatrième édition, BIT, Genève 1996.

## 2. Evaluation des taux d'activité: 1950 - 1990

### 2.1 Données de base:

Tableau 1: Taux d'activité par sexe et par groupe d'âge

| Groupe d'âge | Année 1983 (1) | 1983 (2) | 1983 (3) |
|---|---|---|---|
| **Hommes** | | | |
| 10-14 | 2.24 | 8.62 | 89.75 |
| 15-19 | 26.31 | 47.32 | 51.68 |
| 20-24 | 64.39 | 73.76 | 25.03 |
| 25-29 | 80.72 | 79.34 | 16.82 |
| 30-34 | 86.53 | 82.27 | 14.45 |
| 35-39 | 88.92 | 83.14 | 14.55 |
| 40-44 | 88.68 | 84.18 | 15.11 |
| 45-49 | 86.59 | 82.71 | 16.25 |
| 50-54 | 80.98 | 81.30 | 18.12 |
| 55-59 | 77.62 | 80.19 | 20.08 |
| 60-64 | 63.06 | 72.67 | 29.24 |
| 65+ | 48.42 | 57.09 | 45.56 |
| **Femmes** | | | |
| 10-14 | 2.76 | 8.37 | 88.53 |
| 15-19 | 18.08 | 36.70 | 64.21 |
| 20-24 | 34.15 | 49.10 | 59.92 |
| 25-29 | 43.11 | 50.00 | 59.37 |
| 30-34 | 46.14 | 51.30 | 59.10 |
| 35-39 | 46.15 | 53.40 | 58.36 |
| 40-44 | 48.56 | 53.87 | 57.77 |
| 45-49 | 50.39 | 52.29 | 57.66 |
| 50-54 | 49.00 | 53.64 | 57.90 |
| 55-59 | 47.47 | 51.01 | 59.21 |
| 60-64 | 35.68 | 43.58 | 63.35 |
| 65+ | 20.81 | 27.57 | 75.43 |

Note(s): (1) Urbain; (2) Rural; (3) Total.
Source(s): ADNU88 et STAT.

### 2.2 Méthode(s): interpolation linéaire

#### 2.2.1 Hommes:

- 1950-90, aux taux d'activité 1950-90 tirés du modèle urbain-rural,
application des variations des taux d'activité ajustés tirés du recensement
de 1983 par rapport aux taux interpolés 1983 issus du modèle.

#### 2.2.2 Femmes:

- 1950-90, aux taux d'activité estimés pour la Thaïlande, application des
variations des taux d'activité estimés pour 1983 par rapport aux taux
ajustés du recensement de 1983;
modification des tendances des groupes d'âge [10-14].

## 3. Evaluation des taux de répartition par secteur d'activité: 1950 - 1990

### 3.1 Données de base:

Tableau 2: Répartition de la population active en % par secteur d'activité

| Année | Agriculture | Industrie Total | Manufac. | Services |
|---|---|---|---|---|
| **Hommes** | | | | |
| 1950 (1) | 81.30 | 4.00 | .. | 14.70 |
| 1960 (1) | 78.70 | 6.05 | .. | 15.25 |
| 1970 (1) | 75.10 | 7.35 | .. | 17.55 |
| 1980 (1) | 71.24 | 16.15 | 13.11 | 12.61 |
| 1983 (2) | 71.69 | 9.41 | 6.80 | 18.90 |
| **Femmes** | | | | |
| 1950 (1) | 85.75 | 2.55 | .. | 11.70 |
| 1960 (1) | 84.70 | 3.55 | .. | 11.75 |
| 1970 (1) | 78.25 | 5.55 | .. | 16.20 |
| 1980 (1) | 75.31 | 9.96 | 8.98 | 14.73 |
| 1983 (2) | 79.52 | 7.71 | 7.29 | 12.77 |

Note(s): (1) Viet Nam.
Source(s): (1) EPPA4; (2) STAT.

### 3.2 Méthode(s): interpolation linéaire

#### 3.2.1 Hommes:

- 1950-90, interpolation des taux de répartition 1950-90
estimés pour le Viat Nam;
ajustement des taux interpolés sur la base des 3/4 des variations des taux
interpolés 1983 par rapport aux taux de répartition ajustés
du recensement de 1983.

#### 3.2.2 Femmes:

Méthode, hypothèses et traitements identiques à ceux appliqués aux hommes.

## 4. Projection des taux d'activité: 2000 - 2010

### 4.1 Modèle(s): linéaire, hyperbole et logistique

#### 4.1.1 Hommes:

- A tous les groupes d'âge, application de la fonction F1;
- Modification des tendances des groupes d'âge [10-24] et [60+].

#### 4.1.2 Femmes:

- Aux groupes d'âge [10-19], application de la fonction F1;
- Aux groupes d'âge [20-64], application de la fonction F6;
- Au groupe d'âge [65+], application de la fonction F3;
- Modification des tendances des groupes d'âge [10-64].

*Notes sur les ajustements des taux, voir p. 192-195.*     *Notes sur les fonctions de projection, voir p. 198.*

# Namibie

## 1. Source(s) des données de base

Code(s):     Titre(s):

EPPA3     Evaluations et projections de la population active 1950-2025 - troisième édition, BIT, Genève, 1986.
ASTER     Annuaire des statistiques du travail 1945-89 - Edition rétrospective sur les recensements de population, BIT, Genève, 1990.
R1991     Republic of Namibia, 1991 Population and Housing Census, Report A, Statistical tables, Central Statistical Office, Windhoek, 1993.

## 2. Evaluation des taux d'activité: 1950 - 1990

### 2.1 Données de base:

Tableau 1: Taux d'activité par sexe et par groupe d'âge

| Groupe d'âge | Année 1960 (1) | 1991 (2) |
|---|---|---|
| **Hommes** | | |
| 10-14 | 45.00 | 29.31 |
| 15-19 | 75.00 | 52.96 |
| 20-24 | 95.90 | 80.46 |
| 25-29 | 99.40 | 95.04 |
| 30-34 | 99.25 | 97.29 |
| 35-39 | 99.10 | 97.04 |
| 40-44 | 99.05 | 97.01 |
| 45-49 | 98.75 | 96.61 |
| 50-54 | 98.50 | 94.12 |
| 55-59 | 98.00 | 90.94 |
| 60-64 | 95.60 | 65.16 |
| 65+ | 79.00 | 36.27 |
| **Femmes** | | |
| 10-14 | 43.42 | 18.96 |
| 15-19 | 58.78 | 31.03 |
| 20-24 | 62.84 | 59.51 |
| 25-29 | 54.45 | 67.88 |
| 30-34 | 54.07 | 66.21 |
| 35-39 | 53.09 | 66.60 |
| 40-44 | 53.16 | 64.34 |
| 45-49 | 54.25 | 63.08 |
| 50-54 | 53.01 | 58.67 |
| 55-59 | 48.63 | 52.85 |
| 60-64 | 42.95 | 36.55 |
| 65+ | 30.69 | 20.59 |

**Source(s)**: (1) EPPA3; (2) R1991.

### 2.2 Méthode(s): interpolation et extrapolation linéaires

#### 2.2.1 Hommes:

- 1950-90, interpolation et extrapolation des taux d'activité 1960
tirés des EPPA3 et des taux d'activité tirés du recensement de 1991;
modification des tendances des groupes d'âge [10-14] et [20+] pour 1950
et des tendances des groupes d'âge [20+] pour 1960-90.

#### 2.2.2 Femmes:

Méthode, hypothèses et traitements identiques à ceux appliqués aux hommes.

## 3. Evaluation des taux de répartition par secteur d'activité: 1950 - 1990

### 3.1 Données de base:

Tableau 2: Répartition de la population active en % par secteur d'activité

| Année | Agriculture | Industrie Total | Manufac. | Services |
|---|---|---|---|---|
| **Hommes** | | | | |
| 1960 (1) | 62.68 | 21.71 | 5.34 | 15.61 |
| 1991 (2) | 45.30 | 20.65 | 4.88 | 34.06 |
| **Femmes** | | | | |
| 1960 (1) | 58.62 | 1.94 | 1.38 | 39.43 |
| 1991 (2) | 52.10 | 7.88 | 7.02 | 40.01 |

**Source(s)**: (1) ASTER; (2) R1991.

### 3.2 Méthode(s): moyenne pondérée

#### 3.2.1 Hommes:

- 1950-90, interpolation et extrapolation des taux de répartition 1960 et
1991 tirés respectivement des EPPA3 et du recensement de 1991;
- Application du rapport manufacture/industrie du recensement de 1991.

#### 3.2.2 Femmes:

Méthode, hypothèses et traitements identiques à ceux appliqués aux hommes.

## 4. Projection des taux d'activité: 2000 - 2010

### 4.1 Modèle(s): linéaire, hyperbole et log-linéaire

#### 4.1.1 Hommes:

- Aux groupes d'âge [10-19], application de la fonction F1;
- Aux groupes d'âge [20+], application de la fonction F3;
- Modification des tendances des groupes d'âge [10-14] et [20+].

#### 4.1.2 Femmes:

- Au groupe d'âge [10-14], application de la fonction F2;
- Aux groupes d'âge [15-24] et [60+], application de la fonction F3;
- Aux groupes d'âge [25-59], application de la fonction F1;
- Modification des tendances des groupes d'âge [10-14], [25-29] et [55-59].

*Notes sur les ajustements des taux, voir p. 192-195.*     *Notes sur les fonctions de projection, voir p. 198.*

314

# Népal

## 1. Source(s) des données de base

Code(s): Titre(s):

ADNU84 Annuaire démographique 1984 - Statistiques des recensements de population II, trente-sixième édition, Nations Unies, New York, 1986.
STAT Base de données sur les statistiques du travail - LABORSTA, Bureau de statistique, BIT, Genève.

## 2. Evaluation des taux d'activité: 1950 - 1990

### 2.1 Données de base:

Tableau 1: Taux d'activité par sexe et par groupe d'âge

| Groupe d'âge | Année 1961 | 1971 | 1981 |
|---|---|---|---|
| **Hommes** | | | |
| 10-14 | 74.69 | .. | 61.28 |
| 15-19 | 91.75 | .. | 72.44 |
| 20-24 | 96.74 | .. | 89.71 |
| 25-29 | 98.41 | .. | 96.00 |
| 30-34 | 98.65 | .. | 97.35 |
| 35-39 | 98.85 | .. | 97.56 |
| 40-44 | 98.95 | .. | 97.83 |
| 45-49 | 97.90 | .. | 96.39 |
| 50-54 | 97.74 | .. | 94.27 |
| 55-59 | 95.12 | .. | 92.21 |
| 60-64 | 85.90 | .. | 83.27 |
| 65+ | 70.86 | .. | 68.69 |
| **Femmes** | | | |
| 10-14 | 67.20 | 51.30 | 50.29 |
| 15-19 | 77.47 | 66.00 | 61.50 |
| 20-24 | 69.33 | 62.51 | 59.57 |
| 25-29 | 64.77 | 61.33 | 57.59 |
| 30-34 | 61.04 | 61.45 | 57.11 |
| 35-39 | 59.04 | 61.54 | 58.54 |
| 40-44 | 56.03 | 60.16 | 58.88 |
| 45-49 | 54.03 | 59.60 | 58.87 |
| 50-54 | 51.42 | 56.90 | 58.24 |
| 55-59 | 46.06 | 52.05 | 55.78 |
| 60-64 | 33.49 | 38.72 | 39.92 |
| 65+ | 18.44 | 22.40 | 35.00 |

Source(s): STAT.

### 2.2 Méthode(s): interpolation et extrapolation linéaires

**2.2.1 Hommes:**

- 1950-90, interpolation et extrapolation des taux d'activité tirés des recensements de 1961 et 1981;
modification des tendances de tous les groupes d'âge pour 1950 et 1990.

**2.2.2 Femmes:**

- 1950-90, interpolation et extrapolation des taux d'activité ajustés tirés des recensements de 1961, 1971 et 1981; l'ajustement a été accompli sur la base du rapport hommes/femmes dans l'agriculture tiré du recensement de 1961;
modification des tendances de tous les groupes d'âge pour 1950 et 1990.

## 3. Evaluation des taux de répartition par secteur d'activité: 1950 - 1990

### 3.1 Données de base:

Tableau 2: Répartition de la population active en % par secteur d'activité

| Année | Agriculture | Industrie Total | Manufac. | Services |
|---|---|---|---|---|
| **Hommes** | | | | |
| 1961 | 92.54 | 2.59 | 2.33 | 4.87 |
| 1971 | 92.81 | 1.51 | 1.32 | 5.68 |
| 1981 | 90.64 | 0.77 | 0.64 | 8.60 |
| **Femmes** | | | | |
| 1961 | 97.48 | 1.28 | 1.24 | 1.24 |
| 1971 | 98.17 | 0.47 | 0.46 | 1.36 |
| 1981 | 97.06 | 0.23 | 0.21 | 2.71 |

Source(s): STAT.

### 3.2 Méthode(s): interpolation et extrapolation linéaires

**3.2.1 Hommes:**

- 1950-90, interpolation et extrapolation des taux de répartition tirés des recensements de 1961, 1971 et 1981;
modification des tendances de tous les secteurs pour 1980 et 1990.

**3.2.2 Femmes:**

- 1950-80, interpolation et extrapolation des taux de répartition tirés des recensements de 1961, 1971 et 1981;
- 1990, mêmes niveaux qu'en 1980.

## 4. Projection des taux d'activité: 2000 - 2010

### 4.1 Modèle(s): linéaire et logistique

**4.1.1 Hommes:**

- Aux groupes d'âge [10-54], application de la fonction F1;
- Aux groupes d'âge [55+], application de la fonction F3;
- Modification des tendances des groupes d'âge [20+].

**4.1.2 Femmes:**

- Aux groupes d'âge [10-39] et [60+], application de la fonction F1;
- Aux groupes d'âge [40-59], application de la fonction F6;
- Modification des tendances de tous les groupes d'âge.

*Notes sur les ajustements des taux, voir p. 192-195.*   *Notes sur les fonctions de projection, voir p. 198.*

# Nicaragua

## 1. Source(s) des données de base

| Code(s): | Titre(s): |
|---|---|
| EPPA3 | Evaluations et projections de la population active 1950-2025 - troisième édition, BIT, Genève, 1986. |
| ASTER | Annuaire des statistiques du travail 1945-89 - Edition rétrospective sur les recensements de population, BIT, Genève, 1990. |
| AST91 | Annuaire des statistiques du travail 1991, BIT, Genève, 1991. |
| STAT | Base de données sur les statistiques du travail - LABORSTA, Bureau de statistique, BIT, Genève. |

## 2. Evaluation des taux d'activité: 1950 - 1990

### 2.1 Données de base:

Tableau 1: Taux d'activité par sexe et par groupe d'âge

| Groupe d'âge | Année 1950 (1) | 1960 (1) | 1971 (2) | 1985 (3) | 1990 (3) |
|---|---|---|---|---|---|
| **Hommes** | | | | | |
| 10-14 | 45.00 | 34.70 | 18.74 | .. | .. |
| 15-19 | 91.10 | 78.85 | 54.55 | .. | .. |
| 20-24 | 96.95 | 94.60 | 81.21 | .. | .. |
| 25-29 | 98.65 | 97.60 | 89.78 | .. | .. |
| 30-34 | 98.80 | 97.90 | 91.51 | .. | .. |
| 35-39 | 99.00 | 98.05 | 92.17 | .. | .. |
| 40-44 | 98.90 | 98.00 | 91.43 | .. | .. |
| 45-49 | 98.50 | 97.75 | 91.38 | .. | .. |
| 50-54 | 98.30 | 96.65 | 88.48 | .. | .. |
| 55-59 | 97.80 | 94.60 | 87.30 | .. | .. |
| 60-64 | 96.80 | 93.35 | 80.70 | .. | .. |
| 65+ | 86.30 | 75.05 | 60.73 | .. | .. |
| **Femmes** | | | | | |
| 10-14 | | | 4.01 | 6.34 | 6.92 |
| 15-19 | .. | .. | 17.44 | 23.62 | 25.62 |
| 20-24 | .. | .. | 25.62 | 38.75 | 42.10 |
| 25-29 | .. | .. | 23.70 | 45.61 | 49.45 |
| 30-34 | .. | .. | 22.99 | 50.03 | 54.99 |
| 35-39 | .. | .. | 22.86 | 45.95 | 51.72 |
| 40-44 | .. | .. | 22.32 | 45.79 | 47.69 |
| 45-49 | .. | .. | 20.59 | 41.70 | 45.54 |
| 50-54 | .. | .. | 18.64 | 37.46 | 42.86 |
| 55-59 | .. | .. | 17.27 | 33.84 | 35.43 |
| 60-64 | .. | .. | 13.99 | 22.06 | 23.71 |
| 65+ | .. | .. | 9.05 | 13.30 | 14.77 |

Source(s): (1) EPPA3; (2) ASTER; (3) AST91.

### 2.2 Méthode(s): interpolation et extrapolation linéaires

#### 2.2.1 Hommes:

- 1950-60, taux d'activité 1950-60 tirés des EPPA3;
- 1970-90, interpolation et extrapolation des taux d'activité 1950-60
tirés des EPPA3 et des taux ajustés tirés du recensement de 1971;
aux taux interpolés et extrapolés, application des variations des taux interpolés
1971 par rapport aux taux ajustés tirés du recensement de 1971.

#### 2.2.2 Femmes:

- 1950-70, taux d'activité ajustés 1950-70 tirés des EPPA3;
ajustement des taux sur la base du modèle d'ajustement des taux d'activité
des femmes travaillant dans l'agriculture comme aides familiales;
- 1980-90, interpolation et extrapolation des taux d'activité tirés du
recensement de 1971, de l'enquête de 1985 et des évaluations officielles de
1990; aux interpolés, application des variations des taux interpolés 1985
par rapport aux taux du recensement de 1985.

## 3. Evaluation des taux de répartition par secteur d'activité: 1950 - 1990

### 3.1 Données de base:

Tableau 2: Répartition de la population active en % par secteur d'activité

| Année | Agriculture | Industrie Total | Manufac. | Services |
|---|---|---|---|---|
| **Hommes** | | | | |
| 1960 (1) | 72.25 | 15.20 | .. | 12.55 |
| 1971 (2) | 58.83 | 18.05 | 11.45 | 23.12 |
| 1977 (3) | 53.49 | 22.02 | 14.49 | 24.50 |
| **Femmes** | | | | |
| 1960 (1) | 14.20 | 19.70 | .. | 66.10 |
| 1971 (2) | 8.20 | 17.22 | 16.68 | 74.58 |
| 1977 (3) | 15.73 | 20.85 | 20.32 | 63.42 |

Source(s): (1) EPPA3; (2) ASTER; (3) STAT.

### 3.2 Méthode(s): moyenne pondérée
extrapolation linéaire

#### 3.2.1 Hommes:

- 1950-60, taux de répartition 1950-60 tirés des EPPA3;
- 1970, moyennes pondérées des taux de répartition 1960 tirés des
EPPA3 et des taux de répartition du recensement de 1971;
- 1980-90, extrapolation des taux de répartition du recensement de 1971
et des évaluations officielles de 1977;
modification des tendances de tous les secteurs.

#### 3.2.2 Femmes:

Méthode, hypothèses et traitements identiques à ceux appliqués aux hommes.

## 4. Projection des taux d'activité: 2000 - 2010

### 4.1 Modèle(s): linéaire

#### 4.1.1 Hommes:

- A tous les groupes d'âge, application de la fonction F1;
- Modification des tendances des groupes d'âge [10-19], [30-34],
[40-44] et [65+].

#### 4.1.2 Femmes:

- A tous les groupes d'âge, application de la fonction F1;
- Modification des tendances des groupes d'âge [10-24], [45-54] et [65+].

*Notes sur les ajustements des taux, voir p. 192-195.*     *Notes sur les fonctions de projection, voir p. 198.*

# Niger

## 1. Source(s) des données de base

Code(s):     Titre(s):

EPPA3    Evaluations et projections de la population active 1950-2025 - troisième édition, BIT, Genève, 1986.
ASTER    Annuaire des statistiques du travail 1945-89 - Edition rétrospective sur les recensements de population, BIT, Genève, 1990.
STAT     Base de données sur les statistiques du travail - LABORSTA, Bureau de statistique, BIT, Genève.

## 2. Evaluation des taux d'activité: 1950 - 1990

### 2.1 Données de base:

Tableau 1: Taux d'activité par sexe et par groupe d'âge

| Groupe d'âge | Année 1959 (1) | 1950 (2) | 1960 (2) | 1970 (2) | 1977 (3) | 1980 (2) | 1988 (1) |
|---|---|---|---|---|---|---|---|
| **Hommes** | | | | | | | |
| 10-14 | 56.10 | .. | .. | .. | 20.63 | .. | 53.87 |
| 15-19 | 90.25 | .. | .. | .. | 83.88 | .. | 89.55 |
| 20-24 | 97.30 | .. | .. | .. | 95.90 | .. | 92.64 |
| 25-29 | 97.70 | .. | .. | .. | 98.15 | .. | 97.23 |
| 30-34 | 98.45 | .. | .. | .. | 98.68 | .. | 97.79 |
| 35-39 | 98.65 | .. | .. | .. | 98.95 | .. | 98.29 |
| 40-44 | 98.55 | .. | .. | .. | 98.57 | .. | 98.04 |
| 45-49 | 97.70 | .. | .. | .. | 98.56 | .. | 97.51 |
| 50-54 | 97.45 | .. | .. | .. | 97.05 | .. | 96.91 |
| 55-59 | 96.85 | .. | .. | .. | 96.15 | .. | 95.74 |
| 60-64 | 94.45 | .. | .. | .. | 89.80 | .. | 94.00 |
| 65+ | 82.25 | .. | .. | .. | 72.44 | .. | 87.86 |
| **Femmes** | | | | | | | |
| 10-14 | 50.15 | 50.35 | 50.15 | 49.90 | 2.83 | 46.90 | .. |
| 15-19 | 92.15 | 92.60 | 92.15 | 91.70 | 6.33 | 85.30 | .. |
| 20-24 | 96.35 | 96.80 | 96.35 | 95.90 | 6.49 | 89.70 | .. |
| 25-29 | 97.00 | 97.45 | 97.00 | 96.60 | 6.48 | 90.85 | .. |
| 30-34 | 98.40 | 98.75 | 98.40 | 98.00 | 7.07 | 92.60 | .. |
| 35-39 | 98.05 | 98.45 | 98.05 | 97.70 | 8.02 | 92.65 | .. |
| 40-44 | 97.20 | 97.55 | 97.20 | 96.90 | 9.08 | 92.35 | .. |
| 45-49 | 95.75 | 96.10 | 95.75 | 95.45 | 10.24 | 91.00 | .. |
| 50-54 | 87.90 | 88.20 | 87.90 | 87.65 | 10.13 | 83.95 | .. |
| 55-59 | 77.90 | 78.10 | 77.90 | 77.70 | 10.36 | 75.05 | .. |
| 60-64 | 61.80 | 61.90 | 61.80 | 61.70 | 8.01 | 60.05 | .. |
| 65+ | 35.70 | 35.75 | 35.70 | 35.65 | 6.40 | 35.10 | .. |

Source(s): (1) STAT; (2) EPPA3; (3) ASTER.

### 2.2 Méthode(s): interpolation et extrapolation linéaires

#### 2.2.1 Hommes:

- 1950-90, interpolation et extrapolation des taux d'activité tirés de l'enquête de 1959-60 et des taux d'activité tirés des recensements de 1977 et 1988.

#### 2.2.2 Femmes:

- 1950-90, interpolation et extrapolation des taux d'activité 1950-80 tirés des EPPA3;
ajustement des taux interpolés et extrapolés sur la base des variations des taux interpolés 1977 par rapport aux taux du recensement de 1977;
modification des tendances des groupes d'âge [20-34] de 1950 à 1990.

## 3. Evaluation des taux de répartition par secteur d'activité: 1950 - 1990

### 3.1 Données de base:

Tableau 2: Répartition de la population active en % par secteur d'activité

| Année | Agriculture | Industrie Total | Manufac. | Services |
|---|---|---|---|---|
| **Hommes** | | | | |
| 1950 (1) | 96.00 | 1.20 | .. | 2.80 |
| 1960 (1) | 95.00 | 1.50 | .. | 3.50 |
| 1970 (1) | 92.40 | 2.20 | .. | 5.40 |
| 1977 (2) | 91.91 | 2.83 | 1.73 | 5.26 |
| 1980 (1) | 88.25 | 3.00 | .. | 8.75 |
| **Femmes** | | | | |
| 1950 (1) | 98.00 | 0.05 | .. | 1.95 |
| 1960 (1) | 97.50 | 0.05 | .. | 2.45 |
| 1970 (1) | 96.20 | 0.10 | .. | 3.70 |
| 1977 (2) | 97.40 | 1.39 | 1.36 | 1.21 |
| 1980 (1) | 94.15 | 0.15 | .. | 5.7 |

Source(s): (1) EPPA3; (2) ASTER.

### 3.2 Méthode(s): interpolation et extrapolation linéaires

#### 3.2.1 Hommes:
- 1950-90, interpolation et extrapolation des taux de répartition 1950-80 tirés des EPPA3 et des taux de répartition tirés du recensement de 1977; modification des tendances de tous les secteurs.

#### 3.2.2 Femmes:

Méthode, hypothèses et traitements identiques à ceux appliqués aux hommes.

## 4. Projection des taux d'activité: 2000 - 2010

### 4.1 Modèle(s): linéaire et hyperbole

#### 4.1.1 Hommes:
- A tous les groupes d'âge, application de la fonction F1;
- Modification des tendances des groupes d'âge [10-24] et [65+].

#### 4.1.2 Femmes:

- Aux groupes d'âge [10-19], application de la fonction F1;
- Aux groupes d'âge [20+], application de la fonction F3;
- Modification des tendances des groupes d'âge [20-59].

---

*Notes sur les ajustements des taux, voir p. 192-195.*          *Notes sur les fonctions de projection, voir p. 198.*

# Nigéria

## 1. Source(s) des données de base

Code(s):    Titre(s):

EPPA3      Evaluations et projections de la population active 1950-2025 - troisième édition, BIT, Genève, 1986.
ASTER      Annuaire des statistiques du travail 1945-89 - Edition rétrospective sur les recensements de population, BIT, Genève, 1990.
AST87      Annuaire des statistiques du travail 1987, BIT, Genève, 1987.
AST93      Annuaire des statistiques du travail 1993, BIT, Genève, 1993.

## 2. Evaluation des taux d'activité: 1950 - 1990

### 2.1 Données de base:

Tableau 1: Taux d'activité par sexe et par groupe d'âge

| Groupe d'âge | Année 1950 (1) | 1960 (1) | 1970 (1) | 1983 (2) |
|---|---|---|---|---|
| **Hommes** | | | | |
| 10-14 | 46.85 | 44.60 | 43.10 | 62.04 |
| 15-19 | 77.95 | 74.95 | 72.90 | 29.79 |
| 20-24 | 92.60 | 91.45 | 90.65 | 69.12 |
| 25-29 | 97.00 | 96.85 | 96.70 | 92.52 |
| 30-34 | 97.70 | 97.50 | 97.35 | 96.16 |
| 35-39 | 97.85 | 97.65 | 97.50 | 97.56 |
| 40-44 | 97.65 | 97.45 | 97.30 | 97.94 |
| 45-49 | 96.95 | 96.80 | 96.65 | 98.79 |
| 50-54 | 96.30 | 96.05 | 95.85 | 96.66 |
| 55-59 | 95.05 | 94.65 | 94.35 | 94.63 |
| 60-64 | 91.40 | 90.70 | 90.20 | 91.48 |
| 65+ | 76.95 | 75.65 | 74.75 | 73.57 |
| **Femmes** | | | | |
| 10-14 | 21.25 | 20.20 | 19.50 | 5.36 |
| 15-19 | 46.30 | 44.25 | 42.85 | 13.58 |
| 20-24 | 50.30 | 48.95 | 48.05 | 24.57 |
| 25-29 | 53.90 | 52.40 | 51.35 | 37.21 |
| 30-34 | 57.20 | 55.55 | 54.45 | 40.25 |
| 35-39 | 59.25 | 57.70 | 56.65 | 47.77 |
| 40-44 | 61.60 | 60.05 | 59.00 | 49.31 |
| 45-49 | 65.55 | 63.95 | 62.70 | 55.30 |
| 50-54 | 70.00 | 67.85 | 66.70 | 57.08 |
| 55-59 | 67.15 | 64.90 | 63.35 | 52.55 |
| 60-64 | 59.50 | 56.65 | 54.70 | 43.61 |
| 65+ | 43.85 | 40.90 | 38.95 | 20.57 |

Source(s): (1) EPPA3; (2) AST87.

### 2.2 Méthode(s): interpolation et extrapolation linéaires

#### 2.2.1 Hommes:

- 1950-90, interpolation et extrapolation des taux d'activité 1950-70 tirés des EPPA3 et des taux ajustés tirés de l'enquête de 1983; modification des tendances de tous les groupes d'âge pour 1950.

#### 2.2.2 Femmes:

- 1950-90, interpolation et extrapolation des taux d'activité 1950-70 tirés des EPPA3 et des taux ajustés tirés de l'enquête de 1983; les taux d'activité de l'enquête ont été ajustés pour les groupes d'âge [10-24].

## 3. Evaluation des taux de répartition par secteur d'activité: 1950 - 1990

### 3.1 Données de base:

Tableau 2: Répartition de la population active en % par secteur d'activité

| Année | Agriculture | Industrie Total | Manufac. | Services |
|---|---|---|---|---|
| **Hommes** | | | | |
| 1970 (1) | 71.05 | 13.00 | .. | 15.95 |
| 1983 (2) | 38.74 | 10.74 | 4.35 | 50.52 |
| 1986 (3) | 49.98 | 7.58 | 4.11 | 42.44 |
| **Femmes** | | | | |
| 1970 (1) | 70.80 | 6.25 | .. | 22.95 |
| 1983 (2) | 22.77 | 7.44 | 6.09 | 69.79 |

Source(s): (1) EPPA3; (2) AST87; (3) AST93.

### 3.2 Méthode(s): interpolation et extrapolation linéaires

#### 3.2.1 Hommes:

- 1950-70, taux de répartition 1950-70 tirés des EPPA3;
- 1980-90, interpolation et extrapolation des taux de répartition 1970 tirés des EPPA3 et de la moyenne des taux tirés des sondages de 1983 et 1986;
modification des tendances de tous les secteurs pour 1990.

#### 3.2.2 Femmes:

- 1950-70, taux de répartition 1950-70 tirés des EPPA3;
- 1980-90, interpolation et extrapolation des taux de répartition 1970 et 1983 tirés respectivement des EPPA3 et du sondage du 1983.

## 4. Projection des taux d'activité: 2000 - 2010

### 4.1 Modèle(s): linéaire et hyperbole

#### 4.1.1 Hommes:

- Aux groupes d'âge [10-19], application de la fonction F1;
- Aux groupes d'âge [20+], application de la fonction F3;
- Modification des tendances des groupes d'âge [10-14], [20-24], [40-44] et [60-64].

#### 4.1.2 Femmes:

- A tous les groupes d'âge, application de la fonction F3;
- Modification des tendances des groupes d'âge [10-34] et [45-49].

*Notes sur les ajustements des taux, voir p. 192-195.*          *Notes sur les fonctions de projection, voir p. 198.*

# Norvège

## 1. Source(s) des données de base

Code(s):    Titre(s):
EPPA3      Annuaire des statistiques du travail 1945-89 - Edition rétrospective sur les recensements de population, BIT, Genève, 1990.
STAT       Base de données sur les statistiques du travail - LABORSTA, Bureau de statistique, BIT, Genève.

## 2. Evaluation des taux d'activité: 1950 - 1990

### 2.1 Données de base:

Tableau 1: Taux d'activité par sexe et par groupe d'âge

| Groupe d'âge | Année 1979 | 1980 | 1981 | 1989 | 1990 | 1991 |
|---|---|---|---|---|---|---|
| **Hommes** | | | | | | |
| 10-14 | 0.00 | 0.00 | 0.00 | 0.00 | 0.00 | 0.00 |
| 15-19 | ... | ... | ... | 46.97 | 44.62 | 39.20 |
| 20-24 | 79.49 | 78.52 | 80.29 | 79.89 | 78.49 | 74.42 |
| 25-29 | 88.89 | 88.51 | 89.60 | 90.06 | 88.55 | 86.78 |
| 30-34 | 96.25 | 96.02 | 95.24 | 95.15 | 93.87 | 93.17 |
| 35-39 | 97.76 | 96.73 | 95.72 | 94.97 | 93.51 | 94.12 |
| 40-44 | 96.23 | 96.73 | 96.79 | 94.44 | 93.98 | 93.83 |
| 45-49 | 94.00 | 93.62 | 95.15 | 93.80 | 93.94 | 92.57 |
| 50-54 | 90.91 | 92.63 | 93.67 | 90.53 | 89.22 | 87.13 |
| 55-59 | 88.70 | 86.63 | 87.71 | 83.16 | 82.02 | 81.18 |
| 60-64 | 74.07 | 75.74 | 73.67 | 64.95 | 64.21 | 62.24 |
| 65+ | | | | 14.84 | 13.29 | 11.62 |
| **Femmes** | | | | | | |
| 10-14 | .. | .. | .. | 0.00 | 0.00 | 0.00 |
| 15-19 | .. | .. | .. | 46.03 | 43.55 | 40.83 |
| 20-24 | .. | .. | .. | 70.30 | 67.07 | 66.46 |
| 25-29 | .. | .. | .. | 75.50 | 75.00 | 73.46 |
| 30-34 | .. | .. | .. | 76.92 | 78.21 | 79.74 |
| 35-39 | .. | .. | .. | 82.00 | 81.05 | 80.89 |
| 40-44 | .. | .. | .. | 81.05 | 81.94 | 83.22 |
| 45-49 | .. | .. | .. | 81.97 | 83.46 | 81.34 |
| 50-54 | .. | .. | .. | 75.79 | 74.49 | 75.00 |
| 55-59 | .. | .. | .. | 63.16 | 61.96 | 63.04 |
| 60-64 | .. | .. | .. | 44.12 | 46.53 | 47.47 |
| 65+ | .. | .. | .. | 6.44 | 6.43 | 5.92 |

Source(s): STAT.

### 2.2 Méthode(s): interpolation linéaire / moyenne arithmétique

**2.2.1 Hommes:**
- 1950-70, taux d'activité 1950-70 tirés des EPPA3;
- 1980, interpolation des taux d'activité ajustés tirés des enquêtes de 1980, 1981 et 1982;
ajustement du taux d'activité du groupe d'âge [15-19];
- 1990, moyennes des taux d'activité ajustés tirés des enquêtes de 1989, 1990 et 1991;
ajustement du taux d'activité du groupe d'âge [15-19].

**2.2.2 Femmes:**
- 1950-80, taux d'activité 1950-80 tirés des EPPA3;
- 1990, moyennes des taux d'activité ajustés tirés des enquêtes de 1989, 1990 et 1991;
ajustement du taux d'activité du groupe d'âge [15-19].

## 3. Evaluation des taux de répartition par secteur d'activité: 1950 - 1990

### 3.1 Données de base:

Tableau 2: Répartition de la population active en % par secteur d'activité

| Année | Agriculture | Industrie Total | Manufac. | Services |
|---|---|---|---|---|
| **Hommes** | | | | |
| 1979 | 10.04 | 41.23 | 21.43 | 48.73 |
| 1980 | 9.98 | 40.11 | 20.14 | 49.91 |
| 1981 | 9.86 | 40.31 | 19.72 | 49.83 |
| 1989 | 8.45 | 36.38 | 19.30 | 55.17 |
| 1990 | 8.03 | 37.16 | 19.44 | 54.81 |
| 1991 | 8.27 | 35.77 | 19.67 | 55.96 |
| **Femmes** | | | | |
| 1979 | 6.46 | 14.10 | 11.20 | 79.45 |
| 1980 | 5.98 | 13.74 | 9.92 | 80.28 |
| 1981 | 5.81 | 12.98 | 9.77 | 81.21 |
| 1989 | 4.05 | 11.82 | 8.41 | 84.13 |
| 1990 | 3.73 | 11.67 | 8.21 | 84.60 |
| 1991 | 3.84 | 11.42 | 8.43 | 84.74 |

Source(s): STAT.

### 3.2 Méthode(s): moyenne arithmétique

**3.2.1 Hommes:**
- 1950-70, taux de répartition 1950-70 tirés des EPPA3;
- 1980, moyennes des taux de répartition ajustés tirés des enquêtes de 1979, 1980 et 1981;
ajustement des taux de répartition pour tenir compte des militaires du contingent
- 1990, moyennes des taux de répartition tirés des enquêtes de 1989, 1990 et 1991.

**3.2.2 Femmes:**
- 1950-70, taux de répartition 1950-70 tirés des EPPA3;
- 1980, moyennes des taux de répartition tirés des enquêtes de 1979, 1980 et 1981;
- 1990, moyennes des taux de répartition tirés des enquêtes de 1989, 1990 et 1991.

## 4. Projection des taux d'activité: 2000 - 2010

### 4.1 Modèle(s): hyperbole et logistique

**4.1.1 Hommes:**
- Aux groupes d'âge [15+], application de la fonction F3;
- Modification des tendances des groupes d'âge [25-49].

**4.1.2 Femmes:**
- Aux groupes d'âge [15-64], application de la fonction F6;
- Au groupe d'âge [65+], application de la fonction F3;
- Modification des tendances des groupes d'âge [15-24].

# Nouvelle-Zélande

## 1. Source(s) des données de base

| Code(s): | Titre(s): |
|---|---|
| EPPA3 | Annuaire des statistiques du travail 1945-89 - Edition rétrospective sur les recensements de population, BIT, Genève, 1990. |
| STAT | Base de données sur les statistiques du travail - LABORSTA, Bureau de statistique, BIT, Genève. |

## 2. Evaluation des taux d'activité: 1950 - 1990

### 2.1 Données de base:

Tableau 1: Taux d'activité par sexe et par groupe d'âge

| Groupe d'âge | Année | | | |
|---|---|---|---|---|
| | 1980 (1) | 1989 (2) | 1990 (2) | 1991 (2) |
| **Hommes** | | | | |
| 10-14 | 0.00 | 0.00 | 0.00 | 0.00 |
| 15-19 | 55.65 | 55.81 | 56.09 | 53.79 |
| 20-24 | 89.80 | 86.02 | 84.46 | 82.90 |
| 25-29 | 95.65 | 94.23 | 92.25 | 92.43 |
| 30-34 | 96.90 | 94.98 | 93.02 | 93.86 |
| 35-39 | 97.10 | 94.97 | 93.64 | 94.50 |
| 40-44 | 97.10 | 94.95 | 94.02 | 94.98 |
| 45-49 | 96.30 | 93.33 | 92.73 | 93.17 |
| 50-54 | 94.35 | 91.94 | 90.18 | 91.14 |
| 55-59 | 88.10 | 78.13 | 78.39 | 80.67 |
| 60-64 | 48.50 | 33.76 | 35.34 | 33.19 |
| 65+ | 12.30 | 10.60 | 10.94 | 9.42 |
| **Femmes** | | | | |
| 10-14 | 0.00 | 0.00 | 0.00 | 0.00 |
| 15-19 | 48.80 | 49.38 | 56.68 | 52.22 |
| 20-24 | 62.50 | 69.46 | 69.81 | 71.70 |
| 25-29 | 41.30 | 61.25 | 61.80 | 61.62 |
| 30-34 | 39.70 | 60.49 | 61.54 | 63.05 |
| 35-39 | 49.10 | 72.86 | 71.58 | 72.54 |
| 40-44 | 54.10 | 77.92 | 78.45 | 79.38 |
| 45-49 | 51.80 | 75.78 | 77.32 | 77.73 |
| 50-54 | 43.35 | 69.80 | 69.54 | 69.08 |
| 55-59 | 30.55 | 47.05 | 44.56 | 47.46 |
| 60-64 | 12.40 | 14.41 | 17.34 | 15.48 |
| 65+ | 2.10 | 3.53 | 3.60 | 3.29 |

Source(s): (1) EPPA3; (2) STAT.

### 2.2 Méthode(s): moyenne arithmétique

#### 2.2.1 Hommes:

- 1950-80, taux d'activité 1950-80 tirés des EPPA3;
ajustement du taux d'activité du groupe d'âge [14-19] pour 1980;
- 1990, moyennes des taux d'activité tirés des enquêtes de 1989, 1990 et 1991.

#### 2.2.2 Femmes:

Méthode, hypothèses et traitements identiques à ceux appliqués aux hommes.

## 3. Evaluation des taux de répartition par secteur d'activité: 1950 - 1990

### 3.1 Données de base:

Tableau 2: Répartition de la population active en % par secteur d'activité

| Année | Agriculture | Industrie | | Services |
|---|---|---|---|---|
| | | Total | Manufac. | |
| **Hommes** | | | | |
| 1980 | 13.40 | 39.23 | 26.89 | 47.37 |
| 1991 | 12.59 | 32.32 | 20.81 | 55.09 |
| **Femmes** | | | | |
| 1980 | 6.19 | 21.75 | 19.95 | 72.06 |
| 1991 | 7.42 | 13.43 | 11.61 | 79.15 |

Source(s): STAT.

### 3.2 Méthode(s): moyenne pondérée

#### 3.2.1 Hommes:

- 1950-80, taux de répartition 1950-80 tirés des EPPA3;
- 1990, moyennes pondérées des taux de répartition tirés des enquêtes de 1980 et 1991.

#### 3.2.2 Femmes:

Méthode, hypothèses et traitements identiques à ceux appliqués aux hommes.

## 4. Projection des taux d'activité: 2000 - 2010

### 4.1 Modèle(s): linéaire, hyperbole et logistique

#### 4.1.1 Hommes:

- Au groupe d'âge [15-19], application de la fonction F1;
- Aux groupes d'âge [20+], application de la fonction F3;
- Modification des tendances des groupes d'âge [20-24] et [30-49].

#### 4.1.2 Femmes:

- Aux groupes d'âge [15-24], application de la fonction F1;
- Aux groupes d'âge [25-64], application de la fonction F6;
- Au groupe d'âge [65+], application de la fonction F3.

*Notes sur les ajustements des taux, voir p. 192-195.*

*Notes sur les fonctions de projection, voir p. 198.*

# Oman

## 1. Source(s) des données de base

Code(s):     Titre(s):

EPPA3       Evaluations et projections de la population active 1950-2025 - troisième édition, BIT, Genève, 1986.

## 2. Evaluation des taux d'activité: 1950 - 1990

### 2.1 Données de base:

Tableau 1: Taux d'activité par sexe et par groupe d'âge

| Groupe d'âge | Année | | | |
|---|---|---|---|---|
| | 1950 | 1960 | 1970 | 1980 |
| **Hommes** | | | | |
| 10-14 | 27.00 | 22.00 | 17.00 | 9.00 |
| 15-19 | 87.40 | 73.70 | 60.00 | 46.30 |
| 20-24 | 96.20 | 95.95 | 95.65 | 95.40 |
| 25-29 | 99.20 | 99.25 | 99.25 | 99.30 |
| 30-34 | 99.20 | 99.15 | 99.05 | 99.00 |
| 35-39 | 99.20 | 99.05 | 98.85 | 98.70 |
| 40-44 | 98.20 | 98.00 | 97.80 | 97.60 |
| 45-49 | 97.00 | 96.55 | 96.15 | 95.70 |
| 50-54 | 94.50 | 93.45 | 92.45 | 91.40 |
| 55-59 | 91.00 | 89.35 | 87.75 | 86.10 |
| 60-64 | 80.55 | 78.55 | 76.60 | 74.60 |
| 65+ | 63.00 | 60.10 | 57.20 | 54.30 |
| **Femmes** | | | | |
| 10-14 | 1.00 | 1.35 | 1.70 | 2.05 |
| 15-19 | 2.00 | 2.70 | 3.40 | 4.10 |
| 20-24 | 2.60 | 3.95 | 5.35 | 6.70 |
| 25-29 | 3.00 | 5.50 | 7.90 | 10.30 |
| 30-34 | 3.20 | 5.95 | 8.65 | 11.40 |
| 35-39 | 3.45 | 5.65 | 7.85 | 10.10 |
| 40-44 | 3.55 | 5.15 | 6.80 | 8.40 |
| 45-49 | 3.55 | 4.80 | 6.10 | 7.40 |
| 50-54 | 2.80 | 4.00 | 5.20 | 6.40 |
| 55-59 | 2.70 | 3.40 | 4.10 | 4.80 |
| 60-64 | 2.60 | 2.95 | 3.25 | 3.60 |
| 65+ | 2.50 | 2.65 | 2.75 | 2.90 |

Source(s): EPPA3.

### 2.2 Méthode(s): extrapolation linéaire

#### 2.2.1 Hommes:

- 1950-80, taux d'activité 1950-80 tirés des EPPA3;
- 1990, extrapolation des taux d'activité 1950-80 tirés des EPPA3;
modification des tendances de tous les groupes d'âge.

#### 2.2.2 Femmes:

Méthode, hypothèses et traitements identiques à ceux appliqués aux hommes.

## 3. Evaluation des taux de répartition par secteur d'activité: 1950 - 1990

### 3.1 Données de base:

Tableau 2: Répartition de la population active en % par secteur d'activité

| Année | Agriculture | Industrie | | Services |
|---|---|---|---|---|
| | | Total | Manufac. | |
| **Hommes** | | | | |
| 1950 | 77.00 | 8.50 | .. | 14.50 |
| 1960 | 68.50 | 12.00 | .. | 19.50 |
| 1970 | 58.50 | 17.00 | .. | 24.50 |
| 1980 | 52.00 | 21.00 | .. | 27.00 |
| **Femmes** | | | | |
| 1950 | 55.00 | 15.00 | .. | 30.00 |
| 1960 | 43.00 | 20.00 | .. | 37.00 |
| 1970 | 33.00 | 27.00 | .. | 40.00 |
| 1980 | 25.00 | 33.00 | .. | 42.00 |

Source(s): EPPA3.

### 3.2 Méthode(s): extrapolation linéaire

#### 3.2.1 Hommes:

- 1950-80, taux de répartition 1950-80 tirés des EPPA3;
- 1990, extrapolation des taux de répartition 1950-80 tirés des EPPA3;
modification des tendances de tous les taux de répartition.

#### 3.2.2 Femmes:

Méthode, hypothèses et traitements identiques à ceux appliqués aux hommes.

## 4. Projection des taux d'activité: 2000 - 2010

### 4.1 Modèle(s): linéaire, log-linéaire et hyperbole

#### 4.1.1 Hommes:

- Aux groupes d'âge [15-19] et [25-64], application de la fonction F3;
- Au groupe d'âge [20-24], application de la fonction F2;
- Au groupe d'âge [65+], application de la fonction F1;
- Modification des tendances des groupes d'âge [15-34].

#### 4.1.2 Femmes:

- Aux groupes d'âge [15-19] et [65+], application de la fonction F1;
- Aux groupes d'âge [20-64], application de la fonction F2;
- Modification des tendances de tous les groupes d'âge.

*Notes sur les ajustements des taux, voir p. 192-195.*     *Notes sur les fonctions de projection, voir p. 198.*

# Ouganda

## 1. Source(s) des données de base

Code(s):  Titre(s):

EPPA3  Evaluations et projections de la population active 1950-2025 - troisième édition, BIT, Genève, 1986.

## 2. Evaluation des taux d'activité: 1950 - 1990

### 2.1 Données de base:

Tableau 1: Taux d'activité par sexe et par groupe d'âge

| Groupe d'âge | Année 1950 | 1960 | 1970 | 1980 |
|---|---|---|---|---|
| **Hommes** | | | | |
| 10-14 | 54.40 | 53.45 | 51.75 | 49.95 |
| 15-19 | 87.95 | 86.70 | 84.45 | 82.05 |
| 20-24 | 96.40 | 95.95 | 95.10 | 94.15 |
| 25-29 | 97.55 | 97.50 | 97.35 | 97.25 |
| 30-34 | 98.30 | 98.25 | 98.10 | 97.95 |
| 35-39 | 98.50 | 98.45 | 98.25 | 98.10 |
| 40-44 | 98.35 | 98.25 | 98.10 | 97.95 |
| 45-49 | 97.55 | 97.50 | 97.35 | 97.20 |
| 50-54 | 97.20 | 97.10 | 96.90 | 96.70 |
| 55-59 | 96.50 | 96.35 | 96.00 | 95.65 |
| 60-64 | 93.90 | 93.55 | 93.00 | 92.45 |
| 65+ | 81.25 | 80.70 | 79.75 | 78.70 |
| **Femmes** | | | | |
| 10-14 | 41.10 | 40.40 | 39.10 | 37.75 |
| 15-19 | 66.55 | 65.50 | 63.60 | 61.55 |
| 20-24 | 65.80 | 65.10 | 63.90 | 62.65 |
| 25-29 | 71.00 | 70.25 | 68.85 | 67.40 |
| 30-34 | 75.45 | 74.65 | 73.20 | 71.65 |
| 35-39 | 76.55 | 75.80 | 74.45 | 73.00 |
| 40-44 | 79.00 | 78.25 | 76.90 | 75.40 |
| 45-49 | 78.55 | 77.80 | 76.40 | 74.90 |
| 50-54 | 77.16 | 76.55 | 74.95 | 73.20 |
| 55-59 | 74.75 | 73.85 | 72.15 | 70.35 |
| 60-64 | 69.35 | 68.20 | 66.05 | 63.75 |
| 65+ | 49.10 | 48.00 | 46.00 | 43.90 |

Source(s): EPPA3.

### 2.2 Méthode(s): interpolation et extrapolation linéaires

#### 2.2.1 Hommes:

- 1950-80, taux d'activité 1950-80 tirés des EPPA3;
- 1990, extrapolation des taux d'activité 1950-80 tirés des EPPA3; ajustement des taux extrapolés sur la base des variations des taux interpolés 1980 par rapport aux taux 1980 tirés des EPPA3.

#### 2.2.2 Femmes:

- 1950-90, interpolation et extrapolation des taux d'activité ajustés 1950 et 1980 tirés des EPPA3.

## 3. Evaluation des taux de répartition par secteur d'activité: 1950 - 1990

### 3.1 Données de base:

Tableau 2: Répartition de la population active en % par secteur d'activité

| Année | Agriculture | Industrie Total | Manufac. | Services |
|---|---|---|---|---|
| **Hommes** | | | | |
| 1950 | 91.80 | 3.15 | .. | 5.05 |
| 1960 | 90.10 | 3.80 | .. | 6.10 |
| 1970 | 87.00 | 5.00 | .. | 8.00 |
| 1980 | 83.70 | 6.30 | .. | 10.00 |
| **Femmes** | | | | |
| 1950 | 97.85 | 0.36 | .. | 1.79 |
| 1960 | 95.49 | 0.76 | .. | 3.75 |
| 1970 | 93.13 | 1.16 | .. | 5.71 |
| 1980 | 90.77 | 1.56 | .. | 7.67 |

Source(s): EPPA3.

### 3.2 Méthode(s): interpolation et extrapolation linéaires

#### 3.2.1 Hommes:

- 1950-80, taux de répartition 1950-80 tirés des EPPA3;
- 1990, extrapolation des taux de répartition 1950-80 tirés des EPPA3; ajustement des taux extrapolés sur la base des variations des taux interpolés 1980 par rapport aux taux de répartition 1980 tirés des EPPA3;
- Application du rapport manufacture/industrie estimé pour le Rwanda.

#### 3.2.2 Femmes:

- 1950-90, interpolation extrapolation des taux de répartition ajustés 1950 et 1980 tirés des EPPA3; ajustement des taux de répartition sur la base du rapport hommes/femmes égal à 1 dans l'agriculture; les taux de répartition de manufacture ont été estimés sur la base du rapport manufacture/industrie estimé pour le Rwanda.

## 4. Projection des taux d'activité: 2000 - 2010

### 4.1 Modèle(s): linéaire et hyperbole

#### 4.1.1 Hommes:

- A tous les groupes d'âge, application de la fonction F1;
- Modification des tendances des groupes d'âge [10-14] et [20-24].

#### 4.1.2 Femmes:

- Aux groupes d'âge [10-19], application de la fonction F1;
- Aux groupes d'âge [20+], application de la fonction F3;
- Modification des tendances des groupes d'âge [20-54].

*Notes sur les ajustements des taux, voir p. 192-195.*   *Notes sur les fonctions de projection, voir p. 198.*

# Ouzbékistan

## 1. Source(s) des données de base

Code(s):    Titre(s):

BLT-94-2    Vorobiev A. (1994), "Estimation de la population active pour les quinze pays de l'ex-URSS pour les années 1950, 1959, 1970, 1979 et 1989", dans le Bulletin des statistiques du travail - 1994-2, BIT, Genève.

## 2. Evaluation des taux d'activité: 1950 - 1990

### 2.1 Données de base:

Tableau 1: Taux d'activité par sexe et par groupe d'âge

| | | Année | | | | |
|---|---|---|---|---|---|---|
| | Groupe d'âge | 1950 | 1959 | 1970 | 1979 | 1989 |
| **Hommes** | | | | | | |
| | 10-14 | 0.00 | 0.00 | 0.00 | 0.00 | 0.00 |
| | 15-19 | 53.02 | 52.08 | 37.13 | 37.18 | 28.81 |
| | 20-24 | 81.94 | 82.34 | 80.50 | 84.52 | 80.02 |
| | 25-29 | 94.80 | 95.99 | 94.75 | 97.00 | 95.96 |
| | 30-34 | 95.62 | 95.77 | 97.50 | 98.42 | 97.84 |
| | 35-39 | 95.57 | 96.13 | 98.46 | 98.54 | 97.82 |
| | 40-44 | 94.19 | 93.28 | 96.13 | 98.10 | 97.55 |
| | 45-49 | 91.45 | 92.20 | 97.56 | 97.36 | 96.23 |
| | 50-54 | 88.11 | 89.93 | 90.57 | 93.21 | 92.57 |
| | 55-59 | 83.33 | 86.36 | 82.54 | 82.17 | 84.59 |
| | 60-64 | 71.13 | 72.36 | 45.19 | 30.21 | 34.72 |
| | 65+ | 30.91 | 29.25 | 10.33 | 6.97 | 10.60 |
| **Femmes** | | | | | | |
| | 10-14 | 0.00 | 0.00 | 0.00 | 0.00 | 0.00 |
| | 15-19 | 50.76 | 56.86 | 42.55 | 41.42 | 32.53 |
| | 20-24 | 72.22 | 78.79 | 78.67 | 86.41 | 75.60 |
| | 25-29 | 68.56 | 67.62 | 86.99 | 93.03 | 81.12 |
| | 30-34 | 67.19 | 67.61 | 83.72 | 93.23 | 83.33 |
| | 35-39 | 68.18 | 69.51 | 88.24 | 93.29 | 85.49 |
| | 40-44 | 59.04 | 62.92 | 84.29 | 92.96 | 85.31 |
| | 45-49 | 53.21 | 54.40 | 80.89 | 90.42 | 81.49 |
| | 50-54 | 40.66 | 41.67 | 97.86 | 68.46 | 52.44 |
| | 55-59 | 26.58 | 25.96 | 27.23 | 24.77 | 20.95 |
| | 60-64 | 13.74 | 11.98 | 9.14 | 8.00 | 11.57 |
| | 65+ | 4.64 | 4.56 | 2.80 | 2.04 | 3.65 |

Source(s): BLT-94-2-2

### 2.2 Méthode(s): moyenne pondérée

#### 2.2.1 Hommes:

- 1950-90, moyennes pondérées des taux d'activité 1950, 1959, 1970 et 1989 tirés du Bulletin des statistiques du travail, 1994-2.

#### 2.2.2 Femmes:

Méthode, hypothèses et traitements identiques à ceux appliqués aux hommes.

## 3. Evaluation des taux de répartition par secteur d'activité: 1950 - 1990

### 3.1 Données de base:

Tableau 2: Répartition de la population active en % par secteur d'activité

| | Agriculture | Industrie | | Services |
|---|---|---|---|---|
| Année | | Total | Manufac. | |
| **Hommes** | | | | |
| 1950 | 70.22 | 12.57 | 11.13 | 17.21 |
| 1959 | 53.44 | 20.23 | 9.21 | 26.34 |
| 1970 | 38.72 | 28.36 | 14.79 | 32.93 |
| 1979 | 34.60 | 34.44 | 12.76 | 30.96 |
| 1989 | 34.49 | 30.67 | 12.11 | 34.84 |
| **Femmes** | | | | |
| 1950 | 73.71 | 10.26 | 9.58 | 16.03 |
| 1959 | 65.99 | 13.16 | 9.80 | 20.85 |
| 1970 | 50.57 | 17.32 | 12.83 | 32.12 |
| 1979 | 47.01 | 18.68 | 11.50 | 34.31 |
| 1989 | 36.98 | 19.19 | 12.51 | 43.83 |

Source(s): BLT-94-2.

### 3.2 Méthode(s): moyenne pondérée

#### 3.2.1 Hommes:

- 1950-90, moyennes pondérées des taux de répartition 1950, 1959, 1970, 1979 et 1989 tirés du Bulletin des statistiques du travail - 1994-2.

#### 3.2.2 Femmes:

Méthode, hypothèses et traitements identiques à ceux appliqués aux hommes.

## 4. Projection des taux d'activité: 2000 - 2010

### 4.1 Modèle(s): linéaire, log-linéaire, hyperbole et logistique

#### 4.1.1 Hommes:

- Aux groupes d'âge [15-24] et [55+], application de la fonction F3;
- Aux groupes d'âge [25-54], application de la fonction F1;
- Modification des tendances des groupes d'âge [25-64].

#### 4.1.2 Femmes:

- Au groupe d'âge [15-19], application de la fonction F2;
- Aux groupes d'âge [20-24] et [55+], application de la fonction F3;
- Aux groupes d'âge [25-54], application de la fonction F6;
- Modification des tendances des groupes d'âge [20-59].

---

*Notes sur les ajustements des taux, voir p. 192-195.*

*Notes sur les fonctions de projection, voir p. 198.*

# Pakistan

## 1. Source(s) des données de base

Code(s):    Titre(s):

EPPA3    Evaluations et projections de la population active 1950-2025 - troisième édition, BIT, Genève, 1986.
STAT    Base de données sur les statistiques du travail - LABORSTA, Bureau de statistique, BIT, Genève.

## 2. Evaluation des taux d'activité: 1950 - 1990

### 2.1 Données de base:

Tableau 1: Taux d'activité par sexe et par groupe d'âge

| | Année | | | | | | |
| Groupe d'âge | 1950 | 1960 | 1970 | 1978 | 1981 | 1990 | 1991 |
|---|---|---|---|---|---|---|---|
| **Hommes** | | | | | | | |
| 10-14 | 45.05 | 38.90 | 31.10 | 29.49 | 30.90 | 26.60 | 19.20 |
| 15-19 | 84.65 | 78.80 | 71.25 | 64.60 | 67.70 | 59.40 | 55.20 |
| 20-24 | 93.50 | 90.80 | 90.25 | 88.40 | 88.20 | 86.90 | 87.70 |
| 25-29 | 97.65 | 97.15 | 96.55 | 96.20 | 96.00 | 97.30 | 97.70 |
| 30-34 | 97.70 | 97.50 | 97.30 | 97.94 | 97.10 | 98.80 | 97.80 |
| 35-39 | 97.90 | 97.75 | 97.60 | 98.24 | 97.40 | 98.70 | 97.90 |
| 40-44 | 97.50 | 97.35 | 97.15 | 97.84 | 97.00 | 97.80 | 98.20 |
| 45-49 | 97.25 | 97.15 | 97.00 | 97.50 | 96.80 | 97.40 | 97.60 |
| 50-54 | 96.00 | 95.55 | 95.10 | 95.70 | 94.50 | 94.10 | 94.80 |
| 55-59 | 95.50 | 94.40 | 93.25 | 92.10 | 91.80 | 91.20 | 90.40 |
| 60-64 | 89.70 | 87.45 | 95.20 | 86.70 | 82.30 | 81.00 | 78.50 |
| 65+ | 80.25 | 75.15 | 67.40 | 59.70 | 56.90 | 55.70 | 52.03 |
| **Femmes** | | | | | | | |
| 10-14 | 7.05 | 5.70 | 4.45 | .. | 6.30 | .. | 6.90 |
| 15-19 | 7.65 | 7.45 | 7.25 | .. | 12.10 | .. | 13.10 |
| 20-24 | 7.95 | 8.50 | 9.15 | .. | 12.90 | .. | 14.00 |
| 25-29 | 9.60 | 10.05 | 10.40 | .. | 14.00 | .. | 13.20 |
| 30-34 | 10.75 | 11.25 | 11.65 | .. | 15.70 | .. | 14.10 |
| 35-39 | 9.45 | 9.90 | 10.25 | .. | 13.80 | .. | 13.90 |
| 40-44 | 9.60 | 10.05 | 10.40 | .. | 14.00 | .. | 17.50 |
| 45-49 | 10.95 | 11.05 | 11.15 | .. | 12.70 | .. | 17.80 |
| 50-54 | 10.40 | 10.50 | 10.60 | .. | 11.70 | .. | 16.50 |
| 55-59 | 10.00 | 10.15 | 10.30 | .. | 12.40 | .. | 13.90 |
| 60-64 | 8.20 | 7.95 | 7.60 | .. | 7.40 | .. | 10.70 |
| 65+ | 6.45 | 5.55 | 4.55 | .. | 5.40 | .. | 7.40 |

Source(s): STAT.

### 2.2 Méthode(s): interpolation linéaire

#### 2.2.1 Hommes:

- 1950-90, interpolation des taux d'activité 1950-70 tirés des EPPA3
et des enquêtes de 1978 à 1992.

#### 2.2.2 Femmes:

- 1950-70, taux d'activité ajustés 1950-70 tirés des EPPA3;
ajustement des taux sur la base du modèle d'ajustement des taux d'activité
des femmes travaillant dans l'agriculture comme aides familiales;
- 1980-90, interpolation des taux d'activité tirés des enquêtes
de 1981 et 1991;
ajustement des taux en tenant compte de la sous-énumération
des femmes travaillant dans l'agriculture.

## 3. Evaluation des taux de répartition par secteur d'activité: 1950 - 1990

### 3.1 Données de base:

Tableau 2: Répartition de la population active en % par secteur d'activité

| | | Agriculture | Industrie | | Services |
| Année | | | Total | Manufac. | |
|---|---|---|---|---|---|
| **Hommes** | | | | | |
| | 1981 | 55.98 | 14.94 | 9.40 | 29.08 |
| | 1982 | 44.80 | 20.59 | 12.08 | 34.61 |
| **Femmes** | | | | | |
| | 1981 | 41.18 | 19.02 | 15.98 | 39.80 |
| | 1982 | 66.02 | 14.69 | 13.33 | 19.29 |

Source(s): STAT.

### 3.2 Méthode(s): interpolation et extrapolation linéaires

#### 3.2.1 Hommes:

- 1950-80, taux de répartition 1950-80 tirés des EPPA3;
- 1990, extrapolation des taux de répartition tirés de l'enquête
de 1981 et des estimations officielles de 1991;
modification des tendances de tous les secteurs.

#### 3.2.2 Femmes:

- 1950-70, taux de répartition ajustés 1950-70 tirés des EPPA3;
- 1980-90, interpolation et extrapolation des taux de répartition
tirés de l'enquête de 1981 et des évaluations officielles de 1991;
ajustement des taux des taux de répartition 1950-90 en tenant compte
de la sous-énumération des femmes travaillant dans l'agriculture.

## 4. Projection des taux d'activité: 2000 - 2010

### 4.1 Modèle(s): linéaire, hyperbole et logistique

#### 4.1.1 Hommes:

- Au groupe d'âge [10-14], application de la fonction F1;
- Aux groupes d'âge [15+], application de la fonction F3;
- Modification des tendances des groupes d'âge [10-14] et [30-49].

#### 4.1.2 Femmes:

- Aux groupes d'âge [10-19] et [60+], application de la fonction F1;
- Aux groupes d'âge [20-59], application de la fonction F6;
- Modification des tendances des groupes d'âge [10-19] et [65+].

*Notes sur les ajustements des taux, voir p. 192-195.*

*Notes sur les fonctions de projection, voir p. 198.*

# Panama

## 1. Source(s) des données de base

| Code(s): | Titre(s): |
|---|---|
| EPPA3 | Evaluations et projections de la population active 1950-2025 - troisième édition, BIT, Genève, 1986. |
| STAT | Base de données sur les statistiques du travail - LABORSTA, Bureau de statistique, BIT, Genève. |
| PAN90 | Censos Nacionales de Poblacion y Vivienda, 13 de mayo 1990, Dirección de Estadística y Censo, Controloria General de la República, Panamá. |

## 2. Evaluation des taux d'activité: 1950 - 1990

### 2.1 Données de base:

Tableau 1: Taux d'activité par sexe et par groupe d'âge

| Groupe d'âge | Année 1979 | 1980 | 1985 | 1989 | 1990 | 1991 |
|---|---|---|---|---|---|---|
| **Hommes** | | | | | | |
| 10-14 | .. | .. | .. | ... | 6.49 | ... |
| 15-19 | .. | .. | .. | 46.91 | 42.69 | 45.11 |
| 20-24 | .. | .. | .. | 85.75 | 80.31 | 82.32 |
| 25-29 | .. | .. | .. | 95.82 | 91.39 | 94.93 |
| 30-39 | .. | .. | .. | 96.99 | 94.50 | 96.95 |
| 40-49 | .. | .. | .. | 96.21 | 93.99 | 96.31 |
| 50-59 | .. | .. | .. | 88.93 | 84.89 | 83.65 |
| 60-64 | .. | .. | .. | 43.40 | 47.33 | 42.09 |
| 65+ | .. | .. | .. | ... | ... | ... |
| **Femmes** | | | | | | |
| 10-14 | ... | 2.58 | ... | ... | 2.48 | ... |
| 15-19 | 19.98 | 16.78 | 19.12 | 21.17 | 18.88 | 21.69 |
| 20-24 | 49.49 | 38.29 | 42.44 | 45.71 | 34.66 | 45.70 |
| 25-29 | 50.44 | 41.63 | 50.61 | 52.42 | 40.84 | 51.65 |
| 30-39 | 46.18 | 39.25 | 52.02 | 54.51 | 46.65 | 55.19 |
| 40-49 | 38.54 | 33.28 | 43.06 | 49.75 | 42.36 | 50.90 |
| 50-59 | 24.41 | 19.17 | 24.95 | 25.94 | 23.90 | 25.00 |
| 60-64 | 11.95 | 23.01 | 12.41 | 8.04 | 7.47 | 7.79 |
| 65+ | ... | | | ... | ... | ... |

Source(s): STAT.

### 2.2 Méthode(s): interpolation linéaire
moyenne arithmétique

#### 2.2.1 Hommes:

- 1950-80, taux d'activité 1950-80 tirés des EPPA3;
- 1990, moyennes des taux d'activité ajustés tirés des enquêtes de 1989 et 1991;
pour le groupe d'âge [10-14], taux d'activité tiré du recensement de 1990.

#### 2.2.2 Femmes:

- 1950-70, taux d'activité 1950-70 tirés des EPPA3;
- 1980-90, interpolation des taux d'activité ajustés tirés des enquêtes de 1979, 1985, 1989 et 1991;
pour le groupe d'âge [10-14], taux d'activité tirés des recensements de 1980 et 1990.

## 3. Evaluation des taux de répartition par secteur d'activité: 1950 - 1990

### 3.1 Données de base:

Tableau 2: Répartition de la population active en % par secteur d'activité

| Année | Agriculture | Industrie Total | Manufac. | Services |
|---|---|---|---|---|
| **Hommes** | | | | |
| 1980 | 39.31 | 22.43 | 11.92 | 38.26 |
| 1989 | 39.23 | 19.03 | 11.27 | 41.74 |
| 1991 | 35.08 | 17.78 | 10.14 | 47.13 |
| **Femmes** | | | | |
| 1979 | 4.61 | 12.49 | 11.26 | 82.90 |
| 1985 | 4.53 | 12.34 | 10.70 | 83.13 |
| 1989 | 4.08 | 11.30 | 9.82 | 84.61 |
| 1991 | 2.43 | 10.98 | 9.97 | 86.59 |

Source(s): STAT.

### 3.2 Méthode(s): interpolation et extrapolation linéaires
moyenne arithmétique

#### 3.2.1 Hommes:

- 1950-70, taux de répartition 1950-70 tirés des EPPA3;
- 1980, interpolation des taux de répartition tirés du recensement de 1980 et de l'estimation pour 1990;
- 1990, moyennes des taux de répartition tirés des enquêtes de 1989, et 1991.

#### 3.2.2 Femmes:

- 1950-70, taux de répartition 1950-70 tirés des EPPA3;
- 1980-90, interpolation des taux de répartition tirés des enquêtes de 1979, 1985, 1989 et 1991.

## 4. Projection des taux d'activité: 2000 - 2010

### 4.1 Modèle(s): linéaire, log-linéaire, hyperbole et logistique

#### 4.1.1 Hommes:

- Aux groupes d'âge [10-19], application de la fonction F1;
- Aux groupes d'âge [20-59], application de la fonction F3;
- Aux groupes d'âge [60+], application de la fonction F2;
- Modification des tendances des groupes d'âge [10-19].

#### 4.1.2 Femmes:

- Aux groupes d'âge [10-59], application de la fonction F6;
- Au groupe d'âge [60-64], application de la fonction F1;
- Au groupe d'âge [65+], application de la fonction F3;
- Modification des tendances des groupes d'âge [20-24] et [60-64].

*Notes sur les ajustements des taux, voir p. 192-195.*

*Notes sur les fonctions de projection, voir p. 198.*

# Papouasie-Nouvelle-Guinée

## 1. Source(s) des données de base

Code(s):     Titre(s):

EPPA3       Annuaire des statistiques du travail 1945-89 - Edition rétrospective sur les recensements de population, BIT, Genève, 1990.
STAT        Base de données sur les statistiques du travail - LABORSTA, Bureau de statistique, BIT, Genève.

## 2. Evaluation des taux d'activité: 1950 - 1990

### 2.1 Données de base:

Tableau 1: Taux d'activité par sexe et par groupe d'âge

| Groupe d'âge | Année 1950 (1) | 1960 (1) | 1970 (1) | 1980 (2) |
|---|---|---|---|---|
| **Hommes** | | | | |
| 10-14 | 48.20 | 46.05 | 43.15 | 9.17 |
| 15-19 | 81.20 | 78.25 | 74.25 | 35.45 |
| 20-24 | 97.00 | 95.80 | 95.24 | 59.21 |
| 25-29 | 98.25 | 98.10 | 98.05 | 64.07 |
| 30-34 | 98.50 | 98.30 | 98.30 | 59.65 |
| 35-39 | 98.75 | 98.55 | 98.25 | 57.85 |
| 40-44 | 98.65 | 98.40 | 98.10 | 54.50 |
| 45-49 | 97.15 | 96.95 | 96.70 | 51.35 |
| 50-54 | 94.55 | 94.25 | 93.85 | 47.44 |
| 55-59 | 89.90 | 89.50 | 88.90 | 42.77 |
| 60-64 | 81.90 | 81.20 | 80.30 | 33.20 |
| 65+ | 63.60 | 62.50 | 61.05 | 24.65 |
| **Femmes** | | | | |
| 10-14 | 46.55 | 44.50 | 34.56 | 11.27 |
| 15-19 | 73.60 | 70.60 | 63.76 | 30.04 |
| 20-24 | 77.00 | 75.00 | 71.32 | 35.38 |
| 25-29 | 77.35 | 75.20 | 73.13 | 35.59 |
| 30-34 | 79.35 | 77.15 | 77.67 | 38.14 |
| 35-39 | 80.70 | 78.65 | 78.67 | 38.48 |
| 40-44 | 81.45 | 79.45 | 80.48 | 39.71 |
| 45-49 | 80.60 | 78.55 | 79.53 | 38.69 |
| 50-54 | 78.30 | 76.00 | 76.74 | 90.74 |
| 55-59 | 70.65 | 68.40 | 69.25 | 32.69 |
| 60-64 | 62.15 | 59.40 | 56.59 | 23.52 |
| 65+ | 45.55 | 42.90 | 40.44 | 17.18 |

Source(s): (1) EPPA3; (2) STAT.

### 2.2 Méthode(s): extrapolation linéaire
moyenne pondérée

#### 2.2.1 Hommes:

- 1950-70, taux d'activité 1950-70 tirés des EPPA3;
- 1980, moyennes pondérées des taux d'activité 1960 tirés des EPPA3
et des taux d'activité tirés du recensement de 1980;
- 1990, extrapolation des taux d'activité 1950-80 tirés des EPPA3
et des taux d'activité estimés pour 1980;
modification des tendances de tous les groupes d'âge;
aux taux d'activité extrapolés 1990, application des variations
des taux estimés pour 1980 par rapport aux taux interpolés 1980.

#### 2.2.2 Femmes:

Méthode, hypothèses et traitements identiques à ceux appliqués aux hommes.

## 3. Evaluation des taux de répartition par secteur d'activité: 1950 - 1990

### 3.1 Données de base:

Tableau 2: Répartition de la population active en % par secteur d'activité

| Année | Agriculture | Industrie Total | Manufac. | Services |
|---|---|---|---|---|
| **Hommes** | | | | |
| 1971 | 79.85 | 7.58 | 2.37 | 12.56 |
| 1982 | 75.75 | 8.44 | 3.59 | 15.81 |
| **Femmes** | | | | |
| 1971 | 94.11 | 0.81 | 0.65 | 5.09 |
| 1982 | 91.56 | 2.10 | 1.87 | 6.34 |

Source(s): STAT.

### 3.2 Méthode(s): interpolation et extrapolation linéaires

#### 3.2.1 Hommes:

- 1950-90, interpolation et extrapolation des taux de répartition tirés
des recensements de 1971 et 1981,
modification des tendances de tous les secteurs pour 1990.

#### 3.2.2 Femmes:

- 1950-90, interpolation et extrapolation des aux taux de répartition tirés
des recensements de 1971 et 1981.

## 4. Projection des taux d'activité: 2000 - 2010

### 4.1 Modèle(s): linéaire et hyperbole

#### 4.1.1 Hommes:

- A tous les groupes d'âge, application de la fonction F3;
- Modification des tendances des groupes d'âge [15-49].

#### 4.1.2 Femmes:

- Aux groupes d'âge [10-14] et [20-54], application de la fonction F3;
- Aux groupes d'âge [15-19] et [55+], application de la fonction F1;
- Modification des tendances des groupes d'âge [20-39] et [50-59].

*Notes sur les ajustements des taux, voir p. 192-195.*          *Notes sur les fonctions de projection, voir p. 198.*

# Paraguay

## 1. Source(s) des données de base

Code(s):    Titre(s):

EPPA3    Evaluations et projections de la population active 1950-2025 - troisième édition, BIT, Genève, 1986.
ASTER    Annuaire des statistiques du travail 1945-89 - Edition rétrospective sur les recensements de population, BIT, Genève, 1990.

## 2. Evaluation des taux d'activité: 1950 - 1990

### 2.1 Données de base:

Tableau 1: Taux d'activité par sexe et par groupe d'âge

| | Année | | |
|---|---|---|---|
| Groupe d'âge | 1962 | 1972 | 1982 |
| **Hommes** | | | |
| 10-14 | 16.69 | 25.28 | 19.74 |
| 15-19 | 81.71 | 76.81 | 74.47 |
| 20-24 | 95.74 | 93.28 | 92.14 |
| 25-29 | 98.17 | 97.22 | 97.37 |
| 30-34 | 98.74 | 98.04 | 98.58 |
| 35-39 | 98.86 | 98.11 | 98.84 |
| 40-44 | 98.43 | 97.49 | 98.21 |
| 45-49 | 97.99 | 96.63 | 97.69 |
| 50-54 | 97.32 | 95.30 | 96.47 |
| 55-59 | 95.62 | 91.89 | 94.58 |
| 60-64 | 92.96 | 87.20 | 90.10 |
| 65+ | 74.29 | 65.14 | 54.59 |
| **Femmes** | | | |
| 10-14 | .. | 8.01 | 3.99 |
| 15-19 | .. | 24.67 | 19.99 |
| 20-24 | .. | 30.70 | 27.46 |
| 25-29 | .. | 28.01 | 27.45 |
| 30-34 | .. | 25.67 | 26.35 |
| 35-39 | .. | 23.23 | 24.84 |
| 40-44 | .. | 22.71 | 23.22 |
| 45-49 | .. | 20.69 | 20.66 |
| 50-54 | .. | 18.31 | 18.23 |
| 55-59 | .. | 16.25 | 15.95 |
| 60-64 | .. | 13.89 | 12.70 |
| 65+ | .. | 7.21 | 6.93 |

Source(s): ASTER.

### 2.2 Méthode(s): extrapolation linéaire
moyenne pondérée

#### 2.2.1 Hommes:

- 1950, taux d'activité 1950 tirés des EPPA3;
- 1960-80, moyennes pondérées des taux d'activité tirés des recensements de 1972 et 1982 et des taux ajustés du recensement de 1962;
- 1990, extrapolation des taux d'activité 1950-1980 tirés des EPPA3; aux taux extrapolés, application des variations des taux interpolés 1982 par rapport aux taux tirés du recensement de 1982; modification des tendances de tous les groupes d'âge pour tenir compte du niveau des taux d'activité des enquêtes de 1989 à 1990.

#### 2.2.2 Femmes:

- 1950-80, taux d'activité ajustés 1950-80 tirés des EPPA3; ajustement des taux sur la base du modèle d'ajustement des taux d'activité des femmes travaillant dans l'agriculture comme aides familiales;
- 1990, moyennes pondérées des taux d'activité tirés des recensements de 1972 et 1982.

## 3. Evaluation des taux de répartition par secteur d'activité: 1950 - 1990

### 3.1 Données de base:

Tableau 2: Répartition de la population active en % par secteur d'activité

| | | Agriculture | Industrie | | Services |
|---|---|---|---|---|---|
| Année | | | Total | Manufac. | |
| **Hommes** | | | | | |
| | 1962 | 65.76 | 15.77 | 11.27 | 18.46 |
| | 1972 | 62.60 | 15.92 | 10.39 | 21.48 |
| | 1982 | 55.38 | 20.18 | 10.59 | 24.44 |
| **Femmes** | | | | | |
| | 1962 | 22.66 | 30.42 | 29.47 | 46.93 |
| | 1972 | 13.75 | 28.70 | 28.54 | 57.55 |
| | 1982 | 11.97 | 23.52 | 23.16 | 64.51 |

Source(s): ASTER.

### 3.2 Méthode(s): extrapolation linéaire
moyenne pondérée

#### 3.2.1 Hommes:

- 1950-80, taux de répartition 1950-80 tirés des EPPA3;
- 1990, extrapolation des taux de répartition tirés du recensement de 1972 et 1982;
modification des tendances de tous les secteurs;
- Application du rapport manufacture/industrie tiré du recensement de 1982.

#### 3.2.2 Femmes:

- 1950-60, taux de répartition 1950-60 tirés des EPPA3;
- 1970, moyennes pondérées des taux de répartition tirés des recensements de 1962 et 1972;
- 1980-90, extrapolation des taux de répartition tirés du recensement de 1962, 1972 et 1982;
modification des tendances de tous les secteurs;
application du rapport manufacture/industrie tiré du recensement de 1982.

## 4. Projection des taux d'activité: 2000 - 2010

### 4.1 Modèle(s): linéaire, log-linéaire et hyperbole

#### 4.1.1 Hommes:

- Aux groupes d'âge [10-49], application de la fonction F1;
- Aux groupes d'âge [50-59], application de la fonction F3;
- Aux groupes d'âge [60+], application de la fonction F2;
- Modification des tendances des groupes d'âge [10-49].

#### 4.1.2 Femmes:

- Aux groupes d'âge [10-19] et [55+], application de la fonction F1;
- Aux groupes d'âge [20-54], application de la fonction F2;
- Modification des tendances des groupes d'âge [10-24], [40-44] et [60+].

*Notes sur les ajustements des taux, voir p. 192-195.*    *Notes sur les fonctions de projection, voir p. 198.*

# Pays-Bas

## 1. Source(s) des données de base

Code(s):     Titre(s):

EPPA3     Annuaire des statistiques du travail 1945-89 - Edition rétrospective sur les recensements de population, BIT, Genève, 1990.
STAT     Base de données sur les statistiques du travail - LABORSTA, Bureau de statistique, BIT, Genève.

## 2. Evaluation des taux d'activité: 1950 - 1990

### 2.1 Données de base:

Tableau 1: Taux d'activité par sexe et par groupe d'âge

| Groupe d'âge | Année 1987 | 1988 | 1989 | 1990 | 1991 |
|---|---|---|---|---|---|
| **Hommes** | | | | | |
| 10-14 | 0.00 | 0.00 | 0.00 | 0.00 | 0.00 |
| 15-19 | 41.11 | 42.83 | 42.93 | 44.36 | 45.66 |
| 20-24 | 79.20 | 78.05 | 78.37 | 76.74 | 76.97 |
| 25-29 | 93.32 | 93.25 | 93.21 | 94.14 | 94.42 |
| 30-34 | 96.36 | 96.19 | 96.39 | 96.12 | 96.28 |
| 35-39 | 95.81 | 95.95 | 96.16 | 96.20 | 96.07 |
| 40-44 | 94.64 | 94.91 | 95.02 | 94.40 | 94.44 |
| 45-49 | 91.71 | 91.28 | 91.25 | 91.93 | 92.16 |
| 50-54 | 83.51 | 94.06 | 84.20 | 83.92 | 84.71 |
| 55-59 | 66.17 | 66.57 | 65.27 | 66.30 | 63.66 |
| 60-64 | 27.66 | 26.81 | 24.45 | 22.67 | 21.69 |
| 65+ | 2.96 | 3.32 | 3.20 | 3.08 | 2.96 |
| **Femmes** | | | | | |
| 10-14 | .. | .. | 0.00 | 0.00 | 0.00 |
| 15-19 | .. | .. | 39.18 | 41.86 | 42.89 |
| 20-24 | .. | .. | 75.49 | 77.06 | 76.01 |
| 25-29 | .. | .. | 67.15 | 69.90 | 72.96 |
| 30-34 | .. | .. | 58.35 | 61.30 | 62.52 |
| 35-39 | .. | .. | 59.51 | 61.20 | 62.65 |
| 40-44 | .. | .. | 56.33 | 58.35 | 61.32 |
| 45-49 | .. | .. | 49.38 | 52.49 | 54.31 |
| 50-54 | .. | .. | 37.66 | 39.72 | 42.04 |
| 55-59 | .. | .. | 23.96 | 25.56 | 22.78 |
| 60-64 | .. | .. | 8.94 | 7.82 | 7.80 |
| 65+ | .. | .. | ... | 0.30 | ... |

Source(s): STAT.

### 2.2 Méthode(s): interpolation linéaire
moyenne arithmétique

#### 2.2.1 Hommes:

- 1950-80, taux d'activité ajustés 1960-80 tirés des EPPA3;
ajustement des groupes d'âge [15-29] et [50+] sur la base d'une interpolation des taux d'activité tirés des recensements de 1960, 1971 et 1981;
- 1990, interpolation des taux d'activité tirés des enquêtes de 1987, 1988, 1989, 1990 et 1991;
modification de la tendance du groupe d'âge [65+].

#### 2.2.2 Femmes:

- 1950-80, taux d'activité 1950-80 tirés des EPPA3;
ajustement du taux d'activité du groupe d'âge [15-19];
- 1990, moyennes des taux d'activité tirés des enquêtes de 1989, 1990 et 1991;
modification de la tendance du groupe d'âge [65+].

## 3. Evaluation des taux de répartition par secteur d'activité: 1950 - 1990

### 3.1 Données de base:

Tableau 2: Répartition de la population active en % par secteur d'activité

| Année | Agriculture | Industrie Total | Manufac. | Services |
|---|---|---|---|---|
| **Hommes** | | | | |
| 1989 | 5.45 | 35.05 | 24.19 | 59.50 |
| 1990 | 5.29 | 35.13 | 24.17 | 59.58 |
| 1991 | 5.30 | 34.47 | 23.45 | 60.23 |
| **Femmes** | | | | |
| 1989 | 3.35 | 11.16 | 9.66 | 85.49 |
| 1990 | 3.40 | 11.35 | 10.04 | 85.25 |
| 1991 | 3.28 | 10.96 | 9.48 | 85.76 |

Source(s): (1) STAT.

### 3.2 Méthode(s): moyenne arithmétique

#### 3.2.1 Hommes:

- 1950-80, taux de répartition 1950-80 tirés des EPPA3;
- 1990, moyennes des taux de répartition tirés des enquêtes de 1989, 1990 et 1991.

#### 3.2.2 Femmes:

- 1950-70, taux de répartition 1950-70 tirés des EPPA3;
- 1980, moyennes des taux de répartition tirés des enquêtes de 1979, et 1981;
- 1990, moyennes des taux de répartition tirés des enquêtes de 1989, 1990 et 1991.

## 4. Projection des taux d'activité: 2000 - 2010

### 4.1 Modèle(s): linéaire, log-linéaire, hyperbole et logistique

#### 4.1.1 Hommes:

- Au groupe d'âge [15-19], application de la fonction F2;
- Aux groupes d'âge [20+], application de la fonction F3;
- Modification des tendances des groupes d'âge [30-54].

#### 4.1.2 Femmes:

- Au groupe d'âge [15-19], application de la fonction F1;
- Aux groupes d'âge [20-59], application de la fonction F6;
- Aux groupes d'âge [60+], application de la fonction F3;
- Modification de la tendance du groupe d'âge [20-24].

*Notes sur les ajustements des taux, voir p. 192-195.*

*Notes sur les fonctions de projection, voir p. 198.*

328

# Pérou

## 1. Source(s) des données de base

Code(s):    Titre(s):

EPPA3    Evaluations et projections de la population active 1950-2025 - troisième édition, BIT, Genève, 1986.
ASTER    Annuaire des statistiques du travail 1945-89 - Edition rétrospective sur les recensements de population, BIT, Genève, 1990.

## 2. Evaluation des taux d'activité: 1950 - 1990

### 2.1 Données de base:

Tableau 1: Taux d'activité par sexe et par groupe d'âge

| Groupe d'âge | Année 1950 (1) | 1960 (1) | 1970 (1) | 1981 (2) |
|---|---|---|---|---|
| **Hommes** | | | | |
| 10-14 | 11.95 | 6.75 | 5.00 | 4.92 |
| 15-19 | 59.40 | 55.30 | 42.20 | 37.52 |
| 20-24 | 93.25 | 91.70 | 82.60 | 81.67 |
| 25-29 | 98.00 | 97.50 | 94.90 | 93.43 |
| 30-34 | 98.80 | 98.60 | 97.80 | 97.21 |
| 35-39 | 98.60 | 98.50 | 98.40 | 98.33 |
| 40-44 | 98.50 | 98.40 | 98.30 | 98.30 |
| 45-49 | 98.40 | 98.30 | 98.20 | 98.27 |
| 50-54 | 97.60 | 97.50 | 96.15 | 97.04 |
| 55-59 | 96.50 | 96.05 | 93.65 | 94.50 |
| 60-64 | 91.90 | 91.75 | 85.55 | 88.26 |
| 65+ | 75.00 | 69.30 | 62.65 | 63.46 |
| **Femmes** | | | | |
| 10-14 | 9.50 | 6.60 | 4.10 | 3.94 |
| 15-19 | 29.00 | 27.60 | 19.10 | 18.06 |
| 20-24 | 26.40 | 26.30 | 26.10 | 29.27 |
| 25-29 | 23.50 | 23.50 | 24.15 | 31.09 |
| 30-34 | 20.10 | 21.00 | 21.75 | 30.75 |
| 35-39 | 18.90 | 20.40 | 20.55 | 28.69 |
| 40-44 | 19.80 | 20.50 | 21.10 | 27.28 |
| 45-49 | 20.00 | 20.40 | 19.70 | 26.15 |
| 50-54 | 20.50 | 20.10 | 18.40 | 25.43 |
| 55-59 | 19.70 | 19.40 | 16.60 | 23.23 |
| 60-64 | 19.10 | 18.80 | 14.20 | 22.99 |
| 65+ | 14.25 | 12.10 | 9.00 | 12.02 |

Source(s): (1) EPPA3; (2) ASTER.

### 2.2 Méthode(s): extrapolation linéaire
moyenne pondérée

**2.2.1 Hommes:**

- 1950-70, taux d'activité 1950-70 tirés des EPPA3;
- 1980, moyennes pondérées des taux d'activité 1970 tirés des EPPA3 et des taux ajustés du recensement de 1981;
- 1990, extrapolation des taux d'activité 1950-1970 tirés des EPPA3 et des taux estimés pour 1980;
aux taux extrapolés, application des variations des taux interpolés 1981 par rapport aux taux ajustés tirés du recensement de 1981;
modification des tendances de tous les groupes d'âge.

**2.2.2 Femmes:**

- 1950-70, taux d'activité 1950-70 tirés des EPPA3;
ajustement des taux 1970 sur la base du rapport hommes/femmes dans l'agriculture de 1981;
- 1980, moyennes pondérées des taux d'activité 1970 tirés des EPPA3 et des taux ajustés tirés du recensement de 1981;
- 1990, extrapolation des taux d'activité 1970 tirés des EPPA3 et des taux ajustés du recensement de 1981;
modification des tendances de tous les groupes d'âge.

## 3. Evaluation des taux de répartition par secteur d'activité: 1950 - 1990

### 3.1 Données de base:

Tableau 2: Répartition de la population active en % par secteur d'activité

| Année | Agriculture | Industrie Total | Manufac. | Services |
|---|---|---|---|---|
| **Hommes** | | | | |
| 1950 (1) | 63.85 | 17.95 | .. | 18.20 |
| 1960 (1) | 57.25 | 20.30 | .. | 22.45 |
| 1970 (1) | 53.30 | 17.60 | .. | 29.10 |
| 1980 (1) | 45.05 | 19.75 | .. | 35.20 |
| 1981 (2) | 43.43 | 19.63 | 11.43 | 36.94 |
| **Femmes** | | | | |
| 1972 (2) | 19.28 | 18.89 | 18.41 | 61.82 |
| 1981 (2) | 24.57 | 13.48 | 12.51 | 61.95 |

Source(s): (1) EPPA3; (2) ASTER.

### 3.2 Méthode(s): interpolation et extrapolation linéaires

**3.2.1 Hommes:**

- 1950-80, taux de répartition 1950-80 tirés des EPPA3;
- 1980-90, extrapolation des taux de répartition 1950-80 tirés des EPPA3;
aux taux de répartition extrapolés, application des variations des taux interpolés 1980 par rapport aux taux 1980 tirés des EPPA3;
- Application du rapport manufacture/industrie tiré du recensement de 1981.

**3.2.2 Femmes:**

- 1950-60, taux de répartition 1950-60 tirés des EPPA3;
- 1970-90, interpolation et extrapolation des taux de répartition ajustés tirés du recensement de 1972 et des taux de répartition du recensement de 1981;
les taux de répartition de manufacture ont été estimés sur la base du rapport manufacture/industrie tiré du recensement de 1981.

## 4. Projection des taux d'activité: 2000 - 2010

### 4.1 Modèle(s): linéaire, hyperbole et logistique

**4.1.1 Hommes:**

- Aux groupes d'âge [10-14] et [50+], application de la fonction F1;
- Aux groupes d'âge [15-49], application de la fonction F3;
- Modification des tendances des groupes d'âge [15-34], [40-49] et [65+].

**4.1.2 Femmes:**

- Au groupe d'âge [10-14], application de la fonction F1;
- Au groupe d'âge [15-19], application de la fonction F3;
- Aux groupes d'âge [20+], application de la fonction F6;
- Modification des tendances des groupes d'âge [20-59].

*Notes sur les ajustements des taux, voir p. 192-195.*

*Notes sur les fonctions de projection, voir p. 198.*

# Philippines

## 1. Source(s) des données de base

Code(s):     Titre(s):

EPPA3       Evaluations et projections de la population active 1950-2025 - troisième édition, BIT, Genève, 1986.
STAT        Base de données sur les statistiques du travail - LABORSTA, Bureau de statistique, BIT, Genève.

## 2. Evaluation des taux d'activité: 1950 - 1990

### 2.1 Données de base:

Tableau 1: Taux d'activité par sexe et par groupe d'âge

| Groupe d'âge | Année | | | | |
| --- | --- | --- | --- | --- | --- |
| | 1958 | 1960 | 1970 | 1975 | 1990 |
| **Hommes** | | | | | |
| 10-14 | .. | 30.85 | 28.85 | 20.44 | .. |
| 15-19 | .. | 69.11 | 57.18 | 52.63 | 42.30 |
| 20-24 | .. | 87.89 | 86.35 | 84.35 | 70.74 |
| 25-29 | .. | 95.54 | 95.03 | 93.12 | 86.60 |
| 30-34 | .. | 98.09 | 97.70 | 97.17 | 91.46 |
| 35-39 | .. | 98.18 | 97.91 | 98.29 | 92.69 |
| 40-44 | .. | 98.32 | 97.95 | 98.62 | 92.64 |
| 45-49 | .. | 98.21 | 97.75 | 98.07 | 92.01 |
| 50-54 | .. | 97.95 | 97.34 | 97.28 | 89.94 |
| 55-59 | .. | 95.86 | 96.97 | 95.87 | 86.61 |
| 60-64 | .. | 87.81 | 87.31 | 84.25 | 78.00 |
| 65+ | .. | 69.22 | 63.41 | 62.56 | 59.88 |
| **Femmes** | | | | | |
| 10-14 | 10.12 | .. | .. | .. | .. |
| 15-19 | 21.30 | .. | .. | .. | 31.32 |
| 20-24 | 50.80 | .. | .. | .. | 42.53 |
| 25-29 | 44.00 | .. | .. | .. | 43.25 |
| 30-34 | 47.00 | .. | .. | .. | 42.22 |
| 35-39 | 46.50 | .. | .. | .. | 42.45 |
| 40-44 | 47.00 | .. | .. | .. | 44.27 |
| 45-49 | 50.00 | .. | .. | .. | 42.64 |
| 50-54 | 51.00 | .. | .. | .. | 40.68 |
| 55-59 | 46.00 | .. | .. | .. | 38.87 |
| 60-64 | 33.00 | .. | .. | .. | 35.39 |
| 65+ | 19.20 | .. | .. | .. | 24.85 |

Source(s): STAT.

### 2.2 Méthode(s): interpolation et extrapolation linéaires

#### 2.2.1 Hommes:

- 1950-90, interpolation et extrapolation des taux d'activité tirés des recensements de 1960, 1970 et 1975 et des taux d'activité ajustés tirés du recensement de 1990.

#### 2.2.2 Femmes:

- 1950-90, interpolation et extrapolation des taux d'activité tirés de l'enquête de 1958 et des taux d'activité ajustés tirés du recensement de 1990; ajustement des taux sur la base des résultats des enquêtes de 1989, 1990 et 1991 effectuées au Pakistan; modification des tendances de tous les groupes d'âge.

## 3. Evaluation des taux de répartition par secteur d'activité: 1950 - 1990

### 3.1 Données de base:

Tableau 2: Répartition de la population active en % par secteur d'activité

| Année | Agriculture | Industrie | | Services |
| --- | --- | --- | --- | --- |
| | | Total | Manufac. | |
| **Hommes** | | | | |
| 1960 | 74.55 | 10.09 | 6.54 | 15.35 |
| 1965 | 66.60 | 12.77 | 7.97 | 20.64 |
| 1974 | 64.71 | 13.80 | 8.47 | 21.49 |
| 1975 | 64.45 | 13.93 | 8.56 | 21.62 |
| 1985 | 58.26 | 14.47 | 7.75 | 27.27 |
| 1989 | 53.19 | 16.69 | 8.78 | 30.12 |
| 1990 | 56.57 | 24.56 | 14.88 | 18.87 |
| 1991 | 53.96 | 17.28 | 8.53 | 28.76 |
| **Femmes** | | | | |
| 1989 | 30.94 | 14.20 | 13.58 | 54.87 |
| 1990 | 31.35 | 12.80 | 12.24 | 55.85 |
| 1991 | 30.06 | 13.88 | 13.28 | 56.06 |

Source(s): STAT.

### 3.2 Méthode(s): interpolation et extrapolation linéaires

#### 3.2.1 Hommes:

- 1950-90, interpolation et extrapolation des taux de répartition tirés des recensements de 1960 et 1975 et des enquêtes de 1965, 1974, 1985, 1990 et 1991;
modification des tendances de tous les secteurs pour 1950.

#### 3.2.2 Femmes:

- 1950-80, taux de répartition 1950-80 tirés des EPPA3;
- 1990, moyennes des taux de répartition tirés des enquêtes de 1989, 1990 et 1991.

## 4. Projection des taux d'activité: 2000 - 2010

### 4.1 Modèle(s): linéaire, hyperbole et logistique

#### 4.1.1 Hommes:

- Au groupe d'âge [10-14], application de la fonction F2;
- Aux groupes d'âge [15+], application de la fonction F3;
- Modification des tendances des groupes d'âge [10-14], [35-49] et [65+].

#### 4.1.2 Femmes:

- Au groupe d'âge [10-14], application de la fonction F2;
- Aux groupes d'âge [15-34] et [50+], application de la fonction F3;
- Aux groupes d'âge [35-49], application de la fonction F1;
- Modification des tendances de tous les groupes d'âge.

*Notes sur les ajustements des taux, voir p. 192-195.*

*Notes sur les fonctions de projection, voir p. 198.*

# Pologne

## 1. Source(s) des données de base

Code(s):     Titre(s):

EPPA3       Evaluations et projections de la population active 1950-2025 - troisième édition, BIT, Genève, 1986.
BLT-94-2    Popovic B. (1994), "Nouvelles estimations pour 1980 et 1990 des taux d'activité par âge et répartition sectorielle
            pour certains pays d'Europe orientale et méridionale" dans le Bulletin des statistiques du travail - 1994-2, BIT, Genève.

## 2. Evaluation des taux d'activité: 1950 - 1990

### 2.1 Données de base:

Tableau 1: Taux d'activité par sexe et par groupe d'âge

| Groupe d'âge | Année 1950 (1) | 1960 (1) | 1970 (1) | 1980 (1) | 1980 (2) | 1990 (2) |
|---|---|---|---|---|---|---|
| **Hommes** | | | | | | |
| 10-14 | 2.25 | 0.90 | 0.50 | 0.00 | 0.00 | 0.00 |
| 15-19 | 63.00 | 54.50 | 49.50 | 46.00 | 28.20 | 20.72 |
| 20-24 | 92.90 | 90.40 | 88.95 | 82.50 | 82.25 | 78.19 |
| 25-29 | 97.05 | 96.40 | 96.35 | 96.20 | 95.96 | 93.99 |
| 30-34 | 97.80 | 97.20 | 97.15 | 97.10 | 96.92 | 96.02 |
| 35-39 | 97.80 | 97.15 | 96.90 | 96.20 | 96.07 | 95.53 |
| 40-44 | 97.55 | 96.90 | 96.15 | 94.80 | 94.68 | 94.02 |
| 45-49 | 97.40 | 96.20 | 95.15 | 92.20 | 91.80 | 89.17 |
| 50-54 | 97.00 | 94.85 | 94.05 | 87.30 | 86.36 | 81.70 |
| 55-59 | 96.40 | 91.60 | 90.95 | 82.00 | 79.71 | 70.88 |
| 60-64 | 86.40 | 82.10 | 83.05 | 58.00 | 60.31 | 52.83 |
| 65+ | 59.75 | 57.60 | 55.45 | 30.00 | 34.56 | 32.09 |
| **Femmes** | | | | | | |
| 10-14 | 2.15 | 1.20 | 0.65 | 0.00 | 0.00 | 0.00 |
| 15-19 | 51.10 | 43.25 | 36.65 | 31.20 | 20.71 | 15.92 |
| 20-24 | 68.65 | 69.20 | 69.80 | 68.40 | 67.91 | 63.05 |
| 25-29 | 60.30 | 62.75 | 74.55 | 76.00 | 74.42 | 69.05 |
| 30-34 | 60.85 | 63.30 | 77.15 | 81.00 | 78.92 | 76.37 |
| 35-39 | 64.20 | 66.80 | 79.20 | 82.50 | 82.15 | 83.08 |
| 40-44 | 66.40 | 69.10 | 79.45 | 83.20 | 83.19 | 85.94 |
| 45-49 | 63.20 | 68.10 | 78.70 | 79.00 | 78.87 | 81.78 |
| 50-54 | 60.65 | 65.35 | 75.40 | 72.60 | 71.54 | 71.07 |
| 55-59 | 55.70 | 60.00 | 67.85 | 56.00 | 56.64 | 49.63 |
| 60-64 | 45.25 | 48.70 | 50.90 | 35.00 | 36.65 | 33.99 |
| 65+ | 28.95 | 30.00 | 32.90 | 17.50 | 19.31 | 19.00 |

Source(s): (1) EPPA3; (2) BLT-94-2.

### 2.2 Méthode(s): Données des EPPA3 et du BLT-94-2.

#### 2.2.1 Hommes:

- 1950-80, taux d'activité 1950-80 tirés des EPPA3;
- 1990, aux taux d'activité 1990 tirés du Bulletin des statistiques
du travail 1994-2; application des variations des taux d'activité
1980 tirés des EPPA3 par rapport aux taux d'activité 1980 tirés du
Bulletin.

#### 2.2.2 Femmes:

Méthode, hypothèses et traitements identiques à ceux appliqués aux hommes.

## 3. Evaluation des taux de répartition par secteur d'activité: 1950 - 1990

### 3.1 Données de base:

Tableau 2: Répartition de la population active en % par secteur d'activité

| Année | Agriculture | Industrie Total | Manufac. | Services |
|---|---|---|---|---|
| **Hommes** | | | | |
| 1950 (1) | 49.00 | 30.00 | .. | 20.90 |
| 1960 (1) | 39.50 | 37.80 | .. | 22.60 |
| 1970 (1) | 32.60 | 43.40 | .. | 24.00 |
| 1980 (2) | 28.04 | 45.63 | 28.44 | 26.33 |
| 1990 (2) | 27.44 | 44.88 | 26.86 | 27.68 |
| **Femmes** | | | | |
| 1950 (1) | 69.40 | 13.70 | .. | 16.80 |
| 1960 (1) | 59.40 | 16.90 | .. | 23.70 |
| 1970 (1) | 46.50 | 23.20 | .. | 30.30 |
| 1980 (2) | 31.91 | 28.13 | 24.20 | 39.96 |
| 1990 (2) | 27.50 | 25.01 | 21.19 | 47.49 |

Source(s): (1) EPPA3; (2) BLT-94-2.

### 3.2 Méthode(s): données du BLT-94-2

#### 3.2.1 Hommes:

- 1950-70, taux de répartition 1950-70 tirés des EPPA3;
- 1980-90, taux de répartition tirés du Bulletin des statistiques
du travail - 1994-2.

#### 3.2.2 Femmes:

Méthode, hypothèses et traitements identiques à ceux appliqués aux hommes.

## 4. Projection des taux d'activité: 2000 - 2010

### 4.1 Modèle(s): hyperbole et logistique

#### 4.1.1 Hommes:

- A tous les groupes d'âge, application de la fonction F3;
- Modification des tendances des groupes d'âge [20-24] et [30-49].

#### 4.1.2 Femmes:

- Aux groupes d'âge [15-24] et [55+], application de la fonction F3;
- Aux groupes d'âge [25-54], application de la fonction F6;
- Modification des tendances des groupes d'âge [15-24] et [55-59].

---

*Notes sur les ajustements des taux, voir p. 192-195.*

*Notes sur les fonctions de projection, voir p. 198.*

# Porto Rico

## 1. Source(s) des données de base

Code(s):     Titre(s):

EPPA3     Evaluations et projections de la population active 1950-2025 - troisième édition, BIT, Genève, 1986.
ASTER     Annuaire des statistiques du travail 1945-89 - Edition rétrospective sur les recensements de population, BIT, Genève, 1990.
AST91-93     Editions de 1991 à 1993 de l'Annuaire des statistiques du travail du BIT, Genève.

## 2. Evaluation des taux d'activité: 1950 - 1990

### 2.1 Données de base:

Tableau 1: Taux d'activité par sexe et par groupe d'âge

| Groupe d'âge | Année 1980 (1) | 1990 (2) | 1991 (2) | 1992 (2) |
|---|---|---|---|---|
| **Hommes** | | | | |
| 10-14 | 0.00 | 0.00 | 0.00 | 0.00 |
| 15-19 | 14.81 | 15.24 | 20.16 | 16.84 |
| 20-24 | 58.04 | 67.20 | 67.72 | 65.22 |
| 25-29 | 75.49 | 85.71 | 85.32 | 85.59 |
| 30-34 | 77.34 | 86.73 | 87.13 | 88.57 |
| 35-39 | 77.41 | 86.60 | 86.46 | 86.14 |
| 40-44 | 73.98 | 82.83 | 86.27 | 85.71 |
| 45-49 | 69.00 | 83.33 | 79.31 | 80.21 |
| 50-54 | 62.28 | 72.37 | 77.63 | 75.00 |
| 55-59 | 53.57 | 61.29 | 64.18 | 63.89 |
| 60-64 | 35.93 | 36.21 | 38.98 | 39.06 |
| 65+ | 12.40 | 14.47 | 13.92 | 13.77 |
| **Femmes** | | | | |
| 10-14 | 0.00 | 0.00 | 0.00 | 0.00 |
| 15-19 | 10.15 | 6.87 | 7.22 | 6.40 |
| 20-24 | 37.42 | 34.06 | 31.39 | 33.10 |
| 25-29 | 47.45 | 48.03 | 50.79 | 50.74 |
| 30-34 | 43.34 | 46.77 | 48.39 | 51.52 |
| 35-39 | 40.73 | 51.26 | 51.67 | 48.44 |
| 40-44 | 37.95 | 44.26 | 46.22 | 44.72 |
| 45-49 | 33.46 | 38.00 | 43.69 | 46.60 |
| 50-54 | 25.26 | 35.96 | 33.70 | 36.00 |
| 55-59 | 17.62 | 20.27 | 22.08 | 24.69 |
| 60-64 | 9.96 | 11.76 | 8.82 | 12.99 |
| 65+ | 2.8 | 3.41 | 2.14 | 2.56 |

Source(s): (1) ASTER; (2) AST91-93.

### 2.2 Méthode(s): interpolation et extrapolation linéaires

#### 2.2.1 Hommes:

- 1950-80, taux d'activité 1950-80 tirés des EPPA3;
ajustement des taux d'activité des groupes d'âge [55+] sur la base des résultats des enquêtes de 1979 et 1981;
- 1990, extrapolation des taux d'activité tirés du recensement de 1980 et des enquêtes de 1990, 1991 et 1992;
aux taux extrapolés, application des variations des taux interpolés 1980 par rapport aux taux 1980 tirés des EPPA3.

#### 2.2.2 Femmes:

- 1950-70, taux d'activité 1950-70 tirés des EPPA3;
- 1980-90, interpolation des taux d'activité tirés du recensement de 1980 et des moyennes des taux d'activité tirés des enquêtes de 1990, 1991 et 1992.

## 3. Evaluation des taux de répartition par secteur d'activité: 1950 - 1990

### 3.1 Données de base:

Tableau 2: Répartition de la population active en % par secteur d'activité

| Année | Agriculture | Industrie Total | Manufac. | Services |
|---|---|---|---|---|
| **Hommes** | | | | |
| 1979 (1) | 8.57 | 29.43 | 15.82 | 62.00 |
| 1980 (2) | 5.58 | 33.46 | 17.98 | 60.95 |
| 1981 (1) | 8.09 | 30.38 | 15.88 | 61.53 |
| 1990 (1) | 6.95 | 29.00 | 15.41 | 64.05 |
| 1991 (1) | 6.15 | 28.40 | 15.96 | 65.45 |
| 1992 (1) | 5.60 | 29.31 | 15.61 | 65.10 |
| **Femmes** | | | | |
| 1979 (1) | 0.31 | 27.80 | 26.94 | 71.89 |
| 1980 (2) | 0.48 | 26.14 | 24.40 | 73.38 |
| 1981 (1) | 0.58 | 24.86 | 24.28 | 74.57 |
| 1990 (1) | 0.51 | 21.54 | 20.77 | 77.95 |
| 1991 (1) | 0.51 | 20.51 | 19.24 | 78.99 |
| 1992 (1) | 0.25 | 21.57 | 20.34 | 78.19 |

Source(s): ASTER.

### 3.2 Méthode(s): interpolation linéaire

#### 3.2.1 Hommes:

- 1950-70, taux de répartition 1950-70 tirés des EPPA3;
- 1980-90, interpolation des taux de répartition tirés du recensement de 1980 et des enquêtes de 1979, 1981, 1990, 1991 et 1992.

#### 3.2.2 Femmes:

Méthode, hypothèses et traitements identiques à ceux appliqués aux hommes.

## 4. Projection des taux d'activité: 2000 - 2010

### 4.1 Modèle(s): log-linéaire, hyperbole et logistique

#### 4.1.1 Hommes:

- Aux groupes d'âge [15+], application de la fonction F3;
- Modification des tendances de tous les groupes d'âge.

#### 4.1.2 Femmes:

- Au groupe d'âge [15-19], application de la fonction F3;
- Aux groupes d'âge [20-49], application de la fonction F2;
- Aux groupes d'âge [50+], application de la fonction F6;
- Modification des tendances des groupes d'âge [20+].

*Notes sur les ajustements des taux, voir p. 192-195.*

*Notes sur les fonctions de projection, voir p. 198.*

# Portugal

## 1. Source(s) des données de base

Code(s):   Titre(s):

EPPA3   Annuaire des statistiques du travail 1945-89 - Edition rétrospective sur les recensements de population, BIT, Genève, 1990.
STAT   Base de données sur les statistiques du travail - LABORSTA, Bureau de statistique, BIT, Genève.

## 2. Evaluation des taux d'activité: 1950 - 1990

### 2.1 Données de base:

Tableau 1: Taux d'activité par sexe et par groupe d'âge

| Groupe d'âge | 1950 (1) | 1960 (1) | 1970 (1) | 1980 (1) | 1980 (2) | 1990 (12 |
|---|---|---|---|---|---|---|
| **Hommes** | | | | | | |
| 10-14 | 43.90 | 35.10 | 17.05 | 12.40 | .. | 4.86 |
| 15-19 | 90.70 | 86.85 | 78.85 | 76.15 | .. | 51.12 |
| 20-24 | 94.00 | 92.00 | 93.15 | 92.15 | .. | 73.20 |
| 25-29 | 94.65 | 97.20 | 97.05 | 97.00 | .. | 93.92 |
| 30-34 | 96.35 | 98.40 | 97.70 | 97.50 | .. | 96.32 |
| 35-39 | 96.65 | 98.35 | 97.30 | 96.75 | .. | 96.58 |
| 40-44 | 96.30 | 97.65 | 96.35 | 96.70 | .. | 96.17 |
| 45-49 | 94.55 | 96.00 | 95.05 | 92.40 | .. | 93.57 |
| 50-54 | 92.20 | 93.45 | 92.35 | 88.35 | .. | 86.93 |
| 55-59 | 88.30 | 89.10 | 87.65 | 79.15 | .. | 75.24 |
| 60-64 | 84.10 | 82.55 | 78.95 | 60.60 | .. | 57.08 |
| 65+ | 67.45 | 62.85 | 53.20 | 29.65 | .. | 20.03 |
| **Femmes** | | | | | | |
| 10-14 | 11.30 | 8.70 | 9.50 | .. | 3.01 | 4.84 |
| 15-19 | 34.70 | 27.60 | 44.00 | .. | 54.39 | 39.70 |
| 20-24 | 31.45 | 26.75 | 44.60 | .. | 69.35 | 68.46 |
| 25-29 | 23.15 | 19.95 | 32.50 | .. | 67.49 | 76.53 |
| 30-34 | 20.20 | 16.75 | 25.20 | .. | 63.09 | 77.66 |
| 35-39 | 19.30 | 15.50 | 22.75 | .. | 59.13 | 74.05 |
| 40-44 | 18.70 | 14.95 | 21.20 | .. | 50.51 | 67.77 |
| 45-49 | 19.05 | 14.45 | 19.60 | .. | 44.19 | 61.66 |
| 50-54 | 18.75 | 13.85 | 17.55 | .. | 42.36 | 50.49 |
| 55-59 | 18.05 | 13.55 | 14.60 | .. | 34.46 | 39.84 |
| 60-64 | 16.80 | 12.35 | 12.85 | .. | 29.03 | 24.72 |
| 65+ | 12.40 | 8.05 | 8.05 | .. | 8.50 | 7.77 |

Source(s): (1) EPPA3; (2) STAT.

### 2.2 Méthode(s): données nationales

#### 2.2.1 Hommes:

- 1950-80, taux d'activité 1950-80 tirés des EPPA3;
ajustement des taux d'activité du groupe d'âge [45-49] pour 1980;
- 1990, taux d'activité ajustés tirés de l'enquête de 1990;
ajustement des taux d'activité pour tenir compte des militaires du contingent.

#### 2.2.2 Femmes:

- 1950-70, taux d'activité 1950-70 tirés des EPPA3;
ajustement du taux d'activité du groupe d'âge [65+] pour 1970;
- 1980, taux d'activité ajustés tirés de l'enquête de 1980;
- 1990, taux d'activité tirés de l'enquête de 1990.

## 3. Evaluation des taux de répartition par secteur d'activité: 1950 - 1990

### 3.1 Données de base:

Tableau 2: Répartition de la population active en % par secteur d'activité

| Année | Agriculture | Industrie Total | Manufac. | Services |
|---|---|---|---|---|
| **Hommes** | | | | |
| 1980 | 21.27 | 42.53 | 26.18 | 36.20 |
| 1990 | 15.38 | 40.06 | 24.02 | 44.57 |
| **Femmes** | | | | |
| 1980 | 33.42 | 26.40 | 25.72 | 40.18 |
| 1990 | 21.09 | 25.92 | 24.95 | 52.99 |

Source(s): (1) STAT.

### 3.2 Méthode(s): données nationales

#### 3.2.1 Hommes:

- 1950-70, taux de répartition 1950-70 tirés des EPPA3;
- 1980, taux de répartition tirés de l'enquête de 1980;
- 1980, taux de répartition ajustés tirés de l'enquête de 1980;
ajustement des taux de répartition pour tenir compte des militaires du contingent.

#### 3.2.2 Femmes:

Méthode, hypothèses et traitements identiques à ceux appliqués aux hommes.

## 4. Projection des taux d'activité: 2000 - 2010

### 4.1 Modèle(s): linéaire, hyperbole et logistique

#### 4.1.1 Hommes:

- Au groupe d'âge [15-19], application de la fonction F1;
- Aux groupes d'âge [20+], application de la fonction F3;
- Modification des tendances des groupes d'âge [25-29] et [45-49].

#### 4.1.2 Femmes:

- Au groupe d'âge [10-14], application de la fonction F1;
- Aux groupes d'âge [15-59], application de la fonction F6;
- Aux groupes d'âge [60+], application de la fonction F3;
- Modification des tendances des groupes d'âge [15-64].

*Notes sur les ajustements des taux, voir p. 192-195.*      *Notes sur les fonctions de projection, voir p. 198.*

# Qatar

## 1. Source(s) des données de base

Code(s):     Titre(s):

EPPA3     Evaluations et projections de la population active 1950-2025 - troisième édition, BIT, Genève, 1986.
EPPA4     Population active 1950-2010 - quatrième édition, BIT, Genève 1996.
STAT      Base de données sur les statistiques du travail - LABORSTA, Bureau de statistique, BIT, Genève.

## 2. Evaluation des taux d'activité: 1950 - 1990

### 2.1 Données de base:

Tableau 1: Taux d'activité par sexe et par groupe d'âge

| Groupe d'âge | Année | | | | | | |
|---|---|---|---|---|---|---|---|
| | 1950 (1) | 1970 (1) | 1990 (1) | 1986 (3) | 1950 (2) | 1970 (2) | 1990 (2) |
| **Hommes** | | | | | | | |
| 10-14 | 14.00 | 7.00 | 0.00 | 0.00 | 13.18 | 6.88 | 0.00 |
| 15-19 | 57.35 | 44.50 | 27.84 | 32.16 | 54.00 | 43.75 | 25.44 |
| 20-24 | 92.85 | 88.15 | 84.52 | 88.44 | 87.70 | 88.35 | 87.92 |
| 25-29 | 98.05 | 97.40 | 97.60 | 98.70 | 97.35 | 97.65 | 98.00 |
| 30-34 | 99.45 | 98.90 | 98.67 | 99.61 | 98.35 | 98.65 | 99.20 |
| 35-39 | 99.00 | 98.70 | 98.50 | 99.68 | 97.80 | 98.35 | 99.31 |
| 40-44 | 98.50 | 98.05 | 97.33 | 99.61 | 96.00 | 97.20 | 99.23 |
| 45-49 | 97.00 | 96.40 | 94.89 | 99.04 | 94.90 | 96.20 | 98.81 |
| 50-54 | 92.20 | 91.75 | 90.10 | 96.72 | 90.00 | 91.75 | 95.79 |
| 55-59 | 86.55 | 85.55 | 83.53 | 93.76 | 81.25 | 84.20 | 88.44 |
| 60-64 | 61.75 | 65.70 | 67.16 | 82.32 | 74.35 | 72.20 | 64.99 |
| 65+ | 34.00 | 34.35 | 31.12 | 59.61 | 53.00 | 49.80 | 36.55 |
| **Femmes** | | | | | | | |
| 10-14 | .. | .. | 0.00 | 0.00 | .. | .. | .. |
| 15-19 | .. | .. | 4.66 | 1.37 | .. | .. | .. |
| 20-24 | .. | .. | 46.42 | 13.67 | .. | .. | .. |
| 25-29 | .. | .. | 60.87 | 28.73 | .. | .. | .. |
| 30-34 | .. | .. | 57.34 | 46.91 | .. | .. | .. |
| 35-39 | .. | .. | 45.72 | 47.47 | .. | .. | .. |
| 40-44 | .. | .. | 33.40 | 37.59 | .. | .. | .. |
| 45-49 | .. | .. | 23.39 | 27.09 | .. | .. | .. |
| 50-54 | .. | .. | 10.27 | 15.83 | .. | .. | .. |
| 55-59 | .. | .. | 13.85 | 11.46 | .. | .. | .. |
| 60-64 | .. | .. | 10.70 | 6.83 | .. | .. | .. |
| 65+ | .. | .. | 0.46 | 2.72 | .. | .. | .. |

Note(s): (1) Koweït; (2) Bahreïn.
Source(s): (1)(2) EPPA4; (3) STAT.

### 2.2 Méthode(s): moyenne arithmétique

#### 2.2.1 Hommes:

- 1950-90, aux taux d'activité ajustés tirés du recensement de 1986,
application des variations moyennes des taux d'activité estimés pour
le Koweït et le Bahreïn par rapport aux taux estimés 1986 pour ces deux pays;
modification des tendances des groupes d'âge [10-14] et [50+]

#### 2.2.2 Femmes:

- 1950-80, taux d'activité 1950-80 tirés des EPPA3;
- 1990, aux taux d'activité 1990 estimés le Koweït, application
du quart des variations des taux d'activité ajustés tirés du recensement
de 1986 par rapport aux taux estimés 1986 pour le Koweït.

## 3. Evaluation des taux de répartition par secteur d'activité: 1950 - 1990

### 3.1 Données de base:

Tableau 2: Répartition de la population active en % par secteur d'activité

| Année | Agriculture | Industrie | | Services |
|---|---|---|---|---|
| | | Total | Manufac. | |
| **Hommes** | | | | |
| 1950 (1) | 30.00 | 22.00 | .. | 48.00 |
| 1960 (1) | 18.00 | 24.70 | .. | 57.30 |
| 1970 (1) | 10.00 | 27.30 | .. | 62.70 |
| 1980 (1) | 3.00 | 30.00 | .. | 67.00 |
| 1986 (2) | 3.48 | 35.56 | 7.65 | 60.96 |
| **Femmes** | | | | |
| 1950 (1) | 7.60 | 0.00 | .. | 92.40 |
| 1960 (1) | 4.10 | 0.00 | .. | 95.90 |
| 1970 (1) | 0.25 | 0.00 | .. | 99.75 |
| 1980 (1) | 0.00 | 0.00 | .. | 100.00 |
| 1986 (2) | 0.02 | 2.13 | 0.63 | 97.85 |

Source(s): (1) EPPA3; (2) STAT.

### 3.2 Méthode(s): extrapolation linéaire

#### 3.2.1 Hommes:

- 1950-80, taux de répartition 1950-80 tirés des EPPA3;
- 1990, extrapolation des taux de répartition de l'agriculture 1950-80;
modification de la tendance du secteur;
les taux de répartition de l'industrie, de manufacture et des services
composition par secteur tirée du recensement de 1986.

#### 3.2.2 Femmes:

Méthode, hypothèses et traitements identiques à ceux appliqués aux hommes.

## 4. Projection des taux d'activité: 2000 - 2010

### 4.1 Modèle(s): linéaire, hyperbole et logistique

#### 4.1.1 Hommes:

- Aux groupes d'âge [15-19] et [25-54], application de la fonction F3;
- Aux groupes d'âge [20-24] et [55+], application de la fonction F6;
- Modification des tendances des groupes d'âge [20-49].

#### 4.1.2 Femmes:

- Aux groupes d'âge [15-19], [30-39] et [50-64], application de la fonction F1;
- Aux groupes d'âge [20-29] et [40-49], application de la fonction F6;
- Au groupe d'âge [65+], application de la fonction F3;
- Modification des tendances des groupes d'âge [20-29].

*Notes sur les ajustements des taux, voir p. 192-195.*

*Notes sur les fonctions de projection, voir p. 198.*

# Rép. centrafricaine

## 1. Source(s) des données de base

| Code(s): | Titre(s): |
|---|---|
| EPPA3 | Evaluations et projections de la population active 1950-2025 - troisième édition, BIT, Genève, 1986. |
| R1988 | Recensement de la population 1988 - Tableaux statistiques, Bureau Central du Recensement, Division des Statistiques et des Etudes Economiques, Bangui |
| AST93 | Annuaire des statistiques du travail 1993, BIT, Genève, 1993. |

## 2. Evaluation des taux d'activité: 1950 - 1990

### 2.1 Données de base:

Tableau 1: Taux d'activité par sexe et par groupe d'âge

| Groupe d'âge | Année 1950 (1) | 1960 (1) | 1988 (2) |
|---|---|---|---|
| **Hommes** | | | |
| oct.14 | 54.50 | 53.40 | 23.06 |
| 15-19 | 88.10 | 86.65 | 59.51 |
| 20-24 | 96.50 | 95.90 | 84.42 |
| 25-29 | 97.55 | 97.50 | 94.73 |
| 30-34 | 98.35 | 98.25 | 98.15 |
| 35-39 | 98.50 | 98.40 | 98.53 |
| 40-44 | 98.35 | 98.25 | 98.31 |
| 45-49 | 97.55 | 97.50 | 97.97 |
| 50-54 | 97.25 | 97.10 | 96.71 |
| 55-59 | 96.55 | 96.35 | 94.25 |
| 60-64 | 93.90 | 93.55 | 92.23 |
| 65+ | 81.30 | 80.65 | 82.54 |
| **Femmes** | | | |
| oct.14 | .. | 48.15 | 28.06 |
| 15-19 | .. | 88.00 | 53.79 |
| 20-24 | .. | 92.30 | 62.27 |
| 25-29 | .. | 93.30 | 68.09 |
| 30-34 | .. | 94.85 | 72.10 |
| 35-39 | .. | 94.75 | 76.87 |
| 40-44 | .. | 94.25 | 79.35 |
| 45-49 | .. | 92.90 | 82.03 |
| 50-54 | .. | 85.50 | 81.84 |
| 55-59 | .. | 76.20 | 81.72 |
| 60-64 | .. | 60.75 | 78.22 |
| 65+ | .. | 35.35 | 64.67 |

Source(s): (1) EPPA3; (2) R1988 et AST93.

### 2.2 Méthode(s): interpolation et extrapolation linéaires

#### 2.2.1 Hommes:

- 1950-90, interpolation et extrapolation des taux d'activité 1950-60
tirés des EPPA3 et des taux d'activité ajustés tirés du recensement de 1988;
modification des tendances de tous les groupes d'âge pour 1950.

#### 2.2.2 Femmes:

Méthode, hypothèses et traitements identiques à ceux appliqués aux hommes.

## 3. Evaluation des taux de répartition par secteur d'activité: 1950 - 1990

### 3.1 Données de base:

Tableau 2: Répartition de la population active en % par secteur d'activité

| Année | Agriculture | Industrie Total | Manufac. | Services |
|---|---|---|---|---|
| **Hommes** | | | | |
| 1960 (1) | 90.00 | 3.00 | .. | 7.00 |
| 1988 (2) | 74.82 | 6.14 | 2.88 | 19.04 |
| **Femmes** | | | | |
| 1960 (1) | 96.85 | 0.95 | .. | 2.20 |
| 1988 (2) | 87.63 | 0.37 | 0.24 | 12.00 |

Source(s): (1) EPPA3; (2) R1988 et AST93.

### 3.2 Méthode(s): interpolation et extrapolation linéaires

#### 3.2.1 Hommes:

- 1950-90, interpolation et extrapolation des taux de répartition 1970
et 1988 tirés respectivement des EPPA3 et du recensement de 1988;
- Application du rapport manufacture/industrie tiré du recensement de 1988.

#### 3.2.2 Femmes:

Méthode, hypothèses et traitements identiques à ceux appliqués aux hommes.

## 4. Projection des taux d'activité: 2000 - 2010

### 4.1 Modèle(s): linéaire, log-linéaire et hyperbole

#### 4.1.1 Hommes:

- Aux groupes d'âge [10-14] et [60+], application de la fonction F1;
- Au groupe d'âge [15-19], application de la fonction F2;
- Aux groupes d'âge [20-59], application de la fonction F3;
- Modification des tendances des groupes d'âge [35-49] et [60+].

#### 4.1.2 Femmes:

- Au groupe d'âge [10-14], application de la fonction F1;
- Aux groupes d'âge [15+], application de la fonction F3;
- Modification des tendances de tous les groupes d'âge.

---

*Notes sur les ajustements des taux, voir p. 192-195.*   *Notes sur les fonctions de projection, voir p. 198.*

# Rép. dém. du Congo

## 1. Source(s) des données de base

Code(s):     Titre(s):

EPPA3       Evaluations et projections de la population active 1950-2025 - troisième édition, BIT, Genève, 1986.

## 2. Evaluation des taux d'activité: 1950 - 1990

### 2.1 Données de base:

Tableau 1: Taux d'activité par sexe et par groupe d'âge

| Groupe d'âge | Année 1950 | 1960 | 1970 | 1980 |
|---|---|---|---|---|
| **Hommes** | | | | |
| 10-14 | 45.35 | 43.75 | 40.05 | 35.70 |
| 15-19 | 75.95 | 73.85 | 68.90 | 63.10 |
| 20-24 | 91.80 | 91.00 | 89.10 | 86.90 |
| 25-29 | 96.90 | 96.75 | 96.50 | 96.15 |
| 30-34 | 97.55 | 97.45 | 97.10 | 96.75 |
| 35-39 | 97.70 | 97.55 | 97.20 | 96.85 |
| 40-44 | 97.50 | 97.35 | 97.00 | 96.60 |
| 45-49 | 96.85 | 96.70 | 96.40 | 96.05 |
| 50-54 | 96.15 | 95.95 | 95.50 | 94.95 |
| 55-59 | 94.75 | 94.45 | 93.75 | 92.90 |
| 60-64 | 90.90 | 90.40 | 89.20 | 87.75 |
| 65+ | 76.05 | 75.15 | 73.05 | 70.55 |
| **Femmes** | | | | |
| 10-14 | 37.35 | 35.20 | 30.25 | 24.40 |
| 15-19 | 65.25 | 60.80 | 50.35 | 38.05 |
| 20-24 | 70.10 | 65.75 | 55.55 | 43.55 |
| 25-29 | 72.80 | 68.75 | 59.35 | 48.25 |
| 30-34 | 75.60 | 71.85 | 63.00 | 52.60 |
| 35-39 | 76.75 | 73.20 | 64.95 | 55.20 |
| 40-44 | 78.05 | 74.85 | 67.40 | 58.65 |
| 45-49 | 77.10 | 74.00 | 66.75 | 58.20 |
| 50-54 | 72.35 | 69.75 | 60.70 | 56.60 |
| 55-59 | 66.65 | 64.75 | 60.40 | 55.25 |
| 60-64 | 54.95 | 53.80 | 51.15 | 48.05 |
| 65+ | 33.40 | 33.05 | 32.15 | 31.10 |

Source(s): EPPA3.

### 2.2 Méthode(s): interpolation et extrapolation linéaires

#### 2.2.1 Hommes:

- 1950-80, taux d'activité 1950-80 tirés des EPPA3;
- 1990, extrapolation des taux d'activité 1950-80 tirés des EPPA3;
ajustement des taux extrapolés sur la base des variations des taux
interpolés 1980 par rapport aux taux des EPPA3 de 1980.

#### 2.2.2 Femmes:

- 1950-90, interpolation et extrapolation des taux d'activité 1950-80
tirés des EPPA3;
ajustement des taux interpolés et extrapolés sur la base des variations des
taux interpolés 1980 par rapport aux taux 1980 tirés des EPPA3.

## 3. Evaluation des taux de répartition par secteur d'activité: 1950 - 1990

### 3.1 Données de base:

Tableau 2: Répartition de la population active en % par secteur d'activité

| Année | Agriculture | Industrie Total | Manufac. | Services |
|---|---|---|---|---|
| **Hommes** | | | | |
| 1950 | 75.20 | 13.20 | .. | 11.60 |
| 1980 | 57.50 | 19.80 | .. | 22.70 |
| **Femmes** | | | | |
| 1950 | 99.8 | 0.05 | .. | 0.15 |
| 1980 | 94.7 | 1.45 | .. | 3.85 |

Source(s): EPPA3;

### 3.2 Méthode(s): interpolation et extrapolation linéaires

#### 3.2.1 Hommes:

- 1950 et 1990, taux de répartition 1950 et 1980 tirés des EPPA3;
- 1960-80, interpolation des taux de répartition estimés 1950 et 1990;
- l'industrie et les services, mêmes proportions que celles estimées
dans les EPPA3; moyenne des rapports manufacture/industrie estimés
pour l'Angola et le Zimbabwe.

#### 3.2.2 Femmes:

- 1950-90, interpolation extrapolation des taux de répartition ajustés
1950 et 1980 tirés des EPPA3;
ajustement des taux de répartition sur la base
du rapport hommes/femmes égal à 1 dans l'agriculture;
- 1960-80, interpolation des taux de répartition estimés 1950 et 1990;
- Les taux de répartition de manufacture ont été estimés sur la base des
moyennes des rapports manuf./indust. estimés pour l'Angola et le Zimbabwe.

## 4. Projection des taux d'activité: 2000 - 2010

### 4.1 Modèle(s): hyperbole

#### 4.1.1 Hommes:

- A tous les groupes d'âge, application de la fonction F3;
- Modification des tendances des groupes d'âge [20-54].

#### 4.1.2 Femmes:

- A tous les groupes d'âge, application de la fonction F3;
- Modification des tendances des groupes d'âge [20-59] et [65+]

*Notes sur les ajustements des taux, voir p. 192-195.*

*Notes sur les fonctions de projection, voir p. 198.*

# Rép. pop. dém. de Corée

## 1. Source(s) des données de base

Code(s):     Titre(s):

EPPA3     Evaluations et projections de la population active 1950-2025 - troisième édition, BIT, Genève, 1986.

## 2. Evaluation des taux d'activité: 1950 - 1990

### 2.1 Données de base:

Tableau 1: Taux d'activité par sexe et par groupe d'âge

| | Année | | | |
|---|---|---|---|---|
| Groupe d'âge | 1950 | 1960 | 1970 | 1980 |
| **Hommes** | | | | |
| 10-14 | 13.00 | 7.00 | 4.75 | 2.40 |
| 15-19 | 78.10 | 64.10 | 54.95 | 42.59 |
| 20-24 | 95.00 | 92.00 | 88.75 | 85.35 |
| 25-29 | 97.00 | 96.50 | 96.00 | 95.50 |
| 30-34 | 98.00 | 97.90 | 97.80 | 97.70 |
| 35-39 | 98.10 | 98.00 | 97.90 | 97.80 |
| 40-44 | 98.00 | 97.70 | 97.65 | 97.10 |
| 45-49 | 97.90 | 97.00 | 96.70 | 96.00 |
| 50-54 | 97.70 | 96.40 | 95.60 | 94.30 |
| 55-59 | 96.00 | 92.00 | 90.00 | 85.00 |
| 60-64 | 92.00 | 84.80 | 82.30 | 75.30 |
| 65+ | 73.10 | 61.10 | 51.40 | 37.40 |
| **Femmes** | | | | |
| 10-14 | .. | .. | 6.45 | 3.20 |
| 15-19 | .. | .. | 51.00 | 43.20 |
| 20-24 | .. | .. | 74.55 | 77.00 |
| 25-29 | .. | .. | 75.00 | 75.90 |
| 30-34 | .. | .. | 73.80 | 74.50 |
| 35-39 | .. | .. | 72.90 | 73.60 |
| 40-44 | .. | .. | 72.30 | 73.00 |
| 45-49 | .. | .. | 72.00 | 73.00 |
| 50-54 | .. | .. | 71.50 | 72.50 |
| 55-59 | .. | .. | 52.00 | 51.00 |
| 60-64 | .. | .. | 38.00 | 36.00 |
| 65+ | .. | .. | 25.45 | 21.50 |

Source(s): EPPA3.

### 2.2 Méthode(s): extrapolation linéaire

#### 2.2.1 Hommes:

- 1950-80, taux d'activité 1950-80 tirés des EPPA3;
- 1990, extrapolation des taux d'activité 1950-80 tirés des EPPA3;
ajustement des taux extrapolés sur la base des variations des taux interpolés 1980 par rapport aux taux 1980 tirés des EPPA3;
modification des tendances des groupes d'âge [15-19] et [25+].

#### 2.2.2 Femmes:

Méthode, hypothèses et traitements identiques à ceux appliqués aux hommes.

## 3. Evaluation des taux de répartition par secteur d'activité: 1950 - 1990

### 3.1 Données de base:

Tableau 2: Répartition de la population active en % par secteur d'activité

| | | Agriculture | Industrie | | Services |
|---|---|---|---|---|---|
| Année | | | Total | Manufac. | |
| **Hommes** | | | | | |
| | 1950 | 64.00 | 20.00 | .. | 16.00 |
| | 1960 | 57.00 | 28.00 | .. | 19.00 |
| | 1970 | 48.50 | 33.00 | .. | 22.00 |
| | 1980 | 39.00 | 39.00 | .. | 26.00 |
| **Femmes** | | | | | |
| | 1950 | 79.50 | 8.60 | .. | 11.90 |
| | 1960 | 71.50 | 12.50 | .. | 16.00 |
| | 1970 | 62.20 | 16.80 | .. | 21.00 |
| | 1980 | 52.00 | 20.00 | .. | 28.00 |

Source(s): EPPA3.

### 3.2 Méthode(s): extrapolation linéaire

#### 3.2.1 Hommes:

- 1950-80, taux de répartition 1950-80 tirés des EPPA3;
- 1990, extrapolation des taux de répartition 1950-80 tirés des EPPA3;
modification des tendances des secteurs industriel et des services.

#### 3.2.2 Femmes:

Méthode, hypothèses et traitements identiques à ceux appliqués aux hommes.

## 4. Projection des taux d'activité: 2000 - 2010

### 4.1 Modèle(s): log-linéaire et hyperbole

#### 4.1.1 Hommes:

- Au groupe d'âge [15-19], application de la fonction F2;
- Aux groupes d'âge [20+], application de la fonction F3;
- Modification de la tendance du groupe d'âge [20-24].

#### 4.1.2 Femmes:

- Au groupe d'âge [15-19], application de la fonction F2;
- Aux groupes d'âge [20+], application de la fonction F3;
- Modification des tendances des groupes d'âge [20-64].

# République arabe syrienne

## 1. Source(s) des données de base

Code(s):    Titre(s):

EPPA3    Evaluations et projections de la population active 1950-2025 - troisième édition, BIT, Genève, 1986.

STAT    Base de données sur les statistiques du travail - LABORSTA, Bureau de statistique, BIT, Genève.

## 2. Evaluation des taux d'activité: 1950 - 1990

### 2.1 Données de base:

Tableau 1: Taux d'activité par sexe et par groupe d'âge

| Groupe d'âge | Année | | | | |
| | 1950 (1) | 1960 (1) | 1970 (1) | 1981 (2) | 1983 (2) |
|---|---|---|---|---|---|
| **Hommes** | | | | | |
| 10-14 | 23.25 | 20.65 | .. | 12.53 | .. |
| 15-19 | 71.20 | 65.50 | .. | 53.15 | .. |
| 20-24 | 89.45 | 87.30 | .. | 82.08 | .. |
| 25-29 | 96.45 | 95.95 | .. | 95.50 | .. |
| 30-34 | 97.25 | 97.35 | .. | 98.07 | .. |
| 35-39 | 96.20 | 96.90 | .. | 98.21 | .. |
| 40-44 | 95.55 | 96.10 | .. | 97.15 | .. |
| 45-49 | 94.65 | 94.90 | .. | 94.46 | .. |
| 50-54 | 90.50 | 91.35 | .. | 89.78 | .. |
| 55-59 | 86.95 | 87.30 | .. | 85.27 | .. |
| 60-64 | 75.85 | 76.65 | .. | 68.56 | .. |
| 65+ | 43.35 | 45.55 | .. | 37.44 | .. |
| **Femmes** | | | | | |
| 10-14 | .. | .. | 6.90 | .. | 3.20 |
| 15-19 | .. | .. | 13.35 | .. | 11.20 |
| 20-24 | .. | .. | 16.45 | .. | 15.90 |
| 25-29 | .. | .. | 14.55 | .. | 16.80 |
| 30-34 | .. | .. | 12.60 | .. | 13.50 |
| 35-39 | .. | .. | 12.40 | .. | 12.50 |
| 40-44 | .. | .. | 12.35 | .. | 11.40 |
| 45-49 | .. | .. | 12.65 | .. | 11.10 |
| 50-54 | .. | .. | 11.00 | .. | 9.30 |
| 55-59 | .. | .. | 7.00 | .. | 6.50 |
| 60-64 | .. | .. | 5.50 | .. | 4.80 |
| 65+ | .. | .. | 2.7 | .. | 1.50 |

Source(s): (1) EPPA3; (2) STAT.

### 2.2 Méthode(s): interpolation et extrapolation linéaires
moyenne pondérée

#### 2.2.1 Hommes:

- 1950-80, interpolation des taux d'activité 1950-60 tirés des EPPA3
et des taux du recensement de 1981;
- 1990, aux taux d'activité estimés 1980, application des variations
moyennes des taux d'activité estimés pour l'Egypte et la Jordanie pour 1990.

#### 2.2.2 Femmes:

- 1950-70, taux d'activité ajustés 1950-70 tirés des EPPA3;
ajustement des taux sur la base du modèle d'ajustement des taux d'activité
des femmes travaillant dans l'agriculture comme aides familiales;
- 1980, moyennes pondérées des taux d'activité 1970 tirés des
EPPA3 et des taux d'activité tirés de l'enquêtes de 1983;
- 1990, extrapolation des taux d'activité estimés pour 1970 et 1980;
ajustement des taux d'activité estimés pour 1980 et 1990
en tenant compte de la sous-énumération des femmes travaillant dans l'agriculture

## 3. Evaluation des taux de répartition par secteur d'activité: 1950 - 1990

### 3.1 Données de base:

Tableau 2: Répartition de la population active en % par secteur d'activité

| Année | Agriculture | Industrie | | Services |
| | | Total | Manufac. | |
|---|---|---|---|---|
| **Hommes** | | | | |
| 1979 | 27.48 | 34.70 | 16.63 | 37.82 |
| 1983 | 22.17 | 36.53 | 15.38 | 41.30 |
| 1989 | 19.64 | 31.47 | 15.96 | 48.89 |
| 1991 | 23.06 | 28.42 | 15.55 | 48.52 |
| **Femmes** | | | | |
| 1979 | 60.26 | 14.18 | 12.39 | 25.55 |
| 1983 | 47.80 | 13.83 | 11.47 | 38.37 |
| 1989 | 41.43 | 13.81 | 12.14 | 44.76 |
| 1991 | 54.10 | 7.71 | 6.42 | 38.18 |

Source(s): STAT.

### 3.2 Méthode(s): moyenne pondérée
interpolation et extrapolation linéaires

#### 3.2.1 Hommes:

- 1950-70, taux de répartition 1950-70 tirés des EPPA3;
- 1980, moyennes pondérées des taux de répartition tirés des
enquêtes de 1979 et 1983;
- 1990, moyennes pondérées des taux de répartition tirés des
enquêtes de 1989 et 1991.

#### 3.2.2 Femmes:

- 1950-70, taux de répartition de l'agriculture 1950-70 tirés des EPPA3;
ajustement des taux en tenant compte de la sous-énumération des
femmes travaillant dans l'agriculture;
- 1980-90, interpolation et extrapolation des taux de répartition ajustés
tirés des enquêtes de 1979, 1983, 1989 et 1991;
ajustement des taux pour tenir compte de la sous-énumération des femmes
travaillant dans l'agriculture.

## 4. Projection des taux d'activité: 2000 - 2010

### 4.1 Modèle(s): linéaire et hyperbole

#### 4.1.1 Hommes:

- Aux groupes d'âge [10-14], [30-44] et [50+], application de la fonction F1;
- Aux groupes d'âge [15-29] et [45-49], application de la fonction F3;
- Modification des tendances des groupes d'âge [10-14], [20-44] et [50-59].

#### 4.1.2 Femmes:

- A tous les groupes d'âge, application de la fonction F1;
- Modification des tendances de tous les groupes d'âge.

*Notes sur les ajustements des taux, voir p. 192-195.*    *Notes sur les fonctions de projection, voir p. 198.*

# République de Corée

## 1. Source(s) des données de base

| Code(s): | Titre(s): |
|---|---|
| EPPA3 | Evaluations et projections de la population active 1950-2025 - troisième édition, BIT, Genève, 1986. |
| ADNU | Editions de 1979, 1984 et 1988 de l'Annuaire démographique des Nations Unies, New York. |
| ASTER | Annuaire des statistiques du travail 1945-89 - Edition rétrospective sur les recensements de population, BIT, Genève, 1990. |
| AST90-93 | Editions de 1990 à 1993 de l'Annuaire des statistiques du travail du BIT, Genève. |
| KNSO | Monthly Statistcs of Korea, National Statistical Office, Séoul. |

## 2. Evaluation des taux d'activité: 1950 - 1990

### 2.1 Données de base:

Tableau 1: Taux d'activité par sexe et par groupe d'âge

| Groupe d'âge | Année 1975 (1) | 1980 (2) | 1987 (3) | 1988 (3) | 1989 (3) | 1990 (3) | 1991 (3) | 1992 (3) |
|---|---|---|---|---|---|---|---|---|
| **Hommes** | | | | | | | | |
| 10-14 | .. | 0.70 | 0.00 | 0.00 | 0.00 | 0.00 | .. | .. |
| 15-19 | .. | 26.79 | 17.33 | 15.14 | 12.13 | 11.19 | .. | .. |
| 20-24 | .. | 79.46 | 77.06 | 77.06 | 77.60 | 77.23 | .. | .. |
| 25-29 | .. | 93.02 | 90.34 | 90.57 | 91.51 | 92.53 | .. | .. |
| 30-34 | .. | 97.38 | 96.08 | 96.67 | 97.18 | 97.37 | .. | .. |
| 35-39 | .. | 97.43 | 96.15 | 96.59 | 97.18 | 97.10 | .. | .. |
| 40-44 | .. | 96.86 | 95.30 | 95.70 | 95.40 | 95.70 | .. | .. |
| 45-49 | .. | 95.21 | 92.70 | 93.20 | 93.60 | 94.10 | .. | .. |
| 50-54 | .. | 90.63 | 87.80 | 89.20 | 89.70 | 90.90 | .. | .. |
| 55-59 | .. | 82.52 | 77.40 | 79.70 | 82.40 | 83.60 | .. | .. |
| 60-64 | .. | 68.82 | 64.40 | 65.20 | 65.60 | 67.50 | .. | .. |
| 65+ | .. | 40.63 | 36.20 | 37.00 | 39.00 | 39.60 | .. | .. |
| **Femmes** | | | | | | | | |
| 10-14 | 4.69 | .. | 0.00 | 0.00 | 0.00 | 0.00 | 0.00 | 0.00 |
| 15-19 | 47.48 | .. | 27.68 | 25.06 | 22.32 | 21.46 | 19.67 | 18.49 |
| 20-24 | 62.89 | .. | 63.88 | 65.32 | 67.22 | 67.16 | 67.87 | 67.26 |
| 25-29 | 35.59 | .. | 40.82 | 41.72 | 48.18 | 47.02 | 47.25 | 48.89 |
| 30-34 | 41.63 | .. | 47.53 | 49.48 | 52.42 | 53.11 | 53.98 | 54.52 |
| 35-39 | 51.15 | .. | 57.97 | 57.00 | 57.26 | 58.36 | 60.53 | 59.53 |
| 40-44 | 58.10 | .. | 60.30 | 60.20 | 61.00 | 60.50 | 60.40 | 60.40 |
| 45-49 | 60.08 | .. | 62.10 | 62.70 | 63.50 | 63.90 | 62.00 | 60.90 |
| 50-54 | 57.55 | .. | 57.00 | 58.00 | 60.40 | 60.00 | 60.00 | 60.80 |
| 55-59 | 51.43 | .. | 49.10 | 49.50 | 52.70 | 54.40 | 54.50 | 54.10 |
| 60-64 | 33.00 | .. | 40.30 | 39.70 | 41.60 | 43.60 | 43.20 | 44.90 |
| 65+ | 12.24 | .. | 15.40 | 15.50 | 18.10 | 18.40 | 18.80 | 19.60 |

Source(s): (1) (2) ADNU et ASTER; (3) KNSO et AST90-93.

### 2.2 Méthode(s): interpolation et extrapolation linéaires

**2.2.1 Hommes:**

- 1950-70, taux d'activité 1950-70 tirés des EPPA3;
- 1980-90, extrapolation des taux d'activité ajustés tirés du recensement de 1980 et des enquêtes de 1987 à 1990;
ajustement des taux interpolés sur la base des variations des taux extrapolés 1970 par rapport aux taux de 1970 tirés des EPPA3;
modification des tendances des groupes d'âge [15-29] de 1990.

**2.2.2 Femmes:**

- 1950-80, taux d'activité ajustés 1950-80 tirés des EPPA3;
- 1990, interpolation des taux d'activité tirés du recensement de 1975 et des enquêtes de 1987 à 1992;
ajustement des taux interpolés sur la base des variations des taux extrapolés 1970 par rapport aux taux de 1970 tirés des EPPA3.

## 3. Evaluation des taux de répartition par secteur d'activité: 1950 - 1990

### 3.1 Données de base:

Tableau 2: Répartition de la population active en % par secteur d'activité

| Année | Agriculture | Industrie Total | Manufac. | Services |
|---|---|---|---|---|
| **Hommes** | | | | |
| 1989 | 18.05 | 37.98 | 26.77 | 43.97 |
| 1980 | 16.76 | 38.67 | 26.15 | 44.56 |
| 1991 | 15.42 | 39.63 | 26.01 | 44.95 |
| **Femmes** | | | | |
| 1989 | 21.65 | 30.69 | 28.91 | 47.66 |
| 1990 | 20.41 | 30.00 | 27.93 | 49.60 |
| 1991 | 18.60 | 29.68 | 27.42 | 51.72 |

Source(s): KNSO et AST90-93.

### 3.2 Méthode(s): moyenne arithmétique

**3.2.1 Hommes:**

- 1950-80, taux de répartition 1950-80 tirés des EPPA3;
- 1990, moyennes des taux de répartition tirés des enquêtes de 1989, 1990 et 1991.

**3.2.2 Femmes:**

Méthode, hypothèses et traitements identiques à ceux appliqués aux hommes.

## 4. Projection des taux d'activité: 2000 - 2010

### 4.1 Modèle(s): linéaire, hyperbole et logistique

**4.1.1 Hommes:**

- Aux groupes d'âge [15+], application de la fonction F3;
- Modification des tendances des groupes d'âge [15-49].

**4.1.2 Femmes:**

- Aux groupes d'âge [15-24] et [60+], application de la fonction F1;
- Aux groupes d'âge [25-59], application de la fonction F6;
- Modification des tendances des groupes d'âge [15+].

---

*Notes sur les ajustements des taux, voir p. 192-195.*    *Notes sur les fonctions de projection, voir p. 198.*

# République dém. pop. lao

## 1. Source(s) des données de base

Code(s):   Titre(s):

EPPA4    Population active 1950-2010 - quatrième édition, BIT, Genève 1996.

## 2. Evaluation des taux d'activité: 1950 - 1990

### 2.1 Données de base:

Tableau 1: Taux d'activité par sexe et par groupe d'âge

| Groupe d'âge | 1950 (1) | 1950 (2) | 1970 (1) | 1970 (2) |
|---|---|---|---|---|
| **Hommes** | | | | |
| 10-14 | 37.12 | 38.56 | 28.30 | 29.66 |
| 15-19 | 81.62 | 91.66 | 74.84 | 84.50 |
| 20-24 | 90.30 | 97.38 | 88.80 | 97.38 |
| 25-29 | 95.84 | 98.00 | 96.31 | 98.00 |
| 30-34 | 97.23 | 97.93 | 97.53 | 97.93 |
| 35-39 | 97.42 | 96.85 | 97.85 | 96.85 |
| 40-44 | 97.58 | 94.64 | 97.64 | 94.55 |
| 45-49 | 97.10 | 91.62 | 97.13 | 91.48 |
| 50-54 | 95.50 | 89.96 | 95.41 | 88.17 |
| 55-59 | 92.10 | 80.04 | 91.80 | 84.39 |
| 60-64 | 82.55 | 87.72 | 76.21 | 79.45 |
| 65+ | 55.88 | 81.07 | 48.00 | 65.00 |
| **Femmes** | | | | |
| 10-14 | 43.31 | 29.50 | 32.15 | 26.07 |
| 15-19 | 85.90 | 68.50 | 77.05 | 71.34 |
| 20-24 | 87.06 | 77.59 | 83.57 | 81.17 |
| 25-29 | 84.57 | 76.61 | 83.75 | 80.25 |
| 30-34 | 84.25 | 74.03 | 84.69 | 78.78 |
| 35-39 | 85.81 | 73.25 | 85.98 | 77.39 |
| 40-44 | 86.42 | 72.29 | 86.01 | 75.35 |
| 45-49 | 87.71 | 66.55 | 85.94 | 69.02 |
| 50-54 | 81.61 | 58.64 | 80.24 | 60.64 |
| 55-59 | 78.06 | 53.98 | 73.70 | 52.19 |
| 60-64 | 49.03 | 50.09 | 47.71 | 43.02 |
| 65+ | 34.88 | 39.46 | 27.10 | 31.13 |

Note(s): (1) Thaïlande; (2) Viet Nam.
Source(s): EPPA4.

### 2.2 Méthode(s): interpolation linéaire / moyenne arithmétique

#### 2.2.1 Hommes:

- 1990, moyennes des taux d'activité estimés 1970 pour la Thaïlande et le Viet Nam;
- 1950, aux taux d'activité estimés 1990, application de la moyenne des variations des taux d'activité estimés pour la Thaïlande et le Viet Nam pour 1950 par rapport aux taux estimés 1970 pour ces deux pays;
- 1960-80, interpolation des taux estimés 1950 et 1990; modification des tendances de tous les groupes d'âge.

#### 2.2.2 Femmes:

Méthode, hypothèses et traitements identiques à ceux appliqués aux hommes.

## 3. Evaluation des taux de répartition par secteur d'activité: 1950 - 1990

### 3.1 Données de base:

Tableau 2: Répartition de la population active en % par secteur d'activité

| Année | Agriculture | Industrie Total | Manufac. | Services |
|---|---|---|---|---|
| **Hommes** | | | | |
| 1950 (1) | 82.90 | 3.60 | .. | 13.50 |
| 1950 (2) | 81.30 | 4.00 | .. | 14.70 |
| 1970 (1) | 76.25 | 7.45 | .. | 16.30 |
| 1970 (2) | 75.10 | 7.35 | .. | 17.55 |
| **Femmes** | | | | |
| 1950 (1) | 86.60 | 1.90 | .. | 9.50 |
| 1950 (2) | 85.75 | 2.55 | .. | 11.70 |
| 1970 (1) | 83.65 | 4.45 | .. | 11.90 |
| 1970 (2) | 78.25 | 5.55 | .. | 16.20 |

Note(s): (1) Thaïlande; (2) Viet Nam.
Source(s): EPPA4.

### 3.2 Méthode(s): moyenne pondérée

#### 3.2.1 Hommes:

- 1950, aux taux de répartition estimés 1990, application de la moyenne des variations des taux de répartition 1950 estimées pour la Thaïlande et le Viet Nam par rapport aux taux estimés 1970 pour ces deux pays;
- 1960-80, moyennes pondérées des taux estimés pour 1950 et 1990;
- 1990, moyenne des taux de répartition 1970 estimés pour la Thaïlande et le Viet Nam.

#### 3.2.2 Femmes:

Méthode, hypothèses et traitements identiques à ceux appliqués aux hommes.

## 4. Projection des taux d'activité: 2000 - 2010

### 4.1 Modèle(s): linéaire

#### 4.1.1 Hommes:

- A tous les groupes d'âge, application de la fonction F1;
- Modification des tendances des groupes d'âge [10-19].

#### 4.1.2 Femmes:

- A tous les groupes d'âge, application de la fonction F1;
- Modification des tendances des groupes d'âge [10-54].

*Notes sur les ajustements des taux, voir p. 192-195.*

*Notes sur les fonctions de projection, voir p. 198.*

# République dominicaine

## 1. Source(s) des données de base

Code(s):    Titre(s):

EPPA3    Evaluations et projections de la population active 1950-2025 - troisième édition, BIT, Genève, 1986.
RDR-70    Censos Nacional de Poblacion Y habitacion 1970, Oficina Nacional de Estadìstica (ONE), Santo Domingo.
ASTER    Annuaire des statistiques du travail 1945-89 - Edition rétrospective sur les recensements de population, BIT, Genève, 1990.

## 2. Evaluation des taux d'activité: 1950 - 1990

### 2.1 Données de base:

Tableau 1: Taux d'activité par sexe et par groupe d'âge

| Groupe d'âge | Année 1950 (1) | 1960 (2) | 1970 (3) | 1981 (2) |
|---|---|---|---|---|
| **Hommes** | | | | |
| 10-14 | 53.75 | 48.00 | 41.87 | .. |
| 15-19 | 78.50 | 70.10 | 60.24 | .. |
| 20-24 | 97.00 | 95.05 | 84.94 | .. |
| 25-29 | 98.00 | 97.84 | 92.86 | .. |
| 30-34 | 98.80 | 98.64 | 95.00 | .. |
| 35-39 | 98.80 | 98.65 | 94.61 | .. |
| 40-44 | 98.65 | 98.47 | 93.97 | .. |
| 45-49 | 98.50 | 98.16 | 93.27 | .. |
| 50-54 | 98.25 | 97.86 | 90.95 | .. |
| 55-59 | 97.45 | 96.68 | 90.48 | .. |
| 60-64 | 96.60 | 95.12 | 88.19 | .. |
| 65+ | 84.59 | 83.27 | 79.12 | .. |
| **Femmes** | | | | |
| 10-14 | 2.80 | 2.21 | 25.81 | 11.00 |
| 15-19 | 9.50 | 8.97 | 23.49 | 20.40 |
| 20-24 | 11.55 | 12.23 | 26.53 | 33.30 |
| 25-29 | 11.50 | 12.25 | 25.84 | 38.30 |
| 30-34 | 11.50 | 12.23 | 25.72 | 37.10 |
| 35-39 | 11.65 | 12.39 | 24.72 | 32.40 |
| 40-44 | 11.90 | 12.64 | 25.74 | 33.30 |
| 45-49 | 12.55 | 12.87 | 23.40 | 32.30 |
| 50-54 | 10.00 | 10.25 | 22.52 | 28.90 |
| 55-59 | 11.20 | 11.13 | 21.94 | 28.10 |
| 60-64 | 9.35 | 9.26 | 22.21 | 26.90 |
| 65+ | 4.50 | 4.27 | 10.50 | 10.28 |

Source(s): (1) EPPA3; (2) RDR-70 et ASTER; (3) ASTER.

### 2.2 Méthode(s): interpolation et extrapolation linéaires

#### 2.2.1 Hommes:

- 1950-60, taux d'activité 1950-60 tirés des EPPA3;
ajustement des taux d'activité des groupes d'âge [10-14] et [65+] sur la base
des résultats des recensements de 1970 et 1981;
- 1970, taux d'activité ajustés tirés du recensement de 1970;
- 1980-90, extrapolation des taux d'activité 1950 tirés des EPPA3,
des taux ajustés du recensement de 1960 et des taux du recensement de 1970;
aux taux extrapolés, application des variations des taux interpolés 1970
par rapport aux taux tirés du recensement de 1970.

#### 2.2.2 Femmes:

- 1950-60, taux d'activité 1950-60 tirés des EPPA3;
modification des tendances des groupes d'âge [10-19] pour 1960;
- 1970-80, interpolation des taux d'activité tirés des recensements
de 1970 et 1981;
- 1990, extrapolation des taux d'activité tirés des recensements
de 1970 et 1981;
aux taux extrapolés, application des variations des taux interpolés 1970
par rapport aux taux tirés du recensement de 1970.

## 3. Evaluation des taux de répartition par secteur d'activité: 1950 - 1990

### 3.1 Données de base:

Tableau 2: Répartition de la population active en % par secteur d'activité

| Année | Agriculture | Industrie Total | Manufac. | Services |
|---|---|---|---|---|
| **Hommes** | | | | |
| 1960 | 69.30 | 12.35 | .. | 18.35 |
| 1970 | 58.20 | 14.68 | 11.16 | 27.12 |
| 1981 | 38.61 | 26.64 | 17.02 | 34.76 |
| **Femmes** | | | | |
| 1960 | 13.15 | 16.15 | .. | 70.70 |
| 1970 | 11.91 | 13.02 | 12.43 | 75.07 |
| 1981 | 11.02 | 16.44 | 15.07 | 72.54 |

Source(s): ASTER.

### 3.2 Méthode(s): moyenne pondérée
interpolation et extrapolation linéaires

#### 3.2.1 Hommes:

- 1950-60, taux de répartition 1950-60 tirés des EPPA3;
- 1970, moyennes pondérées des taux de répartition 1960 tirés des
EPPA3 et des taux de répartition du recensement de 1970;
- 1980-90, interpolation et extrapolation des taux de répartition tirés des
recensements de 1970 et 1981;
modification des tendances de tous les secteurs pour 1990.

#### 3.2.2 Femmes:

Méthode, hypothèses et traitements identiques à ceux appliqués aux hommes.

## 4. Projection des taux d'activité: 2000 - 2010

### 4.1 Modèle(s): linéaire, hyperbole et logistique

#### 4.1.1 Hommes:

- Aux groupes d'âge [10-24] et [55+], application de la fonction F1;
- Aux groupes d'âge [25-54], application de la fonction F3;
- Modification des tendances des groupes d'âge [10-24] et [50-59].

#### 4.1.2 Femmes:

- Aux groupes d'âge [10-19] et [40+], application de la fonction F1;
- Aux groupes d'âge [20-39], application de la fonction F6;
- Modification des tendances des groupes d'âge [10-39] et [50+].

*Notes sur les ajustements des taux, voir p. 192-195.*    *Notes sur les fonctions de projection, voir p. 198.*

# République tchèque

## 1. Source(s) des données de base

| Code(s): | Titre(s): |
|---|---|
| BLT-94-2 | Vorobiev A. (1994), "Estimation de la population active pour les quinze pays de l'ex-URSS pour les années 1950, 1959, 1970, 1979 et 1989", dans le Bulletin des statistiques du travail - 1994-2, BIT, Genève. |
| STAT | Base de données sur les statistiques du travail - LABORSTA, Bureau de statistique, BIT, Genève. |

## 2. Evaluation des taux d'activité: 1950 - 1990

### 2.1 Données de base:

Tableau 1: Taux d'activité par sexe et par groupe d'âge

| | | Année | | | | | |
|---|---|---|---|---|---|---|---|
| | Groupe d'âge | 1950 (1)(2) | 1950 (2) | 1961 (2) | 1970 (2) | 1980 (3) | 1990 (3) |
| **Hommes** | | | | | | | |
| | 10-14 | 0.90 | .. | 0.00 | 0.00 | 0.00 | 0.00 |
| | 15-19 | 74.46 | .. | 47.32 | 34.90 | 27.25 | 34.83 |
| | 20-24 | 93.09 | .. | 94.20 | 91.55 | 86.49 | 88.19 |
| | 25-29 | 98.34 | .. | 98.79 | 98.61 | 98.23 | 98.02 |
| | 30-34 | 98.38 | .. | 98.87 | 98.97 | 98.89 | 98.32 |
| | 35-39 | 98.51 | .. | 98.42 | 98.69 | 98.66 | 97.84 |
| | 40-44 | 98.10 | .. | 97.73 | 97.92 | 97.65 | 97.19 |
| | 45-49 | 97.14 | .. | 96.35 | 96.52 | 96.29 | 95.62 |
| | 50-54 | 93.59 | .. | 93.09 | 93.74 | 92.94 | 91.89 |
| | 55-59 | 88.67 | .. | 84.32 | 85.26 | 84.31 | 80.36 |
| | 60-64 | 76.58 | .. | 46.28 | 31.47 | 46.58 | 29.09 |
| | 65+ | 38.38 | .. | 23.87 | 14.66 | 18.96 | 12.38 |
| **Femmes** | | | | | | | |
| | 10-14 | .. | 0.00 | 0.00 | 0.00 | 0.00 | 0.00 |
| | 15-19 | .. | 69.83 | 58.21 | 44.21 | 29.77 | 33.65 |
| | 20-24 | .. | 59.29 | 73.15 | 79.68 | 84.57 | 87.25 |
| | 25-29 | .. | 39.30 | 62.77 | 80.91 | 91.17 | 94.36 |
| | 30-34 | .. | 40.99 | 65.65 | 83.81 | 93.09 | 95.03 |
| | 35-39 | .. | 46.39 | 72.27 | 86.57 | 94.31 | 95.43 |
| | 40-44 | .. | 48.10 | 74.53 | 86.41 | 94.03 | 94.97 |
| | 45-49 | .. | 51.82 | 72.96 | 84.05 | 91.27 | 93.21 |
| | 50-54 | .. | 45.51 | 66.20 | 77.13 | 83.68 | 85.40 |
| | 55-59 | .. | 34.81 | 46.81 | 39.38 | 40.11 | 32.29 |
| | 60-64 | .. | 22.14 | 33.23 | 20.01 | 23.87 | 16.42 |
| | 65+ | .. | 8.80 | 9.10 | 5.89 | 7.24 | 5.09 |

Note(s): (1) Slovaquie.
Source(s): (2) STAT; (3) BLT-94-2.

### 2.2 Méthode(s): moyenne pondérée

#### 2.2.1 Hommes:

- 1950-90, moyennes pondérées des taux d'activité tirés des recensements de 1961 et 1970, des taux d'activité 1980 et 1990 tiré du Bulletin des statistiques du travail 1994-2 et des taux d'activité estimés 1950 sur la base d'une application aux taux d'activité tirés du recensement de 1950 pour la Slovaquie, des variations des taux d'activité du recensement de 1961 par rapport aux taux d'activité du recensement de 1961 pour la Slovaquie;
ajustement des taux d'activité estimés 1950-70 pour le groupe d'âge [10-14].

#### 2.2.2 Femmes:

- 1950-90, moyennes pondérées des taux d'activité tirés des recensements de 1950, 1961 et 1970 et des taux d'activité 1980 et 1990 tiré du Bulletin des statistiques du travail 1994-2;
ajustement des taux d'activité estimés 1950-70 pour le groupe d'âge [10-14].

## 3. Evaluation des taux de répartition par secteur d'activité: 1950 - 1990

### 3.1 Données de base:

Tableau 2: Répartition de la population active en % par secteur d'activité

| | | Agriculture | Industrie | | Services |
|---|---|---|---|---|---|
| | Année | | Total | Manufac. | |
| **Hommes** | | | | | |
| | 1950 | 25.00 | 46.50 | .. | 28.50 |
| | 1961 | 17.75 | 57.47 | 48.22 | 24.78 |
| | 1970 | 14.76 | 56.27 | .. | 28.97 |
| | 1980 | 14.40 | 66.54 | 45.50 | 19.07 |
| | 1991 | 13.03 | 52.55 | 35.42 | 34.41 |
| **Femmes** | | | | | |
| | 1950 | 43.72 | 32.06 | .. | 24.22 |
| | 1961 | 26.99 | 40.36 | 42.31 | 32.65 |
| | 1970 | 14.99 | 41.94 | 0.00 | 43.07 |
| | 1980 | 11.40 | 43.58 | 38.91 | 45.02 |
| | 1991 | 8.91 | 35.75 | 35.53 | 55.34 |

Source(s): STAT.

### 3.2 Méthode(s): moyenne pondérée

#### 3.2.1 Hommes:

- 1950-90, moyennes pondérées des taux de répartition tirés des recensements de 1950, 1961, 1970, 1980 et 1991.

#### 3.2.2 Femmes:

Méthode, hypothèses et traitements identiques à ceux appliqués aux hommes.

## 4. Projection des taux d'activité: 2000 - 2010

### 4.1 Modèle(s): linéaire et hyperbole

#### 4.1.1 Hommes:

- Aux groupes d'âge [15-44] et [60+], application de la fonction F3;
- Aux groupes d'âge [45-59], application de la fonction F1;
- Modification des tendances des groupes d'âge [45-59].

#### 4.1.2 Femmes:

- Aux groupes d'âge [15+], application de la fonction F3;
- Modification des tendances des groupes d'âge [15-54].

*Notes sur les ajustements des taux, voir p. 192-195.*

*Notes sur les fonctions de projection, voir p. 198.*

# Réunion

## 1. Source(s) des données de base

Code(s):  Titre(s):

EPPA3  Evaluations et projections de la population active 1950-2025 - troisième édition, BIT, Genève, 1986.
ASTER  Annuaire des statistiques du travail 1945-89 - Edition rétrospective sur les recensements de population, BIT, Genève, 1990.
AST92  Annuaire des statistiques du travail 1992, BIT, Genève, 1992.

## 2. Evaluation des taux d'activité: 1950 - 1990

### 2.1 Données de base:

Tableau 1: Taux d'activité par sexe et par groupe d'âge

| Groupe d'âge | Année 1982 (1) | 1990 (2) |
|---|---|---|
| **Hommes** | | |
| 10-14 | 0.00 | 0.00 |
| 15-19 | 32.85 | 19.60 |
| 20-24 | 87.28 | 77.50 |
| 25-29 | 93.83 | 92.30 |
| 30-34 | 94.28 | 92.30 |
| 35-39 | 93.82 | 91.50 |
| 40-44 | 91.38 | 89.40 |
| 45-49 | 88.45 | 85.40 |
| 50-54 | 82.81 | 77.50 |
| 55-59 | 72.66 | 58.40 |
| 60-64 | 33.65 | 19.30 |
| 65+ | 22.51 | 3.05 |
| **Femmes** | | |
| 10-14 | 0.00 | 0.00 |
| 15-19 | 25.90 | 14.60 |
| 20-24 | 56.70 | 63.90 |
| 25-29 | 50.30 | 68.10 |
| 30-34 | 46.90 | 63.00 |
| 35-39 | 43.70 | 60.30 |
| 40-44 | 40.40 | 57.40 |
| 45-49 | 37.00 | 51.20 |
| 50-54 | 32.40 | 40.50 |
| 55-59 | 27.90 | 27.50 |
| 60-64 | 11.90 | 8.70 |
| 65+ | 1.34 | 0.80 |

Source(s): (1) ASTER; (2) AST92.

### 2.2 Méthode(s): moyenne pondérée

#### 2.2.1 Hommes:

- 1950-70, taux d'activité 1950-70 tirés des EPPA3;
- 1980-90, moyennes pondérées des taux d'activité ajustés tirés des recensements de 1982 et 1990;
modification des tendances des groupes [20-34] pour 1980.

#### 2.2.2 Femmes:

- 1950-80, taux d'activité 1950-80 tirés des EPPA3;
- 1990, moyennes pondérées des taux d'activité tirés des recensements de 1982 et 1990.

## 3. Evaluation des taux de répartition par secteur d'activité: 1950 - 1990

### 3.1 Données de base:

Tableau 2: Répartition de la population active en % par secteur d'activité

| Année | Agriculture | Industrie Total | Manufac. | Services |
|---|---|---|---|---|
| **Hommes** | | | | |
| 1982 (1) | 36.99 | 29.42 | 8.92 | 33.59 |
| 1990 (2) | 11.12 | 27.64 | 9.51 | 61.25 |
| **Femmes** | | | | |
| 1982 (1) | 7.14 | 4.80 | 3.62 | 88.07 |
| 1990 (2) | 1.94 | 5.09 | 3.64 | 92.97 |

Source(s): (1) ASTER; (2) AST92.

### 3.2 Méthode(s): interpolation et extrapolation linéaires

#### 3.2.1 Hommes:

- 1950-70, taux de répartition 1950-70 tirés des EPPA3;
- 1980-90, interpolation et extrapolation des taux de répartition tirés des recensements de 1982 et 1990;
modification des tendances de tous les secteurs pour 1980.

#### 3.2.2 Femmes:

Méthode, hypothèses et traitements identiques à ceux appliqués aux hommes.

## 4. Projection des taux d'activité: 2000 - 2010

### 4.1 Modèle(s): linéaire, hyperbole et logistique

#### 4.1.1 Hommes:

- Au groupe d'âge [15-19], application de la fonction F1;
- Aux groupes d'âge [20+], application de la fonction F3.

#### 4.1.2 Femmes:

- Aux groupes d'âge [15-19] et [50-54], application de la fonction F1;
- Aux groupes d'âge [20-49], application de la fonction F6;
- Modification de la tendance du groupe d'âge [25-29].

*Notes sur les ajustements des taux, voir p. 192-195.*    *Notes sur les fonctions de projection, voir p. 198.*

# Roumanie

## 1. Source(s) des données de base

| Code(s): | Titre(s): |
|---|---|
| EPPA3 | Evaluations et projections de la population active 1950-2025 - troisième édition, BIT, Genève, 1986. |
| ASTER | Annuaire des statistiques du travail 1945-89 - Edition rétrospective sur les recensements de population, BIT, Genève, 1990. |
| BLT-94-2 | Popovic B. (1994), "Nouvelles estimations pour 1980 et 1990 des taux d'activité par âge et répartition sectorielle pour certains pays d'Europe orientale et méridionale" dans le Bulletin des statistiques du travail - 1994-2, BIT, Genève. |
| AST94 | Annuaire des statistiques du travail 1994, BIT, Genève, 1994. |

## 2. Evaluation des taux d'activité: 1950 - 1990

### 2.1 Données de base:

Tableau 1: Taux d'activité par sexe et par groupe d'âge

| Groupe d'âge | Année 1950 (1) | 1960 (1) | 1970 (1) | 1977 (2) | 1992 (2) |
|---|---|---|---|---|---|
| **Hommes** | | | | | |
| 10-14 | 1.50 | 0.85 | 0.50 | 0.40 | 0.42 |
| 15-19 | 90.00 | 74.10 | 62.10 | 37.50 | 38.60 |
| 20-24 | 95.60 | 93.20 | 90.10 | 87.10 | 86.80 |
| 25-29 | 97.90 | 97.35 | 96.85 | 97.00 | 95.70 |
| 30-34 | 98.40 | 98.35 | 97.90 | 97.90 | 96.70 |
| 35-39 | 98.75 | 98.50 | 98.00 | 97.20 | 96.60 |
| 40-44 | 98.45 | 98.00 | 97.50 | 95.80 | 95.80 |
| 45-49 | 97.95 | 97.70 | 97.50 | 93.80 | 93.20 |
| 50-54 | 96.95 | 95.30 | 94.80 | 88.80 | 79.60 |
| 55-59 | 94.50 | 92.90 | 88.00 | 78.70 | 45.80 |
| 60-64 | 90.85 | 80.40 | 65.00 | 44.70 | 21.00 |
| 65+ | 74.10 | 62.50 | 54.85 | 13.23 | 5.37 |
| **Femmes** | | | | | |
| 10-14 | 2.00 | 1.45 | 0.90 | 0.50 | 0.21 |
| 15-19 | 79.45 | 69.95 | 45.20 | 32.10 | 32.70 |
| 20-24 | 78.55 | 75.90 | 74.15 | 75.60 | 72.10 |
| 25-29 | 74.85 | 76.15 | 80.35 | 83.10 | 78.50 |
| 30-34 | 74.20 | 75.70 | 80.45 | 83.50 | 81.30 |
| 35-39 | 74.05 | 75.85 | 80.80 | 83.60 | 81.60 |
| 40-44 | 75.80 | 76.40 | 79.45 | 81.70 | 79.00 |
| 45-49 | 74.75 | 74.90 | 75.85 | 77.60 | 72.80 |
| 50-54 | 73.85 | 72.10 | 70.70 | 69.70 | 51.00 |
| 55-59 | 67.95 | 63.50 | 55.90 | 72.50 | 28.70 |
| 60-64 | 61.40 | 52.10 | 34.45 | 25.20 | 10.20 |
| 65+ | 40.35 | 29.90 | 15.85 | 10.04 | 4.69 |

Source(s): (1) EPPA3; (2) AST94.

### 2.2 Méthode(s): interpolation linéaire

#### 2.2.1 Hommes:

- 1950-70, taux d'activité 1950-70 tirés des EPPA3;
- 1980-90, interpolation des taux d'activité tirés des recensements de 1977 et 1992.

#### 2.2.2 Femmes:

Méthode, hypothèses et traitements identiques à ceux appliqués aux hommes.

## 3. Evaluation des taux de répartition par secteur d'activité: 1950 - 1990

### 3.1 Données de base:

Tableau 2: Répartition de la population active en % par secteur d'activité

| Année | Agriculture | Industrie Total | Manufac. | Services |
|---|---|---|---|---|
| **Hommes** | | | | |
| 1950 (1) | 61.80 | 21.70 | .. | 16.50 |
| 1960 (1) | 53.00 | 29.50 | .. | 17.40 |
| 1970 (1) | 37.10 | 41.60 | .. | 21.30 |
| 1980 (2) | 25.93 | 50.14 | 33.92 | 23.93 |
| 1990 (2) | 20.95 | 52.91 | 37.39 | 26.14 |
| **Femmes** | | | | |
| 1950 (1) | 84.30 | 6.50 | .. | 9.20 |
| 1960 (1) | 78.40 | 9.40 | .. | 12.10 |
| 1970 (1) | 63.70 | 17.50 | .. | 18.80 |
| 1980 (2) | 45.33 | 29.45 | 26.43 | 25.21 |
| 1990 (2) | 27.75 | 40.04 | 35.94 | 32.21 |

Source(s): (1) EPPA3; (2) BLT-94-2.

### 3.2 Méthode(s): données du BLT-94-2

#### 3.2.1 Hommes:

- 1950-70, taux de répartition 1950-70 tirés des EPPA3;
- 1980-90, taux de répartition tirés du Bulletin des statistiques du travail - 1994-2.

#### 3.2.2 Femmes:

Méthode, hypothèses et traitements identiques à ceux appliqués aux hommes.

## 4. Projection des taux d'activité: 2000 - 2010

### 4.1 Modèle(s): linéaire et hyperbole

#### 4.1.1 Hommes:

- Aux groupes d'âge [15-19] et [25+], application de la fonction F3;
- Aux groupes d'âge [20-24], application de la fonction F1;
- Modification des tendances des groupes d'âge [35-39] et [50-64].

#### 4.1.2 Femmes:

- Aux groupes d'âge [15+], application de la fonction F3;
- Modification des tendances des groupes d'âge [20-24] et [30-39].

*Notes sur les ajustements des taux, voir p. 192-195.*     *Notes sur les fonctions de projection, voir p. 198.*

# Royaume-Uni

## 1. Source(s) des données de base

Code(s):     Titre(s):

EPPA3     Annuaire des statistiques du travail 1945-89 - Edition rétrospective sur les recensements de population, BIT, Genève, 1990.
STAT       Base de données sur les statistiques du travail - LABORSTA, Bureau de statistique, BIT, Genève.

## 2. Evaluation des taux d'activité: 1950 - 1990

### 2.1 Données de base:

Tableau 1: Taux d'activité par sexe et par groupe d'âge

| Groupe d'âge | Année 1950 (1) | 1960 (1) | 1970 (1) | 1980 (1) | 1991 (2) |
|---|---|---|---|---|---|
| **Hommes** | | | | | |
| 10-14 | 0.10 | 0.05 | 0.00 | 0.00 | 0.00 |
| 15-19 | 87.25 | 77.95 | 68.60 | 59.25 | 68.20 |
| 20-24 | 95.40 | 93.65 | 91.85 | 90.10 | 71.55 |
| 25-29 | 98.15 | 97.60 | 97.10 | 96.60 | 95.34 |
| 30-34 | 99.20 | 98.65 | 98.10 | 97.55 | 95.65 |
| 35-39 | 99.35 | 98.75 | 98.10 | 97.50 | 95.31 |
| 40-44 | 99.15 | 98.70 | 98.20 | 97.75 | 94.86 |
| 45-49 | 99.10 | 98.45 | 97.75 | 97.10 | 93.39 |
| 50-54 | 98.60 | 97.55 | 96.45 | 95.40 | 89.23 |
| 55-59 | 97.35 | 95.50 | 93.65 | 91.75 | 79.82 |
| 60-64 | 93.60 | 87.40 | 81.20 | 75.00 | 56.67 |
| 65+ | 34.40 | 26.60 | 18.80 | 11.00 | 8.04 |
| **Femmes** | | | | | |
| 10-14 | 0.10 | 0.05 | 0.05 | 0.00 | 0.00 |
| 15-19 | 80.75 | 71.65 | 62.50 | 53.35 | 61.36 |
| 20-24 | 64.85 | 64.75 | 64.65 | 64.55 | 59.08 |
| 25-29 | 39.55 | 44.25 | 49.00 | 53.70 | 69.09 |
| 30-34 | 26.85 | 36.50 | 46.15 | 55.80 | 65.19 |
| 35-39 | 28.70 | 39.30 | 49.90 | 60.45 | 70.40 |
| 40-44 | 28.50 | 41.45 | 54.40 | 67.35 | 75.24 |
| 45-49 | 29.60 | 42.40 | 55.15 | 67.95 | 74.21 |
| 50-54 | 28.20 | 40.45 | 52.75 | 65.00 | 66.85 |
| 55-59 | 24.60 | 35.00 | 45.45 | 55.85 | 52.61 |
| 60-64 | 15.00 | 18.20 | 21.45 | 24.70 | 22.01 |
| 65+ | 6.05 | 5.40 | 4.75 | 4.15 | 2.95 |

Source(s): (1) EPPA3; (2) STAT.

### 2.2 Méthode(s): interpolation linéaire

#### 2.2.1 Hommes:

- 1950-80, taux d'activité 1950-80 tirés des EPPA3;
- 1990, interpolation des taux d'activité 1980 tirés des EPPA3
et des taux d'activité tirés de l'enquête de 1991;
modification des tendances des groupes d'âge [10-19].

#### 2.2.2 Femmes:

Méthode, hypothèses et traitements identiques à ceux appliqués aux hommes.

## 3. Evaluation des taux de répartition par secteur d'activité: 1950 - 1990

### 3.1 Données de base:

Tableau 2: Répartition de la population active en % par secteur d'activité

| Année | Agriculture | Industrie Total | Manufac. | Services |
|---|---|---|---|---|
| **Hommes** | | | | |
| 1979 | 3.38 | 48.36 | 33.98 | 48.26 |
| 1980 | 3.51 | 47.58 | 33.05 | 48.91 |
| 1981 | 3.24 | 47.40 | 26.75 | 49.36 |
| 1990 | 3.02 | 39.27 | 25.67 | 57.71 |
| **Femmes** | | | | |
| 1979 | 1.22 | 23.52 | 21.57 | 75.26 |
| 1980 | 1.37 | 22.49 | 20.47 | 76.14 |
| 1981 | 0.98 | 22.19 | 17.51 | 76.83 |
| 1990 | 1.01 | 15.33 | 12.93 | 83.67 |

Source(s): (1) STAT.

### 3.2 Méthode(s): données nationales

#### 3.2.1 Hommes:

- 1950-80, taux de répartition 1950-80 tirés des EPPA3;
le taux de répartition 1980 de manufacture a été ajusté sur la base
de l'application aux taux de 1980 de l'industrie du rapport moyen
manufacture/industrie tiré des estimations officielles de 1979 et 1980
et du recensement de 1981;
- 1990, taux de répartition tirés des estimations officielles de 1990.

#### 3.2.2 Femmes:

Méthode, hypothèses et traitements identiques à ceux appliqués aux hommes.

## 4. Projection des taux d'activité: 2000 - 2010

### 4.1 Modèle(s): linéaire, hyperbole et logistique

#### 4.1.1 Hommes:

- Aux groupes d'âge [15-29] et [55+], application de la fonction F1;
- Aux groupes d'âge [30-54], application de la fonction F3;
- Modification des tendances des groupes d'âge [15-44] et [55-64].

#### 4.1.2 Femmes:

- Aux groupes d'âge [15-19] et [55-64], application de la fonction F1;
- Aux groupes d'âge [20-54], application de la fonction F6;
- Au groupe d'âge [65+], application de la fonction F3;
- Modification des tendances des groupes d'âge [15-29] et [55-64].

*Notes sur les ajustements des taux, voir p. 192-195.*

*Notes sur les fonctions de projection, voir p. 198.*

# Russie, Fédération de

## 1. Source(s) des données de base

Code(s):  Titre(s):

BLT-94-2  Vorobiev A. (1994), "Estimation de la population active pour les quinze pays de l'ex-URSS pour les années 1950, 1959, 1970, 1979 et 1989", dans le Bulletin des statistiques du travail - 1994-2, BIT, Genève.

## 2. Evaluation des taux d'activité: 1950 - 1990

### 2.1 Données de base:

Tableau 1: Taux d'activité par sexe et par groupe d'âge

| Groupe d'âge | Année 1950 | 1959 | 1970 | 1979 | 1989 |
|---|---|---|---|---|---|
| **Hommes** | | | | | |
| 10-14 | 0.00 | 0.00 | 0.00 | 0.00 | 0.00 |
| 15-19 | 52.20 | 63.65 | 43.79 | 38.71 | 31.02 |
| 20-24 | 84.87 | 86.31 | 85.24 | 87.28 | 80.97 |
| 25-29 | 96.82 | 97.09 | 96.59 | 96.87 | 96.36 |
| 30-34 | 96.72 | 95.52 | 97.14 | 98.04 | 97.68 |
| 35-39 | 94.99 | 92.85 | 97.69 | 97.97 | 97.69 |
| 40-44 | 94.18 | 94.27 | 97.12 | 97.51 | 97.25 |
| 45-49 | 90.99 | 90.45 | 93.33 | 96.11 | 95.67 |
| 50-54 | 84.98 | 85.56 | 89.86 | 89.68 | 91.49 |
| 55-59 | 71.93 | 77.11 | 78.41 | 75.90 | 78.82 |
| 60-64 | 51.97 | 57.83 | 23.26 | 28.22 | 35.31 |
| 65+ | 21.08 | 25.52 | 10.99 | 10.09 | 13.49 |
| **Femmes** | | | | | |
| 10-14 | 0.00 | 0.00 | 0.00 | 0.00 | 0.00 |
| 15-19 | 50.83 | 44.12 | 37.41 | 33.42 | 24.93 |
| 20-24 | 73.68 | 77.09 | 82.86 | 85.04 | 78.12 |
| 25-29 | 71.61 | 76.16 | 92.01 | 94.42 | 90.14 |
| 30-34 | 68.10 | 72.09 | 93.81 | 95.78 | 93.58 |
| 35-39 | 67.62 | 74.50 | 92.62 | 96.35 | 95.24 |
| 40-44 | 67.46 | 68.18 | 90.32 | 95.72 | 95.47 |
| 45-49 | 62.86 | 64.50 | 90.99 | 92.32 | 92.81 |
| 50-54 | 51.61 | 52.36 | 75.58 | 81.13 | 82.59 |
| 55-59 | 23.57 | 25.81 | 22.47 | 29.11 | 34.30 |
| 60-64 | 20.09 | 21.08 | 9.41 | 11.12 | 20.06 |
| 65+ | 2.35 | 2.35 | 2.01 | 3.01 | 5.86 |

Source(s): BLT-94-2.

### 2.2 Méthode(s): moyenne pondérée

#### 2.2.1 Hommes:

- 1950-90, moyennes pondérées des taux d'activité 1950, 1959, 1970 et 1989 tirés du Bulletin des statistiques du travail, 1994-2;
les taux d'activité 1959, 1970, 1979 tirés du Bulletin ont été ajustés pour les groupes d'âge [15-19] et [60+].

#### 2.2.2 Femmes:

- 1950-90, moyennes pondérées des taux d'activité 1950, 1959, 1970 et 1989 tirés du Bulletin des statistiques du travail, 1994-2;
le taux d'activité 1959 tirés du Bulletin a été ajusté pour le groupe d'âge [15-19].

## 3. Evaluation des taux de répartition par secteur d'activité: 1950 - 1990

### 3.1 Données de base:

Tableau 2: Répartition de la population active en % par secteur d'activité

| Année | Agriculture | Industrie Total | Manufac. | Services |
|---|---|---|---|---|
| **Hommes** | | | | |
| 1950 | 36.27 | 36.23 | 20.01 | 27.50 |
| 1959 | 27.23 | 39.65 | 25.68 | 33.12 |
| 1970 | 20.17 | 49.68 | 31.74 | 30.15 |
| 1979 | 18.81 | 50.33 | 28.71 | 30.86 |
| 1989 | 17.43 | 48.24 | 26.76 | 34.33 |
| **Femmes** | | | | |
| 1950 | 42.63 | 27.67 | 20.30 | 29.70 |
| 1959 | 33.71 | 31.35 | 23.65 | 34.94 |
| 1970 | 17.68 | 35.82 | 28.75 | 46.50 |
| 1979 | 13.19 | 37.00 | 26.86 | 49.81 |
| 1989 | 9.75 | 34.76 | 24.61 | 55.50 |

Source(s): BLT-94-2.

### 3.2 Méthode(s): données du BLT-94-2

#### 3.2.1 Hommes:

- 1950, 1960, 1970, 1980 et 1990, respectivement les taux de répartition 1950, 1959, 1970, 1979 et 1989 tirés du Bulletin des statistiques du travail - 1994-2.

#### 3.2.2 Femmes:

Méthode, hypothèses et traitements identiques à ceux appliqués aux hommes.

## 4. Projection des taux d'activité: 2000 - 2010

### 4.1 Modèle(s): log-linéaire, hyperbole et logistique

#### 4.1.1 Hommes:

- Aux groupes d'âge [15-24], application de la fonction F2;
- Aux groupes d'âge [25+], application de la fonction F3;
- Modification des tendances des groupes d'âge [20+].

#### 4.1.2 Femmes:

- Aux groupes d'âge [15-19] et [60+], application de la fonction F3;
- Aux groupes d'âge [20-59], application de la fonction F6;
- Modification des tendances des groupes d'âge [20-59].

*Notes sur les ajustements des taux, voir p. 192-195.*

*Notes sur les fonctions de projection, voir p. 198.*

# Rwanda

## 1. Source(s) des données de base

**Code(s):** **Titre(s):**

EPPA3    Evaluations et projections de la population active 1950-2025 - troisième édition, BIT, Genève, 1986.
ASTER    Annuaire des statistiques du travail 1945-89 - Edition rétrospective sur les recensements de population, BIT, Genève, 1990.

## 2. Evaluation des taux d'activité: 1950 - 1990

### 2.1 Données de base:

Tableau 1: Taux d'activité par sexe et par groupe d'âge

| Groupe d'âge | Année 1950 (1) | 1960 (1) | 1970 (1) | 1978 (2) | 1980 (1) |
|---|---|---|---|---|---|
| **Hommes** | | | | | |
| 10-14 | 40.35 | 39.70 | 39.05 | 32.34 | 38.50 |
| 15-19 | 90.00 | 88.85 | 87.60 | 86.85 | 86.65 |
| 20-24 | 98.15 | 97.70 | 97.20 | 96.51 | 96.85 |
| 25-29 | 98.35 | 98.30 | 98.20 | 98.16 | 98.15 |
| 30-34 | 98.75 | 98.70 | 98.60 | 98.50 | 98.55 |
| 35-39 | 98.55 | 98.50 | 98.40 | 98.55 | 98.35 |
| 40-44 | 98.50 | 98.45 | 98.35 | 98.27 | 98.30 |
| 45-49 | 98.00 | 97.90 | 97.85 | 97.77 | 97.80 |
| 50-54 | 96.95 | 96.85 | 96.75 | 96.64 | 96.65 |
| 55-59 | 95.00 | 94.85 | 94.65 | 94.55 | 94.55 |
| 60-64 | 89.30 | 89.00 | 88.75 | 88.55 | 88.50 |
| 65+ | 70.15 | 69.75 | 69.30 | 69.00 | 68.95 |
| **Femmes** | | | | | |
| 10-14 | 49.85 | 48.70 | 47.45 | 33.32 | 46.50 |
| 15-19 | 91.55 | 89.15 | 86.55 | 88.19 | 84.55 |
| 20-24 | 95.75 | 93.45 | 90.90 | 96.14 | 88.95 |
| 25-29 | 96.45 | 94.30 | 91.95 | 97.08 | 90.15 |
| 30-34 | 97.85 | 95.85 | 93.65 | 97.43 | 91.95 |
| 35-39 | 97.60 | 95.70 | 93.60 | 97.97 | 92.05 |
| 40-44 | 96.75 | 95.05 | 93.20 | 97.96 | 91.80 |
| 45-49 | 95.35 | 93.70 | 91.85 | 97.25 | 90.50 |
| 50-54 | 87.55 | 86.20 | 84.65 | 95.26 | 83.50 |
| 55-59 | 77.65 | 76.65 | 75.55 | 90.92 | 74.75 |
| 60-64 | 61.65 | 61.05 | 60.35 | 81.67 | 59.85 |
| 65+ | 35.65 | 35.45 | 35.20 | 58.61 | 35.05 |

Source(s): (1) EPPA3; (2) ASTER.

### 2.2 Méthode(s): extrapolation linéaire

**2.2.1 Hommes:**

- 1950-80, taux d'activité 1950-80 tirés des EPPA3;
- 1990, extrapolation des taux d'activité 1950-80 tirés des EPPA3
et des taux d'activité tirés du recensement de 1978;
modification des tendances de tous les groupes d'âge pour 1990;
ajustement des taux extrapolés 1990 sur la base des variations des
taux interpolés 1980 par rapport aux taux 1980 tirés des EPPA3.

**2.2.2 Femmes:**

Méthode, hypothèses et traitements identiques à ceux appliqués aux hommes.

## 3. Evaluation des taux de répartition par secteur d'activité: 1950 - 1990

### 3.1 Données de base:

Tableau 2: Répartition de la population active en % par secteur d'activité

| Année | Agriculture | Industrie Total | Manufac. | Services |
|---|---|---|---|---|
| **Hommes** | | | | |
| 1950 (1) | 92.30 | 3.25 | .. | 4.45 |
| 1960 (1) | 90.75 | 3.90 | .. | 5.35 |
| 1970 (1) | 89.05 | 4.65 | .. | 6.30 |
| 1978 (2) | 88.01 | 5.09 | 2.14 | 6.90 |
| 1980 (1) | 87.75 | 5.20 | .. | 7.05 |
| **Femmes** | | | | |
| 1950 (1) | 99.10 | 0.30 | .. | 0.60 |
| 1960 (1) | 98.70 | 0.40 | .. | 0.90 |
| 1970 (1) | 98.30 | 0.55 | .. | 1.15 |
| 1978 (2) | 97.96 | 0.63 | 0.60 | 1.40 |
| 1980 (1) | 97.95 | 0.65 | .. | 1.40 |

Source(s): (1) EPPA3; (2) ASTER.

### 3.2 Méthode(s): extrapolation linéaire

**3.2.1 Hommes:**

- 1950-80, taux de répartition 1950-80 tirés des EPPA3;
- 1990, extrapolation des taux de répartition 1950-80 tirés des EPPA3;
- Application du rapport manufacture/industrie tiré du recensement de 1978.

**3.2.2 Femmes:**

Méthode, hypothèses et traitements identiques à ceux appliqués aux hommes.

## 4. Projection des taux d'activité: 2000 - 2010

### 4.1 Modèle(s): linéaire et hyperbole

**4.1.1 Hommes:**

- A tous les groupes d'âge, application de la fonction F1.

**4.1.2 Femmes:**

- A tous les groupes d'âge, application de la fonction F3;
- Modification des tendances des groupes d'âge [25-64].

# Sénégal

## 1. Source(s) des données de base

**Code(s):**    **Titre(s):**

EPPA3    Evaluations et projections de la population active 1950-2025 - troisième édition, BIT, Genève, 1986.
R1976    République du Sénégal, Ministère de l'Economie et des Finances, Recensement Général de la Population, avril 1976.
AST93    Annuaire des statistiques du travail 1993, BIT, Genève, 1993.

## 2. Evaluation des taux d'activité: 1950 - 1990

### 2.1 Données de base:

Tableau 1: Taux d'activité par sexe et par groupe d'âge

| Groupe d'âge | Année | | | | | |
|---|---|---|---|---|---|---|
| | 1950 (1) | 1960 (1) | 1970 (1) | 1976 (2) | 1980 (1) | 1988 (3) |
| **Hommes** | | | | | | |
| 10-14 | .. | 58.55 | .. | 47.40 | .. | 37.25 |
| 15-19 | .. | 76.35 | .. | 72.75 | .. | 64.76 |
| 20-24 | .. | 87.25 | .. | 88.39 | .. | 88.39 |
| 25-29 | .. | 95.20 | .. | 96.35 | .. | 94.51 |
| 30-34 | .. | 96.35 | .. | 98.34 | .. | 96.04 |
| 35-39 | .. | 96.90 | .. | 98.63 | .. | 97.07 |
| 40-44 | .. | 96.15 | .. | 98.81 | .. | 96.86 |
| 45-49 | .. | 95.25 | .. | 98.72 | .. | 96.15 |
| 50-54 | .. | 94.10 | .. | 97.37 | .. | 93.99 |
| 55-59 | .. | 86.60 | .. | 90.31 | .. | 86.93 |
| 60-64 | .. | 79.10 | .. | 85.40 | .. | 79.87 |
| 65+ | .. | 59.80 | .. | 74.80 | .. | 61.64 |
| **Femmes** | | | | | | |
| 10-14 | 44.65 | 44.10 | 43.55 | 5.18 | 42.55 | .. |
| 15-19 | 54.40 | 53.80 | 53.20 | 7.26 | 52.10 | .. |
| 20-24 | 57.00 | 56.65 | 56.25 | 5.96 | 55.55 | .. |
| 25-29 | 63.30 | 62.85 | 62.40 | 4.86 | 61.60 | .. |
| 30-34 | 67.30 | 66.85 | 66.35 | 3.84 | 65.45 | .. |
| 35-39 | 69.65 | 69.20 | 68.70 | 3.89 | 67.90 | .. |
| 40-44 | 72.10 | 71.70 | 71.20 | 4.07 | 70.40 | .. |
| 45-49 | 70.80 | 70.35 | 69.85 | 4.75 | 69.00 | .. |
| 50-54 | 67.25 | 66.75 | 66.20 | 4.57 | 65.25 | .. |
| 55-59 | 62.50 | 62.00 | 61.40 | 4.45 | 60.45 | .. |
| 60-64 | 50.05 | 49.50 | 48.85 | 4.61 | 47.75 | .. |
| 65+ | 27.45 | 27.00 | 26.55 | 3.84 | 25.70 | .. |

**Source(s):** (1) EPPA3; (2) R1976; (3) AST93.

### 2.2 Méthode(s): interpolation et extrapolation linéaires

#### 2.2.1 Hommes:

- 1950-90, interpolation et extrapolation des taux d'activité 1960
tirés des EPPA3 et des taux d'activité ajustés tirés des recensements
de 1976 et 1988;
modification des tendances du groupe d'âge [10-14] pour 1960 et 1980.

#### 2.2.2 Femmes:

- 1950-90, interpolation et extrapolation des taux d'activité 1950-80
tirés des EPPA3;
ajustement des taux interpolés et extrapolés sur la base des variations des
taux interpolés 1976 par rapport aux taux ajustés du recensement de 1976;
modification des tendances de tous les groupes d'âge de 1980 à 1990.

## 3. Evaluation des taux de répartition par secteur d'activité: 1950 - 1990

### 3.1 Données de base:

Tableau 2: Répartition de la population active en % par secteur d'activité

| Année | Agriculture | Industrie | | Services |
|---|---|---|---|---|
| | | Total | Manufac. | |
| **Hommes** | | | | |
| 1950 | 78.00 | 7.65 | .. | 14.35 |
| 1960 | 77.00 | 8.00 | .. | 15.00 |
| 1970 | 75.90 | 8.40 | .. | 15.70 |
| 1980 | 74.00 | 9.05 | .. | 16.95 |
| **Femmes** | | | | |
| 1950 | 95.00 | 1.15 | .. | 3.85 |
| 1960 | 93.60 | 1.45 | .. | 4.95 |
| 1970 | 92.30 | 1.75 | .. | 5.95 |
| 1980 | 89.95 | 2.30 | .. | 7.75 |

**Source(s):** EPPA3.

### 3.2 Méthode(s): extrapolation linéaire

#### 3.2.1 Hommes:

- 1950-80, taux de répartition 1950-80 tirés des EPPA3;
- 1990, extrapolation des taux de répartition 1950-80 tirés des EPPA3;
modification des tendances de tous les secteurs;
- Application du rapport manufacture/industrie estimé pour le Niger.

#### 3.2.2 Femmes:

Méthode, hypothèses et traitements identiques à ceux appliqués aux hommes.

## 4. Projection des taux d'activité: 2000 - 2010

### 4.1 Modèle(s): linéaire et hyperbole

#### 4.1.1 Hommes:

- Aux groupes d'âge [10-24], application de la fonction F1;
- Aux groupes d'âge [25+], application de la fonction F3;
- Modification des tendances des groupes d'âge [10-14] et [20-54].

#### 4.1.2 Femmes:

- Au groupe d'âge [10-14], application de la fonction F1;
- Aux groupes d'âge [15+], application de la fonction F3;
- Modification des tendances des groupes d'âge [15-54].

*Notes sur les ajustements des taux, voir p. 192-195.*

*Notes sur les fonctions de projection, voir p. 198.*

# Sierra Leone

## 1. Source(s) des données de base

Code(s):     Titre(s):

EPPA3      Evaluations et projections de la population active 1950-2025 - troisième édition, BIT, Genève, 1986.

## 2. Evaluation des taux d'activité: 1950 - 1990

### 2.1 Données de base:

Tableau 1: Taux d'activité par sexe et par groupe d'âge

| Groupe d'âge | Année 1950 | 1960 | 1970 |
|---|---|---|---|
| **Hommes** | | | |
| 10-14 | 39.00 | 33.00 | 24.55 |
| 15-19 | 71.20 | 66.35 | 59.85 |
| 20-24 | 89.85 | 88.90 | 86.80 |
| 25-29 | 97.15 | 96.95 | 96.70 |
| 30-34 | 97.90 | 97.60 | 97.35 |
| 35-39 | 98.05 | 97.75 | 97.45 |
| 40-44 | 97.90 | 97.55 | 97.25 |
| 45-49 | 97.50 | 97.40 | 96.75 |
| 50-54 | 97.00 | 96.70 | 95.90 |
| 55-59 | 92.90 | 92.80 | 91.00 |
| 60-64 | 88.00 | 87.50 | 84.60 |
| 65+ | 73.45 | 70.35 | 64.30 |
| **Femmes** | | | |
| 10-14 | 26.80 | 23.85 | 19.00 |
| 15-19 | 46.80 | 41.70 | 36.80 |
| 20-24 | 54.00 | 49.00 | 45.25 |
| 25-29 | 54.50 | 50.15 | 47.90 |
| 30-34 | 54.90 | 50.50 | 48.35 |
| 35-39 | 55.40 | 51.00 | 48.80 |
| 40-44 | 55.80 | 51.35 | 49.15 |
| 45-49 | 56.20 | 52.45 | 51.15 |
| 50-54 | 54.40 | 50.75 | 49.50 |
| 55-59 | 48.45 | 47.55 | 46.65 |
| 60-64 | 36.35 | 34.25 | 33.55 |
| 65+ | 23.40 | 22.20 | 20.75 |

Source(s): EPPA3.

### 2.2 Méthode(s): extrapolation linéaire

**2.2.1 Hommes:**

- 1950-70, taux d'activité 1950-70 tirés des EPPA3;
- 1980-90, extrapolation des taux d'activité 1950-70 tirés des EPPA3;
ajustement des taux interpolés et extrapolés sur la base des variations
des taux interpolés 1970 par rapport aux taux 1970 tirés des EPPA3;
modification des tendances de tous les groupes d'âge de 1980 à 1990.

**2.2.2 Femmes:**

Méthode, hypothèses et traitements identiques à ceux appliqués aux hommes.

## 3. Evaluation des taux de répartition par secteur d'activité: 1950 - 1990

### 3.1 Données de base:

Tableau 2: Répartition de la population active en % par secteur d'activité

| Année | Agriculture | Industrie Total | Manufac. | Services |
|---|---|---|---|---|
| **Hommes** | | | | |
| 1950 | 82.00 | 10.55 | .. | 7.45 |
| 1960 | 77.00 | 13.50 | .. | 9.50 |
| 1970 | 70.00 | 17.60 | .. | 12.40 |
| 1980 | 63.00 | 19.65 | .. | 17.35 |
| **Femmes** | | | | |
| 1950 | 91.50 | 1.70 | .. | 6.80 |
| 1960 | 89.00 | 2.20 | .. | 8.80 |
| 1970 | 85.50 | 2.90 | .. | 11.60 |
| 1980 | 82.00 | 3.60 | .. | 14.40 |

Source(s): EPPA3.

### 3.2 Méthode(s): extrapolation linéaire

**3.2.1 Hommes:**

- 1950-80, taux de répartition 1950-80 tirés des EPPA3;
- 1990, extrapolation des taux de répartition 1950-80 tirés des EPPA3;
- Application du rapport manufacture/industrie estimé pour le Libéria.

**3.2.2 Femmes:**

Méthode, hypothèses et traitements identiques à ceux appliqués aux hommes.

## 4. Projection des taux d'activité: 2000 - 2010

### 4.1 Modèle(s): log-linéaire et hyperbole

**4.1.1 Hommes:**

- Au groupe d'âge [10-14], application de la fonction F2;
- Aux groupes d'âge [15+], application de la fonction F3.

**4.1.2 Femmes:**

- Au groupe d'âge [10-14], application de la fonction F2;
- Aux groupes d'âge [15+], application de la fonction F3;
- Modification des tendances des groupes d'âge [20+].

*Notes sur les ajustements des taux, voir p. 192-195.*     *Notes sur les fonctions de projection, voir p. 198.*

# Singapour

## 1. Source(s) des données de base

| Code(s): | Titre(s): |
| --- | --- |
| EPPA3 | Evaluations et projections de la population active 1950-2025 - troisième édition, BIT, Genève, 1986. |
| STAT | Base de données sur les statistiques du travail - LABORSTA, Bureau de statistique, BIT, Genève. |

## 2. Evaluation des taux d'activité: 1950 - 1990

### 2.1 Données de base:

Tableau 1: Taux d'activité par sexe et par groupe d'âge

| Groupe d'âge | Année 1980 (1) | 1980 (2) | 1989 (2) | 1990 (1) | 1991 (2) |
| --- | --- | --- | --- | --- | --- |
| **Hommes** | | | | | |
| 10-14 | 1.64 | 1.64 | 0.00 | 0.00 | 0.00 |
| 15-19 | 47.49 | 45.80 | 25.50 | 28.39 | 31.10 |
| 20-24 | 93.35 | 92.50 | 84.80 | 84.35 | 83.10 |
| 25-29 | 97.23 | 97.30 | 96.60 | 95.42 | 97.00 |
| 30-34 | 97.94 | 98.32 | 98.30 | 96.56 | 98.70 |
| 35-39 | 98.03 | 98.41 | 99.00 | 97.22 | 99.10 |
| 40-44 | 97.62 | 98.00 | 97.80 | 97.65 | 98.40 |
| 45-49 | 95.72 | 96.30 | 96.10 | 95.19 | 96.50 |
| 50-54 | 89.57 | 90.40 | 89.20 | 88.19 | 92.50 |
| 55-59 | 70.69 | 73.20 | 66.60 | 68.35 | 71.00 |
| 60-64 | 52.53 | 55.80 | 48.20 | 31.86 | 46.90 |
| 65+ | 28.61 | 29.80 | 20.74 | ... | 19.80 |
| **Femmes** | | | | | |
| 10-14 | 1.65 | 1.64 | 0.00 | 0.00 | 0.00 |
| 15-19 | 50.73 | 45.80 | 25.50 | 27.84 | 31.10 |
| 20-24 | 78.40 | 92.50 | 84.80 | 79.57 | 83.10 |
| 25-29 | 58.67 | 97.30 | 96.60 | 76.31 | 97.00 |
| 30-34 | 44.20 | 98.32 | 98.30 | 63.06 | 98.70 |
| 35-39 | 37.13 | 98.41 | 99.00 | 54.95 | 99.10 |
| 40-44 | 33.16 | 98.00 | 97.80 | 51.86 | 98.40 |
| 45-49 | 26.47 | 96.30 | 96.10 | 45.01 | 96.50 |
| 50-54 | 20.43 | 90.40 | 89.20 | 34.15 | 92.50 |
| 55-59 | 14.50 | 73.20 | 66.60 | 21.48 | 71.00 |
| 60-64 | 11.30 | 55.80 | 48.20 | 7.70 | 46.90 |
| 65+ | 6.40 | 29.80 | 20.74 | ... | 19.80 |

Note(s): (1) Recensement; (2) Enquêtes.
Source(s): STAT.

### 2.2 Méthode(s): moyenne arithmétique

#### 2.2.1 Hommes:

- 1950-70, taux d'activité 1950-70 tirés des EPPA3;
- 1980, moyennes des taux d'activité tirés du recensement de 1980 et de l'enquête de 1980;
- 1990, moyennes des taux d'activité tirés du recensement de 1990 et des enquêtes de 1989 et 1990.

#### 2.2.2 Femmes:

Méthode, hypothèses et traitements identiques à ceux appliqués aux hommes.

## 3. Evaluation des taux de répartition par secteur d'activité: 1950 - 1990

### 3.1 Données de base:

Tableau 2: Répartition de la population active en % par secteur d'activité

| Année | Agriculture | Industrie Total | Manufac. | Services |
| --- | --- | --- | --- | --- |
| **Hommes** | | | | |
| 1980 (1) | 1.54 | 33.48 | 24.42 | 64.98 |
| 1980 (2) | 1.97 | 35.32 | 24.66 | 62.71 |
| 1989 (1) | 0.62 | 36.81 | 25.93 | 62.56 |
| 1991 (1) | 0.39 | 36.72 | 26.18 | 62.89 |
| **Femmes** | | | | |
| 1980 (1) | 0.95 | 40.33 | 38.56 | 58.72 |
| 1980 (2) | 1.67 | 86.31 | 8.25 | 12.02 |
| 1989 (1) | 0.19 | 35.28 | 33.68 | 64.54 |
| 1991 (1) | 0.11 | 32.85 | 31.22 | 67.04 |

Note(s): (1) Enquête; (2) Recensement.
Source(s): STAT.

### 3.2 Méthode(s): moyenne arithmétique

#### 3.2.1 Hommes:

- 1950-70, taux de répartition 1950-70 tirés des EPPA3;
- 1980, moyennes des taux de répartition tirés du recensement de 1980 et de l'enquête de 1980;
- 1990, moyennes des taux de répartition tirés des enquêtes de 1989 et 1990.

#### 3.2.2 Femmes:

Méthode, hypothèses et traitements identiques à ceux appliqués aux hommes.

## 4. Projection des taux d'activité: 2000 - 2010

### 4.1 Modèle(s): linéaire, hyperbole et logistique

#### 4.1.1 Hommes:

- Au groupe d'âge [15-19], application de la fonction F1;
- Aux groupes d'âge [20+], application de la fonction F6;
- Modification des tendances des groupes d'âge [55-64].

#### 4.1.2 Femmes:

- Aux groupes d'âge [15-19] et [35-54], application de la fonction F1;
- Aux groupes d'âge [20-34], application de la fonction F6;
- Aux groupes d'âge [55+], application de la fonction F3;
- Modification des tendances des groupes d'âge [15-59].

*Notes sur les ajustements des taux, voir p. 192-195.*

*Notes sur les fonctions de projection, voir p. 198.*

# Slovaquie

## 1. Source(s) des données de base

Code(s):     Titre(s):

BLT-94-2     Vorobiev A. (1994), "Estimation de la population active pour les quinze pays de l'ex-URSS pour les années 1950, 1959, 1970, 1979 et 1989", dans le Bulletin des statistiques du travail - 1994-2, BIT, Genève.

## 2. Evaluation des taux d'activité: 1950 - 1990

### 2.1 Données de base:

Tableau 1: Taux d'activité par sexe et par groupe d'âge

| Groupe d'âge | Année 1950 (1) | 1961 | 1970 (1) | 1980 | 1991 (1) |
|---|---|---|---|---|---|
| **Hommes** | | | | | |
| 10-14 | 0.00 | 0.00 | 0.00 | 0.00 | 0.00 |
| 15-19 | 77.05 | 45.71 | 34.90 | 31.58 | 35.28 |
| 20-24 | 94.95 | 91.92 | 91.55 | 86.49 | 88.32 |
| 25-29 | 98.93 | 97.10 | 98.61 | 98.21 | 98.01 |
| 30-34 | 99.14 | 97.53 | 98.97 | 98.36 | 98.26 |
| 35-39 | 98.42 | 97.20 | 98.69 | 97.89 | 97.78 |
| 40-44 | 97.50 | 96.40 | 97.92 | 97.66 | 97.16 |
| 45-49 | 94.75 | 95.25 | 96.52 | 95.45 | 95.58 |
| 50-54 | 91.95 | 92.30 | 93.74 | 92.37 | 91.80 |
| 55-59 | 84.88 | 86.34 | 85.26 | 84.25 | 80.00 |
| 60-64 | 44.19 | 64.53 | 31.47 | 47.83 | 28.22 |
| 65+ | 20.28 | 30.15 | 14.66 | 20.27 | 11.63 |
| **Femmes** | | | | | |
| 10-14 | 0.00 | 0.00 | 0.00 | 0.00 | 0.00 |
| 15-19 | 69.83 | 47.73 | 44.21 | 29.65 | 33.88 |
| 20-24 | 59.29 | 61.32 | 79.68 | 81.43 | 87.46 |
| 25-29 | 39.30 | 47.99 | 80.91 | 89.81 | 94.66 |
| 30-34 | 40.99 | 46.03 | 83.81 | 89.50 | 95.22 |
| 35-39 | 46.39 | 50.74 | 86.57 | 89.12 | 95.50 |
| 40-44 | 48.10 | 52.46 | 86.41 | 86.76 | 95.01 |
| 45-49 | 51.82 | 48.84 | 84.05 | 81.43 | 93.33 |
| 50-54 | 45.51 | 41.90 | 77.13 | 71.33 | 85.56 |
| 55-59 | 34.81 | 32.10 | 39.38 | 36.11 | 31.25 |
| 60-64 | 22.14 | 21.49 | 20.01 | 16.46 | 16.04 |
| 65+ | 8.80 | 6.79 | 5.89 | 4.59 | 4.93 |

Note(s): (1) République tchèque.
Source(s): STAT.

### 2.2 Méthode(s): moyenne pondérée

#### 2.2.1 Hommes:

- 1950-90, moyennes pondérées des taux d'activité tirés des recensements de 1961 et 1980 et des taux d'activité tirés des recensements de 1950, 1970 et 1991 pour la République tchèque;
ajustement des taux d'activité estimés 1950-70 pour le groupe d'âge [10-14].

#### 2.2.2 Femmes:

Méthode, hypothèses et traitements identiques à ceux appliqués aux hommes.

## 3. Evaluation des taux de répartition par secteur d'activité: 1950 - 1990

### 3.1 Données de base:

Tableau 2: Répartition de la population active en % par secteur d'activité

| Année | Agriculture | Industrie Total | Manufac. | Services |
|---|---|---|---|---|
| **Hommes** | | | | |
| 1950 | 44.56 | 33.11 | .. | 22.32 |
| 1961 | 30.12 | 46.54 | .. | 23.34 |
| 1970 | 21.00 | 51.33 | .. | 27.68 |
| 1980 | 14.76 | 37.42 | 30.73 | 47.82 |
| 1991 | 14.39 | 35.32 | 28.66 | 50.29 |
| **Femmes** | | | | |
| 1950 | 62.26 | 18.35 | .. | 19.39 |
| 1961 | 40.70 | 26.84 | .. | 32.46 |
| 1970 | 20.04 | 36.39 | .. | 43.56 |
| 1980 | 12.39 | 33.81 | 30.04 | 53.81 |
| 1991 | 9.20 | 30.62 | 26.93 | 60.18 |

Source(s): STAT.

### 3.2 Méthode(s): moyenne pondérée

#### 3.2.1 Hommes:
- 1950-90, moyennes pondérées des taux de répartition tirés des recensements de 1950, 1961, 1970, 1980 et 1991.

#### 3.2.2 Femmes:

Méthode, hypothèses et traitements identiques à ceux appliqués aux hommes.

## 4. Projection des taux d'activité: 2000 - 2010

### 4.1 Modèle(s): linéaire, hyperbole et logistique

#### 4.1.1 Hommes:

- Aux groupes d'âge [15-19] et [60+], application de la fonction F3;
- Aux groupes d'âge [20-59], application de la fonction F1;
- Modification des tendances des groupes d'âge [25-34].

#### 4.1.2 Femmes:

- Aux groupes d'âge [15-19] et [55+], application de la fonction F3;
- Aux groupes d'âge [20-54], application de la fonction F6;
- Modification des tendances des groupes d'âge [20-54].

*Notes sur les ajustements des taux, voir p. 192-195.*

*Notes sur les fonctions de projection, voir p. 198.*

# Slovénie

## 1. Source(s) des données de base

Code(s):    Titre(s):

BLT-94-2    Popovic B. (1994), "Nouvelles estimations pour 1980 et 1990 des taux d'activité par âge et répartition sectorielle pour certains pays d'Europe orientale et méridionale" dans le Bulletin des statistiques du travail - 1994-2, BIT, Genève.

STAT    Base de données sur les statistiques du travail - LABORSTA, Bureau de statistique, BIT, Genève.

## 2. Evaluation des taux d'activité: 1950 - 1990

### 2.1 Données de base:

Tableau 1: Taux d'activité par sexe et par groupe d'âge

|  | Groupe d'âge | Année 1953 (1) | 1961 (1) | 1971 (1) | 1980 (2) | 1990 (2) |
|---|---|---|---|---|---|---|
| **Hommes** | | | | | | |
| | 10-14 | 9.27 | 1.02 | 0.32 | 0.01 | 0.00 |
| | 15-19 | 84.70 | 71.57 | 44.88 | 33.54 | 25.75 |
| | 20-24 | 92.77 | 90.57 | 88.33 | 86.09 | 79.08 |
| | 25-29 | 95.99 | 96.52 | 85.32 | 97.30 | 94.50 |
| | 30-34 | 97.51 | 97.74 | 90.24 | 98.36 | 97.20 |
| | 35-39 | 98.01 | 97.23 · | 92.40 | 98.23 | 97.06 |
| | 40-44 | 97.85 | 96.83 | 91.50 | 97.17 | 96.28 |
| | 45-49 | 96.62 | 96.11 | 95.32 | 94.54 | 93.69 |
| | 50-54 | 93.34 | 92.24 | 86.80 | 81.35 | 84.60 |
| | 55-59 | 72.85 | 74.50 | 61.55 | 59.18 | 49.85 |
| | 60-64 | 60.78 | 58.83 | 41.89 | 31.41 | 30.64 |
| | 65+ | 45.85 | 42.31 | 33.52 | 19.27 | 14.45 |
| **Femmes** | | | | | | |
| | 10-14 | 7.87 | 0.85 | 0.27 | 0.01 | 0.00 |
| | 15-19 | 71.52 | 62.50 | 38.32 | 28.27 | 21.07 |
| | 20-24 | 72.19 | 77.30 | 68.23 | 82.35 | 75.70 |
| | 25-29 | 54.59 | 67.39 | 74.63 | 91.65 | 92.89 |
| | 30-34 | 45.79 | 59.35 | 71.34 | 90.91 | 93.93 |
| | 35-39 | 43.15 | 55.10 | 68.49 | 88.59 | 92.56 |
| | 40-44 | 41.88 | 51.98 | 64.08 | 82.30 | 89.94 |
| | 45-49 | 41.82 | 48.91 | 56.27 | 73.37 | 82.10 |
| | 50-54 | 37.33 | 42.14 | 44.45 | 57.07 | 45.36 |
| | 55-59 | 34.00 | 35.92 | 30.89 | 28.13 | 22.98 |
| | 60-64 | 31.46 | 31.31 | 25.37 | 19.94 | 17.96 |
| | 65+ | 21.45 | 22.09 | 18.88 | 9.85 | 9.42 |

Source(s): (1) STAT; (2) BLT-94-2.

### 2.2 Méthode(s): interpolation linéaire

#### 2.2.1 Hommes:

- 1950-70, interpolation et extrapolation des taux d'activité tirés des recensements de 1953, 1961 et 1971;
- 1980-90, taux d'activité tirés du Bulletin des statistiques du travail 1994-2.

#### 2.2.2 Femmes:

Méthode, hypothèses et traitements identiques à ceux appliqués aux hommes.

## 3. Evaluation des taux de répartition par secteur d'activité: 1950 - 1990

### 3.1 Données de base:

Tableau 2: Répartition de la population active en % par secteur d'activité

|  | Agriculture | Industrie Total | Manufac. | Services |
|---|---|---|---|---|
| Année | | | | |
| **Hommes** | | | | |
| 1953 (1) | 46.40 | 31.59 | 15.48 | 22.01 |
| 1961 (1) | 35.48 | 39.60 | 34.21 | 24.93 |
| 1971 (1) | 23.93 | 46.67 | 41.15 | 29.40 |
| 1980 (2) | 14.02 | 48.51 | 34.98 | 37.47 |
| 1990 (2) | 5.13 | 52.07 | 41.10 | 42.81 |
| **Femmes** | | | | |
| 1953 (1) | 64.15 | 17.39 | 16.62 | 18.45 |
| 1961 (1) | 45.05 | 28.28 | 27.18 | 26.67 |
| 1971 (1) | 31.49 | 35.12 | 33.80 | 33.39 |
| 1980 (2) | 17.13 | 37.37 | 34.70 | 45.49 |
| 1990 (2) | 6.35 | 39.22 | 36.79 | 54.44 |

Source(s): (1) STAT; (2) BLT-94-2.

### 3.2 Méthode(s): moyenne pondérée
extrapolation linéaire

#### 3.2.1 Hommes:

- 1950, moyennes pondérées des taux de répartition tirés des recensements de 1953 et 1961;
- 1960-70, interpolation et extrapolation des taux de répartition tirés des recensements de 1961 et 1971;
- 1980-90, taux de répartition tirés du Bulletin des statistiques du travail - 1994-2.

#### 3.2.2 Femmes:

Méthode, hypothèses et traitements identiques à ceux appliqués aux hommes.

## 4. Projection des taux d'activité: 2000 - 2010

### 4.1 Modèle(s): linéaire, hyperbole et logistique

#### 4.1.1 Hommes:

- Aux groupes d'âge [15+], application de la fonction F3;
- Modification des tendances des groupes d'âge [40-49].

#### 4.1.2 Femmes:

- Au groupe d'âge [15-19], application de la fonction F3;
- Aux groupes d'âge [20-49], application de la fonction F6;
- Aux groupes d'âge [50+], application de la fonction F1;
- Modification des tendances des groupes d'âge [15-64].

*Notes sur les ajustements des taux, voir p. 192-195.*

*Notes sur les fonctions de projection, voir p. 198.*

# Somalie

## 1. Source(s) des données de base

Code(s):     Titre(s):
EPPA3       Evaluations et projections de la population active 1950-2025 - troisième édition, BIT, Genève, 1986.

## 2. Evaluation des taux d'activité: 1950 - 1990

### 2.1 Données de base:

Tableau 1: Taux d'activité par sexe et par groupe d'âge

| | Année | | | |
|---|---|---|---|---|
| Groupe d'âge | 1950 | 1960 | 1970 | 1980 |
| **Hommes** | | | | |
| 10-14 | 47.40 | 44.95 | 42.80 | 40.35 |
| 15-19 | 78.65 | 75.40 | 72.55 | 69.25 |
| 20-24 | 92.85 | 91.60 | 90.50 | 89.25 |
| 25-29 | 97.05 | 96.85 | 96.70 | 96.50 |
| 30-34 | 97.75 | 97.55 | 97.35 | 97.15 |
| 35-39 | 97.90 | 97.65 | 97.45 | 97.25 |
| 40-44 | 97.70 | 97.45 | 97.25 | 97.05 |
| 45-49 | 97.00 | 96.80 | 96.65 | 96.45 |
| 50-54 | 96.40 | 96.10 | 95.80 | 95.50 |
| 55-59 | 95.15 | 94.70 | 94.25 | 93.80 |
| 60-64 | 91.60 | 90.80 | 90.10 | 89.30 |
| 65+ | 77.25 | 75.85 | 74.60 | 73.20 |
| **Femmes** | | | | |
| 10-14 | 35.85 | 34.00 | 32.35 | 30.50 |
| 15-19 | 58.65 | 55.90 | 53.40 | 50.65 |
| 20-24 | 60.80 | 59.05 | 57.50 | 55.75 |
| 25-29 | 65.30 | 63.35 | 61.55 | 59.60 |
| 30-34 | 69.40 | 67.30 | 65.40 | 63.25 |
| 35-39 | 70.90 | 68.90 | 67.15 | 65.15 |
| 40-44 | 73.35 | 71.35 | 69.60 | 67.65 |
| 45-49 | 72.80 | 70.80 | 69.00 | 66.95 |
| 50-54 | 70.75 | 68.40 | 66.35 | 64.00 |
| 55-59 | 67.80 | 65.35 | 63.15 | 60.70 |
| 60-64 | 60.50 | 57.40 | 54.60 | 51.50 |
| 65+ | 40.85 | 37.95 | 35.35 | 32.45 |

Source(s): EPPA3.

### 2.2 Méthode(s): interpolation et extrapolation linéaires

#### 2.2.1 Hommes:

- 1950-80, taux d'activité 1950-80 tirés des EPPA3;
- 1990, extrapolation des taux d'activité 1950-80 tirés des EPPA3;
ajustement des taux extrapolés sur la base des variations des taux interpolés 1980 par rapport aux taux 1980 tirés des EPPA3.

#### 2.2.2 Femmes:

- 1950-90, interpolation et extrapolation des taux d'activité ajustés 1950 et 1980 tirés des EPPA3;
ajustement des taux d'activité sur la base du rapport hommes/femmes égal à 1 dans l'agriculture;
ajustement des taux interpolés et extrapolés sur la base des variations des taux interpolés 1980 par rapport aux taux ajustés 1980 tirés des EPPA3.

## 3. Evaluation des taux de répartition par secteur d'activité: 1950 - 1990

### 3.1 Données de base:

Tableau 2: Répartition de la population active en % par secteur d'activité

| | | Agriculture | Industrie | | Services |
|---|---|---|---|---|---|
| | Année | | Total | Manufac. | |
| **Hommes** | | | | | |
| | 1950 | 79.00 | 7.00 | .. | 14.00 |
| | 1980 | 66.00 | 13.00 | .. | 21.00 |
| **Femmes** | | | | | |
| | 1950 | 97.00 | 0.50 | .. | 2.50 |
| | 1980 | 89.00 | 1.70 | .. | 8.80 |

Source(s): EPPA3.

### 3.2 Méthode(s): interpolation et extrapolation linéaires

#### 3.2.1 Hommes:

- 1950-80, taux de répartition 1950-80 tirés des EPPA3;
- 1990, extrapolation des taux de répartition 1950-80 tirés des EPPA3;
- Application du rapport manufacture/industrie estimé pour l'Erythrée.

#### 3.2.2 Femmes:

- 1950-90, interpolation extrapolation des taux de répartition ajustés 1950 et 1980 tirés des EPPA3;
ajustement des taux de répartition sur la base du rapport hommes/femmes égal à 1 dans l'agriculture;
les taux de répartition de manufacture ont estimés sur la base du rapport manufacture/industrie estimé pour l'Erythrée.

## 4. Projection des taux d'activité: 2000 - 2010

### 4.1 Modèle(s): linéaire et hyperbole

#### 4.1.1 Hommes:

- Aux groupes d'âge [10-19], application de la fonction F1;
- Aux groupes d'âge [20+], application de la fonction F3;
- Modification des tendances des groupes d'âge [20-49].

#### 4.1.2 Femmes:

- A tous les groupes d'âge, application de la fonction F3;
- Modification des tendances des groupes d'âge [20-59].

# Soudan

## 1. Source(s) des données de base

Code(s):    Titre(s):

EPPA3      Evaluations et projections de la population active 1950-2025 - troisième édition, BIT, Genève, 1986.
R1983      Population and Housing Census of the Sudan 1989, Ministry of Finance and Economic Planning, Department of Statistics, Khartoum, 1989.
ASTER      Annuaire des statistiques du travail 1945-89 - Edition rétrospective sur les recensements de population, BIT, Genève, 1990.

## 2. Evaluation des taux d'activité: 1950 - 1990

### 2.1 Données de base:

Tableau 1: Taux d'activité par sexe et par groupe d'âge

| Groupe d'âge | Année 1950 (1) | 1960 (1) | 1970 (1) | 1973 (2) | 1983 (3) |
|---|---|---|---|---|---|
| **Hommes** | | | | | |
| 10-14 | 46.15 | 42.90 | 42.84 | .. | 39.01 |
| 15-19 | 74.95 | 70.60 | 64.40 | .. | 58.92 |
| 20-24 | 95.55 | 93.60 | 90.85 | .. | 81.27 |
| 25-29 | 97.90 | 97.60 | 97.20 | .. | 92.90 |
| 30-34 | 99.05 | 98.75 | 98.25 | .. | 95.58 |
| 35-39 | 99.50 | 99.15 | 98.65 | .. | 96.90 |
| 40-44 | 99.50 | 99.15 | 98.60 | .. | 96.74 |
| 45-49 | 99.30 | 99.00 | 98.55 | .. | 97.33 |
| 50-54 | 98.40 | 97.95 | 97.25 | .. | 95.63 |
| 55-59 | 98.05 | 97.30 | 96.20 | .. | 95.00 |
| 60-64 | 95.85 | 94.55 | 92.75 | .. | 91.47 |
| 65+ | 78.25 | 76.15 | 78.55 | .. | 78.55 |
| **Femmes** | | | | | |
| 10-14 | 12.15 | 11.30 | 10.05 | ... | 25.29 |
| 15-19 | 19.75 | 18.50 | 16.65 | 16.08 | 28.62 |
| 20-24 | 20.95 | 20.10 | 18.85 | 18.47 | 29.58 |
| 25-29 | 23.25 | 22.20 | 20.75 | 20.32 | 30.49 |
| 30-34 | 24.50 | 23.40 | 21.85 | 21.41 | 31.13 |
| 35-39 | 27.25 | 26.15 | 24.55 | 24.08 | 32.09 |
| 40-44 | 30.40 | 29.20 | 27.50 | 26.98 | 33.44 |
| 45-49 | 31.80 | 30.50 | 28.70 | 28.14 | 35.20 |
| 50-54 | 33.40 | 31.80 | 29.55 | 28.86 | 66.72 |
| 55-59 | 32.15 | 30.50 | 28.15 | 27.45 | 33.22 |
| 60-64 | 33.70 | 31.30 | 27.90 | 26.40 | 33.80 |
| 65+ | 27.60 | 26.00 | 25.00 | 21.35 | ... | 25.44 |

Source(s): (1) EPPA3; (2) ASTER; (3) R1983.

### 2.2 Méthode(s): interpolation et extrapolation linéaires
moyenne pondérée

**2.2.1 Hommes:**

- 1950-90, interpolation et extrapolation des taux d'activité 1950-70 tirés des EPPA3 et des taux ajustés tirés du recensement de 1983; modification des tendances des groupes d'âge [45-49] et [65+] pour les années 1950 à 1990.

**2.2.2 Femmes:**

- 1950-70, taux d'activité ajustés 1950-70 tirés des EPPA3; ajustement des taux sur la base du modèle d'ajustement des taux d'activité des femmes travaillant dans l'agriculture comme aides familiales;
- 1980, moyennes pondérées des taux d'activité ajustés tirés du recensement de 1973 et des taux du recensement de 1983; l'ajustement des taux du recensement de 1973 été accompli sur la base du rapport hommes/femmes dans l'agriculture tiré du recensement de 1983;
- 1990, aux taux estimés 1980, application des variations des taux de 1980 par rapport à ceux de 1990 estimés pour l'Egypte.

## 3. Evaluation des taux de répartition par secteur d'activité: 1950 - 1990

### 3.1 Données de base:

Tableau 2: Répartition de la population active en % par secteur d'activité

| | Agriculture | Industrie Total | Manufac. | Services |
|---|---|---|---|---|
| **Hommes** | | | | |
| 1973 (1) | 65.49 | 8.78 | 4.50 | 25.73 |
| 1983 (2) | 66.47 | 9.68 | 5.17 | 23.85 |
| **Femmes** | | | | |
| 1973 (1) | 88.81 | 3.38 | 3.25 | 7.81 |
| 1983 (2) | 87.11 | 4.51 | 3.85 | 8.38 |

Source(s): (1) ASTER; (2) R1983.

### 3.2 Méthode(s): moyenne pondérée

**3.2.1 Hommes:**

- 1950-70, taux de répartition 1950-70 tirés des EPPA3;
- 1980, moyennes pondérées des taux de répartition tirés des recensements de 1973 et 1983;
- 1990, mêmes variations en terme de pourcentages de points qu'en Egypte pour 1980 et 1990.

**3.2.2 Femmes:**

- 1950-70, taux de répartition 1950-70 tirés des EPPA3;
- 1980, moyennes pondérées des taux de répartition tirés des recensements de 1973 et 1983;
- 1990, mêmes variations en terme de pourcentages de points qu'en Egypte pour 1980 et 1990;
ajustement des taux estimés 1950-90 pour tenir compte de la sous-énumération des femmes travaillant dans l'agriculture.

## 4. Projection des taux d'activité: 2000 - 2010

### 4.1 Modèle(s): linéaire, hyperbole et logistique

**4.1.1 Hommes:**

- Au groupe d'âge [10-14], application de la fonction F1;
- Aux groupes d'âge [15+], application de la fonction F3;
- Modification des tendances des groupes d'âge [10-14], [20-24], [50-54] et [65+].

**4.1.2 Femmes:**

- Aux groupes d'âge [10-19], application de la fonction F1;
- Aux groupes d'âge [20+], application de la fonction F6;
- Modification des tendances de tous les groupes d'âge.

*Notes sur les ajustements des taux, voir p. 192-195.*    *Notes sur les fonctions de projection, voir p. 198.*

# Sri Lanka

## 1. Source(s) des données de base

Code(s): Titre(s):

EPPA3 Evaluations et projections de la population active 1950-2025 - troisième édition, BIT, Genève, 1986.
STAT Base de données sur les statistiques du travail - LABORSTA, Bureau de statistique, BIT, Genève.

## 2. Evaluation des taux d'activité: 1950 - 1990

### 2.1 Données de base:

Tableau 1: Taux d'activité par sexe et par groupe d'âge

| Groupe d'âge | Année 1990 | 1992 | 1993 |
|---|---|---|---|
| **Hommes** | | | |
| 10-14 | 5.30 | 1.80 | .. |
| 15-19 | 36.20 | 30.30 | .. |
| 20-24 | 84.90 | 89.50 | .. |
| 25-29 | 96.40 | 95.20 | .. |
| 30-34 | 97.70 | 98.10 | .. |
| 35-39 | 96.70 | 96.00 | .. |
| 40-44 | 97.90 | 96.20 | .. |
| 45-49 | 95.80 | 91.90 | .. |
| 50-54 | 94.60 | 82.70 | .. |
| 55-59 | 73.90 | 73.90 | .. |
| 60-64 | 49.00 | 38.60 | .. |
| 65+ | 52.90 | 28.70 | .. |
| **Femmes** | | | |
| 10-14 | 4.60 | 1.40 | 1.80 |
| 15-19 | 26.90 | 21.10 | 19.70 |
| 20-24 | 63.80 | 57.10 | 58.47 |
| 25-29 | 58.30 | 56.50 | 50.02 |
| 30-34 | 62.30 | 47.60 | 47.80 |
| 35-39 | 55.60 | 48.70 | 53.71 |
| 40-44 | 51.80 | 43.30 | 45.49 |
| 45-49 | 47.90 | 42.30 | 37.34 |
| 50-54 | 34.50 | 27.10 | 35.13 |
| 55-59 | 31.30 | 20.60 | 19.24 |
| 60-64 | 13.30 | 6.10 | 6.31 |
| 65+ | | | |

Source(s): STAT.

### 2.2 Méthode(s): interpolation linéaire

#### 2.2.1 Hommes:

- 1950-80, taux d'activité 1950-80 tirés des EPPA3;
- 1990, interpolation des taux d'activité 1950-80 tirés des EPPA3
et des moyennes des taux tirés des enquêtes de 1990 et 1992;
ajustement des taux interpolés sur la base des variations des taux interpolés
1980 par rapport aux taux 1980 tirés des EPPA3.

#### 2.2.2 Femmes:

- 1950-80, taux d'activité 1950-80 tirés des EPPA3;
- 1990, interpolation des taux d'activité 1980 tirés des EPPA3
et des moyennes des taux tirés des enquêtes de 1990, 1992 et 1993.

## 3. Evaluation des taux de répartition par secteur d'activité: 1950 - 1990

### 3.1 Données de base:

Tableau 2: Répartition de la population active en % par secteur d'activité

| Année | Agriculture | Industrie Total | Manufac. | Services |
|---|---|---|---|---|
| **Hommes** | | | | |
| 1981 | 49.37 | 18.97 | 10.42 | 31.66 |
| 1985 | 49.75 | 19.27 | 10.58 | 30.98 |
| 1993 | 40.01 | 19.43 | 9.11 | 40.56 |
| **Femmes** | | | | |
| 1981 | 57.30 | 15.84 | 14.61 | 26.86 |
| 1985 | 55.04 | 20.22 | 18.92 | 24.74 |
| 1993 | 39.18 | 26.15 | 23.28 | 34.67 |

Source(s): STAT.

### 3.2 Méthode(s): interpolation linéaire

#### 3.2.1 Hommes:

- 1950-70, taux de répartition 1950-70 tirés des EPPA3;
- 1980-90, interpolation des taux de répartition tirés des recensements
de 1981, 1985 et 1991;
modification des tendances de tous les secteurs.

#### 3.2.2 Femmes:

Méthode, hypothèses et traitements identiques à ceux appliqués aux hommes.

## 4. Projection des taux d'activité: 2000 - 2010

### 4.1 Modèle(s): linéaire, log-linéaire et hyperbole

#### 4.1.1 Hommes:

- Au groupe d'âge [10-14], application de la fonction F2;
- Aux groupes d'âge [15+], application de la fonction F3;
- Modification des tendances des groupes d'âge [10-14] et [35-49].

#### 4.1.2 Femmes:

- Aux groupes d'âge [10-34], application de la fonction F2;
- Aux groupes d'âge [35-59], application de la fonction F1;
- Aux groupes d'âge [60+], application de la fonction F3;
- Modification des tendances des groupes d'âge [10-19] et [30-59].

*Notes sur les ajustements des taux, voir p. 192-195.*     *Notes sur les fonctions de projection, voir p. 198.*

# Suède

## 1. Source(s) des données de base

Code(s):     Titre(s):
EPPA3       Annuaire des statistiques du travail 1945-89 - Edition rétrospective sur les recensements de population, BIT, Genève, 1990.
STAT        Base de données sur les statistiques du travail - LABORSTA, Bureau de statistique, BIT, Genève.

## 2. Evaluation des taux d'activité: 1950 - 1990

### 2.1 Données de base:

Tableau 1: Taux d'activité par sexe et par groupe d'âge

| Groupe d'âge | Année 1970 (1) | 1980 (1) | 1989 (2) | 1990 (2) | 1991 (2) |
|---|---|---|---|---|---|
| **Hommes** | | | | | |
| 10-14 | .. | .. | 0.00 | 0.00 | 0.00 |
| 15-19 | .. | .. | 48.05 | 47.64 | 42.24 |
| 20-24 | .. | .. | 84.86 | 84.57 | 82.89 |
| 25-29 | .. | .. | 92.62 | 92.60 | 91.61 |
| 30-34 | .. | .. | 95.25 | 95.61 | 94.92 |
| 35-39 | .. | .. | 96.05 | 95.33 | 94.98 |
| 40-44 | .. | .. | 96.78 | 96.74 | 96.34 |
| 45-49 | .. | .. | 95.82 | 96.39 | 96.00 |
| 50-54 | .. | .. | 92.92 | 93.59 | 93.72 |
| 55-59 | .. | .. | 86.96 | 87.86 | 86.41 |
| 60-64 | .. | .. | 62.86 | 63.11 | 64.22 |
| 65+ | .. | .. | 8.07 | 7.32 | 8.75 |
| **Femmes** | | | | | |
| 10-14 | 0.35 | 0.00 | 0.00 | 0.00 | 0.00 |
| 15-19 | | | 51.36 | 50.45 | 47.06 |
| 20-24 | 64.05 | 71.30 | 82.00 | 80.68 | 77.32 |
| 25-29 | 55.45 | 73.60 | 87.94 | 87.07 | 86.14 |
| 30-34 | 52.35 | 74.60 | 90.75 | 91.10 | 88.97 |
| 35-39 | 52.85 | 78.60 | 92.10 | 93.03 | 91.96 |
| 40-44 | 53.90 | 82.60 | 93.31 | 93.85 | 93.38 |
| 45-49 | 53.40 | 82.90 | 92.67 | 93.10 | 92.88 |
| 50-54 | 51.15 | 77.00 | 88.34 | 89.08 | 89.27 |
| 55-59 | 44.95 | 66.40 | 78.50 | 79.25 | 80.00 |
| 60-64 | 29.25 | 41.40 | 50.67 | 53.85 | 54.79 |
| 65+ | 3.20 | 2.60 | 3.00 | 2.62 | 2.60 |

Source(s): (1) EPPA3; (2) STAT.

### 2.2 Méthode(s): moyenne arithmétique

#### 2.2.1 Hommes:
- 1950-80, taux d'activité 1950-80 tirés des EPPA3;
ajustement des taux d'activité du groupe d'âge [20-24] pour 1950 et 1960 et du groupe d'âge [15-19] pour 1980;
- 1990, moyennes des taux d'activité tirés des enquêtes de 1989, 1990 et 1991;
modification de la tendance du groupe d'âge [15-19].

#### 2.2.2 Femmes:
- 1950-80, taux d'activité 1950-80 tirés des EPPA3;
ajustement des taux d'activité du groupe d'âge [15-19] pour 1970 et 1980;
- 1990, moyennes des taux d'activité tirés des enquêtes de 1989, 1990 et 1991.

## 3. Evaluation des taux de répartition par secteur d'activité: 1950 - 1990

### 3.1 Données de base:

Tableau 2: Répartition de la population active en % par secteur d'activité

| Année | Agriculture | Industrie Total | Manufac. | Services |
|---|---|---|---|---|
| **Hommes** | | | | |
| 1979 | 8.26 | 49.28 | 34.70 | 42.46 |
| 1980 | 7.89 | 47.72 | 32.54 | 44.39 |
| 1981 | 8.11 | 46.12 | 32.64 | 45.77 |
| 1989 | 7.02 | 42.85 | 32.42 | 50.13 |
| 1990 | 5.64 | 44.30 | 30.96 | 50.07 |
| 1991 | 5.45 | 43.97 | 30.98 | 50.58 |
| **Femmes** | | | | |
| 1979 | 3.94 | 19.01 | 16.73 | 77.05 |
| 1980 | 3.65 | 16.98 | 15.15 | 79.37 |
| 1981 | 3.52 | 16.51 | 15.20 | 79.96 |
| 1989 | 2.98 | 14.16 | 12.96 | 82.86 |
| 1990 | 2.61 | 14.63 | 13.20 | 82.76 |
| 1991 | 2.31 | 14.38 | 13.37 | 83.32 |

Source(s): STAT.

### 3.2 Méthode(s): moyenne arithmétique

#### 3.2.1 Hommes:
- 1950-70, taux de répartition 1950-70 tirés des EPPA3;
- 1980, moyennes des taux de répartition tirés des enquêtes de 1979, 1980 et 1981;
- 1990, moyennes des taux de répartition tirés des enquêtes de 1989, 1990 et 1991.

#### 3.2.2 Femmes:
Méthode, hypothèses et traitements identiques à ceux appliqués aux hommes.

## 4. Projection des taux d'activité: 2000 - 2010

### 4.1 Modèle(s): linéaire, hyperbole et logistique

#### 4.1.1 Hommes:
- Aux groupes d'âge [15-19] et [55+], application de la fonction F3;
- Aux groupes d'âge [20-54], application de la fonction F1;
- Modification des tendances des groupes d'âge [15-39].

#### 4.1.2 Femmes:
- Aux groupes d'âge [15-19] et [65+], application de la fonction F3;
- Aux groupes d'âge [20-64], application de la fonction F6;
- Modification des tendances de tous les groupes d'âge.

*Notes sur les ajustements des taux, voir p. 192-195.*     *Notes sur les fonctions de projection, voir p. 198.*

# Suisse

## 1. Source(s) des données de base

Code(s):    Titre(s):

EPPA3    Annuaire des statistiques du travail 1945-89 - Edition rétrospective sur les recensements de population, BIT, Genève, 1990.
STAT    Base de données sur les statistiques du travail - LABORSTA, Bureau de statistique, BIT, Genève.

## 2. Evaluation des taux d'activité: 1950 - 1990

### 2.1 Données de base:

Tableau 1: Taux d'activité par sexe et par groupe d'âge

| Groupe d'âge | 1950 (1) | 1960 (1) | 1970 (1) | 1980 (1) | 1990 (2) |
|---|---|---|---|---|---|
| **Hommes** | | | | | |
| 10-14 | 1.10 | 0.35 | 0.20 | 0.00 | 0.00 |
| 15-19 | 74.10 | 69.10 | 63.40 | 57.05 | 55.98 |
| 20-24 | 91.00 | 90.50 | 88.55 | 85.20 | 83.80 |
| 25-29 | 96.15 | 96.85 | 96.40 | 94.90 | 93.87 |
| 30-34 | 98.40 | 98.75 | 98.75 | 98.35 | 97.84 |
| 35-39 | 98.70 | 99.00 | 99.10 | 98.95 | 98.56 |
| 40-44 | 98.55 | 98.80 | 98.90 | 98.80 | 98.68 |
| 45-49 | 98.15 | 98.50 | 98.55 | 98.25 | 98.35 |
| 50-54 | 97.15 | 97.55 | 97.45 | 96.85 | 97.44 |
| 55-59 | 94.95 | 95.65 | 95.15 | 93.60 | 94.84 |
| 60-64 | 87.75 | 88.90 | 87.30 | 82.95 | 79.78 |
| 65+ | 50.70 | 43.05 | 31.50 | 16.05 | 9.18 |
| **Femmes** | | | | | |
| 10-14 | 0.65 | 0.35 | 0.20 | 0.00 | 0.00 |
| 15-19 | 64.10 | 63.10 | 58.95 | 51.65 | 49.21 |
| 20-24 | 67.85 | 69.10 | 71.80 | 75.95 | 80.38 |
| 25-29 | 40.45 | 43.70 | 49.75 | 58.70 | 71.39 |
| 30-34 | 27.70 | 33.50 | 40.80 | 49.55 | 60.88 |
| 35-39 | 26.20 | 32.25 | 40.50 | 51.00 | 62.92 |
| 40-44 | 26.85 | 32.40 | 41.20 | 53.20 | 66.79 |
| 45-49 | 27.30 | 33.50 | 41.60 | 51.75 | 66.56 |
| 50-54 | 27.35 | 33.40 | 40.15 | 47.55 | 60.57 |
| 55-59 | 26.15 | 32.00 | 37.20 | 41.75 | 49.88 |
| 60-64 | 22.90 | 27.20 | 27.95 | 25.20 | 24.91 |
| 65+ | 11.65 | 11.50 | 9.35 | 5.15 | 3.22 |

Source(s): (1) EPPA3; (2) STAT.

### 2.2 Méthode(s): moyenne pondérée

#### 2.2.1 Hommes:

- 1950-80, taux d'activité 1950-80 tirés des EPPA3;
- 1990, moyennes pondérées des taux d'activité 1980 tirés des EPPA3 et des taux d'activité tirés du recensement de 1990.

#### 2.2.2 Femmes:

Méthode, hypothèses et traitements identiques à ceux appliqués aux hommes.

## 3. Evaluation des taux de répartition par secteur d'activité: 1950 - 1990

### 3.1 Données de base:

Tableau 2: Répartition de la population active en % par secteur d'activité

| Année | Agriculture | Industrie Total | Manufac. | Services |
|---|---|---|---|---|
| **Hommes** | | | | |
| 1990 | 6.31 | 43.94 | 32.34 | 49.75 |
| **Femmes** | | | | |
| 1990 | 4.29 | 20.31 | 19.38 | 75.40 |

Source(s): (1) STAT.

### 3.2 Méthode(s): données nationales

#### 3.2.1 Hommes:

- 1950-80, taux de répartition 1950-80 tirés des EPPA3;
- 1990, taux de répartition tirés des estimations officielles de 1990.

#### 3.2.2 Femmes:

Méthode, hypothèses et traitements identiques à ceux appliqués aux hommes.

## 4. Projection des taux d'activité: 2000 - 2010

### 4.1 Modèle(s): linéaire, hyperbole et logistique

#### 4.1.1 Hommes:

- Aux groupes d'âge [15-54], application de la fonction F1;
- Aux groupes d'âge [55+], application de la fonction F3;
- Modification des tendances des groupes d'âge [15-19] et [40-49].

#### 4.1.2 Femmes:

- Aux groupes d'âge [15-59], application de la fonction F6;
- Aux groupes d'âge [60+], application de la fonction F3;
- Modification des tendances des groupes d'âge [15-24] et [60-64].

# Suriname

## 1. Source(s) des données de base

| Code(s): | Titre(s): |
|---|---|
| EPPA3 | Evaluations et projections de la population active 1950-2025 - troisième édition, BIT, Genève, 1986. |
| ASTER | Annuaire des statistiques du travail 1945-89 - Edition rétrospective sur les recensements de population, BIT, Genève, 1990. |

## 2. Evaluation des taux d'activité: 1950 - 1990

### 2.1 Données de base:

Tableau 1: Taux d'activité par sexe et par groupe d'âge

| Groupe d'âge | Année 1950 (1) | 1960 (1) | 1964 (2) | 1970 (1) | 1980 (1) | 1980 (2) |
|---|---|---|---|---|---|---|
| **Hommes** | | | | | | |
| 10-14 | 1.80 | 1.00 | .. | 0.70 | 0.50 | .. |
| 15-19 | 66.95 | 48.00 | .. | 43.00 | 35.00 | .. |
| 20-24 | 93.55 | 90.80 | .. | 87.00 | 80.00 | .. |
| 25-29 | 98.25 | 97.05 | .. | 96.90 | 93.50 | .. |
| 30-34 | 98.95 | 97.75 | .. | 97.60 | 97.00 | .. |
| 35-39 | 99.50 | 98.35 | .. | 98.20 | 97.50 | .. |
| 40-44 | 98.30 | 96.85 | .. | 97.00 | 95.00 | .. |
| 45-49 | 96.90 | 96.30 | .. | 95.75 | 93.00 | .. |
| 50-54 | 95.50 | 93.45 | .. | 92.90 | 90.00 | .. |
| 55-59 | 90.65 | 89.00 | .. | 85.00 | 81.00 | .. |
| 60-64 | 80.00 | 75.00 | .. | 72.00 | 65.00 | .. |
| 65+ | 65.60 | 51.90 | .. | 40.60 | 22.00 | .. |
| **Femmes** | | | | | | |
| 10-14 | .. | .. | 0.80 | .. | .. | 0.20 |
| 15-19 | .. | .. | 11.20 | .. | .. | 3.80 |
| 20-24 | .. | .. | 23.90 | .. | .. | 25.30 |
| 25-29 | .. | .. | 20.90 | .. | .. | 32.10 |
| 30-34 | .. | .. | 20.60 | .. | .. | 30.60 |
| 35-39 | .. | .. | 21.40 | .. | .. | 31.80 |
| 40-44 | .. | .. | 22.30 | .. | .. | 29.80 |
| 45-49 | .. | .. | 23.40 | .. | .. | 28.60 |
| 50-54 | .. | .. | 23.70 | .. | .. | 24.50 |
| 55-59 | .. | .. | 16.90 | .. | .. | 20.80 |
| 60-64 | .. | .. | 14.20 | .. | .. | 12.70 |
| 65+ | .. | .. | 8.64 | .. | .. | 4.00 |

Source(s): (1) EPPA3; (2) ASTER.

### 2.2 Méthode(s): interpolation et extrapolation linéaires

#### 2.2.1 Hommes:

- 1950-80, taux d'activité 1950-80 tirés des EPPA3;
- 1990, extrapolation des taux d'activité 1950-80 tirés des EPPA3;
ajustement des taux extrapolés sur la base des variations des
taux interpolés 1980 par rapport aux taux 1980 tirés des EPPA3;
modification des tendances de tous les groupes d'âge.

#### 2.2.2 Femmes:

- 1950-90, interpolation et extrapolation des taux d'activité tirés du
recensement de 1964 et des taux d'activité ajustés tirés du recensement de 1980;
ajustement des taux d'activité sur la base du rapport hommes/femmes
dans l'agriculture tiré du recensement de 1964;
modification des tendances de tous les groupes d'âge pour 1950, 1960 et 1990.

## 3. Evaluation des taux de répartition par secteur d'activité: 1950 - 1990

### 3.1 Données de base:

Tableau 2: Répartition de la population active en % par secteur d'activité

| Année | Agriculture | Industrie Total | Manufac. | Services |
|---|---|---|---|---|
| **Hommes** | | | | |
| 1964 | 28.64 | 26.91 | 11.41 | 44.44 |
| 1980 | 24.83 | 24.94 | 9.42 | 50.22 |
| **Femmes** | | | | |
| 1989 | 27.36 | 7.95 | 6.14 | 64.69 |
| 1990 | 17.50 | 5.39 | 3.62 | 77.12 |

Source(s): ASTER.

### 3.2 Méthode(s): interpolation et extrapolation linéaires

#### 3.2.1 Hommes:

- 1950-90, interpolation et extrapolation des taux de répartition tirés
du recensement de 1964 et des taux de répartition ajustés tirés du recensement
de 1980.

#### 3.2.2 Femmes:

Méthode, hypothèses et traitements identiques à ceux appliqués aux hommes.

## 4. Projection des taux d'activité: 2000 - 2010

### 4.1 Modèle(s): log-linéaire, hyperbole et logistique

#### 4.1.1 Hommes:

- Aux groupes d'âge [15+], application de la fonction F3;
- Modification des tendances des groupes d'âge [15-49].

#### 4.1.2 Femmes:

- Aux groupes d'âge [15-19] et [60+], application de la fonction F3;
- Au groupe d'âge [20-24], application de la fonction F2;
- Aux groupes d'âge [25-59], application de la fonction F6;
- Modification des tendances des groupes d'âge [20-24] et [40-59].

*Notes sur les ajustements des taux, voir p. 192-195.*

*Notes sur les fonctions de projection, voir p. 198.*

# Swaziland

## 1. Source(s) des données de base

| Code(s): | Titre(s): |
|---|---|
| EPPA3 | Evaluations et projections de la population active 1950-2025 - troisième édition, BIT, Genève, 1986. |
| R1966 | Report on the 1966 Swaziland Population Census, Swaziland Government, Mbabane, 1968. |
| ADNU72 | Annuaire démographique 1972 - Statistiques des recensements de population III, vingt-quatrième édition, Nations Unies, New York, 1973. |
| R1986 | Report on the 1986 Swaziland Population Census, 3 Vol., Central Statistical Office, Mbabane, 1986. |

## 2. Evaluation des taux d'activité: 1950 - 1990

### 2.1 Données de base:

Tableau 1: Taux d'activité par sexe et par groupe d'âge

| Groupe d'âge | 1950 (1) | 1960 (1) | 1966 (2) | 1970 (1) | 1980 (1) | 1986 (3) |
|---|---|---|---|---|---|---|
| **Hommes** | | | | | | |
| 10-14 | .. | .. | 26.48 | .. | .. | 20.02 |
| 15-19 | .. | .. | 66.14 | .. | .. | 50.00 |
| 20-24 | .. | .. | 92.53 | .. | .. | 89.18 |
| 25-29 | .. | .. | 98.20 | .. | .. | 97.56 |
| 30-34 | .. | .. | 98.57 | .. | .. | 98.20 |
| 35-39 | .. | .. | 98.62 | .. | .. | 98.25 |
| 40-44 | .. | .. | 97.76 | .. | .. | 97.43 |
| 45-49 | .. | .. | 97.46 | .. | .. | 96.49 |
| 50-54 | .. | .. | 96.04 | .. | .. | 92.55 |
| 55-59 | .. | .. | 94.95 | .. | .. | 85.07 |
| 60-64 | .. | .. | 93.04 | .. | .. | 77.09 |
| 65+ | .. | .. | 83.91 | .. | .. | 40.94 |
| **Femmes** | | | | | | |
| 10-14 | 39.40 | 37.55 | 3.97 | 33.60 | 30.10 | 12.12 |
| 15-19 | 64.05 | 61.30 | 45.63 | 55.45 | 50.15 | 33.08 |
| 20-24 | 64.20 | 62.60 | 51.68 | 59.15 | 55.95 | 49.51 |
| 25-29 | 69.15 | 67.35 | 49.38 | 63.45 | 59.70 | 50.47 |
| 30-34 | 73.50 | 71.55 | 49.66 | 67.40 | 63.40 | 48.35 |
| 35-39 | 74.70 | 72.95 | 49.63 | 69.10 | 65.40 | 44.95 |
| 40-44 | 77.15 | 75.40 | 52.82 | 71.55 | 67.90 | 42.51 |
| 45-49 | 76.70 | 74.90 | 53.05 | 70.95 | 67.20 | 38.25 |
| 50-54 | 75.30 | 73.15 | 53.66 | 68.45 | 64.10 | 34.28 |
| 55-59 | 72.55 | 70.25 | 55.35 | 65.30 | 60.70 | 30.28 |
| 60-64 | 66.60 | 63.45 | 54.28 | 56.70 | 50.75 | 18.90 |
| 65+ | 46.65 | 43.25 | 45.86 | 36.45 | 30.70 | 9.80 |

Source(s): (1) EPPA3; (2) R1966 et ADNU72; (3) R1986.

### 2.2 Méthode(s): interpolation et extrapolation linéaires

#### 2.2.1 Hommes:

- 1950-90, interpolation et extrapolation des taux d'activité ajustés
tirés des recensements de 1966 et 1986;
modification des tendances des groupes d'âge [10-14] et [45+]
pour 1950 et 1960;
modification des tendances des groupes d'âge [55+] pour 1990.

#### 2.2.2 Femmes:

- 1950-90, interpolation et extrapolation des taux d'activité 1950-80 tirés
des EPPA3 et des taux ajustés tirés du recensement de 1986;
ajustement des taux interpolés et extrapolés sur la base des variations
des taux interpolés 1986 par rapport aux taux ajustés tirés
du recensement de 1986.

## 3. Evaluation des taux de répartition par secteur d'activité: 1950 - 1990

### 3.1 Données de base:

Tableau 2: Répartition de la population active en % par secteur d'activité

| Année | Agriculture | Industrie Total | Industrie Manufac. | Services |
|---|---|---|---|---|
| **Hommes** | | | | |
| 1966 (1) | 66.49 | 13.60 | 6.09 | 19.91 |
| 1986 (2) | 33.49 | 29.71 | 12.61 | 36.80 |
| **Femmes** | | | | |
| 1966 (1) | 80.53 | 3.68 | 3.57 | 15.79 |
| 1986 (2) | 55.34 | 7.59 | 6.94 | 37.07 |

Source(s): (1) R1966; (2) R1986.

### 3.2 Méthode(s): interpolation et extrapolation linéaires

#### 3.2.1 Hommes:

- 1950-90, interpolation et extrapolation des taux de répartition ajustés
tirés des recensements de 1966 et 1986;
modification des tendances de tous les secteurs pour 1950, 1960 et 1990.

#### 3.2.2 Femmes:

Méthode, hypothèses et traitements identiques à ceux appliqués aux hommes.

## 4. Projection des taux d'activité: 2000 - 2010

### 4.1 Modèle(s): linéaire et hyperbole

#### 4.1.1 Hommes:

- Au groupe d'âge [10-14], application de la fonction F1;
- Aux groupes d'âge [15+], application de la fonction F3;
- Modification des tendances des groupes d'âge [15-19], [45-49] et [65+].

#### 4.1.2 Femmes:

- A tous les groupes d'âge, application de la fonction F3;
- Modification des tendances des groupes d'âge [10-14] et [20-59].

*Notes sur les ajustements des taux, voir p. 192-195.*     *Notes sur les fonctions de projection, voir p. 198.*

# Tadjikistan

## 1. Source(s) des données de base

**Code(s):** **Titre(s):**

BLT-94-2  Vorobiev A. (1994), "Estimation de la population active pour les quinze pays de l'ex-URSS pour les années 1950, 1959, 1970, 1979 et 1989", dans le Bulletin des statistiques du travail - 1994-2, BIT, Genève.

## 2. Evaluation des taux d'activité: 1950 - 1990

### 2.1 Données de base:

Tableau 1: Taux d'activité par sexe et par groupe d'âge

| Groupe d'âge | 1950 | 1959 | 1970 | 1979 | 1989 |
|---|---|---|---|---|---|
| **Hommes** | | | | | |
| 10-14 | 0.00 | 0.00 | 0.00 | 0.00 | 0.00 |
| 15-19 | 54.44 | 57.14 | 35.11 | 37.28 | 28.90 |
| 20-24 | 83.33 | 86.75 | 83.12 | 85.19 | 79.39 |
| 25-29 | 91.49 | 93.98 | 92.11 | 97.58 | 95.91 |
| 30-34 | 94.29 | 97.44 | 97.66 | 98.70 | 98.77 |
| 35-39 | 92.11 | 97.67 | 98.78 | 98.85 | 98.31 |
| 40-44 | 91.43 | 96.88 | 98.72 | 98.91 | 97.22 |
| 45-49 | 90.32 | 91.43 | 95.24 | 98.70 | 97.50 |
| 50-54 | 89.66 | 93.75 | 92.86 | 95.45 | 93.90 |
| 55-59 | 90.00 | 89.66 | 87.10 | 88.24 | 88.24 |
| 60-64 | 76.47 | 80.00 | 66.67 | 36.00 | 37.50 |
| 65+ | 37.04 | 37.21 | 7.69 | 9.21 | 12.16 |
| **Femmes** | | | | | |
| 10-14 | 0.00 | 0.00 | 0.00 | 0.00 | 0.00 |
| 15-19 | 43.43 | 59.15 | 41.35 | 45.18 | 31.30 |
| 20-24 | 69.05 | 71.43 | 73.86 | 84.21 | 63.14 |
| 25-29 | 70.00 | 73.63 | 76.06 | 86.61 | 66.67 |
| 30-34 | 68.09 | 70.51 | 75.79 | 87.67 | 70.73 |
| 35-39 | 62.79 | 66.07 | 77.38 | 88.46 | 76.86 |
| 40-44 | 58.54 | 63.64 | 76.00 | 88.89 | 77.94 |
| 45-49 | 52.27 | 56.41 | 74.07 | 87.34 | 76.39 |
| 50-54 | 41.18 | 42.11 | 65.00 | 72.86 | 54.22 |
| 55-59 | 23.08 | 26.83 | 26.09 | 27.78 | 22.97 |
| 60-64 | 13.64 | 11.76 | 10.00 | 10.00 | 12.50 |
| 65+ | 5.26 | 5.56 | 2.44 | 2.94 | 5.08 |

Source(s): BLT-94-2-2

### 2.2 Méthode(s): moyenne pondérée

#### 2.2.1 Hommes:

- 1950-90, moyennes pondérées des taux d'activité 1950, 1959, 1970 et 1989 tirés du Bulletin des statistiques du travail, 1994-2.

#### 2.2.2 Femmes:

Méthode, hypothèses et traitements identiques à ceux appliqués aux hommes.

## 3. Evaluation des taux de répartition par secteur d'activité: 1950 - 1990

### 3.1 Données de base:

Tableau 2: Répartition de la population active en % par secteur d'activité

| Année | Agriculture | Industrie Total | Manufac. | Services |
|---|---|---|---|---|
| **Hommes** | | | | |
| 1950 | 73.95 | 8.96 | 6.16 | 17.09 |
| 1959 | 57.11 | 17.83 | 7.22 | 25.05 |
| 1970 | 41.30 | 25.91 | 12.86 | 32.79 |
| 1979 | 35.98 | 28.94 | 13.06 | 35.08 |
| 1989 | 37.01 | 27.97 | 10.66 | 35.01 |
| **Femmes** | | | | |
| 1950 | 77.01 | 8.03 | 6.93 | 14.96 |
| 1959 | 68.73 | 11.83 | 8.73 | 19.44 |
| 1970 | 52.65 | 16.81 | 11.28 | 30.53 |
| 1979 | 55.27 | 16.03 | 9.56 | 28.69 |
| 1989 | 46.74 | 17.19 | 12.24 | 36.07 |

Source(s): BLT-94-2.

### 3.2 Méthode(s): moyenne pondérée

#### 3.2.1 Hommes:

- 1950-90, moyennes pondérées des taux de répartition 1950, 1959, 1970, 1979 et 1989 tirés du Bulletin des statistiques du travail - 1994-2.

#### 3.2.2 Femmes:

Méthode, hypothèses et traitements identiques à ceux appliqués aux hommes.

## 4. Projection des taux d'activité: 2000 - 2010

### 4.1 Modèle(s): linéaire, hyperbole et logistique

#### 4.1.1 Hommes:

- Aux groupes d'âge [15-24] et [60+], application de la fonction F3;
- Aux groupes d'âge [25-59], application de la fonction F1;
- Modification des tendances des groupes d'âge [20-64].

#### 4.1.2 Femmes:

- Au groupe d'âge [15-19], application de la fonction F1;
- Aux groupes d'âge [20-24] et [60+], application de la fonction F3;
- Aux groupes d'âge [25-59], application de la fonction F6;
- Modification des tendances des groupes d'âge [20-49].

*Notes sur les ajustements des taux, voir p. 192-195.*   *Notes sur les fonctions de projection, voir p. 198.*

# Tanzanie, Rép. -Unie de

## 1. Source(s) des données de base

Code(s):     Titre(s):

EPPA3     Evaluations et projections de la population active 1950-2025 - troisième édition, BIT, Genève, 1986.

## 2. Evaluation des taux d'activité: 1950 - 1990

### 2.1 Données de base:

Tableau 1: Taux d'activité par sexe et par groupe d'âge

| Groupe d'âge | Année 1950 | 1960 | 1970 | 1980 |
|---|---|---|---|---|
| **Hommes** | | | | |
| 10-14 | 49.00 | 47.95 | 46.55 | 43.45 |
| 15-19 | 78.70 | 77.35 | 75.45 | 71.40 |
| 20-24 | 87.15 | 86.65 | 85.90 | 84.35 |
| 25-29 | 96.25 | 96.15 | 96.05 | 95.80 |
| 30-34 | 98.15 | 98.05 | 97.90 | 97.60 |
| 35-39 | 99.05 | 98.95 | 98.80 | 98.50 |
| 40-44 | 99.15 | 99.05 | 98.90 | 98.60 |
| 45-49 | 99.35 | 99.25 | 99.15 | 98.85 |
| 50-54 | 98.90 | 98.75 | 98.55 | 98.15 |
| 55-59 | 98.60 | 98.50 | 98.40 | 97.95 |
| 60-64 | 97.75 | 97.35 | 96.85 | 95.65 |
| 65+ | 91.70 | 90.95 | 89.95 | 87.75 |
| **Femmes** | | | | |
| 10-14 | 46.45 | 45.70 | 44.60 | 42.25 |
| 15-19 | 85.80 | 84.25 | 82.00 | 77.20 |
| 20-24 | 90.90 | 89.40 | 87.20 | 82.50 |
| 25-29 | 94.85 | 93.45 | 91.45 | 87.10 |
| 30-34 | 97.35 | 96.05 | 94.15 | 90.05 |
| 35-39 | 98.20 | 97.00 | 95.20 | 91.40 |
| 40-44 | 98.50 | 97.40 | 95.80 | 92.35 |
| 45-49 | 98.30 | 97.20 | 95.65 | 92.30 |
| 50-54 | 95.95 | 95.05 | 93.75 | 90.95 |
| 55-59 | 92.90 | 92.25 | 91.30 | 89.30 |
| 60-64 | 85.30 | 84.90 | 84.35 | 83.10 |
| 65+ | 61.45 | 61.30 | 61.10 | 60.70 |

Source(s): EPPA3.

### 2.2 Méthode(s): extrapolation linéaire

#### 2.2.1 Hommes:

- 1950-80, taux d'activité 1950-80 tirés des EPPA3;
- 1990, extrapolation des taux d'activité 1950-80 tirés des EPPA3;
ajustement des taux extrapolés sur la base des variations des taux
interpolés 1980 par rapport aux taux 1980 tirés des EPPA3;
modification des tendances de tous les groupes d'âge.

#### 2.2.2 Femmes:

Méthode, hypothèses et traitements identiques à ceux appliqués aux hommes.

## 3. Evaluation des taux de répartition par secteur d'activité: 1950 - 1990

### 3.1 Données de base:

Tableau 2: Répartition de la population active en % par secteur d'activité

| Année | Agriculture | Industrie Total | Manufac. | Services |
|---|---|---|---|---|
| **Hommes** | | | | |
| 1950 | 90.60 | 3.40 | .. | 6.00 |
| 1960 | 88.55 | 4.10 | .. | 7.35 |
| 1970 | 85.00 | 5.40 | .. | 9.60 |
| 1980 | 79.75 | 7.25 | .. | 13.00 |
| **Femmes** | | | | |
| 1950 | 97.50 | 0.50 | .. | 2.00 |
| 1960 | 96.45 | 0.75 | .. | 2.80 |
| 1970 | 95.00 | 1.00 | .. | 4.00 |
| 1980 | 91.85 | 1.65 | .. | 6.50 |

Source(s): EPPA3.

### 3.2 Méthode(s): extrapolation linéaire

#### 3.2.1 Hommes:

- 1950-80, taux de répartition 1950-80 tirés des EPPA3;
- 1990, extrapolation des taux de répartition 1950-80 tirés des EPPA3;
modification des tendances de tous les secteurs;
- Application du rapport manufacture/industrie estimé pour l'Ethiopie.

#### 3.2.2 Femmes:

Méthode, hypothèses et traitements identiques à ceux appliqués aux hommes.

## 4. Projection des taux d'activité: 2000 - 2010

### 4.1 Modèle(s): linéaire et hyperbole

#### 4.1.1 Hommes:

- Aux groupes d'âge [10-24], application de la fonction F1;
- Aux groupes d'âge [25+], application de la fonction F3;
- Modification des tendances des groupes d'âge [10-14] et [60+].

#### 4.1.2 Femmes:

- Aux groupes d'âge [10-19], application de la fonction F1;
- Aux groupes d'âge [20+], application de la fonction F3;
- Modification des tendances de tous les groupes d'âge.

*Notes sur les ajustements des taux, voir p. 192-195.*        *Notes sur les fonctions de projection, voir p. 198.*

# Tchad

## 1. Source(s) des données de base

Code(s):    Titre(s):

S1964      Enquête démographique au Tchad, 1964, Vol I et II, Bureau central du Recensement, Ndjamena, 1966.
EPPA3      Evaluations et projections de la population active 1950-2025 - troisième édition, BIT, Genève, 1986.
ASTER      Annuaire des statistiques du travail 1945-89 - Edition rétrospective sur les recensements de population, BIT, Genève, 1990.

## 2. Evaluation des taux d'activité: 1950 - 1990

### 2.1 Données de base:

Tableau 1: Taux d'activité par sexe et par groupe d'âge

| Groupe d'âge | Année | |
|---|---|---|
| | 1964 (1) | 1980 (2) |
| **Hommes** | | |
| 10-14 | 48.42 | 45.61 |
| 15-19 | 75.10 | 70.74 |
| 20-24 | 95.60 | 94.16 |
| 25-29 | 98.60 | 98.08 |
| 30-34 | 98.70 | 98.12 |
| 35-39 | 98.60 | 98.45 |
| 40-44 | 98.10 | 97.70 |
| 45-49 | 98.10 | 97.48 |
| 50-54 | 97.50 | 97.29 |
| 55-59 | 96.30 | 93.35 |
| 60-64 | 95.55 | 86.87 |
| 65+ | 80.82 | 73.48 |
| **Femmes** | | |
| 10-14 | 11.56 | 10.57 |
| 15-19 | 24.10 | 22.03 |
| 20-24 | 29.70 | 28.07 |
| 25-29 | 30.90 | 28.02 |
| 30-34 | 28.60 | 27.97 |
| 35-39 | 30.90 | 27.96 |
| 40-44 | 26.10 | 28.04 |
| 45-49 | 27.70 | 25.21 |
| 50-54 | 25.10 | 25.58 |
| 55-59 | 24.90 | 25.58 |
| 60-64 | 22.76 | 20.37 |
| 65+ | 8.07 | 7.22 |

Source(s): (1) S1964; (2) ASTER.

### 2.2 Méthode(s): interpolation et extrapolation linéaires

#### 2.2.1 Hommes:

- 1950-90, interpolation et extrapolation des taux d'activité
tirés de l'enquête de 1964 et des taux d'activité tirés du recensement de 1980;
modification des tendances des groupes d'âge [15-49] et [55-64] pour 1950;
modification de la tendance du groupe d'âge [25-29] pour 1990.

#### 2.2.2 Femmes:

- 1950-90, interpolation et extrapolation des taux d'activité 1964 et 1980
tirés respectivement de l'enquête de 1964 et du recensement de 1980;
modification des tendances des groupes d'âge [10-14], [30-34]
et [50+] de 1990.

## 3. Evaluation des taux de répartition par secteur d'activité: 1950 - 1990

### 3.1 Données de base:

Tableau 2: Répartition de la population active en % par secteur d'activité

| Année | Agriculture | Industrie | | Services |
|---|---|---|---|---|
| | | Total | Manufac. | |
| **Hommes** | | | | |
| 1970 (1) | 89.00 | 4.10 | .. | 6.90 |
| 1980 (1) | 82.20 | 5.70 | .. | 12.10 |
| **Femmes** | | | | |
| 1964 (2) | 95.25 | 0.40 | .. | 4.35 |
| 1980 (3) | 86.89 | 1.09 | .. | 12.02 |

Source(s): (1) EPPA3; (2) S1964.

### 3.2 Méthode(s): interpolation et extrapolation linéaires
moyenne pondérée

#### 3.2.1 Hommes:

- 1950-80, taux de répartition 1950-80 tirés des EPPA3;
- 1990, extrapolation des taux de répartition 1950-80 tirés des EPPA3.

#### 3.2.2 Femmes:

- 1950-90, interpolation et extrapolation des taux de répartition ajustés
1964 et 1983 tirés respectivement de l'enquête de 1964
et du recensement de 1983.

## 4. Projection des taux d'activité: 2000 - 2010

### 4.1 Modèle(s): linéaire, hyperbole et logistique

#### 4.1.1 Hommes:

- Aux groupes d'âge [10-29], application de la fonction F1;
- Aux groupes d'âge [30+], application de la fonction F3;
- Modification des tendances des groupes d'âge [10-14], [20-24],
[40-44] et [60+].

#### 4.1.2 Femmes:

- Aux groupes d'âge [10-19] et [65+], application de la fonction F1;
- Aux groupes d'âge [20-64], application de la fonction F6;
- Modification des tendances des groupes d'âge [10-19], [35-39] et [50+].

*Notes sur les ajustements des taux, voir p. 192-195.*

*Notes sur les fonctions de projection, voir p. 198.*

# Thaïlande

## 1. Source(s) des données de base

Code(s):    Titre(s):

EPPA3    Evaluations et projections de la population active 1950-2025 - troisième édition, BIT, Genève, 1986.
STAT    Base de données sur les statistiques du travail - LABORSTA, Bureau de statistique, BIT, Genève.

## 2. Evaluation des taux d'activité: 1950 - 1990

### 2.1 Données de base:

Tableau 1: Taux d'activité par sexe et par groupe d'âge

| Groupe d'âge | Année | | | |
|---|---|---|---|---|
| | 1979 | 1980 | 1989 | 1990 |
| **Hommes** | | | | |
| 10-19 | 70.60 | 70.90 | 71.20 | 67.70 |
| 20-24 | 88.80 | 87.80 | 92.80 | 91.60 |
| 25-29 | 97.50 | 97.20 | 97.30 | 96.60 |
| 30-39 | 98.70 | 98.80 | 98.00 | 98.00 |
| 40-49 | 98.40 | 98.50 | 98.10 | 97.90 |
| 50-59 | 94.70 | 95.50 | 94.40 | 94.80 |
| 60+ | 59.20 | 56.70 | 49.50 | 53.00 |
| **Femmes** | | | | |
| 10-19 | 69.90 | 71.00 | 72.20 | 69.40 |
| 20-24 | 81.20 | 80.30 | 83.00 | 81.70 |
| 25-29 | 83.50 | 84.70 | 84.70 | 83.60 |
| 30-39 | 86.00 | 86.80 | 87.00 | 86.60 |
| 40-49 | 85.30 | 87.80 | 86.10 | 86.30 |
| 50-59 | 74.80 | 77.70 | 76.40 | 76.50 |
| 60+ | 29.10 | 31.40 | 28.50 | 32.20 |

Source(s): STAT.

### 2.2 Méthode(s): interpolation linéaire

#### 2.2.1 Hommes:

- 1950-90, interpolation des taux d'activité 1950-80 tirés des EPPA3
et des moyennes des taux d'activité ajustés tirés respectivement des
enquêtes de 1979 et 1980 et des enquêtes de 1989 et 1990.

#### 2.2.2 Femmes:

Méthode, hypothèses et traitements identiques à ceux appliqués aux hommes.

## 3. Evaluation des taux de répartition par secteur d'activité: 1950 - 1990

### 3.1 Données de base:

Tableau 2: Répartition de la population active en % par secteur d'activité

| Année | Agriculture | Industrie | | Services |
|---|---|---|---|---|
| | | Total | Manufac. | |
| **Hommes** | | | | |
| 1980 (1) | 67.95 | 12.50 | .. | 19.55 |
| 1990 (2) | 63.13 | 15.55 | 9.54 | 21.32 |
| **Femmes** | | | | |
| 1980 (1) | 74.20 | 7.75 | .. | 18.05 |
| 1990 (2) | 65.00 | 12.27 | 10.88 | 22.73 |

Source(s): (1) EPPA3; (2) STAT.

### 3.2 Méthode(s): interpolation linéaire

#### 3.2.1 Hommes:

- 1950-80, taux de répartition 1950-80 tirés des EPPA3;
- 1990, interpolation des taux de répartition 1980 tirés des EPPA3,
et des taux de répartition de l'enquête de 1990;
modification des tendances de tous les secteurs;
- Application du rapport manufacture/industrie tiré de l'enquête de 1990.

#### 3.2.2 Femmes:

Méthode, hypothèses et traitements identiques à ceux appliqués aux hommes.

## 4. Projection des taux d'activité: 2000 - 2010

### 4.1 Modèle(s): linéaire, log-linéaire, hyperbole et logistique

#### 4.1.1 Hommes:

- Au groupe d'âge [10-14], application de la fonction F1;
- Au groupe d'âge [15-19], application de la fonction F2;
- Aux groupes d'âge [20+], application de la fonction F3;
- Modification des tendances des groupes d'âge [10-49].

#### 4.1.2 Femmes:

- Aux groupes d'âge [10-19], application de la fonction F1;
- Aux groupes d'âge [20-64], application de la fonction F6;
- Au groupe d'âge [65+], application de la fonction F3;
- Modification des tendances des groupes d'âge [10-59].

*Notes sur les ajustements des taux, voir p. 192-195.*    *Notes sur les fonctions de projection, voir p. 198.*

# Timor oriental

## 1. Source(s) des données de base

Code(s):     Titre(s):

EPPA3       Evaluations et projections de la population active 1950-2025 - troisième édition, BIT, Genève, 1986.

## 2. Evaluation des taux d'activité: 1950 - 1990

### 2.1 Données de base:

Tableau 1: Taux d'activité par sexe et par groupe d'âge

| Groupe d'âge | Année 1950 | 1960 | 1970 | 1980 | 1990 |
|---|---|---|---|---|---|
| **Hommes** | | | | | |
| 10-14 | 28.51 | 26.60 | 24.69 | 22.78 | .. |
| 15-19 | 82.80 | 81.50 | 75.70 | 72.80 | .. |
| 20-24 | 97.50 | 97.00 | 95.25 | 94.00 | .. |
| 25-29 | 97.65 | 97.40 | 97.15 | 97.00 | .. |
| 30-34 | 97.65 | 97.40 | 97.15 | 97.00 | .. |
| 35-39 | 97.60 | 97.35 | 97.10 | 97.00 | .. |
| 40-44 | 97.50 | 97.25 | 97.00 | 96.90 | .. |
| 45-49 | 97.40 | 96.15 | 95.50 | 95.20 | .. |
| 50-54 | 97.00 | 95.70 | 95.00 | 94.65 | .. |
| 55-59 | 95.00 | 93.50 | 91.50 | 90.50 | .. |
| 60-64 | 90.00 | 88.50 | 86.00 | 84.75 | .. |
| 65+ | 78.00 | 76.00 | 70.25 | 67.40 | .. |
| **Femmes** | | | | | |
| 10-14 | 3.00 | .. | .. | .. | 2.20 |
| 15-19 | 10.60 | .. | .. | .. | 12.28 |
| 20-24 | 11.80 | .. | .. | .. | 18.66 |
| 25-29 | 11.45 | .. | .. | .. | 17.36 |
| 30-34 | 10.25 | .. | .. | .. | 15.69 |
| 35-39 | 10.70 | .. | .. | .. | 15.82 |
| 40-44 | 12.00 | .. | .. | .. | 17.40 |
| 45-49 | 11.20 | .. | .. | .. | 15.00 |
| 50-54 | 10.75 | .. | .. | .. | 14.02 |
| 55-59 | 10.00 | .. | .. | .. | 9.86 |
| 60-64 | 8.35 | .. | .. | .. | 7.08 |
| 65+ | 4.50 | .. | .. | .. | 4.15 |

Source(s): EPPA3.

### 2.2 Méthode(s): interpolation linéaire
moyenne pondérée

**2.2.1 Hommes:**

- 1950-80, taux d'activité 1950-80 tirés des EPPA3;
ajustement des taux d'activité du groupe d'âge [10-14];
- 1990, extrapolation des taux d'activité 1950-80 tirés des EPPA3,
ajustement des taux extrapolés sur la base des variations des taux
interpolés 1980 par rapport aux taux 1980 tirés des EPPA3;
modification des tendances des tendances de tous les groupes d'âge.

**2.2.2 Femmes:**

- 1950 et 1990, taux d'activité ajustés 1950 et 1990 tirés des EPPA3;
l'ajustement a été accompli sur la base du modèle d'ajustement des taux d'activité
des femmes travaillant dans l'agriculture comme aides familiales;
- 1960-80, moyennes pondérées des taux d'activité estimés pour 1950
et 1990.

## 3. Evaluation des taux de répartition par secteur d'activité: 1950 - 1990

### 3.1 Données de base:

Tableau 2: Répartition de la population active en % par secteur d'activité

| Année | Agriculture | Industrie Total | Manufac. | Services |
|---|---|---|---|---|
| **Hommes** | | | | |
| 1950 | 80.00 | 7.50 | .. | 12.50 |
| 1960 | 79.00 | 8.00 | .. | 13.00 |
| 1970 | 78.00 | 8.50 | .. | 13.50 |
| 1980 | 77.00 | 8.75 | .. | 14.25 |
| **Femmes** | | | | |
| 1950 | 98.00 | 0.06 | .. | 1.94 |
| 1960 | 96.75 | 0.10 | .. | 3.15 |
| 1970 | 95.50 | 0.14 | .. | 4.36 |
| 1980 | 94.25 | 0.17 | .. | 5.58 |

Source(s): EPPA3.

### 3.2 Méthode(s): extrapolation linéaire

**3.2.1 Hommes:**

- 1950-80, taux de répartition 1950-80 tirés des EPPA3;
- 1990, extrapolation des taux de répartition de l'agriculture 1950-80
des EPPA3;
- Application du rapport industrie/services 1980 tiré des EPPA3.

**3.2.2 Femmes:**

- 1950-80, taux de répartition de l'agriculture 1950-80 tirés des EPPA3;
ajustement sur la base d'un rapport hommes/femmes égal à 1
dans l'agriculture;
application des rapports industrie/services 1950-80 tirés des EPPA3;
- 1990, extrapolation des taux de répartition estimés de l'agriculture
pour 1950-80;
application du rapport industrie/services de 1980 tiré des EPPA3.

## 4. Projection des taux d'activité: 2000 - 2010

### 4.1 Modèle(s): linéaire, hyperbole et logistique

**4.1.1 Hommes:**

- Aux groupes d'âge [10-19] et [55+], application de la fonction F1;
- Aux groupes d'âge [20-54], application de la fonction F3;
- Modification des tendances des groupes d'âge [55+].

**4.1.2 Femmes:**

- Aux groupes d'âge [10-19], application de la fonction F1;
- Aux groupes d'âge [20+], application de la fonction F6;
- Modification des tendances des groupes d'âge [10-19].

*Notes sur les ajustements des taux, voir p. 192-195.*   *Notes sur les fonctions de projection, voir p. 198.*

# Togo

## 1. Source(s) des données de base

| Code(s): | Titre(s): |
|---|---|
| EPPA3 | Evaluations et projections de la population active 1950-2025 - troisième édition, BIT, Genève, 1986. |
| STAT | Base de données sur les statistiques du travail - LABORSTA, Bureau de statistique, BIT, Genève. |
| R1970 | Recensement général de la Population (mars-avril 1970), Direction de la Statistique, Lomé, 1974. |
| AST87 | Annuaire des statistiques du travail 1987, BIT, Genève, 1987. |

## 2. Evaluation des taux d'activité: 1950 - 1990

### 2.1 Données de base:

Tableau 1: Taux d'activité par sexe et par groupe d'âge

| Groupe d'âge | Année 1950 (1) | 1960 (1) | 1961 (2) | 1970 (1) | 1970 (3) | 1981 (4) |
|---|---|---|---|---|---|---|
| **Hommes** | | | | | | |
| 10-14 | 50.60 | 49.30 | .. | 47.70 | .. | 12.72 |
| 15-19 | 74.00 | 72.50 | .. | 70.55 | .. | 36.61 |
| 20-24 | 93.15 | 92.50 | .. | 91.70 | .. | 70.05 |
| 25-29 | 97.20 | 97.10 | .. | 96.95 | .. | 94.59 |
| 30-34 | 97.35 | 97.25 | .. | 97.10 | .. | 98.14 |
| 35-39 | 97.70 | 97.60 | .. | 97.45 | .. | 98.60 |
| 40-44 | 97.45 | 97.30 | .. | 97.15 | .. | 98.12 |
| 45-49 | 97.05 | 96.95 | .. | 96.85 | .. | 97.59 |
| 50-54 | 95.55 | 95.40 | .. | 95.20 | .. | 92.70 |
| 55-59 | 94.30 | 94.05 | .. | 93.75 | .. | 90.12 |
| 60-64 | 90.55 | 90.15 | .. | 89.60 | .. | 87.54 |
| 65+ | 78.30 | 77.55 | .. | 76.65 | .. | 71.52 |
| **Femmes** | | | | | | |
| 10-14 | .. | .. | 36.59 | .. | 47.86 | 12.73 |
| 15-19 | .. | .. | 51.97 | .. | 51.85 | 35.83 |
| 20-24 | .. | .. | 51.73 | .. | 54.01 | 47.66 |
| 25-29 | .. | .. | 55.43 | .. | 57.80 | 55.15 |
| 30-34 | .. | .. | 56.99 | .. | 58.90 | 58.03 |
| 35-39 | .. | .. | 58.50 | .. | 60.52 | 59.59 |
| 40-44 | .. | .. | 60.44 | .. | 60.88 | 60.27 |
| 45-49 | .. | .. | 60.05 | .. | 61.00 | 60.13 |
| 50-54 | .. | .. | 58.76 | .. | 58.86 | 59.94 |
| 55-59 | .. | .. | 55.73 | .. | 55.34 | 56.46 |
| 60-64 | .. | .. | 53.85 | .. | 49.54 | 50.85 |
| 65+ | .. | .. | 37.21 | .. | 33.95 | 34.95 |

Source(s): (1) EPPA3; (2) STAT; (3) R1970; (4) AST87.

### 2.2 Méthode(s): interpolation et extrapolation linéaires

#### 2.2.1 Hommes:

- 1950-70, taux d'activité 1950-70 tirés des EPPA3;
ajustement des taux d'activité des groupes d'âge [30-49] pour 1950 et 1960;
- 1980-90, extrapolation des taux d'activité 1950-70 tirés des EPPA3
et des taux du recensement de 1981;
ajustement des taux interpolés et extrapolés sur la base des variations
des taux interpolés 1970 par rapport aux taux de 1970 tirés des EPPA3;
modification des tendances des groupes d'âge [10-19] pour 1990.

#### 2.2.2 Femmes:

- 1950-90, interpolation et extrapolation des taux d'activité de l'enquête
de 1961 et des taux ajustés des recensements de 1970 et 1981;
modification des tendances de tous les groupes d'âge de 1950.

## 3. Evaluation des taux de répartition par secteur d'activité: 1950 - 1990

### 3.1 Données de base:

Tableau 2: Répartition de la population active en % par secteur d'activité

| Année | Agriculture | Industrie Total | Manufac. | Services |
|---|---|---|---|---|
| **Hommes** | | | | |
| 1961 (1) | 83.50 | 9.50 | .. | 7.00 |
| 1981 (2) | 69.11 | 11.71 | 6.23 | 19.18 |
| **Femmes** | | | | |
| 1961 (1) | 73.50 | 6.00 | .. | 20.50 |
| 1981 (2) | 66.75 | 6.70 | 6.57 | 26.55 |

Source(s): (1) STAT; (2) AST87.

### 3.2 Méthode(s): interpolation et extrapolation linéaires

#### 3.2.1 Hommes:

- 1950-90, interpolation et extrapolation des taux de répartition de
l'enquête de 1961 et du recensement de 1981;
modification des tendances de tous les secteurs;
- Application du rapport manufacture/industrie tiré du recensement de 1981.

#### 3.2.2 Femmes:

Méthode, hypothèses et traitements identiques à ceux appliqués aux hommes.

## 4. Projection des taux d'activité: 2000 - 2010

### 4.1 Modèle(s): log-linéaire et hyperbole

#### 4.1.1 Hommes:

- Au groupe d'âge [10-14], application de la fonction F2;
- Aux groupes d'âge [15+], application de la fonction F1;
- Modification des tendances des groupes d'âge [30-39].

#### 4.1.2 Femmes:

- Au groupe d'âge [10-14], application de la fonction F2;
- Aux groupes d'âge [15+], application de la fonction F1;
- Modification des tendances des groupes d'âge [10-59].

---

*Notes sur les ajustements des taux, voir p. 192-195.*       *Notes sur les fonctions de projection, voir p. 198.*

# Trinité-et-Tobago

## 1. Source(s) des données de base

Code(s):   Titre(s):

EPPA3     Evaluations et projections de la population active 1950-2025 - troisième édition, BIT, Genève, 1986.
AST75-93  Editions de 1975 à 1993 de l'Annuaire des statistiques du travail du BIT, Genève.
TET-LFS   Continuous Sample Survey of Population; Labour Force Report 1989.

## 2. Evaluation des taux d'activité: 1950 - 1990

### 2.1 Données de base:

Tableau 1: Taux d'activité par sexe et par groupe d'âge

| Groupe d'âge | Année 1980 (1) | 1987 (2) | 1988 (2) | 1989 (2) |
|---|---|---|---|---|
| **Hommes** | | | | |
| 10-14 | 1.10 | 0.00 | 0.00 | 0.00 |
| 15-19 | 50.90 | 45.50 | 41.00 | 39.00 |
| 20-24 | 90.20 | 90.30 | 89.40 | 87.70 |
| 25-29 | 95.40 | 96.10 | 93.10 | 94.30 |
| 30-34 | 96.50 | 94.80 | 95.40 | 94.00 |
| 35-39 | 97.00 | 96.40 | 94.70 | 93.60 |
| 40-44 | 95.50 | 93.80 | 94.80 | 94.10 |
| 45-49 | 95.40 | 95.50 | 94.60 | 92.00 |
| 50-54 | 94.00 | 89.50 | 89.70 | 89.00 |
| 55-59 | 89.60 | 85.10 | 81.50 | 79.90 |
| 60-64 | 71.40 | 55.50 | 55.90 | 49.00 |
| 65+ | 21.80 | 20.30 | 21.80 | 18.40 |
| **Femmes** | | | | |
| 10-14 | 0.00 | 0.00 | 0.00 | 0.00 |
| 15-19 | 20.10 | 21.00 | 18.10 | 16.30 |
| 20-24 | 50.03 | 52.20 | 52.10 | 50.70 |
| 25-29 | 49.58 | 51.70 | 50.60 | 51.40 |
| 30-34 | 48.27 | 52.60 | 51.00 | 48.80 |
| 35-39 | 49.01 | 49.30 | 52.50 | 52.50 |
| 40-44 | 43.11 | 52.00 | 50.60 | 49.00 |
| 45-49 | 47.80 | 45.00 | 45.10 | 48.60 |
| 50-54 | 38.06 | 40.70 | 40.20 | 36.90 |
| 55-59 | 34.10 | 30.70 | 33.30 | 26.40 |
| 60-64 | 23.08 | 20.00 | 18.70 | 13.90 |
| 65+ | 7.77 | 6.00 | 5.70 | 5.40 |

Source(s): (1) EPPA3; (2) AST75-93 et TET-LFS.

### 2.2 Méthode(s): extrapolation linéaire

#### 2.2.1 Hommes:

- 1950-80, taux d'activité 1950-80 tirés des EPPA3;
ajustement des taux d'activité des groupes d'âge [15-24] et [65+] pour 1980;
- 1990, extrapolation des taux d'activité 1980 tirés des EPPA3
et des taux des recensements de 1987, 1988 et 1989;
modification des tendances de tous les groupes d'âge.

#### 2.2.2 Femmes:

- 1950-80, taux d'activité 1950-80 tirés des EPPA3;
modification des tendances de tous les groupes d'âge pour 1980;
- 1990, extrapolation des taux d'activité estimés pour 1980
et des moyennes des taux tirés des enquêtes de 1987, 1988 et 1989.

## 3. Evaluation des taux de répartition par secteur d'activité: 1950 - 1990

### 3.1 Données de base:

Tableau 2: Répartition de la population active en % par secteur d'activité

| Année | Agriculture | Industrie Total | Manufac. | Services |
|---|---|---|---|---|
| **Hommes** | | | | |
| 1980 | 10.70 | 45.55 | 16.34 | 43.75 |
| 1989 | 14.81 | 39.69 | 10.73 | 45.50 |
| 1990 | 13.78 | 37.59 | 10.23 | 48.64 |
| 1991 | 13.36 | 39.89 | 11.04 | 46.76 |
| **Femmes** | | | | |
| 1979 | 7.69 | 26.85 | 15.62 | 65.46 |
| 1980 | 7.88 | 24.49 | 14.48 | 67.63 |
| 1981 | 9.96 | 22.51 | 12.47 | 67.53 |
| 1989 | 6.13 | 16.48 | 9.39 | 77.39 |
| 1990 | 5.25 | 16.32 | 9.80 | 78.43 |
| 1991 | 5.16 | 19.61 | 10.54 | 75.23 |

Source(s): AST75-93.

### 3.2 Méthode(s): moyenne arithmétique

#### 3.2.1 Hommes:

- 1950-80, taux de répartition 1950-80 tirés des EPPA3;
- Application du rapport manufacture/industrie tiré de l'enquête de 1980;
- 1990, moyennes des taux de répartition tirés des enquêtes de 1989, 1990 et 1991.

#### 3.2.2 Femmes:

- 1950-70, taux de répartition 1950-70 tirés des EPPA3;
- 1980, moyennes des taux de répartition tirés des enquêtes de 1979, 1980 et 1981;
- 1990, moyennes des taux de répartition tirés des enquêtes de 1989, 1990 et 1991.

## 4. Projection des taux d'activité: 2000 - 2010

### 4.1 Modèle(s): linéaire, log-linéaire, hyperbole et logistique

#### 4.1.1 Hommes:

- Aux groupes d'âge [15-54], application de la fonction F1;
- Aux groupes d'âge [55+], application de la fonction F3;
- Modification des tendances des groupes d'âge [15-54].

#### 4.1.2 Femmes:

- Aux groupes d'âge [15-19] et [55+], application de la fonction F3;
- Au groupe d'âge [20-24], application de la fonction F6;
- Aux groupes d'âge [25-54], application de la fonction F2.

*Notes sur les ajustements des taux, voir p. 192-195.*

*Notes sur les fonctions de projection, voir p. 198.*

# Tunisie

## 1. Source(s) des données de base

| Code(s): | Titre(s): |
|---|---|
| EPPA3 | Evaluations et projections de la population active 1950-2025 - troisième édition, BIT, Genève, 1986. |
| R1984 | Recencement général de la population et de l'habitat, 30 mars 1984, Institut National de la Statistique, Tunis, 1984. |
| ASTER | Annuaire des statistiques du travail 1945-89 - Edition rétrospective sur les recensements de population, BIT, Genève, 1990. |
| ADNU88 | Annuaire démographique 1988 - Statistiques des recensements de population, quarantième édition, Nations Unies, New York, 1990. |

## 2. Evaluation des taux d'activité: 1950 - 1990

### 2.1 Données de base:

Tableau 1: Taux d'activité par sexe et par groupe d'âge

| Groupe d'âge | Année 1950 (1) | 1960 (1) | 1970 (1) | 1975 (2) | 1984 (3) |
|---|---|---|---|---|---|
| **Hommes** | | | | | |
| 10-14 | .. | .. | 18.00 | 17.33 | 0.00 |
| 15-19 | .. | .. | 57.45 | 64.03 | 20.44 |
| 20-24 | .. | .. | 89.40 | 85.39 | 73.25 |
| 25-29 | .. | .. | 97.30 | 99.29 | 95.50 |
| 30-34 | .. | .. | 98.40 | 96.90 | 97.96 |
| 35-39 | .. | .. | 98.30 | 96.90 | 98.76 |
| 40-44 | .. | .. | 97.85 | 99.20 | 98.53 |
| 45-49 | .. | .. | 96.75 | 98.10 | 97.96 |
| 50-54 | .. | .. | 93.60 | 89.70 | 96.83 |
| 55-59 | .. | .. | 86.80 | 68.20 | 94.23 |
| 60-64 | .. | .. | 70.85 | 53.90 | 89.35 |
| 65+ | .. | .. | 49.70 | 38.70 | 40.98 |
| **Femmes** | | | | | |
| 10-14 | 0.00 | 0.00 | 0.00 | 11.80 | 0.00 |
| 15-19 | 9.45 | 11.80 | 16.50 | 29.50 | 25.18 |
| 20-24 | 8.15 | 10.70 | 15.75 | 27.50 | 38.12 |
| 25-29 | 4.00 | 6.65 | 11.85 | 21.80 | 29.41 |
| 30-34 | 2.40 | 4.80 | 9.50 | 15.90 | 23.55 |
| 35-39 | 2.60 | 4.60 | 8.65 | 14.00 | 18.97 |
| 40-44 | 3.35 | 5.25 | 9.00 | 14.60 | 14.57 |
| 45-49 | 3.00 | 4.95 | 8.90 | 14.10 | 12.87 |
| 50-54 | 3.25 | 4.90 | 8.15 | 11.60 | 11.60 |
| 55-59 | 3.05 | 4.35 | 6.95 | 9.20 | 9.83 |
| 60-64 | 3.25 | 4.00 | 5.45 | 7.00 | 4.43 |
| 65+ | 2.10 | 2.40 | 3.00 | 5.40 | 3.46 |

Source(s): (1) EPPA3; (2) ASTER; (3) ADNU88 et R1984.

### 2.2 Méthode(s): extrapolation linéaire

#### 2.2.1 Hommes:

- 1950-70, taux d'activité 1950-70 tirés des EPPA3;
- 1980-90, extrapolation des taux d'activité 1970 tirés des EPPA3 et des taux ajustés des recensements de 1975 et 1984; modification des tendances des groupes d'âge [15-24] pour 1990.

#### 2.2.2 Femmes:

- 1950-70, taux d'activité ajustés 1950-70 tirés des EPPA3;
- 1980, moyennes pondérées des taux d'activité ajustés tirés des recensements de 1975 et 1984;
- 1990, extrapolation des taux d'activité ajustés des recensements de 1975 et 1984;
ajustement des taux extrapolés sur la base des variation des ajustement des taux d'activité sur la base du modèle d'ajustement des taux d'activité des femmes travaillant dans l'agriculture comme aides familiales.

## 3. Evaluation des taux de répartition par secteur d'activité: 1950 - 1990

### 3.1 Données de base:

Tableau 2: Répartition de la population active en % par secteur d'activité

| Année | Agriculture | Industrie Total | Manufac. | Services |
|---|---|---|---|---|
| **Hommes** | | | | |
| 1975 (1) | 45.10 | 22.60 | | 32.30 |
| 1984 (2) | 40.73 | 26.17 | 10.33 | 33.10 |
| **Femmes** | | | | |
| 1975 (1) | 27.10 | 49.56 | 48.73 | 23.34 |
| 1984 (2) | 25.86 | 49.08 | 47.69 | 25.06 |

Source(s): (1) ASTER; (2) R1984.

### 3.2 Méthode(s): moyenne pondérée extrapolation linéaire

#### 3.2.1 Hommes:

- 1950-70, taux de répartition 1950-70 tirés des EPPA3;
- 1980, moyennes pondérées des taux de répartition ajustés tirés des recensements de 1975 et 1984;
- 1990, extrapolation des taux de répartition tirés des recensements de 1975 et 1984;
modification des tendances de tous les secteurs.

#### 3.2.2 Femmes:

- 1950-70, taux de répartition 1950-70 tirés des EPPA3;
- 1980, moyennes pondérées des taux de répartition ajustés tirés des recensements de 1975 et 1984;
- 1990, extrapolation des taux de répartition tirés des recensements de 1975 et 1984; modification des tendances de tous les secteurs; ajustement des taux estimés 1950-90 pour tenir compte de la sous-énumération des femmes travaillant dans l'agriculture.

## 4. Projection des taux d'activité: 2000 - 2010

### 4.1 Modèle(s): linéaire, log-linéaire et hyperbole

#### 4.1.1 Hommes:

- Au groupe d'âge [15-19], application de la fonction F2;
- Aux groupes d'âge [20-59], application de la fonction F1;
- Aux groupes d'âge [60+], application de la fonction F3.

#### 4.1.2 Femmes:

- A tous les groupes d'âge, application de la fonction F1;
- Modification des tendances des groupes d'âge [15-24] et [50+].

*Notes sur les ajustements des taux, voir p. 192-195.*

*Notes sur les fonctions de projection, voir p. 198.*

# Turkménistan

## 1. Source(s) des données de base

Code(s):     Titre(s):

BLT-94-2    Vorobiev A. (1994), "Estimation de la population active pour les quinze pays de l'ex-URSS pour les années 1950, 1959, 1970, 1979 et 1989",
dans le Bulletin des statistiques du travail - 1994-2, BIT, Genève.

## 2. Evaluation des taux d'activité: 1950 - 1990

### 2.1 Données de base:

Tableau 1: Taux d'activité par sexe et par groupe d'âge

| Groupe d'âge | Année 1950 | 1959 | 1970 | 1979 | 1989 |
|---|---|---|---|---|---|
| **Hommes** | | | | | |
| 10-14 | 0.00 | 0.00 | 0.00 | 0.00 | 0.00 |
| 15-19 | 50.75 | 52.38 | 42.86 | 41.32 | 35.64 |
| 20-24 | 82.26 | 85.07 | 85.92 | 90.00 | 85.09 |
| 25-29 | 94.29 | 96.77 | 98.25 | 97.98 | 96.84 |
| 30-34 | 93.10 | 96.49 | 98.63 | 98.36 | 98.39 |
| 35-39 | 90.32 | 93.75 | 98.33 | 98.36 | 97.80 |
| 40-44 | 92.59 | 92.31 | 94.74 | 97.01 | 98.08 |
| 45-49 | 91.30 | 93.10 | 96.88 | 98.18 | 98.15 |
| 50-54 | 89.47 | 91.67 | 91.30 | 93.62 | 94.64 |
| 55-59 | 82.35 | 85.00 | 84.62 | 84.00 | 89.13 |
| 60-64 | 66.67 | 68.42 | 50.00 | 35.00 | 40.54 |
| 65+ | 25.00 | 29.41 | 9.52 | 10.42 | 15.22 |
| **Femmes** | | | | | |
| 10-14 | 0.00 | 0.00 | 0.00 | 0.00 | 0.00 |
| 15-19 | 45.07 | 46.30 | 41.41 | 40.99 | 34.27 |
| 20-24 | 60.87 | 62.32 | 67.65 | 84.85 | 74.55 |
| 25-29 | 62.00 | 66.15 | 92.59 | 88.12 | 77.44 |
| 30-34 | 63.41 | 63.49 | 78.57 | 89.83 | 79.84 |
| 35-39 | 62.50 | 63.04 | 84.48 | 91.53 | 83.16 |
| 40-44 | 62.86 | 62.16 | 81.03 | 90.63 | 83.33 |
| 45-49 | 61.05 | 66.70 | 81.40 | 87.50 | 83.33 |
| 50-54 | 44.00 | 45.16 | 72.73 | 74.07 | 58.62 |
| 55-59 | 28.57 | 26.47 | 29.27 | 30.00 | 27.45 |
| 60-64 | 17.65 | 16.00 | 12.50 | 12.12 | 14.89 |
| 65+ | 4.88 | 4.88 | 3.39 | 4.00 | 4.65 |

Source(s): BLT-94-2-2

### 2.2 Méthode(s): moyenne pondérée

#### 2.2.1 Hommes:

- 1950-90, moyennes pondérées des taux d'activité 1950, 1959, 1970 et 1989
tirés du Bulletin des statistiques du travail, 1994-2.

#### 2.2.2 Femmes:

Méthode, hypothèses et traitements identiques à ceux appliqués aux hommes.

## 3. Evaluation des taux de répartition par secteur d'activité: 1950 - 1990

### 3.1 Données de base:

Tableau 2: Répartition de la population active en % par secteur d'activité

| Année | Agriculture | Industrie Total | Manufac. | Services |
|---|---|---|---|---|
| **Hommes** | | | | |
| 1950 | 58.36 | 17.84 | 9.29 | 23.79 |
| 1959 | 43.84 | 23.21 | 8.60 | 32.95 |
| 1970 | 33.26 | 29.59 | 9.40 | 37.16 |
| 1979 | 32.83 | 31.83 | 8.50 | 35.33 |
| 1989 | 33.76 | 30.04 | 8.34 | 36.20 |
| **Femmes** | | | | |
| 1950 | 60.91 | 13.64 | 9.55 | 25.45 |
| 1959 | 54.72 | 14.57 | 11.02 | 30.71 |
| 1970 | 43.01 | 17.81 | 10.96 | 39.18 |
| 1979 | 46.48 | 16.67 | 9.07 | 36.85 |
| 1989 | 42.01 | 14.58 | 7.84 | 43.42 |

Source(s): BLT-94-2.

### 3.2 Méthode(s): moyenne pondérée

#### 3.2.1 Hommes:

- 1950-90, moyennes pondérées des taux de répartition 1950, 1959,
1970, 1979 et 1989 tirés du Bulletin des statistiques du travail - 1994-2.

#### 3.2.2 Femmes:

Méthode, hypothèses et traitements identiques à ceux appliqués aux hommes.

## 4. Projection des taux d'activité: 2000 - 2010

### 4.1 Modèle(s): linéaire, hyperbole et logistique

#### 4.1.1 Hommes:

- Aux groupes d'âge [15-64], application de la fonction F1;
- Au groupe d'âge [65+], application de la fonction F3;
- Modification des tendances des groupes d'âge [20-64].

#### 4.1.2 Femmes:

- Au groupe d'âge [15-19], application de la fonction F1;
- Aux groupes d'âge [20-59], application de la fonction F6;
- Aux groupes d'âge [60+], application de la fonction F3;
- Modification des tendances des groupes d'âge [15-54].

*Notes sur les ajustements des taux, voir p. 192-195.*

*Notes sur les fonctions de projection, voir p. 198.*

# Turquie

## 1. Source(s) des données de base

**Code(s):**    **Titre(s):**

EPPA3    Evaluations et projections de la population active 1950-2025 - troisième édition, BIT, Genève, 1986.

STAT    Base de données sur les statistiques du travail - LABORSTA, Bureau de statistique, BIT, Genève.

## 2. Evaluation des taux d'activité: 1950 - 1990

### 2.1 Données de base:

Tableau 1: Taux d'activité par sexe et par groupe d'âge

| Groupe d'âge | Année | |
|---|---|---|
| | 1985 | 1990 |
| **Hommes** | | |
| 10-14 | 22.67 | 29.40 |
| 15-19 | 68.12 | 66.11 |
| 20-24 | 90.23 | 89.67 |
| 25-29 | 96.48 | 97.45 |
| 30-34 | 97.41 | 98.34 |
| 35-39 | 97.22 | 98.18 |
| 40-44 | 93.72 | 95.63 |
| 45-49 | 87.05 | 88.00 |
| 50-54 | 79.99 | 77.43 |
| 55-59 | 72.16 | 69.12 |
| 60-64 | 62.95 | 60.60 |
| 65+ | 41.73 | 46.05 |
| **Femmes** | | |
| 10-14 | 22.64 | 22.60 |
| 15-19 | 49.94 | 48.34 |
| 20-24 | 48.18 | 48.27 |
| 25-29 | 43.43 | 43.11 |
| 30-34 | 42.28 | 42.80 |
| 35-39 | 43.33 | 43.43 |
| 40-44 | 46.21 | 43.99 |
| 45-49 | 46.79 | 44.21 |
| 50-54 | 48.18 | 44.77 |
| 55-59 | 44.88 | 44.33 |
| 60-64 | 39.84 | 39.25 |
| 65+ | 23.17 | 27.97 |

**Source(s)**: STAT.

### 2.2 Méthode(s): moyenne pondérée

**2.2.1 Hommes:**

- 1950-80, taux d'activité 1950-80 tirés des EPPA3;
- 1990, moyennes pondérées des taux d'activité tirés des recensements de 1985 et 1990.

**2.2.2 Femmes:**

Méthode, hypothèses et traitements identiques à ceux appliqués aux hommes.

## 3. Evaluation des taux de répartition par secteur d'activité: 1950 - 1990

### 3.1 Données de base:

Tableau 2: Répartition de la population active en % par secteur d'activité

| Année | Agriculture | Industrie | | Services |
|---|---|---|---|---|
| | | Total | Manufac. | |
| **Hommes** | | | | |
| 1975 | 56.40 | 16.85 | 10.90 | 26.75 |
| 1980 | 44.54 | 22.42 | 14.45 | 33.04 |
| 1985 | 43.44 | 21.24 | 14.29 | 35.33 |
| 1990 | 38.02 | 24.23 | 14.96 | 37.75 |
| **Femmes** | | | | |
| 1975 | 89.31 | 4.33 | 4.19 | 6.36 |
| 1980 | 87.86 | 4.60 | 4.48 | 7.55 |
| 1985 | 86.70 | 4.57 | 4.44 | 8.73 |
| 1990 | 82.27 | 6.89 | 6.68 | 10.84 |

**Source(s)**: STAT.

### 3.2 Méthode(s): moyenne pondérée

**3.2.1 Hommes:**

- 1950-70, taux de répartition 1950-70 tirés des EPPA3;
- 1980-90, moyennes pondérées des taux de répartition tirés des recensements de 1975, 1980, 1985 et 1990.

**3.2.2 Femmes:**

Méthode, hypothèses et traitements identiques à ceux appliqués aux hommes.

## 4. Projection des taux d'activité: 2000 - 2010

### 4.1 Modèle(s): linéaire et hyperbole

**4.1.1 Hommes:**

- Aux groupes d'âge [10-44], application de la fonction F1;
- Aux groupes d'âge [45+], application de la fonction F3;
- Modification des tendances des groupes d'âge [10-14], [30-34] et [40+].

**4.1.2 Femmes:**

- Au groupe d'âge [10-14], application de la fonction F1;
- Aux groupes d'âge [15+], application de la fonction F3;
- Modification des tendances des groupes d'âge [10-14] et [20+].

---

*Notes sur les ajustements des taux, voir p. 192-195.*    *Notes sur les fonctions de projection, voir p. 198.*

# Ukraine

## 1. Source(s) des données de base

Code(s):    Titre(s):

BLT-94-2    Vorobiev A. (1994), "Estimation de la population active pour les quinze pays de l'ex-URSS pour les années 1950, 1959, 1970, 1979 et 1989", dans le Bulletin des statistiques du travail - 1994-2, BIT, Genève.

## 2. Evaluation des taux d'activité: 1950 - 1990

### 2.1 Données de base:

Tableau 1: Taux d'activité par sexe et par groupe d'âge

| Groupe d'âge | Année 1959 | 1970 | 1979 | 1989 |
|---|---|---|---|---|
| **Hommes** | | | | |
| 10-14 | 0.00 | 0.00 | 0.00 | 0.00 |
| 15-19 | 62.57 | 40.71 | 36.28 | 27.71 |
| 20-24 | 86.88 | 85.15 | 86.32 | 79.76 |
| 25-29 | 96.22 | 96.37 | 96.77 | 96.09 |
| 30-34 | 95.77 | 98.14 | 98.30 | 97.77 |
| 35-39 | 93.61 | 97.01 | 98.17 | 97.75 |
| 40-44 | 94.96 | 96.39 | 97.73 | 97.22 |
| 45-49 | 90.91 | 94.09 | 96.14 | 95.41 |
| 50-54 | 87.02 | 88.31 | 88.09 | 89.69 |
| 55-59 | 81.38 | 78.71 | 78.73 | 77.74 |
| 60-64 | 60.29 | 31.11 | 26.29 | 31.69 |
| 65+ | 35.31 | 11.14 | 7.09 | 10.54 |
| **Femmes** | | | | |
| 10-14 | 0.00 | 0.00 | 0.00 | 0.00 |
| 15-19 | 60.26 | 38.69 | 34.60 | 25.90 |
| 20-24 | 68.94 | 80.86 | 85.71 | 78.18 |
| 25-29 | 84.82 | 94.38 | 94.01 | 89.33 |
| 30-34 | 71.99 | 91.69 | 95.32 | 92.76 |
| 35-39 | 72.27 | 90.01 | 95.94 | 94.47 |
| 40-44 | 72.47 | 91.94 | 95.34 | 94.41 |
| 45-49 | 62.27 | 81.17 | 91.67 | 92.08 |
| 50-54 | 54.22 | 73.68 | 83.91 | 84.10 |
| 55-59 | 31.62 | 21.59 | 24.92 | 28.43 |
| 60-64 | 22.79 | 10.53 | 7.38 | 14.35 |
| 65+ | 2.73 | 0.89 | 1.66 | 3.66 |

Source(s): BLT-94-2.

### 2.2 Méthode(s): moyenne pondérée

#### 2.2.1 Hommes:

- 1950-70, interpolation et extrapolation des taux d'activité 1950, 1959, 1970, 1979 et 1989 tirés du Bulletin des statistiques du travail 1994-2; aux taux interpolés et extrapolés, application des variations des taux extrapolés 1990 par rapport aux taux tirés du recensement de 1989.

#### 2.2.2 Femmes:

Méthode, hypothèses et traitements identiques à ceux appliqués aux hommes.

## 3. Evaluation des taux de répartition par secteur d'activité: 1950 - 1990

### 3.1 Données de base:

Tableau 2: Répartition de la population active en % par secteur d'activité

| Année | Agriculture | Industrie Total | Manufac. | Services |
|---|---|---|---|---|
| **Hommes** | | | | |
| 1950 | 52.91 | 26.77 | 16.53 | 20.32 |
| 1959 | 39.52 | 32.18 | 18.79 | 28.31 |
| 1970 | 28.74 | 44.50 | 28.65 | 26.76 |
| 1979 | 25.93 | 46.18 | 28.35 | 27.89 |
| 1989 | 23.60 | 45.76 | 28.56 | 30.64 |
| **Femmes** | | | | |
| 1950 | 66.31 | 14.53 | 10.81 | 19.16 |
| 1959 | 55.74 | 19.32 | 14.18 | 24.94 |
| 1970 | 32.81 | 28.85 | 22.73 | 38.34 |
| 1979 | 23.64 | 32.55 | 26.12 | 43.81 |
| 1989 | 16.20 | 33.51 | 27.37 | 50.29 |

Source(s): BLT-94-2.

### 3.2 Méthode(s): données du BLT-94-2

#### 3.2.1 Hommes:

- 1950, 1960, 1970, 1980 et 1990, respectivement les taux de répartition 1950, 1959, 1970, 1979 et 1989 tirés du Bulletin des statistiques du travail - 1994-2.

#### 3.2.2 Femmes:

Méthode, hypothèses et traitements identiques à ceux appliqués aux hommes.

## 4. Projection des taux d'activité: 2000 - 2010

### 4.1 Modèle(s): linéaire, hyperbole et logistique

#### 4.1.1 Hommes:

- Aux groupes d'âge [15-24] et [55+], application de la fonction F3;
- Aux groupes d'âge [25-54], application de la fonction F1;
- Modification des tendances des groupes d'âge [25-54].

#### 4.1.2 Femmes:

- Aux groupes d'âge [15-19] et [55+], application de la fonction F3;
- Aux groupes d'âge [20-54], application de la fonction F6;
- Modification des tendances des groupes d'âge [20-54].

*Notes sur les ajustements des taux, voir p. 192-195.*

*Notes sur les fonctions de projection, voir p. 198.*

# Uruguay

## 1. Source(s) des données de base

Code(s):     Titre(s):

EPPA3       Evaluations et projections de la population active 1950-2025 - troisième édition, BIT, Genève, 1986.
STAT        Base de données sur les statistiques du travail - LABORSTA, Bureau de statistique, BIT, Genève.

## 2. Evaluation des taux d'activité: 1950 - 1990

### 2.1 Données de base:

Tableau 1: Taux d'activité par sexe et par groupe d'âge

| Groupe d'âge | Année 1975 (1) | 1975 (2) | 1985 (1) | 1985 (2) | 1991 (1) | 1992 (1) | 1993 (1) |
|---|---|---|---|---|---|---|---|
| **Hommes** | | | | | | | |
| 10-14 | ... | ... | ... | ... | 2.16 | 1.97 | 3.15 |
| 15-19 | 56.50 | 81.50 | 55.04 | 79.64 | 56.69 | 57.05 | 54.18 |
| 20-24 | 88.80 | 92.50 | 86.50 | 95.30 | 88.52 | 88.76 | 88.25 |
| 25-29 | 95.10 | 94.50 | 95.40 | 97.00 | 97.17 | 96.63 | 96.77 |
| 30-34 | 97.20 | 95.90 | 96.70 | 97.00 | 97.32 | 98.10 | 97.54 |
| 35-39 | 97.20 | 96.60 | 96.50 | 96.70 | 98.02 | 97.44 | 97.45 |
| 40-44 | 96.50 | 96.70 | 96.00 | 96.60 | 97.28 | 97.81 | 97.50 |
| 45-49 | 94.50 | 96.00 | 93.50 | 95.20 | 96.90 | 97.40 | 96.33 |
| 50-54 | 89.10 | 94.30 | 87.30 | 94.50 | 94.06 | 94.09 | 92.64 |
| 55-59 | 78.10 | 90.90 | 78.00 | 81.40 | 87.67 | 87.42 | 86.85 |
| 60-64 | 54.30 | 75.50 | 48.20 | 70.20 | 59.12 | 60.41 | 56.11 |
| 65+ | 17.70 | 35.90 | 13.90 | 33.50 | 17.75 | 17.38 | 16.21 |
| **Femmes** | | | | | | | |
| 10-14 | ... | ... | ... | ... | 1.00 | 1.01 | 1.84 |
| 15-19 | 27.80 | 23.80 | 23.76 | 23.09 | 31.26 | 33.01 | 32.98 |
| 20-24 | 45.00 | 26.50 | 49.60 | 32.30 | 66.60 | 68.39 | 67.61 |
| 25-29 | 45.00 | 24.40 | 55.50 | 31.30 | 67.82 | 71.43 | 70.59 |
| 30-34 | 43.50 | 21.70 | 54.10 | 32.20 | 68.68 | 71.60 | 71.62 |
| 35-39 | 43.30 | 19.80 | 53.60 | 32.10 | 69.75 | 73.00 | 71.25 |
| 40-44 | 41.20 | 20.60 | 52.20 | 29.90 | 66.82 | 69.89 | 67.21 |
| 45-49 | 37.30 | 20.30 | 48.80 | 28.60 | 61.36 | 65.93 | 64.77 |
| 50-54 | 31.10 | 17.90 | 38.30 | 26.10 | 54.49 | 56.30 | 55.22 |
| 55-59 | 22.60 | 14.90 | 26.50 | 19.80 | 37.00 | 36.47 | 37.73 |
| 60-64 | 12.40 | 10.00 | 13.40 | 11.40 | 21.50 | 21.05 | 20.83 |
| 65+ | 3.50 | 4.10 | 3.60 | 4.90 | 5.75 | 6.30 | 5.82 |

Note(s): (1) Urbain; (2) Rural.
Source(s): STAT.

### 2.2 Méthode(s): moyenne pondérée
interpolation et extrapolation linéaires

**2.2.1 Hommes:**

- 1950-70, taux d'activité 1950-70 tirés des EPPA3;
- 1980-90, moyennes pondérées des taux d'activité estimés séparément
pour les zones urbaines et rurales; pour les zones urbaines, estimation
des taux sur la base d'une interpolation des taux d'activité ajustés tirés
des recensements de 1975 et 1985 et de la moyenne des taux d'activité
tirés des enquêtes de 1991, 1992 et 1993; pour les zones rurales, estimation
des taux sur la base d'une interpolation et extrapolation des taux d'activité
tirés des recensements de 1975 et 1985.

**2.2.2 Femmes:**

Méthode, hypothèses et traitements identiques à ceux appliqués aux hommes.

## 3. Evaluation des taux de répartition par secteur d'activité: 1950 - 1990

### 3.1 Données de base:

Tableau 2: Répartition de la population active en % par secteur d'activité

| Année | Agriculture | Industrie Total | Manufac. | Services |
|---|---|---|---|---|
| **Hommes** | | | | |
| 1975 (1) | 23.09 | 30.41 | 19.84 | 46.50 |
| 1985 (1) | 21.64 | 30.83 | 19.74 | 47.53 |
| 1985 (2) | 8.13 | 35.93 | 23.09 | 55.94 |
| 1991 (2) | 7.02 | 33.21 | 21.97 | 59.77 |
| 1992 (2) | 7.12 | 36.20 | 22.36 | 56.68 |
| **Femmes** | | | | |
| 1975 (1) | 3.61 | 23.93 | 23.09 | 72.46 |
| 1985 (1) | 4.00 | 21.30 | 20.27 | 74.70 |
| 1985 (2) | 1.07 | 21.36 | 20.32 | 77.57 |
| 1991 (2) | 1.13 | 22.23 | 21.98 | 76.64 |
| 1992 (2) | 1.07 | 20.89 | 19.82 | 78.04 |

Note(s): (1) Total; (2) Urbain.
Source(s): STAT.

### 3.2 Méthode(s): moyenne pondérée

**3.2.1 Hommes:**

- 1950-60, taux de répartition 1950-60 tirés des EPPA3;
- 1980, moyennes pondérées des taux de répartition tirés des
des recensements de 1975 et 1985;
- 1990, moyennes pondérées des taux de répartition estimés
séparément pour les zones urbaines et rurales; estimation des taux sur la
base des résultats du recensement de 1985 et des enquêtes de 1991 et 1992.

**3.2.2 Femmes:**

Méthode, hypothèses et traitements identiques à ceux appliqués aux hommes.

## 4. Projection des taux d'activité: 2000 - 2010

### 4.1 Modèle(s): linéaire, hyperbole et logistique

**4.1.1 Hommes:**

- Au groupe d'âge [10-14], application de la fonction F1;
- Aux groupes d'âge [15+], application de la fonction F3;
- Modification des tendances des groupes d'âge [15-19] et [25-49].

**4.1.2 Femmes:**

- Au groupe d'âge [10-14], application de la fonction F1;
- Aux groupes d'âge [15-19] et [65+], application de la fonction F3;
- Modification des tendances des groupes d'âge [10-19] et [65+].

*Notes sur les ajustements des taux, voir p. 192-195.*     *Notes sur les fonctions de projection, voir p. 198.*

# Venezuela

## 1. Source(s) des données de base

Code(s):  Titre(s):

EPPA3  Evaluations et projections de la population active 1950-2025 - troisième édition, BIT, Genève, 1986.
ADNU84  Annuaire démographique 1984 - Statistiques des recensements de population II, trente-sixième édition, Nations Unies, New York, 1986.
ASTER  Annuaire des statistiques du travail 1945-89 - Edition rétrospective sur les recensements de population, BIT, Genève, 1990.
AST91-93  Editions de 1991 à 1993 de l'Annuaire des statistiques du travail du BIT, Genève.

## 2. Evaluation des taux d'activité: 1950 - 1990

### 2.1 Données de base:

Tableau 1: Taux d'activité par sexe et par groupe d'âge

| Groupe d'âge | Année 1971 (1) | 1981 (2) | 1990 (3) |
|---|---|---|---|
| **Hommes** | | | |
| 10-14 | 0.00 | 5.30 | .. |
| 15-19 | 50.20 | 47.32 | .. |
| 20-24 | 81.85 | 80.88 | .. |
| 25-29 | 93.58 | 91.15 | .. |
| 30-34 | 95.99 | 93.54 | .. |
| 35-39 | 96.40 | 93.87 | .. |
| 40-44 | 95.74 | 93.47 | .. |
| 45-49 | 94.91 | 91.23 | .. |
| 50-54 | 91.39 | 87.68 | .. |
| 55-59 | 87.24 | 81.16 | .. |
| 60-64 | 63.38 | 70.03 | .. |
| 65+ | 50.14 | 41.94 | .. |
| **Femmes** | | | |
| 10-14 | 0.00 | 1.69 | 0.00 |
| 15-19 | 20.30 | 18.47 | 17.86 |
| 20-24 | 29.40 | 35.78 | 35.80 |
| 25-29 | 29.50 | 39.50 | 42.46 |
| 30-34 | 26.80 | 39.85 | 46.17 |
| 35-39 | 25.00 | 39.02 | 46.02 |
| 40-44 | 23.80 | 35.66 | 43.76 |
| 45-49 | 20.80 | 28.88 | 37.78 |
| 50-54 | 17.00 | 23.35 | 28.78 |
| 55-59 | 13.50 | 16.56 | 20.26 |
| 60-64 | 9.80 | 10.73 | 12.66 |
| 65+ | 5.80 | 5.46 | 6.00 |

Source(s): (1) ASTER; (2) ADNU84 et ASTER; (3) AST91-93.

### 2.2 Méthode(s): interpolation et extrapolation linéaires moyenne pondérée

#### 2.2.1 Hommes:

- 1950-60, taux d'activité 1950-60 tirés des EPPA3;
- 1970, moyennes pondérées des taux d'activité 1960 tirés des EPPA3 et des taux d'activité ajustés tirés du recensement de 1971;
- 1980, interpolation des taux d'activité ajustés tirés des recensements de 1971 et 1981;
- 1990, extrapolation des taux d'activité 1950-60 tirés des EPPA3 et des taux estimés 1970-80; ajustement des taux extrapolés sur la base des variations des taux estimés 1980 par rapport aux taux extrapolés 1980.

#### 2.2.2 Femmes:

- 1950-70, taux d'activité ajustés 1950-70 tirés des EPPA3;
- 1980, moyennes pondérés des taux d'activité tirés des recensements de 1971 et 1981;
- 1990, moyennes pondérées des taux d'activité tirés des recensements de 1981 et 1990.

## 3. Evaluation des taux de répartition par secteur d'activité: 1950 - 1990

### 3.1 Données de base:

Tableau 2: Répartition de la population active en % par secteur d'activité

| Année | Agriculture | Industrie Total | Manufac. | Services |
|---|---|---|---|---|
| **Hommes** | | | | |
| 1981 | 17.48 | 32.76 | 16.74 | 49.75 |
| 1989 | 17.31 | 31.49 | 17.20 | 51.20 |
| 1990 | 16.56 | 32.06 | 16.93 | 51.38 |
| 1991 | 15.95 | 33.00 | 17.48 | 51.05 |
| **Femmes** | | | | |
| 1981 | 1.70 | 16.04 | 12.91 | 82.27 |
| 1989 | 1.82 | 17.19 | 15.30 | 80.99 |
| 1990 | 1.94 | 16.04 | 14.00 | 82.02 |
| 1991 | 1.79 | 16.48 | 14.31 | 81.72 |

Source(s): AST91-93.

### 3.2 Méthode(s): moyenne arithmétique

#### 3.2.1 Hommes:

- 1950-70, taux de répartition 1950-70 tirés des EPPA3;
- 1980-90, moyennes des taux de répartition tirés du recensement de 1981 et des moyennes des taux de répartition tirés des enquêtes de 1989, 1990 et 1991.

#### 3.2.2 Femmes:

Méthode, hypothèses et traitements identiques à ceux appliqués aux hommes.

## 4. Projection des taux d'activité: 2000 - 2010

### 4.1 Modèle(s): hyperbole, exponentiel et logistique

#### 4.1.1 Hommes:

- Aux groupes d'âge [15+], application de la fonction F3;
- Modification des tendances des groupes d'âge [20-24] et [30-59].

#### 4.1.2 Femmes:

- Aux groupes d'âge [15-19] et [55+], application de la fonction F3;
- Au groupe d'âge [20-24], application de la fonction F4;
- Aux groupes d'âge [25-54], application de la fonction F6;
- Modification de la tendance du groupe d'âge [20-24].

---

*Notes sur les ajustements des taux, voir p. 192-195.*  *Notes sur les fonctions de projection, voir p. 198.*

# Viet Nam

## 1. Source(s) des données de base

Code(s):     Titre(s):

EPPA3       Evaluations et projections de la population active 1950-2025 - troisième édition, BIT, Genève, 1986.
STAT        Base de données sur les statistiques du travail - LABORSTA, Bureau de statistique, BIT, Genève.
EPPA4       Population active 1950-2010 - quatrième édition, BIT, Genève 1996.

## 2. Evaluation des taux d'activité: 1950 - 1990

### 2.1 Données de base:

Tableau 1: Taux d'activité par sexe et par groupe d'âge

| Groupe d'âge | Année 1950 (1) | 1960 (1) | 1970 (1) | 1980 (1) | 1989 (2) |
|---|---|---|---|---|---|
| **Hommes** | | | | | |
| 10-14 | 52.00 | 46.00 | 40.00 | 30.00 | 11.73 |
| 15-19 | 87.10 | 83.70 | 80.30 | 74.70 | 67.42 |
| 20-24 | 96.90 | 96.90 | 96.90 | 96.80 | 94.36 |
| 25-29 | 98.75 | 98.75 | 98.75 | 98.70 | 97.41 |
| 30-34 | 98.95 | 98.95 | 98.95 | 98.90 | 97.26 |
| 35-39 | 99.00 | 99.00 | 99.00 | 98.90 | 95.70 |
| 40-44 | 98.90 | 98.85 | 98.80 | 98.75 | 91.78 |
| 45-49 | 97.75 | 97.70 | 97.60 | 97.55 | 86.92 |
| 50-54 | 95.60 | 94.65 | 93.70 | 92.00 | 81.21 |
| 55-59 | 91.70 | 89.80 | 87.90 | 84.30 | 70.86 |
| 60-64 | 81.65 | 77.80 | 73.95 | 66.30 | 53.04 |
| 65+ | 56.00 | 50.45 | 44.90 | 34.00 | 27.19 |
| **Femmes** | | | | | |
| 10-14 | 43.00 | 40.00 | 38.00 | 31.00 | 14.82 |
| 15-19 | 72.40 | 73.90 | 75.40 | 78.60 | 73.33 |
| 20-24 | 82.30 | 84.20 | 86.10 | 89.60 | 88.75 |
| 25-29 | 79.90 | 82.20 | 83.70 | 87.40 | 89.26 |
| 30-34 | 78.00 | 80.90 | 83.00 | 87.10 | 88.11 |
| 35-39 | 77.80 | 80.00 | 82.20 | 86.60 | 86.90 |
| 40-44 | 75.50 | 77.10 | 78.70 | 81.90 | 83.92 |
| 45-49 | 64.70 | 65.90 | 67.10 | 69.50 | 78.67 |
| 50-54 | 47.10 | 47.90 | 48.70 | 50.20 | 69.42 |
| 55-59 | 36.10 | 35.50 | 34.90 | 33.50 | 54.22 |
| 60-64 | 25.50 | 23.70 | 21.90 | 18.40 | 35.54 |
| 65+ | 9.95 | 8.90 | 7.85 | 5.70 | 13.14 |

Note(s): (1) Chine.
Source(s): (1) EPPA4; (2) STAT.

### 2.2 Méthode(s): interpolation et extrapolation linéaires

#### 2.2.1 Hommes:

- 1950-90, interpolation et extrapolation des taux d'activité 1980-90
estimés pour la Chine;
aux taux d'activité 1950-80 estimés pour la Chine, application des variations
des taux interpolés 1989 par rapport aux taux ajustés tirés
du recensement de 1989.

#### 2.2.2 Femmes:

Méthode, hypothèses et traitements identiques à ceux appliqués aux hommes.

## 3. Evaluation des taux de répartition par secteur d'activité: 1950 - 1990

### 3.1 Données de base:

Tableau 2: Répartition de la population active en % par secteur d'activité

| Année | Agriculture | Industrie Total | Manufac. | Services |
|---|---|---|---|---|
| **Hommes** | | | | |
| 1950 (1) | 86.00 | 5.00 | .. | 9.00 |
| 1960 (1) | 81.00 | 6.50 | .. | 12.50 |
| 1970 (1) | 75.00 | 12.00 | .. | 13.00 |
| 1989 (2) | 69.53 | 17.11 | 13.89 | 13.36 |
| **Femmes** | | | | |
| 1950 (1) | 92.00 | 4.00 | .. | 4.00 |
| 1960 (1) | 86.50 | 6.00 | .. | 7.50 |
| 1970 (1) | 83.00 | 7.50 | .. | 9.50 |
| 1989 (2) | 73.15 | 10.84 | 9.77 | 16.02 |

Source(s): (1) EPPA3; (2) STAT.

### 3.2 Méthode(s): rapport proportionnel

#### 3.2.1 Hommes:

- 1950-70, taux de répartition 1950-70 tirés des EPPA3;
- 1980-90, application aux taux de répartition de l'agriculture
tirés du recensement de 1989 des mêmes variations des taux estimées
pour la Chine pour 1980 et 1990; les taux de répartition de l'industrie,
de manufacture et des services ont été estimés sur la base de la
composition par secteur tirée du recensement de 1989.

#### 3.2.2 Femmes:

Méthode, hypothèses et traitements identiques à ceux appliqués aux hommes.

## 4. Projection des taux d'activité: 2000 - 2010

### 4.1 Modèle(s): linéaire et hyperbole

#### 4.1.1 Hommes:

- Aux groupes d'âge [10-34] et [65+], application de la fonction F1;
- Aux groupes d'âge [35-64], application de la fonction F3;
- Modification des tendances des groupes d'âge [15-34] et [65+].

#### 4.1.2 Femmes:

- A tous les groupes d'âge, application de la fonction F1;
- Modification des tendances des groupes d'âge [10-54].

---

*Notes sur les ajustements des taux, voir p. 192-195.*      *Notes sur les fonctions de projection, voir p. 198.*

# Yémen

## 1. Source(s) des données de base

Code(s):     Titre(s):

EPPA3     Evaluations et projections de la population active 1950-2025 - troisième édition, BIT, Genève, 1986.
ESCWA     Compedium of Social Statistics Indicators, Third Issue, December 1993, Economic and Social Commission for Western Asia.
EPPA4     Population active 1950-2010 - quatrième édition, BIT, Genève 1996.
STAT      Base de données sur les statistiques du travail - LABORSTA, Bureau de statistique, BIT, Genève.

## 2. Evaluation des taux d'activité: 1950 - 1990

### 2.1 Données de base:

Tableau 1: Taux d'activité par sexe et par groupe d'âge

| Groupe d'âge | Année | | | | | |
|---|---|---|---|---|---|---|
| | 1950 (1) | 1960 (1) | 1970 (1) | 1980 (1) | 1986 (2) | 1990 (1) |
| **Hommes** | | | | | | |
| 10-14 | 31.55 | 27.84 | 24.12 | 20.41 | 24.87 | 18.56 |
| 15-19 | 79.48 | 69.03 | 58.58 | 48.12 | 52.49 | 42.89 |
| 20-24 | 90.07 | 86.70 | 83.33 | 79.96 | 87.48 | 78.28 |
| 25-29 | 97.41 | 96.86 | 96.31 | 95.76 | 96.61 | 95.49 |
| 30-34 | 97.98 | 97.89 | 97.79 | 97.70 | 97.84 | 97.65 |
| 35-39 | 98.06 | 98.11 | 98.17 | 98.23 | 98.14 | 98.26 |
| 40-44 | 98.08 | 97.82 | 97.57 | 97.32 | 97.71 | 97.19 |
| 45-49 | 97.86 | 97.53 | 97.21 | 96.89 | 97.39 | 96.73 |
| 50-54 | 96.56 | 96.08 | 95.61 | 95.13 | 95.86 | 94.89 |
| 55-59 | 94.92 | 94.23 | 93.55 | 92.86 | 93.92 | 92.52 |
| 60-64 | 90.94 | 84.79 | 78.63 | 72.47 | 79.86 | 69.39 |
| 65+ | 75.53 | 62.13 | 48.73 | 35.33 | 51.41 | 28.63 |
| **Femmes** | | | | | | |
| 10-14 | .. | .. | .. | 16.09 | 21.43 | 7.50 |
| 15-19 | .. | .. | .. | 22.80 | 26.50 | 18.90 |
| 20-24 | .. | .. | .. | 34.33 | 26.91 | 39.17 |
| 25-29 | .. | .. | .. | 33.53 | 32.31 | 38.44 |
| 30-34 | .. | .. | .. | 32.89 | 32.47 | 39.68 |
| 35-39 | .. | .. | .. | 30.77 | 31.44 | 36.43 |
| 40-44 | .. | .. | .. | 30.59 | 31.96 | 35.79 |
| 45-49 | .. | .. | .. | 27.60 | 29.44 | 29.04 |
| 50-54 | .. | .. | .. | 26.70 | 27.96 | 26.52 |
| 55-59 | .. | .. | .. | 24.10 | 24.15 | 23.74 |
| 60-64 | .. | .. | .. | 18.87 | 22.31 | 14.83 |
| 65+ | .. | .. | .. | 9.77 | 6.60 | 8.86 |

Note(s): (1) Egypte.
Source(s): (1) EPPA4; (2) ESCWA et STAT.

### 2.2 Méthode(s): interpolation et extrapolation linéaires

#### 2.2.1 Hommes:

- 1950-90, aux évaluations des taux d'activité 1986 de la ESCWA,
application de la moitié des tendances calculées pour l'Egypte.

#### 2.2.2 Femmes:

- 1950-70, taux d'activité ajustés 1950-70 tirés des EPPA3;
- 1980-90, aux évaluations des taux d'activité 1986 de la ESCWA
application de la moitié des tendances calculées pour l'Egypte
pour la même période.

## 3. Evaluation des taux de répartition par secteur d'activité: 1950 - 1990

### 3.1 Données de base:

Tableau 2: Répartition de la population active en % par secteur d'activité

| Année | Agriculture | Industrie | | Services |
|---|---|---|---|---|
| | | Total | Manufac. | |
| **Hommes** | | | | |
| 1986 | 59.10 | 18.30 | .. | 22.60 |
| **Femmes** | | | | |
| 1986 | 95.66 | 1.96 | .. | 2.38 |

Source(s): ESCWA et STAT.

### 3.2 Méthode(s): extrapolation linéaire

#### 3.2.1 Hommes:

- 1950-70, taux de répartition 1950-70 tirés des EPPA3;
- 1980-90, application aux évaluations des taux de répartition de 1986
de la ESCWA de la moitié des tendances calculées pour l'Egypte
pour la même période.

#### 3.2.2 Femmes:

- 1950-70, taux de répartition 1950-70 tirés des EPPA3;
- 1980-90, application aux évaluations des taux de répartition de 1986
de la ESCWA des mêmes variations que celles estimées pour
les hommes du Yémen pour la même période.

## 4. Projection des taux d'activité: 2000 - 2010

### 4.1 Modèle(s): linéaire et hyperbole

#### 4.1.1 Hommes:

- Au groupe d'âge [10-14], application de la fonction F1;
- Aux groupes d'âge [15+], application de la fonction F3;
- Modification des tendances des groupes d'âge [10-14] et [30-39].

#### 4.1.2 Femmes:

- A tous les groupes d'âge, application de la fonction F1;
- Modification des tendances de tous les groupes d'âge.

---

*Notes sur les ajustements des taux, voir p. 192-195.*     *Notes sur les fonctions de projection, voir p. 198.*

# Yougoslavie, Rép. féd. de

## 1. Source(s) des données de base

Code(s):   Titre(s):

EPPA3      Evaluations et projections de la population active 1950-2025 - troisième édition, BIT, Genève, 1986.
BLT-94-2   Popovic B. (1994), "Nouvelles estimations pour 1980 et 1990 des taux d'activité par âge et répartition sectorielle
           pour certains pays d'Europe orientale et méridionale" dans le Bulletin des statistiques du travail - 1994-2, BIT, Genève.

## 2. Evaluation des taux d'activité: 1950 - 1990

### 2.1 Données de base:

Tableau 1: Taux d'activité par sexe et par groupe d'âge

| Groupe d'âge | Année 1950 (1) | 1960 (1) | 1970 (1) | 1980 (2) | 1990 (2) |
|---|---|---|---|---|---|
| **Hommes** | | | | | |
| 10-14 | 24.10 | 8.85 | 3.25 | 0.25 | 0.01 |
| 15-19 | 86.80 | 67.25 | 48.45 | 21.59 | 25.04 |
| 20-24 | 94.85 | 90.75 | 85.80 | 72.02 | 77.31 |
| 25-29 | 96.10 | 96.55 | 95.80 | 92.87 | 92.16 |
| 30-34 | 97.60 | 97.90 | 98.35 | 97.57 | 98.18 |
| 35-39 | 97.80 | 97.25 | 98.30 | 97.76 | 98.33 |
| 40-44 | 97.60 | 97.00 | 95.55 | 97.05 | 96.39 |
| 45-49 | 97.20 | 96.10 | 96.00 | 95.03 | 91.97 |
| 50-54 | 94.20 | 94.00 | 92.35 | 84.40 | 83.20 |
| 55-59 | 84.65 | 85.60 | 77.05 | 65.39 | 61.20 |
| 60-64 | 79.75 | 75.50 | 65.10 | 55.26 | 40.13 |
| 65+ | 61.60 | 56.70 | 51.30 | 43.30 | 30.63 |
| **Femmes** | | | | | |
| 10-14 | 23.20 | 12.50 | 5.45 | 0.45 | 0.03 |
| 15-19 | 68.80 | 58.35 | 45.15 | 16.18 | 19.15 |
| 20-24 | 60.75 | 60.55 | 60.35 | 53.43 | 60.77 |
| 25-29 | 45.00 | 53.20 | 57.35 | 66.65 | 76.03 |
| 30-34 | 38.85 | 47.65 | 52.25 | 67.14 | 79.56 |
| 35-39 | 35.45 | 45.15 | 50.35 | 58.72 | 78.64 |
| 40-44 | 32.80 | 42.15 | 47.20 | 54.44 | 72.22 |
| 45-49 | 29.50 | 37.80 | 43.40 | 50.19 | 58.33 |
| 50-54 | 24.20 | 31.70 | 36.70 | 41.32 | 42.36 |
| 55-59 | 21.10 | 26.75 | 31.60 | 34.62 | 29.89 |
| 60-64 | 16.50 | 22.10 | 26.80 | 28.84 | 24.58 |
| 65+ | 10.95 | 14.10 | 14.60 | 18.55 | 17.09 |

Source(s): (1) EPPA3; (2) BLT-94-2.

### 2.2 Méthode(s): Données tirées des EPPA3 et du BLT-94-2.

#### 2.2.1 Hommes:

- 1950-70, moyennes pondérées des taux d'activité 1950-70 la Yougoslavie tirés
des EPPA3 et des taux d'activité 1990 tirés du Bulletin des statistiques
du travail -1994-2;
modification des tendances de tous les groupes d'âge;
- 1980-90, taux d'activité tirés du Bulletin des statistiques du travail 1994-2.

#### 2.2.2 Femmes:

- 1950-70, taux d'activité 1950-70 pour la Yougoslavie tirés des EPPA3;
ajustement des taux d'activité des groupes d'âge [10-19];
- 1980-90, taux d'activité tirés du Bulletin des statistiques
du travail 1994-2.

## 3. Evaluation des taux de répartition par secteur d'activité: 1950 - 1990

### 3.1 Données de base:

Tableau 2: Répartition de la population active en % par secteur d'activité

| Année | Agriculture | Industrie Total | Manufac. | Services |
|---|---|---|---|---|
| **Hommes** | | | | |
| 1950 (1) | 68.30 | 17.80 | .. | 13.90 |
| 1960 (1) | 56.00 | 28.00 | .. | 16.00 |
| 1970 (1) | 45.00 | 34.40 | .. | 20.60 |
| 1980 (2) | 33.86 | 34.99 | 21.41 | 31.14 |
| 1990 (2) | 27.82 | 37.97 | 26.31 | 34.22 |
| **Femmes** | | | | |
| 1950 (1) | 83.00 | 5.40 | .. | 11.50 |
| 1960 (1) | 78.10 | 15.00 | .. | 6.80 |
| 1970 (1) | 58.20 | 20.00 | .. | 21.80 |
| 1980 (2) | 47.39 | 19.24 | 16.99 | 33.37 |
| 1990 (2) | 32.33 | 26.25 | 23.15 | 41.42 |

Source(s): (1) EPPA3; (2) BLT-94-2.

### 3.2 Méthode(s): données du BLT-94-2

#### 3.2.1 Hommes:

- 1950-70, taux de répartition 1950-70 tirés des EPPA3;
- 1980-90, taux de répartition tirés du Bulletin des statistiques
du travail - 1994-2.

#### 3.2.2 Femmes:

- 1950-90, moyennes pondérées des taux de répartition 1950-70
tirés des EPPA3 et des taux de répartition 1980-90 tirés du Bulletin.

## 4. Projection des taux d'activité: 2000 - 2010

### 4.1 Modèle(s): linéaire, hyperbole et logistique

#### 4.1.1 Hommes:

- Aux groupes d'âge [15+], application de la fonction F3;
- Modification des tendances des groupes d'âge [15+].

#### 4.1.2 Femmes:

- Aux groupes d'âge [15-19] et [25-54], application de la fonction F6;
- Au groupe d'âge [20-24], application de la fonction F3;
- Aux groupes d'âge [55+], application de la fonction F1;
- Modification des tendances des groupes d'âge [15-24] et [35+].

*Notes sur les ajustements des taux, voir p. 192-195.*

*Notes sur les fonctions de projection, voir p. 198.*

# Zambie

## 1. Source(s) des données de base

Code(s):     Titre(s):

EPPA3     Evaluations et projections de la population active 1950-2025 - troisième édition, BIT, Genève, 1986.
ASTER     Annuaire des statistiques du travail 1945-89 - Edition rétrospective sur les recensements de population, BIT, Genève, 1990.
ADNU88    Annuaire démographique 1988 - Statistiques des recensements de population, quarantième édition, Nations Unies, New York, 1990.
STAT      Base de données sur les statistiques du travail - LABORSTA, Bureau de statistique, BIT, Genève.

## 2. Evaluation des taux d'activité: 1950 - 1990

### 2.1 Données de base:

Tableau 1: Taux d'activité par sexe et par groupe d'âge

| Groupe d'âge | Année 1950 (1) | 1960 (1) | 1970 (1) | 1980 (2) | 1980 (1) | 1990 (3) |
|---|---|---|---|---|---|---|
| **Hommes** | | | | | | |
| 10-14 | 27.60 | 26.40 | 24.85 | 19.39 | .. | 17.90 |
| 15-19 | 74.10 | 71.45 | 68.15 | 37.73 | .. | 69.70 |
| 20-24 | 87.80 | 86.75 | 85.45 | 82.78 | .. | 90.20 |
| 25-29 | 98.65 | 98.50 | 98.30 | 96.76 | .. | 96.40 |
| 30-34 | 99.60 | 99.40 | 99.20 | 98.10 | .. | 97.00 |
| 35-39 | 99.65 | 99.45 | 99.20 | 98.29 | .. | 97.20 |
| 40-44 | 99.55 | 99.35 | 99.05 | 98.23 | .. | 96.00 |
| 45-49 | 99.40 | 99.20 | 99.00 | 98.37 | .. | 95.20 |
| 50-54 | 99.00 | 98.70 | 98.35 | 97.72 | .. | 93.30 |
| 55-59 | 98.75 | 98.30 | 97.75 | 97.77 | .. | 91.30 |
| 60-64 | 97.20 | 96.45 | 95.50 | 96.50 | .. | 78.22 |
| 65+ | 85.90 | 84.55 | 82.85 | 58.68 | .. | 58.68 |
| **Femmes** | | | | | | |
| 10-14 | 23.20 | 22.15 | 20.85 | .. | 19.85 | 15.93 |
| 15-19 | 44.65 | 42.85 | 40.55 | .. | 38.75 | 62.03 |
| 20-24 | 29.80 | 29.05 | 28.10 | .. | 27.35 | 73.29 |
| 25-29 | 25.55 | 24.85 | 24.00 | .. | 23.35 | 73.23 |
| 30-34 | 24.50 | 23.85 | 23.00 | .. | 22.35 | 74.76 |
| 35-39 | 25.65 | 25.00 | 24.20 | .. | 23.60 | 74.24 |
| 40-44 | 28.85 | 28.15 | 27.30 | .. | 26.65 | 68.29 |
| 45-49 | 33.85 | 33.00 | 32.00 | .. | 31.20 | 62.64 |
| 50-54 | 44.30 | 43.05 | 41.45 | .. | 40.15 | 58.20 |
| 55-59 | 53.90 | 52.20 | 50.10 | .. | 48.40 | 49.93 |
| 60-64 | 43.85 | 41.90 | 39.45 | .. | 37.50 | 43.70 |
| 65+ | 21.20 | 19.95 | 18.35 | .. | 17.05 | 32.79 |

Source(s): (1) EPPA3; (2) ADNU88 et ASTER; (3) STAT.

### 2.2 Méthode(s): interpolation et extrapolation linéaires

#### 2.2.1 Hommes:

- 1950-90, interpolation et extrapolation des taux d'activité 1950-70
tirés des EPPA3 et des taux ajustés tirés des recensements de 1980 et 1990;
ajustement des taux extrapolés sur la base des variations des
taux interpolés 1990 par rapport aux taux ajustés du recensement de 1990.

#### 2.2.2 Femmes:

- 1950-90, interpolation et extrapolation des taux d'activité 1950-80
tirés des EPPA3;
ajustement des taux interpolés et extrapolés sur la base des variations des
taux interpolés 1990 par rapport aux taux ajustés du recensement de 1990;
modification des tendances des tendances de tous les groupes d'âge.

## 3. Evaluation des taux de répartition par secteur d'activité: 1950 - 1990

### 3.1 Données de base:

Tableau 2: Répartition de la population active en % par secteur d'activité

| Année | Agriculture | Industrie Total | Manufac. | Services |
|---|---|---|---|---|
| **Hommes** | | | | |
| 1950 (1) | 82.00 | 8.00 | .. | 10.00 |
| 1960 (1) | 78.00 | 9.50 | .. | 12.50 |
| 1970 (1) | 73.00 | 11.00 | .. | 16.00 |
| 1980 (1) | 69.00 | 12.50 | .. | 18.50 |
| 1980 (2) | 47.98 | 18.91 | 6.36 | 33.11 |
| **Femmes** | | | | |
| 1950 (1) | 90.00 | 1.50 | .. | 8.50 |
| 1980 (1) | 84.00 | 2.75 | .. | 13.25 |
| 1980 (2) | 79.22 | 2.63 | 1.97 | 18.15 |

Source(s): (1) EPPA3; (2) STAT.

### 3.2 Méthode(s): interpolation et extrapolation linéaires

#### 3.2.1 Hommes:

- 1950-80, taux de répartition 1950-80 tirés des EPPA3;
- 1990, extrapolation des taux de répartition 1950-80 tirés des EPPA3;
ajustement des taux extrapolés sur la base de 1/4 des variations
des taux interpolés 1980 par rapport aux taux de répartition 1980 tirés
des EPPA3.

#### 3.2.2 Femmes:

- 1950-90, interpolation extrapolation des taux de répartition ajustés
1950 et 1980 tirés des EPPA3;
ajustement des taux de répartition sur la base
du rapport hommes/femmes égal à 1 dans l'agriculture;
les taux de répartition de manufacture ont été estimés sur la base du rapport
manufacture/industrie tiré du recensement de 1980.

## 4. Projection des taux d'activité: 2000 - 2010

### 4.1 Modèle(s): linéaire et hyperbole

#### 4.1.1 Hommes:

- Aux groupes d'âge [10-14] et [25+], application de la fonction F3;
- Au groupe d'âge [15-19], application de la fonction F1;
- Modification des tendances des groupes d'âge [15-24] et [30-54].

#### 4.1.2 Femmes:

- A tous les groupes d'âge, application de la fonction F3;
- Modification des tendances des groupes d'âge [20-54].

*Notes sur les ajustements des taux, voir p. 192-195.*          *Notes sur les fonctions de projection, voir p. 198.*

# Zimbabwe

## 1. Source(s) des données de base

Code(s):     Titre(s):
EPPA3        Evaluations et projections de la population active 1950-2025 - troisième édition, BIT, Genève, 1986.
R1982        Main Demographic Features of Zimbabwe, Population Census 1982, Central Statistical Office, Causeway, 1985.
ASTER        Annuaire des statistiques du travail 1945-89 - Edition rétrospective sur les recensements de population, BIT, Genève, 1990.
AST93        Annuaire des statistiques du travail 1993, BIT, Genève, 1993.

## 2. Evaluation des taux d'activité: 1950 - 1990

### 2.1 Données de base:

Tableau 1: Taux d'activité par sexe et par groupe d'âge

| Groupe d'âge | Année 1950 (1) | 1960 (1) | 1970 (1) | 1980 (1) | 1982 (2) | 1987 (3) |
|---|---|---|---|---|---|---|
| **Hommes** | | | | | | |
| 10-14 | 48.25 | 46.75 | 44.20 | 41.15 | 36.52 | .. |
| 15-19 | 79.75 | 77.80 | 74.40 | 70.35 | 48.16 | .. |
| 20-24 | 93.30 | 92.55 | 91.25 | 89.70 | 83.35 | .. |
| 25-29 | 97.10 | 97.00 | 96.80 | 96.55 | 93.07 | .. |
| 30-34 | 97.80 | 97.70 | 97.45 | 97.20 | 93.96 | .. |
| 35-39 | 97.95 | 97.80 | 97.60 | 97.30 | 94.29 | .. |
| 40-44 | 97.80 | 97.65 | 97.40 | 97.10 | 94.14 | .. |
| 45-49 | 97.05 | 96.95 | 96.75 | 96.50 | 93.85 | .. |
| 50-54 | 96.50 | 96.30 | 96.00 | 95.60 | 92.47 | .. |
| 55-59 | 95.35 | 95.05 | 94.55 | 93.95 | 90.43 | .. |
| 60-64 | 91.85 | 91.40 | 90.55 | 89.55 | 68.97 | .. |
| 65+ | 77.70 | 76.85 | 75.40 | 73.65 | ... | .. |
| **Femmes** | | | | | | |
| 10-14 | .. | .. | .. | .. | .. | 0.00 |
| 15-19 | .. | .. | .. | .. | .. | 44.50 |
| 20-24 | .. | .. | .. | .. | .. | 64.50 |
| 25-29 | .. | .. | .. | .. | .. | 68.70 |
| 30-34 | .. | .. | .. | .. | .. | 83.20 |
| 35-39 | .. | .. | .. | .. | .. | 81.00 |
| 40-44 | .. | .. | .. | .. | .. | 79.28 |
| 45-49 | .. | .. | .. | .. | .. | 78.50 |
| 50-54 | .. | .. | .. | .. | .. | 76.00 |
| 55-59 | .. | .. | .. | .. | .. | 73.12 |
| 60-64 | .. | .. | .. | .. | .. | 67.95 |
| 65+ | .. | .. | .. | .. | .. | 58.84 |

**Source(s)**: (1) EPPA3; (2) R1982 et ASTER; (3) AST93.

### 2.2 Méthode(s): interpolation et extrapolation linéaires

#### 2.2.1 Hommes:

- 1950-90, interpolation et extrapolation des taux d'activité 1950-80
tirés des EPPA3 et des taux d'activité ajustés tirés du recensement de 1982;
ajustement des taux interpolés et extrapolés sur la base des variations
des taux interpolés 1982 par rapport aux taux ajustés du recensement de 1982;
modification des tendances des groupes d'âge [10-19] et [65+] de 1950 à 1990.

#### 2.2.2 Femmes:

- 1950-90, interpolation et extrapolation des taux d'activité 1950-90
estimés pour le Malawi;
ajustement des taux interpolés et extrapolés sur la base des variations
des taux interpolés 1986 par rapport aux taux de l'enquête de 1986-87;
modification des tendances des groupes d'âge [10-14] de 1950 à 1990.

## 3. Evaluation des taux de répartition par secteur d'activité: 1950 - 1990

### 3.1 Données de base:

Tableau 2: Répartition de la population active en % par secteur d'activité

| Année | Agriculture | Industrie Total | Manufac. | Services |
|---|---|---|---|---|
| **Hommes** | | | | |
| 1982 (1) | 54.61 | 23.60 | .. | 21.80 |
| 1986 (2) | 59.87 | 13.67 | 9.01 | 26.45 |
| **Femmes** | | | | |
| 1982 (1) | 76.68 | 5.56 | .. | 17.75 |
| 1986 (2) | 82.71 | 2.33 | 1.83 | 14.96 |

**Source(s)**: R1982; (2) AST93.

### 3.2 Méthode(s): extrapolation linéaire

#### 3.2.1 Hommes:

- 1950-70, taux de répartition 1950-70 tirés des EPPA3;
- 1980-90, extrapolation des taux de répartition 1950-80 tirés des EPPA3,
des taux du recensement de 1982 et des taux de l'enquête de 1986-87;
modification des tendances de tous les secteurs.

#### 3.2.2 Femmes:

Méthode, hypothèses et traitements identiques à ceux appliqués aux hommes.

## 4. Projection des taux d'activité: 2000 - 2010

### 4.1 Modèle(s): linéaire et hyperbole

#### 4.1.1 Hommes:

- Au groupe d'âge [10-14], application de la fonction F1;
- Aux groupes d'âge [15+], application de la fonction F3;
- Modification des tendances des groupes d'âge [10-14] et [60+].

#### 4.1.2 Femmes:

- Aux groupes d'âge [10-59], application de la fonction F3;
- Aux groupes d'âge [60+], application de la fonction F1;
- Modification des tendances des groupes d'âge [25-54] et [60+].

*Notes sur les ajustements des taux, voir p. 192-195.*

*Notes sur les fonctions de projection, voir p. 198.*

# Introducción

El programa de evaluaciones y proyecciones de la población económicamente activa por sexo y grupos de edad es ahora objeto de su cuarta edición. La Oficina de Estadística de la OIT publicó la primera edición[1] en 1971. En lo que se refiere a las otras dos ediciones, la segunda[2] y la tercera[3] se publicaron en 1976 y 1986, respectivamente.

El presente programa tiene por objeto poner a la disposiciones de los Estados Miembros de la Organización Internacional del Trabajo (OIT), de los organismos internacionales y de los usuarios privados un instrumento de trabajo tan completo, detallado y comparable como sea posible a nivel nacional, regional e internacional. Se integra en el marco del programa común de las Naciones Unidas y de los organismos internacionales especializados, en especial la OIT, la Organización de las Naciones Unidas para la Agricultura y la Alimentación (FAO) y la Organización de las Naciones Unidas para la Educación, la Ciencia y la Cultura (UNESCO). Tiene asimismo por objeto facilitar datos demográficos coordinados y compatibles sobre la población, la población económicamente activa, la población agrícola, la población escolar, los hogares, la natalidad, la fecundidad, la mortandad, etc.

**Figura 1: Vínculos entre los programas de la OIT relativos a la población económicamente activa y otros programas**

Una de las características importantes de las estimaciones y proyecciones internacionales relativas a la población económicamente activa reside en el hecho de que permiten comparar los niveles y tendencias de la población económicamente activa de las diferentes regiones y de los diferentes países en los años pasados y futuros.

Para mejorar su comparabilidad a nivel internacional, los datos básicos relativos a la población económicamente activa se han uniformado en la medida de lo posible, en especial en lo que se refiere a los conceptos, en el campo de aplicación considerado, el alcance y la distribución por grupos de edad. Por otra parte, con fines de coherencia de las evaluaciones y proyecciones de la población económicamente activa con los resultados de otros programas demográficos internacionales, se han utilizado las evaluaciones y proyecciones de la población total establecidas por la División de población de las Naciones Unidas en la elaboración de las evaluaciones y proyecciones de la población económicamente activa para la cuarta edición.

El presente suplemento metodológico se divide en dos partes: una primera introductoria de la "Metodología general", en la que se describen las directrices generales utilizadas en la elaboración de las evaluaciones y proyecciones de la población económicamente activa. También se citan ejemplos de los diversos problemas que se han planteado y de las soluciones adoptadas. La segunda parte se titula "Descripciones metodológicas". Contiene una descripción metodológica para cada país y territorio considerados individualmente en las evaluaciones y proyecciones por separado que figuran en la cuarta edición. En cada descripción se indican las fuentes y los datos básicos, así como los métodos de evaluación, los modelos de proyección y las hipótesis específicas relativas al país o territorio de que se trata.

## Metodología general

Como en el caso de las ediciones anteriores, las evaluaciones y las proyecciones de la población económicamente activa se han establecido en esta cuarta edición con la aplicación, a las evaluaciones y proyecciones de la población (variante media) elaboradas por las Naciones Unidas[4], de las evaluaciones y proyecciones de las tasas de actividad de la OIT por sexo y grupos de edad a mediados de cada uno de los años de referencia considerados, a saber, los años 1950, 1960, 1970, 1980, 1990, 2000 y 2010.

En comparación con las tres ediciones anteriores, la cuarta edición incluye innovaciones y cambios en cuanto a los conceptos, definiciones y metodología.

### 1. Conceptos y definiciones

#### 1.2 Población económicamente activa

El concepto de población económicamente activa es el que figura en la Resolución relativa a las estadísticas de la población económicamente activa, del empleo, del desempleo y del subempleo, adoptada por la 13.ª Conferencia Internacional de Estadígrafos del Trabajo — CIET 1982.

[1] OIT, Proyecciones de la fuerza de trabajo 1965-1985, primera edición, Ginebra, 1971.

[2] OIT, Proyecciones de la fuerza de trabajo 1950-2010, segunda edición, Ginebra, 1976.

[3] OIT, Evaluaciones y proyecciones de la población económicamente activa, 1950-2025, tercera edición, Ginebra, 1986

[4] Nations Unies World Population Prospects, the 1994 Revisions, ST/ESA/SER.A/145, Nueva York, 1995.

En esta resolución, la población económicamente activa se define como el conjunto de "todas las personas de uno u otro sexo que aportan su trabajo para producir bienes y servicios económicos, definidos según y como lo hacen los sistemas de cuentas nacionales y de balances de las Naciones Unidas, durante un período de referencia especificado. De acuerdo con estos sistemas la producción de bienes y servicios económicos incluye toda la producción y tratamiento de productos primarios — se destinen éstos al mercado, al trueque o al autoconsumo —, la producción de todos los otros artículos y servicios para el mercado y, en el caso de los hogares que produzcan artículos y servicios para el mercado, la parte de esta producción destinada a su propio consumo"[6].

**Figura 2: Marco conceptual de la población económicamente activa**

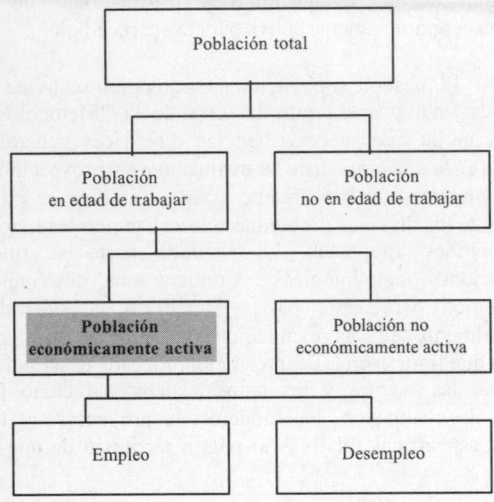

Con arreglo a esta definición, la población económicamente activa comprende: las personas con un "*empleo asalariado*" o "*no asalariado*"[6], *los miembros de las fuerzas armadas* (incluidos los militares de contingente) y los *personas desempleadas* (incluido las personas que buscan su primer empleo).

**1.2.    Tasas de actividad**

La tasa de actividad global (TA) es la proporción de personas activas (PA), según se definen a continuación, en la población total en edad de trabajar (PT).

$$TA = \frac{PA}{PT} \times 100$$

Las tasas de actividad se calculan para cada grupo de edad, para los hombres y las mujeres por separado y para las personas de uno u otro sexo en su conjunto.

**1.3.    Cobertura geográfica**

---

[5] OIT: Recomendaciones internacionales de actualidad en estadísticas del trabajo, edición de 1988, Ginebra, 1988.

[6] Los empleadores, los trabajadores por cuenta propia y miembros de cooperativas de producción, los trabajadores familiares no remunerados, las personas ocupadas en la producción de bienes y servicios económicos para consumo propio del hogar, los aprendices remunerados.

Se incluyen en la cuarta edición todos los países y territorios cuya población total alcanzó o rebasó el umbral de 200.000 habitantes a mediados del año 1990.

En comparación con la tercera edición, el número de países y territorios respecto de los cuales se han llevado a cabo evaluaciones y proyecciones individuales de la población económicamente activa ha aumentado considerablemente. Este aumento se debe en parte a la disminución del umbral de 300.000 a 200.000 habitantes y, por otra parte, a la consideración por separado de cada una de las repúblicas de los antiguos territorios de la URSS, de Yugoslavia y de Checoslovaquia.

**1.3.    Límite de edad y clasificación por grupo de edad**

La edad mínima considerada es de diez años. En la mayor parte de los países, la edad mínima de admisión legal al empleo es superior a este límite. Sin embargo, en muchos países en desarrollo, una proporción elevada de menores de 15 años está ocupada en la agricultura en la categoría de trabajadores familiares no remunerados. Se ha considerado razonable adoptar la edad de diez años como límite de edad inferior y ajustar los datos cada vez que fuere necesario.

En lo que se refiere a los grupos de edad, estos son los mismos que en la tercera edición, a saber, 12 grupos de edad, cada uno de cinco años salvo el último: [10-14], [15-19], [20-24], [25-29], [30-34], [35-39], [40-44], [45-49], [50-54], [55-59], [60-64] y [65+].

**1.5.    Clasificación regional**

La clasificación regional adoptada es la que establecen las Naciones Unidas en su última versión. Comprende seis regiones principales y 20 regiones:

Asia
  *Asia meridional central*
  *Asia meridional oriental*
  *Asia occidental*
  *Asia oriental*
Africa
  *Africa central*
  *Africa meridional*
  *Africa occidental*
  *Africa oriental*
  *Africa septentrional*
América Latina y el Caribe
  *América Central*
  *América del sur*
  *Caribe*
América del Norte
Europa
  *Europa meridional*
  *Europa occidental*
  *Europa oriental*
  *Europa septentrional*
Oceanía
  *Australia, Nueva Zelandia*
  *Melanesia*
  *Micronesia*
  *Polinesia*

Además de estos grupos regionales, se han añadido otros dos grupos basados principalmente en indicadores socioeconómicos[7]: El grupo de las regiones y de los países desarrollados (*América del Norte – Australia, Nueva Zelandia – Europa – Japón*) y el grupo de regiones menos desarrolladas (*África – Asia (con exclusión del Japón) – América Latina y el Caribe – Melanesia – Micronesia – Polinesia*).

En el mundo en su conjunto así como en cada región principal, región, regiones desarrolladas y regiones menos desarrolladas, las tasas respectivas de actividad se evalúan por sexo, grupo de edad y sector de actividad económica.

### 1.6. Sectores de actividad económica

Como en las ediciones anteriores, la cuarta edición presenta también evaluaciones de las tasas de distribución sectorial para el conjunto de la actividad económica. La composición de cada sector se basa en la Clasificación industrial internacional uniforme de todas las actividades económicas (CIIU – Rev. 2, 1968[8]).

La partida 1 (*Agricultura, Caza, Silvicultura y Pesca*) constituye el sector "agricultura".

El sector "industria" comprende las partidas 2, 3, 4 y 5 (*Industrias de extracción – Industrias manufactureras – Electricidad, gas y agua – Construcción y obras públicas*.

El sector de los "servicios" comprende las partidas 6, 7, 8 y 9 (*Comercio al por mayor y al por menor, restaurantes y hoteles – Transportes, almacenes y comunicaciones – Banca, seguros, asuntos inmobiliarios y servicios prestados a las empresas – Servicios prestados a la colectividad, servicios sociales y servicios personales*).

La cuarta edición es innovadora con la presentación por primera vez de evaluaciones por separado para la partida 3 "industrias manufactureras". Habida cuenta de la falta de datos respecto de la mayor parte de los países considerados, estas evaluaciones se limitan solamente a los años 1980 y 1990; en lo que se refiere a los demás sectores, las mismas abarcan el período 1950-1990.

## 2. Metodología

La metodología general adoptada en la cuarta edición se distingue esencialmente de las demás ediciones por su carácter "pragmático". Para cada país o territorio estudiado y con el fin de evaluar las tasas de actividad y las tasas de distribución sectorial, los métodos y las técnicas aplicadas se han elegido en función de la evaluación de diversos criterios que guardan relación con la fuente y la calidad de los datos y las prácticas nacionales en materia de acopio de datos. Esta elección tiene también en cuenta informaciones demográficas específicas sobre un país determinado o una región considerada que figuran en muchas publicaciones

especializadas. También conviene advertir que la experiencia adquirida con las ediciones ha permitido mejorar la selección de los métodos y de las técnicas de evaluación y de proyección.

En los casos en que se carecía total o parcialmente de información sobre estos factores, se ha aplicado la regla de utilizar informaciones o datos sobre países o territorios que han alcanzado un nivel análogo de desarrollo socioeconómico.

El programa de evaluaciones y proyecciones de la población económicamente activa de la OIT comprende dos fases: una fase de evaluación y una fase de proyección.

### 2.1. Fase de evaluación

La fase de evaluación ha consistido en establecer series cronológicas armonizadas de la población económicamente activa, por sexo, grupo de edad y sector de actividad económica en el período 1950-1990.

### 2.1.1. Fuentes y datos básicos

Para establecer las evaluaciones se ha decidido elegir, como punto de partida de la recopilación de datos básicos, los datos extraídos de la tercera edición para los años 1950, 1960 y 1970 y completarlos con datos basados en censos de la población y (o) encuestas por muestreo de la población económicamente activa, o encuestas análogas realizadas entre 1974 y 1994 y publicadas por organismos nacionales o internacionales de estadística.

Con el fin de compensar la falta de datos y comprobar y comparar los datos extraídos de fuentes diferentes, ha sido necesario y útil recurrir a publicaciones específicas de instituciones regionales o internacionales tales como el Centro Latinoamericano de Demografía (CELADE), la Organización de Cooperación y Desarrollo Económicos (OCDE), la Oficina Estadística de las Comunidades Europeas (EUROSTAT), el Nordic Statistics y las comisiones económicas regionales de las Naciones Unidas, a saber, la Comisión Económica para Africa (CEA), la Comisión Económica para Europa (CEE), la Comisión Económica para América Latina y el Caribe (CEPAL), la Comisión Económica y Social para Asia y el Pacífico (CESAP) y la Comisión Económica y Social para Asia Occidental (CESAO).

En comparación con las ediciones anteriores, se concede mayor prioridad en la cuarta edición a las encuestas por muestreo de la población económicamente activa que a los censos de población.

En muchos países, las encuestas por muestreo de la población económicamente activa y su componentes principales, a saber, el empleo y el desempleo, son periódicas y se llevan a cabo con una frecuencia anual o infraanual. Por esta razón permiten recopilar datos más precisos y fiables sobre el tamaño de la población económicamente activa. También ofrecen la ventaja de tener en cuenta las variaciones estacionales en este tamaño cuando se llevan a cabo en diferentes períodos del año. Estas son algunas de las ventajas y no de las menores que presentan tales encuestas en comparación con los censos de población que abarcan varios temas a la vez, se refieren a una fecha única y se efectúan

[7] Naciones Unidas, perspectivas futuras de la población mundial, Nueva York, 1985.

[8] Naciones Unidas, *Informes estadísticos*, scric M, núm. 4, Nueva York, 1969.

generalmente sobre una base decenal para la mayor parte de los países.

Tras haberse seleccionado los datos, el método consiste en ceñirse a las diferentes etapas indicadas en la figura 3 y aplicar los datos básicos, los procedimientos y los tratamientos propios de cada una de estas etapas. Según el país o el territorio de que se trata, una o varias de estas etapas han sido necesarias para las evaluaciones. En total, la fase de evaluación comprendió siete etapas; las de "armonización de las definiciones de la población económicamente activa" y de "ajuste de las distribuciones por grupos de edad" no se aplicaron a las evaluaciones de las tasas de distribución sectorial.

### 2.1.2. Armonización de las definiciones de la población económicamente activa

En esta etapa era preciso cerciorarse de que las definiciones de la población económicamente activa adoptadas en los censos de población y las encuestas por muestreo de la población económicamente activa correspondían a las que había adoptado la CIET en 1982 y, cuando no fuera así, efectuar los ajustes necesarios. El volumen 5 "Población total y población económicamente activa, empleo y desempleo[9] (censos de población)" de la serie *Fuentes y métodos: estadísticas del trabajo* se utilizó como base de referencia para la evaluación de las definiciones.

Las dificultades más frecuentes con que se tropezó en esta fase se refieren a la exclusión de determinadas categorías de personas de la población económicamente activa, ya sea porque se omiten por definición o porque se incluyen en la población inactiva. Se trata principalmente de las fuerzas armadas (en especial los militares de contingente) y las personas que buscan su primer empleo, los aprendices y los trabajadores familiares no remunerados (sobre todo las mujeres ocupadas en la agricultura como auxiliares familiares) y los trabajadores estacionales.

Cuando así lo permitía el desglose de los datos relativos a la población según su situación, o cuando los datos de la categoría considerada eran disponibles, los ajustes se efectuaron integrando los efectivos de la categoría o de las categorías de que se trata en los efectivos de la población económicamente activa por desplazamiento de la categoría o categorías de la población económicamente inactiva hacia la población económicamente activa o mediante una estimación de las personas que habían de integrarse (caso núm. 1).

El ejemplo de la República de Corea es un buen ejemplo del caso núm. 1. Los datos básicos recopilados para este país se han extraído de la tercera edición para los años 1950, 1960 y 1970, y se han utilizado también datos basados en el censo de población de 1980 y en las encuestas por muestreo de la población económicamente activa realizadas entre 1987 y 1990. Ya se trate del censo o de las encuestas, los datos relativos a la población económicamente activa se refieren a toda la población de hogares privados. Por consiguiente, los militares se excluyen de la definición que formuló la CIET en 1982. Para incluir las fuerzas armadas,

---

[9] Población total y población activa, empleo y desempleo (censos de población), vol. 5, *Fuentes y métodos de las estadísticas del trabajo*, primera edición, OIT, 1990.

**Figura 2 : Etapas y procedimientos de la fase de evaluación**

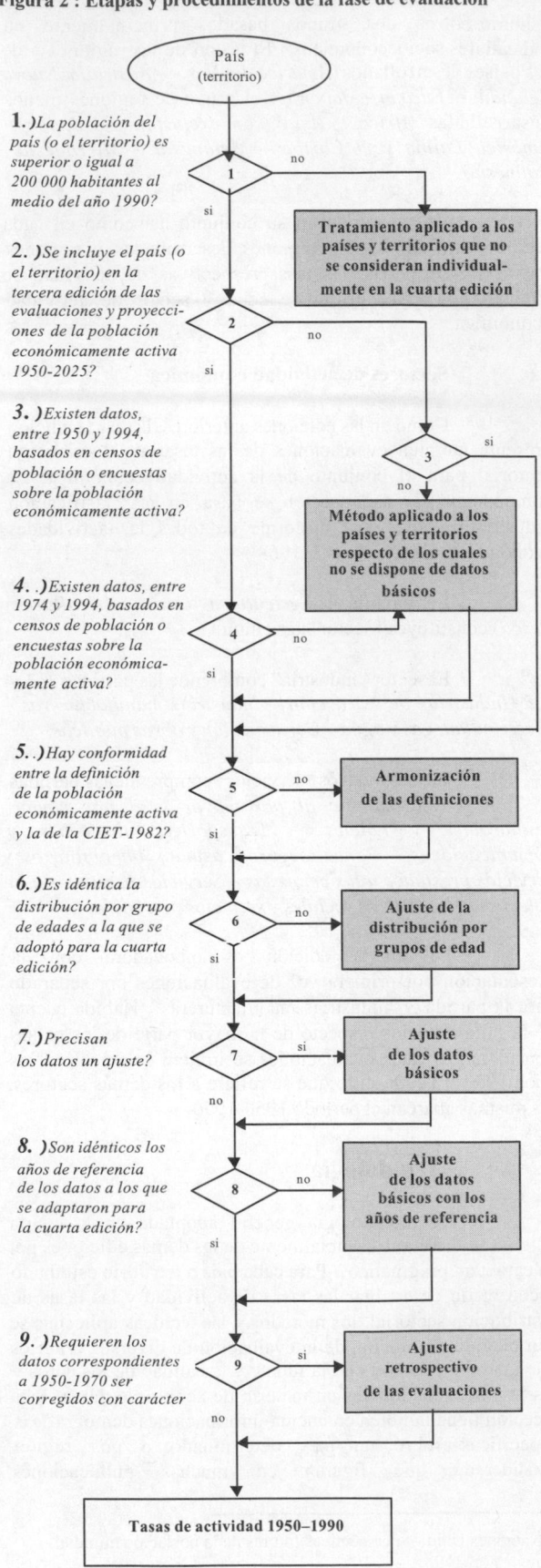

el ajuste ha consistido en agregar a los datos relativos a la población civil económicamente activa los datos estimados relativos a la diferencia existente entre población total y población civil.

En los casos en que no se disponía de datos desglosados, el método de ajuste consistió en agregar a la población activa una proporción estimada de las personas clasificadas en la categoría "Otras" en el grupo de personas económicamente inactivas (caso núm. 2). Las proporciones estimadas se basan en datos extraídos de otras fuentes o de la misma fuente en otro período de referencia y, en otro caso, en los datos de países vecinos en los que existe una situación demográfica, socioeconómica y cultural comparable con la del país estudiado.

El caso núm. 2 fue el más frecuente. En general, el ajuste realizado se limitó a los grupos de edad [15-29] y solamente para los hombres. Por ejemplo, los datos extraídos del censo de 1984 relativos a la población del Congo y que se han utilizado como datos básicos para las evaluaciones se han ajustado con el fin de tener en cuenta los estudiantes ocupados a tiempo parcial u ocasional que no se incluyen la población económicamente activa.

El procedimiento de ajuste ha consistido en agregar a las tasas de personas activas las tasas estimadas de estudiantes ocupados a tiempo parcial o con carácter ocasional que se han clasificado como personas no activas. Por otra parte, como se ha considerado que las tasas de actividad del censo de 1984 eran demasiada bajas para este país en comparación con los datos relativos a países que se encuentran en una situación análoga, la totalidad de las personas incluidas en la categoría "Otras" de las personas inactivas se ha agregado al número de personas económicamente activas. El cuadro 1 (página 382 )da una idea de los ajustes realizados.

### 2.1.3. Ajuste de la distribución por grupos de edad

En la mayor parte de los censos y encuestas estudiados, la distribución de la población activa por grupo de edad corresponde a la distribución de referencia por grupo de edad considerada en la cuarta edición. Sin embargo, en el caso de algunos países, ha resultado necesario armonizar esta distribución.

Los casos más frecuentes observados han sido los casos en que un grupo de edad en la distribución de una población nacional incluye dos o varios grupos de edad de la distribución de referencia. En estos casos se ha aplicado un algoritmo: se considera que la población total y la población activa se distribuyen uniformemente en un grupo de edad determinado y se aplica una técnica que consiste en tener en cuenta los efectos de la distribución de la población total por grupos de edad y los efectos de la tasa de actividad.

En el cuadro 2 (página 382) se indican los diferentes tratamientos aplicados al promedio de las tasas de actividad correspondientes a 1980 y calculado con base en datos extraídos de encuestas por muestreo de la población económicamente activa en *Australia* para los años 1979, 1980 y 1981. Al nivel nacional, la distribución de la población activa por grupo de edad era la siguiente: [15-19], [20-24], [25-34], [35-44], [45-54], [55-59], [60-64] y [65+]. Solamente

los grupos de edad [25-34], [35-44] y [45-54] no corresponden a la distribución estándar; es la tasa de actividad de estos grupos de edad que se ha evaluado.

### 2.1.4. Ajuste de los datos básicos

La labor esencial en esta fase ha consistido en corregir completamente los datos básicos entre los años 1970 y 1994 cuando las tasas de actividad se han considerado demasiado bajas. Estas correcciones se han efectuado principalmente respecto de la tasa de actividad de las mujeres en los países en los que las mujeres trabajan en la agricultura como auxiliares familiares no remunerados y que, por razones socioculturales, se han omitido voluntariamente en las estadísticas oficiales o cuando su evaluación numérica es comparativamente inferior a datos del mismo alcance y naturaleza para países vecinos en que la situación socioeconómica es análoga.

El procedimiento de ajuste ha consistido primero en evaluar el número total de mujeres ocupadas en la agricultura que no se tienen en cuenta y luego en distribuir estas mujeres por grupos de edad con arreglo a un modelo establecido y a la tasa de urbanización del país de que se trata; por último, los resultados obtenidos de esta manera se han agregado a los datos básicos que han sido objeto de un reajuste. Se ha considerado que el número infravalorado de mujeres correspondía a la diferencia entre el número total estimativo de mujeres ocupadas en la agricultura y el número real de mujeres indicado en la fuente cuyos datos han de ser reajustados.

**Modelo de distribución del número infravalorado de mujeres por grupo de edad y por región**

| Grupo de edad | Urbana | Rural |
|---|---|---|
| 10-14 | 3.74 | 26.68 |
| 15-19 | 3.80 | 36.76 |
| 20-24 | 4.20 | 40.36 |
| 25-29 | 3.99 | 42.46 |
| 30-34 | 7.70 | 44.02 |
| 35-39 | 8.20 | 45.29 |
| 40-44 | 10.06 | 46.33 |
| 45-49 | 7.50 | 45.36 |
| 50-54 | 10.29 | 43.47 |
| 55-59 | 9.70 | 39.18 |
| 60-64 | 6.22 | 33.48 |
| 65+ | 2.77 | 17.39 |

**Fuente**: Oficina de Estadística, OIT.

El modelo con arreglo al cual se distribuye el número de mujeres infravalorado se ha establecido en función de las curvas de las tasas de actividad de las mujeres en el sector agrícola para varios países respecto de los cuales se dispone de estadísticas muy detalladas y concretas; la distribución se efectúa por grupos de edad y por regiones urbanas y rurales. El modelo de distribución que figura a continuación se ha aplicado de una manera uniforme a todas las series de datos que convenía reajustar.

El cuadro 3 (página 383) muestra un ejemplo de ajuste de las tasas de actividad de las mujeres del *Malí* con base en datos extraídos del censo de población correspondiente a 1976.

382

**Cuadro 1: Ajuste de las tasas de actividad para hombres con base en el censo de la población de Congo (diciembre de 1984)**

| Grupo de edad | Población económicamente activa en % | Población no económicamente activa en % | | | Tasas estimadas de los estudiantes activos | Tasas adicionales de ajuste | | | Tasas de actividad ajustadas |
|---|---|---|---|---|---|---|---|---|---|
| | | Total | Estudiantes | Otros | | Estudiantes | Otros | Total | |
| c1 | c2 | c3 | c4 | c5 | c6 | c7=c4xc6 | c8=c5 | c9=c7+c8 | c10=c2+c9 |
| 10-14 | 3.10 | 94.26 | 93.14 | 2.64 | 0.25 | 23.28 | 2.64 | 25.92 | 29.02 |
| 15-19 | 18.84 | 77.89 | 75.07 | 3.28 | 0.40 | 30.03 | 3.28 | 33.30 | 52.14 |
| 20-24 | 53.49 | 43.29 | 39.88 | 3.22 | 0.70 | 27.92 | 3.22 | 31.14 | 84.63 |
| 25-29 | 86.04 | 12.16 | 9.98 | 1.81 | 0.90 | 8.98 | 1.81 | 10.79 | 96.82 |
| 30-34 | 96.60 | 2.47 | 1.16 | 0.93 | 0.00 | 0.00 | 0.93 | 0.93 | 97.53 |
| 35-39 | 97.75 | 1.57 | 0.36 | 0.68 | 0.00 | 0.00 | 0.68 | 0.68 | 98.43 |
| 40-44 | 97.61 | 1.71 | 0.20 | 0.68 | 0.00 | 0.00 | 0.68 | 0.68 | 98.29 |
| 45-49 | 96.62 | 2.74 | 0.13 | 0.64 | 0.00 | 0.00 | 0.64 | 0.64 | 97.26 |
| 50-54 | 92.95 | 6.32 | 0.06 | 0.73 | 0.00 | 0.00 | 0.73 | 0.73 | 93.68 |
| 55-59 | 80.96 | 18.19 | 0.19 | 0.85 | 0.00 | 0.00 | 0.85 | 0.85 | 81.81 |
| 60-64 | 81.05 | 17.87 | 0.50 | 1.08 | 0.00 | 0.00 | 0.00 | 0.00 | 81.05 |
| 65+ | 73.79 | 23.37 | 1.63 | 2.84 | 0.00 | 0.00 | 0.00 | 0.00 | 73.79 |

**Fuente**: Oficina de Estadística, OIT.

**Cuadro 2: Evaluación de las tasas de actividad 1980 de los grupos de edad de 25 hasta 44 años para hombres en Australia**

| Grupo de edad | Población económ. activa en % 1980 | Población total 1980 (Millares) | Tasas de actividad 1970 | Tasas de actividad 1980 | | | | | | | | | | | | | | Tasas de actividad ajustadas 1980 |
|---|---|---|---|---|---|---|---|---|---|---|---|---|---|---|---|---|---|---|
| c1 | c2 | c3 | c4 | c5 | c6 | c7 | c8 | c9 | c10 | c11 | c12 | c13 | c14 | c15 | c16 | c17 | c18 | c19 |
| 25-29 | 95.87 | 608 | 95.79 | 94.81 | 1196 | 1147 | 576 | 1138 | 582 | 1150 | 12 | 4 | 0.30 | 0.70 | 28.64 | 66.86 | 95.50 | 95.50 |
| 30-34 | | 588 | 96.55 | 95.54 | | | 562 | | 568 | | | | | 0.70 | 28.86 | 67.39 | 96.25 | 96.25 |
| 35-39 | 95.67 | 961 | 96.44 | 95.36 | 1778 | 1701 | 916 | 1689 | 927 | 1710 | 21 | 9 | 0.42 | 0.58 | 39.59 | 56.40 | 95.99 | 95.99 |
| 40-44 | | 817 | 95.80 | 94.55 | | | 772 | | 783 | | | | | 0.58 | 39.26 | 56.03 | 95.28 | 95.28 |

c6=Suma de los datos de dos grupos de edad adyacentes en c3; c7=(c2xc6)/100; c8=(c3xc5)/100; c9=Suma de los datos de dos grupos de edad adyacentes en c8; c10=(c3xc4)/100; c11=Suma de los datos de dos grupos de edad adyacentes en c10; c12=c11-c9; c13=c11-c7; c14=c13/c12; c15=1-(c13/c12); c16=c5xc14; c17=c4xc15; c18=c16+c17; c19=c18.

**Fuente**: Oficina de Estadística, OIT.

### 2.1.5. Ajuste de los datos básicos con los años de referencia

Como en el caso de la tercera edición, el período de referencia de las evaluaciones se ha fijado en el mes de junio para cada uno de los años de referencia 1950, 1960, 1970, 1980 y 1990.

En los países y territorios para los cuales se han conservado las evaluaciones extraídas de la tercera edición para los años 1950, 1960 y 1970 (y también en algunos casos 1980), los datos básicos entre 1974 y 1994, salvo contadas excepciones, se han ajustado todos para el mes de junio en cada uno de los años de referencia 1980 y 1990.

El procedimiento de ajuste se ha elegido en función del número de años disponibles respecto de los datos básicos y de la importancia del intervalo que separa cada uno de estos años del año de referencia. En general, se ha adoptado el método siguiente para un país o territorio determinado:

- cuando se dispone de dos años de datos básicos próximos al año de referencia (1979 y 1981 o 1989 y 1991), los ajustes se efectúan aplicando promedios aritméticos a las tasas de actividad de los datos básicos. Este ha sido el caso en la mayor parte de los países y regiones desarrollados;

— en los demás casos, se ha efectuado principalmente una interpolación y/o extrapolación de los datos básicos.

Para los países y territorios respecto de los cuales no se han conservado las evaluaciones derivadas de la tercera edición, el ajuste de los datos básicos con los años de referencia se ha efectuado para la mayor parte de estos países por interpolación y/o extrapolación de los datos básicos. Luego, con el fin de precisar más aún la tendencia de las tasas estimadas se han aplicado a las tasas interpoladas y/o extrapoladas las variaciones de las tasas de actividad extraídas

**Cuadro 3: Ajuste de las tasas de actividad para mujeres con base en el censo de la población de Mali (diciembre de 1976)**

| Grupo de edad | Población total | Población económ. activa | Tasas de actividad | Modelo de distribución del número infravalorado de mujeres por rgión | | Parte de las mujeres en el sector de la agricultura en % por región | | | | | | Tasas de actividad que han añadirse | Tasas de actividad ajustadas |
|---|---|---|---|---|---|---|---|---|---|---|---|---|---|
| | | | | Urbana | Rural | Urbana | Rural | | | | | | |
| c1 | c2 | c3 | c4 | c5 | c6 | c7 | c8 | c9 | c10 | c11 | c12 | c13 | |
| 10-14 | 321959 | 47528 | 14.76 | 3.74 | 26.68 | 16.80 | 83.20 | 22.83 | 73497 | 1.66 | 37.79 | 52.55 |
| 15-19 | 333508 | 62813 | 18.83 | 3.80 | 36.76 | 16.80 | 83.20 | 31.22 | 104125 | 1.66 | 51.68 | 70.51 |
| 20-24 | 265842 | 46428 | 17.46 | 4.20 | 40.36 | 16.80 | 83.20 | 34.28 | 91142 | 1.66 | 56.75 | 74.21 |
| 25-29 | 267018 | 48138 | 18.03 | 3.99 | 42.46 | 16.80 | 83.20 | 36.00 | 96123 | 1.66 | 59.58 | 77.61 |
| 30-34 | 225950 | 38859 | 17.20 | 7.70 | 44.02 | 16.80 | 83.20 | 37.92 | 85675 | 1.66 | 62.76 | 79.96 |
| 35-39 | 165949 | 29019 | 17.49 | 8.20 | 45.29 | 16.80 | 83.20 | 39.06 | 64817 | 1.66 | 64.65 | 82.14 |
| 40-44 | 147829 | 25618 | 17.33 | 10.06 | 46.33 | 16.80 | 83.20 | 40.24 | 59480 | 1.66 | 66.60 | 83.93 |
| 45-49 | 98453 | 17225 | 17.50 | 7.50 | 45.36 | 16.80 | 83.20 | 39.00 | 38396 | 1.66 | 64.55 | 82.05 |
| 50-54 | 103607 | 16486 | 15.91 | 10.29 | 43.47 | 16.80 | 83.20 | 37.90 | 39263 | 1.66 | 62.73 | 78.64 |
| 55-59 | 62917 | 9485 | 15.08 | 9.70 | 39.18 | 16.80 | 83.20 | 34.22 | 21532 | 1.66 | 56.65 | 71.72 |
| 60-64 | 81466 | 9897 | 12.15 | 6.22 | 33.48 | 16.80 | 83.20 | 28.90 | 23543 | 1.66 | 47.83 | 59.98 |
| 65+ | 124068 | 10366 | 8.36 | 2.77 | 17.39 | 16.80 | 83.20 | 14.93 | 18524 | 1.66 | 24.71 | 33.07 |

Razón mujeres/hombres en la agricultura con base en el censo de 1976 = 17.94% {(1578948/283107)*100}; Nueva razón mujeres/hombres estimada = 93%;
Número infravalorado de mujeres estimativo = 1185315 {(15789948x0.93) - 283107}. $c9=(c5xc7+c6xc8)/100$; $c10=c2xc9x100$ $c11=185315/716117$; $c12=c9xc11$; $c13=c4+c12$.

**Fuente**: Oficina de Estadística, OIT.

generalmente de los datos del mismo censo (o de la misma encuesta). Por ejemplo, para los grupos de edad de los jóvenes de 10 a 24 años, se ha recurrido a menudo a modificaciones de tendencia de las tasas de actividad estimadas acelerando o frenando estas tendencias según la evaluación del nivel de estas tasas, de conformidad con las hipótesis adoptadas para el país o territorio de que se trata.

El cuadro 4 (página 384 ) presenta un ejemplo de tipo de ajuste de los datos básicos a los años de referencia.

### 2.1.6. Ajuste retrospectivo de las evaluaciones

En una fase inicial, sólo se han ajustado los datos básicos entre los años 1974 y 1994 para los países y territorios en los que las estadísticas omitían mediana o totalmente la contribución de las mujeres a la actividad económica. Para que las evaluaciones y proyecciones fueran comparables en todo el período 1950-2010 y de conformidad con la solicitud de varios organismos, en especial del comité permanente de evaluaciones y proyecciones demográficas del Comité Administrativo en su reunión de los días 25 a 27 de junio de 1996, se decidió proceder a una corrección de los datos básicos extraídos de la tercera edición y conservados en la cuarta edición para los años 1950, 1960 y 1970.

Los métodos y los modelos utilizados para estos ajustes son análogos a los que se han utilizado en la etapa de "ajuste de los datos básicos" (2.1.4)

### 2.1.7. Tratamiento aplicado a los países y territorios que no se consideran individualmente en la cuarta edición

Se trata de países y territorios respecto de los cuales no han podido establecerse evaluaciones por separado por el hecho de que su población total no alcanzaba a mediados del año 1990 el umbral mínimo fijado en 200.000 habitantes. Pese a ello, los datos relativos a estos países y territorios se han incluido en los totales regionales. Ello se ha hecho de la manera siguiente: se calculan las tasas medias de actividad correspondientes a la región sin estos países y

territorios; se aplican luego estas tasas medias a la población total de estos países y territorios y, por último, agregando las poblaciones activas de todos los países y territorios que constituyen la región, se obtiene la población activa de la misma.

En lo que se refiere al mundo en su conjunto, cada región principal y las regiones desarrolladas y menos desarrolladas, el procedimiento aplicado a las evaluaciones y proyecciones de la población económicamente activa es análogo en su desarrollo al que se aplica a la evaluación de la población activa regional.

Los métodos aplicados en esta etapa se aplican, pues, después del tratamiento de los países y territorios que figuraban individualmente en la cuarta edición y que se han conservado.

### 2.1.8. Método aplicado a los países y territorios respecto de los cuales no se dispone de datos básicos

En esta etapa se han resuelto los problemas relacionados con la no disponibilidad total o parcial de los datos básicos utilizados para la elaboración de las evaluaciones. Los países y territorios a los que se aplica este método son los países y territorios que no se han incluido en la tercera edición y/o respecto de los cuales no se dispone de datos posteriores a 1974. Se han clasificado en tres categorías y se ha aplicado a cada una de ellas una solución satisfactoria en la medida de lo posible.

En la primera categoría se agrupan las 22 repúblicas constituidas en los territorios de la URSS (*Armenia, Azerbaiján, Belarús, Estonia, Georgia, Kazajstán, Kirguistán, Letonia, Lituania, Moldova, Federación de Rusia, Tayikistán, Turkmenistán, Ucrania y Uzbekistán*), Yugoslavia (*Bosnia y Herzegovina, Croacia, Macedonia, ex República Yugoslava de Eslovenia, República Federal de Yugoslavia*) y Checoslovaquia (*República Checa, Eslovaquia*). Respecto de estos países, la Oficina de Estadística de la OIT se ha beneficiado de la colaboración de las autoridades nacionales y

384

## Cuadro 4: Evaluación de las tasas de actividad para Perú - Hombres, 1950 - 1990

| Grupo de edad | Tasas de actividad (datos básicos) | | | | Tasas estimadas 1980 | Interpolación y extrapolación de las tasas de actividad 1950, 1960, 1970 et 1980 | | | Tasas extrapoladas 1990 después modificación de las tendencias | Tasas de actividad estimadas 1990 |
|---|---|---|---|---|---|---|---|---|---|---|
| | 1950 | 1960 | 1970 | 1981 | | 1981 | 1985 | 1990 | | |
| c1 | c2 | c3 | c4 | c5 | c6 | c7 | c8 | c9 | c10 | c11 |
| 10-14 | 11.95 | 6.75 | 5.00 | 4.92 | 4.92 | 3.50 | 2.59 | 1.45 | 2.59 | 3.64 |
| 15-19 | 59.40 | 55.30 | 42.20 | 37.52 | 37.94 | 36.31 | 33.22 | 29.34 | 33.22 | 34.31 |
| 20-24 | 93.25 | 91.70 | 82.60 | 81.67 | 81.76 | 80.35 | 78.61 | 76.43 | 78.61 | 79.90 |
| 25-29 | 98.00 | 97.50 | 94.90 | 93.43 | 93.57 | 93.45 | 92.81 | 92.02 | 92.02 | 92.00 |
| 30-34 | 98.80 | 98.60 | 97.80 | 97.21 | 97.26 | 97.25 | 97.03 | 96.76 | 96.76 | 96.72 |
| 35-39 | 98.60 | 98.50 | 98.40 | 98.33 | 98.33 | 98.31 | 98.28 | 98.23 | 98.23 | 98.25 |
| 40-44 | 98.50 | 98.40 | 98.30 | 98.30 | 98.30 | 98.26 | 98.24 | 98.20 | 98.20 | 98.24 |
| 45-49 | 98.40 | 98.30 | 98.20 | 98.27 | 98.26 | 98.21 | 98.19 | 98.16 | 98.16 | 98.22 |
| 50-54 | 97.60 | 97.50 | 96.15 | 97.04 | 96.96 | 96.53 | 96.40 | 96.24 | 96.24 | 96.75 |
| 55-59 | 96.50 | 96.05 | 93.65 | 94.50 | 94.42 | 93.77 | 93.43 | 93.00 | 93.00 | 93.71 |
| 60-64 | 91.90 | 91.75 | 85.55 | 88.26 | 88.01 | 86.44 | 85.73 | 84.84 | 84.84 | 86.62 |
| 65+ | 75.00 | 69.30 | 62.65 | 63.46 | 63.39 | 60.95 | 59.29 | 57.21 | 57.21 | 59.57 |

$c_2$, $c_3$ et $c_4$: tasas de actividad con base en la tercera edición; $c_5$: tasas de actividad con base en el censo de 1981 (julio); $c_6=c_5(10/11)+c_4(1/11)$; $c_{11}=c_{10}(c_5/c_7)$.

**Fuente**: Oficina de Estadística, OIT.

sobre todo de la de expertos[10],[11] de estos países para recopilar datos relativos a la población activa de cada uno de estos países en el período 1950-1990.

La segunda categoría agrupa a los países y territorios respecto de los cuales no se dispone de ningún dato. En esta situación, la solución adoptada ha consistido en elegir como datos básicos para estos países las evaluaciones establecidas para un mínimo de dos países vecinos. Por ejemplo, este ha sido el caso de *Eritrea*; los datos básicos seleccionados para este país corresponden a las estimaciones relativas a *Etiopía* y *Somalia*.

La tercera categoría agrupa a todos los países incluidos en la tercera edición y respecto de los cuales no se dispone de datos entre 1974 y 1994 o respecto de los cuales, en el caso de algunos de ellos, existen datos aunque se hayan preferido los que se incluyen en la tercera edición. Entre estos países figuran: *Arabia Saudita, Bután, Burundi, Camerún, Gabón, Gambia, Guinea, Jordania, Kenya, Líbano, Mauritania, Uganda, República Popular Democrática de Corea, Suriname, Timor Oriental*. Para estos países sólo se han utilizado como datos básicos los relativos a los años 1950, 1960 y 1970 y los de la tercera edición o, en algunos casos, se han agregado también los datos relativos a 1980 y/o 1990.

Los métodos y procedimientos aplicados a las evaluaciones de las tasas de distribución sectorial para la

agricultura, la industria y los servicios son los mismos que se han aplicado a las evaluaciones de las tasas de actividad.

Por carecerse de datos disponibles desglosados por sector industrial en una gran mayoría de países, el procedimiento de evaluación de las tasas de distribución en las industrias manufactureras se ha llevado a cabo de la siguiente manera:

—   En caso de existir datos básicos disponibles para un año próximo a los años de referencia 1980 y 1990 o entre este intervalo, las tasas de distribución en las industrias manufactureras se han obtenido mediante la aplicación a las tasas de distribución estimadas en la industria una razón o razones industria/manufactura extraídas de los datos básicos disponibles.

—   Para los países respecto de los cuales no se dispone de ningún dato, la regla ha consistido en adoptar la razón industria/manufactura estimada para un país que presenta una situación demográfica y económica análogas y aplicarla a las tasas de distribución estimadas en la industria del país de que se trata.

### 2.2.   Fase de proyección

### 2.2.1.   Método

En las ediciones anteriores, las proyecciones de las tasas de actividad de la población activa se establecieron mediante la aplicación de un modelo uniforme a todos los países y territorios considerados. Este método se basaba en la relación entre las variaciones en las tasas de actividad y el grado de desarrollo económico y su evolución medidos con base en la proporción de personas activas de sexo masculino en el sector agrícola. Los resultados obtenidos con este método eran satisfactorios para la gran mayoría de los países y

---

[10]   Popovic, B. (19949, "Nuevas estimaciones para 1980 y 1990 de las tasas de actividad por edad y distribución sectorial en algunos países de Europa oriental y meridional, en *Boletín de estadísticas del trabajo, 1994-2*, OIT, Ginebra, 1994.

[11]   Vorobiev, A. (1994), "Estimación de la población activa para los 15 países de la ex URSS en los años 1950, 1959, 1970, 1979 y 1989", en *Boletín de estadísticas del trabajo, 1994-2*, OIT, Ginebra, 1994.

territorios; sin embargo, principalmente en los países en que la población activa en la agricultura sólo representaba una proporción muy baja, varias dificultades se plantearon con la aplicación de este método. Además, habida cuenta de su mecanismo poco flexible, dicho método sólo permitía tener en cuenta parcialmente cambios importantes ocurridos en el mercado de trabajo, como el desarrollo del trabajo a tiempo parcial o la participación cada vez mayor de las mujeres en la actividad económica.

Por esta razón, se ha decidido en la cuarta edición elegir otro enfoque, a saber, el enfoque histórico. Este se basa en la proyección de las tendencias individuales propias de cada país o territorio. La experiencia adquirida por varios organismos nacionales de estadística y la Oficina de Estadística de la OIT muestra que este método de proyección arroja resultados tan exactos en el plano cualitativo como los que se obtienen con métodos más perfeccionados. Presenta además la ventaja de ser de fácil aplicación y refleja rápidamente las nuevas tendencias que se manifiestan en un país determinado.

El método ha consistido, en primer lugar, en proyectar por medio de funciones de extrapolación las tendencias de las tasas de actividad para cada sexo y grupo de edad y luego, por medio de un gráfico y con arreglo a las hipótesis adoptadas para el país o territorio considerado, en elegir la función apropiada y, por último, cuando ha sido necesario, en introducir modificaciones en las tendencias acelerándolas o desacelerándolas.

### 2.2.2. Hipótesis

Las principales hipótesis adoptadas en la elaboración de las proyecciones son cuatro:

Hipótesis 1: para los países y territorios de las regiones desarrolladas, continuación de la disminución de las tasas de actividad para todos los grupos de edad. Esta disminución es más acentuada en el caso de los grupos de edad [15-19] y [55+].

Hipótesis 2: debería atenuarse el ritmo de disminución de las tasas de actividad de los hombres en las regiones menos desarrolladas.

Hipótesis 3: en las regiones menos desarrolladas, e independientemente de la tendencia observada en el curso del decenio 1980-1990, las tasas de actividad de las mujeres para los grupos de edad [25-54] deberían aproximarse a las correspondientes a los hombres sin rebasarlas.

Hipótesis 4: el ritmo de aumento de los niveles de las tasas de actividad de las mujeres, si lo hubiere, sería más importante para los grupos de edad en que son mayores las disparidades entre estas tasas y las correspondientes a los hombres.

### 2.2.3. Funciones de extrapolación

Las funciones de extrapolación son seis y se enumeran en el cuadro 5 en la página 386.

## Conclusión

Las evaluaciones y proyecciones de la población activa de la OIT se elaboran en promedio a intervalos de ocho años. Este período ha demostrado ser demasiado largo para de la integración de cambios estructurales o de hechos demográficos nuevos en algunos países después de la publicación de una edición. En principio, estos cambios y hechos nuevos se tomarán en cuenta en la edición siguiente; entretanto, la calidad y los niveles de las evaluaciones y proyecciones ya elaboradas se ven afectados. La Oficina de Estadística, consciente de esta situación y deseosa en la medida de lo posible de poner a la disposición de los usuarios estadísticas fiables y comparables sobre la población activa, viene terminando un nuevo programa integrado o estadísticas de la población activa.

Este programa integrado tiene por objeto principal la actualización continuada de las evaluaciones y proyecciones de la población activa: a medida que se disponga de nuevos datos o de que se produzcan hechos demográficos o socioeconómicos nuevos que afecten las hipótesis y los métodos seleccionados, estos factores se integrarían automáticamente en los procedimientos y métodos aplicados a las evaluaciones y proyecciones de la población activa.

Este nuevo programa también tiene por objeto:

—    la integración de las evaluaciones y proyecciones establecidas por los organismos nacionales de estadística;

—    una mayor colaboración entre la OIT y la FAO, así como la UNESCO, para integrar y armonizar mejor los datos elaborados por cada uno de estos organismos;

—    una integración de los resultados de las encuestas realizadas en el marco del Programa Internacional para la Erradicación del Trabajo Infantil (IPEC) de la OIT;

—    una integración de los resultados del programa sobre las estimaciones comparables relativas al empleo y el desempleo de la OIT;

—    una integración de los datos relativos a la población activa por nivel de educación publicadas en las últimas ediciones del *Anuario de estadísticas del trabajo* de la OIT;

—    en el plano técnico e informático, integración de las diferentes bases de datos de los documentos y de los métodos por medio de una interfaz gráfica y de las nuevas tecnologías de la información con el fin de administrar, utilizar y divulgar mejor las evaluaciones y proyecciones de la población activa.

La ejecución de este programa integrado se concretará con la publicación de la quinta edición de las evaluaciones y proyecciones de la población económicamente activa de la OIT.

**Cuadro 5: Funciones extrapoladoras de las proyecciones relativas a las tasas de actividad para 2000-2010**

| N° | Modelo de proyección | Función | Función linear |
|---|---|---|---|
| 1 | **Linear** <br><br> *La variación en la tasa de actividad (y) es proporcional a la variación en el tiempo (x):* <br> $(dy = a dx)$ | $y = ax + b$ | $y = ax + b$ |
| 2 | **Log-linear** <br><br> *La tasa de variación en la tasa de actividad (y) es proporcional a la tasa de variación en el tiempo (x):* <br> $\dfrac{dy}{y} = a\dfrac{dx}{x}$ | $y = Bx^{a}$ | $p = aq + b$ <br><br> con $\quad p = Lny$, <br> $q = Lnx$, <br> $b = LnB$ |
| 3 | **Hyperbole** <br><br> *Posibilidad de establecer un umbral infranqueable en materia de tasa de actividad.* | $y = \dfrac{1}{ax + b}$ | $p = ax + b$ <br><br> con $\quad p = \dfrac{1}{y}$ |
| 4 | **Exponencial** <br><br> *La tasa de variación en la tasa de actividad (y) es proporcional a la tasa de variación en el tiempo (x):* <br> $\dfrac{dy}{y} = a dx$ | $y = e^{ax+b}$ | $p = ax + b$ <br><br> con $\quad p = Lny$ |
| 5 | **Logarítmica** <br><br> *La variación en la tasa de actividad (y) es proporcional a la variación en el tiempo (x):* <br> $dy = a\dfrac{dx}{x}$ | $y = aLnx + b$ | $y = az + b$ <br><br> con $\quad z = Lnx$ |
| 6 | **Logística** <br><br> *Posibilidad de reflejar la transición entre una fase de crecimiento y una fase de autodesaceleración en las tasas de actividad* | $y = y_{min} + \dfrac{y_{max} - y_{min}}{1 + e^{ax+b}}$ | $y = \alpha z + \beta$ <br><br> con $\quad z = \dfrac{1}{1 + e^{ax+b}}$, <br> $\beta = y_{min}$ |

# Afganistán

## 1. Fuente(s) de los datos básicos

Código(s):    Título(s):

EPPA3      Estimaciones y proyecciones de la población económicamente activa, 1950-2025, tercera edición, OIT, Ginebra, 1986.
ADNU84    Annuaire démographique 1984 - Statistiques des recensements de population II, trente-sixième édition, Nations Unies, New York, 1986.
ASTER     Anuario de estadísticas del trabajo 1945-89 - Edición retrospectiva sobre los censos de población, OIT, Ginebra, 1990.

## 2. Evaluación de las tasas de actividad: 1950 - 1990

### 2.1 Datos básicos:

Cuadro 1: Tasas de actividad por sexo y grupo de edad

| Grupo de edad | Año | | | | |
| | 1950 (1) | 1960 (1) | 1970 (1) | 1980 (1) | 1979 (2) |
|---|---|---|---|---|---|
| **Hombres** | | | | | |
| 10-14 | 38.00 | 36.00 | 34.00 | 32.00 | 30.54 |
| 15-19 | 75.85 | 72.20 | 68.55 | 64.90 | 66.00 |
| 20-24 | 92.80 | 91.35 | 89.95 | 88.50 | 88.99 |
| 25-29 | 97.65 | 97.00 | 96.35 | 95.70 | 95.70 |
| 30-34 | 98.05 | 97.55 | 97.00 | 96.50 | 96.84 |
| 35-39 | 98.55 | 98.20 | 97.85 | 97.50 | 97.19 |
| 40-44 | 98.05 | 97.55 | 96.95 | 96.40 | 96.87 |
| 45-49 | 97.55 | 97.05 | 96.60 | 96.10 | 96.48 |
| 50-54 | 96.65 | 95.85 | 95.10 | 94.30 | 94.78 |
| 55-59 | 93.90 | 93.05 | 92.25 | 91.40 | 92.44 |
| 60-64 | 90.50 | 89.35 | 88.25 | 87.10 | 87.84 |
| 65+ | 76.40 | 72.85 | 69.35 | 65.80 | 61.95 |
| **Mujeres** | | | | | |
| 10-14 | 5.00 | 4.50 | 4.00 | 3.50 | 5.06 |
| 15-19 | 8.50 | 8.80 | 9.15 | 9.55 | 9.13 |
| 20-24 | 5.80 | 6.60 | 7.90 | 9.25 | 9.18 |
| 25-29 | 5.45 | 6.20 | 7.40 | 8.70 | 8.22 |
| 30-34 | 5.30 | 5.75 | 6.40 | 7.10 | 6.75 |
| 35-39 | 6.00 | 6.30 | 6.75 | 7.20 | 6.71 |
| 40-44 | 4.55 | 4.75 | 5.05 | 5.30 | 5.17 |
| 45-49 | 4.55 | 4.70 | 4.95 | 5.20 | 4.95 |
| 50-54 | 3.25 | 3.45 | 3.75 | 4.05 | 3.62 |
| 55-59 | 3.25 | 3.50 | 3.80 | 4.10 | 3.80 |
| 60-64 | 2.40 | 2.35 | 2.30 | 2.25 | 2.12 |
| 65+ | 1.80 | 1.75 | 1.65 | 1.60 | 1.18 |

Fuente(s): (1) EPPA3; (2) ADNU84.

### 2.2 Método(s): extrapolación linear

#### 2.2.1 Hombres:

- 1950-80, tasas de actividad ajustadas 1950-80 con base en EPPA3;
ajuste de las tasas de actividad con base en los resultados del censo de 1979;
- 1990, extrapolación de las tasas de actividad 1950-80 con base en EPPA3
modificación de las tendencias de los grupos de edad [25-59].

#### 2.2.2 Mujeres:

- 1950-70, tasas de actividad ajustadas 1950-70 con base en EPPA3;
el ajuste se ha calculado con base en el modelo de ajuste de las tasas de
actividad de las mujeres ocupadas en la agricultura como auxiliares familiares;
- 1980-90, extrapolación de las tasas de actividad 1950-70 con base en EPPA3
y de las tasas de actividad con base en el censo de 1979;
ajuste de las tasas de actividad con base en la razón hombres/mujeres
igual a 2/3 en la agricultura y los resultados de la encuesta de 1989.

## 3. Evaluación de las tasas de distribución por sector de actividad: 1950 - 1990

### 3.1 Datos básicos:

Cuadro 2: Distribución de la población económicamente activa por sector de actividad en %

| Año | Agricultura | Industria | | Servicios |
| | | Total | Manufac. | |
|---|---|---|---|---|
| **Hombres** | | | | |
| 1950 (1) | 80.00 | 5.00 | .. | 15.00 |
| 1960 (1) | 76.00 | 5.50 | .. | 18.50 |
| 1970 (1) | 70.50 | 7.00 | .. | 22.50 |
| 1979 (2) | 66.61 | 7.83 | 4.61 | 25.56 |
| 1980 (1) | 65.50 | 8.50 | .. | 26.00 |
| **Mujeres** | | | | |
| 1950 (1) | 5.00 | 83.50 | .. | 11.50 |
| 1960 (1) | 4.50 | 83.75 | .. | 11.75 |
| 1970 (1) | 4.00 | 84.00 | .. | 12.00 |
| 1979 (2) | 3.53 | 84.44 | 83.60 | 12.03 |

Fuente(s): (1) EPPA3; (2) ASTER.

### 3.2 Método(s): interpolación y extrapolación lineares

#### 3.2.1 Hombres:

- 1950-80, tasas de distribución 1950-80 con base en EPPA3;
- 1990, extrapolación de las tasas de distribución 1950-80 con base en EPPA3;
modificación de las tendencias de todos los sectores;
- Aplicación de la razón manufacturas/industria con base en el censo de 1979.

#### 3.2.2 Mujeres:

- 1950-70, tasas de distribución de la agricultura 1950-70 con base en EPPA3;
ajuste de las tasas sur la base d'un de la razón hombres/mujeres igual a 2/3
en la agricultura;
- 1950-90, interpolación y extrapolación de las tasas ajustadas 1950-70
con base en EPPA3; modificación de las tendencias de todos los sectores;
las tasas de distribución estimadas de manufacturas con base en la razón
manufacturas/industria con base en el censo de 1979.

## 4. Proyección de las tasas de actividad: 2000 - 2010

### 4.1 Modelo(s): linear y hiperbólico

#### 4.1.1 Hombres:

- Para los grupos de edad [10-49], aplicación de la función F1;
- Para los grupos de edad [50+], aplicación de la función F3;
- Modificación de las tendencias de los grupos de edad [10-64].

#### 4.1.2 Mujeres:

- Para todos los grupos de edad, aplicación de la función F1;
- Modificación de las tendencias de todos los grupos de edad.

*Notas sobre los ajustes de las tasas, véase p. 380-384.*      *Notas sobre las funciones de proyección, véase p. 386.*

# Albania

## 1. Fuente(s) de los datos básicos

Código(s):   Título(s):

EPPA3   Estimaciones y proyecciones de la población económicamente activa, 1950-2025, tercera edición, OIT, Ginebra, 1986.
BLT-94-2   Popovic B. (1994), "Nuevas estimaciones de las tasas de actividad para 1980 y 1990, desglosadas por grupos de edad y distribución sectorial, en algunos países de Europa oriental y meridional" en el Boletín de Estadísticas del Trabajol - 1994-2, OIT, Ginebra.

## 2. Evaluación de las tasas de actividad: 1950 - 1990

### 2.1 Datos básicos:

Cuadro 1: Tasas de actividad por sexo y grupo de edad

| Grupo de edad | Año 1950 (1) | 1960 (1) | 1970 (1) | 1980 (2) | 1990 (2) |
|---|---|---|---|---|---|
| **Hombres** | | | | | |
| 10-14 | 13.00 | 8.00 | 5.65 | 3.80 | 2.20 |
| 15-19 | 84.15 | 72.15 | 63.35 | 55.44 | 51.71 |
| 20-24 | 97.25 | 93.25 | 90.35 | 88.06 | 87.32 |
| 25-29 | 97.45 | 95.20 | 94.50 | 94.27 | 94.02 |
| 30-34 | 98.80 | 98.60 | 97.85 | 97.57 | 97.52 |
| 35-39 | 99.40 | 99.20 | 98.45 | 98.17 | 98.12 |
| 40-44 | 99.50 | 99.30 | 98.55 | 98.37 | 98.12 |
| 45-49 | 98.60 | 97.50 | 96.40 | 95.77 | 95.42 |
| 50-54 | 98.45 | 97.35 | 96.30 | 95.57 | 94.82 |
| 55-59 | 96.65 | 90.65 | 86.65 | 83.66 | 81.92 |
| 60-64 | 96.10 | 90.10 | 86.15 | 83.16 | 77.72 |
| 65+ | 75.50 | 60.50 | 51.90 | 43.43 | 36.21 |
| **Mujeres** | | | | | |
| 10-14 | 12.25 | 7.15 | 4.00 | 3.37 | 1.60 |
| 15-19 | 62.15 | 46.95 | 40.25 | 31.06 | 28.73 |
| 20-24 | 75.15 | 67.75 | 65.40 | 68.16 | 70.63 |
| 25-29 | 77.45 | 69.75 | 68.40 | 74.91 | 78.01 |
| 30-34 | 79.00 | 71.15 | 69.80 | 75.70 | 78.81 |
| 35-39 | 81.90 | 73.75 | 72.35 | 77.49 | 80.60 |
| 40-44 | 83.85 | 75.50 | 74.10 | 77.99 | 80.70 |
| 45-49 | 75.75 | 68.60 | 69.40 | 71.54 | 73.62 |
| 50-54 | 74.35 | 67.30 | 68.15 | 67.47 | 68.53 |
| 55-59 | 54.30 | 45.25 | 44.85 | 29.96 | 26.93 |
| 60-64 | 52.85 | 44.05 | 43.65 | 19.65 | 16.56 |
| 65+ | 25.15 | 19.90 | 18.05 | 7.54 | 6.09 |

Fuente(s): (1) EPPA3; (2) BLT-94-2.

### 2.2 Método(s): con base en EPPA3 y BLT-94-2.

#### 2.2.1 Hombres:

- 1950-70, tasas de actividad 1950-70 con base en EPPA3;
- 1980-90, tasas de actividad con base en el Boletín de estadísticas del trabajo 1994-2.

#### 2.2.2 Mujeres:

Métodos, hipótesis y tratamientos idénticos a los que se aplican a los hombres.

## 3. Evaluación de las tasas de distribución por sector de actividad: 1950 - 1990

### 3.1 Datos básicos:

Cuadro 2: Distribución de la población económicamente activa por sector de actividad en %

| Año | Agricultura | Industria Total | Manufac. | Servicios |
|---|---|---|---|---|
| **Hombres** | | | | |
| 1950 (1) | 70.00 | 18.00 | .. | 12.00 |
| 1960 (1) | 63.70 | 23.00 | .. | 13.30 |
| 1970 (1) | 57.30 | 28.10 | .. | 14.50 |
| 1980 (2) | 54.00 | 27.67 | ... | 18.33 |
| 1990 (2) | 50.81 | 25.73 | ... | 23.46 |
| **Mujeres** | | | | |
| 1950 (1) | 85.50 | 8.00 | .. | 6.50 |
| 1960 (1) | 82.50 | 9.40 | .. | 8.00 |
| 1970 (1) | 79.30 | 10.90 | .. | 9.70 |
| 1980 (2) | 62.34 | 16.73 | ... | 20.93 |
| 1990 (2) | 60.19 | 19.35 | ... | 20.46 |

Fuente(s): (1) EPPA3; (2) BLT-94-2.

### 3.2 Método(s): datos de BLT-94-2

#### 3.2.1 Hombres:

- 1950-70, tasas de distribución 1950-70 con base en EPPA3;
- 1980-90, tasas de distribución con base en el boletín de estadísticas del trabajo 1994-2.

#### 3.2.2 Mujeres:

Métodos, hipótesis y tratamientos idénticos a los que se aplican a los hombres.

## 4. Proyección de las tasas de actividad: 2000 - 2010

### 4.1 Modelo(s): linear y hiperbólico

#### 4.1.1 Hombres:

- Para los grupos de edad [15-54], aplicación de la función F1;
- Para los grupos de edad [50+], aplicación de la función F3;
- Modificación de las tendencias de los grupos de edad [15-19] y [45-54].

#### 4.1.2 Mujeres:

- Para los grupos de edad [15-19] y [50+], aplicación de la función F3;
- Para los grupos de edad [20-49], aplicación de la función F1;
- Modificación de la tendencia del grupo de edad [15-19].

*Notas sobre los ajustes de las tasas, véase p.380-384.*   *Notas sobre las funciones de proyección, véase p. 386.*

# Alemania

## 1. Fuente(s) de los datos básicos

Código(s):  Título(s):

EPPA3   Anuario de estadísticas del trabajo 1945-89 - Edición retrospectiva sobre los censos de población, OIT, Ginebra, 1990.

STAT   Base de datos de la OIT sobre estadísticas del trabajo - LABORSTA, Oficina de Estadística, OIT, Ginebra.

## 2. Evaluación de las tasas de actividad: 1950 - 1990

### 2.1 Datos básicos:

Cuadro 1: Tasas de actividad por sexo y grupo de edad

| Grupo de edad | Año 1989 (1) | 1990 (1) | 1991 (1) | 1991 | 1992 (1) | 1992 |
|---|---|---|---|---|---|---|
| **Hombres** | | | | | | |
| 10-14 | 0.00 | 0.00 | 0.00 | 0.00 | 0.00 | 0.00 |
| 15-19 | 43.14 | 43.22 | 40.70 | 44.56 | 39.43 | 41.72 |
| 20-24 | 79.64 | 79.81 | 77.82 | 79.70 | 77.69 | 79.36 |
| 25-29 | 87.00 | 87.38 | 86.76 | 88.50 | 86.84 | 88.24 |
| 30-34 | 95.95 | 95.77 | 95.69 | 96.31 | 95.63 | 96.19 |
| 35-39 | 97.48 | 97.48 | 97.35 | 97.71 | 97.36 | 97.60 |
| 40-44 | 97.50 | 97.41 | 97.22 | 97.56 | 97.34 | 97.56 |
| 45-49 | 96.63 | 96.55 | 95.93 | 96.43 | 95.82 | 96.23 |
| 50-54 | 92.97 | 93.23 | 92.93 | 93.37 | 92.94 | 93.28 |
| 55-59 | 78.63 | 81.09 | 81.45 | 79.75 | 81.51 | 74.21 |
| 60-64 | 34.21 | 35.05 | 34.95 | 33.49 | 34.87 | 31.31 |
| 65+ | 4.50 | 5.25 | 5.13 | 4.54 | 4.91 | 4.36 |
| **Mujeres** | | | | | | |
| 10-14 | 0.00 | 0.00 | 0.00 | 0.00 | 0.00 | 0.00 |
| 15-19 | 38.36 | 37.29 | 34.84 | 37.20 | 34.29 | 36.01 |
| 20-24 | 74.08 | 75.65 | 73.42 | 75.86 | 72.55 | 74.58 |
| 25-29 | 69.26 | 71.58 | 70.77 | 75.57 | 72.47 | 76.56 |
| 30-34 | 62.86 | 66.90 | 66.46 | 72.79 | 67.68 | 73.59 |
| 35-39 | 64.40 | 68.03 | 68.76 | 75.07 | 70.22 | 75.93 |
| 40-44 | 64.81 | 69.46 | 70.52 | 75.35 | 72.59 | 77.12 |
| 45-49 | 61.82 | 66.71 | 67.12 | 72.79 | 68.70 | 73.77 |
| 50-54 | 54.38 | 57.82 | 58.59 | 65.32 | 60.80 | 66.75 |
| 55-59 | 40.89 | 43.82 | 44.36 | 42.84 | 45.51 | 41.70 |
| 60-64 | 11.18 | 12.49 | 12.20 | 10.70 | 11.91 | 9.99 |
| 65+ | 1.64 | 2.00 | 1.99 | 1.73 | 2.00 | 1.71 |

Nota(s): (1) Rep. Fed. de Alemania.
Fuente(s): STAT.

### 2.2 Método(s): promedio aritmético

#### 2.2.1 Hombres:

- 1950-80, tasas de actividad 1950-80 con base en EPPA3;
- 1990, aplicación a las tasas de actividad con base en las encuestas de 1989, 1990 y 1991 para la República Federal de Alemania, de las variaciones medias de las tasas de actividad para Alemania con base las encuestas en de 1991 y 1992, en relación con del promedio de las tasas de actividad para la República Federal de Alemania con base las encuestas en de 1991 y 1992.

#### 2.2.2 Mujeres:

Métodos, hipótesis y tratamientos idénticos a los que se aplican a los hombres.

## 3. Evaluación de las tasas de distribución por sector de actividad: 1950 - 1990

### 3.1 Datos básicos:

Cuadro 2: Distribución de la población económicamente activa por sector de actividad en %

| Año | Agricultura | Industria Total | Manufac. | Servicios |
|---|---|---|---|---|
| **Hombres** | | | | |
| 1989 (1) | 3.39 | 48.50 | 36.59 | 48.11 |
| 1990 (1) | 3.25 | 48.79 | 36.90 | 47.97 |
| 1991 (1) | 3.00 | 46.23 | 35.09 | 50.76 |
| 1991 (2) | 7.27 | 47.95 | 30.58 | 44.79 |
| 1992 (2) | 5.64 | 50.66 | 27.74 | 43.70 |
| 1992 (1) | 3.01 | 47.97 | 36.40 | 49.02 |
| **Mujeres** | | | | |
| 1989 (1) | 4.14 | 24.69 | 22.40 | 71.17 |
| 1990 (1) | 3.82 | 24.58 | 22.27 | 71.60 |
| 1991 (1) | 3.28 | 22.49 | 20.28 | 74.22 |
| 1991 (2) | 4.77 | 24.65 | 20.51 | 70.58 |
| 1992 (2) | 4.07 | 21.51 | 16.75 | 74.41 |
| 1992 (1) | 3.22 | 23.33 | 2.14 | 73.45 |

Notas(s): (1) Rep. Dem. de Alemania; (2) Rep. Fed. de Alemania.
Fuente(s): STAT.

### 3.2 Método(s): promedio aritmético

#### 3.2.1 Hombres:

- 1950-80, tasas de distribución 1950-80 con base en EPPA3;
- 1990, a los promedios de las tasas de distribución con base en las encuestas de 1989, 1990 y 1991 para la República Federal de Alemania, aplicación de las variaciones de los promedios de las tasas con base en las encuestas de 1991 y 1992 para Alemania, en relación con los promedios de las tasas con base en y 1992 para Alemania, en relación con los promedios dc las tasas con base en

#### 3.2.2 Mujeres:

Métodos, hipótesis y tratamientos idénticos a los que se aplican a los hombres.

## 4. Proyección de las tasas de actividad: 2000 - 2010

### 4.1 Modelo(s): linear, log-linear, hiperbólico y logístico

#### 4.1.1 Hombres:

- Para el grupo de edad [15-19], aplicación de la función F1;
- Para el grupo de edad [20-24], aplicación de la función F2;
- Para los grupos de edad [25+], aplicación de la función F3;
- Modificación de las tendencias de los grupos de edad [25-44] y [55+].

#### 4.1.2 Mujeres:

- Para el grupo de edad [15-19], aplicación de la función F1;
- Para el grupo de edad [20-24], aplicación de la función F2;
- Para los grupos de edad [25-54], aplicación de la función F6;
- Para los grupos de edad [55+], aplicación de la función F3;
- Modificación de las tendencias de los grupos de edad [15-24].

*Notas sobre los ajustes de las tasas, véase p.380-384.*

*Notas sobre las funciones de proyección, véase p. 386.*

# Angola

Código(s):  Título(s):

EPPA3  Estimaciones y proyecciones de la población económicamente activa, 1950-2025, tercera edición, OIT, Ginebra, 1986.
ADNU79  Annuaire démographique 1979 - Statistiques des recensements de population, trente et unième édition, Nations Unies, New York, 1980.

## 2. Evaluación de las tasas de actividad: 1950 - 1990

### 2.1 Datos básicos:

Cuadro 1: Tasas de actividad por sexo y grupo de edad

| Grupo de edad | Año 1950 (1) | 1960 (1) | 1970 (1) | 1970 (2) | 1980 (1) |
|---|---|---|---|---|---|
| **Hombres** | | | | | |
| 10-14 | 44.70 | 43.30 | 41.45 | 30.33 | 38.8 |
| 15-19 | 75.05 | 73.20 | 70.70 | 84.63 | 67.25 |
| 20-24 | 91.50 | 90.75 | 89.80 | 87.82 | 88.5 |
| 25-29 | 96.85 | 96.75 | 96.60 | 94.66 | 96.4 |
| 30-34 | 97.50 | 97.40 | 97.25 | 98.22 | 97 |
| 35-39 | 97.65 | 97.50 | 97.35 | 97.44 | 97.1 |
| 40-44 | 97.45 | 97.30 | 97.15 | 96.95 | 96.9 |
| 45-49 | 96.80 | 96.65 | 96.50 | 94.73 | 96.3 |
| 50-54 | 96.05 | 95.90 | 95.65 | 94.58 | 95.35 |
| 55-59 | 94.65 | 94.35 | 94.00 | 90.56 | 93.5 |
| 60-64 | 90.70 | 90.25 | 89.65 | 83.95 | 88.8 |
| 65+ | 75.70 | 74.90 | 73.80 | 73.41 | 72.3 |
| **Mujeres** | | | | | |
| 10-14 | 33.80 | 32.70 | 31.30 | 28.7 | 29.35 |
| 15-19 | 55.60 | 54.00 | 51.90 | 72.05 | 48.95 |
| 20-24 | 58.85 | 57.85 | 56.55 | 76.25 | 54.7 |
| 25-29 | 63.10 | 61.95 | 60.45 | 79.45 | 58.35 |
| 30-34 | 67.05 | 65.80 | 64.20 | 78.03 | 61.95 |
| 35-39 | 68.70 | 67.55 | 66.05 | 81.74 | 63.95 |
| 40-44 | 71.15 | 70.00 | 68.50 | 84.2 | 66.4 |
| 45-49 | 70.55 | 69.40 | 67.85 | 84.8 | 65.7 |
| 50-54 | 68.15 | 66.80 | 65.05 | 82.23 | 62.5 |
| 55-59 | 65.10 | 63.65 | 61.80 | 78.47 | 59.2 |
| 60-64 | 57.05 | 55.25 | 52.90 | 69.15 | 49.55 |
| 65+ | 37.65 | 35.95 | 33.75 | 42.14 | 30.65 |

Fuente(s): (1) EPPA3; (2) ADNU79.

### 2.2 Método(s): interpolación y extrapolación lineares

#### 2.2.1 Hombres:

- 1950-90, interpolación y extrapolación de las tasas de actividad 1950-80 con base en EPPA3;
ajuste de las tasas interpoladas y extrapoladas con base en las variaciones de las tasas interpoladas 1970, en relación con las tasas de actividad con base en el censo 1970;
modificación de las tendencias de los grupos de edad [10-24] para 1950 y 1960 y de todos los grupos de edad para 1980 y 1990.

#### 2.2.2 Mujeres:

- 1950-90, interpolación y extrapolación de las tasas de actividad 1950-80 con base en EPPA3;
ajuste de las tasas interpoladas y extrapoladas con base en las variaciones de las tasas interpoladas 1970, en relación con las tasas de actividad con base en el censo de 1970;
modificación de las tendencias de los grupos de edad [15+] para 1950 y 1960 y de todos los grupos de edad para 1980 y 1990.

## 3. Evaluación de las tasas de distribución por sector de actividad: 1950 - 1990

### 3.1 Datos básicos:

Cuadro 2: Distribución de la población económicamente activa por sector de actividad en %

| Año | Agricultura | Industria Total | Manufac. | Servicios |
|---|---|---|---|---|
| **Hombres** | | | | |
| 1950 (1) | 74.00 | 11.35 | .. | 14.65 |
| 1960 (1) | 71.40 | 12.50 | .. | 16.10 |
| 1970 (1) | 68.00 | 13.50 | .. | 18.50 |
| 1970 (2) | 68.52 | 12.66 | 6.19 | 18.82 |
| 1980 (1) | 63.20 | 15.00 | .. | 21.80 |
| **Mujeres** | | | | |
| 1950 (1) | 94.60 | 0.80 | .. | 4.60 |
| 1960 (1) | 93.30 | 1.00 | .. | 5.70 |
| 1970 (1) | 91.60 | 1.25 | .. | 7.15 |
| 1970 (2) | 88.93 | 1.10 | 1.01 | 9.97 |
| 1980 (1) | 89.20 | 1.60 | .. | 9.20 |

Fuente(s): (1) EPPA3; (2) ADNU79.

### 3.2 Método(s): interpolación y extrapolación lineares

#### 3.2.1 Hombres:

- 1950-90, interpolación y extrapolación de las tasas de distribución 1950-80 con base en EPPA3;
ajuste de las tasas con base en las variaciones de las tasas interpoladas 1970, en relación con las tasas con base en el censo de 1970;
modificación de las tendencias de todos los sectores para 1980 y 1990;
modificación de las tendencias de todos los sectores para 1980 y 1990;

#### 3.2.2 Mujeres:

Métodos, hipótesis y tratamientos idénticos a los que se aplican a los hombres.

## 4. Proyección de las tasas de actividad: 2000 - 2010

### 4.1 Modelo(s): hiperbólico

#### 4.1.1 Hombres:

- Para todos los grupos de edad, aplicación de la función F3.

#### 4.1.2 Mujeres:

- Para todos los grupos de edad, aplicación de la función F3;
- Modificación de las tendencias de los grupos de edad [20-54].

---

# Antillas Neerlandesas

## 1. Fuente(s) de los datos básicos

Código(s):  Título(s):
STAT        Base de datos de la OIT sobre estadísticas del trabajo - LABORSTA, Oficina de Estadística, OIT, Ginebra.

## 2. Evaluación de las tasas de actividad: 1950 - 1990

### 2.1 Datos básicos:

Cuadro 1: Tasas de actividad por sexo y grupo de edad

| Grupo de edad | Año 1972 | 1981 | 1992 |
|---|---|---|---|
| **Hombres** | | | |
| 10-14 | .. | 0.32 | 0.00 |
| 15-19 | .. | 34.10 | 29.76 |
| 20-24 | .. | 85.33 | 80.75 |
| 25-29 | .. | 94.93 | 91.46 |
| 30-34 | .. | 95.79 | 92.59 |
| 35-39 | .. | 96.01 | 93.10 |
| 40-44 | .. | 95.70 | 93.09 |
| 45-49 | .. | 94.83 | 91.54 |
| 50-54 | .. | 89.94 | 86.40 |
| 55-59 | .. | 80.46 | 67.78 |
| 60-64 | .. | 48.37 | 34.32 |
| 65+ | .. | 20.16 | 13.62 |
| **Mujeres** | | | |
| 10-14 | 0.41 | 0.16 | 0.00 |
| 15-19 | 32.11 | 26.20 | 22.00 |
| 20-24 | 66.83 | 73.42 | 70.68 |
| 25-29 | 51.57 | 70.36 | 77.50 |
| 30-34 | 41.25 | 61.34 | 75.90 |
| 35-39 | 35.99 | 53.90 | 73.43 |
| 40-44 | 31.81 | 44.71 | 68.37 |
| 45-49 | 28.51 | 37.66 | 57.96 |
| 50-54 | 24.67 | 29.73 | 43.84 |
| 55-59 | 22.86 | 22.00 | 29.78 |
| 60-64 | 13.54 | 12.73 | 14.31 |
| 65+ | 5.41 | 4.12 | 3.59 |

Fuente(s): STAT.

### 2.2 Método(s): interpolación y extrapolación lineares

#### 2.2.1 Hombres:
- 1950-80, extrapolación de las tasas de actividad ajustadas con base en los censos de 1981 y 1992;
modificación de las tendencias del grupo de edad [50-54];
- 1990, interpolación de las tasas de actividad ajustadas con base en los censos de 1981 y 1992.

#### 2.2.2 Mujeres:
- 1950-70, extrapolación de las tasas de actividad ajustadas con base en los censos de 1972 y 1981;
modificación de las tendencias de todos los grupos de edad;
- 1980, interpolación de las tasas de actividad ajustadas con base en los censos de 1972 y 1981;
modificación de la tendencia del grupo de edad [50-54];
- 1990, interpolación de las tasas de actividad con base en los censos

## 3. Evaluación de las tasas de distribución por sector de actividad: 1950 - 1990

### 3.1 Datos básicos:

Cuadro 2: Distribución de la población económicamente activa por sector de actividad en %

| Año | Agricultura | Industria Total | Manufac. | Servicios |
|---|---|---|---|---|
| **Hombres** | | | | |
| 1960 | 2.83 | 56.86 | 40.51 | 40.31 |
| 1972 | 1.34 | 37.42 | 20.28 | 61.24 |
| 1981 | 0.55 | 30.54 | 14.38 | 68.91 |
| 1992 | 1.07 | 31.37 | 13.57 | 67.56 |
| **Mujeres** | | | | |
| 1960 | 0.21 | 8.09 | 7.32 | 91.70 |
| 1972 | 0.20 | 13.34 | 11.68 | 86.46 |
| 1981 | 0.13 | 5.83 | 3.66 | 94.04 |
| 1992 | 0.28 | 5.20 | 3.76 | 94.52 |

Fuente(s): STAT

### 3.2 Método(s): interpolación y extrapolación lineares

#### 3.2.1 Hombres:
- 1950, extrapolación de las tasas de distribución con base en los censos de 1960 y 1972;
- 1970-90, interpolación de las tasas de distribución con base en los censos de 1960, 1972, 1981 y 1992.

#### 3.2.2 Mujeres:
Métodos, hipótesis y tratamientos idénticos a los que se aplican a los hombres.

## 4. Proyección de las tasas de actividad: 2000 - 2010

### 4.1 Modelo(s): linear, hiperbólico y logístico

#### 4.1.1 Hombres:
- Para los grupos de edad [10-19], aplicación de la función F1;
- Para los grupos de edad [20+], aplicación de la función F3;
- Modificación de las tendencias de todos los grupos de edad.

#### 4.1.2 Mujeres:
- Para el grupo de edad [15-19], aplicación de la función F1;
- Para los grupos de edad [20-64], aplicación de la función F6;
- Para el grupo de edad [65+], aplicación de la función F3;
- Modificación de las tendencias de todos los grupos de edad.

*Notas sobre los ajustes de las tasas, véase p.380-384.*     *Notas sobre las funciones de proyección, véase p. 386.*

# Arabia Saudita

## 1. Fuente(s) de los datos básicos

Código(s):  Título(s):

EPPA3    Estimaciones y proyecciones de la población económicamente activa, 1950-2025, tercera edición, OIT, Ginebra, 1986.

## 2. Evaluación de las tasas de actividad: 1950 - 1990

### 2.1 Datos básicos:

Cuadro 1: Tasas de actividad por sexo y grupo de edad

| Grupo de edad | Año 1975 (1) | 1980 (2) | 1987 (3) | 1988 (3) |
|---|---|---|---|---|
| **Hombres** | | | | |
| 10-14 | 22.00 | 19.30 | 16.20 | 8.10 |
| 15-19 | 86.75 | 81.85 | 69.30 | 49.30 |
| 20-24 | 95.40 | 94.50 | 91.30 | 86.65 |
| 25-29 | 98.00 | 97.80 | 97.30 | 96.55 |
| 30-34 | 98.40 | 98.35 | 98.20 | 98.00 |
| 35-39 | 97.25 | 97.40 | 97.65 | 98.10 |
| 40-44 | 96.80 | 96.85 | 97.00 | 97.20 |
| 45-49 | 96.40 | 96.30 | 96.00 | 97.55 |
| 50-54 | 93.60 | 93.35 | 92.80 | 91.90 |
| 55-59 | 90.35 | 89.90 | 88.50 | 86.40 |
| 60-64 | 81.75 | 80.85 | 78.50 | 74.75 |
| 65+ | 56.15 | 55.30 | 53.05 | 49.50 |
| **Mujeres** | | | | |
| 10-14 | .. | .. | .. | .. |
| 15-19 | .. | .. | .. | .. |
| 20-24 | .. | .. | .. | .. |
| 25-29 | .. | .. | .. | .. |
| 30-34 | .. | .. | .. | .. |
| 35-39 | .. | .. | .. | .. |
| 40-44 | .. | .. | .. | .. |
| 45-49 | .. | .. | .. | .. |
| 50-54 | .. | .. | .. | .. |
| 55-59 | .. | .. | .. | .. |
| 60-64 | .. | .. | .. | .. |
| 65+ | .. | .. | .. | .. |

Fuente(s): EPPA3.

### 2.2 Método(s): extrapolación linear

**2.2.1 Hombres:**

- 1950-80, tasas de actividad 1950-80 con base en EPPA3;
- 1990, extrapolación de las tasas de actividad 1950-80 con base en EPPA3;
ajuste de las tasas extrapoladas con base en las variaciones de las tasas
interpoladas 1980, en relación con las tasas 1980 con base en EPPA3;
modificación de las tendencias de los grupos de edad [10-14], [25-54] y [60+].

**2.2.2 Mujeres:**

- 1950-70, tasas de actividad 1950-70 con base en EPPA3;
- 1980-90, aplicación a las tasas de actividad 1970 con base en EPPA3,
del promedio de las variaciones de las tasas de actividad estimadas para 1980
y 1990 para Bahrein, Kuwait y Omán, en relación con las tasas de actividad
para estos países.

## 3. Evaluación de las tasas de distribución por sector de actividad: 1950 - 1990

### 3.1 Datos básicos:

Cuadro 2: Distribución de la población económicamente activa por sector de actividad en %

| Año | Agricultura | Industria Total | Manufac. | Servicios |
|---|---|---|---|---|
| **Hombres** | | | | |
| 1950 | 76.00 | 9.00 | .. | 15.00 |
| 1960 | 71.00 | 10.00 | .. | 19.00 |
| 1970 | 65.00 | 12.50 | .. | 22.50 |
| 1980 | 45.00 | 16.50 | 5.33 | 38.50 |
| **Mujeres** | | | | |
| 1950 | 87.00 | 2.80 | .. | 10.20 |
| 1960 | 76.00 | 3.60 | .. | 20.40 |
| 1970 | 48.60 | 4.40 | .. | 47.00 |
| 1980 | 25.00 | 5.00 | 2.82 | 70.00 |

Fuente(s): EPPA3.

### 3.2 Método(s): extrapolación linear

**3.2.1 Hombres:**

- 1950-80, tasas de distribución 1950-80 con base en EPPA3;
- 1990, extrapolación de las tasas de distribución 1950-80 con base en EPPA3;
modificación de las tendencias de todos los sectores.

**3.2.2 Mujeres:**

Métodos, hipótesis y tratamientos idénticos a los que se aplican a los hombres.

## 4. Proyección de las tasas de actividad: 2000 - 2010

### 4.1 Modelo(s): linear, log-linear, hiperbólico y logístico

**4.1.1 Hombres:**

- Para el grupo de edad [15-19], aplicación de la función F2;
- Para los grupos de edad [20-59], aplicación de la función F3;
- Para los grupos de edad [60+], aplicación de la función F1;
- Modificación de las tendencias de los grupos de edad [20-24] y [35-54].

**4.1.2 Mujeres:**

- Para los grupos de edad [15-24], aplicación de la función F2;
- Para los grupos de edad [25-39], aplicación de la función F6;
- Para los grupos de edad [40-64], aplicación de la función F2;
- Para el grupo de edad [65+], aplicación de la función F1;
- Modificación de la tendencia del grupo de edad [15-19].

# Argelia

## 1. Fuente(s) de los datos básicos

Código(s): Título(s):

EPPA3 Estimaciones y proyecciones de la población económicamente activa, 1950-2025, tercera edición, OIT, Ginebra, 1986.
R1977 Recensement général de la population et de l'habitat 1977, Office National des Statistiques, Alger, 1979.
R1987 Recensement général de la population et de l'habitat 1987 - Données synthétiques, Office National des Statistiques, Alger, 1989.

## 2. Evaluación de las tasas de actividad: 1950 - 1990

### 2.1 Datos básicos:

Cuadro 1: Tasas de actividad por sexo y grupo de edad

| Grupo de edad | Año 1950 (1) | 1960 (1) | 1970 (1) | 1987 (2) |
|---|---|---|---|---|
| **Hombres** | | | | |
| 10-14 | 28.85 | 20.00 | 13.85 | 0.48 |
| 15-19 | 74.95 | 60.90 | 46.85 | 39.20 |
| 20-24 | 94.75 | 91.75 | 88.80 | 84.44 |
| 25-29 | 97.85 | 96.80 | 95.80 | 95.67 |
| 30-34 | 97.55 | 97.05 | 96.55 | 97.39 |
| 35-39 | 97.10 | 96.80 | 96.45 | 97.70 |
| 40-44 | 96.85 | 96.25 | 95.60 | 96.65 |
| 45-49 | 96.45 | 95.80 | 95.15 | 95.15 |
| 50-54 | 95.15 | 94.40 | 93.65 | 91.99 |
| 55-59 | 93.95 | 90.85 | 87.75 | 86.83 |
| 60-64 | 92.50 | 85.90 | 79.30 | 59.07 |
| 65+ | 76.65 | 60.00 | 43.40 | 25.52 |
| **Mujeres** | | | | |
| 10-14 | .. | .. | 1.25 | 0.08 |
| 15-19 | .. | .. | 4.05 | 3.88 |
| 20-24 | .. | .. | 5.70 | 12.94 |
| 25-29 | .. | .. | 4.95 | 12.92 |
| 30-34 | .. | .. | 4.35 | 8.92 |
| 35-39 | .. | .. | 3.90 | 7.85 |
| 40-44 | .. | .. | 4.45 | 6.78 |
| 45-49 | .. | .. | 5.10 | 6.79 |
| 50-54 | .. | .. | 5.50 | 5.56 |
| 55-59 | .. | .. | 5.30 | 5.12 |
| 60-64 | .. | .. | 3.75 | 3.54 |
| 65+ | .. | .. | 1.85 | 1.71 |

Fuente(s): (1) EPPA3; (2) R1987.

### 2.2 Método(s): interpolación y extrapolación lineares

#### 2.2.1 Hombres:

- 1950-90, interpolación y extrapolación de las tasas de actividad 1950-70 con base en EPPA3 y de las tasas de actividad ajustadas con base el censo de 1987;
modificación de las tendencias de todos los grupos de edad para 1990.

#### 2.2.2 Mujeres:

- 1950-70, tasas de actividad ajustadas 1950-70 con base en EPPA3;
- 1980-90, interpolación y extrapolación de las tasas de actividad 1970 con base en EPPA3 y de las tasas de actividad ajustadas con base en el censo de 1987;
modificación de las tendencias de los grupos de edad [20+] para 1990;
el ajuste se ha calculado con base en el modelo de ajuste de las tasas de actividad de las mujeres ocupadas en la agricultura como auxiliares familiares.

## 3. Evaluación de las tasas de distribución por sector de actividad: 1950 - 1990

### 3.1 Datos básicos:

Cuadro 2: Distribución de la población económicamente activa por sector de actividad en %

| Año | Agricultura | Industria Total | Manufac. | Servicios |
|---|---|---|---|---|
| **Hombres** | | | | |
| 1977 (1) | 32.88 | 33.14 | 11.84 | 33.98 |
| 1987 (2) | 19.54 | 35.68 | 12.76 | 44.78 |
| **Mujeres** | | | | |
| 1977 (1) | 5.09 | 19.39 | 14.21 | 75.52 |
| 1987 (2) | 2.95 | 17.04 | 11.97 | 80.01 |

Fuente(s): (1) R1977; (2) R1987.

### 3.2 Método(s): interpolación y extrapolación lineares

#### 3.2.1 Hombres:

- 1950-70, tasas de distribución 1950-70 con base en EPPA3;
- 1980-90, interpolación y extrapolación de las tasas de distribución con base en los censos de 1977 y 1987;
modificación de las tendencias de todos los sectores para 1990.

#### 3.2.2 Mujeres:

- 1980-90, promedios ponderados de las tasas de distribución ajustadas con base en los censos de 1977 y 1987;
ajuste de las tasas para tener en cuenta a los auxiliares familiares en la agricultura
- 1950-70, interpolación de la diferencia de las tasas de distribución ajustadas y no ajustadas para 1980 y 1990; los resultados obtenidos se han agregado a las tasas de distribución 1950-1970 con base en EPPA3.

## 4. Proyección de las tasas de actividad: 2000 - 2010

### 4.1 Modelo(s): linear y hiperbólico

#### 4.1.1 Hombres:

- Para todos los grupos de edad, aplicación de la función F1;
- Modificación de la tendencia del grupo de edad [20-24].

#### 4.1.2 Mujeres:

- Para los grupos de edad [10-19] y [60+], aplicación de la función F1;
- Para los grupos de edad [20-59], aplicación de la función F6;
- Modificación de las tendencias de los grupos de edad [25-29] y [50-59].

*Notas sobre los ajustes de las tasas, véase p.380-384.*

*Notas sobre las funciones de proyección, véase p. 386.*

# Argentina

## 1. Fuente(s) de los datos básicos

Código(s):   Título(s):

EPPA3     Estimaciones y proyecciones de la población económicamente activa, 1950-2025, tercera edición, OIT, Ginebra, 1986.
STAT      Base de datos de la OIT sobre estadísticas del trabajo - LABORSTA, Oficina de Estadística, OIT, Ginebra.

## 2. Evaluación de las tasas de actividad: 1950 - 1990

### 2.1 Datos básicos:

Cuadro 1: Tasas de actividad por sexo y grupo de edad

| Grupo de edad | 1970 (1) | 1990 (2) |
|---|---|---|
| **Hombres** | | |
| 10-14 | 11.50 | 8.84 |
| 15-19 | 62.20 | 57.54 |
| 20-24 | 87.00 | 86.26 |
| 25-29 | 95.80 | 95.66 |
| 30-34 | 97.50 | 97.77 |
| 35-39 | 98.10 | 97.98 |
| 40-44 | 97.40 | 97.14 |
| 45-49 | 95.40 | 95.04 |
| 50-54 | 91.40 | 90.60 |
| 55-59 | 80.40 | 79.39 |
| 60-64 | 57.20 | 56.07 |
| 65+ | 29.10 | 23.48 |
| **Mujeres** | | |
| 10-14 | 6.20 | 4.41 |
| 15-19 | 31.60 | 24.46 |
| 20-24 | 43.60 | 51.21 |
| 25-29 | 36.00 | 45.09 |
| 30-34 | 31.70 | 40.65 |
| 35-39 | 29.20 | 36.90 |
| 40-44 | 27.20 | 34.89 |
| 45-49 | 25.20 | 31.70 |
| 50-54 | 22.10 | 26.85 |
| 55-59 | 16.40 | 18.41 |
| 60-64 | 10.50 | 9.90 |
| 65+ | 4.70 | 2.89 |

Fuente(s): (1) EPPA3; (2) STAT.

### 2.2 Método(s): promedio aritmético

#### 2.2.1 Hombres:

- 1950-70, tasas de actividad 1950-70 con base en EPPA3;
- 1980, promedios de las tasas de actividad 1970 con base en EPPA3
and de las tasas de actividad con base en estimaciones oficiales de 1990;
- 1990, tasas de actividad con base en estimaciones oficiales 1990.

#### 2.2.2 Mujeres:

Métodos, hipótesis y tratamientos idénticos a los que se aplican a los hombres.

## 3. Evaluación de las tasas de distribución por sector de actividad: 1950 - 1990

### 3.1 Datos básicos:

Cuadro 2: Distribución de la población económicamente activa por sector de actividad en %

| Año | Agricultura | Industria Total | Manufac. | Servicios |
|---|---|---|---|---|
| **Hombres** | | | | |
| 1950 | 23.86 | 38.43 | 28.11 | 37.72 |
| 1970 | 20.24 | 35.67 | 22.11 | 44.09 |
| 1980 | 16.63 | 39.62 | 23.04 | 43.75 |
| **Mujeres** | | | | |
| 1950 | 5.16 | 27.02 | 26.37 | 67.81 |
| 1970 | 4.22 | 20.81 | 19.86 | 74.97 |
| 1980 | 3.06 | 18.22 | 16.91 | 78.72 |

Fuente(s): STAT.

### 3.2 Método(s): extrapolación linear

#### 3.2.1 Hombres:

- 1950-70, tasas de distribución 1950-70 con base en EPPA3;
- 1980-90, extrapolación de las tasas de distribución con base en los censos de 1960, 1970 y 1980;
modificación de las tendencias de todos los sectores;
- Aplicación de la razón manufacturas/industria con base en el censo de 1980.
- Aplicación de la razón manufacturas/industria con base en el censo de 1980.

#### 3.2.2 Mujeres:

Métodos, hipótesis y tratamientos idénticos a los que se aplican a los hombres.

## 4. Proyección de las tasas de actividad: 2000 - 2010

### 4.1 Modelo(s): linear y hiperbólico

#### 4.1.1 Hombres:

- Para los grupos de edad [10-44], aplicación de la función F1;
- Para los grupos de edad [45+], aplicación de la función F3;
- Modificación de la tendencia del grupo de edad [10-14].

#### 4.1.2 Mujeres:

- Para el grupo de edad [10-14], aplicación de la función F1;
- Para los grupos de edad [15+], aplicación de la función F3;
- Modificación de las tendencias de los grupos de edad [10-14], [20-24] y [60-64].

# Armenia

## 1. Fuente(s) de los datos básicos

Código(s):   Título(s):

BLT-94-2   Vorobiev A. (1994), "Estimaciones de la población económicamente activa de los quince países de la ex URSS, en 1950, 1959, 1970, 1979 y 1989", en el Boletín de Estadísticas del Trabajol - 1994-2, OIT, Ginebra.

## 2. Evaluación de las tasas de actividad: 1950 - 1990

### 2.1 Datos básicos:

Cuadro 1: Tasas de actividad por sexo y grupo de edad

| Grupo de edad | Año | | | | |
|---|---|---|---|---|---|
| | 1950 | 1959 | 1970 | 1979 | 1989 |
| **Hombres** | | | | | |
| 10-14 | 0.00 | 0.00 | 0.00 | 0.00 | 0.00 |
| 15-19 | 42.35 | 50.75 | 30.53 | 33.33 | 25.69 |
| 20-24 | 79.01 | 80.68 | 70.73 | 77.64 | 60.87 |
| 25-29 | 90.91 | 93.83 | 98.33 | 95.69 | 77.64 |
| 30-34 | 91.67 | 94.81 | 98.02 | 98.63 | 80.42 |
| 35-39 | 93.75 | 96.77 | 97.59 | 98.63 | 81.90 |
| 40-44 | 93.55 | 95.65 | 96.43 | 97.94 | 79.69 |
| 45-49 | 91.30 | 93.33 | 97.44 | 96.51 | 78.79 |
| 50-54 | 90.48 | 89.66 | 90.48 | 94.74 | 77.38 |
| 55-59 | 92.86 | 86.36 | 86.21 | 86.21 | 70.67 |
| 60-64 | 76.92 | 83.33 | 60.71 | 50.00 | 45.16 |
| 65+ | 36.67 | 33.33 | 16.07 | 16.90 | 19.05 |
| **Mujeres** | | | | | |
| 10-14 | 0.00 | 0.00 | 0.00 | 0.00 | 0.00 |
| 15-19 | 41.57 | 44.12 | 28.00 | 32.98 | 17.91 |
| 20-24 | 58.82 | 60.00 | 63.22 | 73.10 | 50.35 |
| 25-29 | 61.36 | 65.12 | 80.60 | 86.18 | 62.50 |
| 30-34 | 55.56 | 59.26 | 82.24 | 88.31 | 68.46 |
| 35-39 | 58.50 | 59.52 | 83.13 | 91.25 | 72.32 |
| 40-44 | 57.89 | 58.82 | 83.53 | 92.08 | 72.06 |
| 45-49 | 56.76 | 55.00 | 81.25 | 91.76 | 70.42 |
| 50-54 | 40.00 | 41.67 | 64.52 | 79.52 | 62.22 |
| 55-59 | 30.00 | 28.57 | 28.89 | 41.86 | 36.25 |
| 60-64 | 26.32 | 25.00 | 12.20 | 16.22 | 21.62 |
| 65+ | 2.33 | 3.45 | 3.66 | 3.64 | 6.48 |

Fuente(s): BLT-94-2-2

### 2.2 Método(s): promedio ponderado

#### 2.2.1 Hombres:

- 1950-90, promedios ponderados de las tasas de actividad 1950, 1959, 1975 y 1989 con base en el Boletín de estadísticas del trabajo 1994-2.

#### 2.2.2 Mujeres:

Métodos, hipótesis y tratamientos idénticos a los que se aplican a los hombres.

## 3. Evaluación de las tasas de distribución por sector de actividad: 1950 - 1990

### 3.1 Datos básicos:

Cuadro 2: Distribución de la población económicamente activa por sector de actividad en %

| Año | Agricultura | Industria | | Servicios |
|---|---|---|---|---|
| | | Total | Manufac. | |
| **Hombres** | | | | |
| 1950 | 52.63 | 24.91 | 16.84 | 22.46 |
| 1959 | 39.71 | 29.90 | 17.65 | 30.39 |
| 1970 | 25.24 | 43.26 | 26.57 | 31.50 |
| 1979 | 20.92 | 47.77 | 25.78 | 31.31 |
| 1989 | 23.41 | 47.11 | 30.20 | 29.48 |
| **Mujeres** | | | | |
| 1950 | 37.03 | 9.46 | 7.30 | 53.51 |
| 1959 | 59.55 | 21.35 | 18.35 | 19.10 |
| 1970 | 30.02 | 30.91 | 26.71 | 39.07 |
| 1979 | 22.64 | 37.68 | 25.79 | 39.68 |
| 1989 | 12.26 | 38.51 | 34.20 | 49.22 |

Fuente(s): BLT-94-2.

### 3.2 Método(s): promedio ponderado

#### 3.2.1 Hombres:

- 1950-90, promedios ponderados de las tasas de distribución 1950, 1959, 1970, 1979 y 1989 con base en el Boletín de estadísticas del trabajo 1994-2.

#### 3.2.2 Mujeres:

Métodos, hipótesis y tratamientos idénticos a los que se aplican a los hombres.

## 4. Proyección de las tasas de actividad: 2000 - 2010

### 4.1 Modelo(s): hiperbólico y logístico

#### 4.1.1 Hombres:

- Para los grupos de edad [15+], aplicación de la función F3;
- Modificación de las tendencias de los grupos de edad [25-54].

#### 4.1.2 Mujeres:

- Para los grupos de edad [15-24], aplicación de la función F3;
- Para los grupos de edad [25-59], aplicación de la función F6;
- Para los grupos de edad [60+], aplicación de la función F3;
- Modificación de las tendencias de los grupos de edad [20-59].

*Notas sobre los ajustes de las tasas, véase p.380-384.*

*Notas sobre las funciones de proyección, véase p. 386.*

# Australia

## 1. Fuente(s) de los datos básicos

Código(s):  Título(s):

EPPA3  Anuario de estadísticas del trabajo 1945-89 - Edición retrospectiva sobre los censos de población, OIT, Ginebra, 1990.

STAT  Base de datos de la OIT sobre estadísticas del trabajo - LABORSTA, Oficina de Estadística, OIT, Ginebra.

## 2. Evaluación de las tasas de actividad: 1950 - 1990

### 2.1 Datos básicos:

Cuadro 1: Tasas de actividad por sexo y grupo de edad

| Grupo de edad | Año | | | | | |
|---|---|---|---|---|---|---|
| | 1979 | 1980 | 1981 | 1989 | 1990 | 1991 |
| **Hombres** | | | | | | |
| 10-14 | 0.00 | 0.00 | 0.00 | 0.00 | 0.00 | 0.00 |
| 15-19 | 64.10 | 65.30 | 66.00 | 61.90 | 61.40 | 57.10 |
| 20-24 | 90.90 | 91.50 | 91.60 | 89.90 | 89.80 | 88.40 |
| 25-34 | 96.20 | 95.90 | 95.50 | 94.60 | 94.40 | 94.50 |
| 35-44 | 95.90 | 95.60 | 95.50 | 93.80 | 94.40 | 94.10 |
| 45-54 | 91.60 | 91.50 | 90.90 | 89.10 | 89.90 | 89.60 |
| 55-59 | 82.10 | 82.60 | 81.20 | 75.20 | 75.00 | 73.70 |
| 60-64 | 54.40 | 51.50 | 50.50 | 49.80 | 50.60 | 49.90 |
| 65+ | 11.60 | 11.20 | 10.70 | 9.10 | 9.20 | 8.90 |
| **Mujeres** | | | | | | |
| 10-14 | .. | 0.00 | .. | .. | 0.00 | .. |
| 15-19 | .. | 61.50 | .. | .. | 59.30 | .. |
| 20-24 | .. | 71.00 | .. | .. | 78.60 | .. |
| 25-34 | .. | 52.40 | .. | .. | 65.70 | .. |
| 35-44 | .. | 58.20 | .. | .. | 72.00 | .. |
| 45-54 | .. | 47.70 | .. | .. | 61.00 | .. |
| 55-59 | .. | 28.90 | .. | .. | 33.90 | .. |
| 60-64 | .. | 13.40 | .. | .. | 16.00 | .. |
| 65+ | .. | 2.80 | .. | .. | 2.40 | .. |

Fuente(s): STAT.

### 2.2 Método(s):  promedio aritmético

**2.2.1 Hombres:**

- 1950-70, tasas de actividad 1950-70 con base en EPPA3;
ajuste de las tasas de actividad del grupo de edad [15-19] para 1960 y 1970;
- 1980, promedios de las tasas de actividad ajustadas con base en las encuestas de 1979, 1980 y 1981;
- 1990, promedios de las tasas de actividad ajustadas con base en las encuestas de 1989, 1990 y 1991.

**2.2.2 Mujeres:**

- 1950-70, tasas de actividad 1950-70 con base en EPPA3;
ajuste de las tasas de actividad del grupo de edad [15-19];
- 1980 y 1990, promedios de las tasas de actividad ajustadas con base en las encuestas de 1980 y 1990.

## 3. Evaluación de las tasas de distribución por sector de actividad: 1950 - 1990

### 3.1 Datos básicos:

Cuadro 2: Distribución de la población económicamente activa por sector de actividad en %

| Año | Agricultura | Industria | | Servicios |
|---|---|---|---|---|
| | | Total | Manufac. | |
| **Hombres** | | | | |
| 1989 (1) | 7.00 | 35.40 | 20.48 | 57.61 |
| 1990 (1) | 6.39 | 35.65 | 19.72 | 57.95 |
| 1991 (1) | 6.68 | 34.78 | 19.57 | 58.55 |
| **Mujeres** | | | | |
| 1970 (2) | 4.55 | 22.45 | .. | 73.00 |
| 1981 (1) | 3.83 | 17.06 | 14.77 | 79.11 |
| 1989 (1) | 4.16 | 13.77 | 10.87 | 82.07 |
| 1990 (1) | 3.63 | 14.00 | 10.95 | 82.36 |
| 1991 (1) | 3.76 | 13.10 | 10.11 | 83.14 |

Fuente(s): (1) STAT; (2) EPPA3.

### 3.2 Método(s):  promedio aritmético
promedio ponderado

**3.2.1 Hombres:**

- 1950-80, tasas de distribución 1950-80 con base en EPPA3;
- 1990, promedios de las tasas de distribución con base en las encuestas de 1989, 1990 y 1991.

**3.2.2 Mujeres:**

- 1950-70, tasas de distribución 1950-70 con base en EPPA3;
- 1980, promedios ponderados de las tasas de distribución 1970 con base en EPPA3 y de las tasas de distribución con base en el censo de 1981;
- 1990, promedios de las tasas de distribución con base en las encuestas de 1989, 1990 y 1991.

## 4. Proyección de las tasas de actividad: 2000 - 2010

### 4.1 Modelo(s):  linear, hiperbólico y logístico

**4.1.1 Hombres:**

- Para los grupos de edad [15-24], aplicación de la función F1;
- Para los grupos de edad [25+], aplicación de la función F3;
- Modificación de las tendencias de los grupos de edad [25-59].

**4.1.2 Mujeres:**

- Para los grupos de edad [15-24], aplicación de la función F1;
- Para los grupos de edad [25-59], aplicación de la función F6;
- Para los grupos de edad [60+], aplicación de la función F3;
- Modificación de las tendencias de los grupos de edad [15-59].

*Notas sobre los ajustes de las tasas, véase p.380-384.*  *Notas sobre las funciones de proyección, véase p. 386.*

# Austria

## 1. Fuente(s) de los datos básicos

Código(s):   Título(s):

EPPA3   Anuario de estadísticas del trabajo 1945-89 - Edición retrospectiva sobre los censos de población, OIT, Ginebra, 1990.
STAT   Base de datos de la OIT sobre estadísticas del trabajo - LABORSTA, Oficina de Estadística, OIT, Ginebra.

## 2. Evaluación de las tasas de actividad: 1950 - 1990

### 2.1 Datos básicos:

Cuadro 1: Tasas de actividad por sexo y grupo de edad

| Grupo de edad | Año 1989 | 1990 | 1991 |
|---|---|---|---|
| **Hombres** | | | |
| 10-14 | 0.00 | 0.00 | 0.00 |
| 15-19 | 53.39 | 52.81 | 54.46 |
| 20-24 | 76.60 | 77.11 | 76.07 |
| 25-29 | 89.97 | 88.60 | 88.71 |
| 30-34 | 96.75 | 96.98 | 96.74 |
| 35-39 | 97.76 | 98.02 | 97.70 |
| 40-44 | 96.32 | 96.46 | 97.23 |
| 45-49 | 96.04 | 96.11 | 95.05 |
| 50-54 | 89.41 | 91.03 | 91.31 |
| 55-59 | 64.52 | 62.96 | 63.45 |
| 60-64 | 14.48 | 14.13 | 13.84 |
| 65+ | 2.05 | 3.32 | 1.95 |
| **Mujeres** | | | |
| 10-14 | 0.00 | 0.00 | 0.00 |
| 15-19 | 46.49 | 44.84 | 44.53 |
| 20-24 | 72.82 | 72.38 | 73.04 |
| 25-29 | 67.28 | 69.19 | 70.12 |
| 30-34 | 63.88 | 64.09 | 66.33 |
| 35-39 | 63.60 | 66.54 | 67.24 |
| 40-44 | 63.95 | 66.93 | 66.77 |
| 45-49 | 60.28 | 60.62 | 62.07 |
| 50-54 | 51.35 | 53.74 | 54.59 |
| 55-59 | 25.57 | 26.00 | 23.90 |
| 60-64 | 4.60 | 5.00 | 5.32 |
| 65+ | 1.40 | 1.05 | 0.74 |

Fuente(s): STAT.

### 2.2 Método(s):  promedio aritmético

#### 2.2.1 Hombres:

- 1950-80, tasas de actividad 1950-80 con base en EPPA3;
- 1990, promedios de las tasas de actividad ajustadas con base en las encuestas de 1989, 1990 y 1991.

#### 2.2.2 Mujeres:

Métodos, hipótesis y tratamientos idénticos a los que se aplican a los hombres.

## 3. Evaluación de las tasas de distribución por sector de actividad: 1950 - 1990

### 3.1 Datos básicos:

Cuadro 2: Distribución de la población económicamente activa por sector de actividad en %

| Año | Agricultura | Industria Total | Manufac. | Servicios |
|---|---|---|---|---|
| **Hombres** | | | | |
| 1979 | 8.71 | 50.68 | 34.52 | 40.61 |
| 1980 | 8.78 | 50.98 | 34.37 | 40.24 |
| 1981 | 7.49 | 50.79 | 34.88 | 41.72 |
| 1989 | 7.28 | 49.24 | 33.77 | 43.48 |
| 1990 | 7.00 | 49.03 | 33.51 | 43.97 |
| 1991 | 6.61 | 49.19 | 33.64 | 44.20 |
| **Mujeres** | | | | |
| 1979 | 13.16 | 24.56 | 22.21 | 62.28 |
| 1980 | 13.50 | 25.06 | 22.63 | 61.44 |
| 1981 | 10.03 | 26.53 | 23.90 | 63.44 |
| 1989 | 9.13 | 21.05 | 19.02 | 69.82 |
| 1990 | 9.08 | 20.40 | 18.30 | 70.52 |
| 1991 | 8.59 | 20.29 | 18.01 | 71.12 |

Fuente(s): STAT.

### 3.2 Método(s):  promedio aritmético

#### 3.2.1 Hombres:

- 1950-70, tasas de distribución 1950-70 con base en EPPA3;
- 1980, promedios de las tasas de distribución con base en las encuestas de 1979 y 1980 y de las tasas de distribución con base en el censo de 1981;
- 1990, promedios de las tasas de distribución con base en las encuestas de 1989, 1990 y 1991.
de 1989, 1990 y 1991.

#### 3.2.2 Mujeres:

Métodos, hipótesis y tratamientos idénticos a los que se aplican a los hombres.

## 4. Proyección de las tasas de actividad: 2000 - 2010

### 4.1 Modelo(s):  linear y hiperbólico

#### 4.1.1 Hombres:

- Para los grupos de edad [15-19] y [35-49], aplicación de la función F1;
- Para los grupos de edad [20-34] y [50+], aplicación de la función F3;
- Modificación de las tendencias de los grupos de edad [25-29] y [35-49].

#### 4.1.2 Mujeres:

- Para los grupos de edad [15-49], aplicación de la función F1;
- Para los grupos de edad [50+], aplicación de la función F3;
- Modificación de las tendencias de los grupos de edad [15-24].

*Notas sobre los ajustes de las tasas, véase p.380-384.*      *Notas sobre las funciones de proyección, véase p. 386.*

# Azerbaiyán

## 1. Fuente(s) de los datos básicos

Código(s):   Título(s):

BLT-94-2   Vorobiev A. (1994), "Estimaciones de la población económicamente activa de los quince países de la ex URSS, en 1950, 1959, 1970, 1979 y 1989", en el Boletín de Estadísticas del Trabajol - 1994-2, OIT, Ginebra.

## 2. Evaluación de las tasas de actividad: 1950 - 1990

### 2.1 Datos básicos:

Cuadro 1: Tasas de actividad por sexo y grupo de edad

| Grupo de edad | Año 1950 | 1959 | 1970 | 1979 | 1989 |
|---|---|---|---|---|---|
| **Hombres** | | | | | |
| 10-14 | 0.00 | 0.00 | 0.00 | 0.00 | 0.00 |
| 15-19 | 48.91 | 47.26 | 31.67 | 35.48 | 29.59 |
| 20-24 | 82.89 | 84.21 | 80.56 | 80.39 | 75.76 |
| 25-29 | 92.96 | 92.98 | 90.00 | 95.92 | 92.86 |
| 30-34 | 94.74 | 95.04 | 96.89 | 98.33 | 95.59 |
| 35-39 | 94.44 | 96.97 | 97.04 | 98.44 | 95.77 |
| 40-44 | 93.10 | 94.23 | 95.89 | 97.34 | 95.54 |
| 45-49 | 93.33 | 94.03 | 95.71 | 96.79 | 94.31 |
| 50-54 | 91.30 | 90.91 | 90.91 | 93.33 | 90.00 |
| 55-59 | 85.29 | 85.71 | 84.48 | 84.62 | 83.21 |
| 60-64 | 77.78 | 80.49 | 50.00 | 52.50 | 47.42 |
| 65+ | 47.54 | 50.00 | 22.12 | 21.31 | 20.91 |
| **Mujeres** | | | | | |
| 10-14 | 0.00 | 0.00 | 0.00 | 0.00 | 0.00 |
| 15-19 | 45.36 | 45.52 | 30.67 | 37.24 | 28.27 |
| 20-24 | 62.09 | 61.35 | 60.14 | 77.71 | 60.50 |
| 25-29 | 62.24 | 66.86 | 75.41 | 84.95 | 64.96 |
| 30-34 | 62.65 | 61.64 | 69.23 | 86.72 | 69.55 |
| 35-39 | 61.96 | 64.52 | 78.66 | 89.21 | 74.50 |
| 40-44 | 62.96 | 62.82 | 75.00 | 89.80 | 76.67 |
| 45-49 | 61.90 | 63.22 | 74.19 | 88.24 | 75.19 |
| 50-54 | 51.43 | 51.95 | 63.77 | 75.94 | 56.99 |
| 55-59 | 40.35 | 39.24 | 28.13 | 40.70 | 30.87 |
| 60-64 | 32.65 | 40.68 | 13.41 | 18.06 | 19.17 |
| 65+ | 7.53 | 9.38 | 3.41 | 4.50 | 6.70 |

Fuente(s): BLT-94-2-2

### 2.2 Método(s): promedio ponderado

#### 2.2.1 Hombres:

- 1950-90, promedios ponderados de las tasas de actividad 1950, 1959, 1976 y 1989 con base en el Boletín de estadísticas del trabajo 1994-2.

#### 2.2.2 Mujeres:

Métodos, hipótesis y tratamientos idénticos a los que se aplican a los hombres.

## 3. Evaluación de las tasas de distribución por sector de actividad: 1950 - 1990

### 3.1 Datos básicos:

Cuadro 2: Distribución de la población económicamente activa por sector de actividad en %

| Año | Agricultura | Industria Total | Manufac. | Servicios |
|---|---|---|---|---|
| **Hombres** | | | | |
| 1950 | 48.31 | 25.93 | 11.27 | 25.76 |
| 1959 | 42.14 | 25.38 | 11.18 | 32.48 |
| 1970 | 29.01 | 34.79 | 16.84 | 36.21 |
| 1979 | 27.85 | 36.37 | 15.65 | 35.78 |
| 1989 | 27.37 | 35.06 | 14.11 | 37.57 |
| **Mujeres** | | | | |
| 1950 | 59.47 | 17.07 | 12.76 | 23.45 |
| 1959 | 59.19 | 14.20 | 11.06 | 26.61 |
| 1970 | 41.50 | 20.05 | 15.23 | 38.45 |
| 1979 | 43.41 | 19.89 | 12.31 | 36.70 |
| 1989 | 36.85 | 20.60 | 13.31 | 42.55 |

Fuente(s): BLT-94-2.

### 3.2 Método(s): promedio ponderado

#### 3.2.1 Hombres:

- 1950-90, promedios ponderados de las tasas de distribución 1950, 1959, 1970, 1979 y 1989 con base en el Boletín de estadísticas del trabajo 1994-2.

#### 3.2.2 Mujeres:

Métodos, hipótesis y tratamientos idénticos a los que se aplican a los hombres.

## 4. Proyección de las tasas de actividad: 2000 - 2010

### 4.1 Modelo(s): linear, hiperbólico y logístico

#### 4.1.1 Hombres:

- Para los grupos de edad [15-24] y [55+], aplicación de la función F3;
- Para los grupos de edad [25-54], aplicación de la función F1;
- Modificación de las tendencias de los grupos de edad [20-54].

#### 4.1.2 Mujeres:

- Para los grupos de edad [15-24] y [50+], aplicación de la función F3;
- Para los grupos de edad [25-49], aplicación de la función F6;
- Modificación de las tendencias de los grupos de edad [20-54].

*Notas sobre los ajustes de las tasas, véase p.380-384.*     *Notas sobre las funciones de proyección, véase p. 386.*

# Bahamas

## 1. Fuente(s) de los datos básicos

Código(s):  Título(s):

STAT  Base de datos de la OIT sobre estadísticas del trabajo - LABORSTA, Oficina de Estadística, OIT, Ginebra.

## 2. Evaluación de las tasas de actividad: 1950 - 1990

### 2.1 Datos básicos:

Cuadro 1: Tasas de actividad por sexo y grupo de edad

| Grupo de edad | 1953 | 1963 | 1970 | 1980 | 1990 |
|---|---|---|---|---|---|
| **Hombres** | | | | | |
| 10-14 | 1.59 | 3.93 | 2.34 | 0.00 | 0.00 |
| 15-19 | 60.26 | 74.95 | 63.82 | 46.79 | 41.29 |
| 20-24 | 92.04 | 96.42 | 93.10 | 87.23 | 85.68 |
| 25-29 | 95.57 | 97.79 | 96.11 | 92.49 | 90.67 |
| 30-34 | 96.75 | 97.27 | 96.88 | 95.42 | 91.76 |
| 35-39 | 96.92 | 97.41 | 97.04 | 95.08 | 94.11 |
| 40-44 | 96.72 | 96.94 | 96.77 | 94.49 | 94.62 |
| 45-49 | 95.97 | 96.18 | 96.02 | 92.45 | 94.35 |
| 50-54 | 94.69 | 94.35 | 94.60 | 88.79 | 92.07 |
| 55-59 | 90.81 | 94.65 | 91.74 | 83.72 | 88.35 |
| 60-64 | 81.44 | 85.90 | 82.52 | 72.56 | 73.89 |
| 65+ | 50.77 | 63.20 | 53.78 | 39.93 | 36.41 |
| **Mujeres** | | | | | |
| 10-14 | .. | 1.75 | 2.13 | .. | 0.00 |
| 15-19 | .. | 45.04 | 44.55 | 34.54 | 31.26 |
| 20-24 | .. | 61.33 | 71.90 | 72.38 | 75.28 |
| 25-29 | .. | 58.71 | 65.07 | 75.20 | 81.25 |
| 30-34 | .. | 58.33 | 63.39 | 72.19 | 80.69 |
| 35-39 | .. | 58.31 | 62.23 | 72.29 | 80.40 |
| 40-44 | .. | 56.29 | 60.60 | 68.17 | 79.03 |
| 45-49 | .. | 55.54 | 58.38 | 63.53 | 75.94 |
| 50-54 | .. | 54.56 | 56.53 | 59.17 | 68.24 |
| 55-59 | .. | 43.68 | 53.10 | 49.22 | 64.30 |
| 60-64 | .. | 41.05 | 43.73 | 38.00 | 47.48 |
| 65+ | .. | 24.92 | 28.35 | 16.14 | 15.28 |

Fuente(s): STAT.

### 2.2 Método(s): interpolación y extrapolación lineares, promedio ponderado

**2.2.1 Hombres:**

- 1950 y 1970-90, interpolación y extrapolación de las tasas de actividad con base en los censos de 1953 y 1963 y de las tasas de actividad ajustadas con base en los censos de 1980 y 1990.

**2.2.2 Mujeres:**

- 1950-60, interpolación y extrapolación de las tasas de actividad ajustadas con base en los censos 1953 y 1963;
modificación de las tendencias de todos los grupos de edad;
- 1970-90, promedios ponderados de las tasas de actividad ajustadas los censos con base en de 1970 y 1980 y de las tasas de actividad el censo con base en de 1990.

## 3. Evaluación de las tasas de distribución por sector de actividad: 1950 - 1990

### 3.1 Datos básicos:

Cuadro 2: Distribución de la población económicamente activa por sector de actividad en %

| Año | Agricultura | Industria Total | Manufac. | Servicios |
|---|---|---|---|---|
| **Hombres** | | | | |
| 1963 | 18.75 | 34.69 | 8.60 | 46.56 |
| 1970 | 8.57 | 30.84 | 6.40 | 60.59 |
| 1980 | 7.96 | 24.18 | 6.57 | 67.86 |
| 1990 | 8.36 | 24.18 | 4.31 | 67.46 |
| **Mujeres** | | | | |
| 1963 | 11.95 | 7.46 | 6.91 | 80.60 |
| 1970 | 6.23 | 7.41 | 5.68 | 86.36 |
| 1980 | 2.91 | 7.12 | 5.89 | 89.98 |
| 1990 | 1.60 | 5.25 | 3.83 | 93.15 |

Fuente(s): STAT.

### 3.2 Método(s): interpolación y extrapolación lineares

**3.2.1 Hombres:**

- 1950-90, interpolación y extrapolación de las tasas de distribución con base en los censos de 1963, 1970, 1980 y 1990;
modificación de las tendencias de todos los sectores para 1950.

**3.2.2 Mujeres:**

Métodos, hipótesis y tratamientos idénticos a los que se aplican a los hombres.

## 4. Proyección de las tasas de actividad: 2000 - 2010

### 4.1 Modelo(s): linear, hiperbólico y logístico

**4.1.1 Hombres:**

- Para los grupos de edad [15-24], aplicación de la función F1;
- Para los grupos de edad [25+], aplicación de la función F3;
- Modificación de las tendencias de los grupos de edad [50-64].

**4.1.2 Mujeres:**

- Para el grupo de edad [15-19], aplicación de la función F1;
- Para los grupos de edad [20-64], aplicación de la función F6;
- Para el grupo de edad [65+], aplicación de la función F3;
- Modificación de las tendencias de los grupos de edad [55-64].

*Notas sobre los ajustes de las tasas, véase p.380-384.*   *Notas sobre las funciones de proyección, véase p. 386.*

# Bahrein

## 1. Fuente(s) de los datos básicos

Código(s):  Título(s):
EPPA3      Estimaciones y proyecciones de la población económicamente activa, 1950-2025, tercera edición, OIT, Ginebra, 1986.
ASTER      Anuario de estadísticas del trabajo 1945-89 - Edición retrospectiva sobre los censos de población, OIT, Ginebra, 1990.

## 2. Evaluación de las tasas de actividad: 1950 - 1990

### 2.1 Datos básicos:

Cuadro 1: Tasas de actividad por sexo y grupo de edad

| Grupo de edad | 1971 | 1981 | 1991 |
|---|---|---|---|
| **Hombres** | | | |
| 10-14 | 1.87 | 0.00 | 0.00 |
| 15-19 | 42.80 | 30.01 | 24.73 |
| 20-24 | 88.38 | 89.20 | 87.91 |
| 25-29 | 97.66 | 98.10 | 98.01 |
| 30-34 | 98.68 | 99.13 | 99.22 |
| 35-39 | 98.40 | 99.09 | 99.35 |
| 40-44 | 97.29 | 98.80 | 99.35 |
| 45-49 | 96.32 | 97.88 | 98.91 |
| 50-54 | 91.89 | 94.08 | 95.94 |
| 55-59 | 84.48 | 88.17 | 88.60 |
| 60-64 | 72.00 | 69.26 | 64.72 |
| 65+ | 49.52 | 45.46 | 36.05 |
| **Mujeres** | | | |
| 10-14 | 0.04 | 0.00 | 0.00 |
| 15-19 | 3.05 | 8.41 | 8.28 |
| 20-24 | 11.59 | 31.46 | 37.00 |
| 25-29 | 10.19 | 31.09 | 42.03 |
| 30-34 | 7.44 | 24.61 | 41.73 |
| 35-39 | 5.83 | 17.28 | 37.98 |
| 40-44 | 6.15 | 12.81 | 31.87 |
| 45-49 | 4.59 | 9.58 | 18.10 |
| 50-54 | 3.92 | 6.02 | 9.04 |
| 55-59 | 3.67 | 3.63 | 5.10 |
| 60-64 | 2.80 | 1.69 | 1.68 |
| 65+ | 1.69 | 0.78 | 0.72 |

Fuente(s): ASTER

### 2.2 Método(s): interpolación linear

**2.2.1 Hombres:**
- 1950-70, tasas de actividad 1950-70 con base en EPPA3;
- 1980-90, extrapolación de las tasas de actividad con base en los censos de 1971, 1981 y 1991.

**2.2.2 Mujeres:**
Métodos, hipótesis y tratamientos idénticos a los que se aplican a los hombres.

## 3. Evaluación de las tasas de distribución por sector de actividad: 1950 - 1990

### 3.1 Datos básicos:

Cuadro 2: Distribución de la población económicamente activa por sector de actividad en %

| Año | Agricultura | Industria Total | Manufac. | Servicios |
|---|---|---|---|---|
| **Hombres** | | | | |
| 1971 | 7.08 | 36.32 | 14.73 | 56.60 |
| 1981 | 3.04 | 39.16 | 9.15 | 57.80 |
| 1991 | 2.88 | 32.76 | 14.02 | 64.36 |
| **Mujeres** | | | | |
| 1971 | 0.12 | 4.09 | 2.72 | 95.79 |
| 1981 | 0.16 | 5.16 | 1.89 | 94.69 |
| 1991 | 0.21 | 7.23 | 5.90 | 92.57 |

Fuente(s): ASTER.

### 3.2 Método(s): interpolación linear

**3.2.1 Hombres:**
- 1950-70, tasas de distribución 1950-70 con base en EPPA3;
- 1980-90, interpolación de las tasas de distribución con base en los censos de 1971, 1981 y 1991.

**3.2.2 Mujeres:**
Métodos, hipótesis y tratamientos idénticos a los que se aplican a los hombres.

## 4. Proyección de las tasas de actividad: 2000 - 2010

### 4.1 Modelo(s): linear, log-linear y hiperbólico

**4.1.1 Hombres:**
- Para el grupo de edad [15-19], aplicación de la función F2;
- Para los grupos de edad [20+], aplicación de la función F1;
- Modificación de las tendencias de los grupos de edad [20-59].

**4.1.2 Mujeres:**
- Para los grupos de edad [15-59], aplicación de la función F1;
- Para los grupos de edad [60+], aplicación de la función F3;
- Modificación de la tendencia del grupo de edad [15-19].

*Notas sobre los ajustes de las tasas, véase p.380-384.*          *Notas sobre las funciones de proyección, véase p. 386.*

# Bangladesh

## 1. Fuente(s) de los datos básicos

**Código(s):** **Título(s):**

EPPA3     Estimaciones y proyecciones de la población económicamente activa, 1950-2025, tercera edición, OIT, Ginebra, 1986.
BY83-84     Statistical Yearbook of Bangladesh, 1983-84, Bangladesh Bureau of Statistics.
LFS84-85     Report on Labour Force Survey 1984-85, february 1988, GPRB, Bangladesh Bureau of Statistics.
ASTER     Anuario de estadísticas del trabajo 1945-89 - Edición retrospectiva sobre los censos de población, OIT, Ginebra, 1990.
AST85-90     Ediciones de 1985-1993, Anuario de Estadísticas del Trabjo de la OIT, Ginebra.

## 2. Evaluación de las tasas de actividad: 1950 - 1990

### 2.1 Datos básicos:

Cuadro 1: Tasas de actividad por sexo y grupo de edad

| Grupo de edad | Año 1980 (1) | 1983 (1) | 1984 (2) | 1985 (3) | 1989 (3) |
|---|---|---|---|---|---|
| **Hombres** | | | | | |
| 10-14 | 32.77 | 39.86 | 37.70 | 30.40 | 33.76 |
| 15-19 | 72.39 | 69.56 | 70.40 | 67.50 | 70.70 |
| 20-24 | 87.59 | 87.18 | 85.40 | 88.10 | 82.50 |
| 25-29 | 99.53 | 98.58 | 97.70 | 98.70 | 96.50 |
| 30-34 | 99.13 | 98.44 | 99.00 | 99.90 | 98.80 |
| 35-39 | 98.68 | 98.50 | 99.70 | 99.40 | 98.50 |
| 40-44 | 98.78 | 97.05 | 98.40 | 99.50 | 98.30 |
| 45-49 | 98.77 | 98.47 | 98.40 | 99.70 | 98.30 |
| 50-54 | 98.66 | 97.01 | 98.50 | 99.30 | 96.80 |
| 55-59 | 94.89 | 97.63 | 94.70 | 98.00 | 95.70 |
| 60-64 | 90.82 | 90.65 | 91.80 | 93.00 | 89.40 |
| 65+ | 73.34 | 65.73 | 72.90 | 70.40 | 65.00 |
| **Mujeres** | | | | | |
| 10-14 | .. | .. | .. | .. | 31.30 |
| 15-19 | .. | .. | .. | .. | 55.20 |
| 20-24 | .. | .. | .. | .. | 64.90 |
| 25-29 | .. | .. | .. | .. | 68.90 |
| 30-34 | .. | .. | .. | .. | 75.00 |
| 35-39 | .. | .. | .. | .. | 78.00 |
| 40-44 | .. | .. | .. | .. | 76.90 |
| 45-49 | .. | .. | .. | .. | 75.60 |
| 50-54 | .. | .. | .. | .. | 73.50 |
| 55-59 | .. | .. | .. | .. | 67.80 |
| 60-64 | .. | .. | .. | .. | 57.90 |
| 65+ | .. | .. | .. | .. | 33.50 |

Fuente(s): (1) BY83-84; (2) LFS84-85; (3) AST85-90.

### 2.2 Método(s): interpolación y extrapolación lineares

#### 2.2.1 Hombres:

- 1950-70, tasas de actividad 1950-70 con base en EPPA3;
- 1980-90, interpolación y extrapolación de las tasas de actividad con base en las encuestas de 1980, 1983-84, 1984-85, 1985-86 y 1989.

#### 2.2.2 Mujeres:

- 1950-70, tasas de actividad ajustadas 1950-70 con base en EPPA3;
- 1980-90, aplicación a las tasas de actividad con base en la encuesta de 1980, 1/4 de las variaciones de las tasas de actividad estimadas 1980 y 1990 para India.

## 3. Evaluación de las tasas de distribución por sector de actividad: 1950 - 1990

### 3.1 Datos básicos:

Cuadro 2: Distribución de la población económicamente activa por sector de actividad en %

| Año | Agricultura | Industria Total | Manufac. | Servicios |
|---|---|---|---|---|
| **Hombres** | | | | |
| 1983 (1) | 64.11 | 7.93 | 6.20 | 27.96 |
| 1984 (2) | 63.02 | 10.16 | 7.77 | 26.83 |
| 1985 (3) | 62.70 | 9.48 | 7.13 | 27.83 |
| 1989 (3) | 60.00 | 13.60 | 11.41 | 26.40 |
| **Mujeres** | | | | |
| 1989 (3) | 74.34 | 18.61 | 17.96 | 7.05 |

Fuente(s): (1) BY83-84; (2) LFS84-85; (3) AST85-90.

### 3.2 Método(s): extrapolación linear

#### 3.2.1 Hombres:

- 1950-70, tasas de distribución 1950-70 con base en EPPA3;
- 1990, extrapolación de las tasas de distribución con base en las encuestas de 1983-84, 1984-85, 1985-86 y 1989.

#### 3.2.2 Mujeres:

- 1950-70, tasas de distribución 1950-70 con base en EPPA3;
- 1980-90, para la agricultura, aplicación a la tasas tasas de distribución con base en la encuesta de 1989, de las mismas variaciones que las estimadas para los hombres durante el mismo período;
para la industria y los servicios, conservación de la razón industria/servicios con base en la encuesta de 1989.

## 4. Proyección de las tasas de actividad: 2000 - 2010

### 4.1 Modelo(s): linear y hiperbólico

#### 4.1.1 Hombres:

- Para los grupos de edad [10-59], aplicación de la función F3;
- Para los grupos de edad [60+], aplicación de la función F1;
- Modificación de las tendencias de los grupos de edad [20-44].

#### 4.1.2 Mujeres:

- Para todos los grupos de edad, aplicación de la función F1;
- Modificación de las tendencias de todos los grupos de edad.

*Notas sobre los ajustes de las tasas, véase p.380-384.*

*Notas sobre las funciones de proyección, véase p. 386.*

# Barbados

## 1. Fuente(s) de los datos básicos

Código(s):  Título(s):

EPPA3  Estimaciones y proyecciones de la población económicamente activa, 1950-2025, tercera edición, OIT, Ginebra, 1986.
ASTER  Anuario de estadísticas del trabajo 1945-89 - Edición retrospectiva sobre los censos de población, OIT, Ginebra, 1990.
AST82-93  Ediciones de 1982-1993, Anuario de Estadísticas del Trabjo de la OIT, Ginebra.

## 2. Evaluación de las tasas de actividad: 1950 - 1990

### 2.1 Datos básicos:

Cuadro 1: Tasas de actividad por sexo y grupo de edad

| Grupo de edad | Year | | | | | |
|---|---|---|---|---|---|---|
| | 1950 (1) | 1980 (2) | 1986 (3) | 1990 (3) | 191 (3) | 1992 (3) |
| **Hombres** | | | | | | |
| 10-14 | .. | 0.00 | 0.00 | 0.00 | 0.00 | 0.00 |
| 15-19 | .. | 59.54 | 39.64 | 45.16 | 42.73 | 42.20 |
| 20-24 | .. | 92.31 | 88.00 | 91.60 | 80.20 | 89.52 |
| 25-29 | .. | 94.47 | 94.44 | 94.17 | 96.19 | 95.19 |
| 30-34 | .. | 95.78 | 95.05 | 95.83 | 93.64 | 93.64 |
| 35-39 | .. | 95.59 | 94.67 | 95.56 | 95.40 | 93.55 |
| 40-44 | .. | 95.38 | 95.56 | 96.77 | 96.05 | 94.20 |
| 45-49 | .. | 94.89 | 93.33 | 95.65 | 93.33 | 95.65 |
| 50-54 | .. | 93.57 | 91.67 | 94.29 | 90.91 | 92.68 |
| 55-59 | .. | 89.52 | 97.22 | 88.57 | 82.86 | 86.49 |
| 60-64 | .. | 70.82 | 61.76 | 64.52 | 58.33 | 53.49 |
| 65+ | .. | 23.63 | 17.27 | 13.76 | 14.75 | 12.93 |
| **Mujeres** | | | | | | |
| 10-14 | 10.20 | 0.00 | 0.00 | 0.00 | .. | 0.00 |
| 15-19 | 54.15 | 39.89 | 29.46 | 34.99 | .. | 34.62 |
| 20-24 | 63.10 | 70.49 | 79.67 | 85.12 | .. | 85.11 |
| 25-29 | 57.60 | 77.54 | 82.64 | 86.96 | .. | 85.45 |
| 30-34 | 58.10 | 75.45 | 85.45 | 87.16 | .. | 84.68 |
| 35-39 | 58.25 | 71.56 | 83.12 | 90.70 | .. | 85.71 |
| 40-44 | 57.90 | 67.74 | 72.06 | 80.82 | .. | 84.81 |
| 45-49 | 60.05 | 61.27 | 73.08 | 70.91 | .. | 76.19 |
| 50-54 | 57.90 | 53.15 | 58.00 | 67.92 | .. | 72.92 |
| 55-59 | 54.85 | 45.10 | 63.89 | 43.18 | .. | 48.15 |
| 60-64 | 43.65 | 33.53 | 28.89 | 27.45 | .. | 23.91 |
| 65+ | 19.00 | 7.15 | 7.23 | 3.68 | .. | 4.81 |

Fuente(s): (1) EPPA3; (2) ASTER; (3) AST82-93.

### 2.2 Método(s): interpolación y extrapolación lineares

#### 2.2.1 Hombres:

- 1990, interpolación de las tasas de actividad con base en el censo de 1980
y en las encuestas de 1986 to 1992;
modificación de las tendencias de los grupos de edad [20-29];
- 1970, tasas de actividad 1 970 con base en EPPA3;
- 1980, tasas de actividad con base en el censo de 1980;
- 1950-60, extrapolación de las tasas de actividad estimadas para 1970,
1980 y 1990;
modificación de las tendencias de todos los grupos de edad.

#### 2.2.2 Mujeres:

- 1950, tasas de actividad 1950 con base en EPPA3;
- 1970-90, interpolación de las tasas de actividad 1950 con base en EPPA3,
de las tasas de actividad con base en el censo de 1980 y de las tasas de
actividad con base en las encuestas de 1986, 1990 y 1991;
modificación de las tendencias de todos los grupos de edad.

## 3. Evaluación de las tasas de distribución por sector de actividad: 1950 - 1990

### 3.1 Datos básicos:

Cuadro 2: Distribución de la población económicamente activa por sector de actividad en %

| Año | Agricultura | Industria | | Servicios |
|---|---|---|---|---|
| | | Total | Manufac. | |
| **Hombres** | | | | |
| 1960 (1) | 26.42 | 37.74 | .. | 35.85 |
| 1970 (2) | 17.56 | 47.86 | 16.05 | 34.58 |
| 1981 (3) | 10.14 | 23.83 | 10.95 | 66.02 |
| 1989 (3) | 7.12 | 33.03 | 11.50 | 59.85 |
| 1991 (3) | 7.12 | 27.88 | 10.00 | 65.00 |
| **Mujeres** | | | | |
| 1960 (1) | 26.32 | 13.16 | .. | 60.53 |
| 1970 (2) | 16.05 | 30.79 | 14.07 | 53.16 |
| 1981 (3) | 9.20 | 24.14 | 23.22 | 80.46 |
| 1989 (3) | 7.32 | 16.48 | 14.87 | 76.20 |
| 1991 (3) | 4.94 | 14.07 | 12.59 | 80.99 |

Fuente(s): (1) EPPA3; (2) ASTER; (3) AST82-93..

### 3.2 Método(s): interpolación y extrapolación lineares

#### 3.2.1 Hombres:

- 1950-60, tasas de distribución 1950-60 con base en EPPA3;
- 1970, extrapolación de las tasas de distribución 1960 con base en EPPA3
y de las tasas de distribución con base en el censo de 1970;
- 1980, interpolación de las tasas de distribución estimadas para 1970
y de las tasas de distribución con base en la encuesta de 1981;
y de las tasas de distribución con base en la encuesta de 1981;

#### 3.2.2 Mujeres:

Métodos, hipótesis y tratamientos idénticos a los que se aplican a los hombres.

## 4. Proyección de las tasas de actividad: 2000 - 2010

### 4.1 Modelo(s): linear y hiperbólico

#### 4.1.1 Hombres:

- Para los grupos de edad [15-24], aplicación de la función F1;
- Para los grupos de edad [25+], aplicación de la función F3;
- Modificación de las tendencias de los grupos de edad [20-24] y [30-49].

#### 4.1.2 Mujeres:

- Para el grupo de edad [15-19], aplicación de la función F3;
- Para los grupos de edad [20-54], aplicación de la función F6;
- Para los grupos de edad [55+], aplicación de la función F3;
- Modificación de las tendencias de los grupos de edad [45-59].

*Notas sobre los ajustes de las tasas, véase p.380-384.*   *Notas sobre las funciones de proyección, véase p. 386.*

# Belarús

## 1. Fuente(s) de los datos básicos

Código(s):     Título(s):

BLT-94-2      Vorobiev A. (1994), "Estimaciones de la población económicamente activa de los quince países de la ex URSS, en 1950, 1959, 1970, 1979 y 1989", en el Boletín de Estadísticas del Trabajol - 1994-2, OIT, Ginebra.

## 2. Evaluación de las tasas de actividad: 1950 - 1990

### 2.1 Datos básicos:

Cuadro 1: Tasas de actividad por sexo y grupo de edad

| Grupo de edad | Año 1959 | 1970 | 1979 | 1989 |
|---|---|---|---|---|
| **Hombres** | | | | |
| 10-14 | 0.00 | 0.00 | 0.00 | 0.00 |
| 15-19 | 64.15 | 38.64 | 37.45 | 26.97 |
| 20-24 | 86.82 | 83.56 | 86.81 | 81.14 |
| 25-29 | 95.29 | 98.39 | 97.23 | 96.99 |
| 30-34 | 94.76 | 97.99 | 98.14 | 98.33 |
| 35-39 | 96.02 | 97.57 | 98.17 | 98.06 |
| 40-44 | 93.65 | 95.42 | 97.89 | 97.30 |
| 45-49 | 93.75 | 94.82 | 96.26 | 95.74 |
| 50-54 | 91.25 | 91.23 | 91.82 | 92.69 |
| 55-59 | 88.89 | 84.46 | 82.91 | 85.61 |
| 60-64 | 56.20 | 45.07 | 30.48 | 39.91 |
| 65+ | 47.78 | 10.07 | 8.43 | 12.89 |
| **Mujeres** | | | | |
| 10-14 | 0.00 | 0.00 | 0.00 | 0.00 |
| 15-19 | 63.50 | 34.75 | 31.44 | 24.50 |
| 20-24 | 76.87 | 80.95 | 86.10 | 82.30 |
| 25-29 | 84.10 | 94.55 | 94.44 | 92.94 |
| 30-34 | 74.10 | 93.46 | 95.93 | 95.22 |
| 35-39 | 78.68 | 91.97 | 96.19 | 96.16 |
| 40-44 | 77.36 | 92.65 | 96.22 | 96.25 |
| 45-49 | 75.95 | 89.26 | 93.96 | 93.97 |
| 50-54 | 70.09 | 79.79 | 85.71 | 86.69 |
| 55-59 | 58.08 | 28.10 | 29.04 | 36.29 |
| 60-64 | 53.18 | 14.35 | 9.64 | 20.42 |
| 65+ | 17.45 | 2.43 | 4.40 | 4.90 |

Fuente(s): BLT-94-2.

**2.2 Método(s):** interpolación y extrapolación lineares
promedio ponderado

### 2.2.1 Hombres:

- 1950-90, interpolación y extrapolación de las tasas de actividad 1950, 1959, 1970 y 1989 con base en el Boletín de estadísticas del trabajo 1994-2; modificación de las tendencias de todos los grupos de edad para 1950.

### 2.2.2 Mujeres:

- 1950, extrapolación de las tasas de actividad 1959 y 1970 con base en el Boletín de estadísticas del trabajo 1994-2; modificación de las tendencias de todos los grupos de edad;
- 1960-90, promedios ponderados de las tasas de actividad 1959, 1970, 1979 y 1989 con base en el Boletín.

## 3. Evaluación de las tasas de distribución por sector de actividad: 1950 - 1990

### 3.1 Datos básicos:

Cuadro 2: Distribución de la población económicamente activa por sector de actividad en %

| Año | Agricultura | Industria Total | Manufac. | Servicios |
|---|---|---|---|---|
| **Hombres** | | | | |
| 1950 | 65.60 | 15.43 | 8.81 | 18.97 |
| 1959 | 51.06 | 22.35 | 14.08 | 26.59 |
| 1970 | 33.84 | 39.01 | 24.58 | 27.15 |
| 1979 | 28.99 | 43.43 | 26.38 | 27.58 |
| 1989 | 26.16 | 44.62 | 27.38 | 29.23 |
| **Mujeres** | | | | |
| 1950 | 75.37 | 9.45 | 7.30 | 15.19 |
| 1959 | 65.49 | 14.45 | 11.78 | 20.06 |
| 1970 | 36.43 | 27.77 | 22.89 | 35.80 |
| 1979 | 24.42 | 32.89 | 26.06 | 42.69 |
| 1989 | 14.84 | 35.20 | 28.44 | 49.96 |

Fuente(s): BLT-94-2.

**3.2 Método(s):** datos de BLT-94-2

### 3.2.1 Hombres:

- 1950-90, promedios ponderados de las tasas de distribución 1950, 1959, 1970, 1979 y 1989 con base en el Boletín de estadísticas del trabajo 1994-2.

### 3.2.2 Mujeres:

Métodos, hipótesis y tratamientos idénticos a los que se aplican a los hombres.

## 4. Proyección de las tasas de actividad: 2000 - 2010

### 4.1 Modelo(s): linear y hiperbólico

### 4.1.1 Hombres:

- Para los grupos de edad [15-24] y [60+], aplicación de la función F3;
- Para los grupos de edad [25-59], aplicación de la función F1;
- Modificación de las tendencias de los grupos de edad [15-19] y [25-54].

### 4.1.2 Mujeres:

- Para los grupos de edad [15+], aplicación de la función F3;
- Modificación de las tendencias de los grupos de edad [15-19] y [25-54].

*Notas sobre los ajustes de las tasas, véase p.380-384.*

*Notas sobre las funciones de proyección, véase p. 386.*

# Bélgica

## 1. Fuente(s) de los datos básicos

Código(s):   Título(s):

EPPA3      Anuario de estadísticas del trabajo 1945-89 - Edición retrospectiva sobre los censos de población, OIT, Ginebra, 1990.
STAT       Base de datos de la OIT sobre estadísticas del trabajo - LABORSTA, Oficina de Estadística, OIT, Ginebra.

## 2. Evaluación de las tasas de actividad: 1950 - 1990

### 2.1 Datos básicos:

Cuadro 1: Tasas de actividad por sexo y grupo de edad

| Grupo de edad | Año | |
|---|---|---|
| | 1988 | 1991 |
| **Hombres** | | |
| 10-14 | 0.00 | 0.00 |
| 15-19 | 11.30 | 12.86 |
| 20-24 | 67.10 | 66.50 |
| 25-29 | 94.50 | 94.09 |
| 30-34 | 96.10 | 95.98 |
| 35-39 | 96.40 | 95.72 |
| 40-44 | 94.80 | 94.39 |
| 45-49 | 90.90 | 92.97 |
| 50-54 | 79.10 | 80.49 |
| 55-59 | 51.30 | 50.56 |
| 60-64 | 20.50 | 18.17 |
| 65+ | 2.30 | 1.93 |
| **Mujeres** | | |
| 10-14 | 0.00 | 0.00 |
| 15-19 | 9.72 | 9.04 |
| 20-24 | 60.90 | 61.55 |
| 25-29 | 78.20 | 80.40 |
| 30-34 | 71.00 | 74.97 |
| 35-39 | 66.00 | 70.63 |
| 40-44 | 55.40 | 61.89 |
| 45-49 | 43.30 | 50.04 |
| 50-54 | 29.00 | 31.75 |
| 55-59 | 16.30 | 17.64 |
| 60-64 | 4.10 | 3.74 |
| 65+ | 0.70 | 0.47 |

Fuente(s): STAT.

### 2.2 Método(s): promedio ponderado

**2.2.1 Hombres:**

- 1950-80, tasas de actividad 1950-80 con base en EPPA3;
- 1990, promedios ponderados de las tasas de actividad con base en las encuestas de 1988 y 1991.

**2.2.2 Mujeres:**

Métodos, hipótesis y tratamientos idénticos a los que se aplican a los hombres.

## 3. Evaluación de las tasas de distribución por sector de actividad: 1950 - 1990

### 3.1 Datos básicos:

Cuadro 2: Distribución de la población económicamente activa por sector de actividad en %

| | Agricultura | Industria | | Servicios |
|---|---|---|---|---|
| Año | | Total | Manufac. | |
| **Hombres** | | | | |
| 1990 | 3.21 | 37.04 | 25.94 | 59.75 |
| **Mujeres** | | | | |
| 1990 | 1.75 | 13.62 | 12.40 | 84.63 |

Fuente(s): STAT.

### 3.2 Método(s): datos del país

**3.2.1 Hombres:**

- 1950-80, tasas de distribución 1950-80 con base en EPPA3;
- 1990, tasas de distribución ajustadas con base en la encuesta de 1990; ajuste de las tasas de distribución para tener en cuenta los efectivos del servicio militar obligatorio.

**3.2.2 Mujeres:**

Métodos, hipótesis y tratamientos idénticos a los que se aplican a los hombres.

## 4. Proyección de las tasas de actividad: 2000 - 2010

### 4.1 Modelo(s): hiperbólico y logístico

**4.1.1 Hombres:**

- Para los grupos de edad [15+], aplicación de la función F3;
- Modificación de las tendencias de los grupos de edad [15-24].

**4.1.2 Mujeres:**

- Para el grupo de edad [15-19], aplicación de la función F3;
- Para los grupos de edad [20+], aplicación de la función F6;
- Modificación de las tendencias de los grupos de edad [15-29].

---

*Notas sobre los ajustes de las tasas, véase p.380-384.*          *Notas sobre las funciones de proyección, véase p. 386.*

# Belice

## 1. Fuente(s) de los datos básicos

Código(s): Título(s):

EPPA3      Estimaciones y proyecciones de la población económicamente activa, 1950-2025, tercera edición, OIT, Ginebra, 1986.
ASTER      Anuario de estadísticas del trabajo 1945-89 - Edición retrospectiva sobre los censos de población, OIT, Ginebra, 1990.
STAT        Base de datos de la OIT sobre estadísticas del trabajo - LABORSTA, Oficina de Estadística, OIT, Ginebra.

## 2. Evaluación de las tasas de actividad: 1950 - 1990

### 2.1 Datos básicos:

Cuadro 1: Tasas de actividad por sexo y grupo de edad

| Grupo de edad | Año 1960 (1) | 1970 (1) | 1980 (1) | 1991 (2) |
|---|---|---|---|---|
| **Hombres** | | | | |
| 10-14 | .. | 9.20 | .. | 17.34 |
| 15-19 | .. | 70.95 | .. | 54.43 |
| 20-24 | .. | 96.70 | .. | 88.92 |
| 25-29 | .. | 97.77 | .. | 93.03 |
| 30-34 | .. | 97.90 | .. | 93.00 |
| 35-39 | .. | 98.20 | .. | 93.37 |
| 40-44 | .. | 96.80 | .. | 93.88 |
| 45-49 | .. | 97.63 | .. | 92.18 |
| 50-54 | .. | 95.21 | .. | 90.63 |
| 55-59 | .. | 91.43 | .. | 81.67 |
| 60-64 | .. | 86.70 | .. | 72.79 |
| 65+ | .. | 59.39 | .. | 45.81 |
| **Mujeres** | | | | |
| 10-14 | 0.26 | 0.99 | 0.00 | 3.26 |
| 15-19 | 19.88 | 29.10 | 27.00 | 15.13 |
| 20-24 | 24.00 | 31.20 | 34.37 | 32.82 |
| 25-29 | 19.04 | 21.70 | 28.70 | 30.69 |
| 30-34 | 18.66 | 19.80 | 26.94 | 29.62 |
| 35-39 | 18.30 | 18.70 | 22.93 | 31.52 |
| 40-44 | 17.84 | 17.70 | 23.12 | 29.03 |
| 45-49 | 19.10 | 18.20 | 20.56 | 25.31 |
| 50-54 | 18.60 | 17.50 | 17.27 | 21.62 |
| 55-59 | 18.00 | 16.90 | 17.53 | 14.64 |
| 60-64 | 17.00 | 14.30 | 15.72 | 11.63 |
| 65+ | 9.70 | 7.50 | 8.36 | 5.04 |

Fuente(s): (1) ASTER; (2) STAT.

### 2.2 Método(s): interpolación y extrapolación lineares

**2.2.1 Hombres:**

- 1950-60, tasas de actividad 1950-60 con base en EPPA3;
- 1970-90, interpolación y extrapolación de las tasas de actividad ajustadas con base en de 1970 y 1991 los censos.

**2.2.2 Mujeres:**

- 1960-70, tasas de actividad con base en los censos de 1960 y 1970;
- 1950 y 1980-90, interpolación de las tasas de actividad ajustadas con base en los censos de 1960, 1970, 1980 y 1991.

## 3. Evaluación de las tasas de distribución por sector de actividad: 1950 - 1990

### 3.1 Datos básicos:

Cuadro 2: Distribución de la población económicamente activa por sector de actividad en %

| Año | Agricultura | Industria Total | Manufac. | Servicios |
|---|---|---|---|---|
| **Hombres** | | | | |
| 1943 (1) | 51.38 | 20.69 | 13.16 | 27.92 |
| 1960 (1) | 49.00 | 26.64 | 16.09 | 24.36 |
| 1980 (1) | 46.44 | 17.71 | 10.06 | 35.85 |
| 1991 (2) | 41.06 | 20.37 | 9.11 | 38.56 |
| **Mujeres** | | | | |
| 1943 (1) | 15.72 | 14.91 | 14.86 | 69.37 |
| 1960 (1) | 10.84 | 11.57 | 11.20 | 77.60 |
| 1980 (1) | 8.69 | 15.39 | 14.24 | 75.92 |
| 1991 (2) | 3.95 | 13.33 | 12.13 | 82.72 |

Fuente(s): (1) ASTER; (2) STAT.

### 3.2 Método(s): interpolación linear

**3.2.1 Hombres:**

- 1960 y 1980, tasas de distribución con base en los censos de 1960 y 1980;
- 1950, 1970 y 1990, interpolación de las tasas de distribución con base en los censos de 1946, 1960, 1980 y 1991.

**3.2.2 Mujeres:**

Métodos, hipótesis y tratamientos idénticos a los que se aplican a los hombres.

## 4. Proyección de las tasas de actividad: 2000 - 2010

### 4.1 Modelo(s): linear, log-linear y hiperbólico

**4.1.1 Hombres:**

- Para el grupo de edad [10-14], aplicación de la función F2;
- Para los grupos de edad [15-29], aplicación de la función F1;
- Para los grupos de edad [30+], aplicación de la función F3;
- Modificación de las tendencias de los grupos de edad [25-29] y [40-44].

**4.1.2 Mujeres:**

- Para el grupo de edad [10-14], aplicación de la función F2;
- Para el grupo de edad [15-19], aplicación de la función F1;
- Para los grupos de edad [20+], aplicación de la función F3;
- Modificación de las tendencias de los grupos de edad [15-59].

---

*Notas sobre los ajustes de las tasas, véase p.380-384.*        *Notas sobre las funciones de proyección, véase p. 386.*

# Benin

## 1. Fuente(s) de los datos básicos

Código(s):   Título(s):

EPPA3      Estimaciones y proyecciones de la población económicamente activa, 1950-2025, tercera edición, OIT, Ginebra, 1986.
S1960      Enquête démographique 1960-61, Institut National de la Statistique et de l'Analyse Economique, Cotonou, 1961.
ADNU84   Annuaire démographique 1984 - Statistiques des recensements de population II, trente-sixième édition, Nations Unies, New York, 1986.
ASTER    Anuario de estadísticas del trabajo 1945-89 - Edición retrospectiva sobre los censos de población, OIT, Ginebra, 1990.

## 2. Evaluación de las tasas de actividad: 1950 - 1990

### 2.1 Datos básicos:

Cuadro 1: Tasas de actividad por sexo y grupo de edad

| Grupo de edad | Año 1950 (1) | 1960 (2) | 1960 (1) | 1970 (1) | 1979 (3) | 1980 (1) |
|---|---|---|---|---|---|---|
| **Hombres** | | | | | | |
| 10-14 | 46.55 | ... | .. | 42.50 | 36.78 | 36.75 |
| 15-19 | 90.00 | 87.06 | .. | 83.60 | 62.70 | 74.60 |
| 20-24 | 97.00 | 95.95 | .. | 94.70 | 87.68 | 91.40 |
| 25-29 | 97.80 | 97.66 | . | 97.50 | 96.29 | 97.00 |
| 30-34 | 99.00 | 98.84 | .. | 98.65 | 97.49 | 98.10 |
| 35-39 | 99.20 | 98.98 | .. | 98.75 | 97.61 | 98.20 |
| 40-44 | 98.15 | 97.94 | .. | 97.70 | 97.12 | 97.10 |
| 45-49 | 97.25 | 97.09 | .. | 96.90 | 96.39 | 96.40 |
| 50-54 | 95.65 | 95.41 | .. | 95.10 | 94.37 | 94.35 |
| 55-59 | 94.05 | 93.66 | .. | 93.20 | 92.14 | 92.00 |
| 60-64 | 90.45 | 89.78 | .. | 89.00 | 88.11 | 87.00 |
| 65+ | 81.30 | 80.11 | .. | 78.70 | 75.12 | 75.00 |
| **Mujeres** | | | | | | |
| 10-14 | 30.50 | .. | 29.10 | 28.55 | 27.16 | 27.60 |
| 15-19 | 87.90 | .. | 84.25 | 82.75 | 33.48 | 80.30 |
| 20-24 | 93.50 | .. | 91.20 | 90.25 | 37.67 | 88.70 |
| 25-29 | 97.00 | .. | 96.50 | 96.00 | 40.93 | 95.40 |
| 30-34 | 98.50 | .. | 98.00 | 97.50 | 41.87 | 97.30 |
| 35-39 | 97.80 | .. | 96.40 | 95.45 | 43.31 | 94.80 |
| 40-44 | 94.25 | .. | 93.00 | 92.10 | 44.03 | 91.60 |
| 45-49 | 84.30 | .. | 82.30 | 81.45 | 45.10 | 80.10 |
| 50-54 | 80.30 | .. | 78.00 | 77.05 | 43.02 | 75.50 |
| 55-59 | 75.50 | .. | 73.15 | 72.15 | 42.30 | 70.55 |
| 60-64 | 60.75 | .. | 58.00 | 56.85 | 37.00 | 55.00 |
| 65+ | 44.45 | .. | 41.60 | 40.45 | 27.50 | 38.50 |

Fuente(s): (1) EPPA3; (2) S1960; (3) ADNU84 y ASTER.

### 2.2 Método(s): interpolación y extrapolación lineares

#### 2.2.1 Hombres:

- 1950-90, interpolación y extrapolación de las tasas de actividad con base en la encuesta de 1960 y de las tasas de actividad con base en el censo de 1979; modificación de las tendencias de todos los grupos de edad para 1950 y 1990.

#### 2.2.2 Mujeres:

- 1950-90, interpolación y extrapolación de las tasas de actividad 1950-90 con base en EPPA3; modificación de las tendencias de todos los grupos de edad para 1950 y 1990.

## 3. Evaluación de las tasas de distribución por sector de actividad: 1950 - 1990

### 3.1 Datos básicos:

Cuadro 2: Distribución de la población económicamente activa por sector de actividad en %

| Año | Agricultura | Industria Total | Manufac. | Servicios |
|---|---|---|---|---|
| **Hombres** | | | | |
| 1950 | 85.79 | 5.00 | .. | 9.25 |
| 1960 | 82.00 | 6.50 | .. | 11.50 |
| 1970 | 77.55 | 8.00 | .. | 14.45 |
| 1980 | 66.00 | 10.00 | .. | 24.00 |
| **Mujeres** | | | | |
| 1950 | 91.60 | 1.10 | .. | 7.30 |
| 1960 | 88.40 | 1.55 | .. | 10.05 |
| 1970 | 84.55 | 2.10 | .. | 13.35 |
| 1980 | 68.80 | 3.20 | .. | 22.20 |

Fuente(s): EPPA3.

### 3.2 Método(s): extrapolación linear

#### 3.2.1 Hombres:

- 1950-80, tasas de distribución 1950-80 con base en EPPA3;
- 1990, extrapolación de las tasas de distribución 1950-80 con base en EPPA3;
- Las razones manufacturas/industria con base en las razones manufacturas/industria estimadas para Togo.

#### 3.2.2 Mujeres:

Métodos, hipótesis y tratamientos idénticos a los que se aplican a los hombres.

## 4. Proyección de las tasas de actividad: 2000 - 2010

### 4.1 Modelo(s): logístico, linear y hiperbólico

#### 4.1.1 Hombres:

- Para el grupo de edad [10-14], aplicación de la función F6;
- Para el grupo de edad [15-19], aplicación de la función F1;
- Para los grupos de edad [20+], aplicación de la función F3;
- Modificación de las tendencias de los grupos de edad [55+].

#### 4.1.2 Mujeres:

- Para los grupos de edad [10-14] y [20-64], aplicación de la función F3;
- Para el grupo de edad [15-19], aplicación de la función F6;
- Para el grupo de edad [65+], aplicación de la función F1;
- Modificación de las tendencias de los grupos de edad [20+].

*Notas sobre los ajustes de las tasas, véase p.380-384.*       *Notas sobre las funciones de proyección, véase p. 386.*

# Bhután

## 1. Fuente(s) de los datos básicos

Código(s):   Título(s):
EPPA3   Estimaciones y proyecciones de la población económicamente activa, 1950-2025, tercera edición, OIT, Ginebra, 1986.
EPPA4   Población económicamente activa 1950-2010 - cuarta edición, OIT, Ginebra, 1996.

## 2. Evaluación de las tasas de actividad: 1950 - 1990

### 2.1 Datos básicos:

Cuadro 1: Tasas de actividad por sexo y grupo de edad

| Grupo de edad | Año 1950 | 1975 |
|---|---|---|
| **Hombres** | | |
| 10-14 | 77.04 | 65.31 |
| 15-19 | 95.13 | 78.23 |
| 20-24 | 97.97 | 91.82 |
| 25-29 | 98.84 | 96.72 |
| 30-34 | 98.88 | 97.74 |
| 35-39 | 99.08 | 97.95 |
| 40-44 | 99.15 | 98.16 |
| 45-49 | 98.16 | 96.84 |
| 50-54 | 98.34 | 95.31 |
| 55-59 | 95.63 | 93.08 |
| 60-64 | 86.37 | 84.06 |
| 65+ | 71.24 | 69.35 |
| **Mujeres** | | |
| 10-14 | 67.68 | 52.88 |
| 15-19 | 79.11 | 65.13 |
| 20-24 | 70.39 | 61.85 |
| 25-29 | 66.08 | 59.79 |
| 30-34 | 62.52 | 59.08 |
| 35-39 | 60.04 | 59.61 |
| 40-44 | 56.44 | 58.93 |
| 45-49 | 54.24 | 58.47 |
| 50-54 | 50.91 | 56.88 |
| 55-59 | 44.74 | 53.24 |
| 60-64 | 33.03 | 38.66 |
| 65+ | 14.10 | 28.59 |

Fuente(s): EPPA4.

### 2.2 Método(s): interpolación linear

#### 2.2.1 Hombres:
- 1950 y 1990, tasas de actividad estimadas 1950 y 1990 para Nepal;
- 1960-80, interpolación de las tasas de actividad estimadas para 1950 y 1990.

#### 2.2.2 Mujeres:
Métodos, hipótesis y tratamientos idénticos a los que se aplican a los hombres.

## 3. Evaluación de las tasas de distribución por sector de actividad: 1950 - 1990

### 3.1 Datos básicos:

Cuadro 2: Distribución de la población económicamente activa por sector de actividad en %

| Año | Agricultura | Industria Total | Manufac. | Servicios |
|---|---|---|---|---|
| **Hombres** | | | | |
| 1950 (1) | 93.50 | 3.08 | 2.78 | 3.42 |
| 1975 (1) | 91.60 | 1.26 | 1.09 | 7.14 |
| **Mujeres** | | | | |
| 1950 (1) | 97.83 | 1.73 | 1.69 | 0.44 |
| 1975 (1) | 98.00 | 0.37 | 0.35 | 1.64 |

Nota(s): Nepal.
Fuente(s): EPPA4.

### 3.2 Método(s): interpolación linear

#### 3.2.1 Hombres:
- 1950 y 1990, tasas de distribución 1950 y 1975 estimadas para Nepal;
- 1960-80, interpolación de las tasas de distribución estimadas para 1950 y 1990.

#### 3.2.2 Mujeres:
Métodos, hipótesis y tratamientos idénticos a los que se aplican a los hombres.

## 4. Proyección de las tasas de actividad: 2000 - 2010

### 4.1 Modelo(s): linear

#### 4.1.1 Hombres:
- Para todos los grupos de edad, aplicación de la función F1;
- Modificación de las tendencias de los grupos de edad [10-19] y [60+].

#### 4.1.2 Mujeres:
- Para todos los grupos de edad, aplicación de la función F1;
- Modificación de las tendencias de todos los grupos de edad.

408

# Bolivia

## 1. Fuente(s) de los datos básicos

Código(s):   Título(s):

EPPA3     Estimaciones y proyecciones de la población económicamente activa, 1950-2025, tercera edición, OIT, Ginebra, 1986.
ASTER     Anuario de estadísticas del trabajo 1945-89 - Edición retrospectiva sobre los censos de población, OIT, Ginebra, 1990.
AST94     Anuario de Estadísticas del Trabjo 1994, OIT, Ginebra, 1994.

## 2. Evaluación de las tasas de actividad: 1950 - 1990

### 2.1 Datos básicos:

Cuadro 1: Tasas de actividad por sexo y grupo de edad

| Grupo de edad | 1950 (1) | 1976 (1) | 1992 (2) |
|---|---|---|---|
| **Hombres** | | | |
| 10-14 | 44.17 | 15.99 | 16.12 |
| 15-19 | 78.27 | 54.97 | 44.58 |
| 20-24 | 92.90 | 83.80 | 76.97 |
| 25-29 | 96.73 | 94.75 | 91.03 |
| 30-34 | 97.30 | 98.10 | 95.48 |
| 35-39 | 97.28 | 98.65 | 96.34 |
| 40-44 | 96.82 | 98.44 | 96.28 |
| 45-49 | 96.58 | 98.25 | 95.69 |
| 50-54 | 95.54 | 97.18 | 93.79 |
| 55-59 | 94.58 | 94.77 | 87.26 |
| 60-64 | 92.23 | 89.73 | 80.98 |
| 65+ | 78.13 | 80.49 | 69.49 |
| **Mujeres** | | | |
| 10-14 | 51.91 | 10.09 | 15.28 |
| 15-19 | 66.74 | 22.11 | 35.61 |
| 20-24 | 64.80 | 25.16 | 45.70 |
| 25-29 | 64.22 | 25.44 | 50.16 |
| 30-34 | 66.28 | 23.62 | 52.05 |
| 35-39 | 64.56 | 22.76 | 54.27 |
| 40-44 | 68.30 | 22.88 | 55.20 |
| 45-49 | 65.36 | 22.49 | 54.27 |
| 50-54 | 66.67 | 20.58 | 51.18 |
| 55-59 | 43.29 | 18.63 | 46.97 |
| 60-64 | 29.67 | 16.75 | 43.48 |
| 65+ | 21.68 | 14.06 | 37.18 |

Fuente(s): (1) ASTER; (2) AST94.

### 2.2 Método(s): interpolación y extrapolación lineares

#### 2.2.1 Hombres:

- 1950-70, tasas de actividad 1950-70 con base en EPPA3;
- 1980-90, extrapolación de las tasas de actividad ajustadas con base en el censo de 1976 y de las tasas de actividad ajustadas con base en el censo de 1992.

#### 2.2.2 Mujeres:

- 1950-70, interpolación de las tasas de actividad con base en los censos de 1950 y 1976;
ajuste de las tasas de actividad con base en la razón hombres/mujeres en la agricultura con base en el censo de 1992;
- 1980-90, interpolación de las tasas de actividad con base en los censos de 1976 y 1992.

## 3. Evaluación de las tasas de distribución por sector de actividad: 1950 - 1990

### 3.1 Datos básicos:

Cuadro 2: Distribución de la población económicamente activa por sector de actividad en %

| Año | Agricultura | Industria Total | Manufac. | Servicios |
|---|---|---|---|---|
| **Hombres** | | | | |
| 1950 (1) | 54.44 | 31.55 | 12.79 | 14.02 |
| 1976 (1) | 54.21 | 20.65 | 7.98 | 25.15 |
| 1992 (2) | 44.22 | 23.47 | 10.70 | 32.31 |
| **Mujeres** | | | | |
| 1950 (1) | 74.34 | 11.23 | 8.42 | 14.42 |
| 1976 (1) | 27.21 | 18.51 | 17.26 | 54.28 |
| 1992 (2) | 43.57 | 9.37 | 8.62 | 47.07 |

Fuente(s): (1) ASTER; (2) AST94.

### 3.2 Método(s): interpolación linear

#### 3.2.1 Hombres:

- 1950-90, interpolación de las tasas de distribución con base en los censos de 1950, 1976 y 1992;
ajuste de las tasas estimadas para 1950-60 para tener en cuenta a los auxiliares familiares en la agricultura.

#### 3.2.2 Mujeres:

Métodos, hipótesis y tratamientos idénticos a los que se aplican a los hombres.

## 4. Proyección de las tasas de actividad: 2000 - 2010

### 4.1 Modelo(s): linear, log-linear y hiperbólico

#### 4.1.1 Hombres:

- Para los grupos de edad [10-14] y [60+], aplicación de la función F1;
- Para los grupos de edad [15-59], aplicación de la función F3;
- Modificación de las tendencias de los grupos de edad [10-14], [20-34] y [40-49].

#### 4.1.2 Mujeres:

- Para los grupos de edad [10-19] y [55+], aplicación de la función F1;
- Para los grupos de edad [20-54], aplicación de la función F2;
- Modificación de las tendencias de los grupos de edad [10-19] y [55+].

# Bosnia y Herzegovina

## 1. Fuente(s) de los datos básicos

Código(s): Título(s):

EPPA3     Estimaciones y proyecciones de la población económicamente activa, 1950-2025, tercera edición, OIT, Ginebra, 1986.

BLT-94-2   Popovic B. (1994), "Nuevas estimaciones de las tasas de actividad para 1980 y 1990, desglosadas por grupos de edad y distribución sectorial, en algunos países de Europa oriental y meridional" en el Boletín de Estadísticas del Trabajol - 1994-2, OIT, Ginebra.

## 2. Evaluación de las tasas de actividad: 1950 - 1990

### 2.1 Datos básicos:

Cuadro 1: Tasas de actividad por sexo y grupo de edad

| Grupo de edad | Año | | | | |
| | 1950 (1) | 1960 (1) | 1970 (1) | 1980 (2) | 1990 (2) |
| --- | --- | --- | --- | --- | --- |
| **Hombres** | | | | | |
| 10-14 | 24.10 | 8.85 | 3.25 | 0.31 | 0.02 |
| 15-19 | 86.80 | 67.25 | 48.45 | 25.07 | 22.47 |
| 20-24 | 94.85 | 90.75 | 85.80 | 80.53 | 81.67 |
| 25-29 | 96.10 | 96.55 | 95.80 | 95.53 | 96.06 |
| 30-34 | 97.60 | 97.90 | 98.35 | 97.79 | 98.01 |
| 35-39 | 97.80 | 97.25 | 98.30 | 97.34 | 97.97 |
| 40-44 | 97.60 | 97.00 | 95.55 | 96.11 | 96.85 |
| 45-49 | 97.20 | 96.10 | 96.00 | 92.38 | 93.97 |
| 50-54 | 94.20 | 94.00 | 92.35 | 77.71 | 80.28 |
| 55-59 | 84.65 | 85.60 | 77.05 | 59.83 | 60.51 |
| 60-64 | 79.75 | 75.50 | 65.10 | 51.19 | 38.79 |
| 65+ | 61.60 | 56.70 | 51.30 | 38.36 | 27.42 |
| **Mujeres** | | | | | |
| 10-14 | 23.20 | 12.50 | 5.45 | 1.02 | 0.07 |
| 15-19 | 68.80 | 58.35 | 45.15 | 20.99 | 18.13 |
| 20-24 | 60.75 | 60.55 | 60.35 | 54.68 | 61.95 |
| 25-29 | 45.00 | 53.20 | 57.35 | 56.44 | 68.73 |
| 30-34 | 38.85 | 47.65 | 52.25 | 50.93 | 64.91 |
| 35-39 | 35.45 | 45.15 | 50.35 | 40.73 | 64.17 |
| 40-44 | 32.80 | 42.15 | 47.20 | 35.00 | 56.15 |
| 45-49 | 29.50 | 37.80 | 43.40 | 28.17 | 43.69 |
| 50-54 | 24.20 | 31.70 | 36.70 | 20.12 | 29.67 |
| 55-59 | 21.10 | 26.75 | 31.60 | 15.34 | 17.94 |
| 60-64 | 16.50 | 22.10 | 26.80 | 12.68 | 12.32 |
| 65+ | 10.95 | 14.10 | 14.60 | 7.45 | 7.23 |

Fuente(s): (1) EPPA3; (2) BLT-94-2.

### 2.2 Método(s): con base en EPPA3 y BLT-94-2.

#### 2.2.1 Hombres:

- 1950-70, tasas de actividad 1950-70 para Yugoslavia con base en EPPA3;
- 1980-90, 1980 y 1990 tasas de actividad con base en el Boletín de estadísticas del trabajo 1994-2.

#### 2.2.2 Mujeres:

Métodos, hipótesis y tratamientos idénticos a los que se aplican a los hombres.

## 3. Evaluación de las tasas de distribución por sector de actividad: 1950 - 1990

### 3.1 Datos básicos:

Cuadro 2: Distribución de la población económicamente activa por sector de actividad en %

| Año | Agricultura | Industria | | Servicios |
| | | Total | Manufac. | |
| --- | --- | --- | --- | --- |
| **Hombres** | | | | |
| 1950 (1) | 68.30 | 17.80 | .. | 13.90 |
| 1960 (1) | 56.00 | 28.00 | .. | 16.00 |
| 1970 (1) | 45.00 | 34.40 | .. | 20.60 |
| 1980 (2) | 25.60 | 44.67 | 22.28 | 29.73 |
| 1990 (2) | 8.78 | 53.95 | 31.08 | 37.27 |
| **Mujeres** | | | | |
| 1950 (1) | 83.00 | 5.40 | .. | 11.50 |
| 1960 (1) | 78.10 | 15.00 | .. | 6.80 |
| 1970 (1) | 58.20 | 20.00 | .. | 21.80 |
| 1980 (2) | 37.49 | 23.92 | 20.51 | 38.58 |
| 1990 (2) | 15.55 | 36.83 | 32.57 | 47.62 |

Fuente(s): (1) EPPA3; (2) BLT-94-2.

### 3.2 Método(s): datos de BLT-94-2

#### 3.2.1 Hombres:

- 1950-70, tasas de distribución 1950-70 para Yugoslavia con base en EPPA3;
- 1980-90, tasas de distribución con base en el boletín de estadísticas del trabajo 1994-2.

#### 3.2.2 Mujeres:

Métodos, hipótesis y tratamientos idénticos a los que se aplican a los hombres.

## 4. Proyección de las tasas de actividad: 2000 - 2010

### 4.1 Modelo(s): linear y hiperbólico

#### 4.1.1 Hombres:

- Para los grupos de edad [15-24] y [50+], aplicación de la función F3;
- Para los grupos de edad [25-49], aplicación de la función F1;
- Modificación de las tendencias de los grupos de edad [15-24].

#### 4.1.2 Mujeres:

- Para los grupos de edad [15-24] y [50+], aplicación de la función F3;
- Para los grupos de edad [25-49], aplicación de la función F1;
- Modificación de la tendencia del grupo de edad [15-19].

---

*Notas sobre los ajustes de las tasas, véase p.380-384.*      *Notas sobre las funciones de proyección, véase p. 386.*

# Botswana

## 1. Fuente(s) de los datos básicos

Código(s): Título(s):
ASTER     Anuario de estadísticas del trabajo 1945-89 - Edición retrospectiva sobre los censos de población, OIT, Ginebra, 1990.
R1991     1991 Population and Housing Census Administrative/Technical Report and National Statistical Tables, Central Statistical Office, Gaborone, 1994.

## 2. Evaluación de las tasas de actividad: 1950 - 1990

### 2.1 Datos básicos:

Cuadro 1: Tasas de actividad por sexo y grupo de edad

| Grupo de edad | Año 1964 (1) | 1971 (1) | 1991 (2) |
|---|---|---|---|
| **Hombres** | | | |
| 10-14 | 37.95 | 40.18 | 18.16 |
| 15-19 | 63.98 | 66.26 | 43.78 |
| 20-24 | 92.32 | 92.92 | 86.92 |
| 25-29 | 99.15 | 99.20 | 98.71 |
| 30-34 | 99.07 | 99.10 | 98.81 |
| 35-39 | 99.03 | 99.05 | 98.87 |
| 40-44 | 98.99 | 99.01 | 98.85 |
| 45-49 | 98.82 | 98.82 | 98.82 |
| 50-54 | 98.70 | 98.70 | 98.78 |
| 55-59 | 98.44 | 98.42 | 98.69 |
| 60-64 | 89.85 | 90.70 | 82.33 |
| 65+ | 74.31 | 75.08 | 67.54 |
| **Mujeres** | | | |
| 10-14 | .. | 27.64 | 18.14 |
| 15-19 | .. | 58.54 | 41.26 |
| 20-24 | .. | 83.12 | 75.68 |
| 25-29 | .. | 87.20 | 82.50 |
| 30-34 | .. | 87.49 | 80.84 |
| 35-39 | .. | 87.35 | 77.83 |
| 40-44 | .. | 85.69 | 73.46 |
| 45-49 | .. | 83.54 | 67.01 |
| 50-54 | .. | 80.22 | 60.05 |
| 55-59 | .. | 77.68 | 54.74 |
| 60-64 | .. | 72.40 | 46.65 |
| 65+ | .. | 59.24 | 27.12 |

Fuente(s): (1) ASTER; (2) R1991.

### 2.2 Método(s): interpolación y extrapolación lineares

#### 2.2.1 Hombres:

- 1950-90, interpolación y extrapolación de las tasas de actividad con base en los censos de 1964, 1971 y 1991;
distribución por grupos de edad de la población activa de los censos de 1964 y 1971 con base en la distribución por grupos de edad de la población activa para Namibia.

#### 2.2.2 Mujeres:

Métodos, hipótesis y tratamientos idénticos a los que se aplican a los hombres.

## 3. Evaluación de las tasas de distribución por sector de actividad: 1950 - 1990

### 3.1 Datos básicos:

Cuadro 2: Distribución de la población económicamente activa por sector de actividad en %

| Año | Agricultura | Industria Total | Manufac. | Servicios |
|---|---|---|---|---|
| **Hombres** | | | | |
| 1964 (1) | 87.41 | 5.04 | 1.28 | 7.55 |
| 1981 (1) | 51.14 | 19.26 | 2.05 | 29.60 |
| 1991 (2) | 37.27 | 31.65 | 5.29 | 31.08 |
| **Mujeres** | | | | |
| 1964 (1) | 95.11 | 0.73 | 0.66 | 4.15 |
| 1981 (1) | 72.91 | 1.75 | 0.67 | 25.34 |
| 1991 (2) | 52.85 | 9.98 | 5.97 | 37.17 |

Fuente(s): (1) ASTER; (2) R1991.

### 3.2 Método(s): interpolación y extrapolación lineares
promedio ponderado

#### 3.2.1 Hombres:

- 1950-60, interpolación y extrapolación de las tasas de distribución con base en los censos de 1964, 1981 y 1991;
modificación de las tendencias de todos los sectores;
- 1970-90, promedios ponderados de las tasas de distribución con base en los censos de 1964, 1981 y 1991.
los censos de 1964, 1981 y 1991.

#### 3.2.2 Mujeres:

Métodos, hipótesis y tratamientos idénticos a los que se aplican a los hombres.

## 4. Proyección de las tasas de actividad: 2000 - 2010

### 4.1 Modelo(s): logístico, log-linear, hiperbólico y logaritímico

#### 4.1.1 Hombres:

- Para los grupos de edad [10-14] y [65+], aplicación de la función F6;
- Para el grupo de edad [15-19], aplicación de la función F2;
- Para los grupos de edad [20-64], aplicación de la función F3;
- Modificación de las tendencias de los grupos de edad [35-39] y [45-59].

#### 4.1.2 Mujeres:

- Para el grupo de edad [10-14], aplicación de la función F5;
- Para el grupo de edad [15-19], aplicación de la función F2;
- Para los grupos de edad [20+], aplicación de la función F3;
- Modificación de las tendencias de los grupos de edad [20-64].

*Notas sobre los ajustes de las tasas, véase p.380-384.*     *Notas sobre las funciones de proyección, véase p. 386.*

# Brasil

## 1. Fuente(s) de los datos básicos

Código(s):   Título(s):
EPPA3    Estimaciones y proyecciones de la población económicamente activa, 1950-2025, tercera edición, OIT, Ginebra, 1986.
ASTER    Anuario de estadísticas del trabajo 1945-89 - Edición retrospectiva sobre los censos de población, OIT, Ginebra, 1990.
AST93    Anuario de Estadísticas del Trabjo 1993, OIT, Ginebra, 1993.

## 2. Evaluación de las tasas de actividad: 1950 - 1990

### 2.1 Datos básicos:

Cuadro 1: Tasas de actividad por sexo y grupo de edad

| Grupo de edad | Año 1980 (1) | 1989 (2) | 1990 (2) |
|---|---|---|---|
| **Hombres** | | | |
| 10-14 | 20.24 | 25.51 | 24.32 |
| 15-19 | 64.80 | 73.27 | 71.76 |
| 20-24 | 90.03 | 92.50 | 92.14 |
| 25-29 | 96.05 | 96.30 | 96.16 |
| 30-39 | 96.53 | 97.31 | 96.85 |
| 40-49 | 93.16 | 94.62 | 94.46 |
| 50-59 | 82.30 | 81.51 | 82.33 |
| 60+ | 44.39 | 45.51 | 46.03 |
| **Women** | | | |
| 10-14 | 8.61 | 11.77 | 10.61 |
| 15-19 | 31.21 | 40.93 | 41.42 |
| 20-24 | 39.07 | 52.02 | 52.86 |
| 25-29 | 35.95 | 52.45 | 52.75 |
| 30-39 | 34.20 | 53.27 | 54.66 |
| 40-49 | 30.04 | 48.63 | 49.50 |
| 50-59 | 21.38 | 33.85 | 34.54 |
| 60+ | 7.38 | 11.29 | 11.55 |

Fuente(s): (1) ASTER; (2) AST93.

### 2.2 Método(s): promedio ponderado

#### 2.2.1 Hombres:
- 1950-70, tasas de actividad ajustadas 1950-70 con base en EPPA3;
ajuste de las tasas de actividad con base en los resultados del censo de 1980
y de las encuestas de 1989 y 1990;
- 1980, promedios ponderados de las tasas de actividad 1970 con base
en EPPA3 y de las tasas de actividad ajustadas con base en el censo de 1980;
- 1990, promedios ponderados de las tasas de actividad con base en
las encuestas de 1989 y 1990.

#### 2.2.2 Mujeres:
Métodos, hipótesis y tratamientos idénticos a los que se aplican a los hombres.

## 3. Evaluación de las tasas de distribución por sector de actividad: 1950 - 1990

### 3.1 Datos básicos:

Cuadro 2: Distribución de la población económicamente activa por sector de actividad en %

| Año | Agricultura | Industria Total | Manufac. | Servicios |
|---|---|---|---|---|
| **Hombres** | | | | |
| 1980 (1) | 37.54 | 29.32 | 19.11 | 33.14 |
| 1989 (2) | 29.36 | 29.04 | .. | 41.60 |
| 1990 (3) | 28.08 | 28.15 | 16.93 | 43.78 |
| **Mujeres** | | | | |
| 1980 (1) | 15.27 | 15.76 | 15.27 | 68.98 |
| 1989 (2) | 14.68 | 12.72 | 0.00 | 72.60 |
| 1990 (3) | 13.34 | 12.82 | 11.94 | 73.85 |

Fuente(s): (1) ASTER; (2) AST93.

### 3.2 Método(s): promedio ponderado

#### 3.2.1 Hombres:
- 1950-70, tasas de distribución ajustadas 1950-70 con base en EPPA3;
ajuste de las tasas con base en los resultados del censo de 1980
y de las encuestas de 1989 y 1990;
- 1980-90, promedios ponderados de las tasas de distribución con base en
el censo de 1980 y de las tasas de distribución con base en la encuesta
el censo de 1980 y de las tasas de distribución con base en la encuesta

#### 3.2.2 Mujeres:
Métodos, hipótesis y tratamientos idénticos a los que se aplican a los hombres.

## 4. Proyección de las tasas de actividad: 2000 - 2010

### 4.1 Modelo(s): linear, hiperbólico y logístico

#### 4.1.1 Hombres:
- Para los grupos de edad [10-44], aplicación de la función F1;
- Para los grupos de edad [45+], aplicación de la función F3;
- Modificación de las tendencias de los grupos de edad [10-24] y [35-49].

#### 4.1.2 Mujeres:
- Para el grupo de edad [10-14], aplicación de la función F1;
- Para los grupos de edad [15-64], aplicación de la función F6;
- Para el grupo de edad [65+], aplicación de la función F3;
- Modificación de las tendencias de los grupos de edad [10-64].

# Brunéi Darussalam

## 1. Fuente(s) de los datos básicos

Código(s):   Título(s):
ADNU79   Annuaire démographique 1979 - Statistiques des recensements de population, trente et unième édition, Nations Unies, New York, 1980.
ASTER   Anuario de estadísticas del trabajo 1945-89 - Edición retrospectiva sobre los censos de población, OIT, Ginebra, 1990.
ADNU93   Annuaire démographique 1993 - Statistiques des recensements de population, trente et unième édition, Nations Unies, New York.
STAT   Base de datos de la OIT sobre estadísticas del trabajo - LABORSTA, Oficina de Estadística, OIT, Ginebra.

## 2. Evaluación de las tasas de actividad: 1950 - 1990

### 2.1 Datos básicos:

Cuadro 1: Tasas de actividad por sexo y grupo de edad

| Grupo de edad | Año 1960 (1) | 1971 (1) | 1981 (1) | 1986 (1) | 1991 (2) |
|---|---|---|---|---|---|
| **Hombres** | | | | | |
| 10-14 | 0.00 | 0.00 | 0.00 | .. | 0.00 |
| 15-19 | 46.47 | 32.90 | 38.18 | .. | 23.80 |
| 20-24 | 91.30 | 86.55 | 86.40 | .. | 84.22 |
| 25-29 | 99.02 | 97.10 | 97.30 | .. | 97.10 |
| 30-34 | 99.29 | 97.33 | 98.71 | .. | 98.13 |
| 35-39 | 99.97 | 98.08 | 98.91 | .. | 98.35 |
| 40-44 | 99.36 | 97.66 | 98.32 | .. | 98.25 |
| 45-49 | 97.96 | 97.12 | 98.27 | .. | 96.34 |
| 50-54 | 95.89 | 94.87 | 96.40 | .. | 93.95 |
| 55-59 | 90.92 | 88.11 | 88.86 | .. | 72.08 |
| 60-64 | 82.44 | 80.88 | 82.70 | .. | 71.03 |
| 65+ | 56.66 | 58.61 | 51.94 | .. | 32.23 |
| **Mujeres** | | | | | |
| 10-14 | 0.00 | 0.00 | 0.00 | 0.00 | 0.00 |
| 15-19 | 18.82 | 17.92 | 17.02 | 14.45 | 13.74 |
| 20-24 | 19.83 | 30.23 | 47.13 | 52.68 | 58.19 |
| 25-29 | 16.68 | 24.36 | 43.37 | 57.18 | 63.89 |
| 30-34 | 18.49 | 21.78 | 36.73 | 48.01 | 60.67 |
| 35-39 | 21.89 | 18.35 | 32.92 | 46.93 | 56.66 |
| 40-44 | 25.03 | 19.76 | 28.56 | 41.79 | 51.50 |
| 45-49 | 26.42 | 20.26 | 22.74 | 36.07 | 43.36 |
| 50-54 | 30.64 | 21.55 | 20.55 | 24.89 | 34.89 |
| 55-59 | 27.76 | 22.83 | 14.49 | 16.75 | 17.56 |
| 60-64 | 20.68 | 18.80 | 10.44 | 12.49 | 13.18 |
| 65+ | 7.71 | 11.48 | 5.95 | 5.77 | 4.16 |

Fuente(s): (1) ADNU79 y ASTER; (2) STAT.

### 2.2 Método(s): interpolación linear
promedio ponderado

**2.2.1 Hombres:**

- 1950-80, interpolación de las tasas de actividad con base en
los censos de 1960, 1971 y 1981;
modificación de las tendencias de todos los grupos de edad para 1950;
- 1990, promedios ponderados de las tasas de actividad con base en
los censos de 1981 y 1990.

**2.2.2 Mujeres:**

- 1950-70, interpolación de las tasas de actividad con base en
los censos de 1960 y 1971;
- 1980-90, interpolación de las tasas de actividad con base en los censo
de 1981, 1986 y 1991;
aplicación a las tasas de actividad del grupo de edad [10-14], la razón de
las tasas de actividad del grupo de edad [10-14] y [15-19] estimadas para Kuwait

## 3. Evaluación de las tasas de distribución por sector de actividad: 1950 - 1990

### 3.1 Datos básicos:

Cuadro 2: Distribución de la población económicamente activa por sector de actividad en %

| Año | Agricultura | Industria Total | Manufac. | Servicios |
|---|---|---|---|---|
| **Hombres** | | | | |
| 1960 (1) | 28.68 | 40.69 | 5.75 | 30.63 |
| 1971 (1) | 9.84 | 39.32 | 4.37 | 50.85 |
| 1981 (1) | 4.72 | 37.23 | 4.23 | 58.05 |
| 1991 (2) | 2.21 | 31.43 | 6.44 | 66.35 |
| **Mujeres** | | | | |
| 1960 (1) | 57.35 | 10.07 | 5.56 | 32.58 |
| 1971 (1) | 23.01 | 10.36 | 4.43 | 66.63 |
| 1981 (1) | 6.25 | 11.00 | 3.66 | 82.75 |
| 1991 (2) | 1.63 | 8.87 | 4.24 | 89.49 |

Fuente(s): (1) ASTER; (2) STAT.

### 3.2 Método(s): promedio ponderado
extrapolación linear

**3.2.1 Hombres:**

- 1950, extrapolación de las tasas de distribución con base en los censos
de 1960 y 1971;
- 1960-90, promedios ponderados de las tasas de distribución con base en
los censos de 1960, 1971, 1981 y 1991.

**3.2.2 Mujeres:**

- 1950, tasas de distribución de la agricultura estimada con base en la razón
hombres/mujeres en la agricultura con base en el censo de 1960;
la tasa de distribución de la industria con base en el censo de 1960;
la tasa de distribución de los servicios se calcula como residuo;
- 1960-90, promedios ponderados de las tasas de distribución con base en
los censos de 1960, 1971, 1981 y 1991.

## 4. Proyección de las tasas de actividad: 2000 - 2010

### 4.1 Modelo(s): linear, log-linear, hiperbólico y logístico

**4.1.1 Hombres:**

- Para los grupos de edad [15-54], aplicación de la función F1;
- Para los grupos de edad [55+], aplicación de la función F3;
- Modificación de las tendencias de los grupos de edad [15-19], [25-34],
[40-44] y [55-64].

**4.1.2 Mujeres:**

- Para los grupos de edad [15-24], [30-39] y [45-64], aplicación de la función F1
- Para el grupo de edad [25-29], aplicación de la función F6;
- Para el grupo de edad [40-44], aplicación de la función F2;
- Para el grupo de edad [65+], aplicación de la función F3;
- Modificación de las tendencias de los grupos de edad [15-64].

---

*Notas sobre los ajustes de las tasas, véase p.380-384.*   *Notas sobre las funciones de proyección, véase p. 386.*

# Bulgaria

## 1. Fuente(s) de los datos básicos

Código(s):   Título(s):

EPPA3        Estimaciones y proyecciones de la población económicamente activa, 1950-2025, tercera edición, OIT, Ginebra, 1986.
ASTER        Anuario de estadísticas del trabajo 1945-89 - Edición retrospectiva sobre los censos de población, OIT, Ginebra, 1990.
BLT-94-2     Popovic B. (1994), "Nuevas estimaciones de las tasas de actividad para 1980 y 1990, desglosadas por grupos de edad y distribución sectorial, en algunos países de Europa oriental y meridional" en el Boletín de Estadísticas del Trabajol - 1994-2, OIT, Ginebra.

## 2. Evaluación de las tasas de actividad: 1950 - 1990

### 2.1 Datos básicos:

Cuadro 1: Tasas de actividad por sexo y grupo de edad

| Grupo de edad | Año 1950 (1) | 1960 (1) | 1970 (1) | 1985 (2) |
|---|---|---|---|---|
| **Hombres** | | | | |
| 10-14 | 2.00 | 0.85 | 0.45 | 0.00 |
| 15-19 | 60.00 | 45.55 | 31.15 | 17.69 |
| 20-24 | 92.70 | 90.00 | 83.30 | 81.90 |
| 25-29 | 95.55 | 95.35 | 95.15 | 95.07 |
| 30-34 | 98.00 | 97.90 | 97.80 | 97.80 |
| 35-39 | 98.35 | 98.10 | 97.80 | 95.80 |
| 40-44 | 98.50 | 97.90 | 97.35 | 95.50 |
| 45-49 | 98.40 | 97.25 | 96.15 | 94.60 |
| 50-54 | 97.80 | 95.30 | 92.80 | 88.10 |
| 55-59 | 95.50 | 90.80 | 86.05 | 80.90 |
| 60-64 | 93.20 | 70.00 | 46.80 | 39.20 |
| 65+ | 69.00 | 38.35 | 20.60 | 15.17 |
| **Mujeres** | | | | |
| 10-14 | 3.50 | 1.30 | 0.85 | 0.07 |
| 15-19 | 56.25 | 44.50 | 32.20 | 34.47 |
| 20-24 | 72.50 | 69.80 | 73.35 | 87.04 |
| 25-29 | 71.70 | 78.10 | 85.05 | 95.00 |
| 30-34 | 74.05 | 80.90 | 88.35 | 96.40 |
| 35-39 | 77.15 | 83.25 | 89.90 | 94.80 |
| 40-44 | 78.55 | 83.35 | 88.50 | 94.60 |
| 45-49 | 76.55 | 79.55 | 82.70 | 91.00 |
| 50-54 | 71.55 | 71.40 | 71.25 | 83.60 |
| 55-59 | 68.95 | 46.40 | 31.20 | 32.00 |
| 60-64 | 62.80 | 28.45 | 12.90 | 16.50 |
| 65+ | 20.40 | 8.60 | 3.60 | 4.35 |

Fuente(s): (1) EPPA3; (2) STAT.

### 2.2 Método(s): promedio ponderado
extrapolación linear

#### 2.2.1 Hombres:

- 1950-70, tasas de actividad 1950-70 con base en EPPA3;
- 1980, promedios ponderados de las tasas de actividad 1970 con base en EPPA3 y de las tasas de actividad ajustadas con base en el censo de 1985;
- 1990, extrapolación de las tasas de actividad 1950-70 con base en EPPA3 y de las tasas de actividad estimadas para 1980 y de las tasas de actividad ajustadas con base en el censo de 1985; modificación de las tendencias de todos los grupos de edad; aplicación a las tasas extrapoladas, de las variaciones de las tasas interpoladas 1985, en relación con las tasas ajustadas del censo de 1985.

#### 2.2.2 Mujeres:

Métodos, hipótesis y tratamientos idénticos a los que se aplican a los hombres.

## 3. Evaluación de las tasas de distribución por sector de actividad: 1950 - 1990

### 3.1 Datos básicos:

Cuadro 2: Distribución de la población económicamente activa por sector de actividad en %

| Año | Agricultura | Industria Total | Manufac. | Servicios |
|---|---|---|---|---|
| **Hombres** | | | | |
| 1950 (1) | 63.20 | 18.30 | .. | 18.40 |
| 1960 (1) | 47.60 | 31.30 | .. | 21.10 |
| 1970 (1) | 29.10 | 44.30 | .. | 26.60 |
| 1980 (2) | 18.72 | 49.90 | 34.99 | 31.38 |
| 1990 (2) | 13.83 | 53.96 | 40.81 | 32.21 |
| **Mujeres** | | | | |
| 1950 (1) | 85.50 | 7.00 | .. | 7.40 |
| 1960 (1) | 68.60 | 15.60 | .. | 15.80 |
| 1970 (1) | 41.90 | 29.50 | .. | 28.50 |
| 1980 (2) | 21.94 | 38.64 | 33.90 | 39.42 |
| 1990 (2) | 13.05 | 42.09 | 36.62 | 44.86 |

Fuente(s): (1) EPPA3; (2) BLT-94-2.

### 3.2 Método(s): datos de BLT-94-2

#### 3.2.1 Hombres:

- 1950-70, tasas de distribución 1950-70 con base en EPPA3;
- 1980-90, tasas de distribución con base en el boletín de estadísticas del trabajo 1994-2.

#### 3.2.2 Mujeres:

Métodos, hipótesis y tratamientos idénticos a los que se aplican a los hombres.

## 4. Proyección de las tasas de actividad: 2000 - 2010

### 4.1 Modelo(s): linear y hiperbólico

#### 4.1.1 Hombres:

- Para los grupos de edad [15+], aplicación de la función F3;
- Modificación de las tendencias de los grupos de edad [20-24] y [30-34].

#### 4.1.2 Mujeres:

- Para el grupo de edad [15-19], aplicación de la función F1;
- Para los grupos de edad [20+], aplicación de la función F3;
- Modification des tendances du groupe d'âge [15-54].

*Notas sobre los ajustes de las tasas, véase p.380-384.*

*Notas sobre las funciones de proyección, véase p. 386.*

# Burkina Faso

## 1. Fuente(s) de los datos básicos

Código(s):     Título(s):
S1960          Enquête démographique 1960-61, Institut National de la Statistique et de la Démographie, Ouagadougou, 1961.
R1985          Recensement général de la population 1985, Institut National de la Statistique et de la Démographie, Ouagadougou, 1985.
S1991          Enquête démographique, 1991, Institut National de la Statistique et de la Démographie, Ouagadougou, 1991.

## 2. Evaluación de las tasas de actividad: 1950 - 1990

### 2.1 Datos básicos:

Cuadro 1: Tasas de actividad por sexo y grupo de edad

| Grupo de edad | Año 1960 (1) | 1985 (2) | 1991 (3) |
|---|---|---|---|
| **Hombres** | | | |
| 10-14 | 79.00 | 71.18 | 63.25 |
| 15-19 | 87.00 | 86.02 | 77.75 |
| 20-24 | 96.05 | 92.24 | 85.99 |
| 25-29 | 97.50 | 96.78 | 93.45 |
| 30-34 | 98.25 | 97.72 | 97.60 |
| 35-39 | 98.45 | 98.06 | 98.13 |
| 40-44 | 98.30 | 97.62 | 98.33 |
| 45-49 | 97.50 | 97.47 | 98.49 |
| 50-54 | 97.15 | 95.78 | 96.24 |
| 55-59 | 96.40 | 94.05 | 93.73 |
| 60-64 | 93.65 | 91.01 | 92.33 |
| 65+ | 80.85 | 73.31 | 78.19 |
| **Mujeres** | | | |
| 10-14 | 79.80 | 68.18 | 60.63 |
| 15-19 | 88.75 | 76.33 | 71.58 |
| 20-24 | 93.05 | 76.82 | 75.27 |
| 25-29 | 93.95 | 80.07 | 80.89 |
| 30-34 | 95.50 | 81.20 | 83.56 |
| 35-39 | 95.40 | 82.44 | 84.02 |
| 40-44 | 94.80 | 82.08 | 86.60 |
| 45-49 | 93.40 | 82.32 | 85.51 |
| 50-54 | 92.04 | 81.12 | 87.24 |
| 55-59 | 86.37 | 74.46 | 78.47 |
| 60-64 | 80.38 | 64.13 | 67.88 |
| 65+ | 65.46 | 40.32 | 44.05 |

**Fuente(s):** (1) S1960; (2) R1985; (3) S1991.

### 2.2 Método(s): interpolación y extrapolación lineares

#### 2.2.1 Hombres:
- 1950-90, interpolación y extrapolación de las tasas de actividad con base en el censo de 1985 y de las tasas de actividad con base en las encuestas de 1960 y 1991; ajuste de las tasas extrapoladas 1950 con base en las variaciones de las tasas interpoladas 1960, en relación con las tasas de actividad con base en la encuesta de 1960; ajuste las tasas extrapoladas con base en las variaciones de las tasas interpoladas 1985, en relación con las tasas de actividad con base en el censo de 1985; modificación de las tendencias de todos los grupos de edad para 1950 y de los grupos de edad [10-19] para 1990.

#### 2.2.2 Mujeres:
- 1950-90, interpolación y extrapolación de las tasas de actividad con base en la encuesta de 1960 y de los promedios de las tasas de actividad con base en el censo de 1985 y la encuesta de 1991; modificación de las tendencias de todos los grupos de edad para 1950 y de los grupos de edad [10-14] y [20+] para 1990.

## 3. Evaluación de las tasas de distribución por sector de actividad: 1950 - 1990

### 3.1 Datos básicos:

Cuadro 2: Distribución de la población económicamente activa por sector de actividad en %

| Año | Agricultura | Industria Total | Manufac. | Servicios |
|---|---|---|---|---|
| **Hombres** | | | | |
| 1960 (1) | 92.00 | 3.00 | .. | 5.00 |
| 1985 (2) | 91.18 | 3.64 | .. | 5.18 |
| 1991 (3) | 91.85 | 1.84 | 1.15 | 6.31 |
| **Mujeres** | | | | |
| 1960 (1) | 91.50 | 2.10 | .. | 6.40 |
| 1985 (2) | 92.32 | 2.08 | .. | 5.60 |
| 1991 (3) | 94.40 | 1.14 | 1.09 | 4.45 |

**Fuente(s):** (1) S1960; (2) R1985; (3) S1991.

### 3.2 Método(s): interpolación y extrapolación lineares

#### 3.2.1 Hombres:
- 1950-90, interpolación de las tasas de distribución con base en las encuestas de 1960 y 1991 y el censo de 1985;
- Aplicación de la razón manufacturas/industria con base en la encuesta de 1991

#### 3.2.2 Mujeres:
Métodos, hipótesis y tratamientos idénticos a los que se aplican a los hombres.

## 4. Proyección de las tasas de actividad: 2000 - 2010

### 4.1 Modelo(s): linear, hiperbólico y exponencial

#### 4.1.1 Hombres:
- Para los grupos de edad [10-24], aplicación de la función F1;
- Para los grupos de edad [25+], aplicación de la función F3;
- Modificación de las tendencias de los grupos de edad [20-24] y [40-44].

#### 4.1.2 Mujeres:
- Para el grupo de edad [10-14], aplicación de la función F4;
- Para los grupos de edad [15+], aplicación de la función F3;
- Modificación de las tendencias de los grupos de edad [10-14] y [20-64].

*Notas sobre los ajustes de las tasas, véase p.380-384.*          *Notas sobre las funciones de proyección, véase p. 386.*

# Burundi

## 1. Fuente(s) de los datos básicos

Código(s):  Título(s):

EPPA3   Estimaciones y proyecciones de la población económicamente activa, 1950-2025, tercera edición, OIT, Ginebra, 1986.
ASTER   Anuario de estadísticas del trabajo 1945-89 - Edición retrospectiva sobre los censos de población, OIT, Ginebra, 1990.

## 2. Evaluación de las tasas de actividad: 1950 - 1990

### 2.1 Datos básicos:

Cuadro 1: Tasas de actividad por sexo y grupo de edad

| Grupo de edad | Año 1950 | 1960 | 1970 | 1980 |
|---|---|---|---|---|
| **Hombres** | | | | |
| 10-14 | 56.35 | 55.25 | 54.15 | 53.45 |
| 15-19 | 89.35 | 87.90 | 86.45 | 85.55 |
| 20-24 | 96.25 | 95.65 | 95.10 | 94.80 |
| 25-29 | 97.80 | 97.75 | 97.65 | 97.60 |
| 30-34 | 98.55 | 98.45 | 98.35 | 98.30 |
| 35-39 | 98.55 | 98.45 | 98.35 | 98.30 |
| 40-44 | 98.15 | 98.05 | 97.95 | 97.90 |
| 45-49 | 98.05 | 97.95 | 97.85 | 97.80 |
| 50-54 | 96.85 | 96.70 | 96.60 | 96.50 |
| 55-59 | 95.65 | 95.40 | 95.20 | 95.10 |
| 60-64 | 92.60 | 92.25 | 91.90 | 91.70 |
| 65+ | 76.25 | 75.70 | 75.10 | 74.75 |
| **Mujeres** | | | | |
| 10-14 | 50.35 | 48.90 | 47.45 | 46.55 |
| 15-19 | 92.60 | 89.55 | 86.45 | 84.60 |
| 20-24 | 96.80 | 93.80 | 90.80 | 89.00 |
| 25-29 | 97.45 | 94.65 | 91.90 | 90.25 |
| 30-34 | 98.75 | 96.15 | 93.55 | 92.00 |
| 35-39 | 98.45 | 96.00 | 93.55 | 92.10 |
| 40-44 | 97.55 | 95.35 | 93.15 | 91.85 |
| 45-49 | 96.10 | 93.95 | 91.80 | 90.55 |
| 50-54 | 88.20 | 86.40 | 84.65 | 83.55 |
| 55-59 | 78.10 | 76.80 | 75.55 | 74.75 |
| 60-64 | 61.90 | 61.15 | 60.35 | 59.90 |
| 65+ | 35.75 | 35.45 | 35.20 | 35.05 |

Fuente: EPPA3.

### 2.2 Método(s): interpolación y extrapolación lineares

**2.2.1 Hombres:**
- 1950-90, interpolación y extrapolación de las tasas de actividad 1950-80 con base en EPPA3;
modificación de las tendencias de todos los grupos de edad;
ajuste de las tasas extrapoladas 1990 con base en las variaciones
de las tasas interpoladas 1980, en relación con las tasas de actividad 1980
con base en EPPA3.

**2.2.2 Mujeres:**
Métodos, hipótesis y tratamientos idénticos a los que se aplican a los hombres.

## 3. Evaluación de las tasas de distribución por sector de actividad: 1950 - 1990

### 3.1 Datos básicos:

Cuadro 2: Distribución de la población económicamente activa por sector de actividad en %

| Año | Agricultura | Industria Total | Manufac. | Servicios |
|---|---|---|---|---|
| **Hombres** | | | | |
| 1950 (1) | 93.00 | 2.20 | .. | 4.80 |
| 1960 (1) | 91.00 | 2.85 | .. | 6.15 |
| 1970 (1) | 89.00 | 3.30 | .. | 7.70 |
| 1979 (2) | 87.90 | 3.66 | 2.11 | 8.43 |
| 1980 (1) | 87.80 | 3.70 | .. | 8.50 |
| **Mujeres** | | | | |
| 1950 (1) | 98.30 | 0.80 | .. | 0.90 |
| 1960 (1) | 98.15 | 0.90 | .. | 0.95 |
| 1970 (1) | 98.00 | 0.95 | .. | 1.05 |
| 1979 (2) | 97.89 | 1.02 | 1.01 | 1.10 |
| 1980 (1) | 97.85 | 1.05 | .. | 1.10 |

Fuente(s): (1) EPPA3; (2) ASTER.

### 3.2 Método(s): extrapolación linear

**3.2.1 Hombres:**
- 1950-80, tasas de distribución 1950-80 con base en EPPA3;
- 1990, extrapolación de las tasas de distribución 1950-80 con base en EPPA3;
- Aplicación de la razón manufacturas/industria con base en el censo de 1979.

**3.2.2 Mujeres:**
Métodos, hipótesis y tratamientos idénticos a los que se aplican a los hombres.

## 4. Proyección de las tasas de actividad: 2000 - 2010

### 4.1 Modelo(s): linear y hiperbólico

**4.1.1 Hombres:**
- Para todos los grupos de edad, aplicación de la función F1.

**4.1.2 Mujeres:**
- Para todos los grupos de edad, aplicación de la función F3;
- Modificación de las tendencias de los grupos de edad [20-54].

*Notas sobre los ajustes de las tasas, véase p.380-384.*   *Notas sobre las funciones de proyección, véase p. 386.*

# Cabo Verde

## 1. Fuente(s) de los datos básicos

Código(s):   Título(s):

EPPA3        Estimaciones y proyecciones de la población económicamente activa, 1950-2025, tercera edición, OIT, Ginebra, 1986.
R1980        Recenseamento Geral da Populacao e Habitacao 1980, III Volume: Populacao Activa, Ministerio do Plano e das Finanças, Paraia, 1983.
R1990        Recenseamento da Populacao e Habitacao 1990, Ministerio do Plano e das Finanças, Paraia, 1992.

## 2. Evaluación de las tasas de actividad: 1950 - 1990

### 2.1 Datos básicos:

Cuadro 1: Tasas de actividad por sexo y grupo de edad

| Grupo de edad | Año 1950 (1) | 1960 (1) | 1970 (1) | 1980 (1) | 1980 (2) | 1990 (3) |
|---|---|---|---|---|---|---|
| **Hombres** | | | | | | |
| 10-14 | 52.05 | 52.00 | 51.85 | 51.60 | .. | 17.89 |
| 15-19 | 84.80 | 84.75 | 84.60 | 84.25 | .. | 72.65 |
| 20-24 | 95.25 | 95.20 | 95.15 | 95.00 | .. | 94.27 |
| 25-29 | 97.40 | 97.40 | 97.40 | 97.35 | .. | 96.83 |
| 30-34 | 98.15 | 98.10 | 98.10 | 98.10 | .. | 96.69 |
| 35-39 | 98.30 | 98.30 | 98.30 | 98.25 | .. | 95.78 |
| 40-44 | 98.15 | 98.15 | 98.10 | 98.10 | .. | 95.11 |
| 45-49 | 97.35 | 97.35 | 97.35 | 97.35 | .. | 95.63 |
| 50-54 | 96.95 | 96.95 | 96.90 | 96.90 | .. | 93.57 |
| 55-59 | 96.05 | 96.05 | 96.05 | 96.00 | .. | 91.54 |
| 60-64 | 93.10 | 93.10 | 93.05 | 92.95 | .. | 86.64 |
| 65+ | 79.90 | 79.85 | 79.80 | 79.65 | .. | 59.42 |
| **Mujeres** | | | | | | |
| 10-14 | 7.50 | 6.80 | 6.20 | .. | 5.48 | 10.97 |
| 15-19 | 29.70 | 32.10 | 34.50 | .. | 36.32 | 43.19 |
| 20-24 | 31.40 | 35.70 | 40.00 | .. | 44.49 | 52.56 |
| 25-29 | 27.05 | 30.50 | 34.00 | .. | 37.98 | 51.66 |
| 30-34 | 24.80 | 28.55 | 32.20 | .. | 34.14 | 51.24 |
| 35-39 | 22.10 | 24.50 | 27.80 | .. | 30.35 | 50.02 |
| 40-44 | 19.20 | 21.20 | 23.20 | .. | 25.14 | 42.84 |
| 45-49 | 18.70 | 19.50 | 20.45 | .. | 21.20 | 38.52 |
| 50-54 | 18.00 | 19.00 | 20.00 | .. | 20.95 | 33.96 |
| 55-59 | 15.80 | 16.30 | 17.80 | .. | 17.36 | 27.95 |
| 60-64 | 13.00 | 13.10 | 13.20 | .. | 13.30 | 24.58 |
| 65+ | 11.80 | 10.50 | 9.20 | .. | 7.75 | 11.87 |

Fuente(s): (1) EPPA3; (2) R1980; (3) R1990.

### 2.2 Método(s): interpolación y extrapolación lineares

#### 2.2.1 Hombres:

- 1950-80, interpolación de la tasas de actividad 1950-80 con base en EPPA3;
ajuste de las tasas interpoladas con base en las variaciones de las
tasas extrapoladas 1990, en relación con las tasas de actividad ajustadas
con base en el censo de 1990;
- 1990, tasas de actividad ajustadas con base en el censo de 1990;
modificación de las tendencias de los grupos de edad [10-14] y [60+] para 1980
y 1990.

#### 2.2.2 Mujeres:

- 1950-70, extrapolación de las tasas de actividad ajustadas con base en
los censos de 1980 y 1990;
- 1980-90, tasas de actividad ajustadas con base en los censos de 1980 y 1990;
modificación de las tendencias de todos los grupos de edad.

## 3. Evaluación de las tasas de distribución por sector de actividad: 1950 - 1990

### 3.1 Datos básicos:

Cuadro 2: Distribución de la población económicamente activa por sector de actividad en %

| Año | Agricultura | Industria Total | Manufac. | Servicios |
|---|---|---|---|---|
| **Hombres** | | | | |
| 1980 (1) | 34.76 | 37.08 | 2.55 | 28.17 |
| 1990 (2) | 29.92 | 37.54 | 6.50 | 32.54 |
| **Mujeres** | | | | |
| 1980 (1) | 40.35 | 18.63 | 2.88 | 41.03 |
| 1990 (2) | 31.63 | 17.43 | 4.18 | 50.94 |

Fuente(s): (1) R1980; (2) R1990.

### 3.2 Método(s): extrapolación linear

#### 3.2.1 Hombres:
- 1980 y 90, tasas de distribución con base en los censos de 1980 y 1990;
- 1950-70, para los servicios, extrapolación de las tasas de distribución
con base en los censos de 1980 y 1990;
para la industria, aplicación de la razón industria/servicios con base en
el censo de 1980;
el censo de 1980;

#### 3.2.2 Mujeres:
- 1980-90, tasas de distribución con base en los censos de 1980 y 1990;
- 1950-70, para los servicios, extrapolación de las tasas de distribución
con base en los censos de 1980 y 1990;
modificación de la tendencia del sector;
para la industria, aplicación de la razón industria/servicios con base en el censo
de 1980 y para la agricultura, se calcula como residuo.

## 4. Proyección de las tasas de actividad: 2000 - 2010

### 4.1 Modelo(s): linear

#### 4.1.1 Hombres:
- Para todos los grupos de edad, aplicación de la función F1;
- Modificación de las tendencias de los grupos de edad [15-24].

#### 4.1.2 Mujeres:
- Para todos los grupos de edad, aplicación de la función F1;
- Modificación de las tendencias de los grupos de edad [60+].

*Notas sobre los ajustes de las tasas, véase p.380-384.*    *Notas sobre las funciones de proyección, véase p. 386.*

# Camboya

## 1. Fuente(s) de los datos básicos

Código(s):  Título(s):

EPPA3  Estimaciones y proyecciones de la población económicamente activa, 1950-2025, tercera edición, OIT, Ginebra, 1986.
STAT  Base de datos de la OIT sobre estadísticas del trabajo - LABORSTA, Oficina de Estadística, OIT, Ginebra.
AST93  Anuario de Estadísticas del Trabjo 1993, OIT, Ginebra, 1993.

## 2. Evaluación de las tasas de actividad: 1950 - 1990

### 2.1 Datos básicos:

Cuadro 1: Tasas de actividad por sexo y grupo de edad

| Grupo de edad | Año 1962 (1) | 1992 (2) |
|---|---|---|
| **Hombres** | | |
| 10-14 | 17.87 | 24.31 |
| 15-19 | 58.08 | 54.00 |
| 20-24 | 87.99 | 88.00 |
| 25-29 | 97.45 | 96.77 |
| 30-34 | 98.81 | 98.30 |
| 35-39 | 98.85 | 98.75 |
| 40-44 | 98.76 | 98.12 |
| 45-49 | 98.35 | 97.42 |
| 50-54 | 96.54 | 95.83 |
| 55-59 | 91.09 | 91.43 |
| 60-64 | 78.11 | 68.11 |
| 65+ | 49.61 | 41.10 |
| **Mujeres** | | |
| 10-14 | 28.48 | 26.49 |
| 15-19 | 66.96 | 68.82 |
| 20-24 | 63.76 | 87.89 |
| 25-29 | 58.40 | 88.82 |
| 30-34 | 58.94 | 91.73 |
| 35-39 | 61.49 | 92.28 |
| 40-44 | 62.71 | 92.76 |
| 45-49 | 63.58 | 91.41 |
| 50-54 | 57.98 | 89.29 |
| 55-59 | 49.47 | 85.46 |
| 60-64 | 32.42 | 56.01 |
| 65+ | 16.23 | 26.63 |

Fuente(s): (1) STAT; (2) AST93.

### 2.2 Método(s): interpolación y extrapolación lineares

#### 2.2.1 Hombres:

- 1950-90, interpolación y extrapolación de las tasas de actividad con base en el censo de 1962 y de las tasas de actividad con base en estimaciones oficiales de 1992.

#### 2.2.2 Mujeres:

- 1950-90, aplicación a las tasas de actividad estimadas para Tailandia, de las variaciones de las tasas de actividad estimadas 1992, en relación con las tasas de actividad con base en estimaciones oficiales de 1992; modificación de las tendencias de todos los grupos de edad.

## 3. Evaluación de las tasas de distribución por sector de actividad: 1950 - 1990

### 3.1 Datos básicos:

Cuadro 2: Distribución de la población económicamente activa por sector de actividad en %

| Año | Agricultura | Industria Total | Manufac. | Servicios |
|---|---|---|---|---|
| **Hombres** | | | | |
| 1950 (1) | 79.90 | 2.55 | 0.00 | 17.55 |
| 1960 (1) | 77.20 | 4.65 | 0.00 | 18.15 |
| 1962 (2) | 76.74 | 5.01 | 3.34 | 18.25 |
| 1970 (1) | 73.80 | 5.35 | 0.00 | 20.85 |
| 1980 (1) | 70.30 | 6.80 | 4.77 | 22.90 |
| **Mujeres** | | | | |
| 1950 (1) | 89.35 | 0.85 | 0.00 | 9.80 |
| 1960 (1) | 88.35 | 1.90 | 0.00 | 9.75 |
| 1962 (2) | 88.19 | 2.21 | 2.01 | 9.61 |
| 1970 (1) | 84.55 | 2.60 | 0.00 | 12.85 |
| 1980 (1) | 80.00 | 6.50 | 5.98 | 13.50 |

Fuente(s): (1) EPPA3; (2) STAT.

### 3.2 Método(s): extrapolación linear

#### 3.2.1 Hombres:

- 1950-80, tasas de distribución 1950-80 con base en EPPA3;
- 1990, extrapolación de las tasas de distribución 1950-80 con base en EPPA3; modificación de las tendencias de todos los sectores;
- Aplicación de la razón manufacturas/industria con base en el censo de 1962.

#### 3.2.2 Mujeres:

Métodos, hipótesis y tratamientos idénticos a los que se aplican a los hombres.

## 4. Proyección de las tasas de actividad: 2000 - 2010

### 4.1 Modelo(s): linear, log-linear, hiperbólico y logístico

#### 4.1.1 Hombres:

- Para los grupos de edad [10-59], aplicación de la función F1;
- Para los grupos de edad [60+], aplicación de la función F3;
- Modificación de la tendencia del grupo de edad [35-39].

#### 4.1.2 Mujeres:

- Para el grupo de edad [10-14], aplicación de la función F1;
- Para los grupos de edad [15-24], aplicación de la función F2;
- Para los grupos de edad [25-59], aplicación de la función F6;
- Para los grupos de edad [60+], aplicación de la función F3;
- Modificación de la tendencia del grupo de edad [10-14].

*Notas sobre los ajustes de las tasas, véase p.380-384.*

*Notas sobre las funciones de proyección, véase p. 386.*

# Camerún

## 1. Fuente(s) de los datos básicos

Código(s):   Título(s):

EPPA3      Estimaciones y proyecciones de la población económicamente activa, 1950-2025, tercera edición, OIT, Ginebra, 1986.
ASTER      Anuario de estadísticas del trabajo 1945-89 - Edición retrospectiva sobre los censos de población, OIT, Ginebra, 1990.

## 2. Evaluación de las tasas de actividad: 1950 - 1990

### 2.1 Datos básicos:

Cuadro 1: Tasas de actividad por sexo y grupo de edad

| Grupo de edad | Año 1950 (1) | 1960 (1) | 1970 (1) | 1980 (1) | 1976 (2) |
|---|---|---|---|---|---|
| **Hombres** | | | | | |
| 10-14 | 52.05 | 50.35 | 47.35 | 40.00 | .. |
| 15-19 | 84.80 | 82.60 | 78.60 | 68.85 | .. |
| 20-24 | 95.25 | 94.35 | 92.85 | 89.10 | .. |
| 25-29 | 97.40 | 97.25 | 97.05 | 96.50 | .. |
| 30-34 | 98.15 | 98.00 | 97.75 | 97.10 | .. |
| 35-39 | 98.30 | 98.15 | 97.90 | 97.20 | .. |
| 40-44 | 98.15 | 98.00 | 97.70 | 97.00 | .. |
| 45-49 | 97.35 | 97.25 | 97.00 | 96.40 | .. |
| 50-54 | 96.95 | 96.75 | 96.35 | 95.50 | .. |
| 55-59 | 96.05 | 95.75 | 95.15 | 93.75 | .. |
| 60-64 | 93.10 | 92.55 | 91.60 | 89.15 | .. |
| 65+ | 79.90 | 78.95 | 77.20 | 73.00 | .. |
| **Mujeres** | | | | | |
| 10-14 | 31.65 | 30.65 | 28.80 | 24.35 | 13.26 |
| 15-19 | 42.30 | 41.00 | 38.80 | 33.30 | 35.42 |
| 20-24 | 49.55 | 48.65 | 47.00 | 42.95 | 44.40 |
| 25-29 | 53.15 | 52.10 | 50.20 | 45.65 | 47.40 |
| 30-34 | 55.90 | 54.75 | 52.80 | 47.90 | 49.78 |
| 35-39 | 62.00 | 60.85 | 58.85 | 53.90 | 55.79 |
| 40-44 | 62.75 | 61.65 | 59.65 | 54.85 | 56.64 |
| 45-49 | 70.35 | 69.10 | 66.80 | 61.25 | 63.38 |
| 50-54 | 66.25 | 64.85 | 62.30 | 56.10 | 58.48 |
| 55-59 | 60.85 | 59.40 | 56.90 | 50.70 | 61.64 |
| 60-64 | 57.90 | 56.05 | 52.70 | 44.55 | 47.68 |
| 65+ | 40.80 | 39.05 | 35.90 | 28.25 | 31.21 |

Fuente(s): (1) EPPA3; (2) ASTER.

### 2.2 Método(s): interpolación y extrapolación lineares

**2.2.1 Hombres:**

- 1950-90, interpolación y extrapolación de las tasas de actividad 1950-80
con base en EPPA3;
modificación de las tendencias de los grupos de edad [10-14] y [15-19] para 1990

**2.2.2 Mujeres:**

- 1950-90, interpolación y extrapolación de las tasas de actividad 1950-80
con base en EPPA3;
ajuste de las tasas interpoladas 1980 con base en las variaciones de las tasas
interpoladas 1970, en relación con las tasas de actividad ajustadas con base en
el censo de 1976;
modificación de las tendencias de los grupos de edad [15+] para 1990.

## 3. Evaluación de las tasas de distribución por sector de actividad: 1950 - 1990

### 3.1 Datos básicos:

Cuadro 2: Distribución de la población económicamente activa por sector de actividad en %

| Año | Agricultura | Industria Total | Manufac. | Servicios |
|---|---|---|---|---|
| **Hombres** | | | | |
| 1950 (1) | 87.50 | 4.50 | .. | 8.00 |
| 1960 (1) | 84.40 | 5.40 | .. | 10.20 |
| 1970 (1) | 78.90 | 7.00 | .. | 14.10 |
| 1976 (2) | 70.61 | 9.62 | 6.35 | 19.77 |
| 1980 (1) | 65.40 | 11.15 | .. | 23.45 |
| **Mujeres** | | | | |
| 1950 (1) | 99.00 | 0.30 | .. | 0.70 |
| 1960 (1) | 97.00 | 1.00 | .. | 2.00 |
| 1970 (1) | 95.00 | 1.20 | .. | 3.80 |
| 1976 (2) | 92.14 | 2.56 | 2.48 | 5.29 |
| 1980 (1) | 86.50 | 2.25 | .. | 11.25 |

Fuente(s): (1) EPPA3; (2) ASTER.

### 3.2 Método(s): extrapolación linear

**3.2.1 Hombres:**

- 1950-80, tasas de distribución 1950-80 con base en EPPA3;
- 1990, extrapolación de las tasas de distribución 1950-80 con base en
EPPA3 y de las tasas de distribución con base en el censo de 1976;
- Aplicación de la razón manufacturas/industria con base en el censo de 1976.

**3.2.2 Mujeres:**

Métodos, hipótesis y tratamientos idénticos a los que se aplican a los hombres.

## 4. Proyección de las tasas de actividad: 2000 - 2010

### 4.1 Modelo(s): linear y hiperbólico

**4.1.1 Hombres:**

- Para los grupos de edad [10-24], aplicación de la función F1;
- Para los grupos de edad [25+], aplicación de la función F3;
- Modificación de las tendencias de los grupos de edad [25-64].

**4.1.2 Mujeres:**

- Para el grupo de edad [10-14], aplicación de la función F1;
- Para los grupos de edad [15+], aplicación de la función F3;
- Modificación de las tendencias de los grupos de edad [10-44] y [60-64].

*Notas sobre los ajustes de las tasas, véase p.380-384.*          *Notas sobre las funciones de proyección, véase p. 386.*

# Canadá

## 1. Fuente(s) de los datos básicos

Código(s):   Título(s):

EPPA3   Estimaciones y proyecciones de la población económicamente activa, 1950-2025, tercera edición, OIT, Ginebra, 1986.
STAT   Base de datos de la OIT sobre estadísticas del trabajo - LABORSTA, Oficina de Estadística, OIT, Ginebra.

## 2. Evaluación de las tasas de actividad: 1950 - 1990

### 2.1 Datos básicos:

Cuadro 1: Tasas de actividad por sexo y grupo de edad

| Grupo de edad | Año 1979 | 1980 | 1981 | 1989 | 1990 | 1991 |
|---|---|---|---|---|---|---|
| **Hombres** | | | | | | |
| 10-14 | 0.00 | 0.00 | 0.00 | 0.00 | 0.00 | 0.00 |
| 15-19 | 57.20 | 58.00 | 58.17 | 60.51 | 58.90 | 55.82 |
| 20-24 | 86.40 | 86.20 | 86.52 | 84.79 | 82.80 | 81.45 |
| 25-29 | 94.43 | 94.23 | 94.20 | 93.64 | 93.11 | 91.86 |
| 30-34 | 97.05 | 96.65 | 96.60 | 94.66 | 94.22 | 93.19 |
| 35-39 | 96.72 | 96.38 | 96.50 | 95.02 | 94.49 | 93.73 |
| 40-44 | 95.85 | 95.59 | 95.69 | 94.47 | 94.18 | 93.76 |
| 45-49 | 94.58 | 94.49 | 94.64 | 93.32 | 92.98 | 92.82 |
| 50-54 | 90.77 | 90.66 | 90.85 | 89.84 | 88.61 | 88.02 |
| 55-59 | 85.27 | 85.04 | 84.16 | 78.11 | 77.35 | 75.97 |
| 60-64 | 65.65 | 65.25 | 63.66 | 53.44 | 51.58 | 48.19 |
| 65+ | 15.30 | 14.70 | 14.09 | 10.97 | 11.41 | 11.33 |
| **Mujeres** | | | | | | |
| 10-14 | 0.00 | 0.00 | 0.00 | 0.00 | 0.00 | 0.00 |
| 15-19 | 50.80 | 52.20 | 53.03 | 56.49 | 55.93 | 53.82 |
| 20-24 | 71.30 | 73.00 | 72.96 | 77.24 | 76.46 | 75.55 |
| 25-29 | 62.28 | 64.45 | 67.11 | 77.30 | 78.15 | 77.99 |
| 30-34 | 58.39 | 60.83 | 63.84 | 75.14 | 76.26 | 76.35 |
| 35-39 | 58.73 | 60.94 | 63.85 | 76.57 | 77.74 | 77.67 |
| 40-44 | 60.22 | 62.41 | 65.30 | 77.80 | 79.08 | 79.09 |
| 45-49 | 54.77 | 57.04 | 58.85 | 71.81 | 73.02 | 74.41 |
| 50-54 | 49.42 | 51.16 | 52.55 | 62.42 | 63.45 | 64.48 |
| 55-59 | 41.81 | 41.20 | 41.25 | 46.37 | 45.23 | 46.60 |
| 60-64 | 24.71 | 24.78 | 24.78 | 22.25 | 25.95 | 24.49 |
| 65+ | 4.2 | 4.3 | 4.48 | 3.96 | 3.79 | 3.50 |

Fuente(s): STAT.

### 2.2 Método(s): promedio aritmético

#### 2.2.1 Hombres:

- 1950-70, tasas de actividad 1950-70 con base en EPPA3;
- 1980, promedios de las tasas de actividad con base en las encuestas de 1979, 1980 y 1981;
- 1990, promedios de las tasas de actividad con base en las encuestas de 1989, 1990 and 1991;
ajuste para tener en cuenta de las fuerzas armadas.

#### 2.2.2 Mujeres:

Métodos, hipótesis y tratamientos idénticos a los que se aplican a los hombres.

## 3. Evaluación de las tasas de distribución por sector de actividad: 1950 - 1990

### 3.1 Datos básicos:

Cuadro 2: Distribución de la población económicamente activa por sector de actividad en %

| Año | Agricultura | Industria Total | Manufac. | Servicios |
|---|---|---|---|---|
| **Hombres** | | | | |
| 1979 | 7.51 | 36.44 | 23.20 | 56.05 |
| 1980 | 6.88 | 36.20 | 23.80 | 56.92 |
| 1981 | 6.73 | 36.36 | 24.10 | 56.91 |
| 1989 | 4.08 | 35.58 | 21.41 | 60.34 |
| 1990 | 4.01 | 34.90 | 20.34 | 61.09 |
| 1991 | 4.18 | 33.89 | 19.68 | 61.93 |
| **Mujeres** | | | | |
| 1979 | 3.37 | 15.25 | 12.96 | 81.38 |
| 1980 | 3.16 | 15.76 | 13.68 | 81.08 |
| 1981 | 11.74 | 56.40 | 47.31 | 31.86 |
| 1989 | 2.44 | 13.52 | 11.34 | 84.04 |
| 1990 | 2.38 | 12.97 | 10.69 | 84.64 |
| 1991 | 2.57 | 12.36 | 10.17 | 85.07 |

Fuente(s): STAT.

### 3.2 Método(s): promedio aritmético

#### 3.2.1 Hombres:

- 1950-70, tasas de distribución 1950-70 con base en EPPA3;
- 1980, promedios de las tasas de distribución con base en las encuestas de 1979, 1980 y 1981;
- 1990, promedios de las tasas de distribución con base en las encuestas de 1989, 1990 y 1991.
de 1989, 1990 y 1991.

#### 3.2.2 Mujeres:

Métodos, hipótesis y tratamientos idénticos a los que se aplican a los hombres.

## 4. Proyección de las tasas de actividad: 2000 - 2010

### 4.1 Modelo(s): linear, hiperbólico y logístico

#### 4.1.1 Hombres:

- Para el grupo de edad [15-19], aplicación de la función F1;
- Para los grupos de edad [20+], aplicación de la función F3;
- Modificación de las tendencias de los grupos de edad [15-19] y [25-54].

#### 4.1.2 Mujeres:

- Para los grupos de edad [15-64], aplicación de la función F6;
- Para el grupo de edad [65+], aplicación de la función F3;
- Modificación de las tendencias de los grupos de edad [15-64].

*Notas sobre los ajustes de las tasas, véase p.380-384.*     *Notas sobre las funciones de proyección, véase p. 386.*

# Chad

## 1. Fuente(s) de los datos básicos

**Código(s):** **Título(s):**

S1964 Enquête démographique au Tchad, 1964, Vol I et II, Bureau central du Recensement, Ndjamena, 1966.
EPPA3 Estimaciones y proyecciones de la población económicamente activa, 1950-2025, tercera edición, OIT, Ginebra, 1986.
ASTER Anuario de estadísticas del trabajo 1945-89 - Edición retrospectiva sobre los censos de población, OIT, Ginebra, 1990.

## 2. Evaluación de las tasas de actividad: 1950 - 1990

### 2.1 Datos básicos:

Cuadro 1: Tasas de actividad por sexo y grupo de edad

| | Año | |
|---|---|---|
| Grupo de edad | 1964 (1) | 1980 (2) |
| **Hombres** | | |
| 10-14 | 48.42 | 45.61 |
| 15-19 | 75.10 | 70.74 |
| 20-24 | 95.60 | 94.16 |
| 25-29 | 98.60 | 98.08 |
| 30-34 | 98.70 | 98.12 |
| 35-39 | 98.60 | 98.45 |
| 40-44 | 98.10 | 97.70 |
| 45-49 | 98.10 | 97.48 |
| 50-54 | 97.50 | 97.29 |
| 55-59 | 96.30 | 93.35 |
| 60-64 | 95.55 | 86.87 |
| 65+ | 80.82 | 73.48 |
| **Mujeres** | | |
| 10-14 | 11.56 | 10.57 |
| 15-19 | 24.10 | 22.03 |
| 20-24 | 29.70 | 28.07 |
| 25-29 | 30.90 | 28.02 |
| 30-34 | 28.60 | 27.97 |
| 35-39 | 30.90 | 27.96 |
| 40-44 | 26.10 | 28.04 |
| 45-49 | 27.70 | 25.21 |
| 50-54 | 25.10 | 25.58 |
| 55-59 | 24.90 | 25.58 |
| 60-64 | 22.76 | 20.37 |
| 65+ | 8.07 | 7.22 |

**Fuente(s):** (1) S1964; (2) ASTER.

### 2.2 Método(s): interpolación y extrapolación lineares

#### 2.2.1 Hombres:

- 1950-90, interpolación y extrapolación de las tasas de actividad con base en la encuesta de 1964 y el censo de 1980;
modificación de las tendencias de los grupos de edad [15-49] y [55-64] para 1950
modificación de la tendencia del grupo de edad [25-29] para 1990.

#### 2.2.2 Mujeres:

- 1950-90, interpolación y extrapolación de las tasas de actividad con base en la encuesta de 1964 y el censo de 1980;
modificación de las tendencias de los grupos de edad [10-14], [30-34] y [50+] para 1990.

## 3. Evaluación de las tasas de distribución por sector de actividad: 1950 - 1990

### 3.1 Datos básicos:

Cuadro 2: Distribución de la población económicamente activa por sector de actividad en %

| | Agricultura | Industria | | Servicios |
|---|---|---|---|---|
| Año | | Total | Manufac. | |
| **Hombres** | | | | |
| 1970 (1) | 89.00 | 4.10 | .. | 6.90 |
| 1980 (1) | 82.20 | 5.70 | .. | 12.10 |
| **Mujeres** | | | | |
| 1964 (2) | 95.25 | 0.40 | .. | 4.35 |
| 1980 (3) | 86.89 | 1.09 | .. | 12.02 |

**Fuente(s):** (1) EPPA3; (2) S1964.

### 3.2 Método(s): interpolación y extrapolación lineares promedio ponderado

#### 3.2.1 Hombres:

- 1950-80, tasas de distribución 1950-80 con base en EPPA3;
- 1990, extrapolación de las tasas de distribución 1950-80 con base en EPPA3.

#### 3.2.2 Mujeres:

- 1950-90, interpolación y extrapolación de las tasas de distribución ajustadas con base en la encuesta de 1964 y el censo de 1983.

## 4. Proyección de las tasas de actividad: 2000 - 2010

### 4.1 Modelo(s): linear, hiperbólico y logístico

#### 4.1.1 Hombres:

- Para los grupos de edad [10-29], aplicación de la función F1;
- Para los grupos de edad [30+], aplicación de la función F3;
- Modificación de las tendencias de los grupos de edad [10-14], [20-24], [40-44] y [60+].

#### 4.1.2 Mujeres:

- Para los grupos de edad [10-19] y [65+], aplicación de la función F1;
- Para los grupos de edad [20-64], aplicación de la función F6;
- Modificación de las tendencias de los grupos de edad [10-19], [35-39] y [50+].

*Notas sobre los ajustes de las tasas, véase p.380-384.*

*Notas sobre las funciones de proyección, véase p. 386.*

# Chile

## 1. Fuente(s) de los datos básicos

Código(s):   Título(s):

EPPA3   Estimaciones y proyecciones de la población económicamente activa, 1950-2025, tercera edición, OIT, Ginebra, 1986.
ASTER   Anuario de estadísticas del trabajo 1945-89 - Edición retrospectiva sobre los censos de población, OIT, Ginebra, 1990.
AST90-92   Ediciones de 1990-1992, Anuario de Estadísticas del Trabjo de la OIT, Ginebra.
INE   Indicatores de empleo por sexo y grupos de edad, Total Nacional, Instituto Nacional de Estadísticas, Santiago.

## 2. Evaluación de las tasas de actividad: 1950 - 1990

### 2.1 Datos básicos:

Cuadro 1: Tasas de actividad por sexo y grupo de edad

| Grupo de edad | Año 1952 (1) | 1970 (1) | 1980 (1) | 1989 (2) | 1990 (2) | 1991 (2) |
|---|---|---|---|---|---|---|
| **Hombres** | | | | | | |
| 10-14 | .. | 4.17 | 0.00 | 0.00 | 0.00 | 0.00 |
| 15-19 | .. | 46.87 | 39.24 | 30.10 | 30.00 | 29.70 |
| 20-24 | .. | 86.07 | 81.94 | 79.20 | 80.90 | 78.25 |
| 25-29 | .. | 96.88 | 95.04 | 94.50 | 94.20 | 93.50 |
| 30-34 | .. | 97.92 | 97.69 | 97.40 | 97.50 | 97.10 |
| 35-39 | .. | 97.72 | 97.64 | 97.90 | 98.00 | 97.70 |
| 40-44 | .. | 96.51 | 97.33 | 97.30 | 96.80 | 97.00 |
| 45-49 | .. | 94.79 | 93.68 | 94.80 | 95.10 | 95.20 |
| 50-54 | .. | 89.72 | 87.13 | 89.50 | 89.20 | 90.30 |
| 55-59 | .. | 84.31 | 78.24 | 80.50 | 79.80 | 80.60 |
| 60-64 | .. | 75.03 | 68.64 | 67.50 | 64.60 | 62.60 |
| 65+ | .. | 48.40 | 32.51 | 29.25 | 28.69 | 28.71 |
| **Mujeres** | | | | | | |
| 10-14 | 3.38 | 1.79 | 0.00 | 0.00 | 0.00 | 0.00 |
| 15-19 | 28.40 | 17.26 | 15.30 | 18.40 | 15.90 | 19.50 |
| 20-24 | 35.10 | 32.47 | 34.57 | 38.10 | 38.40 | 38.20 |
| 25-29 | 30.40 | 30.13 | 35.89 | 40.90 | 41.95 | 42.45 |
| 30-34 | 28.00 | 26.04 | 33.28 | 42.63 | 41.48 | 41.08 |
| 35-39 | 27.60 | 25.04 | 31.51 | 42.55 | 43.38 | 41.50 |
| 40-44 | 27.60 | 23.64 | 29.49 | 42.55 | 42.93 | 42.83 |
| 45-49 | 26.60 | 22.07 | 26.71 | 38.70 | 38.50 | 39.45 |
| 50-54 | 24.60 | 20.26 | 22.88 | 30.78 | 31.88 | 32.18 |
| 55-59 | 22.40 | 16.59 | 17.38 | 25.40 | 28.45 | 26.98 |
| 60-64 | 19.50 | 12.76 | 11.55 | 15.88 | 15.40 | 15.43 |
| 65+ | 13.24 | 6.45 | 4.51 | 3.33 | 3.95 | 4.03 |

Fuente(s): (1) ASTER; (2) AST90-92 y INE.

### 2.2 Método(s): interpolación y extrapolación lineares / promedio ponderado

#### 2.2.1 Hombres:

- 1950-60, tasas de actividad 1950-60 con base en EPPA3;
- 1970-80, interpolación de las tasas de actividad ajustadas con base en los censos de 1970 y 1982;
- 1990, promedios de las tasas de actividad con base en las encuestas de 1989, 1990 and 1991;
ajuste de las tasas de actividad de los grupos de edad [15-24].

#### 2.2.2 Mujeres:

- 1950-70, extrapolación de las tasas de actividad con base en el censo de 1952 y de las tasas de actividad ajustadas con base en el censo 1970;
- 1980, promedios ponderados de las tasas de actividad ajustadas con base en el censo de 1982 y las tasas de actividad estimadas para 1990;
- 1980, promedios de las tasas de actividad con base en las encuestas de 1989, 1990 y 1991

## 3. Evaluación de las tasas de distribución por sector de actividad: 1950 - 1990

### 3.1 Datos básicos:

Cuadro 2: Distribución de la población económicamente activa por sector de actividad en %

| Año | Agricultura | Industria Total | Manufac. | Servicios |
|---|---|---|---|---|
| **Hombres** | | | | |
| 1970 (1) | 29.13 | 32.06 | 17.80 | 38.81 |
| 1982 (1) | 25.53 | 29.10 | 15.75 | 45.37 |
| 1989 (2) | 24.42 | 30.12 | 17.14 | 45.45 |
| 1991 (2) | 24.40 | 29.27 | 16.82 | 46.33 |
| 1990 (2) | 23.98 | 30.30 | 17.24 | 45.72 |
| **Mujeres** | | | | |
| 1952 (1) | 8.00 | 25.87 | 25.07 | 66.12 |
| 1970 (1) | 6.81 | 19.89 | 18.79 | 73.30 |
| 1982 (1) | 6.31 | 12.45 | 11.53 | 81.24 |
| 1989 (2) | 5.89 | 15.70 | 14.81 | 78.41 |
| 1991 (2) | 5.88 | 13.93 | 13.02 | 80.20 |
| 1990 (2) | 6.02 | 14.77 | 13.72 | 79.21 |

Fuente(s): (1) ASTER; (2) AST90-92 y INE.

### 3.2 Método(s): promedio ponderado / promedio aritmético

#### 3.2.1 Hombres:
- 1950-60, tasas de distribución 1950-60 con base en EPPA3;
- 1970-80, promedios ponderados de las tasas de distribución con base en los censos de 1970 y 1982;
- 1990, promedios de las tasas de distribución con base en las encuestas de 1989, 1990 y 1991.
de 1989, 1990 y 1991.

#### 3.2.2 Mujeres:
- 1960-80, promedios ponderados de las tasas de distribución con base en el censo de 1952 y de las tasas ajustadas con base en los censos de 1970 y 1982;
- 1990, promedios de las tasas de distribución con base en las encuestas de 1989, 1990 y 1991.

## 4. Proyección de las tasas de actividad: 2000 - 2010

### 4.1 Modelo(s): linear y hiperbólico

#### 4.1.1 Hombres:
- Para los grupos de edad [15+], aplicación de la función F3;
- Modificación de las tendencias de los grupos de edad [15-44].

#### 4.1.2 Mujeres:
- Para los grupos de edad [15+], aplicación de la función F3;
- Modificación de las tendencias de todos los grupos de edad.

*Notas sobre los ajustes de las tasas, véase p.380-384.*   *Notas sobre las funciones de proyección, véase p. 386.*

# China

## 1. Fuente(s) de los datos básicos

| Código(s): | Título(s): |
|---|---|
| EPPA3 | Estimaciones y proyecciones de la población económicamente activa, 1950-2025, tercera edición, OIT, Ginebra, 1986. |
| ASTER | Anuario de estadísticas del trabajo 1945-89 - Edición retrospectiva sobre los censos de población, OIT, Ginebra, 1990. |
| R1990 | Population Statistics of China, I.D.A, Statistical Data Series No. 55, State Statistical Bureau, Beijing. |

## 2. Evaluación de las tasas de actividad: 1950 - 1990

### 2.1 Datos básicos:

Cuadro 1: Tasas de actividad por sexo y grupo de edad

| Grupo de edad | Año 1950 (1) | 1960 (1) | 1970 (1) | 1980 (1) | 1990 (2) |
|---|---|---|---|---|---|
| **Hombres** | | | | | |
| 10-14 | 52.00 | 46.00 | 40.00 | 30.00 | 0.00 |
| 15-19 | 87.10 | 83.70 | 80.30 | 74.70 | 63.76 |
| 20-24 | 96.90 | 96.90 | 96.90 | 96.80 | 94.10 |
| 25-29 | 98.75 | 98.75 | 98.75 | 98.70 | 98.51 |
| 30-34 | 98.95 | 98.95 | 98.95 | 98.90 | 98.90 |
| 35-39 | 99.00 | 99.00 | 99.00 | 98.90 | 99.00 |
| 40-44 | 98.90 | 98.85 | 98.80 | 98.75 | 98.74 |
| 45-49 | 97.75 | 97.70 | 97.60 | 97.55 | 97.65 |
| 50-54 | 95.60 | 94.65 | 93.70 | 92.00 | 93.29 |
| 55-59 | 91.70 | 89.80 | 87.90 | 84.30 | 83.55 |
| 60-64 | 81.65 | 77.80 | 73.95 | 66.30 | 63.19 |
| 65+ | 56.00 | 50.45 | 44.90 | 34.00 | 32.72 |
| **Mujeres** | | | | | |
| 10-14 | 43.00 | 40.00 | 38.00 | 31.00 | 0.00 |
| 15-19 | 72.40 | 73.90 | 75.40 | 78.60 | 70.52 |
| 20-24 | 82.30 | 84.20 | 86.10 | 89.60 | 91.22 |
| 25-29 | 79.90 | 82.20 | 83.70 | 87.40 | 91.43 |
| 30-34 | 78.00 | 80.90 | 83.00 | 87.10 | 91.29 |
| 35-39 | 77.80 | 80.00 | 82.20 | 86.60 | 91.25 |
| 40-44 | 75.50 | 77.10 | 78.70 | 81.90 | 88.36 |
| 45-49 | 64.70 | 65.90 | 67.10 | 69.50 | 81.14 |
| 50-54 | 47.10 | 47.90 | 48.70 | 50.20 | 62.00 |
| 55-59 | 36.10 | 35.50 | 34.90 | 33.50 | 45.08 |
| 60-64 | 25.50 | 23.70 | 21.90 | 18.40 | 27.29 |
| 65+ | 9.95 | 8.90 | 7.85 | 5.70 | 8.03 |

Fuente(s): (1) EPPA3; (2) R1990.

### 2.2 Método(s): datos del país

#### 2.2.1 Hombres:

- 1950-80, tasas de actividad 1950-80 con base en EPPA3;
- 1990, tasas de actividad con base en el censo 1990;
ajuste de las tasas de actividad del grupo de edad [10-14].

#### 2.2.2 Mujeres:

Métodos, hipótesis y tratamientos idénticos a los que se aplican a los hombres.

## 3. Evaluación de las tasas de distribución por sector de actividad: 1950 - 1990

### 3.1 Datos básicos:

Cuadro 2: Distribución de la población económicamente activa por sector de actividad en %

| Año | Agricultura | Industria Total | Manufac. | Servicios |
|---|---|---|---|---|
| **Hombres** | | | | |
| 1980 (1) | 71.00 | 15.50 | .. | 13.50 |
| 1982 (2) | 70.36 | 17.70 | 11.75 | 11.94 |
| 1990 (3) | 69.10 | 16.52 | .. | 14.38 |
| **Mujeres** | | | | |
| 1980 (1) | 78.50 | 12.00 | .. | 9.50 |
| 1982 (2) | 78.01 | 13.82 | 11.94 | 8.17 |
| 1990 (3) | 76.09 | 13.34 | .. | 10.56 |

Fuente(s): (1) EPPA3; (2) ASTER; (3) R1990.

### 3.2 Método(s): datos del país

#### 3.2.1 Hombres:

- 1950-80, tasas de distribución 1950-80 con base en EPPA3;
- 1990, tasa de distribución de la agricultura con base en el censo de 1982;
- Aplicación de la razón industria/servicios 1980 con base en EPPA3;
- Aplicación de la razón manufacturas/industria con base en el censo de 1982.

#### 3.2.2 Mujeres:

Métodos, hipótesis y tratamientos idénticos a los que se aplican a los hombres.

## 4. Proyección de las tasas de actividad: 2000 - 2010

### 4.1 Modelo(s): linear, hiperbólico y logístico

#### 4.1.1 Hombres:

- Para los grupos de edad [10-49], aplicación de la función F1;
- Para los grupos de edad [50+], aplicación de la función F3;
- Modificación de las tendencias de los grupos de edad [10-54] y [65+].

#### 4.1.2 Mujeres:

- Para los grupos de edad [10-19], aplicación de la función F1;
- Para los grupos de edad [20+], aplicación de la función F6;
- Modificación de las tendencias de todos los grupos de edad.

*Notas sobre los ajustes de las tasas, véase p.380-384.*

*Notas sobre las funciones de proyección, véase p. 386.*

# Chipre

## 1. Fuente(s) de los datos básicos

Código(s):  Título(s):

EPPA3      Estimaciones y proyecciones de la población económicamente activa, 1950-2025, tercera edición, OIT, Ginebra, 1986.
CHY-OE1    Labour force and migration surveys, 19886/87, DSRMF, Series III, Report No. 6, Department of Statistics and Research, Nicosia.
CHY-OE2    Labour Statistics 1987-1992, DSRMF, Series II, Department of Statistics and Research, Nicosia.

## 2. Evaluación de las tasas de actividad: 1950 - 1990

### 2.1 Datos básicos:

Cuadro 1: Tasas de actividad por sexo y grupo de edad

| Grupo de edad | Año 1987 | 1988 | 1989 | 1990 |
|---|---|---|---|---|
| **Hombres** | | | | |
| 10-14 | 0.00 | 0.00 | 0.00 | 0.00 |
| 15-19 | 57.21 | 55.50 | 66.50 | 64.40 |
| 20-24 | 80.60 | 85.80 | 83.50 | 81.10 |
| 25-29 | 94.01 | 93.70 | 93.70 | 93.90 |
| 30-34 | 98.02 | 99.10 | 99.60 | 99.60 |
| 35-39 | 99.08 | 99.50 | 99.50 | 99.50 |
| 40-44 | 98.52 | 98.40 | 99.50 | 99.50 |
| 45-49 | 97.82 | 97.20 | 99.30 | 98.70 |
| 50-54 | 96.92 | 93.90 | 97.10 | 97.30 |
| 55-59 | 92.78 | 92.70 | 95.50 | 92.90 |
| 60-64 | 82.37 | 80.20 | 77.30 | 77.50 |
| 65+ | 27.62 | 28.00 | 28.00 | 28.00 |
| **Mujeres** | | | | |
| 10-14 | 0.00 | 0.00 | 0.00 | 0.00 |
| 15-19 | 36.88 | 29.70 | 33.70 | 34.00 |
| 20-24 | 61.30 | 56.60 | 63.80 | 65.10 |
| 25-29 | 61.12 | 57.90 | 63.10 | 64.20 |
| 30-34 | 59.68 | 58.50 | 63.10 | 64.00 |
| 35-39 | 62.04 | 61.60 | 63.40 | 64.00 |
| 40-44 | 58.62 | 58.90 | 63.10 | 64.00 |
| 45-49 | 61.04 | 61.80 | 50.50 | 00.10 |
| 50-54 | 55.12 | 54.70 | 49.00 | 49.70 |
| 55-59 | 45.37 | 46.00 | 38.10 | 39.20 |
| 60-64 | 33.58 | 36.00 | 24.60 | 25.20 |
| 65+ | 10.82 | 10.80 | 8.80 | 8.70 |

Fuente(s): CHY-OE1 y CHY-OE2.

### 2.2 Método(s): interpolación y extrapolación lineares

#### 2.2.1 Hombres:

- 1950-90, interpolación de las tasas de actividad 1950-80 con base en EPPA3 y de las tasas de actividad con base en estimaciones oficiales de 1987 to 1990; para del grupo de edad [10-14], tasas de actividad con base en EPPA3.

#### 2.2.2 Mujeres:

- 1950-80, tasas de actividad 1950-80 con base en EPPA3;
- 1990, extrapolación de las tasas de actividad 1950-80 con base en EPPA3; ajuste de las tasas extrapoladas con base en las variaciones de las tasas interpoladas 1980, en relación con las tasas 1980 con base en EPPA3.

## 3. Evaluación de las tasas de distribución por sector de actividad: 1950 - 1990

### 3.1 Datos básicos:

Cuadro 2: Distribución de la población económicamente activa por sector de actividad en %

| Año | Agricultura | Industria Total | Manufac. | Servicios |
|---|---|---|---|---|
| **Hombres** | | | | |
| 1981 | 19.15 | 36.91 | 19.33 | 43.94 |
| 1989 | 13.36 | 33.13 | 17.42 | 53.51 |
| **Mujeres** | | | | |
| 1981 | 34.80 | 29.09 | 25.73 | 36.11 |
| 1989 | 18.00 | 26.33 | 24.72 | 55.68 |

Fuente(s): CHY-OE1 y CHY-OE2.

### 3.2 Método(s): promedio aritmético

#### 3.2.1 Hombres:

- 1950-70, tasas de distribución 1950-70 con base en EPPA3;
- 1980, promedios de las tasas de distribución con base en las encuestas de 1979, 1980 y 1981;
- 1990, promedios de las tasas de distribución con base en estimaciones oficiales de 1989, 1990 y 1991.
oficiales de 1989, 1990 y 1991.

#### 3.2.2 Mujeres:

Métodos, hipótesis y tratamientos idénticos a los que se aplican a los hombres.

## 4. Proyección de las tasas de actividad: 2000 - 2010

### 4.1 Modelo(s): linear, hiperbólico y logístico

#### 4.1.1 Hombres:

- Para el grupo de edad [15-19], aplicación de la función F1;
- Para los grupos de edad [20+], aplicación de la función F3;
- Modificación de las tendencias de los grupos de edad [15-49] y [65+].

#### 4.1.2 Mujeres:

- Para los grupos de edad [15-19] y [60+], aplicación de la función F3;
- Para los grupos de edad [20-54], aplicación de la función F6;
- Para el grupo de edad [55-59], aplicación de la función F1;
- Modificación de las tendencias de los grupos de edad [15-19] y [55-59].

---

*Notas sobre los ajustes de las tasas, véase p.380-384.*

*Notas sobre las funciones de proyección, véase p. 386.*

# Colombia

## 1. Fuente(s) de los datos básicos

Código(s):  Título(s):

EPPA3  Estimaciones y proyecciones de la población económicamente activa, 1950-2025, tercera edición, OIT, Ginebra, 1986.
CELADE  CELADE, Bulletin Démographique, No. 49, janvier 1992.
STAT  Base de datos de la OIT sobre estadísticas del trabajo - LABORSTA, Oficina de Estadística, OIT, Ginebra.

## 2. Evaluación de las tasas de actividad: 1950 - 1990

### 2.1 Datos básicos:

Cuadro 1: Tasas de actividad por sexo y grupo de edad

| Grupo de edad | Año 1985 (1) | 1985 (2) | 1985 (3) | 1991 (1) | 1991 (2) | 1991 (3) |
|---|---|---|---|---|---|---|
| **Hombres** | | | | | | |
| 10-14 | 16.36 | 10.50 | 25.50 | 12.56 | 4.35 | 37.19 |
| 15-19 | 45.71 | 37.00 | 60.50 | 47.40 | 38.17 | 75.07 |
| 20-24 | 68.22 | 63.00 | 79.50 | 84.74 | 81.78 | 93.64 |
| 25-29 | 85.81 | 85.50 | 86.50 | 95.65 | 94.86 | 97.99 |
| 30-34 | 90.22 | 91.00 | 88.50 | 98.11 | 97.75 | 99.18 |
| 35-39 | 91.03 | 92.00 | 89.00 | 97.97 | 97.99 | 97.89 |
| 40-44 | 90.32 | 91.00 | 89.00 | 97.95 | 97.58 | 99.05 |
| 45-49 | 89.64 | 90.00 | 89.00 | 96.70 | 96.65 | 96.84 |
| 50-54 | 86.10 | 85.00 | 88.00 | 90.65 | 88.57 | 96.88 |
| 55-59 | 79.24 | 75.50 | 85.50 | 83.78 | 80.50 | 93.60 |
| 60-64 | 69.41 | 63.80 | 78.50 | 74.05 | 68.42 | 90.92 |
| 65+ | 46.73 | 40.02 | 57.37 | 32.57 | 20.92 | 67.52 |
| **Mujeres** | | | | | | |
| 10-14 | 8.77 | 7.00 | 11.90 | 4.91 | 2.17 | 11.31 |
| 15-19 | 21.86 | 21.80 | 22.00 | 30.51 | 31.51 | 28.19 |
| 20-24 | 35.83 | 37.30 | 31.50 | 54.90 | 61.30 | 39.97 |
| 25-29 | 46.67 | 49.99 | 36.63 | 58.17 | 63.96 | 44.66 |
| 30-34 | 44.17 | 46.90 | 36.26 | 60.64 | 67.03 | 45.75 |
| 35-39 | 41.04 | 43.00 | 35.90 | 57.41 | 61.67 | 47.46 |
| 40-44 | 37.48 | 38.50 | 35.06 | 52.82 | 54.52 | 48.83 |
| 45-49 | 33.32 | 33.06 | 33.91 | 49.77 | 54.80 | 38.03 |
| 50-54 | 28.93 | 27.30 | 32.70 | 33.96 | 33.73 | 34.50 |
| 55-59 | 24.25 | 21.50 | 30.70 | 29.22 | 27.73 | 32.71 |
| 60-64 | 19.51 | 15.78 | 28.50 | 22.18 | 17.16 | 33.89 |
| 65+ | 12.63 | 9.16 | 21.34 | 8.85 | 4.73 | 18.47 |

Nota(s): (1) Total; (2) Urbana; (3) Rural.
Fuente(s): CELADE y STAT.

### 2.2 Método(s): promedio ponderado
interpolación y extrapolación lineares

#### 2.2.1 Hombres:

- 1950-70, tasas de actividad 1950-70 con base en EPPA3;
ajuste de las tasas de actividad de los grupos de edad de edad para 1970;
- 1980, promedios ponderados de las tasas de actividad estimadas 1970 y 1990;
- 1990, extrapolación de las tasas de actividad para las áreas urbanas
con base en la encuesta de 1990 y el censo de 1991;
aplicación a las tasas extrapoladas, de las variaciones de los promedios
ponderados de las tasas de actividad en áreas rurales y urbanas con base en
el censo de 1991, en relación con las tasas de actividad 1991 en urbanas áreas.

#### 2.2.2 Mujeres:

- 1950-70, interpolación y extrapolación de las tasas de actividad ajustadas
1950-70 con base en EPPA3;
el ajuste se ha calculado con base en el modelo de ajuste de las tasas de
actividad de las mujeres ocupadas en la agricultura como auxiliares familiares;
- 1980-90, promedios ponderados de las tasas de actividad estimadas
por separado de las áreas urbanas y rurales con base en la interpolación
y extrapolación de las tasas de actividad con base en los censos de 1986

## 3. Evaluación de las tasas de distribución por sector de actividad: 1950 - 1990

### 3.1 Datos básicos:

Cuadro 2: Distribución de la población económicamente activa por sector de actividad en %

| Año | Agricultura | Industria Total | Manufac. | Servicios |
|---|---|---|---|---|
| **Hombres** | | | | |
| 1980 (1) | 46.72 | 22.81 | 15.24 | 30.47 |
| 1991 (2) | 1.94 | 34.68 | 23.97 | 63.38 |
| 1991 (3) | 70.59 | 10.70 | 4.66 | 18.71 |
| **Mujeres** | | | | |
| 1980 (1) | 5.55 | 21.57 | 19.94 | 72.88 |
| 1991 (2) | 0.64 | 25.03 | 23.65 | 74.33 |
| 1991 (3) | 29.73 | 17.07 | 14.83 | 53.20 |

Nota(s): (1) Total; (2) Urbana; (3) Rural.
Fuente(s): STAT.

### 3.2 Método(s): promedio ponderado

#### 3.2.1 Hombres:

- 1950-70, tasas de distribución 1950-70 con base en EPPA3;
- 1980, tasas de distribución con base en la encuesta de 1980;
- 1990, promedios ponderados de las tasas de distribución con base en
la encuesta de 1980 y de las tasas de distribución con base en estimaciones
oficiales de 1991 para las áreas urbanas y rurales.
oficiales de 1991 para las áreas urbanas y rurales.

#### 3.2.2 Mujeres:

- 1950-70, tasas de distribución ajustadas 1950-70 con base en EPPA3;
- 1980, tasas de distribución ajustadas con base en la encuesta de 1980;
- 1990, promedios ponderados de las tasas de distribución ajustadas
con base en la encuesta de 1980 y de las tasas de distribución con base en
estimaciones oficiales de 1991 para las áreas urbanas y rurales.

## 4. Proyección de las tasas de actividad: 2000 - 2010

### 4.1 Modelo(s): log-linear, hiperbólico y logístico

#### 4.1.1 Hombres:

- Para el grupo de edad [10-14], aplicación de la función F2;
- Para los grupos de edad [20+], aplicación de la función F3;
- Modificación de las tendencias de los grupos de edad [15-24] y [35-49].

#### 4.1.2 Mujeres:

- Para el grupo de edad [10-14], aplicación de la función F2;
- Para los grupos de edad [15-19] y [65+], aplicación de la función F3;
- Para el grupo de edad [20-24], aplicación de la función F1;
- Para los grupos de edad [25-64], aplicación de la función F6;
- Modificación de las tendencias de los grupos de edad [20-24] y [65+].

---

# Comoras

## 1. Fuente(s) de los datos básicos

Código(s):  Título(s):

EPPA3  Estimaciones y proyecciones de la población económicamente activa, 1950-2025, tercera edición, OIT, Ginebra, 1986.
ASTER  Anuario de estadísticas del trabajo 1945-89 - Edición retrospectiva sobre los censos de población, OIT, Ginebra, 1990.

## 2. Evaluación de las tasas de actividad: 1950 - 1990

### 2.1 Datos básicos:

Cuadro 1: Tasas de actividad por sexo y grupo de edad

| | Año | | | | |
|---|---|---|---|---|---|
| Grupo de edad | 1950 (1) | 1960 (1) | 1970 (1) | 1980 (1) | 1980 (2) |
| **Hombres** | | | | | |
| 10-14 | 51.75 | 50.90 | 49.65 | 47.75 | 48.12 |
| 15-19 | 84.45 | 83.30 | 81.65 | 79.10 | 60.94 |
| 20-24 | 95.10 | 94.65 | 94.00 | 93.05 | 84.25 |
| 25-29 | 97.35 | 97.30 | 97.20 | 97.05 | 96.41 |
| 30-34 | 98.10 | 98.05 | 97.90 | 97.75 | 98.35 |
| 35-39 | 98.25 | 98.20 | 98.10 | 97.90 | 98.66 |
| 40-44 | 98.10 | 98.05 | 97.90 | 97.75 | 98.24 |
| 45-49 | 97.35 | 97.30 | 97.20 | 97.05 | 97.78 |
| 50-54 | 96.90 | 96.80 | 96.65 | 96.40 | 96.89 |
| 55-59 | 96.00 | 95.85 | 95.60 | 95.25 | 96.56 |
| 60-64 | 93.00 | 92.75 | 92.35 | 91.70 | 93.43 |
| 65+ | 79.75 | 79.25 | 78.50 | 77.45 | 81.31 |
| **Mujeres** | | | | | |
| 10-14 | 39.10 | 38.45 | 37.50 | 36.10 | 41.05 |
| 15-19 | 63.60 | 62.60 | 61.20 | 59.05 | 55.55 |
| 20-24 | 63.90 | 63.30 | 62.40 | 61.05 | 63.30 |
| 25-29 | 68.85 | 68.15 | 67.15 | 65.60 | 67.13 |
| 30-34 | 73.20 | 72.45 | 71.35 | 69.70 | 70.67 |
| 35-39 | 74.45 | 73.75 | 72.70 | 71.15 | 72.85 |
| 40-44 | 76.90 | 76.15 | 75.15 | 73.60 | 75.44 |
| 45-49 | 76.40 | 75.65 | 74.65 | 73.05 | 73.11 |
| 50-54 | 74.95 | 74.10 | 72.90 | 71.10 | 72.75 |
| 55-59 | 72.15 | 71.30 | 70.05 | 68.15 | 66.41 |
| 60-64 | 66.05 | 64.95 | 63.35 | 60.90 | 58.71 |
| 65+ | 46.00 | 45.00 | 43.50 | 41.25 | 37.59 |

Fuente(s): (1) EPPA3; (2) ASTER.

### 2.2 Método(s): interpolación y extrapolación lineares

#### 2.2.1 Hombres:

- 1950-90, interpolación y extrapolación de las tasas de actividad 1950-80 con base en EPPA3;
ajuste de las tasas interpoladas y extrapoladas con base en las variaciones de las tasas interpoladas 1980, en relación con las tasas de actividad ajustadas con base en el censo 1980.

#### 2.2.2 Mujeres:

- 1950-90, interpolación y extrapolación de las tasas de actividad ajustadas 1950-80 con base en EPPA3;
ajuste de las tasas interpoladas y extrapoladas habida cuenta de la subenumeración censal de las mujeres ocupadas en la agricultura;
ajuste de las tasas interpoladas y extrapoladas con base en las variaciones de las tasas interpoladas 1980, en relación con las tasas de actividad con base en el censo de 1980.

## 3. Evaluación de las tasas de distribución por sector de actividad: 1950 - 1990

### 3.1 Datos básicos:

Cuadro 2: Distribución de la población económicamente activa por sector de actividad en %

| | Agricultura | Industria | | Servicios |
|---|---|---|---|---|
| Año | | Total | Manufac. | |
| **Hombres** | | | | |
| 1950 (1) | 87.00 | 5.20 | .. | 7.80 |
| 1960 (1) | 85.40 | 5.85 | .. | 8.75 |
| 1970 (1) | 83.10 | 6.80 | .. | 10.10 |
| 1980 (1) | 79.60 | 8.15 | .. | 12.25 |
| 1980 (2) | 70.65 | 11.01 | 4.69 | 18.34 |
| **Mujeres** | | | | |
| 1950 (1) | 95.70 | 0.95 | .. | 3.35 |
| 1960 (1) | 93.95 | 1.20 | .. | 4.85 |
| 1970 (1) | 91.40 | 1.70 | .. | 6.90 |
| 1980 (1) | 87.55 | 2.50 | .. | 9.95 |
| 1980 (2) | 93.33 | 3.41 | 3.34 | 3.25 |

Fuente(s): (1) EPPA3; (2) ASTER.

### 3.2 Método(s): interpolación y extrapolación lineares

#### 3.2.1 Hombres:

- 1950-90, interpolación y extrapolación de las tasas de distribución 1950-80 con base en EPPA3;
modificación de las tendencias de todos los sectores;
ajuste de las tasas con base en las variaciones de las tasas interpoladas 1980, en relación con las tasas de distribución con base en el censo de 1980.
en relación con las tasas de distribución con base en el censo de 1980.

#### 3.2.2 Mujeres:

- 1950-90, interpolación y extrapolación de las tasas de distribución 1950-80 con base en EPPA3;
modificación de las tendencias de todos los sectores;
a las tasas interpoladas y extrapoladas, aplicación de las variaciones de las tasas interpoladas 1980, en relación con las tasas de distribución con base en el censo de 1980.

## 4. Proyección de las tasas de actividad: 2000 - 2010

### 4.1 Modelo(s): linear y hiperbólico

#### 4.1.1 Hombres:

- Para todos los grupos de edad, aplicación de la función F1.

#### 4.1.2 Mujeres:

- Para los grupos de edad [10-19], aplicación de la función F1;
- Para los grupos de edad [20+], aplicación de la función F3;
- Modificación de las tendencias de los grupos de edad [20-59].

*Notas sobre los ajustes de las tasas, véase p.380-384.*

*Notas sobre las funciones de proyección, véase p. 386.*

# Congo

## 1. Fuente(s) de los datos básicos

Código(s):  Título(s):

EPPA3      Estimaciones y proyecciones de la población económicamente activa, 1950-2025, tercera edición, OIT, Ginebra, 1986.
ASTER      Anuario de estadísticas del trabajo 1945-89 - Edición retrospectiva sobre los censos de población, OIT, Ginebra, 1990.
AST89-90   Anuario de Estadísticas del Trabjo 1989-90, OIT, Ginebra, 1990.

## 2. Evaluación de las tasas de actividad: 1950 - 1990

### 2.1 Datos básicos:

Cuadro 1: Tasas de actividad por sexo y grupo de edad

| Grupo de edad | Año 1950 (1) | 1960 (1) | 1970 (1) | 1984 (2) |
|---|---|---|---|---|
| **Hombres** | | | | |
| 10-14 | 32.10 | 31.45 | 30.70 | 3.10 |
| 15-19 | 58.35 | 57.45 | 56.45 | 18.84 |
| 20-24 | 84.70 | 84.35 | 83.95 | 53.49 |
| 25-29 | 97.55 | 97.50 | 97.45 | 86.04 |
| 30-34 | 99.45 | 99.35 | 99.30 | 96.60 |
| 35-39 | 99.55 | 99.50 | 99.40 | 97.75 |
| 40-44 | 99.05 | 99.00 | 98.90 | 97.61 |
| 45-49 | 98.75 | 98.70 | 98.65 | 96.62 |
| 50-54 | 96.55 | 96.50 | 96.40 | 92.95 |
| 55-59 | 93.35 | 93.20 | 93.05 | 80.96 |
| 60-64 | 90.45 | 90.20 | 89.95 | 81.05 |
| 65+ | 69.00 | 68.65 | 68.20 | 73.79 |
| **Mujeres** | | | | |
| 10-14 | .. | .. | 22.10 | 4.67 |
| 15-19 | .. | .. | 37.65 | 17.84 |
| 20-24 | .. | .. | 40.90 | 32.98 |
| 25-29 | .. | .. | 49.00 | 51.02 |
| 30-34 | .. | .. | 55.40 | 59.26 |
| 35-39 | .. | .. | 61.40 | 64.39 |
| 40-44 | .. | .. | 69.50 | 67.97 |
| 45-49 | .. | .. | 72.95 | 70.90 |
| 50-54 | .. | .. | 75.95 | 73.56 |
| 55-59 | .. | .. | 76.55 | 72.47 |
| 60-64 | .. | .. | 71.95 | 69.74 |
| 65+ | .. | .. | 59.84 | 58.00 |

Fuente(s): (1) EPPA3; (2) AST89-90.

### 2.2 Método(s): interpolación y extrapolación lineares

#### 2.2.1 Hombres:

- 1950-90, interpolación y extrapolación de las tasas de actividad 1950-70
con base en EPPA3 y de las tasas de actividad ajustadas con base
el censo de 1984;
modificación de las tendencias de los grupos de edad [10-19] y [25-64] para 1950
y de los grupos de edad [20-24] y [65+] para 1980.

#### 2.2.2 Mujeres:

- 1950-90, interpolación y extrapolación de las tasas de actividad 1970
con base en EPPA3 y de las tasas de actividad con base en el censo 1984;
modificación de las tendencias del grupo de edad [10-14] para 1950-70.

## 3. Evaluación de las tasas de distribución por sector de actividad: 1950 - 1990

### 3.1 Datos básicos:

Cuadro 2: Distribución de la población económicamente activa por sector de actividad en %

| Año | Agricultura | Industria Total | Manufac. | Servicios |
|---|---|---|---|---|
| **Hombres** | | | | |
| 1974 (1) | 47.95 | 18.15 | 12.77 | 33.91 |
| 1984 (2) | 36.40 | 22.05 | 10.95 | 41.55 |
| **Mujeres** | | | | |
| 1974 (1) | 89.55 | 1.27 | 1.20 | 9.18 |
| 1984 (2) | 73.37 | 3.08 | 2.51 | 23.56 |

Fuente(s): (1) ASTER; (2) AST89-90.

### 3.2 Método(s): interpolación y extrapolación lineares

#### 3.2.1 Hombres:

- 1950-90, interpolación y extrapolación de las tasas de distribución
con base en los censos de 1974 y 1984;
modificación de las tendencias de todos los sectores para 1950-70 y 1990.

#### 3.2.2 Mujeres:

Métodos, hipótesis y tratamientos idénticos a los que se aplican a los hombres.

## 4. Proyección de las tasas de actividad: 2000 - 2010

### 4.1 Modelo(s): log-linear, hiperbólico y linear

#### 4.1.1 Hombres:

- Para el grupo de edad [10-14], aplicación de la función F2;
- Para los grupos de edad [15-19] y [65+], aplicación de la función F1;
- Para los grupos de edad [20-64], aplicación de la función F3;
- Modificación de las tendencias de los grupos de edad [30-34] y [65+].

#### 4.1.2 Mujeres:

- Para el grupo de edad [10-14], aplicación de la función F2;
- Para los grupos de edad [15+], aplicación de la función F1;
- Modificación de las tendencias de los grupos de edad [10-19], [40-44] y [55+].

*Notas sobre los ajustes de las tasas, véase p.380-384.*          *Notas sobre las funciones de proyección, véase p. 386.*

# Costa Rica

## 1. Fuente(s) de los datos básicos

Código(s):    Título(s):

EPPA3    Estimaciones y proyecciones de la población económicamente activa, 1950-2025, tercera edición, OIT, Ginebra, 1986.
ADNU88    Anuario de estadísticas del trabajo 1945-89 - Edición retrospectiva sobre los censos de población, OIT, Ginebra, 1990.
ASTER    Annuaire démographique 1988 - Statistiques des recensements de population, quarantième édition, Nations Unies, New York, 1990.
AST90-92    Ediciones de 1990-1992, Anuario de Estadísticas del Trabjo de la OIT, Ginebra.

## 2. Evaluación de las tasas de actividad: 1950 - 1990

### 2.1 Datos básicos:

Cuadro 1: Tasas de actividad por sexo y grupo de edad

| Grupo de edad | Año 1984 (1) | 1989 (2) | 1990 (2) | 1991 (2) |
|---|---|---|---|---|
| **Hombres** | | | | |
| 10-14 | 3.80 | 10.36 | 11.16 | 9.52 |
| 15-19 | 17.09 | 61.98 | 59.37 | 55.63 |
| 20-24 | 28.25 | 86.42 | 89.78 | 88.09 |
| 25-29 | 29.97 | 95.26 | 95.93 | 96.43 |
| 30-39 | 29.96 | 97.08 | 97.05 | 97.01 |
| 40-49 | 24.26 | 95.82 | 94.93 | 94.46 |
| 50-59 | 13.77 | 87.10 | 87.12 | 84.58 |
| 60-64 | 6.95 | 60.90 | 59.63 | 55.27 |
| 65+ | 3.08 | ... | ... | ... |
| **Mujeres** | | | | |
| 10-14 | 12.72 | 3.00 | 3.05 | 3.36 |
| 15-19 | 59.43 | 27.05 | 27.14 | 23.90 |
| 20-24 | 83.74 | 42.43 | 44.04 | 44.07 |
| 25-29 | 92.65 | 40.35 | 35.49 | 38.64 |
| 30-39 | 94.53 | 43.12 | 43.22 | 42.89 |
| 40-49 | 93.11 | 34.39 | 39.60 | 37.92 |
| 50-59 | 86.16 | 19.20 | 21.04 | 22.05 |
| 60-64 | 69.63 | 9.64 | 11.94 | 7.74 |
| 65+ | 38.91 | ... | ... | ... |

Fuente(s): (1) ASTER y ADNU88; (2) AST90-92.

### 2.2 Método(s): promedio ponderado / promedio aritmético

**2.2.1 Hombres:**

- 1950-70, tasas de actividad 1950-70 con base en EPPA3;
- 1980, promedios ponderados de las tasas de actividad 1970 con base en EPPA3 y de las tasas de actividad ajustadas con base en el censo de 1984;
- 1990, promedios de las tasas de actividad con base en las encuestas de 1989, 1990 and 1991.

**2.2.2 Mujeres:**

Métodos, hipótesis y tratamientos idénticos a los que se aplican a los hombres.

## 3. Evaluación de las tasas de distribución por sector de actividad: 1950 - 1990

### 3.1 Datos básicos:

Cuadro 2: Distribución de la población económicamente activa por sector de actividad en %

| Año | Agricultura | Industria Total | Manufac. | Servicios |
|---|---|---|---|---|
| **Hombres** | | | | |
| 1983 (1) | 36.26 | 22.63 | 15.25 | 41.11 |
| 1984 (1) | 43.56 | 22.74 | 13.54 | 33.70 |
| 1985 (1) | 35.44 | 29.83 | 14.87 | 34.73 |
| 1989 (2) | 34.45 | 26.67 | 16.77 | 38.88 |
| 1991 (2) | 33.39 | 27.25 | 16.87 | 39.36 |
| 1990 (2) | 33.23 | 27.36 | 17.93 | 39.41 |
| **Mujeres** | | | | |
| 1983 (1) | 5.15 | 21.76 | 21.57 | 73.10 |
| 1984 (1) | 4.81 | 20.46 | 19.68 | 74.73 |
| 1985 (1) | 4.52 | 20.69 | 26.53 | 74.79 |
| 1989 (2) | 6.06 | 26.67 | 28.37 | 67.27 |
| 1991 (2) | 6.40 | 24.40 | 25.85 | 69.20 |
| 1990 (2) | 6.70 | 26.76 | 23.46 | 66.54 |

Fuente(s): (1) ASTER y ADNU88; (2) AST90-92.

### 3.2 Método(s): promedio ponderado / promedio aritmético

**3.2.1 Hombres:**
- 1950-60, tasas de distribución 1950-60 con base en EPPA3;
- 1980, promedios ponderados de las tasas de distribución 1970 con base en EPPA3 y de los promedios de las tasas de distribución con base en las encuestas de 1983 y 1985 y el censo de 1984;
- 1990, promedios de las tasas de distribución con base en las encuestas
- 1990, promedios de las tasas de distribución con base en las encuestas

**3.2.2 Mujeres:**
Métodos, hipótesis y tratamientos idénticos a los que se aplican a los hombres.

## 4. Proyección de las tasas de actividad: 2000 - 2010

### 4.1 Modelo(s): linear, log-linear, hiperbólico y logístico

**4.1.1 Hombres:**
- Para el grupo de edad [10-14], aplicación de la función F2;
- Para los grupos de edad [15-29], aplicación de la función F1;
- Para los grupos de edad [30+], aplicación de la función F3;
- Modificación de las tendencias de los grupos de edad [10-14] y [30-34].

**4.1.2 Mujeres:**
- Para los grupos de edad [10-19], aplicación de la función F1;
- Para los grupos de edad [20-49], aplicación de la función F6;
- Para los grupos de edad [50-64], aplicación de la función F2;
- Para el grupo de edad [65+], aplicación de la función F3;
- Modificación de las tendencias de los grupos de edad [10-14] y [50-64].

*Notas sobre los ajustes de las tasas, véase p.380-384.*    *Notas sobre las funciones de proyección, véase p. 386.*

# Côte d'Ivoire

## 1. Fuente(s) de los datos básicos

Código(s):     Título(s):
EPPA3          Estimaciones y proyecciones de la población económicamente activa, 1950-2025, tercera edición, OIT, Ginebra, 1986.
ADNU84         Annuaire démographique 1984 - Statistiques des recensements de population II, trente-sixième édition, Nations Unies, New York, 1986.
AST93          Anuario de Estadísticas del Trabjo 1993, OIT, Ginebra, 1993.

## 2. Evaluación de las tasas de actividad: 1950 - 1990

### 2.1 Datos básicos:

Cuadro 1: Tasas de actividad por sexo y grupo de edad

| Grupo de edad | Año 1960 (1) | 1970 (1) | 1975 (2) | 1988 (3) |
|---|---|---|---|---|
| **Hombres** | | | | |
| 10-14 | 47.75 | .. | 32.35 | 26.20 |
| 15-19 | 84.40 | .. | 70.38 | 62.74 |
| 20-24 | 95.30 | .. | 93.94 | 87.65 |
| 25-29 | 97.65 | .. | 98.07 | 96.18 |
| 30-34 | 98.40 | .. | 98.18 | 98.14 |
| 35-39 | 98.55 | .. | 98.50 | 98.54 |
| 40-44 | 98.35 | .. | 97.80 | 98.53 |
| 45-49 | 98.15 | .. | 97.50 | 97.76 |
| 50-54 | 97.60 | .. | 97.28 | 97.17 |
| 55-59 | 96.05 | .. | 93.20 | 91.87 |
| 60-64 | 92.70 | .. | 90.22 | 89.49 |
| 65+ | 78.20 | .. | 74.78 | 74.17 |
| **Mujeres** | | | | |
| 10-14 | 40.45 | 33.80 | 27.93 | 20.67 |
| 15-19 | 76.25 | 61.40 | 39.45 | 35.07 |
| 20-24 | 79.50 | 65.35 | 43.97 | 39.25 |
| 25-29 | 81.75 | 68.70 | 46.00 | 42.81 |
| 30-34 | 84.00 | 71.80 | 48.73 | 46.59 |
| 35-39 | 84.55 | 73.15 | 50.29 | 48.16 |
| 40-44 | 85.00 | 74.80 | 51.49 | 49.87 |
| 45-49 | 80.00 | 70.55 | 51.64 | 50.14 |
| 50-54 | 74.85 | 66.90 | 49.94 | 48.65 |
| 55-59 | 58.50 | 53.60 | 47.46 | 46.30 |
| 60-64 | 47.95 | 44.95 | 43.31 | 39.85 |
| 65+ | 28.95 | 27.95 | 26.22 | 24.19 |

Fuente(s):  (1) EPPA3; (2) ASTER y ADNU84; (3) AST93.

### 2.2 Método(s): interpolación y extrapolación lineares

**2.2.1 Hombres:**

- 1950-90, interpolación y extrapolación de las tasas de actividad 1960 con base en EPPA3 y de las tasas de actividad con base en los censos de 1975 y 1988; modificación de las tendencias de todos los grupos de edad para 1950.

**2.2.2 Mujeres:**

- 1950-90, interpolación y extrapolación de las tasas de actividad 1960-70 con base en EPPA3 y de las tasas de actividad con base en los censos de 1975 y 1988.

## 3. Evaluación de las tasas de distribución por sector de actividad: 1950 - 1990

### 3.1 Datos básicos:

Cuadro 2: Distribución de la población económicamente activa por sector de actividad en %

| Año | Agricultura | Industria Total | Manufac. | Servicios |
|---|---|---|---|---|
| **Hombres** | | | | |
| 1950 | 86.00 | 3.50 | .. | 10.50 |
| 1960 | 79.00 | 5.25 | .. | 15.75 |
| 1970 | 70.00 | 7.50 | .. | 22.50 |
| 1980 | 60.00 | 10.00 | .. | 30.00 |
| **Mujeres** | | | | |
| 1950 | 96.50 | 0.70 | .. | 2.80 |
| 1960 | 93.35 | 1.35 | .. | 5.30 |
| 1970 | 87.00 | 2.60 | .. | 10.40 |
| 1980 | 75.00 | 5.00 | .. | 20.00 |

Fuente(s): EPPA3.

### 3.2 Método(s): extrapolación linear

**3.2.1 Hombres:**

- 1950-80, tasas de distribución 1950-80 con base en EPPA3;
- 1990, extrapolación de las tasas de distribución 1950-80 con base en EPPA3;
- 1980-90, aplicación de las razones manufacturas/industria estimadas para Camerún.

**3.2.2 Mujeres:**

Métodos, hipótesis y tratamientos idénticos a los que se aplican a los hombres.

## 4. Proyección de las tasas de actividad: 2000 - 2010

### 4.1 Modelo(s): log-linear y hiperbólico

**4.1.1 Hombres:**

- Para los grupos de edad [10-19], aplicación de la función F2;
- Para los grupos de edad [20+], aplicación de la función F3;
- Modificación de las tendencias de los grupos de edad [30-34] y [50-54].

**4.1.2 Mujeres:**

- Para los grupos de edad [10-19], aplicación de la función F2;
- Para los grupos de edad [20+], aplicación de la función F3;
- Modificación de las tendencias de los grupos de edad [15+].

*Notas sobre los ajustes de las tasas, véase p.380-384.*     *Notas sobre las funciones de proyección, véase p. 386.*

# Croacia

## 1. Fuente(s) de los datos básicos

Código(s): Título(s):

BLT-94-2    Popovic B. (1994), "Nuevas estimaciones de las tasas de actividad para 1980 y 1990, desglosadas por grupos de edad y distribución sectorial, en algunos países de Europa oriental y meridional" en el Boletín de Estadísticas del Trabajol - 1994-2, OIT, Ginebra.

STAT    Base de datos de la OIT sobre estadísticas del trabajo - LABORSTA, Oficina de Estadística, OIT, Ginebra.

## 2. Evaluación de las tasas de actividad: 1950 - 1990

### 2.1 Datos básicos:

Cuadro 1: Tasas de actividad por sexo y grupo de edad

| Grupo de edad | Año 1953 (1) | 1961 (1) | 1971 (1) | 1980 (2) | 1990 (2) |
|---|---|---|---|---|---|
| **Hombres** | | | | | |
| 10-14 | 19.19 | 2.52 | 1.46 | 0.07 | 0.00 |
| 15-19 | 82.87 | 64.93 | 38.43 | 23.90 | 21.81 |
| 20-24 | 93.57 | 90.85 | 82.88 | 78.82 | 77.23 |
| 25-29 | 95.61 | 96.45 | 95.00 | 95.25 | 92.98 |
| 30-34 | 97.34 | 97.57 | 97.60 | 97.57 | 96.52 |
| 35-39 | 96.63 | 96.61 | 97.36 | 97.53 | 96.45 |
| 40-44 | 97.19 | 96.26 | 93.77 | 96.33 | 96.17 |
| 45-49 | 96.23 | 95.36 | 84.70 | 93.93 | 93.76 |
| 50-54 | 92.76 | 92.62 | 80.75 | 82.58 | 86.04 |
| 55-59 | 82.87 | 82.66 | 68.90 | 63.39 | 60.84 |
| 60-64 | 76.95 | 71.09 | 56.70 | 49.04 | 30.26 |
| 65+ | 59.76 | 54.26 | 45.43 | 36.74 | 17.49 |
| **Mujeres** | | | | | |
| 10-14 | 18.38 | 3.52 | 2.06 | 0.08 | 0.00 |
| 15-19 | 66.09 | 54.87 | 35.33 | 20.48 | 18.64 |
| 20-24 | 62.20 | 67.15 | 61.98 | 69.45 | 65.49 |
| 25-29 | 48.59 | 59.84 | 66.77 | 78.92 | 79.48 |
| 30-34 | 43.47 | 54.20 | 60.06 | 76.81 | 82.68 |
| 35-39 | 40.99 | 50.71 | 56.93 | 71.27 | 81.62 |
| 40-44 | 36.55 | 49.29 | 52.21 | 60.50 | 77.31 |
| 45-49 | 32.61 | 43.64 | 45.54 | 51.77 | 66.95 |
| 50-54 | 27.55 | 36.55 | 38.86 | 38.38 | 43.98 |
| 55-59 | 22.94 | 29.98 | 28.93 | 24.92 | 23.92 |
| 60-64 | 19.85 | 24.56 | 23.44 | 19.53 | 14.66 |
| 65+ | 12.69 | 15.51 | 14.76 | 10.75 | 7.85 |

Fuente(s): (1) STAT; (2) BLT-94-2.

### 2.2 Método(s): extrapolación linear
promedio ponderado

#### 2.2.1 Hombres:

- 1950, extrapolación de las tasas de actividad ajustadas con base en los censos 1953 y 1971, de las tasas de actividad con base en el censo de 1961 y de las tasas de actividad con base en estimaciones oficiales de 1980; aplicación a las tasas extrapoladas, de las variaciones tasas interpoladas 1953, en relación con las tasas de actividad con base en el censo de 1953;
- 1960-70, promedios ponderados de las tasas de actividad ajustadas con base en los censos de 1953 y 1971 y de las tasas con base en el censo de 1961;
- 1980-90, tasas de actividad 1980 y 1990 con base en el Boletín (BLT-94-2).

#### 2.2.2 Mujeres:

- 1950, extrapolación de las tasas de actividad con base en los censos de 1953, 1961, 1971 y 1981; aplicación a las tasas extrapoladas, de las variaciones de las tasas interpoladas 1953, en relación con las tasas de actividad con base en el censo de 1953;
- 1960-70, promedios ponderados de las tasas de actividad con base en los censos de 1953, 1961 y 1971;
- 1980-90, tasas de actividad 1980 y 1990 con base en el Boletín

## 3. Evaluación de las tasas de distribución por sector de actividad: 1950 - 1990

### 3.1 Datos básicos:

Cuadro 2: Distribución de la población económicamente activa por sector de actividad en %

| Año | Agricultura | Industria Total | Manufac. | Servicios |
|---|---|---|---|---|
| **Hombres** | | | | |
| 1953 (1) | 56.04 | 15.12 | .. | 28.83 |
| 1961 (1) | 45.81 | 22.88 | .. | 31.31 |
| 1971 (1) | 34.47 | 29.20 | .. | 36.33 |
| 1980 (2) | 23.14 | 38.36 | 24.58 | 38.50 |
| 1990 (2) | 16.68 | 37.90 | 26.97 | 45.42 |
| **Mujeres** | | | | |
| 1953 (1) | 80.61 | 8.00 | .. | 11.39 |
| 1961 (1) | 62.74 | 14.59 | .. | 22.67 |
| 1971 (1) | 44.83 | 20.78 | .. | 34.39 |
| 1980 (2) | 27.73 | 27.45 | 24.93 | 44.83 |
| 1990 (2) | 15.21 | 28.27 | 25.72 | 56.52 |

Fuente(s): (1) STAT; (2) BLT-94-2.

### 3.2 Método(s): promedio ponderado
extrapolación linear

#### 3.2.1 Hombres:

- 1950, extrapolación de las tasas de distribución con base en los censos de 1953, 1961 y 1971 y de las tasas con base en el boletín de estadísticas del trabajo 1994-2; modificación de las tendencias de todos los sectores;
- 1960-70, promedios ponderados de las tasas de distribución con base en los censos de 1953, 1961 y 1971;
los censos de 1953, 1961 y 1971;

#### 3.2.2 Mujeres:

Métodos, hipótesis y tratamientos idénticos a los que se aplican a los hombres.

## 4. Proyección de las tasas de actividad: 2000 - 2010

### 4.1 Modelo(s): linear, hiperbólico y logístico

#### 4.1.1 Hombres:

- Para los grupos de edad [15+], aplicación de la función F3;
- Modificación de las tendencias de los grupos de edad [15-24] y [50-54].

#### 4.1.2 Mujeres:

- Para los grupos de edad [15-19] y [60+], aplicación de la función F3;
- Para los grupos de edad [25-54], aplicación de la función F6;
- Para el grupo de edad [55-59], aplicación de la función F1;
- Modificación de las tendencias de los grupos de edad [15-24] y [55-59].

*Notas sobre los ajustes de las tasas, véase p.380-384.*    *Notas sobre las funciones de proyección, véase p. 386.*

# Cuba

## 1. Fuente(s) de los datos básicos

Código(s):  Título(s):

CB-R70   Censo de Poblacion y viviendas, 1970, Oficina Nacional del Censo, Comité Estatal de Estadísticas, La Habana.
EPPA3   Estimaciones y proyecciones de la población económicamente activa, 1950-2025, tercera edición, OIT, Ginebra, 1986.
ASTER   Anuario de estadísticas del trabajo 1945-89 - Edición retrospectiva sobre los censos de población, OIT, Ginebra, 1990.
STAT   Base de datos de la OIT sobre estadísticas del trabajo - LABORSTA, Oficina de Estadística, OIT, Ginebra.

## 2. Evaluación de las tasas de actividad: 1950 - 1990

### 2.1 Datos básicos:

Cuadro 1: Tasas de actividad por sexo y grupo de edad

| Grupo de edad | Año 1953 (1) | 1970 (2) | 1981 (1) | 1988 (3) |
|---|---|---|---|---|
| **Hombres** | | | | |
| 10-14 | 8.00 | 1.04 | 0.00 | 0.00 |
| 15-19 | 76.70 | 51.03 | 32.79 | 38.60 |
| 20-24 | 91.60 | 85.73 | 82.79 | 85.65 |
| 25-29 | 94.20 | 92.45 | 94.79 | 93.74 |
| 30-34 | 94.80 | 93.54 | 96.76 | 98.41 |
| 35-39 | 95.10 | 93.80 | 96.95 | 98.28 |
| 40-44 | 94.90 | 93.19 | 96.34 | 97.63 |
| 45-49 | 94.40 | 92.07 | 95.15 | 96.45 |
| 50-54 | 92.50 | 88.83 | 92.07 | 93.68 |
| 55-59 | 89.20 | 82.22 | 86.08 | 88.28 |
| 60-64 | 82.20 | 65.45 | 60.91 | 50.63 |
| 65+ | 57.10 | 27.84 | 21.44 | 12.77 |
| **Mujeres** | | | | |
| 10-14 | 2.00 | 0.39 | 0.00 | 0.00 |
| 15-19 | 17.20 | 16.41 | 15.53 | 15.44 |
| 20-24 | 22.30 | 25.26 | 45.59 | 51.07 |
| 25-29 | 22.10 | 24.17 | 51.73 | 57.10 |
| 30-34 | 21.30 | 23.03 | 52.79 | 65.94 |
| 35-39 | 21.10 | 22.18 | 52.06 | 65.50 |
| 40-44 | 20.90 | 21.09 | 48.89 | 61.56 |
| 45-49 | 19.60 | 18.91 | 40.83 | 53.43 |
| 50-54 | 18.20 | 15.92 | 30.95 | 41.88 |
| 55-59 | 15.50 | 12.01 | 18.11 | 22.38 |
| 60-64 | 12.90 | 6.75 | 7.78 | 8.69 |
| 65+ | 8.50 | 1.89 | 2.03 | 1.78 |

Fuente(s): (1) ASTER; (2) ASTER y CB-R70; (3) STAT

### 2.2 Método(s): interpolación y extrapolación lineares

**2.2.1 Hombres:**

- 1950-70, interpolación y extrapolación de las tasas de actividad ajustadas con base en los censos de 1953 y 1970;
- 1980-90, extrapolación de las tasas de actividad ajustadas con base en el censo de 1982 y la encuesta de 1988.

**2.2.2 Mujeres:**

- 1950-70, interpolación y extrapolación de las tasas de actividad ajustadas con base en los censos de 1953 y 1970;
- 1980-90, extrapolación de las tasas de actividad ajustadas con base en el censo de 1981 y la encuesta de 1988;
modificación de las tendencias de todos los grupos de edad.

## 3. Evaluación de las tasas de distribución por sector de actividad: 1950 - 1990

### 3.1 Datos básicos:

Cuadro 2: Distribución de la población económicamente activa por sector de actividad en %

| Año | Agricultura | Industria Total | Manufac. | Servicios |
|---|---|---|---|---|
| **Hombres** | | | | |
| 1960 (1) | 42.00 | 24.20 | .. | 33.80 |
| 1970 (2) | 35.42 | 27.61 | 19.32 | 36.97 |
| 1981 (2) | 28.88 | 32.04 | 18.57 | 39.08 |
| **Mujeres** | | | | |
| 1960 (1) | 6.80 | 20.80 | .. | 72.40 |
| 1970 (2) | 8.24 | 22.10 | 21.19 | 69.66 |
| 1981 (2) | 10.62 | 21.55 | 17.59 | 67.82 |

Fuente(s): (1) EPPA3; (2) ASTER.

### 3.2 Método(s): promedio ponderado extrapolación linear

**3.2.1 Hombres:**

- 1950-60, tasas de distribución 1950-60 con base en EPPA3;
- 1970, promedios ponderados de las tasas de distribución 1960 con base en EPPA3 y de las tasas de distribución con base en el censo de 1970;
- 1980-90, promedios ponderados de las tasas de distribución con base en los censos de 1970 y 1981.
los censos de 1970 y 1981.

**3.2.2 Mujeres:**

- 1950-60, tasas de distribución 1950-60 con base en EPPA3;
- 1970, promedios ponderados de las tasas de distribución 1960 con base en EPPA3 y de las tasas de distribución con base en el censo de 1970;
- 1980, promedios ponderados de las tasas de distribución con base en los censos de 1970 y 1981;
- 1990, extrapolación de las tasas de distribución 1970 estimadas y de las tasas con base en el censo de 1981. modificación de las tendencias.

## 4. Proyección de las tasas de actividad: 2000 - 2010

### 4.1 Modelo(s): hiperbólico y logístico

**4.1.1 Hombres:**

- Para los grupos de edad [15+], aplicación de la función F3;
- Modificación de las tendencias de los grupos de edad [30-59].

**4.1.2 Mujeres:**

- Para los grupos de edad [15-19] y [60+], aplicación de la función F3;
- Para los grupos de edad [20-59], aplicación de la función F6;
- Modificación de la tendencia del grupo de edad [20-24].

# Dinamarca

## 1. Fuente(s) de los datos básicos

Código(s):   Título(s):

EPPA3       Anuario de estadísticas del trabajo 1945-89 - Edición retrospectiva sobre los censos de población, OIT, Ginebra, 1990.
STAT        Base de datos de la OIT sobre estadísticas del trabajo - LABORSTA, Oficina de Estadística, OIT, Ginebra.

## 2. Evaluación de las tasas de actividad: 1950 - 1990

### 2.1 Datos básicos:

Cuadro 1: Tasas de actividad por sexo y grupo de edad

| Grupo de edad | 1989 | 1990 | 1991 |
|---|---|---|---|
| **Hombres** | | | |
| 10-14 | 0.00 | 0.00 | 0.00 |
| 15-19 | 73.20 | 71.60 | 69.90 |
| 20-24 | 88.40 | 86.80 | 85.80 |
| 25-29 | 93.00 | 92.90 | 92.20 |
| 30-34 | 94.20 | 95.30 | 95.70 |
| 35-39 | 96.00 | 95.40 | 94.90 |
| 40-44 | 95.90 | 96.10 | 95.10 |
| 45-49 | 96.40 | 94.80 | 94.30 |
| 50-54 | 90.70 | 91.60 | 92.40 |
| 55-59 | 85.30 | 84.50 | 81.90 |
| 60-64 | 49.50 | 50.50 | 47.10 |
| 65+ | 10.32 | 12.46 | 10.97 |
| **Mujeres** | | | |
| 10-14 | 0.00 | 0.00 | 0.00 |
| 15-19 | 65.20 | 65.20 | 64.40 |
| 20-24 | 80.10 | 79.30 | 81.70 |
| 25-29 | 86.70 | 86.90 | 85.10 |
| 30-34 | 91.90 | 90.70 | 90.30 |
| 35-39 | 89.30 | 90.30 | 90.50 |
| 40-44 | 88.70 | 89.60 | 91.00 |
| 45-49 | 82.80 | 87.30 | 87.00 |
| 50-54 | 76.60 | 79.50 | 79.40 |
| 55-59 | 59.00 | 62.10 | 64.50 |
| 60-64 | 23.40 | 26.40 | 26.80 |
| 65+ | 3.23 | 3.17 | 3.02 |

Fuente(s): STAT

### 2.2 Método(s): promedio aritmético

#### 2.2.1 Hombres:

- 1950-80, tasas de actividad 1950-80 con base en EPPA3;
ajuste de las tasas de actividad del grupo de edad [15-19] para 1980;
- 1990, promedios de las tasas de actividad con base en las encuestas de 1989, 1990 y 1991.

#### 2.2.2 Mujeres:

Métodos, hipótesis y tratamientos idénticos a los que se aplican a los hombres.

## 3. Evaluación de las tasas de distribución por sector de actividad: 1950 - 1990

### 3.1 Datos básicos:

Cuadro 2: Distribución de la población económicamente activa por sector de actividad en %

| Año | Agricultura | Industria Total | Manufac. | Servicios |
|---|---|---|---|---|
| **Hombres** | | | | |
| 1979 | 10.22 | 40.96 | 27.06 | 48.81 |
| 1981 | 10.06 | 43.13 | 28.33 | 46.82 |
| 1989 | 7.83 | 38.00 | 23.87 | 54.17 |
| 1990 | 7.69 | 37.84 | 24.89 | 54.46 |
| 1991 | 7.89 | 37.94 | 25.13 | 54.18 |
| **Mujeres** | | | | |
| 1979 | 5.27 | 16.87 | 14.87 | 77.86 |
| 1981 | 3.28 | 17.57 | 15.68 | 79.15 |
| 1989 | 2.98 | 16.47 | 14.40 | 80.55 |
| 1990 | 2.81 | 16.62 | 14.78 | 80.58 |
| 1991 | 2.99 | 17.08 | 15.14 | 79.94 |

Fuente(s): STAT.

### 3.2 Método(s): promedio ponderado / promedio aritmético

#### 3.2.1 Hombres:

- 1950-70, tasas de distribución 1950-70 con base en EPPA3;
- 1980, promedios ponderados de las tasas de distribución con base en las encuestas de 1979 y 1981;
- 1990, promedios de las tasas de distribución con base en las encuestas de 1989, 1990 y 1991.
de 1989, 1990 y 1991.

#### 3.2.2 Mujeres:

Métodos, hipótesis y tratamientos idénticos a los que se aplican a los hombres.

## 4. Proyección de las tasas de actividad: 2000 - 2010

### 4.1 Modelo(s): linear, hiperbólico y logístico

#### 4.1.1 Hombres:

- Para los grupos de edad [15-24], aplicación de la función F1;
- Para los grupos de edad [25+], aplicación de la función F3;
- Modificación de las tendencias de los grupos de edad [15-39] y [45-49].

#### 4.1.2 Mujeres:

- Para los grupos de edad [15-34] y [60-64], aplicación de la función F1;
- Para los grupos de edad [35-59], aplicación de la función F6;
- Para el grupo de edad [65+], aplicación de la función F3;
- Modificación de las tendencias de los grupos de edad [15-64].

# Ecuador

## 1. Fuente(s) de los datos básicos

Código(s):  Título(s):

EPPA3    Estimaciones y proyecciones de la población económicamente activa, 1950-2025, tercera edición, OIT, Ginebra, 1986.
STAT     Base de datos de la OIT sobre estadísticas del trabajo - LABORSTA, Oficina de Estadística, OIT, Ginebra.

## 2. Evaluación de las tasas de actividad: 1950 - 1990

### 2.1 Datos básicos:

Cuadro 1: Tasas de actividad por sexo y grupo de edad

| Grupo de edad | Año 1970 (1) | 1982 (2) | 1990 (2) |
|---|---|---|---|
| **Hombres** | | | |
| 10-14 | 25.00 | 9.34 | 17.06 |
| 15-19 | 68.00 | 47.78 | 52.43 |
| 20-24 | 88.85 | 75.31 | 79.32 |
| 25-29 | 96.70 | 90.04 | 90.83 |
| 30-34 | 98.65 | 91.98 | 94.97 |
| 35-39 | 98.90 | 92.97 | 95.87 |
| 40-44 | 98.80 | 92.98 | 95.57 |
| 45-49 | 98.45 | 92.13 | 95.02 |
| 50-54 | 97.55 | 90.53 | 93.36 |
| 55-59 | 96.00 | 88.30 | 91.02 |
| 60-64 | 93.90 | 82.69 | 85.68 |
| 65+ | 83.40 | 64.77 | 64.34 |
| **Mujeres** | | | |
| 10-14 | 5.00 | 3.97 | 6.69 |
| 15-19 | 17.70 | 14.55 | 19.04 |
| 20-24 | 21.70 | 22.75 | 29.35 |
| 25-29 | 19.40 | 26.18 | 34.06 |
| 30-34 | 17.50 | 24.18 | 35.91 |
| 35-39 | 16.60 | 22.09 | 35.38 |
| 40-44 | 16.65 | 20.44 | 33.34 |
| 45-49 | 16.20 | 18.91 | 30.37 |
| 50-54 | 15.70 | 17.35 | 27.21 |
| 55-59 | 14.55 | 15.57 | 24.44 |
| 60-64 | 13.15 | 13.15 | 20.98 |
| 65+ | 10.15 | 9.11 | 13.95 |

Fuente(s): (1) EPPA3; (2) STAT.

### 2.2 Método(s):  interpolación linear
promedio ponderado

#### 2.2.1 Hombres:

- 1950-70, tasas de actividad 1950-70 con base en EPPA3;
- 1980-90, promedios ponderados de las tasas de actividad 1970 con base en EPPA3 y de las tasas de actividad ajustadas con base en los censos de 1982 y 1990.

#### 2.2.2 Mujeres:

- 1950-70, tasas de actividad ajustadas 1950-70 con base en EPPA3; el ajuste se ha calculado con base en el modelo de ajuste de las tasas de actividad de las mujeres ocupadas en la agricultura como auxiliares familiares;
- 1980-90, interpolación y extrapolación de las tasas de actividad ajustadas con base en el censo de 1982 y de las tasas de actividad ajustadas con base en el censo de 1990.

## 3. Evaluación de las tasas de distribución por sector de actividad: 1950 - 1990

### 3.1 Datos básicos:

Cuadro 2: Distribución de la población económicamente activa por sector de actividad en %

| Año | Agricultura | Industria Total | Manufac. | Servicios |
|---|---|---|---|---|
| **Hombres** | | | | |
| 1970 (1) | 57.60 | 19.60 | .. | 22.80 |
| 1982 (2) | 41.11 | 21.89 | 12.09 | 36.99 |
| 1990 (2) | 38.79 | 20.14 | 10.64 | 41.06 |
| **Mujeres** | | | | |
| 1982 (2) | 13.02 | 17.08 | 15.96 | 69.90 |
| 1990 (2) | 15.75 | 15.73 | 14.69 | 68.52 |

Fuente(s): (1) EPPA3; (2) STAT.

### 3.2 Método(s):  promedio ponderado
interpolación y extrapolación lineares

#### 3.2.1 Hombres:

- 1950-70, tasas de distribución 1950-70 con base en EPPA3;
- 1980-90, promedios ponderados de las tasas de distribución 1970 con base en EPPA3 y de las tasas de distribución con base en los censos de 1982 y 1990.

#### 3.2.2 Mujeres:

- 1950, tasas de distribución 1950 con base en EPPA3;
- 1960-70, interpolación de las tasas de distribución estimadas para 1950 y 1980;
- 1980-90, interpolación y extrapolación de las tasas de distribución con base en los censos de 1982 y 1990.

## 4. Proyección de las tasas de actividad: 2000 - 2010

### 4.1 Modelo(s):  linear, log-linear y hiperbólico

#### 4.1.1 Hombres:

- Para los grupos de edad [10-19], aplicación de la función F2;
- Para los grupos de edad [20-59], aplicación de la función F3;
- Para los grupos de edad [60+], aplicación de la función F3;
- Modificación de las tendencias de los grupos de edad [20-49].

#### 4.1.2 Mujeres:

- Para los grupos de edad [10-24], aplicación de la función F3;
- Para los grupos de edad [25+], aplicación de la función F2;
- Modificación de las tendencias de los grupos de edad [10-14] y [20-24].

*Notas sobre los ajustes de las tasas, véase p.380-384.*

*Notas sobre las funciones de proyección, véase p. 386.*

# Egipto

## 1. Fuente(s) de los datos básicos

Código(s):  Título(s):

EPPA3    Estimaciones y proyecciones de la población económicamente activa, 1950-2025, tercera edición, OIT, Ginebra, 1986.
ASTER    Anuario de estadísticas del trabajo 1945-89 - Edición retrospectiva sobre los censos de población, OIT, Ginebra, 1990.
AST91    Anuario de Estadísticas del Trabjo 1991, OIT, Ginebra, 1991.
AST93    Anuario de Estadísticas del Trabjo 1993, OIT, Ginebra, 1993.

## 2. Evaluación de las tasas de actividad: 1950 - 1990

### 2.1 Datos básicos:

Cuadro 1: Tasas de actividad por sexo y grupo de edad

| Grupo de edad | Año 1950 (1) | 1960 (1) | 1970 (1) | 1976 (2) | 1986 (3) | 1989 (4) |
|---|---|---|---|---|---|---|
| **Hombres** | | | | | | |
| 10-14 | 30.50 | 26.15 | .. | 26.30 | 12.44 | .. |
| 15-19 | 78.95 | 68.75 | .. | 49.85 | 39.45 | .. |
| 20-24 | 90.35 | 86.70 | .. | 71.69 | 78.52 | .. |
| 25-29 | 97.75 | 96.05 | .. | 92.84 | 94.96 | .. |
| 30-34 | 98.25 | 97.80 | .. | 96.98 | 98.21 | .. |
| 35-39 | 98.05 | 98.10 | .. | 98.27 | 98.23 | .. |
| 40-44 | 97.90 | 97.90 | .. | 97.86 | 96.80 | .. |
| 45-49 | 97.40 | 97.70 | .. | 98.23 | 95.74 | .. |
| 50-54 | 96.00 | 96.30 | .. | 96.76 | 93.70 | .. |
| 55-59 | 94.20 | 94.50 | .. | 95.02 | 90.95 | .. |
| 60-64 | 90.00 | 85.30 | .. | 76.71 | 66.82 | .. |
| 65+ | 74.80 | 62.80 | .. | 40.92 | 25.79 | .. |
| **Mujeres** | | | | | | |
| 10-14 | 8.50 | 8.20 | 4.90 | 7.22 | 1.44 | 5.80 |
| 15-19 | 10.20 | 8.65 | 6.25 | 5.13 | 5.91 | 17.10 |
| 20-24 | 6.15 | 7.25 | 10.05 | 12.42 | 18.85 | 38.50 |
| 25-29 | 3.70 | 4.75 | 7.85 | 10.79 | 16.83 | 38.10 |
| 30-34 | 3.75 | 4.45 | 6.30 | 7.81 | 14.17 | 40.24 |
| 35-39 | 4.10 | 4.40 | 5.05 | 5.47 | 9.56 | 38.00 |
| 40-44 | 5.65 | 5.30 | 4.65 | 4.39 | 7.47 | 37.87 |
| 45-49 | 4.75 | 4.40 | 3.85 | 3.53 | 5.36 | 29.60 |
| 50-54 | 5.20 | 4.60 | 3.60 | 3.14 | 3.51 | 26.99 |
| 55-59 | 3.65 | 3.40 | 2.95 | 2.75 | 2.64 | 24.38 |
| 60-64 | 3.60 | 3.20 | 2.55 | 2.20 | 1.40 | 13.70 |
| 65+ | 2.25 | 1.90 | 1.35 | 1.03 | 0.63 | 8.90 |

Fuente(s): (1) EPPA3; (2) ASTER; (3) AST91; (4) AST93.

### 2.2 Método(s): interpolación y extrapolación lineares

#### 2.2.1 Hombres:

- 1950-90, interpolación y extrapolación de las tasas de actividad 1950-60 con base en EPPA3 y de las tasas de actividad ajustadas con base los censos de 1976 y 1986.

#### 2.2.2 Mujeres:

- 1950-70, tasas de actividad ajustadas 1950-70 con base en EPPA3;
- 1980-90, interpolación y extrapolación de las tasas de actividad ajustadas con base en los censos de 1980 y 1985 y de las tasas de actividad con base en de 1988 la encuesta;
el ajuste se ha calculado con base en el modelo de ajuste de las tasas de actividad de las mujeres ocupadas en la agricultura como auxiliares familiares.

## 3. Evaluación de las tasas de distribución por sector de actividad: 1950 - 1990

### 3.1 Datos básicos:

Cuadro 2: Distribución de la población económicamente activa por sector de actividad en %

| Año | Agricultura | Industria Total | Manufac. | Servicios |
|---|---|---|---|---|
| **Hombres** | | | | |
| 1976 (1) | 50.35 | 19.00 | 13.61 | 30.65 |
| 1986 (2) | 43.83 | 22.45 | 13.22 | 33.73 |
| 1989 (3) | 34.58 | 25.16 | 14.94 | 40.26 |
| **Mujeres** | | | | |
| 1976 (1) | 23.34 | 15.40 | 13.44 | 61.26 |
| 1986 (2) | 10.82 | 12.61 | 10.43 | 76.58 |
| 1989 (3) | 63.16 | 9.09 | 8.37 | 27.75 |

Fuente(s): (1) ASTER; (2) AST91; (3) AST93.

### 3.2 Método(s): promedio ponderado

#### 3.2.1 Hombres:

- 1950-70, tasas de distribución 1950-70 con base en EPPA3;
- 1980-90, promedios ponderados de las tasas de distribución ajustadas con base en el censo de 1976, de las tasas con base en el censo de 1986 y de las tasas de distribución con base en la encuesta de 1989.

#### 3.2.2 Mujeres:

Métodos, hipótesis y tratamientos idénticos a los que se aplican a los hombres.

## 4. Proyección de las tasas de actividad: 2000 - 2010

### 4.1 Modelo(s): linear y hiperbólico

#### 4.1.1 Hombres:

- Para el grupo de edad [10-14], aplicación de la función F1;
- Para los grupos de edad [15+], aplicación de la función F3;
- Modificación de las tendencias de los grupos de edad [10-24].

#### 4.1.2 Mujeres:

- Para todos los grupos de edad, aplicación de la función F1;
- Modificación de las tendencias de los grupos de edad [10-19], [30-34] y [30+].

*Notas sobre los ajustes de las tasas, véase p.380-384.*

*Notas sobre las funciones de proyección, véase p. 386.*

# El Salvador

## 1. Fuente(s) de los datos básicos

Código(s):   Título(s):

EPPA3      Estimaciones y proyecciones de la población económicamente activa, 1950-2025, tercera edición, OIT, Ginebra, 1986.
CELADE    CELADE, Bulletin Démographique, No. 49, janvier 1992.
STAT       Base de datos de la OIT sobre estadísticas del trabajo - LABORSTA, Oficina de Estadística, OIT, Ginebra.

## 2. Evaluación de las tasas de actividad: 1950 - 1990

### 2.1 Datos básicos:

Cuadro 1: Tasas de actividad por sexo y grupo de edad

| Grupo de edad | Año 1970 (1) | 1990 (2)(3) | 1990 (4)(5) |
|---|---|---|---|
| **Hombres** | | | |
| 10-14 | 30.00 | 39.73 | 35.77 |
| 15-19 | 71.00 | 78.73 | 75.97 |
| 20-24 | 93.30 | 93.83 | 92.67 |
| 25-29 | 97.40 | 99.00 | 99.00 |
| 30-34 | 97.90 | 99.00 | 99.00 |
| 35-39 | 98.00 | 99.00 | 99.00 |
| 40-44 | 98.10 | 99.00 | 99.00 |
| 45-49 | 98.10 | 99.00 | 99.00 |
| 50-54 | 97.30 | 98.60 | 98.60 |
| 55-59 | 96.80 | 97.00 | 96.00 |
| 60-64 | 94.10 | 94.17 | 92.33 |
| 65+ | 71.80 | ... | 73.21 |
| **Mujeres** | | | |
| 10-14 | 5.20 | 4.80 | 4.78 |
| 15-19 | 26.10 | 20.33 | 20.33 |
| 20-24 | 34.65 | 24.80 | 39.34 |
| 25-29 | 26.35 | 13.20 | 20.78 |
| 30-34 | 24.00 | 11.10 | 17.58 |
| 35-39 | 22.20 | 10.30 | 16.27 |
| 40-44 | 21.55 | 10.10 | 15.87 |
| 45-49 | 19.85 | 9.50 | 14.57 |
| 50-54 | 18.45 | 9.00 | 13.44 |
| 55-59 | 16.50 | 8.50 | 12.11 |
| 60-64 | 15.25 | 7.83 | 10.81 |
| 65+ | 9.70 | ... | 4.80 |

Nota(s): (2) Rural; (5) Urbana.
Fuente(s): (1) EPPA3; (2) CELADE; (4) STAT.

### 2.2 Método(s): promedio aritmético

#### 2.2.1 Hombres:

- 1950-70, tasas de actividad 1950-70 con base en EPPA3;
- 1980, promedios de las tasas de actividad estimadas para 1970 y 1990;
- 1990, tasas de actividad ajustadas con base en la encuesta de 1990;
ajuste tasas de actividad estimadas con base en las áreas rurales.

#### 2.2.2 Mujeres:

Métodos, hipótesis y tratamientos idénticos a los que se aplican a los hombres.

## 3. Evaluación de las tasas de distribución por sector de actividad: 1950 - 1990

### 3.1 Datos básicos:

Cuadro 2: Distribución de la población económicamente activa por sector de actividad en %

| Año | Agricultura | Industria Total | Manufac. | Servicios |
|---|---|---|---|---|
| **Hombres** | | | | |
| 1950 (1) | 75.70 | 13.60 | .. | 10.70 |
| 1960 (1) | 72.35 | 15.65 | .. | 12.00 |
| 1970 (1) | 69.00 | 13.40 | .. | 17.60 |
| 1980 (1) | 55.80 | 19.80 | .. | 24.40 |
| **Mujeres** | | | | |
| 1950 (1) | 12.40 | 24.85 | .. | 62.75 |
| 1961 (2) | 71.72 | 15.89 | 10.53 | 12.39 |
| 1971 (2) | 69.57 | 12.67 | 8.49 | 17.76 |
| 1991 (2) | 15.30 | 33.55 | 22.44 | 51.15 |

Fuente(s): (1) EPPA3; (2) STAT.

### 3.2 Método(s): interpolación y extrapolación lineares

#### 3.2.1 Hombres:

- 1950-80, tasas de distribución 1950-80 con base en EPPA3;
- 1990, extrapolación de las tasas de distribución 1950-80 con base en EPPA3; ajuste de las tasas extrapoladas con base en las variaciones de las tasas interpoladas 1980, en relación con las tasas 1980 con base en EPPA3.

#### 3.2.2 Mujeres:

- 1950, tasas de distribución 1950 con base en EPPA3;
- 1960, 1970 y 1990, interpolación y extrapolación de las tasas de distribución con base en los censos de 1961 y 1971 y de las tasas de distribución ajustadas con base en el censo de 1991;
- 1980, promedios de las tasas de distribución estimadas para 1970 y 1990.

## 4. Proyección de las tasas de actividad: 2000 - 2010

### 4.1 Modelo(s): linear, hiperbólico y logístico

#### 4.1.1 Hombres:

- Para los grupos de edad [10-54], aplicación de la función F1;
- Para los grupos de edad [55+], aplicación de la función F3;
- Modificación de las tendencias de los grupos de edad [10-14], [25-49] y [60+].

#### 4.1.2 Mujeres:

- Para los grupos de edad [10-14] y [20-44], aplicación de la función F1;
- Para el grupo de edad [15-19], aplicación de la función F3;
- Para los grupos de edad [45+], aplicación de la función F6;
- Modificación de las tendencias de todos los grupos de edad.

# Emiratos Arabes Unidos

## 1. Fuente(s) de los datos básicos

Código(s):    Título(s):

EPPA3    Estimaciones y proyecciones de la población económicamente activa, 1950-2025, tercera edición, OIT, Ginebra, 1986.
STAT    Base de datos de la OIT sobre estadísticas del trabajo - LABORSTA, Oficina de Estadística, OIT, Ginebra.

## 2. Evaluación de las tasas de actividad: 1950 - 1990

### 2.1 Datos básicos:

Cuadro 1: Tasas de actividad por sexo y grupo de edad

| | Año | | |
|---|---|---|---|
| Grupo de edad | 1975 | 1980 | 1985 |
| **Hombres** | | | |
| 10-14 | 12.54 | 0.00 | 0.00 |
| 15-19 | 65.81 | 45.32 | 28.03 |
| 20-24 | 96.38 | 94.57 | 88.88 |
| 25-29 | 99.01 | 99.03 | 98.60 |
| 30-34 | 99.18 | 99.50 | 99.40 |
| 35-39 | 98.88 | 99.38 | 99.46 |
| 40-44 | 98.37 | 99.04 | 99.27 |
| 45-49 | 96.87 | 97.94 | 98.62 |
| 50-54 | 92.05 | 94.39 | 96.24 |
| 55-59 | 86.74 | 90.74 | 91.99 |
| 60-64 | 72.81 | 76.02 | 78.06 |
| 65+ | 31.78 | 27.90 | 25.98 |
| **Mujeres** | | | |
| 10-14 | 0.95 | 0.00 | 0.00 |
| 15-19 | 3.94 | 4.47 | 5.99 |
| 20-24 | 12.12 | 14.63 | 26.43 |
| 25-29 | 16.51 | 21.91 | 30.34 |
| 30-34 | 14.59 | 24.74 | 33.21 |
| 35-39 | 11.73 | 19.41 | 31.34 |
| 40-44 | 9.62 | 18.32 | 27.13 |
| 45-49 | 7.70 | 13.18 | 19.18 |
| 50-54 | 6.54 | 9.47 | 12.61 |
| 55-59 | 4.95 | 5.89 | 6.60 |
| 60-64 | 2.75 | 3.39 | 3.26 |
| 65+ | 1.36 | 1.07 | 0.86 |

Fuente(s): STAT.

### 2.2 Método(s):  extrapolación linear
promedio ponderado

**2.2.1 Hombres:**

- 1950-70, tasas de actividad 1950-70 con base en EPPA3;
- 1980, promedios ponderados de las tasas de actividad 1970 con base
en EPPA3 y de las tasas de actividad con base en el censo de 1980;
- 1990, extrapolación de las tasas de actividad con base en los censos
de 1975, 1980 y 1985;
ajuste de las tasas extrapoladas con base en de las variaciones de las tasas
interpoladas 1985, en relación con las tasas de actividad con base en
el censo de 1985; modificación de las tendencias de todos los grupos de edad.

**2.2.2 Mujeres:**

- 1950-80, tasas de actividad 1950-80 con base en EPPA3;
- 1990, extrapolación de las tasas de actividad con base en
los censos de 1975, 1980 y 1985;
ajuste de las tasas extrapoladas con base en las variaciones de las tasas
interpoladas 1985, en relación con las tasas de actividad con base en
el censo de 1985.

## 3. Evaluación de las tasas de distribución por sector de actividad: 1950 - 1990

### 3.1 Datos básicos:

Cuadro 2: Distribución de la población económicamente activa por sector de actividad en %

| | Agricultura | Industria | | Servicios |
|---|---|---|---|---|
| Año | | Total | Manufac. | |
| **Hombres** | | | | |
| 1975 | 4.76 | 43.98 | 6.08 | 51.26 |
| 1980 | 4.83 | 39.81 | 6.51 | 55.35 |
| 1985 | 8.43 | 30.86 | 8.13 | 60.72 |
| **Mujeres** | | | | |
| 1975 | 0.32 | 5.80 | 1.06 | 93.88 |
| 1980 | 0.08 | 6.71 | 1.48 | 93.21 |
| 1985 | 0.06 | 3.32 | 1.05 | 96.62 |

Fuente(s): STAT.

### 3.2 Método(s):  extrapolación linear

**3.2.1 Hombres:**

- 1950-80, tasas de distribución 1950-80 con base en EPPA3;
ajuste de las tasas de 1970 con base en los resultados del censo de 1975;
- 1990, extrapolación de las tasas de distribución con base en los censos
de 1980 y 1985;
modificación de las tendencias de todos los sectores.
modificación de las tendencias de todos los sectores.

**3.2.2 Mujeres:**

- 1950-80, tasas de distribución 1950-80 con base en EPPA3;
- 1990, extrapolación de las tasas de distribución con base en los censos
de 1980 y 1985;
modificación de las tendencias de todos los sectores.

## 4. Proyección de las tasas de actividad: 2000 - 2010

### 4.1 Modelo(s):  linear, log-linear y hiperbólico

**4.1.1 Hombres:**

- Para el grupo de edad [15-19], aplicación de la función F2;
- Para los grupos de edad [20-59], aplicación de la función F1;
- Para los grupos de edad [60+], aplicación de la función F3;
- Modificación de las tendencias de los grupos de edad [20-59].

**4.1.2 Mujeres:**

- Para los grupos de edad [15+], aplicación de la función F1;
- Modificación de la tendencia del grupo de edad [15-19].

---

*Notas sobre los ajustes de las tasas, véase p.380-384.*

*Notas sobre las funciones de proyección, véase p. 386.*

# Eritrea

## 1. Fuente(s) de los datos básicos

Código(s):   Título(s):
FSEE94      ILO, Foundation For Sustained Employment in Eritrea, EAMAT Addis Ababa, 1994.
EPPA4       Población económicamente activa 1950-2010 - cuarta edición, OIT, Ginebra, 1996.

## 2. Evaluación de las tasas de actividad: 1950 - 1990

### 2.1 Datos básicos:

Cuadro 1: Tasas de actividad por sexo y grupo de edad

| Grupo de edad | Año 1950 (1) | 1970 (1) | 1990 (1) | 1950 (2) | 1970 (2) | 1990 (2) |
|---|---|---|---|---|---|---|
| **Hombres** | | | | | | |
| 10-14 | 55.69 | 51.05 | 45.02 | 47.40 | 42.80 | 38.02 |
| 15-19 | 71.92 | 67.03 | 62.13 | 78.65 | 72.55 | 66.15 |
| 20-24 | 83.93 | 81.97 | 80.45 | 92.85 | 90.50 | 88.06 |
| 25-29 | 94.75 | 94.43 | 94.10 | 97.05 | 96.70 | 96.32 |
| 30-34 | 97.21 | 96.85 | 96.49 | 97.75 | 97.35 | 96.95 |
| 35-39 | 98.26 | 97.87 | 97.52 | 97.90 | 97.45 | 97.03 |
| 40-44 | 98.19 | 97.78 | 97.38 | 97.70 | 97.25 | 96.83 |
| 45-49 | 98.00 | 97.65 | 97.29 | 97.00 | 96.65 | 96.27 |
| 50-54 | 96.29 | 95.76 | 95.24 | 96.40 | 95.80 | 95.20 |
| 55-59 | 95.66 | 94.80 | 93.94 | 95.15 | 94.25 | 93.35 |
| 60-64 | 93.95 | 92.51 | 91.07 | 91.60 | 90.10 | 88.54 |
| 65+ | 80.93 | 78.37 | 75.81 | 77.25 | 74.60 | 71.86 |
| **Mujeres** | | | | | | |
| 10-14 | 50.19 | 46.02 | 41.85 | 41.00 | 37.00 | 31.00 |
| 15-19 | 61.10 | 57.45 | 54.54 | 65.71 | 59.76 | 56.05 |
| 20-24 | 64.17 | 61.77 | 59.86 | 68.56 | 64.51 | 61.99 |
| 25-29 | 65.16 | 62.60 | 60.54 | 73.45 | 68.93 | 66.11 |
| 30-34 | 65.21 | 62.62 | 60.54 | 77.95 | 73.15 | 70.15 |
| 35-39 | 65.85 | 63.47 | 61.56 | 79.70 | 75.15 | 72.31 |
| 40-44 | 67.12 | 64.76 | 62.86 | 82.40 | 77.89 | 75.07 |
| 45-49 | 67.66 | 65.21 | 63.26 | 81.59 | 76.97 | 74.08 |
| 50-54 | 66.09 | 63.27 | 61.02 | 79.26 | 74.11 | 70.88 |
| 55-59 | 64.45 | 61.48 | 59.10 | 75.48 | 70.16 | 66.84 |
| 60-64 | 59.79 | 55.91 | 52.81 | 67.01 | 60.48 | 56.40 |
| 65+ | 46.41 | 41.30 | 36.18 | 44.22 | 38.34 | 34.66 |

Nota(s): (1) Ethiopie; (2) Somalie. Fuente(s): EPPA4.

### 2.2 Método(s): promedio aritmético

**2.2.1 Hombres:**
- 1950-90, promedios de las tasas de actividad estimadas 1950-90
para Somalia y Etiopía.

**2.2.2 Mujeres:**
- 1990, promedios de las tasas de actividad estimadas para Somalia y Etiopía;
ajuste de los promedios de las tasas de actividad con base en
en la razón hombres/mujeres igual a 1 en la agricultura;
- 1950-80, promedios ajustados de las tasas de actividad 1950-90 estimadas
para Somalia y Etiopía;
ajuste de las tasas de actividad con base en de las variaciones de los promedios
de las tasas, en relación con las tasas estimadas;

## 3. Evaluación de las tasas de distribución por sector de actividad: 1950 - 1990

### 3.1 Datos básicos:

Cuadro 2: Distribución de la población económicamente activa por sector de actividad en %

| Año | Agricultura | Industria Total | Manufac. | Servicios |
|---|---|---|---|---|
| **Hombres** | | | | |
| 1993 | 50.13 | 14.04 | 12.39 | 35.83 |
| **Mujeres** | | | | |
| 1993 | 60.87 | 15.24 | 13.35 | 23.89 |

Fuente(s): FSSE94.

### 3.2 Método(s): promedio aritmético

**3.2.1 Hombres:**
- 1950-80, promedios de las tasas estimadas para Somalia y Etiopía
para 1950-80;
- 1990, tasas estimadas con base en FSEE94;
- La razón industria/servicios estimada con base en las estimaciones
para Somalia y Etiopía;
para Somalia y Etiopía;

**3.2.2 Mujeres:**
Métodos, hipótesis y tratamientos idénticos a los que se aplican a los hombres.

## 4. Proyección de las tasas de actividad: 2000 - 2010

### 4.1 Modelo(s): linear y hiperbólico

**4.1.1 Hombres:**
- Para los grupos de edad [10-29], aplicación de la función F1;
- Para los grupos de edad [30+], aplicación de la función F3;
- Modificación de las tendencias de los grupos de edad [30-59].

**4.1.2 Mujeres:**
- Para los grupos de edad [10-19], aplicación de la función F1;
- Para los grupos de edad [20+], aplicación de la función F3;
- Modificación de las tendencias de los grupos de edad [20-49].

*Notas sobre los ajustes de las tasas, véase p.380-384.*          *Notas sobre las funciones de proyección, véase p. 386.*

# Eslovaquia

## 1. Fuente(s) de los datos básicos

Código(s):    Título(s):

BLT-94-2    Vorobiev A. (1994), "Estimaciones de la población económicamente activa de los quince países de la ex URSS, en 1950, 1959, 1970, 1979 y 1989", en el Boletín de Estadísticas del Trabajol - 1994-2, OIT, Ginebra.

## 2. Evaluación de las tasas de actividad: 1950 - 1990

### 2.1 Datos básicos:

Cuadro 1: Tasas de actividad por sexo y grupo de edad

| Grupo de edad | Año | | | | |
|---|---|---|---|---|---|
| | 1950 (1) | 1961 | 1970 (1) | 1980 | 1991 (1) |
| **Hombres** | | | | | |
| 10-14 | 0.00 | 0.00 | 0.00 | 0.00 | 0.00 |
| 15-19 | 77.05 | 45.71 | 34.90 | 31.58 | 35.28 |
| 20-24 | 94.95 | 91.92 | 91.55 | 86.49 | 88.32 |
| 25-29 | 98.93 | 97.10 | 98.61 | 98.21 | 98.01 |
| 30-34 | 99.14 | 97.53 | 98.97 | 98.36 | 98.26 |
| 35-39 | 98.42 | 97.20 | 98.69 | 97.89 | 97.78 |
| 40-44 | 97.50 | 96.40 | 97.92 | 97.66 | 97.16 |
| 45-49 | 94.75 | 95.25 | 96.52 | 95.45 | 95.58 |
| 50-54 | 91.95 | 92.30 | 93.74 | 92.37 | 91.80 |
| 55-59 | 84.88 | 86.34 | 85.26 | 84.25 | 80.00 |
| 60-64 | 44.19 | 64.53 | 31.47 | 47.83 | 28.22 |
| 65+ | 20.28 | 30.15 | 14.66 | 20.27 | 11.63 |
| **Mujeres** | | | | | |
| 10-14 | 0.00 | 0.00 | 0.00 | 0.00 | 0.00 |
| 15-19 | 69.83 | 47.73 | 44.21 | 29.65 | 33.88 |
| 20-24 | 59.29 | 61.32 | 79.68 | 81.43 | 87.46 |
| 25-29 | 39.30 | 47.99 | 80.91 | 89.81 | 94.66 |
| 30-34 | 40.99 | 46.03 | 83.81 | 89.50 | 95.22 |
| 35-39 | 46.39 | 50.74 | 86.57 | 89.12 | 95.50 |
| 40-44 | 48.10 | 52.46 | 86.41 | 86.76 | 95.01 |
| 45-49 | 51.82 | 48.84 | 84.05 | 81.43 | 93.33 |
| 50-54 | 45.51 | 41.90 | 77.13 | 71.33 | 85.56 |
| 55-59 | 34.81 | 32.10 | 39.38 | 36.11 | 31.25 |
| 60-64 | 22.14 | 21.49 | 20.01 | 16.46 | 16.04 |
| 65+ | 8.80 | 6.79 | 5.89 | 4.59 | 4.93 |

Nota(s): (1) República Checa.
Fuente(s): STAT.

### 2.2 Método(s): promedio ponderado

#### 2.2.1 Hombres:

- 1950-90, promedios ponderados de las tasas de actividad con base en el censo de 1961 y 1980 y de las tasas de actividad para República Checa con base en los censos de 1950, 1970 y 1991;
ajuste de las tasas de actividad estimadas 1950-70 del grupo de edad [10-14].

#### 2.2.2 Mujeres:

Métodos, hipótesis y tratamientos idénticos a los que se aplican a los hombres.

## 3. Evaluación de las tasas de distribución por sector de actividad: 1950 - 1990

### 3.1 Datos básicos:

Cuadro 2: Distribución de la población económicamente activa por sector de actividad en %

| Año | Agricultura | Industria | | Servicios |
|---|---|---|---|---|
| | | Total | Manufac. | |
| **Hombres** | | | | |
| 1950 | 44.56 | 33.11 | .. | 22.32 |
| 1961 | 30.12 | 46.54 | .. | 23.34 |
| 1970 | 21.00 | 51.33 | .. | 27.68 |
| 1980 | 14.76 | 37.42 | 30.73 | 47.82 |
| 1991 | 14.39 | 35.32 | 28.66 | 50.29 |
| **Mujeres** | | | | |
| 1950 | 62.26 | 18.35 | .. | 19.39 |
| 1961 | 40.70 | 26.84 | .. | 32.46 |
| 1970 | 20.04 | 36.39 | .. | 43.56 |
| 1980 | 12.39 | 33.81 | 30.04 | 53.81 |
| 1991 | 9.20 | 30.62 | 26.93 | 60.18 |

Fuente(s): STAT.

### 3.2 Método(s): promedio ponderado

#### 3.2.1 Hombres:

- 1950-90, promedios ponderados de las tasas de distribución con base en los censos de 1950, 1961, 1970, 1980 y 1991.

#### 3.2.2 Mujeres:

Métodos, hipótesis y tratamientos idénticos a los que se aplican a los hombres.

## 4. Proyección de las tasas de actividad: 2000 - 2010

### 4.1 Modelo(s): linear, hiperbólico y logístico

#### 4.1.1 Hombres:

- Para los grupos de edad [15-19] y [60+], aplicación de la función F3;
- Para los grupos de edad [20-59], aplicación de la función F1;
- Modificación de las tendencias de los grupos de edad [25-34].

#### 4.1.2 Mujeres:

- Para los grupos de edad [15-19] y [55+], aplicación de la función F3;
- Para los grupos de edad [20-54], aplicación de la función F6;
- Modificación de las tendencias de los grupos de edad [20-54].

*Notas sobre los ajustes de las tasas, véase p.380-384.*

*Notas sobre las funciones de proyección, véase p. 386.*

# Eslovenia

## 1. Fuente(s) de los datos básicos

Código(s):   Título(s):

BLT-94-2    Popovic B. (1994), "Nuevas estimaciones de las tasas de actividad para 1980 y 1990, desglosadas por grupos de edad y distribución sectorial,
en algunos países de Europa oriental y meridional" en el Boletín de Estadísticas del Trabajol - 1994-2, OIT, Ginebra.

STAT        Base de datos de la OIT sobre estadísticas del trabajo - LABORSTA, Oficina de Estadística, OIT, Ginebra.

## 2. Evaluación de las tasas de actividad: 1950 - 1990

### 2.1 Datos básicos:

Cuadro 1: Tasas de actividad por sexo y grupo de edad

| Grupo de edad | Año | | | | |
|---|---|---|---|---|---|
| | 1953 (1) | 1961 (1) | 1971 (1) | 1980 (2) | 1990 (2) |
| **Hombres** | | | | | |
| 10-14 | 9.27 | 1.02 | 0.32 | 0.01 | 0.00 |
| 15-19 | 84.70 | 71.57 | 44.88 | 33.54 | 25.75 |
| 20-24 | 92.77 | 90.57 | 88.33 | 86.09 | 79.08 |
| 25-29 | 95.99 | 96.52 | 85.32 | 97.30 | 94.50 |
| 30-34 | 97.51 | 97.74 | 90.24 | 98.36 | 97.20 |
| 35-39 | 98.01 | 97.23 | 92.40 | 98.23 | 97.06 |
| 40-44 | 97.85 | 96.83 | 91.50 | 97.17 | 96.28 |
| 45-49 | 96.62 | 96.11 | 95.32 | 94.54 | 93.69 |
| 50-54 | 93.34 | 92.24 | 86.80 | 81.35 | 84.60 |
| 55-59 | 72.85 | 74.50 | 61.55 | 59.18 | 49.85 |
| 60-64 | 60.78 | 58.83 | 41.89 | 31.41 | 30.64 |
| 65+ | 45.85 | 42.31 | 33.52 | 19.27 | 14.45 |
| **Mujeres** | | | | | |
| 10-14 | 7.87 | 0.85 | 0.27 | 0.01 | 0.00 |
| 15-19 | 71.52 | 62.50 | 38.32 | 28.27 | 21.07 |
| 20-24 | 72.19 | 77.30 | 68.23 | 82.35 | 75.70 |
| 25-29 | 54.59 | 67.39 | 74.63 | 91.65 | 92.89 |
| 30-34 | 45.79 | 59.35 | 71.34 | 90.91 | 93.93 |
| 35-39 | 43.15 | 55.10 | 68.49 | 88.59 | 92.56 |
| 40-44 | 41.88 | 51.98 | 64.08 | 82.30 | 89.94 |
| 45-49 | 41.82 | 48.91 | 56.27 | 73.37 | 82.10 |
| 50-54 | 37.33 | 42.14 | 44.45 | 57.07 | 45.36 |
| 55-59 | 34.00 | 35.92 | 30.89 | 28.13 | 22.98 |
| 60-64 | 31.46 | 31.31 | 25.37 | 19.94 | 17.96 |
| 65+ | 21.45 | 22.09 | 18.88 | 9.85 | 9.42 |

Fuente(s): (1) STAT; (2) BLT-94-2.

### 2.2 Método(s): interpolación linear

#### 2.2.1 Hombres:

- 1950-70, interpolación y extrapolación de las tasas de actividad con base en
los censos de 1953, 1961 y 1971;
- 1980-90, 1980 y 1990 tasas de actividad con base en el Boletín
de estadísticas del trabajo 1994-2.

#### 2.2.2 Mujeres:

Métodos, hipótesis y tratamientos idénticos a los que se aplican a los hombres.

## 3. Evaluación de las tasas de distribución por sector de actividad: 1950 - 1990

### 3.1 Datos básicos:

Cuadro 2: Distribución de la población económicamente activa por sector de actividad en %

| Año | Agricultura | Industria | | Servicios |
|---|---|---|---|---|
| | | Total | Manufac. | |
| **Hombres** | | | | |
| 1953 (1) | 46.40 | 31.59 | 15.48 | 22.01 |
| 1961 (1) | 35.48 | 39.60 | 34.21 | 24.93 |
| 1971 (1) | 23.93 | 46.67 | 41.15 | 29.40 |
| 1980 (2) | 14.02 | 48.51 | 34.98 | 37.47 |
| 1990 (2) | 5.13 | 52.07 | 41.10 | 42.81 |
| **Mujeres** | | | | |
| 1953 (1) | 64.15 | 17.39 | 16.62 | 18.45 |
| 1961 (1) | 45.05 | 28.28 | 27.18 | 26.67 |
| 1971 (1) | 31.49 | 35.12 | 33.80 | 33.39 |
| 1980 (2) | 17.13 | 37.37 | 34.70 | 45.49 |
| 1990 (2) | 6.35 | 39.22 | 36.79 | 54.44 |

Fuente(s): (1) STAT; (2) BLT-94-2.

### 3.2 Método(s): promedio ponderado
extrapolación linear

#### 3.2.1 Hombres:

- 1950, promedios ponderados de las tasas de distribución con base en
los censos de 1953 y 1961;
- 1960-70, interpolación y extrapolación de las tasas de distribución
con base en los censos de 1961 y 1971;
- 1980-90, tasas de distribución con base en el boletín de estadísticas
- 1980-90, tasas de distribución con base en el boletín de estadísticas

#### 3.2.2 Mujeres:

Métodos, hipótesis y tratamientos idénticos a los que se aplican a los hombres.

## 4. Proyección de las tasas de actividad: 2000 - 2010

### 4.1 Modelo(s): linear, hiperbólico y logístico

#### 4.1.1 Hombres:

- Para los grupos de edad [15+], aplicación de la función F3;
- Modificación de las tendencias de los grupos de edad [40-49].

#### 4.1.2 Mujeres:

- Para el grupo de edad [15-19], aplicación de la función F3;
- Para los grupos de edad [20-49], aplicación de la función F6;
- Para los grupos de edad [50+], aplicación de la función F1;
- Modificación de las tendencias de los grupos de edad [15-64].

*Notas sobre los ajustes de las tasas, véase p.380-384.*                *Notas sobre las funciones de proyección, véase p. 386.*

# España

## 1. Fuente(s) de los datos básicos

Código(s):  Título(s):

EPPA3   Anuario de estadísticas del trabajo 1945-89 - Edición retrospectiva sobre los censos de población, OIT, Ginebra, 1990.
STAT    Base de datos de la OIT sobre estadísticas del trabajo - LABORSTA, Oficina de Estadística, OIT, Ginebra.

## 2. Evaluación de las tasas de actividad: 1950 - 1990

### 2.1 Datos básicos:

Cuadro 1: Tasas de actividad por sexo y grupo de edad

| Grupo de edad | Año 1970 (1) | 1980 (2) | 1981 (2) | 1989 (2) | 1990 (2) | 1991 (2) |
|---|---|---|---|---|---|---|
| **Hombres** | | | | | | |
| 10-14 | .. | .. | .. | 0.00 | 0.00 | 0.00 |
| 15-19 | .. | .. | .. | 34.82 | 33.31 | 32.25 |
| 20-24 | .. | .. | .. | 71.87 | 72.53 | 71.15 |
| 25-29 | .. | .. | .. | 91.58 | 91.99 | 91.82 |
| 30-34 | .. | .. | .. | 96.08 | 96.55 | 96.08 |
| 35-39 | .. | .. | .. | 96.20 | 96.70 | 96.88 |
| 40-44 | .. | .. | .. | 95.46 | 95.67 | 95.76 |
| 45-49 | .. | .. | .. | 94.14 | 94.06 | 93.57 |
| 50-54 | .. | .. | .. | 88.43 | 89.30 | 88.96 |
| 55-59 | .. | .. | .. | 75.70 | 76.53 | 76.26 |
| 60-64 | .. | .. | .. | 48.19 | 46.94 | 46.59 |
| 65+ | .. | .. | .. | 4.27 | 3.77 | 3.68 |
| **Mujeres** | | | | | | |
| 10-14 | 3.45 | 0.00 | 0.00 | 0.00 | 0.00 | 0.00 |
| 15-19 | 36.15 | 40.52 | 38.67 | 32.70 | 31.20 | 27.80 |
| 20-24 | 38.90 | 55.21 | 55.42 | 62.22 | 61.45 | 60.62 |
| 25-29 | 20.70 | 42.13 | 42.91 | 64.00 | 65.15 | 65.90 |
| 30-34 | 13.75 | 30.34 | 31.25 | 53.79 | 56.26 | 58.51 |
| 35-39 | 13.35 | 30.01 | 28.72 | 45.14 | 48.96 | 51.95 |
| 40-44 | 14.15 | 28.26 | 27.87 | 38.92 | 41.11 | 42.72 |
| 45-49 | 14.65 | 27.82 | 28.40 | 33.27 | 34.53 | 35.96 |
| 50-54 | 15.25 | 26.79 | 25.15 | 28.16 | 29.15 | 30.60 |
| 55-59 | 14.90 | 24.61 | 23.05 | 23.64 | 23.24 | 22.66 |
| 60-64 | 12.00 | 17.27 | 17.29 | 15.34 | 15.54 | 15.84 |
| 65+ | 4.4 | 7.88 | 6.73 | 1.84 | 1.66 | 1.46 |

Fuente(s): (1) EPPA3, (2) STAT.

**2.2 Método(s):** interpolación y extrapolación lineares
promedio aritmético

**2.2.1 Hombres:**

- 1950-80, tasas de actividad 1950-80 con base en EPPA3;
ajuste de las tasas de actividad de los grupos de edad [30+] para 1980;
- 1990, promedios ajustadas de las tasas de actividad con base en
las encuestas de 1989, 1990 y 1991;
ajuste para tener en cuenta los efectivos del servicio militar obligatorio.

**2.2.2 Mujeres:**

- 1950-80, interpolación y extrapolación 1970 de las tasas de actividad
con base en EPPA3 y de las tasas de actividad con base en las encuestas
1980 y 1982;
modificación de las tendencias de todos los grupos de edad;
- 1990, promedios de las tasas de actividad con base en
las encuestas de 1990 y 1991;
ajuste de las tasas de actividad del grupo de edad [15-19].

## 3. Evaluación de las tasas de distribución por sector de actividad: 1950 - 1990

### 3.1 Datos básicos:

Cuadro 2: Distribución de la población económicamente activa por sector de actividad en %

| Año | Agricultura | Industria Total | Manufac. | Servicios |
|---|---|---|---|---|
| **Hombres** | | | | |
| 1950 | 54.75 | 25.20 | .. | 20.05 |
| 1960 | 46.80 | 32.05 | .. | 21.15 |
| 1970 | 28.90 | 39.05 | .. | 32.05 |
| **Mujeres** | | | | |
| 1950 | 24.94 | 25.00 | .. | 50.06 |
| 1960 | 20.81 | 28.50 | .. | 50.69 |
| 1970 | 13.93 | 31.36 | .. | 54.70 |

Fuente(s): EPPA3.

**3.2 Método(s):** interpolación y extrapolación lineares

**3.2.1 Hombres:**
- 1950-90, promedios ponderados de las tasas interpoladas y extrapoladas
con base en la interpolación y extrapolación de las tasas de distribución
1950-70 con base en EPPA3.

**3.2.2 Mujeres:**
Métodos, hipótesis y tratamientos idénticos a los que se aplican a los hombres.

## 4. Proyección de las tasas de actividad: 2000 - 2010

**4.1 Modelo(s):** linear, hiperbólico y logístico

**4.1.1 Hombres:**
- Para los grupos de edad [15+], aplicación de la función F3;
- Modificación de la tendencia del grupo de edad [45-49].

**4.1.2 Mujeres:**
- Para los grupos de edad [15-54], aplicación de la función F6;
- Para los grupos de edad [55-64], aplicación de la función F1;
- Para el grupo de edad [65+], aplicación de la función F3;
- Modificación de las tendencias de los grupos de edad [15-19] y [55-64].

*Notas sobre los ajustes de las tasas, véase p.380-384.*    *Notas sobre las funciones de proyección, véase p. 386.*

# Estados Unidos

## 1. Fuente(s) de los datos básicos

Código(s):   Título(s):

EPPA3       Estimaciones y proyecciones de la población económicamente activa, 1950-2025, tercera edición, OIT, Ginebra, 1986.
STAT        Base de datos de la OIT sobre estadísticas del trabajo - LABORSTA, Oficina de Estadística, OIT, Ginebra.

## 2. Evaluación de las tasas de actividad: 1950 - 1990

### 2.1 Datos básicos:

Cuadro 1: Tasas de actividad por sexo y grupo de edad

| Grupo de edad | Año | | |
| --- | --- | --- | --- |
| | 1989 | 1990 | 1991 |
| **Hombres** | | | |
| 10-14 | 0.00 | 0.00 | 0.00 |
| 15-19 | 45.50 | 44.52 | 40.62 |
| 20-24 | 79.61 | 84.30 | 74.37 |
| 25-29 | 89.56 | 93.80 | 89.32 |
| 30-34 | 91.84 | 94.60 | 93.03 |
| 35-39 | 92.25 | 94.90 | 92.99 |
| 40-44 | 92.18 | 93.90 | 90.66 |
| 45-49 | 91.61 | 92.30 | 93.02 |
| 50-54 | 88.44 | 88.80 | 89.02 |
| 55-59 | 78.75 | 79.80 | 79.65 |
| 60-64 | 54.14 | 55.50 | 55.15 |
| 65+ | 15.96 | | 15.55 |
| **Mujeres** | | | |
| 10-14 | 0.00 | 0.00 | 0.00 |
| 15-19 | 43.78 | 41.40 | 39.78 |
| 20-24 | 72.01 | 71.60 | 68.37 |
| 25-29 | 73.41 | 73.80 | 73.48 |
| 30-34 | 72.69 | 73.40 | 73.66 |
| 35-39 | 74.67 | 75.50 | 75.73 |
| 40-44 | 76.79 | 77.60 | 76.74 |
| 45-49 | 74.28 | 74.80 | 76.96 |
| 50-54 | 65.75 | 66.90 | 68.88 |
| 55-59 | 54.50 | 55.30 | 56.49 |
| 60-64 | 35.23 | 35.50 | 35.14 |
| 65+ | 7.79 | … | 7.97 |

Fuente(s): STAT.

### 2.2 Método(s):  promedio aritmético

#### 2.2.1 Hombres:

- 1950-80, tasas de actividad 1950-80 con base en EPPA3;
- 1990, promedios ponderados de las tasas de actividad con base en las encuestas de 1989, 1990 y 1991;
ajuste para tener en cuenta de las fuerzas armadas.

#### 2.2.2 Mujeres:

Métodos, hipótesis y tratamientos idénticos a los que se aplican a los hombres.

## 3. Evaluación de las tasas de distribución por sector de actividad: 1950 - 1990

### 3.1 Datos básicos:

Cuadro 2: Distribución de la población económicamente activa por sector de actividad en %

| Año | Agricultura | Industria | | Servicios |
| --- | --- | --- | --- | --- |
| | | Total | Manufac. | |
| **Hombres** | | | | |
| 1989 | 3.99 | 35.12 | 21.61 | 60.89 |
| 1990 | 3.96 | 34.98 | 21.28 | 61.06 |
| 1991 | 4.09 | 33.70 | 20.83 | 62.20 |
| **Mujeres** | | | | |
| 1989 | 1.38 | 15.61 | 13.54 | 83.01 |
| 1990 | 1.35 | 15.13 | 13.09 | 83.53 |
| 1991 | 1.34 | 14.85 | 12.86 | 83.81 |

Fuente(s): STAT.

### 3.2 Método(s):  promedio aritmético

#### 3.2.1 Hombres:

- 1950-70, tasas de distribución 1950-70 con base en EPPA3;
- 1990, promedios de las tasas de distribución con base en las encuestas de 1989, 1990 y 1991.

#### 3.2.2 Mujeres:

Métodos, hipótesis y tratamientos idénticos a los que se aplican a los hombres.

## 4. Proyección de las tasas de actividad: 2000 - 2010

### 4.1 Modelo(s):  linear, hiperbólico y logístico

#### 4.1.1 Hombres:

- Para el grupo de edad [15-19], aplicación de la función F1;
- Para los grupos de edad [20+], aplicación de la función F3;
- Modificación de las tendencias de los grupos de edad [15-19] y [25-54].

#### 4.1.2 Mujeres:

- Para los grupos de edad [15-64], aplicación de la función F6;
- Para el grupo de edad [65+], aplicación de la función F3;
- Modificación de las tendencias de los grupos de edad [15-64].

---

*Notas sobre los ajustes de las tasas, véase p.380-384.*        *Notas sobre las funciones de proyección, véase p. 386.*

# Estonia

## 1. Fuente(s) de los datos básicos

Código(s):  Título(s):

BLT-94-2  Vorobiev A. (1994), "Estimaciones de la población económicamente activa de los quince países de la ex URSS, en 1950, 1959, 1970, 1979 y 1989", en el Boletín de Estadísticas del Trabajol - 1994-2, OIT, Ginebra.

## 2. Evaluación de las tasas de actividad: 1950 - 1990

### 2.1 Datos básicos:

Cuadro 1: Tasas de actividad por sexo y grupo de edad

| Grupo de edad | Año | | | |
|---|---|---|---|---|
| | 1959 | 1970 | 1979 | 1989 |
| **Hombres** | | | | |
| 10-14 | 0.00 | 0.00 | 0.00 | 0.00 |
| 15-19 | 48.84 | 43.40 | 33.93 | 32.20 |
| 20-24 | 88.00 | 88.68 | 86.67 | 81.13 |
| 25-29 | 93.88 | 95.83 | 98.31 | 96.67 |
| 30-34 | 95.24 | 96.36 | 97.92 | 96.67 |
| 35-39 | 93.33 | 98.04 | 99.98 | 98.21 |
| 40-44 | 92.31 | 97.87 | 96.08 | 97.78 |
| 45-49 | 93.75 | 96.88 | 95.83 | 95.65 |
| 50-54 | 90.00 | 91.67 | 90.24 | 91.30 |
| 55-59 | 88.46 | 86.21 | 81.48 | 85.37 |
| 60-64 | 78.95 | 34.62 | 42.86 | 51.52 |
| 65+ | 38.46 | 18.37 | 15.79 | 22.22 |
| **Mujeres** | | | | |
| 10-14 | 0.00 | 0.00 | 0.00 | 0.00 |
| 15-19 | 37.21 | 35.42 | 27.45 | 26.42 |
| 20-24 | 73.47 | 82.98 | 83.64 | 76.47 |
| 25-29 | 74.07 | 91.49 | 94.74 | 91.53 |
| 30-34 | 71.43 | 92.86 | 95.92 | 93.44 |
| 35-39 | 71.74 | 92.59 | 96.15 | 96.55 |
| 40-44 | 72.97 | 92.86 | 96.36 | 93.88 |
| 45-49 | 71.74 | 91.67 | 94.44 | 94.12 |
| 50-54 | 68.18 | 82.35 | 85.45 | 88.68 |
| 55-59 | 50.00 | 40.00 | 43.18 | 53.85 |
| 60-64 | 55.56 | 20.93 | 26.47 | 37.25 |
| 65+ | 6.90 | 8.26 | 8.73 | 12.80 |

Fuente(s): BLT-94-2.

### 2.2 Método(s): extrapolación linear
promedio ponderado

#### 2.2.1 Hombres:

- 1950-60, extrapolación de las tasas de actividad 1970, 1979 y 1989 con base el Boletín de estadísticas del trabajo 1994-2;
modificación de las tendencias de todos los grupos de edad;
aplicación a las tasas estimadas 1990, de las variaciones de las tasas interpoladas 1970, en relación con las tasas de actividad 1970 con base en el Boletín;
- 1970-90, promedios ponderados de las tasas de actividad 1970, 1979 y 1989 con base en el Boletín.

#### 2.2.2 Mujeres:

- 1950-90, promedios ponderados de las tasas de actividad 1950, 1959, 1978 y 1989 con base en el Boletín de estadísticas del trabajo 1994-2;
ajuste de la tasa de actividad del grupo de edad [15-19] para 1950;
ajuste de las tasas de actividad de los grupos de edad [55-64] para 1959, 1970 y 1979.

## 3. Evaluación de las tasas de distribución por sector de actividad: 1950 - 1990

### 3.1 Datos básicos:

Cuadro 2: Distribución de la población económicamente activa por sector de actividad en %

| Año | Agricultura | Industria | | Servicios |
|---|---|---|---|---|
| | | Total | Manufac. | |
| **Hombres** | | | | |
| 1950 | 32.42 | 33.98 | 16.41 | 33.59 |
| 1959 | 26.84 | 41.85 | 25.24 | 31.31 |
| 1970 | 20.22 | 50.69 | 31.30 | 29.09 |
| 1979 | 18.64 | 50.63 | 29.47 | 30.73 |
| 1989 | 17.88 | 48.71 | 28.00 | 33.41 |
| **Mujeres** | | | | |
| 1950 | 51.81 | 19.20 | 14.49 | 28.99 |
| 1959 | 33.11 | 28.48 | 22.52 | 38.41 |
| 1970 | 15.79 | 36.29 | 29.92 | 47.92 |
| 1979 | 12.25 | 36.75 | 29.00 | 51.00 |
| 1989 | 11.14 | 34.36 | 27.25 | 54.50 |

Fuente(s): BLT-94-2.

### 3.2 Método(s): datos de BLT-94-2

#### 3.2.1 Hombres:

- 1950-90, promedios ponderados de las tasas de distribución 1950, 1959, 1970, 1979 y 1989 con base en el Boletín de estadísticas del trabajo 1994-2.

#### 3.2.2 Mujeres:

Métodos, hipótesis y tratamientos idénticos a los que se aplican a los hombres.

## 4. Proyección de las tasas de actividad: 2000 - 2010

### 4.1 Modelo(s): linear, hiperbólico y logístico

#### 4.1.1 Hombres:

- Para los grupos de edad [15-19], [25-39] y [65+], aplicación de la función F1;
- Para los grupos de edad [20-24] y [40-59], aplicación de la función F3;
- Modificación de las tendencias de los grupos de edad [15-44].

#### 4.1.2 Mujeres:

- Para los grupos de edad [15-19] y [65+], aplicación de la función F1;
- Para los grupos de edad [20-24] y [55-64], aplicación de la función F3;
- Para los grupos de edad [25-54], aplicación de la función F6;
- Modificación de las tendencias de los grupos de edad [15-24] y [65+].

*Notas sobre los ajustes de las tasas, véase p.380-384.*

*Notas sobre las funciones de proyección, véase p. 386.*

# Etiopía

## 1. Fuente(s) de los datos básicos

Código(s):  Título(s):

EPPA3  Estimaciones y proyecciones de la población económicamente activa, 1950-2025, tercera edición, OIT, Ginebra, 1986.
AST91  Anuario de Estadísticas del Trabjo 1991, OIT, Ginebra, 1991.

## 2. Evaluación de las tasas de actividad: 1950 - 1990

### 2.1 Datos básicos:

Cuadro 1: Tasas de actividad por sexo y grupo de edad

| Grupo de edad | Año 1950 (1) | 1960 (1) | 1970 (1) | 1980 (1) | 1984 (2) |
|---|---|---|---|---|---|
| **Hombres** | | | | | |
| 10-14 | 57.85 | 55.45 | 53.65 | 50.40 | 47.80 |
| 15-19 | 85.05 | 82.20 | 80.05 | 76.10 | 63.60 |
| 20-24 | 92.85 | 91.80 | 91.00 | 89.50 | 80.60 |
| 25-29 | 96.60 | 96.45 | 96.30 | 96.10 | 94.20 |
| 30-34 | 97.75 | 97.60 | 97.45 | 97.20 | 96.60 |
| 35-39 | 97.80 | 97.80 | 97.70 | 97.40 | 97.60 |
| 40-44 | 97.30 | 97.10 | 96.90 | 96.70 | 97.50 |
| 45-49 | 96.90 | 96.70 | 96.60 | 96.35 | 97.40 |
| 50-54 | 96.00 | 95.75 | 95.55 | 95.20 | 95.40 |
| 55-59 | 94.80 | 94.40 | 94.05 | 93.50 | 94.20 |
| 60-64 | 90.65 | 89.95 | 89.45 | 88.50 | 91.50 |
| 65+ | 67.60 | 66.55 | 65.75 | 64.30 | 76.58 |
| **Mujeres** | | | | | |
| 10-14 | 38.10 | 36.50 | 35.35 | 33.20 | 43.10 |
| 15-19 | 66.40 | 63.85 | 61.95 | 58.50 | 54.90 |
| 20-24 | 66.50 | 64.90 | 63.70 | 61.50 | 60.10 |
| 25-29 | 69.85 | 68.05 | 66.75 | 64.30 | 60.80 |
| 30-34 | 71.85 | 70.00 | 68.60 | 66.10 | 60.80 |
| 35-39 | 68.50 | 66.90 | 65.70 | 63.50 | 61.80 |
| 40-44 | 66.10 | 64.60 | 63.45 | 61.40 | 63.10 |
| 45-49 | 61.70 | 60.25 | 59.15 | 57.20 | 63.50 |
| 50-54 | 55.25 | 53.70 | 52.60 | 50.50 | 61.30 |
| 55-59 | 45.85 | 44.50 | 43.50 | 41.60 | 59.40 |
| 60-64 | 39.25 | 37.65 | 36.40 | 34.20 | 53.20 |
| 65+ | 14.10 | 13.35 | 12.75 | 11.70 | 37.71 |

Fuente(s):  (1) EPPA3; (2) AST91.

### 2.2 Método(s): interpolación y extrapolación lineares

**2.2.1 Hombres:**
- 1950-90, interpolación y extrapolación de las tasas de actividad 1950-80 con base en EPPA3 y de las tasas de actividad ajustadas con base el censo de 1984;
ajuste de las tasas interpoladas y extrapoladas con base en las variaciones de las tasas extrapoladas 1984, en relación con las tasas de actividad con base en el censo de 1984;
modificación de las tendencias de los grupos de edad [10-14] y [20-24] para 1990

**2.2.2 Mujeres:**
- 1950-90, interpolación y extrapolación de las tasas de actividad 1950-80 con base en EPPA3 y de las tasas de actividad ajustadas con base el censo de 1984;
ajuste de las tasas interpoladas y extrapoladas con base en las variaciones de las tasas extrapoladas 1984, en relación con las tasas de actividad con base en el censo de 1984;
modificación de las tendencias de los grupos de edad [15-64] para 1950-90.

## 3. Evaluación de las tasas de distribución por sector de actividad: 1950 - 1990

### 3.1 Datos básicos:

Cuadro 2: Distribución de la población económicamente activa por sector de actividad en %

| Año | Agricultura | Industria Total | Manufac. | Servicios |
|---|---|---|---|---|
| **Hombres** | | | | |
| 1950 (1) | 89.00 | 4.00 | .. | 7.00 |
| 1960 (1) | 85.00 | 5.50 | .. | 9.50 |
| 1970 (1) | 82.00 | 7.00 | .. | 11.00 |
| 1980 (1) | 76.50 | 9.00 | .. | 14.50 |
| 1984 (2) | 89.28 | 2.16 | 1.58 | 8.56 |
| **Mujeres** | | | | |
| 1950 (1) | 93.50 | 2.80 | .. | 3.70 |
| 1960 (1) | 90.95 | 3.70 | .. | 5.35 |
| 1970 (1) | 89.40 | 4.30 | .. | 6.30 |
| 1980 (1) | 84.90 | 6.10 | .. | 9.00 |
| 1984 (2) | 87.56 | 1.70 | 1.58 | 10.74 |

Fuente(s): (1) EPPA3; (2) AST91

### 3.2 Método(s): interpolación y extrapolación lineares

**3.2.1 Hombres:**
- 1950-90, interpolación y extrapolación de las tasas de distribución 1950-80 con base en EPPA3;
para la agricultura, ajuste de las tasas interpoladas y extrapoladas con base en las variaciones de las tasas interpoladas 1984, en relación con las tasas con base en el censo de 1984; las tasas de distribución estimadas de la con base en el censo de 1984; las tasas de distribución estimadas de la

**3.2.2 Mujeres:**
 Métodos, hipótesis y tratamientos idénticos a los que se aplican a los hombres.

## 4. Proyección de las tasas de actividad: 2000 - 2010

### 4.1 Modelo(s): linear y hiperbólico

**4.1.1 Hombres:**
- Para los grupos de edad [10-19], aplicación de la función F1;
- Para los grupos de edad [20+], aplicación de la función F3;
- Modificación de la tendencia del grupo de edad [20-24].

**4.1.2 Mujeres:**
- Para los grupos de edad [10-19], aplicación de la función F1;
- Para los grupos de edad [20+], aplicación de la función F3;
- Modificación de las tendencias de los grupos de edad [15-59].

# Fiji

## 1. Fuente(s) de los datos básicos

Código(s):  Título(s):

EPPA3   Anuario de estadísticas del trabajo 1945-89 - Edición retrospectiva sobre los censos de población, OIT, Ginebra, 1990.
STAT    Base de datos de la OIT sobre estadísticas del trabajo - LABORSTA, Oficina de Estadística, OIT, Ginebra.

## 2. Evaluación de las tasas de actividad: 1950 - 1990

### 2.1 Datos básicos:

Cuadro 1: Tasas de actividad por sexo y grupo de edad

| Grupo de edad | Año 1950 (1) | 1960 (1) | 1970 (1) | 1976 (2) | 1986 (2) |
|---|---|---|---|---|---|
| **Hombres** | | | | | |
| 10-14 | 31.00 | 21.00 | 15.00 | 0.00 | 0.00 |
| 15-19 | 86.60 | 75.90 | 65.20 | 56.84 | 57.90 |
| 20-24 | 97.00 | 96.30 | 93.60 | 91.28 | 91.00 |
| 25-29 | 98.85 | 98.00 | 97.20 | 96.34 | 95.97 |
| 30-34 | 98.75 | 98.30 | 97.85 | 97.31 | 97.32 |
| 35-39 | 98.45 | 98.15 | 97.90 | 97.37 | 97.41 |
| 40-44 | 98.55 | 98.10 | 97.60 | 97.35 | 97.57 |
| 45-49 | 97.30 | 97.70 | 96.35 | 95.39 | 95.83 |
| 50-54 | 98.05 | 95.80 | 93.55 | 92.37 | 92.04 |
| 55-59 | 96.00 | 92.65 | 89.30 | 84.94 | 83.71 |
| 60-64 | 91.50 | 86.60 | 81.75 | 76.14 | 71.64 |
| 65+ | 60.70 | 54.55 | 48.40 | 48.41 | 48.42 |
| **Mujeres** | | | | | |
| 10-14 | 1.60 | 2.00 | 1.50 | .. | 0.00 |
| 15-19 | 4.05 | 6.30 | 10.85 | .. | 21.40 |
| 20-24 | 5.75 | 9.75 | 17.70 | .. | 29.11 |
| 25-29 | 3.95 | 7.40 | 14.35 | .. | 26.19 |
| 30-34 | 3.05 | 6.35 | 12.90 | .. | 26.32 |
| 35-39 | 2.80 | 5.80 | 11.85 | .. | 25.31 |
| 40-44 | 3.30 | 6.00 | 11.35 | .. | 23.32 |
| 45-49 | 3.20 | 5.65 | 10.50 | .. | 21.32 |
| 50-54 | 2.75 | 5.05 | 9.60 | .. | 19.14 |
| 55-59 | 2.55 | 4.50 | 8.45 | .. | 16.71 |
| 60-64 | 1.45 | 3.10 | 6.40 | .. | 13.53 |
| 65+ | 0.90 | 1.95 | 4.10 | .. | 8.32 |

Fuente(s): (1) EPPA3; (2) STAT.

### 2.2 Método(s):  extrapolación linear
promedio ponderado

#### 2.2.1 Hombres:

- 1950-70, tasas de actividad 1950-70 con base en EPPA3;
- 1980, promedios ponderados de las tasas de actividad con base en los censos de 1976 y 1986;
- 1990, extrapolación de las tasas de actividad 1950-70 con base en EPPA3 y de las tasas de actividad estimadas para 1980 y de las tasas de actividad con base en el censo de 1986.

#### 2.2.2 Mujeres:

- 1950-80, tasas de actividad 1950-80 con base en EPPA3;
- 1990, promedios ponderados de las tasas de actividad 1980 con base en EPPA3 y de las tasas de actividad con base en el censo de 1986.

## 3. Evaluación de las tasas de distribución por sector de actividad: 1950 - 1990

### 3.1 Datos básicos:

Cuadro 2: Distribución de la población económicamente activa por sector de actividad en %

| Año | Agricultura | Industria Total | Manufac. | Servicios |
|---|---|---|---|---|
| **Hombres** | | | | |
| 1976 | 50.69 | 18.45 | 8.16 | 30.86 |
| 1986 | 52.69 | 15.99 | 7.66 | 31.33 |
| **Mujeres** | | | | |
| 1976 | 27.07 | 8.02 | 6.96 | 64.90 |
| 1986 | 28.42 | 11.28 | 10.33 | 60.30 |

Fuente(s): STAT.

### 3.2 Método(s):  interpolación y extrapolación lineares

#### 3.2.1 Hombres:

- 1950-70, tasas de distribución 1950-70 con base en EPPA3;
- 1980, interpolación de las tasas de distribución con base en los censos de 1976 y 1986;
- 1990, extrapolación de las tasas de distribución 1950-70 con base en EPPA3, de las tasas estimadas para 1980 y de las tasas con base en el censo de 1986;
de las tasas estimadas para 1980 y de las tasas con base en el censo de 1986;

#### 3.2.2 Mujeres:

Métodos, hipótesis y tratamientos idénticos a los que se aplican a los hombres.

## 4. Proyección de las tasas de actividad: 2000 - 2010

### 4.1 Modelo(s):  linear, hiperbólico y logístico

#### 4.1.1 Hombres:

- Para los grupos de edad [15-19] y [30+], aplicación de la función F3;
- Para los grupos de edad [20-29], aplicación de la función F1;
- Modificación de las tendencias de los grupos de edad [15-24] y [30-44].

#### 4.1.2 Mujeres:

- Para los grupos de edad [15-19] y [65+], aplicación de la función F1;
- Para los grupos de edad [20-64], aplicación de la función F6;
- Modificación de las tendencias de los grupos de edad [20-59].

*Notas sobre los ajustes de las tasas, véase p.380-384.*

*Notas sobre las funciones de proyección, véase p. 386.*

# Filipinas

## 1. Fuente(s) de los datos básicos

Código(s):  Título(s):

EPPA3  Estimaciones y proyecciones de la población económicamente activa, 1950-2025, tercera edición, OIT, Ginebra, 1986.
STAT  Base de datos de la OIT sobre estadísticas del trabajo - LABORSTA, Oficina de Estadística, OIT, Ginebra.

## 2. Evaluación de las tasas de actividad: 1950 - 1990

### 2.1 Datos básicos:

Cuadro 1: Tasas de actividad por sexo y grupo de edad

| Grupo de edad | Año 1958 | 1960 | 1970 | 1975 | 1990 |
|---|---|---|---|---|---|
| **Hombres** | | | | | |
| 10-14 | .. | 30.85 | 28.85 | 20.44 | .. |
| 15-19 | .. | 69.11 | 57.18 | 52.63 | 42.30 |
| 20-24 | .. | 87.89 | 86.35 | 84.35 | 70.74 |
| 25-29 | .. | 95.54 | 95.03 | 93.12 | 86.60 |
| 30-34 | .. | 98.09 | 97.70 | 97.17 | 91.46 |
| 35-39 | .. | 98.18 | 97.91 | 98.29 | 92.69 |
| 40-44 | .. | 98.32 | 97.95 | 98.62 | 92.64 |
| 45-49 | .. | 98.21 | 97.75 | 98.07 | 92.01 |
| 50-54 | .. | 97.95 | 97.34 | 97.28 | 89.94 |
| 55-59 | .. | 95.86 | 96.97 | 95.87 | 86.61 |
| 60-64 | .. | 87.81 | 87.31 | 84.25 | 78.00 |
| 65+ | .. | 69.22 | 63.41 | 62.56 | 59.88 |
| **Mujeres** | | | | | |
| 10-14 | 10.12 | .. | .. | .. | .. |
| 15-19 | 21.30 | .. | .. | .. | 31.32 |
| 20-24 | 50.80 | .. | .. | .. | 42.53 |
| 25-29 | 44.00 | .. | .. | .. | 43.25 |
| 30-34 | 47.00 | .. | .. | .. | 42.22 |
| 35-39 | 46.50 | .. | .. | .. | 42.45 |
| 40-44 | 47.00 | .. | .. | .. | 44.27 |
| 45-49 | 50.00 | .. | .. | .. | 42.64 |
| 50-54 | 54.00 | .. | .. | .. | 40.68 |
| 55-59 | 46.00 | .. | .. | .. | 38.87 |
| 60-64 | 33.00 | .. | .. | .. | 35.39 |
| 65+ | 19.20 | .. | .. | .. | 24.85 |

Fuente(s): STAT.

### 2.2 Método(s): interpolación y extrapolación lineares

**2.2.1 Hombres:**
- 1950-90, interpolación y extrapolación de las tasas de actividad con base en los censos de 1960, 1970 y 1975 y de las tasas de actividad ajustadas con base en el censo de 1990.

**2.2.2 Mujeres:**
- 1950-90, interpolación y extrapolación de las tasas de actividad con base en la encuesta de 1958 y de las tasas de actividad ajustadas con base en el censo de 1990;
ajuste de las tasas de actividad con base en los resultados de las encuestas de 1989, 1990 y 1991 realizadas en Pakistán;
modificación de las tendencias de todos los grupos de edad.

## 3. Evaluación de las tasas de distribución por sector de actividad: 1950 - 1990

### 3.1 Datos básicos:

Cuadro 2: Distribución de la población económicamente activa por sector de actividad en %

| Año | Agricultura | Industria Total | Manufac. | Servicios |
|---|---|---|---|---|
| **Hombres** | | | | |
| 1960 | 74.55 | 10.09 | 6.54 | 15.35 |
| 1965 | 66.60 | 12.77 | 7.97 | 20.64 |
| 1974 | 64.71 | 13.80 | 8.47 | 21.49 |
| 1975 | 64.45 | 13.93 | 8.56 | 21.62 |
| 1985 | 58.26 | 14.47 | 7.75 | 27.27 |
| 1989 | 53.19 | 16.69 | 8.78 | 30.12 |
| 1990 | 56.57 | 24.56 | 14.88 | 18.87 |
| 1991 | 53.96 | 17.28 | 8.53 | 28.76 |
| **Mujeres** | | | | |
| 1989 | 30.94 | 14.20 | 13.58 | 54.87 |
| 1990 | 31.35 | 12.80 | 12.24 | 55.85 |
| 1991 | 30.06 | 13.88 | 13.28 | 56.06 |

Fuente(s): STAT.

### 3.2 Método(s): interpolación y extrapolación lineares

**3.2.1 Hombres:**
- 1950-90, interpolación y extrapolación de las tasas de distribución con base en los censos de 1960 y 1975 y las encuestas de 1965, 1974, 1985, 1990 y 1991;
modificación de las tendencias de todos los sectores para 1950.

**3.2.2 Mujeres:**
- 1950-80, tasas de distribución 1950-80 con base en EPPA3;
- 1990, promedios de las tasas de distribución con base en las encuestas de 1989, 1990 y 1991.

## 4. Proyección de las tasas de actividad: 2000 - 2010

### 4.1 Modelo(s): linear, hiperbólico y logístico

**4.1.1 Hombres:**
- Para el grupo de edad [10-14], aplicación de la función F2;
- Para los grupos de edad [15+], aplicación de la función F3;
- Modificación de las tendencias de los grupos de edad [10-14], [35-49] y [65+].

**4.1.2 Mujeres:**
- Para el grupo de edad [10-14], aplicación de la función F2;
- Para los grupos de edad [15-34] y [50+], aplicación de la función F3;
- Para los grupos de edad [35-49], aplicación de la función F1;
- Modificación de las tendencias de todos los grupos de edad.

# Finlandia

## 1. Fuente(s) de los datos básicos

Código(s):   Título(s):

EPPA3   Anuario de estadísticas del trabajo 1945-89 - Edición retrospectiva sobre los censos de población, OIT, Ginebra, 1990.
STAT   Base de datos de la OIT sobre estadísticas del trabajo - LABORSTA, Oficina de Estadística, OIT, Ginebra.

## 2. Evaluación de las tasas de actividad: 1950 - 1990

### 2.1 Datos básicos:

Cuadro 1: Tasas de actividad por sexo y grupo de edad

| Grupo de edad | Año 1989 | 1990 | 1991 |
|---|---|---|---|
| **Hombres** | | | |
| 10-14 | 0.00 | 0.00 | 0.00 |
| 15-19 | 42.21 | 40.26 | 36.94 |
| 20-24 | 81.97 | 80.79 | 79.07 |
| 25-29 | 92.23 | 92.23 | 91.67 |
| 30-34 | 95.48 | 95.43 | 94.87 |
| 35-39 | 95.28 | 94.71 | 94.69 |
| 40-44 | 94.93 | 94.74 | 94.64 |
| 45-49 | 91.95 | 91.50 | 90.53 |
| 50-54 | 86.03 | 84.89 | 84.40 |
| 55-59 | 59.68 | 61.79 | 61.48 |
| 60-64 | 27.83 | 28.21 | 29.66 |
| 65+ | 5.60 | 4.66 | 4.55 |
| **Mujeres** | | | |
| 10-14 | 0.00 | 0.00 | 0.00 |
| 15-19 | 36.49 | 38.10 | 32.89 |
| 20-24 | 69.89 | 67.84 | 66.87 |
| 25-29 | 82.16 | 80.98 | 79.89 |
| 30-34 | 85.79 | 83.96 | 82.26 |
| 35-39 | 88.61 | 88.44 | 86.87 |
| 40-44 | 90.82 | 89.86 | 89.67 |
| 45-49 | 89.80 | 89.93 | 90.24 |
| 50-54 | 82.61 | 82.98 | 83.22 |
| 55-59 | 58.65 | 60.77 | 60.47 |
| 60-64 | 22.06 | 19.71 | 20.44 |
| 65+ | 1.88 | 1.62 | 1.61 |

Fuente(s): STAT.

### 2.2 Método(s): promedio aritmético

#### 2.2.1 Hombres:

- 1950-80, tasas de actividad 1950-80 con base en EPPA3;
ajuste de las tasas de actividad del grupo de edad [15-19] para 1980;
- 1990, promedios de las tasas de actividad con base en las encuestas de 1989, 1990 y 1991;
ajuste de las tasas de actividad estimadas del grupo de edad [15-19].

#### 2.2.2 Mujeres:

- 1950-80, tasas de actividad 1950-80 con base en EPPA3;
ajuste de las tasas de actividad del grupo de edad [15-19] para 1980;
- 1990, promedios de las tasas de actividad con base en las encuestas de 1989, 1990 y 1991;
ajuste de las tasas de actividad estimadas de los grupos de edad [15-24].

## 3. Evaluación de las tasas de distribución por sector de actividad: 1950 - 1990

### 3.1 Datos básicos:

Cuadro 2: Distribución de la población económicamente activa por sector de actividad en %

| Año | Agricultura | Industria Total | Manufac. | Servicios |
|---|---|---|---|---|
| **Hombres** | | | | |
| 1989 | 10.83 | 42.59 | 23.29 | 46.57 |
| 1990 | 10.12 | 42.84 | 23.34 | 47.05 |
| 1991 | 10.02 | 42.03 | 23.64 | 47.94 |
| **Mujeres** | | | | |
| 1989 | 6.28 | 17.77 | 12.89 | 75.95 |
| 1990 | 6.21 | 17.56 | 12.92 | 76.22 |
| 1991 | 6.23 | 16.84 | 13.13 | 76.94 |

Fuente(s): STAT.

### 3.2 Método(s): promedio aritmético

#### 3.2.1 Hombres:

- 1950-80, tasas de distribución 1950-80 con base en EPPA3;
la tasa de distribución 1980 de los manufacturas ajustada con base en la aplicación a la tasa de 1980 de la industria del promedio de la razón manufacturas/industria con base en las encuestas de 1979, 1980 y 1981;
- 1990, promedios de las tasas de distribución con base en las encuestas
- 1990, promedios de las tasas de distribución con base en las encuestas

#### 3.2.2 Mujeres:

Métodos, hipótesis y tratamientos idénticos a los que se aplican a los hombres.

## 4. Proyección de las tasas de actividad: 2000 - 2010

### 4.1 Modelo(s): linear, hiperbólico y logístico

#### 4.1.1 Hombres:

- Para los grupos de edad [15-19] y [30+], aplicación de la función F3;
- Para los grupos de edad [20-29], aplicación de la función F1;
- Modificación de las tendencias de los grupos de edad [45-59].

#### 4.1.2 Mujeres:

- Para los grupos de edad [15-29], aplicación de la función F1;
- Para los grupos de edad [30-59], aplicación de la función F6;
- Para los grupos de edad [60+], aplicación de la función F3;
- Modificación de las tendencias de los grupos de edad [20-59].

*Notas sobre los ajustes de las tasas, véase p.380-384.*   *Notas sobre las funciones de proyección, véase p. 386.*

# Francia

## 1. Fuente(s) de los datos básicos

Código(s):   Título(s):

EPPA3    Anuario de estadísticas del trabajo 1945-89 - Edición retrospectiva sobre los censos de población, OIT, Ginebra, 1990.
STAT      Base de datos de la OIT sobre estadísticas del trabajo - LABORSTA, Oficina de Estadística, OIT, Ginebra.

## 2. Evaluación de las tasas de actividad: 1950 - 1990

### 2.1 Datos básicos:

Cuadro 1: Tasas de actividad por sexo y grupo de edad

| Grupo de edad | Año 1979 | 1980 | 1981 | 1989 | 1990 | 1991 |
|---|---|---|---|---|---|---|
| **Hombres** | | | | | | |
| 10-14 | 0.00 | 0.00 | 0.00 | 0.00 | 0.00 | 0.00 |
| 15-19 | 26.50 | 25.70 | 24.30 | 14.90 | 14.60 | 12.20 |
| 20-24 | 81.10 | 80.10 | 78.10 | 69.30 | 65.00 | 62.10 |
| 25-29 | 95.40 | 95.40 | 94.90 | 94.40 | 94.00 | 93.90 |
| 30-34 | 98.10 | 98.10 | 98.00 | 97.20 | 96.80 | 96.80 |
| 35-39 | 98.10 | 98.30 | 97.90 | 97.30 | 97.00 | 97.20 |
| 40-44 | 97.60 | 97.60 | 97.60 | 97.20 | 97.00 | 96.80 |
| 45-49 | 95.60 | 96.60 | 96.40 | 95.50 | 96.10 | 95.60 |
| 50-54 | 93.00 | 92.90 | 92.40 | 90.10 | 90.00 | 89.40 |
| 55-59 | 82.30 | 81.00 | 79.80 | 68.10 | 67.70 | 68.60 |
| 60-64 | 45.30 | 47.90 | 43.10 | 24.20 | 22.80 | 19.70 |
| 65+ | 6.80 | 6.00 | 5.30 | 3.51 | 2.77 | 2.60 |
| **Mujeres** | | | | | | |
| 10-14 | 0.00 | 0.00 | 0.00 | 0.00 | 0.00 | 0.00 |
| 15-19 | 20.00 | 18.40 | 17.30 | 9.40 | 8.10 | 6.80 |
| 20-24 | 68.90 | 68.00 | 67.50 | 59.90 | 57.60 | 54.00 |
| 25-29 | 70.10 | 70.50 | 70.30 | 76.40 | 77.70 | 78.10 |
| 30-34 | 66.50 | 66.90 | 67.70 | 73.50 | 74.60 | 74.50 |
| 35-39 | 63.70 | 65.00 | 66.90 | 73.50 | 73.10 | 74.70 |
| 40-44 | 61.30 | 63.00 | 64.80 | 74.10 | 75.40 | 76.10 |
| 45-49 | 59.20 | 59.10 | 59.30 | 69.00 | 69.10 | 71.30 |
| 50-54 | 53.80 | 55.40 | 57.20 | 62.10 | 62.70 | 64.40 |
| 55-59 | 46.60 | 47.80 | 47.20 | 44.60 | 45.30 | 45.40 |
| 60-64 | 24.60 | 27.60 | 26.00 | 17.60 | 17.00 | 16.00 |
| 65+ | 3.7 | 2.9 | 2.6 | 1.72 | 1.53 | 1.36 |

Fuente(s): STAT.

### 2.2 Método(s): promedio ponderado

**2.2.1 Hombres:**

- 1950-70, tasas de actividad 1950-70 con base en EPPA3;
- 1980, promedios ponderados de las tasas de actividad con base en las encuestas de 1979, 1980 y 198;
- 1990, promedios ponderados de las tasas de actividad con base en las encuestas 1989, 1990 y 1991.

**2.2.2 Mujeres:**

Métodos, hipótesis y tratamientos idénticos a los que se aplican a los hombres.

## 3. Evaluación de las tasas de distribución por sector de actividad: 1950 - 1990

### 3.1 Datos básicos:

Cuadro 2: Distribución de la población económicamente activa por sector de actividad en %

| Año | Agricultura | Industria Total | Manufac. | Servicios |
|---|---|---|---|---|
| **Hombres** | | | | |
| 1979 | 9.11 | 43.36 | .. | 47.53 |
| 1980 | 8.86 | 43.16 | .. | 47.98 |
| 1981 | 8.60 | 42.65 | .. | 48.75 |
| 1989 | 6.45 | 37.49 | .. | 56.06 |
| 1990 | 6.23 | 38.13 | .. | 55.63 |
| 1991 | 6.10 | 37.79 | .. | 56.11 |
| **Mujeres** | | | | |
| 1979 | 7.67 | 22.56 | .. | 69.78 |
| 1980 | 7.35 | 22.18 | .. | 70.47 |
| 1981 | 7.08 | 21.31 | .. | 71.62 |
| 1989 | 4.83 | 17.22 | .. | 77.95 |
| 1990 | 4.51 | 17.14 | .. | 78.35 |
| 1991 | 4.15 | 16.73 | .. | 79.12 |

Fuente(s): STAT.

### 3.2 Método(s): promedio aritmético

**3.2.1 Hombres:**

- 1950-70, tasas de distribución 1950-70 con base en EPPA3;
- 1980, promedios de las tasas de distribución con base en las encuestas de 1979, 1980 y 1981;
- 1990, promedios de las tasas de distribución con base en las encuestas de 1989, 1990 y 1991.
de 1989, 1990 y 1991.

**3.2.2 Mujeres:**

Métodos, hipótesis y tratamientos idénticos a los que se aplican a los hombres.

## 4. Proyección de las tasas de actividad: 2000 - 2010

### 4.1 Modelo(s): linear, hiperbólico y logístico

**4.1.1 Hombres:**

- Para todos los grupos de edad, aplicación de la función F3;
- Modificación de las tendencias de los grupos de edad [20-24] y [30-44].

**4.1.2 Mujeres:**

- Para los grupos de edad [15-24] y [60+], aplicación de la función F3;
- Para los grupos de edad [25-54], aplicación de la función F6;
- Para el grupo de edad [55-59], aplicación de la función F1;
- Modificación de las tendencias de los grupos de edad [15-59].

*Notas sobre los ajustes de las tasas, véase p.380-384.*        *Notas sobre las funciones de proyección, véase p. 386.*

# Gabón

## 1. Fuente(s) de los datos básicos

Código(s):　Título(s):

EPPA3　　Estimaciones y proyecciones de la población económicamente activa, 1950-2025, tercera edición, OIT, Ginebra, 1986.

## 2. Evaluación de las tasas de actividad: 1950 - 1990

### 2.1 Datos básicos:

Cuadro 1: Tasas de actividad por sexo y grupo de edad

| Grupo de edad | Año 1950 | 1960 | 1970 | 1980 |
|---|---|---|---|---|
| **Hombres** | | | | |
| 10-14 | 38.90 | 36.60 | 33.60 | 31.85 |
| 15-19 | 48.35 | 46.00 | 43.00 | 41.25 |
| 20-24 | 91.10 | 89.65 | 87.75 | 86.60 |
| 25-29 | 96.20 | 96.00 | 95.70 | 95.55 |
| 30-34 | 97.25 | 97.00 | 96.70 | 96.50 |
| 35-39 | 97.25 | 97.00 | 96.65 | 96.45 |
| 40-44 | 97.30 | 97.00 | 96.65 | 96.45 |
| 45-49 | 95.35 | 95.10 | 94.80 | 94.60 |
| 50-54 | 94.35 | 94.00 | 93.55 | 93.30 |
| 55-59 | 92.25 | 91.70 | 91.00 | 90.55 |
| 60-64 | 81.85 | 81.00 | 79.90 | 79.25 |
| 65+ | 72.70 | 71.15 | 69.10 | 67.90 |
| **Mujeres** | | | | |
| 10-14 | 41.10 | 40.40 | 39.10 | 37.75 |
| 15-19 | 66.55 | 65.50 | 63.60 | 61.55 |
| 20-24 | 65.80 | 65.10 | 63.90 | 62.65 |
| 25-29 | 71.00 | 70.25 | 68.85 | 67.40 |
| 30-34 | 75.45 | 74.65 | 73.20 | 71.65 |
| 35-39 | 76.55 | 75.80 | 74.45 | 73.00 |
| 40-44 | 79.00 | 78.25 | 76.90 | 75.40 |
| 45-49 | 78.55 | 77.00 | 76.40 | 74.00 |
| 50-54 | 77.45 | 76.55 | 74.95 | 73.20 |
| 55-59 | 74.75 | 73.85 | 72.15 | 70.35 |
| 60-64 | 69.35 | 68.20 | 66.05 | 63.75 |
| 65+ | 49.10 | 48.00 | 46.00 | 43.90 |

Fuente(s): EPPA3.

### 2.2 Método(s): interpolación y extrapolación lineares

**2.2.1 Hombres:**

- 1950 y 1970-90, interpolación y extrapolación de las tasas de actividad 1950-80 con base en EPPA3;
ajuste de las tasas interpoladas y extrapoladas con base en las variaciones de las tasas interpoladas 1960, en relación con las tasas de actividad 1960 con base en EPPA3;
modificación de las tendencias de los grupos de edad [10-14], [25-49] y [65+] para 1980 y 1990;
- 1960, tasas de actividad 1960 con base en EPPA3.

**2.2.2 Mujeres:**

- 1960, tasas de actividad 1960 con base en EPPA3;
- 1950 y 1970-90, interpolación y extrapolación de las tasas de actividad 1950-80 con base en EPPA3;
ajuste de las tasas interpoladas y extrapoladas con base en las variaciones interpoladas 1960, en relación con las tasas de actividad 1960 con base en EPPA3;
modificación de las tendencias de todos los grupos de edad para 1950

## 3. Evaluación de las tasas de distribución por sector de actividad: 1950 - 1990

### 3.1 Datos básicos:

Cuadro 2: Distribución de la población económicamente activa por sector de actividad en %

| Año | Agricultura | Industria Total | Manufac. | Servicios |
|---|---|---|---|---|
| **Hombres** | | | | |
| 1950 | 84.00 | 8.40 | .. | 7.60 |
| 1960 | 78.50 | 11.00 | .. | 10.50 |
| 1970 | 71.40 | 14.60 | .. | 14.00 |
| **Mujeres** | | | | |
| 1950 | 97.50 | 0.35 | .. | 2.15 |
| 1960 | 95.00 | 0.70 | .. | 4.30 |
| 1970 | 92.00 | 1.40 | .. | 6.60 |

Fuente(s): (1) EPPA3.

### 3.2 Método(s): promedio ponderado

**3.2.1 Hombres:**

- 1950-70, tasas de distribución 1950-70 con base en EPPA3;
- 1980, promedios ponderados de las tasas de distribución 1970 con base en EPPA3 y de las tasas estimadas para 1990;
- 1990, extrapolación de las tasas de distribución 1950-70 con base en EPPA3; modificación de las tendencias de todos los sectores.
modificación de las tendencias de todos los sectores.

**3.2.2 Mujeres:**

Métodos, hipótesis y tratamientos idénticos a los que se aplican a los hombres.

## 4. Proyección de las tasas de actividad: 2000 - 2010

### 4.1 Modelo(s): linear y hiperbólico

**4.1.1 Hombres:**

- Para los grupos de edad [10-19] y [65+], aplicación de la función F1;
- Para los grupos de edad [20-64], aplicación de la función F3;
- Modificación de la tendencia del grupo de edad [10-14].

**4.1.2 Mujeres:**

- Para el grupo de edad [10-14], aplicación de la función F1;
- Para los grupos de edad [15+], aplicación de la función F3;
- Modificación de las tendencias de los grupos de edad [15-64].

---

*Notas sobre los ajustes de las tasas, véase p.380-384.*　　　*Notas sobre las funciones de proyección, véase p. 386.*

# Gambia

## 1. Fuente(s) de los datos básicos

Código(s):    Título(s):
EPPA3        Estimaciones y proyecciones de la población económicamente activa, 1950-2025, tercera edición, OIT, Ginebra, 1986.
ASTER        Anuario de estadísticas del trabajo 1945-89 - Edición retrospectiva sobre los censos de población, OIT, Ginebra, 1990.

## 2. Evaluación de las tasas de actividad: 1950 - 1990

### 2.1 Datos básicos:

Cuadro 1: Tasas de actividad por sexo y grupo de edad

| Grupo de edad | Año 1950 (1) | 1960 (1) | 1970 (1) | 1980 (1) | 1983 (2) |
|---|---|---|---|---|---|
| **Hombres** | | | | | |
| 10-14 | 50.70 | 49.70 | 48.35 | 46.55 | .. |
| 15-19 | 83.00 | 81.70 | 79.95 | 77.55 | .. |
| 20-24 | 94.55 | 94.05 | 93.35 | 92.45 | .. |
| 25-29 | 97.30 | 97.20 | 97.10 | 97.00 | .. |
| 30-34 | 98.00 | 97.95 | 97.80 | 97.65 | .. |
| 35-39 | 98.20 | 98.10 | 97.95 | 97.80 | .. |
| 40-44 | 98.00 | 97.90 | 97.80 | 97.60 | .. |
| 45-49 | 97.25 | 97.20 | 97.10 | 96.95 | .. |
| 50-54 | 96.80 | 96.65 | 96.50 | 96.30 | .. |
| 55-59 | 95.80 | 95.60 | 95.35 | 95.00 | .. |
| 60-64 | 92.65 | 92.35 | 91.90 | 91.30 | .. |
| 65+ | 79.10 | 78.55 | 77.80 | 76.75 | .. |
| **Mujeres** | | | | | |
| 10-14 | 38.30 | 37.55 | 36.55 | 35.20 | 41.91 |
| 15-19 | 62.35 | 61.25 | 59.75 | 57.70 | 61.89 |
| 20-24 | 63.15 | 62.45 | 61.50 | 60.20 | 68.30 |
| 25-29 | 67.95 | 67.20 | 66.10 | 64.65 | 71.14 |
| 30-34 | 72.25 | 71.40 | 70.25 | 68.65 | 73.90 |
| 35-39 | 73.55 | 72.75 | 71.70 | 70.2 | 74.58 |
| 40-44 | 76.00 | 75.20 | 74.10 | 72.65 | 77.22 |
| 45-49 | 75.50 | 74.70 | 73.60 | 72.1 | 75.31 |
| 50-54 | 73.90 | 72.95 | 71.70 | 69.95 | 73.86 |
| 55-59 | 71.05 | 70.10 | 68.75 | 66.95 | 72.41 |
| 60-64 | 64.65 | 63.40 | 61.70 | 59.45 | 71.49 |
| 65+ | 44.70 | 43.55 | 42.00 | 39.85 | 60.74 |

Fuente(s): (1) EPPA3; (2) ASTER.

### 2.2 Método(s): interpolación y extrapolación lineares

#### 2.2.1 Hombres:

- 1950-80, tasas de actividad 1950-80 con base en EPPA3;
- 1990, extrapolación de las tasas de actividad 1950-80 con base en EPPA3;
ajuste de las tasas extrapoladas con base en las variaciones de las tasas
interpoladas 1980, en relación con las tasas 1980 con base en EPPA3;
modificación de las tendencias de los grupos de edad [10-14], [15-24]
y del grupo de edad [65+] para 1990.

#### 2.2.2 Mujeres:

- 1950-90, interpolación y extrapolación de las tasas de actividad 1950-80
con base en EPPA3;
ajuste de las tasas interpoladas y extrapoladas con base en las variaciones
de las tasas extrapoladas 1983, en relación con las tasas de actividad con base
en el censo en de 1983;
modificación de las tendencias de todos los grupos de edad para 1970 y 1980
y de los grupos de edad [10-14] y [60-64] para 1990.

## 3. Evaluación de las tasas de distribución por sector de actividad: 1950 - 1990

### 3.1 Datos básicos:

Cuadro 2: Distribución de la población económicamente activa por sector de actividad en %

| Año | Agricultura | Industria Total | Manufac. | Servicios |
|---|---|---|---|---|
| **Hombres** | | | | |
| 1950 | 85.00 | 6.60 | .. | 8.40 |
| 1960 | 83.20 | 7.40 | .. | 9.40 |
| 1970 | 80.75 | 8.50 | .. | 10.75 |
| 1980 | 77.45 | 10.00 | .. | 12.55 |
| **Mujeres** | | | | |
| 1950 | 97.00 | 1.00 | .. | 2.00 |
| 1960 | 96.00 | 1.30 | .. | 2.70 |
| 1970 | 94.50 | 1.80 | .. | 3.70 |
| 1980 | 93.00 | 2.30 | .. | 4.70 |

Fuente(s): EPPA3.

### 3.2 Método(s): extrapolación linear

#### 3.2.1 Hombres:

- 1950-80, tasas de distribución 1950-80 con base en EPPA3;
- 1990, extrapolación de las tasas de distribución 1950-80 con base en EPPA3;
ajuste de las tasas extrapoladas 1990 con base en las variaciones de las tasas
interpoladas 1980, en relación con las tasas 1980 con base en EPPA3;
- Aplicación de las razones manufacturas/industria estimada para Níger.
- Aplicación de las razones manufacturas/industria estimada para Níger.

#### 3.2.2 Mujeres:

Métodos, hipótesis y tratamientos idénticos a los que se aplican a los hombres.

## 4. Proyección de las tasas de actividad: 2000 - 2010

### 4.1 Modelo(s): linear y hiperbólico

#### 4.1.1 Hombres:

- Para todos los grupos de edad, aplicación de la función F1;
- Modificación de las tendencias de los grupos de edad [10-19].

#### 4.1.2 Mujeres:

- Para los grupos de edad [10-19], aplicación de la función F1;
- Para los grupos de edad [20+], aplicación de la función F3;
- Modificación de las tendencias de los grupos de edad [20-59].

*Notas sobre los ajustes de las tasas, véase p.380-384.*          *Notas sobre las funciones de proyección, véase p. 386.*

# Georgia

## 1. Fuente(s) de los datos básicos

Código(s):   Título(s):

BLT-94-2    Vorobiev A. (1994), "Estimaciones de la población económicamente activa de los quince países de la ex URSS, en 1950, 1959, 1970, 1979 y 1989", en el Boletín de Estadísticas del Trabajol - 1994-2, OIT, Ginebra.

## 2. Evaluación de las tasas de actividad: 1950 - 1990

### 2.1 Datos básicos:

Cuadro 1: Tasas de actividad por sexo y grupo de edad

| Grupo de edad | Año 1950 | 1959 | 1970 | 1979 | 1989 |
|---|---|---|---|---|---|
| **Hombres** | | | | | |
| 10-14 | 0.00 | 0.00 | 0.00 | 0.00 | 0.00 |
| 15-19 | 50.56 | 51.53 | 32.51 | 34.40 | 29.36 |
| 20-24 | 82.02 | 81.62 | 82.76 | 80.60 | 74.38 |
| 25-29 | 92.13 | 91.38 | 85.83 | 94.77 | 47.79 |
| 30-34 | 93.83 | 94.19 | 96.84 | 97.64 | 96.02 |
| 35-39 | 92.63 | 94.32 | 96.41 | 97.18 | 96.55 |
| 40-44 | 92.94 | 93.15 | 96.05 | 96.67 | 95.20 |
| 45-49 | 91.55 | 91.67 | 90.63 | 95.57 | 93.53 |
| 50-54 | 90.91 | 89.19 | 89.06 | 90.91 | 90.85 |
| 55-59 | 86.79 | 87.10 | 83.33 | 82.43 | 84.40 |
| 60-64 | 78.00 | 86.79 | 71.01 | 50.00 | 55.38 |
| 65+ | 42.06 | 41.83 | 14.09 | 18.90 | 25.95 |
| **Mujeres** | | | | | |
| 10-14 | 0.00 | 0.00 | 0.00 | 0.00 | 0.00 |
| 15-19 | 42.86 | 42.20 | 31.12 | 35.86 | 27.23 |
| 20-24 | 56.68 | 56.28 | 59.87 | 75.35 | 59.05 |
| 25-29 | 62.69 | 62.50 | 83.22 | 86.17 | 70.54 |
| 30-34 | 62.18 | 61.46 | 80.00 | 89.29 | 75.93 |
| 35-39 | 62.39 | 64.18 | 81.03 | 90.30 | 80.85 |
| 40-44 | 64.08 | 65.22 | 80.75 | 90.77 | 82.35 |
| 45-49 | 62.93 | 63.16 | 82.17 | 88.55 | 81.01 |
| 50-54 | 53.49 | 57.14 | 73.27 | 81.61 | 75.27 |
| 55-59 | 48.81 | 50.00 | 40.00 | 48.03 | 50.31 |
| 60-64 | 42.50 | 48.15 | 22.94 | 23.64 | 34.13 |
| 65+ | 18.56 | 17.61 | 6.44 | 6.83 | 12.19 |

Fuente(s): BLT-94-2-2

### 2.2 Método(s): promedio ponderado

**2.2.1 Hombres:**

- 1950-90, promedios ponderados de las tasas de actividad 1950, 1959, 1977 y 1989 con base en el Boletín de estadísticas del trabajo 1994-2.

**2.2.2 Mujeres:**

Métodos, hipótesis y tratamientos idénticos a los que se aplican a los hombres.

## 3. Evaluación de las tasas de distribución por sector de actividad: 1950 - 1990

### 3.1 Datos básicos:

Cuadro 2: Distribución de la población económicamente activa por sector de actividad en %

| Año | Agricultura | Industria Total | Manufac. | Servicios |
|---|---|---|---|---|
| **Hombres** | | | | |
| 1950 | 57.65 | 20.56 | 11.87 | 21.79 |
| 1959 | 44.18 | 24.26 | 13.51 | 31.56 |
| 1970 | 33.73 | 30.71 | 18.97 | 35.56 |
| 1979 | 31.08 | 31.55 | 17.93 | 37.37 |
| 1989 | 27.91 | 37.42 | 21.17 | 34.66 |
| **Mujeres** | | | | |
| 1950 | 66.85 | 11.14 | 8.04 | 22.00 |
| 1959 | 45.51 | 18.58 | 9.12 | 35.91 |
| 1970 | 40.85 | 19.98 | 17.01 | 39.17 |
| 1979 | 35.46 | 20.48 | 17.45 | 44.06 |
| 1989 | 25.83 | 23.01 | 19.04 | 51.16 |

Fuente(s): BLT-94-2.

### 3.2 Método(s): promedio ponderado

**3.2.1 Hombres:**

- 1950-90, promedios ponderados de las tasas de distribución 1950, 1959, 1970, 1979 y 1989 con base en el Boletín de estadísticas del trabajo 1994-2.

**3.2.2 Mujeres:**

Métodos, hipótesis y tratamientos idénticos a los que se aplican a los hombres.

## 4. Proyección de las tasas de actividad: 2000 - 2010

### 4.1 Modelo(s): linear, hiperbólico y logístico

**4.1.1 Hombres:**

- Para los grupos de edad [15-24] y [55+], aplicación de la función F3;
- Para los grupos de edad [25-54], aplicación de la función F1;
- Modificación de las tendencias de los grupos de edad [20-54].

**4.1.2 Mujeres:**

- Para los grupos de edad [15-19] y [55+], aplicación de la función F3;
- Para los grupos de edad [20-24] y [50-54], aplicación de la función F1;
- Para los grupos de edad [25-49], aplicación de la función F6;
- Modificación de la tendencia del grupo de edad [50-54].

*Notas sobre los ajustes de las tasas, véase p.380-384.*   *Notas sobre las funciones de proyección, véase p. 386.*

# Ghana

## 1. Fuente(s) de los datos básicos

Código(s):   Título(s):

EPPA3   Estimaciones y proyecciones de la población económicamente activa, 1950-2025, tercera edición, OIT, Ginebra, 1986.
ADNU64   Annuaire démographique 1964 - Statistiques des recensements de population III, seizième édition, Nations Unies, New York, 1965.
ASTER   Anuario de estadísticas del trabajo 1945-89 - Edición retrospectiva sobre los censos de población, OIT, Ginebra, 1990.

## 2. Evaluación de las tasas de actividad: 1950 - 1990

### 2.1 Datos básicos:

Cuadro 1: Tasas de actividad por sexo y grupo de edad

| Grupo de edad | Año 1950 (1) | 1960 (2) | 1970 (3) | 1984 (3) |
|---|---|---|---|---|
| **Hombres** | | | | |
| 10-14 | 27.80 | 0.00 | 0.00 | 0.00 |
| 15-19 | 63.40 | 61.49 | 42.31 | 42.10 |
| 20-24 | 90.00 | 91.00 | 82.60 | 82.51 |
| 25-29 | 97.25 | 96.48 | 95.53 | 95.52 |
| 30-34 | 98.25 | 97.50 | 97.52 | 97.52 |
| 35-39 | 98.35 | 97.54 | 97.93 | 97.93 |
| 40-44 | 98.15 | 97.34 | 97.82 | 97.83 |
| 45-49 | 97.75 | 96.92 | 97.52 | 97.52 |
| 50-54 | 96.75 | 96.03 | 96.57 | 96.58 |
| 55-59 | 96.00 | 93.73 | 95.23 | 95.25 |
| 60-64 | 95.20 | 89.12 | 91.61 | 91.64 |
| 65+ | 82.00 | 71.52 | 75.41 | 75.45 |
| **Mujeres** | | | | |
| 10-14 | .. | ... | .. | ... |
| 15-19 | .. | 53.71 | .. | 64.59 |
| 20-24 | .. | 52.32 | .. | 83.94 |
| 25-29 | .. | 51.50 | .. | 86.62 |
| 30-34 | .. | 57.05 | .. | 88.96 |
| 35-39 | .. | 59.32 | .. | 90.91 |
| 40-44 | .. | 65.35 | .. | 91.26 |
| 45-49 | .. | 67.00 | .. | 91.73 |
| 50-54 | .. | 69.63 | .. | 90.95 |
| 55-59 | .. | 70.61 | .. | 89.53 |
| 60-64 | .. | 64.03 | .. | 85.66 |
| 65+ | .. | 43.20 | .. | 73.57 |

**Fuente(s):** (1) EPPA3; (2) ASTER y ADNU64; (3) ASTER.

### 2.2 Método(s): interpolación y extrapolación lineares
promedio ponderado

#### 2.2.1 Hombres:

- 1950-90, interpolación y extrapolación de las tasas de actividad con base en los censos de 1960 y 1984;
aplicación a las tasas de actividad 1950 con base en EPPA3,
de las variaciones de las tasas extrapoladas 1960, en relación con las tasas de actividad con base en el censo de 1960;
- 1960-90, promedios ponderados de las tasas de actividad con base en el censos de 1960 y 1984.

#### 2.2.2 Mujeres:

- 1950-90, interpolación y extrapolación de las tasas de actividad con base en los censos de 1960 y 1984;
modificación de las tendencias de los grupos de edad [60+] para 1950-90, de los grupos de edad [10-59] para 1950 y de los grupos de edad [10-19] para 1980 y 1990.

## 3. Evaluación de las tasas de distribución por sector de actividad: 1950 - 1990

### 3.1 Datos básicos:

Cuadro 2: Distribución de la población económicamente activa por sector de actividad en %

| Año | Agricultura | Industria Total | Manufac. | Servicios |
|---|---|---|---|---|
| **Hombres** | | | | |
| 1960 (1) | 65.42 | 17.16 | 8.27 | 17.42 |
| 1984 (2) | 66.36 | 11.30 | 7.52 | 22.33 |
| **Mujeres** | | | | |
| 1960 (1) | 58.26 | 10.56 | 10.01 | 31.18 |
| 1984 (2) | 56.04 | 14.26 | 14.00 | 29.70 |

**Fuente(s):** (1) ADNU64; (2) ASTER.

### 3.2 Método(s): promedio ponderado

#### 3.2.1 Hombres:

- 1950-60, tasas de distribución 1950-60 con base en EPPA3;
- 1980, promedios ponderados de las tasas de distribución 1960 con base en EPPA3 y de las tasas de distribución con base en el censo de 1984;
- 1970, promedios de las tasas estimadas para 1960 y 1980;
- 1990, estimación basada en una disminución de 0,25 punto por año en
- 1990, estimación basada en una disminución de 0,25 punto por año en

#### 3.2.2 Mujeres:

- 1950-70, tasas de distribución 1950-70 con base en EPPA3;
- 1980, promedios ponderados de las tasas de distribución 1960 con base en EPPA3 y de las tasas de distribución con base en el censo de 1984;
- 1990, extrapolación de las tasas estimadas para 1970 y 1980.

## 4. Proyección de las tasas de actividad: 2000 - 2010

### 4.1 Modelo(s): linear y hiperbólico

#### 4.1.1 Hombres:

- Para los grupos de edad [10-59], aplicación de la función F1;
- Para los grupos de edad [60+], aplicación de la función F3;
- Modificación de las tendencias de los grupos de edad [15-59].

#### 4.1.2 Mujeres:

- Para todos los grupos de edad, aplicación de la función F1;
- Modificación de las tendencias de los grupos de edad [15+].

# Grecia

## 1. Fuente(s) de los datos básicos

Código(s):  Título(s):

EPPA3   Anuario de estadísticas del trabajo 1945-89 - Edición retrospectiva sobre los censos de población, OIT, Ginebra, 1990.
STAT    Base de datos de la OIT sobre estadísticas del trabajo - LABORSTA, Oficina de Estadística, OIT, Ginebra.

## 2. Evaluación de las tasas de actividad: 1950 - 1990

### 2.1 Datos básicos:

Cuadro 1: Tasas de actividad por sexo y grupo de edad

| Grupo de edad | Año 1970 (1) | 1981 (2) | 1989 (2) | 1990 (2) | 1991 (2) |
|---|---|---|---|---|---|
| **Hombres** | | | | | |
| 10-14 | .. | .. | 0.00 | 0.00 | 0.00 |
| 15-19 | .. | .. | 20.00 | 19.10 | 18.60 |
| 20-24 | .. | .. | 72.00 | 70.40 | 68.30 |
| 25-29 | .. | .. | 94.30 | 93.70 | 92.30 |
| 30-34 | .. | .. | 97.20 | 96.70 | 96.50 |
| 35-39 | .. | .. | 97.10 | 97.30 | 97.00 |
| 40-44 | .. | .. | 96.70 | 96.30 | 96.10 |
| 45-49 | .. | .. | 94.50 | 94.00 | 93.90 |
| 50-54 | .. | .. | 86.90 | 87.70 | 86.40 |
| 55-59 | .. | .. | 73.50 | 72.30 | 71.50 |
| 60-64 | .. | .. | 48.10 | 46.00 | 45.60 |
| 65+ | .. | .. | 11.70 | 11.80 | 11.00 |
| **Mujeres** | | | | | |
| 10-14 | 6.50 | 3.04 | 0.00 | 0.00 | 0.00 |
| 15-19 | 28.10 | 23.24 | 15.40 | 15.60 | 14.10 |
| 20-24 | 36.00 | 39.02 | 53.90 | 54.00 | 53.00 |
| 25-29 | 31.85 | 37.50 | 59.10 | 60.20 | 58.70 |
| 30-34 | 29.80 | 33.56 | 58.40 | 58.50 | 55.70 |
| 35-39 | 29.70 | 30.82 | 57.10 | 57.10 | 54.20 |
| 40-44 | 29.55 | 30.64 | 50.00 | 49.90 | 49.10 |
| 45-49 | 27.35 | 28.80 | 45.60 | 45.40 | 41.30 |
| 50-54 | 25.40 | 25.77 | 38.90 | 37.80 | 34.70 |
| 55-59 | 21.95 | 19.91 | 30.20 | 28.50 | 26.60 |
| 60-64 | 16.40 | 13.38 | 19.60 | 19.90 | 15.90 |
| 65+ | 8.20 | 4.96 | 4.1 | 4.5 | 3.9 |

Fuente(s): (1) EPPA3; (2) STAT.

### 2.2 Método(s): promedio ponderado, promedio aritmético

#### 2.2.1 Hombres:

- 1950-80, tasas de actividad 1950-80 con base en EPPA3;
- 1990, promedios de las tasas de actividad ajustadas con base en las encuestas de 1989, 1990 y 1991;
ajuste de las tasas de actividad estimadas de los grupos de edad [15-29] para tener en cuenta los efectivos del servicio militar obligatorio.

#### 2.2.2 Mujeres:

- 1950-70, tasas de actividad 1950-70 con base en EPPA3;
- 1980, promedios ponderados de las tasas de actividad 1970 con base en EPPA3 y de las tasas de actividad con base en el censo de 1981;
- 1990, promedios de las tasas de actividad con base en las encuestas de 1989, 1990 and 1991;
ajuste de las tasas de actividad estimadas del grupo de edad [15-19] para 1990.

## 3. Evaluación de las tasas de distribución por sector de actividad: 1950 - 1990

### 3.1 Datos básicos:

Cuadro 2: Distribución de la población económicamente activa por sector de actividad en %

| Año | Agricultura | Industria Total | Manufac. | Servicios |
|---|---|---|---|---|
| **Hombres** | | | | |
| 1981 | 27.46 | 34.29 | 19.52 | 38.24 |
| 1989 | 21.22 | 33.28 | 21.06 | 45.50 |
| 1990 | 20.19 | 33.60 | 20.98 | 46.21 |
| 1991 | 19.56 | 33.00 | 20.65 | 47.44 |
| **Mujeres** | | | | |
| 1981 | 32.69 | 21.19 | 20.23 | 46.12 |
| 1989 | 31.39 | 18.22 | 17.51 | 50.39 |
| 1990 | 29.52 | 18.11 | 17.26 | 52.37 |
| 1991 | 25.85 | 18.53 | 17.67 | 55.63 |

Fuente(s): STAT.

### 3.2 Método(s): promedio aritmético

#### 3.2.1 Hombres:

- 1950-80, tasas de distribución 1950-80 con base en EPPA3;
- Aplicación de la razón manufacturas/industria con base en el censo de 1981;
- 1990, promedios ajustadas de las tasas de distribución con base en las encuestas de 1989, 1990 y 1991;
ajuste de las tasas de distribución para tener en cuenta los efectivos
ajuste de las tasas de distribución para tener en cuenta los efectivos

#### 3.2.2 Mujeres:

Métodos, hipótesis y tratamientos idénticos a los que se aplican a los hombres.

## 4. Proyección de las tasas de actividad: 2000 - 2010

### 4.1 Modelo(s): linear, hiperbólico y logístico

#### 4.1.1 Hombres:

- Para los grupos de edad [15-19] y [35+], aplicación de la función F1;
- Para los grupos de edad [20-34], aplicación de la función F3;
- Modificación de las tendencias de los grupos de edad [25-34].

#### 4.1.2 Mujeres:

- Para los grupos de edad [15-19] y [60+], aplicación de la función F3;
- Para el grupo de edad [20-24], aplicación de la función F1;
- Para los grupos de edad [25-59], aplicación de la función F6;
- Modificación de las tendencias de los grupos de edad [15-19] y [50-64].

*Notas sobre los ajustes de las tasas, véase p.380-384.*  *Notas sobre las funciones de proyección, véase p. 386.*

# Guadalupe

## 1. Fuente(s) de los datos básicos

Código(s):  Título(s):

EPPA3      Estimaciones y proyecciones de la población económicamente activa, 1950-2025, tercera edición, OIT, Ginebra, 1986.
ADNU       Ediciones de 1984 et 1988 del Annuaire démographique des Nations Unies, New York.
ASTER      Anuario de estadísticas del trabajo 1945-89 - Edición retrospectiva sobre los censos de población, OIT, Ginebra, 1990.
STAT       Base de datos de la OIT sobre estadísticas del trabajo - LABORSTA, Oficina de Estadística, OIT, Ginebra.

## 2. Evaluación de las tasas de actividad: 1950 - 1990

### 2.1 Datos básicos:

Cuadro 1: Tasas de actividad por sexo y grupo de edad

| | Año | | |
|---|---|---|---|
| Grupo de edad | 1974 (1) | 1982 (1) | 1990 (2) |
| **Hombres** | | | |
| 10-14 | 0.00 | 0.00 | 0.00 |
| 15-19 | 37.26 | 24.12 | 18.31 |
| 20-24 | 76.83 | 83.50 | 75.69 |
| 25-29 | 94.73 | 93.44 | 92.49 |
| 30-34 | 94.75 | 95.55 | 94.06 |
| 35-39 | 94.45 | 96.11 | 93.24 |
| 40-44 | 93.58 | 94.92 | 93.05 |
| 45-49 | 90.96 | 93.32 | 91.83 |
| 50-54 | 87.31 | 90.56 | 85.04 |
| 55-59 | 79.94 | 83.11 | 72.60 |
| 60-64 | 53.03 | 52.34 | 37.50 |
| 65+ | 15.74 | 10.05 | 5.53 |
| **Mujeres** | | | |
| 10-14 | 0.00 | 0.00 | 0.00 |
| 15-19 | 29.22 | 15.38 | 12.61 |
| 20-24 | 65.18 | 66.74 | 67.66 |
| 25-29 | 59.27 | 69.70 | 81.48 |
| 30-34 | 54.17 | 66.91 | 77.61 |
| 35-39 | 50.35 | 64.85 | 75.88 |
| 40-44 | 48.67 | 61.47 | 73.45 |
| 45-49 | 47.66 | 57.07 | 68.10 |
| 50-54 | 45.48 | 51.48 | 59.11 |
| 55-59 | 40.89 | 46.70 | 45.79 |
| 60-64 | 24.93 | 25.34 | 21.77 |
| 65+ | 6.16 | 3.82 | 2.55 |

Fuente(s): (1) ADNU; (2) EPPA3.

### 2.2 Método(s): interpolación y extrapolación lineares promedio ponderado

**2.2.1 Hombres:**

- 1950-60, tasas de actividad 1950-60 con base en EPPA3;
ajuste de las tasas de actividad del grupo de edad [25-29];
- 1970 y 1990, interpolación y extrapolación de las tasas de actividad ajustadas con base en los censos de 1974, 1982 y 1990.

**2.2.2 Mujeres:**

- 1950-70, tasas de actividad 1950-70 con base en EPPA3;
- 1980, promedios ponderados de las tasas de actividad con base en los censos de 1974 y 1982;
- 1990, promedios ponderados de las tasas de actividad con base en los censos de 1982 y 1990.

## 3. Evaluación de las tasas de distribución por sector de actividad: 1950 - 1990

### 3.1 Datos básicos:

Cuadro 2: Distribución de la población económicamente activa por sector de actividad en %

| | Agricultura | Industria | | Servicios |
|---|---|---|---|---|
| Año | | Total | Manufac. | |
| **Hombres** | | | | |
| 1974 | 27.49 | 32.01 | 12.21 | 40.50 |
| 1982 | 24.06 | 24.52 | 5.14 | 51.42 |
| 1990 | 10.11 | 30.63 | 11.26 | 59.26 |
| **Mujeres** | | | | |
| 1974 | 13.15 | 7.40 | 6.03 | 79.45 |
| 1982 | 9.78 | 3.46 | 2.10 | 86.77 |
| 1990 | 3.03 | 5.46 | 3.94 | 91.51 |

Fuente(s): STAT.

### 3.2 Método(s): promedio ponderado

**3.2.1 Hombres:**

- 1950-70, tasas de distribución 1950-70 con base en EPPA3;
- 1980-90, promedios ponderados de las tasas de distribución con base en los censos de 1974, 1982 y 1990.

**3.2.2 Mujeres:**

Métodos, hipótesis y tratamientos idénticos a los que se aplican a los hombres.

## 4. Proyección de las tasas de actividad: 2000 - 2010

### 4.1 Modelo(s): linear, hiperbólico y logístico

**4.1.1 Hombres:**

- Para los grupos de edad [15-19], [40-44] y [50+], aplicación de la función F3;
- Para los grupos de edad [20-39] y [45-49], aplicación de la función F1;
- Modificación de las tendencias de los grupos de edad [30-39] y [45-49].

**4.1.2 Mujeres:**

- Para los grupos de edad [15-19], [45-49] y [55+], aplicación de la función F3;
- Para los grupos de edad [20-24] y [50-54], aplicación de la función F1;
- Para los grupos de edad [25-44], aplicación de la función F6;
- Modificación de las tendencias de los grupos de edad [20-24] y [50-54].

*Notas sobre los ajustes de las tasas, véase p.380-384.*

*Notas sobre las funciones de proyección, véase p. 386.*

# Guatemala

## 1. Fuente(s) de los datos básicos

Código(s):  Título(s):

EPPA3  Estimaciones y proyecciones de la población económicamente activa, 1950-2025, tercera edición, OIT, Ginebra, 1986.
INEG-81  Censos Nacionales de 1981, Tomo I, Cifras definitivas, Instituto Nacional de Estadística, Guatemala.
ADNU  Ediciones de 1979 et 1988 del Annuaire démographique des Nations Unies, New York.
ASTER  Anuario de estadísticas del trabajo 1945-89 - Edición retrospectiva sobre los censos de población, OIT, Ginebra, 1990.
AST-93  Anuario de Estadísticas del Trabjo 1993, OIT, Ginebra, 1993.

## 2. Evaluación de las tasas de actividad: 1950 - 1990

### 2.1 Datos básicos:

Cuadro 1: Tasas de actividad por sexo y grupo de edad

| Grupo de edad | Año 1973 (1) | 1981 (1) | 1989 (2) |
|---|---|---|---|
| **Hombres** | | | |
| 10-14 | 26.39 | 17.57 | 28.01 |
| 15-19 | 72.04 | 63.29 | 74.01 |
| 20-24 | 90.04 | 85.80 | 93.96 |
| 25-29 | 94.59 | 92.19 | 97.93 |
| 30-34 | 95.52 | 93.69 | 97.99 |
| 35-39 | 95.62 | 93.80 | 98.53 |
| 40-44 | 95.38 | 93.41 | 98.70 |
| 45-49 | 95.02 | 93.16 | 97.80 |
| 50-54 | 93.73 | 91.75 | 96.44 |
| 55-59 | 91.95 | 90.31 | 94.84 |
| 60-64 | 87.15 | 85.85 | 89.53 |
| 65+ | 68.60 | 66.83 | 62.93 |
| **Mujeres** | | | |
| 10-14 | 4.10 | 3.44 | 7.80 |
| 15-19 | 14.99 | 13.27 | 25.63 |
| 20-24 | 17.38 | 17.18 | 29.83 |
| 25-29 | 15.00 | 15.96 | 29.72 |
| 30-34 | 14.09 | 15.39 | 33.81 |
| 35-39 | 13.87 | 13.99 | 31.46 |
| 40-44 | 14.05 | 13.59 | 30.89 |
| 45-49 | 13.54 | 12.26 | 30.32 |
| 50-54 | 12.92 | 11.69 | 28.93 |
| 55-59 | 11.93 | 10.05 | 23.36 |
| 60-64 | 10.13 | 8.81 | 20.62 |
| 65+ | 7.06 | 6.49 | 13.73 |

Fuente(s): (1) ADNU, ASTER, INEG-81; (2) AST-93.

### 2.2 Método(s): interpolación y extrapolación lineares

#### 2.2.1 Hombres:

- 1950-60, tasas de actividad 1950-60 con base en EPPA3;
ajuste de las tasas de actividad del grupo de edad [10-14];
- 1970-90, interpolación y extrapolación de las tasas de actividad ajustadas los censos de 1973 y 1981.

#### 2.2.2 Mujeres:

- 1950-70, tasas de actividad ajustadas 1950-70 con base en EPPA3;
el ajuste se ha calculado con base en el modelo de ajuste de las tasas de actividad de las mujeres ocupadas en la agricultura como auxiliares familiares;
- 1980-90, interpolación y extrapolación de las tasas de actividad ajustadas con base en el censo de 1981 y de las tasas de actividad con base el censo en de 1989.

## 3. Evaluación de las tasas de distribución por sector de actividad: 1950 - 1990

### 3.1 Datos básicos:

Cuadro 2: Distribución de la población económicamente activa por sector de actividad en %

| Año | Agricultura | Industria Total | Manufac. | Servicios |
|---|---|---|---|---|
| **Hombres** | | | | |
| 1980 (1) | 64.45 | 16.55 | .. | 19.00 |
| 1981 (2) | 64.07 | 16.58 | 9.77 | 19.34 |
| 1989 (3) | 61.35 | 16.53 | 10.45 | 22.13 |
| **Mujeres** | | | | |
| 1981 (2) | 9.70 | 19.68 | 18.82 | 70.62 |
| 1989 (3) | 15.99 | 23.58 | 23.24 | 60.43 |

Fuente(s): (1) EPPA3; (2) ASTER; (3) AST93.

### 3.2 Método(s): promedio ponderado
extrapolación linear

#### 3.2.1 Hombres:

- 1950-80, tasas de distribución 1950-80 con base en EPPA3;
- Aplicación de la razón manufacturas/industria con base en el censo de 1981;
- 1990, promedios ponderados de las tasas de distribución 1980 con base en EPPA3 y de las tasas de distribución con base en la encuesta de 1989;
- Aplicación de la razón manufacturas/industria con base en la encuesta de 1989
- Aplicación de la razón manufacturas/industria con base en la encuesta de 1989

#### 3.2.2 Mujeres:

- 1950-70, tasas de distribución ajustadas 1950-70 con base en EPPA3;
ajuste de las tasas con base en la razón hombres/mujeres igual a 1/10 en la agricultura;
- 1980-90, extrapolación de las tasas de distribución ajustadas con base en el censo de 1981 y de las tasas de distribución con base en la encuesta de 1989.

## 4. Proyección de las tasas de actividad: 2000 - 2010

### 4.1 Modelo(s): linear, log-linear y logístico

#### 4.1.1 Hombres:

- Para los grupos de edad [10-14] y [25+], aplicación de la función F1;
- Para los grupos de edad [19-24], aplicación de la función F6;
- Modificación de las tendencias de los grupos de edad [10-54] y [65+].

#### 4.1.2 Mujeres:

- Para los grupos de edad [10-14] y [65+], aplicación de la función F1;
- Para los grupos de edad [15-64], aplicación de la función F2;
- Modificación de las tendencias de los grupos de edad [15+].

*Notas sobre los ajustes de las tasas, véase p.380-384.*      *Notas sobre las funciones de proyección, véase p. 386.*

# Guinea

## 1. Fuente(s) de los datos básicos

Código(s):   Título(s):

EPPA3     Estimaciones y proyecciones de la población económicamente activa, 1950-2025, tercera edición, OIT, Ginebra, 1986.
AST91     Anuario de Estadísticas del Trabjo 1991, OIT, Ginebra, 1991.

## 2. Evaluación de las tasas de actividad: 1950 - 1990

### 2.1 Datos básicos:

Cuadro 1: Tasas de actividad por sexo y grupo de edad

| Grupo de edad | Año 1950 (1) | 1960 (1) | 1970 (1) | 1980 (1) | 1983 (2) |
|---|---|---|---|---|---|
| **Hombres** | | | | | |
| 10-14 | 52.30 | 50.00 | 48.05 | 45.35 | .. |
| 15-19 | 85.20 | 82.15 | 79.55 | 75.95 | .. |
| 20-24 | 95.35 | 94.20 | 93.20 | 91.85 | .. |
| 25-29 | 97.40 | 97.25 | 97.10 | 96.90 | .. |
| 30-34 | 98.15 | 97.95 | 97.80 | 97.55 | .. |
| 35-39 | 98.30 | 98.10 | 97.95 | 97.70 | .. |
| 40-44 | 98.15 | 97.95 | 97.75 | 97.50 | .. |
| 45-49 | 97.40 | 97.20 | 97.05 | 96.85 | .. |
| 50-54 | 96.95 | 96.70 | 96.45 | 96.15 | .. |
| 55-59 | 96.10 | 95.70 | 95.30 | 94.80 | .. |
| 60-64 | 93.20 | 92.45 | 91.80 | 90.95 | .. |
| 65+ | 80.05 | 78.75 | 77.60 | 76.10 | .. |
| **Mujeres** | | | | | |
| 10-14 | 39.50 | 37.80 | 36.30 | 34.30 | 28.40 |
| 15-19 | 64.20 | 61.60 | 59.40 | 56.35 | 41.20 |
| 20-24 | 64.30 | 62.70 | 61.30 | 59.35 | 44.80 |
| 25-29 | 69.30 | 67.45 | 65.85 | 63.65 | 50.40 |
| 30-34 | 73.65 | 71.70 | 70.00 | 67.65 | 51.70 |
| 35-39 | 74.90 | 73.05 | 71.45 | 69.25 | 51.20 |
| 40-44 | 77.30 | 75.45 | 73.90 | 71.7 | 51.00 |
| 45-49 | 76.85 | 74.95 | 73.35 | 71.1 | 51.20 |
| 50-54 | 75.45 | 73.25 | 71.40 | 68.8 | 49.30 |
| 55-59 | 72.70 | 70.40 | 68.45 | 65.75 | 46.00 |
| 60-64 | 66.75 | 63.85 | 61.35 | 57.9 | 34.00 |
| 65+ | 46.65 | 43.95 | 41.60 | 38.45 | 16.95 |

Fuente(s): (1) EPPA3; (2) AST91.

### 2.2 Método(s): interpolación y extrapolación lineares

#### 2.2.1 Hombres:

- 1950-80, tasas de actividad 1950-80 con base en EPPA3;
- 1990, extrapolación de las tasas de actividad 1950-80 con base en EPPA3;
ajuste de las tasas extrapoladas con base en las variaciones de las tasas interpoladas 1980, en relación con las tasas 1980 con base en EPPA3;
modificación de las tendencias de todos los grupos de edad para 1990.

#### 2.2.2 Mujeres:

- 1950-90, interpolación y extrapolación de las tasas de actividad 1950-80 con base en EPPA3;
ajuste de las tasas interpoladas y extrapoladas con base en las variaciones de las tasas extrapoladas 1983, en relación con las tasas de actividad con base en el censo en de 1983;
modificación de las tendencias de todos los grupos de edad para 1950-80.

## 3. Evaluación de las tasas de distribución por sector de actividad: 1950 - 1990

### 3.1 Datos básicos:

Cuadro 2: Distribución de la población económicamente activa por sector de actividad en %

| Año | Agricultura | Industria Total | Manufac. | Servicios |
|---|---|---|---|---|
| **Hombres** | | | | |
| 1950 (1) | 88.00 | 5.80 | .. | 6.20 |
| 1960 (1) | 83.80 | 7.85 | .. | 8.35 |
| 1970 (1) | 80.20 | 9.60 | .. | 10.20 |
| 1980 (1) | 75.25 | 11.95 | .. | 12.80 |
| 1983 (2) | 85.44 | 2.11 | 0.67 | 12.45 |
| **Mujeres** | | | | |
| 1950 (1) | 97.30 | 1.90 | .. | 0.80 |
| 1960 (1) | 96.15 | 2.70 | .. | 1.15 |
| 1970 (1) | 92.00 | 3.50 | .. | 4.50 |
| 1980 (1) | 88.30 | 4.90 | .. | 6.80 |
| 1983 (2) | 85.30 | 2.20 | 0.68 | 12.50 |

Fuente(s): (1) EPPA3; (2) AST91.

### 3.2 Método(s): interpolación y extrapolación lineares

#### 3.2.1 Hombres:

- 1950-90, interpolación y extrapolación de las tasas de distribución con base en EPPA3;
ajuste de las tasas interpoladas y extrapoladas 1950-90 con base en las variaciones de las tasas interpoladas 1983, en relación con las tasas de distribución con base en el censo de 1983;
de distribución con base en el censo de 1983;

#### 3.2.2 Mujeres:

- 1950-90, interpolación extrapolación de las tasas de distribución ajustadas 1950 y 1980 con base en EPPA3;
ajuste de las tasas de distribución con base en la razón hombres/mujeres igual a 1 en la agricultura; a las tasas de distribución de la industria y los servicios, aplicación de la razón industria/servicios con base en el censo de 1983; las tasas de distribución estimadas de manufacturas con base en la razón manufacturas/industria con base en el censo de 1983.

## 4. Proyección de las tasas de actividad: 2000 - 2010

### 4.1 Modelo(s): linear y hiperbólico

#### 4.1.1 Hombres:

- Para los grupos de edad [10-29], aplicación de la función F1;
- Modificación de la tendencia del grupo de edad [10-14].

#### 4.1.2 Mujeres:

- Para los grupos de edad [10-19] y [60+], aplicación de la función F1;
- Para los grupos de edad [20-59], aplicación de la función F3;
- Modificación de las tendencias de los grupos de edad [10-19] y [60+].

# Guinea Ecuatorial

## 1. Fuente(s) de los datos básicos

Código(s):  Título(s):

EPPA3  Estimaciones y proyecciones de la población económicamente activa, 1950-2025, tercera edición, OIT, Ginebra, 1986.
AST91  Anuario de Estadísticas del Trabjo 1991, OIT, Ginebra, 1991.
R1983  Republica de Guinea Ecuatorial, Censos Nacionales I de Poblacion I de Vivienda,  Caractristica de la Poblacion, 4/07/1983, Malabo.

## 2. Evaluación de las tasas de actividad: 1950 - 1990

### 2.1 Datos básicos:

Cuadro 1: Tasas de actividad por sexo y grupo de edad

| Grupo de edad | Año 1950 (1) | 1960 (1) | 1970 (1) | 1980 (1) | 1983 (2) |
|---|---|---|---|---|---|
| **Hombres** | | | | | |
| 10-14 | 49.30 | 44.95 | 39.80 | 32.75 | 8.97 |
| 15-19 | 81.20 | 75.40 | 68.55 | 59.15 | 77.54 |
| 20-24 | 93.85 | 91.60 | 89.00 | 85.35 | 96.37 |
| 25-29 | 97.20 | 96.85 | 96.45 | 95.95 | 96.92 |
| 30-34 | 97.90 | 97.55 | 97.10 | 96.50 | 96.89 |
| 35-39 | 98.05 | 97.65 | 97.20 | 96.55 | 97.03 |
| 40-44 | 97.90 | 97.45 | 97.00 | 96.30 | 97.15 |
| 45-49 | 97.15 | 96.80 | 96.40 | 95.80 | 96.68 |
| 50-54 | 96.60 | 96.10 | 95.45 | 94.60 | 96.54 |
| 55-59 | 95.55 | 94.70 | 93.70 | 92.30 | 96.00 |
| 60-64 | 92.20 | 90.80 | 89.10 | 86.80 | 93.83 |
| 65+ | 78.35 | 75.85 | 72.90 | 68.85 | 52.17 |
| **Mujeres** | | | | | |
| 10-14 | 36.35 | 34.20 | 31.75 | 28.85 | 9.17 |
| 15-19 | 59.45 | 56.20 | 52.50 | 48.20 | 48.55 |
| 20-24 | 61.30 | 59.25 | 56.95 | 54.20 | 37.82 |
| 25-29 | 65.90 | 63.55 | 60.90 | 57.80 | 37.18 |
| 30-34 | 70.00 | 67.50 | 64.65 | 61.35 | 41.96 |
| 35-39 | 71.50 | 69.15 | 66.50 | 63.40 | 44.62 |
| 40-44 | 73.95 | 71.60 | 68.95 | 65.85 | 46.95 |
| 45-49 | 73.40 | 71.00 | 08.30 | 05.15 | 48.71 |
| 50-54 | 71.45 | 68.70 | 65.55 | 61.90 | 48.02 |
| 55-59 | 68.50 | 65.60 | 62.35 | 58.55 | 47.55 |
| 60-64 | 61.40 | 57.75 | 53.60 | 48.75 | 48.71 |
| 65+ | 41.70 | 38.25 | 34.40 | 29.90 | 22.45 |

FuenteSource(s): (1) EPPA3; (2) AST91 y R1983.

### 2.2 Método(s): interpolación y extrapolación lineares

**2.2.1 Hombres:**

- 1950-90, interpolación y extrapolación de las tasas de actividad 1950-80
con base en EPPA3 y de las tasas de actividad ajustadas con base
el censo de 1983;
ajuste de las tasas interpoladas y extrapoladas con base en las variaciones
de las tasas interpoladas 1983, en relación con las tasas de actividad
con basc cn cl ccnso dc 1983;
modificación de las tendencias de todos los grupos de edad.

**2.2.2 Mujeres:**

Métodos, hipótesis y tratamientos idénticos a los que se aplican a los hombres.

## 3. Evaluación de las tasas de distribución  por sector de actividad: 1950 - 1990

### 3.1 Datos básicos:

Cuadro  2: Distribución de la población económicamente activa por sector de actividad en %

| Año | Agricultura | Industria Total | Manufac. | Servicios |
|---|---|---|---|---|
| **Hombres** | | | | |
| 1950 (1) | 82.50 | 6.25 | .. | 11.15 |
| 1960 (1) | 74.50 | 9.25 | .. | 16.25 |
| 1970 (1) | 65.00 | 12.70 | .. | 22.30 |
| 1980 (1) | 52.00 | 17.4 | | 30.60 |
| 1983 (2) | 69.10 | 7.34 | 2.63 | 23.55 |
| **Mujeres** | | | | |
| 1950 (1) | 96.00 | 0.70 | .. | 3.30 |
| 1960 (1) | 93.00 | 1.25 | .. | 5.75 |
| 1970 (1) | 89.00 | 2.00 | .. | 9.00 |
| 1980 (1) | 85.50 | 2.60 | .. | 11.90 |
| 1983 (2) | 92.05 | 0.88 | 0.70 | 7.07 |

Fuente(s): (1) EPPA3; (2) AST91.

### 3.2 Método(s): interpolación y extrapolación lineares

**3.2.1 Hombres:**

- 1950-90, interpolación y extrapolación de las tasas de distribución 1950-80
con base en EPPA3 y de las tasas de distribución con base en el censo de 1983;
ajuste de las tasas interpoladas y extrapoladas con base en 1/3 de las variaciones
de las tasas interpoladas 1983, en relación con las tasas de distribución
con base en el censo de 1983;
con base en el censo de 1983;

**3.2.2 Mujeres:**

Métodos, hipótesis y tratamientos idénticos a los que se aplican a los hombres.

## 4. Proyección de las tasas de actividad: 2000 - 2010

### 4.1 Modelo(s): linear y hiperbólico

**4.1.1 Hombres:**

- Para los grupos de edad [10-29] y [55+], aplicación de la función F1;
- Para los grupos de edad [30-54], aplicación de la función F3;
- Modificación de la tendencia del grupo de edad [10-14].

**4.1.2 Mujeres:**

- Para el grupo de edad [10-14], aplicación de la función F1;
- Para los grupos de edad [15+], aplicación de la función F3;
- Modificación de las tendencias de los grupos de edad [15-54].

*Notas sobre los ajustes de las tasas, véase p.380-384.*

*Notas sobre las funciones de proyección, véase p. 386.*

# Guinea-Bissau

## 1. Fuente(s) de los datos básicos

Código(s):  Título(s):
EPPA3   Estimaciones y proyecciones de la población económicamente activa, 1950-2025, tercera edición, OIT, Ginebra, 1986.
ADNU84  Annuaire démographique 1984 - Statistiques des recensements de population II, trente-sixième édition, Nations Unies, New York, 1986.
ASTER   Anuario de estadísticas del trabajo 1945-89 - Edición retrospectiva sobre los censos de población, OIT, Ginebra, 1990.

## 2. Evaluación de las tasas de actividad: 1950 - 1990

### 2.1 Datos básicos:

Cuadro 1: Tasas de actividad por sexo y grupo de edad

| Grupo de edad | Año 1950 (1) | 1960 (1) | 1970 (1) | 1979 (2) |
|---|---|---|---|---|
| **Hombres** | | | | |
| 10-14 | 50.95 | 49.10 | 46.75 | 48.22 |
| 15-19 | 83.40 | 80.90 | 77.80 | 55.21 |
| 20-24 | 94.65 | 93.75 | 92.55 | 86.87 |
| 25-29 | 97.30 | 97.15 | 97.00 | 97.46 |
| 30-34 | 98.05 | 97.90 | 97.70 | 98.86 |
| 35-39 | 98.20 | 98.05 | 97.80 | 99.02 |
| 40-44 | 98.05 | 97.85 | 97.65 | 98.80 |
| 45-49 | 97.30 | 97.15 | 96.95 | 98.95 |
| 50-54 | 96.80 | 96.60 | 96.30 | 98.18 |
| 55-59 | 95.85 | 95.50 | 95.05 | 97.95 |
| 60-64 | 92.75 | 92.15 | 91.40 | 96.87 |
| 65+ | 79.25 | 78.20 | 76.85 | 89.46 |
| **Mujeres** | | | | |
| 10-14 | 38.50 | 37.10 | 35.35 | 2.63 |
| 15-19 | 62.65 | 60.55 | 57.90 | 2.22 |
| 20-24 | 63.35 | 62.00 | 60.35 | 3.96 |
| 25-29 | 68.20 | 66.70 | 64.80 | 3.22 |
| 30-34 | 72.50 | 70.85 | 68.85 | 2.68 |
| 35-39 | 73.80 | 72.25 | 70.40 | 2.35 |
| 40-44 | 76.20 | 74.70 | 72.80 | 2.26 |
| 45-49 | 75.70 | 74.20 | 72.25 | 2.25 |
| 50-54 | 74.15 | 72.40 | 70.15 | 1.83 |
| 55-59 | 71.35 | 69.50 | 67.15 | 2.18 |
| 60-64 | 65.00 | 62.65 | 59.65 | 1.70 |
| 65+ | 45.05 | 42.85 | 40.10 | 1.45 |

Fuente(s): (1) EPPA3; (2) ADNU84 y ASTER.

### 2.2 Método(s): interpolación y extrapolación lineares

#### 2.2.1 Hombres:

- 1950-90, interpolación y extrapolación de las tasas de actividad 1950-80
con base en EPPA3 y de las tasas de actividad ajustadas con base
el censo de 1979;
ajuste de las tasas interpoladas y extrapoladas con base en las variaciones
de las tasas interpoladas 1979, en relación con las tasas de actividad
con base en el censo de 1979;
modificación de las tendencias de todos los grupos de edad.

#### 2.2.2 Mujeres:

Métodos, hipótesis y tratamientos idénticos a los que se aplican a los hombres.

## 3. Evaluación de las tasas de distribución por sector de actividad: 1950 - 1990

### 3.1 Datos básicos:

Cuadro 2: Distribución de la población económicamente activa por sector de actividad en %

| Año | Agricultura | Industria Total | Manufac. | Servicios |
|---|---|---|---|---|
| **Hombres** | | | | |
| 1950 (1) | 85.50 | 1.85 | .. | 12.65 |
| 1960 (1) | 82.10 | 2.55 | .. | 15.35 |
| 1970 (1) | 77.80 | 4.10 | .. | 18.10 |
| 1979 (2) | 81.08 | 2.45 | 1.42 | 16.47 |
| 1980 (1) | 75.20 | 5.00 | .. | 19.80 |
| **Mujeres** | | | | |
| 1950 (1) | 95.00 | 0.65 | . | 4.35 |
| 1960 (1) | 94.00 | 1.00 | .. | 5.00 |
| 1970 (1) | 92.70 | 1.40 | .. | 5.90 |
| 1979 (2) | 97.64 | 0.23 | 0.18 | 2.13 |
| 1980 (1) | 91.90 | 1.65 | .. | 6.45 |

Fuente(s): (1) EPPA3; (2) ASTER.

### 3.2 Método(s): interpolación y extrapolación lineares

#### 3.2.1 Hombres:

- 1950-90, interpolación y extrapolación de las tasas de distribución 1950-80
con base en EPPA3 y de las tasas de distribución con base en el censo de 1979;
ajuste de las tasas interpoladas y extrapoladas con base en 1/3 de las variaciones
de las tasas interpoladas 1979, en relación con las tasas de distribución
con base en el censo de 1979;
con base en el censo de 1979;

#### 3.2.2 Mujeres:

- 1950-90, interpolación y extrapolación de las tasas de distribución 1950-80
con base en EPPA3 y de las tasas de distribución con base en el censo de 1979;
ajuste de las tasas interpoladas y extrapoladas con base en la mitad
(total para 1990) de las variaciones de las tasas interpoladas 1979,
en relación con las tasas de distribución con base en el censo de 1979;
- Aplicación de la razón manufacturas/industria con base en el censo de 1979.

## 4. Proyección de las tasas de actividad: 2000 - 2010

### 4.1 Modelo(s): linear y hiperbólico

#### 4.1.1 Hombres:

- Para los grupos de edad [10-29], aplicación de la función F1;
- Para los grupos de edad [30+], aplicación de la función F3;
- Modificación de la tendencia del grupo de edad [10-14].

#### 4.1.2 Mujeres:

- Para los grupos de edad [10-19], aplicación de la función F1;
- Para los grupos de edad [20+], aplicación de la función F3;
- Modificación de las tendencias de los grupos de edad [10-19] y [60+].

---

*Notas sobre los ajustes de las tasas, véase p.380-384.*     *Notas sobre las funciones de proyección, véase p. 386.*

# Guyana

## 1. Fuente(s) de los datos básicos

Código(s): Título(s):

EPPA3    Estimaciones y proyecciones de la población económicamente activa, 1950-2025, tercera edición, OIT, Ginebra, 1986.
STAT     Base de datos de la OIT sobre estadísticas del trabajo - LABORSTA, Oficina de Estadística, OIT, Ginebra.

## 2. Evaluación de las tasas de actividad: 1950 - 1990

### 2.1 Datos básicos:

Cuadro 1: Tasas de actividad por sexo y grupo de edad

| | Año | | |
|---|---|---|---|
| Grupo de edad | 1970 (1) | 1980 (2) | 1987 (2) |
| **Hombres** | | | |
| 10-14 | 4.40 | 0.00 | 0.00 |
| 15-19 | 67.00 | 64.77 | 61.42 |
| 20-24 | 94.20 | 94.22 | 91.98 |
| 25-29 | 97.90 | 97.77 | 94.40 |
| 30-34 | 98.55 | 97.96 | 97.79 |
| 35-39 | 97.95 | 97.97 | 97.81 |
| 40-44 | 97.30 | 97.70 | 97.35 |
| 45-49 | 96.75 | 96.51 | 95.66 |
| 50-54 | 93.50 | 93.72 | 93.44 |
| 55-59 | 91.90 | 88.92 | 86.79 |
| 60-64 | 67.75 | 65.66 | 64.17 |
| 65+ | 41.35 | 34.36 | 32.27 |
| **Mujeres** | | | |
| 10-14 | 1.40 | 0.00 | |
| 15-19 | 26.25 | 21.28 | 22.56 |
| 20-24 | 29.10 | 36.57 | 42.30 |
| 25-29 | 20.50 | 33.26 | 41.70 |
| 30-34 | 18.50 | 30.21 | 43.70 |
| 35-39 | 19.95 | 27.37 | 39.61 |
| 40-44 | 22.00 | 27.04 | 37.06 |
| 45-49 | 22.25 | 26.90 | 34.50 |
| 50-54 | 20.40 | 25.44 | 31.05 |
| 55-59 | 18.05 | 21.77 | 26.82 |
| 60-64 | 12.10 | 15.07 | 17.93 |
| 65+ | 5.15 | 5.55 | 5.24 |

Fuente(s): (1) EPPA3; (2) STAT.

### 2.2 Método(s): promedio ponderado

#### 2.2.1 Hombres:

- 1950-70, tasas de actividad 1950-70 con base en EPPA3;
- 1980, promedios ponderados de las tasas de actividad 1970 con base en EPPA3 y de las tasas de actividad ajustadas con base en el censo de 1980; modificación de las tendencias de los grupos de edad [55-64];
- 1990, promedios ponderados de las tasas de actividad ajustadas con base en de 1980 el censo y de las tasas de actividad con base en la encuesta de 1987;
modificación de la tendencia del grupo de edad [65+].

#### 2.2.2 Mujeres:

- 1950-70, tasas de actividad 1950-70 con base en EPPA3;
- 1980, promedios ponderados de las tasas de actividad 1970 con base en EPPA3 y de las tasas de actividad ajustadas con base en el censo de 1980;
- 1990, promedios ponderados de las tasas de actividad ajustadas con base en el censo de 1980 y de las tasas de actividad ajustadas con base en la encuesta de 1987;
modificación de las tendencias del grupo de edad [65+].

## 3. Evaluación de las tasas de distribución por sector de actividad: 1950 - 1990

### 3.1 Datos básicos:

Cuadro 2: Distribución de la población económicamente activa por sector de actividad en %

| | | Agricultura | Industria | | Servicios |
|---|---|---|---|---|---|
| | Año | | Total | Manufac. | |
| **Hombres** | | | | | |
| | 1960 | 40.95 | 30.25 | .. | 28.80 |
| | 1970 | 35.85 | 32.05 | .. | 32.10 |
| | 1980 | 31.60 | 28.90 | 16.39 | 39.50 |
| **Mujeres** | | | | | |
| | 1960 | 25.80 | 15.00 | .. | 59.20 |
| | 1970 | 16.85 | 15.00 | .. | 68.15 |
| | 1980 | 11.80 | 16.25 | 12.79 | 71.95 |

Fuente(s): EPPA3.

### 3.2 Método(s): extrapolación linear

#### 3.2.1 Hombres:

- 1950-80, tasas de distribución 1950-80 con base en EPPA3;
- 1990, extrapolación de las tasas de distribución 1960-80 con base en EPPA3; modificación de las tendencias de todos los sectores.

#### 3.2.2 Mujeres:

Métodos, hipótesis y tratamientos idénticos a los que se aplican a los hombres.

## 4. Proyección de las tasas de actividad: 2000 - 2010

### 4.1 Modelo(s): linear, log-linear, hiperbólico y logístico

#### 4.1.1 Hombres:

- Para los grupos de edad [15-24], aplicación de la función F1;
- Para los grupos de edad [25+], aplicación de la función F3.

#### 4.1.2 Mujeres:

- Para los grupos de edad [15-24], aplicación de la función F2;
- Para los grupos de edad [25-64], aplicación de la función F6;
- Para el grupo de edad [65+], aplicación de la función F3.

---

*Notas sobre los ajustes de las tasas, véase p.380-384.*        *Notas sobre las funciones de proyección, véase p. 386.*

# Haití

## 1. Fuente(s) de los datos básicos

Código(s): Título(s):
EPPA3       Estimaciones y proyecciones de la población económicamente activa, 1950-2025, tercera edición, OIT, Ginebra, 1986.
ASTER       Anuario de estadísticas del trabajo 1945-89 - Edición retrospectiva sobre los censos de población, OIT, Ginebra, 1990.

## 2. Evaluación de las tasas de actividad: 1950 - 1990

### 2.1 Datos básicos:

Cuadro 1: Tasas de actividad por sexo y grupo de edad

| Grupo de edad | Año 1950 (1) | 1960 (1) | 1970 (1) | 1982 (2) |
|---|---|---|---|---|
| **Hombres** | | | | |
| 10-14 | 53.00 | 47.50 | 42.00 | 25.70 |
| 15-19 | 83.70 | 75.00 | 66.40 | 43.87 |
| 20-24 | 95.60 | 92.60 | 89.75 | 76.99 |
| 25-29 | 98.40 | 98.00 | 97.55 | 91.85 |
| 30-34 | 98.80 | 98.80 | 98.75 | 94.13 |
| 35-39 | 99.00 | 99.10 | 99.20 | 96.18 |
| 40-44 | 98.90 | 98.90 | 98.95 | 95.23 |
| 45-49 | 98.80 | 98.75 | 98.75 | 94.21 |
| 50-54 | 98.35 | 98.25 | 98.10 | 91.14 |
| 55-59 | 97.75 | 97.60 | 97.50 | 92.68 |
| 60-64 | 96.50 | 95.90 | 95.30 | 87.47 |
| 65+ | 87.20 | 84.25 | 81.00 | 70.32 |
| **Mujeres** | | | | |
| 10-14 | 51.50 | 45.00 | 41.00 | 22.29 |
| 15-19 | 81.10 | 73.05 | 64.85 | 35.14 |
| 20-24 | 85.80 | 80.65 | 75.40 | 53.49 |
| 25-29 | 85.25 | 80.05 | 74.75 | 56.71 |
| 30-34 | 85.70 | 80.00 | 74.20 | 55.50 |
| 35-39 | 86.30 | 80.85 | 75.35 | 58.42 |
| 40-44 | 87.15 | 82.35 | 77.50 | 57.51 |
| 45-49 | 87.10 | 82.35 | 77.45 | 60.16 |
| 50-54 | 85.15 | 81.20 | 77.20 | 57.83 |
| 55-59 | 83.50 | 79.55 | 75.50 | 54.15 |
| 60-64 | 79.75 | 74.90 | 69.85 | 46.55 |
| 65+ | 59.00 | 52.25 | 45.40 | 35.80 |

Fuente(s): (1) EPPA3; (2) ASTER.

### 2.2 Método(s): extrapolación linear
promedio ponderado

#### 2.2.1 Hombres:

- 1950-70, tasas de actividad 1950-70 con base en EPPA3;
- 1980, promedios ponderados de las tasas de actividad 1970 con base
en EPPA3 y de las tasas de actividad ajustadas con base en el censo de 1982;
- 1990, extrapolación de las tasas de actividad 1950-70 con base en EPPA3
y de las tasas de actividad estimadas para 1980;
aplicación a las tasas extrapoladas, de las variaciones de las tasas interpoladas,
1982, en relación con las tasas de actividad ajustadas con base en el censo
de 1982; modificación de las tendencias de todos los grupos de edad.

#### 2.2.2 Mujeres:

Métodos, hipótesis y tratamientos idénticos a los que se aplican a los hombres.

## 3. Evaluación de las tasas de distribución por sector de actividad: 1950 - 1990

### 3.1 Datos básicos:

Cuadro 2: Distribución de la población económicamente activa por sector de actividad en %

| Año | Agricultura | Industria Total | Manufac. | Servicios |
|---|---|---|---|---|
| **Hombres** | | | | |
| 1950 | 88.70 | 5.60 | 4.30 | 5.70 |
| 1971 | 83.97 | 6.84 | 4.96 | 9.19 |
| 1982 | 77.92 | 8.71 | 6.02 | 13.37 |
| **Mujeres** | | | | |
| 1950 | 82.25 | 5.84 | 5.78 | 11.91 |
| 1971 | 61.85 | 7.67 | 7.62 | 30.48 |
| 1982 | 51.31 | 9.59 | 7.64 | 39.10 |

Fuente(s): (1) ASTER.

### 3.2 Método(s): promedio ponderado
extrapolación linear

#### 3.2.1 Hombres:

- 1950-70, tasas de distribución 1950-70 con base en EPPA3;
- 1980, promedios ponderados de las tasas de distribución 1970 con base en
EPPA3 y de las tasas de distribución con base en el censo de 1982;
- 1990, extrapolación de las tasas de distribución con base en los censos
de 1950, 1971 y 1982;
de 1950, 1971 y 1982;

#### 3.2.2 Mujeres:

Métodos, hipótesis y tratamientos idénticos a los que se aplican a los hombres.

## 4. Proyección de las tasas de actividad: 2000 - 2010

### 4.1 Modelo(s): linear y hiperbólico

#### 4.1.1 Hombres:

- Para los grupos de edad [10-14] y [20+], aplicación de la función F1;
- Para el grupo de edad [15-19], aplicación de la función F3;
- Modificación de las tendencias de los grupos de edad [10-34] y [45-54].

#### 4.1.2 Mujeres:

- Para el grupo de edad [10-14], aplicación de la función F1;
- Para los grupos de edad [15+], aplicación de la función F3;
- Modificación de las tendencias de los grupos de edad [10-64].

---

*Notas sobre los ajustes de las tasas, véase p.380-384.*     *Notas sobre las funciones de proyección, véase p. 386.*

# Honduras

## 1. Fuente(s) de los datos básicos

Código(s):  Título(s):

EPPA3   Estimaciones y proyecciones de la población económicamente activa, 1950-2025, tercera edición, OIT, Ginebra, 1986.
STAT    Base de datos de la OIT sobre estadísticas del trabajo - LABORSTA, Oficina de Estadística, OIT, Ginebra.

## 2. Evaluación de las tasas de actividad: 1950 - 1990

### 2.1 Datos básicos:

Cuadro 1: Tasas de actividad por sexo y grupo de edad

| Grupo de edad | Año 1974 | 1991 | 1992 |
|---|---|---|---|
| **Hombres** | | | |
| 10-14 | 28.88 | 13.95 | 15.18 |
| 15-19 | 77.75 | 63.47 | 63.80 |
| 20-24 | 92.38 | 90.93 | 89.17 |
| 25-29 | 96.58 | 94.90 | 94.03 |
| 30-34 | 98.07 | 97.61 | 97.65 |
| 35-39 | 98.22 | 97.83 | 97.86 |
| 40-44 | 97.53 | 97.67 | 97.66 |
| 45-49 | 97.24 | 96.74 | 97.92 |
| 50-54 | 95.38 | 95.22 | 95.58 |
| 55-59 | 94.08 | 95.26 | 94.06 |
| 60-64 | 89.07 | 88.23 | 88.44 |
| 65+ | 65.21 | 57.34 | 59.24 |
| **Mujeres** | | | |
| 10-14 | .. | 3.63 | 3.82 |
| 15-19 | .. | 21.16 | 24.51 |
| 20-24 | .. | 38.55 | 37.57 |
| 25-29 | .. | 36.11 | 35.17 |
| 30-34 | .. | 42.78 | 46.24 |
| 35-39 | .. | 43.79 | 46.60 |
| 40-44 | .. | 41.01 | 45.12 |
| 45-49 | .. | 39.10 | 41.37 |
| 50-54 | .. | 34.22 | 37.84 |
| 55-59 | .. | 29.99 | 32.31 |
| 60-64 | .. | 22.22 | 22.52 |
| 65+ | .. | 13.61 | 14.44 |

Fuente(s): STAT.

### 2.2 Método(s): interpolación linear
promedio aritmético

#### 2.2.1 Hombres:

- 1950-60, tasas de actividad 1950-60 con base en EPPA3;
- 1970-90, interpolación de las tasas de actividad ajustadas con base en el censo de 1974 y de los promedios de las tasas de actividad con base en las encuestas de 1991 y 1992.

#### 2.2.2 Mujeres:

- 1950-70, tasas de actividad 1950-70 con base en EPPA3;
- 1980-90, aplicación a los promedios de las tasas de actividad con base en las encuestas en de 1991 y 1992, 3/4 de las variaciones tasas de actividad estimadas para Mexico.

## 3. Evaluación de las tasas de distribución por sector de actividad: 1950 - 1990

### 3.1 Datos básicos:

Cuadro 2: Distribución de la población económicamente activa por sector de actividad en %

| Año | Agricultura | Industria Total | Manufac. | Servicios |
|---|---|---|---|---|
| **Hombres** | | | | |
| 1974 (1) | 71.76 | 12.84 | 8.30 | 15.41 |
| 1991 (2) | 45.27 | 23.69 | 16.34 | 31.03 |
| **Mujeres** | | | | |
| 1980 (1) | 7.10 | 30.18 | .. | 62.72 |
| 1991 (2) | 22.09 | 12.00 | 11.82 | 65.91 |

Fuente(s): (1) STAT; (2) EPPA3.

### 3.2 Método(s): interpolación linear
promedio ponderado

#### 3.2.1 Hombres:

- 1950-70, tasas de distribución 1950-70 con base en EPPA3;
- 1980-90, promedios ponderados de las tasas de distribución con base en el censo de 1974 y de los promedios de las tasas con base en las encuestas de 1991 y 1992.

#### 3.2.2 Mujeres:

- 1950-70, tasas de distribución 1950-70 con base en EPPA3;
- 1980-90, interpolación de las tasas de distribución 1980 con base en EPPA3 y del promedio de las tasas con base en las encuestas de 1991 y 1992; ajuste de las tasas con base en la razón hombres/mujeres de la agricultura con base en la encuesta de 1991.

## 4. Proyección de las tasas de actividad: 2000 - 2010

### 4.1 Modelo(s): linear, log-linear, hiperbólico y logístico

#### 4.1.1 Hombres:

- Para el grupo de edad [10-14], aplicación de la función F2;
- Para los grupos de edad [15+], aplicación de la función F3;
- Modificación de la tendencia del grupo de edad [10-14].

#### 4.1.2 Mujeres:

- Para los grupos de edad [10-14] y [30+], aplicación de la función F1;
- Para los grupos de edad [15-29], aplicación de la función F6;
- Modificación de las tendencias de los grupos de edad [15+].

*Notas sobre los ajustes de las tasas, véase p.380-384.*

*Notas sobre las funciones de proyección, véase p. 386.*

# Hong Kong, China

## 1. Fuente(s) de los datos básicos

Código(s):  Título(s):

EPPA3  Estimaciones y proyecciones de la población económicamente activa, 1950-2025, tercera edición, OIT, Ginebra, 1986.
STAT  Base de datos de la OIT sobre estadísticas del trabajo - LABORSTA, Oficina de Estadística, OIT, Ginebra.

## 2. Evaluación de las tasas de actividad: 1950 - 1990

### 2.1 Datos básicos:

Cuadro 1: Tasas de actividad por sexo y grupo de edad

| Grupo de edad | Año 1979 | 1980 | 1981 | 1989 | 1990 | 1991 |
|---|---|---|---|---|---|---|
| **Hombres** | | | | | | |
| 10-14 | 0.00 | 0.00 | 0.00 | 0.00 | 0.00 | 0.00 |
| 15-19 | 35.80 | 39.60 | 45.50 | 31.10 | 29.80 | 29.30 |
| 20-24 | 87.40 | 89.00 | 91.90 | 86.30 | 86.00 | 84.50 |
| 25-29 | 98.50 | 97.90 | 98.30 | 98.30 | 98.40 | 97.50 |
| 30-34 | 98.70 | 99.10 | 98.80 | 98.90 | 98.90 | 98.80 |
| 35-39 | 99.10 | 98.90 | 98.90 | 98.90 | 98.80 | 98.70 |
| 40-44 | 98.40 | 98.60 | 98.30 | 99.00 | 98.90 | 98.40 |
| 45-49 | 97.50 | 97.40 | 97.40 | 97.70 | 97.80 | 97.80 |
| 50-54 | 93.90 | 93.60 | 93.80 | 93.30 | 92.80 | 92.40 |
| 55-59 | 83.30 | 84.00 | 83.00 | 81.20 | 81.20 | 81.60 |
| 60-64 | 64.40 | 64.10 | 67.00 | 56.80 | 54.70 | 54.60 |
| 65+ | 32.50 | 32.10 | 35.20 | 22.50 | 21.40 | 20.80 |
| **Mujeres** | | | | | | |
| 10-14 | 0.00 | 0.00 | 0.00 | 0.00 | 0.00 | 0.00 |
| 15-19 | 39.50 | 39.00 | 42.70 | 31.10 | 29.80 | 29.30 |
| 20-24 | 78.00 | 79.70 | 80.00 | 86.30 | 86.00 | 84.50 |
| 25-29 | 58.40 | 60.30 | 61.30 | 76.40 | 77.90 | 79.60 |
| 30-34 | 41.60 | 44.70 | 49.20 | 54.10 | 55.30 | 59.10 |
| 35-39 | 41.60 | 44.70 | 49.20 | 52.20 | 52.30 | 52.30 |
| 40-44 | 44.80 | 48.00 | 54.10 | 53.40 | 53.50 | 53.90 |
| 45-49 | 41.20 | 44.20 | 49.40 | 51.00 | 52.30 | 52.20 |
| 50-54 | 36.80 | 36.00 | 44.60 | 39.50 | 38.10 | 41.60 |
| 55-59 | 33.70 | 31.50 | 36.90 | 28.30 | 27.10 | 27.50 |
| 60-64 | 19.60 | 19.80 | 22.20 | 19.50 | 18.40 | 17.20 |
| 65+ | 11.30 | 11.90 | 13.70 | 7.60 | 5.90 | 6.40 |

Fuente(s): STAT.

### 2.2 Método(s): interpolación linear

**2.2.1 Hombres:**

- 1950-80, tasas de actividad 1950-80 con base en EPPA3;
- 1990, interpolación de las tasas de actividad ajustadas con base en las encuestas de 1979 to 1992;
ajuste de las tasas interpoladas con base en las variaciones de las tasas interpoladas 1980, en relación con las tasas de actividad 1980 con base en EPPA3.

**2.2.2 Mujeres:**

- 1950-70, tasas de actividad 1950-70 con base en EPPA3;
- 1980-90, extrapolación de las tasas de actividad con base en las encuestas de 1979 to 1992.

## 3. Evaluación de las tasas de distribución por sector de actividad: 1950 - 1990

### 3.1 Datos básicos:

Cuadro 2: Distribución de la población económicamente activa por sector de actividad en %

| Año | Agricultura | Industria Total | Manufac. | Servicios |
|---|---|---|---|---|
| **Hombres** | | | | |
| 1979 | 1.42 | 46.69 | 36.02 | 51.89 |
| 1980 | 1.44 | 47.21 | 35.05 | 51.36 |
| 1981 | 1.31 | 45.52 | 31.85 | 53.18 |
| 1989 | 1.14 | 40.16 | 26.52 | 58.69 |
| 1990 | 0.95 | 38.85 | 25.31 | 60.20 |
| 1991 | 0.84 | 38.13 | 24.68 | 61.03 |
| **Mujeres** | | | | |
| 1979 | 0.89 | 57.72 | 56.30 | 41.39 |
| 1980 | 1.08 | 56.15 | 54.76 | 42.77 |
| 1981 | 1.59 | 54.27 | 52.82 | 44.13 |
| 1989 | 1.08 | 36.39 | 35.27 | 62.53 |
| 1990 | 0.71 | 33.04 | 31.86 | 66.25 |
| 1991 | 0.43 | 29.56 | 28.39 | 70.01 |

Fuente(s): STAT.

### 3.2 Método(s): promedio aritmético

**3.2.1 Hombres:**

- 1950-70, tasas de distribución 1950-70 con base en EPPA3;
- 1980, promedios de las tasas de distribución con base en las encuestas de 1979, 1980 y 1981;
- 1990, promedios de las tasas de distribución con base en las encuestas de 1989, 1990 y 1991.
de 1989, 1990 y 1991.

**3.2.2 Mujeres:**

Métodos, hipótesis y tratamientos idénticos a los que se aplican a los hombres.

## 4. Proyección de las tasas de actividad: 2000 - 2010

### 4.1 Modelo(s): linear, hiperbólico y logístico

**4.1.1 Hombres:**

- Para los grupos de edad [15-54], aplicación de la función F1;
- Para los grupos de edad [55+], aplicación de la función F3;
- Modificación de las tendencias de los grupos de edad [15+].

**4.1.2 Mujeres:**

- Para los grupos de edad [15-24], aplicación de la función F1;
- Para los grupos de edad [25-54], aplicación de la función F6;
- Para los grupos de edad [55+], aplicación de la función F3;
- Modificación de las tendencias de los grupos de edad [15-54].

*Notas sobre los ajustes de las tasas, véase p.380-384.*   *Notas sobre las funciones de proyección, véase p. 386.*

# Hungría

## 1. Fuente(s) de los datos básicos

Código(s):    Título(s):

EPPA3        Estimaciones y proyecciones de la población económicamente activa, 1950-2025, tercera edición, OIT, Ginebra, 1986.
BLT-94-2     Popovic B. (1994), "Nuevas estimaciones de las tasas de actividad para 1980 y 1990, desglosadas por grupos de edad y distribución sectorial, en algunos países de Europa oriental y meridional" en el Boletín de Estadísticas del Trabajol - 1994-2, OIT, Ginebra.

## 2. Evaluación de las tasas de actividad: 1950 - 1990

### 2.1 Datos básicos:

Cuadro 1: Tasas de actividad por sexo y grupo de edad

| Grupo de edad | Año 1950 (1) | 1960 (1) | 1970 (1) | 1980 (2) | 1990 (2) |
|---|---|---|---|---|---|
| **Hombres** | | | | | |
| 10-14 | 6.65 | 2.20 | 0.75 | 0.26 | 0.23 |
| 15-19 | 79.20 | 75.00 | 64.00 | 60.02 | 52.69 |
| 20-24 | 93.60 | 93.05 | 92.50 | 91.77 | 88.27 |
| 25-29 | 97.65 | 98.00 | 98.35 | 98.14 | 96.72 |
| 30-34 | 98.70 | 98.65 | 98.60 | 98.35 | 97.11 |
| 35-39 | 98.25 | 98.15 | 98.10 | 97.68 | 96.15 |
| 40-44 | 98.05 | 97.55 | 97.00 | 95.95 | 94.31 |
| 45-49 | 97.20 | 96.05 | 95.00 | 92.79 | 90.75 |
| 50-54 | 95.75 | 93.15 | 91.00 | 86.02 | 81.39 |
| 55-59 | 92.45 | 88.00 | 84.50 | 71.72 | 60.46 |
| 60-64 | 83.20 | 76.00 | 75.00 | 12.53 | 3.55 |
| 65+ | 64.40 | 57.00 | 54.00 | 3.82 | 0.98 |
| **Mujeres** | | | | | |
| 10-14 | 6.50 | 3.00 | 2.50 | 0.64 | 0.47 |
| 15-19 | 55.55 | 54.00 | 53.00 | 46.81 | 41.97 |
| 20-24 | 45.00 | 55.40 | 66.00 | 59.96 | 61.22 |
| 25-29 | 35.50 | 48.70 | 65.30 | 69.61 | 64.34 |
| 30-34 | 33.00 | 49.10 | 68.70 | 80.96 | 78.86 |
| 35-39 | 30.00 | 50.70 | 71.00 | 85.03 | 86.62 |
| 40-44 | 29.00 | 51.80 | 69.40 | 83.33 | 87.74 |
| 45-49 | 28.00 | 49.70 | 64.00 | 77.74 | 83.58 |
| 50-54 | 27.00 | 46.30 | 56.60 | 67.49 | 68.49 |
| 55-59 | 28.50 | 30.60 | 29.20 | 18.22 | 5.07 |
| 60-64 | 27.00 | 26.00 | 23.00 | 8.20 | 1.63 |
| 65+ | 20.00 | 20.00 | 18.00 | 3.05 | 0.21 |

Fuente(s): (1) EPPA3; (2) BLT-94-2.

### 2.2 Método(s):  con base en EPPA3 y BLT-94-2.

#### 2.2.1 Hombres:

- 1950-70, tasas de actividad 1950-70 con base en EPPA3;
- 1980-90, tasas de actividad con base en el Boletín de estadísticas
del trabajo 1994-2;
ajuste de las tasas de actividad del grupo de edad [15-19].

#### 2.2.2 Mujeres:

Métodos, hipótesis y tratamientos idénticos a los que se aplican a los hombres.

## 3. Evaluación de las tasas de distribución por sector de actividad: 1950 - 1990

### 3.1 Datos básicos:

Cuadro 2: Distribución de la población económicamente activa por sector de actividad en %

| Año | Agricultura | Industria Total | Manufac. | Servicios |
|---|---|---|---|---|
| **Hombres** | | | | |
| 1950 (1) | 51.30 | 26.40 | .. | 22.30 |
| 1960 (1) | 36.60 | 38.40 | .. | 24.90 |
| 1970 (1) | 26.80 | 47.80 | .. | 25.40 |
| 1980 (2) | 20.86 | 47.49 | 28.90 | 31.65 |
| 1990 (2) | 18.91 | 42.36 | 29.30 | 38.73 |
| **Mujeres** | | | | |
| 1950 (1) | 52.90 | 17.30 | ... | 29.80 |
| 1960 (1) | 40.60 | 28.40 | ... | 30.90 |
| 1970 (1) | 22.60 | 40.30 | ... | 37.00 |
| 1980 (2) | 15.21 | 38.15 | 32.51 | 46.64 |
| 1990 (2) | 10.53 | 32.12 | 28.76 | 57.34 |

Fuente(s): (1) EPPA3; (2) BLT-94-2.

### 3.2 Método(s):  datos de BLT-94-2

#### 3.2.1 Hombres:

- 1950-70, tasas de distribución 1950-70 con base en EPPA3;
- 1980-90, tasas de distribución con base en el boletín de estadísticas
del trabajo 1994-2.

#### 3.2.2 Mujeres:

Métodos, hipótesis y tratamientos idénticos a los que se aplican a los hombres.

## 4. Proyección de las tasas de actividad: 2000 - 2010

### 4.1 Modelo(s):  linear, hiperbólico y logístico

#### 4.1.1 Hombres:

- Para el grupo de edad [15-19], aplicación de la función F1;
- Para los grupos de edad [20+], aplicación de la función F3;
- Modificación de las tendencias de los grupos de edad [35+].

#### 4.1.2 Mujeres:

- Para el grupo de edad [15-19], aplicación de la función F1;
- Para los grupos de edad [20-54], aplicación de la función F6;
- Para los grupos de edad [55+], aplicación de la función F3;
- Modificación de las tendencias de los grupos de edad [20+].

*Notas sobre los ajustes de las tasas, véase p.380-384.*      *Notas sobre las funciones de proyección, véase p. 386.*

# India

## 1. Fuente(s) de los datos básicos

Código(s):   Título(s):

EPPA3      Estimaciones y proyecciones de la población económicamente activa, 1950-2025, tercera edición, OIT, Ginebra, 1986.
ADNU       Ediciones de 1984 et 1988 del Annuaire démographique des Nations Unies, New York.
STAT       Base de datos de la OIT sobre estadísticas del trabajo - LABORSTA, Oficina de Estadística, OIT, Ginebra.

## 2. Evaluación de las tasas de actividad: 1950 - 1990

### 2.1 Datos básicos:

Cuadro 1: Tasas de actividad por sexo y grupo de edad

| Grupo de edad | Año 1950 (1) | 1960 (1) | 1970 (1) | 1981 (2) | 1983 (2) | 1990 (3) |
|---|---|---|---|---|---|---|
| **Hombres** | | | | | | |
| 10-14 | 41.40 | 33.60 | 25.80 | 22.14 | 22.77 | 12.40 |
| 15-19 | 76.95 | 69.40 | 62.40 | 61.69 | 65.18 | 54.63 |
| 20-24 | 93.55 | 90.35 | 89.20 | 88.42 | 89.65 | 86.18 |
| 25-29 | 97.50 | 97.35 | 96.65 | 96.80 | 96.89 | 96.47 |
| 30-34 | 97.80 | 97.70 | 97.70 | 98.32 | 98.54 | 97.03 |
| 35-39 | 97.80 | 97.70 | 97.70 | 98.61 | 98.80 | 98.02 |
| 40-44 | 97.70 | 97.60 | 97.60 | 98.66 | 98.69 | 97.90 |
| 45-49 | 97.35 | 96.95 | 97.20 | 97.48 | 97.48 | 97.76 |
| 50-54 | 96.60 | 95.95 | 95.50 | 95.31 | 94.99 | 96.30 |
| 55-59 | 96.00 | 94.00 | 92.50 | 91.85 | 90.81 | 92.97 |
| 60-64 | 89.60 | 85.25 | 81.65 | 75.62 | 74.32 | 76.48 |
| 65+ | 71.65 | 68.65 | 63.65 | 57.96 | 56.53 | 58.92 |
| **Mujeres** | | | | | | |
| 10-14 | 28.05 | 25.30 | 20.75 | 15.15 | 20.16 | 11.68 |
| 15-19 | 38.25 | 35.40 | 31.00 | 32.36 | 39.70 | 25.05 |
| 20-24 | 45.40 | 42.40 | 36.35 | 35.34 | 44.33 | 34.47 |
| 25-29 | 51.40 | 48.50 | 42.15 | 35.98 | 45.52 | 34.66 |
| 30-34 | 52.40 | 49.50 | 44.30 | 37.09 | 54.71 | 38.70 |
| 35-39 | 53.40 | 51.00 | 45.65 | 38.03 | 47.78 | 36.60 |
| 40-44 | 52.05 | 49.85 | 44.60 | 37.59 | 59.68 | 42.61 |
| 45-49 | 50.25 | 48.30 | 43.50 | 36.36 | 58.52 | 45.17 |
| 50-54 | 46.25 | 44.20 | 39.60 | 31.87 | 43.77 | 36.06 |
| 55-59 | 41.25 | 38.35 | 34.55 | 28.25 | 42.46 | 31.40 |
| 60-64 | 32.70 | 30.45 | 27.15 | 22.11 | 30.07 | 24.24 |
| 65+ | 19.75 | 15.50 | 13.20 | 9.81 | 15.16 | 11.24 |

Fuente(s): (1) EPPA3; (2) ADNU; (3) STAT.

### 2.2 Método(s): interpolación linear

**2.2.1 Hombres:**

- 1950-90, interpolación de las tasas de actividad 1950-70 con base en EPPA3 y de las tasas de actividad con base en el censo de 1981 y las encuestas 1983 y 1989/90.

**2.2.2 Mujeres:**

- 1950-70, tasas de actividad ajustadas 1950-70 con base en EPPA3; el ajuste se ha calculado con base en el modelo de ajuste de las tasas de actividad de las mujeres ocupadas en la agricultura como auxiliares familiares;
- 1980-90, interpolación de las tasas de actividad con base en el censo de 1981 y de las tasas de actividad con base en las encuestas de 1983 y 1989/90.

## 3. Evaluación de las tasas de distribución por sector de actividad: 1950 - 1990

### 3.1 Datos básicos:

Cuadro 2: Distribución de la población económicamente activa por sector de actividad en %

| Año | Agricultura | Industria Total | Manufac. | Servicios |
|---|---|---|---|---|
| **Hombres** | | | | |
| 1981 | 65.89 | 15.05 | 12.01 | 19.07 |
| 1983 | 62.41 | 15.58 | .. | 22.00 |
| 1990 | 58.35 | 16.37 | .. | 25.28 |
| **Mujeres** | | | | |
| 1981 | 84.07 | 8.60 | 7.58 | 7.32 |
| 1983 | 81.12 | 10.18 | .. | 8.69 |
| 1990 | 74.82 | 14.47 | .. | 10.71 |

Fuente(s): STAT.

### 3.2 Método(s): interpolación y extrapolación lineares

**3.2.1 Hombres:**

- 1970-90, interpolación de las tasas de distribución 1950-70 con base en EPPA3 y de las tasas de distribución con base en las encuestas de 1983 y 1989/90;
- Aplicación de la razón manufacturas/industria con base en el censo de 1981.

**3.2.2 Mujeres:**

- 1950-70, tasas de distribución 1950-70 con base en EPPA3;
- 1980-90, interpolación y extrapolación de las tasas de distribución con base en el censo de 1983 y la encuesta de 1989/90;
- Aplicación de la razón manufacturas/industria con base en el censo de 1981.

## 4. Proyección de las tasas de actividad: 2000 - 2010

### 4.1 Modelo(s): linear, log-linear y hiperbólico

**4.1.1 Hombres:**

- Para el grupo de edad [10-14], aplicación de la función F2;
- Para los grupos de edad [15+], aplicación de la función F1;
- Modificación de las tendencias de los grupos de edad [10-54].

**4.1.2 Mujeres:**

- Para los grupos de edad [10-19] y [40-59], aplicación de la función F1;
- Para los grupos de edad [20-39] y [60+], aplicación de la función F3;
- Para los grupos de edad [10-59], aplicación de la función F1.

*Notas sobre los ajustes de las tasas, véase p.380-384.*          *Notas sobre las funciones de proyección, véase p. 386.*

# Indonesia

## 1. Fuente(s) de los datos básicos

Código(s):  Título(s):

EPPA3    Estimaciones y proyecciones de la población económicamente activa, 1950-2025, tercera edición, OIT, Ginebra, 1986.
STAT     Base de datos de la OIT sobre estadísticas del trabajo - LABORSTA, Oficina de Estadística, OIT, Ginebra.

## 2. Evaluación de las tasas de actividad: 1950 - 1990

### 2.1 Datos básicos:

Cuadro 1: Tasas de actividad por sexo y grupo de edad

| Grupo de edad | 1978 | 1982 | 1988 | 1992 |
|---|---|---|---|---|
| **Hombres** | | | | |
| 10-14 | .. | .. | 13.70 | 12.52 |
| 15-19 | .. | .. | 45.60 | 47.76 |
| 20-24 | .. | .. | 77.30 | 76.75 |
| 25-29 | .. | .. | 94.10 | 93.60 |
| 30-34 | .. | .. | 97.80 | 97.52 |
| 35-39 | .. | .. | 98.60 | 98.68 |
| 40-44 | .. | .. | 98.40 | 98.04 |
| 45-49 | .. | .. | 97.80 | 97.58 |
| 50-54 | .. | .. | 95.40 | 93.84 |
| 55-59 | .. | .. | 89.10 | 89.55 |
| 60-64 | .. | .. | 79.20 | 79.67 |
| 65+ | .. | .. | 56.30 | 56.84 |
| **Mujeres** | | | | |
| 10-14 | .. | 9.00 | 10.90 | 7.97 |
| 15-19 | 36.20 | 33.20 | 36.20 | 34.86 |
| 20-24 | 38.30 | 41.40 | 52.70 | 46.31 |
| 25-29 | 44.40 | 43.90 | 56.50 | 52.18 |
| 30-34 | 52.60 | 47.00 | 58.80 | 54.43 |
| 35-39 | .. | 51.80 | 62.10 | 58.00 |
| 40-44 | | 54.70 | 64.20 | 59.56 |
| 45-49 | .. | 56.70 | 63.60 | 60.55 |
| 50-54 | 52.90 | 51.10 | 60.70 | 57.65 |
| 55-59 | 49.20 | 50.40 | 55.60 | 52.17 |
| 60-64 | 42.30 | 39.30 | 46.10 | 42.73 |
| 65+ | 27 | 23.2 | 25.40 | 25.09 |

Fuente(s): STAT.

### 2.2 Método(s): promedio aritmético

**2.2.1 Hombres:**

- 1950-70, tasas de actividad 1950-70 con base en EPPA3;
- 1990, interpolación de las tasas de actividad con base en las encuestas de 1988 y 1992.

**2.2.2 Mujeres:**

- 1950-70, tasas de actividad 1950-70 con base en EPPA3;
- 1980, promedios de las tasas de actividad ajustadas con base en las encuestas de 1978 y 1982;
- 1990, promedios de las tasas de actividad con base en las encuestas de 1988 y 1992.

## 3. Evaluación de las tasas de distribución por sector de actividad: 1950 - 1990

### 3.1 Datos básicos:

Cuadro 2: Distribución de la población económicamente activa por sector de actividad en %

| Año | Agricultura | Industria Total | Manufac. | Servicios |
|---|---|---|---|---|
| **Hombres** | | | | |
| 1978 | 62.75 | 8.63 | 5.88 | 28.61 |
| 1982 | 55.16 | 15.16 | 8.47 | 29.68 |
| 1989 | 55.72 | 14.08 | 8.90 | 30.19 |
| 1992 | 53.74 | 15.09 | 8.92 | 31.17 |
| **Mujeres** | | | | |
| 1978 | 57.74 | 10.37 | 10.17 | 31.89 |
| 1982 | 53.77 | 14.47 | 13.90 | 31.77 |
| 1989 | 57.09 | 12.05 | 13.01 | 30.86 |
| 1992 | 55.06 | 13.51 | 12.85 | 31.43 |

Fuente(s): STAT.

### 3.2 Método(s): promedio ponderado / promedio aritmético

**3.2.1 Hombres:**

- 1950-70, tasas de distribución 1950-70 con base en EPPA3;
- 1980, promedios de las tasas de distribución con base en las encuestas de 1978 y 1982;
- 1990, promedios ponderados de las tasas de distribución con base en las encuestas de 1989 y 1992.
las encuestas de 1989 y 1992.

**3.2.2 Mujeres:**

Métodos, hipótesis y tratamientos idénticos a los que se aplican a los hombres.

## 4. Proyección de las tasas de actividad: 2000 - 2010

### 4.1 Modelo(s): linear, log-linear, hiperbólico y logístico

**4.1.1 Hombres:**

- Para los grupos de edad [10-14] y [50+], aplicación de la función F1;
- Para el grupo de edad [15-19], aplicación de la función F2;
- Para los grupos de edad [20-49], aplicación de la función F3;
- Modificación de las tendencias de los grupos de edad [20-44].

**4.1.2 Mujeres:**

- Para los grupos de edad [10-19] y [65+], aplicación de la función F3;
- Para el grupo de edad [20-24], aplicación de la función F1;
- Para los grupos de edad [25-64], aplicación de la función F6;
- Modificación de la tendencia del grupo de edad [15-19].

*Notas sobre los ajustes de las tasas, véase p.380-384.*    *Notas sobre las funciones de proyección, véase p. 386.*

# Irán, Rep. Islámica del

## 1. Fuente(s) de los datos básicos

| Código(s): | Título(s): |
|---|---|
| EPPA3 | Estimaciones y proyecciones de la población económicamente activa, 1950-2025, tercera edición, OIT, Ginebra, 1986. |
| ADNU84 | Ediciones de 1984 et 1988 del Annuaire démographique des Nations Unies, New York. |
| ASTER | Anuario de estadísticas del trabajo 1945-89 - Edición retrospectiva sobre los censos de población, OIT, Ginebra, 1990. |
| AST92 | Anuario de Estadísticas del Trabjo 1992, OIT, Ginebra, 1992. |
| STAT | Base de datos de la OIT sobre estadísticas del trabajo - LABORSTA, Oficina de Estadística, OIT, Ginebra. |

## 2. Evaluación de las tasas de actividad: 1950 - 1990

### 2.1 Datos básicos:

Cuadro 1: Tasas de actividad por sexo y grupo de edad

| Grupo de edad | Año 1976 (1) | 1986 (2) | 1991 (3) |
|---|---|---|---|
| **Hombres** | | | |
| 10-14 | 18.41 | 11.44 | 6.86 |
| 15-19 | 53.34 | 50.41 | 42.49 |
| 20-24 | 86.44 | 86.34 | 82.95 |
| 25-29 | 95.74 | 94.08 | 94.28 |
| 30-34 | 97.84 | 96.14 | 97.02 |
| 35-39 | 98.38 | 96.64 | 97.46 |
| 40-44 | 97.72 | 95.84 | 96.76 |
| 45-49 | 96.02 | 93.27 | 94.86 |
| 50-54 | 92.44 | 89.65 | 90.94 |
| 55-59 | 86.25 | 84.05 | 86.96 |
| 60-64 | 77.04 | 76.34 | 78.97 |
| 65+ | 56.40 | 53.10 | 59.48 |
| **Mujeres** | | | |
| 10-14 | 10.75 | 4.49 | 3.90 |
| 15-19 | 15.74 | 9.40 | 11.10 |
| 20-24 | 17.90 | 12.01 | 14.01 |
| 25-29 | 16.11 | 11.15 | 11.50 |
| 30-34 | 14.14 | 11.16 | 11.16 |
| 35-39 | 12.75 | 9.46 | 10.84 |
| 40-44 | 11.72 | 7.79 | 8.79 |
| 45-49 | 10.89 | 6.21 | 6.84 |
| 50-54 | 9.73 | 5.44 | 4.96 |
| 55-59 | 8.10 | 4.84 | 4.13 |
| 60-64 | 6.62 | 4.24 | 3.75 |
| 65+ | 4.48 | 2.80 | 3.45 |

Fuente(s): (1) ASTER y ADNU84; (2) AST92; (3) STAT.

### 2.2 Método(s): interpolación linear

**2.2.1 Hombres:**

- 1950-70, tasas de actividad 1950-70 con base en EPPA3;
- 1980-90, extrapolación de las tasas de actividad ajustadas con base en los censos de 1976 y 1991.

**2.2.2 Mujeres:**

- 1950-70, tasas de actividad ajustadas 1950-70 con base en EPPA3; el ajuste se ha calculado con base en el modelo de ajuste de las tasas de actividad de las mujeres ocupadas en la agricultura como auxiliares familiares;
- 1980-90, interpolación de las tasas de actividad ajustadas con base en los censos de 1986 y 1991; ajuste de las tasas de actividad con base en la razón hombres/mujeres igual a 2/3 en la agricultura;

## 3. Evaluación de las tasas de distribución por sector de actividad: 1950 - 1990

### 3.1 Datos básicos:

Cuadro 2: Distribución de la población económicamente activa por sector de actividad en %

| Año | Agricultura | Industria Total | Manufac. | Servicios |
|---|---|---|---|---|
| **Hombres** | | | | |
| 1976 | 36.88 | 31.27 | 13.69 | 31.84 |
| 1986 | 30.27 | 26.33 | 12.78 | 43.40 |
| **Mujeres** | | | | |
| 1976 | 45.45 | 36.92 | 35.65 | 17.63 |
| 1986 | 27.97 | 24.33 | 23.02 | 47.70 |

Fuente(s): ASTER.

### 3.2 Método(s): interpolación y extrapolación lineares

**3.2.1 Hombres:**

- 1950-70, tasas de distribución 1950-70 con base en EPPA3;
- 1980-90, interpolación y extrapolación de las tasas de distribución con base en los censos de 1976 y 1986; modificación de las tendencias de todos los sectores.

**3.2.2 Mujeres:**

- 1950-70, tasas de distribución de la agricultura 1950-70 con base en EPPA3; ajuste de las tasas habida cuenta de la subenumeración censal de las mujeres ocupadas en la agricultura;
- 1980-90, interpolación y extrapolación de las tasas de distribución ajustadas con base en los censos de 1976 y 1986; ajuste de las tasas con base en la razón hombres/mujeres igual a 2/3 en la agricultura;
- Aplicación de la razón manufacturas/industria con base en el censo de 1986.

## 4. Proyección de las tasas de actividad: 2000 - 2010

### 4.1 Modelo(s): linear, log-linear, hiperbólico y logístico

**4.1.1 Hombres:**

- Para el grupo de edad [10-14], aplicación de la función F1;
- Para los grupos de edad [15+], aplicación de la función F3;
- Modificación de las tendencias de los grupos de edad [20-24] y [50-54].

**4.1.2 Mujeres:**

- Para el grupo de edad [10-14], aplicación de la función F1;
- Para los grupos de edad [15-19] y [54+], aplicación de la función F6;
- Para los grupos de edad [20-49], aplicación de la función F2;
- Modificación de las tendencias de los grupos de edad [10-59].

# Iraq

## 1. Fuente(s) de los datos básicos

Código(s):   Título(s):

EPPA3     Estimaciones y proyecciones de la población económicamente activa, 1950-2025, tercera edición, OIT, Ginebra, 1986.
ASTER     Anuario de estadísticas del trabajo 1945-89 - Edición retrospectiva sobre los censos de población, OIT, Ginebra, 1990.
ADNU88   Annuaire démographique 1988 - Statistiques des recensements de population, quarantième édition, Nations Unies, New York, 1990.
STAT      Base de datos de la OIT sobre estadísticas del trabajo - LABORSTA, Oficina de Estadística, OIT, Ginebra.

## 2. Evaluación de las tasas de actividad: 1950 - 1990

### 2.1 Datos básicos:

Cuadro 1: Tasas de actividad por sexo y grupo de edad

| Grupo de edad | Año 1950 (1) | 1960 (1) | 1970 (1) | 1977 (2) | 1987 (3) |
|---|---|---|---|---|---|
| **Hombres** | | | | | |
| 10-14 | 35.50 | 29.00 | 24.00 | 10.97 | 6.18 |
| 15-19 | 80.00 | 67.00 | 50.00 | 39.87 | 41.59 |
| 20-24 | 92.00 | 88.50 | 86.00 | 84.93 | 80.70 |
| 25-29 | 96.00 | 96.25 | 96.50 | 96.65 | 94.81 |
| 30-34 | 97.60 | 97.45 | 97.35 | 97.52 | 95.52 |
| 35-39 | 96.75 | 96.75 | 96.80 | 96.79 | 95.43 |
| 40-44 | 96.50 | 96.00 | 95.50 | 94.86 | 94.27 |
| 45-49 | 96.00 | 94.65 | 93.35 | 92.17 | 87.58 |
| 50-54 | 95.00 | 93.00 | 90.00 | 87.75 | 77.98 |
| 55-59 | 94.00 | 90.00 | 86.00 | 82.88 | 72.07 |
| 60-64 | 92.50 | 86.00 | 79.50 | 74.71 | 70.00 |
| 65+ | 80.00 | 68.00 | 59.00 | 54.01 | 47.98 |
| **Mujeres** | | | | | |
| 10-14 | .. | .. | .. | 9.84 | 1.06 |
| 15-19 | .. | .. | .. | 10.86 | 3.57 |
| 20-24 | .. | .. | .. | 15.45 | 14.16 |
| 25-29 | .. | .. | .. | 18.99 | 20.14 |
| 30-34 | .. | .. | .. | 20.84 | 15.28 |
| 35-39 | .. | .. | .. | 19.17 | 12.50 |
| 40-44 | .. | .. | .. | 19.25 | 13.33 |
| 45-49 | .. | .. | .. | 18.60 | 10.14 |
| 50-54 | .. | .. | .. | 18.31 | 7.35 |
| 55-59 | .. | .. | .. | 16.48 | 5.27 |
| 60-64 | .. | .. | .. | 12.96 | 3.81 |
| 65+ | .. | .. | .. | 6.71 | 2.54 |

Fuente(s): (1) EPPA3; (2) ASTER y ADNU88; (3) STAT.

### 2.2 Método(s): extrapolación linear
                  promedio ponderado

#### 2.2.1 Hombres:

- 1950-70, tasas de actividad 1950-70 con base en EPPA3;
- 1980-90, extrapolación de las tasas de actividad ajustadas con base en los censos de 1977 y 1987;
ajuste de las tasas interpoladas con base en las variaciones de las tasas interpoladas 1970, en relación con las tasas de actividad 1970 con base en EPPA3.

#### 2.2.2 Mujeres:

- 1950-70, tasas de actividad ajustadas 1950-70 con base en EPPA3;
- 1980, promedios ponderados de las tasas de actividad con base en los censos de 1977 y 1987;
- 1990, aplicación a las tasas de actividad estimadas 1980, de las variaciones de las tasas de actividad ajustadas con base en el censo de 1977, en relación con las tasas ajustadas con base en el censo de 1987; ajuste de las tasas interpoladas y extrapoladas habida cuenta de la

## 3. Evaluación de las tasas de distribución por sector de actividad: 1950 - 1990

### 3.1 Datos básicos:

Cuadro 2: Distribución de la población económicamente activa por sector de actividad en %

| Año | Agricultura | Industria Total | Manufac. | Servicios |
|---|---|---|---|---|
| **Hombres** | | | | |
| 1977 (1) | 23.84 | 24.58 | 9.51 | 51.58 |
| 1987 (2) | 13.21 | 19.81 | 7.14 | 66.98 |
| **Mujeres** | | | | |
| 1977 (1) | 67.60 | 10.89 | 9.31 | 21.52 |
| 1987 (2) | 17.35 | 13.84 | 9.50 | 68.81 |

Fuente(s): (1) ASTER; (2) STAT.

### 3.2 Método(s): promedio ponderado

#### 3.2.1 Hombres:

- 1950-70, tasas de distribución 1950-70 con base en EPPA3;
- 1980, promedios ponderados de las tasas de distribución ajustadas con base er los censos de 1977 y 1987;
- 1990, aplicación a las tasas estimadas 1980 de las variaciones de las tasas ajustadas con base en el censo de 1977, en relación con las tasas ajustadas ajustadas con base en el censo de 1977, en relación con las tasas ajustadas

#### 3.2.2 Mujeres:

Métodos, hipótesis y tratamientos idénticos a los que se aplican a los hombres.

## 4. Proyección de las tasas de actividad: 2000 - 2010

### 4.1 Modelo(s): linear, log-linear, hiperbólico y logístico

#### 4.1.1 Hombres:

- Para el grupo de edad [10-14], aplicación de la función F2;
- Para los grupos de edad [15-24] y [60+], aplicación de la función F3;
- Para los grupos de edad [25-59], aplicación de la función F1;
- Modificación de las tendencias de los grupos de edad [10-14] y [20-59].

#### 4.1.2 Mujeres:

- Para los grupos de edad [10-19] y [65+], aplicación de la función F1;
- Para los grupos de edad [20-64], aplicación de la función F6;
- Modificación de las tendencias de todos los grupos de edad.

*Notas sobre los ajustes de las tasas, véase p.380-384.*           *Notas sobre las funciones de proyección, véase p. 386.*

# Irlanda

## 1. Fuente(s) de los datos básicos

Código(s):  Título(s):

EPPA3   Anuario de estadísticas del trabajo 1945-89 - Edición retrospectiva sobre los censos de población, OIT, Ginebra, 1990.
STAT    Base de datos de la OIT sobre estadísticas del trabajo - LABORSTA, Oficina de Estadística, OIT, Ginebra.

## 2. Evaluación de las tasas de actividad: 1950 - 1990

### 2.1 Datos básicos:

Cuadro 1: Tasas de actividad por sexo y grupo de edad

| Grupo de edad | Año 1989 | 1990 | 1991 |
|---|---|---|---|
| **Hombres** | | | |
| 10-14 | 0.00 | 0.00 | 0.00 |
| 15-19 | 30.35 | 29.98 | 29.25 |
| 20-24 | 82.40 | 82.08 | 81.12 |
| 25-29 | 96.20 | 95.58 | 95.23 |
| 30-34 | 96.86 | 96.96 | 97.01 |
| 35-39 | 96.01 | 96.03 | 96.44 |
| 40-44 | 95.00 | 95.59 | 95.39 |
| 45-49 | 93.19 | 92.72 | 93.50 |
| 50-54 | 88.62 | 89.78 | 89.39 |
| 55-59 | 79.44 | 79.42 | 79.80 |
| 60-64 | 60.93 | 57.19 | 59.37 |
| 65+ | 16.82 | 15.88 | 15.79 |
| **Mujeres** | | | |
| 10-14 | 0.00 | 0.00 | 0.00 |
| 15-19 | 23.39 | 23.57 | 21.11 |
| 20-24 | 73.68 | 73.28 | 73.37 |
| 25-29 | 62.14 | 64.79 | 65.96 |
| 30-34 | 42.05 | 44.65 | 49.43 |
| 35-39 | 30.75 | 34.00 | 38.53 |
| 40-44 | 27.99 | 30.83 | 32.26 |
| 45-49 | 27.00 | 29.28 | 29.50 |
| 50-54 | 23.57 | 26.19 | 27.97 |
| 55-59 | 19.83 | 21.80 | 22.13 |
| 60-64 | 13.27 | 14.51 | 14.04 |
| 65+ | 3.07 | 3.07 | 2.99 |

Fuente(s): STAT.

### 2.2 Método(s): interpolación linear

#### 2.2.1 Hombres:

- 1950-80, tasas de actividad 1950-80 con base en EPPA3;
- 1990, interpolación de las tasas de actividad con base en las encuestas de 1989, 1990 y 1991;
aplicación a las tasas interpoladas, los promedios de las variaciones tasas de actividad con base en las encuestas de 1989, 1990 y 1991, en relación con las tasas de actividad con base en la encuesta de 1990.

#### 2.2.2 Mujeres:

Métodos, hipótesis y tratamientos idénticos a los que se aplican a los hombres.

## 3. Evaluación de las tasas de distribución por sector de actividad: 1950 - 1990

### 3.1 Datos básicos:

Cuadro 2: Distribución de la población económicamente activa por sector de actividad en %

| Año | Agricultura | Industria Total | Manufac. | Servicios |
|---|---|---|---|---|
| **Hombres** | | | | |
| 1981 | 20.68 | 39.76 | 22.22 | 39.56 |
| 1989 | 20.56 | 32.18 | 20.16 | 47.26 |
| 1990 | 20.44 | 33.17 | 20.56 | 46.38 |
| 1991 | 19.03 | 33.87 | 21.12 | 47.10 |
| **Mujeres** | | | | |
| 1981 | 3.74 | 21.93 | 20.45 | 74.33 |
| 1989 | 3.45 | 19.58 | 18.38 | 76.97 |
| 1990 | 3.70 | 18.76 | 17.57 | 77.53 |
| 1991 | 3.27 | 18.39 | 16.92 | 78.34 |

Fuente(s): STAT.

### 3.2 Método(s): promedio aritmético

#### 3.2.1 Hombres:

- 1950-80, tasas de distribución 1950-80 con base en EPPA3;
la tasa de distribución 1980 de los manufacturas ajustada con base en la aplicación a la tasa de distribución 1980 de la industria de la razón manufacturas/industria con base en el censo de 1981;
- 1990, promedios ajustadas de las tasas de distribución con base en
- 1990, promedios ajustadas de las tasas de distribución con base en

#### 3.2.2 Mujeres:

Métodos, hipótesis y tratamientos idénticos a los que se aplican a los hombres.

## 4. Proyección de las tasas de actividad: 2000 - 2010

### 4.1 Modelo(s): linear, log-linear, hiperbólico y logístico

#### 4.1.1 Hombres:

- Para los grupos de edad [15-24] y [55+], aplicación de la función F3;
- Para los grupos de edad [25-54], aplicación de la función F1;
- Modificación de las tendencias de los grupos de edad [35-49].

#### 4.1.2 Mujeres:

- Para los grupos de edad [15-19] y [55+], aplicación de la función F3;
- Para los grupos de edad [20-29], aplicación de la función F1;
- Para los grupos de edad [30-54], aplicación de la función F2;
- Modificación de las tendencias de los grupos de edad [15-24] y [30-54].

*Notas sobre los ajustes de las tasas, véase p.380-384.*    *Notas sobre las funciones de proyección, véase p. 386.*

# Islandia

## 1. Fuente(s) de los datos básicos

Código(s):   Título(s):

EPPA3        Estimaciones y proyecciones de la población económicamente activa, 1950-2025, tercera edición, OIT, Ginebra, 1986.
YNS-94       Yearbook of Nordic Statistics 1994

## 2. Evaluación de las tasas de actividad: 1950 - 1990

### 2.1 Datos básicos:

Cuadro 1: Tasas de actividad por sexo y grupo de edad

| Grupo de edad | Año 1950 (1) | 1960 (1) | 1970 (1) | 1980 (1) | 1992 (2) |
|---|---|---|---|---|---|
| **Hombres** | | | | | |
| 10-14 | 7.50 | 3.00 | 2.05 | 0.00 | 0.00 |
| 15-19 | 80.70 | 65.65 | 62.50 | 57.42 | 48.40 |
| 20-24 | 91.90 | 90.00 | 90.00 | 89.62 | 77.30 |
| 25-29 | 94.20 | 94.45 | 95.50 | 96.92 | 95.00 |
| 30-34 | 98.80 | 97.70 | 97.45 | 96.89 | 97.00 |
| 35-39 | 98.60 | 97.50 | 97.25 | 96.83 | 97.00 |
| 40-44 | 97.75 | 97.70 | 97.55 | 97.49 | 97.50 |
| 45-49 | 97.80 | 97.20 | 97.60 | 97.34 | 97.35 |
| 50-54 | 97.30 | 95.85 | 95.35 | 94.59 | 94.75 |
| 55-59 | 97.15 | 94.90 | 93.05 | 91.79 | 92.47 |
| 60-64 | 93.25 | 92.20 | 91.45 | 90.85 | 91.16 |
| 65+ | 63.00 | 53.00 | 43.00 | 33.00 | 43.48 |
| **Mujeres** | | | | | |
| 10-14 | 3.00 | 1.25 | 0.80 | 0.00 | 0.00 |
| 15-19 | 61.55 | 55.20 | 57.45 | 59.80 | 60.40 |
| 20-24 | 51.35 | 45.30 | 59.30 | 79.00 | 67.60 |
| 25-29 | 34.65 | 29.00 | 46.45 | 76.50 | 76.72 |
| 30-34 | 25.90 | 24.85 | 41.00 | 70.50 | 81.60 |
| 35-39 | 27.80 | 24.85 | 41.05 | 70.70 | 85.12 |
| 40-44 | 29.65 | 28.75 | 44.00 | 68.50 | 88.47 |
| 45-49 | 32.10 | 33.75 | 47.90 | 69.00 | 87.23 |
| 50-54 | 33.35 | 35.60 | 47.75 | 65.40 | 81.23 |
| 55-59 | 34.75 | 36.50 | 43.55 | 52.00 | 79.76 |
| 60-64 | 31.90 | 33.95 | 40.90 | 50.00 | 76.87 |
| 65+ | 12.95 | 15.05 | 14.15 | 13.3 | 23.14 |

Fuente(s): (1) EPPA3; (2) YNS-94.

### 2.2 Método(s): interpolación linear

#### 2.2.1 Hombres:

- 1950-80, tasas de actividad 1950-80 con base en EPPA3;
- 1980, interpolación de las tasas de actividad 1980 con base en EPPA3
y de las tasas de actividad ajustadas 1992 con base en
el "Yearbook of Nordic Statistics, 1994".

#### 2.2.2 Mujeres:

Métodos, hipótesis y tratamientos idénticos a los que se aplican a los hombres.

## 3. Evaluación de las tasas de distribución por sector de actividad: 1950 - 1990

### 3.1 Datos básicos:

Cuadro 2: Distribución de la población económicamente activa por sector de actividad en %

| Año | Agricultura | Industria Total | Manufac. | Servicios |
|---|---|---|---|---|
| **Hombres** | | | | |
| 1980 (1) | 14.71 | 45.59 | 27.35 | 39.71 |
| 1992 (2) | 16.25 | 32.50 | 18.75 | 51.25 |
| **Mujeres** | | | | |
| 1980 (1) | 4.17 | 25.00 | 25.00 | 70.83 |
| 1992 (2) | 4.92 | 14.75 | 14.75 | 80.33 |

Fuente(s): (1) EPPA3; (2) YNS-94.

### 3.2 Método(s): interpolación linear

#### 3.2.1 Hombres:

- 1950-80, tasas de distribución 1950-80 con base en EPPA3;
la tasa de distribución 1980 de los manufacturas ajustada con base en
la tasa de distribución con base en "Yearbook of Nordic Statistics, 1994";
- 1990, interpolación de las tasas de distribución 1980 con base en EPPA3
y de las tasas de distribución 1992 con base en "Yearbook".
y de las tasas de distribución 1992 con base en "Yearbook".

#### 3.2.2 Mujeres:

Métodos, hipótesis y tratamientos idénticos a los que se aplican a los hombres.

## 4. Proyección de las tasas de actividad: 2000 - 2010

### 4.1 Modelo(s): linear, hiperbólico y logístico

#### 4.1.1 Hombres:

- Para los grupos de edad [15-19] y [25-29], aplicación de la función F1;
- Para los grupos de edad [20-54] y [30+], aplicación de la función F3;
- Modificación de la tendencia del grupo de edad [25-29].

#### 4.1.2 Mujeres:

- Para el grupo de edad [15-19], aplicación de la función F1;
- Para los grupos de edad [20-24] y [60+], aplicación de la función F3;
- Para los grupos de edad [25-59], aplicación de la función F6;
- Modificación de las tendencias de los grupos de edad [15-24] y [60+].

*Notas sobre los ajustes de las tasas, véase p.380-384.*

*Notas sobre las funciones de proyección, véase p. 386.*

# Islas Salomón

## 1. Fuente(s) de los datos básicos

Código(s):  Título(s):

EPPA3  Anuario de estadísticas del trabajo 1945-89 - Edición retrospectiva sobre los censos de población, OIT, Ginebra, 1990.
STAT  Base de datos de la OIT sobre estadísticas del trabajo - LABORSTA, Oficina de Estadística, OIT, Ginebra.

## 2. Evaluación de las tasas de actividad: 1950 - 1990

### 2.1 Datos básicos:

Cuadro 1: Tasas de actividad por sexo y grupo de edad

| Grupo de edad | Año 1950 (1) | 1960 (1) | 1970 (1) | 1980 (1) | 1986 (2) |
|---|---|---|---|---|---|
| **Hombres** | | | | | |
| 10-14 | 45.48 | 41.48 | 37.49 | 33.61 | 33.60 |
| 15-19 | 81.99 | 77.86 | 72.45 | 65.23 | 77.27 |
| 20-24 | 97.00 | 95.88 | 94.01 | 91.23 | 96.33 |
| 25-29 | 98.33 | 98.09 | 97.74 | 97.24 | 97.50 |
| 30-34 | 98.54 | 98.30 | 97.98 | 97.52 | 97.57 |
| 35-39 | 98.71 | 98.49 | 98.20 | 97.72 | 97.52 |
| 40-44 | 98.64 | 98.36 | 98.03 | 97.53 | 96.54 |
| 45-49 | 97.17 | 97.06 | 96.65 | 96.04 | 96.01 |
| 50-54 | 94.99 | 94.44 | 93.80 | 92.98 | 92.24 |
| 55-59 | 90.73 | 89.91 | 88.96 | 87.61 | 86.26 |
| 60-64 | 83.42 | 81.90 | 80.49 | 78.43 | 79.31 |
| 65+ | 63.18 | 61.14 | 59.04 | 62.39 | 68.98 |
| **Mujeres** | | | | | |
| 10-14 | 38.84 | 36.20 | 33.33 | 31.03 | 41.86 |
| 15-19 | 62.38 | 58.54 | 54.99 | 50.60 | 81.77 |
| 20-24 | 66.44 | 63.56 | 61.43 | 59.13 | 87.81 |
| 25-29 | 66.86 | 64.58 | 61.16 | 58.34 | 86.15 |
| 30-34 | 68.09 | 66.33 | 63.26 | 60.85 | 89.49 |
| 35-39 | 70.01 | 67.90 | 65.04 | 60.76 | 88.54 |
| 40-44 | 72.15 | 68.36 | 66.65 | 63.24 | 88.50 |
| 45-49 | 71.75 | 68.61 | 65.31 | 61.45 | 88.70 |
| 50-54 | 70.48 | 67.89 | 63.18 | 60.28 | 87.10 |
| 55-59 | 63.48 | 61.55 | 56.08 | 53.33 | 86.27 |
| 60-64 | 54.56 | 54.04 | 48.61 | 43.77 | 74.11 |
| 65+ | 42.92 | 37.78 | 33.57 | 24.81 | 56.38 |

Fuente(s): (1) EPPA3; (2) STAT.

### 2.2 Método(s): interpolación y extrapolación lineares

**2.2.1 Hombres:**

- 1950-90, interpolación y extrapolación de las tasas de actividad 1950-80
con base en EPPA3;
modificación de las tendencias de todos los grupos de edad;
aplicación a las tasas extrapoladas 1990, de las variaciones de las tasas
extrapoladas 1986, en relación con las tasas de actividad el censo de 1986.

**2.2.2 Mujeres:**

Métodos, hipótesis y tratamientos idénticos a los que se aplican a los hombres.

## 3. Evaluación de las tasas de distribución por sector de actividad: 1950 - 1990

### 3.1 Datos básicos:

Cuadro 2: Distribución de la población económicamente activa por sector de actividad en %

| Año | Agricultura | Industria Total | Manufac. | Servicios |
|---|---|---|---|---|
| **Hombres** | | | | |
| 1986 | 69.05 | 10.15 | 4.22 | 20.80 |
| **Mujeres** | | | | |
| 1986 | 86.19 | 2.96 | 2.36 | 10.85 |

Fuente(s): STAT.

### 3.2 Método(s): interpolación linear

**3.2.1 Hombres:**

- 1950-90, interpolación de las a las tasas estimadas 1950-90
para Papua Nueva Guinea;
modificación de las tendencias de todos los sectores para 1980 y 1990;
a las tasas interpoladas 1950-90, aplicación de las variaciones de las tasas
interpoladas para 1986, en relación con las tasas con base en el censo de 1986;
interpoladas para 1986, en relación con las tasas con base en el censo de 1986;

**3.2.2 Mujeres:**

Métodos, hipótesis y tratamientos idénticos a los que se aplican a los hombres.

## 4. Proyección de las tasas de actividad: 2000 - 2010

### 4.1 Modelo(s): linear y hiperbólico

**4.1.1 Hombres:**

- Para todos los grupos de edad, aplicación de la función F3;
- Modificación de las tendencias de los grupos de edad [10-44].

**4.1.2 Mujeres:**

- Para los grupos de edad [10-19] y [60+], aplicación de la función F1;
- Para los grupos de edad [20-59], aplicación de la función F3;
- Modificación de las tendencias de los grupos de edad [10-19] y [50+].

# Israel

## 1. Fuente(s) de los datos básicos

Código(s):  Título(s):

EPPA3  Estimaciones y proyecciones de la población económicamente activa, 1950-2025, tercera edición, OIT, Ginebra, 1986.
AST75-93  Ediciones de 1975-1993, Anuario de Estadísticas del Trabjo de la OIT, Ginebra.
ISRCBS  Labour force surveys 1979, special series No. 662, CBS, Jerusalem, 1981.

## 2. Evaluación de las tasas de actividad: 1950 - 1990

### 2.1 Datos básicos:

Cuadro 1: Tasas de actividad por sexo y grupo de edad

| Grupo de edad | Año | | | | | |
|---|---|---|---|---|---|---|
| | 1975 | 1980 | 1985 | 1990 | 1991 | 1992 |
| **Hombres** | | | | | | |
| 10-14 | 0.00 | 0.00 | 0.00 | 0.00 | 0.00 | 0.00 |
| 15-19 | 18.50 | 14.30 | 13.60 | 14.10 | 13.9 | 13.50 |
| 20-24 | 40.30 | 41.30 | 42.80 | 40.30 | 42.1 | 42.40 |
| 25-29 | 86.70 | 84.70 | 83.60 | 82.60 | 82.5 | 81.90 |
| 30-39 | 93.80 | 91.10 | 90.20 | 88.00 | 87.4 | 86.90 |
| 40-49 | 92.80 | 90.40 | 89.70 | 87.70 | 86.9 | 87.90 |
| 50-59 | 84.30 | 82.50 | 76.10 | 73.70 | 71.5 | 71.40 |
| 60+ | 29.20 | 27.90 | 21.40 | 20.20 | 18.7 | 18.70 |
| **Mujeres** | | | | | | |
| 10-14 | 0.00 | 0.00 | 0.00 | 0.00 | 0.00 | 0.00 |
| 15-19 | 11.30 | 10.90 | 8.30 | 10.00 | 7.90 | 7.90 |
| 20-24 | 40.40 | 39.90 | 39.30 | 40.70 | 40.10 | 40.00 |
| 25-29 | 44.20 | 52.60 | 55.60 | 58.40 | 58.50 | 58.50 |
| 30-39 | 40.60 | 50.10 | 57.40 | 62.90 | 63.20 | 63.20 |
| 40-49 | 36.80 | 41.70 | 46.40 | 53.10 | 56.90 | 57.00 |
| 50-59 | 22.40 | 26.00 | 24.80 | 28.60 | 30.90 | 30.90 |
| 60+ | 6.00 | 6.60 | 5.60 | 6.30 | 5.50 | 5.60 |

Fuente(s): AST75-93.

### 2.2 Método(s): interpolación linear

**2.2.1 Hombres:**

- 1950-80, tasas de actividad 1950-80 con base en EPPA3;
- 1990, interpolación de las tasas de actividad con base en las encuestas de 1975 to 1992;
ajuste de las tasas interpoladas con base en las variaciones de las tasas interpoladas 1980, en relación con las tasas de actividad 1980 con base en EPPA3.

**2.2.2 Mujeres:**

- 1950-80, tasas de actividad 1950-80 con base en EPPA3;
modificación de las tendencias de los grupos de edad [35-54] para 1980;
- 1990, interpolación de las tasas de actividad ajustadas con base en las encuestas de 1975 to 1992 ;
ajuste de las tasas interpoladas con base en las variaciones de las tasas interpoladas 1980, en relación con las tasas de actividad 1980 con base en EPPA3.

## 3. Evaluación de las tasas de distribución por sector de actividad: 1950 - 1990

### 3.1 Datos básicos:

Cuadro 2: Distribución de la población económicamente activa por sector de actividad en %

| Año | Agricultura | Industria | | Servicios |
|---|---|---|---|---|
| | | Total | Manufac. | |
| **Hombres** | | | | |
| 1979 | 6.91 | 39.91 | 24.85 | 53.19 |
| 1980 | 7.52 | 39.90 | 24.51 | 52.58 |
| 1981 | 7.47 | 39.67 | 24.05 | 52.87 |
| 1989 | 5.99 | 36.72 | 21.67 | 57.29 |
| 1990 | 6.32 | 37.23 | 21.31 | 57.45 |
| 1991 | 4.53 | 38.50 | 20.12 | 56.96 |
| **Mujeres** | | | | |
| 1979 | 3.88 | 17.65 | 12.01 | 78.47 |
| 1980 | 4.06 | 15.94 | 11.55 | 80.00 |
| 1981 | 3.41 | 15.54 | 11.26 | 81.05 |
| 1989 | 2.44 | 15.32 | 8.76 | 82.24 |
| 1990 | 2.37 | 15.39 | 8.57 | 82.24 |
| 1991 | 1.91 | 15.21 | 8.06 | 82.88 |

Fuente(s): (1) AST75-93.

### 3.2 Método(s): promedio aritmético

**3.2.1 Hombres:**

- 1950-70, tasas de distribución 1950-70 con base en EPPA3;
- 1980-90, promedios de las tasas de distribución con base en las encuestas de 1979, 1980 y 1981 para 1980, las encuestas de 1989, 1990 y 1991 para 1990.

**3.2.2 Mujeres:**

Métodos, hipótesis y tratamientos idénticos a los que se aplican a los hombres.

## 4. Proyección de las tasas de actividad: 2000 - 2010

### 4.1 Modelo(s): linear, log-linear y hiperbólico

**4.1.1 Hombres:**

- Para los grupos de edad [15-24] y [65+], aplicación de la función F2;
- Para los grupos de edad [20-64], aplicación de la función F3.

**4.1.2 Mujeres:**

- Para el grupo de edad [15-19], aplicación de la función F3;
- Para los grupos de edad [20+], aplicación de la función F1.

*Notas sobre los ajustes de las tasas, véase p.380-384.*

*Notas sobre las funciones de proyección, véase p. 386.*

# Italia

## 1. Fuente(s) de los datos básicos

Código(s):  Título(s):,

EPPA3  Anuario de estadísticas del trabajo 1945-89 - Edición retrospectiva sobre los censos de población, OIT, Ginebra, 1990.
STAT  Base de datos de la OIT sobre estadísticas del trabajo - LABORSTA, Oficina de Estadística, OIT, Ginebra.

## 2. Evaluación de las tasas de actividad: 1950 - 1990

### 2.1 Datos básicos:

Cuadro 1: Tasas de actividad por sexo y grupo de edad

| Grupo de edad | Año | | | | | |
|---|---|---|---|---|---|---|
| | 1979 | 1980 | 1981 | 1989 | 1990 | 1991 |
| **Hombres** | | | | | | |
| 10-14 | 0.00 | 0.00 | 0.00 | 1.12 | 0.00 | 0.00 |
| 15-19 | 33.04 | 33.30 | 33.10 | 30.58 | 24.73 | 23.23 |
| 20-24 | 71.65 | 72.52 | 74.10 | 71.49 | 70.16 | 69.55 |
| 25-29 | 93.72 | 93.00 | 93.00 | 90.65 | 90.39 | 89.46 |
| 30-34 | 98.50 | 98.60 | 98.30 | 96.85 | 96.65 | 96.62 |
| 35-39 | 98.50 | 98.60 | 98.50 | 97.97 | 97.59 | 97.63 |
| 40-44 | 97.90 | 97.70 | 98.00 | 97.27 | 97.31 | 97.19 |
| 45-49 | 96.50 | 96.30 | 96.50 | 95.59 | 95.19 | 95.05 |
| 50-54 | 90.70 | 90.70 | 91.10 | 87.53 | 87.35 | 87.23 |
| 55-59 | 74.20 | 74.80 | 74.90 | 67.76 | 68.51 | 68.92 |
| 60-64 | 37.56 | 39.60 | 39.60 | 35.21 | 35.87 | 37.16 |
| 65+ | 12.56 | 12.62 | 11.90 | 7.90 | 7.97 | 8.10 |
| **Mujeres** | | | | | | |
| 10-14 | 0.00 | 0.00 | 0.00 | 0.38 | 0.00 | 0.00 |
| 15-19 | 28.59 | 28.94 | 29.00 | 26.41 | 21.38 | 19.06 |
| 20-24 | 55.42 | 57.87 | 58.50 | 63.91 | 62.75 | 61.19 |
| 25-29 | 52.94 | 54.64 | 56.50 | 64.83 | 65.29 | 65.06 |
| 30-34 | 46.50 | 48.40 | 50.20 | 62.15 | 62.04 | 62.59 |
| 35-39 | 42.20 | 44.50 | 45.30 | 58.95 | 58.84 | 59.52 |
| 40-44 | 39.20 | 40.30 | 41.90 | 51.64 | 52.76 | 53.76 |
| 45-49 | 36.50 | 36.00 | 37.50 | 44.69 | 44.87 | 45.83 |
| 50-54 | 32.10 | 32.00 | 32.20 | 34.06 | 34.98 | 36.07 |
| 55-59 | 21.10 | 21.40 | 21.30 | 20.20 | 20.38 | 21.15 |
| 60-64 | 10.50 | 11.00 | 11.50 | 9.76 | 10.05 | 10.02 |
| 65+ | 3.63 | 3.48 | 3.4 | 2.00 | 2.18 | 2.24 |

Fuente(s): STAT.

### 2.2 Método(s): promedio aritmético

#### 2.2.1 Hombres:

- 1950-70, tasas de actividad 1950-70 con base en EPPA3;
ajuste de las tasas de actividad de los grupos de edad [25+] para 1970;
- 1980, promedios de las tasas de actividad con base en
1980 y 1981 las encuestas;
modificación de las tendencias de los grupos de edad [10-25];
- 1990, promedios de las tasas de actividad con base en las encuestas
1989, 1990 y 1991;
modificación de las tendencias de los grupos de edad [15-24].

#### 2.2.2 Mujeres:

- 1950-70, tasas de actividad 1950-70 con base en EPPA3;
- 1980, promedios de las tasas de actividad con base en
las encuestas de 1979, 1980 y 1981;
modificación de las tendencias de los grupos de edad [10-19];
- 1990, promedios de las tasas de actividad con base en
las encuestas de 1989, 1990 y 1991;
modificación de las tendencias de los grupos de edad [10-19].

## 3. Evaluación de las tasas de distribución por sector de actividad: 1950 - 1990

### 3.1 Datos básicos:

Cuadro 2: Distribución de la población económicamente activa por sector de actividad en %

| Año | Agricultura | Industria | | Servicios |
|---|---|---|---|---|
| | | Total | Manufac. | |
| **Hombres** | | | | |
| 1979 | 13.24 | 40.86 | 25.86 | 45.90 |
| 1980 | 10.07 | 41.88 | 26.43 | 48.05 |
| 1981 | 11.79 | 43.36 | 23.94 | 44.85 |
| 1989 | 8.63 | 36.20 | 22.65 | 55.18 |
| 1990 | 8.25 | 36.59 | 22.65 | 55.16 |
| 1991 | 8.14 | 36.73 | 22.35 | 55.13 |
| **Mujeres** | | | | |
| 1979 | 17.20 | 27.38 | 26.26 | 55.42 |
| 1980 | 12.97 | 29.19 | 27.78 | 57.85 |
| 1981 | 13.20 | 28.51 | 24.57 | 58.29 |
| 1989 | 9.40 | 22.86 | 21.29 | 67.73 |
| 1990 | 8.97 | 22.93 | 21.26 | 68.10 |
| 1991 | 8.79 | 22.11 | 20.44 | 69.10 |

Fuente(s): STAT.

### 3.2 Método(s): promedio aritmético

#### 3.2.1 Hombres:

- 1950-80, tasas de distribución 1950-80 con base en EPPA3;
- 1980, promedios de las tasas de distribución con base en las encuestas
de 1979, 1980 y 1981;
- 1990, promedios de las tasas de distribución con base en las encuestas
de 1989, 1990 y 1991.
de 1989, 1990 y 1991.

#### 3.2.2 Mujeres:

Métodos, hipótesis y tratamientos idénticos a los que se aplican a los hombres.

## 4. Proyección de las tasas de actividad: 2000 - 2010

### 4.1 Modelo(s): hiperbólico y logístico

#### 4.1.1 Hombres:

- Para todos los grupos de edad, aplicación de la función F3;
- Modificación de las tendencias de los grupos de edad [20-54].

#### 4.1.2 Mujeres:

- Para los grupos de edad [10-19] y [55+], aplicación de la función F3;
- Para los grupos de edad [20-54], aplicación de la función F6;
- Modificación de las tendencias de los grupos de edad [20-24] y [55-59].

*Notas sobre los ajustes de las tasas, véase p.380-384.*  *Notas sobre las funciones de proyección, véase p. 386.*

# Jamahiriya Arabe Libia

## 1. Fuente(s) de los datos básicos

Código(s):  Título(s):

EPPA3     Estimaciones y proyecciones de la población económicamente activa, 1950-2025, tercera edición, OIT, Ginebra, 1986.
ASTER     Anuario de estadísticas del trabajo 1945-89 - Edición retrospectiva sobre los censos de población, OIT, Ginebra, 1990.
ADNU88    Annuaire démographique 1988 - Statistiques des recensements de population, quarantième édition, Nations Unies, New York, 1990.
STAT      Base de datos de la OIT sobre estadísticas del trabajo - LABORSTA, Oficina de Estadística, OIT, Ginebra.

## 2. Evaluación de las tasas de actividad: 1950 - 1990

### 2.1 Datos básicos:

Cuadro 1: Tasas de actividad por sexo y grupo de edad

| Grupo de edad | Año 1950 (1) | 1960 (1) | 1970 (1) | 1973 (2) | 1984 (3) |
|---|---|---|---|---|---|
| **Hombres** | | | | | |
| 10-14 | 46.75 | 26.50 | 16.00 | 1.90 | 0.00 |
| 15-19 | 72.65 | 58.50 | 57.06 | 27.21 | 20.44 |
| 20-24 | 95.00 | 88.05 | 87.19 | 75.79 | 73.25 |
| 25-29 | 96.30 | 95.40 | 96.55 | 95.96 | 95.50 |
| 30-34 | 96.85 | 96.95 | 97.05 | 97.87 | 97.96 |
| 35-39 | 97.00 | 97.20 | 97.70 | 98.48 | 98.76 |
| 40-44 | 96.70 | 97.05 | 97.40 | 98.23 | 98.53 |
| 45-49 | 96.60 | 96.55 | 96.50 | 96.96 | 97.96 |
| 50-54 | 95.55 | 94.90 | 94.25 | 94.87 | 96.83 |
| 55-59 | 93.05 | 91.40 | 89.75 | 90.63 | 94.23 |
| 60-64 | 91.80 | 86.10 | 80.40 | 80.73 | 89.35 |
| 65+ | 72.85 | 61.55 | 50.25 | 49.35 | 40.98 |
| **Mujeres** | | | | | |
| 10-14 | 6.75 | 5.05 | 2.65 | 1.74 | 0.00 |
| 15-19 | 4.55 | 4.50 | 4.40 | 4.09 | 5.86 |
| 20-24 | 3.65 | 4.75 | 6.30 | 7.38 | 23.08 |
| 25-29 | 2.95 | 4.45 | 6.60 | 8.09 | 19.71 |
| 30-34 | 3.25 | 4.50 | 6.30 | 7.79 | 9.68 |
| 35-39 | 3.60 | 4.75 | 6.40 | 7.40 | 7.68 |
| 40-44 | 4.25 | 5.40 | 7.05 | 7.74 | 7.42 |
| 45-49 | 5.00 | 6.15 | 7.80 | 9.08 | 8.26 |
| 50-54 | 4.75 | 5.90 | 7.55 | 8.83 | 8.93 |
| 55-59 | 3.25 | 4.60 | 6.55 | 7.85 | 9.64 |
| 60-64 | 2.85 | 3.40 | 4.20 | 4.72 | 7.10 |
| 65+ | 2.00 | 1.85 | 1.65 | 1.67 | 1.55 |

Fuente(s): (1) EPPA3; (2) ASTER; (3) ADNU88 y STAT.

### 2.2 Método(s): interpolación y extrapolación lineares

#### 2.2.1 Hombres:

- 1950-90, interpolación y extrapolación de las tasas de actividad 1950-70 con base en EPPA3 y de las tasas de actividad ajustadas con base el censo de 1973 y de las tasas de actividad con base en el censo 1984.

#### 2.2.2 Mujeres:

- 1950-70, tasas de actividad ajustadas 1950-70 con base en EPPA3;
- 1980-90, interpolación y extrapolación de las tasas de actividad 1970 con base en EPPA3 y de las tasas de actividad ajustadas con base en los censos de 1973 y 1984;
el ajuste se ha calculado con base en el modelo de ajuste de las tasas de actividad de las mujeres ocupadas en la agricultura como auxiliares familiares.

## 3. Evaluación de las tasas de distribución por sector de actividad: 1950 - 1990

### 3.1 Datos básicos:

Cuadro 2: Distribución de la población económicamente activa por sector de actividad en %

| Año | Agricultura | Industria Total | Manufac. | Servicios |
|---|---|---|---|---|
| **Hombres** | | | | |
| 1973 (1) | 22.54 | 27.21 | 4.28 | 50.24 |
| 1984 (2) | 12.60 | 29.27 | 6.12 | 58.13 |
| **Mujeres** | | | | |
| 1976 (1) | 38.85 | 6.37 | 4.61 | 54.78 |
| 1984 (2) | 12.12 | 6.49 | 3.99 | 81.39 |

Fuente(s): (1) ASTER; (2) STAT.

### 3.2 Método(s): promedio ponderado
extrapolación linear

#### 3.2.1 Hombres:

- 1950-70, tasas de distribución 1950-70 con base en EPPA3;
- 1980, promedios ponderados de las tasas de distribución ajustadas con base en el censo de 1973 y de las tasas con base en el censo de 1984;
- 1990, extrapolación de las tasas de distribución ajustadas con base en el censo de 1973 y de las tasas con base en el censo de 1984;
el censo de 1973 y de las tasas con base en el censo de 1984;

#### 3.2.2 Mujeres:

Métodos, hipótesis y tratamientos idénticos a los que se aplican a los hombres.

## 4. Proyección de las tasas de actividad: 2000 - 2010

### 4.1 Modelo(s): linear y hiperbólico

#### 4.1.1 Hombres:

- Para los grupos de edad [15+], aplicación de la función F3;
- Modificación de las tendencias de los grupos de edad [20-59].

#### 4.1.2 Mujeres:

- Para los grupos de edad [15+], aplicación de la función F1;
- Modificación de las tendencias de todos los grupos de edad.

*Notas sobre los ajustes de las tasas, véase p.380-384.*

*Notas sobre las funciones de proyección, véase p. 386.*

# Jamaica

## 1. Fuente(s) de los datos básicos

Código(s): Título(s):

EPPA3 Estimaciones y proyecciones de la población económicamente activa, 1950-2025, tercera edición, OIT, Ginebra, 1986.
STAT Base de datos de la OIT sobre estadísticas del trabajo - LABORSTA, Oficina de Estadística, OIT, Ginebra.

## 2. Evaluación de las tasas de actividad: 1950 - 1990

### 2.1 Datos básicos:

Cuadro 1: Tasas de actividad por sexo y grupo de edad

| Grupo de edad | Año 1980 (1) | 1990 (2) |
|---|---|---|
| **Hombres** | | |
| 10-14 | 0.60 | 0.30 |
| 15-19 | 52.00 | 39.66 |
| 20-24 | 94.50 | 92.57 |
| 25-29 | 96.60 | 93.91 |
| 30-34 | 97.90 | 96.14 |
| 35-39 | 97.90 | 96.24 |
| 40-44 | 98.00 | 96.33 |
| 45-49 | 97.40 | 95.74 |
| 50-54 | 96.30 | 93.93 |
| 55-59 | 92.50 | 88.80 |
| 60-64 | 84.00 | 78.78 |
| 65+ | 58.90 | 53.64 |
| **Mujeres** | | |
| 10-14 | 0.30 | 0.10 |
| 15-19 | 40.00 | 31.70 |
| 20-24 | 82.50 | 80.33 |
| 25-29 | 87.80 | 82.83 |
| 30-34 | 87.70 | 85.95 |
| 35-39 | 87.60 | 88.46 |
| 40-44 | 87.30 | 88.16 |
| 45-49 | 87.00 | 88.00 |
| 50-54 | 77.00 | 77.89 |
| 55-59 | 70.00 | 72.10 |
| 60-64 | 47.00 | 46.06 |
| 65+ | 9.90 | 23.58 |

Fuente(s): (1) EPPA3; (2) STAT.

### 2.2 Método(s): interpolación linear

#### 2.2.1 Hombres:

- 1950-80, tasas de actividad 1950-80 con base en EPPA3;
- 1990, interpolación de las tasas de actividad 1980 con base en EPPA3
y de las tasas de actividad ajustadas con base en la encuesta de 1990 .

#### 2.2.2 Mujeres:

- 1950-80, tasas de actividad ajustadas 1950-80 con base en EPPA3;
ajuste de las tasas de actividad de los grupos de edad [65+] para 1970 y 1980;
- 1990, interpolación de las tasas de actividad ajustadas 1980 con base
en EPPA3 y de las tasas de actividad con base en la encuesta de 1990.

## 3. Evaluación de las tasas de distribución por sector de actividad: 1950 - 1990

### 3.1 Datos básicos:

Cuadro 2: Distribución de la población económicamente activa por sector de actividad en %

| Año | Agricultura | Industria Total | Manufac. | Servicios |
|---|---|---|---|---|
| **Hombres** | | | | |
| 1981 | 44.78 | 22.38 | 13.88 | 32.85 |
| 1990 | 33.56 | 32.04 | 18.88 | 34.39 |
| **Mujeres** | | | | |
| 1981 | 20.78 | 7.35 | 6.90 | 71.87 |
| 1990 | 14.53 | 13.11 | 12.42 | 72.36 |

Fuente(s): STAT.

### 3.2 Método(s): datos del país

#### 3.2.1 Hombres:

- 1950-80, tasas de distribución 1950-80 con base en EPPA3;
- 1990, tasas de distribución con base en la encuesta de 1981;
- Aplicación de la razón manufacturas/industria con base en la encuesta de 1981

#### 3.2.2 Mujeres:

Métodos, hipótesis y tratamientos idénticos a los que se aplican a los hombres.

## 4. Proyección de las tasas de actividad: 2000 - 2010

### 4.1 Modelo(s): linear, log-linear, hiperbólico y logístico

#### 4.1.1 Hombres:

- Para el grupo de edad [15-19], aplicación de la función F2;
- Para los grupos de edad [20-24] y [65+], aplicación de la función F1;
- Para los grupos de edad [25-64], aplicación de la función F3;
- Modificación de las tendencias de los grupos de edad [20-59].

#### 4.1.2 Mujeres:

- Para el grupo de edad [15-19], aplicación de la función F2;
- Para los grupos de edad [20-59], aplicación de la función F6;
- Para los grupos de edad [60+], aplicación de la función F1;
- Modificación de las tendencias de los grupos de edad [20+].

*Notas sobre los ajustes de las tasas, véase p.380-384.*     *Notas sobre las funciones de proyección, véase p. 386.*

# Japón

## 1. Fuente(s) de los datos básicos

Código(s):  Título(s):

EPPA3   Estimaciones y proyecciones de la población económicamente activa, 1950-2025, tercera edición, OIT, Ginebra, 1986.
STAT    Base de datos de la OIT sobre estadísticas del trabajo - LABORSTA, Oficina de Estadística, OIT, Ginebra.

## 2. Evaluación de las tasas de actividad: 1950 - 1990

### 2.1 Datos básicos:

Cuadro 1: Tasas de actividad por sexo y grupo de edad

| Grupo de edad | Año 1980 (1) | 1980 (2) | 1990 (1) | 1990 (2) |
|---|---|---|---|---|
| **Hombres** | | | | |
| 10-14 | 0.00 | .. | 0.00 | .. |
| 15-19 | 20.34 | .. | 19.94 | .. |
| 20-24 | 74.74 | .. | 75.40 | .. |
| 25-29 | 97.58 | .. | 96.69 | .. |
| 30-34 | 98.60 | .. | 98.06 | .. |
| 35-39 | 98.68 | .. | 98.15 | .. |
| 40-44 | 98.42 | .. | 98.13 | .. |
| 45-49 | 97.99 | .. | 97.90 | .. |
| 50-54 | 97.30 | .. | 97.05 | .. |
| 55-59 | 93.99 | .. | 93.99 | .. |
| 60-64 | 81.45 | .. | 76.14 | .. |
| 65+ | 46.01 | .. | 39.44 | .. |
| **Mujeres** | | | | |
| 10-14 | 0.00 | 0.00 | 0.00 | 0.00 |
| 15-19 | 18.76 | 18.50 | 17.35 | 17.80 |
| 20-24 | 71.13 | 70.00 | 75.54 | 75.10 |
| 25-29 | 49.43 | 49.20 | 61.25 | 61.40 |
| 30-34 | 46.47 | 48.35 | 50.71 | 51.70 |
| 35-39 | 55.54 | 57.77 | 59.42 | 62.60 |
| 40-44 | 61.82 | 64.31 | 66.74 | 69.60 |
| 45-49 | 62.27 | 64.40 | 68.33 | 71.70 |
| 50-54 | 58.73 | 59.30 | 62.96 | 65.50 |
| 55-59 | 50.66 | 50.50 | 51.51 | 53.90 |
| 60-64 | 38.85 | 38.80 | 37.35 | 39.50 |
| 65+ | 16.14053 | 15.50 | 14.93 | 16.20 |

Nota(s): (1) Censos; (2) Encuesta.
Fuente(s): STAT.

### 2.2 Método(s): promedio ponderado
promedio aritmético

**2.2.1 Hombres:**

- 1950-80, tasas de actividad 1950-80 con base en EPPA3;
- 1990, promedios ponderados de las tasas de actividad con base en los censos de 1980 y 1990.

**2.2.2 Mujeres:**

- 1950-70, tasas de actividad 1950-70 con base en EPPA3;
- 1980, promedios de las tasas de actividad con base en el censo de 1980 y la encuesta de 1980;
- 1990, promedios de las tasas de actividad con base en la encuesta de 1990 y el censo de 1990.

## 3. Evaluación de las tasas de distribución por sector de actividad: 1950 - 1990

### 3.1 Datos básicos:

Cuadro 2: Distribución de la población económicamente activa por sector de actividad en %

| Año | Agricultura | Industria Total | Manufac. | Servicios |
|---|---|---|---|---|
| **Hombres** | | | | |
| 1985 (1) | 8.22 | 38.39 | 24.47 | 53.39 |
| 1990 (1) | 6.50 | 39.00 | 24.67 | 54.50 |
| **Mujeres** | | | | |
| 1980 (1) | 13.74 | 26.37 | 22.72 | 59.89 |
| 1980 (2) | 13.24 | 28.48 | 24.65 | 58.28 |
| 1990 (1) | 8.17 | 26.45 | 22.63 | 65.39 |
| 1990 (2) | 8.51 | 27.56 | 23.56 | 63.92 |

Nota(s): (1) Censo; (2) Encuesta.
Fuente(s): STAT.

### 3.2 Método(s): promedio ponderado
promedio aritmético

**3.2.1 Hombres:**

- 1950-80, tasas de distribución 1950-80 con base en EPPA3;
- 1980, promedios ponderados de las tasas de distribución ajustadas con base en los censos de 1985 y 1990.

**3.2.2 Mujeres:**

- 1950-70, tasas de distribución 1950-70 con base en EPPA3;
- 1980, promedios de las tasas de distribución con base en la encuesta de 1980 y el censo de 1980;
- 1990, promedios de las tasas de distribución con base en la encuesta de 1990 y el censo de 1990.

## 4. Proyección de las tasas de actividad: 2000 - 2010

### 4.1 Modelo(s): linear y hiperbólico

**4.1.1 Hombres:**

- Para los grupos de edad [15-24], aplicación de la función F3;
- Para los grupos de edad [25+], aplicación de la función F1;
- Modificación de las tendencias de los grupos de edad [25+].

**4.1.2 Mujeres:**

- Para los grupos de edad [15-44], [50-59] y [65+], aplicación de la función F3;
- Para los grupos de edad [45-49] y [60-64], aplicación de la función F1;
- Modificación de las tendencias de los grupos de edad [20-64].

*Notas sobre los ajustes de las tasas, véase p.380-384.*     *Notas sobre las funciones de proyección, véase p. 386.*

# Jordania

## 1. Fuente(s) de los datos básicos

Código(s):  Título(s):
EPPA3       Estimaciones y proyecciones de la población económicamente activa, 1950-2025, tercera edición, OIT, Ginebra, 1986.
ASTER       Anuario de estadísticas del trabajo 1945-89 - Edición retrospectiva sobre los censos de población, OIT, Ginebra, 1990.
ESCWA       Compedium of Social Statistics Indicators, Third Issue, December 1993, Economic and Social Commission for Western Asia.

## 2. Evaluación de las tasas de actividad: 1950 - 1990

### 2.1 Datos básicos:

Cuadro 1: Tasas de actividad por sexo y grupo de edad

| Grupo de edad | Año | | | | | |
|---|---|---|---|---|---|---|
| | 1970 (1) | 1960 (1) | 1970 (1) | 1979 (2) | 1980 (1) | 1987 (3) |
| **Hombres** | | | | | | |
| 10-14 | 17.70 | 13.90 | 10.30 | .. | 6.40 | .. |
| 15-19 | 60.00 | 55.00 | 52.00 | .. | 37.00 | .. |
| 20-24 | 88.20 | 87.30 | 86.70 | .. | 84.50 | .. |
| 25-29 | 96.90 | 96.70 | 96.40 | .. | 96.25 | .. |
| 30-34 | 98.10 | 97.90 | 97.70 | .. | 97.50 | .. |
| 35-39 | 98.10 | 97.90 | 97.70 | .. | 97.50 | .. |
| 40-44 | 96.80 | 96.55 | 96.30 | .. | 96.30 | .. |
| 45-49 | 96.80 | 96.20 | 95.40 | .. | 94.90 | .. |
| 50-54 | 94.10 | 93.40 | 92.70 | .. | 92.20 | .. |
| 55-59 | 90.00 | 89.00 | 88.00 | .. | 87.20 | .. |
| 60-64 | 83.60 | 81.50 | 79.20 | .. | 76.00 | .. |
| 65+ | 55.80 | 51.60 | 47.90 | | 38.70 | |
| **Mujeres** | | | | | | |
| 10-14 | .. | .. | .. | 1.20 | .. | 0.24 |
| 15-19 | .. | .. | .. | 3.44 | .. | 2.15 |
| 20-24 | .. | .. | .. | 15.69 | .. | 20.06 |
| 25-29 | .. | .. | .. | 13.51 | .. | 16.83 |
| 30-34 | .. | .. | .. | 8.66 | .. | 12.03 |
| 35-39 | .. | .. | .. | 5.15 | .. | 8.38 |
| 40-44 | .. | .. | .. | 3.26 | .. | 6.68 |
| 45-49 | .. | .. | .. | 2.38 | .. | 5.72 |
| 50-54 | .. | .. | .. | 2.04 | .. | 4.80 |
| 55-59 | .. | .. | .. | 1.81 | .. | 3.91 |
| 60-64 | .. | .. | .. | 1.06 | .. | 1.23 |
| 65+ | | | | 0.49 | | 0.54 |

Fuente(s): (1) EPPA3; (2) ASTER; (3) ESCWA.

### 2.2 Método(s): interpolación y extrapolación lineares

**2.2.1 Hombres:**

- 1950-80, tasas de actividad 1950-80 con base en EPPA3;
- 1990, extrapolación de las tasas de actividad 1950-80 con base en EPPA3;
ajuste de las tasas extrapoladas con base en las variaciones de las tasas
interpoladas 1980, en relación con las tasas 1980 con base en EPPA3.

**2.2.2 Mujeres:**

- 1950-70, tasas de actividad 1950-70 con base en EPPA3;
- 1980-90, interpolación y extrapolación de las tasas de actividad
con base en el censo de 1979 y de las tasas con base en estimaciones
de 1986 del ESCWA ;
el ajuste se ha calculado con base en el modelo de ajuste de las tasas de
actividad de las mujeres ocupadas en la agricultura como auxiliares familiares.

## 3. Evaluación de las tasas de distribución por sector de actividad: 1950 - 1990

### 3.1 Datos básicos:

Cuadro 2: Distribución de la población económicamente activa por sector de actividad en %

| Año | Agricultura | Industria | | Servicios |
|---|---|---|---|---|
| | | Total | Manufac. | |
| **Hombres** | | | | |
| 1950 (1) | 55.00 | 25.70 | .. | 19.30 |
| 1960 (1) | 46.00 | 26.00 | .. | 28.00 |
| 1970 (1) | 28.50 | 26.60 | .. | 44.90 |
| 1979 (2) | 12.13 | 27.17 | 8.05 | 60.69 |
| 1980 (1) | 11.00 | 27.20 | | 61.80 |
| **Mujeres** | | | | |
| 1950 (1) | 44.00 | 24.00 | | 32.00 |
| 1960 (1) | 35.00 | 24.00 | | 41.00 |
| 1970 (1) | 18.00 | 15.50 | .. | 66.50 |
| 1979 (2) | 1.23 | 7.42 | 6.43 | 91.34 |

Fuente(s): (1) EPPA3; (2) ASTER.

### 3.2 Método(s): extrapolación linear

**3.2.1 Hombres:**

- 1950-80, tasas de distribución 1950-80 con base en EPPA3;
- 1990, extrapolación de las tasas de distribución 1950-80 con base en EPPA3
y de las tasas de distribución con base en el censo de 1979;
modificación de las tendencias de todos los sectores.

**3.2.2 Mujeres:**

- 1950-70, tasas de distribución 1950-70 con base en EPPA3;
- 1980-90, extrapolación de las tasas de distribución 1950-70 con base en EPP/
y de las tasas de distribución con base en el censo de 1979;
modificación de las tendencias de todos los sectores.

## 4. Proyección de las tasas de actividad: 2000 - 2010

### 4.1 Modelo(s): linear y hiperbólico

**4.1.1 Hombres:**

- Para los grupos de edad [15+], aplicación de la función F3;
- Modificación de las tendencias de los grupos de edad [35-39] y [45-54].

**4.1.2 Mujeres:**

- Para los grupos de edad [15+], aplicación de la función F1;
- Modificación de las tendencias de los grupos de edad [15+].

# Kazakstán

## 1. Fuente(s) de los datos básicos

Código(s):    Título(s):

BLT-94-2    Vorobiev A. (1994), "Estimaciones de la población económicamente activa de los quince países de la ex URSS, en 1950, 1959, 1970, 1979 y 1989", en el Boletín de Estadísticas del Trabajol - 1994-2, OIT, Ginebra.

## 2. Evaluación de las tasas de actividad: 1950 - 1990

### 2.1 Datos básicos:

Cuadro 1: Tasas de actividad por sexo y grupo de edad

| Grupo de edad | Año 1950 | 1959 | 1970 | 1979 | 1989 |
|---|---|---|---|---|---|
| **Hombres** | | | | | |
| 10-14 | 0.00 | 0.00 | 0.00 | 0.00 | 0.00 |
| 15-19 | 51.92 | 60.15 | 41.55 | 39.04 | 34.45 |
| 20-24 | 83.05 | 87.40 | 87.53 | 88.83 | 82.82 |
| 25-29 | 94.68 | 97.61 | 96.85 | 97.55 | 96.77 |
| 30-34 | 94.22 | 95.66 | 98.30 | 98.71 | 98.09 |
| 35-39 | 93.41 | 95.58 | 98.14 | 98.30 | 98.03 |
| 40-44 | 94.01 | 93.41 | 97.20 | 97.91 | 97.95 |
| 45-49 | 91.67 | 92.13 | 96.08 | 96.72 | 96.64 |
| 50-54 | 85.83 | 86.93 | 88.51 | 90.97 | 92.50 |
| 55-59 | 16.00 | 79.28 | 80.12 | 78.23 | 80.74 |
| 60-64 | 54.69 | 70.10 | 34.56 | 24.59 | 28.94 |
| 65+ | 30.35 | 26.84 | 7.32 | 9.69 | 9.16 |
| **Mujeres** | | | | | |
| 10-14 | 0.00 | 0.00 | 0.00 | 0.00 | 0.00 |
| 15-19 | 48.29 | 50.67 | 33.28 | 33.04 | 25.04 |
| 20-24 | 58.06 | 59.21 | 80.74 | 82.41 | 73.42 |
| 25-29 | 62.36 | 67.69 | 84.42 | 90.69 | 84.70 |
| 30-34 | 60.50 | 59.24 | 82.46 | 92.33 | 88.87 |
| 35-39 | 52.78 | 55.09 | 93.61 | 93.04 | 91.62 |
| 40-44 | 47.64 | 49.79 | 83.11 | 92.36 | 91.85 |
| 45-49 | 46.41 | 46.64 | 82.09 | 88.47 | 88.32 |
| 50-54 | 33.33 | 32.86 | 65.47 | 74.07 | 71.85 |
| 55-59 | 19.83 | 19.91 | 21.71 | 25.10 | 25.95 |
| 60-64 | 9.38 | 11.18 | 8.23 | 7.27 | 12.89 |
| 65+ | 2.94 | 2.10 | 1.76 | 1.66 | 3.12 |

Fuente(s): BLT-94-2-2

### 2.2 Método(s):  promedio ponderado

#### 2.2.1 Hombres:

- 1950-90, promedios ponderados de las tasas de actividad 1950, 1959, 1970 y 1989 con base en el Boletín de estadísticas del trabajo 1994-2.

#### 2.2.2 Mujeres:

Métodos, hipótesis y tratamientos idénticos a los que se aplican a los hombres.

## 3. Evaluación de las tasas de distribución  por sector de actividad: 1950 - 1990

### 3.1 Datos básicos:

Cuadro  2: Distribución de la población económicamente activa por sector de actividad en %

| Año | Agricultura | Industria Total | Manufac. | Servicios |
|---|---|---|---|---|
| **Hombres** | | | | |
| 1950 | 53.30 | 21.94 | 10.57 | 24.76 |
| 1959 | 38.25 | 24.35 | 10.55 | 37.40 |
| 1970 | 29.30 | 38.08 | 16.09 | 32.62 |
| 1979 | 28.38 | 37.97 | 16.13 | 33.65 |
| 1989 | 28.16 | 37.41 | 15.03 | 34.43 |
| **Mujeres** | | | | |
| 1950 | 58.18 | 14.68 | 9.28 | 27.14 |
| 1959 | 40.44 | 21.20 | 11.98 | 38.36 |
| 1970 | 24.34 | 21.18 | 16.69 | 54.49 |
| 1979 | 20.79 | 24.80 | 15.94 | 54.41 |
| 1989 | 16.00 | 24.78 | 15.78 | 59.22 |

Fuente(s): BLT-94-2.

### 3.2 Método(s):  promedio ponderado

#### 3.2.1 Hombres:

- 1950-90, promedios ponderados de las tasas de distribución 1950, 1959, 1970,  1979 y 1989 con base en el Boletín de estadísticas del trabajo 1994-2.

#### 3.2.2 Mujeres:

Métodos, hipótesis y tratamientos idénticos a los que se aplican a los hombres.

## 4. Proyección de las tasas de actividad: 2000 - 2010

### 4.1 Modelo(s):  linear, log-linear, hiperbólico y logístico

#### 4.1.1 Hombres:

- Para el grupo de edad [15-19], aplicación de la función F2;
- Para los grupos de edad [20-24] y [60+], aplicación de la función F3;
- Para los grupos de edad [25-59], aplicación de la función F1;
- Modificación de las tendencias de los grupos de edad [25-59].

#### 4.1.2 Mujeres:

- Para el grupo de edad [15-19], aplicación de la función F3;
- Para los grupos de edad [20-24] y [50+], aplicación de la función F1;
- Para los grupos de edad [25-49], aplicación de la función F6;
- Modificación de las tendencias de los grupos de edad [15+].

---

*Notas sobre los ajustes de las tasas, véase p.380-384.*    *Notas sobre las funciones de proyección, véase p. 386.*

# Kenya

## 1. Fuente(s) de los datos básicos

Código(s):    Título(s):

EPPA3    Estimaciones y proyecciones de la población económicamente activa, 1950-2025, tercera edición, OIT, Ginebra, 1986.

## 2. Evaluación de las tasas de actividad: 1950 - 1990

### 2.1 Datos básicos:

Cuadro 1: Tasas de actividad por sexo y grupo de edad

| Grupo de edad | Año | | | |
|---|---|---|---|---|
| | 1950 | 1960 | 1970 | 1980 |
| **Hombres** | | | | |
| 10-14 | 50.70 | 49.75 | 48.40 | 46.45 |
| 15-19 | 83.00 | 81.80 | 80.00 | 77.35 |
| 20-24 | 94.55 | 94.05 | 93.35 | 92.35 |
| 25-29 | 97.30 | 97.20 | 97.10 | 96.95 |
| 30-34 | 98.00 | 97.95 | 97.80 | 97.65 |
| 35-39 | 98.20 | 98.10 | 97.95 | 97.80 |
| 40-44 | 98.00 | 97.90 | 97.80 | 97.60 |
| 45-49 | 97.25 | 97.20 | 97.10 | 96.90 |
| 50-54 | 96.80 | 96.65 | 96.50 | 96.25 |
| 55-59 | 95.80 | 95.65 | 95.35 | 95.00 |
| 60-64 | 92.65 | 92.35 | 91.90 | 91.25 |
| 65+ | 79.10 | 78.60 | 77.80 | 76.70 |
| **Mujeres** | | | | |
| 10-14 | 38.30 | 37.60 | 36.55 | 35.10 |
| 15-19 | 62.35 | 61.30 | 59.75 | 57.55 |
| 20-24 | 63.15 | 62.50 | 61.50 | 60.10 |
| 25-29 | 67.95 | 67.20 | 66.10 | 64.55 |
| 30-34 | 72.25 | 71.45 | 70.25 | 68.55 |
| 35-39 | 73.55 | 72.80 | 71.70 | 70.10 |
| 40-44 | 76.00 | 75.25 | 74.15 | 72.55 |
| 45-49 | 75.50 | 74.75 | 73.60 | 72.00 |
| 50-54 | 73.90 | 73.00 | 71.70 | 69.85 |
| 55-59 | 71.05 | 70.15 | 68.80 | 66.80 |
| 60-64 | 64.65 | 63.50 | 61.75 | 59.25 |
| 65+ | 44.70 | 43.60 | 42.00 | 39.70 |

Fuente(s): EPPA3.

### 2.2 Método(s): interpolación y extrapolación lineares

#### 2.2.1 Hombres:

- 1950-80, tasas de actividad 1950-80 con base en EPPA3;
- 1990, extrapolación de las tasas de actividad 1950-80 con base en EPPA3;
ajuste de las tasas extrapoladas con base en las variaciones de las tasas interpoladas 1980, en relación con las tasas 1980 con base en EPPA3.

#### 2.2.2 Mujeres:

- 1950-90, interpolación y extrapolación de las tasas de actividad 1950-80 con base en EPPA3;
ajuste de las tasas interpoladas y extrapoladas con base en las variaciones de las tasas interpoladas 1980, en relación con las tasas de actividad ajustadas 1980 con base en EPPA3;
ajuste de las tasas de actividad 1980 con base en la razón hombres/mujeres igual a 1 en la agricultura;

## 3. Evaluación de las tasas de distribución por sector de actividad: 1950 - 1990

### 3.1 Datos básicos:

Cuadro 2: Distribución de la población económicamente activa por sector de actividad en %

| Año | Agricultura | Industria | | Servicios |
|---|---|---|---|---|
| | | Total | Manufac. | |
| **Hombres** | | | | |
| 1950 | 85.00 | 6.50 | .. | 8.50 |
| 1960 | 83.30 | 7.15 | .. | 9.55 |
| 1970 | 80.80 | 8.20 | .. | 11.00 |
| 1980 | 77.20 | 9.80 | .. | 13.00 |
| **Mujeres** | | | | |
| 1950 | 95.00 | 1.00 | .. | 4.00 |
| 1960 | 92.00 | 1.45 | .. | 5.75 |
| 1970 | 90.30 | 1.95 | .. | 7.75 |
| 1980 | 86.30 | 2.75 | .. | 10.95 |

Fuente(s): EPPA3.

### 3.2 Método(s): interpolación y extrapolación lineares

#### 3.2.1 Hombres:

- 1950-80, tasas de distribución 1950-80 con base en EPPA3;
- 1990, extrapolación de las tasas de distribución 1950-80 con base en EPPA3; ajuste de las tasas extrapoladas 1990 con base en las variaciones de las tasas interpoladas 1980, en relación con las tasas 1980 con base en EPPA3;
- Aplicación de la razón manufacturas/industria estimada para Malawi.
- Aplicación de la razón manufacturas/industria estimada para Malawi.

#### 3.2.2 Mujeres:

- 1980, tasas de distribución estimadas con base en la razón hombres/mujeres igual a 1 en la agricultura;
- 1950-70 y 1990, interpolación y extrapolación de las tasas de distribución 1950-70 con base en EPPA3 y de las tasas estimadas 1980; ajuste de las tasas extrapoladas 1990 con base en las variaciones de las tasas interpoladas 1980, en relación con las tasas 1980 estimadas;
- Aplicación de la razón manufacturas/industria estimada para Malawi.

## 4. Proyección de las tasas de actividad: 2000 - 2010

### 4.1 Modelo(s): linear y hiperbólico

#### 4.1.1 Hombres:

- Para todos los grupos de edad, aplicación de la función F1;
- Modificación de las tendencias de los grupos de edad [10-24] y [60+].

#### 4.1.2 Mujeres:

- Para los grupos de edad [10-19], aplicación de la función F1;
- Para los grupos de edad [20+], aplicación de la función F3;
- Modificación de las tendencias de los grupos de edad [10-14] y [65+].

# Kirguistán

## 1. Fuente(s) de los datos básicos

Código(s):   Título(s):

BLT-94-2   Vorobiev A. (1994), "Estimaciones de la población económicamente activa de los quince países de la ex URSS, en 1950, 1959, 1970, 1979 y 1989", en el Boletín de Estadísticas del Trabajol - 1994-2, OIT, Ginebra.

## 2. Evaluación de las tasas de actividad: 1950 - 1990

### 2.1 Datos básicos:

Cuadro 1: Tasas de actividad por sexo y grupo de edad

| Grupo de edad | Año 1950 | 1959 | 1970 | 1979 | 1989 |
|---|---|---|---|---|---|
| **Hombres** | | | | | |
| 10-14 | 0.00 | 0.00 | 0.00 | 0.00 | 0.00 |
| 15-19 | 48.89 | 51.85 | 35.04 | 37.44 | 27.88 |
| 20-24 | 82.14 | 84.88 | 84.52 | 87.80 | 80.66 |
| 25-29 | 91.84 | 95.35 | 94.44 | 96.88 | 96.28 |
| 30-34 | 92.11 | 95.00 | 98.08 | 98.65 | 98.08 |
| 35-39 | 93.18 | 95.24 | 97.73 | 97.53 | 98.35 |
| 40-44 | 94.29 | 93.75 | 96.55 | 97.87 | 97.01 |
| 45-49 | 90.63 | 91.89 | 95.74 | 96.30 | 95.95 |
| 50-54 | 87.88 | 90.00 | 90.32 | 90.41 | 91.36 |
| 55-59 | 76.92 | 81.48 | 82.86 | 80.56 | 82.61 |
| 60-64 | 64.00 | 74.07 | 46.67 | 26.92 | 28.81 |
| 65+ | 26.79 | 33.93 | 7.25 | 6.67 | 10.29 |
| **Mujeres** | | | | | |
| 10-14 | 0.00 | 0.00 | 0.00 | 0.00 | 0.00 |
| 15-19 | 43.75 | 47.30 | 31.21 | 33.17 | 25.50 |
| 20-24 | 61.70 | 66.67 | 79.57 | 84.05 | 74.03 |
| 25-29 | 68.57 | 76.67 | 85.92 | 90.70 | 84.29 |
| 30-34 | 66.07 | 69.32 | 87.62 | 92.00 | 87.42 |
| 35-39 | 66.10 | 70.49 | 88.76 | 92.50 | 90.32 |
| 40-44 | 59.18 | 63.83 | 87.23 | 92.55 | 91.30 |
| 45-49 | 55.00 | 56.00 | 84.85 | 89.66 | 89.19 |
| 50-54 | 40.43 | 42.86 | 70.21 | 73.86 | 62.07 |
| 55-59 | 26.32 | 28.85 | 27.59 | 26.23 | 23.17 |
| 60-64 | 15.15 | 14.63 | 10.00 | 8.51 | 12.82 |
| 65+ | 2.70 | 3.95 | 1.77 | 2.19 | 3.45 |

Fuente(s): BLT-94-2-2

### 2.2 Método(s): promedio ponderado

**2.2.1 Hombres:**

- 1950-90, promedios ponderados de las tasas de actividad 1950, 1959, 1971 y 1989 con base en el Boletín de estadísticas del trabajo 1994-2.

**2.2.2 Mujeres:**

Métodos, hipótesis y tratamientos idénticos a los que se aplican a los hombres.

## 3. Evaluación de las tasas de distribución por sector de actividad: 1950 - 1990

### 3.1 Datos básicos:

Cuadro 2: Distribución de la población económicamente activa por sector de actividad en %

| Año | Agricultura | Industria Total | Manufac. | Servicios |
|---|---|---|---|---|
| **Hombres** | | | | |
| 1950 | 69.15 | 13.30 | 9.57 | 17.55 |
| 1959 | 61.37 | 3.01 | 15.89 | 35.62 |
| 1970 | 35.00 | 35.00 | 17.59 | 30.00 |
| 1979 | 34.28 | 34.28 | 15.59 | 31.44 |
| 1989 | 35.57 | 30.78 | 13.74 | 33.65 |
| **Mujeres** | | | | |
| 1950 | 71.74 | 9.32 | 7.76 | 18.94 |
| 1959 | 57.14 | 16.17 | 11.32 | 26.68 |
| 1970 | 36.40 | 23.90 | 17.65 | 39.71 |
| 1979 | 33.66 | 23.46 | 17.32 | 42.88 |
| 1989 | 28.59 | 22.65 | 16.46 | 48.76 |

Fuente(s): BLT-94-2.

### 3.2 Método(s): promedio ponderado

**3.2.1 Hombres:**

- 1950-90, promedios ponderados de las tasas de distribución 1950, 1959, 1970, 1979 y 1989 con base en el Boletín de estadísticas del trabajo 1994-2.

**3.2.2 Mujeres:**

Métodos, hipótesis y tratamientos idénticos a los que se aplican a los hombres.

## 4. Proyección de las tasas de actividad: 2000 - 2010

### 4.1 Modelo(s): linear, hiperbólico y logístico

**4.1.1 Hombres:**

- Para los grupos de edad [15-24] y [60+], aplicación de la función F3;
- Para los grupos de edad [25-59], aplicación de la función F1;
- Modificación de las tendencias de los grupos de edad [25-59].

**4.1.2 Mujeres:**

- Para los grupos de edad [15-24] y [65+], aplicación de la función F3;
- Para los grupos de edad [25-64], aplicación de la función F6;
- Modificación de las tendencias de los grupos de edad [20+];
- Modificación de las tendencias de los grupos de edad [15+].

*Notas sobre los ajustes de las tasas, véase p.380-384.*

*Notas sobre las funciones de proyección, véase p. 386.*

# Kuwait

## 1. Fuente(s) de los datos básicos

Código(s):   Título(s):

EPPA3     Estimaciones y proyecciones de la población económicamente activa, 1950-2025, tercera edición, OIT, Ginebra, 1986.
ASTER     Anuario de estadísticas del trabajo 1945-89 - Edición retrospectiva sobre los censos de población, OIT, Ginebra, 1990.
AST92     Anuario de Estadísticas del Trabjo 1992, OIT, Ginebra, 1992.

## 2. Evaluación de las tasas de actividad: 1950 - 1990

### 2.1 Datos básicos:

Cuadro 1: Tasas de actividad por sexo y grupo de edad

| Grupo de edad | Año 1975 (1) | 1980 (1) | 1985 (1) | 1988 (2) |
|---|---|---|---|---|
| **Hombres** | | | | |
| 10-14 | .. | 0.00 | 0.00 | 0.00 |
| 15-19 | .. | 34.74 | 14.20 | 9.04 |
| 20-24 | .. | 86.16 | 79.67 | 73.32 |
| 25-29 | .. | 97.64 | 97.72 | 97.61 |
| 30-34 | .. | 98.69 | 99.15 | 99.52 |
| 35-39 | .. | 98.49 | 98.96 | 99.33 |
| 40-44 | .. | 97.52 | 96.34 | 97.59 |
| 45-49 | .. | 95.57 | 91.20 | 91.87 |
| 50-54 | .. | 90.92 | 86.61 | 84.83 |
| 55-59 | .. | 84.39 | 79.45 | 79.90 |
| 60-64 | .. | 67.20 | 63.97 | 58.46 |
| 65+ | .. | 33.61 | 20.64 | 15.71 |
| **Mujeres** | | | | |
| 10-14 | 0.00 | 0.00 | 0.00 | 0.00 |
| 15-19 | 4.62 | 4.99 | 6.28 | 4.59 |
| 20-24 | 15.31 | 21.36 | 37.07 | 42.13 |
| 25-29 | 19.81 | 29.92 | 47.38 | 55.32 |
| 30-34 | 18.90 | 27.35 | 45.19 | 52.10 |
| 35-39 | 19.16 | 23.88 | 37.59 | 42.04 |
| 40-44 | 21.42 | 24.13 | 29.54 | 31.77 |
| 45-49 | 19.99 | 21.83 | 24.29 | 22.88 |
| 50-54 | 15.89 | 18.93 | 18.19 | 18.89 |
| 55-59 | 10.41 | 13.21 | 13.14 | 13.44 |
| 60-64 | 6.37 | 7.63 | 7.23 | 10.19 |
| 65+ | 2.61 | 2.80 | 1.48 | 0.69 |

**Fuente(s)**: (1) ASTER; (2) AST92.

### 2.2 Método(s):   interpolación y extrapolación lineares

#### 2.2.1 Hombres:

- 1950-70, tasas de actividad 1950-70 con base en EPPA3;
- 1980-90, interpolación y extrapolación de las tasas de actividad con base en los censos de 1977 y 1986 y de las tasas de actividad con base en la encuesta de 1989;
ajuste de las tasas interpoladas y extrapoladas con base en las variaciones de las tasas interpoladas 1980, en relación con las tasas de actividad con base en el censo de 1980.

#### 2.2.2 Mujeres:

- 1950-70, tasas de actividad 1950-70 con base en EPPA3;
- 1980-90, interpolación y extrapolación de las tasas de actividad con base en los censos de 1975, 1980 y 1985 y la encuesta de 1988;
ajuste de las tasas interpoladas y extrapoladas con base en las variaciones de las tasas interpoladas 1980, en relación con las tasas de actividad con base en el censo de 1980.

## 3. Evaluación de las tasas de distribución por sector de actividad: 1950 - 1990

### 3.1 Datos básicos:

Cuadro 2: Distribución de la población económicamente activa por sector de actividad en %

| Año | Agricultura | Industria Total | Manufac. | Servicios |
|---|---|---|---|---|
| **Hombres** | | | | |
| 1975 (1) | 2.84 | 25.88 | 9.15 | 71.28 |
| 1980 (1) | 2.15 | 35.93 | 9.61 | 61.92 |
| 1985 (1) | 2.35 | 35.07 | 9.35 | 62.58 |
| 1988 (2) | 1.67 | 32.99 | 9.76 | 65.34 |
| **Mujeres** | | | | |
| 1975 (1) | 0.06 | 1.83 | 0.98 | 98.11 |
| 1980 (1) | 0.13 | 2.52 | 1.16 | 97.35 |
| 1985 (1) | 0.09 | 2.21 | 0.98 | 97.70 |
| 1988 (2) | 0.08 | 1.92 | 0.83 | 98.00 |

**Fuente(s)**: (1) ASTER; (2) AST91; (3) AST93.

### 3.2 Método(s):   extrapolación linear

#### 3.2.1 Hombres:

- 1950-80, tasas de distribución 1950-80 con base en EPPA3;
- 1990, extrapolación de las tasas de distribución con base en los censos de 1975, 1980 y 1985 y de las tasas con base en la encuesta de 1988; modificación de las tendencias de todos los sectores;
- Aplicación de la razón manufacturas/industria con base en la encuesta de 1988
- Aplicación de la razón manufacturas/industria con base en la encuesta de 1988

#### 3.2.2 Mujeres:

Métodos, hipótesis y tratamientos idénticos a los que se aplican a los hombres.

## 4. Proyección de las tasas de actividad: 2000 - 2010

### 4.1 Modelo(s):   linear, hiperbólico y logístico

#### 4.1.1 Hombres:

- Para el grupo de edad [15-19], aplicación de la función F3;
- Para los grupos de edad [20+], aplicación de la función F1;
- Modificación de las tendencias de los grupos de edad [20-24] y [60+].

#### 4.1.2 Mujeres:

- Para los grupos de edad [15-39], aplicación de la función F1;
- Para los grupos de edad [40-64], aplicación de la función F6;
- Para el grupo de edad [65+], aplicación de la función F3;
- Modificación de las tendencias de los grupos de edad [15-64].

*Notas sobre los ajustes de las tasas, véase p.380-384.*          *Notas sobre las funciones de proyección, véase p. 386.*

# La Faja de Gaza

## 1. Fuente(s) de los datos básicos

Código(s):　Título(s):

EPPA3　　Estimaciones y proyecciones de la población económicamente activa, 1950-2025, tercera edición, OIT, Ginebra, 1986.

LFS-97-93　Labour Force Statistics in the West Bank and Gaza Strip, Curent Status Report Series (No.3), Palestinian Central Bureau of Statistics, Ramallah-West Bank, 1995.

## 2. Evaluación de las tasas de actividad: 1950 - 1990

### 2.1 Datos básicos:

Cuadro 1: Tasas de actividad por sexo y grupo de edad

| Grupo de edad | Año | | | |
|---|---|---|---|---|
| | 1987 | 1989 | 1991 | 1993 |
| **Hombres** | | | | |
| Total | 71.00 | 67.00 | 68.00 | 68.00 |
| 15-24 | 34.00 | 32.00 | 30.00 | 30.00 |
| 25-64 | 85.00 | 83.00 | 87.00 | 86.00 |
| 65+ | 29.00 | 19.00 | 20.00 | 14.00 |
| **Mujeres** | | | | |
| Total | 3.00 | 2.00 | 1.70 | 1.80 |
| 15-24 | 1.50 | 0.60 | 0.60 | 0.30 |
| 25-64 | 4.00 | 3.10 | 2.50 | 2.90 |
| 65+ | 1.30 | 0.10 | 0.20 | 0.30 |

Fuente(s): LFS-87-93.

### 2.2 Método(s): interpolación y extrapolación lineares

#### 2.2.1 Hombres:

- 1950-90, interpolación y extrapolación de las tasas de actividad ajustadas con base en las encuestas de 1987, 1989, 1991 y 1993; modificación de las tendencias de todos los grupos de edad.

#### 2.2.2 Mujeres:

Métodos, hipótesis y tratamientos idénticos a los que se aplican a los hombres.

## 3. Evaluación de las tasas de distribución por sector de actividad: 1950 - 1990

### 3.1 Datos básicos:

Cuadro 2: Distribución de la población económicamente activa por sector de actividad en %

| Año | Agricultura | Industria | | Servicios |
|---|---|---|---|---|
| | | Total | Manufac. | |
| **Hombres** | | | | |
| 1950 | 40.50 | 25.00 | .. | 34.50 |
| 1960 | 32.00 | 31.40 | .. | 36.60 |
| 1970 | 31.70 | 32.80 | .. | 35.50 |
| **Mujeres** | | | | |
| 1950 | 64.00 | 22.00 | .. | 14.00 |
| 1960 | 62.00 | 18.50 | .. | 19.50 |
| 1970 | 51.90 | 18.00 | .. | 30.10 |

Fuente(s): EPPA3.

### 3.2 Método(s): extrapolación linear

#### 3.2.1 Hombres:

- 1950-70, tasas de distribución 1950-70 con base en EPPA3;
- 1980, promedios de las tasas de distribución con base en las encuestas de 1979, 1980 y 1981;
- 1990, promedios de las tasas de distribución con base en estimaciones oficiales de 1989, 1990 y 1991.
oficiales de 1989, 1990 y 1991.

#### 3.2.2 Mujeres:

Métodos, hipótesis y tratamientos idénticos a los que se aplican a los hombres.

## 4. Proyección de las tasas de actividad: 2000 - 2010

### 4.1 Modelo(s): linear y hiperbólico

#### 4.1.1 Hombres:

- Para los grupos de edad [15+], aplicación de la función F3;
- Modificación de las tendencias de todos los grupos de edad.

#### 4.1.2 Mujeres:

- Para los grupos de edad [15+], aplicación de la función F1;
- Modificación de las tendencias de todos los grupos de edad.

---

*Notas sobre los ajustes de las tasas, véase p.380-384.*     *Notas sobre las funciones de proyección, véase p. 386.*

# Lesotho

## 1. Fuente(s) de los datos básicos

Código(s):   Título(s):

EPPA3    Estimaciones y proyecciones de la población económicamente activa, 1950-2025, tercera edición, OIT, Ginebra, 1986.
ASTER    Anuario de estadísticas del trabajo 1945-89 - Edición retrospectiva sobre los censos de población, OIT, Ginebra, 1990.
R1986    1986 Population Census, Statistical tables, Vol II., Bureau of Statistics, Maseru, 1987.

## 2. Evaluación de las tasas de actividad: 1950 - 1990

### 2.1 Datos básicos:

Cuadro 1: Tasas de actividad por sexo y grupo de edad

| Grupo de edad | Año 1950 (1) | 1960 (1) | 1970 (1) | 1980 (1) | 1986 (2) |
|---|---|---|---|---|---|
| **Hombres** | | | | | |
| 10-14 | 51.35 | 44.10 | 40.00 | 32.30 | 34.36 |
| 15-19 | 86.75 | 83.50 | 80.45 | 74.70 | 54.24 |
| 20-24 | 97.85 | 96.80 | 96.00 | 94.30 | 88.65 |
| 25-29 | 98.90 | 98.70 | 98.50 | 98.20 | 97.58 |
| 30-34 | 99.40 | 99.20 | 99.00 | 98.65 | 98.31 |
| 35-39 | 99.45 | 99.30 | 99.10 | 98.75 | 98.22 |
| 40-44 | 99.40 | 99.20 | 99.00 | 98.70 | 97.80 |
| 45-49 | 99.35 | 99.15 | 98.95 | 98.30 | 97.23 |
| 50-54 | 99.25 | 99.05 | 98.85 | 98.20 | 95.79 |
| 55-59 | 99.20 | 97.10 | 97.10 | 95.80 | 93.56 |
| 60-64 | 98.45 | 97.10 | 96.05 | 93.75 | 89.78 |
| 65+ | 83.35 | 83.00 | 80.90 | 73.60 | 77.45 |
| **Mujeres** | | | | | |
| 10-14 | 19.00 | 16.00 | 15.00 | 12.00 | 16.98 |
| 15-19 | 39.50 | 36.50 | 34.75 | 31.10 | 39.04 |
| 20-24 | 81.10 | 78.65 | 75.70 | 71.45 | 53.07 |
| 25-29 | 87.70 | 86.35 | 83.40 | 80.15 | 53.16 |
| 30-34 | 89.75 | 88.35 | 85.35 | 82.00 | 53.67 |
| 35-39 | 90.05 | 88.70 | 85.65 | 82.30 | 54.49 |
| 40-44 | 90.15 | 88.75 | 85.70 | 82.40 | 53.66 |
| 45-49 | 92.60 | 91.50 | 88.80 | 85.05 | 51.42 |
| 50-54 | 90.25 | 89.15 | 86.55 | 82.90 | 47.14 |
| 55-59 | 89.80 | 88.20 | 85.90 | 81.35 | 43.93 |
| 60-64 | 85.85 | 84.35 | 82.15 | 77.80 | 37.25 |
| 65+ | 81.25 | 78.80 | 75.90 | 68.00 | 22.63 |

**Fuente(s)**: (1) EPPA3; (2) R1986.

### 2.2 Método(s): interpolación y extrapolación lineares

#### 2.2.1 Hombres:
- 1950-90, interpolación y extrapolación de las tasas de actividad 1950-80 con base en EPPA3;
ajuste de las tasas interpoladas y extrapoladas con base en las variaciones de las tasas interpoladas 1986, en relación con las tasas de actividad con base en el censo 1986;
modificación de las tendencias de todos los grupos de edad para 1950-90.

#### 2.2.2 Mujeres:
- 1950-90, interpolación y extrapolación de las tasas de actividad 1950-80 con base en EPPA3;
ajuste de las tasas interpoladas y extrapoladas con base en las variaciones de las tasas interpoladas 1986, en relación con la tasas de actividad ajustadas con base en el censo de 1986.

## 3. Evaluación de las tasas de distribución por sector de actividad: 1950 - 1990

### 3.1 Datos básicos:

Cuadro 2: Distribución de la población económicamente activa por sector de actividad en %

| Año | Agricultura | Industria Total | Manufac. | Servicios |
|---|---|---|---|---|
| **Hombres** | | | | |
| 1976 (1) | 23.62 | 57.92 | 2.33 | 18.46 |
| 1986 (2) | 28.87 | 43.44 | 1.76 | 27.69 |
| **Mujeres** | | | | |
| 1976 (1) | 65.80 | 5.57 | 3.52 | 28.63 |
| 1986 (2) | 61.19 | 5.05 | 2.89 | 33.76 |

**Fuente(s)**: (1) ASTER; (2) R1986.

### 3.2 Método(s): promedio ponderado

#### 3.2.1 Hombres:
- 1950-90, interpolación y extrapolación de las tasas de distribución con base en los censos de 1976 y 1986;
modificación de la tendencia del sector de la agricultura para 1950;
- Aplicación a la industria y los servicios para 1950-60, las mismas proporcione como en 1970.
como en 1970.

#### 3.2.2 Mujeres:
Métodos, hipótesis y tratamientos idénticos a los que se aplican a los hombres.

## 4. Proyección de las tasas de actividad: 2000 - 2010

### 4.1 Modelo(s): linear y hiperbólico

#### 4.1.1 Hombres:
- Para todos los grupos de edad, aplicación de la función F1;
- Modificación de la tendencia del grupo de edad [65+].

#### 4.1.2 Mujeres:
- Para los grupos de edad [10-19], aplicación de la función F1;
- Para los grupos de edad [20+], aplicación de la función F3;
- Modificación de las tendencias de los grupos de edad [10-49].

*Notas sobre los ajustes de las tasas, véase p.380-384.*     *Notas sobre las funciones de proyección, véase p. 386.*

# Letonia

## 1. Fuente(s) de los datos básicos

Código(s):   Título(s):

BLT-94-2   Vorobiev A. (1994), "Estimaciones de la población económicamente activa de los quince países de la ex URSS, en 1950, 1959, 1970, 1979 y 1989",
en el Boletín de Estadísticas del Trabajol - 1994-2, OIT, Ginebra.

## 2. Evaluación de las tasas de actividad: 1950 - 1990

### 2.1 Datos básicos:

Cuadro 1: Tasas de actividad por sexo y grupo de edad

| Grupo de edad | Año | | | | |
|---|---|---|---|---|---|
| | 1950 | 1959 | 1970 | 1979 | 1989 |
| **Hombres** | | | | | |
| 10-14 | 0.00 | 0.00 | 0.00 | 0.00 | 0.00 |
| 15-19 | 55.56 | 57.14 | 40.23 | 33.33 | 32.63 |
| 20-24 | 84.21 | 85.37 | 84.52 | 85.15 | 82.11 |
| 25-29 | 92.73 | 96.47 | 96.59 | 96.77 | 96.19 |
| 30-34 | 93.48 | 94.37 | 96.88 | 98.75 | 97.98 |
| 35-39 | 93.65 | 96.08 | 98.85 | 98.89 | 97.78 |
| 40-44 | 92.31 | 93.02 | 96.25 | 96.63 | 96.05 |
| 45-49 | 92.00 | 93.10 | 96.36 | 96.39 | 98.78 |
| 50-54 | 89.74 | 91.53 | 92.68 | 92.65 | 92.50 |
| 55-59 | 85.19 | 89.13 | 90.38 | 86.67 | 86.11 |
| 60-64 | 56.00 | 72.73 | 43.14 | 42.86 | 51.79 |
| 65+ | 28.57 | 42.47 | 21.74 | 16.67 | 20.62 |
| **Mujeres** | | | | | |
| 10-14 | 0.00 | 0.00 | 0.00 | 0.00 | 0.00 |
| 15-19 | 43.01 | 45.24 | 35.44 | 31.52 | 29.21 |
| 20-24 | 62.50 | 67.42 | 82.28 | 83.33 | 81.11 |
| 25-29 | 71.59 | 79.35 | 92.05 | 93.48 | 90.48 |
| 30-34 | 69.57 | 71.29 | 92.93 | 95.12 | 94.06 |
| 35-39 | 69.32 | 70.37 | 92.47 | 94.79 | 94.68 |
| 40-44 | 92.77 | 69.84 | 91.09 | 95.88 | 95.06 |
| 45-49 | 67.11 | 71.25 | 89.66 | 93.55 | 93.62 |
| 50-54 | 59.70 | 63.64 | 81.36 | 88.78 | 88.17 |
| 55-59 | 41.51 | 44.44 | 40.51 | 43.59 | 50.00 |
| 60-64 | 29.17 | 32.79 | 24.00 | 22.41 | 33.33 |
| 65+ | 10.62 | 12.24 | 6.35 | 7.31 | 11.01 |

Fuente(s): BLT-94-2.

### 2.2 Método(s):   promedio ponderado

#### 2.2.1 Hombres:

- 1950-90, promedios ponderados de las tasas de actividad 1950, 1959,
1983 y 1989 con base en el Boletín de estadísticas del trabajo 1994-2;
modificación de las tendencias del grupo de edad [30-34] para 1950 y 1960;
modificación de las tendencias de los grupos de edad [60+] para 1960-80.

#### 2.2.2 Mujeres:

- 1950-90, promedios ponderados de las tasas de actividad 1950, 1959,
1980 y 1989 con base en el Boletín de estadísticas del trabajo 1994-2;
modificación de la tendencia del grupo de edad [65+] para 1950.

## 3. Evaluación de las tasas de distribución por sector de actividad: 1950 - 1990

### 3.1 Datos básicos:

Cuadro 2: Distribución de la población económicamente activa por sector de actividad en %

| Año | Agricultura | Industria | | Servicios |
|---|---|---|---|---|
| | | Total | Manufac. | |
| **Hombres** | | | | |
| 1950 | 39.22 | 30.50 | 18.95 | 30.28 |
| 1959 | 30.84 | 39.93 | 24.42 | 29.23 |
| 1970 | 19.30 | 50.40 | 30.62 | 30.30 |
| 1979 | 18.44 | 49.41 | 31.12 | 32.15 |
| 1989 | 19.18 | 46.85 | 29.73 | 33.97 |
| **Mujeres** | | | | |
| 1950 | 57.29 | 16.91 | 14.16 | 25.79 |
| 1959 | 38.65 | 25.77 | 21.92 | 35.58 |
| 1970 | 18.99 | 34.97 | 30.22 | 46.04 |
| 1979 | 14.27 | 35.45 | 30.69 | 50.29 |
| 1989 | 12.33 | 32.55 | 28.12 | 55.12 |

Fuente(s): BLT-94-2.

### 3.2 Método(s):   datos de BLT-94-2

#### 3.2.1 Hombres:

- 1950, 1960, 1970, 1980 y 1990, respectivamente las tasas de distribución
1950, 1959, 1970, 1979 y 1989 con base en el boletín de estadísticas
del trabajo 1994-2.

#### 3.2.2 Mujeres:

Métodos, hipótesis y tratamientos idénticos a los que se aplican a los hombres.

## 4. Proyección de las tasas de actividad: 2000 - 2010

### 4.1 Modelo(s):   linear, hiperbólico y logístico

#### 4.1.1 Hombres:

- Para los grupos de edad [15-54], aplicación de la función F1;
- Para los grupos de edad [55+], aplicación de la función F3;
- Modificación de las tendencias de los grupos de edad [25-54].

#### 4.1.2 Mujeres:

- Para el grupo de edad [15-19], aplicación de la función F1;
- Para los grupos de edad [20-54], aplicación de la función F6;
- Para los grupos de edad [55+], aplicación de la función F3;
- Modificación de las tendencias de los grupos de edad [20+].

*Notas sobre los ajustes de las tasas, véase p.380-384.*

*Notas sobre las funciones de proyección, véase p. 386.*

# Líbano

## 1. Fuente(s) de los datos básicos

Código(s):  Título(s):

EPPA3  Estimaciones y proyecciones de la población económicamente activa, 1950-2025, tercera edición, OIT, Ginebra, 1986.

## 2. Evaluación de las tasas de actividad: 1950 - 1990

### 2.1 Datos básicos:

Cuadro 1: Tasas de actividad por sexo y grupo de edad

| Grupo de edad | Año | | | |
|---|---|---|---|---|
| | 1950 | 1960 | 1970 | 1980 |
| **Hombres** | | | | |
| 10-14 | 22.55 | 12.15 | 6.55 | 5.35 |
| 15-19 | 46.65 | 42.20 | 38.20 | 35.00 |
| 20-24 | 79.75 | 76.25 | 72.90 | 72.00 |
| 25-29 | 96.65 | 95.50 | 94.00 | 93.80 |
| 30-34 | 97.20 | 97.00 | 96.35 | 96.30 |
| 35-39 | 97.50 | 97.20 | 96.90 | 96.80 |
| 40-44 | 97.05 | 96.00 | 96.00 | 95.70 |
| 45-49 | 96.90 | 95.20 | 94.00 | 94.50 |
| 50-54 | 94.00 | 92.00 | 89.00 | 89.00 |
| 55-59 | 92.00 | 86.15 | 80.70 | 79.05 |
| 60-64 | 82.35 | 75.70 | 69.55 | 68.40 |
| 65+ | 58.50 | 46.70 | 42.20 | 41.40 |
| **Mujeres** | | | | |
| 10-14 | 8.00 | 6.40 | 5.90 | 4.20 |
| 15-19 | 9.00 | 10.60 | 16.70 | 17.75 |
| 20-24 | 11.50 | 17.45 | 28.35 | 33.15 |
| 25-29 | 11.00 | 15.50 | 25.00 | 30.05 |
| 30-34 | 10.50 | 13.50 | 20.35 | 24.10 |
| 35-39 | 10.30 | 11.90 | 16.35 | 18.90 |
| 40-44 | 9.50 | 11.30 | 15.10 | 17.05 |
| 45-49 | 9.20 | 10.80 | 13.95 | 15.50 |
| 50-54 | 9.00 | 9.50 | 11.60 | 13.05 |
| 55-59 | 8.70 | 8.50 | 9.10 | 9.90 |
| 60-64 | 8.40 | 8.10 | 8.30 | 8.80 |
| 65+ | 4.20 | 3.40 | 2.85 | 3.00 |

Fuente(s): EPPA3.

### 2.2 Método(s): extrapolación linear

#### 2.2.1 Hombres:

- 1950-90, tasas de actividad ajustadas 1950-90 con base en EPPA3;
ajuste de las tasas de actividad con base en evaluaciones
de las fuerzas armadas.

#### 2.2.2 Mujeres:

- 1950-80, tasas de actividad 1950-80 con base en EPPA3;
- 1990, extrapolación de las tasas de actividad 1950-80 con base en EPPA3.

## 3. Evaluación de las tasas de distribución por sector de actividad: 1950 - 1990

### 3.1 Datos básicos:

Cuadro 2: Distribución de la población económicamente activa por sector de actividad en %

| Año | Agricultura | Industria | | Servicios |
|---|---|---|---|---|
| | | Total | Manufac. | |
| **Hombres** | | | | |
| 1950 | 52.60 | 21.80 | | 25.60 |
| 1960 | 36.50 | 24.30 | | 39.20 |
| 1970 | 18.90 | 26.40 | | 54.70 |
| 1980 | 12.60 | 29.20 | | 58.20 |
| **Mujeres** | | | | |
| 1950 | 76.20 | 8.50 | | 15.30 |
| 1960 | 49.90 | 14.25 | | 35.85 |
| 1970 | 23.60 | 20.00 | | 56.40 |
| 1980 | 20.00 | 21.00 | | 59.00 |

Fuente(s): EPPA3.

### 3.2 Método(s): extrapolación linear

#### 3.2.1 Hombres:

- 1950-80, tasas de distribución 1950-80 con base en EPPA3;
- 1990, extrapolación de las tasas de distribución de la agricultura 1970-80 con base en EPPA3;
la diferencia en las tasas de distribución de la agricultura entre 1980 y 1990
se ha repartido entre la industria (80 por ciento) y los servicios ( 20 por ciento).
se ha repartido entre la industria (80 por ciento) y los servicios ( 20 por ciento).

#### 3.2.2 Mujeres:

- 1950-80, tasas de distribución 1950-80 con base en EPPA3;
- 1990, extrapolación de las tasas de distribución de la agricultura 1970-80 con base en EPPA3;
la diferencia en las tasas de distribución de la agricultura entre 1980 y 1990
se ha repartido entre la industria (10 por ciento) y los servicios ( 90 por ciento).

## 4. Proyección de las tasas de actividad: 2000 - 2010

### 4.1 Modelo(s): linear, log-linear, hiperbólico y logístico

#### 4.1.1 Hombres:

- Para los grupos de edad [15-19] y [55+], aplicación de la función F3;
- Para los grupos de edad [20-54], aplicación de la función F1;
- Modificación de las tendencias de los grupos de edad [20-54].

#### 4.1.2 Mujeres:

- Para los grupos de edad [15-29], aplicación de la función F6;
- Para los grupos de edad [30-59], aplicación de la función F2;
- Para los grupos de edad [60+], aplicación de la función F3;
- Modificación de las tendencias de los grupos de edad [15-59].

*Notas sobre los ajustes de las tasas, véase p.380-384.*   *Notas sobre las funciones de proyección, véase p. 386.*

# Liberia

## 1. Fuente(s) de los datos básicos

Código(s):  Título(s):

ASTER  Anuario de estadísticas del trabajo 1945-89 - Edición retrospectiva sobre los censos de población, OIT, Ginebra, 1990.

## 2. Evaluación de las tasas de actividad: 1950 - 1990

### 2.1 Datos básicos:

Cuadro 1: Tasas de actividad por sexo y grupo de edad

| Grupo de edad | Año | | |
|---|---|---|---|
| | 1962 | 1974 | 1984 |
| **Hombres** | | | |
| 10-14 | 22.39 | 8.60 | .. |
| 15-19 | 46.45 | 21.07 | .. |
| 20-24 | 74.78 | 51.33 | .. |
| 25-29 | 87.30 | 78.36 | .. |
| 30-34 | 92.99 | 88.10 | .. |
| 35-39 | 94.44 | 91.26 | .. |
| 40-44 | 93.91 | 91.65 | .. |
| 45-49 | 93.76 | 91.75 | .. |
| 50-54 | 92.12 | 90.43 | .. |
| 55-59 | 91.13 | 89.61 | .. |
| 60-64 | 81.51 | 80.33 | .. |
| 65+ | 64.30 | 65.97 | .. |
| **Mujeres** | | | |
| 10-14 | 20.12 | 6.75 | 14.18 |
| 15-19 | 34.93 | 15.37 | 25.37 |
| 20-24 | 41.20 | 21.57 | 37.80 |
| 25-29 | 44.25 | 25.42 | 48.47 |
| 30-34 | 47.90 | 28.65 | 56.17 |
| 35-39 | 49.76 | 30.67 | 59.93 |
| 40-44 | 51.05 | 33.51 | 63.74 |
| 45-49 | 49.87 | 33.86 | 63.90 |
| 50-54 | 46.94 | 31.44 | 62.76 |
| 55-59 | 44.35 | 30.38 | 59.09 |
| 60-64 | 31.98 | 23.69 | 49.49 |
| 65+ | 20.38 | 16.20 | 32.47 |

Fuente(s): ASTER.

### 2.2 Método(s): interpolación y extrapolación lineares

#### 2.2.1 Hombres:

- 1950-90, interpolación y extrapolación de las tasas de actividad con base en el censo de 1962 y 1974;
modificación de las tendencias de los grupos de edad [35-44] para 1980 y de los grupos de edad [20-29] para 1990.

#### 2.2.2 Mujeres:

- 1950-90, interpolación y extrapolación de las tasas de actividad con base en los censos de 1962, 1974 y 1984;
modificación de las tendencias de todos los grupos de edad.

## 3. Evaluación de las tasas de distribución por sector de actividad: 1950 - 1990

### 3.1 Datos básicos:

Cuadro 2: Distribución de la población económicamente activa por sector de actividad en %

| Año | Agricultura | Industria | | Servicios |
|---|---|---|---|---|
| | | Total | Manufac. | |
| **Hombres** | | | | |
| 1962 | 74.52 | 13.03 | 2.96 | 12.45 |
| 1974 | 71.01 | 10.34 | 1.78 | 18.65 |
| 1984 | 67.08 | 9.03 | 2.74 | 23.89 |
| **Mujeres** | | | | |
| 1962 | 95.03 | 0.72 | 0.41 | 4.26 |
| 1974 | 94.19 | 0.50 | 0.13 | 5.31 |
| 1984 | 85.89 | 0.75 | 0.24 | 13.35 |

Fuente(s): ASTER.

### 3.2 Método(s): promedio ponderado

#### 3.2.1 Hombres:

- 1960-80, promedios ponderados de las tasas de distribución con base en los censos de 1962, 1974 y 1984;
- 1990, extrapolación de las tasas con base en los censos de 1974 y 1984;
- 1950, aplicación a la tasa de distribución de la agricultura 1980 con base en EPPA3, 3/4 de la tendencia estimada para 1980-90;
en EPPA3, 3/4 de la tendencia estimada para 1980-90;

#### 3.2.2 Mujeres:

- 1960-80, promedios ponderados de las tasas de distribución con base en los censos de 1962, 1974 y 1984;
- 1990, extrapolación de las tasas de distribución con base en los censos de 1974 y 1984;
- 1950, aplicación a la tasa de distribución de la agricultura 1980 con base en EPPA3, 1/2 de la tendencia estimada para 1980-90;
para la industria y los servicios, las mismas proporciones como en 1960.

## 4. Proyección de las tasas de actividad: 2000 - 2010

### 4.1 Modelo(s): log-linear, hiperbólico y linear

#### 4.1.1 Hombres:

- Para los grupos de edad [10-19], aplicación de la función F2;
- Para los grupos de edad [20-64], aplicación de la función F3;
- Para los grupos de edad [60+], aplicación de la función F1;
- Modificación de las tendencias de los grupos de edad [25-29] y [35-39].

#### 4.1.2 Mujeres:

- Para los grupos de edad [10-54], aplicación de la función F1;
- Para los grupos de edad [55+], aplicación de la función F3;
- Modificación de la tendencia del grupo de edad [15-19].

*Notas sobre los ajustes de las tasas, véase p.380-384.*

*Notas sobre las funciones de proyección, véase p. 386.*

# Lituania

## 1. Fuente(s) de los datos básicos

Código(s):   Título(s):

BLT-94-2   Vorobiev A. (1994), "Estimaciones de la población económicamente activa de los quince países de la ex URSS, en 1950, 1959, 1970, 1979 y 1989",
en el Boletín de Estadísticas del Trabajol - 1994-2, OIT, Ginebra.

## 2. Evaluación de las tasas de actividad: 1950 - 1990

### 2.1 Datos básicos:

Cuadro 1: Tasas de actividad por sexo y grupo de edad

| Grupo de edad | Año | | | | |
|---|---|---|---|---|---|
| | 1950 | 1959 | 1970 | 1979 | 1989 |
| **Hombres** | | | | | |
| 10-14 | 0.00 | 0.00 | 0.00 | 0.00 | 0.00 |
| 15-19 | 55.74 | 58.62 | 33.88 | 27.10 | 26.90 |
| 20-24 | 92.59 | 81.98 | 84.11 | 84.17 | 79.17 |
| 25-29 | 93.75 | 94.64 | 97.32 | 97.56 | 96.82 |
| 30-34 | 91.07 | 95.74 | 98.26 | 99.06 | 97.83 |
| 35-39 | 92.19 | 94.37 | 98.21 | 98.25 | 97.50 |
| 40-44 | 91.84 | 93.88 | 97.00 | 97.32 | 97.03 |
| 45-49 | 90.77 | 94.74 | 96.00 | 97.20 | 95.33 |
| 50-54 | 89.09 | 92.94 | 93.62 | 94.25 | 92.08 |
| 55-59 | 84.78 | 89.29 | 88.68 | 89.06 | 86.02 |
| 60-64 | 66.67 | 80.43 | 55.56 | 39.02 | 44.59 |
| 65+ | 48.08 | 52.63 | 20.34 | 12.41 | 14.71 |
| **Mujeres** | | | | | |
| 10-14 | 0.00 | 0.00 | 0.00 | 0.00 | 0.00 |
| 15-19 | 44.60 | 49.17 | 28.70 | 21.53 | 20.00 |
| 20-24 | 68.09 | 70.73 | 80.56 | 80.30 | 72.79 |
| 25-29 | 71.17 | 74.02 | 88.70 | 95.08 | 87.74 |
| 30-34 | 65.85 | 68.00 | 88.00 | 95.54 | 91.43 |
| 35-39 | 65.66 | 66.67 | 88.71 | 95.90 | 93.65 |
| 40-44 | 63.74 | 67.14 | 87.90 | 95.20 | 93.64 |
| 45-49 | 62.96 | 65.88 | 84.31 | 93.50 | 90.83 |
| 50-54 | 57.81 | 60.24 | 75.38 | 86.44 | 85.00 |
| 55-59 | 42.37 | 46.15 | 38.10 | 36.17 | 42.37 |
| 60-64 | 23.08 | 50.75 | 16.87 | 15.63 | 25.66 |
| 65+ | 8.13 | 9.77 | 6.22 | 7.86 | 7.06 |

Fuente(s): BLT-94-2.

### 2.2 Método(s):  promedio ponderado

#### 2.2.1 Hombres:

- 1950-90, promedios ponderados de las tasas de actividad 1950, 1959, 1984 y 1989 con base en el Boletín de estadísticas del trabajo 1994-2;
ajuste de las tasas de actividad 1950, 1959, 1970 y 1979 con base en el Boletín para los grupos de edad [15-19] y [55+];
ajuste de las tasas de actividad estimadas del grupo de edad [20-24] para 1960.

#### 2.2.2 Mujeres:

- 1950-90, promedios ponderados de las tasas de actividad 1950, 1959, 1981 y 1989 con base en el Boletín de estadísticas del trabajo 1994-2;
ajuste de las tasas de actividad 1950, 1959, 1970 y 1979 con base en el Boletín para los grupos de edad [55+].

## 3. Evaluación de las tasas de distribución  por sector de actividad: 1950 - 1990

### 3.1 Datos básicos:

Cuadro 2: Distribución de la población económicamente activa por sector de actividad en %

| Año | Agricultura | Industria | | Servicios |
|---|---|---|---|---|
| | | Total | Manufac. | |
| **Hombres** | | | | |
| 1950 | 61.38 | 16.01 | 11.62 | 22.61 |
| 1959 | 48.49 | 27.20 | 16.76 | 24.31 |
| 1970 | 31.26 | 43.96 | 24.78 | 24.78 |
| 1979 | 26.36 | 46.82 | 27.05 | 26.82 |
| 1989 | 23.21 | 46.93 | 27.61 | 29.86 |
| **Mujeres** | | | | |
| 1950 | 73.04 | 9.29 | 8.01 | 17.67 |
| 1959 | 56.80 | 16.64 | 13.76 | 26.56 |
| 1970 | 31.59 | 29.70 | 24.87 | 38.71 |
| 1979 | 29.34 | 29.55 | 24.28 | 41.12 |
| 1989 | 13.35 | 33.70 | 28.01 | 52.95 |

Fuente(s): BLT-94-2.

### 3.2 Método(s):  datos de BLT-94-2

#### 3.2.1 Hombres:

- 1950, 1960, 1970, 1980 y 1990, respectivamente las tasas de distribución 1950, 1959, 1970, 1979 y 1989 con base en el boletín de estadísticas del trabajo 1994-2.

#### 3.2.2 Mujeres:

Métodos, hipótesis y tratamientos idénticos a los que se aplican a los hombres.

## 4. Proyección de las tasas de actividad: 2000 - 2010

### 4.1 Modelo(s):  linear, hiperbólico y logístico

#### 4.1.1 Hombres:

- Para los grupos de edad [15-19] y [50+], aplicación de la función F3;
- Para los grupos de edad [20-49], aplicación de la función F1;
- Modificación de las tendencias de los grupos de edad [25-54].

#### 4.1.2 Mujeres:

- Para los grupos de edad [15-19] y [55+], aplicación de la función F3;
- Para el grupo de edad [20-24], aplicación de la función F1;
- Para los grupos de edad [25-54], aplicación de la función F6;
- Modificación de las tendencias de los grupos de edad [20-54].

*Notas sobre los ajustes de las tasas, véase p.380-384.*          *Notas sobre las funciones de proyección, véase p. 386.*

# Luxemburgo

## 1. Fuente(s) de los datos básicos

Código(s):  Título(s):

EPPA3  Anuario de estadísticas del trabajo 1945-89 - Edición retrospectiva sobre los censos de población, OIT, Ginebra, 1990.
STAT  Base de datos de la OIT sobre estadísticas del trabajo - LABORSTA, Oficina de Estadística, OIT, Ginebra.

## 2. Evaluación de las tasas de actividad: 1950 - 1990

### 2.1 Datos básicos:

Cuadro 1: Tasas de actividad por sexo y grupo de edad

| Grupo de edad | Año | | | | |
|---|---|---|---|---|---|
| | 1950 (1) | 1960 (1) | 1970 (1) | 1980 (1) | 1991 (2) |
| **Hombres** | | | | | |
| 10-14 | 3.25 | 1.65 | 1.00 | 0.00 | 0.00 |
| 15-19 | 73.05 | 58.80 | 53.10 | 47.45 | 29.63 |
| 20-24 | 90.55 | 92.75 | 86.95 | 81.15 | 75.34 |
| 25-29 | 95.15 | 96.45 | 96.05 | 95.60 | 94.02 |
| 30-34 | 96.70 | 97.95 | 98.15 | 98.35 | 97.27 |
| 35-39 | 96.05 | 96.95 | 97.80 | 98.70 | 97.80 |
| 40-44 | 95.30 | 96.90 | 97.35 | 97.80 | 96.86 |
| 45-49 | 95.10 | 95.45 | 95.70 | 95.95 | 94.78 |
| 50-54 | 91.65 | 92.35 | 91.30 | 90.30 | 85.92 |
| 55-59 | 88.45 | 85.65 | 72.75 | 59.85 | 54.78 |
| 60-64 | 58.35 | 55.70 | 43.35 | 31.00 | 19.04 |
| 65+ | 34.45 | 21.15 | 13.35 | 5.50 | 2.09 |
| **Mujeres** | | | | | |
| 10-14 | 2.50 | 1.60 | 1.05 | 0.00 | 0.00 |
| 15-19 | 56.00 | 56.80 | 54.80 | 45.20 | 25.75 |
| 20-24 | 50.00 | 50.60 | 52.90 | 68.70 | 71.04 |
| 25-29 | 34.40 | 30.45 | 33.75 | 55.50 | 68.39 |
| 30-34 | 29.30 | 26.20 | 26.35 | 43.95 | 56.78 |
| 35-39 | 31.30 | 28.30 | 24.50 | 39.70 | 54.60 |
| 40-44 | 33.30 | 30.20 | 24.75 | 35.25 | 51.94 |
| 45-49 | 31.95 | 29.60 | 25.40 | 29.45 | 44.20 |
| 50-54 | 28.65 | 26.50 | 23.80 | 25.10 | 32.86 |
| 55-59 | 27.95 | 21.60 | 19.95 | 19.85 | 19.83 |
| 60-64 | 21.95 | 17.20 | 13.40 | 12.20 | 9.38 |
| 65+ | 13.65 | 9.8 | 4.8 | 2.75 | 0.70 |

Fuente(s): STAT.

### 2.2 Método(s): promedio ponderado

#### 2.2.1 Hombres:

- 1950-80, tasas de actividad 1950-80 con base en EPPA3;
- 1990, promedios ponderados de las tasas de actividad 1980 con base en EPPA3 y de las tasas de actividad con base en el censo de 1991.

#### 2.2.2 Mujeres:

Métodos, hipótesis y tratamientos idénticos a los que se aplican a los hombres.

## 3. Evaluación de las tasas de distribución por sector de actividad: 1950 - 1990

### 3.1 Datos básicos:

Cuadro 2: Distribución de la población económicamente activa por sector de actividad en %

| Año | Agricultura | Industria | | Servicios |
|---|---|---|---|---|
| | | Total | Manufac. | |
| **Hombres** | | | | |
| 1981 | 4.85 | 44.97 | 30.47 | 50.18 |
| 1991 | 3.56 | 36.07 | 30.19 | 60.37 |
| **Mujeres** | | | | |
| 1981 | 5.38 | 10.84 | 8.96 | 83.78 |
| 1991 | 3.26 | 9.27 | 7.39 | 87.47 |

Fuente(s): (1) STAT.

### 3.2 Método(s): promedio ponderado

#### 3.2.1 Hombres:

- 1950-80, tasas de distribución 1950-80 con base en EPPA3;
- 1990, promedios ponderados de las tasas de distribución con base en los censos de 1981 y 1991.

#### 3.2.2 Mujeres:

Métodos, hipótesis y tratamientos idénticos a los que se aplican a los hombres.

## 4. Proyección de las tasas de actividad: 2000 - 2010

### 4.1 Modelo(s): linear, hiperbólico y logístico

#### 4.1.1 Hombres:

- Para los grupos de edad [15-34] y [50+], aplicación de la función F3;
- Para los grupos de edad [35-49], aplicación de la función F3;
- Modificación de las tendencias de los grupos de edad [30-49].

#### 4.1.2 Mujeres:

- Para los grupos de edad [15-19] y [50+], aplicación de la función F3;
- Para los grupos de edad [20-29], aplicación de la función F6;
- Para los grupos de edad [30-49], aplicación de la función F1;
- Modificación de la tendencia del grupo de edad [20-24].

*Notas sobre los ajustes de las tasas, véase p.380-384.*   *Notas sobre las funciones de proyección, véase p. 386.*

# Macao, China

## 1. Fuente(s) de los datos básicos

Código(s): Título(s):

STAT        Base de datos de la OIT sobre estadísticas del trabajo - LABORSTA, Oficina de Estadística, OIT, Ginebra.

## 2. Evaluación de las tasas de actividad: 1950 - 1990

### 2.1 Datos básicos:

Cuadro 1: Tasas de actividad por sexo y grupo de edad

| | Año | | | |
|---|---|---|---|---|
| Grupo de edad | 1960 | 1981 | 1991 | 1992 |
| **Hombres** | | | | |
| 10-14 | .. | 5.97 | 3.86 | .. |
| 15-19 | .. | 57.31 | 59.50 | .. |
| 20-24 | .. | 94.62 | 92.11 | .. |
| 25-29 | .. | 98.49 | 97.94 | .. |
| 30-34 | .. | 98.76 | 98.02 | .. |
| 35-39 | .. | 98.25 | 99.98 | .. |
| 40-44 | .. | 97.17 | 97.24 | .. |
| 45-49 | .. | 95.07 | 95.54 | .. |
| 50-54 | .. | 87.95 | 86.87 | .. |
| 55-59 | .. | 79.85 | 78.08 | .. |
| 60-64 | .. | 72.01 | 57.60 | .. |
| 65+ | | ... | 29.29 | |
| **Mujeres** | | | | |
| 10-14 | 3.95 | 8.18 | ... | ... |
| 15-19 | 16.40 | 57.32 | 29.26 | 29.26 |
| 20-24 | 20.57 | 83.50 | 56.90 | 56.90 |
| 25-29 | 17.13 | 69.71 | 59.53 | 59.53 |
| 30-34 | 18.36 | 53.98 | 53.86 | 53.86 |
| 35-39 | 21.27 | 50.00 | 59.13 | 59.13 |
| 40-44 | 22.84 | 45.97 | 58.33 | 58.33 |
| 45-49 | 21.97 | 39.58 | 52.12 | 52.12 |
| 50-54 | 22.89 | 31.39 | 47.69 | 47.69 |
| 55-59 | 19.49 | 27.58 | 23.54 | 23.54 |
| 60-64 | 17.37 | 19.97 | 21.94 | 21.94 |
| 65+ | 8.26 | 12.30 | 5.11 | 5.11 |

Fuente(s): STAT.

### 2.2 Método(s): promedio ponderado

#### 2.2.1 Hombres:

- 1950-90, promedios ponderados de las tasas de actividad ajustadas
con base en de 1981 y 1991 el censo;
modificación de las tendencias del grupo de edad [25-29] para 1950-70.

#### 2.2.2 Mujeres:

- 1960, 1980 y 1990, promedios ponderados de las tasas de actividad con
base en los censos de 1960 y 1980 y en estimaciones oficiales de 1992;
- 1950 y 1970, promedios ponderados de las tasas de actividad estimadas
1960 y 1980;
modificación de las tendencias de todos los grupos de edad para 1950.

## 3. Evaluación de las tasas de distribución por sector de actividad: 1950 - 1990

### 3.1 Datos básicos:

Cuadro 2: Distribución de la población económicamente activa por sector de actividad en %

| | Agricultura | Industria | | Servicios |
|---|---|---|---|---|
| Año | | Total | Manufac. | |
| **Hombres** | | | | |
| 1960 | 6.08 | 30.82 | 25.14 | 63.09 |
| 1981 | 6.50 | 47.47 | 34.46 | 46.03 |
| 1991 | 1.50 | 34.28 | 20.77 | 64.22 |
| **Mujeres** | | | | |
| 1960 | 3.36 | 49.43 | 47.19 | 47.21 |
| 1981 | 5.25 | 64.26 | 62.80 | 30.49 |
| 1991 | 1.23 | 48.63 | 46.52 | 50.14 |

Fuente(s): STAT.

### 3.2 Método(s): promedio ponderado

#### 3.2.1 Hombres:

- 1960 y 1980-90, promedios ponderados de las tasas de distribución
con base en los censos de 1960, 1981 y 1991;
- 1950 y 1970, promedios ponderados de las tasas de distribución estimadas
para 1960 y 1980.

#### 3.2.2 Mujeres:

Métodos, hipótesis y tratamientos idénticos a los que se aplican a los hombres.

## 4. Proyección de las tasas de actividad: 2000 - 2010

### 4.1 Modelo(s): linear, log-linear, hiperbólico y logístico

#### 4.1.1 Hombres:

- Para los grupos de edad [15-19] y [55+], aplicación de la función F3;
- Para el grupo de edad [20-24], aplicación de la función F2;
- Para los grupos de edad [25-54], aplicación de la función F1;
- Modificación de la tendencia del grupo de edad [30-34].

#### 4.1.2 Mujeres:

- Para los grupos de edad [15-24] y [60+], aplicación de la función F1;
- Para los grupos de edad [25-59], aplicación de la función F6;
- Modificación de las tendencias de los grupos de edad [15-54].

---

# Macedonia, Ex República Yugos

## 1. Fuente(s) de los datos básicos

Código(s):   Título(s):

BLT-94-2   Popovic B. (1994), "Nuevas estimaciones de las tasas de actividad para 1980 y 1990, desglosadas por grupos de edad y distribución sectorial, en algunos países de Europa oriental y meridional" en el Boletín de Estadísticas del Trabajol - 1994-2, OIT, Ginebra.

STAT   Base de datos de la OIT sobre estadísticas del trabajo - LABORSTA, Oficina de Estadística, OIT, Ginebra.

## 2. Evaluación de las tasas de actividad: 1950 - 1990

### 2.1 Datos básicos:

Cuadro 1: Tasas de actividad por sexo y grupo de edad

| Grupo de edad | Año | | | | | |
|---|---|---|---|---|---|---|
| | 1948 (1) | 1953 (1) | 1961 (1) | 1971 (1) | 1980 (2) | 1990 (2) |
| **Hombres** | | | | | | |
| 10-14 | 20.84 | 17.03 | 9.84 | 3.30 | 0.63 | 0.04 |
| 15-19 | 89.34 | 79.29 | 56.27 | 40.69 | 27.13 | 21.91 |
| 20-24 | 96.01 | 93.56 | 89.27 | 77.27 | 76.89 | 76.52 |
| 25-29 | 99.87 | 97.06 | 94.67 | 95.45 | 92.01 | 92.64 |
| 30-34 | 99.99 | 98.78 | 96.95 | 98.31 | 98.12 | 96.30 |
| 35-39 | 99.82 | 98.80 | 98.42 | 97.58 | 98.69 | 96.79 |
| 40-44 | 98.92 | 97.17 | 96.47 | 96.84 | 98.04 | 96.02 |
| 45-49 | 99.18 | 99.96 | 97.98 | 90.83 | 96.28 | 94.91 |
| 50-54 | 96.42 | 96.62 | 97.08 | 87.33 | 88.83 | 85.97 |
| 55-59 | 94.44 | 92.78 | 90.61 | 83.95 | 73.93 | 64.83 |
| 60-64 | 92.46 | 88.73 | 85.01 | 67.87 | 59.77 | 41.20 |
| 65+ | 71.06 | 60.08 | 59.48 | 50.97 | 39.52 | 25.55 |
| **Mujeres** | | | | | | |
| 10-14 | .. | 13.69 | 9.08 | 4.66 | 1.05 | 0.07 |
| 15-19 | .. | 58.59 | 54.39 | 37.98 | 22.34 | 17.73 |
| 20-24 | .. | 50.49 | 49.63 | 48.78 | 50.60 | 61.03 |
| 25-29 | .. | 37.11 | 43.52 | 45.29 | 61.65 | 67.08 |
| 30-34 | .. | 34.75 | 36.34 | 38.44 | 64.34 | 69.04 |
| 35-39 | .. | 30.52 | 32.04 | 36.88 | 59.78 | 69.03 |
| 40-44 | .. | 28.93 | 31.64 | 32.14 | 53.19 | 66.87 |
| 45-49 | .. | 22.07 | 26.52 | 28.70 | 46.39 | 60.54 |
| 50-54 | .. | 17.05 | 22.26 | 26.00 | 36.12 | 50.42 |
| 55-59 | .. | 11.58 | 18.07 | 21.72 | 28.84 | 26.43 |
| 60-64 | .. | 12.44 | 14.41 | 16.39 | 22.77 | 20.89 |
| 65+ | .. | 4.94 | 7.58 | 8.04 | 12.20 | 9.99 |

Fuente(s): (1) STAT; (2) BLT-94-2.

### 2.2 Método(s): extrapolación linear

#### 2.2.1 Hombres:

- 1950-70, extrapolación de las tasas de actividad con base en los censos de 1948, 1953, 1961 y 1971;
- 1980-90, 1980 y 1990 tasas de actividad con base en el Boletín de estadísticas del trabajo 1994-2.

#### 2.2.2 Mujeres:

- 1950-70, extrapolación de las tasas de actividad con base en el censo 1953 y de las tasas de actividad ajustadas con base en los censos de 1961 y 1971;
- 1980-90, tasas de actividad 1980 y 1990 con base en el Boletín de estadísticas del trabajo 1994-2.

## 3. Evaluación de las tasas de distribución por sector de actividad: 1950 - 1990

### 3.1 Datos básicos:

Cuadro 2: Distribución de la población económicamente activa por sector de actividad en %

| Año | Agricultura | Industria | | Servicios |
|---|---|---|---|---|
| | | Total | Manufac. | |
| **Hombres** | | | | |
| 1950 (1) | 72.22 | 11.71 | 3.52 | 16.08 |
| 1960 (1) | 61.01 | 19.78 | 10.18 | 19.21 |
| 1970 (1) | 49.63 | 27.01 | .. | 23.36 |
| 1980 (2) | 29.89 | 38.10 | 20.58 | 32.01 |
| 1990 (2) | 20.84 | 39.88 | 24.46 | 39.27 |
| **Mujeres** | | | | |
| 1950 (1) | 88.70 | 3.55 | 3.20 | 7.75 |
| 1960 (1) | 76.13 | 9.53 | 8.78 | 14.34 |
| 1970 (1) | 62.21 | 16.47 | .. | 21.32 |
| 1980 (2) | 46.88 | 23.01 | 21.04 | 30.10 |
| 1990 (2) | 22.54 | 41.05 | 37.59 | 36.41 |

Fuente(s): (1) EPPA3; (2) BLT-94-2.

### 3.2 Método(s): datos de BLT-94-2

#### 3.2.1 Hombres:

- 1950-70, tasas de distribución 1950-70 con base en EPPA3;
- 1980-90, tasas de distribución con base en el boletín de estadísticas del trabajo 1994-2.

#### 3.2.2 Mujeres:

Métodos, hipótesis y tratamientos idénticos a los que se aplican a los hombres.

## 4. Proyección de las tasas de actividad: 2000 - 2010

### 4.1 Modelo(s): linear, hiperbólico y logístico

#### 4.1.1 Hombres:

- Para los grupos de edad [15+], aplicación de la función F3;
- Modificación de las tendencias de los grupos de edad [15-39].

#### 4.1.2 Mujeres:

- Para los grupos de edad [15-19] y [65+], aplicación de la función F3;
- Para los grupos de edad [20-54], aplicación de la función F6;
- Para los grupos de edad [55-64], aplicación de la función F1;
- Modificación de las tendencias de los grupos de edad [15-24] y [50+].

*Notas sobre los ajustes de las tasas, véase p.380-384.*

*Notas sobre las funciones de proyección, véase p. 386.*

# Madagascar

## 1. Fuente(s) de los datos básicos

Código(s):  Título(s):
EPPA3     Estimaciones y proyecciones de la población económicamente activa, 1950-2025, tercera edición, OIT, Ginebra, 1986.
ASTER     Anuario de estadísticas del trabajo 1945-89 - Edición retrospectiva sobre los censos de población, OIT, Ginebra, 1990.

## 2. Evaluación de las tasas de actividad: 1950 - 1990

### 2.1 Datos básicos:

Cuadro 1: Tasas de actividad por sexo y grupo de edad

| Grupo de edad | Año 1950 (1) | 1960 (1) | 1970 (1) | 1980 (1) | 1975 (2) | 1980 (1) |
|---|---|---|---|---|---|---|
| **Hombres** | | | | | | |
| 10-14 | 49.05 | 47.40 | 45.50 | 45.50 | 43.98 | 43.60 |
| 15-19 | 80.85 | 78.65 | 76.15 | 76.15 | 75.21 | 73.60 |
| 20-24 | 93.70 | 92.85 | 91.90 | 91.90 | 89.96 | 90.95 |
| 25-29 | 97.15 | 97.05 | 96.90 | 96.90 | 98.30 | 96.75 |
| 30-34 | 97.85 | 97.75 | 97.60 | 97.60 | 98.99 | 97.40 |
| 35-39 | 98.05 | 97.90 | 97.70 | 97.70 | 99.03 | 97.55 |
| 40-44 | 97.85 | 97.70 | 97.50 | 97.50 | 98.97 | 97.35 |
| 45-49 | 97.15 | 97.00 | 96.85 | 96.85 | 98.90 | 96.70 |
| 50-54 | 96.60 | 96.40 | 96.15 | 96.15 | 98.61 | 95.90 |
| 55-59 | 95.50 | 95.15 | 94.80 | 94.80 | 95.62 | 94.45 |
| 60-64 | 92.15 | 91.60 | 90.95 | 90.95 | 94.14 | 90.35 |
| 65+ | 78.20 | 77.25 | 76.15 | 76.15 | 83.84 | 75.05 |
| **Mujeres** | | | | | | |
| 10-14 | 37.05 | 35.85 | 34.40 | 34.40 | 38.99 | 32.95 |
| 15-19 | 60.50 | 58.65 | 56.50 | 56.50 | 58.20 | 54.35 |
| 20-24 | 62.00 | 60.80 | 59.45 | 59.45 | 69.33 | 58.10 |
| 25-29 | 66.65 | 65.30 | 63.80 | 63.80 | 78.10 | 62.25 |
| 30-34 | 70.85 | 69.40 | 67.75 | 67.75 | 78.42 | 66.10 |
| 35-39 | 72.25 | 70.90 | 69.35 | 69.35 | 79.00 | 67.80 |
| 40-44 | 74.70 | 73.35 | 71.80 | 71.80 | 79.45 | 70.25 |
| 45-49 | 74.15 | 72.80 | 71.25 | 71.25 | 82.55 | 69.65 |
| 50-54 | 72.35 | 70.75 | 68.95 | 68.95 | 82.86 | 67.10 |
| 55-59 | 69.45 | 67.80 | 65.90 | 65.90 | 76.67 | 64.00 |
| 60-64 | 62.60 | 60.50 | 58.10 | 58.10 | 76.73 | 55.65 |
| 65+ | 42.80 | 40.85 | 38.60 | 38.60 | 46.32 | 36.35 |

Fuente(s): (1) EPPA3; (2) ASTER.

### 2.2 Método(s): interpolación y extrapolación lineares

**2.2.1 Hombres:**
- 1950-90, interpolación y extrapolación de las tasas de actividad 1950-80 con base en EPPA3;
ajuste de las tasas interpoladas y extrapoladas con base en las variaciones de las tasas interpoladas 1975, en relación con las tasas de actividad con base en el censo 1975;
modificación de las tendencias de todos los grupos de edad para 1950-70 and de los grupos de edad [10-19] y [65+] para 1980 y 1990.

**2.2.2 Mujeres:**
- 1950-90, interpolación y extrapolación de las tasas de actividad 1950-80 con base en EPPA3;
ajuste de las tasas interpoladas y extrapoladas con base en las variaciones de las tasas interpoladas 1975, en relación con las tasas de actividad con base en el censo de 1975;
modificación de las tendencias de todos los grupos de edad para 1950-70;
modificación de las tendencias de los grupos de edad [20-64] para 1980 y 1990.

## 3. Evaluación de las tasas de distribución por sector de actividad: 1950 - 1990

### 3.1 Datos básicos:

Cuadro 2: Distribución de la población económicamente activa por sector de actividad en %

| Año | Agricultura | Industria Total | Manufac. | Servicios |
|---|---|---|---|---|
| **Hombres** | | | | |
| 1950 (1) | 82.00 | 5.00 | .. | 13.00 |
| 1960 (1) | 79.00 | 6.00 | .. | 15.00 |
| 1970 (1) | 75.50 | 7.50 | .. | 17.00 |
| 1975 (2) | 73.75 | 8.25 | .. | 18.00 |
| 1980 (1) | 72.00 | 9.00 | .. | 19.00 |
| **Mujeres** | | | | |
| 1950 (1) | 98.50 | 0.35 | .. | 1.15 |
| 1960 (1) | 97.00 | 0.75 | .. | 2.25 |
| 1970 (1) | 95.25 | 1.20 | .. | 3.55 |
| 1975 (2) | 95.00 | 1.70 | .. | 3.30 |
| 1980 (1) | 93.50 | 1.65 | .. | 4.85 |

Fuente(s): (1) EPPA3; (2) ASTER.

### 3.2 Método(s): interpolación y extrapolación lineares

**3.2.1 Hombres:**
- 1950-90, interpolación y extrapolación de las tasas de distribución 1950-80 con base en EPPA3;
ajuste de las tasas interpoladas y extrapoladas con base en 3/4 de las variaciones de las tasas interpoladas 1975, en relación con las tasas de distribución con base en el censo de 1975.
de distribución con base en el censo de 1975.

**3.2.2 Mujeres:**
- 1950-90, interpolación extrapolación de las tasas de distribución ajustadas 1950 y 1980 con base en EPPA3;
ajuste de las tasas de distribución con base en
la razón hombres/mujeres en la agricultura con base en el censo de 1975;
las tasas de distribución de manufacturas estimada con base en los razones manufacturas/industria estimadas para Mauricio.

## 4. Proyección de las tasas de actividad: 2000 - 2010

### 4.1 Modelo(s): linear

**4.1.1 Hombres:**
- Para todos los grupos de edad, aplicación de la función F1;
- Modificación de las tendencias de los grupos de edad [10-19] y [60+].

**4.1.2 Mujeres:**
- Para todos los grupos de edad, aplicación de la función F1;
- Modificación de las tendencias de los grupos de edad [10-59].

---

*Notas sobre los ajustes de las tasas, véase p.380-384.*          *Notas sobre las funciones de proyección, véase p. 386.*

# Malasia

## 1. Fuente(s) de los datos básicos

Código(s):   Título(s):

EPPA3   Estimaciones y proyecciones de la población económicamente activa, 1950-2025, tercera edición, OIT, Ginebra, 1986.
STAT   Base de datos de la OIT sobre estadísticas del trabajo - LABORSTA, Oficina de Estadística, OIT, Ginebra.

## 2. Evaluación de las tasas de actividad: 1950 - 1990

### 2.1 Datos básicos:

Cuadro 1: Tasas de actividad por sexo y grupo de edad

| Grupo de edad | Año 1950 (3) | 1960 (3) | 1970 (3) | 1980 (1)(4) | 1980 (2)(4) | 1990 (4) |
|---|---|---|---|---|---|---|
| **Hombres** | | | | | | |
| 10-14 | .. | .. | .. | 8.84 | ... | ... |
| 15-19 | .. | .. | .. | 49.05 | 50.10 | 40.20 |
| 20-24 | .. | .. | .. | 89.76 | 92.20 | 83.20 |
| 25-29 | .. | .. | .. | 95.55 | 97.70 | 95.10 |
| 30-34 | .. | .. | .. | 96.29 | 98.30 | 97.10 |
| 35-39 | .. | .. | .. | 96.54 | 97.80 | 97.80 |
| 40-44 | .. | .. | .. | 96.24 | 98.30 | 97.20 |
| 45-49 | .. | .. | .. | 95.19 | 97.60 | 96.60 |
| 50-54 | .. | .. | .. | 91.47 | 94.80 | 92.60 |
| 55-59 | .. | .. | .. | 77.63 | 79.90 | 71.40 |
| 60-64 | .. | .. | .. | 69.03 | 70.50 | 61.40 |
| 65+ | .. | .. | .. | 49.37 | ... | ... |
| **Mujeres** | | | | | | |
| 10-14 | 10.90 | 9.20 | 8.55 | .. | ... | ... |
| 15-19 | 33.20 | 33.75 | 34.25 | .. | 33.70 | 27.60 |
| 20-24 | 35.20 | 38.90 | 42.65 | .. | 56.70 | 57.70 |
| 25-29 | 30.00 | 30.70 | 37.80 | .. | 46.50 | 51.40 |
| 30-34 | 32.95 | 33.70 | 39.25 | .. | 44.30 | 49.30 |
| 35-39 | 36.95 | 37.80 | 42.85 | .. | 48.20 | 48.30 |
| 40-44 | 38.25 | 39.15 | 42.30 | .. | 50.20 | 49.60 |
| 45-49 | 39.90 | 41.10 | 42.30 | .. | 49.40 | 49.60 |
| 50-54 | 37.00 | 37.75 | 38.45 | .. | 44.10 | 42.40 |
| 55-59 | 32.00 | 31.95 | 31.90 | .. | 35.40 | 32.50 |
| 60-64 | 24.25 | 24.25 | 24.20 | .. | 27.90 | 26.60 |
| 65+ | 12.85 | 11.85 | 13.70 | .. | ... | ... |

Nota(s): (1) Censo; (2) Encuesta.
Fuente(s): (3) EPPA3; (4) STAT.

### 2.2 Método(s):   interpolación linear
promedio aritmético

#### 2.2.1 Hombres:

- 1950-70, tasas de actividad 1950-70 con base en EPPA3;
ajuste de las tasas de actividad del grupo de edad [20-24];
- 1980, promedios de las tasas de actividad con base en
el censo de 1980 y la encuesta de 1980;
tasas de actividad de los grupos de edad [10-14] y [65+] con base en
el censo de 1980;
- 1990, las tasas de actividad ajustadas con base en la encuesta de 1990.

#### 2.2.2 Mujeres:

- 1950-80, tasas de actividad 1950-80 con base en EPPA3;
- 1990, interpolación de las tasas de actividad 1950-70 con base en EPPA3
y de las tasas de actividad con base en las encuestas de 1980 y 1990.

## 3. Evaluación de las tasas de distribución por sector de actividad: 1950 - 1990

### 3.1 Datos básicos:

Cuadro 2: Distribución de la población económicamente activa por sector de actividad en %

| Año | Agricultura | Industria Total | Manufac. | Servicios |
|---|---|---|---|---|
| **Hombres** | | | | |
| 1980 | 37.49 | 19.86 | 11.83 | 42.65 |
| 1988 | 29.95 | 22.57 | 13.12 | 47.48 |
| **Mujeres** | | | | |
| 1980 | 49.33 | 17.69 | 16.31 | 32.98 |
| 1988 | 30.31 | 21.68 | 20.61 | 48.01 |

Fuente(s): STAT.

### 3.2 Método(s):   extrapolación linear

#### 3.2.1 Hombres:

- 1950-70, tasas de distribución 1950-70 con base en EPPA3;
- 1980, tasas de distribución ajustadas con base en el censo de 1980;
- 1990, extrapolación de las tasas de distribución ajustadas con base en
el censo de 1980 y de las tasas de distribución con base en la encuesta de 1988.

#### 3.2.2 Mujeres:

- 1950-70, tasas de distribución 1950-70 con base en EPPA3;
- 1980, tasas de distribución con base en el censo de 1980;
- 1990, extrapolación de las tasas de distribución con base en el censo
de 1980 y la encuesta de 1988.

## 4. Proyección de las tasas de actividad: 2000 - 2010

### 4.1 Modelo(s):   linear, log-linear y hiperbólico

#### 4.1.1 Hombres:

- Para los grupos de edad [10-24], aplicación de la función F1;
- Para los grupos de edad [25+], aplicación de la función F3;
- Modificación de las tendencias de los grupos de edad [10-49].

#### 4.1.2 Mujeres:

- Para los grupos de edad [10-39], aplicación de la función F1;
- Para los grupos de edad [40-59], aplicación de la función F2;
- Para los grupos de edad [60+], aplicación de la función F3;
- Modificación de las tendencias de los grupos de edad [10-14], [20-44] y [65+].

*Notas sobre los ajustes de las tasas, véase p.380-384.*   *Notas sobre las funciones de proyección, véase p. 386.*

# Malawi

## 1. Fuente(s) de los datos básicos

Código(s):   Título(s):

EPPA3       Estimaciones y proyecciones de la población económicamente activa, 1950-2025, tercera edición, OIT, Ginebra, 1986.
ASTER       Anuario de estadísticas del trabajo 1945-89 - Edición retrospectiva sobre los censos de población, OIT, Ginebra, 1990.
R1987       Population Census 1987, National Statistical Office, Zomba.

## 2. Evaluación de las tasas de actividad: 1950 - 1990

### 2.1 Datos básicos:

Cuadro 1: Tasas de actividad por sexo y grupo de edad

| Grupo de edad | Año 1950 (1) | 1960 (1) | 1970 (1) | 1977 (2) | 1980 (1) | 1987 (3) |
|---|---|---|---|---|---|---|
| **Hombres** | | | | | | |
| 10-14 | 49.45 | 47.65 | 45.70 | .. | 40.35 | 10.85 |
| 15-19 | 80.50 | 78.05 | 75.45 | .. | 68.25 | 34.28 |
| 20-24 | 93.05 | 92.05 | 91.00 | .. | 88.05 | 72.48 |
| 25-29 | 98.90 | 98.75 | 98.60 | .. | 98.10 | 92.42 |
| 30-34 | 99.15 | 98.95 | 98.75 | .. | 98.25 | 96.17 |
| 35-39 | 99.30 | 99.10 | 98.90 | .. | 98.35 | 96.96 |
| 40-44 | 99.40 | 99.20 | 99.00 | .. | 98.45 | 97.13 |
| 45-49 | 99.20 | 99.05 | 98.85 | .. | 98.35 | 97.14 |
| 50-54 | 99.10 | 99.00 | 98.85 | .. | 98.10 | 96.83 |
| 55-59 | 99.00 | 98.90 | 98.80 | .. | 97.65 | 96.89 |
| 60-64 | 98.55 | 97.85 | 97.10 | .. | 95.05 | 95.12 |
| 65+ | 88.80 | 87.55 | 86.20 | .. | 82.45 | 87.91 |
| **Mujeres** | | | | | | |
| 10-14 | .. | .. | .. | 16.50 | .. | 10.72 |
| 15-19 | .. | .. | .. | 43.81 | .. | 49.57 |
| 20-24 | .. | .. | .. | 60.71 | .. | 73.51 |
| 25-29 | .. | .. | .. | 65.24 | .. | 78.72 |
| 30-34 | .. | .. | .. | 69.00 | .. | 82.23 |
| 35-39 | .. | .. | .. | 71.42 | .. | 84.59 |
| 40-44 | .. | .. | .. | 73.49 | .. | 87.04 |
| 45-49 | .. | .. | .. | 73.29 | .. | 88.72 |
| 50-54 | .. | .. | .. | 72.96 | .. | 89.50 |
| 55-59 | .. | .. | .. | 76.45 | .. | 89.94 |
| 60-64 | .. | .. | .. | 68.60 | .. | 83.93 |
| 65+ | .. | .. | .. | 55.19 | .. | 71.35 |

Fuente(s): (1) EPPA3; (2) ASTER; (3) R1987.

### 2.2 Método(s): interpolación y extrapolación lineares

#### 2.2.1 Hombres:

- 1950-90, interpolación y extrapolación de las tasas de actividad 1950-80 con base en EPPA3;
ajuste de las tasas interpoladas y extrapoladas con base en las variaciones de las tasas interpoladas 1987, en relación con las tasas de actividad con base en el censo 1987;
modificación de las tendencias de los grupos de edad [10+] para 1990.

#### 2.2.2 Mujeres:

- 1950-90, interpolación y extrapolación de las tasas de actividad ajustadas con base en los censos de 1977 y 1987.

## 3. Evaluación de las tasas de distribución por sector de actividad: 1950 - 1990

### 3.1 Datos básicos:

Cuadro 2: Distribución de la población económicamente activa por sector de actividad en %

| Año | Agricultura | Industria Total | Manufac. | Servicios |
|---|---|---|---|---|
| **Hombres** | | | | |
| 1950 (1) | 93.75 | 2.60 | .. | 3.65 |
| 1960 (1) | 90.00 | 4.00 | .. | 6.00 |
| 1970 (1) | 86.00 | 6.00 | .. | 8.00 |
| 1977 (2) | 78.08 | 9.91 | 5.65 | 12.00 |
| 1987 (3) | 78.39 | 8.46 | 4.81 | 13.15 |
| **Mujeres** | | | | |
| 1950 (1) | 98.50 | 0.50 | .. | 1.00 |
| 1960 (1) | 97.50 | 0.80 | .. | 1.70 |
| 1970 (1) | 96.00 | 1.30 | .. | 2.70 |
| 1977 (2) | 96.31 | 1.38 | 1.17 | 2.31 |
| 1987 (3) | 95.66 | 1.20 | 1.06 | 3.14 |

Fuente(s): (1) EPPA3; (2) ASTER; (3) R1987.

### 3.2 Método(s): interpolación y extrapolación lineares
promedio ponderado

#### 3.2.1 Hombres:

- 1950-70, tasas de distribución 1950-70 con base en EPPA3;
- 1980, promedios ponderados de las tasas con base en los censos de 1977 de 1979 y 1987;
- 1990, estimación de la tasa de distribución de la agricultura con base en los resultados del censo de 1987 y aplicación a las tasas de la industria los resultados del censo de 1987 y aplicación a las tasas de la industria

#### 3.2.2 Mujeres:

- 1950-90, interpolación y extrapolación de las tasas de distribución con base en los censos de 1977 y 1987;
modificación de las tendencias de todos los sectores para 1950 y 1960.

## 4. Proyección de las tasas de actividad: 2000 - 2010

### 4.1 Modelo(s): linear y hiperbólico

#### 4.1.1 Hombres:

- Para el grupo de edad [10-14], aplicación de la función F1;
- Para los grupos de edad [15+], aplicación de la función F3;
- Modificación de la tendencia del grupo de edad [65+].

#### 4.1.2 Mujeres:

- Para los grupos de edad [10-19] y [60+], aplicación de la función F1;
- Para los grupos de edad [20-59], aplicación de la función F3;
- Modificación de las tendencias de todos los grupos de edad.

---

*Notas sobre los ajustes de las tasas, véase p.380-384.*    *Notas sobre las funciones de proyección, véase p. 386.*

# Maldivas

## 1. Fuente(s) de los datos básicos

Código(s):    Título(s):

ADNU84    Annuaire démographique 1984 - Statistiques des recensements de population II, trente-sixième édition, Nations Unies, New York, 1986.
ADNU88    Annuaire démographique 1988 - Statistiques des recensements de population, quarantième édition, Nations Unies, New York, 1990.

## 2. Evaluación de las tasas de actividad: 1950 - 1990

### 2.1 Datos básicos:

Cuadro 1: Tasas de actividad por sexo y grupo de edad

|  | Año | |
| --- | --- | --- |
| Grupo de edad | 1977 | 1985 |
| **Hombres** | | |
| 10-14 | 37.23 | 5.08 |
| 15-19 | 77.95 | 56.40 |
| 20-24 | 93.39 | 84.59 |
| 25-29 | 95.04 | 87.83 |
| 30-34 | 95.69 | 88.89 |
| 35-39 | 96.50 | 88.93 |
| 40-44 | 96.80 | 86.84 |
| 45-49 | 97.05 | 86.87 |
| 50-54 | 95.54 | 83.33 |
| 55-59 | 93.77 | 80.55 |
| 60-64 | 87.47 | 72.89 |
| 65+ | 65.13 | 49.38 |
| **Mujeres** | | |
| 10-14 | 24.13 | 1.81 |
| 15-19 | 52.23 | 19.80 |
| 20-24 | 62.14 | 23.76 |
| 25-29 | 64.73 | 23.27 |
| 30-34 | 64.76 | 25.48 |
| 35-39 | 70.70 | 26.53 |
| 40-44 | 71.93 | 27.82 |
| 45-49 | 73.33 | 28.34 |
| 50-54 | 68.14 | 28.15 |
| 55-59 | 61.47 | 26.87 |
| 60-64 | 52.26 | 22.44 |
| 65+ | 35.07 | 16.37 |

Fuente(s): ADNU88 y STAT.

### 2.2 Método(s): promedio ponderado

#### 2.2.1 Hombres:

- 1980, promedios ponderados de las tasas de actividad ajustadas con base en los censos de 1977 y 1985;
modificación de las tendencias de los grupos de edad [10-14] y [60+];
- 1990, aplicación a las tasas de actividad estimadas 1980, de las variaciones de la interpolación de las tasas de actividad ajustadas con base en los censos de 1975 y 1985;
- 1950-70, aplicación a las tasas estimadas 1980, de las variaciones estimadas para Indonesia.

#### 2.2.2 Mujeres:

- 1980, promedios ponderados de las tasas de actividad con base en el censo de 1977 y de las tasas de actividad ajustadas con base en el censo de 1985;
modificación de las tendencias de los grupos de edad [10-14] y [60+];
- 1990, aplicación a las tasas de actividad estimadas, de las variaciones de la interpolación de las tasas de actividad con base en el censo de 1975 y de las tasas de actividad ajustadas con base en el censo de 1985;

## 3. Evaluación de las tasas de distribución por sector de actividad: 1950 - 1990

### 3.1 Datos básicos:

Cuadro 2: Distribución de la población económicamente activa por sector de actividad en %

|  | Agricultura | Industria | | Servicios |
| --- | --- | --- | --- | --- |
| Año | | Total | Manufac. | |
| **Hombres** | | | | |
| 1975 | 63.32 | 13.39 | 7.89 | 23.29 |
| 1985 | 43.01 | 19.46 | 11.38 | 37.52 |
| **Mujeres** | | | | |
| 1975 | 44.02 | 48.13 | 47.90 | 7.84 |
| 1985 | 32.49 | 56.65 | 55.97 | 10.86 |

Fuente(s): STAT.

### 3.2 Método(s): interpolación y extrapolación lineares

#### 3.2.1 Hombres:

- 1950-90, interpolación y extrapolación de las tasas de distribución con base en los censos de 1977 y 1985;
modificación de las tendencias de todos los sectores.

#### 3.2.2 Mujeres:

- 1950-90, interpolación y extrapolación de las tasas de distribución con base en los censos de 1977 y 1985;
las tasas de distribución de la agricultura estimadas con base en la razón hombres/mujeres con base en el censo de 1977;
- Aplicación de la razón manufacturas/industria con base en el censo de 1977.

## 4. Proyección de las tasas de actividad: 2000 - 2010

### 4.1 Modelo(s): linear, log-linear, hiperbólico y logístico

#### 4.1.1 Hombres:

- Para los grupos de edad [10-14], [20-29] y [60+], aplicación de la función F1;
- Para los grupos de edad [15-19] y [30-59], aplicación de la función F3;
- Modificación de las tendencias de los grupos de edad [10-29].

#### 4.1.2 Mujeres:

- Para los grupos de edad [10-19], aplicación de la función F2;
- Para los grupos de edad [20-59], aplicación de la función F6;
- Para los grupos de edad [60+], aplicación de la función F3;
- Modificación de las tendencias de los grupos de edad [10-64].

*Notas sobre los ajustes de las tasas, véase p.380-384.*

*Notas sobre las funciones de proyección, véase p. 386.*

# Malí

## 1. Fuente(s) de los datos básicos

Código(s): Título(s):

EPPA3    Estimaciones y proyecciones de la población económicamente activa, 1950-2025, tercera edición, OIT, Ginebra, 1986.
ASTER    Anuario de estadísticas del trabajo 1945-89 - Edición retrospectiva sobre los censos de población, OIT, Ginebra, 1990.

## 2. Evaluación de las tasas de actividad: 1950 - 1990

### 2.1 Datos básicos:

Cuadro 1: Tasas de actividad por sexo y grupo de edad

| Grupo de edad | Año 1950 (1) | 1960 (1) | 1970 (1) | 1976 (2) |
|---|---|---|---|---|
| **Hombres** | | | | |
| 10-14 | 70.75 | 69.05 | 67.35 | 66.17 |
| 15-19 | 86.20 | 84.50 | 82.75 | 81.59 |
| 20-24 | 92.60 | 91.95 | 91.30 | 90.84 |
| 25-29 | 97.55 | 97.45 | 97.35 | 97.27 |
| 30-34 | 98.25 | 98.10 | 98.00 | 97.92 |
| 35-39 | 98.25 | 98.15 | 98.00 | 97.93 |
| 40-44 | 98.00 | 97.85 | 97.75 | 97.64 |
| 45-49 | 97.75 | 97.65 | 97.55 | 97.47 |
| 50-54 | 96.65 | 96.50 | 96.35 | 96.22 |
| 55-59 | 95.20 | 94.95 | 94.70 | 94.49 |
| 60-64 | 90.30 | 89.90 | 89.45 | 89.17 |
| 65+ | 74.40 | 73.70 | 73.00 | 72.51 |
| **Mujeres** | | | | |
| 10-14 | 15.80 | 15.40 | 15.00 | 14.76 |
| 15-19 | 20.00 | 19.55 | 19.10 | 18.83 |
| 20-24 | 18.15 | 17.90 | 17.65 | 17.46 |
| 25-29 | 18.80 | 18.50 | 18.20 | 18.03 |
| 30-34 | 17.95 | 17.65 | 17.40 | 17.20 |
| 35-39 | 18.20 | 17.95 | 17.65 | 17.49 |
| 40-44 | 18.00 | 17.75 | 17.50 | 17.33 |
| 45-49 | 18.20 | 17.95 | 17.70 | 17.50 |
| 50-54 | 16.65 | 16.35 | 16.10 | 15.91 |
| 55-59 | 15.85 | 15.55 | 15.30 | 15.08 |
| 60-64 | 13.00 | 12.65 | 12.35 | 12.15 |
| 65+ | 9.10 | 8.85 | 8.55 | 8.36 |

Fuente(s): (1) EPPA3; (2) ASTER.

### 2.2 Método(s): interpolación y extrapolación lineares

#### 2.2.1 Hombres:

- 1950-70, tasas de actividad 1950-70 con base en EPPA3;
- 1980-90, interpolación de las tasas de actividad 1950-70 con base en EPPA3 y de las tasas de actividad con base en el censo de 1976; ajuste de las tasas extrapoladas con base en las variaciones de las tasas interpoladas 1976, en relación con las tasas de actividad con base en el censo de 1976.

#### 2.2.2 Mujeres:

- 1950-90, interpolación y extrapolación de las tasas de actividad 1950-80 con base en EPPA3 y de las tasas de actividad ajustadas con base el censo de 1976; ajuste de las tasas interpoladas y extrapoladas con base en las variaciones de las tasas interpoladas 1976, en relación con las tasas de actividad con base en el censo de 1976.

## 3. Evaluación de las tasas de distribución por sector de actividad: 1950 - 1990

### 3.1 Datos básicos:

Cuadro 2: Distribución de la población económicamente activa por sector de actividad en %

| Año | Agricultura | Industria Total | Manufac. | Servicios |
|---|---|---|---|---|
| **Hombres** | | | | |
| 1976 | 88.99 | 1.32 | 0.39 | 9.69 |
| **Mujeres** | | | | |
| 1976 | 43.15 | 8.00 | .. | 48.85 |

Fuente(s): ASTER.

### 3.2 Método(s): interpolación y extrapolación lineares

#### 3.2.1 Hombres:

- 1950-90, interpolación y extrapolación de las tasas de distribución 1990 con base en EPPA3 y de las tasas distribución con base en el censo de 1976;
- Aplicación de la razón manufacturas/industria con base en el censo de 1976.

#### 3.2.2 Mujeres:

Métodos, hipótesis y tratamientos idénticos a los que se aplican a los hombres.

## 4. Proyección de las tasas de actividad: 2000 - 2010

### 4.1 Modelo(s): linear

#### 4.1.1 Hombres:

- Para todos los grupos de edad, aplicación de la función F1;
- Modificación de las tendencias de los grupos de edad [10-19], [30-34] y [65+].

#### 4.1.2 Mujeres:

- Para los grupos de edad [10-19] y [45+], aplicación de la función F1;
- Para los grupos de edad [20-44], aplicación de la función F3;
- Modificación de las tendencias de los grupos de edad [20-34] y [45+].

*Notas sobre los ajustes de las tasas, véase p.380-384.*  *Notas sobre las funciones de proyección, véase p. 386.*

# Malta

## 1. Fuente(s) de los datos básicos

Código(s):  Título(s):

EPPA3  Anuario de estadísticas del trabajo 1945-89 - Edición retrospectiva sobre los censos de población, OIT, Ginebra, 1990.
STAT  Base de datos de la OIT sobre estadísticas del trabajo - LABORSTA, Oficina de Estadística, OIT, Ginebra.

## 2. Evaluación de las tasas de actividad: 1950 - 1990

### 2.1 Datos básicos:

Cuadro 1: Tasas de actividad por sexo y grupo de edad

| Grupo de edad | Año 1950 (1) | 1960 (1) | 1970 (1) | 1980 (1) | 1985 (2) |
|---|---|---|---|---|---|
| **Hombres** | | | | | |
| 10-14 | 4.30 | 3.00 | 1.80 | 1.50 | 0.00 |
| 15-19 | 68.65 | 64.35 | 60.30 | 56.50 | 23.20 |
| 20-24 | 92.30 | 91.15 | 90.05 | 88.90 | 72.15 |
| 25-29 | 96.35 | 95.90 | 95.50 | 95.05 | 81.89 |
| 30-34 | 97.35 | 97.60 | 97.90 | 98.15 | 87.19 |
| 35-39 | 96.20 | 97.05 | 97.90 | 98.75 | 87.82 |
| 40-44 | 96.35 | 96.65 | 96.95 | 97.25 | 88.16 |
| 45-49 | 93.65 | 94.05 | 94.45 | 94.80 | 85.68 |
| 50-54 | 91.25 | 90.30 | 89.35 | 88.45 | 78.67 |
| 55-59 | 86.95 | 84.80 | 82.70 | 80.65 | 66.98 |
| 60-64 | 63.30 | 62.10 | 60.90 | 59.70 | 19.51 |
| 65+ | 31.45 | 23.60 | 17.70 | 13.30 | 2.49 |
| **Mujeres** | | | | | |
| 10-14 | 1.35 | 1.35 | 0.95 | 0.75 | 0.00 |
| 15-19 | 24.00 | 30.05 | 32.20 | 30.35 | 36.99 |
| 20-24 | 22.75 | 29.15 | 32.95 | 34.25 | 59.60 |
| 25-29 | 14.85 | 18.25 | 21.75 | 25.35 | 28.36 |
| 30-34 | 13.50 | 13.50 | 15.60 | 19.85 | 14.62 |
| 35-39 | 14.80 | 13.25 | 13.55 | 15.65 | 13.31 |
| 40-44 | 16.30 | 13.70 | 13.15 | 14.75 | 13.94 |
| 45-49 | 16.60 | 15.00 | 14.85 | 16.30 | 12.59 |
| 50-54 | 15.65 | 12.40 | 12.90 | 17.05 | 9.78 |
| 55-59 | 14.60 | 12.75 | 13.00 | 15.45 | 7.24 |
| 60-64 | 12.10 | 9.95 | 10.00 | 12.20 | 1.40 |
| 65+ | 6.45 | 4.05 | 2.75 | 2.50 | 0.42 |

Fuente(s): (1) EPPA3; (2) STAT.

### 2.2 Método(s): extrapolación linear

**2.2.1 Hombres:**

- 1950-80, tasas de actividad 1950-80 con base en EPPA3;
- 1990, extrapolación de las tasas de actividad 1950-80 con base en EPPA3
y de las tasas de actividad con base en el censo de 1985 ;
modificación de las tendencias de todos los grupos de edad;
aplicación a las tasas extrapoladas, de las variaciones de las tasas interpoladas
1985, en relación con las tasas de actividad con base en el censo de 1985 .

**2.2.2 Mujeres:**

Métodos, hipótesis y tratamientos idénticos a los que se aplican a los hombres.

## 3. Evaluación de las tasas de distribución por sector de actividad: 1950 - 1990

### 3.1 Datos básicos:

Cuadro 2: Distribución de la población económicamente activa por sector de actividad en %

| Año | Agricultura | Industria Total | Manufac. | Servicios |
|---|---|---|---|---|
| **Hombres** | | | | |
| 1968 | 10.38 | 54.17 | 32.30 | 35.45 |
| 1972 | 6.98 | 38.93 | 26.61 | 54.09 |
| 1979 | 10.14 | 48.47 | 37.95 | 41.39 |
| 1980 | 9.64 | 48.36 | 37.27 | 42.00 |
| 1981 | 8.87 | 48.84 | 37.52 | 42.29 |
| 1990 | 3.01 | 34.66 | 25.88 | 62.33 |
| **Mujeres** | | | | |
| 1968 | 4.85 | 29.82 | 29.76 | 65.32 |
| 1972 | 3.10 | 35.80 | 35.87 | 61.01 |
| 1979 | 2.88 | 55.87 | 55.45 | 41.26 |
| 1980 | 2.88 | 54.99 | 54.59 | 42.13 |
| 1981 | 3.66 | 54.32 | 53.83 | 42.02 |
| 1990 | 1.25 | 34.35 | 33.64 | 64.40 |

Fuente(s): STAT.

### 3.2 Método(s): promedio aritmético

**3.2.1 Hombres:**

- 1950-60, tasas de distribución 1950-60 con base en EPPA3;
- 1970, promedios de las tasas de distribución con base en estimaciones
oficiales de 1968 y 1970 y de las tasas con base en la encuesta de 1972;
- 1980, promedios de las tasas de distribución con base en estimaciones
oficiales de 1979, 1980 y 1981;
oficiales de 1979, 1980 y 1981;

**3.2.2 Mujeres:**

Métodos, hipótesis y tratamientos idénticos a los que se aplican a los hombres.

## 4. Proyección de las tasas de actividad: 2000 - 2010

### 4.1 Modelo(s): linear, hiperbólico y logístico

**4.1.1 Hombres:**

- Para el grupo de edad [15-19], aplicación de la función F1;
- Para los grupos de edad [20+], aplicación de la función F3;
- Modificación de las tendencias de los grupos de edad [25-59].

**4.1.2 Mujeres:**

- Para los grupos de edad [15-64], aplicación de la función F6;
- Para el grupo de edad [65+], aplicación de la función F3;
- Modificación de las tendencias de los grupos de edad [15-54].

*Notas sobre los ajustes de las tasas, véase p.380-384.*

*Notas sobre las funciones de proyección, véase p. 386.*

# Marruecos

## 1. Fuente(s) de los datos básicos

Código(s):   Título(s):

EPPA3       Estimaciones y proyecciones de la población económicamente activa, 1950-2025, tercera edición, OIT, Ginebra, 1986.
R1971       Recensement général de la population et de l'habitat 1971: résultats de l'exhaustif, niveau national, Direction de la statistique, Rabat, 1976.
R1982       Caractéristiques socio-économiques de la population d'après le recensement général de la population et de l'habitat de 1982,
            Direction de la statistique, Rabat, 1984.

## 2. Evaluación de las tasas de actividad: 1950 - 1990

### 2.1 Datos básicos:

Cuadro 1: Tasas de actividad por sexo y grupo de edad

| Grupo de edad | Año | | | | |
|---|---|---|---|---|---|
| | 1950 (1) | 1960 (1) | 1970 (1) | 1980 (1) | 1982 (2) |
| **Hombres** | | | | | |
| 10-14 | 33.50 | 25.50 | 17.50 | 16.50 | 16.51 |
| 15-19 | 80.00 | 70.00 | 60.00 | 57.00 | 57.03 |
| 20-24 | 95.40 | 93.00 | 85.40 | 81.10 | 80.32 |
| 25-29 | 97.20 | 97.10 | 96.20 | 95.30 | 95.17 |
| 30-34 | 97.40 | 97.50 | 97.25 | 97.70 | 98.14 |
| 35-39 | 97.00 | 97.00 | 97.00 | 98.00 | 98.37 |
| 40-44 | 96.50 | 96.60 | 96.70 | 97.80 | 98.06 |
| 45-49 | 96.20 | 96.30 | 96.40 | 96.60 | 96.56 |
| 50-54 | 95.80 | 95.00 | 94.30 | 93.60 | 93.27 |
| 55-59 | 95.10 | 94.00 | 92.00 | 90.00 | 89.53 |
| 60-64 | 94.00 | 91.00 | 86.00 | 81.00 | 68.94 |
| 65+ | 84.00 | 68.00 | 55.70 | 43.50 | 42.12 |
| **Mujeres** | | | | | |
| 10-14 | 5.30 | 5.80 | 8.70 | 11.95 | 11.91 |
| 15-19 | 6.00 | 8.80 | 15.70 | 18.40 | 18.97 |
| 20-24 | 5.80 | 6.20 | 13.00 | 19.00 | 20.42 |
| 25-29 | 5.60 | 6.00 | 9.90 | 19.00 | 20.94 |
| 30-34 | 5.90 | 7.30 | 9.90 | 16.50 | 17.72 |
| 35-39 | 6.00 | 8.50 | 10.70 | 15.00 | 16.16 |
| 40-44 | 6.30 | 9.70 | 12.70 | 14.50 | 14.65 |
| 45-49 | 7.00 | 10.60 | 12.30 | 14.50 | 14.09 |
| 50-54 | 7.20 | 10.60 | 12.60 | 14.50 | 14.64 |
| 55-59 | 7.20 | 10.60 | 12.60 | 14.50 | 14.63 |
| 60-64 | 7.00 | 9.20 | 10.20 | 11.00 | 11.16 |
| 65+ | 6.50 | 6.30 | 5.90 | 5.50 | 5.30 |

Fuente(s): (1) EPPA3; (2) R1982.

### 2.2 Método(s): interpolación y extrapolación lineares

**2.2.1 Hombres:**

- 1950-80, tasas de actividad 1950-80 con base en EPPA3;
- 1990, extrapolación de las tasas de actividad 1950-80 con base en EPPA3
y de las tasas de actividad ajustadas con base en el censo de 1982;
modificación de las tendencias de los grupos de edad [10-14], [25-54] y [65+].

**2.2.2 Mujeres:**

- 1950-80, tasas de actividad ajustadas 1950-80 con base en EPPA3;
- 1990, extrapolación de las tasas de actividad 1950-80 con base en EPPA3
y de las tasas de actividad con base en el censo de 1982 ;
ajuste de las tasas extrapoladas con base en las variaciones de las tasas
interpoladas 1980, en relación con las tasas de actividad 1980
con base en EPPA3;
modificación de las tendencias de los grupos de edad [10-14], [20-49] y [55+];

## 3. Evaluación de las tasas de distribución por sector de actividad: 1950 - 1990

### 3.1 Datos básicos:

Cuadro 2: Distribución de la población económicamente activa por sector de actividad en %

| Año | Agricultura | Industria | | Servicios |
|---|---|---|---|---|
| | | Total | Manufac. | |
| **Hombres** | | | | |
| 1971 (1) | 59.44 | 16.51 | .. | 24.05 |
| 1982 (2) | 44.84 | 25.02 | 13.38 | 30.14 |
| **Mujeres** | | | | |
| 1971 (1) | 44.23 | 23.20 | .. | 32.56 |
| 1982 (2) | 35.70 | 33.87 | 33.19 | 30.43 |

Fuente(s): (1) R1971; (2) R1982.

### 3.2 Método(s): interpolación y extrapolación lineares

**3.2.1 Hombres:**

- 1950-70, tasas de distribución 1950-70 con base en EPPA3;
- 1980-90, interpolación y extrapolación de las tasas de distribución ajustadas
con base en el censo de 1971 y de las tasas con base en el censo de 1982;
modificación de las tendencias de todos los sectores.

**3.2.2 Mujeres:**

- 1950-70, tasas de distribución 1950-70 con base en EPPA3;
- 1980-90, interpolación y extrapolación de las tasas de distribución ajustadas
con base en el censo de 1971 y de las tasas con base en el censo de 1982;
modificación de las tendencias de todos los sectores;
ajuste de las tasas estimadas 1950-90 habida cuenta de la subenumeración
censal de las mujeres ocupadas en la agricultura.

## 4. Proyección de las tasas de actividad: 2000 - 2010

### 4.1 Modelo(s): linear y hiperbólico

**4.1.1 Hombres:**

- Para los grupos de edad [10-24], aplicación de la función F1;
- Para los grupos de edad [25+], aplicación de la función F3;
- Modificación de las tendencias de los grupos de edad [20-24] y [30-49].

**4.1.2 Mujeres:**

- Para todos los grupos de edad, aplicación de la función F1;
- Modificación de las tendencias de todos los grupos de edad.

*Notas sobre los ajustes de las tasas, véase p.380-384.*          *Notas sobre las funciones de proyección, véase p. 386.*

# Martinica

## 1. Fuente(s) de los datos básicos

Código(s):   Título(s):

EPPA3      Estimaciones y proyecciones de la población económicamente activa, 1950-2025, tercera edición, OIT, Ginebra, 1986.
STAT      Base de datos de la OIT sobre estadísticas del trabajo - LABORSTA, Oficina de Estadística, OIT, Ginebra.

## 2. Evaluación de las tasas de actividad: 1950 - 1990

### 2.1 Datos básicos:

Cuadro 1: Tasas de actividad por sexo y grupo de edad

| Grupo de edad | Año | | | | | |
|---|---|---|---|---|---|---|
| | 1950 (1) | 1970 (1) | 1974 (2) | 1980 (1) | 1982 (2) | 1990 (2) |
| **Hombres** | | | | | | |
| 10-14 | 4.00 | 1.05 | .. | .. | 0.00 | .. |
| 15-19 | 55.00 | 43.20 | .. | .. | 25.24 | .. |
| 20-24 | 87.60 | 86.70 | .. | .. | 81.85 | .. |
| 25-29 | 96.50 | 94.60 | .. | .. | 91.37 | .. |
| 30-34 | 97.90 | 95.95 | .. | .. | 93.51 | .. |
| 35-39 | 97.95 | 96.00 | .. | .. | 93.97 | .. |
| 40-44 | 97.45 | 95.55 | .. | .. | 91.81 | .. |
| 45-49 | 96.70 | 93.25 | .. | .. | 88.87 | .. |
| 50-54 | 93.60 | 90.25 | .. | .. | 83.91 | .. |
| 55-59 | 88.35 | 82.10 | .. | .. | 74.44 | .. |
| 60-64 | 72.00 | 66.90 | .. | .. | 43.08 | .. |
| 65+ | 52.90 | 28.70 | .. | .. | 6.16 | .. |
| **Mujeres** | | | | | | |
| 10-14 | 2.00 | 0.55 | 0.00 | 0.35 | 0.00 | 0.00 |
| 15-19 | 33.70 | 29.20 | 29.35 | 28.10 | 17.61 | 9.49 |
| 20-24 | 47.55 | 57.60 | 69.34 | 69.10 | 70.03 | 66.25 |
| 25-29 | 48.50 | 53.00 | 64.73 | 72.50 | 76.96 | 85.08 |
| 30-34 | 49.35 | 47.40 | 59.22 | 69.35 | 74.19 | 83.85 |
| 35-39 | 51.85 | 44.70 | 53.22 | 66.50 | 71.94 | 82.13 |
| 40-44 | 53.65 | 45.10 | 50.01 | 62.10 | 66.66 | 80.52 |
| 45-49 | 53.15 | 44.60 | 46.91 | 56.70 | 60.83 | 75.39 |
| 50-54 | 54.30 | 40.45 | 45.50 | 48.95 | 52.11 | 65.60 |
| 55-59 | 45.45 | 37.10 | 35.90 | 40.30 | 44.82 | 49.89 |
| 60-64 | 32.15 | 18.45 | 18.36 | 20.60 | 25.26 | 22.28 |
| 65+ | 16.95 | 4.50 | 4.08 | 4.05 | 3.32 | 2.40 |

Fuente(s): (1) EPPA3; (2) STAT.

### 2.2 Método(s): interpolación y extrapolación lineares

#### 2.2.1 Hombres:

- 1950-70, tasas de actividad 1950-70 con base en EPPA3;
- 1980, extrapolación de las tasas de actividad 1970 con base en EPPA3
y de las tasas de actividad ajustadas con base en el censo de 1982;
- 1990, extrapolación de las tasas de actividad 1950-80 con base en EPPA3
y de las tasas de actividad ajustadas con base en el censo de 1982;
ajuste de las tasas de actividad con base en de las variaciones de las tasas
interpoladas 1980, en relación con las tasas de actividad ajustadas con base en
el censo de 1982; modificación de la tendencia del grupo de edad [65+].

#### 2.2.2 Mujeres:

- 1950-60, tasas de actividad 1950-60 con base en EPPA3;
- 1970-90, interpolación y extrapolación de las tasas de actividad 1960
con base en EPPA3 y de las tasas de actividad con base en los censos
de 1974, 1982 y 1990.

## 3. Evaluación de las tasas de distribución por sector de actividad: 1950 - 1990

### 3.1 Datos básicos:

Cuadro 2: Distribución de la población económicamente activa por sector de actividad en %

| Año | Agricultura | Industria | | Servicios |
|---|---|---|---|---|
| | | Total | Manufac. | |
| **Hombres** | | | | |
| 1960 (1) | 45.16 | 27.42 | .. | 27.42 |
| 1974 (2) | 23.35 | 27.64 | 9.59 | 49.01 |
| 1982 (2) | 14.92 | 26.40 | 5.04 | 58.68 |
| 1990 (2) | 10.20 | 26.37 | 12.07 | 63.43 |
| **Mujeres** | | | | |
| 1960 (1) | 33.33 | 11.11 | 0.00 | 55.56 |
| 1974 (2) | 10.83 | 7.09 | 5.69 | 82.09 |
| 1982 (2) | 6.87 | 5.11 | 4.06 | 88.03 |
| 1990 (2) | 4.62 | 6.29 | 4.90 | 89.09 |

Fuente(s): (1) EPPA3; (2) STAT.

### 3.2 Método(s): interpolación y extrapolación lineares

#### 3.2.1 Hombres:

- 1950-70, tasas de distribución 1950-70 con base en EPPA3;
- 1980-90, interpolación y extrapolación de las tasas de distribución 1960
con base en EPPA3 y de las tasas con base en los censos de 1974, 1982 y 1990.

#### 3.2.2 Mujeres:

Métodos, hipótesis y tratamientos idénticos a los que se aplican a los hombres.

## 4. Proyección de las tasas de actividad: 2000 - 2010

### 4.1 Modelo(s): linear, log-linear, hiperbólico y logístico

#### 4.1.1 Hombres:

- Para el grupo de edad [10-14], aplicación de la función F2;
- Para los grupos de edad [15-29], aplicación de la función F1;
- Para los grupos de edad [30+], aplicación de la función F3;
- Modificación de las tendencias de los grupos de edad [40-49].

#### 4.1.2 Mujeres:

- Para los grupos de edad [15-19] y [55+], aplicación de la función F3;
- Para el grupo de edad [20-24], aplicación de la función F1;
- Para los grupos de edad [25-54], aplicación de la función F6;
- Modificación de las tendencias de los grupos de edad [20-29] y [40-49].

*Notas sobre los ajustes de las tasas, véase p.380-384.*      *Notas sobre las funciones de proyección, véase p. 386.*

# Mauricio

## 1. Fuente(s) de los datos básicos

Código(s):   Título(s):

EPPA3   Estimaciones y proyecciones de la población económicamente activa, 1950-2025, tercera edición, OIT, Ginebra, 1986.
ASTER   Anuario de estadísticas del trabajo 1945-89 - Edición retrospectiva sobre los censos de población, OIT, Ginebra, 1990.
R1983   1983 Housing and Population Census, Analysis Report, Vol IV, Central Statistical Office, Port Louis, April 1987.
R1990   1990 Housing and Population Census of Mauritius - Economic Characteristics, Central Statistical Office, Port Louis, 1991.

## 2. Evaluación de las tasas de actividad: 1950 - 1990

### 2.1 Datos básicos:

Cuadro 1: Tasas de actividad por sexo y grupo de edad

| Grupo de edad | Año 1950 (1) | 1960 (1) | 1970 (1) | 1972 (2) | 1983 (3) | 1990 (4) |
|---|---|---|---|---|---|---|
| **Hombres** | | | | | | |
| 10-14 | 11.80 | 10.40 | 9.05 | 15.73 | 10.13 | 11.21 |
| 15-19 | 82.45 | 73.30 | 65.75 | 64.72 | 61.88 | 50.71 |
| 20-24 | 97.80 | 96.30 | 94.75 | 94.58 | 95.98 | 90.43 |
| 25-29 | 98.60 | 97.90 | 97.25 | 97.60 | 97.85 | 95.46 |
| 30-34 | 98.70 | 98.00 | 97.35 | 97.36 | 97.65 | 96.79 |
| 35-39 | 98.60 | 97.90 | 97.25 | 97.25 | 97.28 | 97.10 |
| 40-44 | 98.55 | 97.85 | 97.20 | 96.54 | 95.81 | 96.55 |
| 45-49 | 97.70 | 96.65 | 95.65 | 95.22 | 94.49 | 94.61 |
| 50-54 | 94.60 | 93.30 | 92.00 | 91.68 | 91.05 | 91.19 |
| 55-59 | 93.55 | 90.00 | 88.00 | 85.25 | 82.30 | 81.70 |
| 60-64 | 91.00 | 68.00 | 50.00 | 41.93 | 22.53 | 29.74 |
| 65+ | 49.07 | 34.80 | 24.15 | 22.37 | 12.13 | 16.39 |
| **Mujeres** | | | | | | |
| 10-14 | 4.20 | 3.25 | 2.30 | 3.69 | 3.15 | 3.41 |
| 15-19 | 13.95 | 14.35 | 14.75 | 15.15 | 24.30 | 25.72 |
| 20-24 | 18.10 | 19.80 | 21.50 | 21.97 | 38.68 | 43.63 |
| 25-29 | 19.10 | 19.25 | 19.40 | 20.20 | 33.33 | 41.90 |
| 30-34 | 22.15 | 22.30 | 22.45 | 23.20 | 31.21 | 45.58 |
| 35-39 | 25.80 | 26.00 | 26.15 | 26.01 | 32.87 | 45.94 |
| 40-44 | 26.50 | 26.70 | 26.90 | 27.81 | 32.87 | 41.81 |
| 45-49 | 31.60 | 29.95 | 28.30 | 28.22 | 31.26 | 37.04 |
| 50-54 | 31.25 | 29.60 | 28.00 | 27.98 | 27.89 | 32.42 |
| 55-59 | 29.00 | 27.00 | 25.00 | 24.31 | 23.48 | 24.61 |
| 60-64 | 27.00 | 21.00 | 15.00 | 12.95 | 6.03 | 9.00 |
| 65+ | 7.55 | 6.85 | 5.35 | 5.26 | 2.57 | 4.09 |

Fuente(s): (1) EPPA3; (2) ASTER; (3) ASTER y R1983; (4) R1990.

### 2.2 Método(s): interpolación linear

**2.2.1 Hombres:**

- 1950-70, tasas de actividad 1950-70 con base en EPPA3;
- 1980, interpolación de las tasas de actividad con base en los censos de 1972, 1983 y 1990;
modificación de las tendencias de todos los grupos de edad;
- 1990, tasas de actividad con base en el censo de 1990.

**2.2.2 Mujeres:**

Métodos, hipótesis y tratamientos idénticos a los que se aplican a los hombres.

## 3. Evaluación de las tasas de distribución por sector de actividad: 1950 - 1990

### 3.1 Datos básicos:

Cuadro 2: Distribución de la población económicamente activa por sector de actividad en %

| Año | Agricultura | Industria Total | Manufac. | Servicios |
|---|---|---|---|---|
| **Hombres** | | | | |
| 1972 (1) | 31.99 | 28.23 | 14.40 | 39.77 |
| 1983 (2) | 25.36 | 27.45 | 15.84 | 47.18 |
| 1990 (3) | 17.75 | 40.14 | 24.51 | 42.11 |
| **Mujeres** | | | | |
| 1972 (1) | 37.18 | 11.02 | 10.41 | 51.80 |
| 1983 (2) | 23.33 | 33.58 | 32.94 | 43.09 |
| 1990 (3) | 14.32 | 50.19 | 49.72 | 35.50 |

Fuente(s): (1) ASTER; (2) R1983; (3) R1990.

### 3.2 Método(s): promedio ponderado

**3.2.1 Hombres:**

- 1950-70, tasas de distribución 1950-70 con base en EPPA3;
- 1980, promedios ponderados de las tasas de distribución con base en los censos de 1972 y 1983;
- 1990, tasas de distribución con base en el censo de 1990.

**3.2.2 Mujeres:**

Métodos, hipótesis y tratamientos idénticos a los que se aplican a los hombres.

## 4. Proyección de las tasas de actividad: 2000 - 2010

### 4.1 Modelo(s): linear, log-linear y hiperbólico

**4.1.1 Hombres:**

- Para los grupos de edad [10-14] y [20-29], aplicación de la función F1;
- Para el grupo de edad [15-19], aplicación de la función F2;
- Para los grupos de edad [30+], aplicación de la función F3;
- Modificación de las tendencias de los grupos de edad [15-19] y [30-49].

**4.1.2 Mujeres:**

- Para los grupos de edad [10-19] y [45-49], aplicación de la función F1;
- Para los grupos de edad [20-44], aplicación de la función F2;
- Para los grupos de edad [50+], aplicación de la función F3;
- Modificación de la tendencia del grupo de edad [20-24].

*Notas sobre los ajustes de las tasas, véase p.380-384.*

*Notas sobre las funciones de proyección, véase p. 386.*

# Mauritania

## 1. Fuente(s) de los datos básicos

Código(s):  Título(s):

EPPA3       Estimaciones y proyecciones de la población económicamente activa, 1950-2025, tercera edición, OIT, Ginebra, 1986.
R1977       Recensement de la population 1977, Direction de la Statistique et de la Comptabilité Nationale, Nouakchott.

## 2. Evaluación de las tasas de actividad: 1950 - 1990

### 2.1 Datos básicos:

Cuadro 1: Tasas de actividad por sexo y grupo de edad

| Grupo de edad | Año 1950 | 1960 | 1970 | 1980 |
|---|---|---|---|---|
| **Hombres** | | | | |
| 10-14 | 39.60 | 38.60 | 35.15 | 28.20 |
| 15-19 | 91.75 | 89.90 | 83.25 | 70.00 |
| 20-24 | 97.75 | 98.30 | 95.35 | 91.10 |
| 25-29 | 99.00 | 98.50 | 97.55 | 96.80 |
| 30-34 | 99.25 | 99.15 | 98.70 | 97.90 |
| 35-39 | 99.45 | 99.30 | 98.85 | 97.95 |
| 40-44 | 99.50 | 99.35 | 98.90 | 97.95 |
| 45-49 | 98.80 | 98.70 | 98.30 | 97.50 |
| 50-54 | 97.35 | 97.15 | 96.60 | 95.40 |
| 55-59 | 97.25 | 96.95 | 96.00 | 94.10 |
| 60-64 | 81.15 | 80.80 | 79.40 | 76.65 |
| 65+ | 66.75 | 66.10 | 63.85 | 59.30 |
| **Mujeres** | | | | |
| 10-14 | 16.50 | 16.10 | 14.65 | 11.75 |
| 15-19 | 31.20 | 30.50 | 27.95 | 22.90 |
| 20-24 | 27.35 | 26.95 | 25.50 | 22.65 |
| 25-29 | 25.25 | 24.85 | 23.45 | 20.70 |
| 30-34 | 25.85 | 25.45 | 24.05 | 21.15 |
| 35-39 | 24.20 | 23.85 | 22.65 | 20.15 |
| 40-44 | 25.50 | 25.15 | 23.85 | 21.35 |
| 45-49 | 24.20 | 23.85 | 22.60 | 20.15 |
| 50-54 | 25.50 | 25.10 | 23.55 | 20.50 |
| 55-59 | 23.10 | 22.70 | 21.20 | 18.25 |
| 60-64 | 17.55 | 17.10 | 15.60 | 12.50 |
| 65+ | 14.05 | 13.60 | 12.00 | 8.80 |

Fuente(s): EPPA3.

### 2.2 Método(s): interpolación y extrapolación lineares

#### 2.2.1 Hombres:

- 1950-80, tasas de actividad 1950-80 con base en EPPA3;
- 1990, extrapolación de las tasas de actividad 1950-80 con base en EPPA3; ajuste de las tasas extrapoladas con base en las variaciones de las tasas interpoladas 1980, en relación con las tasas 1980 con base en EPPA3; modificación de las tendencias de los grupos de edad [25-54] para 1990.

#### 2.2.2 Mujeres:

- 1950-90, interpolación y extrapolación de las tasas de actividad 1950-80 con base en EPPA3; ajuste de las tasas interpoladas y extrapoladas habida cuenta de la subenumeración censal de las mujeres ocupadas en la agricultura; ajuste con base en la razón hombres/mujeres igual a 1 en la agricultura.

## 3. Evaluación de las tasas de distribución por sector de actividad: 1950 - 1990

### 3.1 Datos básicos:

Cuadro 2: Distribución de la población económicamente activa por sector de actividad en %

| Año | Agricultura | Industria Total | Manufac. | Servicios |
|---|---|---|---|---|
| **Hombres** | | | | |
| 1950 (1) | 94.50 | 1.60 | .. | 3.90 |
| 1960 (1) | 92.00 | 2.40 | .. | 5.60 |
| 1970 (1) | 83.00 | 5.00 | .. | 12.00 |
| 1977 (2) | 65.82 | 8.88 | 4.38 | 25.31 |
| 1980 (1) | 65.00 | 10.50 | .. | 24.50 |
| **Mujeres** | | | | |
| 1977 (2) | 70.67 | 2.92 | 0.00 | 26.41 |

Fuente(s): (1) EPPA3; (2) R1977.

### 3.2 Método(s): interpolación y extrapolación lineares

#### 3.2.1 Hombres:

- 1950-80, tasas de distribución 1950-80 con base en EPPA3;
- 1990, extrapolación de las tasas de distribución 1950-80 con base en EPPA3; modificación de las tendencias de todos los sectores.

#### 3.2.2 Mujeres:

- 1950 y 1980-90, tasa de distribución de la agricultura con base en la razón hombres/mujeres igual a 1 en la agricultura; tasas de distribución de la industria y los servicios con base en la razón industria/servicios con base en el censo de 1977;
- Aplicación de la razón manufacturas/industria estimada para Marruecos;
- 1960-70, interpolación de las tasas estimadas 1950 y de las tasas con base en el censo de 1977.

## 4. Proyección de las tasas de actividad: 2000 - 2010

### 4.1 Modelo(s): linear

#### 4.1.1 Hombres:

- Para todos los grupos de edad, aplicación de la función F1;
- Modificación de las tendencias de los grupos de edad [10-19] y [60+].

#### 4.1.2 Mujeres:

- Para todos los grupos de edad, aplicación de la función F1;
- Modificación de las tendencias de los grupos de edad [15-54].

---

*Notas sobre los ajustes de las tasas, véase p.380-384.*

*Notas sobre las funciones de proyección, véase p. 386.*

# México

## 1. Fuente(s) de los datos básicos

Código(s):   Título(s):
EPPA3    Estimaciones y proyecciones de la población económicamente activa, 1950-2025, tercera edición, OIT, Ginebra, 1986.
ASTER    Anuario de estadísticas del trabajo 1945-89 - Edición retrospectiva sobre los censos de población, OIT, Ginebra, 1990.
AST93    Anuario de Estadísticas del Trabjo 1993, OIT, Ginebra, 1993.

## 2. Evaluación de las tasas de actividad: 1950 - 1990

### 2.1 Datos básicos:

Cuadro 1: Tasas de actividad por sexo y grupo de edad

| Grupo de edad | Año 1980 (1) | 1990 (2) | 1991 (2) |
|---|---|---|---|
| **Hombres** | | | |
| 10-14 | 11.69 | 6.72 | .. |
| 15-19 | 55.89 | 47.05 | .. |
| 20-24 | 83.45 | 77.10 | .. |
| 25-29 | 94.16 | 89.32 | .. |
| 30-34 | 96.12 | 92.11 | .. |
| 35-39 | 96.20 | 92.18 | .. |
| 40-44 | 95.92 | 91.17 | .. |
| 45-49 | 95.27 | 89.04 | .. |
| 50-54 | 93.83 | 84.68 | .. |
| 55-59 | 91.42 | 78.75 | .. |
| 60-64 | 85.64 | 68.55 | .. |
| 65+ | 68.58 | 45.90 | .. |
| **Mujeres** | | | |
| 10-14 | 2.09 | .. | 6.19 |
| 15-19 | 17.95 | .. | 30.11 |
| 20-24 | 29.10 | .. | 40.42 |
| 25-29 | 28.42 | .. | 37.92 |
| 30-34 | 26.87 | .. | 40.71 |
| 35-39 | 24.85 | .. | 42.48 |
| 40-44 | 22.56 | .. | 38.40 |
| 45-49 | 18.71 | .. | 36.27 |
| 50-54 | 15.20 | .. | 28.85 |
| 55-59 | 12.01 | .. | 26.54 |
| 60-64 | 9.33 | .. | 21.77 |
| 65+ | 5.42 | .. | 12.40 |

Fuente(s): (1) ASTER; (2) AST93,

### 2.2 Método(s): promedio ponderado

#### 2.2.1 Hombres:
- 1950-70, tasas de actividad 1950-70 con base en EPPA3;
ajuste de las tasas de actividad de los grupos de edad [10-19] y [40-59] para 197(
- 1980, tasas de actividad ajustadas con base en el censo de 1980;
- 1990, promedios ponderados de las tasas de actividad ajustadas con base en los censos de 1980 y 1990.

#### 2.2.2 Mujeres:
- 1950-70, tasas de actividad 1950-70 con base en EPPA3;
- 1980, tasas de actividad con base en el censo 1980;
- 1990, promedios ponderados de las tasas de actividad con base en el censo de 1980 y la encuesta de 1991.

## 3. Evaluación de las tasas de distribución por sector de actividad: 1950 - 1990

### 3.1 Datos básicos:

Cuadro 2: Distribución de la población económicamente activa por sector de actividad en %

| Año | Agricultura | Industria Total | Manufac. | Servicios |
|---|---|---|---|---|
| **Hombres** | | | | |
| 1980 (1) | 42.58 | 29.53 | 16.31 | 27.89 |
| 1990 (2) | 29.40 | 30.81 | 19.77 | 39.79 |
| 1991 (2) | 34.05 | 24.98 | 14.84 | 40.97 |
| **Mujeres** | | | | |
| 1980 (1) | 19.18 | 27.87 | 17.60 | 52.95 |
| 1990 (2) | 3.63 | 22.00 | 20.26 | 74.38 |
| 1991 (2) | 10.86 | 19.20 | 18.11 | 69.94 |

Fuente(s): (1) ASTER; (2) AST93.

### 3.2 Método(s): promedio ponderado

#### 3.2.1 Hombres:
- 1950-70, tasas de distribución 1950-70 con base en EPPA3;
- 1980, tasas de distribución con base en el censo de 1980;
- 1970-90, promedios ponderados de las tasas de distribución con base en el censo de 1980 y la encuesta de 1991.

#### 3.2.2 Mujeres:
Métodos, hipótesis y tratamientos idénticos a los que se aplican a los hombres.

## 4. Proyección de las tasas de actividad: 2000 - 2010

### 4.1 Modelo(s): linear, hiperbólico y logístico

#### 4.1.1 Hombres:
- Para los grupos de edad [10-54] y [65+], aplicación de la función F1;
- Para los grupos de edad [55-64], aplicación de la función F3;
- Modificación de las tendencias de los grupos de edad [20-24] y [40-54].

#### 4.1.2 Mujeres:
- Para los grupos de edad [10-29] y [50-59], aplicación de la función F6;
- Para los grupos de edad [30-49] y [60+], aplicación de la función F1;
- Modificación de las tendencias de los grupos de edad [10-34] y [50+].

# Moldava, Rep. de

## 1. Fuente(s) de los datos básicos

Código(s):  Título(s):

BLT-94-2   Vorobiev A. (1994), "Estimaciones de la población económicamente activa de los quince países de la ex URSS, en 1950, 1959, 1970, 1979 y 1989", en el Boletín de Estadísticas del Trabajol - 1994-2, OIT, Ginebra.

## 2. Evaluación de las tasas de actividad: 1950 - 1990

### 2.1 Datos básicos:

Cuadro 1: Tasas de actividad por sexo y grupo de edad

| Grupo de edad | Año 1950 | 1959 | 1970 | 1979 | 1989 |
|---|---|---|---|---|---|
| **Hombres** | | | | | |
| 10-14 | 0.00 | 0.00 | 0.00 | 0.00 | 0.00 |
| 15-19 | 53.04 | 75.86 | 46.99 | 40.93 | 29.94 |
| 20-24 | 91.02 | 88.98 | 86.92 | 89.53 | 82.76 |
| 25-29 | 95.65 | 99.08 | 95.33 | 97.66 | 96.07 |
| 30-34 | 93.94 | 96.12 | 82.68 | 98.00 | 97.19 |
| 35-39 | 96.10 | 97.70 | 99.13 | 99.13 | 97.63 |
| 40-44 | 94.83 | 98.39 | 97.25 | 98.39 | 96.77 |
| 45-49 | 95.65 | 97.22 | 96.70 | 97.22 | 95.28 |
| 50-54 | 91.18 | 94.55 | 94.92 | 92.93 | 92.66 |
| 55-59 | 92.31 | 93.02 | 91.43 | 87.18 | 84.95 |
| 60-64 | 77.27 | 87.10 | 58.82 | 31.37 | 28.75 |
| 65+ | 32.35 | 60.00 | 15.48 | 8.70 | 9.23 |
| **Mujeres** | | | | | |
| 10-14 | 0.00 | 0.00 | 0.00 | 0.00 | 0.00 |
| 15-19 | 71.32 | 80.00 | 49.72 | 40.00 | 28.93 |
| 20-24 | 81.34 | 84.03 | 86.40 | 90.27 | 80.39 |
| 25-29 | 81.51 | 89.76 | 95.20 | 96.69 | 90.00 |
| 30-34 | 81.18 | 81.89 | 93.92 | 96.33 | 93.05 |
| 35-39 | 79.35 | 81.08 | 96.12 | 98.46 | 94.44 |
| 40-44 | 76.06 | 79.49 | 91.60 | 95.77 | 94.23 |
| 45-49 | 72.60 | 76.74 | 89.74 | 92.68 | 90.98 |
| 50-54 | 70.18 | 70.77 | 80.00 | 78.74 | 75.78 |
| 55-59 | 59.52 | 61.19 | 38.95 | 22.73 | 21.37 |
| 60-64 | 38.89 | 64.00 | 14.49 | 8.11 | 9.65 |
| 65+ | 9.09 | 13.19 | 5.63 | 1.61 | 3.15 |

Fuente(s): BLT-94-2.

## 2.2 Método(s): interpolación y extrapolación lineares promedio ponderado

### 2.2.1 Hombres:

- 1950-90, para los grupos de edad [10-19] y [60+], promedios ponderados de las tasas de actividad 1950, 1959, 1970, 1979 y 1989 con base en el Boletín de estadísticas del trabajo 1994-2; ajuste de las tasas de actividad estimadas 1950-80 del grupo de edad [10-14]; para los grupos de edad [10-59], interpolación y extrapolación de las tasas de actividad 1950, 1959, 1970, 1979 y 1989 con base en el Boletín; ajuste de las tasas de actividad de los grupos de edad [60+] para 1959.

### 2.2.2 Mujeres:

- 1950-90, promedios ponderados de las tasas de actividad 1950, 1959, 1979 y 1989 con base en el Boletín de estadísticas del trabajo 1994-2; ajuste de las tasas de actividad de los grupos de edad [15-19] y [60+] para 1959; modificación de las tendencias del grupo de edad [10-14] para 1950 to 1980.

## 3. Evaluación de las tasas de distribución por sector de actividad: 1950 - 1990

### 3.1 Datos básicos:

Cuadro 2: Distribución de la población económicamente activa por sector de actividad en %

| Año | Agricultura | Industria Total | Manufac. | Servicios |
|---|---|---|---|---|
| **Hombres** | | | | |
| 1950 | 75.99 | 8.78 | 5.73 | 15.23 |
| 1959 | 66.23 | 13.35 | 8.64 | 20.42 |
| 1970 | 52.07 | 25.46 | 15.44 | 22.47 |
| 1979 | 45.51 | 29.49 | 17.29 | 25.00 |
| 1989 | 38.13 | 33.58 | 18.09 | 28.29 |
| **Mujeres** | | | | |
| 1950 | 86.61 | 3.15 | 2.52 | 10.24 |
| 1959 | 77.90 | 7.58 | 6.57 | 14.52 |
| 1970 | 56.41 | 17.17 | 13.91 | 26.41 |
| 1979 | 40.91 | 22.73 | 18.09 | 36.36 |
| 1989 | 27.56 | 26.00 | 20.06 | 46.45 |

Fuente(s): BLT-94-2.

### 3.2 Método(s): datos de BLT-94-2

#### 3.2.1 Hombres:

- 1950, 1960, 1970, 1980 y 1990, respectivamente las tasas de distribución 1950, 1959, 1970, 1979 y 1989 con base en el boletín de estadísticas del trabajo 1994-2.

#### 3.2.2 Mujeres:

Métodos, hipótesis y tratamientos idénticos a los que se aplican a los hombres.

## 4. Proyección de las tasas de actividad: 2000 - 2010

### 4.1 Modelo(s): hiperbólico y logístico

#### 4.1.1 Hombres:

- Para los grupos de edad [15+], aplicación de la función F3;
- Modificación de las tendencias de los grupos de edad [20-49].

#### 4.1.2 Mujeres:

- Para los grupos de edad [15-24] y [55+], aplicación de la función F3;
- Para los grupos de edad [25-54], aplicación de la función F6;
- Modificación de las tendencias de los grupos de edad [20-54].

# Mongolia

## 1. Fuente(s) de los datos básicos

Código(s):    Título(s):

EPPA3        Estimaciones y proyecciones de la población económicamente activa, 1950-2025, tercera edición, OIT, Ginebra, 1986.

## 2. Evaluación de las tasas de actividad: 1950 - 1990

### 2.1 Datos básicos:

Cuadro 1: Tasas de actividad por sexo y grupo de edad

| Grupo de edad | Año 1950 | 1960 | 1970 | 1980 |
|---|---|---|---|---|
| **Hombres** | | | | |
| 10-14 | 5.75 | 5.40 | 4.65 | 4.00 |
| 15-19 | 84.90 | 82.40 | 76.50 | 71.45 |
| 20-24 | 95.40 | 94.70 | 93.05 | 91.65 |
| 25-29 | 96.80 | 96.80 | 96.85 | 96.90 |
| 30-34 | 98.00 | 98.00 | 98.05 | 98.10 |
| 35-39 | 98.25 | 98.20 | 98.15 | 98.05 |
| 40-44 | 98.40 | 98.30 | 98.05 | 97.80 |
| 45-49 | 98.35 | 98.15 | 97.65 | 97.20 |
| 50-54 | 98.35 | 97.90 | 96.75 | 95.75 |
| 55-59 | 98.35 | 97.30 | 94.90 | 92.85 |
| 60-64 | 95.80 | 92.60 | 85.25 | 78.95 |
| 65+ | 69.20 | 65.90 | 58.35 | 51.85 |
| **Mujeres** | | | | |
| 10-14 | 6.45 | 4.90 | 3.80 | 3.05 |
| 15-19 | 88.50 | 72.90 | 66.75 | 60.80 |
| 20-24 | 78.40 | 79.15 | 79.45 | 79.70 |
| 25-29 | 67.95 | 75.50 | 78.50 | 81.40 |
| 30-34 | 66.00 | 75.05 | 78.60 | 82.10 |
| 35-39 | 68.20 | 76.65 | 80.00 | 83.20 |
| 40-44 | 70.00 | 77.40 | 80.35 | 83.20 |
| 45-49 | 70.50 | 76.80 | 79.30 | 81.75 |
| 50-54 | 71.50 | 75.25 | 76.70 | 78.15 |
| 55-59 | 79.75 | 74.10 | 72.00 | 69.80 |
| 60-64 | 83.90 | 66.95 | 60.30 | 53.80 |
| 65+ | 58.40 | 43.05 | 37.00 | 31.10 |

Fuente(s): EPPA3.

### 2.2 Método(s): extrapolación linear

**2.2.1 Hombres:**

- 1950-80, tasas de actividad 1950-80 con base en EPPA3;
- 1990, extrapolación de las tasas de actividad 1950-80 con base en EPPA3;
modificación de las tendencias de los grupos de edad [10-24] y [65+].

**2.2.2 Mujeres:**

- 1950-80, tasas de actividad 1950-80 con base en EPPA3;
- 1990, extrapolación de las tasas de actividad 1950-80 con base en EPPA3;
ajuste de las tasas extrapoladas con base en las variaciones de las tasas interpoladas 1980, en relación con las tasas 1980 con base en EPPA3;
modificación de las tendencias de los grupos de edad [10-19] y [65+].

## 3. Evaluación de las tasas de distribución por sector de actividad: 1950 - 1990

### 3.1 Datos básicos:

Cuadro 2: Distribución de la población económicamente activa por sector de actividad en %

| Año | Agricultura | Industria Total | Manufac. | Servicios |
|---|---|---|---|---|
| **Hombres** | | | | |
| 1950 | 70.00 | 17.00 | .. | 13.00 |
| 1960 | 64.00 | 19.00 | .. | 17.00 |
| 1970 | 51.00 | 21.00 | .. | 28.00 |
| 1980 | 43.00 | 21.00 | .. | 36.00 |
| **Mujeres** | | | | |
| 1950 | 67.00 | 17.00 | .. | 16.00 |
| 1960 | 57.00 | 19.00 | .. | 24.00 |
| 1970 | 44.00 | 21.00 | .. | 25.00 |
| 1980 | 36.00 | 21.00 | .. | 43.00 |

Fuente(s): EPPA3.

### 3.2 Método(s): extrapolación linear

**3.2.1 Hombres:**

- 1950-80, tasas de distribución 1950-80 con base en EPPA3;
- 1990, extrapolación de las tasas de distribución 1950-80 con base en EPPA3.

**3.2.2 Mujeres:**

- 1950-80, tasas de distribución 1950-80 con base en EPPA3;
- 1980-90, extrapolación de las tasas de distribución 1950-80 con base en EPPA3;
modificación de las tendencias de todos los sectores.

## 4. Proyección de las tasas de actividad: 2000 - 2010

### 4.1 Modelo(s): linear, log-linear, hiperbólico y logístico

**4.1.1 Hombres:**

- Para los grupos de edad [10-59], aplicación de la función F1;
- Para los grupos de edad [60+], aplicación de la función F3;
- Modificación de las tendencias de los grupos de edad [10-34].

**4.1.2 Mujeres:**

- Para los grupos de edad [10-19], aplicación de la función F2;
- Para los grupos de edad [20-49], aplicación de la función F6;
- Para los grupos de edad [50+], aplicación de la función F3;
- Modificación de la tendencia del grupo de edad [10-14].

*Notas sobre los ajustes de las tasas, véase p.380-384.*    *Notas sobre las funciones de proyección, véase p. 386.*

# Mozambique

## 1. Fuente(s) de los datos básicos

Código(s):     Título(s):

EPPA3          Estimaciones y proyecciones de la población económicamente activa, 1950-2025, tercera edición, OIT, Ginebra, 1986.
ASTER          Anuario de estadísticas del trabajo 1945-89 - Edición retrospectiva sobre los censos de población, OIT, Ginebra, 1990.
ADNU88         Annuaire démographique 1988 - Statistiques des recensements de population, quarantième édition, Nations Unies, New York, 1990.
STAT           Base de datos de la OIT sobre estadísticas del trabajo - LABORSTA, Oficina de Estadística, OIT, Ginebra.

## 2. Evaluación de las tasas de actividad: 1950 - 1990

### 2.1 Datos básicos:

Cuadro 1: Tasas de actividad por sexo y grupo de edad

| Grupo de edad | Año 1950 (1) | 1960 (1) | 1970 (1) | 1980 (1) | 1980 (2) |
|---|---|---|---|---|---|
| **Hombres** | | | | | |
| 10-14 | 57.90 | 55.80 | 53.65 | 51.50 | 24.52 |
| 15-19 | 79.35 | 77.00 | 74.60 | 72.25 | 52.90 |
| 20-24 | 94.20 | 93.25 | 92.35 | 91.40 | 91.41 |
| 25-29 | 98.60 | 98.50 | 98.35 | 98.20 | 97.73 |
| 30-34 | 98.85 | 98.70 | 98.55 | 98.40 | 98.74 |
| 35-39 | 99.10 | 98.95 | 98.75 | 98.60 | 98.87 |
| 40-44 | 99.30 | 99.15 | 98.95 | 98.80 | 98.86 |
| 45-49 | 99.35 | 99.20 | 99.05 | 98.90 | 98.85 |
| 50-54 | 99.30 | 99.15 | 98.95 | 98.70 | 98.53 |
| 55-59 | 99.20 | 99.00 | 98.70 | 98.60 | 98.16 |
| 60-64 | 98.90 | 98.25 | 97.65 | 97.00 | 97.01 |
| 65+ | 94.75 | 93.50 | 92.25 | 91.00 | 92.06 |
| **Mujeres** | | | | | |
| 10-14 | 52.50 | 51.65 | 50.85 | 50.00 | 33.33 |
| 15-19 | 83.10 | 81.40 | 79.70 | 78.00 | 68.88 |
| 20-24 | 92.50 | 90.85 | 89.15 | 87.50 | 87.56 |
| 25-29 | 93.60 | 92.05 | 90.55 | 89.00 | 90.02 |
| 30-34 | 95.35 | 93.90 | 92.45 | 91.00 | 91.47 |
| 35-39 | 95.55 | 94.20 | 92.85 | 91.50 | 93.05 |
| 40-44 | 95.65 | 94.45 | 93.20 | 92.00 | 93.01 |
| 45-49 | 96.05 | 94.85 | 93.70 | 92.50 | 93.43 |
| 50-54 | 94.50 | 93.50 | 92.50 | 91.50 | 92.28 |
| 55-59 | 91.65 | 90.95 | 90.20 | 89.50 | 91.41 |
| 60-64 | 88.10 | 87.75 | 87.35 | 87.00 | 87.80 |
| 65+ | 76.45 | 76.30 | 76.15 | 76.00 | 78.46 |

Fuente(s): (1) EPPA3; (2) ASTER y ADNU88.

### 2.2 Método(s): interpolación y extrapolación lineares

#### 2.2.1 Hombres:

- 1980, tasas de actividad ajustadas con base en el censo de 1980;
- 1950-70 y 1990, interpolación y extrapolación de las tasas de actividad 1950-70 y 1990 con base en EPPA3;
ajuste de las tasas interpoladas y extrapoladas con base en las variaciones interpoladas 1980, en relación con las tasas de actividad 1980 con base en EPPA3;
modificación de las tendencias de todos los grupos de edad para 1950-80 y de los grupos de edad [60+] para 1990.

#### 2.2.2 Mujeres:

Métodos, hipótesis y tratamientos idénticos a los que se aplican a los hombres.

## 3. Evaluación de las tasas de distribución por sector de actividad: 1950 - 1990

### 3.1 Datos básicos:

Cuadro 2: Distribución de la población económicamente activa por sector de actividad en %

| Año | Agricultura | Industria Total | Manufac. | Servicios |
|---|---|---|---|---|
| **Hombres** | | | | |
| 1950 (1) | 82.00 | 7.10 | .. | 10.90 |
| 1960 (1) | 78.70 | 9.40 | .. | 11.90 |
| 1970 (1) | 75.40 | 11.60 | .. | 13.00 |
| 1980 (1) | 72.00 | 13.90 | .. | 14.10 |
| 1980 (2) | 71.99 | 13.93 | 12.35 | 14.08 |
| **Mujeres** | | | | |
| 1950 (1) | 98.15 | 0.40 | .. | 1.45 |
| 1960 (1) | 97.80 | 0.50 | .. | 1.70 |
| 1970 (1) | 97.40 | 0.70 | .. | 1.90 |
| 1980 (1) | 97.05 | 0.80 | .. | 2.15 |
| 1980 (2) | 97.05 | 0.80 | 0.78 | 2.15 |

Fuente(s): (1) EPPA3; (2) STAT.

### 3.2 Método(s): extrapolación linear

#### 3.2.1 Hombres:

- 1950-80, tasas de distribución 1950-80 con base en EPPA3;
- 1990, tasas de distribución estimadas con base en la extrapolación de las tasas de distribución 1950-80 con base en EPPA3;
modificación de las tendencias de todos los sectores;
- Aplicación de la razón manufacturas/industria con base en el censo de 1980.
- Aplicación de la razón manufacturas/industria con base en el censo de 1980.

#### 3.2.2 Mujeres:

Métodos, hipótesis y tratamientos idénticos a los que se aplican a los hombres.

## 4. Proyección de las tasas de actividad: 2000 - 2010

### 4.1 Modelo(s): linear

#### 4.1.1 Hombres:

- Para todos los grupos de edad, aplicación de la función F1;
- Modificación de las tendencias de los grupos de edad [10-29] y [60+].

#### 4.1.2 Mujeres:

- Para todos los grupos de edad, aplicación de la función F1;
- Modificación de las tendencias de los grupos de edad [25-49] y [60+].

*Notas sobre los ajustes de las tasas, véase p.380-384.*          *Notas sobre las funciones de proyección, véase p. 386.*

# Myanmar

## 1. Fuente(s) de los datos básicos

Código(s):   Título(s):

ADNU84    Annuaire démographique 1984 - Statistiques des recensements de population II, trente-sixième édition, Nations Unies, New York, 1986.
STAT       Base de datos de la OIT sobre estadísticas del trabajo - LABORSTA, Oficina de Estadística, OIT, Ginebra.
EPPA4     Población económicamente activa 1950-2010 - cuarta edición, OIT, Ginebra, 1996.

## 2. Evaluación de las tasas de actividad: 1950 - 1990

### 2.1 Datos básicos:

Cuadro 1: Tasas de actividad por sexo y grupo de edad

| Grupo de edad | Año 1983 (1) | 1983 (2) | 1983 (3) |
|---|---|---|---|
| **Hombres** | | | |
| 10-14 | 2.24 | 8.62 | 89.75 |
| 15-19 | 26.31 | 47.32 | 51.68 |
| 20-24 | 64.39 | 73.76 | 25.03 |
| 25-29 | 80.72 | 79.34 | 16.82 |
| 30-34 | 86.53 | 82.27 | 14.45 |
| 35-39 | 88.92 | 83.14 | 14.55 |
| 40-44 | 88.68 | 84.18 | 15.11 |
| 45-49 | 86.59 | 82.71 | 16.25 |
| 50-54 | 80.98 | 81.30 | 18.12 |
| 55-59 | 77.62 | 80.19 | 20.08 |
| 60-64 | 63.06 | 72.67 | 29.24 |
| 65+ | 48.42 | 57.09 | 45.56 |
| **Mujeres** | | | |
| 10-14 | 2.76 | 8.37 | 88.53 |
| 15-19 | 18.08 | 36.70 | 64.21 |
| 20-24 | 34.15 | 49.10 | 59.92 |
| 25-29 | 43.11 | 50.00 | 59.37 |
| 30-34 | 46.14 | 51.30 | 59.10 |
| 35-39 | 46.15 | 53.40 | 58.36 |
| 40-44 | 48.56 | 53.87 | 57.77 |
| 45-49 | 50.39 | 52.29 | 57.66 |
| 50-54 | 49.00 | 53.64 | 57.90 |
| 55-59 | 47.47 | 51.01 | 59.21 |
| 60-64 | 35.68 | 43.58 | 63.35 |
| 65+ | 20.81 | 27.57 | 75.43 |

Nota(s): (1) Urbana; (2) Rural; (3) Total.
Fuente(s): ADNU88 y STAT.

### 2.2 Método(s): interpolación linear

#### 2.2.1 Hombres:

- 1950-90, aplicación a las tasas de actividad 1950-90 con base en modelo
urbana-rural, de las variaciones de las tasas de actividad ajustadas con base
en el censo 1983, en relación con las tasas interpoladas 1983.

#### 2.2.2 Mujeres:

- 1950-90, aplicación a las tasas de actividad estimadas para Tailandia,
de las variaciones de las tasas de actividad estimadas 1983, en relación con
las tasas de actividad ajustadas con base en el censo 1983;
modificación de las tendencias del grupo de edad [10-14].

## 3. Evaluación de las tasas de distribución por sector de actividad: 1950 - 1990

### 3.1 Datos básicos:

Cuadro 2: Distribución de la población económicamente activa por sector de actividad en %

| Año | Agricultura | Industria Total | Manufac. | Servicios |
|---|---|---|---|---|
| **Hommes** | | | | |
| 1950 (1) | 81.30 | 4.00 | .. | 14.70 |
| 1960 (1) | 78.70 | 6.05 | .. | 15.25 |
| 1970 (1) | 75.10 | 7.35 | .. | 17.55 |
| 1980 (1) | 71.24 | 16.15 | 13.11 | 12.61 |
| 1983 (2) | 71.69 | 9.41 | 6.80 | 18.90 |
| **Mujeres** | | | | |
| 1950 (1) | 85.75 | 2.55 | .. | 11.70 |
| 1960 (1) | 84.70 | 3.55 | .. | 11.75 |
| 1970 (1) | 78.25 | 5.55 | .. | 16.20 |
| 1980 (1) | 75.31 | 9.96 | 8.98 | 14.73 |
| 1983 (2) | 79.52 | 7.71 | 7.29 | 12.77 |

Nota(s): (1) Viet Nam.
Fuente(s): (1) EPPA4; (2) STAT.

### 3.2 Método(s): interpolación linear

#### 3.2.1 Hombres:

- 1950-90, interpolación de las tasas de distribución 1950-90
estimadas para Viat Nam;
ajuste de las tasas interpoladas con base en 3/4 de las variaciones de las tasas
interpoladas 1983, en relación con las tasas de distribución ajustadas
con base en el censo de 1983.
con base en el censo de 1983.

#### 3.2.2 Mujeres:

Métodos, hipótesis y tratamientos idénticos a los que se aplican a los hombres.

## 4. Proyección de las tasas de actividad: 2000 - 2010

### 4.1 Modelo(s): linear, hiperbólico y logístico

#### 4.1.1 Hombres:

- Para todos los grupos de edad, aplicación de la función F1;
- Modificación de las tendencias de los grupos de edad [10-24] y [60+].

#### 4.1.2 Mujeres:

- Para los grupos de edad [10-19], aplicación de la función F1;
- Para los grupos de edad [20-64], aplicación de la función F6;
- Para el grupo de edad [65+], aplicación de la función F3;
- Modificación de las tendencias de los grupos de edad [10-64].

---

# Namibia

## 1. Fuente(s) de los datos básicos

Código(s): Título(s):

EPPA3     Estimaciones y proyecciones de la población económicamente activa, 1950-2025, tercera edición, OIT, Ginebra, 1986.
ASTER     Anuario de estadísticas del trabajo 1945-89 - Edición retrospectiva sobre los censos de población, OIT, Ginebra, 1990.
R1991     Republic of Namibia, 1991 Population and Housing Census, Report A, Statistical tables, Central Statistical Office, Windhoek, 1993.

## 2. Evaluación de las tasas de actividad: 1950 - 1990

### 2.1 Datos básicos:

Cuadro 1: Tasas de actividad por sexo y grupo de edad

| Grupo de edad | Año | |
|---|---|---|
| | 1960 (1) | 1991 (2) |
| **Hombres** | | |
| 10-14 | 45.00 | 29.31 |
| 15-19 | 75.00 | 52.96 |
| 20-24 | 95.90 | 80.46 |
| 25-29 | 99.40 | 95.04 |
| 30-34 | 99.25 | 97.29 |
| 35-39 | 99.10 | 97.04 |
| 40-44 | 99.05 | 97.01 |
| 45-49 | 98.75 | 96.61 |
| 50-54 | 98.50 | 94.12 |
| 55-59 | 98.00 | 90.94 |
| 60-64 | 95.60 | 65.16 |
| 65+ | 79.00 | 36.27 |
| **Mujeres** | | |
| 10-14 | 43.42 | 18.96 |
| 15-19 | 58.78 | 31.03 |
| 20-24 | 62.84 | 59.51 |
| 25-29 | 54.45 | 67.88 |
| 30-34 | 54.07 | 66.21 |
| 35-39 | 53.09 | 65.69 |
| 40-44 | 53.16 | 64.34 |
| 45-49 | 54.25 | 63.08 |
| 50-54 | 53.01 | 58.67 |
| 55-59 | 48.63 | 52.85 |
| 60-64 | 42.95 | 36.55 |
| 65+ | 30.69 | 20.59 |

Fuente(s): (1) EPPA3; (2) R1991.

### 2.2 Método(s): interpolación y extrapolación lineares

#### 2.2.1 Hombres:

- 1950-90, interpolación y extrapolación de las tasas de actividad 1960
con base en EPPA3 y de las tasas de actividad ajustadas on base en
el censo de 1991 ;
modificación de las tendencias de los grupos de edad [10-14] y [20+] para 1950
y de los grupos de edad [20+] para 1960-90.

#### 2.2.2 Mujeres:

Métodos, hipótesis y tratamientos idénticos a los que se aplican a los hombres.

## 3. Evaluación de las tasas de distribución por sector de actividad: 1950 - 1990

### 3.1 Datos básicos:

Cuadro 2: Distribución de la población económicamente activa por sector de actividad en %

| Año | Agricultura | Industria | | Servicios |
|---|---|---|---|---|
| | | Total | Manufac. | |
| **Hombres** | | | | |
| 1960 (1) | 62.68 | 21.71 | 5.34 | 15.61 |
| 1991 (2) | 45.30 | 20.65 | 4.88 | 34.06 |
| **Mujeres** | | | | |
| 1960 (1) | 58.62 | 1.94 | 1.38 | 39.43 |
| 1991 (2) | 52.10 | 7.88 | 7.02 | 40.01 |

Fuente(s): (1) ASTER; (2) R1991.

### 3.2 Método(s): promedio ponderado

#### 3.2.1 Hombres:

- 1950-90, interpolación y extrapolación de las tasas de distribución 1960
con base en EPPA3 y de las tasas distribución con base en el censo de 1991;
- Aplicación de la razón manufacturas/industria con base en el censo de 1991.

#### 3.2.2 Mujeres:

Métodos, hipótesis y tratamientos idénticos a los que se aplican a los hombres.

## 4. Proyección de las tasas de actividad: 2000 - 2010

### 4.1 Modelo(s): linear, hiperbólico y log-linear

#### 4.1.1 Hombres:

- Para los grupos de edad [10-19], aplicación de la función F1;
- Para los grupos de edad [20+], aplicación de la función F3;
- Modificación de las tendencias de los grupos de edad [10-14] y [20+].

#### 4.1.2 Mujeres:

- Para el grupo de edad [10-14], aplicación de la función F2;
- Para los grupos de edad [15-24] y [60+], aplicación de la función F3;
- Para los grupos de edad [25-59], aplicación de la función F1;
- Modificación de las tendencias de los grupos de edad [10-14],
[25-29] y [55-59].

*Notas sobre los ajustes de las tasas, véase p.380-384.*

*Notas sobre las funciones de proyección, véase p. 386.*

# Nepal

## 1. Fuente(s) de los datos básicos

Código(s):  Título(s):

ADNU84  Annuaire démographique 1984 - Statistiques des recensements de population II, trente-sixième édition, Nations Unies, New York, 1986.
STAT  Base de datos de la OIT sobre estadísticas del trabajo - LABORSTA, Oficina de Estadística, OIT, Ginebra.

## 2. Evaluación de las tasas de actividad: 1950 - 1990

### 2.1 Datos básicos:

Cuadro 1: Tasas de actividad por sexo y grupo de edad

| Grupo de edad | Año 1961 | 1971 | 1981 |
|---|---|---|---|
| **Hombres** | | | |
| 10-14 | 74.69 | .. | 61.28 |
| 15-19 | 91.75 | .. | 72.44 |
| 20-24 | 96.74 | .. | 89.71 |
| 25-29 | 98.41 | .. | 96.00 |
| 30-34 | 98.65 | .. | 97.35 |
| 35-39 | 98.85 | .. | 97.56 |
| 40-44 | 98.95 | .. | 97.83 |
| 45-49 | 97.90 | .. | 96.39 |
| 50-54 | 97.74 | .. | 94.27 |
| 55-59 | 95.12 | .. | 92.21 |
| 60-64 | 85.90 | .. | 83.27 |
| 65+ | 70.86 | .. | 68.69 |
| **Mujeres** | | | |
| 10-14 | 67.20 | 51.30 | 50.29 |
| 15-19 | 77.47 | 66.00 | 61.50 |
| 20-24 | 69.33 | 62.51 | 59.57 |
| 25-29 | 64.77 | 61.33 | 57.59 |
| 30-34 | 61.04 | 61.45 | 57.11 |
| 35-39 | 59.04 | 61.54 | 58.54 |
| 40-44 | 56.03 | 60.16 | 58.88 |
| 45-49 | 54.03 | 59.60 | 58.87 |
| 50-54 | 51.42 | 56.90 | 58.24 |
| 55-59 | 46.06 | 52.05 | 55.78 |
| 60-64 | 33.49 | 38.72 | 39.92 |
| 65+ | 18.44 | 22.40 | 35.00 |

Fuente(s): STAT.

### 2.2 Método(s): interpolación y extrapolación lineares

#### 2.2.1 Hombres:

- 1950-90, interpolación y extrapolación de las tasas de actividad con base en los censos de 1961 y 1981;
modificación de las tendencias de todos los grupos de edad para 1950 y 1990.

#### 2.2.2 Mujeres:

- 1950-90, interpolación y extrapolación de las tasas de actividad ajustadas con base en los censos de 1961, 1971 y 1981;
ajuste de las tasas de actividad con base en la razón hombres/mujeres en la agricultura con base en el censo de 1961;
modificación de las tendencias de todos los grupos de edad para 1950 y 1990.

## 3. Evaluación de las tasas de distribución por sector de actividad: 1950 - 1990

### 3.1 Datos básicos:

Cuadro 2: Distribución de la población económicamente activa por sector de actividad en %

| Año | Agricultura | Industria Total | Manufac. | Servicios |
|---|---|---|---|---|
| **Hombres** | | | | |
| 1961 | 92.54 | 2.59 | 2.33 | 4.87 |
| 1971 | 92.81 | 1.51 | 1.32 | 5.68 |
| 1981 | 90.64 | 0.77 | 0.64 | 8.60 |
| **Mujeres** | | | | |
| 1961 | 97.48 | 1.28 | 1.24 | 1.24 |
| 1971 | 98.17 | 0.47 | 0.46 | 1.36 |
| 1981 | 97.06 | 0.23 | 0.21 | 2.71 |

Fuente(s): STAT.

### 3.2 Método(s): interpolación y extrapolación lineares

#### 3.2.1 Hombres:

- 1950-90, interpolación y extrapolación de las tasas de distribución con base en los censos de 1961, 1971 y 1981;
modificación de las tendencias de todos los sectores para 1980 y 1990.

#### 3.2.2 Mujeres:

- 1950-80, interpolación y extrapolación de las tasas de distribución con base en los censos de 1961, 1971 y 1981;
- 1990, tasas de distribución estimadas para 1980.

## 4. Proyección de las tasas de actividad: 2000 - 2010

### 4.1 Modelo(s): linear y logístico

#### 4.1.1 Hombres:

- Para los grupos de edad [10-54], aplicación de la función F1;
- Para los grupos de edad [55+], aplicación de la función F3;
- Modificación de las tendencias de los grupos de edad [20+].

#### 4.1.2 Mujeres:

- Para los grupos de edad [10-39] y [60+], aplicación de la función F1;
- Para los grupos de edad [40-59], aplicación de la función F6;
- Modificación de las tendencias de todos los grupos de edad.

*Notas sobre los ajustes de las tasas, véase p.380-384.*     *Notas sobre las funciones de proyección, véase p. 386.*

# Nicaragua

## 1. Fuente(s) de los datos básicos

Código(s):    Título(s):

EPPA3    Estimaciones y proyecciones de la población económicamente activa, 1950-2025, tercera edición, OIT, Ginebra, 1986.
ASTER    Anuario de estadísticas del trabajo 1945-89 - Edición retrospectiva sobre los censos de población, OIT, Ginebra, 1990.
AST91    Anuario de Estadísticas del Trabjo 1991, OIT, Ginebra, 1991.
STAT    Base de datos de la OIT sobre estadísticas del trabajo - LABORSTA, Oficina de Estadística, OIT, Ginebra.

## 2. Evaluación de las tasas de actividad: 1950 - 1990

### 2.1 Datos básicos:

Cuadro 1: Tasas de actividad por sexo y grupo de edad

| Grupo de edad | Año 1950 (1) | 1960 (1) | 1971 (2) | 1985 (3) | 1990 (3) |
|---|---|---|---|---|---|
| **Hombres** | | | | | |
| 10-14 | 45.00 | 34.70 | 18.74 | .. | .. |
| 15-19 | 91.10 | 78.85 | 54.55 | .. | .. |
| 20-24 | 96.95 | 94.60 | 81.21 | .. | .. |
| 25-29 | 98.65 | 97.60 | 89.78 | .. | .. |
| 30-34 | 98.80 | 97.90 | 91.51 | .. | .. |
| 35-39 | 99.00 | 98.05 | 92.17 | .. | .. |
| 40-44 | 98.90 | 98.00 | 91.43 | .. | .. |
| 45-49 | 98.50 | 97.75 | 91.38 | .. | .. |
| 50-54 | 98.30 | 96.65 | 88.48 | .. | .. |
| 55-59 | 97.80 | 94.60 | 87.30 | .. | .. |
| 60-64 | 96.80 | 93.35 | 80.70 | .. | .. |
| 65+ | 86.30 | 75.05 | 60.73 | | |
| **Mujeres** | | | | | |
| 10-14 | | | 4.01 | 6.34 | 6.92 |
| 15-19 | .. | .. | 17.44 | 23.62 | 25.62 |
| 20-24 | .. | .. | 25.62 | 38.75 | 42.10 |
| 25-29 | .. | .. | 23.70 | 45.61 | 49.45 |
| 30-34 | .. | .. | 22.99 | 50.03 | 54.99 |
| 35-39 | .. | .. | 22.86 | 45.95 | 51.72 |
| 40-44 | .. | .. | 22.32 | 45.79 | 47.69 |
| 45-49 | .. | .. | 20.59 | 41.70 | 45.54 |
| 50-54 | .. | .. | 18.64 | 37.46 | 42.86 |
| 55-59 | .. | .. | 17.27 | 33.84 | 35.43 |
| 60-64 | .. | .. | 13.99 | 22.06 | 23.71 |
| 65+ | .. | .. | 9.05 | 13.30 | 14.77 |

Fuente(s): (1) EPPA3; (2) ASTER; (3) AST91.

### 2.2 Método(s): interpolación y extrapolación lineares

#### 2.2.1 Hombres:

- 1950-60, tasas de actividad 1950-60 con base en EPPA3;
- 1970-90, interpolación y extrapolación de las tasas de actividad 1950-60 con base en EPPA3 y de las tasas de actividad ajustadas con base en el censo de 1971;
aplicación a las tasas interpoladas y extrapoladas, de las variaciones de las tasas interpoladas 1971, en relación con las tasas de actividad ajustadas con base en el censo de 1971.

#### 2.2.2 Mujeres:

- 1950-70, tasas de actividad ajustadas 1950-70 con base en EPPA3;
el ajuste se ha calculado con base en el modelo de ajuste de las tasas de actividad de las mujeres ocupadas en la agricultura como auxiliares familiares;
- 1980-90, interpolación y extrapolación de las tasas de actividad con base en el censo de 1971, de las tasas de actividad con base en la encuesta de 1985 y estimaciones oficiales de 1990;
aplicación a las tasas interpoladas, de las variaciones de las tasas interpoladas

## 3. Evaluación de las tasas de distribución por sector de actividad: 1950 - 1990

### 3.1 Datos básicos:

Cuadro 2: Distribución de la población económicamente activa por sector de actividad en %

| Año | Agricultura | Industria Total | Manufac. | Servicios |
|---|---|---|---|---|
| **Mujeres** | | | | |
| 1960 (1) | 72.25 | 15.20 | .. | 12.55 |
| 1971 (2) | 58.83 | 18.05 | 11.45 | 23.12 |
| 1977 (3) | 53.49 | 22.02 | 14.49 | 24.50 |
| **Mujeres** | | | | |
| 1960 (1) | 14.20 | 19.70 | .. | 66.10 |
| 1971 (2) | 8.20 | 17.22 | 16.68 | 74.58 |
| 1977 (3) | 15.73 | 20.85 | 20.32 | 63.42 |

Fuente(s): (1) EPPA3; (2) ASTER; (3) STAT.

### 3.2 Método(s): promedio ponderado extrapolación linear

#### 3.2.1 Hombres:

- 1950-60, tasas de distribución 1950-60 con base en EPPA3;
- 1970, promedios ponderados de las tasas de distribución 1960 con base en EPPA3 y de las tasas de distribución con base en el censo de 1971;
- 1980-90, extrapolación de las tasas de distribución con base en el censo de 1971 y de las tasas de distribución con base en estimaciones oficiales de 1977 de 1971 y de las tasas de distribución con base en estimaciones oficiales de 1977.

#### 3.2.2 Mujeres:

Métodos, hipótesis y tratamientos idénticos a los que se aplican a los hombres.

## 4. Proyección de las tasas de actividad: 2000 - 2010

### 4.1 Modelo(s): linear

#### 4.1.1 Hombres:

- Para todos los grupos de edad, aplicación de la función F1;
- Modificación de las tendencias de los grupos de edad [10-19], [30-34], [40-44] y [65+].

#### 4.1.2 Mujeres:

- Para todos los grupos de edad, aplicación de la función F1;
- Modificación de las tendencias de los grupos de edad [10-24], [45-54] y [65+].

# Níger

## 1. Fuente(s) de los datos básicos

Código(s):  Título(s):

EPPA3     Estimaciones y proyecciones de la población económicamente activa, 1950-2025, tercera edición, OIT, Ginebra, 1986.
ASTER     Anuario de estadísticas del trabajo 1945-89 - Edición retrospectiva sobre los censos de población, OIT, Ginebra, 1990.
STAT      Base de datos de la OIT sobre estadísticas del trabajo - LABORSTA, Oficina de Estadística, OIT, Ginebra.

## 2. Evaluación de las tasas de actividad: 1950 - 1990

### 2.1 Datos básicos:

Cuadro 1: Tasas de actividad por sexo y grupo de edad

| Grupo de edad | Año 1959 (1) | 1950 (2) | 1960 (2) | 1970 (2) | 1977 (3) | 1980 (2) | 1988 (1) |
|---|---|---|---|---|---|---|---|
| **Hombres** | | | | | | | |
| 10-14 | 56.10 | .. | .. | .. | 20.63 | .. | 53.87 |
| 15-19 | 90.25 | .. | .. | .. | 83.88 | .. | 89.55 |
| 20-24 | 97.30 | .. | .. | .. | 95.90 | .. | 92.64 |
| 25-29 | 97.70 | .. | .. | .. | 98.15 | .. | 97.23 |
| 30-34 | 98.45 | .. | .. | .. | 98.68 | .. | 97.79 |
| 35-39 | 98.65 | .. | .. | .. | 98.95 | .. | 98.29 |
| 40-44 | 98.55 | .. | .. | .. | 98.57 | .. | 98.04 |
| 45-49 | 97.70 | .. | .. | .. | 98.56 | .. | 97.51 |
| 50-54 | 97.45 | .. | .. | .. | 97.05 | .. | 96.91 |
| 55-59 | 96.85 | .. | .. | .. | 96.15 | .. | 95.74 |
| 60-64 | 94.45 | .. | .. | .. | 89.80 | .. | 94.00 |
| 65+ | 82.25 | .. | .. | .. | 72.44 | .. | 87.86 |
| **Mujeres** | | | | | | | |
| 10-14 | 50.15 | 50.35 | 50.15 | 49.90 | 2.83 | 46.90 | .. |
| 15-19 | 92.15 | 92.60 | 92.15 | 91.70 | 6.33 | 85.30 | .. |
| 20-24 | 96.35 | 96.80 | 96.35 | 95.90 | 6.49 | 89.70 | .. |
| 25-29 | 97.00 | 97.45 | 97.00 | 96.60 | 6.48 | 90.85 | .. |
| 30-34 | 98.40 | 98.75 | 98.40 | 98.00 | 7.07 | 92.60 | .. |
| 35-39 | 98.05 | 98.45 | 98.05 | 97.70 | 8.02 | 92.65 | .. |
| 40-44 | 97.20 | 97.55 | 97.20 | 96.90 | 9.08 | 92.35 | .. |
| 45-49 | 95.75 | 96.10 | 95.75 | 95.45 | 10.24 | 91.00 | .. |
| 50-54 | 87.90 | 88.20 | 87.90 | 87.65 | 10.13 | 83.95 | .. |
| 55-59 | 77.90 | 78.10 | 77.90 | 77.70 | 10.36 | 75.05 | .. |
| 60-64 | 61.80 | 61.90 | 61.80 | 61.70 | 8.01 | 60.05 | .. |
| 65+ | 35.70 | 35.75 | 35.70 | 35.65 | 6.40 | 35.10 | .. |

Fuente(s): (1) STAT; (2) EPPA3; (3) ASTER.

### 2.2 Método(s): interpolación y extrapolación lineares

#### 2.2.1 Hombres:

- 1950-90, interpolación y extrapolación de las tasas de actividad con base en la encuesta de 1959-60 y de las tasas de actividad con base en los censos de 1977 y 1988.

#### 2.2.2 Mujeres:

- 1950-90, interpolación y extrapolación de las tasas de actividad 1950-80 con base en EPPA3;
ajuste de las tasas interpoladas y extrapoladas con base en las variaciones de las tasas interpoladas 1977, en relación con las tasas de actividad con base en el censo de 1977;
modificación de las tendencias de los grupos de edad [20-34] para 1950 to 1990.

## 3. Evaluación de las tasas de distribución por sector de actividad: 1950 - 1990

### 3.1 Datos básicos:

Cuadro 2: Distribución de la población económicamente activa por sector de actividad en %

| Año | Agricultura | Industria Total | Manufac. | Servicios |
|---|---|---|---|---|
| **Hombres** | | | | |
| 1950 (1) | 96.00 | 1.20 | .. | 2.80 |
| 1960 (1) | 95.00 | 1.50 | .. | 3.50 |
| 1970 (1) | 92.40 | 2.20 | .. | 5.40 |
| 1977 (2) | 91.91 | 2.83 | 1.73 | 5.26 |
| 1980 (1) | 88.25 | 3.00 | .. | 8.75 |
| **Mujeres** | | | | |
| 1950 (1) | 98.00 | 0.05 | .. | 1.95 |
| 1960 (1) | 97.50 | 0.05 | .. | 2.45 |
| 1970 (1) | 96.20 | 0.10 | .. | 3.70 |
| 1977 (2) | 97.40 | 1.39 | 1.36 | 1.21 |
| 1980 (1) | 94.15 | 0.15 | .. | 5.7 |

Fuente(s): (1) EPPA3; (2) ASTER.

### 3.2 Método(s): interpolación y extrapolación lineares

#### 3.2.1 Hombres:

- 1950-90, interpolación y extrapolación de las tasas de distribución 1950-80 con base en EPPA3 y de las tasas de distribución con base en el censo de 1977; modificación de las tendencias de todos los sectores.

#### 3.2.2 Mujeres:

Métodos, hipótesis y tratamientos idénticos a los que se aplican a los hombres.

## 4. Proyección de las tasas de actividad: 2000 - 2010

### 4.1 Modelo(s): linear y hiperbólico

#### 4.1.1 Hombres:

- Para todos los grupos de edad, aplicación de la función F1;
- Modificación de las tendencias de los grupos de edad [10-24] y [65+].

#### 4.1.2 Mujeres:

- Para los grupos de edad [10-19], aplicación de la función F1;
- Para los grupos de edad [20+], aplicación de la función F3;
- Modificación de las tendencias de los grupos de edad [20-59].

---

*Notas sobre los ajustes de las tasas, véase p.380-384.*     *Notas sobre las funciones de proyección, véase p. 386.*

# Nigeria

## 1. Fuente(s) de los datos básicos

Código(s):  Título(s):

EPPA3  Estimaciones y proyecciones de la población económicamente activa, 1950-2025, tercera edición, OIT, Ginebra, 1986.
ASTER  Anuario de estadísticas del trabajo 1945-89 - Edición retrospectiva sobre los censos de población, OIT, Ginebra, 1990.
AST87  Anuario de Estadísticas del Trabjo 1987, OIT, Ginebra, 1987.
AST93  Anuario de Estadísticas del Trabjo 1993, OIT, Ginebra, 1993.

## 2. Evaluación de las tasas de actividad: 1950 - 1990

### 2.1 Datos básicos:

Cuadro 1: Tasas de actividad por sexo y grupo de edad

| Grupo de edad | Año | | | |
|---|---|---|---|---|
| | 1950 (1) | 1960 (1) | 1970 (1) | 1983 (2) |
| **Hombres** | | | | |
| 10-14 | 46.85 | 44.60 | 43.10 | 62.04 |
| 15-19 | 77.95 | 74.95 | 72.90 | 29.79 |
| 20-24 | 92.60 | 91.45 | 90.65 | 69.12 |
| 25-29 | 97.00 | 96.85 | 96.70 | 92.52 |
| 30-34 | 97.70 | 97.50 | 97.35 | 96.16 |
| 35-39 | 97.85 | 97.65 | 97.50 | 97.56 |
| 40-44 | 97.65 | 97.45 | 97.30 | 97.94 |
| 45-49 | 96.95 | 96.80 | 96.65 | 98.79 |
| 50-54 | 96.30 | 96.05 | 95.85 | 96.66 |
| 55-59 | 95.05 | 94.65 | 94.35 | 94.63 |
| 60-64 | 91.40 | 90.70 | 90.20 | 91.48 |
| 65+ | 76.95 | 75.65 | 74.75 | 73.57 |
| **Mujeres** | | | | |
| 10-14 | 21.25 | 20.20 | 19.50 | 5.36 |
| 15-19 | 46.30 | 44.25 | 42.85 | 13.58 |
| 20-24 | 50.30 | 48.95 | 48.05 | 24.57 |
| 25-29 | 53.90 | 52.40 | 51.35 | 37.21 |
| 30-34 | 57.20 | 55.55 | 54.45 | 40.25 |
| 35-39 | 59.25 | 57.70 | 56.65 | 47.77 |
| 40-44 | 61.60 | 60.05 | 59.00 | 49.31 |
| 45-49 | 65.55 | 63.85 | 62.70 | 55.38 |
| 50-54 | 70.00 | 67.85 | 66.70 | 57.08 |
| 55-59 | 67.15 | 64.90 | 63.35 | 52.55 |
| 60-64 | 59.50 | 56.65 | 54.70 | 43.61 |
| 65+ | 43.85 | 40.90 | 38.95 | 20.57 |

Fuente(s): (1) EPPA3; (2) AST87.

### 2.2 Método(s): interpolación y extrapolación lineares

#### 2.2.1 Hombres:

- 1950-90, interpolación y extrapolación de las tasas de actividad 1950-70
con base en EPPA3 y de las tasas de actividad ajustadas con base
la encuesta de 1983;
modificación de las tendencias de todos los grupos de edad para 1950.

#### 2.2.2 Mujeres:

- 1950-90, interpolación y extrapolación de las tasas de actividad 1950-70
con base en EPPA3 y de las tasas de actividad ajustadas con base
la encuesta de 1983;
ajuste de las tasas de actividad del grupo de edad [10-24].

## 3. Evaluación de las tasas de distribución por sector de actividad: 1950 - 1990

### 3.1 Datos básicos:

Cuadro 2: Distribución de la población económicamente activa por sector de actividad en %

| Año | Agricultura | Industria | | Servicios |
|---|---|---|---|---|
| | | Total | Manufac. | |
| **Hombres** | | | | |
| 1970 (1) | 71.05 | 13.00 | .. | 15.95 |
| 1983 (2) | 38.74 | 10.74 | 4.35 | 50.52 |
| 1986 (3) | 49.98 | 7.58 | 4.11 | 42.44 |
| **Mujeres** | | | | |
| 1970 (1) | 70.80 | 6.25 | .. | 22.95 |
| 1983 (2) | 22.77 | 7.44 | 6.09 | 69.79 |

Fuente(s): (1) EPPA3; (2) AST87; (3) AST93.

### 3.2 Método(s): interpolación y extrapolación lineares

#### 3.2.1 Hombres:

- 1950-70, tasas de distribución 1950-70 con base en EPPA3;
- 1980-90, interpolación y extrapolación de las tasas de distribución 1970
con base en EPPA3 y del promedio de las tasas con base en las encuestas
de 1983 y 1986;
modificación de las tendencias de todos los sectores para 1990.
modificación de las tendencias de todos los sectores para 1990.

#### 3.2.2 Mujeres:

- 1950-70, tasas de distribución 1950-70 con base en EPPA3;
- 1980-90, interpolación y extrapolación de las tasas de distribución 1970
con base en EPPA3 y de las tasas de distribución con base en
la encuesta de 1983.

## 4. Proyección de las tasas de actividad: 2000 - 2010

### 4.1 Modelo(s): linear y hiperbólico

#### 4.1.1 Hombres:

- Para los grupos de edad [10-19], aplicación de la función F1;
- Para los grupos de edad [20+], aplicación de la función F3;
- Modificación de las tendencias de los grupos de edad [10-14], [20-24],
[40-44] y [60-64].

#### 4.1.2 Mujeres:

- Para todos los grupos de edad, aplicación de la función F3;
- Modificación de las tendencias de los grupos de edad [10-34] y [45-49].

*Notas sobre los ajustes de las tasas, véase p.380-384.*  *Notas sobre las funciones de proyección, véase p. 386.*

# Noruega

## 1. Fuente(s) de los datos básicos

Código(s):  Título(s):

EPPA3      Anuario de estadísticas del trabajo 1945-89 - Edición retrospectiva sobre los censos de población, OIT, Ginebra, 1990.
STAT       Base de datos de la OIT sobre estadísticas del trabajo - LABORSTA, Oficina de Estadística, OIT, Ginebra.

## 2. Evaluación de las tasas de actividad: 1950 - 1990

### 2.1 Datos básicos:

Cuadro 1: Tasas de actividad por sexo y grupo de edad

| Grupo de edad | Año | | | | | |
|---|---|---|---|---|---|---|
| | 1979 | 1980 | 1981 | 1989 | 1990 | 1991 |
| **Hombres** | | | | | | |
| 10-14 | 0.00 | 0.00 | 0.00 | 0.00 | 0.00 | 0.00 |
| 15-19 | ... | ... | ... | 46.97 | 44.62 | 39.20 |
| 20-24 | 79.49 | 78.52 | 80.29 | 79.89 | 78.49 | 74.42 |
| 25-29 | 88.89 | 88.51 | 89.60 | 90.06 | 88.55 | 86.78 |
| 30-34 | 96.25 | 96.02 | 95.24 | 95.15 | 93.87 | 93.17 |
| 35-39 | 97.76 | 96.73 | 95.72 | 94.97 | 93.51 | 94.12 |
| 40-44 | 96.23 | 96.73 | 96.79 | 94.44 | 93.98 | 93.83 |
| 45-49 | 94.00 | 93.62 | 95.15 | 93.80 | 93.94 | 92.57 |
| 50-54 | 90.91 | 92.63 | 93.67 | 90.53 | 89.22 | 87.13 |
| 55-59 | 88.70 | 86.63 | 87.71 | 83.16 | 82.02 | 81.18 |
| 60-64 | 74.07 | 75.74 | 73.67 | 64.95 | 64.21 | 62.24 |
| 65+ | | | | 14.84 | 13.29 | 11.62 |
| **Mujeres** | | | | | | |
| 10-14 | .. | .. | .. | 0.00 | 0.00 | 0.00 |
| 15-19 | .. | .. | .. | 46.03 | 43.55 | 40.83 |
| 20-24 | .. | .. | .. | 70.30 | 67.07 | 66.46 |
| 25-29 | .. | .. | .. | 75.50 | 75.00 | 73.46 |
| 30-34 | .. | .. | .. | 76.92 | 78.21 | 79.74 |
| 35-39 | .. | .. | .. | 82.00 | 81.05 | 80.89 |
| 40-44 | .. | .. | .. | 81.05 | 81.94 | 83.22 |
| 45-49 | .. | .. | .. | 81.97 | 83.46 | 81.34 |
| 50-54 | .. | .. | .. | 75.79 | 74.49 | 75.00 |
| 55-59 | .. | .. | .. | 63.16 | 61.96 | 63.04 |
| 60-64 | .. | .. | .. | 44.12 | 46.53 | 47.47 |
| 65+ | .. | .. | .. | 6.44 | 6.43 | 5.92 |

Fuente(s): STAT.

### 2.2 Método(s): interpolación linear
promedio aritmético

#### 2.2.1 Hombres:

- 1950-70, tasas de actividad 1950-70 con base en EPPA3;
- 1980, interpolación de las tasas de actividad ajustadas con base en las encuestas de 1980, 1981 y 1982;
ajuste de las tasas de actividad del grupo de edad [15-19];
- 1990, promedios de las tasas de actividad ajustadas con base en las encuestas de 1989, 1990 y 1991;
ajuste de las tasas de actividad del grupo de edad [15-19].

#### 2.2.2 Mujeres:

- 1950-80, tasas de actividad 1950-80 con base en EPPA3;
- 1990, promedios de las tasas de actividad ajustadas con base en las encuestas de 1989, 1990 y 1991;
ajuste de las tasas de actividad del grupo de edad [15-19].

## 3. Evaluación de las tasas de distribución por sector de actividad: 1950 - 1990

### 3.1 Datos básicos:

Cuadro 2: Distribución de la población económicamente activa por sector de actividad en %

| Año | Agricultura | Industria | | Servicios |
|---|---|---|---|---|
| | | Total | Manufac. | |
| **Hombres** | | | | |
| 1979 | 10.04 | 41.23 | 21.43 | 48.73 |
| 1980 | 9.98 | 40.11 | 20.14 | 49.91 |
| 1981 | 9.86 | 40.31 | 19.72 | 49.83 |
| 1989 | 8.45 | 36.38 | 19.30 | 55.17 |
| 1990 | 8.03 | 37.16 | 19.44 | 54.81 |
| 1991 | 8.27 | 35.77 | 19.67 | 55.96 |
| **Mujeres** | | | | |
| 1979 | 6.46 | 14.10 | 11.20 | 79.45 |
| 1980 | 5.98 | 13.74 | 9.92 | 80.28 |
| 1981 | 5.81 | 12.98 | 9.77 | 81.21 |
| 1989 | 4.05 | 11.82 | 8.41 | 84.13 |
| 1990 | 3.73 | 11.67 | 8.21 | 84.60 |
| 1991 | 3.84 | 11.42 | 8.43 | 84.74 |

Fuente(s): STAT.

### 3.2 Método(s): promedio aritmético

#### 3.2.1 Hombres:

- 1950-70, tasas de distribución 1950-70 con base en EPPA3;
- 1980, promedios de las tasas de distribución ajustadas con base en las encuestas de 1979,1980 y 1981; ajuste de las tasas de distribución para tener en cuenta los efectivos del servicio militar obligatorio;
- 1990, promedios de las tasas de distribución con base en las encuestas
- 1990, promedios de las tasas de distribución con base en las encuestas

#### 3.2.2 Mujeres:

- 1950-70, tasas de distribución 1950-70 con base en EPPA3;
- 1980, promedios de las tasas de distribución con base en las encuestas de 1979, 1980 y 1981;
- 1990, promedios de las tasas de distribución con base en las encuestas de 1989, 1990 y 1991.

## 4. Proyección de las tasas de actividad: 2000 - 2010

### 4.1 Modelo(s): hiperbólico y logístico

#### 4.1.1 Hombres:

- Para los grupos de edad [15+], aplicación de la función F3;
- Modificación de las tendencias de los grupos de edad [25-49].

#### 4.1.2 Mujeres:

- Para los grupos de edad [15-64], aplicación de la función F6;
- Para el grupo de edad [65+], aplicación de la función F3;
- Modificación de las tendencias de los grupos de edad [15-24].

*Notas sobre los ajustes de las tasas, véase p.380-384.*    *Notas sobre las funciones de proyección, véase p. 386.*

# Nueva Zelandia

## 1. Fuente(s) de los datos básicos

Código(s):    Título(s):

EPPA3    Anuario de estadísticas del trabajo 1945-89 - Edición retrospectiva sobre los censos de población, OIT, Ginebra, 1990.
STAT    Base de datos de la OIT sobre estadísticas del trabajo - LABORSTA, Oficina de Estadística, OIT, Ginebra.

## 2. Evaluación de las tasas de actividad: 1950 - 1990

### 2.1 Datos básicos:

Cuadro 1: Tasas de actividad por sexo y grupo de edad

| Grupo de edad | 1980 (1) | 1989 (2) | 1990 (2) | 1991 (2) |
|---|---|---|---|---|
| **Hombres** | | | | |
| 10-14 | 0.00 | 0.00 | 0.00 | 0.00 |
| 15-19 | 55.65 | 55.81 | 56.09 | 53.79 |
| 20-24 | 89.80 | 86.02 | 84.46 | 82.90 |
| 25-29 | 95.65 | 94.23 | 92.25 | 92.43 |
| 30-34 | 96.90 | 94.98 | 93.02 | 93.86 |
| 35-39 | 97.10 | 94.97 | 93.64 | 94.50 |
| 40-44 | 97.10 | 94.95 | 94.02 | 94.98 |
| 45-49 | 96.30 | 93.33 | 92.73 | 93.17 |
| 50-54 | 94.35 | 91.94 | 90.18 | 91.14 |
| 55-59 | 88.10 | 78.13 | 78.39 | 80.67 |
| 60-64 | 48.50 | 33.76 | 35.34 | 33.19 |
| 65+ | 12.30 | 10.60 | 10.94 | 9.42 |
| **Mujeres** | | | | |
| 10-14 | 0.00 | 0.00 | 0.00 | 0.00 |
| 15-19 | 48.80 | 49.38 | 56.68 | 52.22 |
| 20-24 | 62.50 | 69.46 | 69.81 | 71.70 |
| 25-29 | 41.30 | 61.25 | 61.80 | 61.62 |
| 30-34 | 39.70 | 60.49 | 61.54 | 63.05 |
| 35-39 | 49.10 | 72.86 | 71.58 | 72.54 |
| 40-44 | 54.10 | 77.92 | 78.45 | 79.38 |
| 45-49 | 51.80 | 75.78 | 77.32 | 77.73 |
| 50-54 | 43.35 | 69.80 | 69.54 | 69.08 |
| 55-59 | 30.55 | 47.05 | 44.56 | 47.46 |
| 60-64 | 12.40 | 14.41 | 17.34 | 15.48 |
| 65+ | 2.10 | 3.53 | 3.60 | 3.29 |

Fuente(s): (1) EPPA3; (2) STAT.

### 2.2 Método(s):   promedio aritmético

#### 2.2.1 Hombres:

- 1950-80, tasas de actividad 1950-80 con base en EPPA3;
ajuste de las tasas de actividad del grupo de edad [15-19] para 1980;
- 1990, promedios de las tasas de actividad con base en las encuestas de 1989, 1990 y 1991.

#### 2.2.2 Mujeres:

Métodos, hipótesis y tratamientos idénticos a los que se aplican a los hombres.

## 3. Evaluación de las tasas de distribución por sector de actividad: 1950 - 1990

### 3.1 Datos básicos:

Cuadro 2: Distribución de la población económicamente activa por sector de actividad en %

| Año | Agricultura | Industria Total | Manufac. | Servicios |
|---|---|---|---|---|
| **Hombres** | | | | |
| 1980 | 13.40 | 39.23 | 26.89 | 47.37 |
| 1991 | 12.59 | 32.32 | 20.81 | 55.09 |
| **Mujeres** | | | | |
| 1980 | 6.19 | 21.75 | 19.95 | 72.06 |
| 1991 | 7.42 | 13.43 | 11.61 | 79.15 |

Fuente(s): STAT.

### 3.2 Método(s):   promedio ponderado

#### 3.2.1 Hombres:

- 1950-80, tasas de distribución 1950-80 con base en EPPA3;
- 1990, promedios ponderados de las tasas de distribución con base en las encuestas de 1980 y 1991.

#### 3.2.2 Mujeres:

Métodos, hipótesis y tratamientos idénticos a los que se aplican a los hombres.

## 4. Proyección de las tasas de actividad: 2000 - 2010

### 4.1 Modelo(s):   linear, hiperbólico y logístico

#### 4.1.1 Hombres:

- Para el grupo de edad [15-19], aplicación de la función F1;
- Para los grupos de edad [20+], aplicación de la función F3;
- Modificación de las tendencias de los grupos de edad [20-24] y [30-49].

#### 4.1.2 Mujeres:

- Para los grupos de edad [15-24], aplicación de la función F1;
- Para los grupos de edad [25-64], aplicación de la función F6;
- Para el grupo de edad [65+], aplicación de la función F3.

*Notas sobre los ajustes de las tasas, véase p.380-384.*

*Notas sobre las funciones de proyección, véase p. 386.*

# Omán

## 1. Fuente(s) de los datos básicos

Código(s):    Título(s):
EPPA3        Estimaciones y proyecciones de la población económicamente activa, 1950-2025, tercera edición, OIT, Ginebra, 1986.

## 2. Evaluación de las tasas de actividad: 1950 - 1990

### 2.1 Datos básicos:

Cuadro 1: Tasas de actividad por sexo y grupo de edad

| Grupo de edad | Año 1950 | 1960 | 1970 | 1980 |
|---|---|---|---|---|
| **Hombres** | | | | |
| 10-14 | 27.00 | 22.00 | 17.00 | 9.00 |
| 15-19 | 87.40 | 73.70 | 60.00 | 46.30 |
| 20-24 | 96.20 | 95.95 | 95.65 | 95.40 |
| 25-29 | 99.20 | 99.25 | 99.25 | 99.30 |
| 30-34 | 99.20 | 99.15 | 99.05 | 99.00 |
| 35-39 | 99.20 | 99.05 | 98.85 | 98.70 |
| 40-44 | 98.20 | 98.00 | 97.80 | 97.60 |
| 45-49 | 97.00 | 96.55 | 96.15 | 95.70 |
| 50-54 | 94.50 | 93.45 | 92.45 | 91.40 |
| 55-59 | 91.00 | 89.35 | 87.75 | 86.10 |
| 60-64 | 80.55 | 78.55 | 76.60 | 74.60 |
| 65+ | 63.00 | 60.10 | 57.20 | 54.30 |
| **Mujeres** | | | | |
| 10-14 | 1.00 | 1.35 | 1.70 | 2.05 |
| 15-19 | 2.00 | 2.70 | 3.40 | 4.10 |
| 20-24 | 2.60 | 3.95 | 5.35 | 6.70 |
| 25-29 | 3.00 | 5.50 | 7.90 | 10.30 |
| 30-34 | 3.20 | 5.95 | 8.65 | 11.40 |
| 35-39 | 3.45 | 5.65 | 7.85 | 10.10 |
| 40-44 | 3.55 | 5.15 | 6.80 | 8.40 |
| 45-49 | 3.55 | 4.80 | 6.10 | 7.40 |
| 50-54 | 2.80 | 4.00 | 5.20 | 6.40 |
| 55-59 | 2.70 | 3.40 | 4.10 | 4.80 |
| 60-64 | 2.60 | 2.95 | 3.25 | 3.60 |
| 65+ | 2.50 | 2.65 | 2.75 | 2.90 |

Fuente(s): EPPA3.

### 2.2 Método(s): extrapolación linear

#### 2.2.1 Hombres:

- 1950-80, tasas de actividad 1950-80 con base en EPPA3;
- 1990, extrapolación de las tasas de actividad 1950-80 con base en EPPA3; modificación de las tendencias de todos los grupos de edad.

#### 2.2.2 Mujeres:

Métodos, hipótesis y tratamientos idénticos a los que se aplican a los hombres.

## 3. Evaluación de las tasas de distribución por sector de actividad: 1950 - 1990

### 3.1 Datos básicos:

Cuadro 2: Distribución de la población económicamente activa por sector de actividad en %

| Año | Agricultura | Industria Total | Manufac. | Servicios |
|---|---|---|---|---|
| **Hombres** | | | | |
| 1950 | 77.00 | 8.50 | .. | 14.50 |
| 1960 | 68.50 | 12.00 | .. | 19.50 |
| 1970 | 58.50 | 17.00 | .. | 24.50 |
| 1980 | 52.00 | 21.00 | .. | 27.00 |
| **Mujeres** | | | | |
| 1950 | 55.00 | 15.00 | .. | 30.00 |
| 1960 | 43.00 | 20.00 | .. | 37.00 |
| 1970 | 33.00 | 27.00 | .. | 40.00 |
| 1980 | 25.00 | 33.00 | .. | 42.00 |

Fuente(s): EPPA3.

### 3.2 Método(s): extrapolación linear

#### 3.2.1 Hombres:

- 1950-80, tasas de distribución 1950-80 con base en EPPA3;
- 1990, extrapolación de las tasas de distribución 1950-80 con base en EPPA3; modificación de las tendencias de todos los sectores.

#### 3.2.2 Mujeres:

Métodos, hipótesis y tratamientos idénticos a los que se aplican a los hombres.

## 4. Proyección de las tasas de actividad: 2000 - 2010

### 4.1 Modelo(s): linear, log-linear y hiperbólico

#### 4.1.1 Hombres:

- Para los grupos de edad [15-19] y [25-64], aplicación de la función F3;
- Para el grupo de edad [20-24], aplicación de la función F2;
- Para el grupo de edad [65+], aplicación de la función F1;
- Modificación de las tendencias de los grupos de edad [15-34].

#### 4.1.2 Mujeres:

- Para los grupos de edad [15-19] y [65+], aplicación de la función F1;
- Para los grupos de edad [20-64], aplicación de la función F2;
- Modificación de las tendencias de todos los grupos de edad.

*Notas sobre los ajustes de las tasas, véase p.380-384.*    *Notas sobre las funciones de proyección, véase p. 386.*

# Otros Melanesia

## 1. Fuente(s) de los datos básicos

Código(s): Título(s):

EPPA3     Anuario de estadísticas del trabajo 1945-89 - Edición retrospectiva sobre los censos de población, OIT, Ginebra, 1990.
STAT     Base de datos de la OIT sobre estadísticas del trabajo - LABORSTA, Oficina de Estadística, OIT, Ginebra.

## 2. Evaluación de las tasas de actividad: 1950 - 1990

### 2.1 Datos básicos:

Cuadro 1: Tasas de actividad por sexo y grupo de edad

| Grupo de edad | 1976 (1) | 1979 (2) | 1983 (1) | 1989 (1) | 1989 (2) |
|---|---|---|---|---|---|
| **Hombres** | | | | | |
| 10-14 | 1.51 | 0.00 | 0.00 | ... | 0.00 |
| 15-19 | 36.03 | 61.72 | 38.70 | ... | 73.16 |
| 20-24 | 74.53 | 92.87 | 82.99 | 86.34 | 91.19 |
| 25-29 | 93.98 | 97.33 | 91.62 | 93.25 | 95.03 |
| 30-34 | 95.48 | 98.69 | 95.11 | 95.13 | 95.33 |
| 35-39 | 95.77 | 98.65 | 95.31 | 94.81 | 94.93 |
| 40-44 | 95.21 | 98.70 | 94.57 | 94.56 | 94.53 |
| 45-49 | 93.76 | 98.78 | 93.43 | 92.23 | 93.76 |
| 50-54 | 90.91 | 98.17 | 81.23 | 81.36 | 94.75 |
| 55-59 | 79.17 | 97.11 | 61.90 | 56.18 | 94.11 |
| 60-64 | 56.18 | 93.97 | 36.67 | 26.72 | 88.63 |
| 65+ | 36.12 | 85.88 | ... | 11.99 | 74.45 |
| **Mujeres** | | | | | |
| 10-14 | 1.58 | 0.00 | 0.00 | ... | 0.00 |
| 15-19 | 29.57 | 64.90 | 17.87 | ... | 70.66 |
| 20-24 | 55.94 | 80.12 | 50.63 | 65.53 | 80.42 |
| 25-29 | 53.17 | 79.81 | 54.76 | 61.94 | 81.64 |
| 30-34 | 50.75 | 81.26 | 53.24 | 59.45 | 79.67 |
| 35-39 | 48.97 | 84.32 | 50.95 | 58.19 | 84.01 |
| 40-44 | 47.80 | 83.30 | 48.41 | 54.97 | 85.04 |
| 45-49 | 47.02 | 85.70 | 44.68 | 50.19 | 86.98 |
| 50-54 | 47.48 | 85.83 | 37.06 | 41.06 | 87.11 |
| 55-59 | 41.46 | 86.07 | 33.19 | 29.32 | 83.82 |
| 60-64 | 32.14 | 82.35 | 12.15 | 16.07 | 79.42 |
| 65+ | 19.43 | 71.87 | ... | 5.74 | 64.48 |

Nota(s): (1) Nueva Caledonia; (2) Vanuatu.
Fuente(s): STAT.

### 2.2 Método(s): interpolación y extrapolación lineares
promedio ponderado

#### 2.2.1 Hombres:

- 1950-90, promedios ponderados de las tasas de actividad estimadas por separado para Nueva Caledonia y Vanuatu;
las tasas de actividad estimadas con base en la interpolación y extrapolación de las tasas de actividad ajustadas para Nueva Caledonia con base en los censos de 1976, 1983 y 1989 y de las tasas de actividad para Vanuatu con base en el censo de 1979 and 1989.

#### 2.2.2 Mujeres:

Métodos, hipótesis y tratamientos idénticos a los que se aplican a los hombres.

## 3. Evaluación de las tasas de distribución por sector de actividad: 1950 - 1990

### 3.1 Datos básicos:

Cuadro 2: Distribución de la población económicamente activa por sector de actividad en %

| Año | Agricultura | Industria Total | Manufac. | Servicios |
|---|---|---|---|---|
| **Hombres** | | | | |
| 1976 (1) | 25.93 | 37.70 | 15.89 | 36.37 |
| 1979 (2) | 71.56 | 6.18 | 2.01 | 22.26 |
| 1983 (1) | 21.45 | 25.08 | 14.01 | 53.47 |
| 1989 (1) | 14.38 | 27.72 | 13.51 | 57.89 |
| 1989 (2) | 70.56 | 6.27 | 2.35 | 23.16 |
| **Mujeres** | | | | |
| 1976 (1) | 35.32 | 6.24 | 3.64 | 58.44 |
| 1979 (2) | 84.71 | 2.06 | 1.87 | 13.23 |
| 1983 (1) | 23.24 | 4.98 | 3.80 | 71.78 |
| 1989 (1) | 14.20 | 6.26 | 4.92 | 79.54 |
| 1989 (2) | 83.65 | 1.35 | 1.25 | 15.00 |

Nota(s): (1) Nueva Caledonia; (2) Vanuatu.
Fuente(s): STAT.

### 3.2 Método(s): promedio ponderado
interpolación y extrapolación lineares

#### 3.2.1 Hombres:
- 1950-90, promedios ponderados de las tasas de distribución estimadas separado para Nueva Caledonia y Vanuatu; las tasas estimadas con base en la interpolación y extrapolación de las tasas de distribución con base en los censos de 1976, 1983 y 1989 para Nueva Caledonia y de las tasas de distribución con base en los censos de 1979 y 1989 para Vanuatu. de distribución con base en los censos de 1979 y 1989 para Vanuatu.

#### 3.2.2 Mujeres:
Métodos, hipótesis y tratamientos idénticos a los que se aplican a los hombres.

## 4. Proyección de las tasas de actividad: 2000 - 2010

### 4.1 Modelo(s): linear y hiperbólico

#### 4.1.1 Hombres:
- Para los grupos de edad [10-29], aplicación de la función F1;
- Para los grupos de edad [30+], aplicación de la función F3;
- Modificación de las tendencias de los grupos de edad [10-14], [20-24] y [30-49].

#### 4.1.2 Mujeres:
- Para todos los grupos de edad, aplicación de la función F1;
- Modificación de las tendencias de los grupos de edad [20+].

*Notas sobre los ajustes de las tasas, véase p.380-384.*     *Notas sobre las funciones de proyección, véase p. 386.*

# Países Bajos

## 1. Fuente(s) de los datos básicos

Código(s):   Título(s):

EPPA3   Anuario de estadísticas del trabajo 1945-89 - Edición retrospectiva sobre los censos de población, OIT, Ginebra, 1990.
STAT   Base de datos de la OIT sobre estadísticas del trabajo - LABORSTA, Oficina de Estadística, OIT, Ginebra.

## 2. Evaluación de las tasas de actividad: 1950 - 1990

### 2.1 Datos básicos:

Cuadro 1: Tasas de actividad por sexo y grupo de edad

| Grupo de edad | Año | | | | |
|---|---|---|---|---|---|
| | 1987 | 1988 | 1989 | 1990 | 1991 |
| **Hombres** | | | | | |
| 10-14 | 0.00 | 0.00 | 0.00 | 0.00 | 0.00 |
| 15-19 | 41.11 | 42.83 | 42.93 | 44.36 | 45.66 |
| 20-24 | 79.20 | 78.05 | 78.37 | 76.74 | 76.97 |
| 25-29 | 93.32 | 93.25 | 93.21 | 94.14 | 94.42 |
| 30-34 | 96.36 | 96.19 | 96.39 | 96.12 | 96.28 |
| 35-39 | 95.81 | 95.95 | 96.16 | 96.20 | 96.07 |
| 40-44 | 94.64 | 94.91 | 95.02 | 94.40 | 94.44 |
| 45-49 | 91.71 | 91.28 | 91.25 | 91.93 | 92.16 |
| 50-54 | 83.51 | 94.06 | 84.20 | 83.92 | 84.71 |
| 55-59 | 66.17 | 66.57 | 65.27 | 66.30 | 63.66 |
| 60-64 | 27.66 | 26.81 | 24.45 | 22.67 | 21.69 |
| 65+ | 2.96 | 3.32 | 3.20 | 3.08 | 2.96 |
| **Mujeres** | | | | | |
| 10-14 | .. | .. | 0.00 | 0.00 | 0.00 |
| 15-19 | .. | .. | 39.18 | 41.86 | 42.89 |
| 20-24 | .. | .. | 75.49 | 77.06 | 76.01 |
| 25-29 | .. | .. | 67.15 | 69.90 | 72.96 |
| 30-34 | .. | .. | 58.35 | 61.30 | 62.52 |
| 35-39 | .. | .. | 59.51 | 61.20 | 62.65 |
| 40-44 | .. | .. | 56.33 | 58.35 | 61.32 |
| 45-49 | .. | .. | 49.38 | 52.49 | 54.31 |
| 50-54 | .. | .. | 37.66 | 38.72 | 42.04 |
| 55-59 | .. | .. | 23.96 | 25.56 | 22.78 |
| 60-64 | .. | .. | 8.94 | 7.82 | 7.80 |
| 65+ | .. | .. | ... | 0.30 | ... |

Fuente(s): STAT.

### 2.2 Método(s):   interpolación linear
promedio aritmético

#### 2.2.1 Hombres:

- 1950-80, tasas de actividad ajustadas 1950-80 con base en EPPA3;
ajuste de las tasas de actividad de los grupos de edad [15-29] y [50+] con base en la interpolación de las tasas de actividad con base en los censos de 1960, 1971 y 1981;
- 1990, interpolación de las tasas de actividad ajustadas con base en las encuestas de 1987, 1988, 1989, 1990 y 1991;
modificación de la tendencia del grupo de edad [65+].

#### 2.2.2 Mujeres:

- 1950-80, tasas de actividad 1950-80 con base en EPPA3;
ajuste de las tasas de actividad del grupo de edad [15-19];
- 1990, promedios de las tasas de actividad con base en las encuestas de 1989, 1990 y 1991;
modificación de la tendencia del grupo de edad [65+].

## 3. Evaluación de las tasas de distribución por sector de actividad: 1950 - 1990

### 3.1 Datos básicos:

Cuadro 2: Distribución de la población económicamente activa por sector de actividad en %

| Año | Agricultura | Industria | | Servicios |
|---|---|---|---|---|
| | | Total | Manufac. | |
| **Hombres** | | | | |
| 1989 | 5.45 | 35.05 | 24.19 | 59.50 |
| 1990 | 5.29 | 35.13 | 24.17 | 59.58 |
| 1991 | 5.30 | 34.47 | 23.45 | 60.23 |
| **Mujeres** | | | | |
| 1989 | 3.35 | 11.16 | 9.66 | 85.49 |
| 1990 | 3.40 | 11.35 | 10.04 | 85.25 |
| 1991 | 3.28 | 10.96 | 9.48 | 85.76 |

Fuente(s): (1) STAT.

### 3.2 Método(s):   promedio aritmético

#### 3.2.1 Hombres:

- 1950-80, tasas de distribución 1950-80 con base en EPPA3;
- 1990, promedios de las tasas de distribución con base en las encuestas de 1989, 1990 y 1991.

#### 3.2.2 Mujeres:

- 1950-70, tasas de distribución 1950-70 con base en EPPA3;
- 1980, promedios de las tasas de distribución con base en las encuestas 1979 y 1981;
- 1990, promedios de las tasas de distribución con base en las encuestas de 1989, 1990 y 1991.

## 4. Proyección de las tasas de actividad: 2000 - 2010

### 4.1 Modelo(s):   linear, log-linear, hiperbólico y logístico

#### 4.1.1 Hombres:

- Para el grupo de edad [15-19], aplicación de la función F2;
- Para los grupos de edad [20+], aplicación de la función F3;
- Modificación de las tendencias de los grupos de edad [30-54].

#### 4.1.2 Mujeres:

- Para el grupo de edad [15-19], aplicación de la función F1;
- Para los grupos de edad [20-59], aplicación de la función F6;
- Para los grupos de edad [60+], aplicación de la función F3;
- Modificación de la tendencia del grupo de edad [20-24].

*Notas sobre los ajustes de las tasas, véase p.380-384.*      *Notas sobre las funciones de proyección, véase p. 386.*

# Pakistán

## 1. Fuente(s) de los datos básicos

Código(s):    Título(s):

EPPA3    Estimaciones y proyecciones de la población económicamente activa, 1950-2025, tercera edición, OIT, Ginebra, 1986.
STAT    Base de datos de la OIT sobre estadísticas del trabajo - LABORSTA, Oficina de Estadística, OIT, Ginebra.

## 2. Evaluación de las tasas de actividad: 1950 - 1990

### 2.1 Datos básicos:

Cuadro 1: Tasas de actividad por sexo y grupo de edad

| Grupo de edad | Año | | | | | | |
|---|---|---|---|---|---|---|---|
| | 1950 | 1960 | 1970 | 1978 | 1981 | 1990 | 1991 |
| **Hombres** | | | | | | | |
| 10-14 | 45.05 | 38.90 | 31.10 | 29.49 | 30.90 | 26.60 | 19.20 |
| 15-19 | 84.65 | 78.80 | 71.25 | 64.60 | 67.70 | 59.40 | 55.20 |
| 20-24 | 93.50 | 90.80 | 90.25 | 88.40 | 88.20 | 86.90 | 87.70 |
| 25-29 | 97.65 | 97.15 | 96.55 | 96.20 | 96.00 | 97.30 | 97.70 |
| 30-34 | 97.70 | 97.50 | 97.30 | 97.94 | 97.10 | 98.80 | 97.80 |
| 35-39 | 97.90 | 97.75 | 97.60 | 98.24 | 97.40 | 98.70 | 97.90 |
| 40-44 | 97.50 | 97.35 | 97.15 | 97.84 | 97.00 | 97.80 | 98.20 |
| 45-49 | 97.25 | 97.15 | 97.00 | 97.50 | 96.80 | 97.40 | 97.60 |
| 50-54 | 96.00 | 95.55 | 95.10 | 95.70 | 94.50 | 94.10 | 94.80 |
| 55-59 | 95.50 | 94.40 | 93.25 | 92.10 | 91.80 | 91.20 | 90.40 |
| 60-64 | 89.70 | 87.45 | 95.20 | 86 70 | 82.30 | 81.00 | 78.50 |
| 65+ | 80.25 | 75.15 | 67.40 | 59.70 | 56.90 | 55.70 | 52.03 |
| **Mujeres** | | | | | | | |
| 10-14 | 7.05 | 5.70 | 4.45 | .. | 6.30 | .. | 6.90 |
| 15-19 | 7.65 | 7.45 | 7.25 | .. | 12.10 | .. | 13.10 |
| 20-24 | 7.95 | 8.50 | 9.15 | .. | 12.90 | .. | 14.00 |
| 25-29 | 9.60 | 10.05 | 10.40 | .. | 14.00 | .. | 13.20 |
| 30-34 | 10.75 | 11.25 | 11.65 | .. | 15.70 | .. | 14.10 |
| 35-39 | 9.45 | 9.90 | 10.25 | .. | 13.80 | .. | 13.90 |
| 40-44 | 9.60 | 10.05 | 10.40 | .. | 14.00 | .. | 17.50 |
| 45-49 | 10.95 | 11.05 | 11.15 | .. | 12.70 | .. | 17.80 |
| 50-54 | 10.40 | 10.50 | 10.60 | .. | 11.70 | .. | 16.50 |
| 55-59 | 10.00 | 10.15 | 10.30 | .. | 12.40 | .. | 13.90 |
| 60-64 | 8.20 | 7.95 | 7.60 | .. | 7.40 | .. | 10.70 |
| 65+ | 6.45 | 5.55 | 4.55 | .. | 5.40 | .. | 7.40 |

Fuente(s): STAT.

### 2.2 Método(s): interpolación linear

#### 2.2.1 Hombres:

- 1950-90, interpolación de las tasas de actividad 1950-70 con base en EPPA3 y de las tasas de actividad con base en las encuestas de 1978 to 1992.

#### 2.2.2 Mujeres:

- 1950-70, tasas de actividad ajustadas 1950-70 con base en EPPA3; el ajuste se ha calculado con base en el modelo de ajuste de las tasas de actividad de las mujeres ocupadas en la agricultura como auxiliares familiares;
- 1980-90, interpolación de las tasas de actividad con base en las encuestas de 1981 y 1991;
ajuste de las tasas interpoladas y extrapoladas habida cuenta de la subenumeración censal de las mujeres ocupadas en la agricultura;

## 3. Evaluación de las tasas de distribución por sector de actividad: 1950 - 1990

### 3.1 Datos básicos:

Cuadro 2: Distribución de la población económicamente activa por sector de actividad en %

| Año | Agricultura | Industria | | Servicios |
|---|---|---|---|---|
| | | Total | Manufac. | |
| **Hombres** | | | | |
| 1981 | 55.98 | 14.94 | 9.40 | 29.08 |
| 1982 | 44.80 | 20.59 | 12.08 | 34.61 |
| **Mujeres** | | | | |
| 1981 | 41.18 | 19.02 | 15.98 | 39.80 |
| 1982 | 66.02 | 14.69 | 13.33 | 19.29 |

Fuente(s): STAT.

### 3.2 Método(s): interpolación y extrapolación lineares

#### 3.2.1 Hombres:

- 1950-80, tasas de distribución 1950-80 con base en EPPA3;
- 1990, extrapolación de las tasas de distribución con base en la encuesta de 1981 y de las tasas con base en estimaciones oficiales de 1991; modificación de las tendencias de todos los sectores.

#### 3.2.2 Mujeres:

- 1950-70, tasas de distribución ajustadas 1950-70 con base en EPPA3;
- 1980-90, interpolación y extrapolación de las tasas de distribución con base en la encuesta de 1981 y estimaciones oficiales de 1991; ajuste de las tasas habida cuenta de la subenumeración censal de las mujeres ocupadas en la agricultura.

## 4. Proyección de las tasas de actividad: 2000 - 2010

### 4.1 Modelo(s): linear, hiperbólico y logístico

#### 4.1.1 Hombres:

- Para el grupo de edad [10-14], aplicación de la función F1;
- Para los grupos de edad [15+], aplicación de la función F3;
- Modificación de las tendencias de los grupos de edad [10-14] y [30-49].

#### 4.1.2 Mujeres:

- Para los grupos de edad [10-19] y [60+], aplicación de la función F1;
- Para los grupos de edad [20-59], aplicación de la función F6;
- Modificación de las tendencias de los grupos de edad [10-19] y [65+].

# Panamá

## 1. Fuente(s) de los datos básicos

Código(s):  Título(s):

EPPA3   Estimaciones y proyecciones de la población económicamente activa, 1950-2025, tercera edición, OIT, Ginebra, 1986.
STAT    Base de datos de la OIT sobre estadísticas del trabajo - LABORSTA, Oficina de Estadística, OIT, Ginebra.
PAN90   Censos Nacionales de Poblacion y Vivienda, 13 de mayo 1990, Dirección de Estadística y Censo, Controloria General de la República, Panamá.

## 2. Evaluación de las tasas de actividad: 1950 - 1990

### 2.1 Datos básicos:

Cuadro 1: Tasas de actividad por sexo y grupo de edad

| Grupo de edad | Año | | | | | |
|---|---|---|---|---|---|---|
| | 1979 | 1980 | 1985 | 1989 | 1990 | 1991 |
| **Hombres** | | | | | | |
| 10-14 | .. | .. | .. | ... | 6.49 | ... |
| 15-19 | .. | .. | .. | 46.91 | 42.69 | 45.11 |
| 20-24 | .. | .. | .. | 85.75 | 80.31 | 82.32 |
| 25-29 | .. | .. | .. | 95.82 | 91.39 | 94.93 |
| 30-39 | .. | .. | .. | 96.99 | 94.50 | 96.95 |
| 40-49 | .. | .. | .. | 96.21 | 93.99 | 96.31 |
| 50-59 | .. | .. | .. | 88.93 | 84.89 | 83.65 |
| 60-64 | .. | .. | .. | 43.40 | 47.33 | 42.09 |
| 65+ | .. | .. | .. | ... | ... | ... |
| **Mujeres** | | | | | | |
| 10-14 | ... | 2.58 | ... | ... | 2.48 | ... |
| 15-19 | 19.98 | 16.78 | 19.12 | 21.17 | 18.88 | 21.69 |
| 20-24 | 49.49 | 38.29 | 42.44 | 45.71 | 34.66 | 45.70 |
| 25-29 | 50.44 | 41.63 | 50.61 | 52.42 | 40.84 | 51.65 |
| 30-39 | 46.18 | 39.25 | 52.02 | 54.51 | 46.65 | 55.19 |
| 40-49 | 38.54 | 33.28 | 43.06 | 49.75 | 42.36 | 50.90 |
| 50-59 | 24.41 | 19.17 | 24.95 | 25.94 | 23.90 | 25.00 |
| 60-64 | 11.95 | 23.01 | 12.41 | 8.04 | 7.47 | 7.79 |
| 65+ | ... | ... | ... | ... | ... | ... |

Fuente(s): STAT.

### 2.2 Método(s): interpolación linear / promedio aritmético

#### 2.2.1 Hombres:

- 1950-80, tasas de actividad 1950-80 con base en EPPA3;
- 1990, promedios de las tasas de actividad ajustadas con base en las encuestas de 1989 y 1991;
para el grupo de edad [10-14], tasas de actividad con base en el censo de 1990.

#### 2.2.2 Mujeres:

- 1950-70, tasas de actividad 1950-70 con base en EPPA3;
- 1980-90, extrapolación de las tasas de actividad ajustadas con base en las encuestas de 1979, 1985, 1989 y 1991;
para el grupo de edad [10-14], tasas de actividad con base en los censos de 1980 y 1990.

## 3. Evaluación de las tasas de distribución por sector de actividad: 1950 - 1990

### 3.1 Datos básicos:

Cuadro 2: Distribución de la población económicamente activa por sector de actividad en %

| Año | Agricultura | Industria | | Servicios |
|---|---|---|---|---|
| | | Total | Manufac. | |
| **Hombres** | | | | |
| 1980 | 39.31 | 22.43 | 11.92 | 38.26 |
| 1989 | 39.23 | 19.03 | 11.27 | 41.74 |
| 1991 | 35.08 | 17.78 | 10.14 | 47.13 |
| **Mujeres** | | | | |
| 1979 | 4.61 | 12.49 | 11.26 | 82.90 |
| 1985 | 4.53 | 12.34 | 10.70 | 83.13 |
| 1989 | 4.08 | 11.30 | 9.82 | 84.61 |
| 1991 | 2.43 | 10.98 | 9.97 | 86.59 |

Fuente(s): STAT.

### 3.2 Método(s): interpolación y extrapolación lineares / promedio aritmético

#### 3.2.1 Hombres:

- 1950-70, tasas de distribución 1950-70 con base en EPPA3;
- 1980, interpolación de las tasas de distribución con base en el censo de 1980 y de las tasas de distribución estimadas para 1990;
- 1990, promedios de las tasas de distribución con base en las encuestas de 1989 y 1991.
de 1989 y 1991.

#### 3.2.2 Mujeres:

- 1950-70, tasas de distribución 1950-70 con base en EPPA3;
- 1980-90, interpolación de las tasas de distribución con base en las encuestas de 1979, 1985, 1989 y 1991.

## 4. Proyección de las tasas de actividad: 2000 - 2010

### 4.1 Modelo(s): linear, log-linear, hiperbólico y logístico

#### 4.1.1 Hombres:

- Para los grupos de edad [10-19], aplicación de la función F1;
- Para los grupos de edad [20-59], aplicación de la función F3;
- Para los grupos de edad [60+], aplicación de la función F2;
- Modificación de las tendencias de los grupos de edad [10-19].

#### 4.1.2 Mujeres:

- Para los grupos de edad [10-59], aplicación de la función F6;
- Para el grupo de edad [60-64], aplicación de la función F1;
- Para el grupo de edad [65+], aplicación de la función F3;
- Modificación de las tendencias de los grupos de edad [20-24] y [60-64].

*Notas sobre los ajustes de las tasas, véase p.380-384.*     *Notas sobre las funciones de proyección, véase p. 386.*

# Papua Nueva Guinea

## 1. Fuente(s) de los datos básicos

Código(s):     Título(s):
EPPA3          Anuario de estadísticas del trabajo 1945-89 - Edición retrospectiva sobre los censos de población, OIT, Ginebra, 1990.
STAT           Base de datos de la OIT sobre estadísticas del trabajo - LABORSTA, Oficina de Estadística, OIT, Ginebra.

## 2. Evaluación de las tasas de actividad: 1950 - 1990

### 2.1 Datos básicos:

Cuadro 1: Tasas de actividad por sexo y grupo de edad

| Grupo de edad | Año 1950 (1) | 1960 (1) | 1970 (1) | 1980 (2) |
|---|---|---|---|---|
| **Hombres** | | | | |
| 10-14 | 48.20 | 46.05 | 43.15 | 9.17 |
| 15-19 | 81.20 | 78.25 | 74.25 | 35.45 |
| 20-24 | 97.00 | 95.80 | 95.24 | 59.21 |
| 25-29 | 98.25 | 98.10 | 98.05 | 64.07 |
| 30-34 | 98.50 | 98.30 | 98.30 | 59.65 |
| 35-39 | 98.75 | 98.55 | 98.25 | 57.85 |
| 40-44 | 98.65 | 98.40 | 98.10 | 54.50 |
| 45-49 | 97.15 | 96.95 | 96.70 | 51.35 |
| 50-54 | 94.55 | 94.25 | 93.85 | 47.44 |
| 55-59 | 89.90 | 89.50 | 88.90 | 42.77 |
| 60-64 | 81.90 | 81.20 | 80.30 | 33.20 |
| 65+ | 63.60 | 62.50 | 61.05 | 24.65 |
| **Mujeres** | | | | |
| 10-14 | 46.55 | 44.50 | 34.56 | 11.27 |
| 15-19 | 73.60 | 70.60 | 63.76 | 30.04 |
| 20-24 | 77.00 | 75.00 | 71.32 | 35.38 |
| 25-29 | 77.35 | 75.20 | 73.13 | 35.59 |
| 30-34 | 79.35 | 77.15 | 77.67 | 38.14 |
| 35-39 | 80.70 | 78.65 | 78.67 | 38.48 |
| 40-44 | 81.45 | 79.45 | 80.48 | 39.71 |
| 45-49 | 80.60 | 78.55 | 79.53 | 38.69 |
| 50-54 | 78.30 | 76.00 | 76.74 | 36.74 |
| 55-59 | 70.65 | 68.40 | 69.25 | 32.69 |
| 60-64 | 62.15 | 59.40 | 56.59 | 23.52 |
| 65+ | 45.55 | 42.90 | 40.44 | 17.18 |

Fuente(s): (1) EPPA3; (2) STAT.

### 2.2 Método(s):   extrapolación linear
promedio ponderado

#### 2.2.1 Hombres:

- 1950-70, tasas de actividad 1950-70 con base en EPPA3;
- 1980, promedios ponderados de las tasas de actividad 1970 con base en EPPA3 y de las tasas de actividad con base en el censo de 1980;
- 1990, extrapolación de las tasas de actividad 1950-80 con base en EPPA3 y de las tasas de actividad estimadas para 1980;
modificación de las tendencias de todos los grupos de edad;
aplicación a las tasas extrapoladas, de las variaciones de las tasas interpoladas 1980, en relación con las tasas de actividad estimadas para 1980.

#### 2.2.2 Mujeres:

Métodos, hipótesis y tratamientos idénticos a los que se aplican a los hombres.

## 3. Evaluación de las tasas de distribución por sector de actividad: 1950 - 1990

### 3.1 Datos básicos:

Cuadro 2: Distribución de la población económicamente activa por sector de actividad en %

| Año | Agricultura | Industria Total | Manufac. | Servicios |
|---|---|---|---|---|
| **Hombres** | | | | |
| 1971 | 79.85 | 7.58 | 2.37 | 12.56 |
| 1982 | 75.75 | 8.44 | 3.59 | 15.81 |
| **Mujeres** | | | | |
| 1971 | 94.11 | 0.81 | 0.65 | 5.09 |
| 1982 | 91.56 | 2.10 | 1.87 | 6.34 |

Fuente(s): STAT.

### 3.2 Método(s):   interpolación y extrapolación lineares

#### 3.2.1 Hombres:

- 1950-90, interpolación y extrapolación de las tasas de distribución con base en los censos de 1971 y 1981;
modificación de las tendencias de todos los sectores para 1990.

#### 3.2.2 Mujeres:

- 1950-90, interpolación y extrapolación de las tasas de distribución con base en los censos de 1971 y 1981.

## 4. Proyección de las tasas de actividad: 2000 - 2010

### 4.1 Modelo(s):   linear y hiperbólico

#### 4.1.1 Hombres:

- Para todos los grupos de edad, aplicación de la función F3;
- Modificación de las tendencias de los grupos de edad [15-49].

#### 4.1.2 Mujeres:

- Para los grupos de edad [10-14] y [20-54], aplicación de la función F3;
- Para los grupos de edad [15-19] y [55+], aplicación de la función F1;
- Modificación de las tendencias de los grupos de edad [20-39] y [50-59].

---

*Notas sobre los ajustes de las tasas, véase p.380-384.*          *Notas sobre las funciones de proyección, véase p. 386.*

# Paraguay

## 1. Fuente(s) de los datos básicos

Código(s): Título(s):

EPPA3 Estimaciones y proyecciones de la población económicamente activa, 1950-2025, tercera edición, OIT, Ginebra, 1986.
ASTER Anuario de estadísticas del trabajo 1945-89 - Edición retrospectiva sobre los censos de población, OIT, Ginebra, 1990.

## 2. Evaluación de las tasas de actividad: 1950 - 1990

### 2.1 Datos básicos:

Cuadro 1: Tasas de actividad por sexo y grupo de edad

| Grupo de edad | Año 1962 | 1972 | 1982 |
|---|---|---|---|
| **Hombres** | | | |
| 10-14 | 16.69 | 25.28 | 19.74 |
| 15-19 | 81.71 | 76.81 | 74.47 |
| 20-24 | 95.74 | 93.28 | 92.14 |
| 25-29 | 98.17 | 97.22 | 97.37 |
| 30-34 | 98.74 | 98.04 | 98.58 |
| 35-39 | 98.86 | 98.11 | 98.84 |
| 40-44 | 98.43 | 97.49 | 98.21 |
| 45-49 | 97.99 | 96.63 | 97.69 |
| 50-54 | 97.32 | 95.30 | 96.47 |
| 55-59 | 95.62 | 91.89 | 94.58 |
| 60-64 | 92.96 | 87.20 | 90.10 |
| 65+ | 74.29 | 65.14 | 54.59 |
| **Mujeres** | | | |
| 10-14 | .. | 8.01 | 3.99 |
| 15-19 | .. | 24.67 | 19.99 |
| 20-24 | .. | 30.70 | 27.46 |
| 25-29 | .. | 28.01 | 27.45 |
| 30-34 | .. | 25.67 | 26.35 |
| 35-39 | .. | 23.23 | 24.84 |
| 40-44 | .. | 22.71 | 23.22 |
| 45-49 | .. | 20.69 | 20.66 |
| 50-54 | .. | 18.31 | 18.23 |
| 55-59 | .. | 16.25 | 15.95 |
| 60-64 | .. | 13.89 | 12.70 |
| 65+ | .. | 7.21 | 6.93 |

Fuente(s): ASTER.

### 2.2 Método(s): extrapolación linear / promedio ponderado

**2.2.1 Hombres:**

- 1950, tasas de actividad 1950 con base en EPPA3;
- 1960-80, promedios ponderados de las tasas de actividad con base en los censos 1972 y 1982 y de las tasas de actividad ajustadas con base en el censo de 1962;
- 1990, extrapolación de las tasas de actividad 1950-80 con base en EPPA3; aplicación a las tasas extrapoladas, de las variaciones de las tasas interpoladas, 1982, en relación con las tasas con base en el censo de 1982; modificación de las tendencias de todos los grupos de edad con base en las encuestas de 1989-92.

**2.2.2 Mujeres:**

- 1950-80, tasas de actividad ajustadas 1950-80 con base en EPPA3; el ajuste se ha calculado con base en el modelo de ajuste de las tasas de actividad de las mujeres ocupadas en la agricultura como auxiliares familiares;
- 1990, promedios ponderados de las tasas de actividad con base en los censos de 1972 y 1982.

## 3. Evaluación de las tasas de distribución por sector de actividad: 1950 - 1990

### 3.1 Datos básicos:

Cuadro 2: Distribución de la población económicamente activa por sector de actividad en %

| Año | Agricultura | Industria Total | Manufac. | Servicios |
|---|---|---|---|---|
| **Hombres** | | | | |
| 1962 | 65.76 | 15.77 | 11.27 | 18.46 |
| 1972 | 62.60 | 15.92 | 10.39 | 21.48 |
| 1982 | 55.38 | 20.18 | 10.59 | 24.44 |
| **Mujeres** | | | | |
| 1962 | 22.66 | 30.42 | 29.47 | 46.93 |
| 1972 | 13.75 | 28.70 | 28.54 | 57.55 |
| 1982 | 11.97 | 23.52 | 23.16 | 64.51 |

Fuente(s): ASTER.

### 3.2 Método(s): extrapolación linear / promedio ponderado

**3.2.1 Hombres:**

- 1950-80, tasas de distribución 1950-80 con base en EPPA3;
- 1990, extrapolación de las tasas de distribución con base en el censo de 1972 y 1982;
modificación de las tendencias de todos los sectores;
- Aplicación de la razón manufacturas/industria con base en el censo de 1982.
- Aplicación de la razón manufacturas/industria con base en el censo de 1982.

**3.2.2 Mujeres:**

- 1950-60, tasas de distribución 1950-60 con base en EPPA3;
- 1970, promedios ponderados de las tasas de distribución con base en los censos de 1962 y 1972;
- 1980-90, extrapolación de las tasas de distribución con base en el censo de 1962, 1972 y 1982;
modificación de las tendencias de todos los sectores;
- Aplicación de la razón manufacturas/industria con base en el censo de 1982.

## 4. Proyección de las tasas de actividad: 2000 - 2010

### 4.1 Modelo(s): linear, log-linear y hiperbólico

**4.1.1 Hombres:**

- Para los grupos de edad [10-49], aplicación de la función F1;
- Para los grupos de edad [50-59], aplicación de la función F3;
- Para los grupos de edad [60+], aplicación de la función F2;
- Modificación de las tendencias de los grupos de edad [10-49].

**4.1.2 Mujeres:**

- Para los grupos de edad [10-19] y [55+], aplicación de la función F1;
- Para los grupos de edad [20-54], aplicación de la función F2;
- Modificación de las tendencias de los grupos de edad [10-24], [40-44] y [60+].

# Perú

## 1. Fuente(s) de los datos básicos

Código(s):  Título(s):

EPPA3      Estimaciones y proyecciones de la población económicamente activa, 1950-2025, tercera edición, OIT, Ginebra, 1986.
ASTER      Anuario de estadísticas del trabajo 1945-89 - Edición retrospectiva sobre los censos de población, OIT, Ginebra, 1990.

## 2. Evaluación de las tasas de actividad: 1950 - 1990

### 2.1 Datos básicos:

Cuadro 1: Tasas de actividad por sexo y grupo de edad

| Grupo de edad | Año 1950 (1) | 1960 (1) | 1970 (1) | 1981 (2) |
|---|---|---|---|---|
| **Hombres** | | | | |
| 10-14 | 11.95 | 6.75 | 5.00 | 4.92 |
| 15-19 | 59.40 | 55.30 | 42.20 | 37.52 |
| 20-24 | 93.25 | 91.70 | 82.60 | 81.67 |
| 25-29 | 98.00 | 97.50 | 94.90 | 93.43 |
| 30-34 | 98.80 | 98.60 | 97.80 | 97.21 |
| 35-39 | 98.60 | 98.50 | 98.40 | 98.33 |
| 40-44 | 98.50 | 98.40 | 98.30 | 98.30 |
| 45-49 | 98.40 | 98.30 | 98.20 | 98.27 |
| 50-54 | 97.60 | 97.50 | 96.15 | 97.04 |
| 55-59 | 96.50 | 96.05 | 93.65 | 94.50 |
| 60-64 | 91.90 | 91.75 | 85.55 | 88.26 |
| 65+ | 75.00 | 69.30 | 62.65 | 63.46 |
| **Mujeres** | | | | |
| 10-14 | 9.50 | 6.60 | 4.10 | 3.94 |
| 15-19 | 29.00 | 27.60 | 19.10 | 18.06 |
| 20-24 | 26.40 | 26.30 | 26.10 | 29.27 |
| 25-29 | 23.50 | 23.50 | 24.15 | 31.09 |
| 30-34 | 20.10 | 21.00 | 21.75 | 30.75 |
| 35-39 | 18.90 | 20.40 | 20.55 | 28.69 |
| 40-44 | 19.80 | 20.50 | 21.10 | 27.28 |
| 45-49 | 20.00 | 20.40 | 19.70 | 26.15 |
| 50-54 | 20.50 | 20.10 | 18.40 | 25.43 |
| 55-59 | 19.70 | 19.40 | 16.60 | 23.23 |
| 60-64 | 19.10 | 18.80 | 14.20 | 22.99 |
| 65+ | 14.25 | 12.10 | 9.00 | 12.02 |

Fuente(s): (1) EPPA3; (2) ASTER.

### 2.2 Método(s): extrapolación linear
promedio ponderado

#### 2.2.1 Hombres:

- 1950-70, tasas de actividad 1950-70 con base en EPPA3;
- 1980, promedios ponderados de las tasas de actividad 1970 con base en EPPA3 y de las tasas de actividad ajustadas con base en el censo de 1981;
- 1990, extrapolación de las tasas de actividad 1950-70 con base en EPPA3 y de las tasas de actividad estimadas para 1980;
aplicación a las tasas extrapoladas, de las variaciones de las tasas interpoladas 1981, en relación con las tasas de actividad ajustadas con base en el censo de 1981; modificación de las tendencias de todos los grupos de edad.

#### 2.2.2 Mujeres:

- 1950-70, tasas de actividad 1950-70 con base en EPPA3;
ajuste de las tasas de actividad 1970 con base en la razón hombres/mujeres en la agricultura con base en el censo de 1981;
- 1980, promedios ponderados de las tasas de actividad 1970 con base en EPPA3 y de las tasas de actividad ajustadas con base en el censo de 1981;
- 1990, extrapolación de las tasas de actividad 1970 con base en EPPA3 y de las tasas de actividad ajustadas con base en el censo de 1981;

## 3. Evaluación de las tasas de distribución por sector de actividad: 1950 - 1990

### 3.1 Datos básicos:

Cuadro 2: Distribución de la población económicamente activa por sector de actividad en %

| Año | Agricultura | Industria Total | Manufac. | Servicios |
|---|---|---|---|---|
| **Hombres** | | | | |
| 1950 (1) | 63.85 | 17.95 | .. | 18.20 |
| 1960 (1) | 57.25 | 20.30 | .. | 22.45 |
| 1970 (1) | 53.30 | 17.60 | .. | 29.10 |
| 1980 (1) | 45.05 | 19.75 | .. | 35.20 |
| 1981 (2) | 43.43 | 19.63 | 11.43 | 36.94 |
| **Mujeres** | | | | |
| 1972 (2) | 19.28 | 18.89 | 18.41 | 61.82 |
| 1981 (2) | 24.57 | 13.48 | 12.51 | 61.95 |

Fuente(s): (1) EPPA3; (2) ASTER.

### 3.2 Método(s): interpolación y extrapolación lineares

#### 3.2.1 Hombres:

- 1950-80, tasas de distribución 1950-80 con base en EPPA3;
- 1980-90, extrapolación de las tasas de distribución 1950-80 con base en EPPA3 a las tasas de distribución extrapoladas, aplicación de las variaciones de las tasas interpoladas 1980, en relación con las tasas 1980 con base en EPPA3;
con base en EPPA3;

#### 3.2.2 Mujeres:

- 1950-60, tasas de distribución 1950-60 con base en EPPA3;
- 1970-90, interpolación y extrapolación de las tasas de distribución ajustadas con base en el censo de 1972 y de las tasas de distribución con base en el censo de 1981;
las tasas de distribución de manufacturas estimada con base en la razón manufacturas/industria con base en el censo de 1981.

## 4. Proyección de las tasas de actividad: 2000 - 2010

### 4.1 Modelo(s): linear, hiperbólico y logístico

#### 4.1.1 Hombres:

- Para los grupos de edad [10-14] y [50+], aplicación de la función F1;
- Para los grupos de edad [15-49], aplicación de la función F3;
- Modificación de las tendencias de los grupos de edad [15-34], [40-49] y [65+].

#### 4.1.2 Mujeres:

- Para el grupo de edad [10-14], aplicación de la función F1;
- Para el grupo de edad [15-19], aplicación de la función F3;
- Para los grupos de edad [20+], aplicación de la función F6;
- Modificación de las tendencias de los grupos de edad [20-59].

---

*Notas sobre los ajustes de las tasas, véase p.380-384.*     *Notas sobre las funciones de proyección, véase p. 386.*

# Polonia

## 1. Fuente(s) de los datos básicos

Código(s):    Título(s):

EPPA3         Estimaciones y proyecciones de la población económicamente activa, 1950-2025, tercera edición, OIT, Ginebra, 1986.
BLT-94-2      Popovic B. (1994), "Nuevas estimaciones de las tasas de actividad para 1980 y 1990, desglosadas por grupos de edad y distribución sectorial,
              en algunos países de Europa oriental y meridional" en el Boletín de Estadísticas del Trabajol - 1994-2, OIT, Ginebra.

## 2. Evaluación de las tasas de actividad: 1950 - 1990

### 2.1 Datos básicos:

Cuadro 1: Tasas de actividad por sexo y grupo de edad

| Grupo de edad | Año 1950 (1) | 1960 (1) | 1970 (1) | 1980 (1) | 1980 (2) | 1990 (2) |
|---|---|---|---|---|---|---|
| **Hombres** | | | | | | |
| 10-14 | 2.25 | 0.90 | 0.50 | 0.00 | 0.00 | 0.00 |
| 15-19 | 63.00 | 54.50 | 49.50 | 46.00 | 28.20 | 20.72 |
| 20-24 | 92.90 | 90.40 | 88.95 | 82.50 | 82.25 | 78.19 |
| 25-29 | 97.05 | 96.40 | 96.35 | 96.20 | 95.96 | 93.99 |
| 30-34 | 97.80 | 97.20 | 97.15 | 97.10 | 96.92 | 96.02 |
| 35-39 | 97.80 | 97.15 | 96.90 | 96.20 | 96.07 | 95.53 |
| 40-44 | 97.55 | 96.90 | 96.15 | 94.80 | 94.68 | 94.02 |
| 45-49 | 97.40 | 96.20 | 95.15 | 92.20 | 91.80 | 89.17 |
| 50-54 | 97.00 | 94.85 | 94.05 | 87.30 | 86.36 | 81.70 |
| 55-59 | 96.40 | 91.60 | 90.95 | 82.00 | 79.71 | 70.88 |
| 60-64 | 86.40 | 82.10 | 83.05 | 58.00 | 60.31 | 52.83 |
| 65+ | 59.75 | 57.60 | 55.45 | 30.00 | 34.56 | 32.09 |
| **Mujeres** | | | | | | |
| 10-14 | 2.15 | 1.20 | 0.65 | 0.00 | 0.00 | 0.00 |
| 15-19 | 51.10 | 43.25 | 36.65 | 31.20 | 20.71 | 15.92 |
| 20-24 | 68.65 | 69.20 | 69.80 | 68.40 | 67.91 | 63.05 |
| 25-29 | 60.30 | 62.75 | 74.55 | 76.00 | 74.42 | 69.05 |
| 30-34 | 60.85 | 63.30 | 77.15 | 81.00 | 78.92 | 76.37 |
| 35-39 | 64.20 | 66.80 | 79.20 | 82.50 | 82.15 | 83.08 |
| 40-44 | 66.40 | 69.10 | 79.45 | 83.20 | 83.19 | 85.94 |
| 45-49 | 63.20 | 68.10 | 78.70 | 79.00 | 78.87 | 81.78 |
| 50-54 | 60.65 | 65.35 | 75.40 | 72.60 | 71.54 | 71.07 |
| 55-59 | 55.70 | 60.00 | 67.85 | 56.00 | 56.64 | 49.63 |
| 60-64 | 45.25 | 48.70 | 50.90 | 35.00 | 36.65 | 33.99 |
| 65+ | 28.95 | 30.00 | 32.90 | 17.50 | 19.31 | 19.00 |

Fuente(s): (1) EPPA3; (2) BLT-94-2.

### 2.2 Método(s): con base en EPPA3 y BLT-94-2.

#### 2.2.1 Hombres:

- 1950-80, tasas de actividad 1950-80 con base en EPPA3;
- 1990, aplicación a las tasas de actividad 1990 con base en el Boletín
de estadísticas del trabajo 1994-2, las variaciones tasas de actividad 1980
con base en EPPA3, en relación con las tasas de actividad 1980 con base
en el Boletín.

#### 2.2.2 Mujeres:

Métodos, hipótesis y tratamientos idénticos a los que se aplican a los hombres.

## 3. Evaluación de las tasas de distribución por sector de actividad: 1950 - 1990

### 3.1 Datos básicos:

Cuadro 2: Distribución de la población económicamente activa por sector de actividad en %

| Año | Agricultura | Industria Total | Manufac. | Servicios |
|---|---|---|---|---|
| **Hombres** | | | | |
| 1950 (1) | 49.00 | 30.00 | .. | 20.90 |
| 1960 (1) | 39.50 | 37.80 | .. | 22.60 |
| 1970 (1) | 32.60 | 43.40 | .. | 24.00 |
| 1980 (2) | 28.04 | 45.63 | 28.44 | 26.33 |
| 1990 (2) | 27.44 | 44.88 | 26.86 | 27.68 |
| **Mujeres** | | | | |
| 1950 (1) | 69.40 | 13.70 | .. | 16.80 |
| 1960 (1) | 59.40 | 16.90 | .. | 23.70 |
| 1970 (1) | 46.50 | 23.20 | .. | 30.30 |
| 1980 (2) | 31.91 | 28.13 | 24.20 | 39.96 |
| 1990 (2) | 27.50 | 25.01 | 21.19 | 47.49 |

Fuente(s): (1) EPPA3; (2) BLT-94-2.

### 3.2 Método(s): datos de BLT-94-2

#### 3.2.1 Hombres:

- 1950-70, tasas de distribución 1950-70 con base en EPPA3;
- 1980-90, tasas de distribución con base en el boletín de estadísticas
del trabajo 1994-2.

#### 3.2.2 Mujeres:

Métodos, hipótesis y tratamientos idénticos a los que se aplican a los hombres.

## 4. Proyección de las tasas de actividad: 2000 - 2010

### 4.1 Modelo(s): hiperbólico y logístico

#### 4.1.1 Hombres:

- Para todos los grupos de edad, aplicación de la función F3;
- Modificación de las tendencias de los grupos de edad [20-24] y [30-49].

#### 4.1.2 Mujeres:

- Para los grupos de edad [15-24] y [55+], aplicación de la función F3;
- Para los grupos de edad [25-54], aplicación de la función F6;
- Modificación de las tendencias de los grupos de edad [15-24] y [55-59].

*Notas sobre los ajustes de las tasas, véase p.380-384.*

*Notas sobre las funciones de proyección, véase p. 386.*

# Portugal

## 1. Fuente(s) de los datos básicos

Código(s):  Título(s):

EPPA3    Anuario de estadísticas del trabajo 1945-89 - Edición retrospectiva sobre los censos de población, OIT, Ginebra, 1990.
STAT     Base de datos de la OIT sobre estadísticas del trabajo - LABORSTA, Oficina de Estadística, OIT, Ginebra.

## 2. Evaluación de las tasas de actividad: 1950 - 1990

### 2.1 Datos básicos:

Cuadro 1: Tasas de actividad por sexo y grupo de edad

| Grupo de edad | Año 1950 (1) | 1960 (1) | 1970 (1) | 1980 (1) | 1980 (2) | 1990 (12 |
|---|---|---|---|---|---|---|
| **Hombres** | | | | | | |
| 10-14 | 43.90 | 35.10 | 17.05 | 12.40 | .. | 4.86 |
| 15-19 | 90.70 | 86.85 | 78.85 | 76.15 | .. | 51.12 |
| 20-24 | 94.00 | 92.00 | 93.15 | 92.15 | .. | 73.20 |
| 25-29 | 94.65 | 97.20 | 97.05 | 97.00 | .. | 93.92 |
| 30-34 | 96.35 | 98.40 | 97.70 | 97.50 | .. | 96.32 |
| 35-39 | 96.65 | 98.35 | 97.30 | 96.75 | .. | 96.58 |
| 40-44 | 96.30 | 97.65 | 96.35 | 96.70 | .. | 96.17 |
| 45-49 | 94.55 | 96.00 | 95.05 | 92.40 | .. | 93.57 |
| 50-54 | 92.20 | 93.45 | 92.35 | 88.35 | .. | 86.93 |
| 55-59 | 88.30 | 89.10 | 87.65 | 79.15 | .. | 75.24 |
| 60-64 | 84.10 | 82.55 | 78.95 | 60.60 | .. | 57.08 |
| 65+ | 67.45 | 62.85 | 53.20 | 29.65 | .. | 20.03 |
| **Mujeres** | | | | | | |
| 10-14 | 11.30 | 8.70 | 9.50 | .. | 3.01 | 4.84 |
| 15-19 | 34.70 | 27.60 | 44.00 | .. | 54.39 | 39.70 |
| 20-24 | 31.45 | 26.75 | 44.60 | .. | 69.35 | 68.46 |
| 25-29 | 23.15 | 19.95 | 32.50 | .. | 67.49 | 76.53 |
| 30-34 | 20.20 | 16.75 | 25.20 | .. | 63.09 | 77.66 |
| 35-39 | 19.30 | 15.50 | 22.75 | .. | 59.13 | 74.05 |
| 40-44 | 18.70 | 14.95 | 21.20 | .. | 50.51 | 67.77 |
| 45-49 | 19.05 | 14.45 | 19.60 | .. | 44.19 | 61.66 |
| 50-54 | 18.75 | 13.85 | 17.55 | .. | 42.36 | 50.49 |
| 55-59 | 18.05 | 13.55 | 14.60 | .. | 34.46 | 39.84 |
| 60-64 | 16.80 | 12.35 | 12.85 | .. | 29.03 | 24.72 |
| 65+ | 12.40 | 8.05 | 8.05 | .. | 8.50 | 7.77 |

Fuente(s): (1) EPPA3; (2) STAT.

### 2.2 Método(s): datos del país

**2.2.1 Hombres:**

- 1950-80, tasas de actividad 1950-80 con base en EPPA3;
ajuste de las tasas de actividad de los grupos de edad [45-49] para 1980;
- 1990, tasas de actividad ajustadas con base en la encuesta de 1990;
ajuste para tener en cuenta los efectivos del servicio militar obligatorio.

**2.2.2 Mujeres:**

- 1950-70, tasas de actividad 1950-70 con base en EPPA3;
ajuste de las tasas de actividad de los grupos de edad [65+] para 1970;
- 1980, tasas de actividad ajustadas con base en la encuesta de 1980;
- 1990, tasas de actividad con base en la encuesta de 1990.

## 3. Evaluación de las tasas de distribución por sector de actividad: 1950 - 1990

### 3.1 Datos básicos:

Cuadro 2: Distribución de la población económicamente activa por sector de actividad en %

| Año | Agricultura | Industria Total | Manufac. | Servicios |
|---|---|---|---|---|
| **Hombres** | | | | |
| 1980 | 21.27 | 42.53 | 26.18 | 36.20 |
| 1990 | 15.38 | 40.06 | 24.02 | 44.57 |
| **Mujeres** | | | | |
| 1980 | 33.42 | 26.40 | 25.72 | 40.18 |
| 1990 | 21.09 | 25.92 | 24.95 | 52.99 |

Fuente(s): (1) STAT.

### 3.2 Método(s): datos del país

**3.2.1 Hombres:**

- 1950-70, tasas de distribución 1950-70 con base en EPPA3;
- 1980, tasas de distribución con base en la encuesta de 1980;
- 1980, tasas de distribución ajustadas con base en la encuesta de 1980;
ajuste de las tasas de distribución para tener en cuenta los efectivos
del servicio militar obligatorio.
del servicio militar obligatorio.

**3.2.2 Mujeres:**

Métodos, hipótesis y tratamientos idénticos a los que se aplican a los hombres.

## 4. Proyección de las tasas de actividad: 2000 - 2010

### 4.1 Modelo(s): linear, hiperbólico y logístico

**4.1.1 Hombres:**

- Para el grupo de edad [15-19], aplicación de la función F1;
- Para los grupos de edad [20+], aplicación de la función F3;
- Modificación de las tendencias de los grupos de edad [25-29] y [45-49].

**4.1.2 Mujeres:**

- Para el grupo de edad [10-14], aplicación de la función F1;
- Para los grupos de edad [15-59], aplicación de la función F6;
- Para los grupos de edad [60+], aplicación de la función F3;
- Modificación de las tendencias de los grupos de edad [15-64].

*Notas sobre los ajustes de las tasas, véase p.380-384.*    *Notas sobre las funciones de proyección, véase p. 386.*

# Puerto Rico

## 1. Fuente(s) de los datos básicos

Código(s):  Título(s):

EPPA3    Estimaciones y proyecciones de la población económicamente activa, 1950-2025, tercera edición, OIT, Ginebra, 1986.
ASTER    Anuario de estadísticas del trabajo 1945-89 - Edición retrospectiva sobre los censos de población, OIT, Ginebra, 1990.
AST91-93  Ediciones de 1991-1993, Anuario de Estadísticas del Trabjo de la OIT, Ginebra.

## 2. Evaluación de las tasas de actividad: 1950 - 1990

### 2.1 Datos básicos:

Cuadro 1: Tasas de actividad por sexo y grupo de edad

| Grupo de edad | Año 1980 (1) | 1990 (2) | 1991 (2) | 1992 (2) |
|---|---|---|---|---|
| **Hombres** | | | | |
| 10-14 | 0.00 | 0.00 | 0.00 | 0.00 |
| 15-19 | 14.81 | 15.24 | 20.16 | 16.84 |
| 20-24 | 58.04 | 67.20 | 67.72 | 65.22 |
| 25-29 | 75.49 | 85.71 | 85.32 | 85.59 |
| 30-34 | 77.34 | 86.73 | 87.13 | 88.57 |
| 35-39 | 77.41 | 86.60 | 86.46 | 86.14 |
| 40-44 | 73.98 | 82.83 | 86.27 | 85.71 |
| 45-49 | 69.00 | 83.33 | 79.31 | 80.21 |
| 50-54 | 62.28 | 72.37 | 77.63 | 75.00 |
| 55-59 | 53.57 | 61.29 | 64.18 | 63.89 |
| 60-64 | 35.93 | 36.21 | 38.98 | 39.06 |
| 65+ | 12.40 | 14.47 | 13.92 | 13.77 |
| **Mujeres** | | | | |
| 10-14 | 0.00 | 0.00 | 0.00 | 0.00 |
| 15-19 | 10.15 | 6.87 | 7.22 | 6.40 |
| 20-24 | 37.42 | 34.06 | 31.39 | 33.10 |
| 25-29 | 47.45 | 48.03 | 50.79 | 50.74 |
| 30-34 | 43.34 | 46.77 | 48.39 | 51.52 |
| 35-39 | 40.73 | 51.26 | 51.67 | 48.44 |
| 40-44 | 37.95 | 44.26 | 46.22 | 44.72 |
| 45-49 | 33.46 | 38.00 | 43.69 | 45.69 |
| 50-54 | 25.26 | 35.96 | 33.70 | 36.00 |
| 55-59 | 17.62 | 20.27 | 22.08 | 24.69 |
| 60-64 | 9.96 | 11.76 | 8.82 | 12.99 |
| 65+ | 2.8 | 3.41 | 2.14 | 2.56 |

Fuente(s): (1) ASTER; (2) AST91-93.

### 2.2 Método(s): interpolación y extrapolación lineares

#### 2.2.1 Hombres:

- 1950-80, tasas de actividad 1950-80 con base en EPPA3;
ajuste de las tasas de actividad de los grupos de edad [55+] con base
en las encuestas de 1979 y 1981;
- 1990, extrapolación de las tasas de actividad con base en
y las encuestas de 1990, 1991 y 1992;
aplicación a las tasas extrapoladas, de las variaciones tasas interpoladas 1980,
en relación con las tasas de actividad 1980 con base en EPPA3.

#### 2.2.2 Mujeres:

- 1950-70, tasas de actividad 1950-70 con base en EPPA3;
- 1980-90, extrapolación de las tasas de actividad con base en
el censo de 1980 y de los promedios de las tasas de actividad con base en
las encuestas de 1990, 1991 y 1992.

## 3. Evaluación de las tasas de distribución por sector de actividad: 1950 - 1990

### 3.1 Datos básicos:

Cuadro 2: Distribución de la población económicamente activa por sector de actividad en %

| Año | Agricultura | Industria Total | Manufac. | Servicios |
|---|---|---|---|---|
| **Hombres** | | | | |
| 1979 (1) | 8.57 | 29.43 | 15.82 | 62.00 |
| 1980 (2) | 5.58 | 33.46 | 17.98 | 60.95 |
| 1981 (1) | 8.09 | 30.38 | 15.88 | 61.53 |
| 1990 (1) | 6.95 | 29.00 | 15.41 | 64.05 |
| 1991 (1) | 6.15 | 28.40 | 15.96 | 65.45 |
| 1992 (1) | 5.60 | 29.31 | 15.61 | 65.10 |
| **Mujeres** | | | | |
| 1979 (1) | 0.31 | 27.80 | 26.94 | 71.89 |
| 1980 (2) | 0.48 | 26.14 | 24.40 | 73.38 |
| 1981 (1) | 0.58 | 24.86 | 24.28 | 74.57 |
| 1990 (1) | 0.51 | 21.54 | 20.77 | 77.95 |
| 1991 (1) | 0.51 | 20.51 | 19.24 | 78.99 |
| 1992 (1) | 0.25 | 21.57 | 20.34 | 78.19 |

Fuente(s): ASTER.

### 3.2 Método(s): interpolación linear

#### 3.2.1 Hombres:

- 1950-70, tasas de distribución 1950-70 con base en EPPA3;
- 1980-90, interpolación de las tasas de distribución con base en el censo de
1980 y las tasas con base en las encuestas de 1979, 1981, 1990, 1991 et 1992.

#### 3.2.2 Mujeres:

Métodos, hipótesis y tratamientos idénticos a los que se aplican a los hombres.

## 4. Proyección de las tasas de actividad: 2000 - 2010

### 4.1 Modelo(s): log-linear, hiperbólico y logístico

#### 4.1.1 Hombres:

- Para los grupos de edad [15+], aplicación de la función F3;
- Modificación de las tendencias de todos los grupos de edad.

#### 4.1.2 Mujeres:

- Para el grupo de edad [15-19], aplicación de la función F3;
- Para los grupos de edad [20-49], aplicación de la función F2;
- Para los grupos de edad [50+], aplicación de la función F6;
- Modificación de las tendencias de los grupos de edad [20+].

*Notas sobre los ajustes de las tasas, véase p.380-384.*          *Notas sobre las funciones de proyección, véase p. 386.*

# Qatar

## 1. Fuente(s) de los datos básicos

Código(s):    Título(s):

EPPA3    Estimaciones y proyecciones de la población económicamente activa, 1950-2025, tercera edición, OIT, Ginebra, 1986.
EPPA4    Población económicamente activa 1950-2010 - cuarta edición, OIT, Ginebra, 1996.
STAT    Base de datos de la OIT sobre estadísticas del trabajo - LABORSTA, Oficina de Estadística, OIT, Ginebra.

## 2. Evaluación de las tasas de actividad: 1950 - 1990

### 2.1 Datos básicos:

Cuadro 1: Tasas de actividad por sexo y grupo de edad

| Grupo de edad | Año | | | | | | |
|---|---|---|---|---|---|---|---|
| | 1950 (1) | 1970 (1) | 1990 (1) | 1986 (3) | 1950 (2) | 1970 (2) | 1990 (2) |
| **Hombres** | | | | | | | |
| 10-14 | 14.00 | 7.00 | 0.00 | 0.00 | 13.18 | 6.88 | 0.00 |
| 15-19 | 57.35 | 44.50 | 27.84 | 32.16 | 54.00 | 43.75 | 25.44 |
| 20-24 | 92.85 | 88.15 | 84.52 | 88.44 | 87.70 | 88.35 | 87.92 |
| 25-29 | 98.05 | 97.40 | 97.60 | 98.70 | 97.35 | 97.65 | 98.00 |
| 30-34 | 99.45 | 98.90 | 98.67 | 99.61 | 98.35 | 98.65 | 99.20 |
| 35-39 | 99.00 | 98.70 | 98.50 | 99.68 | 97.80 | 98.35 | 99.31 |
| 40-44 | 98.50 | 98.05 | 97.33 | 99.61 | 96.00 | 97.20 | 99.23 |
| 45-49 | 97.00 | 96.40 | 94.89 | 99.04 | 94.90 | 96.20 | 98.81 |
| 50-54 | 92.20 | 91.75 | 90.10 | 96.72 | 90.00 | 91.75 | 95.79 |
| 55-59 | 86.55 | 85.55 | 83.53 | 93.76 | 81.25 | 84.20 | 88.44 |
| 60-64 | 61.75 | 65.70 | 67.16 | 82.32 | 74.35 | 72.20 | 64.99 |
| 65+ | 34.00 | 34.35 | 31.12 | 59.61 | 53.00 | 49.80 | 36.55 |
| **Mujeres** | | | | | | | |
| 10-14 | .. | .. | 0.00 | 0.00 | .. | .. | .. |
| 15-19 | .. | .. | 4.66 | 1.37 | .. | .. | .. |
| 20-24 | .. | .. | 46.42 | 13.67 | .. | .. | .. |
| 25-29 | .. | .. | 60.87 | 28.73 | .. | .. | .. |
| 30-34 | .. | .. | 57.34 | 46.91 | .. | .. | .. |
| 35-39 | .. | .. | 45.72 | 47.47 | .. | .. | .. |
| 40-44 | .. | .. | 33.40 | 37.59 | .. | .. | .. |
| 45-49 | .. | .. | 23.39 | 27.09 | .. | .. | .. |
| 50-54 | .. | .. | 19.27 | 15.95 | .. | .. | .. |
| 55-59 | .. | .. | 13.85 | 11.46 | .. | .. | .. |
| 60-64 | .. | .. | 10.70 | 6.83 | .. | .. | .. |
| 65+ | .. | .. | 0.46 | 2.72 | .. | .. | .. |

Nota(s): (1) Kuwait; (2) Bahrein.
Fuente(s): (1)(2) EPPA4; (3) STAT.

### 2.2 Método(s): promedio aritmético

#### 2.2.1 Hombres:

- 1950-90, aplicación a las de las tasas de actividad ajustadas con base en
el censo 1986, de las variaciones medias de las tasas estimadas para Kuwait
y Bahrein, en relación con las tasas estimadas 1986 para estos países;
modificación de las tendencias de los grupos de edad [10-14] y [50+].

#### 2.2.2 Mujeres:

- 1950-80, tasas de actividad 1950-80 con base en EPPA3;
- 1990, aplicación a las tasas de actividad 1990 estimadas para Kuwait,
1/4 de las variaciones de las tasas de actividad ajustadas con base en el censo
de 1986, en relación con las tasas de actividad estimadas 1986 para Kuwait.

## 3. Evaluación de las tasas de distribución por sector de actividad: 1950 - 1990

### 3.1 Datos básicos:

Cuadro 2: Distribución de la población económicamente activa por sector de actividad en %

| Año | Agricultura | Industria | | Servicios |
|---|---|---|---|---|
| | | Total | Manufac. | |
| **Hombres** | | | | |
| 1950 (1) | 30.00 | 22.00 | .. | 48.00 |
| 1960 (1) | 18.00 | 24.70 | .. | 57.30 |
| 1970 (1) | 10.00 | 27.30 | .. | 62.70 |
| 1980 (1) | 3.00 | 30.00 | .. | 67.00 |
| 1986 (2) | 3.48 | 35.56 | 7.65 | 60.96 |
| **Mujeres** | | | | |
| 1950 (1) | 7.60 | 0.00 | .. | 92.40 |
| 1960 (1) | 4.10 | 0.00 | .. | 95.90 |
| 1970 (1) | 0.25 | 0.00 | .. | 99.75 |
| 1980 (1) | 0.00 | 0.00 | .. | 100.00 |
| 1986 (2) | 0.02 | 2.13 | 0.63 | 97.85 |

Fuente(s): (1) EPPA3; (2) STAT.

### 3.2 Método(s): extrapolación linear

#### 3.2.1 Hombres:

- 1950-80, tasas de distribución 1950-80 con base en EPPA3;
- 1990, extrapolación de las tasas de distribución de la agricultura 1950-80
modificación de la tendencia del sector;
las tasas de distribución de la industria, de manufacturas y los servicios
con base en el censo de 1986.
con base en el censo de 1986.

#### 3.2.2 Mujeres:

Métodos, hipótesis y tratamientos idénticos a los que se aplican a los hombres.

## 4. Proyección de las tasas de actividad: 2000 - 2010

### 4.1 Modelo(s): linear, hiperbólico y logístico

#### 4.1.1 Hombres:

- Para los grupos de edad [15-19] y [25-54], aplicación de la función F3;
- Para los grupos de edad [20-24] y [55+], aplicación de la función F6;
- Modificación de las tendencias de los grupos de edad [20-49].

#### 4.1.2 Mujeres:

- Para los grupos de edad [15-19], [30-39] y [50-64], aplicación de la función F1
- Para los grupos de edad [20-29] y [40-49], aplicación de la función F6;
- Para el grupo de edad [65+], aplicación de la función F3;
- Modificación de las tendencias de los grupos de edad [20-29].

*Notas sobre los ajustes de las tasas, véase p.380-384.*

*Notas sobre las funciones de proyección, véase p. 386.*

# Reino Unido

## 1. Fuente(s) de los datos básicos

Código(s):   Título(s):

EPPA3      Anuario de estadísticas del trabajo 1945-89 - Edición retrospectiva sobre los censos de población, OIT, Ginebra, 1990.
STAT       Base de datos de la OIT sobre estadísticas del trabajo - LABORSTA, Oficina de Estadística, OIT, Ginebra.

## 2. Evaluación de las tasas de actividad: 1950 - 1990

### 2.1 Datos básicos:

Cuadro 1: Tasas de actividad por sexo y grupo de edad

| Grupo de edad | Año | | | | |
|---|---|---|---|---|---|
| | 1950 (1) | 1960 (1) | 1970 (1) | 1980 (1) | 1991 (2) |
| **Hombres** | | | | | |
| 10-14 | 0.10 | 0.05 | 0.00 | 0.00 | 0.00 |
| 15-19 | 87.25 | 77.95 | 68.60 | 59.25 | 68.20 |
| 20-24 | 95.40 | 93.65 | 91.85 | 90.10 | 71.55 |
| 25-29 | 98.15 | 97.60 | 97.10 | 96.60 | 95.34 |
| 30-34 | 99.20 | 98.65 | 98.10 | 97.55 | 95.65 |
| 35-39 | 99.35 | 98.75 | 98.10 | 97.50 | 95.31 |
| 40-44 | 99.15 | 98.70 | 98.20 | 97.75 | 94.86 |
| 45-49 | 99.10 | 98.45 | 97.75 | 97.10 | 93.39 |
| 50-54 | 98.60 | 97.55 | 96.45 | 95.40 | 89.23 |
| 55-59 | 97.35 | 95.50 | 93.65 | 91.75 | 79.82 |
| 60-64 | 93.60 | 87.40 | 81.20 | 75.00 | 56.67 |
| 65+ | 34.40 | 26.60 | 18.80 | 11.00 | 8.04 |
| **Mujeres** | | | | | |
| 10-14 | 0.10 | 0.05 | 0.05 | 0.00 | 0.00 |
| 15-19 | 80.75 | 71.65 | 62.50 | 53.35 | 61.36 |
| 20-24 | 64.85 | 64.75 | 64.65 | 64.55 | 59.08 |
| 25-29 | 39.55 | 44.25 | 49.00 | 53.70 | 69.09 |
| 30-34 | 26.85 | 36.50 | 46.15 | 55.80 | 65.19 |
| 35-39 | 28.70 | 39.30 | 49.90 | 60.45 | 70.40 |
| 40-44 | 28.50 | 41.45 | 54.40 | 67.35 | 75.24 |
| 45-49 | 29.60 | 42.40 | 55.15 | 67.95 | 74.21 |
| 50-54 | 28.20 | 40.45 | 52.75 | 65.00 | 66.85 |
| 55-59 | 24.60 | 35.00 | 45.45 | 55.85 | 52.61 |
| 60-64 | 15.00 | 18.20 | 21.45 | 24.70 | 22.01 |
| 65+ | 6.05 | 5.40 | 4.75 | 4.15 | 2.95 |

Fuente(s): (1) EPPA3; (2) STAT.

### 2.2 Método(s): interpolación linear

#### 2.2.1 Hombres:

- 1950-80, tasas de actividad 1950-80 con base en EPPA3;
- 1990, interpolación de las tasas de actividad 1980 con base en EPPA3
y de las tasas de actividad con base en la encuesta de 1991;
modificación de las tendencias de los grupos de edad [10-19].

#### 2.2.2 Mujeres:

Métodos, hipótesis y tratamientos idénticos a los que se aplican a los hombres.

## 3. Evaluación de las tasas de distribución por sector de actividad: 1950 - 1990

### 3.1 Datos básicos:

Cuadro 2: Distribución de la población económicamente activa por sector de actividad en %

| Año | Agricultura | Industria | | Servicios |
|---|---|---|---|---|
| | | Total | Manufac. | |
| **Hombres** | | | | |
| 1979 | 3.38 | 48.36 | 33.98 | 48.26 |
| 1980 | 3.51 | 47.58 | 33.05 | 48.91 |
| 1981 | 3.24 | 47.40 | 26.75 | 49.36 |
| 1990 | 3.02 | 39.27 | 25.67 | 57.71 |
| **Mujeres** | | | | |
| 1979 | 1.22 | 23.52 | 21.57 | 75.26 |
| 1980 | 1.37 | 22.49 | 20.47 | 76.14 |
| 1981 | 0.98 | 22.19 | 17.51 | 76.83 |
| 1990 | 1.01 | 15.33 | 12.93 | 83.67 |

Fuente(s): (1) STAT.

### 3.2 Método(s): datos del país

#### 3.2.1 Hombres:

- 1950-80, tasas de distribución 1950-80 con base en EPPA3;
la tasa de distribución 1980 de los manufacturas ajustada con base en
la aplicación a la tasa de 1980 de la industria del promedio de la razón
manufacturas/industria con base en estimaciones oficiales de 1979 y 1980
y el censo de 1981;
y el censo de 1981;

#### 3.2.2 Mujeres:

Métodos, hipótesis y tratamientos idénticos a los que se aplican a los hombres.

## 4. Proyección de las tasas de actividad: 2000 - 2010

### 4.1 Modelo(s): linear, hiperbólico y logístico

#### 4.1.1 Hombres:

- Para los grupos de edad [15-29] y [55+], aplicación de la función F1;
- Para los grupos de edad [30-54], aplicación de la función F3;
- Modificación de las tendencias de los grupos de edad [15-44] y [55-64].

#### 4.1.2 Mujeres:

- Para los grupos de edad [15-19] y [55-64], aplicación de la función F1;
- Para los grupos de edad [20-54], aplicación de la función F6;
- Para el grupo de edad [65+], aplicación de la función F3;
- Modificación de las tendencias de los grupos de edad [15-29] y [55-64].

---

*Notas sobre los ajustes de las tasas, véase p.380-384.*          *Notas sobre las funciones de proyección, véase p. 386.*

# Rep. Centroafricana

## 1. Fuente(s) de los datos básicos

Código(s):   Título(s):

EPPA3      Estimaciones y proyecciones de la población económicamente activa, 1950-2025, tercera edición, OIT, Ginebra, 1986.
R1988      Recensement de la population 1988 - Tableaux statistiques, Bureau Central du Recensement, Division des Statistiques et des Etudes Economiques, Bangui
AST93      Anuario de Estadísticas del Trabjo 1993, OIT, Ginebra, 1993.

## 2. Evaluación de las tasas de actividad: 1950 - 1990

### 2.1 Datos básicos:

Cuadro 1: Tasas de actividad por sexo y grupo de edad

| Grupo de edad | Año 1950 (1) | 1960 (1) | 1988 (2) |
|---|---|---|---|
| **Hombres** | | | |
| 10-14 | 54.50 | 53.40 | 23.06 |
| 15-19 | 88.10 | 86.65 | 59.51 |
| 20-24 | 96.50 | 95.90 | 84.42 |
| 25-29 | 97.55 | 97.50 | 94.73 |
| 30-34 | 98.35 | 98.25 | 98.15 |
| 35-39 | 98.50 | 98.40 | 98.53 |
| 40-44 | 98.35 | 98.25 | 98.31 |
| 45-49 | 97.55 | 97.50 | 97.97 |
| 50-54 | 97.25 | 97.10 | 96.71 |
| 55-59 | 96.55 | 96.35 | 94.25 |
| 60-64 | 93.90 | 93.55 | 92.23 |
| 65+ | 81.30 | 80.65 | 82.54 |
| **Mujeres** | | | |
| 10-14 | .. | 48.15 | 28.06 |
| 15-19 | .. | 88.00 | 53.79 |
| 20-24 | .. | 92.30 | 62.27 |
| 25-29 | .. | 93.30 | 68.09 |
| 30-34 | .. | 94.85 | 72.10 |
| 35-39 | .. | 94.75 | 76.87 |
| 40-44 | .. | 94.25 | 79.35 |
| 45-49 | .. | 92.90 | 82.03 |
| 50-54 | .. | 85.50 | 81.84 |
| 55-59 | .. | 76.20 | 81.72 |
| 60-64 | .. | 60.75 | 78.22 |
| 65+ | .. | 35.35 | 64.67 |

Fuente(s): (1) EPPA3; (2) R1988 y AST93.

### 2.2 Método(s): interpolación y extrapolación lineares

#### 2.2.1 Hombres:

- 1950-90, interpolación y extrapolación de las tasas de actividad 1950-60
con base en EPPA3 y de las tasas de actividad ajustadas con base
el censo de 1988;
modificación de las tendencias de todos los grupos de edad para 1950.

#### 2.2.2 Mujeres:

Métodos, hipótesis y tratamientos idénticos a los que se aplican a los hombres.

## 3. Evaluación de las tasas de distribución por sector de actividad: 1950 - 1990

### 3.1 Datos básicos:

Cuadro 2: Distribución de la población económicamente activa por sector de actividad en %

| Año | Agricultura | Industria Total | Manufac. | Servicios |
|---|---|---|---|---|
| **Hombres** | | | | |
| 1960 (1) | 90.00 | 3.00 | .. | 7.00 |
| 1988 (2) | 74.82 | 6.14 | 2.88 | 19.04 |
| **Mujeres** | | | | |
| 1960 (1) | 96.85 | 0.95 | .. | 2.20 |
| 1988 (2) | 87.63 | 0.37 | 0.24 | 12.00 |

Fuente(s): (1) EPPA3; (2) R1988 y AST93.

### 3.2 Método(s): interpolación y extrapolación lineares

#### 3.2.1 Hombres:

- 1950-90, interpolación y extrapolación de las tasas de distribución 1970
con base en EPPA3 y de las tasas distribución con base en el censo de 1988;
- Aplicación de la razón manufacturas/industria con base en el censo de 1988.

#### 3.2.2 Mujeres:

Métodos, hipótesis y tratamientos idénticos a los que se aplican a los hombres.

## 4. Proyección de las tasas de actividad: 2000 - 2010

### 4.1 Modelo(s): linear, log-linear y hiperbólico

#### 4.1.1 Hombres:

- Para los grupos de edad [10-14] y [60+], aplicación de la función F1;
- Para el grupo de edad [15-19], aplicación de la función F2;
- Para los grupos de edad [20-59], aplicación de la función F3;
- Modificación de las tendencias de los grupos de edad [35-49] y [60+].

#### 4.1.2 Mujeres:

- Para el grupo de edad [10-14], aplicación de la función F1;
- Para los grupos de edad [15+], aplicación de la función F3;
- Modificación de las tendencias de todos los grupos de edad.

*Notas sobre los ajustes de las tasas, véase p.380-384.*     *Notas sobre las funciones de proyección, véase p. 386.*

# Rep. Dem. del Congo

## 1. Fuente(s) de los datos básicos

Código(s):  Título(s):

EPPA3    Estimaciones y proyecciones de la población económicamente activa, 1950-2025, tercera edición, OIT, Ginebra, 1986.

## 2. Evaluación de las tasas de actividad: 1950 - 1990

### 2.1 Datos básicos:

Cuadro 1: Tasas de actividad por sexo y grupo de edad

| Grupo de edad | Año | | | |
|---|---|---|---|---|
| | 1950 | 1960 | 1970 | 1980 |
| **Hombres** | | | | |
| 10-14 | 45.35 | 43.75 | 40.05 | 35.70 |
| 15-19 | 75.95 | 73.85 | 68.90 | 63.10 |
| 20-24 | 91.80 | 91.00 | 89.10 | 86.90 |
| 25-29 | 96.90 | 96.75 | 96.50 | 96.15 |
| 30-34 | 97.55 | 97.45 | 97.10 | 96.75 |
| 35-39 | 97.70 | 97.55 | 97.20 | 96.85 |
| 40-44 | 97.50 | 97.35 | 97.00 | 96.60 |
| 45-49 | 96.85 | 96.70 | 96.40 | 96.05 |
| 50-54 | 96.15 | 95.95 | 95.50 | 94.95 |
| 55-59 | 94.75 | 94.45 | 93.75 | 92.90 |
| 60-64 | 90.90 | 90.40 | 89.20 | 87.75 |
| 65+ | 76.05 | 75.15 | 73.05 | 70.55 |
| **Mujeres** | | | | |
| 10-14 | 37.35 | 35.20 | 30.25 | 24.40 |
| 15-19 | 65.25 | 60.80 | 50.35 | 38.05 |
| 20-24 | 70.10 | 65.75 | 55.55 | 43.55 |
| 25-29 | 72.80 | 68.75 | 59.35 | 48.25 |
| 30-34 | 75.60 | 71.85 | 63.00 | 52.60 |
| 35-39 | 76.75 | 73.20 | 64.95 | 55.20 |
| 40-44 | 78.05 | 74.85 | 67.40 | 58.65 |
| 45-49 | 77.10 | 74.00 | 66.75 | 58.20 |
| 50-54 | 72.35 | 69.75 | 63.70 | 56.60 |
| 55-59 | 66.65 | 64.75 | 60.40 | 55.25 |
| 60-64 | 54.95 | 53.80 | 51.15 | 48.05 |
| 65+ | 33.40 | 33.05 | 32.15 | 31.10 |

Fuente(s): EPPA3.

### 2.2 Método(s): interpolación y extrapolación lineares

#### 2.2.1 Hombres:

- 1950-80, tasas de actividad 1950-80 con base en EPPA3;
- 1990, extrapolación de las tasas de actividad 1950-80 con base en EPPA3;
ajuste de las tasas extrapoladas con base en las variaciones de las tasas interpoladas 1980, en relación con las tasas 1980 con base en EPPA3.

#### 2.2.2 Mujeres:

- 1950-90, interpolación y extrapolación de las tasas de actividad 1950-80 con base en EPPA3;
ajuste de las tasas interpoladas y extrapoladas con base en las variaciones de las tasas interpoladas 1980, en relación con las tasas de actividad 1980 con base en EPPA3.

## 3. Evaluación de las tasas de distribución  por sector de actividad: 1950 - 1990

### 3.1 Datos básicos:

Cuadro  2: Distribución de la población económicamente activa por sector de actividad en %

| Año | Agricultura | Industria | | Servicios |
|---|---|---|---|---|
| | | Total | Manufac. | |
| **Hombres** | | | | |
| 1950 | 75.20 | 13.20 | .. | 11.60 |
| 1980 | 57.50 | 19.80 | .. | 22.70 |
| **Mujeres** | | | | |
| 1950 | 99.8 | 0.05 | .. | 0.15 |
| 1980 | 94.7 | 1.45 | .. | 3.85 |

Fuente(s): EPPA3;

### 3.2 Método(s): interpolación y extrapolación lineares

#### 3.2.1 Hombres:

- 1950 y 1990, tasas de distribución 1950 y 1980 con base en EPPA3;
- 1960-80, interpolación de las tasas de distribución estimadas 1950 y 1990;
la industria y los servicios, mismas proporciones como en EPPA3;
promedios de las razones manufacturas/industria estimadas para Angola y Zimbabwe.
y Zimbabwe.

#### 3.2.2 Mujeres:

- 1950-90, interpolación extrapolación de las tasas de distribución ajustadas 1950 y 1980 con base en EPPA3;
ajuste de las tasas de distribución con base en
la razón hombres/mujeres igual a 1 en la agricultura;
- 1960-80, interpolación de las tasas de distribución estimadas 1950 y 1990;
- Las tasas de distribución de manufacturas estimadas con base en los promedios de las razones manuf/indust. estimadas para Angola y Zimbabwe.

## 4. Proyección de las tasas de actividad: 2000 - 2010

### 4.1 Modelo(s): hiperbólico

#### 4.1.1 Hombres:

- Para todos los grupos de edad, aplicación de la función F3;
- Modificación de las tendencias de los grupos de edad [20-54].

#### 4.1.2 Mujeres:

- Para todos los grupos de edad, aplicación de la función F3;
- Modificación de las tendencias de los grupos de edad [20-59] y [65+]

---

*Notas sobre los ajustes de las tasas, véase p.380-384.*     *Notas sobre las funciones de proyección, véase p. 386.*

# Rep. Pop. Dem. de Corea

## 1. Fuente(s) de los datos básicos

Código(s):  Título(s):

EPPA3  Estimaciones y proyecciones de la población económicamente activa, 1950-2025, tercera edición, OIT, Ginebra, 1986.

## 2. Evaluación de las tasas de actividad: 1950 - 1990

### 2.1 Datos básicos:

Cuadro 1: Tasas de actividad por sexo y grupo de edad

| Grupo de edad | Año 1950 | 1960 | 1970 | 1980 |
|---|---|---|---|---|
| **Hombres** | | | | |
| 10-14 | 13.00 | 7.00 | 4.75 | 2.40 |
| 15-19 | 78.10 | 64.10 | 54.95 | 42.59 |
| 20-24 | 95.00 | 92.00 | 88.75 | 85.35 |
| 25-29 | 97.00 | 96.50 | 96.00 | 95.50 |
| 30-34 | 98.00 | 97.90 | 97.80 | 97.70 |
| 35-39 | 98.10 | 98.00 | 97.90 | 97.80 |
| 40-44 | 98.00 | 97.70 | 97.65 | 97.10 |
| 45-49 | 97.90 | 97.00 | 96.70 | 96.00 |
| 50-54 | 97.70 | 96.40 | 95.60 | 94.30 |
| 55-59 | 96.00 | 92.00 | 90.00 | 85.00 |
| 60-64 | 92.00 | 84.80 | 82.30 | 75.30 |
| 65+ | 73.10 | 61.10 | 51.40 | 37.40 |
| **Mujeres** | | | | |
| 10-14 | .. | .. | 6.45 | 3.20 |
| 15-19 | .. | .. | 51.00 | 43.20 |
| 20-24 | .. | .. | 74.55 | 77.00 |
| 25-29 | .. | .. | 75.00 | 75.90 |
| 30-34 | .. | .. | 73.80 | 74.50 |
| 35-39 | .. | .. | 72.90 | 73.60 |
| 40-44 | .. | .. | 72.30 | 73.00 |
| 45-49 | .. | .. | 72.00 | 73.00 |
| 50-54 | .. | .. | 71.50 | 72.50 |
| 55-59 | .. | .. | 52.00 | 51.00 |
| 60-64 | .. | .. | 38.00 | 36.00 |
| 65+ | .. | .. | 25.45 | 21.50 |

Fuente(s): EPPA3.

### 2.2 Método(s): extrapolación linear

#### 2.2.1 Hombres:

- 1950-80, tasas de actividad 1950-80 con base en EPPA3;
- 1990, extrapolación de las tasas de actividad 1950-80 con base en EPPA3; ajuste de las tasas extrapoladas con base en las variaciones de las tasas interpoladas 1980, en relación con las tasas 1980 con base en EPPA3; modificación de las tendencias de los grupos de edad [15-19] y [25+].

#### 2.2.2 Mujeres:

Métodos, hipótesis y tratamientos idénticos a los que se aplican a los hombres.

## 3. Evaluación de las tasas de distribución por sector de actividad: 1950 - 1990

### 3.1 Datos básicos:

Cuadro 2: Distribución de la población económicamente activa por sector de actividad en %

| Año | Agricultura | Industria Total | Manufac. | Servicios |
|---|---|---|---|---|
| **Hombres** | | | | |
| 1950 | 64.00 | 20.00 | .. | 16.00 |
| 1960 | 57.00 | 28.00 | .. | 19.00 |
| 1970 | 48.50 | 33.00 | .. | 22.00 |
| 1980 | 39.00 | 39.00 | .. | 26.00 |
| **Mujeres** | | | | |
| 1950 | 79.50 | 8.60 | .. | 11.90 |
| 1960 | 71.50 | 12.50 | .. | 16.00 |
| 1970 | 62.20 | 16.80 | .. | 21.00 |
| 1980 | 52.00 | 20.00 | .. | 28.00 |

Fuente(s): EPPA3.

### 3.2 Método(s): extrapolación linear

#### 3.2.1 Hombres:

- 1950-80, tasas de distribución 1950-80 con base en EPPA3;
- 1990, extrapolación de las tasas de distribución 1950-80 con base en EPPA3; modificación de las tendencias de los sectores de la industria y los servicios.

#### 3.2.2 Mujeres:

Métodos, hipótesis y tratamientos idénticos a los que se aplican a los hombres.

## 4. Proyección de las tasas de actividad: 2000 - 2010

### 4.1 Modelo(s): log-linear y hiperbólico

#### 4.1.1 Hombres:

- Para el grupo de edad [15-19], aplicación de la función F2;
- Para los grupos de edad [20+], aplicación de la función F3;
- Modificación de la tendencia del grupo de edad [20-24].

#### 4.1.2 Mujeres:

- Para el grupo de edad [15-19], aplicación de la función F2;
- Para los grupos de edad [20+], aplicación de la función F3;
- Modificación de las tendencias de los grupos de edad [20-64].

*Notas sobre los ajustes de las tasas, véase p.380-384.*

*Notas sobre las funciones de proyección, véase p. 386.*

# República Arabe Siria

## 1. Fuente(s) de los datos básicos

Código(s):   Título(s):

EPPA3      Estimaciones y proyecciones de la población económicamente activa, 1950-2025, tercera edición, OIT, Ginebra, 1986.
STAT       Base de datos de la OIT sobre estadísticas del trabajo - LABORSTA, Oficina de Estadística, OIT, Ginebra.

## 2. Evaluación de las tasas de actividad: 1950 - 1990

### 2.1 Datos básicos:

Cuadro 1: Tasas de actividad por sexo y grupo de edad

| Grupo de edad | Año | | | | |
|---|---|---|---|---|---|
| | 1950 (1) | 1960 (1) | 1970 (1) | 1981 (2) | 1983 (2) |
| **Hombres** | | | | | |
| 10-14 | 23.25 | 20.65 | .. | 12.53 | .. |
| 15-19 | 71.20 | 65.50 | .. | 53.15 | .. |
| 20-24 | 89.45 | 87.30 | .. | 82.08 | .. |
| 25-29 | 96.45 | 95.95 | .. | 95.50 | .. |
| 30-34 | 97.25 | 97.35 | .. | 98.07 | .. |
| 35-39 | 96.20 | 96.90 | .. | 98.21 | .. |
| 40-44 | 95.55 | 96.10 | .. | 97.15 | .. |
| 45-49 | 94.65 | 94.90 | .. | 94.46 | .. |
| 50-54 | 90.50 | 91.35 | .. | 89.78 | .. |
| 55-59 | 86.95 | 87.30 | .. | 85.27 | .. |
| 60-64 | 75.85 | 76.65 | .. | 68.56 | .. |
| 65+ | 43.35 | 45.55 | .. | 37.44 | .. |
| **Mujeres** | | | | | |
| 10-14 | .. | .. | 6.90 | .. | 3.20 |
| 15-19 | .. | .. | 13.35 | .. | 11.20 |
| 20-24 | .. | .. | 16.45 | .. | 15.90 |
| 25-29 | .. | .. | 14.55 | .. | 16.80 |
| 30-34 | .. | .. | 12.60 | .. | 13.50 |
| 35-39 | .. | .. | 12.40 | .. | 12.50 |
| 40-44 | .. | .. | 12.35 | .. | 11.40 |
| 45-49 | .. | .. | 12.65 | .. | 11.10 |
| 50-54 | .. | .. | 11.00 | .. | 8.30 |
| 55-59 | .. | .. | 7.00 | .. | 6.50 |
| 60-64 | .. | .. | 5.50 | .. | 4.80 |
| 65+ | .. | .. | 2.7 | .. | 1.50 |

Fuente(s): (1) EPPA3; (2) STAT.

### 2.2 Método(s): interpolación y extrapolación lineares
                 promedio ponderado

**2.2.1 Hombres:**

- 1950-80, interpolación de la tasas de actividad 1950-60 con base en EPPA3 y de las tasas de actividad con base en el censo 1981;
- 1990, aplicación a las tasas estimadas 1980, del promedio de las variaciones de las tasas de actividad estimadas 1990 para Egipto y Jordania.

**2.2.2 Mujeres:**

- 1950-70, tasas de actividad ajustadas 1950-70 con base en EPPA3; el ajuste se ha calculado con base en el modelo de ajuste de las tasas de actividad de las mujeres ocupadas en la agricultura como auxiliares familiares;
- 1980, promedios ponderados de las tasas de actividad 1970 con base en EPPA3 y de las tasas de actividad con base en el censo de 1983 ;
- 1990, extrapolación de las tasas de actividad estimadas para 1970 y 1980; ajuste de las tasas interpoladas y extrapoladas habida cuenta de la

## 3. Evaluación de las tasas de distribución por sector de actividad: 1950 - 1990

### 3.1 Datos básicos:

Cuadro 2: Distribución de la población económicamente activa por sector de actividad en %

| Año | Agricultura | Industria | | Servicios |
|---|---|---|---|---|
| | | Total | Manufac. | |
| **Hombres** | | | | |
| 1979 | 27.48 | 34.70 | 16.63 | 37.82 |
| 1983 | 22.17 | 36.53 | 15.38 | 41.30 |
| 1989 | 19.64 | 31.47 | 15.96 | 48.89 |
| 1991 | 23.06 | 28.42 | 15.55 | 48.52 |
| **Mujeres** | | | | |
| 1979 | 60.26 | 14.18 | 12.39 | 25.55 |
| 1983 | 47.80 | 13.83 | 11.47 | 38.37 |
| 1989 | 41.43 | 13.81 | 12.14 | 44.76 |
| 1991 | 54.10 | 7.71 | 6.42 | 38.18 |

Fuente(s): STAT.

### 3.2 Método(s): promedio ponderado
                 interpolación y extrapolación lineares

**3.2.1 Hombres:**

- 1950-70, tasas de distribución 1950-70 con base en EPPA3;
- 1980, promedios ponderados de las tasas de distribución con base en las encuestas de 1979 y 1983;
- 1990, promedios ponderados de las tasas de distribución con base en las encuestas de 1989 y 1991.
las encuestas de 1989 y 1991.

**3.2.2 Mujeres:**

- 1950-70, tasas de distribución de la agricultura 1950-70 con base en EPPA3; ajuste de las tasas habida cuenta de la subenumeración censal de las mujeres ocupadas en la agricultura;
- 1980-90, interpolación y extrapolación de las tasas de distribución ajustadas con base en las encuestas de 1979, 1983, 1989 y 1991; ajuste de las tasas estimadas 1950-90 habida cuenta de la subenumeración censal de las mujeres ocupadas en la agricultura.

## 4. Proyección de las tasas de actividad: 2000 - 2010

### 4.1 Modelo(s): linear y hiperbólico

**4.1.1 Hombres:**

- Para los grupos de edad [10-14], [30-44] y [50+], aplicación de la función F1;
- Para los grupos de edad [15-29] y [45-49], aplicación de la función F3;
- Modificación de las tendencias de los grupos de edad [10-14], [20-44] y [50-59].

**4.1.2 Mujeres:**

- Para todos los grupos de edad, aplicación de la función F1;
- Modificación de las tendencias de todos los grupos de edad.

---

*Notas sobre los ajustes de las tasas, véase p.380-384.*      *Notas sobre las funciones de proyección, véase p. 386.*

# República Checa

## 1. Fuente(s) de los datos básicos

**Código(s):** **Título(s):**

BLT-94-2  Vorobiev A. (1994), "Estimaciones de la población económicamente activa de los quince países de la ex URSS, en 1950, 1959, 1970, 1979 y 1989", en el Boletín de Estadísticas del Trabajol - 1994-2, OIT, Ginebra.

STAT  Base de datos de la OIT sobre estadísticas del trabajo - LABORSTA, Oficina de Estadística, OIT, Ginebra.

## 2. Evaluación de las tasas de actividad: 1950 - 1990

### 2.1 Datos básicos:

**Cuadro 1: Tasas de actividad por sexo y grupo de edad**

| Grupo de edad | Año 1950 (1)(2) | 1950 (2) | 1961 (2) | 1970 (2) | 1980 (3) | 1990 (3) |
|---|---|---|---|---|---|---|
| **Hombres** | | | | | | |
| 10-14 | 0.90 | .. | 0.00 | 0.00 | 0.00 | 0.00 |
| 15-19 | 74.46 | .. | 47.32 | 34.90 | 27.25 | 34.83 |
| 20-24 | 93.09 | .. | 94.20 | 91.55 | 86.49 | 88.19 |
| 25-29 | 98.34 | .. | 98.79 | 98.61 | 98.23 | 98.02 |
| 30-34 | 98.38 | .. | 98.87 | 98.97 | 98.89 | 98.32 |
| 35-39 | 98.51 | .. | 98.42 | 98.69 | 98.66 | 97.84 |
| 40-44 | 98.10 | .. | 97.73 | 97.92 | 97.65 | 97.19 |
| 45-49 | 97.14 | .. | 96.35 | 96.52 | 96.29 | 95.62 |
| 50-54 | 93.59 | .. | 93.09 | 93.74 | 92.94 | 91.89 |
| 55-59 | 88.67 | .. | 84.32 | 85.26 | 84.31 | 80.36 |
| 60-64 | 76.58 | .. | 46.28 | 31.47 | 46.58 | 29.09 |
| 65+ | 38.38 | .. | 23.87 | 14.66 | 18.96 | 12.38 |
| **Mujeres** | | | | | | |
| 10-14 | .. | 0.00 | 0.00 | 0.00 | 0.00 | 0.00 |
| 15-19 | .. | 69.83 | 58.21 | 44.21 | 29.77 | 33.65 |
| 20-24 | .. | 59.29 | 73.15 | 79.68 | 84.57 | 87.25 |
| 25-29 | .. | 39.30 | 62.77 | 80.91 | 91.17 | 94.36 |
| 30-34 | .. | 40.99 | 65.65 | 83.81 | 93.09 | 95.03 |
| 35-39 | .. | 46.39 | 72.27 | 86.57 | 94.31 | 95.43 |
| 40-44 | .. | 48.10 | 74.53 | 86.41 | 94.03 | 94.97 |
| 45-49 | .. | 51.82 | 72.96 | 84.05 | 91.27 | 93.21 |
| 50-54 | .. | 45.51 | 66.20 | 77.13 | 83.68 | 85.40 |
| 55-59 | .. | 34.81 | 46.81 | 39.38 | 43.11 | 32.29 |
| 60-64 | .. | 22.14 | 33.23 | 20.01 | 23.87 | 16.42 |
| 65+ | .. | 8.80 | 9.10 | 5.89 | 7.24 | 5.09 |

**Nota(s):** (1) Eslovaquia.
**Fuente(s):** (2) STAT; (3) BLT-94-2.

### 2.2 Método(s): promedio ponderado

#### 2.2.1 Hombres:

- 1950-90, promedios ponderados de las tasas de actividad con base en los censos de 1961 y 1970, de las tasas de actividad 1980 y 1990 con base en el Boletín de estadísticas del trabajo 1994-2 y de las tasas de actividad estimadas 1950 con base de la aplicación a las tasas de actividad para Eslovaquia con base en el censo de 1950, de las variaciones de las tasas de actividad con base en el censo de 1961, en relación con las tasas de actividad para Eslovaquia con base en el censo de 1961;
ajuste de las tasas de actividad estimadas 1950-70 del grupo de edad [10-14].

#### 2.2.2 Mujeres:

- 1950-90, promedios ponderados de las tasas de actividad con base en los censos de 1950, 1961 y 1970 y las tasas de actividad 1980 y 1990 con base en el Boletín de estadísticas del trabajo 1994-2;
ajuste de las tasas de actividad estimadas 1950-70 del grupo de edad [10-14].

## 3. Evaluación de las tasas de distribución por sector de actividad: 1950 - 1990

### 3.1 Datos básicos:

**Cuadro 2: Distribución de la población económicamente activa por sector de actividad en %**

| Año | Agricultura | Industria Total | Manufac. | Servicios |
|---|---|---|---|---|
| **Hombres** | | | | |
| 1950 | 25.00 | 46.50 | .. | 28.50 |
| 1961 | 17.75 | 57.47 | 48.22 | 24.78 |
| 1970 | 14.76 | 56.27 | .. | 28.97 |
| 1980 | 14.40 | 66.54 | 45.50 | 19.07 |
| 1991 | 13.03 | 52.55 | 35.42 | 34.41 |
| **Mujeres** | | | | |
| 1950 | 43.72 | 32.06 | .. | 24.22 |
| 1961 | 26.99 | 40.36 | 42.31 | 32.65 |
| 1970 | 14.99 | 41.94 | 0.00 | 43.07 |
| 1980 | 11.40 | 43.58 | 38.91 | 45.02 |
| 1991 | 8.91 | 35.75 | 35.53 | 55.34 |

**Fuente(s):** STAT.

### 3.2 Método(s): promedio ponderado

#### 3.2.1 Hombres:
- 1950-90, promedios ponderados de las tasas de distribución con base en los censos de 1950, 1961, 1970, 1980 y 1991.

#### 3.2.2 Mujeres:
Métodos, hipótesis y tratamientos idénticos a los que se aplican a los hombres.

## 4. Proyección de las tasas de actividad: 2000 - 2010

### 4.1 Modelo(s): linear y hiperbólico

#### 4.1.1 Hombres:
- Para los grupos de edad [15-44] y [60+], aplicación de la función F3;
- Para los grupos de edad [45-59], aplicación de la función F1;
- Modificación de las tendencias de los grupos de edad [45-59].

#### 4.1.2 Mujeres:
- Para los grupos de edad [15+], aplicación de la función F3;
- Modificación de las tendencias de los grupos de edad [15-54].

---

*Notas sobre los ajustes de las tasas, véase p.380-384.*      *Notas sobre las funciones de proyección, véase p. 386.*

# República de Corea

## 1. Fuente(s) de los datos básicos

Código(s):    Título(s):

EPPA3    Estimaciones y proyecciones de la población económicamente activa, 1950-2025, tercera edición, OIT, Ginebra, 1986.
ADNU    Ediciones de 1979, 1984 et 1988 del Annuaire démographique des Nations Unies, New York.
ASTER    Anuario de estadísticas del trabajo 1945-89 - Edición retrospectiva sobre los censos de población, OIT, Ginebra, 1990.
AST90-93    Ediciones de 1990-1993, Anuario de Estadísticas del Trabjo de la OIT, Ginebra.
KNSO    Monthly Statistcs of Korea, National Statistical Office, Séoul.

## 2. Evaluación de las tasas de actividad: 1950 - 1990

### 2.1 Datos básicos:

Cuadro 1: Tasas de actividad por sexo y grupo de edad

| Grupo de edad | Año | | | | | | | |
|---|---|---|---|---|---|---|---|---|
| | 1975 (1) | 1980 (2) | 1987 (3) | 1988 (3) | 1989 (3) | 1990 (3) | 1991 (3) | 1992 (3) |
| **Hombres** | | | | | | | | |
| 10-14 | .. | 0.70 | 0.00 | 0.00 | 0.00 | 0.00 | .. | .. |
| 15-19 | .. | 26.79 | 17.33 | 15.14 | 12.13 | 11.19 | .. | .. |
| 20-24 | .. | 79.46 | 77.06 | 77.06 | 77.60 | 77.23 | .. | .. |
| 25-29 | .. | 93.02 | 90.34 | 90.57 | 91.51 | 92.53 | .. | .. |
| 30-34 | .. | 97.38 | 96.08 | 96.67 | 97.18 | 97.37 | .. | .. |
| 35-39 | .. | 97.43 | 96.15 | 96.59 | 97.18 | 97.10 | .. | .. |
| 40-44 | .. | 96.86 | 95.30 | 95.70 | 95.40 | 95.70 | .. | .. |
| 45-49 | .. | 95.21 | 92.70 | 93.20 | 93.60 | 94.10 | .. | .. |
| 50-54 | .. | 90.63 | 87.80 | 89.20 | 89.70 | 90.90 | .. | .. |
| 55-59 | .. | 82.52 | 77.40 | 79.70 | 82.40 | 83.60 | .. | .. |
| 60-64 | .. | 68.82 | 64.40 | 65.20 | 65.60 | 67.50 | .. | .. |
| 65+ | .. | 40.63 | 36.20 | 37.00 | 39.00 | 39.60 | .. | .. |
| **Mujeres** | | | | | | | | |
| 10-14 | 4.69 | .. | 0.00 | 0.00 | 0.00 | 0.00 | 0.00 | 0.00 |
| 15-19 | 47.48 | .. | 27.68 | 25.06 | 22.32 | 21.46 | 19.67 | 18.49 |
| 20-24 | 62.89 | .. | 63.88 | 65.32 | 67.22 | 67.16 | 67.87 | 67.26 |
| 25-29 | 35.59 | .. | 40.82 | 41.72 | 48.18 | 47.02 | 47.25 | 48.89 |
| 30-34 | 41.63 | .. | 47.53 | 49.48 | 52.42 | 53.11 | 53.98 | 54.52 |
| 35-39 | 51.15 | .. | 57.97 | 57.00 | 57.26 | 58.36 | 60.53 | 59.53 |
| 40-44 | 58.10 | .. | 60.30 | 60.20 | 61.00 | 60.50 | 60.40 | 60.40 |
| 45-49 | 60.08 | .. | 62.10 | 62.70 | 63.50 | 63.90 | 62.00 | 60.90 |
| 50-54 | 57.55 | .. | 57.00 | 58.00 | 60.40 | 60.00 | 60.00 | 60.80 |
| 55-59 | 51.43 | .. | 49.10 | 49.50 | 52.70 | 54.40 | 54.50 | 54.10 |
| 60-64 | 33.00 | .. | 40.30 | 39.70 | 41.60 | 43.60 | 43.20 | 44.90 |
| 65+ | 12.24 | .. | 15.40 | 15.50 | 18.10 | 18.40 | 18.80 | 19.60 |

Fuente(s): (1) (2) ADNU et ASTER; (3) KNSO y AST90-93.

### 2.2 Método(s): interpolación y extrapolación lineares

**2.2.1 Hombres:**

- 1950-70, tasas de actividad 1950-70 con base en EPPA3;
- 1980-90, extrapolación de las tasas de actividad ajustadas con base en el censo de 1980 y las encuestas de 1987 to 1990;
ajuste de las tasas interpoladas con base en las variaciones de las tasas extrapoladas 1970, en relación con las tasas de actividad 1970 con base en EPPA3;
modificación de las tendencias de los grupos de edad [15-29] para 1990.

**2.2.2 Mujeres:**

- 1950-80, tasas de actividad ajustadas 1950-80 con base en EPPA3;
- 1990, interpolación de las tasas de actividad con base en de 1975 el censo y las encuestas de 1987 to 1992;
ajuste de las tasas interpoladas con base en las variaciones de las tasas interpoladas 1970, en relación con las tasas de actividad 1970 con base en EPPA3.

## 3. Evaluación de las tasas de distribución por sector de actividad: 1950 - 1990

### 3.1 Datos básicos:

Cuadro 2: Distribución de la población económicamente activa por sector de actividad en %

| Año | Agricultura | Industria | | Servicios |
|---|---|---|---|---|
| | | Total | Manufac. | |
| **Hombres** | | | | |
| 1989 | 18.05 | 37.98 | 26.77 | 43.97 |
| 1980 | 16.76 | 38.67 | 26.15 | 44.56 |
| 1991 | 15.42 | 39.63 | 26.01 | 44.95 |
| **Mujeres** | | | | |
| 1989 | 21.65 | 30.69 | 28.91 | 47.66 |
| 1990 | 20.41 | 30.00 | 27.93 | 49.60 |
| 1991 | 18.60 | 29.68 | 27.42 | 51.72 |

Fuente(s): KNSO y AST90-93.

### 3.2 Método(s): promedio aritmético

**3.2.1 Hombres:**

- 1950-80, tasas de distribución 1950-80 con base en EPPA3;
- 1990, promedios de las tasas de distribución con base en las encuestas de 1989, 1990 y 1991.

**3.2.2 Mujeres:**

Métodos, hipótesis y tratamientos idénticos a los que se aplican a los hombres.

## 4. Proyección de las tasas de actividad: 2000 - 2010

### 4.1 Modelo(s): linear, hiperbólico y logístico

**4.1.1 Hombres:**

- Para los grupos de edad [15+], aplicación de la función F3;
- Modificación de las tendencias de los grupos de edad [15-49].

**4.1.2 Mujeres:**

- Para los grupos de edad [15-24] y [60+], aplicación de la función F1;
- Para los grupos de edad [25-59], aplicación de la función F6;
- Modificación de las tendencias de los grupos de edad [15+].

*Notas sobre los ajustes de las tasas, véase p.380-384.*          *Notas sobre las funciones de proyección, véase p. 386.*

# República Dem. Pop. Lao

## 1. Fuente(s) de los datos básicos

Código(s):   Título(s):

EPPA4        Población económicamente activa 1950-2010 - cuarta edición, OIT, Ginebra, 1996.

## 2. Evaluación de las tasas de actividad: 1950 - 1990

### 2.1 Datos básicos:

Cuadro 1: Tasas de actividad por sexo y grupo de edad

| Grupo de edad | Año 1950 (1) | 1950 (2) | 1970 (1) | 1970 (2) |
|---|---|---|---|---|
| **Hombres** | | | | |
| 10-14 | 37.12 | 38.56 | 28.30 | 29.66 |
| 15-19 | 81.62 | 91.66 | 74.84 | 84.50 |
| 20-24 | 90.30 | 97.38 | 88.80 | 97.38 |
| 25-29 | 95.84 | 98.00 | 96.31 | 98.00 |
| 30-34 | 97.23 | 97.93 | 97.53 | 97.93 |
| 35-39 | 97.42 | 96.85 | 97.85 | 96.85 |
| 40-44 | 97.58 | 94.64 | 97.64 | 94.55 |
| 45-49 | 97.10 | 91.62 | 97.13 | 91.48 |
| 50-54 | 95.50 | 89.96 | 95.41 | 88.17 |
| 55-59 | 92.10 | 88.04 | 91.80 | 84.39 |
| 60-64 | 82.55 | 87.72 | 76.21 | 79.45 |
| 65+ | 55.88 | 81.07 | 48.00 | 65.00 |
| **Mujeres** | | | | |
| 10-14 | 43.31 | 29.50 | 32.15 | 26.07 |
| 15-19 | 85.90 | 68.50 | 77.05 | 71.34 |
| 20-24 | 87.06 | 77.59 | 83.57 | 81.17 |
| 25-29 | 84.57 | 76.61 | 83.75 | 80.25 |
| 30-34 | 84.25 | 74.03 | 84.69 | 78.78 |
| 35-39 | 85.81 | 73.25 | 85.98 | 77.39 |
| 40-44 | 86.42 | 72.29 | 86.01 | 75.35 |
| 45-49 | 87.71 | 66.55 | 85.94 | 69.02 |
| 50-54 | 81.61 | 58.64 | 80.24 | 60.64 |
| 55-59 | 78.86 | 53.98 | 73.78 | 52.19 |
| 60-64 | 49.03 | 50.09 | 47.71 | 43.02 |
| 65+ | 34.88 | 39.46 | 27.10 | 31.13 |

Nota(s): (1) Tailandia; (2) Viet Nam.
Fuente(s): EPPA4.

### 2.2 Método(s): interpolación linear
promedio aritmético

**2.2.1 Hombres:**

- 1990, promedios de las tasas de actividad 1990 estimadas
para Tailandia y Viet Nam;
- 1950, aplicación a las tasas de actividad estimadas 1990, del promedio
de las variaciones de las tasas de actividad estimadas 1950 para Tailandia
y Viet Nam, en relación con las tasas de actividad estimadas 1970
para estos países;
- 1960-80, interpolación de las tasas de actividad estimadas para 1950 y 1990;
modificación de las tendencias de todos los grupos de edad.

**2.2.2 Mujeres:**

Métodos, hipótesis y tratamientos idénticos a los que se aplican a los hombres.

## 3. Evaluación de las tasas de distribución por sector de actividad: 1950 - 1990

### 3.1 Datos básicos:

Cuadro 2: Distribución de la población económicamente activa por sector de actividad en %

| Año | Agricultura | Industria Total | Manufac. | Servicios |
|---|---|---|---|---|
| **Hombres** | | | | |
| 1950 (1) | 82.90 | 3.60 | .. | 13.50 |
| 1950 (2) | 81.30 | 4.00 | .. | 14.70 |
| 1970 (1) | 76.25 | 7.45 | .. | 16.30 |
| 1970 (2) | 75.10 | 7.35 | .. | 17.55 |
| **Mujeres** | | | | |
| 1950 (1) | 86.60 | 1.90 | .. | 9.50 |
| 1950 (2) | 85.75 | 2.55 | .. | 11.70 |
| 1970 (1) | 83.65 | 4.45 | .. | 11.90 |
| 1970 (2) | 78.25 | 5.55 | .. | 16.20 |

Nota(s): (1) Tailandia; (2) Viet Nam.
Fuente(s): EPPA4.

### 3.2 Método(s): promedio ponderado

**3.2.1 Hombres:**

- 1950, a las tasas de distribución estimadas 1990, aplicación a el promedio
de las variaciones de las tasas de distribución 1950 estimadas para Tailandia
y le Viet Nam, en relación con las tasas estimadas 1970 para estos países;
- 1960-80, promedios ponderados de las tasas estimadas para 1950 y 1990;
- 1990, promedios de las tasas de distribución 1970 estimadas para la Tailandia
- 1990, promedios de las tasas de distribución 1970 estimadas para la Tailandia

**3.2.2 Mujeres:**

Métodos, hipótesis y tratamientos idénticos a los que se aplican a los hombres.

## 4. Proyección de las tasas de actividad: 2000 - 2010

### 4.1 Modelo(s): linear

**4.1.1 Hombres:**

- Para todos los grupos de edad, aplicación de la función F1;
- Modificación de las tendencias de los grupos de edad [10-19].

**4.1.2 Mujeres:**

- Para todos los grupos de edad, aplicación de la función F1;
- Modificación de las tendencias de los grupos de edad [10-54].

*Notas sobre los ajustes de las tasas, véase p.380-384.*     *Notas sobre las funciones de proyección, véase p. 386.*

# República Dominicana

## 1. Fuente(s) de los datos básicos

Código(s):   Título(s):

EPPA3   Estimaciones y proyecciones de la población económicamente activa, 1950-2025, tercera edición, OIT, Ginebra, 1986.
RDR-70   Censos Nacional de Poblacion Y habitacion 1970, Oficina Nacional de Estadística (ONE), Santo Domingo.
ASTER   Anuario de estadísticas del trabajo 1945-89 - Edición retrospectiva sobre los censos de población, OIT, Ginebra, 1990.

## 2. Evaluación de las tasas de actividad: 1950 - 1990

### 2.1 Datos básicos:

Cuadro 1: Tasas de actividad por sexo y grupo de edad

| Grupo de edad | Año 1950 (1) | 1960 (2) | 1970 (3) | 1981 (2) |
|---|---|---|---|---|
| **Hombres** | | | | |
| 10-14 | 53.75 | 48.00 | 41.87 | .. |
| 15-19 | 78.50 | 70.10 | 60.24 | .. |
| 20-24 | 97.00 | 95.05 | 84.94 | .. |
| 25-29 | 98.00 | 97.84 | 92.86 | .. |
| 30-34 | 98.80 | 98.64 | 95.00 | .. |
| 35-39 | 98.80 | 98.65 | 94.61 | .. |
| 40-44 | 98.65 | 98.47 | 93.97 | .. |
| 45-49 | 98.50 | 98.16 | 93.27 | .. |
| 50-54 | 98.25 | 97.86 | 90.95 | .. |
| 55-59 | 97.45 | 96.68 | 90.48 | .. |
| 60-64 | 96.60 | 95.12 | 88.19 | .. |
| 65+ | 84.59 | 83.27 | 79.12 | .. |
| **Mujeres** | | | | |
| 10-14 | 2.80 | 2.21 | 25.81 | 11.00 |
| 15-19 | 9.50 | 8.97 | 23.49 | 20.40 |
| 20-24 | 11.55 | 12.23 | 26.53 | 33.30 |
| 25-29 | 11.50 | 12.25 | 25.84 | 38.30 |
| 30-34 | 11.50 | 12.23 | 25.72 | 37.10 |
| 35-39 | 11.65 | 12.39 | 24.72 | 32.40 |
| 40-44 | 11.90 | 12.64 | 25.74 | 33.30 |
| 45-49 | 12.55 | 12.87 | 23.40 | 32.30 |
| 50-54 | 10.00 | 10.25 | 22.52 | 28.90 |
| 55-59 | 11.20 | 11.13 | 21.94 | 28.10 |
| 60-64 | 9.35 | 9.26 | 22.21 | 26.90 |
| 65+ | 4.50 | 4.27 | 10.50 | 10.28 |

Fuente(s): (1) EPPA3; (2) RDR-70 y ASTER; (3) ASTER.

### 2.2 Método(s): interpolación y extrapolación lineares

#### 2.2.1 Hombres:

- 1950-60, tasas de actividad 1950-60 con base en EPPA3;
ajuste de las tasas de actividad de los grupos de edad [10-14] y [65+] con base en los resultados de los censos de 1970 y 1981;
- 1970, tasas de actividad ajustadas con base en el censo de 1970;
- 1980-90, extrapolación de las tasas de actividad 1950 con base en EPPA3, de las tasas ajustadas con base en el censo de 1960 y de las tasas con base en el censo de 1970; aplicación a las tasas extrapoladas, de las variaciones de las tasas interpoladas 1970, en relación con las tasas con base en el censo de 1970.

#### 2.2.2 Mujeres:

- 1950-60, tasas de actividad 1950-60 con base en EPPA3;
modificación de las tendencias de los grupos de edad [10-19] para 1960;
- 1970-80, interpolación de las tasas de actividad con base en los censos de 1970 y 1981;
- 1990, extrapolación de las tasas de actividad con base en los censos de 1970 y 1981;
aplicación a las tasas extrapoladas, de las variaciones tasas interpoladas 1970,

## 3. Evaluación de las tasas de distribución por sector de actividad: 1950 - 1990

### 3.1 Datos básicos:

Cuadro 2: Distribución de la población económicamente activa por sector de actividad en %

| Año | Agricultura | Industria Total | Manufac. | Servicios |
|---|---|---|---|---|
| **Hombres** | | | | |
| 1960 | 69.30 | 12.35 | .. | 18.35 |
| 1970 | 58.20 | 14.68 | 11.16 | 27.12 |
| 1981 | 38.61 | 26.64 | 17.02 | 34.76 |
| **Mujeres** | | | | |
| 1960 | 13.15 | 16.15 | .. | 70.70 |
| 1970 | 11.91 | 13.02 | 12.43 | 75.07 |
| 1981 | 11.02 | 16.44 | 15.07 | 72.54 |

Fuente(s): ASTER.

### 3.2 Método(s): promedio ponderado
interpolación y extrapolación lineares

#### 3.2.1 Hombres:

- 1950-60, tasas de distribución 1950-60 con base en EPPA3;
- 1970, promedios ponderados de las tasas de distribución 1960 con base en EPPA3 y de las tasas de distribución con base en el censo de 1970;
- 1980-90, interpolación y extrapolación de las tasas de distribución con base en los censos de 1970 y 1981;
los censos de 1970 y 1981;

#### 3.2.2 Mujeres:

Métodos, hipótesis y tratamientos idénticos a los que se aplican a los hombres.

## 4. Proyección de las tasas de actividad: 2000 - 2010

### 4.1 Modelo(s): linear, hiperbólico y logístico

#### 4.1.1 Hombres:

- Para los grupos de edad [10-24] y [55+], aplicación de la función F1;
- Para los grupos de edad [25-54], aplicación de la función F3;
- Modificación de las tendencias de los grupos de edad [10-24] y [50-59].

#### 4.1.2 Mujeres:

- Para los grupos de edad [10-19] y [40+], aplicación de la función F1;
- Para los grupos de edad [20-39], aplicación de la función F6;
- Modificación de las tendencias de los grupos de edad [10-39] y [50+].

*Notas sobre los ajustes de las tasas, véase p.380-384.*   *Notas sobre las funciones de proyección, véase p. 386.*

# Reunión

## 1. Fuente(s) de los datos básicos

Código(s):    Título(s):

EPPA3    Estimaciones y proyecciones de la población económicamente activa, 1950-2025, tercera edición, OIT, Ginebra, 1986.
ASTER    Anuario de estadísticas del trabajo 1945-89 - Edición retrospectiva sobre los censos de población, OIT, Ginebra, 1990.
AST92    Anuario de Estadísticas del Trabjo 1992, OIT, Ginebra, 1992.

## 2. Evaluación de las tasas de actividad: 1950 - 1990

### 2.1 Datos básicos:

Cuadro 1: Tasas de actividad por sexo y grupo de edad

| Grupo de edad | Año 1982 (1) | 1990 (2) |
|---|---|---|
| **Hombres** | | |
| 10-14 | 0.00 | 0.00 |
| 15-19 | 32.85 | 19.60 |
| 20-24 | 87.28 | 77.50 |
| 25-29 | 93.83 | 92.30 |
| 30-34 | 94.28 | 92.30 |
| 35-39 | 93.82 | 91.50 |
| 40-44 | 91.38 | 89.40 |
| 45-49 | 88.45 | 85.40 |
| 50-54 | 82.81 | 77.50 |
| 55-59 | 72.66 | 58.40 |
| 60-64 | 33.65 | 19.30 |
| 65+ | 22.51 | 3.05 |
| **Mujeres** | | |
| 10-14 | 0.00 | 0.00 |
| 15-19 | 25.90 | 14.60 |
| 20-24 | 56.70 | 63.90 |
| 25-29 | 50.30 | 68.10 |
| 30-34 | 46.90 | 63.00 |
| 35-39 | 43.70 | 60.30 |
| 40-44 | 40.40 | 57.40 |
| 45-49 | 37.00 | 51.20 |
| 50-54 | 32.40 | 40.50 |
| 55-59 | 27.90 | 27.50 |
| 60-64 | 11.90 | 8.70 |
| 65+ | 1.34 | 0.80 |

Fuente(s): (1) ASTER; (2) AST92.

### 2.2 Método(s): promedio ponderado

**2.2.1 Hombres:**

- 1950-70, tasas de actividad 1950-70 con base en EPPA3;
- 1980-90, promedios ponderados de las tasas de actividad ajustadas con base los censos en de 1982 y 1990;
modificación de las tendencias de los grupos de edad [20-34] para 1980.

**2.2.2 Mujeres:**

- 1950-80, tasas de actividad 1950-80 con base en EPPA3;
- 1990, promedios ponderados de las tasas de actividad con base en los censos de 1982 y 1990.

## 3. Evaluación de las tasas de distribución por sector de actividad: 1950 - 1990

### 3.1 Datos básicos:

Cuadro 2: Distribución de la población económicamente activa por sector de actividad en %

| Año | Agricultura | Industria Total | Manufac. | Servicios |
|---|---|---|---|---|
| **Hombres** | | | | |
| 1982 (1) | 36.99 | 29.42 | 8.92 | 33.59 |
| 1990 (2) | 11.12 | 27.64 | 9.51 | 61.25 |
| **Mujeres** | | | | |
| 1982 (1) | 7.14 | 4.80 | 3.62 | 88.07 |
| 1990 (2) | 1.94 | 5.09 | 3.64 | 92.97 |

Fuente(s): (1) ASTER; (2) AST92.

### 3.2 Método(s): interpolación y extrapolación lineares

**3.2.1 Hombres:**

- 1950-70, tasas de distribución 1950-70 con base en EPPA3;
- 1980-90, interpolación y extrapolación de las tasas de distribución con base en los censos de 1982 y 1990;
modificación de las tendencias de todos los sectores para 1980.

**3.2.2 Mujeres:**

Métodos, hipótesis y tratamientos idénticos a los que se aplican a los hombres.

## 4. Proyección de las tasas de actividad: 2000 - 2010

### 4.1 Modelo(s): linear, hiperbólico y logístico

**4.1.1 Hombres:**

- Para el grupo de edad [15-19], aplicación de la función F1;
- Para los grupos de edad [20+], aplicación de la función F3.

**4.1.2 Mujeres:**

- Para los grupos de edad [15-19] y [50-54], aplicación de la función F1;
- Para los grupos de edad [20-49], aplicación de la función F6;
- Modificación de la tendencia del grupo de edad [25-29].

*Notas sobre los ajustes de las tasas, véase p.380-384.*

*Notas sobre las funciones de proyección, véase p. 386.*

# Rumania

## 1. Fuente(s) de los datos básicos

Código(s):  Título(s):

EPPA3    Estimaciones y proyecciones de la población económicamente activa, 1950-2025, tercera edición, OIT, Ginebra, 1986.
ASTER    Anuario de estadísticas del trabajo 1945-89 - Edición retrospectiva sobre los censos de población, OIT, Ginebra, 1990.
BLT-94-2    Popovic B. (1994), "Nuevas estimaciones de las tasas de actividad para 1980 y 1990, desglosadas por grupos de edad y distribución sectorial, en algunos países de Europa oriental y meridional" en el Boletín de Estadísticas del Trabajol - 1994-2, OIT, Ginebra.
AST94    Anuario de Estadísticas del Trabjo 1994, OIT, Ginebra, 1994.

## 2. Evaluación de las tasas de actividad: 1950 - 1990

### 2.1 Datos básicos:

Cuadro 1: Tasas de actividad por sexo y grupo de edad

| Grupo de edad | Año 1950 (1) | 1960 (1) | 1970 (1) | 1977 (2) | 1992 (2) |
|---|---|---|---|---|---|
| **Hombres** | | | | | |
| 10-14 | 1.50 | 0.85 | 0.50 | 0.40 | 0.42 |
| 15-19 | 90.00 | 74.10 | 62.10 | 37.50 | 38.60 |
| 20-24 | 95.60 | 93.20 | 90.10 | 87.10 | 86.80 |
| 25-29 | 97.90 | 97.35 | 96.85 | 97.00 | 95.70 |
| 30-34 | 98.40 | 98.35 | 97.90 | 97.90 | 96.70 |
| 35-39 | 98.75 | 98.50 | 98.00 | 97.20 | 96.60 |
| 40-44 | 98.45 | 98.00 | 97.50 | 95.80 | 95.80 |
| 45-49 | 97.95 | 97.70 | 97.50 | 93.80 | 93.20 |
| 50-54 | 96.95 | 95.30 | 94.80 | 88.80 | 79.60 |
| 55-59 | 94.50 | 92.90 | 88.00 | 78.70 | 45.80 |
| 60-64 | 90.85 | 80.40 | 65.00 | 44.70 | 21.00 |
| 65+ | 74.10 | 62.50 | 54.85 | 13.23 | 5.37 |
| **Mujeres** | | | | | |
| 10-14 | 2.00 | 1.45 | 0.90 | 0.50 | 0.21 |
| 15-19 | 79.45 | 69.95 | 45.20 | 32.10 | 32.70 |
| 20-24 | 78.55 | 75.90 | 74.15 | 75.60 | 72.10 |
| 25-29 | 74.85 | 76.15 | 80.35 | 83.10 | 78.50 |
| 30-34 | 74.20 | 75.70 | 80.45 | 83.50 | 81.30 |
| 35-39 | 74.05 | 75.85 | 80.80 | 83.60 | 81.60 |
| 40-44 | 75.80 | 76.40 | 79.45 | 81.70 | 79.00 |
| 45-49 | 74.75 | 74.90 | 75.85 | 77.60 | 72.80 |
| 50-54 | 73.85 | 72.10 | 70.70 | 69.70 | 51.00 |
| 55-59 | 67.95 | 63.50 | 55.90 | 72.50 | 28.70 |
| 60-64 | 61.40 | 52.10 | 34.45 | 25.20 | 10.20 |
| 65+ | 40.35 | 29.90 | 15.85 | 10.04 | 4.69 |

Fuente(s): (1) EPPA3; (2) AST94.

### 2.2 Método(s): interpolación linear

#### 2.2.1 Hombres:

- 1950-70, tasas de actividad 1950-70 con base en EPPA3;
- 1980-90, extrapolación de las tasas de actividad con base en los censos de 1977 y 1992.

#### 2.2.2 Mujeres:

Métodos, hipótesis y tratamientos idénticos a los que se aplican a los hombres.

## 3. Evaluación de las tasas de distribución por sector de actividad: 1950 - 1990

### 3.1 Datos básicos:

Cuadro 2: Distribución de la población económicamente activa por sector de actividad en %

| Año | Agricultura | Industria Total | Manufac. | Servicios |
|---|---|---|---|---|
| **Hombres** | | | | |
| 1950 (1) | 61.80 | 21.70 | .. | 16.50 |
| 1960 (1) | 53.00 | 29.50 | .. | 17.40 |
| 1970 (1) | 37.10 | 41.60 | .. | 21.30 |
| 1980 (2) | 25.93 | 50.14 | 33.92 | 23.93 |
| 1990 (2) | 20.95 | 52.91 | 37.39 | 26.14 |
| **Mujeres** | | | | |
| 1950 (1) | 84.30 | 6.50 | .. | 9.20 |
| 1960 (1) | 78.40 | 9.40 | .. | 12.10 |
| 1970 (1) | 63.70 | 17.50 | .. | 18.80 |
| 1980 (2) | 45.33 | 29.45 | 26.43 | 25.21 |
| 1990 (2) | 27.75 | 40.04 | 35.94 | 32.21 |

Fuente(s): (1) EPPA3; (2) BLT-94-2.

### 3.2 Método(s): datos de BLT-94-2

#### 3.2.1 Hombres:

- 1950-70, tasas de distribución 1950-70 con base en EPPA3;
- 1980-90, tasas de distribución con base en el boletín de estadísticas del trabajo 1994-2.

#### 3.2.2 Mujeres:

Métodos, hipótesis y tratamientos idénticos a los que se aplican a los hombres.

## 4. Proyección de las tasas de actividad: 2000 - 2010

### 4.1 Modelo(s): linear y hiperbólico

#### 4.1.1 Hombres:

- Para los grupos de edad [15-19] y [25+], aplicación de la función F3;
- Para los grupos de edad [20-24], aplicación de la función F1;
- Modificación de las tendencias de los grupos de edad [35-39] y [50-64].

#### 4.1.2 Mujeres:

- Para los grupos de edad [15+], aplicación de la función F3;
- Modificación de las tendencias de los grupos de edad [20-24] y [30-39].

# Rusia, Federación de

## 1. Fuente(s) de los datos básicos

Código(s):   Título(s):

BLT-94-2    Vorobiev A. (1994), "Estimaciones de la población económicamente activa de los quince países de la ex URSS, en 1950, 1959, 1970, 1979 y 1989", en el Boletín de Estadísticas del Trabajol - 1994-2, OIT, Ginebra.

## 2. Evaluación de las tasas de actividad: 1950 - 1990

### 2.1 Datos básicos:

Cuadro 1: Tasas de actividad por sexo y grupo de edad

| Grupo de edad | Año | | | | |
|---|---|---|---|---|---|
| | 1950 | 1959 | 1970 | 1979 | 1989 |
| **Hombres** | | | | | |
| 10-14 | 0.00 | 0.00 | 0.00 | 0.00 | 0.00 |
| 15-19 | 52.20 | 63.65 | 43.79 | 38.71 | 31.02 |
| 20-24 | 84.87 | 86.31 | 85.24 | 87.28 | 80.97 |
| 25-29 | 96.82 | 97.09 | 96.59 | 96.87 | 96.36 |
| 30-34 | 96.72 | 95.52 | 97.14 | 98.04 | 97.68 |
| 35-39 | 94.99 | 92.85 | 97.69 | 97.97 | 97.69 |
| 40-44 | 94.18 | 94.27 | 97.12 | 97.51 | 97.25 |
| 45-49 | 90.99 | 90.45 | 93.33 | 96.11 | 95.67 |
| 50-54 | 84.98 | 85.56 | 89.86 | 89.68 | 91.49 |
| 55-59 | 71.93 | 77.11 | 78.41 | 75.90 | 78.82 |
| 60-64 | 51.97 | 57.83 | 23.26 | 28.22 | 35.31 |
| 65+ | 21.08 | 25.52 | 10.99 | 10.09 | 13.49 |
| **Mujeres** | | | | | |
| 10-14 | 0.00 | 0.00 | 0.00 | 0.00 | 0.00 |
| 15-19 | 50.83 | 44.12 | 37.41 | 33.42 | 24.93 |
| 20-24 | 73.68 | 77.09 | 82.86 | 85.04 | 78.12 |
| 25-29 | 71.61 | 76.16 | 92.01 | 94.42 | 90.14 |
| 30-34 | 68.10 | 72.09 | 93.81 | 95.78 | 93.58 |
| 35-39 | 67.62 | 74.50 | 92.62 | 96.35 | 95.24 |
| 40-44 | 67.46 | 68.18 | 90.32 | 95.72 | 95.47 |
| 45-49 | 62.86 | 64.50 | 90.99 | 92.32 | 92.81 |
| 50-54 | 51.61 | 52.36 | 75.58 | 81.13 | 82.59 |
| 55-59 | 23.57 | 25.81 | 22.47 | 29.11 | 34.30 |
| 60-64 | 20.09 | 21.08 | 9.41 | 11.12 | 20.06 |
| 65+ | 2.35 | 2.35 | 2.01 | 3.01 | 5.86 |

Fuente(s): BLT-94-2.

### 2.2 Método(s):  promedio ponderado

#### 2.2.1 Hombres:

- 1950-90, promedios ponderados de las tasas de actividad 1950, 1959, 1985 y 1989 con base en el Boletín de estadísticas del trabajo 1994-2; ajuste de las tasas de actividad 1950, 1970 y 1979 con base en el Boletín para los grupos de edad [15-19] y [60+].

#### 2.2.2 Mujeres:

- 1950-90, promedios ponderados de las tasas de actividad 1950, 1959, 1982 y 1989 con base en el Boletín de estadísticas del trabajo 1994-2; ajuste de la tasa de actividad 1959 con base en el Boletín para el grupo de edad [15-19].

## 3. Evaluación de las tasas de distribución  por sector de actividad: 1950 - 1990

### 3.1 Datos básicos:

Cuadro  2: Distribución de la población económicamente activa por sector de actividad en %

| Año | Agricultura | Industria | | Servicios |
|---|---|---|---|---|
| | | Total | Manufac. | |
| **Hombres** | | | | |
| 1950 | 36.27 | 36.23 | 20.01 | 27.50 |
| 1959 | 27.23 | 39.65 | 25.68 | 33.12 |
| 1970 | 20.17 | 49.68 | 31.74 | 30.15 |
| 1979 | 18.81 | 50.33 | 28.71 | 30.86 |
| 1989 | 17.43 | 48.24 | 26.76 | 34.33 |
| **Mujeres** | | | | |
| 1950 | 42.63 | 27.67 | 20.30 | 29.70 |
| 1959 | 33.71 | 31.35 | 23.65 | 34.94 |
| 1970 | 17.68 | 35.82 | 28.75 | 46.50 |
| 1979 | 13.19 | 37.00 | 26.86 | 49.81 |
| 1989 | 9.75 | 34.76 | 24.61 | 55.50 |

Fuente(s): BLT-94-2.

### 3.2 Método(s):  datos de BLT-94-2

#### 3.2.1 Hombres:

- 1950, 1960, 1970, 1980 y 1990, respectivamente las tasas de distribución 1950, 1959, 1970, 1979 y 1989 con base en el boletín de estadísticas del trabajo 1994-2.

#### 3.2.2 Mujeres:

Métodos, hipótesis y tratamientos idénticos a los que se aplican a los hombres.

## 4. Proyección de las tasas de actividad: 2000 - 2010

### 4.1 Modelo(s):  log-linear, hiperbólico y logístico

#### 4.1.1 Hombres:

- Para los grupos de edad [15-24], aplicación de la función F2;
- Para los grupos de edad [25+], aplicación de la función F3;
- Modificación de las tendencias de los grupos de edad [20+].

#### 4.1.2 Mujeres:

- Para los grupos de edad [15-19] y [60+], aplicación de la función F3;
- Para los grupos de edad [20-59], aplicación de la función F6;
- Modificación de las tendencias de los grupos de edad [20-59].

*Notas sobre los ajustes de las tasas, véase p.380-384.*

*Notas sobre las funciones de proyección, véase p. 386.*

# Rwanda

## 1. Fuente(s) de los datos básicos

Código(s):  Título(s):

EPPA3    Estimaciones y proyecciones de la población económicamente activa, 1950-2025, tercera edición, OIT, Ginebra, 1986.
ASTER    Anuario de estadísticas del trabajo 1945-89 - Edición retrospectiva sobre los censos de población, OIT, Ginebra, 1990.

## 2. Evaluación de las tasas de actividad: 1950 - 1990

### 2.1 Datos básicos:

Cuadro 1: Tasas de actividad por sexo y grupo de edad

| Age group | Año 1950 (1) | 1960 (1) | 1970 (1) | 1978 (2) | 1980 (1) |
|---|---|---|---|---|---|
| **Men** | | | | | |
| 10-14 | 40.35 | 39.70 | 39.05 | 32.34 | 38.50 |
| 15-19 | 90.00 | 88.85 | 87.60 | 86.85 | 86.65 |
| 20-24 | 98.15 | 97.70 | 97.20 | 96.51 | 96.85 |
| 25-29 | 98.35 | 98.30 | 98.20 | 98.16 | 98.15 |
| 30-34 | 98.75 | 98.70 | 98.60 | 98.50 | 98.55 |
| 35-39 | 98.55 | 98.50 | 98.40 | 98.55 | 98.35 |
| 40-44 | 98.50 | 98.45 | 98.35 | 98.27 | 98.30 |
| 45-49 | 98.00 | 97.90 | 97.85 | 97.77 | 97.80 |
| 50-54 | 96.95 | 96.85 | 96.75 | 96.64 | 96.65 |
| 55-59 | 95.00 | 94.85 | 94.65 | 94.55 | 94.55 |
| 60-64 | 89.30 | 89.00 | 88.75 | 88.55 | 88.50 |
| 65+ | 70.15 | 69.75 | 69.30 | 69.00 | 68.95 |
| **Women** | | | | | |
| 10-14 | 49.85 | 48.70 | 47.45 | 33.32 | 46.50 |
| 15-19 | 91.55 | 89.15 | 86.55 | 88.19 | 84.55 |
| 20-24 | 95.75 | 93.45 | 90.90 | 96.14 | 88.95 |
| 25-29 | 96.45 | 94.30 | 91.95 | 97.08 | 90.15 |
| 30-34 | 97.85 | 95.85 | 93.65 | 97.43 | 91.95 |
| 35-39 | 97.60 | 95.70 | 93.60 | 97.97 | 92.05 |
| 40-44 | 96.75 | 95.05 | 93.20 | 97.96 | 91.80 |
| 45-49 | 95.35 | 93.70 | 91.85 | 97.25 | 90.50 |
| 50-54 | 87.55 | 86.20 | 84.65 | 95.26 | 83.50 |
| 55-59 | 77.65 | 76.65 | 75.55 | 90.92 | 74.75 |
| 60-64 | 61.65 | 61.05 | 60.35 | 81.67 | 59.85 |
| 65+ | 35.65 | 35.45 | 35.20 | 58.61 | 35.05 |

Fuente(s): (1) EPPA3; (2) ASTER.

### 2.2 Método(s): extrapolación linear

#### 2.2.1 Hombres:

- 1950-80, tasas de actividad 1950-80 con base en EPPA3;
- 1990, extrapolación de las tasas de actividad 1950-80 con base en EPPA3
y de las tasas de actividad con base en el censo de 1978 ;
modificación de las tendencias de todos los grupos de edad para 1990;
ajuste de las tasas extrapoladas 1990 con base en las variaciones
de la tasas interpoladas 1980, en relación con las tasas de actividad 1980
con base en EPPA3.

#### 2.2.2 Mujeres:

Métodos, hipótesis y tratamientos idénticos a los que se aplican a los hombres.

## 3. Evaluación de las tasas de distribución por sector de actividad: 1950 - 1990

### 3.1 Datos básicos:

Cuadro 2: Distribución de la población económicamente activa por sector de actividad en %

| Año | Agricultura | Industria Total | Manufac. | Servicios |
|---|---|---|---|---|
| **Hombres** | | | | |
| 1950 (1) | 92.30 | 3.25 | .. | 4.45 |
| 1960 (1) | 90.75 | 3.90 | .. | 5.35 |
| 1970 (1) | 89.05 | 4.65 | .. | 6.30 |
| 1978 (2) | 88.01 | 5.09 | 2.14 | 6.90 |
| 1980 (1) | 87.75 | 5.20 | .. | 7.05 |
| **Mujeres** | | | | |
| 1950 (1) | 99.10 | 0.30 | .. | 0.60 |
| 1960 (1) | 98.70 | 0.40 | .. | 0.90 |
| 1970 (1) | 98.30 | 0.55 | .. | 1.15 |
| 1978 (2) | 97.96 | 0.63 | 0.60 | 1.40 |
| 1980 (1) | 97.95 | 0.65 | .. | 1.40 |

Fuente(s): (1) EPPA3; (2) ASTER.

### 3.2 Método(s): extrapolación linear

#### 3.2.1 Hombres:

- 1950-80, tasas de distribución 1950-80 con base en EPPA3;
- 1990, extrapolación de las tasas de distribución 1950-80 con base en EPPA3;
- Aplicación de la razón manufacturas/industria con base en el censo de 1978.

#### 3.2.2 Mujeres:

Métodos, hipótesis y tratamientos idénticos a los que se aplican a los hombres.

## 4. Proyección de las tasas de actividad: 2000 - 2010

### 4.1 Modelo(s): linear y hiperbólico

#### 4.1.1 Hombres:

- Para todos los grupos de edad, aplicación de la función F1.

#### 4.1.2 Mujeres:

- Para todos los grupos de edad, aplicación de la función F3;
- Modificación de las tendencias de los grupos de edad [25-64].

*Notas sobre los ajustes de las tasas, véase p.380-384.*      *Notas sobre las funciones de proyección, véase p. 386.*

# Senegal

## 1. Fuente(s) de los datos básicos

Código(s):  Título(s):

EPPA3  Estimaciones y proyecciones de la población económicamente activa, 1950-2025, tercera edición, OIT, Ginebra, 1986.
R1976  République du Sénégal, Ministère de l'Economie et des Finances, Recensement Général de la Population, avril 1976.
AST93  Anuario de Estadísticas del Trabjo 1993, OIT, Ginebra, 1993.

## 2. Evaluación de las tasas de actividad: 1950 - 1990

### 2.1 Datos básicos:

Cuadro 1: Tasas de actividad por sexo y grupo de edad

| Grupo de edad | Año | | | | | |
|---|---|---|---|---|---|---|
| | 1950 (1) | 1960 (1) | 1970 (1) | 1976 (2) | 1980 (1) | 1988 (3) |
| **Hombres** | | | | | | |
| 10-14 | .. | 58.55 | .. | 47.40 | .. | 37.25 |
| 15-19 | .. | 76.35 | .. | 72.75 | .. | 64.76 |
| 20-24 | .. | 87.25 | .. | 88.39 | .. | 88.39 |
| 25-29 | .. | 95.20 | .. | 96.35 | .. | 94.51 |
| 30-34 | .. | 96.35 | .. | 98.34 | .. | 96.04 |
| 35-39 | .. | 96.90 | .. | 98.63 | .. | 97.07 |
| 40-44 | .. | 96.15 | .. | 98.81 | .. | 96.86 |
| 45-49 | .. | 95.25 | .. | 98.72 | .. | 96.15 |
| 50-54 | .. | 94.10 | .. | 97.37 | .. | 93.99 |
| 55-59 | .. | 86.60 | .. | 90.31 | .. | 86.93 |
| 60-64 | .. | 79.10 | .. | 85.40 | .. | 79.87 |
| 65+ | .. | 59.80 | .. | 74.80 | .. | 61.64 |
| **Mujeres** | | | | | | |
| 10-14 | 44.65 | 44.10 | 43.55 | 5.18 | 42.55 | .. |
| 15-19 | 54.40 | 53.80 | 53.20 | 7.26 | 52.10 | .. |
| 20-24 | 57.00 | 56.65 | 56.25 | 5.96 | 55.55 | .. |
| 25-29 | 63.30 | 62.85 | 62 40 | 4.86 | 61.60 | .. |
| 30-34 | 67.30 | 66.85 | 66.35 | 3.84 | 65.45 | .. |
| 35-39 | 69.65 | 69.20 | 68.70 | 3.89 | 67.90 | .. |
| 40-44 | 72.10 | 71.70 | 71.20 | 4.07 | 70.40 | .. |
| 45-49 | 70.80 | 70.35 | 69.85 | 4.75 | 69.00 | .. |
| 50-54 | 67.25 | 66.75 | 66.20 | 4.57 | 65.25 | .. |
| 55-59 | 62.50 | 62.00 | 61.40 | 4.45 | 60.45 | .. |
| 60-64 | 50.05 | 49.50 | 48.85 | 4.61 | 47.75 | .. |
| 65+ | 27.45 | 27.00 | 26.55 | 3.84 | 25.70 | .. |

Fuente(s): (1) EPPA3; (2) R1976; (3) AST93.

### 2.2 Método(s): interpolación y extrapolación lineares

#### 2.2.1 Hombres:
- 1950-90, interpolación y extrapolación de las tasas de actividad 1960
con base en EPPA3 y de las tasas de actividad ajustadas on base en
los censos de 1976 y 1988;
modificación de las tendencias del grupo de edad [10-14] para 1960 y 1980.

#### 2.2.2 Mujeres:
- 1950-90, interpolación y extrapolación de las tasas de actividad 1950-80
con base en EPPA3;
ajuste de las tasas interpoladas y extrapoladas con base en las variaciones
de las tasas interpoladas 1976, en relación con las tasas de actividad con base
en el censo de 1976;
modificación de las tendencias de todos los grupos de edad para 1980 y 1990.

## 3. Evaluación de las tasas de distribución por sector de actividad: 1950 - 1990

### 3.1 Datos básicos:

Cuadro 2: Distribución de la población económicamente activa por sector de actividad en %

| Año | Agricultura | Industria | | Servicios |
|---|---|---|---|---|
| | | Total | Manufac. | |
| **Hombres** | | | | |
| 1950 | 78.00 | 7.65 | .. | 14.35 |
| 1960 | 77.00 | 8.00 | .. | 15.00 |
| 1970 | 75.90 | 8.40 | .. | 15.70 |
| 1980 | 74.00 | 9.05 | .. | 16.95 |
| **Mujeres** | | | | |
| 1950 | 95.00 | 1.15 | .. | 3.85 |
| 1960 | 93.60 | 1.45 | .. | 4.95 |
| 1970 | 92.30 | 1.75 | .. | 5.95 |
| 1980 | 89.95 | 2.30 | .. | 7.75 |

Fuente(s): EPPA3.

### 3.2 Método(s): extrapolación linear

#### 3.2.1 Hombres:
- 1950-80, tasas de distribución 1950-80 con base en EPPA3;
- 1990, extrapolación de las tasas de distribución 1950-80 con base en EPPA3;
modificación de las tendencias de todos los sectores;
- Aplicación de la razón manufacturas/industria estimada para le Níger.

#### 3.2.2 Mujeres:
Métodos, hipótesis y tratamientos idénticos a los que se aplican a los hombres.

## 4. Proyección de las tasas de actividad: 2000 - 2010

### 4.1 Modelo(s): linear y hiperbólico

#### 4.1.1 Hombres:
- Para los grupos de edad [10-24], aplicación de la función F1;
- Para los grupos de edad [25+], aplicación de la función F3;
- Modificación de las tendencias de los grupos de edad [10-14] y [20-54].

#### 4.1.2 Mujeres:
- Para el grupo de edad [10-14], aplicación de la función F1;
- Para los grupos de edad [15+], aplicación de la función F3;
- Modificación de las tendencias de los grupos de edad [15-54].

*Notas sobre los ajustes de las tasas, véase p.380-384.*

*Notas sobre las funciones de proyección, véase p. 386.*

# Sierrra Leona

## 1. Fuente(s) de los datos básicos

Código(s):  Título(s):

EPPA3    Estimaciones y proyecciones de la población económicamente activa, 1950-2025, tercera edición, OIT, Ginebra, 1986.

## 2. Evaluación de las tasas de actividad: 1950 - 1990

### 2.1 Datos básicos:

Cuadro 1: Tasas de actividad por sexo y grupo de edad

| Grupo de edad | Año 1950 | 1960 | 1970 |
|---|---|---|---|
| **Hombres** | | | |
| 10-14 | 39.00 | 33.00 | 24.55 |
| 15-19 | 71.20 | 66.35 | 59.85 |
| 20-24 | 89.85 | 88.90 | 86.80 |
| 25-29 | 97.15 | 96.95 | 96.70 |
| 30-34 | 97.90 | 97.60 | 97.35 |
| 35-39 | 98.05 | 97.75 | 97.45 |
| 40-44 | 97.90 | 97.55 | 97.25 |
| 45-49 | 97.50 | 97.40 | 96.75 |
| 50-54 | 97.00 | 96.70 | 95.90 |
| 55-59 | 92.90 | 92.80 | 91.00 |
| 60-64 | 88.00 | 87.50 | 84.60 |
| 65+ | 73.45 | 70.35 | 64.30 |
| **Mujeres** | | | |
| 10-14 | 26.80 | 23.85 | 19.00 |
| 15-19 | 46.80 | 41.70 | 36.80 |
| 20-24 | 54.00 | 49.00 | 45.25 |
| 25-29 | 54.50 | 50.15 | 47.90 |
| 30-34 | 54.90 | 50.50 | 48.35 |
| 35-39 | 55.40 | 51.00 | 48.80 |
| 40-44 | 55.80 | 51.35 | 49.15 |
| 45-49 | 56.20 | 52.45 | 51.15 |
| 50-54 | 54.40 | 50.75 | 49.50 |
| 55-59 | 48.45 | 47.55 | 46.65 |
| 60-64 | 36.35 | 34.25 | 33.55 |
| 65+ | 23.40 | 22.20 | 20.75 |

Fuente(s): EPPA3.

### 2.2 Método(s):  extrapolación linear

#### 2.2.1 Hombres:

- 1950-70, tasas de actividad 1950-70 con base en EPPA3;
- 1980-90, extrapolación de las tasas de actividad 1950-70 con base en EPPA3;
ajuste de las tasas interpoladas y extrapoladas con base en las variaciones de las tasas interpoladas 1970, en relación con las tasas 1970 con base en EPPA3;
modificación de las tendencias de todos los grupos de edad para 1980-90.

#### 2.2.2 Mujeres:

Métodos, hipótesis y tratamientos idénticos a los que se aplican a los hombres.

## 3. Evaluación de las tasas de distribución por sector de actividad: 1950 - 1990

### 3.1 Datos básicos:

Cuadro 2: Distribución de la población económicamente activa por sector de actividad en %

| Año | Agricultura | Industria Total | Manufac. | Servicios |
|---|---|---|---|---|
| **Hombres** | | | | |
| 1950 | 82.00 | 10.55 | .. | 7.45 |
| 1960 | 77.00 | 13.50 | .. | 9.50 |
| 1970 | 70.00 | 17.60 | .. | 12.40 |
| 1980 | 63.00 | 19.65 | .. | 17.35 |
| **Mujeres** | | | | |
| 1950 | 91.50 | 1.70 | .. | 6.80 |
| 1960 | 89.00 | 2.20 | .. | 8.80 |
| 1970 | 85.50 | 2.90 | .. | 11.60 |
| 1980 | 82.00 | 3.60 | .. | 14.40 |

Fuente(s): EPPA3.

### 3.2 Método(s):  extrapolación linear

#### 3.2.1 Hombres:

- 1950-80, tasas de distribución 1950-80 con base en EPPA3;
- 1990, extrapolación de las tasas de distribución 1950-80 con base en EPPA3;
- Aplicación de la razón manufacturas/industria estimada para le Liberia.

#### 3.2.2 Mujeres:

Métodos, hipótesis y tratamientos idénticos a los que se aplican a los hombres.

## 4. Proyección de las tasas de actividad: 2000 - 2010

### 4.1 Modelo(s):  log-linear y hiperbólico

#### 4.1.1 Hombres:

- Para el grupo de edad [10-14], aplicación de la función F2;
- Para los grupos de edad [15+], aplicación de la función F3.

#### 4.1.2 Mujeres:

- Para el grupo de edad [10-14], aplicación de la función F2;
- Para los grupos de edad [15+], aplicación de la función F3;
- Modificación de las tendencias de los grupos de edad [20+].

---

*Notas sobre los ajustes de las tasas, véase p.380-384.*   *Notas sobre las funciones de proyección, véase p. 386.*

# Singapur

## 1. Fuente(s) de los datos básicos

Código(s):   Título(s):

EPPA3    Estimaciones y proyecciones de la población económicamente activa, 1950-2025, tercera edición, OIT, Ginebra, 1986.
STAT     Base de datos de la OIT sobre estadísticas del trabajo - LABORSTA, Oficina de Estadística, OIT, Ginebra.

## 2. Evaluación de las tasas de actividad: 1950 - 1990

### 2.1 Datos básicos:

Cuadro 1: Tasas de actividad por sexo y grupo de edad

| Grupo de edad | Año 1980 (1) | 1980 (2) | 1989 (2) | 1990 (1) | 1991 (2) |
|---|---|---|---|---|---|
| **Hombres** | | | | | |
| 10-14 | 1.64 | 1.64 | 0.00 | 0.00 | 0.00 |
| 15-19 | 47.49 | 45.80 | 25.50 | 28.39 | 31.10 |
| 20-24 | 93.35 | 92.50 | 84.80 | 84.35 | 83.10 |
| 25-29 | 97.23 | 97.30 | 96.60 | 95.42 | 97.00 |
| 30-34 | 97.94 | 98.32 | 98.30 | 96.56 | 98.70 |
| 35-39 | 98.03 | 98.41 | 99.00 | 97.22 | 99.10 |
| 40-44 | 97.62 | 98.00 | 97.80 | 97.65 | 98.40 |
| 45-49 | 95.72 | 96.30 | 96.10 | 95.19 | 96.50 |
| 50-54 | 89.57 | 90.40 | 89.20 | 88.19 | 92.50 |
| 55-59 | 70.69 | 73.20 | 66.60 | 68.35 | 71.00 |
| 60-64 | 52.53 | 55.80 | 48.20 | 31.86 | 46.90 |
| 65+ | 28.61 | 29.80 | 20.74 | ... | 19.80 |
| **Mujeres** | | | | | |
| 10-14 | 1.65 | 1.64 | 0.00 | 0.00 | 0.00 |
| 15-19 | 50.73 | 45.80 | 25.50 | 27.84 | 31.10 |
| 20-24 | 78.40 | 92.50 | 84.80 | 79.57 | 83.10 |
| 25-29 | 58.67 | 97.30 | 96.60 | 76.31 | 97.00 |
| 30-34 | 44.20 | 98.32 | 98.30 | 63.06 | 98.70 |
| 35-39 | 37.13 | 98.41 | 99.00 | 54.95 | 99.10 |
| 40-44 | 33.16 | 98.00 | 97.80 | 51.86 | 98.40 |
| 45-49 | 26.47 | 96.30 | 96.10 | 45.01 | 96.50 |
| 50-54 | 20.43 | 90.40 | 89.20 | 34.15 | 92.50 |
| 55-59 | 14.50 | 73.20 | 66.60 | 21.48 | 71.00 |
| 60-64 | 11.30 | 55.80 | 48.20 | 7.70 | 46.90 |
| 65+ | 6.40 | 29.80 | 20.74 | ... | 19.80 |

**Nota(s):** (1) Censo; (2) Encuesta.
**Fuente(s):** STAT.

### 2.2 Método(s): promedio aritmético

#### 2.2.1 Hombres:

- 1950-70, tasas de actividad 1950-70 con base en EPPA3;
- 1980, promedios de las tasas de actividad con base en
el censo de 1980 y la encuesta de 1980;
- 1990, promedios de las tasas de actividad con base en el censo de 1990
y de las tasas de actividad con base en las encuestas de 1989 y 1990.

#### 2.2.2 Mujeres:

Métodos, hipótesis y tratamientos idénticos a los que se aplican a los hombres.

## 3. Evaluación de las tasas de distribución por sector de actividad: 1950 - 1990

### 3.1 Datos básicos:

Cuadro 2: Distribución de la población económicamente activa por sector de actividad en %

| Año | Agricultura | Industria Total | Manufac. | Servicios |
|---|---|---|---|---|
| **Hombres** | | | | |
| 1980 (1) | 1.54 | 33.48 | 24.42 | 64.98 |
| 1980 (2) | 1.97 | 35.32 | 24.66 | 62.71 |
| 1989 (1) | 0.62 | 36.81 | 25.93 | 62.56 |
| 1991 (1) | 0.39 | 36.72 | 26.18 | 62.89 |
| **Mujeres** | | | | |
| 1980 (1) | 0.95 | 40.33 | 38.56 | 58.72 |
| 1980 (2) | 1.67 | 86.31 | 8.25 | 12.02 |
| 1989 (1) | 0.19 | 35.28 | 33.68 | 64.54 |
| 1991 (1) | 0.11 | 32.85 | 31.22 | 67.04 |

**Nota(s):** (1) Encuesta; (2) Censo.
**Fuente(s):** STAT.

### 3.2 Método(s): promedio aritmético

#### 3.2.1 Hombres:

- 1950-70, tasas de distribución 1950-70 con base en EPPA3;
- 1980, promedios de las tasas de distribución con base en el censo de 1980
y la encuesta de 1980;
- 1990, promedios de las tasas de distribución con base en las encuestas
de 1989 y 1990.
de 1989 y 1990.

#### 3.2.2 Mujeres:

Métodos, hipótesis y tratamientos idénticos a los que se aplican a los hombres.

## 4. Proyección de las tasas de actividad: 2000 - 2010

### 4.1 Modelo(s): linear, hiperbólico y logístico

#### 4.1.1 Hombres:

- Para el grupo de edad [15-19], aplicación de la función F1;
- Para los grupos de edad [20+], aplicación de la función F6;
- Modificación de las tendencias de los grupos de edad [55-64].

#### 4.1.2 Mujeres:

- Para los grupos de edad [15-19] y [35-54], aplicación de la función F1;
- Para los grupos de edad [20-34], aplicación de la función F6;
- Para los grupos de edad [55+], aplicación de la función F3;
- Modificación de las tendencias de los grupos de edad [15-59].

*Notas sobre los ajustes de las tasas, véase p.380-384.*          *Notas sobre las funciones de proyección, véase p. 386.*

# Somalia

## 1. Fuente(s) de los datos básicos

Código(s):   Título(s):

EPPA3   Estimaciones y proyecciones de la población económicamente activa, 1950-2025, tercera edición, OIT, Ginebra, 1986.

## 2. Evaluación de las tasas de actividad: 1950 - 1990

### 2.1 Datos básicos:

Cuadro 1: Tasas de actividad por sexo y grupo de edad

| Grupo de edad | Año 1950 | 1960 | 1970 | 1980 |
|---|---|---|---|---|
| **Hombres** | | | | |
| 10-14 | 47.40 | 44.95 | 42.80 | 40.35 |
| 15-19 | 78.65 | 75.40 | 72.55 | 69.25 |
| 20-24 | 92.85 | 91.60 | 90.50 | 89.25 |
| 25-29 | 97.05 | 96.85 | 96.70 | 96.50 |
| 30-34 | 97.75 | 97.55 | 97.35 | 97.15 |
| 35-39 | 97.90 | 97.65 | 97.45 | 97.25 |
| 40-44 | 97.70 | 97.45 | 97.25 | 97.05 |
| 45-49 | 97.00 | 96.80 | 96.65 | 96.45 |
| 50-54 | 96.40 | 96.10 | 95.80 | 95.50 |
| 55-59 | 95.15 | 94.70 | 94.25 | 93.80 |
| 60-64 | 91.60 | 90.80 | 90.10 | 89.30 |
| 65+ | 77.25 | 75.85 | 74.60 | 73.20 |
| **Mujeres** | | | | |
| 10-14 | 35.85 | 34.00 | 32.35 | 30.50 |
| 15-19 | 58.65 | 55.90 | 53.40 | 50.65 |
| 20-24 | 60.80 | 59.05 | 57.50 | 55.75 |
| 25-29 | 65.30 | 63.35 | 61.55 | 59.60 |
| 30-34 | 69.40 | 67.30 | 65.40 | 63.25 |
| 35-39 | 70.90 | 68.90 | 67.15 | 65.15 |
| 40-44 | 73.35 | 71.35 | 69.60 | 67.65 |
| 45-49 | 72.80 | 70.80 | 69.00 | 66.95 |
| 50-54 | 70.75 | 68.40 | 66.35 | 64.00 |
| 55-59 | 67.80 | 65.35 | 63.15 | 60.70 |
| 60-64 | 60.50 | 57.40 | 54.60 | 51.50 |
| 65+ | 40.85 | 37.95 | 35.35 | 32.45 |

Fuente(s): EPPA3.

### 2.2 Método(s): interpolación y extrapolación lineares

#### 2.2.1 Hombres:

- 1950-80, tasas de actividad 1950-80 con base en EPPA3;
- 1990, extrapolación de las tasas de actividad 1950-80 con base en EPPA3;
ajuste de las tasas extrapoladas con base en las variaciones de las tasas interpoladas 1980, en relación con las tasas 1980 con base en EPPA3.

#### 2.2.2 Mujeres:

- 1950-90, interpolación y extrapolación de las tasas de actividad ajustadas 1950 y 1980 con base en EPPA3;
ajuste de los promedios de las tasas de actividad con base en
en la razón hombres/mujeres igual a 1 en la agricultura;
ajuste de las tasas interpoladas y extrapoladas con base en las variaciones de las tasas interpoladas 1980, en relación con las tasas de actividad ajustadas 1980 con base en EPPA3.

## 3. Evaluación de las tasas de distribución por sector de actividad: 1950 - 1990

### 3.1 Datos básicos:

Cuadro 2: Distribución de la población económicamente activa por sector de actividad en %

| Año | Agricultura | Industria Total | Manufac. | Servicios |
|---|---|---|---|---|
| **Hombres** | | | | |
| 1950 | 79.00 | 7.00 | .. | 14.00 |
| 1980 | 66.00 | 13.00 | .. | 21.00 |
| **Mujeres** | | | | |
| 1950 | 97.00 | 0.50 | .. | 2.50 |
| 1980 | 89.00 | 1.70 | .. | 8.80 |

Fuente(s): EPPA3.

### 3.2 Método(s): interpolación y extrapolación lineares

#### 3.2.1 Hombres:

- 1950-80, tasas de distribución 1950-80 con base en EPPA3;
- 1990, extrapolación de las tasas de distribución 1950-80 con base en EPPA3;
- Aplicación de la razón manufacturas/industria estimada para Eritrea.

#### 3.2.2 Mujeres:

- 1950-90, interpolación extrapolación de las tasas de distribución ajustadas 1950 y 1980 con base en EPPA3;
ajuste de las tasas de distribución con base en
la razón hombres/mujeres igual a 1 en la agricultura;
las tasas de distribución de manufacturas estimada con base en los razones manufacturas/industria estimadas para Eritrea.

## 4. Proyección de las tasas de actividad: 2000 - 2010

### 4.1 Modelo(s): linear y hiperbólico

#### 4.1.1 Hombres:

- Para los grupos de edad [10-19], aplicación de la función F1;
- Para los grupos de edad [20+], aplicación de la función F3;
- Modificación de las tendencias de los grupos de edad [20-49].

#### 4.1.2 Mujeres:

- Para todos los grupos de edad, aplicación de la función F3;
- Modificación de las tendencias de los grupos de edad [20-59].

*Notas sobre los ajustes de las tasas, véase p.380-384.*   *Notas sobre las funciones de proyección, véase p. 386.*

# Sri Lanka

## 1. Fuente(s) de los datos básicos

Código(s):   Título(s):

EPPA3   Estimaciones y proyecciones de la población económicamente activa, 1950-2025, tercera edición, OIT, Ginebra, 1986.
STAT   Base de datos de la OIT sobre estadísticas del trabajo - LABORSTA, Oficina de Estadística, OIT, Ginebra.

## 2. Evaluación de las tasas de actividad: 1950 - 1990

### 2.1 Datos básicos:

Cuadro 1: Tasas de actividad por sexo y grupo de edad

| Grupo de edad | Año | | |
|---|---|---|---|
| | 1990 | 1992 | 1993 |
| **Hombres** | | | |
| 10-14 | 5.30 | 1.80 | .. |
| 15-19 | 36.20 | 30.30 | .. |
| 20-24 | 84.90 | 89.50 | .. |
| 25-29 | 96.40 | 95.20 | .. |
| 30-34 | 97.70 | 98.10 | .. |
| 35-39 | 96.70 | 96.00 | .. |
| 40-44 | 97.90 | 96.20 | .. |
| 45-49 | 95.80 | 91.90 | .. |
| 50-54 | 94.60 | 82.70 | .. |
| 55-59 | 73.90 | 73.90 | .. |
| 60-64 | 49.00 | 38.60 | .. |
| 65+ | 52.90 | 28.70 | .. |
| **Mujeres** | | | |
| 10-14 | 4.60 | 1.40 | 1.80 |
| 15-19 | 26.90 | 21.10 | 19.70 |
| 20-24 | 63.80 | 57.10 | 58.47 |
| 25-29 | 58.30 | 56.50 | 50.02 |
| 30-34 | 62.30 | 47.60 | 47.80 |
| 35-39 | 55.60 | 48.70 | 53.71 |
| 40-44 | 51.80 | 43.30 | 45.49 |
| 45-49 | 47.90 | 42.30 | 37.34 |
| 50-54 | 34.50 | 27.10 | 35.13 |
| 55-59 | 31.30 | 20.60 | 19.24 |
| 60-64 | 13.30 | 6.10 | 6.31 |
| 65+ | | | |

Fuente(s): STAT.

### 2.2 Método(s):   interpolación linear

#### 2.2.1 Hombres:

- 1950-80, tasas de actividad 1950-80 con base en EPPA3;
- 1990, interpolación de las tasas de actividad 1950-80 con base en EPPA3
y de los promedios de las tasas de actividad con base en las encuestas
de 1990 y 1992;
ajuste de las tasas interpoladas con base en las variaciones de las tasas
interpoladas 1980, en relación con las tasas de actividad 1980
con base en EPPA3.

#### 2.2.2 Mujeres:

- 1950-80, tasas de actividad 1950-80 con base en EPPA3;
- 1990, interpolación de las tasas de actividad 1980 con base en EPPA3
y de los promedios de las tasas de actividad con base en las encuestas
de 1990, 1992 y 1992.

## 3. Evaluación de las tasas de distribución por sector de actividad: 1950 - 1990

### 3.1 Datos básicos:

Cuadro 2: Distribución de la población económicamente activa por sector de actividad en %

| Año | Agricultura | Industria | | Servicios |
|---|---|---|---|---|
| | | Total | Manufac. | |
| **Hombres** | | | | |
| 1981 | 49.37 | 18.97 | 10.42 | 31.66 |
| 1985 | 49.75 | 19.27 | 10.58 | 30.98 |
| 1993 | 40.01 | 19.43 | 9.11 | 40.56 |
| **Mujeres** | | | | |
| 1981 | 57.30 | 15.84 | 14.61 | 26.86 |
| 1985 | 55.04 | 20.22 | 18.92 | 24.74 |
| 1993 | 39.18 | 26.15 | 23.28 | 34.67 |

Fuente(s): STAT.

### 3.2 Método(s):   interpolación linear

#### 3.2.1 Hombres:

- 1950-70, tasas de distribución 1950-70 con base en EPPA3;
- 1980-90, interpolación de las tasas de distribución con base en los censos
de 1981, 1985 y 1991;
modificación de las tendencias de todos los sectores.

#### 3.2.2 Mujeres:

Métodos, hipótesis y tratamientos idénticos a los que se aplican a los hombres.

## 4. Proyección de las tasas de actividad: 2000 - 2010

### 4.1 Modelo(s):   linear, log-linear y hiperbólico

#### 4.1.1 Hombres:

- Para el grupo de edad [10-14], aplicación de la función F2;
- Para los grupos de edad [15+], aplicación de la función F3;
- Modificación de las tendencias de los grupos de edad [10-14] y [35-49].

#### 4.1.2 Mujeres:

- Para los grupos de edad [10-34], aplicación de la función F2;
- Para los grupos de edad [35-59], aplicación de la función F1;
- Para los grupos de edad [60+], aplicación de la función F3;
- Modificación de las tendencias de los grupos de edad [10-19] y [30-59].

*Notas sobre los ajustes de las tasas, véase p.380-384.*   *Notas sobre las funciones de proyección, véase p. 386.*

# Sudáfrica

## 1. Fuente(s) de los datos básicos

Código(s):    Título(s):

EPPA3       Estimaciones y proyecciones de la población económicamente activa, 1950-2025, tercera edición, OIT, Ginebra, 1986.
ASTER       Anuario de estadísticas del trabajo 1945-89 - Edición retrospectiva sobre los censos de población, OIT, Ginebra, 1990.
ADNU88      Annuaire démographique 1988 - Statistiques des recensements de population, quarantième édition, Nations Unies, New York, 1990.
AST93       Anuario de Estadísticas del Trabjo 1993, OIT, Ginebra, 1993.

## 2. Evaluación de las tasas de actividad: 1950 - 1990

### 2.1 Datos básicos:

Cuadro 1: Tasas de actividad por sexo y grupo de edad

| Grupo de edad | Año 1950 (1) | 1960 (1) | 1970 (1) | 1980 (1) | 1985 (2) |
|---|---|---|---|---|---|
| **Hombres** | | | | | |
| 10-14 | 22.30 | 7.80 | 3.85 | 0.30 | 0.00 |
| 15-19 | 74.40 | 67.60 | 59.50 | 35.90 | 47.94 |
| 20-24 | 95.70 | 98.00 | 92.65 | 83.45 | 81.70 |
| 25-29 | 97.50 | 96.60 | 95.45 | 93.35 | 95.37 |
| 30-34 | 99.25 | 98.60 | 97.85 | 96.40 | 97.79 |
| 35-39 | 99.40 | 98.75 | 98.00 | 96.50 | 97.85 |
| 40-44 | 98.90 | 98.25 | 97.65 | 96.40 | 97.49 |
| 45-49 | 98.55 | 98.00 | 97.25 | 94.50 | 97.13 |
| 50-54 | 98.00 | 97.00 | 95.85 | 91.50 | 95.62 |
| 55-59 | 95.55 | 94.65 | 90.35 | 80.00 | 87.09 |
| 60-64 | 90.00 | 87.15 | 80.25 | 62.10 | 73.75 |
| 65+ | 69.65 | 53.05 | 44.30 | 14.30 | 30.29 |
| **Mujeres** | | | | | |
| 10-14 | 4.00 | 2.60 | 1.50 | 0.15 | 0.00 |
| 15-19 | 35.45 | 35.30 | 46.80 | 28.25 | 41.91 |
| 20-24 | 35.40 | 38.60 | 58.45 | 59.65 | 54.07 |
| 25-29 | 23.40 | 29.55 | 49.65 | 50.50 | 58.92 |
| 30-34 | 20.20 | 25.55 | 43.50 | 44.30 | 51.69 |
| 35-39 | 19.95 | 25.25 | 39.55 | 40.25 | 51.19 |
| 40-44 | 19.75 | 24.95 | 37.55 | 38.20 | 48.25 |
| 45-49 | 18.40 | 23.50 | 36.85 | 37.55 | 47.84 |
| 50-54 | 17.90 | 22.85 | 34.40 | 35.55 | 44.36 |
| 55-59 | 15.15 | 18.90 | 25.95 | 25.30 | 29.43 |
| 60-64 | 11.25 | 13.80 | 20.05 | 14.90 | 22.72 |
| 65+ | 8.15 | 6.00 | 5.60 | 2.00 | 5.61 |

Fuente(s): (1) EPPA3; (2) ADNU88 y ASTER.

### 2.2 Método(s): extrapolación linear
promedio ponderado

#### 2.2.1 Hombres:

- 1950-70, tasas de actividad 1950-70 con base en EPPA3;
- 1980, promedios ponderados de las tasas de actividad 1970 con base en EPPA3 y de las tasas de actividad ajustadas con base en el censo de 1985;
- 1990, extrapolación de las tasas de actividad 1950-70 con base en EPPA3 y de las tasas de actividad ajustadas con base en el censo de 1985;
ajuste de las tasas extrapoladas con base en de las variaciones de las tasas interpoladas 1985, en relación con las tasas de actividad ajustadas con base en el censo de 1985.

#### 2.2.2 Mujeres:

- 1950-70, tasas de actividad 1950-70 con base en EPPA3;
ajuste de las tasas de actividad 1950 y 1960;
- 1980, promedios ponderados de las tasas de actividad 1970 con base en EPPA3 y de las tasas de actividad ajustadas con base en el censo de 1985;
- 1990, extrapolación de las tasas de actividad 1950-70 con base en EPPA3 y de las tasas de actividad ajustadas con base en el censo de 1985;
ajuste de las tasas extrapoladas con base en las variaciones de las tasas

## 3. Evaluación de las tasas de distribución por sector de actividad: 1950 - 1990

### 3.1 Datos básicos:

Cuadro 2: Distribución de la población económicamente activa por sector de actividad en %

| Año | Agricultura | Industria Total | Manufac. | Servicios |
|---|---|---|---|---|
| **Hombres** | | | | |
| 1980 (1) | 18.12 | 44.69 | 20.25 | 37.19 |
| 1985 (1) | 17.07 | 46.55 | 19.79 | 36.38 |
| 1991 (2) | 15.42 | 41.58 | 17.41 | 43.00 |
| **Women** | | | | |
| 1985 (1) | 12.49 | 17.16 | 14.94 | 70.35 |
| 1991 (2) | 9.99 | 14.44 | 12.31 | 75.57 |

Fuente(s): (1) ASTER; (2) AST93.

### 3.2 Método(s): promedio ponderado

#### 3.2.1 Hombres:

- 1950-70, tasas de distribución 1950-70 con base en EPPA3;
- 1980-90, promedios ponderados de las tasas de distribución con base en los censos de 1980, 1985 y 1991.

#### 3.2.2 Mujeres:

- 1950-80, tasas de distribución 1950-80 con base en EPPA3;
ajuste de las tasas para tener en cuenta a los auxiliares familiares en la agricultura
- 1990, promedios ponderados de las tasas de distribución con base en los censos de 1985 y 1991.

## 4. Proyección de las tasas de actividad: 2000 - 2010

### 4.1 Modelo(s): linear, log-linear, hiperbólico y logístico

#### 4.1.1 Hombres:

- Para el grupo de edad [15-19], aplicación de la función F2;
- Para los grupos de edad [20+], aplicación de la función F3.

#### 4.1.2 Mujeres:

- Para los grupos de edad [15-19] y [60+], aplicación de la función F3;
- Para los grupos de edad [20-24], aplicación de la función F1;
- Para los grupos de edad [25-59], aplicación de la función F6;
- Modificación de las tendencias de los grupos de edad [15-19], [25-29] y [60-64].

---

*Notas sobre los ajustes de las tasas, véase p.380-384.*    *Notas sobre las funciones de proyección, véase p. 386.*

# Sudán

## 1. Fuente(s) de los datos básicos

Código(s):    Título(s):

EPPA3       Estimaciones y proyecciones de la población económicamente activa, 1950-2025, tercera edición, OIT, Ginebra, 1986.
R1983        Population and Housing Census ofthe Sudan 1989, Ministry ofFinance and Economic Planning, Department of Statistics, Khartoum, 1989.
ASTER       Anuario de estadísticas del trabajo 1945-89 - Edición retrospectiva sobre los censos de población, OIT, Ginebra, 1990.

## 2. Evaluación de las tasas de actividad: 1950 - 1990

### 2.1 Datos básicos:

Cuadro 1: Tasas de actividad por sexo y grupo de edad

| Grupo de edad | Año 1950 (1) | 1960 (1) | 1970 (1) | 1973 (2) | 1983 (3) |
|---|---|---|---|---|---|
| **Hombres** | | | | | |
| 10-14 | 46.15 | 42.90 | 42.84 | .. | 39.01 |
| 15-19 | 74.95 | 70.60 | 64.40 | .. | 58.92 |
| 20-24 | 95.55 | 93.60 | 90.85 | .. | 81.27 |
| 25-29 | 97.90 | 97.60 | 97.20 | .. | 92.90 |
| 30-34 | 99.05 | 98.75 | 98.25 | .. | 95.58 |
| 35-39 | 99.50 | 99.15 | 98.65 | .. | 96.90 |
| 40-44 | 99.50 | 99.15 | 98.60 | .. | 96.74 |
| 45-49 | 99.30 | 99.00 | 98.55 | .. | 97.33 |
| 50-54 | 98.40 | 97.95 | 97.25 | .. | 95.63 |
| 55-59 | 98.05 | 97.30 | 96.20 | .. | 95.00 |
| 60-64 | 95.85 | 94.55 | 92.75 | .. | 91.47 |
| 65+ | 78.25 | 76.15 | 78.55 | .. | 78.55 |
| **Mujeres** | | | | | |
| 10-14 | 12.15 | 11.30 | 10.05 | ... | 25.29 |
| 15-19 | 19.75 | 18.50 | 16.65 | 16.08 | 28.62 |
| 20-24 | 20.95 | 20.10 | 18.85 | 18.47 | 29.58 |
| 25-29 | 23.25 | 22.20 | 20.75 | 20.32 | 30.49 |
| 30-34 | 24.50 | 23.40 | 21.85 | 21.41 | 31.13 |
| 35-39 | 27.25 | 26.15 | 24.55 | 24.08 | 32.09 |
| 40-44 | 30.40 | 29.20 | 27.50 | 26.98 | 33.44 |
| 45-49 | 31.80 | 30.50 | 28.70 | 28.14 | 35.20 |
| 50-54 | 33.40 | 31.80 | 29.55 | 28.85 | 36.72 |
| 55-59 | 32.15 | 30.50 | 28.15 | 27.45 | 33.22 |
| 60-64 | 33.70 | 31.30 | 27.90 | 26.40 | 33.80 |
| 65+ | 27.60 | 25.00 | 21.35 | ... | 25.44 |

Fuente(s): (1) EPPA3; (2) ASTER; (3) R1983.

### 2.2 Método(s): interpolación y extrapolación lineares
promedio ponderado

#### 2.2.1 Hombres:

- 1950-90, interpolación y extrapolación de las tasas de actividad 1950-70
con base en EPPA3 y de las tasas de actividad ajustadas con base
el censo de 1983;
modificación de las tendencias de los grupos de edad [45-49] y [65+]
para 1950-90.

#### 2.2.2 Mujeres:

- 1950-70, tasas de actividad ajustadas 1950-70 con base en EPPA3;
el ajuste se ha calculado con base en el modelo de ajuste de las tasas de
actividad de las mujeres ocupadas en la agricultura como auxiliares familiares;
- 1980, promedios ponderados de las tasas de actividad ajustadas con base
en el censo en de 1973 y de las tasas de actividad con base en el censo de 1983;
ajuste de las tasas de actividad con base en la razón hombres/mujeres
en la agricultura con base en el censo de 1983;

## 3. Evaluación de las tasas de distribución por sector de actividad: 1950 - 1990

### 3.1 Datos básicos:

Cuadro 2: Distribución de la población económicamente activa por sector de actividad en %

| Año | Agricultura | Industria Total | Manufac. | Servicios |
|---|---|---|---|---|
| **Hombres** | | | | |
| 1973 (1) | 65.49 | 8.78 | 4.50 | 25.73 |
| 1983 (2) | 66.47 | 9.68 | 5.17 | 23.85 |
| **Mujeres** | | | | |
| 1973 (1) | 88.81 | 3.38 | 3.25 | 7.81 |
| 1983 (2) | 87.11 | 4.51 | 3.85 | 8.38 |

Fuente(s): (1) ASTER; (2) R1983.

### 3.2 Método(s): promedio ponderado

#### 3.2.1 Hombres:

- 1950-70, tasas de distribución 1950-70 con base en EPPA3;
- 1980, promedios ponderados de las tasas de distribución con base en
los censos de 1973 y 1983;
- 1990, mismas variaciones en porcentajes como en la distribución de las tasas
en Egipto para 1980 y 1990.
en Egipto para 1980 y 1990.

#### 3.2.2 Mujeres:

- 1950-70, tasas de distribución 1950-70 con base en EPPA3;
- 1980, promedios ponderados de las tasas de distribución con base en
los censos de 1973 y 1983;
- 1990, mismas variaciones en porcentajes como en la distribución de las tasas
en Egipto para 1980 y 1990;
ajuste de las tasas estimadas 1950-90 habida cuenta de la subenumeración
censal de las mujeres ocupadas en la agricultura.

## 4. Proyección de las tasas de actividad: 2000 - 2010

### 4.1 Modelo(s): linear, hiperbólico y logístico

#### 4.1.1 Hombres:

- Para el grupo de edad [10-14], aplicación de la función F1;
- Para los grupos de edad [15+], aplicación de la función F3;
- Modificación de las tendencias de los grupos de edad [10-14], [20-24],
[50-54] y [65+].

#### 4.1.2 Mujeres:

- Para los grupos de edad [10-19], aplicación de la función F1;
- Para los grupos de edad [20+], aplicación de la función F6;
- Modificación de las tendencias de todos los grupos de edad.

*Notas sobre los ajustes de las tasas, véase p.380-384.*          *Notas sobre las funciones de proyección, véase p. 386.*

# Suecia

## 1. Fuente(s) de los datos básicos

Código(s):    Título(s):

EPPA3       Anuario de estadísticas del trabajo 1945-89 - Edición retrospectiva sobre los censos de población, OIT, Ginebra, 1990.
STAT        Base de datos de la OIT sobre estadísticas del trabajo - LABORSTA, Oficina de Estadística, OIT, Ginebra.

## 2. Evaluación de las tasas de actividad: 1950 - 1990

### 2.1 Datos básicos:

Cuadro 1: Tasas de actividad por sexo y grupo de edad

| Grupo de edad | Année 1970 (1) | 1980 (1) | 1989 (2) | 1990 (2) | 1991 (2) |
|---|---|---|---|---|---|
| **Hombres** | | | | | |
| 10-14 | .. | .. | 0.00 | 0.00 | 0.00 |
| 15-19 | .. | .. | 48.05 | 47.64 | 42.24 |
| 20-24 | .. | .. | 84.86 | 84.57 | 82.89 |
| 25-29 | .. | .. | 92.62 | 92.60 | 91.61 |
| 30-34 | .. | .. | 95.25 | 95.61 | 94.92 |
| 35-39 | .. | .. | 96.05 | 95.33 | 94.98 |
| 40-44 | .. | .. | 96.78 | 96.74 | 96.34 |
| 45-49 | .. | .. | 95.82 | 96.39 | 96.00 |
| 50-54 | .. | .. | 92.92 | 93.59 | 93.72 |
| 55-59 | .. | .. | 86.96 | 87.86 | 86.41 |
| 60-64 | .. | .. | 62.86 | 63.11 | 64.22 |
| 65+ | .. | .. | 8.07 | 7.32 | 8.75 |
| **Mujeres** | | | | | |
| 10-14 | 0.35 | 0.00 | 0.00 | 0.00 | 0.00 |
| 15-19 | | | 51.36 | 50.45 | 47.06 |
| 20-24 | 64.05 | 71.30 | 82.00 | 80.68 | 77.32 |
| 25-29 | 55.45 | 73.60 | 87.94 | 87.07 | 86.14 |
| 30-34 | 52.35 | 74.60 | 90.75 | 91.10 | 88.97 |
| 35-39 | 52.85 | 78.60 | 92.10 | 93.03 | 91.96 |
| 40-44 | 53.90 | 82.60 | 93.31 | 93.85 | 93.38 |
| 45-49 | 53.40 | 82.90 | 92.67 | 93.10 | 92.88 |
| 50-54 | 51.15 | 77.80 | 88.34 | 89.08 | 89.27 |
| 55-59 | 44.95 | 66.40 | 78.50 | 79.25 | 80.00 |
| 60-64 | 29.25 | 41.40 | 50.67 | 53.85 | 54.79 |
| 65+ | 3.20 | 2.60 | 3.00 | 2.62 | 2.60 |

Fuente(s): (1) EPPA3; (2) STAT.

### 2.2 Método(s):  promedio aritmético

#### 2.2.1 Hombres:

- 1950-80, tasas de actividad 1950-80 con base en EPPA3;
ajuste de las tasas de actividad del grupo de edad [20-24] para 1950 y 1960
y del grupo de edad [15-19] para 1980;
- 1990, promedios de las tasas de actividad con base en las encuestas
de 1989, 1990 and 1991;
modificación de la tendencia del grupo de edad [15-19].

#### 2.2.2 Mujeres:

- 1950-80, tasas de actividad 1950-80 con base en EPPA3;
ajuste de las tasas de actividad del grupo de edad [15-19] para 1970 y 1980;
- 1990, promedios de las tasas de actividad con base en las encuestas
de 1989, 1990 y 1991.

## 3. Evaluación de las tasas de distribución por sector de actividad: 1950 - 1990

### 3.1 Datos básicos:

Cuadro 2: Distribución de la población económicamente activa por sector de actividad en %

| Año | Agricultura | Industria Total | Manufac. | Servicios |
|---|---|---|---|---|
| **Hombres** | | | | |
| 1979 | 8.26 | 49.28 | 34.70 | 42.46 |
| 1980 | 7.89 | 47.72 | 32.54 | 44.39 |
| 1981 | 8.11 | 46.12 | 32.64 | 45.77 |
| 1989 | 7.02 | 42.85 | 32.42 | 50.13 |
| 1990 | 5.64 | 44.30 | 30.96 | 50.07 |
| 1991 | 5.45 | 43.97 | 30.98 | 50.58 |
| **Mujeres** | | | | |
| 1979 | 3.94 | 19.01 | 16.73 | 77.05 |
| 1980 | 3.65 | 16.98 | 15.15 | 79.37 |
| 1981 | 3.52 | 16.51 | 15.20 | 79.96 |
| 1989 | 2.98 | 14.16 | 12.96 | 82.86 |
| 1990 | 2.61 | 14.63 | 13.20 | 82.76 |
| 1991 | 2.31 | 14.38 | 13.37 | 83.32 |

Fuente(s): STAT.

### 3.2 Método(s):  promedio aritmético

#### 3.2.1 Hombres:

- 1950-70, tasas de distribución 1950-70 con base en EPPA3;
- 1980, promedios de las tasas de distribución con base en las encuestas
de 1979, 1980 y 1981;
- 1990, promedios de las tasas de distribución con base en las encuestas
de 1989, 1990 y 1991.
de 1989, 1990 y 1991.

#### 3.2.2 Mujeres:

Métodos, hipótesis y tratamientos idénticos a los que se aplican a los hombres.

## 4. Proyección de las tasas de actividad: 2000 - 2010

### 4.1 Modelo(s):  linear, hiperbólico y logístico

#### 4.1.1 Hombres:

- Para los grupos de edad [15-19] y [55+], aplicación de la función F3;
- Para los grupos de edad [20-54], aplicación de la función F1;
- Modificación de las tendencias de los grupos de edad [15-39].

#### 4.1.2 Mujeres:

- Para los grupos de edad [15-19] y [65+], aplicación de la función F3;
- Para los grupos de edad [20-64], aplicación de la función F6;
- Modificación de las tendencias de todos los grupos de edad.

*Notas sobre los ajustes de las tasas, véase p.380-384.*        *Notas sobre las funciones de proyección, véase p. 386.*

# Suiza

## 1. Fuente(s) de los datos básicos

Código(s):  Título(s):

EPPA3  Anuario de estadísticas del trabajo 1945-89 - Edición retrospectiva sobre los censos de población, OIT, Ginebra, 1990.
STAT  Base de datos de la OIT sobre estadísticas del trabajo - LABORSTA, Oficina de Estadística, OIT, Ginebra.

## 2. Evaluación de las tasas de actividad: 1950 - 1990

### 2.1 Datos básicos:

Cuadro 1: Tasas de actividad por sexo y grupo de edad

| Grupo de edad | Año | | | | |
|---|---|---|---|---|---|
| | 1950 (1) | 1960 (1) | 1970 (1) | 1980 (1) | 1990 (2) |
| **Hombres** | | | | | |
| 10-14 | 1.10 | 0.35 | 0.20 | 0.00 | 0.00 |
| 15-19 | 74.10 | 69.10 | 63.40 | 57.05 | 55.98 |
| 20-24 | 91.00 | 90.50 | 88.55 | 85.20 | 83.80 |
| 25-29 | 96.15 | 96.85 | 96.40 | 94.90 | 93.87 |
| 30-34 | 98.40 | 98.75 | 98.75 | 98.35 | 97.84 |
| 35-39 | 98.70 | 99.00 | 99.10 | 98.95 | 98.56 |
| 40-44 | 98.55 | 98.80 | 98.90 | 98.80 | 98.68 |
| 45-49 | 98.15 | 98.50 | 98.55 | 98.25 | 98.35 |
| 50-54 | 97.15 | 97.55 | 97.45 | 96.85 | 97.44 |
| 55-59 | 94.95 | 95.65 | 95.15 | 93.60 | 94.84 |
| 60-64 | 87.75 | 88.90 | 87.30 | 82.95 | 79.78 |
| 65+ | 50.70 | 43.05 | 31.50 | 16.05 | 9.18 |
| **Mujeres** | | | | | |
| 10-14 | 0.65 | 0.35 | 0.20 | 0.00 | 0.00 |
| 15-19 | 64.10 | 63.10 | 58.95 | 51.65 | 49.21 |
| 20-24 | 67.85 | 69.10 | 71.80 | 75.95 | 80.38 |
| 25-29 | 40.45 | 43.70 | 49.75 | 58.70 | 71.39 |
| 30-34 | 27.70 | 33.50 | 40.80 | 49.55 | 60.88 |
| 35-39 | 26.20 | 32.25 | 40.50 | 51.00 | 62.92 |
| 40-44 | 26.85 | 32.40 | 41.20 | 53.20 | 66.79 |
| 45-49 | 27.30 | 33.50 | 41.60 | 61.76 | 66.50 |
| 50-54 | 27.35 | 33.40 | 40.15 | 47.55 | 60.57 |
| 55-59 | 26.15 | 32.00 | 37.20 | 41.75 | 49.88 |
| 60-64 | 22.90 | 27.20 | 27.95 | 25.20 | 24.91 |
| 65+ | 11.65 | 11.50 | 9.35 | 5.15 | 3.22 |

Fuente(s): (1) EPPA3; (2) STAT.

### 2.2 Método(s): promedio ponderado

#### 2.2.1 Hombres:

- 1950-80, tasas de actividad 1950-80 con base en EPPA3;
- 1990, promedios ponderados de las tasas de actividad 1980 con base en EPPA3 y de las tasas de actividad con base en el censo de 1990.

#### 2.2.2 Mujeres:

Métodos, hipótesis y tratamientos idénticos a los que se aplican a los hombres.

## 3. Evaluación de las tasas de distribución por sector de actividad: 1950 - 1990

### 3.1 Datos básicos:

Cuadro 2: Distribución de la población económicamente activa por sector de actividad en %

| Año | Agricultura | Industria | | Servicios |
|---|---|---|---|---|
| | | Total | Manufac. | |
| **Men** | | | | |
| 1990 | 6.31 | 43.94 | 32.34 | 49.75 |
| **Women** | | | | |
| 1990 | 4.29 | 20.31 | 19.38 | 75.40 |

Fuente(s): (1) STAT.

### 3.2 Método(s): datos del país

#### 3.2.1 Hombres:

- 1950-80, tasas de distribución 1950-80 con base en EPPA3;
- 1990, tasas de distribución con base en estimaciones oficiales de 1990.

#### 3.2.2 Mujeres:

Métodos, hipótesis y tratamientos idénticos a los que se aplican a los hombres.

## 4. Proyección de las tasas de actividad: 2000 - 2010

### 4.1 Modelo(s): linear, hiperbólico y logístico

#### 4.1.1 Hombres:

- Para los grupos de edad [15-54], aplicación de la función F1;
- Para los grupos de edad [55+], aplicación de la función F3;
- Modificación de las tendencias de los grupos de edad [15-19] y [40-49].

#### 4.1.2 Mujeres:

- Para los grupos de edad [15-59], aplicación de la función F6;
- Para los grupos de edad [60+], aplicación de la función F3;
- Modificación de las tendencias de los grupos de edad [15-24] y [60-64].

*Notas sobre los ajustes de las tasas, véase p.380-384.*    *Notas sobre las funciones de proyección, véase p. 386.*

# Suriname

## 1. Fuente(s) de los datos básicos

Código(s):   Título(s):

EPPA3   Estimaciones y proyecciones de la población económicamente activa, 1950-2025, tercera edición, OIT, Ginebra, 1986.
ASTER   Anuario de estadísticas del trabajo 1945-89 - Edición retrospectiva sobre los censos de población, OIT, Ginebra, 1990.

## 2. Evaluación de las tasas de actividad: 1950 - 1990

### 2.1 Datos básicos:

Cuadro 1: Tasas de actividad por sexo y grupo de edad

| Grupo de edad | Año 1950 (1) | 1960 (1) | 1964 (2) | 1970 (1) | 1980 (1) | 1980 (2) |
|---|---|---|---|---|---|---|
| **Hombres** | | | | | | |
| 10-14 | 1.80 | 1.00 | .. | 0.70 | 0.50 | .. |
| 15-19 | 66.95 | 48.00 | .. | 43.00 | 35.00 | .. |
| 20-24 | 93.55 | 90.80 | .. | 87.00 | 80.00 | .. |
| 25-29 | 98.25 | 97.05 | .. | 96.90 | 93.50 | .. |
| 30-34 | 98.95 | 97.75 | .. | 97.60 | 97.00 | .. |
| 35-39 | 99.50 | 98.35 | .. | 98.20 | 97.50 | .. |
| 40-44 | 98.30 | 96.85 | .. | 97.00 | 95.00 | .. |
| 45-49 | 96.90 | 96.30 | .. | 95.75 | 93.00 | .. |
| 50-54 | 95.50 | 93.45 | .. | 92.90 | 90.00 | .. |
| 55-59 | 90.65 | 89.00 | .. | 85.00 | 81.00 | .. |
| 60-64 | 80.00 | 75.00 | .. | 72.00 | 65.00 | .. |
| 65+ | 65.60 | 51.90 | .. | 40.60 | 22.00 | .. |
| **Mujeres** | | | | | | |
| 10-14 | .. | .. | 0.80 | .. | .. | 0.20 |
| 15-19 | .. | .. | 11.20 | .. | .. | 3.80 |
| 20-24 | .. | .. | 23.90 | .. | .. | 25.30 |
| 25-29 | .. | .. | 20.90 | .. | .. | 32.10 |
| 30-34 | .. | .. | 20.60 | .. | .. | 30.60 |
| 35-39 | .. | .. | 21.40 | .. | .. | 31.80 |
| 40-44 | .. | .. | 22.30 | .. | .. | 29.80 |
| 45-49 | .. | .. | 23.40 | .. | .. | 28.60 |
| 50-54 | .. | .. | 23.20 | .. | .. | 24.50 |
| 55-59 | .. | .. | 16.90 | .. | .. | 20.80 |
| 60-64 | .. | .. | 14.20 | .. | .. | 12.70 |
| 65+ | .. | .. | 8.64 | .. | .. | 4.00 |

Fuente(s): (1) EPPA3; (2) ASTER.

### 2.2 Método(s): interpolación y extrapolación lineares

**2.2.1 Hombres:**

- 1950-80, tasas de actividad 1950-80 con base en EPPA3;
- 1990, extrapolación de las tasas de actividad 1950-80 con base en EPPA3;
ajuste de las tasas extrapoladas con base en las variaciones de las tasas
interpoladas 1980, en relación con las tasas 1980 con base en EPPA3;
modificación de las tendencias de todos los grupos de edad.

**2.2.2 Mujeres:**

- 1950-90, interpolación y extrapolación de las tasas de actividad con base en
el censo de 1977 y de las tasas de actividad ajustadas con base en
el censo de 1985;
ajuste de las tasas de actividad 1970 con base en la razón hombres/mujeres
en la agricultura con base en el censo de 1964;
modificación de las tendencias de todos los grupos de edad para 1950,
1960 y 1990.

## 3. Evaluación de las tasas de distribución por sector de actividad: 1950 - 1990

### 3.1 Datos básicos:

Cuadro 2: Distribución de la población económicamente activa por sector de actividad en %

| Año | Agricultura | Industria Total | Manufac. | Servicios |
|---|---|---|---|---|
| **Hombres** | | | | |
| 1964 | 28.64 | 26.91 | 11.41 | 44.44 |
| 1980 | 24.83 | 24.94 | 9.42 | 50.22 |
| **Mujeres** | | | | |
| 1989 | 27.36 | 7.95 | 6.14 | 64.69 |
| 1990 | 17.50 | 5.39 | 3.62 | 77.12 |

Fuente(s): ASTER.

### 3.2 Método(s): interpolación y extrapolación lineares

**3.2.1 Hombres:**

- 1950-90, interpolación y extrapolación de las tasas de distribución
con base en el censo de 1964 y las tasas de distribución ajustadas
con base en el censo de 1980.

**3.2.2 Mujeres:**

Métodos, hipótesis y tratamientos idénticos a los que se aplican a los hombres.

## 4. Proyección de las tasas de actividad: 2000 - 2010

### 4.1 Modelo(s): log-linear, hiperbólico y logístico

**4.1.1 Hombres:**

- Para los grupos de edad [15+], aplicación de la función F3;
- Modificación de las tendencias de los grupos de edad [15-49].

**4.1.2 Mujeres:**

- Para los grupos de edad [15-19] y [60+], aplicación de la función F3;
- Para el grupo de edad [20-24], aplicación de la función F2;
- Para los grupos de edad [25-59], aplicación de la función F6;
- Modificación de las tendencias de los grupos de edad [20-24] y [40-59].

*Notas sobre los ajustes de las tasas, véase p.380-384.*   *Notas sobre las funciones de proyección, véase p. 386.*

# Swazilandia

## 1. Fuente(s) de los datos básicos

Código(s):    Título(s):

EPPA3    Estimaciones y proyecciones de la población económicamente activa, 1950-2025, tercera edición, OIT, Ginebra, 1986.
R1966    Report on the 1966 Swaziland Population Census, Swaziland Government, Mbabane, 1968.
ADNU72    Annuaire démographique 1972 - Statistiques des recensements de population III, vingt-quatrième édition, Nations Unies, New York, 1973.
R1986    Report on the 1986 Swaziland Population Census, 3 Vol., Central Statistical Office, Mbabane, 1986.

## 2. Evaluación de las tasas de actividad: 1950 - 1990

### 2.1 Datos básicos:

Cuadro 1: Tasas de actividad por sexo y grupo de edad

| Grupo de edad | Año 1950 (1) | 1960 (1) | 1966 (2) | 1970 (1) | 1980 (1) | 1986 (3) |
|---|---|---|---|---|---|---|
| **Hombres** | | | | | | |
| 10-14 | .. | .. | 26.48 | .. | .. | 20.02 |
| 15-19 | .. | .. | 66.14 | .. | .. | 50.00 |
| 20-24 | .. | .. | 92.53 | .. | .. | 89.18 |
| 25-29 | .. | .. | 98.20 | .. | .. | 97.56 |
| 30-34 | .. | .. | 98.57 | .. | .. | 98.20 |
| 35-39 | .. | .. | 98.62 | .. | .. | 98.25 |
| 40-44 | .. | .. | 97.76 | .. | .. | 97.43 |
| 45-49 | .. | .. | 97.46 | .. | .. | 96.49 |
| 50-54 | .. | .. | 96.04 | .. | .. | 92.55 |
| 55-59 | .. | .. | 94.95 | .. | .. | 85.07 |
| 60-64 | .. | .. | 93.04 | .. | .. | 77.09 |
| 65+ | .. | .. | 83.91 | .. | .. | 40.94 |
| **Mujeres** | | | | | | |
| 10-14 | 39.40 | 37.55 | 3.97 | 33.60 | 30.10 | 12.12 |
| 15-19 | 64.05 | 61.30 | 45.63 | 55.45 | 50.15 | 33.08 |
| 20-24 | 64.20 | 62.60 | 51.68 | 59.15 | 55.95 | 49.51 |
| 25-29 | 60.15 | 67.35 | 40.38 | 63.45 | 59.70 | 50.47 |
| 30-34 | 73.50 | 71.55 | 49.66 | 67.40 | 63.40 | 48.35 |
| 35-39 | 74.70 | 72.95 | 49.63 | 69.10 | 65.40 | 44.95 |
| 40-44 | 77.15 | 75.40 | 52.82 | 71.55 | 67.90 | 42.51 |
| 45-49 | 76.70 | 74.90 | 53.05 | 70.95 | 67.20 | 38.25 |
| 50-54 | 75.30 | 73.15 | 53.66 | 68.45 | 64.10 | 34.28 |
| 55-59 | 72.55 | 70.25 | 55.35 | 65.30 | 60.70 | 30.28 |
| 60-64 | 66.60 | 63.45 | 54.28 | 56.70 | 50.75 | 18.90 |
| 65+ | 46.65 | 43.25 | 45.86 | 36.45 | 30.70 | 9.80 |

Fuente(s): (1) EPPA3; (2) R1966 y ADNU72; (3) R1986.

### 2.2 Método(s): interpolación y extrapolación lineares

**2.2.1 Hombres:**

- 1950-90, interpolación y extrapolación de las tasas de actividad ajustadas con base en los censos de 1966 y 1986;
modificación de las tendencias de los grupos de edad [10-14] y [45+] para 1950 y 1960;
modificación de las tendencias de los grupos de edad [55+] para 1990.

**2.2.2 Mujeres:**

- 1950-90, interpolación y extrapolación de las tasas de actividad 1950-80 con base en EPPA3 y de las tasas de actividad ajustadas con base en el censo de 1986;
ajuste de las tasas interpoladas y extrapoladas con base en las variaciones de las tasas interpoladas 1986, en relación con las tasas de actividad ajustadas con base en el censo de 1986.

## 3. Evaluación de las tasas de distribución por sector de actividad: 1950 - 1990

### 3.1 Datos básicos:

Cuadro 2: Distribución de la población económicamente activa por sector de actividad en %

| Año | Agricultura | Industria Total | Manufac. | Servicios |
|---|---|---|---|---|
| **Hombres** | | | | |
| 1966 (1) | 66.49 | 13.60 | 6.09 | 19.91 |
| 1986 (2) | 33.49 | 29.71 | 12.61 | 36.80 |
| **Mujeres** | | | | |
| 1966 (1) | 80.53 | 3.68 | 3.57 | 15.79 |
| 1986 (2) | 55.34 | 7.59 | 6.94 | 37.07 |

Fuente(s): (1) R1966; (2) R1986.

### 3.2 Método(s): interpolación y extrapolación lineares

**3.2.1 Hombres:**
- 1950-90, interpolación y extrapolación de las tasas de distribución ajustadas con base en los censos de 1966 y 1986;
modificación de las tendencias de todos los sectores para 1950, 1960 y 1990.

**3.2.2 Mujeres:**
Métodos, hipótesis y tratamientos idénticos a los que se aplican a los hombres.

## 4. Proyección de las tasas de actividad: 2000 - 2010

### 4.1 Modelo(s): linear y hiperbólico

**4.1.1 Hombres:**
- Para el grupo de edad [10-14], aplicación de la función F1;
- Para los grupos de edad [15+], aplicación de la función F3;
- Modificación de las tendencias de los grupos de edad [15-19], [45-49] y [65+].

**4.1.2 Mujeres:**
- Para todos los grupos de edad, aplicación de la función F3;
- Modificación de las tendencias de los grupos de edad [10-14] y [20-59].

---

*Notas sobre los ajustes de las tasas, véase p.380-384.*    *Notas sobre las funciones de proyección, véase p. 386.*

# Tailandia

## 1. Fuente(s) de los datos básicos

Código(s):   Título(s):
EPPA3      Estimaciones y proyecciones de la población económicamente activa, 1950-2025, tercera edición, OIT, Ginebra, 1986.
STAT       Base de datos de la OIT sobre estadísticas del trabajo - LABORSTA, Oficina de Estadística, OIT, Ginebra.

## 2. Evaluación de las tasas de actividad: 1950 - 1990

### 2.1 Datos básicos:

Cuadro 1: Tasas de actividad por sexo y grupo de edad

| Grupo de edad | Año 1979 | 1980 | 1989 | 1990 |
|---|---|---|---|---|
| **Hombres** | | | | |
| 10-19 | 70.60 | 70.90 | 71.20 | 67.70 |
| 20-24 | 88.80 | 87.80 | 92.80 | 91.60 |
| 25-29 | 97.50 | 97.20 | 97.30 | 96.60 |
| 30-39 | 98.70 | 98.80 | 98.00 | 98.00 |
| 40-49 | 98.40 | 98.50 | 98.10 | 97.90 |
| 50-59 | 94.70 | 95.50 | 94.40 | 94.80 |
| 60+ | 59.20 | 56.70 | 49.50 | 53.00 |
| **Mujeres** | | | | |
| 10-19 | 69.90 | 71.00 | 72.20 | 69.40 |
| 20-24 | 81.20 | 80.30 | 83.00 | 81.70 |
| 25-29 | 83.50 | 84.70 | 84.70 | 83.60 |
| 30-39 | 86.00 | 86.80 | 87.00 | 86.60 |
| 40-49 | 85.30 | 87.80 | 86.10 | 86.30 |
| 50-59 | 74.80 | 77.70 | 76.40 | 76.50 |
| 60+ | 29.10 | 31.40 | 28.50 | 32.20 |

Fuente(s): STAT.

### 2.2 Método(s): interpolación linear

**2.2.1 Hombres:**
- 1950-90, interpolación de las tasas de actividad 1950-80 con base en EPPA3, de los promedios de las tasas de actividad ajustadas con base en las encuestas de 1979 y 1980 y de los promedios de las tasas de actividad ajustadas con base en las encuestas de 1989 y 1990.

**2.2.2 Mujeres:**
Métodos, hipótesis y tratamientos idénticos a los que se aplican a los hombres.

## 3. Evaluación de las tasas de distribución por sector de actividad: 1950 - 1990

### 3.1 Datos básicos:

Cuadro 2: Distribución de la población económicamente activa por sector de actividad en %

| Año | Agricultura | Industria Total | Manufac. | Servicios |
|---|---|---|---|---|
| **Hombres** | | | | |
| 1980 (1) | 67.95 | 12.50 | .. | 19.55 |
| 1990 (2) | 63.13 | 15.55 | 9.54 | 21.32 |
| **Mujeres** | | | | |
| 1980 (1) | 74.20 | 7.75 | .. | 18.05 |
| 1990 (2) | 65.00 | 12.27 | 10.88 | 22.73 |

Fuente(s): (1) EPPA3; (2) STAT.

### 3.2 Método(s): interpolación linear

**3.2.1 Hombres:**
- 1950-80, tasas de distribución 1950-80 con base en EPPA3;
- 1990, interpolación de las tasas de distribución 1980 con base en EPPA3, et de las tasas de distribución con base en la encuesta de 1990; modificación de las tendencias de todos los sectores;
- Aplicación de la razón manufacturas/industria con base en la encuesta de 1990
- Aplicación de la razón manufacturas/industria con base en la encuesta de 1990

**3.2.2 Mujeres:**
Métodos, hipótesis y tratamientos idénticos a los que se aplican a los hombres.

## 4. Proyección de las tasas de actividad: 2000 - 2010

### 4.1 Modelo(s): linear, log-linear, hiperbólico y logístico

**4.1.1 Hombres:**
- Para el grupo de edad [10-14], aplicación de la función F1;
- Para el grupo de edad [15-19], aplicación de la función F2;
- Para los grupos de edad [20+], aplicación de la función F3;
- Modificación de las tendencias de los grupos de edad [10-49].

**4.1.2 Mujeres:**
- Para los grupos de edad [10-19], aplicación de la función F1;
- Para los grupos de edad [20-64], aplicación de la función F6;
- Para el grupo de edad [65+], aplicación de la función F3;
- Modificación de las tendencias de los grupos de edad [10-59].

*Notas sobre los ajustes de las tasas, véase p.380-384.*          *Notas sobre las funciones de proyección, véase p. 386.*

# Tajikistán

## 1. Fuente(s) de los datos básicos

Código(s):   Título(s):
BLT-94-2    Vorobiev A. (1994), "Estimaciones de la población económicamente activa de los quince países de la ex URSS, en 1950, 1959, 1970, 1979 y 1989", en el Boletín de Estadísticas del Trabajol - 1994-2, OIT, Ginebra.

## 2. Evaluación de las tasas de actividad: 1950 - 1990

### 2.1 Datos básicos:

Cuadro 1: Tasas de actividad por sexo y grupo de edad

| Grupo de edad | 1950 | 1959 | 1970 | 1979 | 1989 |
|---|---|---|---|---|---|
| **Hombres** | | | | | |
| 10-14 | 0.00 | 0.00 | 0.00 | 0.00 | 0.00 |
| 15-19 | 54.44 | 57.14 | 35.11 | 37.28 | 28.90 |
| 20-24 | 83.33 | 86.75 | 83.12 | 85.19 | 79.39 |
| 25-29 | 91.49 | 93.98 | 92.11 | 97.58 | 95.91 |
| 30-34 | 94.29 | 97.44 | 97.66 | 98.70 | 98.77 |
| 35-39 | 92.11 | 97.67 | 98.78 | 98.85 | 98.31 |
| 40-44 | 91.43 | 96.88 | 98.72 | 98.91 | 97.22 |
| 45-49 | 90.32 | 91.43 | 95.24 | 98.70 | 97.50 |
| 50-54 | 89.66 | 93.75 | 92.86 | 95.45 | 93.90 |
| 55-59 | 90.00 | 89.66 | 87.10 | 88.24 | 88.24 |
| 60-64 | 76.47 | 80.00 | 66.67 | 36.00 | 37.50 |
| 65+ | 37.04 | 37.21 | 7.69 | 9.21 | 12.16 |
| **Mujeres** | | | | | |
| 10-14 | 0.00 | 0.00 | 0.00 | 0.00 | 0.00 |
| 15-19 | 43.43 | 59.15 | 41.35 | 45.18 | 31.30 |
| 20-24 | 69.05 | 71.43 | 73.86 | 84.21 | 63.14 |
| 25-29 | 70.00 | 73.63 | 76.06 | 86.61 | 66.67 |
| 30-34 | 68.09 | 70.51 | 75.79 | 87.67 | 70.73 |
| 35-39 | 62.79 | 66.07 | 77.38 | 88.46 | 76.86 |
| 40-44 | 58.54 | 63.64 | 76.00 | 88.89 | 77.94 |
| 45-49 | 52.27 | 56.41 | 74.07 | 87.34 | 76.39 |
| 50-54 | 41.18 | 42.11 | 65.00 | 72.86 | 54.22 |
| 55-59 | 23.08 | 26.83 | 26.09 | 27.78 | 22.97 |
| 60-64 | 13.64 | 11.76 | 10.00 | 10.00 | 12.50 |
| 65+ | 5.26 | 5.56 | 2.44 | 2.94 | 5.08 |

Fuente(s): BLT-94-2-2

### 2.2 Método(s): promedio ponderado

#### 2.2.1 Hombres:
- 1950-90, promedios ponderados de las tasas de actividad 1950, 1959, 1973 y 1989 con base en el Boletín de estadísticas del trabajo 1994-2.

#### 2.2.2 Mujeres:
Métodos, hipótesis y tratamientos idénticos a los que se aplican a los hombres.

## 3. Evaluación de las tasas de distribución por sector de actividad: 1950 - 1990

### 3.1 Datos básicos:

Cuadro 2: Distribución de la población económicamente activa por sector de actividad en %

| Año | Agricultura | Industria Total | Manufac. | Servicios |
|---|---|---|---|---|
| **Hombres** | | | | |
| 1950 | 73.95 | 8.96 | 6.16 | 17.09 |
| 1959 | 57.11 | 17.83 | 7.22 | 25.05 |
| 1970 | 41.30 | 25.91 | 12.86 | 32.79 |
| 1979 | 35.98 | 28.94 | 13.06 | 35.08 |
| 1989 | 37.01 | 27.97 | 10.66 | 35.01 |
| **Mujeres** | | | | |
| 1950 | 77.01 | 8.03 | 6.93 | 14.96 |
| 1959 | 68.73 | 11.83 | 8.73 | 19.44 |
| 1970 | 52.65 | 16.81 | 11.28 | 30.53 |
| 1979 | 55.27 | 16.03 | 9.56 | 28.69 |
| 1989 | 46.74 | 17.19 | 12.24 | 36.07 |

Fuente(s): BLT-94-2.

### 3.2 Método(s): promedio ponderado

#### 3.2.1 Hombres:
- 1950-90, promedios ponderados de las tasas de distribución 1950, 1959, 1970, 1979 y 1989 con base en el Boletín de estadísticas del trabajo 1994-2.

#### 3.2.2 Mujeres:
Métodos, hipótesis y tratamientos idénticos a los que se aplican a los hombres.

## 4. Proyección de las tasas de actividad: 2000 - 2010

### 4.1 Modelo(s): linear, hiperbólico y logístico

#### 4.1.1 Hombres:
- Para los grupos de edad [15-24] y [60+], aplicación de la función F3;
- Para los grupos de edad [25-59], aplicación de la función F1;
- Modificación de las tendencias de los grupos de edad [20-64].

#### 4.1.2 Mujeres:
- Para el grupo de edad [15-19], aplicación de la función F1;
- Para los grupos de edad [20-24] y [60+], aplicación de la función F3;
- Para los grupos de edad [25-59], aplicación de la función F6;
- Modificación de las tendencias de los grupos de edad [20-49].

*Notas sobre los ajustes de las tasas, véase p.380-384.*     *Notas sobre las funciones de proyección, véase p. 386.*

# Tanzanía, Rep. Unida de

## 1. Fuente(s) de los datos básicos

Código(s):   Título(s):

EPPA3      Estimaciones y proyecciones de la población económicamente activa, 1950-2025, tercera edición, OIT, Ginebra, 1986.

## 2. Evaluación de las tasas de actividad: 1950 - 1990

### 2.1 Datos básicos:

Cuadro 1: Tasas de actividad por sexo y grupo de edad

| Grupo de edad | Año 1950 | 1960 | 1970 | 1980 |
|---|---|---|---|---|
| **Hombres** | | | | |
| 10-14 | 49.00 | 47.95 | 46.55 | 43.45 |
| 15-19 | 78.70 | 77.35 | 75.45 | 71.40 |
| 20-24 | 87.15 | 86.65 | 85.90 | 84.35 |
| 25-29 | 96.25 | 96.15 | 96.05 | 95.80 |
| 30-34 | 98.15 | 98.05 | 97.90 | 97.60 |
| 35-39 | 99.05 | 98.95 | 98.80 | 98.50 |
| 40-44 | 99.15 | 99.05 | 98.90 | 98.60 |
| 45-49 | 99.35 | 99.25 | 99.15 | 98.85 |
| 50-54 | 98.90 | 98.75 | 98.55 | 98.15 |
| 55-59 | 98.60 | 98.50 | 98.40 | 97.95 |
| 60-64 | 97.75 | 97.35 | 96.85 | 95.65 |
| 65+ | 91.70 | 90.95 | 89.95 | 87.75 |
| **Mujeres** | | | | |
| 10-14 | 46.45 | 45.70 | 44.60 | 42.25 |
| 15-19 | 85.80 | 84.25 | 82.00 | 77.20 |
| 20-24 | 90.90 | 89.40 | 87.20 | 82.50 |
| 25-29 | 94.85 | 93.45 | 91.45 | 87.10 |
| 30-34 | 97.35 | 96.05 | 94.15 | 90.05 |
| 35-39 | 98.20 | 97.00 | 95.20 | 91.40 |
| 40-44 | 98.50 | 97.40 | 95.80 | 92.35 |
| 45-49 | 98.30 | 97.20 | 95.65 | 92.30 |
| 50-54 | 95.95 | 95.05 | 93.75 | 90.95 |
| 55-59 | 92.90 | 92.25 | 91.30 | 89.30 |
| 60-64 | 85.30 | 84.90 | 84.35 | 83.10 |
| 65+ | 61.45 | 61.30 | 61.10 | 60.70 |

Fuente(s): EPPA3.

### 2.2 Método(s): extrapolación linear

#### 2.2.1 Hombres:

- 1950-80, tasas de actividad 1950-80 con base en EPPA3;
- 1990, extrapolación de las tasas de actividad 1950-80 con base en EPPA3; ajuste de las tasas extrapoladas con base en las variaciones de las tasas interpoladas 1980, en relación con las tasas 1980 con base en EPPA3; modificación de las tendencias de todos los grupos de edad.

#### 2.2.2 Mujeres:

Métodos, hipótesis y tratamientos idénticos a los que se aplican a los hombres.

## 3. Evaluación de las tasas de distribución por sector de actividad: 1950 - 1990

### 3.1 Datos básicos:

Cuadro 2: Distribución de la población económicamente activa por sector de actividad en %

| Año | Agricultura | Industria Total | Manufac. | Servicios |
|---|---|---|---|---|
| **Hombres** | | | | |
| 1950 | 90.60 | 3.40 | .. | 6.00 |
| 1960 | 88.55 | 4.10 | .. | 7.35 |
| 1970 | 85.00 | 5.40 | .. | 9.60 |
| 1980 | 79.75 | 7.25 | .. | 13.00 |
| **Mujeres** | | | | |
| 1950 | 97.50 | 0.50 | .. | 2.00 |
| 1960 | 96.45 | 0.75 | .. | 2.80 |
| 1970 | 95.00 | 1.00 | .. | 4.00 |
| 1980 | 91.85 | 1.65 | .. | 6.50 |

Fuente(s): EPPA3.

### 3.2 Método(s): extrapolación linear

#### 3.2.1 Hombres:

- 1950-80, tasas de distribución 1950-80 con base en EPPA3;
- 1990, extrapolación de las tasas de distribución 1950-80 con base en EPPA3; modificación de las tendencias de todos los sectores;
- Aplicación de la razón manufacturas/industria estimada para Etiopía.

#### 3.2.2 Mujeres:

Métodos, hipótesis y tratamientos idénticos a los que se aplican a los hombres.

## 4. Proyección de las tasas de actividad: 2000 - 2010

### 4.1 Modelo(s): linear y hiperbólico

#### 4.1.1 Hombres:

- Para los grupos de edad [10-24], aplicación de la función F1;
- Para los grupos de edad [25+], aplicación de la función F3;
- Modificación de las tendencias de los grupos de edad [10-14] y [60+].

#### 4.1.2 Mujeres:

- Para los grupos de edad [10-19], aplicación de la función F1;
- Para los grupos de edad [20+], aplicación de la función F3;
- Modificación de las tendencias de todos los grupos de edad.

*Notas sobre los ajustes de las tasas, véase p.380-384.*

*Notas sobre las funciones de proyección, véase p. 386.*

# Timor oriental

## 1. Fuente(s) de los datos básicos

Código(s):  Título(s):

EPPA3    Estimaciones y proyecciones de la población económicamente activa, 1950-2025, tercera edición, OIT, Ginebra, 1986.

## 2. Evaluación de las tasas de actividad: 1950 - 1990

### 2.1 Datos básicos:

Cuadro 1: Tasas de actividad por sexo y grupo de edad

| Grupo de edad | Año | | | | |
|---|---|---|---|---|---|
| | 1950 | 1960 | 1970 | 1980 | 1990 |
| **Hombres** | | | | | |
| 10-14 | 28.51 | 26.60 | 24.69 | 22.78 | .. |
| 15-19 | 82.80 | 81.50 | 75.70 | 72.80 | .. |
| 20-24 | 97.50 | 97.00 | 95.25 | 94.00 | .. |
| 25-29 | 97.65 | 97.40 | 97.15 | 97.00 | .. |
| 30-34 | 97.65 | 97.40 | 97.15 | 97.00 | .. |
| 35-39 | 97.60 | 97.35 | 97.10 | 97.00 | .. |
| 40-44 | 97.50 | 97.25 | 97.00 | 96.90 | .. |
| 45-49 | 97.40 | 96.15 | 95.50 | 95.20 | .. |
| 50-54 | 97.00 | 95.70 | 95.00 | 94.65 | .. |
| 55-59 | 95.00 | 93.50 | 91.50 | 90.50 | .. |
| 60-64 | 90.00 | 88.50 | 86.00 | 84.75 | .. |
| 65+ | 78.00 | 76.00 | 70.25 | 67.40 | .. |
| **Mujeres** | | | | | |
| 10-14 | 3.00 | .. | .. | .. | 2.20 |
| 15-19 | 10.60 | .. | .. | .. | 12.28 |
| 20-24 | 11.80 | .. | .. | .. | 18.66 |
| 25-29 | 11.45 | .. | .. | .. | 17.36 |
| 30-34 | 10.25 | .. | .. | .. | 15.69 |
| 35-39 | 10.70 | .. | .. | .. | 15.82 |
| 40-44 | 12.00 | .. | .. | .. | 17.40 |
| 45-49 | 11.20 | .. | .. | .. | 15.00 |
| 50-54 | 10.75 | .. | .. | .. | 14.02 |
| 55-59 | 10.00 | .. | .. | .. | 9.86 |
| 60-64 | 8.35 | .. | .. | .. | 7.08 |
| 65+ | 4.50 | .. | .. | .. | 4.15 |

Fuente(s): EPPA3.

### 2.2 Método(s):  interpolación linear
promedio ponderado

#### 2.2.1 Hombres:

- 1950-80, tasas de actividad 1950-80 con base en EPPA3;
ajuste de las tasas de actividad del grupo de edad [10-14];
- 1990, extrapolación de las tasas de actividad 1950-80 con base en EPPA3
ajúste de las tasas extrapoladas con base en las variaciones de las tasas
interpoladas 1980, en relación con las tasas de actividad 1980 con base en
EPPA3;
modificación de las tendencias de todos los grupos de edad para 1970.

#### 2.2.2 Mujeres:

- 1950 y 1990, tasas de actividad ajustadas 1950 y 1990 con base en EPPA3;
el ajuste se ha calculado con base en el modelo de ajuste de las tasas de
actividad de las mujeres ocupadas en la agricultura como auxiliares familiares;
- 1960-80, promedios ponderados de las tasas de actividad estimadas
para 1950 y 1990.

## 3. Evaluación de las tasas de distribución por sector de actividad: 1950 - 1990

### 3.1 Datos básicos:

Cuadro 2: Distribución de la población económicamente activa por sector de actividad en %

| Año | Agricultura | Industria | | Servicios |
|---|---|---|---|---|
| | | Total | Manufac. | |
| **Hombres** | | | | |
| 1950 | 80.00 | 7.50 | .. | 12.50 |
| 1960 | 79.00 | 8.00 | .. | 13.00 |
| 1970 | 78.00 | 8.50 | .. | 13.50 |
| 1980 | 77.00 | 8.75 | .. | 14.25 |
| **Mujeres** | | | | |
| 1950 | 98.00 | 0.06 | .. | 1.94 |
| 1960 | 96.75 | 0.10 | .. | 3.15 |
| 1970 | 95.50 | 0.14 | .. | 4.36 |
| 1980 | 94.25 | 0.17 | .. | 5.58 |

Fuente(s): EPPA3.

### 3.2 Método(s):  extrapolación linear

#### 3.2.1 Hombres:

- 1950-80, tasas de distribución 1950-80 con base en EPPA3;
- 1990, extrapolación de las tasas de distribución de la agricultura 1950-80
con base en EPPA3;
- Aplicación de la razón industria/servicios 1980 con base en EPPA3.

#### 3.2.2 Mujeres:

- 1950-80, tasas de distribución de la agricultura 1950-80 con base en EPPA3;
ajuste de las tasas con base en la razón hombres/mujeres igual a 1
en la agricultura;
- Aplicación de las razones industria/servicios 1950-80 con base en EPPA3;
- 1990, extrapolación de las tasas de distribución estimadas de la agricultura
para 1950-80;
- Aplicación de la razón industria/servicios de 1980 con base en EPPA3.

## 4. Proyección de las tasas de actividad: 2000 - 2010

### 4.1 Modelo(s):  linear, hiperbólico y logístico

#### 4.1.1 Hombres:

- Para los grupos de edad [10-19] y [55+], aplicación de la función F1;
- Para los grupos de edad [20-54], aplicación de la función F3;
- Modificación de las tendencias de los grupos de edad [55+].

#### 4.1.2 Mujeres:

- Para los grupos de edad [10-19], aplicación de la función F1;
- Para los grupos de edad [20+], aplicación de la función F6;
- Modificación de las tendencias de los grupos de edad [10-19].

*Notas sobre los ajustes de las tasas, véase p.380-384.*

*Notas sobre las funciones de proyección, véase p. 386.*

# Togo

## 1. Fuente(s) de los datos básicos

Código(s):   Título(s):

EPPA3   Estimaciones y proyecciones de la población económicamente activa, 1950-2025, tercera edición, OIT, Ginebra, 1986.
STAT   Base de datos de la OIT sobre estadísticas del trabajo - LABORSTA, Oficina de Estadística, OIT, Ginebra.
R1970   Recensement général de la Population (mars-avril 1970), Direction de la Statistique, Lomé, 1974.
AST87   Anuario de Estadísticas del Trabjo 1987, OIT, Ginebra, 1987.

## 2. Evaluación de las tasas de actividad: 1950 - 1990

### 2.1 Datos básicos:

Cuadro 1: Tasas de actividad por sexo y grupo de edad

| Grupo de edad | Año 1950 (1) | 1960 (1) | 1961 (2) | 1970 (1) | 1970 (3) | 1981 (4) |
|---|---|---|---|---|---|---|
| **Hombres** | | | | | | |
| 10-14 | 50.60 | 49.30 | .. | 47.70 | .. | 12.72 |
| 15-19 | 74.00 | 72.50 | .. | 70.55 | .. | 36.61 |
| 20-24 | 93.15 | 92.50 | .. | 91.70 | .. | 70.05 |
| 25-29 | 97.20 | 97.10 | .. | 96.95 | .. | 94.59 |
| 30-34 | 97.35 | 97.25 | .. | 97.10 | .. | 98.14 |
| 35-39 | 97.70 | 97.60 | .. | 97.45 | .. | 98.60 |
| 40-44 | 97.45 | 97.30 | .. | 97.15 | .. | 98.12 |
| 45-49 | 97.05 | 96.95 | .. | 96.85 | .. | 97.59 |
| 50-54 | 95.55 | 95.40 | .. | 95.20 | .. | 92.70 |
| 55-59 | 94.30 | 94.05 | .. | 93.75 | .. | 90.12 |
| 60-64 | 90.55 | 90.15 | .. | 89.60 | .. | 87.54 |
| 65+ | 78.30 | 77.55 | .. | 76.65 | .. | 71.52 |
| **Mujeres** | | | | | | |
| 10-14 | .. | .. | 36.59 | .. | 47.86 | 12.73 |
| 15-19 | .. | .. | 51.97 | .. | 51.85 | 35.83 |
| 20-24 | .. | .. | 51.73 | .. | 54.01 | 47.66 |
| 25-29 | .. | .. | 55.43 | .. | 57.80 | 55.15 |
| 30-34 | .. | .. | 56.99 | .. | 58.90 | 58.03 |
| 35-39 | .. | .. | 58.50 | .. | 60.52 | 59.59 |
| 40-44 | .. | .. | 60.44 | .. | 60.88 | 60.27 |
| 45-49 | .. | .. | 60.05 | .. | 61.00 | 60.13 |
| 50-54 | .. | .. | 58.76 | .. | 58.86 | 59.94 |
| 55-59 | .. | .. | 55.73 | .. | 55.34 | 56.46 |
| 60-64 | .. | .. | 53.85 | .. | 49.54 | 50.85 |
| 65+ | .. | .. | 37.21 | .. | 33.95 | 34.95 |

Fuente(s): (1) EPPA3; (2) STAT; (3) R1970; (4) AST87.

### 2.2 Método(s): interpolación y extrapolación lineares

**2.2.1 Hombres:**

- 1950-70, tasas de actividad 1950-70 con base en EPPA3;
ajuste de las tasas de actividad de los grupos de edad [30-49] para 1950 y 1960;
- 1980-90, extrapolación de las tasas de actividad 1950-70 con base en EPPA3
y de las tasas de actividad con base en el censo de 1981;
ajuste de las tasas interpoladas y extrapoladas con base en las variaciones
de las tasas interpoladas 1970, en relación con de 1970 tasas de actividad
con base en EPPA3;
modificación de las tendencias de los grupos de edad [10-19] para 1990.

**2.2.2 Mujeres:**

- 1950-90, interpolación y extrapolación de las tasas de actividad con base en
el censo de 1961 y de las tasas de actividad ajustadas con base en
los censos de 1970 y 1981;
modificación de las tendencias de todos los grupos de edad para 1950.

## 3. Evaluación de las tasas de distribución por sector de actividad: 1950 - 1990

### 3.1 Datos básicos:

Cuadro 2: Distribución de la población económicamente activa por sector de actividad en %

| Año | Agricultura | Industria Total | Manufac. | Servicios |
|---|---|---|---|---|
| **Hombres** | | | | |
| 1961 (1) | 83.50 | 9.50 | .. | 7.00 |
| 1981 (2) | 69.11 | 11.71 | 6.23 | 19.18 |
| **Mujeres** | | | | |
| 1961 (1) | 73.50 | 6.00 | .. | 20.50 |
| 1981 (2) | 66.75 | 6.70 | 6.57 | 26.55 |

Fuente(s): (1) STAT; (2) AST87.

### 3.2 Método(s): interpolación y extrapolación lineares

**3.2.1 Hombres:**

- 1950-90, interpolación y extrapolación de las tasas de distribución
con base en la encuesta de 1961 y el censo de 1981;
modificación de las tendencias de todos los sectores;
- Aplicación de la razón manufacturas/industria con base en el censo de 1981.

**3.2.2 Mujeres:**

Métodos, hipótesis y tratamientos idénticos a los que se aplican a los hombres.

## 4. Proyección de las tasas de actividad: 2000 - 2010

### 4.1 Modelo(s): log-linear y hiperbólico

**4.1.1 Hombres:**

- Para el grupo de edad [10-14], aplicación de la función F2;
- Para los grupos de edad [15+], aplicación de la función F1;
- Modificación de las tendencias de los grupos de edad [30-39].

**4.1.2 Mujeres:**

- Para el grupo de edad [10-14], aplicación de la función F2;
- Para los grupos de edad [15+], aplicación de la función F1;
- Modificación de las tendencias de los grupos de edad [10-59].

*Notas sobre los ajustes de las tasas, véase p.380-384.*   *Notas sobre las funciones de proyección, véase p. 386.*

# Trinidad y Tabago

## 1. Fuente(s) de los datos básicos

Código(s):  Título(s):

EPPA3  Estimaciones y proyecciones de la población económicamente activa, 1950-2025, tercera edición, OIT, Ginebra, 1986.
AST75-93  Ediciones de 1975-1993, Anuario de Estadísticas del Trabjo de la OIT, Ginebra.
TET-LFS  Continuous Sample Survey of Population; Labour Force Report 1989.

## 2. Evaluación de las tasas de actividad: 1950 - 1990

### 2.1 Datos básicos:

Cuadro 1: Tasas de actividad por sexo y grupo de edad

| Grupo de edad | Año 1980 (1) | 1987 (2) | 1988 (2) | 1989 (2) |
|---|---|---|---|---|
| **Hombres** | | | | |
| 10-14 | 1.10 | 0.00 | 0.00 | 0.00 |
| 15-19 | 50.90 | 45.50 | 41.00 | 39.00 |
| 20-24 | 90.20 | 90.30 | 89.40 | 87.70 |
| 25-29 | 95.40 | 96.10 | 93.10 | 94.30 |
| 30-34 | 96.50 | 94.80 | 95.40 | 94.00 |
| 35-39 | 97.00 | 96.40 | 94.70 | 93.60 |
| 40-44 | 95.50 | 93.80 | 94.80 | 94.10 |
| 45-49 | 95.40 | 95.50 | 94.60 | 92.00 |
| 50-54 | 94.00 | 89.50 | 89.70 | 89.00 |
| 55-59 | 89.60 | 85.10 | 81.50 | 79.90 |
| 60-64 | 71.40 | 55.50 | 55.90 | 49.00 |
| 65+ | 21.80 | 20.30 | 21.80 | 18.40 |
| **Mujeres** | | | | |
| 10-14 | 0.00 | 0.00 | 0.00 | 0.00 |
| 15-19 | 20.10 | 21.00 | 18.10 | 16.30 |
| 20-24 | 50.03 | 52.20 | 52.10 | 50.70 |
| 25-29 | 49.58 | 51.70 | 50.60 | 51.40 |
| 30-34 | 48.27 | 52.60 | 51.00 | 48.80 |
| 35-39 | 49.01 | 49.30 | 52.50 | 52.50 |
| 40-44 | 43.11 | 52.00 | 50.60 | 49.00 |
| 45-49 | 47.80 | 45.00 | 45.10 | 48.60 |
| 50-54 | 38.95 | 40.70 | 40.20 | 36.90 |
| 55-59 | 34.10 | 30.70 | 33.30 | 26.40 |
| 60-64 | 23.08 | 20.00 | 18.70 | 13.90 |
| 65+ | 7.77 | 6.00 | 5.70 | 5.40 |

Fuente(s): (1) EPPA3; (2) AST75-93 y TET-LFS.

### 2.2 Método(s): extrapolación linear

**2.2.1 Hombres:**

- 1950-80, tasas de actividad 1950-80 con base en EPPA3;
ajuste de las tasas de actividad de los grupos de edad [15-24] y [65+] para 1980;
- 1990, extrapolación de la tasas de actividad 1980 con base en EPPA3
y de las tasas de actividad con base en los censos de 1987, 1988 y 1989;
modificación de las tendencias de todos los grupos de edad.

**2.2.2 Mujeres:**

- 1950-80, tasas de actividad 1950-80 con base en EPPA3;
modificación de las tendencias de todos los grupos de edad para 1980;
- 1990, extrapolación de las tasas de actividad estimadas 1980 y de los
promedios de las tasas de actividad con base en las encuestas
de 1987, 1988 y 1989.

## 3. Evaluación de las tasas de distribución por sector de actividad: 1950 - 1990

### 3.1 Datos básicos:

Cuadro 2: Distribución de la población económicamente activa por sector de actividad en %

| Año | Agricultura | Industria Total | Manufac. | Servicios |
|---|---|---|---|---|
| **Hombres** | | | | |
| 1980 | 10.70 | 45.55 | 16.34 | 43.75 |
| 1989 | 14.81 | 39.69 | 10.73 | 45.50 |
| 1990 | 13.78 | 37.59 | 10.23 | 48.64 |
| 1991 | 13.36 | 39.89 | 11.04 | 46.76 |
| **Mujeres** | | | | |
| 1979 | 7.69 | 26.85 | 15.62 | 65.46 |
| 1980 | 7.88 | 24.49 | 14.48 | 67.63 |
| 1981 | 9.96 | 22.51 | 12.47 | 67.53 |
| 1989 | 6.13 | 16.48 | 9.39 | 77.39 |
| 1990 | 5.25 | 16.32 | 9.80 | 78.43 |
| 1991 | 5.16 | 19.61 | 10.54 | 75.23 |

Fuente(s): AST75-93.

### 3.2 Método(s): promedio aritmético

**3.2.1 Hombres:**

- 1950-80, tasas de distribución 1950-80 con base en EPPA3;
- Aplicación de la razón manufacturas/industria con base en la encuesta de 1980
- 1990, promedios de las tasas de distribución con base en
las encuestas de 1989, 1990 y 1991.

**3.2.2 Mujeres:**

- 1950-70, tasas de distribución 1950-70 con base en EPPA3;
- 1980, promedios de las tasas de distribución con base en las encuestas
de 1979, 1980 y 1981;
- 1990, promedios de las tasas de distribución con base en las encuestas
de 1989, 1990 y 1991.

## 4. Proyección de las tasas de actividad: 2000 - 2010

### 4.1 Modelo(s): linear, log-linear, hiperbólico y logístico

**4.1.1 Hombres:**

- Para los grupos de edad [15-54], aplicación de la función F1;
- Para los grupos de edad [55+], aplicación de la función F3;
- Modificación de las tendencias de los grupos de edad [15-54].

**4.1.2 Mujeres:**

- Para los grupos de edad [15-19] y [55+], aplicación de la función F3;
- Para el grupo de edad [20-24], aplicación de la función F6;
- Para los grupos de edad [25-54], aplicación de la función F2.

*Notas sobre los ajustes de las tasas, véase p.380-384.*

*Notas sobre las funciones de proyección, véase p. 386.*

# Túnez

## 1. Fuente(s) de los datos básicos

Código(s):  Título(s):

EPPA3 . Estimaciones y proyecciones de la población económicamente activa, 1950-2025, tercera edición, OIT, Ginebra, 1986.
R1984 Recencement général de la population et de l'habitat, 30 mars 1984, Institut National de la Statistique, Tunis, 1984.
ASTER Anuario de estadísticas del trabajo 1945-89 - Edición retrospectiva sobre los censos de población, OIT, Ginebra, 1990.
ADNU88 Annuaire démographique 1988 - Statistiques des recensements de population, quarantième édition, Nations Unies, New York, 1990.

## 2. Evaluación de las tasas de actividad: 1950 - 1990

### 2.1 Datos básicos:

Cuadro 1: Tasas de actividad por sexo y grupo de edad

| Grupo de edad | Año | | | | |
|---|---|---|---|---|---|
| | 1950 (1) | 1960 (1) | 1970 (1) | 1975 (2) | 1984 (3) |
| **Hombres** | | | | | |
| 10-14 | .. | .. | 18.00 | 17.33 | 0.00 |
| 15-19 | .. | .. | 57.45 | 64.03 | 20.44 |
| 20-24 | .. | .. | 89.40 | 85.39 | 73.25 |
| 25-29 | .. | .. | 97.30 | 99.29 | 95.50 |
| 30-34 | .. | .. | 98.40 | 96.90 | 97.96 |
| 35-39 | .. | .. | 98.30 | 96.90 | 98.76 |
| 40-44 | .. | .. | 97.85 | 99.20 | 98.53 |
| 45-49 | .. | .. | 96.75 | 98.10 | 97.96 |
| 50-54 | .. | .. | 93.60 | 89.70 | 96.83 |
| 55-59 | .. | .. | 86.80 | 68.20 | 94.23 |
| 60-64 | .. | .. | 70.85 | 53.90 | 89.35 |
| 65+ | .. | .. | 49.70 | 38.70 | 40.98 |
| **Mujeres** | | | | | |
| 10-14 | 0.00 | 0.00 | 0.00 | 11.80 | 0.00 |
| 15-19 | 9.45 | 11.80 | 16.50 | 29.50 | 25.18 |
| 20-24 | 8.15 | 10.70 | 15.75 | 27.50 | 38.12 |
| 25-29 | 4.00 | 6.65 | 11.85 | 21.80 | 29.41 |
| 30-34 | 2.40 | 4.80 | 9.50 | 15.90 | 23.55 |
| 35-39 | 2.60 | 4.60 | 8.65 | 14.00 | 18.97 |
| 40-44 | 3.35 | 5.25 | 9.00 | 14.60 | 14.57 |
| 45-49 | 3.00 | 4.95 | 8.90 | 14.10 | 12.87 |
| 50-54 | 3.25 | 4.90 | 8.15 | 11.60 | 11.60 |
| 55-59 | 3.05 | 4.35 | 6.95 | 9.20 | 9.83 |
| 60-64 | 3.25 | 4.00 | 5.45 | 7.00 | 4.43 |
| 65+ | 2.10 | 2.40 | 3.00 | 5.40 | 3.46 |

Fuente(s): (1) EPPA3; (2) ASTER; (3) ADNU88 y R1984.

### 2.2 Método(s): extrapolación linear

#### 2.2.1 Hombres:

- 1950-70, tasas de actividad 1950-70 con base en EPPA3;
- 1980-90, extrapolación de las tasas de actividad 1970 con base en EPPA3 y de las tasas de actividad con base en los censos de 1975 y 1984; modificación de las tendencias de los grupos de edad [15-24] para 1990.

#### 2.2.2 Mujeres:

- 1950-70, tasas de actividad ajustadas 1950-70 con base en EPPA3;
- 1980, promedios ponderados de las tasas de actividad ajustadas con base en los censos de 1975 y 1984;
- 1990, extrapolación de las tasas de actividad ajustadas con base en los censos de 1975 y 1984; ajuste de las tasas extrapoladas con base en de las variaciones de las tasas interpoladas 1980, en relación con las tasas de actividad estimadas para 1980;

## 3. Evaluación de las tasas de distribución por sector de actividad: 1950 - 1990

### 3.1 Datos básicos:

Cuadro 2: Distribución de la población económicamente activa por sector de actividad en %

| Año | Agricultura | Industria | | Servicios |
|---|---|---|---|---|
| | | Total | Manufac. | |
| **Hombres** | | | | |
| 1975 (1) | 45.10 | 22.60 | | 32.30 |
| 1984 (2) | 40.73 | 26.17 | 10.33 | 33.10 |
| **Mujeres** | | | | |
| 1975 (1) | 27.10 | 49.56 | 48.73 | 23.34 |
| 1984 (2) | 25.86 | 49.08 | 47.69 | 25.06 |

Fuente(s): (1) ASTER; (2) R1984.

### 3.2 Método(s): promedio ponderado
extrapolación linear

#### 3.2.1 Hombres:

- 1950-70, tasas de distribución 1950-70 con base en EPPA3;
- 1980, promedios ponderados de las tasas de distribución ajustadas con base en los censos de 1975 y 1984;
- 1990, extrapolación de las tasas de distribución con base en los censos de 1975 y 1984;
de 1975 y 1984;

#### 3.2.2 Mujeres:

- 1950-70, tasas de distribución 1950-70 con base en EPPA3;
- 1980, promedios ponderados de las tasas de distribución ajustadas con base en los censos de 1975 y 1984;
- 1990, extrapolación de las tasas de distribución con base en los censos de 1975 y 1984; modificación de las tendencias de todos los sectores; ajuste de las tasas estimadas 1950-90 habida cuenta de la subenumeración censal de las mujeres ocupadas en la agricultura.

## 4. Proyección de las tasas de actividad: 2000 - 2010

### 4.1 Modelo(s): linear, log-linear y hiperbólico

#### 4.1.1 Hombres:

- Para el grupo de edad [15-19], aplicación de la función F2;
- Para los grupos de edad [20-59], aplicación de la función F1;
- Para los grupos de edad [60+], aplicación de la función F3.

#### 4.1.2 Mujeres:

- Para todos los grupos de edad, aplicación de la función F1;
- Modificación de las tendencias de los grupos de edad [15-24] y [50+].

---

*Notas sobre los ajustes de las tasas, véase p.380-384.*     *Notas sobre las funciones de proyección, véase p. 386.*

# Turkmenistán

## 1. Fuente(s) de los datos básicos

Código(s):   Título(s):

BLT-94-2   Vorobiev A. (1994), "Estimaciones de la población económicamente activa de los quince países de la ex URSS, en 1950, 1959, 1970, 1979 y 1989", en el Boletín de Estadísticas del Trabajol - 1994-2, OIT, Ginebra.

## 2. Evaluación de las tasas de actividad: 1950 - 1990

### 2.1 Datos básicos:

Cuadro 1: Tasas de actividad por sexo y grupo de edad

| Grupo de edad | Año | | | | |
|---|---|---|---|---|---|
| | 1950 | 1959 | 1970 | 1979 | 1989 |
| **Hombres** | | | | | |
| 10-14 | 0.00 | 0.00 | 0.00 | 0.00 | 0.00 |
| 15-19 | 50.75 | 52.38 | 42.86 | 41.32 | 35.64 |
| 20-24 | 82.26 | 85.07 | 85.92 | 90.00 | 85.09 |
| 25-29 | 94.29 | 96.77 | 98.25 | 97.98 | 96.84 |
| 30-34 | 93.10 | 96.49 | 98.63 | 98.36 | 98.39 |
| 35-39 | 90.32 | 93.75 | 98.33 | 98.36 | 97.80 |
| 40-44 | 92.59 | 92.31 | 94.74 | 97.01 | 98.08 |
| 45-49 | 91.30 | 93.10 | 96.88 | 98.18 | 98.15 |
| 50-54 | 89.47 | 91.67 | 91.30 | 93.62 | 94.64 |
| 55-59 | 82.35 | 85.00 | 84.62 | 84.00 | 89.13 |
| 60-64 | 66.67 | 68.42 | 50.00 | 35.00 | 40.54 |
| 65+ | 25.00 | 29.41 | 9.52 | 10.42 | 15.22 |
| **Mujeres** | | | | | |
| 10-14 | 0.00 | 0.00 | 0.00 | 0.00 | 0.00 |
| 15-19 | 45.07 | 46.30 | 41.41 | 40.99 | 34.27 |
| 20-24 | 60.87 | 62.32 | 67.65 | 84.85 | 74.55 |
| 25-29 | 62.00 | 66.15 | 92.59 | 88.12 | 77.44 |
| 30-34 | 63.41 | 63.49 | 78.57 | 89.83 | 79.84 |
| 35-39 | 62.50 | 63.04 | 84.48 | 91.53 | 83.16 |
| 40-44 | 62.86 | 62.16 | 81.03 | 90.63 | 83.33 |
| 45-49 | 54.05 | 56.76 | 81.40 | 87.50 | 83.33 |
| 50-54 | 44.00 | 45.16 | 72.73 | 74.07 | 58.62 |
| 55-59 | 28.57 | 26.47 | 29.27 | 30.00 | 27.45 |
| 60-64 | 17.65 | 16.00 | 12.50 | 12.12 | 14.89 |
| 65+ | 4.88 | 4.88 | 3.39 | 4.00 | 4.65 |

Fuente(s): BLT-94-2-2

### 2.2 Método(s): promedio ponderado

#### 2.2.1 Hombres:

- 1950-90, promedios ponderados de las tasas de actividad 1950, 1959, 1974 y 1989 con base en el Boletín de estadísticas del trabajo 1994-2.

#### 2.2.2 Mujeres:

Métodos, hipótesis y tratamientos idénticos a los que se aplican a los hombres.

## 3. Evaluación de las tasas de distribución por sector de actividad: 1950 - 1990

### 3.1 Datos básicos:

Cuadro 2: Distribución de la población económicamente activa por sector de actividad en %

| Año | Agricultura | Industria | | Servicios |
|---|---|---|---|---|
| | | Total | Manufac. | |
| **Hombres** | | | | |
| 1950 | 58.36 | 17.84 | 9.29 | 23.79 |
| 1959 | 43.84 | 23.21 | 8.60 | 32.95 |
| 1970 | 33.26 | 29.59 | 9.40 | 37.16 |
| 1979 | 32.83 | 31.83 | 8.50 | 35.33 |
| 1989 | 33.76 | 30.04 | 8.34 | 36.20 |
| **Mujeres** | | | | |
| 1950 | 60.91 | 13.64 | 9.55 | 25.45 |
| 1959 | 54.72 | 14.57 | 11.02 | 30.71 |
| 1970 | 43.01 | 17.81 | 10.96 | 39.18 |
| 1979 | 46.48 | 16.67 | 9.07 | 36.85 |
| 1989 | 42.01 | 14.58 | 7.84 | 43.42 |

Fuente(s): BLT-94-2.

### 3.2 Método(s): promedio ponderado

#### 3.2.1 Hombres:

- 1950-90, promedios ponderados de las tasas de distribución 1950, 1959, 1970, 1979 y 1989 con base en el Boletín de estadísticas del trabajo 1994-2.

#### 3.2.2 Mujeres:

Métodos, hipótesis y tratamientos idénticos a los que se aplican a los hombres.

## 4. Proyección de las tasas de actividad: 2000 - 2010

### 4.1 Modelo(s): linear, hiperbólico y logístico

#### 4.1.1 Hombres:

- Para los grupos de edad [15-64], aplicación de la función F1;
- Para el grupo de edad [65+], aplicación de la función F3;
- Modificación de las tendencias de los grupos de edad [20-64].

#### 4.1.2 Mujeres:

- Para el grupo de edad [15-19], aplicación de la función F1;
- Para los grupos de edad [20-59], aplicación de la función F6;
- Para los grupos de edad [60+], aplicación de la función F3;
- Modificación de las tendencias de los grupos de edad [15-54].

*Notas sobre los ajustes de las tasas, véase p.380-384.*

*Notas sobre las funciones de proyección, véase p. 386.*

# Turquía

## 1. Fuente(s) de los datos básicos

Código(s):     Título(s):

EPPA3      Estimaciones y proyecciones de la población económicamente activa, 1950-2025, tercera edición, OIT, Ginebra, 1986.
STAT       Base de datos de la OIT sobre estadísticas del trabajo - LABORSTA, Oficina de Estadística, OIT, Ginebra.

## 2. Evaluación de las tasas de actividad: 1950 - 1990

### 2.1 Datos básicos:

Cuadro 1: Tasas de actividad por sexo y grupo de edad

| Grupo de edad | Año 1985 | 1990 |
|---|---|---|
| **Hombres** | | |
| 10-14 | 22.67 | 29.40 |
| 15-19 | 68.12 | 66.11 |
| 20-24 | 90.23 | 89.67 |
| 25-29 | 96.48 | 97.45 |
| 30-34 | 97.41 | 98.34 |
| 35-39 | 97.22 | 98.18 |
| 40-44 | 93.72 | 95.63 |
| 45-49 | 87.05 | 88.00 |
| 50-54 | 79.99 | 77.43 |
| 55-59 | 72.16 | 69.12 |
| 60-64 | 62.95 | 60.60 |
| 65+ | 41.73 | 46.05 |
| **Mujeres** | | |
| 10-14 | 22.64 | 22.60 |
| 15-19 | 49.94 | 48.34 |
| 20-24 | 48.18 | 48.27 |
| 25-29 | 43.43 | 43.11 |
| 30-34 | 42.28 | 42.80 |
| 35-39 | 43.33 | 43.43 |
| 40-44 | 46.21 | 43.99 |
| 45-49 | 46.79 | 44.21 |
| 50-54 | 48.18 | 44.77 |
| 55-59 | 44.88 | 44.33 |
| 60-64 | 39.84 | 39.25 |
| 65+ | 23.17 | 27.97 |

Fuente(s): STAT.

### 2.2 Método(s): promedio ponderado

#### 2.2.1 Hombres:

- 1950-80, tasas de actividad 1950-80 con base en EPPA3;
- 1990, promedios ponderados de las tasas de actividad con base en los censos de 1985 y 1990.

#### 2.2.2 Mujeres:

Métodos, hipótesis y tratamientos idénticos a los que se aplican a los hombres.

## 3. Evaluación de las tasas de distribución por sector de actividad: 1950 - 1990

### 3.1 Datos básicos:

Cuadro 2: Distribución de la población económicamente activa por sector de actividad en %

| Año | Agricultura | Industria Total | Manufac. | Servicios |
|---|---|---|---|---|
| **Hombres** | | | | |
| 1975 | 56.40 | 16.85 | 10.90 | 26.75 |
| 1980 | 44.54 | 22.42 | 14.45 | 33.04 |
| 1985 | 43.44 | 21.24 | 14.29 | 35.33 |
| 1990 | 38.02 | 24.23 | 14.96 | 37.75 |
| **Mujeres** | | | | |
| 1975 | 89.31 | 4.33 | 4.19 | 6.36 |
| 1980 | 87.86 | 4.60 | 4.48 | 7.55 |
| 1985 | 86.70 | 4.57 | 4.44 | 8.73 |
| 1990 | 82.27 | 6.89 | 6.68 | 10.84 |

Fuente(s): STAT.

### 3.2 Método(s): promedio ponderado

#### 3.2.1 Hombres:

- 1950-70, tasas de distribución 1950-70 con base en EPPA3;
- 1980-90, promedios ponderados de las tasas de distribución con base en los censos de 1975, 1980, 1985 y 1990.

#### 3.2.2 Mujeres:

Métodos, hipótesis y tratamientos idénticos a los que se aplican a los hombres.

## 4. Proyección de las tasas de actividad: 2000 - 2010

### 4.1 Modelo(s): linear y hiperbólico

#### 4.1.1 Hombres:

- Para los grupos de edad [10-44], aplicación de la función F1;
- Para los grupos de edad [45+], aplicación de la función F3;
- Modificación de las tendencias de los grupos de edad [10-14], [30-34] y [40+].

#### 4.1.2 Mujeres:

- Para el grupo de edad [10-14], aplicación de la función F1;
- Para los grupos de edad [15+], aplicación de la función F3;
- Modificación de las tendencias de los grupos de edad [10-14] y [20+].

*Notas sobre los ajustes de las tasas, véase p.380-384.*     *Notas sobre las funciones de proyección, véase p. 386.*

# Ucrania

## 1. Fuente(s) de los datos básicos

Código(s):  Título(s):

BLT-94-2   Vorobiev A. (1994), "Estimaciones de la población económicamente activa de los quince países de la ex URSS, en 1950, 1959, 1970, 1979 y 1989", en el Boletín de Estadísticas del Trabajol - 1994-2, OIT, Ginebra.

## 2. Evaluación de las tasas de actividad: 1950 - 1990

### 2.1 Datos básicos:

Cuadro 1: Tasas de actividad por sexo y grupo de edad

| Grupo de edad | Año 1959 | 1970 | 1979 | 1989 |
|---|---|---|---|---|
| **Hombres** | | | | |
| 10-14 | 0.00 | 0.00 | 0.00 | 0.00 |
| 15-19 | 62.57 | 40.71 | 36.28 | 27.71 |
| 20-24 | 86.88 | 85.15 | 86.32 | 79.76 |
| 25-29 | 96.22 | 96.37 | 96.77 | 96.09 |
| 30-34 | 95.77 | 98.14 | 98.30 | 97.77 |
| 35-39 | 93.61 | 97.01 | 98.17 | 97.75 |
| 40-44 | 94.96 | 96.39 | 97.73 | 97.22 |
| 45-49 | 90.91 | 94.09 | 96.14 | 95.41 |
| 50-54 | 87.02 | 88.31 | 88.09 | 89.69 |
| 55-59 | 81.38 | 78.71 | 78.73 | 77.74 |
| 60-64 | 60.29 | 31.11 | 26.29 | 31.69 |
| 65+ | 35.31 | 11.14 | 7.09 | 10.54 |
| **Mujeres** | | | | |
| 10-14 | 0.00 | 0.00 | 0.00 | 0.00 |
| 15-19 | 60.26 | 38.69 | 34.60 | 25.90 |
| 20-24 | 68.94 | 80.86 | 85.71 | 78.18 |
| 25-29 | 84.82 | 94.38 | 94.01 | 89.33 |
| 30-34 | 71.99 | 91.69 | 95.32 | 92.76 |
| 35-39 | 72.27 | 90.01 | 95.94 | 94.47 |
| 40-44 | 72.47 | 91.94 | 95.34 | 94.41 |
| 45-49 | 62.27 | 81.17 | 91.67 | 92.08 |
| 50-54 | 54.22 | 73.68 | 83.91 | 84.18 |
| 55-59 | 31.62 | 21.59 | 24.92 | 28.43 |
| 60-64 | 22.79 | 10.53 | 7.38 | 14.35 |
| 65+ | 2.73 | 0.89 | 1.66 | 3.66 |

Fuente(s): BLT-94-2.

### 2.2 Método(s): promedio ponderado

#### 2.2.1 Hombres:

- 1950-70, interpolación y extrapolación de las tasas de actividad 1950, 1959, 1970, 1979 y 1989 con base en el Boletín de estadísticas del trabajo 1994-2; aplicación a las tasas interpoladas y extrapoladas, de las variaciones de las tasas extrapoladas 1990, en relación con las tasas de actividad con base en el censo de 1989.

#### 2.2.2 Mujeres:

Métodos, hipótesis y tratamientos idénticos a los que se aplican a los hombres.

## 3. Evaluación de las tasas de distribución por sector de actividad: 1950 - 1990

### 3.1 Datos básicos:

Cuadro 2: Distribución de la población económicamente activa por sector de actividad en %

| Año | Agricultura | Industria Total | Manufac. | Servicios |
|---|---|---|---|---|
| **Hombres** | | | | |
| 1950 | 52.91 | 26.77 | 16.53 | 20.32 |
| 1959 | 39.52 | 32.18 | 18.79 | 28.31 |
| 1970 | 28.74 | 44.50 | 28.65 | 26.76 |
| 1979 | 25.93 | 46.18 | 28.35 | 27.89 |
| 1989 | 23.60 | 45.76 | 28.56 | 30.64 |
| **Mujeres** | | | | |
| 1950 | 66.31 | 14.53 | 10.81 | 19.16 |
| 1959 | 55.74 | 19.32 | 14.18 | 24.94 |
| 1970 | 32.81 | 28.85 | 22.73 | 38.34 |
| 1979 | 23.64 | 32.55 | 26.12 | 43.81 |
| 1989 | 16.20 | 33.51 | 27.37 | 50.29 |

Fuente(s): BLT-94-2.

### 3.2 Método(s): datos de BLT-94-2

#### 3.2.1 Hombres:

- 1950, 1960, 1970, 1980 y 1990, respectivamente las tasas de distribución 1950, 1959, 1970, 1979 y 1989 con base en el boletín de estadísticas del trabajo 1994-2.

#### 3.2.2 Mujeres:

Métodos, hipótesis y tratamientos idénticos a los que se aplican a los hombres.

## 4. Proyección de las tasas de actividad: 2000 - 2010

### 4.1 Modelo(s): linear, hiperbólico y logístico

#### 4.1.1 Hombres:

- Para los grupos de edad [15-24] y [55+], aplicación de la función F3;
- Para los grupos de edad [25-54], aplicación de la función F1;
- Modificación de las tendencias de los grupos de edad [25-54].

#### 4.1.2 Mujeres:

- Para los grupos de edad [15-19] y [55+], aplicación de la función F3;
- Para los grupos de edad [20-54], aplicación de la función F6;
- Modificación de las tendencias de los grupos de edad [20-54].

*Notas sobre los ajustes de las tasas, véase p.380-384.*   *Notas sobre las funciones de proyección, véase p. 386.*

# Uganda

## 1. Fuente(s) de los datos básicos

Código(s):    Título(s):

EPPA3        Estimaciones y proyecciones de la población económicamente activa, 1950-2025, tercera edición, OIT, Ginebra, 1986.

## 2. Evaluación de las tasas de actividad: 1950 - 1990

### 2.1 Datos básicos:

Cuadro 1: Tasas de actividad por sexo y grupo de edad

| Grupo de edad | Año | | | |
|---|---|---|---|---|
| | 1950 | 1960 | 1970 | 1980 |
| **Hombres** | | | | |
| 10-14 | 54.40 | 53.45 | 51.75 | 49.95 |
| 15-19 | 87.95 | 86.70 | 84.45 | 82.05 |
| 20-24 | 96.40 | 95.95 | 95.10 | 94.15 |
| 25-29 | 97.55 | 97.50 | 97.35 | 97.25 |
| 30-34 | 98.30 | 98.25 | 98.10 | 97.95 |
| 35-39 | 98.50 | 98.45 | 98.25 | 98.10 |
| 40-44 | 98.35 | 98.25 | 98.10 | 97.95 |
| 45-49 | 97.55 | 97.50 | 97.35 | 97.20 |
| 50-54 | 97.20 | 97.10 | 96.90 | 96.70 |
| 55-59 | 96.50 | 96.35 | 96.00 | 95.65 |
| 60-64 | 93.90 | 93.55 | 93.00 | 92.45 |
| 65+ | 81.25 | 80.70 | 79.75 | 78.70 |
| **Mujeres** | | | | |
| 10-14 | 41.10 | 40.40 | 39.10 | 37.75 |
| 15-19 | 66.55 | 65.50 | 63.60 | 61.55 |
| 20-24 | 65.80 | 65.10 | 63.90 | 62.65 |
| 25-29 | 71.00 | 70.25 | 68.85 | 67.40 |
| 30-34 | 75.45 | 74.65 | 73.20 | 71.65 |
| 35-39 | 76.55 | 75.80 | 74.45 | 73.00 |
| 40-44 | 79.00 | 78.25 | 76.90 | 75.40 |
| 45-49 | 78.55 | 77.80 | 76.40 | 74.90 |
| 50-54 | 77.45 | 76.55 | 74.95 | 73.20 |
| 55-59 | 74.75 | 73.85 | 72.15 | 70.35 |
| 60-64 | 69.35 | 68.20 | 66.05 | 63.75 |
| 65+ | 49.10 | 48.00 | 46.00 | 43.90 |

Fuente(s): EPPA3.

### 2.2 Método(s): interpolación y extrapolación lineares

#### 2.2.1 Hombres:

- 1950-80, tasas de actividad 1950-80 con base en EPPA3;
- 1990, extrapolación de las tasas de actividad 1950-80 con base en EPPA3;
ajuste de las tasas extrapoladas con base en las variaciones de las tasas
interpoladas 1980, en relación con las tasas 1980 con base en EPPA3.

#### 2.2.2 Mujeres:

- 1950-90, interpolación y extrapolación de las tasas de actividad ajustadas
1950 y 1980 con base en EPPA;
ajuste de los promedios de las tasas de actividad con base en
en la razón hombres/mujeres igual a 1 en la agricultura.

## 3. Evaluación de las tasas de distribución por sector de actividad: 1950 - 1990

### 3.1 Datos básicos:

Cuadro 2: Distribución de la población económicamente activa por sector de actividad en %

| Año | Agricultura | Industria | | Servicios |
|---|---|---|---|---|
| | | Total | Manufac. | |
| **Hombres** | | | | |
| 1950 | 91.80 | 3.15 | .. | 5.05 |
| 1960 | 90.10 | 3.80 | .. | 6.10 |
| 1970 | 87.00 | 5.00 | .. | 8.00 |
| 1980 | 83.70 | 6.30 | .. | 10.00 |
| **Mujeres** | | | | |
| 1950 | 97.85 | 0.36 | .. | 1.79 |
| 1960 | 95.49 | 0.76 | .. | 3.75 |
| 1970 | 93.13 | 1.16 | .. | 5.71 |
| 1980 | 90.77 | 1.56 | .. | 7.67 |

Fuente(s): EPPA3.

### 3.2 Método(s): interpolación y extrapolación lineares

#### 3.2.1 Hombres:

- 1950-80, tasas de distribución 1950-80 con base en EPPA3;
- 1990, extrapolación de las tasas de distribución 1950-80 con base en EPPA3;
ajuste de las tasas extrapoladas con base en las variaciones de las tasas
interpoladas 1980, en relación con las tasas de distribución 1980 con base en EI
- Aplicación de la razón manufacturas/industria estimada para le Rwanda.
- Aplicación de la razón manufacturas/industria estimada para le Rwanda.

#### 3.2.2 Mujeres:

- 1950-90, interpolación extrapolación de las tasas de distribución ajustadas
1950 y 1980 con base en EPPA3;
ajuste de las tasas de distribución con base en
la razón hombres/mujeres igual a 1 en la agricultura;
las tasas de distribución de manufacturas estimada con base en los razones
manufacturas/industria estimadas para le Rwanda.

## 4. Proyección de las tasas de actividad: 2000 - 2010

### 4.1 Modelo(s): linear y hiperbólico

#### 4.1.1 Hombres:

- Para todos los grupos de edad, aplicación de la función F1;
- Modificación de las tendencias de los grupos de edad [10-14] y [20-24].

#### 4.1.2 Mujeres:

- Para los grupos de edad [10-19], aplicación de la función F1;
- Para los grupos de edad [20+], aplicación de la función F3;
- Modificación de las tendencias de los grupos de edad [20-54].

*Notas sobre los ajustes de las tasas, véase p.380-384.*          *Notas sobre las funciones de proyección, véase p. 386.*

# Uruguay

## 1. Fuente(s) de los datos básicos

Código(s):    Título(s):

EPPA3    Estimaciones y proyecciones de la población.económicamente activa, 1950-2025, tercera edición, OIT, Ginebra, 1986.
STAT    Base de datos de la OIT sobre estadísticas del trabajo - LABORSTA, Oficina de Estadística, OIT, Ginebra.

## 2. Evaluación de las tasas de actividad: 1950 - 1990

### 2.1 Datos básicos:

Cuadro 1: Tasas de actividad por sexo y grupo de edad

| Grupo de edad | Año 1975 (1) | 1975 (2) | 1985 (1) | 1985 (2) | 1991 (1) | 1992 (1) | 1993 (1) |
|---|---|---|---|---|---|---|---|
| **Hombres** | | | | | | | |
| 10-14 | ... | ... | ... | ... | 2.16 | 1.97 | 3.15 |
| 15-19 | 56.50 | 81.50 | 55.04 | 79.64 | 56.69 | 57.05 | 54.18 |
| 20-24 | 88.80 | 92.50 | 86.50 | 95.30 | 88.52 | 88.76 | 88.25 |
| 25-29 | 95.10 | 94.50 | 95.40 | 97.00 | 97.17 | 96.63 | 96.77 |
| 30-34 | 97.20 | 95.90 | 96.70 | 97.00 | 97.32 | 98.10 | 97.54 |
| 35-39 | 97.20 | 96.60 | 96.50 | 96.70 | 98.02 | 97.44 | 97.45 |
| 40-44 | 96.50 | 96.70 | 96.00 | 96.60 | 97.28 | 97.81 | 97.50 |
| 45-49 | 94.50 | 96.00 | 93.50 | 95.20 | 96.90 | 97.40 | 96.33 |
| 50-54 | 89.10 | 94.30 | 87.30 | 94.50 | 94.06 | 94.09 | 92.64 |
| 55-59 | 78.10 | 90.90 | 78.00 | 81.40 | 87.67 | 87.42 | 86.85 |
| 60-64 | 54.30 | 75.50 | 48.20 | 70.20 | 59.12 | 60.41 | 56.11 |
| 65+ | 17.70 | 35.90 | 13.90 | 33.50 | 17.75 | 17.38 | 16.21 |
| **Mujeres** | | | | | | | |
| 10-14 | ... | ... | ... | ... | 1.00 | 1.01 | 1.84 |
| 15-19 | 27.80 | 23.80 | 23.76 | 23.09 | 31.26 | 33.01 | 32.98 |
| 20-24 | 45.00 | 26.50 | 49.60 | 32.30 | 66.60 | 68.39 | 67.61 |
| 25-29 | 45.00 | 24.40 | 55.50 | 31.30 | 67.82 | 71.43 | 70.59 |
| 30-34 | 43.50 | 21.70 | 54.10 | 32.20 | 68.68 | 71.60 | 71.62 |
| 35-39 | 43.30 | 19.80 | 53.60 | 32.10 | 69.75 | 73.00 | 71.25 |
| 40-44 | 41.20 | 20.60 | 52.20 | 29.90 | 66.82 | 69.89 | 67.21 |
| 45-49 | 37.30 | 20.30 | 48.80 | 28.60 | 61.36 | 65.93 | 64.77 |
| 50-54 | 31.10 | 17.90 | 38.30 | 26.10 | 54.49 | 56.30 | 55.22 |
| 55-59 | 22.60 | 14.90 | 26.50 | 19.80 | 37.00 | 36.47 | 37.73 |
| 60-64 | 12.40 | 10.00 | 13.40 | 11.40 | 21.50 | 21.05 | 20.83 |
| 65+ | 3.50 | 4.10 | 3.60 | 4.90 | 5.75 | 6.30 | 5.82 |

**Nota(s):** (1) Urbana; (2) Rural.
**Fuente(s):** STAT.

### 2.2 Método(s): promedio ponderado
interpolación y extrapolación lineares

#### 2.2.1 Hombres:

- 1950-70, tasas de actividad 1950-70 con base en EPPA3;
- 1980-90, promedios ponderados de las tasas de actividad estimadas por separado de las areas urbanas y rurales; para las áreas urbanas, las tasas estimadas se han obtenido con base en la interpolción de las tasas de actividad ajustadas con base en los censos de 1975 y 1985 con base en y del promedio de las tasas con base en las encuestas de 1991, 1992 y 1993; para áreas rurales, las tasas estimadas se han obtenido con base en la interpolación y extrapolación de las tasas de actividad con base en los censos de 1975 y 1985.

#### 2.2.2 Mujeres:

Métodos, hipótesis y tratamientos idénticos a los que se aplican a los hombres.

## 3. Evaluación de las tasas de distribución por sector de actividad: 1950 - 1990

### 3.1 Datos básicos:

Cuadro 2: Distribución de la población económicamente activa por sector de actividad en %

| Año | Agricultura | Industria Total | Manufac. | Servicios |
|---|---|---|---|---|
| **Hombres** | | | | |
| 1975 (1) | 23.09 | 30.41 | 19.84 | 46.50 |
| 1985 (1) | 21.64 | 30.83 | 19.74 | 47.53 |
| 1985 (2) | 8.13 | 35.93 | 23.09 | 55.94 |
| 1991 (2) | 7.02 | 33.21 | 21.97 | 59.77 |
| 1992 (2) | 7.12 | 36.20 | 22.36 | 56.68 |
| **Mujeres** | | | | |
| 1975 (1) | 3.61 | 23.93 | 23.09 | 72.46 |
| 1985 (1) | 4.00 | 21.30 | 20.27 | 74.70 |
| 1985 (2) | 1.07 | 21.36 | 20.32 | 77.57 |
| 1991 (2) | 1.13 | 22.23 | 21.98 | 76.64 |
| 1992 (2) | 1.07 | 20.89 | 19.82 | 78.04 |

**Nota(s):** (1) Total; (2) Urban.
**Fuente(s):** STAT.

### 3.2 Método(s): promedio ponderado

#### 3.2.1 Hombres:

- 1950-60, tasas de distribución 1950-60 con base en EPPA3;
- 1980, promedios ponderados de las tasas de distribución con base en los censos de 1975 y 1985;
- 1990, promedios ponderados dc las tasas dc distribución estimadas por separado para las áreas urbanas y rurales; estimación de las tasas por separado para las áreas urbanas y rurales; estimación de las tasas

#### 3.2.2 Mujeres:

Métodos, hipótesis y tratamientos idénticos a los que se aplican a los hombres.

## 4. Proyección de las tasas de actividad: 2000 - 2010

### 4.1 Modelo(s): linear, hiperbólico y logístico

#### 4.1.1 Hombres:

- Para el grupo de edad [10-14], aplicación de la función F1;
- Para los grupos de edad [15+], aplicación de la función F3;
- Modificación de las tendencias de los grupos de edad [15-19] y [25-49].

#### 4.1.2 Mujeres:

- Para el grupo de edad [10-14], aplicación de la función F1;
- Para los grupos de edad [15-19] y [65+], aplicación de la función F3;
- Modificación de las tendencias de los grupos de edad [10-19] y [65+].

*Notas sobre los ajustes de las tasas, véase p.380-384.*          *Notas sobre las funciones de proyección, véase p. 386.*

# Uzbekistán

## 1. Fuente(s) de los datos básicos

Código(s):   Título(s):

BLT-94-2   Vorobiev A. (1994), "Estimaciones de la población económicamente activa de los quince países de la ex URSS, en 1950, 1959, 1970, 1979 y 1989", en el Boletín de Estadísticas del Trabajol - 1994-2, OIT, Ginebra.

## 2. Evaluación de las tasas de actividad: 1950 - 1990

### 2.1 Datos básicos:

Cuadro 1: Tasas de actividad por sexo y grupo de edad

| Grupo de edad | Año | | | | |
|---|---|---|---|---|---|
| | 1950 | 1959 | 1970 | 1979 | 1989 |
| **Hombres** | | | | | |
| 10-14 | 0.00 | 0.00 | 0.00 | 0.00 | 0.00 |
| 15-19 | 53.02 | 52.08 | 37.13 | 37.18 | 28.81 |
| 20-24 | 81.94 | 82.34 | 80.50 | 84.52 | 80.02 |
| 25-29 | 94.80 | 95.99 | 94.75 | 97.00 | 95.96 |
| 30-34 | 95.62 | 95.77 | 97.50 | 98.42 | 97.84 |
| 35-39 | 95.57 | 96.13 | 98.46 | 98.54 | 97.82 |
| 40-44 | 94.19 | 93.28 | 96.13 | 98.10 | 97.55 |
| 45-49 | 91.45 | 92.20 | 97.56 | 97.36 | 96.23 |
| 50-54 | 88.11 | 89.93 | 90.57 | 93.21 | 92.57 |
| 55-59 | 83.33 | 86.36 | 82.54 | 82.17 | 84.59 |
| 60-64 | 71.13 | 72.36 | 45.19 | 30.21 | 34.72 |
| 65+ | 30.91 | 29.25 | 10.33 | 6.97 | 10.60 |
| **Mujeres** | | | | | |
| 10-14 | 0.00 | 0.00 | 0.00 | 0.00 | 0.00 |
| 15-19 | 50.76 | 56.86 | 42.55 | 41.42 | 32.53 |
| 20-24 | 72.22 | 78.79 | 78.67 | 86.41 | 75.60 |
| 25-29 | 68.56 | 67.62 | 86.99 | 93.03 | 81.12 |
| 30-34 | 67.19 | 67.61 | 83.72 | 93.23 | 83.33 |
| 35-39 | 68.18 | 69.51 | 88.24 | 93.29 | 85.49 |
| 40-44 | 59.04 | 62.92 | 84.29 | 92.96 | 85.31 |
| 45-49 | 53.21 | 54.40 | 80.89 | 90.42 | 81.49 |
| 50-54 | 40.66 | 41.67 | 97.86 | 68.46 | 52.44 |
| 55-59 | 26.58 | 25.96 | 27.23 | 24.77 | 20.95 |
| 60-64 | 13.74 | 11.98 | 9.14 | 8.00 | 11.57 |
| 65+ | 4.64 | 4.56 | 2.80 | 2.04 | 3.65 |

Fuente(s): BLT-94-2-2

### 2.2 Método(s): promedio ponderado

**2.2.1 Hombres:**

- 1950-90, promedios ponderados de las tasas de actividad 1950, 1959, 1972 y 1989 con base en el Boletín de estadísticas del trabajo 1994-2.

**2.2.2 Mujeres:**

Métodos, hipótesis y tratamientos idénticos a los que se aplican a los hombres.

## 3. Evaluación de las tasas de distribución por sector de actividad: 1950 - 1990

### 3.1 Datos básicos:

Cuadro 2: Distribución de la población económicamente activa por sector de actividad en %

| Año | Agricultura | Industria | | Servicios |
|---|---|---|---|---|
| | | Total | Manufac. | |
| **Hombres** | | | | |
| 1950 | 70.22 | 12.57 | 11.13 | 17.21 |
| 1959 | 53.44 | 20.23 | 9.21 | 26.34 |
| 1970 | 38.72 | 28.36 | 14.79 | 32.93 |
| 1979 | 34.60 | 34.44 | 12.76 | 30.96 |
| 1989 | 34.49 | 30.67 | 12.11 | 34.84 |
| **Mujeres** | | | | |
| 1950 | 73.71 | 10.26 | 9.58 | 16.03 |
| 1959 | 65.99 | 13.16 | 9.80 | 20.85 |
| 1970 | 50.57 | 17.32 | 12.83 | 32.12 |
| 1979 | 47.01 | 18.68 | 11.50 | 34.31 |
| 1989 | 36.98 | 19.19 | 12.51 | 43.83 |

Fuente(s): BLT-94-2.

### 3.2 Método(s): promedio ponderado

**3.2.1 Hombres:**

- 1950-90, promedios ponderados de las tasas de distribución 1950, 1959, 1970, 1979 y 1989 con base en el Boletín de estadísticas del trabajo 1994-2.

**3.2.2 Mujeres:**

Métodos, hipótesis y tratamientos idénticos a los que se aplican a los hombres.

## 4. Proyección de las tasas de actividad: 2000 - 2010

### 4.1 Modelo(s): linear, log-linear, hiperbólico y logístico

**4.1.1 Hombres:**

- Para los grupos de edad [15-24] y [55+], aplicación de la función F3;
- Para los grupos de edad [25-54], aplicación de la función F1;
- Modificación de las tendencias de los grupos de edad [25-64].

**4.1.2 Mujeres:**

- Para el grupo de edad [15-19], aplicación de la función F2;
- Para los grupos de edad [20-24] y [55+], aplicación de la función F3;
- Para los grupos de edad [25-54], aplicación de la función F6;
- Modificación de las tendencias de los grupos de edad [20-59].

*Notas sobre los ajustes de las tasas, véase p.380-384.*      *Notas sobre las funciones de proyección, véase p. 386.*

# Venezuela

## 1. Fuente(s) de los datos básicos

Código(s):    Título(s):

EPPA3       Estimaciones y proyecciones de la población económicamente activa, 1950-2025, tercera edición, OIT, Ginebra, 1986.
ADNU84      Annuaire démographique 1984 - Statistiques des recensements de population II, trente-sixième édition, Nations Unies, New York, 1986.
ASTER       Anuario de estadísticas del trabajo 1945-89 - Edición retrospectiva sobre los censos de población, OIT, Ginebra, 1990.
AST91-93    Ediciones de 1991-1993, Anuario de Estadísticas del Trabjo de la OIT, Ginebra.

## 2. Evaluación de las tasas de actividad: 1950 - 1990

### 2.1 Datos básicos:

Cuadro 1: Tasas de actividad por sexo y grupo de edad

|  | Año | | |
|---|---|---|---|
| Grupo de edad | 1971 (1) | 1981 (2) | 1990 (3) |
| **Hombres** | | | |
| 10-14 | 0.00 | 5.30 | .. |
| 15-19 | 50.20 | 47.32 | .. |
| 20-24 | 81.85 | 80.88 | .. |
| 25-29 | 93.58 | 91.15 | .. |
| 30-34 | 95.99 | 93.54 | .. |
| 35-39 | 96.40 | 93.87 | .. |
| 40-44 | 95.74 | 93.47 | .. |
| 45-49 | 94.91 | 91.23 | .. |
| 50-54 | 91.39 | 87.68 | .. |
| 55-59 | 87.24 | 81.16 | .. |
| 60-64 | 63.38 | 70.03 | .. |
| 65+ | 50.14 | 41.94 | .. |
| **Mujeres** | | | |
| 10-14 | 0.00 | 1.69 | 0.00 |
| 15-19 | 20.30 | 18.47 | 17.86 |
| 20-24 | 29.40 | 35.78 | 36.80 |
| 25-29 | 29.50 | 39.50 | 42.46 |
| 30-34 | 26.80 | 39.85 | 46.17 |
| 35-39 | 25.00 | 39.02 | 46.02 |
| 40-44 | 23.80 | 35.66 | 43.76 |
| 45-49 | 20.80 | 28.88 | 37.78 |
| 50-54 | 17.00 | 23.35 | 28.78 |
| 55-59 | 13.50 | 16.56 | 20.26 |
| 60-64 | 9.80 | 10.73 | 12.66 |
| 65+ | 5.80 | 5.46 | 6.00 |

Fuente(s): (1) ASTER; (2) ADNU84 y ASTER; (3) AST91-93.

### 2.2 Método(s):   interpolación y extrapolación lineares
                     promedio ponderado

#### 2.2.1 Hombres:

- 1950-60, tasas de actividad 1950-60 con base en EPPA3;
- 1970, promedios ponderados de las  tasas de actividad 1970 con base
en EPPA3 y de las tasas de actividad ajustadas con base en el censo de 1971;
- 1980, interpolación de las tasas de actividad ajustadas con base en
los censos de 1971 y 1981;
- 1990, extrapolación de las tasas de actividad 1950-60 con base en EPPA3
y de las tasas de actividad estimadas para 1970 y 1980;
ajuste de las tasas extrapoladas;

#### 2.2.2 Mujeres:

- 1950-70, tasas de actividad ajustadas 1950-70 con base en EPPA3;
- 1980, promedios ponderados de las tasas de actividad con base en
los censos de 1971 y 1981;
- 1990, promedios ponderados de las tasas de actividad con base en
los censos de 1981 y 1990.

## 3. Evaluación de las tasas de distribución  por sector de actividad: 1950 - 1990

### 3.1 Datos básicos:

Cuadro  2: Distribución de la población económicamente activa por sector de actividad en %

|  | Agricultura | Industria | | Servicios |
|---|---|---|---|---|
| Año |  | Total | Manufac. |  |
| **Hombres** | | | | |
| 1981 | 17.48 | 32.76 | 16.74 | 49.75 |
| 1989 | 17.31 | 31.49 | 17.20 | 51.20 |
| 1990 | 16.56 | 32.06 | 16.93 | 51.38 |
| 1991 | 15.95 | 33.00 | 17.48 | 51.05 |
| **Mujeres** | | | | |
| 1981 | 1.70 | 16.04 | 12.91 | 82.27 |
| 1989 | 1.82 | 17.19 | 15.30 | 80.99 |
| 1990 | 1.94 | 16.04 | 14.00 | 82.02 |
| 1991 | 1.79 | 16.48 | 14.31 | 81.72 |

Fuente(s): AST91-93.

### 3.2 Método(s):   promedio aritmético

#### 3.2.1 Hombres:

- 1950-70, tasas de distribución 1950-70 con base en EPPA3;
- 1980-90, promedios de las tasas de distribución con base en el censo
de 1981 y de los promedios de las tasas de distribución con base en
las encuestas de 1989, 1990 y 1991.

#### 3.2.2 Mujeres:

Métodos, hipótesis y tratamientos idénticos a los que se aplican a los hombres.

## 4. Proyección de las tasas de actividad: 2000 - 2010

### 4.1 Modelo(s):   hiperbólico, exponencial y logístico

#### 4.1.1 Hombres:

- Para los grupos de edad [15+], aplicación de la función F3;
- Modificación de las tendencias de los grupos de edad [20-24] y [30-59].

#### 4.1.2 Mujeres:

- Para los grupos de edad [15-19] y [55+], aplicación de la función F3;
- Para el grupo de edad [20-24], aplicación de la función F4;
- Para los grupos de edad [25-54], aplicación de la función F6;
- Modificación de la tendencia del grupo de edad [20-24].

*Notas sobre los ajustes de las tasas, véase p.380-384.*          *Notas sobre las funciones de proyección, véase p. 386.*

# Viet Nam

## 1. Fuente(s) de los datos básicos

Código(s):   Título(s):

EPPA3      Estimaciones y proyecciones de la población económicamente activa, 1950-2025, tercera edición, OIT, Ginebra, 1986.
STAT       Base de datos de la OIT sobre estadísticas del trabajo - LABORSTA, Oficina de Estadística, OIT, Ginebra.
EPPA4      Población económicamente activa 1950-2010 - cuarta edición, OIT, Ginebra, 1996.

## 2. Evaluación de las tasas de actividad: 1950 - 1990

### 2.1 Datos básicos:

Cuadro 1: Tasas de actividad por sexo y grupo de edad

| Grupo de edad | Año 1950 (1) | 1960 (1) | 1970 (1) | 1980 (1) | 1989 (2) |
|---|---|---|---|---|---|
| **Hombres** | | | | | |
| 10-14 | 52.00 | 46.00 | 40.00 | 30.00 | 11.73 |
| 15-19 | 87.10 | 83.70 | 80.30 | 74.70 | 67.42 |
| 20-24 | 96.90 | 96.90 | 96.90 | 96.80 | 94.36 |
| 25-29 | 98.75 | 98.75 | 98.75 | 98.70 | 97.41 |
| 30-34 | 98.95 | 98.95 | 98.95 | 98.90 | 97.26 |
| 35-39 | 99.00 | 99.00 | 99.00 | 98.90 | 95.70 |
| 40-44 | 98.90 | 98.85 | 98.80 | 98.75 | 91.78 |
| 45-49 | 97.75 | 97.70 | 97.60 | 97.55 | 86.92 |
| 50-54 | 95.60 | 94.65 | 93.70 | 92.00 | 81.21 |
| 55-59 | 91.70 | 89.80 | 87.90 | 84.30 | 70.86 |
| 60-64 | 81.65 | 77.80 | 73.95 | 66.30 | 53.04 |
| 65+ | 56.00 | 50.45 | 44.90 | 34.00 | 27.19 |
| **Mujeres** | | | | | |
| 10-14 | 43.00 | 40.00 | 38.00 | 31.00 | 14.82 |
| 15-19 | 72.40 | 73.90 | 75.40 | 78.60 | 73.33 |
| 20-24 | 82.30 | 84.20 | 86.10 | 89.60 | 88.75 |
| 25-29 | 79.90 | 82.20 | 83.70 | 87.40 | 89.26 |
| 30-34 | 78.00 | 80.90 | 83.00 | 87.10 | 88.11 |
| 35-39 | 77.80 | 80.00 | 82.20 | 86.60 | 86.90 |
| 40-44 | 75.50 | 77.10 | 78.70 | 81.90 | 83.92 |
| 45-49 | 64.70 | 65.90 | 67.10 | 69.50 | 78.67 |
| 50-54 | 47.10 | 47.90 | 48.70 | 50.20 | 69.42 |
| 55-59 | 36.10 | 35.50 | 34.90 | 33.50 | 54.22 |
| 60-64 | 25.50 | 23.70 | 21.90 | 18.40 | 35.54 |
| 65+ | 9.95 | 8.90 | 7.85 | 5.70 | 13.14 |

Nota(s): (1) China.
Fuente(s): (1) EPPA4; (2) STAT.

### 2.2 Método(s): interpolación y extrapolación lineares

**2.2.1 Hombres:**

- 1950-90, interpolación y extrapolación de las tasas de actividad estimadas 1980-90 pora China;
aplicación a las tasas de actividad estimadas 1950-80 para China,
de las variaciones de las tasas interpoladas 1989, en relación con las tasas
de actividad ajustadas con base en el censo de 1989.

**2.2.2 Mujeres:**

Métodos, hipótesis y tratamientos idénticos a los que se aplican a los hombres.

## 3. Evaluación de las tasas de distribución por sector de actividad: 1950 - 1990

### 3.1 Datos básicos:

Cuadro 2: Distribución de la población económicamente activa por sector de actividad en %

| Año | Agricultura | Industria Total | Manufac. | Servicios |
|---|---|---|---|---|
| **Hombres** | | | | |
| 1950 (1) | 86.00 | 5.00 | .. | 9.00 |
| 1960 (1) | 81.00 | 6.50 | .. | 12.50 |
| 1970 (1) | 75.00 | 12.00 | .. | 13.00 |
| 1989 (2) | 69.53 | 17.11 | 13.89 | 13.36 |
| **Mujeres** | | | | |
| 1950 (1) | 92.00 | 4.00 | .. | 4.00 |
| 1960 (1) | 86.50 | 6.00 | .. | 7.50 |
| 1970 (1) | 83.00 | 7.50 | .. | 9.50 |
| 1989 (2) | 73.15 | 10.84 | 9.77 | 16.02 |

Fuente(s): (1) EPPA3; (2) STAT.

### 3.2 Método(s): razón proprocional

**3.2.1 Hombres:**

- 1950-70, tasas de distribución 1950-70 con base en EPPA3;
- 1980-90, aplicación a las tasas de distribución de la agricultura
con base en el censo de 1989, de las mismas variaciones que las tasas
estimadas para China para 1980 y 1990; las tasas de distribución de la industria,
de las manufacturas y de los servicios estimadas con base en la
de las manufacturas y de los servicios estimadas con base en la

**3.2.2 Mujeres:**

Métodos, hipótesis y tratamientos idénticos a los que se aplican a los hombres.

## 4. Proyección de las tasas de actividad: 2000 - 2010

### 4.1 Modelo(s): linear y hiperbólico

**4.1.1 Hombres:**

- Para los grupos de edad [10-34] y [65+], aplicación de la función F1;
- Para los grupos de edad [35-64], aplicación de la función F3;
- Modificación de las tendencias de los grupos de edad [15-34] y [65+].

**4.1.2 Mujeres:**

- Para todos los grupos de edad, aplicación de la función F1;
- Modificación de las tendencias de los grupos de edad [10-54].

---

*Notas sobre los ajustes de las tasas, véase p.380-384.*        *Notas sobre las funciones de proyección, véase p. 386.*

# Yemen

## 1. Fuente(s) de los datos básicos

Código(s):   Título(s):

EPPA3   Estimaciones y proyecciones de la población económicamente activa, 1950-2025, tercera edición, OIT, Ginebra, 1986.
ESCWA   Compedium of Social Statistics Indicators, Third Issue, December 1993, Economic and Social Commission for Western Asia.
EPPA4   Población económicamente activa 1950-2010 - cuarta edición, OIT, Ginebra, 1996.
STAT   Base de datos de la OIT sobre estadísticas del trabajo - LABORSTA, Oficina de Estadística, OIT, Ginebra.

## 2. Evaluación de las tasas de actividad: 1950 - 1990

### 2.1 Datos básicos:

Cuadro 1: Tasas de actividad por sexo y grupo de edad

| Grupo de edad | Año 1950 (1) | 1960 (1) | 1970 (1) | 1980 (1) | 1986 (2) | 1990 (1) |
|---|---|---|---|---|---|---|
| **Hombres** | | | | | | |
| 10-14 | 31.55 | 27.84 | 24.12 | 20.41 | 24.87 | 18.56 |
| 15-19 | 79.48 | 69.03 | 58.58 | 48.12 | 52.49 | 42.89 |
| 20-24 | 90.07 | 86.70 | 83.33 | 79.96 | 87.48 | 78.28 |
| 25-29 | 97.41 | 96.86 | 96.31 | 95.76 | 96.61 | 95.49 |
| 30-34 | 97.98 | 97.89 | 97.79 | 97.70 | 97.84 | 97.65 |
| 35-39 | 98.06 | 98.11 | 98.17 | 98.23 | 98.14 | 98.26 |
| 40-44 | 98.08 | 97.82 | 97.57 | 97.32 | 97.71 | 97.19 |
| 45-49 | 97.86 | 97.53 | 97.21 | 96.89 | 97.39 | 96.73 |
| 50-54 | 96.56 | 96.08 | 95.61 | 95.13 | 95.86 | 94.89 |
| 55-59 | 94.92 | 94.23 | 93.55 | 92.86 | 93.92 | 92.52 |
| 60-64 | 90.94 | 84.79 | 78.63 | 72.47 | 79.86 | 69.39 |
| 65+ | 75.53 | 62.13 | 48.73 | 35.33 | 51.41 | 28.63 |
| **Mujeres** | | | | | | |
| 10-14 | .. | .. | .. | 16.09 | 21.43 | 7.50 |
| 15-19 | .. | .. | .. | 22.80 | 26.50 | 18.90 |
| 20-24 | .. | .. | .. | 34.33 | 26.91 | 39.17 |
| 25-29 | .. | .. | .. | 33.53 | 32.31 | 38.44 |
| 30-34 | .. | .. | .. | 32.89 | 32.47 | 39.68 |
| 35-39 | .. | .. | .. | 30.77 | 31.44 | 36.43 |
| 40-44 | .. | .. | .. | 30.59 | 31.96 | 36.70 |
| 45-49 | .. | .. | .. | 27.60 | 29.44 | 29.04 |
| 50-54 | .. | .. | .. | 26.78 | 27.96 | 26.52 |
| 55-59 | .. | .. | .. | 24.10 | 24.15 | 23.74 |
| 60-64 | .. | .. | .. | 18.87 | 22.31 | 14.83 |
| 65+ | .. | .. | .. | 9.77 | 6.60 | 8.86 |

Nota(s): (1) Egipto.
Fuente(s): (1) EPPA4; (2) ESCWA and STAT.

### 2.2 Método(s): interpolación y extrapolación lineares

#### 2.2.1 Hombres:

- 1950-90, aplicación a las tasas de actividad estimadas 1986 del ESCWA, de la mitad de las tendencias estimadas para Egipto.

#### 2.2.2 Mujeres:

- 1950-70, tasas de actividad ajustadas 1950-70 con base en EPPA3;
- 1980-90, aplicación a las tasas de actividad estimadas 1986 del ESCWA, de la mitad de las tendencias estimadas para Egipto.

## 3. Evaluación de las tasas de distribución por sector de actividad: 1950 - 1990

### 3.1 Datos básicos:

Cuadro 2: Distribución de la población económicamente activa por sector de actividad en %

| Año | Agricultura | Industria Total | Manufac. | Servicios |
|---|---|---|---|---|
| **Hombres** | | | | |
| 1986 | 59.10 | 18.30 | .. | 22.60 |
| **Mujeres** | | | | |
| 1986 | 95.66 | 1.96 | .. | 2.38 |

Fuente(s): ESCWA y STAT.

### 3.2 Método(s): extrapolación linear

#### 3.2.1 Hombres:

- 1950-70, tasas de distribución 1950-70 con base en EPPA3;
- 1980-90, aplicación a las tasas de distribución 1986 con base en estimaciones de la ESCWA de la mitad de las tendencias estimadas para Egipto.

#### 3.2.2 Mujeres:

- 1950-70, tasas de distribución 1950-70 con base en EPPA3;
- 1980-90, aplicación a las tasas de distribución 1986 con base en estimaciones de la ESCWA, de las mismas variaciones que las estimadas para los hombres en el Yemen durante el mismo período.

## 4. Proyección de las tasas de actividad: 2000 - 2010

### 4.1 Modelo(s): linear y hiperbólico

#### 4.1.1 Hombres:

- Para el grupo de edad [10-14], aplicación de la función F1;
- Para los grupos de edad [15+], aplicación de la función F3;
- Modificación de las tendencias de los grupos de edad [10-14] y [30-39].

#### 4.1.2 Mujeres:

- Para todos los grupos de edad, aplicación de la función F1;
- Modificación de las tendencias de todos los grupos de edad.

*Notas sobre los ajustes de las tasas, véase p.380-384.*   *Notas sobre las funciones de proyección, véase p. 386.*

# Yugoslavia, Rep. Fed. de

## 1. Fuente(s) de los datos básicos

**Código(s):** **Título(s):**

EPPA3   Estimaciones y proyecciones de la población económicamente activa, 1950-2025, tercera edición, OIT, Ginebra, 1986.

BLT-94-2   Popovic B. (1994), "Nuevas estimaciones de las tasas de actividad para 1980 y 1990, desglosadas por grupos de edad y distribución sectorial, en algunos países de Europa oriental y meridional" en el Boletín de Estadísticas del Trabajo1 - 1994-2, OIT, Ginebra.

## 2. Evaluación de las tasas de actividad: 1950 - 1990

### 2.1 Datos básicos:

Cuadro 1: Tasas de actividad por sexo y grupo de edad

| Grupo de edad | Año 1950 (1) | 1960 (1) | 1970 (1) | 1980 (2) | 1990 (2) |
|---|---|---|---|---|---|
| **Hombres** | | | | | |
| 10-14 | 24.10 | 8.85 | 3.25 | 0.25 | 0.01 |
| 15-19 | 86.80 | 67.25 | 48.45 | 21.59 | 25.04 |
| 20-24 | 94.85 | 90.75 | 85.80 | 72.02 | 77.31 |
| 25-29 | 96.10 | 96.55 | 95.80 | 92.87 | 92.16 |
| 30-34 | 97.60 | 97.90 | 98.35 | 97.57 | 98.18 |
| 35-39 | 97.80 | 97.25 | 98.30 | 97.76 | 98.33 |
| 40-44 | 97.60 | 97.00 | 95.55 | 97.05 | 96.39 |
| 45-49 | 97.20 | 96.10 | 96.00 | 95.03 | 91.97 |
| 50-54 | 94.20 | 94.00 | 92.35 | 84.40 | 83.20 |
| 55-59 | 84.65 | 85.60 | 77.05 | 65.39 | 61.20 |
| 60-64 | 79.75 | 75.50 | 65.10 | 55.26 | 40.13 |
| 65+ | 61.60 | 56.70 | 51.30 | 43.30 | 30.63 |
| **Mujeres** | | | | | |
| 10-14 | 23.20 | 12.50 | 5.45 | 0.45 | 0.03 |
| 15-19 | 68.80 | 58.35 | 45.15 | 16.18 | 19.15 |
| 20-24 | 60.75 | 60.55 | 60.35 | 53.43 | 60.77 |
| 25-29 | 45.00 | 53.20 | 57.35 | 66.65 | 76.03 |
| 30-34 | 38.85 | 47.65 | 52.25 | 67.14 | 79.56 |
| 35-39 | 35.45 | 45.15 | 50.35 | 58.72 | 78.64 |
| 40-44 | 32.80 | 42.15 | 47.20 | 54.44 | 72.22 |
| 45-49 | 29.50 | 37.80 | 43.40 | 50.19 | 58.33 |
| 50-54 | 24.20 | 31.70 | 36.70 | 41.32 | 42.36 |
| 55-59 | 21.10 | 26.75 | 31.60 | 34.62 | 29.89 |
| 60-64 | 16.50 | 22.10 | 26.80 | 28.84 | 24.58 |
| 65+ | 10.95 | 14.10 | 14.60 | 18.55 | 17.09 |

**Fuente(s)**: (1) EPPA3; (2) BLT-94-2.

### 2.2 Método(s): con base en EPPA3 y BLT-94-2.

#### 2.2.1 Hombres:

- 1950-70, 1950-70 tasas de actividad para Yugoslavia
con base en EPPA3 y of 1990 tasas de actividad con base en
el Boletín de estadísticas del trabajo 1994-2;
F
- 1980-90, tasas de actividad 1980-90 con base en el Boletín.

#### 2.2.2 Mujeres:

- 1950-70, tasas de actividad 1950-70 para Yugoslavia
con base en EPPA3;
ajuste de las tasas de actividad de los grupos de edad [10-19];
- 1980-90, tasas de actividad 1980 y 1990 con base en el Boletín
de estadísticas del trabajo 1994-2.

## 3. Evaluación de las tasas de distribución por sector de actividad: 1950 - 1990

### 3.1 Datos básicos:

Cuadro 2: Distribución de la población económicamente activa por sector de actividad en %

| Año | Agricultura | Industria Total | Manufac. | Servicios |
|---|---|---|---|---|
| **Hombres** | | | | |
| 1950 (1) | 68.30 | 17.80 | .. | 13.90 |
| 1960 (1) | 56.00 | 28.00 | .. | 16.00 |
| 1970 (1) | 45.00 | 34.40 | .. | 20.60 |
| 1980 (2) | 33.86 | 34.99 | 21.41 | 31.14 |
| 1990 (2) | 27.82 | 37.97 | 26.31 | 34.22 |
| **Mujeres** | | | | |
| 1950 (1) | 83.00 | 5.40 | .. | 11.50 |
| 1960 (1) | 78.10 | 15.00 | .. | 6.80 |
| 1970 (1) | 58.20 | 20.00 | .. | 21.80 |
| 1980 (2) | 47.39 | 19.24 | 16.99 | 33.37 |
| 1990 (2) | 32.33 | 26.25 | 23.15 | 41.42 |

**Fuente(s)**: (1) EPPA3; (2) BLT-94-2.

### 3.2 Método(s): datos de BLT-94-2

#### 3.2.1 Hombres:

- 1950-70, tasas de distribución 1950-70 con base en EPPA3;
- 1980-90, tasas de distribución con base en el boletín de estadísticas
del trabajo 1994-2.

#### 3.2.2 Mujeres:

- 1950-90, promedios ponderados de las tasas de distribución 1950-70
con base en EPPA3 y de las tasas de distribución 1980-90 con base en el boletín

## 4. Proyección de las tasas de actividad: 2000 - 2010

### 4.1 Modelo(s): linear, hiperbólico y logístico

#### 4.1.1 Hombres:

- Para los grupos de edad [15+], aplicación de la función F3;
- Modificación de las tendencias de los grupos de edad [15+].

#### 4.1.2 Mujeres:

- Para los grupos de edad [15-19] y [25-54], aplicación de la función F6;
- Para el grupo de edad [20-24], aplicación de la función F3;
- Para los grupos de edad [55+], aplicación de la función F1;
- Modificación de las tendencias de los grupos de edad [15-24] y [35+].

*Notas sobre los ajustes de las tasas, véase p.380-384.*    *Notas sobre las funciones de proyección, véase p. 386.*

# Zambia

## 1. Fuente(s) de los datos básicos

Código(s):    Título(s):

EPPA3        Estimaciones y proyecciones de la población económicamente activa, 1950-2025, tercera edición, OIT, Ginebra, 1986.
ASTER        Anuario de estadísticas del trabajo 1945-89 - Edición retrospectiva sobre los censos de población, OIT, Ginebra, 1990.
ADNU88       Annuaire démographique 1988 - Statistiques des recensements de population, quarantième édition, Nations Unies, New York, 1990.
STAT         Base de datos de la OIT sobre estadísticas del trabajo - LABORSTA, Oficina de Estadística, OIT, Ginebra.

## 2. Evaluación de las tasas de actividad: 1950 - 1990

### 2.1 Datos básicos:

Cuadro 1: Tasas de actividad por sexo y grupo de edad

| Grupo de edad | Año 1950 (1) | 1960 (1) | 1970 (1) | 1980 (2) | 1980 (1) | 1990 (3) |
|---|---|---|---|---|---|---|
| **Hombres** | | | | | | |
| 10-14 | 27.60 | 26.40 | 24.85 | 19.39 | .. | 17.90 |
| 15-19 | 74.10 | 71.45 | 68.15 | 37.73 | .. | 69.70 |
| 20-24 | 87.80 | 86.75 | 85.45 | 82.78 | .. | 90.20 |
| 25-29 | 98.65 | 98.50 | 98.30 | 96.76 | .. | 96.40 |
| 30-34 | 99.60 | 99.40 | 99.20 | 98.10 | .. | 97.00 |
| 35-39 | 99.65 | 99.45 | 99.20 | 98.29 | .. | 97.20 |
| 40-44 | 99.55 | 99.35 | 99.05 | 98.23 | .. | 96.00 |
| 45-49 | 99.40 | 99.20 | 99.00 | 98.37 | .. | 95.20 |
| 50-54 | 99.00 | 98.70 | 98.35 | 97.72 | .. | 93.30 |
| 55-59 | 98.75 | 98.30 | 97.75 | 97.77 | .. | 91.30 |
| 60-64 | 97.20 | 96.45 | 95.50 | 96.50 | .. | 78.22 |
| 65+ | 85.90 | 84.55 | 82.85 | 58.68 | .. | 58.68 |
| **Mujeres** | | | | | | |
| 10-14 | 23.20 | 22.15 | 20.85 | .. | 19.85 | 15.93 |
| 15-19 | 44.65 | 42.85 | 40.55 | .. | 38.75 | 62.03 |
| 20-24 | 29.80 | 29.05 | 28.10 | .. | 27.35 | 73.29 |
| 25-29 | 25.55 | 24.85 | 24.00 | .. | 23.35 | 73.23 |
| 30-34 | 24.50 | 23.85 | 23.00 | .. | 22.35 | 74.76 |
| 35-39 | 25.65 | 25.00 | 24.20 | .. | 23.60 | 74.24 |
| 40-44 | 28.85 | 28.15 | 27.30 | .. | .26.65 | 68.29 |
| 45-49 | 33.85 | 33.00 | 32.00 | .. | 31.20 | 62.64 |
| 50-54 | 44.30 | 43.05 | 41.45 | .. | 40.15 | 58.20 |
| 55-59 | 53.90 | 52.20 | 50.10 | .. | 48.40 | 49.93 |
| 60-64 | 43.85 | 41.90 | 39.45 | .. | 37.50 | 43.70 |
| 65+ | 21.20 | 19.95 | 18.35 | .. | 17.05 | 32.79 |

Fuente(s): (1) EPPA3; (2) ADNU88 y ASTER; (3) STAT.

### 2.2 Método(s):   interpolación y extrapolación lineares

#### 2.2.1 Hombres:

- 1950-90, interpolación y extrapolación de las tasas de actividad 1950-70 con base en EPPA3 y de las tasas de actividad ajustadas con base los censos de 1980 y 1990;
ajuste de las tasas extrapoladas con base en las variaciones de las tasas interpoladas 1990, en relación con las tasas de actividad ajustadas con base en el censo de 1990.

#### 2.2.2 Mujeres:

- 1950-90, interpolación y extrapolación de las tasas de actividad 1950-80 con base en EPPA3;
ajuste de las tasas interpoladas y extrapoladas con base en las variaciones de las tasas interpoladas 1990, en relación con las tasas de actividad ajustadas con base en el censo de 1990;
modificación de las tendencias de todos los grupos de edad.

## 3. Evaluación de las tasas de distribución por sector de actividad: 1950 - 1990

### 3.1 Datos básicos:

Cuadro 2: Distribución de la población económicamente activa por sector de actividad en %

| Año | Agricultura | Industria Total | Manufac. | Servicios |
|---|---|---|---|---|
| **Hombres** | | | | |
| 1950 (1) | 82.00 | 8.00 | .. | 10.00 |
| 1960 (1) | 78.00 | 9.50 | .. | 12.50 |
| 1970 (1) | 73.00 | 11.00 | .. | 16.00 |
| 1980 (1) | 69.00 | 12.50 | .. | 18.50 |
| 1980 (2) | 47.98 | 18.91 | 6.36 | 33.11 |
| **Mujeres** | | | | |
| 1950 (1) | 90.00 | 1.50 | .. | 8.50 |
| 1980 (1) | 84.00 | 2.75 | .. | 13.25 |
| 1980 (2) | 79.22 | 2.63 | 1.97 | 18.15 |

Fuente(s): (1) EPPA3; (2) STAT.

### 3.2 Método(s):   interpolación y extrapolación lineares

#### 3.2.1 Hombres:

- 1950-80, tasas de distribución 1950-80 con base en EPPA3;
- 1990, extrapolación de las tasas de distribución 1950-80 con base en EPPA3;
ajuste de las tasas extrapoladas con base en 1/4 de las variaciones de las tasas interpoladas 1980, en relación con las tasas de distribución 1980 con base en EPPA3.
con base en EPPA3.

#### 3.2.2 Mujeres:

- 1950-90, interpolación extrapolación de las tasas de distribución ajustadas 1950 y 1980 con base en EPPA3;
ajuste de las tasas de distribución con base en
la razón hombres/mujeres igual a 1 en la agricultura;
las tasas de distribución de manufacturas estimada con base en la razón manufacturas/industria con base en el censo de 1980.

## 4. Proyección de las tasas de actividad: 2000 - 2010

### 4.1 Modelo(s):   linear y hiperbólico

#### 4.1.1 Hombres:

- Para los grupos de edad [10-14] y [25+], aplicación de la función F3;
- Para el grupo de edad [15-19], aplicación de la función F1;
- Modificación de las tendencias de los grupos de edad [15-24] y [30-54].

#### 4.1.2 Mujeres:

- Para todos los grupos de edad, aplicación de la función F3;
- Modificación de las tendencias de los grupos de edad [20-54].

*Notas sobre los ajustes de las tasas, véase p.380-384.*

*Notas sobre las funciones de proyección, véase p. 386.*

# Zimbabwe

## 1. Fuente(s) de los datos básicos

| Código(s): | Título(s): |
|---|---|
| EPPA3 | Estimaciones y proyecciones de la población económicamente activa, 1950-2025, tercera edición, OIT, Ginebra, 1986. |
| R1982 | Main Demographic Features of Zimbabwe, Population Census 1982, Central Statistical Office, Causeway, 1985. |
| ASTER | Anuario de estadísticas del trabajo 1945-89 - Edición retrospectiva sobre los censos de población, OIT, Ginebra, 1990. |
| AST93 | Anuario de Estadísticas del Trabjo 1993, OIT, Ginebra, 1993. |

## 2. Evaluación de las tasas de actividad: 1950 - 1990

### 2.1 Datos básicos:

Cuadro 1: Tasas de actividad por sexo y grupo de edad

| Grupo de edad | Año 1950 (1) | 1960 (1) | 1970 (1) | 1980 (1) | 1982 (2) | 1987 (3) |
|---|---|---|---|---|---|---|
| **Hombres** | | | | | | |
| 10-14 | 48.25 | 46.75 | 44.20 | 41.15 | 36.52 | .. |
| 15-19 | 79.75 | 77.80 | 74.40 | 70.35 | 48.16 | .. |
| 20-24 | 93.30 | 92.55 | 91.25 | 89.70 | 83.35 | .. |
| 25-29 | 97.10 | 97.00 | 96.80 | 96.55 | 93.07 | .. |
| 30-34 | 97.80 | 97.70 | 97.45 | 97.20 | 93.96 | .. |
| 35-39 | 97.95 | 97.80 | 97.60 | 97.30 | 94.29 | .. |
| 40-44 | 97.80 | 97.65 | 97.40 | 97.10 | 94.14 | .. |
| 45-49 | 97.05 | 96.95 | 96.75 | 96.50 | 93.85 | .. |
| 50-54 | 96.50 | 96.30 | 96.00 | 95.60 | 92.47 | .. |
| 55-59 | 95.35 | 95.05 | 94.55 | 93.95 | 90.43 | .. |
| 60-64 | 91.85 | 91.40 | 90.55 | 89.55 | 68.97 | .. |
| 65+ | 77.70 | 76.85 | 75.40 | 73.65 | ... | .. |
| **Mujeres** | | | | | | |
| 10-14 | .. | .. | .. | .. | .. | 0.00 |
| 15-19 | .. | .. | .. | .. | .. | 44.50 |
| 20-24 | .. | .. | .. | .. | .. | 64.50 |
| 25-29 | .. | .. | .. | .. | .. | 68.70 |
| 30-34 | .. | .. | .. | .. | .. | 83.20 |
| 35-39 | .. | .. | .. | .. | .. | 81.00 |
| 40-44 | .. | .. | .. | .. | .. | 79.28 |
| 45-49 | .. | .. | .. | .. | .. | 78.50 |
| 50-54 | .. | .. | .. | .. | .. | 76.00 |
| 55-59 | .. | .. | .. | .. | .. | 73.12 |
| 60-64 | .. | .. | .. | .. | .. | 67.95 |
| 65+ | .. | .. | .. | .. | .. | 58.84 |

Fuente(s): (1) EPPA3; (2) R1982 y ASTER; (3) AST93.

### 2.2 Método(s): interpolación y extrapolación lineares

#### 2.2.1 Hombres:

- 1950-90, interpolación y extrapolación de las tasas de actividad 1950-80 con base en EPPA3 y de las tasas de actividad ajustadas con base el censo de 1982;
ajuste de las tasas interpoladas y extrapoladas con base en las variaciones de las tasas interpoladas 1982, en relación con las tasas de actividad ajustadas con base en el censo de 1982;
modificación de las tendencias de los grupos de edad [10-19] y [65+] para 1950-90.

#### 2.2.2 Mujeres:

- 1950-90, interpolación y extrapolación de las tasas de actividad estimadas 1950-90 para el Malawi;
ajuste de las tasas interpoladas y extrapoladas con base en las variaciones de las tasas interpoladas 1986, en relación con las tasas de actividad con base en la encuesta de 1986/87;
modificación de las tendencias del grupo de edad [10-14] para 1950-90.

## 3. Evaluación de las tasas de distribución por sector de actividad: 1950 - 1990

### 3.1 Datos básicos:

Cuadro 2: Distribución de la población económicamente activa por sector de actividad en %

| Año | Agricultura | Industria Total | Manufac. | Servicios |
|---|---|---|---|---|
| **Hombres** | | | | |
| 1982 (1) | 54.61 | 23.60 | .. | 21.80 |
| 1986 (2) | 59.87 | 13.67 | 9.01 | 26.45 |
| **Mujeres** | | | | |
| 1982 (1) | 76.68 | 5.56 | .. | 17.75 |
| 1986 (2) | 82.71 | 2.33 | 1.83 | 14.96 |

Fuente(s): R1982; (2) AST93.

### 3.2 Método(s): extrapolación linear

#### 3.2.1 Hombres:

- 1950-70, tasas de distribución 1950-70 con base en EPPA3;
- 1980-90, extrapolación de las tasas de distribución 1950-80 con base en EPP/ de las tasas de distribución con base en el censo de 1982 y de las tasas de distribución con base en la encuesta de 1986-87;
modificación de las tendencias de todos los sectores.
modificación de las tendencias de todos los sectores.

#### 3.2.2 Mujeres:

Métodos, hipótesis y tratamientos idénticos a los que se aplican a los hombres.

## 4. Proyección de las tasas de actividad: 2000 - 2010

### 4.1 Modelo(s): linear y hiperbólico

#### 4.1.1 Hombres:

- Para el grupo de edad [10-14], aplicación de la función F1;
- Para los grupos de edad [15+], aplicación de la función F3;
- Modificación de las tendencias de los grupos de edad [10-14] y [60+].

#### 4.1.2 Mujeres:

- Para los grupos de edad [10-59], aplicación de la función F3;
- Para los grupos de edad [60+], aplicación de la función F1;
- Modificación de las tendencias de los grupos de edad [25-54] y [60+].

*Notas sobre los ajustes de las tasas, véase p.380-384.*

*Notas sobre las funciones de proyección, véase p. 386.*